Topic relevant selected content from the highest rated entries, typeset, printed and shipped.

Combine the advantages of up-to-date and in-depth knowledge with the convenience of printed books.

A portion of the proceeds of each book will be donated to the Wikimedia Foundation to support their mission: to empower and engage people around the world to collect and develop educational content under a free license or in the public domain, and to disseminate it effectively and globally.

The content within this book was generated collaboratively by volunteers. Please be advised that nothing found here has necessarily been reviewed by people with the expertise required to provide you with complete, accurate or reliable information. Some information in this book maybe misleading or simply wrong. The publisher does not guarantee the validity of the information found here. If you need specific advice (for example, medical, legal, financial, or risk management) please seek a professional who is licensed or knowledgeable in that area.

Contents

Articles

References

Article Licenses

Bioinformatics

Bioinformatics ◀ /ˌbaɪ.oʊˌɪnfərˈmætɪks/ is the application of computer science and information technology to the field of biology and medicine. Bioinformatics deals with algorithms, databases and information systems, web technologies, artificial intelligence and soft computing, information and computation theory, software engineering, data mining, image processing, modeling and simulation, signal processing, discrete mathematics, control and system theory, circuit theory, and statistics, for generating new knowledge of biology and medicine, and improving & discovering new models of computation (e.g. DNA computing, neural computing, evolutionary computing, immuno-computing, swarm-computing, cellular-computing). Java, XML, Perl, C, C++, Python, R, SQL and MatLab are the some of the more prominent software technologies used in this field.

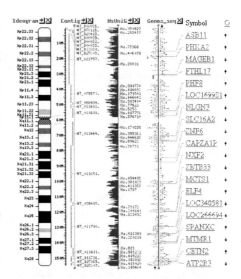

Map of the human X chromosome (from the NCBI website). Assembly of the human genome is one of the greatest achievements of bioinformatics.

Introduction

Bioinformatics was applied in the creation and maintenance of a database to store biological information at the beginning of the "genomic revolution", such as nucleotide and amino acid sequences. Development of this type of database involved not only design issues but the development of complex interfaces whereby researchers could both access existing data as well as submit new or revised data.

In order to study how normal cellular activities are altered in different disease states, the biological data must be combined to form a comprehensive picture of these activities. Therefore, the field of bioinformatics has evolved such that the most pressing task now involves the analysis and interpretation of various types of data, including nucleotide and amino acid sequences, protein domains, and protein structures. The actual process of analyzing and interpreting data is referred to as computational biology. Important sub-disciplines within bioinformatics and computational biology include:

- the development and implementation of tools that enable efficient access to, and use and management of, various types of information.
- the development of new algorithms (mathematical formulas) and statistics with which to assess relationships among members of large data sets, such as methods to locate a gene within a sequence, predict protein structure and/or function, and cluster protein sequences into families of related sequences.

The primary goal of bioinformatics is to increase the understanding of biological processes. What sets it apart from other approaches, however, is its focus on developing and applying computationally intensive techniques (e.g., pattern recognition, data mining, machine learning algorithms, and visualization) to achieve this goal. Major research efforts in the field include sequence alignment, gene finding, genome assembly, drug design, drug discovery, protein structure alignment, protein structure prediction, prediction of gene expression and protein–protein interactions, genome-wide association studies and the modeling of evolution.

The term *bioinformatics* was coined by Paulien Hogeweg and Ben Hesper in 1978 for the study of informatic processes in biotic systems.[1] [2] Its primary use since at least the late 1980s has been in genomics and genetics, particularly in those areas of genomics involving large-scale DNA sequencing.

Bioinformatics now entails the creation and advancement of databases, algorithms, computational and statistical techniques and theory to solve formal and practical problems arising from the management and analysis of biological data.

Over the past few decades rapid developments in genomic and other molecular research technologies and developments in information technologies have combined to produce a tremendous amount of information related to molecular biology. It is the name given to these mathematical and computing approaches used to glean understanding of biological processes.

Common activities in bioinformatics include mapping and analyzing DNA and protein sequences, aligning different DNA and protein sequences to compare them and creating and viewing 3-D models of protein structures.

There are two fundamental ways of modelling a Biological system (e.g. living cell) both coming under Bioinformatic approaches.

- Static
  - Sequences – Proteins, Nucleic acids and Peptides
  - Structures – Proteins, Nucleic acids, Ligands (including metabolites and drugs) and Peptides
  - Interaction data among the above entities including microarray data and Networks of proteins, metabolites
- Dynamic
  - Systems Biology comes under this category including reaction fluxes and variable concentrations of metabolites
  - Multi-Agent Based modelling approaches capturing cellular events such as signalling, transcription and reaction dynamics

A broad sub-category under bioinformatics is structural bioinformatics.

Major research areas

Sequence analysis

Since the Phage Φ-X174 was sequenced in 1977,[3] the DNA sequences of thousands of organisms have been decoded and stored in databases. This sequence information is analyzed to determine genes that encode polypeptides (proteins), RNA genes, regulatory sequences, structural motifs, and repetitive sequences. A comparison of genes within a species or between different species can show similarities between protein functions, or relations between species (the use of molecular systematics to construct phylogenetic trees). With the growing amount of data, it long ago became impractical to analyze DNA sequences manually. Today, computer programs such as BLAST are used daily to search sequences from more than 260 000 organisms, containing over 190 billion nucleotides.[4] These programs can compensate for mutations (exchanged, deleted or inserted bases) in the DNA sequence, to identify sequences that are related, but not identical. A variant of this sequence alignment is used in the sequencing process itself. The so-called shotgun sequencing technique (which was used, for example, by The Institute for Genomic Research to sequence the first bacterial genome, *Haemophilus influenzae*)[5] does not produce entire chromosomes, but instead generates the sequences of many thousands of small DNA fragments (ranging from 35 to 900 nucleotides long, depending on the sequencing technology). The ends of these fragments overlap and, when aligned properly by a genome assembly program, can be used to reconstruct the complete genome. Shotgun sequencing yields sequence data quickly, but the task of assembling the fragments can be quite complicated for larger genomes. For a genome as large as the human genome, it may take many days of CPU time on large-memory, multiprocessor computers to assemble the fragments, and the resulting assembly will usually contain numerous gaps that have to be filled in later. Shotgun sequencing is the method of choice for virtually all genomes sequenced today, and genome assembly algorithms are a critical area of bioinformatics research.

Another aspect of bioinformatics in sequence analysis is annotation, which involves computational gene finding to search for protein-coding genes, RNA genes, and other functional sequences within a genome. Not all of the nucleotides within a genome are part of genes. Within the genome of higher organisms, large parts of the DNA do not serve any obvious purpose. This so-called junk DNA may, however, contain unrecognized functional elements. Bioinformatics helps to bridge the gap between genome and proteome projects — for example, in the use of DNA sequences for protein identification.

Genome annotation

In the context of genomics, annotation is the process of marking the genes and other biological features in a DNA sequence. The first genome annotation software system was designed in 1995 by Dr. Owen White, who was part of the team at The Institute for Genomic Research that sequenced and analyzed the first genome of a free-living organism to be decoded, the bacterium *Haemophilus influenzae*. Dr. White built a software system to find the genes (places in the DNA sequence that encode a protein), the transfer RNA, and other features, and to make initial assignments of function to those genes. Most current genome annotation systems work similarly, but the programs available for analysis of genomic DNA are constantly changing and improving.

Computational evolutionary biology

Evolutionary biology is the study of the origin and descent of species, as well as their change over time. Informatics has assisted evolutionary biologists in several key ways; it has enabled researchers to:

- trace the evolution of a large number of organisms by measuring changes in their DNA, rather than through physical taxonomy or physiological observations alone,
- more recently, compare entire genomes, which permits the study of more complex evolutionary events, such as gene duplication, horizontal gene transfer, and the prediction of factors important in bacterial speciation,
- build complex computational models of populations to predict the outcome of the system over time
- track and share information on an increasingly large number of species and organisms

Future work endeavours to reconstruct the now more complex tree of life.

The area of research within computer science that uses genetic algorithms is sometimes confused with computational evolutionary biology, but the two areas are not necessarily related.

Literature analysis

The growth in the number of published literature makes it virtually impossible to read every paper, resulting in disjointed subfields of research. Literature analysis aims to employ computational and statistical linguistics to mine this growing library of text resources. For example:

- abbreviation recognition - identify the long-form and abbreviation of biological terms,
- named entity recognition - recognizing biological terms such as gene names
- protein-protein interaction - identify which proteins interact with which proteins from text

The area of research uses statistics and computational linguistics, and is substantially influenced by them.

Analysis of gene expression

The expression of many genes can be determined by measuring mRNA levels with multiple techniques including microarrays, expressed cDNA sequence tag (EST) sequencing, serial analysis of gene expression (SAGE) tag sequencing, massively parallel signature sequencing (MPSS), RNA-Seq, also known as "Whole Transcriptome Shotgun Sequencing" (WTSS), or various applications of multiplexed in-situ hybridization. All of these techniques are extremely noise-prone and/or subject to bias in the biological measurement, and a major research area in computational biology involves developing statistical tools to separate signal from noise in high-throughput gene expression studies. Such studies are often used to determine the genes implicated in a disorder: one might compare microarray data from cancerous epithelial cells to data from non-cancerous cells to determine the transcripts that are up-regulated and down-regulated in a particular population of cancer cells.

Analysis of regulation

Regulation is the complex orchestration of events starting with an extracellular signal such as a hormone and leading to an increase or decrease in the activity of one or more proteins. Bioinformatics techniques have been applied to explore various steps in this process. For example, promoter analysis involves the identification and study of sequence motifs in the DNA surrounding the coding region of a gene. These motifs influence the extent to which that region is transcribed into mRNA. Expression data can be used to infer gene regulation: one might compare microarray data from a wide variety of states of an organism to form hypotheses about the genes involved in each state. In a single-cell organism, one might compare stages of the cell cycle, along with various stress conditions (heat shock, starvation, etc.). One can then apply clustering algorithms to that expression data to determine which genes are co-expressed. For example, the upstream regions (promoters) of co-expressed genes can be searched for over-represented regulatory elements.

Analysis of protein expression

Protein microarrays and high throughput (HT) mass spectrometry (MS) can provide a snapshot of the proteins present in a biological sample. Bioinformatics is very much involved in making sense of protein microarray and HT MS data; the former approach faces similar problems as with microarrays targeted at mRNA, the latter involves the problem of matching large amounts of mass data against predicted masses from protein sequence databases, and the complicated statistical analysis of samples where multiple, but incomplete peptides from each protein are detected.

Analysis of mutations in cancer

In cancer, the genomes of affected cells are rearranged in complex or even unpredictable ways. Massive sequencing efforts are used to identify previously unknown point mutations in a variety of genes in cancer. Bioinformaticians continue to produce specialized automated systems to manage the sheer volume of sequence data produced, and they create new algorithms and software to compare the sequencing results to the growing collection of human genome sequences and germline polymorphisms. New physical detection technologies are employed, such as oligonucleotide microarrays to identify chromosomal gains and losses (called comparative genomic hybridization), and single-nucleotide polymorphism arrays to detect known *point mutations*. These detection methods simultaneously measure several hundred thousand sites throughout the genome, and when used in high-throughput to measure thousands of samples, generate terabytes of data per experiment. Again the massive amounts and new types of data generate new opportunities for bioinformaticians. The data is often found to contain considerable variability, or noise, and thus Hidden Markov model and change-point analysis methods are being developed to infer real copy number changes.

Another type of data that requires novel informatics development is the analysis of lesions found to be recurrent among many tumors.

Comparative genomics

The core of comparative genome analysis is the establishment of the correspondence between genes (orthology analysis) or other genomic features in different organisms. It is these intergenomic maps that make it possible to trace the evolutionary processes responsible for the divergence of two genomes. A multitude of evolutionary events acting at various organizational levels shape genome evolution. At the lowest level, point mutations affect individual nucleotides. At a higher level, large chromosomal segments undergo duplication, lateral transfer, inversion, transposition, deletion and insertion. Ultimately, whole genomes are involved in processes of hybridization, polyploidization and endosymbiosis, often leading to rapid speciation. The complexity of genome evolution poses many exciting challenges to developers of mathematical models and algorithms, who have recourse to a spectra of algorithmic, statistical and mathematical techniques, ranging from exact, heuristics, fixed parameter and approximation algorithms for problems based on parsimony models to Markov Chain Monte Carlo algorithms for Bayesian analysis of problems based on probabilistic models.

Many of these studies are based on the homology detection and protein families computation.

Modeling biological systems

Systems biology involves the use of computer simulations of cellular subsystems (such as the networks of metabolites and enzymes which comprise metabolism, signal transduction pathways and gene regulatory networks) to both analyze and visualize the complex connections of these cellular processes. Artificial life or virtual evolution attempts to understand evolutionary processes via the computer simulation of simple (artificial) life forms.

High-throughput image analysis

Computational technologies are used to accelerate or fully automate the processing, quantification and analysis of large amounts of high-information-content biomedical imagery. Modern image analysis systems augment an observer's ability to make measurements from a large or complex set of images, by improving accuracy, objectivity, or speed. A fully developed analysis system may completely replace the observer. Although these systems are not unique to biomedical imagery, biomedical imaging is becoming more important for both diagnostics and research. Some examples are:

- high-throughput and high-fidelity quantification and sub-cellular localization (high-content screening, cytohistopathology, Bioimage informatics)
- morphometrics
- clinical image analysis and visualization
- determining the real-time air-flow patterns in breathing lungs of living animals
- quantifying occlusion size in real-time imagery from the development of and recovery during arterial injury
- making behavioral observations from extended video recordings of laboratory animals
- infrared measurements for metabolic activity determination
- inferring clone overlaps in DNA mapping, e.g. the Sulston score

Structural Bioinformatic Approaches

Prediction of protein structure

Protein structure prediction is another important application of bioinformatics. The amino acid sequence of a protein, the so-called primary structure, can be easily determined from the sequence on the gene that codes for it. In the vast majority of cases, this primary structure uniquely determines a structure in its native environment. (Of course, there are exceptions, such as the bovine spongiform encephalopathy – a.k.a. Mad Cow Disease – prion.) Knowledge of this structure is vital in understanding the function of the protein. For lack of better terms, structural information is usually classified as one of *secondary*, *tertiary* and *quaternary* structure. A viable general solution to such predictions remains an open problem. As of now, most efforts have been directed towards heuristics that work most of the time.

One of the key ideas in bioinformatics is the notion of homology. In the genomic branch of bioinformatics, homology is used to predict the function of a gene: if the sequence of gene *A*, whose function is known, is homologous to the sequence of gene *B*, whose function is unknown, one could infer that B may share A's function. In the structural branch of bioinformatics, homology is used to determine which parts of a protein are important in structure formation and interaction with other proteins. In a technique called homology modeling, this information is used to predict the structure of a protein once the structure of a homologous protein is known. This currently remains the only way to predict protein structures reliably.

One example of this is the similar protein homology between hemoglobin in humans and the hemoglobin in legumes (leghemoglobin). Both serve the same purpose of transporting oxygen in the organism. Though both of these proteins have completely different amino acid sequences, their protein structures are virtually identical, which reflects their near identical purposes.

Other techniques for predicting protein structure include protein threading and *de novo* (from scratch) physics-based modeling.

See also: structural motif and structural domain.

Molecular Interaction

Efficient software is available today for studying interactions among proteins, ligands and peptides. Types of interactions most often encountered in the field include – Protein–ligand (including drug), protein–protein and protein–peptide.

Molecular dynamic simulation of movement of atoms about rotatable bonds is the fundamental principle behind computational algorithms, termed **docking algorithms** for studying molecular interactions.

See also: protein–protein interaction prediction.

Docking algorithms

In the last two decades, tens of thousands of protein three-dimensional structures have been determined by X-ray crystallography and Protein nuclear magnetic resonance spectroscopy (protein NMR). One central question for the biological scientist is whether it is practical to predict possible protein–protein interactions only based on these 3D shapes, without doing protein–protein interaction experiments. A variety of methods have been developed to tackle the Protein–protein docking problem, though it seems that there is still much work to be done in this field.

Software and tools

Software tools for bioinformatics range from simple command-line tools, to more complex graphical programs and standalone web-services available from various bioinformatics companies or public institutions.

Open source bioinformatics software

Many free and open source software tools have existed and continued to grow since the 1980s.[6] The combination of a continued need for new algorithms for the analysis of emerging types of biological readouts, the potential for innovative *in silico* experiments, and freely available open code bases have helped to create opportunities for all research groups to contribute to both bioinformatics and the range of open source software available, regardless of their funding arrangements. The open source tools often act as incubators of ideas, or community-supported plug-ins in commercial applications. They may also provide *de facto* standards and shared object models for assisting with the challenge of bioinformation integration.

The range of open source software packages includes titles such as Bioconductor, BioPerl, BioJava, BioRuby, Bioclipse, EMBOSS, Taverna workbench, and UGENE. In order to maintain this tradition and create further opportunities, the non-profit Open Bioinformatics Foundation[6] have supported the annual Bioinformatics Open Source Conference (BOSC) since 2000.[6]

Web services in bioinformatics

SOAP and REST-based interfaces have been developed for a wide variety of bioinformatics applications allowing an application running on one computer in one part of the world to use algorithms, data and computing resources on servers in other parts of the world. The main advantages derive from the fact that end users do not have to deal with software and database maintenance overheads.

Basic bioinformatics services are classified by the EBI into three categories: SSS (Sequence Search Services), MSA (Multiple Sequence Alignment) and BSA (Biological Sequence Analysis). The availability of these service-oriented bioinformatics resources demonstrate the applicability of web based bioinformatics solutions, and range from a collection of standalone tools with a common data format under a single, standalone or web-based interface, to integrative, distributed and extensible bioinformatics workflow management systems.

References

[1] Hogeweg, P. (1978). "Simulating the growth of cellular forms". *Simulation* **31** (3): 90–96. doi:10.1177/003754977803100305.
[2] Hogeweg, P. (2011). Searls, David B.. ed. "The Roots of Bioinformatics in Theoretical Biology". *PLoS Computational Biology* **7** (3): e1002021. Bibcode 2011PLSCB...7E0020H. doi:10.1371/journal.pcbi.1002021. PMC 3068925. PMID 21483479.
[3] Sanger F, Air GM, Barrell BG, Brown NL, Coulson AR, Fiddes CA, Hutchison CA, Slocombe PM, Smith M (February 1977). "Nucleotide sequence of bacteriophage phi X174 DNA". *Nature* **265** (5596): 687–95. doi:10.1038/265687a0. PMID 870828.
[4] Benson DA, Karsch-Mizrachi I, Lipman DJ, Ostell J, Wheeler DL (January 2008). "GenBank". *Nucleic Acids Res.* **36** (Database issue): D25–30. doi:10.1093/nar/gkm929. PMC 2238942. PMID 18073190.
[5] Fleischmann RD, Adams MD, White O, Clayton RA, Kirkness EF, Kerlavage AR, Bult CJ, Tomb JF, Dougherty BA, Merrick JM (July 1995). "Whole-genome random sequencing and assembly of Haemophilus influenzae Rd". *Science* **269** (5223): 496–512. doi:10.1126/science.7542800. PMID 7542800.
[6] "Open Bioinformatics Foundation: About us" (http://www.open-bio.org/wiki/Main_Page). *Official website*. Open Bioinformatics Foundation. . Retrieved 10 May 2011.

Further reading

- Achuthsankar S Nair Computational Biology & Bioinformatics – A gentle Overview (http://print.achuth.googlepages.com/BINFTutorialV5.0CSI07.pdf), Communications of Computer Society of India, January 2007
- Aluru, Srinivas, ed. *Handbook of Computational Molecular Biology*. Chapman & Hall/Crc, 2006. ISBN 1584884061 (Chapman & Hall/Crc Computer and Information Science Series)
- Baldi, P and Brunak, S, *Bioinformatics: The Machine Learning Approach*, 2nd edition. MIT Press, 2001. ISBN 0-262-02506-X
- Barnes, M.R. and Gray, I.C., eds., *Bioinformatics for Geneticists*, first edition. Wiley, 2003. ISBN 0-470-84394-2
- Baxevanis, A.D. and Ouellette, B.F.F., eds., *Bioinformatics: A Practical Guide to the Analysis of Genes and Proteins*, third edition. Wiley, 2005. ISBN 0-471-47878-4
- Baxevanis, A.D., Petsko, G.A., Stein, L.D., and Stormo, G.D., eds., *Current Protocols in Bioinformatics*. Wiley, 2007. ISBN 0-471-25093-7
- Claverie, J.M. and C. Notredame, *Bioinformatics for Dummies*. Wiley, 2003. ISBN 0-7645-1696-5
- Cristianini, N. and Hahn, M. *Introduction to Computational Genomics* (http://www.computational-genomics.net/), Cambridge University Press, 2006. (ISBN 9780521671910 I ISBN 0521671914)
- Durbin, R., S. Eddy, A. Krogh and G. Mitchison, *Biological sequence analysis*. Cambridge University Press, 1998. ISBN 0-521-62971-3
- Gilbert, D. *Bioinformatics software resources* (http://bib.oxfordjournals.org/cgi/content/abstract/5/3/300). Briefings in Bioinformatics, Briefings in Bioinformatics, 2004 5(3):300–304.
- Keedwell, E., *Intelligent Bioinformatics: The Application of Artificial Intelligence Techniques to Bioinformatics Problems*. Wiley, 2005. ISBN 0-470-02175-6
- Kohane, et al. *Microarrays for an Integrative Genomics*. The MIT Press, 2002. ISBN 0-262-11271-X
- Lund, O. et al. *Immunological Bioinformatics*. The MIT Press, 2005. ISBN 0-262-12280-4

- Michael S. Waterman, *Introduction to Computational Biology: Sequences, Maps and Genomes*. CRC Press, 1995. ISBN 0-412-99391-0
- Mount, David W. *Bioinformatics: Sequence and Genome Analysis* Spring Harbor Press, May 2002. ISBN 0-87969-608-7
- Pachter, Lior and Sturmfels, Bernd. "Algebraic Statistics for Computational Biology" Cambridge University Press, 2005. ISBN 0-521-85700-7
- Pevzner, Pavel A. *Computational Molecular Biology: An Algorithmic Approach* The MIT Press, 2000. ISBN 0-262-16197-4
- Soinov, L. Bioinformatics and Pattern Recognition Come Together (http://jprr.org/index.php/jprr/article/view/8/5) Journal of Pattern Recognition Research (JPRR (http://www.jprr.org)), Vol 1 (1) 2006 p. 37–41
- Tisdall, James. "Beginning Perl for Bioinformatics" O'Reilly, 2001. ISBN 0-596-00080-4
- Dedicated issue of *Philosophical Transactions B* on Bioinformatics freely available (http://publishing.royalsociety.org/bioinformatics)
- Catalyzing Inquiry at the Interface of Computing and Biology (2005) CSTB report (http://www.nap.edu/catalog/11480.html)
- Calculating the Secrets of Life: Contributions of the Mathematical Sciences and computing to Molecular Biology (1995) (http://www.nap.edu/catalog/2121.html)
- Foundations of Computational and Systems Biology MIT Course (http://ocw.mit.edu/OcwWeb/Biology/7-91JSpring2004/LectureNotes/index.htm)
- Computational Biology: Genomes, Networks, Evolution Free MIT Course (http://compbio.mit.edu/6.047/)
- Algorithms for Computational Biology Free MIT Course (http://ocw.mit.edu/OcwWeb/Electrical-Engineering-and-Computer-Science/6-096Spring-2005/CourseHome/index.htm)
- Zhang, Z., Cheung, K.H. and Townsend, J.P. Bringing Web 2.0 to bioinformatics, Briefing in Bioinformatics. In press (http://www.ncbi.nlm.nih.gov/pubmed/18842678)

External links

- Bioinformatics Organization (http://bioinformatics.org/)
- EMBnet (http://www.embnet.org/)
- Open Bioinformatics Foundation (http://www.open-bio.org/)
- The Center for Modeling Immunity to Enteric Pathogens (MIEP) (http://www.modelingimmunity.org)

Gene prediction

In computational biology **gene prediction** or **gene finding** refers to the process of identifying the regions of genomic DNA that encode genes. This includes protein-coding genes as well as RNA genes, but may also include prediction of other functional elements such as regulatory regions. Gene finding is one of the first and most important steps in understanding the genome of a species once it has been sequenced.

In its earliest days, "gene finding" was based on painstaking experimentation on living cells and organisms. Statistical analysis of the rates of homologous recombination of several different genes could determine their order on a certain chromosome, and information from many such experiments could be combined to create a genetic map specifying the rough location of known genes relative to each other. Today, with comprehensive genome sequence and powerful computational resources at the disposal of the research community, gene finding has been redefined as a largely computational problem.

Determining that a sequence *is functional* should be distinguished from determining *the function* of the gene or its product. The latter still demands *in vivo* experimentation through gene knockout and other assays, although frontiers of bioinformatics research are making it increasingly possible to predict the function of a gene based on its sequence alone.

Extrinsic approaches

In extrinsic (or evidence-based) gene finding systems, the target genome is searched for sequences that are similar to extrinsic evidence in the form of the known sequence of a messenger RNA (mRNA) or protein product. Given an mRNA sequence, it is trivial to derive a unique genomic DNA sequence from which it had to have been transcribed. Given a protein sequence, a family of possible coding DNA sequences can be derived by reverse translation of the genetic code. Once candidate DNA sequences have been determined, it is a relatively straightforward algorithmic problem to efficiently search a target genome for matches, complete or partial, and exact or inexact. BLAST is a widely used system designed for this purpose.

A high degree of similarity to a known messenger RNA or protein product is strong evidence that a region of a target genome is a protein-coding gene. However, to apply this approach systemically requires extensive sequencing of mRNA and protein products. Not only is this expensive, but in complex organisms, only a subset of all genes in the organism's genome are expressed at any given time, meaning that extrinsic evidence for many genes is not readily accessible in any single cell culture. Thus, in order to collect extrinsic evidence for most or all of the genes in a complex organism, many hundreds or thousands of different cell types must be studied, which itself presents further difficulties. For example, some human genes may be expressed only during development as an embryo or fetus , which might be difficult to study for ethical reasons.

Despite these difficulties, extensive transcript and protein sequence databases have been generated for human as well as other important model organisms in biology, such as mice and yeast. For example, the RefSeq database contains transcript and protein sequence from many different species, and the Ensembl system comprehensively maps this evidence to human and several other genomes. It is, however, likely that these databases are both incomplete and contain small but significant amounts of erroneous data..

Ab initio approaches

Because of the inherent expense and difficulty in obtaining extrinsic evidence for many genes, it is also necessary to resort to *Ab initio* gene finding, in which genomic DNA sequence alone is systematically searched for certain tell-tale signs of protein-coding genes. These signs can be broadly categorized as either *signals*, specific sequences that indicate the presence of a gene nearby, or *content*, statistical properties of protein-coding sequence itself. *Ab initio* gene finding might be more accurately characterized as gene *prediction*, since extrinsic evidence is generally required to conclusively establish that a putative gene is functional.

In the genomes of prokaryotes, genes have specific and relatively well-understood promoter sequences (signals), such as the Pribnow box and transcription factor binding sites, which are easy to systematically identify. Also, the sequence coding for a protein occurs as one contiguous open reading frame (ORF), which is typically many hundred or thousands of base pairs long. The statistics of stop codons are such that even finding an open reading frame of this length is a fairly informative sign. (Since 3 of the 64 possible codons in the genetic code are stop codons, one would expect a stop codon approximately every 20–25 codons, or 60–75 base pairs, in a random sequence.) Furthermore, protein-coding DNA has certain periodicities and other statistical properties that are easy to detect in sequence of this length. These characteristics make prokaryotic gene finding relatively straightforward, and well-designed systems are able to achieve high levels of accuracy.

Ab initio gene finding in eukaryotes, especially complex organisms like humans, is considerably more challenging for several reasons. First, the promoter and other regulatory signals in these genomes are more complex and less well-understood than in prokaryotes, making them more difficult to reliably recognize. Two classic examples of signals identified by eukaryotic gene finders are CpG islands and binding sites for a poly(A) tail.

Second, splicing mechanisms employed by eukaryotic cells mean that a particular protein-coding sequence in the genome is divided into several parts (exons), separated by non-coding sequences (introns). (Splice sites are themselves another signal that eukaryotic gene finders are often designed to identify.) A typical protein-coding gene in humans might be divided into a dozen exons, each less than two hundred base pairs in length, and some as short as twenty to thirty. It is therefore much more difficult to detect periodicities and other known content properties of protein-coding DNA in eukaryotes.

Advanced gene finders for both prokaryotic and eukaryotic genomes typically use complex probabilistic models, such as hidden Markov models, in order to combine information from a variety of different signal and content measurements. The GLIMMER system is a widely used and highly accurate gene finder for prokaryotes. GeneMark is another popular approach. Eukaryotic *ab initio* gene finders, by comparison, have achieved only limited success; notable examples are the GENSCAN and geneid programs. The SNAP gene finder is HMM-based like Genscan and attempts to be more adaptable to different organisms, addressing problems related to using a gene finder on a genome sequence that it was not trained against.[1] A few recent approaches like mSplicer,[2] CONTRAST,[3] or mGene[4] also use machine learning techniques like support vector machines for successful gene prediction. They build a discriminative model using hidden Markov support vector machines or conditional random fields to learn an accurate gene prediction scoring function.

Other signals

Among the derived signals used for prediction are statistics resulting from the sub-sequence statistics like k-mer statistics, Fourier transform of a pseudo-number-coded DNA, Z-curve parameters and certain run features.[5]

It has been suggested that signals other than those directly detectable in sequences may improve gene prediction. For example, the role of secondary structure in the identification of regulatory motifs has been reported.[6] In addition, it has been suggested that RNA secondary structure prediction helps splice site prediction.[7] [8] [9] [10]

Comparative genomics approaches

As the entire genomes of many different species are sequenced, a promising direction in current research on gene finding is a comparative genomics approach. This is based on the principle that the forces of natural selection cause genes and other functional elements to undergo mutation at a slower rate than the rest of the genome, since mutations in functional elements are more likely to negatively impact the organism than mutations elsewhere. Genes can thus be detected by comparing the genomes of related species to detect this evolutionary pressure for conservation. This approach was first applied to the mouse and human genomes, using programs such as SLAM, SGP and

Twinscan/N-SCAN.

Comparative gene finding can also be used to project high quality annotations from one genome to another. Notable examples include Projector, GeneWise and GeneMapper. Such techniques now play a central role in the annotation of all genomes.

External links

- http://www.geneprediction.org
- FGENESH [11]
- Bibliography on computational gene recognition by Wentian Li [12]
- geneid [13]
- SGP2 [14]
- http://cbcb.umd.edu/software/glimmer
- http://cbcb.umd.edu/software/GlimmerHMM
- http://bio.math.berkeley.edu/genemapper/
- http://www.genomethreader.org
- GENSCAN [15]
- Twinscan/N-SCAN [16]
- CHEMGENOME [17]
- GeneMark [18]
- Gismo [19]
- mGene [20]
- StarORF [21] — A multi-platform and web tool for predicting ORFs and obtaining reverse complement sequence

References

[1] Korf I. (2004-05-14). "Gene finding in novel genomes". *BMC Bioinformatics* **5**: 59–67. doi:10.1186/1471-2105-5-59. PMC 421630. PMID 15144565.

[2] Rätsch, Gunnar; Sonnenburg, S; Srinivasan, J; Witte, H; Müller, KR; Sommer, RJ; Schölkopf, B (2007-02-23). "Improving the *C. elegans* genome annotation using machine learning". *PLoS Computational Biology* **3** (2): e20. doi:10.1371/journal.pcbi.0030020. PMC 1808025. PMID 17319737.

[3] Gross, Samuel S; Do, CB; Sirota, M; Batzoglou, S (2007-12-20). "CONTRAST: A Discriminative, Phylogeny-free Approach to Multiple Informant De Novo Gene Prediction". *Genome Biology* **8** (12): R269. doi:10.1186/gb-2007-8-12-r269. PMC 2246271. PMID 18096039.

[4] Schweikert G, Behr J, Zien A, *et al.* (July 2009). "mGene.web: a web service for accurate computational gene finding" (http://nar. oxfordjournals.org/cgi/pmidlookup?view=long&pmid=19494180). *Nucleic Acids Res.* **37** (Web Server issue): W312–6. doi:10.1093/nar/gkp479. PMC 2703990. PMID 19494180. .

[5] Saeys Y, Rouzé P, Van de Peer Y (2007). "In search of the small ones: improved prediction of short exons in vertebrates, plants, fungi and protists" (http://bioinformatics.oxfordjournals.org/cgi/content/abstract/23/4/414). *Bioinformatics* **23** (4): 414–420. doi:10.1093/bioinformatics/btl639. PMID 17204465. .

[6] Hiller M, Pudimat R, Busch A, Backofen R (2006). "Using RNA secondary structures to guide sequence motif finding towards single-stranded regions". *Nucleic Acids Res* **34** (17): e117. doi:10.1093/nar/gkl544. PMC 1903381. PMID 16987907.

[7] Patterson DJ, Yasuhara K, Ruzzo WL (2002). "Pre-mRNA secondary structure prediction aids splice site prediction". *Pac Symp Biocomput*: 223–234. PMID 11928478.

[8] Marashi SA, Goodarzi H, Sadeghi M, Eslahchi C, Pezeshk H (2006). "Importance of RNA secondary structure information for yeast donor and acceptor splice site predictions by neural networks". *Comput Biol Chem* **30** (1): 50–7. doi:10.1016/j.compbiolchem.2005.10.009. PMID 16386465.

[9] Marashi SA, Eslahchi C, Pezeshk H, Sadeghi M (2006). "Impact of RNA structure on the prediction of donor and acceptor splice sites". *BMC Bioinformatics* **7**: 297. doi:10.1186/1471-2105-7-297. PMC 1526458. PMID 16772025.

[10] Rogic, S (2006) (PDF). *The role of pre-mRNA secondary structure in gene splicing in* Saccharomyces cerevisiae (http://www.cs.ubc.ca/ grads/resources/thesis/Nov06/Rogic_Sanja.pdf) (PhD thesis). University of British Columbia. .

[11] http://linux1.softberry.com/berry.phtml?topic=fgenesh&group=programs&subgroup=gfind

[12] http://www.nslij-genetics.org/gene/

[13] http://genome.imim.es/software/geneid/

[14] http://genome.imim.es/software/sgp2/

[15] http://genes.mit.edu/GENSCAN.html

[16] http://mblab.wustl.edu/software/twinscan/

[17] http://www.scfbio-iitd.res.in/research/genepredictor.htm

[18] http://opal.biology.gatech.edu/GeneMark/

[19] http://www.cebitec.uni-bielefeld.de/groups/brf/software/gismo/

[20] http://www.mgene.org/

[21] http://web.mit.edu/star/orf/

Premier Biosoft

Premier Biosoft

PREMIER Biosoft International	
Type	Private
Founded	1994
Headquarters	Palo Alto, California
Key people	Kay Brown (CEO)
Website	www.premierbiosoft.com [1]

PREMIER Biosoft International ("PBI" for short) is a California, United States based bioinformatics company. The company specializes in developing software for use in life science research. In addition to developing software products, the company offers assay design services and consultancy for bioinformatics projects.[2]

Company Background

PREMIER Biosoft, established in 1994, is one of the earliest bioinformatics company, founded by Ms. Kay Brown with a mission to serve the life science research labs all over the world. The mission statement for PBI reads as follows:"Accelerating Research in Life Sciences" The company serves research labs, pharmaceuticals, core facilities and biotechnology companies with its products. The company's first product, Primer Premier, was authored over 12 years ago, for designing PCR assays.

Products & Services

After the launch of Primer Premier the company released SimVector, a plasmid drawing and cloning simulation tool, and Array Designer, for designing microarray probes.

The trend in the PCR market was soon shifting towards a new and powerful technique called real time PCR. PREMIER Biosoft caught up early and authored Beacon Designer, supporting the most popular real time PCR chemistries The company later came out with a pathogen detection system called AlleleID with support for real time PCR and microarray probe design for designing cross species, species specific, intron-exon spanning assays and splice variant microarrays.

The company has ventured into proteomics, glycomics and lipidomics research with the launch of Xpression Primer (tagged primer design tool), SimGlycan (MS/MS data analysis tool) and SimLipid (lipid characterization tool). The company's latest offerings, TMA Foresight, analyzes tissue microarray data [3] and PrimerPlex, designs oligos for xMAP® based multiplex systems.

References

[1] http://www.premierbiosoft.com

[2] Link Details - Bioinformatics Companies -premier Biosoft (http://lifesciencedirectory.com/link.php?n=1394)

[3] PREMIER Biosoft : PREMIER Biosoft enters the new arena of Tissue Microarrays (http://bioitalliance.org/blogs/premier_biosoft/archive/2008/04/03/291.aspx)

External links

- Premier Biosoft Homepage (http://www.premierbiosoft.com)
- Bio-IT alliance page (http://bioitalliance.org/blogs/premier_biosoft/default.aspx)

3D-Jury

3D-Jury is a metaserver that aggregates and compares models from various protein structure prediction servers. It takes in groups of predictions made by a collection of servers and assigns each pair a 3D-Jury score, based on structural similarity. The score is generated by counting the number of C_α atoms in the two predictions within 3.5 Å of each other after being superpositioned. To improve accuracy of the final model, users can select the prediction servers from which to aggregate results.[1]

The Robetta automatic protein structure prediction server incorporates 3D-Jury into its prediction pipeline.[2]

References

[1] Ginalski K et al. (2003). "3D-Jury: a simple approach to improve protein structure predictions" (http://bioinformatics.oxfordjournals.org/cgi/reprint/19/8/1015). *Bioinformatics* **19** (8): 1015–1018. doi:10.1093/bioinformatics/btg124. PMID 12761065. .

[2] Chivian D et al. (2005). "Prediction of CASP6 structures using automated Robetta protocols" (http://www3.interscience.wiley.com/cgi-bin/fulltext/112097083/HTMLSTART). *Proteins* **61** (S7): 157–166. doi:10.1002/prot.20733. PMID 16187358. .

External links

- BioInfoBank Meta Server (http://meta.bioinfo.pl/submit_wizard.pl) 3D-Jury web interface

ABCD Schema

The **Access to Biological Collections Data (ABCD) schema** is a highly-structured data exchange and access model for taxon occurrence data (specimens, observations, etc. of living organisms), i.e. primary biodiversity data.

In 2006, the schema was extended, to include an 'Extension For Geosciences', to form the ABCDEFG Schema[1]

References

[1] http://www.geocase.eu/documentation/efg_schema.pdf

External links

- http://www.tdwg.org/activities/abcd/
- http://www.codata.org/
- http://www.wfcc.nig.ac.jp/NEWSLETTER/newsletter36/a6.pdf the ABCD database schema

ABCdb

ABCdb

Content	
Description	ABCdb database on ABC transporter systems in prokaryotic genomes.
Data types captured	ATP-binding Cassette (ABC) transporters
Organism(s)	prokaryotes
Contact	
Research center	University of Toulouse, CNRS
Laboratory	LMGM [1]
Primary Citation	PMID 16499625
Access	
Website	http://www-abcdb.biotoul.fr/
Tools	
Web	advanced search, BLAST
Miscellaneous	
Curation policy	yes - automatic and manual
Bookmarkable entities	yes

ABCdb is a database for the ATP-binding Cassette (ABC) transporters encoded by completely sequenced archaeal and (eu)bacterial genomes.

biological function of ABC systems

Most ABC systems function in the transport of a compound across a membrane into the cell (importer) or to the exterior (exporter), for which the system generates energy by the hydrolysis of adenosine triphosphate (ATP). The ABC transporters occur in all living organisms.

An ABC transporter system consist minimally of two components: an ATP binding cassette (ABC) and a TransMembrane domain (TMD) or Membrane Spanning Domain (MSD). These are usually separate proteins or can occur as protein domains. A typical ABC transporter is composed of two Nucleotide Binding Domains (NBD) that energize transport via ATP hydrolysis and of two Membrane Spanning Domains (MSD) that act as a membrane channel for the substrate. Importers require a Solute Binding Protein (SBP) that recognizes and binds the substrate.

The different partners of an ABC system are generally encoded by neighboring genes.

Features

The ABC proteins form a superfamily encoded by large families of paralogous genes. Sequence analysis shows that members of the ABC superfamily may have diverged from common ancestral forms and permits to organize ABC proteins into sub-families. The classification of ABC systems into (sub-)families can help to predict which substrates may be transported by the system.

ABCdb is a public resource[2] , from which one can:

- select a strain from the tree of species and view all its ABC systems, classified into (sub-)families.
- for a particular ABC (sub-)family, compare all the proteins of completely sequenced prokaryotes.
- use a sequence and blast it against ABCdb to find annotations for similar proteins

References

[1] http://www-lmgm.biotoul.fr/uk/index.html
[2] Fichant G, Basse MJ, Quentin Y (Mar 2006). "ABCdb: an online resource for ABC transporter repertories from sequenced archaeal and bacterial genomes". *FEMS Microbiol Lett.* **256(2)**: 333–9. doi:10.1111/j.1574-6968.2006.00139.x. PMID 16499625.

External link

- http://www-abcdb.biotoul.fr/ABCdb website

Accession number (bioinformatics)

An **accession number** in bioinformatics is a unique identifier given to a DNA or protein sequence record to allow for tracking of different versions of that sequence record and the associated sequence over time in a single data repository. Because of its relative stability, accession numbers can be utilized as foreign keys for referring to a sequence object, but not necessarily to a unique sequence. All sequence information repositories implement the concept of "accession number" but might do so with subtle variations.

Accession numbers in specific data resources

UniProt (SwissProt) Knowledgebase

In UniProt documentation, the stated role of the accession number is "to provide a stable way of identifying entries from release to release." One entry (or record) might be associated with multiple accession numbers. Thus, in UniProt, there is no specific relationship between accession number and sequence; the primary relationship is between accession number and knowledgebase record, and a single knowledgebase record can refer to multiple sequences. In the flat version of the data, **AC** is the field delimiter for the accession number, the first being the "primary accession number" and all subsequent values being "secondary accession numbers". The proper key field for tracking a UniProt record is the primary accession number. The group of accession numbers associated with a knowledgebase record depends on the history of the record with respect to mergers and splits. New accession numbers arise in two main ways: new sequences (common) and knowledgebase record splits (rare).[uniprot]

LRG

Locus Reference Genomic (LRG) records have unique accession numbers starting with LRG_ followed by a number. They are recommended in the Human Genome Variation Society Nomenclature guidelines [1] as stable genomic reference sequences to report sequence variants in LSDBs and the literature.

Commonly encountered accession numbers

- Uniprot ID [2]
- Unified Uniprot Accession
- Uniprot-Swissprot Accession [3]
- Uniprot-Swissprot ID [3]
- Unified Uniprot ID
- Refseq DNA ID [4]
- Entrez Gene ID [5]
- CCDS ID [6]
- Vega translation ID
- Vega Transcript ID [7]
- Vega Peptide ID [7]
- Vega Gene ID [7]
- HUGO ID [8]
- MIM ID [9]
- LRG ID [10]

Notes and references

1. Amos Bairoch, Rolf Apweiler, Cathy H. Wu. "User Manual" [11]. *UniProt Knowledgebase.* Retrieved October 20, 2005.
2. ⓔ *This article incorporates public domain material from the National Center for Biotechnology Information document "NCBI Handbook"* [12].

References

[1] http://www.hgvs.org/mutnomen/
[2] http://www.pir.uniprot.org/database/knowledgebase.shtml
[3] http://ca.expasy.org/
[4] http://www.ncbi.nlm.nih.gov/RefSeq/
[5] http://www.ncbi.nlm.nih.gov/entrez/query.fcgi?db=gene
[6] http://www.ncbi.nlm.nih.gov/CCDS/CcdsBrowse.cgi
[7] http://vega.sanger.ac.uk/index.html
[8] http://www.gene.ucl.ac.uk/cgi-bin/nomenclature/searchgenes.pl
[9] http://www.ncbi.nlm.nih.gov/entrez/query.fcgi?db=OMIM
[10] http://www.lrg-sequence.org
[11] http://www.expasy.org/sprot/userman.html#AC_line
[12] http://www.ncbi.nlm.nih.gov/books/bv.fcgi?call=bv.View..ShowTOC&rid=handbook.TOC&depth=2

Accomplishment by a Senior Scientist Award

The **Accomplishment by a Senior Scientist Award**[1] is an annual prize awarded by the International Society for Computational Biology for contributions to the field of computational biology.

Laureates

- 2011 - Michael Ashburner[2]
- 2010 - Chris Sander [3]
- 2009 - Webb Miller[4]
- 2008 - David Haussler[5]
- 2007 - Temple F. Smith[6]
- 2006 - Michael Waterman[7]
- 2005 - Janet Thornton[8]
- 2004 - David J. Lipman[9]
- 2003 - David Sankoff [10]

Sources

[1] http://www.iscb.org/iscb-awards/accomplishment-senior-scientist-award Accomplishment by a Senior Scientist Award

[2] Mullins, J.; Morrison Mckay, B. (2011). "International Society for Computational Biology Honors Michael Ashburner and Olga Troyanskaya with Top Bioinformatics/Computational Biology Awards for 2011". *PLoS Computational Biology* **7** (6): e1002081. doi:10.1371/journal.pcbi.1002081. PMC 3107244. PMID 21673867.

[3] http://www.mskcc.org/mskcc/html/11655.cfm

[4] Morrison Mckay, B. J.; Sansom, C. (2009). "Webb Miller and Trey Ideker to Receive Top International Bioinformatics Awards for 2009 from the International Society for Computational Biology". *PLoS Computational Biology* **5** (4): e1000375. doi:10.1371/journal.pcbi.1000375. PMC 2666155. PMID 19390599.

[5] Sansom, C.; Morrison Mckay, B. J. (2008). Bourne, Philip E.. ed. "ISCB Honors David Haussler and Aviv Regev". *PLoS Computational Biology* **4** (7): e1000101. doi:10.1371/journal.pcbi.1000101. PMC 2536508. PMID 18795145.

[6] Maisel, M. (2007). "ISCB Honors Temple F. Smith and Eran Segal". *PLoS Computational Biology* **3** (6): e128. Bibcode 2007PLSCB...3..128M. doi:10.1371/journal.pcbi.0030128. PMC 1904388. PMID 17604447.

[7] Maisel, M. (2006). "ISCB Honors Michael S. Waterman and Mathieu Blanchette". *PLoS Computational Biology* **2** (8): e105. Bibcode 2006PLSCB...2..105M. doi:10.1371/journal.pcbi.0020105. PMC 1526462.

[8] http://www.iscb.org/cms_addon/conferences/ismb2005/keynotes.html 2005 ISCB Senior Scientist Accomplishment Award: Janet Thorton, EMBL-EBI

[9] http://www.iscb.org/images/stories/newsletter/newsletter7-3/ssaa.html ISCB Names 2004 Senior Scientist Accomplishment Award Winner, Dr. David Lipman

[10] http://albuquerque.bioinformatics.uottawa.ca/bio.html

Syed I. Ahson

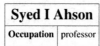

Syed I Ahson	
Occupation	professor

Syed I Ahson is a computer science professor, education management professional,[1] researcher, and author.[2] He specialises in multiple areas, including bioinformatics, computational biology,[3] and Web 2.0. Ahson graduated from University of Sheffield in the United Kingdom. He was a National Merit Scholarship Award, India (1959-1965). He also won a British Council Overseas Scholarship Award for Ph.D. (1973-1975). He later taught in Saudi Arabia and India. His recent posting was at Patna University, Bihar as pro-Vice chancellor. While there he enacted educational reforms amide political chaos and bureaucracy.[4]

Work

- Pro-Vice-Chancellor of Patna University, Bihar, India
- Professor of Computer Science, Jamia Millia Islamia, New Delhi, India (2001-2007).
- Professor, King Saud University, Riyadh, Saudi Arabia (1993-2000).
- Professor, Indian Institute of Technology, Delhi, India (1991-1992).
- Chairman and Professor, Computer Engineering Department, King Saud University, Riyadh, Saudi Arabia (1988-1990).
- Assistant Professor and Professor, Indian Institute of Technology, Delhi, India (1978-1987).
- Lecturer, Patna University, Bihar, India.

Books

- R. A. Khan, K. Mustafa and S. I. Ahson, "Software Quality Concepts and Practices", Narosa Publications, 2006 Alpha Science/Oxford 2007.
- S. I. Ahson, "Microprocessors", Tata McGraw-Hill, 1986.
- D.P.Kothari, A. K. Mahalanabis and S. I. Ahson, "Computer-Aided System Analysis and Design", Tata McGraw-Hill, 1988.
- S. I. Ahson (Editor-in-Chief), "Recent Advances in Servomechanisms Design and Realization in India", Indian Space Research Organization (ISRO), Bangalore, 1984.
- S.I.Ahson and R.Prasad, "Swachalit Niyantran Nikayon ke Siddhant",(Hindi),Madhya Pradesh Hindi Granth Academy,Bhopal,1980
- S.I.Ahson and S.M.Bhaskar, "Information Security-A Practical Approach", -Narosa Publications – 2008,Alpha Science/Oxford
- S.I.Ahson and Monica Mehrotra (Editors), "Proceedings of National Workshop on Software Security(NWSS-2007)", 13-14 Sept. 2007,I.K.International Publishing House Pvt Lmtd.,New Delhi

References

[1] "www.bbscindia.com/ScienceConference/profile.php" (http://www.bbscindia.com/ScienceConference/profile.php). .

[2] "www.allbookstores.com/Syed-A-Ahson/author" (http://www.allbookstores.com/Syed-A-Ahson/author). .

[3] "www.i-isc.com/advisoryboard.html" (http://www.i-isc.com/advisoryboard.html). .

[4] "articles.timesofindia.indiatimes.com/2010-05-06/patna/28302938_1_s-i-ahson-pu-pro-vc-patna-university" (http://articles.timesofindia. indiatimes.com/2010-05-06/patna/28302938_1_s-i-ahson-pu-pro-vc-patna-university). *The Times Of India*. .

Align-m

Align-m is a multiple sequence alignment program written by Ivo Van Walle.

Align-m has the ability to accomplish the following tasks:

- Multiple sequence alignment
- Include extra information to guide the sequence alignment
- Multiple structural alignment
- Homology modeling by (iteratively) combining sequence and structure alignment data
- 'Filtering' of BLAST or other pairwise alignments
- Combining many alignments into one consensus sequence
- Multiple genome alignment (can cope with rearrangements)

External links

- Official website [1]

References

[1] http://bioinformatics.vub.ac.be/software/software.html

ANOVA-simultaneous component analysis

ASCA, ANOVA-SCA, or **analysis of variance – simultaneous component analysis** is a method that partitions variation and enables interpretation of these partitions by SCA, a method that is similar to PCA. This method is a multi or even megavariate extension of ANOVA. The variation partitioning is similar to Analysis of variance (ANOVA). Each partition matches all variation induced by an effect or factor, usually a treatment regime or experimental condition. The calculated effect partitions are called effect estimates. Because even the effect estimates are multivariate, interpretation of these effects estimates is not intuitive. By applying SCA on the effect estimates one gets a simple interpretable result.[1] [2] [3] In case of more than one effect this method estimates the effects in such a way that the different effects are not correlated.

Details

Many research areas see increasingly large numbers of variables in only few samples. The low sample to variable ratio creates problems known as multicollinearity and singularity. Because of this, most traditional multivariate statistical methods cannot be applied.

ASCA algorithm

This section details how to calculate the ASCA model on a case of two main effects with one interaction effect. It is easy to extend the declared rationale to more main effects and more interaction effects. If the first effect is time and the second effect is dosage, only the interaction between time and dosage exist. We assume there are four time points and three dosage levels.

Let X be a matrix that holds the data. X is mean centered, thus having zero mean columns. Let A and B denote the main effects and AB the interaction of these effects. Two main effects in a biological experiment can be time (A) and pH (B), and these two effects may interact. In designing such experiments one controls the main effects to several (at least two) levels. The different levels of an effect can be referred to as A1, A2, A3 and A4, representing 2, 3, 4, 5 hours from the start of the experiment. The same thing holds for effect B, for example, pH 6, pH 7 and pH 8 can be considered effect levels.

A and B are required to be balanced if the effect estimates need to be orthogonal and the partitioning unique. Matrix E holds the information that is not assigned to any effect. The partitioning gives the following notation:

$$X = A + B + AB + E$$

Calculating main effect estimate A (or B)

Find all rows that correspond to effect A level 1 and averages these rows. The result is a vector. Repeat this for the other effect levels. Make a new matrix of the same size of X and place the calculated averages in the matching rows. That is, give all rows that match effect (i.e.) A level 1 the average of effect A level 1. After completing the level estimates for the effect, perform an SCA. The scores of this SCA are the sample deviations for the effect, the important variables of this effect are in the weights of the SCA loading vector.

Calculating interaction effect estimate AB

Estimating the interaction effect is similar to estimating main effects. The difference is that for interaction estimates the rows that match effect A level 1 are combined with the effect B level 1 and all combinations of effects and levels are cycled through. In our example setting, with four time point and three dosage levels there are 12 interaction sets {A1-B1, A1B2, A2B1, A2B2 and so on}. It is important to deflate (remove) the main effects before estimating the interaction effect.

SCA on partitions A, B and AB

Simultaneous component analysis is mathematically identical to PCA, but is semantically different in that it models different objects or subjects at the same time. The standard notation for a SCA – and PCA – model is:

$$X = TP' + E$$

where X is the data, T are the component scores and P are the component loadings. E is the residual or error matrix. Because ASCA models the variation partitions by SCA, the model for effect estimates looks like this:

$$A = T_a P'_a + E_a$$
$$B = T_b P'_b + E_b$$
$$AB = T_{ab} P'_{ab} + E_{ab}$$
$$E = T_e P'_e + E_e$$

Note that every partition has its own error matrix. However, algebra dictates that in a balanced mean centered data set every two level system is of rank one. This results in zero errors, since any rank 1 matrix can be written as the product of a single component score and loading vector.

The full ASCA model with two effects and interaction including the SCA looks like this:

Decomposition:

$$X = A + B + AB + E$$
$$X = T_a P'_a + T_b P'_b + T_{ab} P'_{ab} + T_e P'_e + E_a + E_b + E_{ab} + E_e + E$$

Time as an Effect

Because 'time' is treated as a qualitative factor in the ANOVA decomposition preceding ASCA, a nonlinear multivariate time trajectory can be modeled. An example of this is shown in Figure 10 of this reference.[4]

References

[1] Smilde1, Age K.; Jansen, Jeroen J.; Hoefsloot, Huub C. J.; Lamers, Robert-Jan A. N.; van der Greef, Jan; Timmerman, Marieke E. (2005) "ANOVA-simultaneous component analysis (ASCA): a new tool for analyzing designed metabolomics data", *Bioinformatics*, 21 (13), 3043-3048. doi:10.1093/bioinformatics/bti476

[2] Jansen, J. J.; Hoefsloot, H. C. J.; van der Greef, J.; Timmerman, M. E.; Westerhuis, J. A.;Smilde, A. K. (2005) "ASCA: analysis of multivariate data obtained from an experimental design". *Journal of Chemometrics*, 19: 469–481. doi:10.1002/cem.952

[3] Daniel J Vis , Johan A Westerhuis , Age K Smilde: Jan van der Greef (2007) "Statistical validation of megavariate effects in ASCA", *BMC Bioinformatics"* , 8:322 doi:10.1186/1471-2105-8-322

[4] Smilde, A. K., Hoefsloot, H. C. and Westerhuis, J. A. (2008), "The geometry of ASCA". *Journal of Chemometrics*, 22, 464–471. doi:10.1002/cem.1175

Archaeopteryx (evolutionary tree visualization and analysis)

Archaeopteryx

Developer(s)	Christian M. Zmasek
Stable release	0.901 beta / 2009.08.21
Operating system	Windows, Linux, Mac OS X
Type	Bioinformatics
License	LGPL
Website	www.phylosoft.org/archaeopteryx [1]

Archaeopteryx is an interactive computer software program, written in Java, for viewing, editing, and analyzing phylogenetic trees. This type of program can be used for a variety of analyses of molecular data sets, but is particularly designed for phylogenomics. Besides tree description formats with limited expressiveness (such as Newick/New Hamphshire, Nexus), ATV also implements the phyloXML[2] format. Archaeopteryx is the successor to the tree viewer ATV.[3]

References

[1] http://www.phylosoft.org/archaeopteryx

[2] Han, Mira V.; Zmasek, Christian M. (2009). "phyloXML: XML for evolutionary biology and comparative genomics" (http://www. biomedcentral.com/1471-2105/10/356). *BMC Bioinformatics* (United Kingdom: BioMed Central) **10**: 356. doi:10.1186/1471-2105-10-356. PMC 2774328. PMID 19860910. .

[3] Zmasek, Christian M.; Eddy, Sean R. (2001). "ATV: display and manipulation of annotated phylogenetic trees" (http://bioinformatics. oxfordjournals.org/cgi/reprint/17/4/383). *Bioinformatics* (United Kingdom: Oxford Journals) **17** (4): 383–384. doi:10.1093/bioinformatics/17.4.383. PMID 11301314. .

External links

- phyloXML (http://www.phyloxml.org)
- List of phylogeny software, hosted at the University of Washington (http://evolution.genetics.washington.edu/ phylip/software.html)
- Archaeopteryx (http://phylosoft.org/archaeopteryx/)

Arlequin

Arlequin is a free population genetics software. It performs several types of tests and calculations, including Fst, computing genetic distance, Hardy-Weinberg equilibrium, linkage disequilibrium, mismatch distribution, and pairwise difference tests.

It is currently in version 3.5 and is only available for Windows, though the previous version is still available for Windows, Mac OS X PPC, and Linux.

External links

- Official site [1]
- About [2]

References

[1] http://cmpg.unibe.ch/software/arlequin3/
[2] http://cmpg.unibe.ch/software/arlequin35/Arlequin35.html

ArrayTrack

ArrayTrack

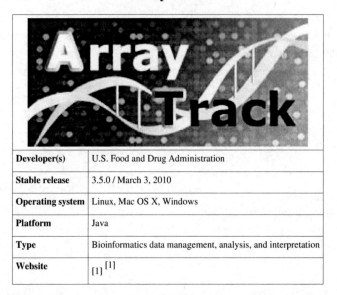

Developer(s)	U.S. Food and Drug Administration
Stable release	3.5.0 / March 3, 2010
Operating system	Linux, Mac OS X, Windows
Platform	Java
Type	Bioinformatics data management, analysis, and interpretation
Website	[1] [1]

ArrayTrack is a multi-purpose bioinformatics tool primarily used for microarray data management, analysis, and interpretation. ArrayTrack was developed to support in-house filter array research for the U.S. Food and Drug Administration in 2001 and was made freely available to the public as an integrated research tool for microarrays in 2003.[2] Since then, ArrayTrack has averaged about 5,000 users per year. It is regularly updated by the National Center for Toxicological Research.

Features

ArrayTrack is composed of three major components: Study Database, Tools, and Libraries, which primarily handle data management, analysis, and interpretation, respectively. Each of these components can be directly accessed from the other two, e.g., analysis Tools can be used directly on experimental data stored in the Study Database, and significant genes discovered from the results can be queried in the Libraries to view additional annotations and associated proteins, pathways, Gene Ontology terms, etc.[3]

- **Study Database:** The Study Database contains user-imported experiment data, including both raw data and annotation data. It is mainly used to manage microarray data, but also supports proteomics and metabolomics data. Imported data are initially private to the owner but can be made available to other users. The Study Database also stores significant gene lists, which can be created directly from data analysis results in ArrayTrack.
- **Tools:** A wide variety of analysis and visualization Tools are available in ArrayTrack, including but are not limited to: statistical analysis Tools including T-Test, ANOVA, and SAM-Test; unsupervised pattern discovery Tools including Hierarchical Clustering Analysis and Principal Component Analysis; and model prediction Tools including K-Nearest Neighbors and Linear Discriminant Analysis. Although ArrayTrack's Tools are designed to accommodate imported data, they are also compatible with external data.
- **Libraries:** ArrayTrack hosts a collection of Libraries which store specific annotation data, viewable in a dynamic spreadsheet format. There is a Library specific for genes, proteins, pathways, Gene Ontology terms, chemical compounds, SNPs, QTL, chip types, and more. Each Library supports multi-input searching, sorting, filtering, copy-pasting, and exporting. Libraries can be directly queried for the desired contents of stored gene lists, analysis results, and other Libraries. A specific entry in any Library can be linked to the equivalent entry in many

popular public knowledge bases, including the original sources of data.

ArrayTrack is directly integrated with a variety of other bioinformatics software, such as pathway analysis tools GeneGo MetaCore and Ingenuity Pathway Analysis.[4] [5]

Accessibility

ArrayTrack is freely available to the public and can be accessed online. It is run on the client's computer using a Java-based interface that connects to an Oracle database hosted by the FDA. As a Java-based application, ArrayTrack is compatible with Windows, Mac, and Linux machines.

References

[1] http://www.fda.gov/ScienceResearch/BioinformaticsTools/Arraytrack/
[2] Weida Tong, Xiaoxi Cao, Stephen Harris, Hongmei Sun, Hong Fang, James Fuscoe, Angela Harris, Huixiao Hong, Qian Xie, Roger Perkins, Leming Shi, and Dan Casciano. ArrayTrack—supporting toxicogenomic research at the U.S. Food and Drug Administration National Center for Toxicological Research (http://www.ncbi.nlm.nih.gov/pmc/articles/PMC1241745/). Environmental Health Perspectives. 2003 November; 111(15): 1819–1826.
[3] Fang H, Harris SC, Su Z, Chen M, Qian F, Shi L, Perkins R, Tong W ArrayTrack: an FDA and public genomic tool (http://www.ncbi.nlm.nih.gov/pubmed/19597796). Methods in Molecular Biology. 2009;563:379-98.
[4] "The U.S. Food and Drug Administration will use GeneGo's Metacore for "omics" research and reviewing of genomics data." (http://www.genego.com/pdf/FDA_Oct_05.pdf) (PDF). . Retrieved 2011-04-13.
[5] "The U.S. Food and Drug Administration to use Ingenuity Pathway Analysis in review of Pharmacogenomics Submissions." (http://www.ingenuity.com/news/pdf/IngenuityFDARelease6.21.05.pdf) (PDF). . Retrieved 2011-04-13.

External links

* ArrayTrack main page (http://www.fda.gov/ScienceResearch/BioinformaticsTools/Arraytrack/default.htm)

Astrid Research

Astrid Research Inc.

Type	Privately held company
Industry	Bioinformatics Software
Headquarters	Debrecen, Hungary
Area served	Worldwide
Products	GenoMiner, GenoViewer
Website	Astrid Research Inc. [1]

Astrid Research Inc. is a bioinformatics company that provides software products and services for genome research, including Microarray, Sanger and next generation sequencing as well as 3rd generation sequencing.

History

Astrid Research was incorporated in 2004.

Products

• **GenoMiner** is high-performance IT platform for next generation sequencing data analysis.

Services

• **NGS data analysis** for all sequencing platforms.

References

[1] http://www.astrid.hu

External links

• Official site (http://www.astrid.hu)

Aureus Sciences

Aureus Sciences

Type	Private
Industry	Life Sciences Pharmacokinetic modelling & simulation
Founded	Paris, France (2000)
Website	www.aureus-sciences.com [1]

Aureus Sciences is a research-based company which provides solutions to the pharmaceutical industry for drug development.

The company's range of products includes therapeutic target knowledgebases, ADME-based databases and software applications.

Aureus Sciences was formerly known as Aureus Pharma.[2]

Products

Aureus' software applications allow *in silico* prediction of drug absorption, distribution, metabolism and excretion (ADME) and potential drug-drug interactions.

- Knowledgebases : AurSCOPE Kinases, GPCR, Ion Channels, Proteases, Nuclear Receptors, ADME.[3]
- Applications : AurQUEST, DDI Predict, AurPROFILER, AurPASS.[4]

The scientific background to Aureus' process is detailed in recent publications.[5] [6]

References

[1] http://www.aureus-sciences.com/

[2] "Aureus Pharma changes its name to Aureus Sciences ® and launches a new, comprehensive life science applications webportal" (http://www.aureus-sciences.com/aureus/web/guest/news-events?p_p_id=latest_news&p_p_lifecycle=0&p_p_state=normal&p_p_mode=view&p_p_col_id=content_primary&p_p_col_count=1&_latest_news_struts_action=/ext/latest_news/view_content&_latest_news_assetId=48043&_latest_news_returnToFullPageURL=/aureus/web/guest/news-events?p_p_id=latest_news&p_p_lifecycle=0&p_p_state=normal&p_p_mode=view&p_p_col_id=content_primary&p_p_col_count=1&_latest_news_delta=6&_latest_news_keywords=&_latest_news_advancedSearch=false&_latest_news_andOperator=true&cur=4) (press release). Aureus Sciences. 2011-01-20. .

[3] Aureus knowledgebases (http://www.aureus-sciences.com/aureus/web/guest/databases)

[4] Aureus applications (http://www.aureus-sciences.com/aureus/web/guest/applications)

[5] Faure P, Dubus E, Ijjaali I, Morlière C, Barberan O, Petitet F (December 2010). "Knowledge-based analysis of multi-potent G-protein coupled receptors ligands" (http://www.sciencedirect.com/science/article/pii/S0223523410006756). *Eur. J. Med. Chem.* **45** (12): 5708–5717. doi:10.1016/j.ejmech.2010.09.027. PMID 20933307. .

[6] Dubus E, Ijjaali I, Barberan O, Petitet F (December 2009). "Drug repositioning using in silico compound profiling.". *Future Med. Chem.* **1** (9): 1723–36. PMID 21425988.

External links

- Aureus Sciences web portal (http://www.aureus-sciences.com/)

Automated species identification

Automated species identification is a method of making the expertise of taxonomists available to ecologists, parataxonomists and others via computers, PDA's and other digital technology.

Introduction

The **automated identification** of biological objects such as insects (individuals) and/or groups (e.g., species, guilds, characters) has been a dream among systematists for centuries. The goal of some of the first multivariate biometric methods was to address the perennial problem of group discrimination and inter-group characterization. Despite much preliminary work in the 1950s and '60s, progress in designing and implementing practical systems for fully automated object biological identification has proven frustratingly slow. As recently as 2004 Dan Janzen updated the dream for a new audience:

> The spaceship lands. He steps out. He points it around. It says 'friendly–unfriendly—edible–poisonous—safe– dangerous—living–inanimate'. On the next sweep it says '*Quercus oleoides—Homo sapiens—Spondias mombin—Solanum nigrum—Crotalus durissus—Morpho peleides*— serpentine'. This has been in my head since reading science fiction in ninth grade half a century ago.

The species identification problem

Janzen's preferred solution to this classic problem involved building machines to identify species from their DNA. His predicted budget and proposed research team is "US$1 million and five bright people." However, recent developments in computer architectures, as well as innovations in software design, have placed the tools needed to realize Janzen's vision in the hands of the systematics community not in several years hence, but now; and not just for DNA barcodes, but for digital images of organisms too. A recent survey of results accuracy results for small-scale trials (<50 taxa) obtained by such systems shows an average reproducible accuracy of over 85 percent with no significant correlation between accuracy and the number of included taxa or the type of group being assessed (e.g., butterflies, moths, bees, pollen, spores, foraminifera, dinoflagellates, vertebrates).[1] Moreover, these identifications, often involving thousands of individual specimens, can be made in a fraction of the time required by human experts and can be done on site, on demand, anywhere in the world.

These developments could not have come at a better time. As the taxonomic community already knows, the world is running out of specialists who can identify the very biodiversity whose preservation has become a global concern. In commenting on this problem in palaeontology as long ago as 1993, Roger Kaesler recognized:

> "... we are running out of systematic palaeontologists who have anything approaching synoptic knowledge of a major group of organisms ... Palaeontologists of the next century are unlikely to have the luxury of dealing at length with taxonomic problems ... Palaeontology will have to sustain its level of excitement without the aid of systematists, who have contributed so much to its success."

This expertise deficiency cuts as deeply into those commercial industries that rely on accurate identifications (e.g., agriculture, biostratigraphy) as it does into a wide range of pure and applied research programmes (e.g., conservation, biological oceanography, climatology, ecology). It is also commonly, though informally, acknowledged that the technical, taxonomic literature of all organismal groups is littered with examples of inconsistent and incorrect identifications. This is due to a variety of factors, including taxonomists being insufficiently trained and skilled in making identifications (e.g., using different rules-of-thumb in recognizing the boundaries between similar groups), insufficiently detailed original group descriptions and/or illustrations, inadequate access to current monographs and well-curated collections and, of course, taxonomists having different opinions regarding group concepts. Peer review only weeds out the most obvious errors of commission or omission in this area, and then only when an author provides adequate representations (e.g., illustrations, recordings, gene sequences) of the specimens in question.

Systematics too has much to gain, both practically and theoretically, from the further development and use of automated identification systems. It is now widely recognized that the days of systematics as a field populated by mildly eccentric individuals pursuing knowledge in splendid isolation from funding priorities and economic imperatives are rapidly drawing to a close. In order to attract both personnel and resources, systematics must transform itself into a "large, coordinated, international scientific enterprise" [2] Many have identified use of the Internet— especially via the World Wide Web — as the medium through which this transformation can be made. While establishment of a virtual, GenBank-like system for accessing morphological data, audio clips, video files and so forth would be a significant step in the right direction, improved access to observational information and/or text-based descriptions alone will not address either the taxonomic impediment or low identification reproducibility issues successfully. Instead, the inevitable subjectivity associated with making critical decisions on the basis of qualitative criteria must be reduced or, at the very least, embedded within a more formally analytic context.

Properly designed, flexible, and robust, automated identification systems, organized around distributed computing architectures and referenced to authoritatively identified collections of training set data (e.g., images, gene sequences) can, in principle, provide all systematists with access to the electronic data archives and the necessary analytic tools to handle routine identifications of common taxa. Properly designed systems can also recognize when their algorithms cannot make a reliable identification and refer that image to a specialist (whose address can be accessed from another database). Such systems can also include elements of artificial intelligence and so improve their performance the more they are used. Most tantalizingly, once morphological (or molecular) models of a species have been developed and demonstrated to be accurate, these models can be queried to determine which aspects of the observed patterns of variation and variation limits are being used to achieve the identification, thus opening the way for the discovery of new and (potentially) more reliable taxonomic characters.

References cited

[1] Gaston, Kevin J.; O'Neill, Mark A. (March 22, 2004). "Automated species recognition: why not?". *Philosophical Transactions of the Royal Society of London*. B **359**: 655–667. doi:10.1098/rstb.2003.1442.

[2] Wheeler, Quentin D. (2003) (PDF). *Transforming taxonomy* (http://www.systass.org/newsletter/newsletter1203.pdf). The Systematist. pp. 3–5. .

• Janzen, Daniel H. (2004). "Now is the time". *Philosophical Transactions of the Royal Society of London*. B (359): 731–732. doi:10.1098/rstb.2003.1444.

• Kaesler, Roger L (1993). "A window of opportunity: peering into a new century of palaeontology". *Journal of Palaeontology* **67** (3): 329–333. JSTOR 1306022.

External links

Here are some links to the home pages of species identification systems. While all were initially designed to identify specious invertebrate groups, the **SPIDA** and **DAISY** system are essentially generic and capable of classifying any image material presented. The **ABIS** and **DrawWing** system are restricted to insects with membranous wings as it operates by matching a specific set of characters based on wing venation.

• The SPIDA system (http://research.amnh.org/invertzoo/spida/common/index.htm)
• ABIS (http://www.informatik.uni-bonn.de/projects/ABIS)
• DAISY (http://www.tumblingdice.co.uk/daisy)
• DrawWing (http://drawwing.org)

Bayesian inference in phylogeny

Bayesian inference in phylogeny generates a posterior distribution for a parameter, composed of a phylogenetic tree and a model of evolution, based on the prior for that parameter and the likelihood of the data, generated by a multiple alignment. The Bayesian approach has become more popular due to advances in computational machinery, especially, Markov chain Monte Carlo algorithms. Bayesian inference has a number of applications in molecular phylogenetics, for example, estimation of species phylogeny and species divergence times.

Basic Bayesian theory

Recall that for Bayesian inference:

$$p(\theta|D) = \frac{p(D|\theta)p(\theta)}{p(D)}$$

The denominator $p(D)$ is the *marginal probability of the data*, averaged over all possible parameter values weighted by their prior distribution. Formally,

$$p(D) = \int_\Theta p(D|\theta)p(\theta)d\theta$$

where Θ is the parameter space for θ.

In the original Metropolis algorithm, given a current θ-value x, and a new θ-value y, the new value is accepted with probability:

$$h(y)/h(x) = \frac{p(D|y)p(y)}{p(D|x)p(x)}$$

The LOCAL algorithm of Larget and Simon

The LOCAL algorithm begins by selecting an internal branch of the tree at random. The nodes at the ends of this branch are each connected to two other branches. One of each pair is chosen at random. Imagine taking these three selected edges and stringing them like a clothesline from left to right, where the direction (left/right) is also selected at random. The two endpoints of the first branch selected will have a sub-tree hanging like a piece of clothing strung to the line. The algorithm proceeds by multiplying the three selected branches by a common random amount, akin to stretching or shrinking the clothesline. Finally the leftmost of the two hanging sub-trees is disconnected and reattached to the clothesline at a location selected uniformly at random. *This is the candidate tree.*

Suppose we began by selecting the internal branch with length t_8 (in Figure (a) (to be added)) that separates taxa A and B from the rest. Suppose also that we have (randomly) selected branches with lengths t_1 and t_9 from each side, and that we oriented these branches as shown in Figure(b). Let $m = t_1 + t_8 + t_9$, be the current length of the clothesline. We select the new length to be $m^\star = m \exp(\lambda(U_1 - 0.5))$, where U_1 is a uniform random variable on $(0, 1)$. Then for the LOCAL algorithm, the acceptance probability can be computed to be:

$$\frac{h(y)}{h(x)} \times \frac{m^{\star 3}}{m^3}$$

Assessing convergence

Suppose we want to estimate a branch length of a 2-taxon tree under JC, in which n_1 sites are unvaried and n_2 are variable. Assume exponential prior distribution with rate λ. The density is $p(t) = \lambda e^{-\lambda t}$. The probabilities of the possible site patterns are:

$$1/4 \left(1/4 + 3/4 e^{-4/3t} \right)$$

for unvaried sites, and

$$1/4 \left(1/4 - 1/4 e^{-4/3t} \right)$$

Thus the unnormalized posterior distribution is:

$$h(t) = (1/4)^{n_1+n_2} \left(1/4 + 3/4 e^{-4/3t^{n_1}} \right)$$

or, alternately,

$$h(t) = \left(1/4 - 1/4 e^{-4/3t^{n_2}} \right) \left(\lambda e^{-\lambda t} \right)$$

Update branch length by choosing new value uniformly at random from a window of half-width w centered at the current value:

$$t^{\star} = |t + U|$$

where U is uniformly distributed between $-w$ and w. The acceptance probability is:

$$h(t^{\star})/h(t)$$

Example: $n_1 = 70$, $n_2 = 30$. We will compare results for two values of w, $w = 0.1$ and $w = 0.5$. In each case, we will begin with an initial length of 5 and update the length 2000 times. (See Figure 3.2 (to be added) for results.)

Metropolis-coupled MCMC (Geyer)

If the target distribution has multiple peaks, separated by low valleys, the Markov chain may have difficulty in moving from one peak to another. As a result, the chain may get stuck on one peak and the resulting samples will not approximate the posterior density correctly. This is a serious practical concern for phylogeny reconstruction, as multiple local peaks are known to exist in the tree space during heuristic tree search under maximum parsimony (MP), maximum likelihood (ML), and minimum evolution (ME) criteria, and the same can be expected for stochastic tree search using MCMC. Many strategies have been proposed to improve mixing of Markov chains in presence of multiple local peaks in the posterior density. One of the most successful algorithms is the Metropolis-coupled MCMC (or MC^3).

In this algorithm, m chains are run in parallel, with different stationary distributions $\pi_j(.)$, $j = 1, 2, \ldots, m$, where the first one, $\pi_1 = \pi$ is the target density, while π_j, $j = 2, 3, \ldots, m$ are chosen to improve mixing. For example, one can choose incremental heating of the form:

$$\pi_j(\theta) = \pi(\theta)^{1/[1+\lambda(j-1)]}, \quad \lambda > 0,$$

so that the first chain is the cold chain with the correct target density, while chains $2, 3, \ldots, m$ are heated chains. Note that raising the density $\pi(.)$ to the power $1/T$ with $T > 1$ has the effect of flattening out the distribution, similar to heating a metal. In such a distribution, it is easier to traverse between peaks (separated by valleys) than in the original distribution. After each iteration, a swap of states between two randomly chosen chains is proposed through a Metropolis-type step. Let $\theta^{(j)}$ be the current state in chain j, $j = 1, 2, \ldots, m$. A swap between the states of chains i and j is accepted with probability:

$$\alpha = \frac{\pi_i(\theta^{(j)})\pi_j(\theta^{(i)})}{\pi_i(\theta^{(i)})\pi_j(\theta^{(j)})}$$

At the end of the run, output from only the cold chain is used, while those from the hot chains are discarded. Heuristically, the hot chains will visit the local peaks rather easily, and swapping states between chains will let the cold chain occasionally jump valleys, leading to better mixing. However, if $\pi_i(\theta)/\pi_j(\theta)$ is unstable, proposed swaps will seldom be accepted. This is the reason for using several chains which differ only incrementally. (See Figure3.3 (to be added)).

An obvious disadvantage of the algorithm is that m chains are run and only one chain is used for inference. For this reason, MC^3 is ideally suited for implementation on parallel machines, since each chain will in general require the same amount of computation per iteration.

References

- Geyer, C.J. (1991) Markov chain Monte Carlo maximum likelihood. In *Computing Science and Statistics: Proceedings of the 23rd Symposium of the Interface* (ed. E.M. Keramidas), pp. 156–163. Interface Foundation, Fairfax Station, VA.
- Yang, Z. and B. Rannala. (1997) Bayesian phylogenetic inference using DNA sequences: A Markov chain Monte Carlo method. *Molecular Biology and Evolution*, **14**, 717–724.
- Larget, B. and D.L. Simon. (1999) Markov chain Monte Carlo algorithms for the Bayesian analysis of phylogenetic trees. *Molecular Biology and Evolution*, **16**, 750–759.
- Huelsenbeck, J.P. and F. Ronquist. (2001) MrBayes: Bayesian inference in phylogenetic trees. *Bioinformatics*, **17**, 754–755.
- Ronquist, F. and J.P. Huelsenbeck. (2003) MrBayes3: Bayesian phylogenetic inference under mixed models. *Bioinformatics*, **19**, 1572–1574.
- Rannala, B. and Z. Yang. (2003) Bayes estimation of species divergence times and ancestral population sizes using DNA sequences from multiple loci. *Genetics*, **164**, 1645–1656.

Benjamin Franklin Award (Bioinformatics)

The **Benjamin Franklin Award** is an award for Open Access in the Life Sciences presented by the Bioinformatics Organization[1]

Laureates

- 2002 - Michael B. Eisen
- 2003 - Jim Kent
- 2004 - Lincoln D. Stein
- 2005 - Ewan Birney
- 2006 - Michael Ashburner
- 2007 - Sean Eddy
- 2008 - Robert Gentleman
- 2009 - Philip E. Bourne
- 2010 - Alex Bateman
- 2011 - Jonathan Eisen

Sources

[1] (http://www.bioinformatics.org/franklin/)

Biclustering

Biclustering, **co-clustering**, or **two-mode clustering**[1] is a data mining technique which allows simultaneous clustering of the rows and columns of a matrix. The term was first introduced by Mirkin[2] (recently by Cheng and Church[3] in gene expression analysis), although the technique was originally introduced much earlier[2] (i.e., by J.A. Hartigan[4]).

Given a set of m rows in n columns (i.e., an $m \times n$ matrix), the biclustering algorithm generates biclusters - a subset of rows which exhibit similar behavior across a subset of columns, or vice versa.

Complexity

The complexity of the biclustering problem depends on the exact problem formulation, and particularly on the merit function used to evaluate the quality of a given bicluster. However most interesting variants of this problem are NP-complete requiring either large computational effort or the use of lossy heuristics to short-circuit the calculation.[]

Type of Bicluster

Different biclustering algorithms have different definitions of bicluster. [5]

They are:

1. Bicluster with constant values (a),
2. Bicluster with constant values on rows (b) or columns (c),
3. Bicluster with coherent values (d, e).

2.0	2.0	2.0	2.0	2.0
2.0	2.0	2.0	2.0	2.0
2.0	2.0	2.0	2.0	2.0
2.0	2.0	2.0	2.0	2.0
2.0	2.0	2.0	2.0	2.0

1.0	1.0	1.0	1.0	1.0
2.0	2.0	2.0	2.0	2.0
3.0	3.0	3.0	3.0	3.0
4.0	4.0	4.0	4.0	4.0
4.0	4.0	4.0	4.0	4.0

1.0	2.0	3.0	4.0	5.0
1.0	2.0	3.0	4.0	5.0
1.0	2.0	3.0	4.0	5.0
1.0	2.0	3.0	4.0	5.0
1.0	2.0	3.0	4.0	5.0

1.0	4.0	5.0	0.0	1.5
4.0	7.0	8.0	3.0	4.5
3.0	6.0	7.0	2.0	3.5
5.0	8.0	9.0	4.0	5.5
2.0	5.0	6.0	1.0	2.5

1.0	0.5	2.0	0.2	0.8
2.0	1.0	4.0	0.4	1.6
3.0	1.5	6.0	0.6	2.4
4.0	2.0	8.0	0.8	3.2
5.0	2.5	10.0	1.0	4.0

The relationship between these cluster models and other types of clustering such as correlation clustering is discussed in.[6]

Algorithms

There are many biclustering algorithms developed for bioinformatics, including: block clustering, CTWC (Coupled Two-Way Clustering), ITWC (Interrelated Two-Way Clustering), δ-bicluster, δ-pCluster, δ-pattern, FLOC, OPC, Plaid Model, OPSMs (Order-preserving submatrixes), Gibbs, SAMBA (Statistical-Algorithmic Method for Bicluster Analysis),[7] , Robust Biclustering Algorithm (RoBA), Crossing Minimization [8] , cMonkey,[9] PRMs, DCC, LEB (Localize and Extract Biclusters), QUBIC (QUalitative BIClustering), BCCA (Bi-Correlation Clustering Algorithm) and FABIA (Factor Analysis for Bicluster Acquisition).[10] Biclustering algorithms have also been proposed and used in other application fields under the names coclustering, bidimentional clustering, and subspace clustering.[]

Given the known importance of discovering local patterns in time series data, recent proposals have addressed the biclustering problem in the specific case of time series gene expression data. In this case, the interesting biclusters can be restricted to those with contiguous columns. This restriction leads to a tractable problem and enables the development of efficient exaustive enumeration algorithms such as CCC-Biclustering [11] and e-CCC-Biclustering [12] . These algorithms find and report all maximal biclusters with coherent and contiguous columns with perfect/approximate expression patterns, in time linear/polynomial in the size of the time series gene expression matrix using efficient string processing techniques based on suffix trees.

Some recent algorithms have attempted to include additional support for biclustering rectangular matrices in the form of other datatypes, including cMonkey.

There is an ongoing debate about how to judge the results of these methods, as biclustering allows overlap between clusters and some algorithms allow the exclusion of hard-to-reconcile columns/conditions. Not all of the available algorithms are deterministic and the analyst must pay attention to the degree to which results represent stable minima. Because this is an unsupervised-classification problem, the lack of a gold standard makes it difficult to spot errors in the results. One approach is to utilize multiple biclustering algorithms, with majority or super-majority voting amongst them deciding the best result. Another way is to analyse the quality of shifting and scaling patterns in biclusters.[13] Biclustering has been used in the domain of text mining (or classification) where it is popularly known as co-clustering .[14] Text corpora are represented in a vectorial form as a matrix D whose rows denote the documents and whose columns denote the words in the dictionary. Matrix elements D_{ij} denote occurrence of word j in document i. Co-clustering algorithms are then applied to discover blocks in D that correspond to a group of documents (rows) characterized by a group of words(columns).

Several approaches have been proposed based on the information contents of the resulting blocks: matrix-based approaches such as SVD and BVD, and graph-based approaches. Information-theoretic algorithms iteratively assign each row to a cluster of documents and each column to a cluster of words such that the mutual information is maximized. Matrix-based methods focus on the decomposition of matrices into blocks such that the error between the original matrix and the regenerated matrices from the decomposition is minimized. Graph-based methods tend to minimize the cuts between the clusters. Given two groups of documents d_1 and d_2, the number of cuts can be measured as the number of words that occur in documents of groups d_1 and d_2.

More recently (Bisson and Hussain)[14] have proposed a new approach of using the similarity between words and the similarity between documents to co-cluster the matrix. Their method (known as **χ-Sim**, for cross similarity) is based on finding document-document similarity and word-word similarity, and then using classical clustering methods such as hierarchical clustering. Instead of explicitly clustering rows and columns alternately, they consider higher-order occurrences of words, inherently taking into account the documents in which they occur. Thus, the similarity between two words is calculated based on the documents in which they occur and also the documents in which "similar" words occur. The idea here is that two documents about the same topic do not necessarily use the same set of words to describe it but a subset of the words and other similar words that are characteristic of that topic. This approach of taking higher-order similarities takes the latent semantic structure of the whole corpus into consideration with the result of generating a better clustering of the documents and words.

In contrast to other approaches, FABIA is a multiplicative model that assumes realistic non-Gaussian signal distributions with heavy tails. FABIA utilizes well understood model selection techniques like variational approaches and applies the Bayesian framework. The generative framework allows FABIA to determine the information content of each bicluster to separate spurious biclusters from true biclusters.

References

[1] Van Mechelen I, Bock HH, De Boeck P (2004). "Two-mode clustering methods:a structured overview". *Statistical Methods in Medical Research* **13** (5): 363–94. doi:10.1191/0962280204sm373ra. PMID 15516031.

[2] Mirkin, Boris (1996). *Mathematical Classification and Clustering*. Kluwer Academic Publishers. ISBN 0792341597.

[3] Cheng Y, Church GM (2000). "Biclustering of expression data". *Proceedings of the 8th International Conference on Intelligent Systems for Molecular Biology*: 93–103.

[4] Hartigan JA (1972). "Direct clustering of a data matrix". *Journal of the American Statistical Association* (American Statistical Association) **67** (337): 123–9. doi:10.2307/2284710. JSTOR 2284710.

[5] Madeira SC, Oliveira AL (2004). "Biclustering Algorithms for Biological Data Analysis: A Survey". *IEEE Transactions on Computational Biology and Bioinformatics* **1** (1): 24–45. doi:10.1109/TCBB.2004.2. PMID 17048406.

[6] Kriegel, H.-P.; Kröger, P., Zimek, A. (March 2009). "Clustering High Dimensional Data: A Survey on Subspace Clustering, Pattern-based Clustering, and Correlation Clustering" (http://doi.acm.org/10.1145/1497577.1497578). *ACM Transactions on Knowledge Discovery from Data (TKDD)* **3** (1): 1–58. doi:10.1145/1497577.1497578. .

[7] Tanay A, Sharan R, Kupiec M and Shamir R (2004). "Revealing modularity and organization in the yeast molecular network by integrated analysis of highly heterogeneous genomewide data". *Proc Natl Acad Sci USA* **101** (9): 2981–2986. doi:10.1073/pnas.0308661100. PMC 365731. PMID 14973197.

[8] Abdullah, Ahsan; Hussain, Amir (2006). "A new biclustering technique based on crossing minimization" (http://linkinghub.elsevier.com/retrieve/pii/S0925231206001615). *Neurocomputing, vol. 69 issue 16-18* **69** (16–18): 1882–1896. doi:10.1016/j.neucom.2006.02.018. .

[9] Reiss DJ, Baliga NS, Bonneau R (2006). "Integrated biclustering of heterogeneous genome-wide datasets for the inference of global regulatory networks". *BMC Bioinformatics* **2**: 280–302. doi:10.1186/1471-2105-7-280. PMC 1502140. PMID 16749936.

[10] Hochreiter S, Bodenhofer U, Heusel M, Mayr A, Mitterecker A, Kasim A, Khamiakova T, Van Sanden S, Lin D, Talloen W, Bijnens L, Gohlmann HWH, Shkedy Z, Clevert DA (2010). "FABIA: factor analysis for bicluster acquisition". *Bioinformatics* **26** (12): 1520–1527. doi:10.1093/bioinformatics/btq227. PMC 2881408. PMID 20418340.

[11] Madeira SC, Teixeira MC, Sá-Correia I, Oliveira AL (2010). "Identification of Regulatory Modules in Time Series Gene Expression Data using a Linear Time Biclustering Algorithm". *IEEE Transactions on Computational Biology and Bioinformatics* **1** (7): 153–165. doi:10.1109/TCBB.2008.34.

[12] Madeira SC, Oliveira AL (2009). "A polynomial time biclustering algorithm for finding approximate expression patterns in gene expression time series". *Algorithms for Molecular Biology* **4** (8).

[13]   Aguilar-Ruiz JS (2005). "Shifting and scaling patterns from gene expression data". *Bioinformatics* **21** (10): 3840–3845.
      doi:10.1093/bioinformatics/bti641. PMID 16144809.

[14]   Bission G. and Hussain F. (2008). "Chi-Sim: A new similarity measure for the co-clustering task". *ICMLA*: 211–217.
      doi:10.1109/ICMLA.2008.103.

Others

- A. Tanay. R. Sharan, and R. Shamir, "Biclustering Algorithms: A Survey", In *Handbook of Computational Molecular Biology*, Edited by Srinivas Aluru, Chapman (2004)
- Kluger Y, Basri R, Chang JT, Gerstein MB (2003). "Spectral Biclustering of Microarray Data: Coclustering Genes and Conditions". *Genome Research* **13** (4): 703–716. doi:10.1101/gr.648603. PMC 430175. PMID 12671006.

External links

- FABIA: Factor Analysis for Bicluster Acquisition, an R package (http://www.bioinf.jku.at/software/fabia/fabia.html) —software

Biochip

The development of **biochips** is a major thrust of the rapidly growing biotechnology industry, which encompasses a very diverse range of research efforts including genomics, proteomics, and pharmaceuticals, among other activities. Advances in these areas are giving scientists new methods for unravelling the complex biochemical processes occurring inside cells, with the larger goal of understanding and treating human diseases. At the same time, the semiconductor industry has been steadily perfecting the science of micro-miniaturization. The merging of these two fields in recent years has enabled biotechnologists to begin packing their traditionally bulky sensing

Hundreds of gel drops are visible on the biochip

tools into smaller and smaller spaces, onto so-called biochips. These chips are essentially miniaturized laboratories that can perform hundreds or thousands of simultaneous biochemical reactions. Biochips enable researchers to quickly screen large numbers of biological analytes for a variety of purposes, from disease diagnosis to detection of bioterrorism agents.

History

The development of bioc has a long history, starting with early work on the underlying sensor technology. One of the first portable, chemistry-based sensors was the glass pH electrode, invented in 1922 by Hughes (Hughes, 1922). Measurement of pH was accomplished by detecting the potential difference developed across a thin glass membrane selective to the permeation of hydrogen ions; this selectivity was achieved by exchanges between H^+ and SiO sites in the glass. The basic concept of using exchange sites to create permselective membranes was used to develop other ion sensors in subsequent years. For example, a K^+ sensor was produced by incorporating valinomycin into a thin membrane (Schultz, 1996). Over thirty years elapsed before the first true biosensor (*i.e.* a sensor utilizing biological molecules) emerged. In 1956, Leland Clark published a paper on an oxygen sensing electrode (Clark, 1956_41). This device became the basis for a glucose sensor developed in 1962 by Clark and colleague Lyons which utilized glucose oxidase molecules embedded in a dialysis membrane (Clark, 1962). The enzyme functioned in the presence of glucose to decrease the amount of oxygen available to the oxygen electrode, thereby relating oxygen levels to glucose concentration. This and similar biosensors became known as enzyme electrodes, and are still in use today.

In 1953, Watson and Crick announced their discovery of the now familiar double helix structure of DNA molecules and set the stage for genetics research that continues to the present day (Nelson, 2000). The development of sequencing techniques in 1977 by Gilbert (Maxam, 1977) and Sanger (Sanger, 1977) (working separately) enabled researchers to directly read the genetic codes that provide instructions for protein synthesis. This research showed how hybridization of complementary single oligonucleotide strands could be used as a basis for DNA sensing. Two additional developments enabled the technology used in modern DNA-based biosensors. First, in 1983 Kary Mullis invented the polymerase chain reaction (PCR) technique (Nelson, 2000), a method for amplifying DNA concentrations. This discovery made possible the detection of extremely small quantities of DNA in samples. Second, in 1986 Hood and co-workers devised a method to label DNA molecules with fluorescent tags instead of radiolabels (Smith, 1986), thus enabling hybridization experiments to be observed optically.

The rapid technological advances of the biochemistry and semiconductor fields in the 1980s led to the large scale development of biochips in the 1990s. At this time, it became clear that biochips were largely a "platform" technology which consisted of several separate, yet integrated components. Figure 1 shows the make up of a typical biochip platform. The actual sensing component (or "chip") is just one piece of a complete analysis system. Transduction must be done to translate the actual sensing event (DNA binding, oxidation/reduction, *etc.*) into a format understandable by a computer (voltage, light intensity, mass, *etc.*), which then enables additional analysis and processing to produce a final, human-readable output. The multiple technologies needed to make a successful biochip — from sensing chemistry, to microarraying, to signal processing — require a true multidisciplinary approach, making the barrier to entry steep. One of the first commercial biochips was introduced by Affymetrix. Their "GeneChip" products contain thousands of individual DNA sensors for use in sensing defects, or single nucleotide polymorphisms (SNPs), in genes such as p53 (a tumor suppressor) and BRCA1 and BRCA2 (related to breast cancer) (Cheng, 2001). The chips are produced using microlithography techniques traditionally used to fabricate integrated circuits (see below).

Today, a large variety of biochip technologies are either in development or being commercialized. Numerous advancements continue to be made in sensing research that enable new platforms to be developed for new applications. Cancer diagnosis through DNA typing is just one market opportunity. A variety of industries currently desire the ability to simultaneously screen for a wide range of chemical and biological agents, with

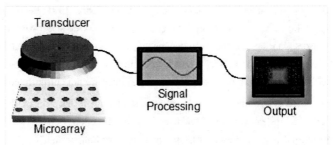

Figure 1. Biochips are a platform that require, in addition to microarray technology, transduction and signal processing technologies to output the results of sensing experiments.

purposes ranging from testing public water systems for disease agents to screening airline cargo for explosives. Pharmaceutical companies wish to combinatorially screen drug candidates against target enzymes. To achieve these ends, DNA, RNA, proteins, and even living cells are being employed as sensing mediators on biochips (Potera, 2008). Numerous transduction methods can be employed including surface plasmon resonance, fluorescence, and chemiluminescence. The particular sensing and transduction techniques chosen depend on factors such as price, sensitivity, and reusability.

Microarray fabrication

The microarray — the dense, two-dimensional grid of biosensors — is the critical component of a biochip platform. Typically, the sensors are deposited on a flat substrate, which may either be passive (*e.g.* silicon or glass) or active, the latter consisting of integrated electronics or micromechanical devices that perform or assist signal transduction. Surface chemistry is used to covalently bind the sensor molecules to the substrate medium. The fabrication of microarrays is non-trivial and is a major economic and technological hurdle that may ultimately decide the

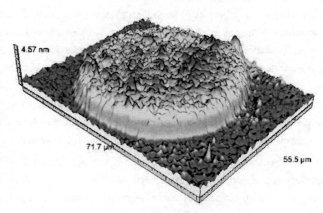

3D Sarfus image of a DNA biochip.

success of future biochip platforms. The primary manufacturing challenge is the process of placing each sensor at a specific position (typically on a Cartesian grid) on the substrate. Various means exist to achieve the placement, but typically robotic micro-pipetting (Schena, 1995) or micro-printing (MacBeath, 1999) systems are used to place tiny spots of sensor material on the chip surface. Because each sensor is unique, only a few spots can be placed at a time. The low-throughput nature of this process results in high manufacturing costs.

Fodor and colleagues developed a unique fabrication process (later used by Affymetrix) in which a series of microlithography steps is used to combinatorially synthesize hundreds of thousands of unique, single-stranded DNA sensors on a substrate one nucleotide at a time (Fodor, 1991; Pease, 1994). One lithography step is needed per base type; thus, a total of four steps is required per nucleotide level. Although this technique is very powerful in that many sensors can be created simultaneously, it is currently only feasible for creating short DNA strands (15–25 nucleotides). Reliability and cost factors limit the number of photolithography steps that can be done. Furthermore, light-directed combinatorial synthesis techniques are not currently possible for proteins or other sensing molecules.

As noted above, most microarrays consist of a Cartesian grid of sensors. This approach is used chiefly to map or "encode" the coordinate of each sensor to its function. Sensors in these arrays typically use a universal signalling technique (*e.g.* fluorescence), thus making coordinates their only identifying feature. These arrays must be made using a serial process (*i.e.* requiring multiple, sequential steps) to ensure that each sensor is placed at the correct position.

"Random" fabrication, in which the sensors are placed at arbitrary positions on the chip, is an alternative to the serial method. The tedious and expensive positioning process is not required, enabling the use of parallelized self-assembly techniques. In this approach, large batches of identical sensors can be produced; sensors from each batch are then combined and assembled into an array. A non-coordinate based encoding scheme must be used to identify each sensor. As the figure shows, such a design was first demonstrated (and later commercialized by Illumina) using functionalized beads placed randomly in the wells of an etched fiber optic cable (Steemers, 2000; Michael, 1998) Each bead was uniquely encoded with a fluorescent signature. However, this encoding scheme is limited in the number of unique dye combinations that can be used and successfully differentiated.

Protein biochip array and other microarray technologies

Microarrays are not limited to DNA analysis; protein microarrays, antibody microarray, chemical compound microarray can also be produced using biochips. Randox [1] Laboratories Ltd. launched Evidence, the first protein Biochip Array Technology analyzer in 2003. In protein Biochip Array Technology, the biochip replaces the ELISA plate or cuvette as the reaction platform. The biochip is used to simultaneously analyze a panel of related tests in a single sample, producing a patient profile. The patient profile can be used in disease screening, diagnosis, monitoring disease progression or monitoring treatment. Performing multiple analyses simultaneously, described as multiplexing, allows a significant reduction in processing time and the amount of patient sample required. Biochip Array Technology is a novel application of a familiar methodology, using sandwich, competitive and antibody-capture immunoassays. The difference from conventional immunoassays is that the capture ligands are covalently attached to the surface of the biochip in an ordered array rather than in solution.

In sandwich assays an enzyme-labelled antibody is used; in competitive assays an enzyme-labelled antigen is used. On antibody-antigen binding a chemiluminescence reaction produces light. Detection is by a charge-coupled device (CCD) camera. The CCD camera is a sensitive and high-resolution sensor able to accurately detect and quantify very low levels of light. The test regions are located using a grid pattern then the chemiluminescence signals are analysed by imaging software to rapidly and simultaneously quantify the individual analytes.

Details about other array technologies can be found in the following page: Antibody microarray

References

- Vahid Bemanian, Frøydis D. Blystad, Live Bruseth, Gunn A. Hildrestrand, Lise Holden, Endre Kjærland, Pål Puntervoll, Hanne Ravneberg and Morten Ruud, "What is Bioethics?" Dec 1998.
- M. Burnham, R. Mitchell, " Bioethics — An Introduction" 1992.
- Cady, NC (2009). "Microchip-based PCR Amplification Systems". *Lab-on-a-Chip Technology: Biomolecular Separation and Analysis*. Caister Academic Press. ISBN 978-1-904455-47-9.
- L. C. Clark, Jr., "Monitor and control of blood tissue O2 tensions," *Transactions of the American Society for Artificial Internal Organs* 2, pp. 41–84, 1956.
- L. C. Clark, Jr. and C. Lyons, "Electrode system for continuous monitoring in cardiovascular surgery," *Annals of the New York Academy of Sciences* 148, pp. 133–153, 1962.
- Fan et al. (2009). "Two-Dimensional Electrophoresis in a Chip". *Lab-on-a-Chip Technology: Biomolecular Separation and Analysis*. Caister Academic Press. ISBN 978-1-904455-47-9.
- S. P. Fodor, J. L. Read, M. C. Pirrung, L. Stryer, A. T. Lu, and D. Solas, "Light-directed, spatially addressable parallel chemical analysis," *Science* 251, pp. 767–773, 1991.
- P. Fortina, D. Graves, C. Stoeckert, Jr., S. McKenzie, and S. Surrey in *Biochip Technology*, J. Cheng and L. J. Kricka, eds., ch. Technology Options and Applications of DNA Microarrays, pp. 185–216, Harwood Academic Publishers, Philadelphia, 2001.
- K. L. Gunderson, S. Kruglyak, M. S. Graige, F. Garcia, B. G. Kermani, C. Zhao, D. Che, T. Dickinson, E. Wickham, J. Bierle, D. Doucet, M. Milewski, R. Yang, C. Siegmund, J. Haas, L. Zhou, A. Oliphant, J.-B. Fan, S. Barnard, and M. S. Chee, "Decoding randomly ordered DNA arrays," *Genome Research* 14(5), pp. 870–877, 2004.
- Herold, KE; Rasooly, A (editor) (2009). *Lab-on-a-Chip Technology: Fabrication and Microfluidics*. Caister Academic Press. ISBN 978-1-904455-46-2.
- Herold, KE; Rasooly, A (editor) (2009). *Lab-on-a-Chip Technology: Biomolecular Separation and Analysis*. Caister Academic Press. ISBN 978-1-904455-47-9.
- W. S. Hughes, "The potential difference between glass and electrolytes in contact with water," *J. Am. Chem. Soc.* 44, pp. 2860–2866, 1922.

- A. M. Maxam and W. Gilbert, "A new method for sequencing DNA," *Proc. Nat. Acad. Sci.* 74, pp. 560–564, 1977.
- G. MacBeath, A. N. Koehler, and S. L. Schreiber, "Printing small molecules as microarrays and detecting protein-ligand interactions en masse," *J. Am. Chem. Soc.* 121, pp. 7967–7968, 1999.
- K. L. Michael, L. C. Taylor, S. L. Schultz, and D. R. Walt, "Randomly ordered addressable high-density optical sensor arrays," *Analytical Chemistry* 70, pp. 1242–1248, 1998.
- D. L. Nelson and M. M. Cox, *Lehninger Principles of Biochemistry*, Worth Publishers, New York, 2000.
- Potera, Carol (1 September 2008). "Delivery of Time-Lapsed Live-Cell Imaging" [2]. *Genetic Engineering & Biotechnology News* **28** (15): pp. 14. ISSN 1935-472X. Retrieved 29 April 2009.
- A. C. Pease, D. Solas, E. J. Sullivan, M. T. Cronin, C. P. Holmes, and S. P. Fodor, "Light-generated oligonucleotide arrays for rapid DNA sequence analysis," *Proc. Natl. Acad. Sci.* 91, pp. 5022–5026, 1994.
- C. Roberts, C. S. Chen, M. Mrksich, V. Martichonok, D. E. Ingber, and G. M. Whitesides, "Using mixed self-assembled monolayers presenting RGD and (EG)3OH groups to characterize long-term attachment of bovine capillary endothelial cells to surfaces," *J. Am. Chem. Soc.* 120, pp. 6548–6555, 1998.
- F. Sanger, S. Nicklen, and A. R. Coulson, "DNA sequencing with chainterminating inhibitors," *Proc. Nat. Acad. Sci.* 74, pp. 5463–5467, 1977.
- M. Schena, D. Shalon, R. W. Davis, and P. O. Brown, "Quantitative monitoring of gene expression patterns with a complementary DNA microarray," *Science* 270, pp. 467–470, 1995.
- H. Schmeck, "Blazing the Genetic Trail." Bethesda, MD: Howard Hughes Medical Institute, 1991.
- J. S. Schultz and R. F. Taylor in *Handbook of Chemical and Biological Sensors*, J. S. Schultz and R. F. Taylor, eds., ch. Introduction to Chemical and Biological Sensors, pp. 1–10, Institute of Physics Publishing, Philadelphia, 1996.
- L. M. Smith, J. Z. Sanders, R. J. Kaiser, P. Hughes, C. Dodd, C. R. Connell, C. Heiner, S. B. H. Kent, and L. E. Hood, "Fluorescence detection in automated DNA sequence analysis," *Nature* 321, pp. 61–67, 1986.
- F. J. Steemers, J. A. Ferguson, and D. R. Walt, "Screening unlabeled DNA targets with randomly-ordered fiber-optic gene arrays," *Nature Biotechnology* 18, pp. 91–94, 2000.
- The Future of Genetic Research [3]
- Interview of A. Caplan, "Should We or Shouldn't We?" [4]
- Bioethics Intro [5]
- NBIAP NEWS REPORT, U.S. Department of Agriculture, "To Regulate or Not to Regulate" Forum: To Rationalize U.S. Biotech Regs. June 1994
- To Regulate or Not to Regulate [6]
- What is a Biochip? [7]

References

[1] http://www.randox.com
[2] http://www.genengnews.com/biobusiness/cpitem.aspx?aid=2576
[3] http://www.accessexcellence.org/RC/AB/IE/Future_Of_Genetic_Research.html
[4] http://web.reed.edu/reed_magazine/spring06/features/life_in_venice/should_we.html
[5] http://www.woodrow.org/teachers/bi/1992/bioethics_intro.html
[6] http://www.accessexcellence.org/RC/AB/IE/To_Regulate_or_Not.html
[7] http://searchcio-midmarket.techtarget.com/sDefinition/0,,sid183_gci211664,00.html

Bioclipse

Bioclipse

Developer(s)	The Bioclipse Project
Stable release	(August 30, 2010) [1] [+/–]
Preview release	(July 27, 2011) [2] [+/–]
Operating system	Cross-platform
Type	Cheminformatics/Bioinformatics
License	Eclipse Public License
Website	www.bioclipse.net [3]

The **Bioclipse** project is a Java-based, open source, visual platform for chemo- and bioinformatics based on the Eclipse Rich Client Platform (RCP).[4] It recently gained scripting functionality.[5]

Like any RCP application, Bioclipse uses a plugin architecture that inherits basic functionality and visual interfaces from Eclipse, such as help system, software updates, preferences, cross-platform deployment etc. Via its plugins, Bioclipse provides functionality for chemo- and bioinformatics, and extension points that easily can be extended by other, possibly proprietary, plugins to provide additional functionality.

The first stable release of Bioclipse includes a Chemistry Development Kit (CDK) plugin to provide a chemoinformatic backend, a Jmol plugin for 3D-visualization of molecules, and a BioJava plugin for sequence analysis.

Bioclipse is developed as a collaboration between the Proteochemometric Group, Dept. of Pharmaceutical Biosciences, Uppsala University, Sweden, the Steinbeck Group at the European Bioinformatics Institute, and the Analytical Chemistry Department at Leiden University, but also includes extensions developed at other academic institutes, including the Karolinska Institutet.[6] The development is backed up by the International Bioclipse Association.[7]

Bioclipse Scripting Language

The Bioclipse Scripting Language (BSL) is a scripting environment, currently based on JavaScript. It extends the scripting language with managers that wrap the functionality of third party libraries, as mentioned above. These scripts thus provide means to make analyses in Bioclipse sharable, for example, on MyExperiment.org. Bioclipse defines a number of core data types that managers support, allowing information to be used between these managers.

References

[1] http://en.wikipedia.org/wiki/Template%3Alatest_stable_software_release%2Fbioclipse?action=edit&preload=Template:LSR/syntax

[2] http://en.wikipedia.org/wiki/Template%3Alatest_preview_software_release%2Fbioclipse?action=edit&preload=Template:LSR/syntax

[3] http://www.bioclipse.net/

[4] Ola Spjuth, Tobias Helmus, Egon L Willighagen, Stefan Kuhn, Martin Eklund, Johannes Wagener, P. Murray-Rust, Christoph Steinbeck, Jarl E.S. Wikberg, *Bioclipse: An open source workbench for chemo- and bioinformatics*, BMC Bioinformatics, **2007**, *8*. doi:10.1186/1471-2105-8-59

[5] Ola Spjuth, Jonathan Alvarsson, Arvid Berg, Martin Eklund, Stefan Kuhn, Carl Mäsak, Gilleain Torrance, Johannes Wagener, Egon L Willighagen, Christoph Steinbeck, and Jarl ES Wikberg, *Bioclipse 2: A scriptable integration platform for the life sciences*, BMC Bioinformatics, **2009**, *10*, doi:10.1186/1471-2105-10-397

[6] Bioclipse Labs (http://wiki.bioclipse.net/index.php?title=Category:BioclipseLabs)

[7] Uppsala University Pressmedelanden: *Dubbla utmärkelser för IT/bioteknik-system* (http://info.uu.se/press.nsf/pm/dubbla.utmarkelser. id6E0.html)

External links

- www.bioclipse.net homepage (http://www.bioclipse.net/)
- SourceForge project page (http://sf.net/projects/bioclipse)
- Wiki (http://wiki.bioclipse.net/)
- Planet Bioclipse (RSS Aggregator) (http://planet.bioclipse.net/)
- Bug Tracker (http://bugs.bioclipse.net/)
- BSL scripts on MyExperiment.org (http://www.myexperiment.org/workflows?filter=TYPE_ID("51"))

Bioconductor

Bioconductor

Stable release	2.8 / April 14, 2011
Operating system	Linux, Mac OS X, Windows
Platform	R programming language
Type	Analysis of genomic information
License	Artistic License 2.0
Website	www.bioconductor.org [1]

Bioconductor is a free, open source and open development software project for the analysis and comprehension of genomic data generated by wet lab experiments in molecular biology.

Bioconductor is based primarily on the statistical R programming language, but does contain contributions in other programming languages. It has two releases each year that follow the semiannual releases of R. At any one time there is a release version, which corresponds to the released version of R, and a development version, which corresponds to the development version of R. Most users will find the release version appropriate for their needs. In addition there are a large number of genome annotation packages available that are mainly, but not solely, oriented towards different types of microarrays.

The project was started in the Fall of 2001 and is overseen by the Bioconductor core team, based primarily at the Fred Hutchinson Cancer Research Center with other members coming from various US and international institutions.

Bioconductor Packages

Most Bioconductor components are distributed as R packages, which are add-on modules for R. Initially most of the Bioconductor software packages focused on the analysis of single channel Affymetrix and two or more channel cDNA/Oligo microarrays. As the project has matured, the functional scope of the software packages broadened to include the analysis of all types of genomic data, such as SAGE, sequence, or SNP data.

Goals

The broad goals of the projects are to:

- Provide widespread access to a broad range of powerful statistical and graphical methods for the analysis of genomic data.
- Facilitate the inclusion of biological metadata in the analysis of genomic data, e.g. literature data from PubMed, annotation data from LocusLink.
- Provide a common software platform that enables the rapid development and deployment of plug-able, scalable, and interoperable software.
- Further scientific understanding by producing high-quality documentation and reproducible research.
- Train researchers on computational and statistical methods for the analysis of genomic data.

Main Features

- **The R Project for Statistical Computing.** R and the R package system provides a broad range of advantages to the Bioconductor project including:

  - It contains a high-level interpreted language in which one can easily and quickly prototype new computational methods.
  - It includes a well established system for packaging together software components and documentation.
  - It can address the diversity and complexity of computational biology and bioinformatics problems in a common object-oriented framework.
  - It provides access to on-line computational biology and bioinformatics data sources.
  - It supports a rich set of statistical simulation and modeling activities.
  - It contains cutting edge data and model visualization capabilities.
  - It has been the basis for pathbreaking research in parallel statistical computing.
  - It is under very active development by a dedicated team of researchers with a strong commitment to good documentation and software design.

- **Documentation and reproducible research.** Each Bioconductor package contains at least one vignette, which is a document that provides a textual, task-oriented description of the package's functionality. These vignettes come in several forms. Many are simple "How-to"s that are designed to demonstrate how a particular task can be accomplished with that package's software. Others provide a more thorough overview of the package or might even discuss general issues related to the package. In the future, the bioconductor project is looking towards providing vignettes that are not specifically tied to a package, but rather are demonstrating more complex concepts. As with all aspects of the Bioconductor project, users are encouraged to participate in this effort.

- **Statistical and graphical methods.** The Bioconductor project aims to provide access to a wide range of powerful statistical and graphical methods for the analysis of genomic data. Analysis packages are available for: pre-processing Affymetrix and cDNA array data; identifying differentially expressed genes; graph theoretical analyses; plotting genomic data. In addition, the R package system itself provides implementations for a broad range of state-of-the-art statistical and graphical techniques, including linear and non-linear modeling, cluster analysis, prediction, resampling, survival analysis, and time series analysis.

- **Genome Annotation.** The Bioconductor project provides software for associating microarray and other genomic data in real time to biological metadata from web databases such as GenBank, LocusLink and PubMed (annotate package). Functions are also provided for incorporating the results of statistical analysis in HTML reports with links to annotation WWW resources. Software tools are available for assembling and processing genomic annotation data, from databases such as GenBank, the Gene Ontology Consortium, LocusLink, UniGene, the UCSC Human Genome Project (AnnotationDbi package). Data packages are distributed to provide mappings between different probe identifiers (e.g. Affy IDs, LocusLink, PubMed). Customized annotation libraries can also be assembled.

- **Open source.** The Bioconductor project has a commitment to full open source discipline, with distribution via a SourceForge.net-like platform. All contributions are expected to exist under an open source license such as Artistic 2.0, GPL2, or BSD. There are many different reasons why open—source software is beneficial to the analysis of microarray data and to computational biology in general. The reasons include:

  - To provide full access to algorithms and their implementation
  - To facilitate software improvements through bug fixing and plug-ins
  - To encourage good scientific computing and statistical practice by providing appropriate tools and instruction
  - To provide a workbench of tools that allow researchers to explore and expand the methods used to analyze biological data
  - To ensure that the international scientific community is the owner of the software tools needed to carry out research

- To lead and encourage commercial support and development of those tools that are successful
- To promote reproducible research by providing open and accessible tools with which to carry out that research (reproducible research is distinct from independent verification)
- **Open development.** Users are encouraged to become developers, either by contributing Bioconductor compliant packages or documentation. Additionally Bioconductor provides a mechanism for linking together different groups with common goals to foster collaboration on software, possibly at the level of shared development.

Milestones

Version	Release Date	Package Count	Dependency
1.0	May 1, 2002	15	R 1.5
1.1	November 19, 2002	20	R 1.6
1.2	May 29, 2003	30	R 1.7
1.3	October 30, 2003	49	R 1.8
1.4	May 17, 2004	81	R 1.9
1.5	October 25, 2004	100	R 2.0
1.6	May 18, 2005	123	R 2.1
1.7	October 14, 2005	141	R 2.2
1.8	April 27, 2006	172	R 2.3
1.9	October 4, 2006	188	R 2.4
2.0	April 26, 2007	214	R 2.5
2.1	October 8, 2007	233	R 2.6
2.2	May 1, 2008	260	R 2.7
2.3	October 22, 2008	294	R 2.8
2.4	April 21, 2009	320	R 2.9
2.5	October 28, 2009	352	R 2.10
2.6	April 23, 2010	389	R 2.11
2.7	October 18, 2010	418	R 2.12
2.8	April 14, 2011	466	R 2.13

Resources

- Gentleman, R.; Carey, V.; Huber, W.; Irizarry, R.; Dudoit, S. (2005). *Bioinformatics and Computational Biology Solutions Using R and Bioconductor*. Springer. ISBN 978-0-387-25146-2
- Gentleman, R. (2008). *R Programming for Bioinformatics*. Chapman & Hall/CRC. ISBN 1-4200-6367-7
- Hahne, F.; Huber, W.; Gentleman, R.; Falcon, S. (2008). *Bioconductor Case Studies*. Springer. ISBN 978-0-387-77239-4

External links

- Official Website [2]
- Genome Biology 2004 article: Bioconductor: open software development for computational biology and bioinformatics [3]
- The R Project [4] GNU R is a programming language for statistical computing.
- The community of the Debian GNU/Linux distribution strives towards an automated building of BioConductor packages [5] for their distribution. BioKnoppix [6] and Quantian [7] are projects extending Knoppix that have contributed bootable Debian GNU/Linux CDs providing BioConductor installations.

References

[1] http://www.bioconductor.org/
[2] http://www.bioconductor.org
[3] http://genomebiology.com/content/pdf/gb-2004-5-10-r80.pdf
[4] http://www.r-project.org
[5] http://wiki.debian.org/AliothPkgBioc
[6] http://bioknoppix.hpcf.upr.edu/
[7] http://dirk.eddelbuettel.com/quantian.html

BioCreative

BioCreAtIvE (A critical assessment of text mining methods in molecular biology) consists in a community-wide effort for evaluating information extraction and text mining developments in the biological domain[1] .

Three main tasks were posed at the first BioCreAtIvE challenge: the entity extraction task[2] , the gene name normalization task[3] [4] , and the functional annotation of gene products task[5] . The data sets produced by this contest serve as a Gold Standard training and test set to evaluate and train Bio-NER tools and annotation extraction tools.

The second BioCreAtIvE included three tasks organized by Lynette Hirschman and Alex Morgan of MITRE; Alfonso Valencia and Martin Krallinger of CNIO in Spain; and W. John Wilbur, Lorrie Tanabe and Larry Smith of NIH.

External links

- BioCreAtIve 2, 2006-2007 [6]
- First BioCreAtIvE workshop, 2004 [7]
- BMC Bioinformatics special issue : BioCreAtIvE [8]
- First BioCreAtIvE data download request [9]

References

[1] Hirschman, L.; Yeh, A.; Blaschke, C.; Valencia, A. (2005). "Overview of BioCreAtIvE: Critical assessment of information extraction for biology". *BMC Bioinformatics* **6**: S1. doi:10.1186/1471-2105-6-S1-S1. PMC 1869002. PMID 15960821.
[2] Yeh, A.; Morgan, A.; Colosimo, M.; Hirschman, L. (2005). "BioCreAtIvE Task 1A: Gene mention finding evaluation". *BMC Bioinformatics* **6**: S2. doi:10.1186/1471-2105-6-S1-S2. PMC 1869012. PMID 15960832.
[3] Hirschman, L.; Colosimo, M.; Morgan, A.; Yeh, A. (2005). "Overview of BioCreAtIvE task 1B: Normalized gene lists". *BMC Bioinformatics* **6**: S11. doi:10.1186/1471-2105-6-S1-S11. PMC 1869004. PMID 15960823.
[4] Colosimo, M. E.; Morgan, A. A.; Yeh, A. S.; Colombe, J. B.; Hirschman, L. (2005). "Data preparation and interannotator agreement: BioCreAtIvE Task 1B". *BMC Bioinformatics* **6**: S12. doi:10.1186/1471-2105-6-S1-S12. PMC 1869005. PMID 15960824.
[5] Blaschke, C.; Leon, E.; Krallinger, M.; Valencia, A. (2005). "Evaluation of BioCreAtIvE assessment of task 2". *BMC Bioinformatics* **6**: S16. doi:10.1186/1471-2105-6-S1-S16. PMC 1869008. PMID 15960828.

[6] http://biocreative.sourceforge.net
[7] http://www.pdg.cnb.uam.es/BioLINK/workshop_BioCreative_04/
[8] http://www.biomedcentral.com/1471-2105/6?issue=S1
[9] http://www.pdg.cnb.uam.es/BioLINK/workshop_BioCreative_04/results/agreetment.html

Biocurator

A **biocurator** is a professional scientist who collects, annotates, and validates information that is disseminated by biological and model organism databases. The role of a biocurator encompasses quality control of primary biological research data intended for publication, extracting and organizing data from original scientific literature, and describing the data with standard annotation protocols and vocabularies that enable powerful queries and biological database inter-operability. Biocurators communicate with researchers to ensure the accuracy of curated information and to foster data exchanges with research laboratories.

Biocurators (also called **scientific curators**, **data curators** or **annotators**) have been recognized as the "museum catalogers of the Internet age".[1]

To annotate data, biocurators commonly employ—and take part in the creation and development of—shared biomedical ontologies: structured, controlled vocabularies that encompass many biological and medical knowledge domains. These domains include genomics and proteomics, anatomy, animal and plant development, biochemistry, metabolic pathways, taxonomic classification, and mutant phenotypes.

Biocurators enforce the consistent use of gene nomenclature guidelines and participate in the genetic nomenclature committees of various model organisms, often in collaboration with the HUGO Gene Nomenclature Committee (HGNC [2]). They also enforce other nomenclature guidelines like those provided by the Nomenclature Committee of the International Union of Biochemistry and Molecular Biology (IUBMB), one example of which is the Enzyme Commission EC number.

The International Society for Biocuration (ISB) was founded in 2008; the non-profit organisation "promotes the field of biocuration and provides a forum for information exchange through meetings and workshops." International Biocurator Conferences have been held in Pacific Grove, California (2005), San José, CA (2007), and Berlin (2009), Chiba, Japan (2010), and a meeting has been scheduled for Washington in 2012.

References

[1] Bourne and McEntyre (2006). Biocurators: contributors to the world of science. (http://dx.doi.org/10.1371/journal.pcbi.0020142) *PLoS Comput Biol* 2(10):e142.
[2] http://www.genenames.org/

External links

- International Society for Biocuration (http://www.biocurator.org/)
- XTractor (http://www.xtractor.in/) - Discovering Newer Scientific Relations Across PubMed Abstracts. A tool to obtain manually annotated relationships for Proteins, Diseases, Drugs and Biological Processes as they get published in PubMed.
- Open Biomedical Ontologies (OBO) Foundry (http://obofoundry.org/)
- Comparative Toxicogenomics Database (http://ctd.mdibl.org/)
- TexFlame (http://texflame.com) - An online tool that renders a single PubMed abstract as a Systems Biology Graphical Notation (SBGN)-like graph. Provides biocurators a starting point for creation of pathway maps.

Bioimage informatics

Bioimage informatics is a subfield of bioinformatics and computational biology. It is most related to using computational techniques to analyze bioimages, especially cellular and molecular images, at large scale and high throughput, with the goal to mine useful knowledge out of complicated and heterogeneous image and related metadata. There has been an increasing focus on developing novel image processing, data mining, database and visualization techniques to extract, compare, search and manage the biological knowledge in these data-intensive problems.[1]

This field is in quick growth in recent years, apparently due to the flood of complicated molecular and cellular microscopic images produced in a series of projects that create compelling challenges for the image computing community.

References

[1] Peng H (September 2008). "Bioimage informatics: a new area of engineering biology". *Bioinformatics* **24** (17): 1827–36. doi:10.1093/bioinformatics/btn346. PMC 2519164. PMID 18603566.

Bioinformatic Harvester

The **Bioinformatic Harvester** is a bioinformatic meta search engine at KIT Karlsruhe Institute of Technology for genes and protein-associated information. Harvester currently works for human, mouse, rat, zebrafish, drosophila and arabidopsis thaliana based information. Harvester cross-links >50 popular bioinformatic resources and allows cross searches. Harvester serves 10.000s of pages every day to scientists and physicians.

Bioinformatic Harvester

Developer(s)	Urban Liebel, Björn Kindler
Stable release	4 / May 24, 2011
Operating system	Web based
Type	Bioinformatics tool
License	Public Domain
Website	http://harvester.kit.edu

How Harvester works

Harvester collects information from protein and gene databases along with information from so called "prediction servers." Prediction server e.g. provide online sequence analysis for a single protein. Harvesters search index is based on the IPI and UniProt protein information collection. The collections consists of:

- ~72.000 human, ~57.000 mouse, ~41.000 rat, ~51.000 zebrafish, ~35.000 arabidopsis protein pages, which cross-link ~50 major bioinfiormatic resources.

Harvester crosslinks several types of information

Text based information

...from the following databases:

- UniProt, world largest protein database
- SOURCE, convenient gene information overview
- Simple Modular Architecture Research Tool (SMART),
- SOSUI, predicts transmembrane domains
- PSORT, predicts protein localisation
- HomoloGene, compares proteins from different species
- gfp-cdna, protein localisation with fluorescence microscopy
- International Protein Index (IPI).

A screenshot of the Harvester search engine [1]

Databases rich in graphical elements

...are not collected, but crosslinked via iframes. Iframes are transparent windows within a HTML pages. The iframe windows allows up-to-date viewing of the "iframed," linked databases. Several such iframes are combined on a Harvester protein page. This method allows convenient comparison of information from several databases.

- NCBI-BLAST, an algorithm for comparing biological sequences from the NCBI.
- Ensembl, automatic gene annotation by the EMBL-EBI and Sanger Institute
- FlyBase is a database of model organism *Drosophila melanogaster*.
- GoPubMed is a knowledge-based search engine for biomedical texts.
- iHOP, information hyperlinked over proteins via gene/protein synonyms
- Mendelian Inheritance in Man project catalogues all the known diseases.
- RZPD, German resources Center for genome research in Berlin/Heidelberg.
- STRING, Search Tool for the Retrieval of Interacting Genes/Proteins, developed by EMBL, SIB and UZH.
- Zebrafish Information Network.
- LOCATE [2] subcellular localization database (mouse).

"linkouts"

- Genome browser, working draft assemblies for genomes UCSC
- Google Scholar
- Mitocheck
- PolyMeta, meta search engine for Google, Yahoo, MSN, Ask, Exalead, AllTheWeb, GigaBlast

What one can find

Harvester allows a combination of different search terms and single words.

Search Examples:

- Gene-name: "golga3"
- Gene-alias: "ADAP-S ADAS ADHAPS ADPS" (one gene name is sufficient)
- Gene-Ontologies: "Enzyme linked receptor protein signaling pathway"
- Unigene-Cluster: "Hs.449360"
- Go-annotation: "intra-Golgi transport"

- Molecular function: "protein kinase binding"
- Protein: "Q9NPD3"
- Protein domain: "SH2 sar"
- Protein Localisation: "endoplasmic reticulum"

- Chromosome: "2q31"
- Disease relevant: use the word "diseaselink"
- Combinations: "golgi diseaselink" (finds all golgi proteins associated with a disease)
- mRNA: "AL136897"

- Word: "Cancer"
- Comment: "highly expressed in heart"
- Author: "Merkel, Schmidt"
- Publication or project: "cDNA sequencing project"

Literature

- Liebel U, Kindler B, Pepperkok R (August 2004). "'Harvester': a fast meta search engine of human protein resources" [3]. *Bioinformatics* **20** (12): 1962–3. doi:10.1093/bioinformatics/bth146. PMID 14988114.
- Liebel U, Kindler B, Pepperkok R (2005). "Bioinformatic "Harvester": a search engine for genome-wide human, mouse, and rat protein resources" [4]. *Meth. Enzymol.* **404**: 19–26. doi:10.1016/S0076-6879(05)04003-6. PMID 16413254.

External links

- http://harvester.kit.edu Bioinformatic Harvester V at KIT Karlsruhe Institute of Technology
- Harvester42 [5] at KIT - integrating 50 general search engines

References

[1] http://harvester.kit.edu/
[2] http://locate.imb.uq.edu.au/
[3] http://bioinformatics.oxfordjournals.org/cgi/pmidlookup?view=long&pmid=14988114
[4] http://linkinghub.elsevier.com/retrieve/pii/S0076-6879(05)04003-6
[5] http://harvester42.fzk.de

Bioinformatics (journal)

Bioinformatics	
Abbreviated title (ISO)	*Bioinformatics*
Discipline	Computational biology
Language	English
Publication details	
Publisher	Oxford University Press
Publication history	1998-present
Frequency	24 issues/year
Impact factor (2009)	4.926
Indexing	
ISSN	1367-4803 [1] (print) 1460-2059 [2] (web)
Links	
• Journal homepage [3]	

Bioinformatics is a peer-reviewed scientific journal publishing original research and software in computational biology. It is the official journal of the International Society for Computational Biology, together with *PLoS Computational Biology*. Authors can pay extra for open access and are allowed to self-archive after 1 year. *Bioinformatics* was established in 1998 and has been published since by Oxford University Press.

The editors are Alex Bateman and Alfonso Valencia.[4]

References

[1] http://www.worldcat.org/issn/1367-4803
[2] http://www.worldcat.org/issn/1460-2059
[3] http://bioinformatics.oxfordjournals.org/
[4] http://www.oxfordjournals.org/our_journals/bioinformatics/editorial_board.html Bioinformatics Editorial Board

External links

- Official website (http://bioinformatics.oxfordjournals.org/)

Bioinformatics workflow management systems

A **bioinformatics workflow management system** is a specialized form of workflow management system designed specifically to compose and execute a series of computational or data manipulation steps, or a workflow, in a specific domain of science, bioinformatics.

There are currently many different workflow systems. Some have been developed more generally as scientific workflow systems for use by scientists from many different disciplines like astronomy and earth science.

Examples

- Anduril is an open source component-based workflow framework for scientific data analysis developed at the University of Helsinki.[1] Anduril provides an execution engine written in Java, a large number of components for bioinformatics analysis, and the AndurilScript language to create and manage workflows.
- BioBike[2] is a biocomputing platform based upon the KnowOS (Knowledge Operating System) e-science technology. Written entirely in Lisp, KnowOS's main distinguishing feature is "through-the-browser" programmability.
- BioExtract harnesses the power of online informatics tools for creating and customizing workflows. Users can query online sequence data, analyze it using an array of informatics tools, create and share custom workflows for repeated analysis, and save the resulting data and workflows in standardized reports.
- BioManager is a bioinformatic data management and analysis workflow developed by the University of Sydney.
- CellProfiler[3] is an open source modular image analysis software developed at the Broad Institute. Capable of handling hundreds of thousands of images, it contains advanced algorithms for image analysis of cell-based assays and is optimized for high-throughput work. The software allows the user to construct a pipeline of individual modules; each module performs a image processing step, such as image loading, object identification, and feature extraction.
- Discovery Net (circa 2000) is one of the earliest examples of scientific workflow systems. It was the winner of the "Most Innovative Data Intensive Application Award" at the ACM SC02 (Supercomputing 2002) conference and exhibition, based on a demonstration of a fully interactive distributed genome annotation pipeline for a Malaria genome case study. The Discovery Net system originated from a £2m EPSRC-funded project with the same name investigating the development of an e-Science platform for scientific discovery from the data generated by a wide variety of high throughput devices at Imperial College London. Many of the features of the system (architecture features, visual front-end, simplified access to remote Web and Grid Services and inclusion of a workflow store) were considered novel at the time, and have since found their way into other academic and commercial systems.
- Ergatis[4] is a web-based system used to create, run, and monitor reusable bioinformatics analysis pipelines. It contains pre-built components for common bioinformatics analysis tasks, such as blast searches or storing data in a Chado database. These components can be arranged graphically to create highly-configurable pipelines.
- Galaxy[5] is an open source workflow system developed at Penn State and Emory University. Galaxy is available as a free public web server[6] and as downloadable software.[7] Galaxy stresses ease of use and sharing and persisting analyses.
- GenePattern is a genomic analysis platform developed at the Broad Institute of MIT & Harvard that provides access to more than 150 tools for gene expression analysis, proteomics, SNP analysis, RNA-seq, flow cytometry, and common data processing tasks. A web-based interface provides access to these tools and allows the creation of multi-step analysis pipelines that enable reproducible in silico research.
- Geodise (Grid Enabled Optimisation and Design Search for Engineering) was developed at the University of Southampton.
- Kepler enables scientists in a variety of disciplines like biology, ecology and astronomy to compose and execute workflows. Kepler is based on the Ptolemy II system for heterogeneous, concurrent modeling and design.

Ptolemy II was developed by the members of the Ptolemy project at University of California Berkeley. Although not originally intended for scientific workflows, it provides a mature platform for building and executing workflows, and supports multiple models of computation.

- LONI Pipeline is a Java-based distributed graphical data-analysis environment for constructing, validating, executing and disseminating scientific workflows. As the LONI Pipeline references all data, services and tools as external objects, it directly allows resource interoperability without the need for rebuilding the software.
- Medicel Integrator Workflow is a cluster-enabled bioinformatics workflow design and execution application. It can be used stand-alone or integrated with a biology data warehouse.
- Pegasus is a flexible framework that enables the mapping of complex scientific workflows onto the grid developed at the Information Sciences Institute at the University of Southern California.
- Pegasys is a software for executing and integrating analyses of biological sequences, developed by the University of British Columbia.
- Pipeline Pilot is Accelrys' scientific informatics platform that streamlines the data integration and analysis by using a Visual Programming Language (similar to LabVIEW) to build a pipeline to transform any number of inputs (raw data) into any number of outputs.
- Taverna workbench is an open source workflow system that enables scientists (typically, though not exclusively, in bioinformatics) to compose and execute scientific workflows. It has been developed as part of a £5.5m EPSRC project called myGrid based at the University of Manchester. Independently, other researchers have created Programming by example workflow development tools that are interoperable with Taverna.[8]
- Triana is an open source problem solving environment developed at Cardiff University that combines an intuitive visual interface with powerful data analysis tools.
- Wildfire is a distributed, Grid-enabled workflow construction and execution environment. It has a graphical user interface for constructing and running workflows. Wildfire borrows user interface features from Jemboss and adds a drag-and-drop interface allowing the user to compose EMBOSS (and other) programs into workflows. For execution, Wildfire uses GEL, the underlying workflow execution engine, which can exploit available parallelism on multiple CPU machines including Beowulf-class clusters and Grids.
- Sight is a web agent – oriented workflow platform that historically has extensive means to integrate websites with ordinary web forms and HTML responses (there is also support for WSDL as well). The system has a GUI-based workflow composer that supports modules with multiple ports and allows to access data from the modules that stand earlier in workflow. Sight was developed in Ulm university using java and it currently released under GPL.
- RetroGuide is a query framework for querying retrospective bioinformatics data.
- UGENE Workflow Designer is an open source visual environment designed for building and executing bioinformatics workflows. The main purpose of the system is providing user-friendly GUI for creating computational workflows that can be executed as well as on commodity hardware as on high-performance clusters and supercomputers.
- HCDC is an open source workflow system developed at ETH Zurich that is focus on large scale image based biological experiments. Include large collection of components for multiwell plate handling (96, 384, ...).
- Mobyle is a framework and web portal specifically aimed at the integration of bioinformatics software and databanks. Mobyle is the successor of Pise and the RPBS server, previous systems that provided web environments to define and execute bioinformatics analyses.
- Remora is a web server implemented according to the BioMoby web-service specifications, providing life science researchers with an easy-to-use workflow generator and launcher, a repository of predefined workflows and a survey system.

References

[1] Ovaska, K.; Laakso, M.; Haapa-Paananen, S.; Louhimo, R.; Chen, P.; Aittomäki, V.; Valo, E.; Núñez-Fontarnau, J. et al. (2010). "Large-scale data integration framework provides a comprehensive view on glioblastoma multiforme". *Genome Medicine* **2** (9): 65. doi:10.1186/gm186. PMID 20822536.

[2] Elhai, J.; Taton, A.; Massar, J.; Myers, J. K.; Travers, M.; Casey, J.; Slupesky, M.; Shrager, J. (2009). "BioBIKE: A Web-based, programmable, integrated biological knowledge base". *Nucleic Acids Research* **37** (Web Server issue): W28–W32. doi:10.1093/nar/gkp354. PMC 2703918. PMID 19433511.

[3] Kamentsky, L.; Jones, T. R.; Fraser, A.; Bray, M. -A.; Logan, D. J.; Madden, K. L.; Ljosa, V.; Rueden, C. et al. (2011). "Improved structure, function and compatibility for CellProfiler: Modular high-throughput image analysis software". *Bioinformatics* **27** (8): 1179–1180. doi:10.1093/bioinformatics/btr095. PMC 3072555. PMID 21349861.

[4] Orvis, J.; Crabtree, J.; Galens, K.; Gussman, A.; Inman, J. M.; Lee, E.; Nampally, S.; Riley, D. et al. (2010). "Ergatis: A web interface and scalable software system for bioinformatics workflows". *Bioinformatics* **26** (12): 1488–1492. doi:10.1093/bioinformatics/btq167. PMC 2881353. PMID 20413634.

[5] Goecks, J.; Nekrutenko, A.; Taylor, J.; Galaxy Team, T. (2010). "Galaxy: A comprehensive approach for supporting accessible, reproducible, and transparent computational research in the life sciences". *Genome Biology* **11** (8): R86. doi:10.1186/gb-2010-11-8-r86. PMC 2945788. PMID 20738864.

[6] http://usegalaxy.org/

[7] http://getgalaxy.org/

[8] Hull, Duncan; Wolstencroft, Katy; Stevens, Robert; Goble, Carole A.; Pocock, Matthew R.; Li, Peter; Oinn, Tom (2006). "Taverna: A tool for building and running workflows of services". *Nucleic Acids Research* **34** (Web Server issue): W729–W732. doi:10.1093/nar/gkl320. PMC 1538887. PMID 16845108.

External links

• Oinn, T.; Greenwood, M.; Addis, M.; Alpdemir, M. N.; Ferris, J.; Glover, K.; Goble, C.; Goderis, A. et al. (2006). "Taverna: Lessons in creating a workflow environment for the life sciences". *Concurrency and Computation: Practice and Experience* **18** (10): 1067–1100. doi:10.1002/cpe.993. This paper reviews some of the above workflow systems

• Yu, J.; Buyya, R. (2005). "A taxonomy of scientific workflow systems for grid computing". *ACM SIGMOD Record* **34** (3): 44. doi:10.1145/1084805.1084814. from the ACM SIGMOD Record

• Portal of a joint European Grid and web-services project called EMBRACE (http://www.embracegrid.info/). Provides much information and many work-out bioinformatics examples and web-services.

• Galaxy (http://galaxy.psu.edu/)

• GenePattern Website (http://www.genepattern.org) and Reich, M.; Liefeld, T.; Gould, J.; Lerner, J.; Tamayo, P.; Mesirov, J. P. (2006). "GenePattern 2.0". *Nature Genetics* **38** (5): 500–501. doi:10.1038/ng0506-500. PMID 16642009. (Nature Genetics)

• Curcin, V.; Ghanem, M. (2008). *Scientific workflow systems - can one size fit all?*. pp. 1–9. doi:10.1109/CIBEC.2008.4786077. paper in CIBEC'08 comparing multiple workflow systems for bioinformatics applications

• Workflow technology based Solutions for Bioinformatics (http://openwetware.org/wiki/Abhishek_Tiwari:Workflow_technology#Workflow_technology_based_Solutions_for_Bioinformatics)

• Mobyle (http://mobyle.pasteur.fr)

• Remora (http://lipm-bioinfo.toulouse.inra.fr/remora)

BioJava

The **BioJava** Project is an open source project dedicated to providing Java tools for processing biological data. This includes include objects for manipulating sequences, protein structures, file parsers, CORBA interoperability, DAS, access to ACeDB, dynamic programming, and simple statistical routines.

The BioJava library is useful for automating many daily and mundane bioinformatics tasks. As the library matures, the BioJava libraries will provide a foundation upon which both free software and commercial packages can be developed.

External links

- BioJava Website [1]

References

- BioJava: an Open-Source Framework for Bioinformatics [2]

R.C.G. Holland; T. Down; M. Pocock; A. Prlić; D. Huen; K. James; S. Foisy; A. Dräger; A. Yates; M. Heuer; M.J. Schreiber Bioinformatics 2008; doi: 10.1093/bioinformatics/btn397

References

[1] http://biojava.org/
[2] http://bioinformatics.oxfordjournals.org/cgi/content/abstract/btn397v1?ijkey=jIKd6VUGPrgshbv&keytype=ref

BioLinux

BioLinux is a term used in a variety of projects involved in making access to bioinformatics software on a Linux platform easier using one or more of the following methods:

- Provision of complete systems
- Provision of bioinformatics software repositories
- Addition of bioinformatics packages to standard distributions
- Live DVD/CDs with bioinformatics software added
- Community building and support systems

There are now various projects with similar aims, on both Linux systems and other Unices, and a selection of these are given below. There is also an overview in the Canadian Bioinformatics Helpdesk Newsletter [1] that details some of the Linux-based projects.

Complete systems

Various complete distributions that integrate bioinformatics software are available, in various stages of development.

- BioBrew [2]
- BioLand [3]
- BioLinuxBR [4]
- BioSLAX [5]
- Debian Med [6]
- NEBC Bio-Linux [7]

Package repositories

Red Hat

Package repositories are generally specific to the distribution of Linux the bioinformatician is using. A number of Linux variants are prevalent in bioinformatics work. Fedora is a freely-distributed version of the commercial Red Hat system. Red Hat is widely used in the corporate world as they offer commercial support and training packages. Fedora Core is a community supported derivative of Red Hat and is popular amongst those who like Red Hat's system but don't require commercial support. Many users of bioinformatics applications have produced RPMs (Red Hat's package format) designed to work with Fedora, which you can potentially also install on Red Hat Enterprise Linux systems. Other distributions such as Mandriva and SUSE use RPMs, so these packages may also work on these distributions.

- BioRPMs [8] (RedHat and Fedora)
- RPMfind.net [9] (Various RPM-based distributions, indexed by category)

Debian

Debian is another very popular Linux distribution in use in many academic institutions, and some bioinformaticians have made their own software packages available for this distribution in the deb format.

- Debian Med [10] (Debian contains a lot of medical software internally)
- NEBC Bio-Linux [11] (Non-standard Debian)

Slackware

Slackware is one of the less used Linux distributions. It is popular with those who have better knowledge of the Linux operating system and who prefer the command line over the various GUIs available. Packages are in the tgz or tgx format. The most widely known live distribution based on Slackware is Slax and it has been used as a base for many of the bioinformatics distributions.

- BioSLAX

Apple/Mac

Many Linux packages are compatible with Mac OS X and there are several projects which attempt to make it easy to install selected Linux packages (including bioinformatics software) on a computer running Mac OS X. These include:

- Fink scientific packages [12]
- Homebrew [13]

Similarly, eBioinformatics [14] provides a Mac OS GUI for over 300 open source bioinformatics programs.

Live DVDs/CDs

Live DVDs or CDs are not an ideal way to provide bioinformatics computing, as they run from a CD/DVD drive. This means they are slower than a traditional hard disk installation and have limited ability to be configured. However, they can be suitable for providing ad-hoc solutions where no other Linux access is available, and may even be used as the basis for a Linux installation (e.g. BioKnoppix).

- BioKnoppix [6]
- DNALinux [15]
- Quantian [7]
- Vigyaan [16]
- VLinux [17]
- NEBC Bio-Linux [18]
- BioSlax [19]

Standard distributions with good bioinformatics support

In general, Linux distributions have a wide range of official packages available, but this does not usually include much in the way of scientific support. There are exceptions, such as those detailed below.

Gentoo Linux

Gentoo Linux provides over 50 bioinformatics applications (see packages.gentoo.org [20] and Gentoo Science Overlay [21]) in the form of ebuilds, which build the applications from source code.

Although a very flexible system with excellent community support, the requirement to install from source means that Gentoo systems are often slow to install, and require considerable maintenance. It is possible to reduce some of the compilation time by using a central server to generate binary packages.

FreeBSD

FreeBSD is not a Linux distribution, but as it is a version of Unix it is very similar. Its ports are like Gentoo's ebuilds, and the same caveats apply. However, there are also pre-complied binary packages available. There are over 60 biological sciences applications, and they're listed on the Fresh Ports [22] site.

Debian

There are more than a hundred bioinformatics packages provided as part of the standard Debian installation. NEBC Bio-Linux [7] packages can also be installed on a standard Debian system as long as the bio-linux-base package is also installed. This creates a /usr/local/bioinf directory where our other packages install their software. Debian packages may also work on Ubuntu Linux or other Debian-derived installations.

Community building and support systems

Providing support and documentation should be an important part of any BioLinux project, that scientists who are not IT specialists may quickly find answers to their specific problems. Support forums or mailing lists are also useful to disseminate knowledge within the research community. Some of these resources are linked to here.

- Bio-Linux BR [23]
- BioLinux Grupo [24]
- NEBC Bio-Linux [25]
- EMBnet.News [26] Two issues (2007) dedicated to Bioinformatics Linux distributions

References

[1] http://gchelpdesk.ualberta.ca/news/03mar05/cbhd_news_03mar05.php#GearingUp
[2] http://bioinformatics.org/biobrew/
[3] http://bioland.cbi.pku.edu.cn/
[4] http://biolinux.df.ibilce.unesp.br/
[5] http://www.bioslax.org/
[6] http://www.debian.org/devel/debian-med/
[7] http://envgen.nox.ac.uk/biolinux.html
[8] http://uberh4x0r.org/~yax/biorpm/
[9] http://www.rpmfind.net/linux/RPM/Groups.html
[10] http://www.debian.org/devel/debian-med
[11] http://envgen.nox.ac.uk/repository.html
[12] http://pdb.finkproject.org/pdb/sections.php
[13] http://github.com/mxcl/homebrew
[14] http://www.ebioinformatics.org
[15] http://www.dnalinux.com/
[16] http://www.vigyaancd.org/
[17] http://bioinformatics.org/vlinux
[18] http://nebc.nox.ac.uk/tools/bio-linux
[19] http://www.bioslax.com
[20] http://packages.gentoo.org/packages/?category=sci-biology
[21] http://overlays.gentoo.org/proj/science
[22] http://www.freshports.org/biology/
[23] http://biolinux.df.ibilce.unesp.br
[24] http://biolinux.ourproject.org
[25] http://envgen.nox.ac.uk/biolinux_doc.html
[26] http://www.embnet.org

Biological data visualization

Biology Data Visualization is a branch of bioinformatics concerned with the application of computer graphics, scientific visualization, and information visualization to different areas of the life sciences. This includes visualization of sequences, genomes, alignments, phylogenies, macromolecular structures, systems biology, microscopy, and magnetic resonance imaging data. Software tools used for visualizing biological data range from simple, stand-alone programs to complex, integrated systems.

State-of-the-art and perspectives

Today we are experiencing a rapid growth in volume and diversity of biological data, presenting an increasing challenge for biologists. A key step in understanding and learning from these data is visualization. Thus, there has been a corresponding increase in the number and diversity of systems for visualizing biological data.

An emerging trend is the blurring of boundaries between the visualization of 3D structures at atomic resolution, visualization of larger complexes by cryo-electron microscopy, and visualization of the location of proteins and complexes within whole cells and tissues.[1] [2]

A second emerging trend is an increase in the availability and importance of time-resolved data from systems biology, electron microscopy[3] [4] and cell and tissue imaging. In contrast, visualization of trajectories has long been a prominent part of molecular dynamics.

Finally, as datasets are increasing in size, complexity, and interconnectness, biological visualization systems are improving in usability, data integration and standardization.

List of visualization systems

A large number of software systems are available for visualization biological data. The links below link lists of such systems, grouped by application areas.

Genomic and assembly data

Alignments, phylogeny and evolution

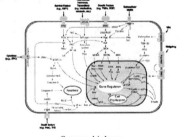

Systems biology

Molecular Graphics Molecular Dynamics

Microscopy

Magnetic resonance imaging

Related conferences

- BioVis: IEEE Symposium on Biological Data Visualization [5]
- Applications of Information Visualization in Bioinformatics [6]
- CIBDV: Computational Intelligence for Biological Data Visualization [7]
- IVBI: Information Visualization in Biomedical Informatics Symposium [8]
- VMLS: Visualization in Medicine & Life Sciences [9]
- VIZBI: Workshop on Visualizing Biological Data [10]

References

[1] Lucić (2005). "Structural studies by electron tomography: from cells to molecules". *Annual review of biochemistry* **74**: 833–65. doi:10.1146/annurev.biochem.73.011303.074112. PMID 15952904.

[2] Steven (2008). "The future is hybrid". *Journal of structural biology* **163** (3): 186–95. doi:10.1016/j.jsb.2008.06.002. PMID 18602011.

[3] Plattner (2006). "Sub-second cellular dynamics: time-resolved electron microscopy and functional correlation". *International review of cytology* **255**: 133–76. doi:10.1016/S0074-7696(06)55003-X. PMID 17178466.

[4] Frank (2004). "Time-resolved imaging of macromolecular processes and interactions". *Journal of structural biology* **147** (3): 209–10. doi:10.1016/j.jsb.2004.06.003. PMID 15450290.

[5] http://www.biovis.net

[6] http://www.sbforum.org/earchive.php?e_id=45

[7] http://www.pa.icar.cnr.it/sscibb2008/

[8] http://www.graphicslink.co.uk/IV09/IVbm.htm

[9] http://www.faculty.jacobs-university.de/llinsen/vmls/2009

[10] http://vizbi.org

Biological database

Biological databases are libraries of life sciences information, collected from scientific experiments, published literature, high-throughput experiment technology, and computational analyses. They contain information from research areas including genomics, proteomics, metabolomics, microarray gene expression, and phylogenetics.[1] Information contained in biological databases includes gene function, structure, localization (both cellular and chromosomal), clinical effects of mutations as well as similarities of biological sequences and structures.

Relational database concepts of computer science and Information retrieval concepts of digital libraries are important for understanding biological databases. Biological database design, development, and long-term management is a core area of the discipline of bioinformatics.[2] Data contents include gene sequences, textual descriptions, attributes and ontology classifications, citations, and tabular data. These are often described as semi-structured data, and can be represented as tables, key delimited records, and XML structures. Cross-references among databases are common, using database accession numbers.

Overview

Biological databases are an important tool in assisting scientists to understand and explain a host of biological phenomena from the structure of biomolecules and their interaction, to the whole metabolism of organisms and to understanding the evolution of species. This knowledge helps facilitate the fight against diseases, assists in the development of medications and in discovering basic relationships amongst species in the history of life.

Biological knowledge is distributed amongst many different general and specialized databases. This sometimes makes it difficult to ensure the consistency of information. Biological databases cross-reference other databases with accession numbers as one way of linking their related knowledge together.

An important resource for finding biological databases is a special yearly issue of the journal *Nucleic Acids Research* (NAR). The Database Issue of NAR [3] is freely available, and categorizes many of the publicly available online databases related to biology and bioinformatics.

Output

Biological data comes in many formats. These formats include text, sequence data, protein structure and links. Each of these can be found from certain sources, for example:

- Text formats are provided by PubMed and OMIM.
- Sequence data are provide by GenBank, in terms of DNA, and UniProt, in terms of protein.
- Protein structures are provided by PDB, SCOP, and CATH.

Problems associated with protein databases

Since discovery in the area of protein structure has not evolved quite as quickly as discoveries in the area sequence data, due to the 3D nature of protein structure, less information is available for it. Nonetheless, data can be accessed through members of the wwPDB (PDBe [4], PDBj [5] and RCSB PDB [6], SCOP-Structural Classification of Proteins- at ([7]), and CATH at ([8]).

Species-specific databases

Species-specific databases are available for some species, mainly those that are often used in research. For example, Colibase ([9]) is an *E. coli* database. Other popular species specific databases include, Flybase ([10]) for *Drosophila*, and WormBase ([11]) for the nematodes *Caenorhabditis elegans* and *Caenorhabditis briggsae*.

References

[1] Altman RB (March 2004). "Building successful biological databases" (http://bib.oxfordjournals.org/cgi/pmidlookup?view=long&
     pmid=15153301). *Brief. Bioinformatics* **5** (1): 4–5. doi:10.1093/bib/5.1.4. PMID 15153301. .

[2] Bourne P (August 2005). "Will a biological database be different from a biological journal?". *PLoS Comput. Biol.* **1** (3): 179–81.
     doi:10.1371/journal.pcbi.0010034. PMC 1193993. PMID 16158097.

[3] http://www3.oup.co.uk/nar/database/c/

[4] http://www.pdbe.org

[5] http://www.pdbj.org

[6] http://www.pdb.org

[7] http://scop.berkeley.edu/

[8] http://www.cathdb.info/

[9] http://colibase.bham.ac.uk/

[10] http://flybase.bio.indiana.edu/

[11] http://www.wormbase.org/

* http://www.avatar.se/molbioinfo2001/databases.html

External links

* Wiki of biological databases (http://biodatabase.org/index.php/Main_Page)
* Interactive list of biological databases (http://www.oxfordjournals.org/nar/database/c/), classified by categories, from Nucleic Acids Research, 2010
* Genome Proteome Search Engine (http://www.gpse.org) to search across biological databases
* DBD: Database of Biological Databases (http://www.biodbs.info)
* CAMERA (http://camera.calit2.net/index.php) Cyberinfrastructure for Metagenomics, free data repository and bioinformatics tools for metagenomics.

Biological network inference

Biological network inference is the process of making inferences and predictions about biological networks.

Biological networks

Many types of biological networks exist. Few such networks are known in anything approaching their complete structure, even in the simplest bacteria. Still less is known on the parameters governing the behavior of such networks over time, how the networks at different levels in a cell interact, and how to predict the complete state description of a eukaryotic cell or bacterial organism at a given point in the future. Systems biology, in this sense, is still in its infancy. Prediction is the subject of dynamic modeling. This article focuses on a necessary prerequisite to dynamic modeling of a network: inference of the topology, that is, prediction of the "wiring diagram" of the network. More specifically, we focus here on inference of biological network structure using the growing sets of high-throughput expression data for genes, proteins, and metabolites.

Briefly, methods using high-throughput data for inference of regulatory networks rely on searching for patterns of partial correlation or conditional probabilities that indicate causal influence.[1] Such patterns of partial correlations found in the high-throughput data, possibly combined with other supplemental data on the genes or proteins in the proposed networks, or combined with other information on the organism, form the basis upon which such algorithms work. Such algorithms can be of use in inferring the topology of any network where the change in state of one node can affect the state of other nodes.

Computational inference methods

In a topological sense, a network is a set of nodes and a set of directed or undirected edges between the nodes. Biological networks currently under study using such computational inference methods include:

1) Transcriptional regulatory networks. Genes are the nodes and the edges are directed. A gene serves as the source of a direct regulatory edge to a target gene by producing an RNA or protein molecule that functions as a transcriptional activator or inhibitor of the target gene. If the gene is an activator, then it is the source of a positive regulatory connection; if an inhibitor, then it is the source of a negative regulatory connection. Computational algorithms used to infer the topology take as primary input the data from a set of microarray runs measuring the mRNA expression levels of the genes under consideration for inclusion in the network.

As of 2007, the great bulk of high-throughput data being fed into correlation-based algorithms comes from microarray experiments, and such analysis is the most fruitful point of biological application for such algorithms. (This is reflected in the reference list at bottom, where almost all bioinformatic algorithm references are directed toward use of microarray data.) Clustering or some form of statistical classification is typically employed to perform an initial organization of the high-throughput mRNA expression values derived from microarray experiments. The question then arises: how can the clustering or classification results be connected to the underlying biology? Such results can be useful for pattern classification – for example, to classify subtypes of cancer, or to predict differential responses to a drug (pharmacogenomics). But to understand the relationships between the genes, that is, to more precisely define the influence of each gene on the others, the scientist typically attempts to reconstruct the transcriptional regulatory network. This can be done by using background literature, or information in public databases, combined with the clustering results. It can also be done by the application of a correlation-based inference algorithm, as will be discussed below, an approach which is having increased success as the size of the available microarray sets keeps increasing [2] [3]

2) Signal transduction networks (very important in the biology of cancer). Proteins are the nodes and the edges are directed. Primary input into the inference algorithm would be data from a set of experiments measuring protein activation / inactivation (e.g., phosphorylation / dephosphorylation) across a set of proteins.

3) Metabolite networks. Metabolites are the nodes and the edges are directed. Primary input into an algorithm would be data from a set of experiments measuring metabolite levels.

4) Intraspecies or interspecies communication networks in microbial communities. Nodes are excreted organic compounds and the edges are directed. Input into an inference algorithm is data from a set of experiments measuring levels of excreted molecules.

Protein-protein interaction networks are also under very active study. However, reconstruction of these networks does not use correlation-based inference in the sense discussed for the networks already described (interaction does not necessarily imply a change in protein state), and a description of such interaction network reconstruction is left to other articles.

References

[1] Sprites, P; Glymour, C; Scheines, R (2000). *Causation, Prediction, and Search: Adaptive Computation and Machine Learning* (2nd ed.). MIT Press.

[2] Faith, JJ *et al.* (2007). "Large-Scale Mapping and Validation of Escherichia coli Transcriptional Regulation from a Compendium of Expression Profiles". *PLoS Biology* 5 (1): 54–66. doi:10.1371/journal.pbio.0050008. PMC 1764438. PMID 17214507.

[3] Hayete, B; Gardner, TS; Collins, JJ (2007). "Size matters: network inference tackles the genome scale". *Molecular Systems Biology* 3 (1): 77. doi:10.1038/msb4100118. PMC 1828748. PMID 17299414.

Biomax Informatics AG

Biomax Informatics AG

Type	Private
Industry	Bioinformatics, software, services
Founded	1997
Headquarters	Martinsried, Munich, Germany
Key people	Klaus Heumann, CEO
Products	See detailed listing
Website	www.biomax.com [1]

Biomax Informatics is a Munich-based software company specializing in research software for bioinformatics. Biomax was founded in 1997 and has its roots in the Munich Information Center for Protein Sequences (MIPS). The company's customer base consists of companies and research organizations in the areas of drug discovery, diagnostics, fine chemicals, food and plant production. In addition to exclusive software tools, Biomax Informatics provides services and curated knowledge bases.

In September 2007, Biomax Informatics acquired the Viscovery software business of the Austrian data mining specialist Eudaptics Software[2] .

Biomax Informatics and Sophic Systems Alliance Inc. (USA) participate in the Cancer Gene Data Curation Project with the National Cancer Institute (USA)[3] . This project maintains a public data set of cancer-related genes and drugs. This data set has been integrated with the NCI's caBIO (cancer Bioinformatics Infrastructure Objects) domain model which is part of the CaBIG Integrative Cancer Research (ICR) workspace. This Cancer Gene Index[4] [5] can be obtained separately from an NCI web site.

Products

- BioXM Knowledge Management Environment[6] [7]
- BioRS Integration and Retrieval System[8]
- Pedant-Pro Sequence Analysis Suite

Subsidiaries

- Viscovery Software GmbH

References

[1] http://www.biomax.com
[2] Biomax Informatics AG acquires data mining business from eudaptics (http://www.kdnuggets.com/news/2007/n18/28i.html)
[3] "No gene left behind" by Amy Swinderman in Drug Discovery News Informatics (http://www.drugdiscoverynews.com/index.php?newsarticle=2347)
[4] Cancer Gene Index End User Documentation (https://wiki.nci.nih.gov/display/ICR/Cancer+Gene+Index+End+User+Documentation)
[5] Creation of the Cancer Gene Index (https://wiki.nci.nih.gov/display/ICR/Creation+of+the+Cancer+Gene+Index)
[6] Losko, Sascha; Wenger, Karsten; Kalus, Wenzel; Ramge, Andrea; Wiehler, Jens; Heumann, Klaus (2006). *Knowledge Networks of Biological and Medical Data: an Exhaustive and Flexible Solution to Model Life Science Domains*. **4075**. pp. 232. doi:10.1007/11799511_21.

[7] Losko, Sascha; Heumann, Klaus (20092009). "Semantic Data Integration and Knowledge Management to Represent Biological Network
     Associations". *Methods in molecular biology (Clifton, N.J.)* **563**: 241. doi:10.1007/978-1-60761-175-2_13. PMID 19597789.

[8] . doi:10.2390/biecoll-jib-2006-44.

External links

- Biomax Informatics official homepage (http://www.biomax.com)
- Viscovery Software official homepage (http://www.viscovery.net)
- Cancer Gene Data Curation Project (http://ncicb.nci.nih.gov/projects/cgdcp)

Biomedical text mining

Biomedical text mining (also known as **BioNLP**) refers to text mining applied to texts and literature of the biomedical and molecular biology domain. It is a rather recent research field on the edge of natural language processing, bioinformatics, medical informatics and computational linguistics.

There is an increasing interest in text mining and information extraction strategies applied to the biomedical and molecular biology literature due to the increasing number of electronically available publications stored in databases such as PubMed.

Main applications

The main developments in this area have been related to the identification of biological entities (named entity recognition), such as protein and gene names in free text, the association of gene clusters obtained by microarray experiments with the biological context provided by the corresponding literature, automatic extraction of protein interactions and associations of proteins to functional concepts (e.g. gene ontology terms). Even the extraction of kinetic parameters from text or the subcellular location of proteins have been addressed by information extraction and text mining technology.

Examples

- KLEIO [1] - an advanced information retrieval system providing knowledge enriched searching for biomedicine.
- FACTA+ [2] - a MEDLINE search engine for finding associations between biomedical concepts. The FACTA+ Visualizer [3] helps intuitive understanding of FACTA+ search results through graphical visualization of the results.[4]
- U-Compare [5] - U-Compare is an integrated text mining/natural language processing system based on the UIMA Framework, with an emphasis on components for biomedical text mining.[6]
- TerMine [7] - a term management system that identifies key terms in biomedical and other text types.
- MEDIE [8] - an intelligent search engine to retrieve biomedical correlations from MEDLINE, based on indexing by Natural Language Processing and Text Mining techniques [9]
- AcroMine [10] - an acronym dictionary which can be used to find distinct expanded forms of acronyms from MEDLINE.[11]
- AcroMine Disambiguator [12] - Disambiguates abbreviations in biomedical text with their correct full forms.[13]
- GENIA tagger [14] - Analyses biomedical text and outputs base forms, part-of-speech tags, chunk tags, and named entity tags
- NEMine [15] - Recognises gene/protein names in text
- Yeast MetaboliNER [16] - Recognizes yeast metabolite names in text.
- Smart Dictionary Lookup [17] - machine learning-based gene/protein name lookup.
- Chilibot [18] — A tool for finding relationships between genes or gene products.

- EBIMed [19] - EBIMed is a web application that combines Information Retrieval and Extraction from Medline.[20]
- FABLE [21] — A gene-centric text-mining search engine for MEDLINE
- GOAnnotator [22], an online tool that uses Semantic similarity for verification of electronic protein annotations using GO terms automatically extracted from literature.
- GoPubMed [23] — retrieves PubMed abstracts for your search query, then detects ontology terms from the Gene Ontology and Medical Subject Headings in the abstracts and allows the user to browse the search results by exploring the ontologies and displaying only papers mentioning selected terms, their synonyms or descendants.
- Anne O'Tate [24] Retrieves sets of PubMed records, using a standard PubMed interface, and analyzes them, arranging content of PubMed record fields (MeSH, author, journal, words from title and abtsracts, and others) in order of frequency.
- Information Hyperlinked Over Proteins (iHOP) [25][26] : "A network of concurring genes and proteins extends through the scientific literature touching on phenotypes, pathologies and gene function. iHOP provides this network as a natural way of accessing millions of PubMed abstracts. By using genes and proteins as hyperlinks between sentences and abstracts, the information in PubMed can be converted into one navigable resource, bringing all advantages of the internet to scientific literature research."
- LitInspector [27] — Gene and signal transduction pathway data mining in PubMed abstracts.
- NextBio [28]- Life sciences search engine with a text mining functionality that utilizes PubMed abstracts (ex: literature search) [29] and clinical trials (example) [30] to return concepts relevant to the query based on a number of heuristics including ontology relationships, journal impact, publication date, and authorship.
- PubAnatomy [31] — An interactive visual search engine that provides new ways to explore relationships among Medline literature, text mining results, anatomical structures, gene expression and other background information.
- PubGene [32] — Co-occurrence networks display of gene and protein symbols as well as MeSH, GO, PubChem and interaction terms (such as "binds" or "induces") as these appear in MEDLINE records (that is, PubMed titles and abstracts).
- Whatizit [33] - Whatizit is great at identifying molecular biology terms and linking them to publicly available databases.[34]
- XTractor [35] — Discovering Newer Scientific Relations Across PubMed Abstracts. A tool to obtain manually annotated,expert curated relationships for Proteins [36], Diseases [37], Drugs [38] and Biological Processes [39] as they get published in PubMed.
- Medical Abstract [40] — Medical Abstract is an aggregator for medical abstract journal from PubMed Abstracts.
- MuGeX [41] — MuGeX is a tool for finding disease specific mutation-gene pairs.
- MedCase [42] — MedCase is an experimental tool of Faculties of Veterinary Medicine and Computer Science in Cluj-Napoca, designed as a homeostatic serving sistem with natural language support for medical applications.

Conferences at which BioNLP research is presented

BioNLP is presented at a variety of meetings:

- Pacific Symposium on Biocomputing: in plenary session
- Intelligent Systems for Molecular Biology: in plenary session and also in the BioLINK and Bio-ontologies workshops
- Association for Computational Linguistics and North American Association for Computational Linguistics annual meetings and associated workshops: in plenary session and as part of the BioNLP workshop (see below)
- BioNLP 2010 [43]
- American Medical Informatics Association annual meeting: in plenary session

External links

- Bio-NLP resources, systems and application database collection [44]
- The BioNLP mailing list archives [45]
- Corpora for biomedical text mining [46]
- The BioCreative evaluations of biomedical text mining technologies [6]
- Directory of people involved in BioNLP [47]
- National Centre for Text Mining (NaCTeM) [48]

References

[1] http://www.nactem.ac.uk/software/kleio/

[2] http://refine1-nactem.mc.man.ac.uk/facta/

[3] http://refine1-nactem.mc.man.ac.uk/facta-visualizer/

[4] Tsuruoka Y, Tsujii J and Ananiadou S (2008). "FACTA: a text search engine for finding associated biomedical concepts". *Bioinformatics* **24** (21): 2559–2560. doi:10.1093/bioinformatics/btn469. PMC 2572701. PMID 18772154.

[5] http://u-compare.org/index.html

[6] Kano Y, Baumgartner Jr WA, McCrohon L, Ananiadou S, Cohen KB, Hunter L and Tsujii J (2009). "U-Compare: share and compare text mining tools with UIMA". *Bioinformatics* **25** (15): 1997–1998. doi:10.1093/bioinformatics/btp289. PMC 2712335. PMID 19414535.

[7] http://www.nactem.ac.uk/software/termine/

[8] http://www-tsujii.is.s.u-tokyo.ac.jp/medie/

[9] Miyao Y, Ohta T, Masuda K, Tsuruoka Y, Yoshida K, Ninomiya T and Tsujii J (2006). "Semantic Retrieval for the Accurate Identification of Relational Concepts in Massive Textbases" (http://www-tsujii.is.s.u-tokyo.ac.jp/~yusuke/paper/acl2006.pdf). *Proceedings of COLING-ACL 2006.* pp. 1017–1024. .

[10] http://www.nactem.ac.uk/software/acromine/

[11] Okazaki N and Ananiadou S (2006). "Building an abbreviation dictionary using a term recognition approach". *Bioinformatics* **22** (24): 3089–3095. doi:10.1093/bioinformatics/btl534. PMID 17050571.

[12] http://www.nactem.ac.uk/software/acromine_disambiguation/

[13] Okazaki N, Ananiadou S and Tsujii J (2010). "Building a high-quality sense inventory for improved abbreviation disambiguation". *Bioinformatics* **26** (9): 1246–1253. doi:10.1093/bioinformatics/btq129. PMC 2859134. PMID 20360059.

[14] http://www-tsujii.is.s.u-tokyo.ac.jp/GENIA/tagger/

[15] http://text0.mib.man.ac.uk/~sasaki/bootstrep/nemine.html

[16] http://nactem-t1.mib.man.ac.uk/metaboliner/

[17] http://text0.mib.man.ac.uk/software/mldic/

[18] http://www.chilibot.net/

[19] http://www.ebi.ac.uk/Rebholz-srv/ebimed/

[20] Rebholz-Schuhmann D, Kirsch H, Arregui M, Gaudan S, Riethoven M and Stoehr P (2007). "EBIMed—text crunching to gather facts for proteins from Medline". *Bioinformatics* **23** (2): e237–e244. doi:10.1093/bioinformatics/btl302. PMID 17237098.

[21] http://fable.chop.edu

[22] http://xldb.fc.ul.pt/biotools/rebil/goa/

[23] http://www.gopubmed.org

[24] http://arrowsmith.psych.uic.edu/cgi-bin/arrowsmith_uic/AnneOTate.cgi

[25] http://www.ihop-net.org/UniPub/iHOP/

[26] Hoffmann R, Valencia A (September 2005). "Implementing the iHOP concept for navigation of biomedical literature" (http://bioinformatics.oxfordjournals.org/cgi/pmidlookup?view=long&pmid=16204114). *Bioinformatics* **21** (Suppl 2): ii252–8. doi:10.1093/bioinformatics/bti1142. PMID 16204114. .

[27] http://www.litinspector.org

[28] http://www.nextbio.com

[29] http://www.nextbio.com/b/home/generalSearch.nb?q=breast+cancer

[30] http://www.nextbio.com/b/home/generalSearch.nb?q=breast+cancer#sitype=TRIALS

[31] http://brainarray.mbni.med.umich.edu/Brainarray/prototype/PubAnatomy/

[32] http://www.pubgene.org

[33] http://www.ebi.ac.uk/webservices/whatizit/

[34] Rebholz-Schuhmann D, Arregui M, Gaudan S, Kirsch H, Jimeno A (November 2008). "Text processing through Web services: calling Whatizit". *Bioinformatics* **24** (2): 296–298. doi:10.1093/bioinformatics/btm557. PMID 18006544.

[35] http://www.xtractor.in/

[36] http://www.xtractor.in/insta_search.do?entity_type=SWISSPROT&search_id=P00533&entity_id=EGFR

[37] http://www.xtractor.in/insta_search.do?entity_type=MESH&search_id=D001943&entity_id=Breast%20Neoplasms

[38] http://www.xtractor.in/insta_search.do?entity_type=DRUG&search_id=APRD01148&entity_id=Oseltamivir%20Phosphate

[39] http://www.xtractor.in/insta_search.do?entity_type=GO&search_id=GO:0006915&entity_id=apoptosis

[40] http://medicalabstract.com/

[41] http://bioapps.sabanciuniv.edu/mugex/

[42] http://www.profivet.ro/sim

[43] http://compbio.ucdenver.edu/BioNLP2010

[44] http://zope.bioinfo.cnio.es/bionlp_tools

[45] https://lists.ccs.neu.edu/pipermail/bionlp/

[46] http://compbio.ucdenver.edu/ccp/corpora/index.shtml

[47] http://compbio.ucdenver.edu/Hunter_lab/Cohen/bioNlpPeople.html

[48] http://www.nactem.ac.uk

- Krallinger M, Valencia A (2005). "Text-mining and information-retrieval services for molecular biology" (http:// genomebiology.com/1465-6906/6/224). *Genome Biol.* **6** (7): 224. doi:10.1186/gb-2005-6-7-224. PMC 1175978. PMID 15998455.

- Hoffmann R, Krallinger M, Andres E, Tamames J, Blaschke C, Valencia A (May 2005). "Text mining for metabolic pathways, signaling cascades, and protein networks" (http://stke.sciencemag.org/cgi/ pmidlookup?view=long&pmid=15886388). *Sci. STKE* **2005** (283): pe21. doi:10.1126/stke.2832005pe21. PMID 15886388.

- Krallinger M, Erhardt RA, Valencia A (March 2005). "Text-mining approaches in molecular biology and biomedicine" (http://linkinghub.elsevier.com/retrieve/pii/S1359644605033763). *Drug Discov. Today* **10** (6): 439–45. doi:10.1016/S1359-6446(05)03376-3. PMID 15808823.

- Biomedical Literature Mining Publications (BLIMP) (http://blimp.cs.queensu.ca/): A comprehensive and regularly updated index of publications on (bio)medical text mining

BioMOBY

BioMOBY is a registry of web services used in bioinformatics. It allows interoperability between biological data hosts and analytical services by annotating services with terms taken from standard ontologies.

The BioMOBY project

The BioMoby [1] project began at the **Model Organism Bring Your own Database Interface Conference (MOBY-DIC)**, held in Emma Lake [2], Saskatchewan on September 21, 2001. It stemmed from a conversation between Mark D Wilkinson [3] and Suzanna Lewis [4] during a [5] Gene Ontology developers meeting at the Carnegie Institute, Stanford, where the functionalities of the Genquire and Apollo genome annotation tools were being discussed and compared. The lack of a simple standard that would allow these tools to interact with the myriad of data-sources required to accurately annotate a genome was a critical need of both systems.

Funding for the BioMOBY project was subsequently adopted by Genome Prairie [6] (2002-2005), Genome Alberta [7](2005-date), in part through Genome Canada [8], a not-for-profit institution leading the Canadian X-omic initiatives.

There are two main branches of the BioMOBY project. One is a web-service-based approach, while the other utilizes Semantic Web technologies. This article will refer only to the Web Service specifications. The other branch of the project, Semantic Moby, is described in a separate entry.

Moby

The Moby project defines three Ontologies that describe biological data-types [9], biological data-formats [10], and bioinformatics analysis types [11]. Most of the interoperable behaviours seen in Moby are achieved through the Object (data-format) and Namespace (data-type) ontologies.

The MOBY Namespace Ontology [9] is derived from the Cross-Reference Abbreviations List of the Gene Ontology [5] project. It is simply a list of abbreviations for the different types of identifiers that are used in bioinformatics. For example, Genbank has "gi" identifiers that are used to enumerate all of their sequence records - this is defined as "NCBI_gi" in the Namespace Ontology.

The MOBY Object Ontology [10] is an ontology consisting of IS-A, HAS-A, and HAS relationships between data formats. For example a DNASequence IS-A GenericSequence and HAS-A String representing the text of the sequence. All data in Moby must be represented as some type of MOBY Object. An XML serialization of this ontology is defined in the Moby API such that any given ontology node has a predictable XML structure.

Thus, between these two ontologies, a service provider and/or a client program can receive a piece of Moby XML, and immediately know both its structure, and its "intent" (semantics).

The final core component of Moby is the MOBY Central [12] web service registry. MOBY Central [12] is aware of the Object, Namespace and Service ontologies, and thus can match consumers who have in-hand Moby data, with service providers who claim to consume that data-type (or some compatible ontological data-type) or to perform a particular operation on it. This "semantic matching" helps ensure that only relevant service providers are identified in a registry query, and moreover, ensures that the in-hand data can be passed to that service provider *verbatim*. As such, the interaction between a consumer and a service provider can be partially or fully automated, as shown in the Gbrowse Moby [13] and Ahab [14] clients respectively.

BioMOBY and RDF/OWL

BioMOBY does not, for its core operations, utilize the RDF or OWL standards from the W3C. This is in part because neither of these standards were stable in 2001, when the project began, and in part because the library support for these standards were not "commodity" in any of the most common languages (i.e. Perl and Java) at that time.

Nevertheless, the BioMOBY system exhibits what can only be described as Semantic Web-like behaviours. The BioMOBY Object Ontology [10] controls the valid data structures in exactly the same way as an OWL ontology defines an RDF data instance. BioMOBY Web Services consume and generate BioMOBY XML [15], the structure of which is defined by the BioMOBY Object Ontology [10]. As such, BioMOBY Web Services have been acting as prototypical Semantic Web Services since 2001, despite not using the eventual RDF/OWL standards.

However, BioMOBY does utilize the RDF/OWL standards, as of 2006, for the description of its Objects [10], Namespaces [9],Service [11], and Registry [16]. Increasingly these ontologies are being used to govern the behaviour of all BioMOBY functions using DL reasoners.

BioMOBY clients

There are several client applications that can search and browse the BioMOBY registry of services. One of the most popular is the Taverna workbench built as part of the MyGrid project. The first BioMOBY client was Gbrowse Moby [17], written in 2001 to allow access to the prototype version of BioMoby Services. Gbrowse Moby [18], in addition to being a BioMoby browser, now works in tandem with the Taverna workbench to create SCUFL workflows reflecting the Gbrowse Moby browsing session that can then be run in a high-throughput environment. The Seahawk [19] [20] applet also provides the ability to export a session history as a Taverna workflow, in what constitutes a programming by example functionality.

The Ahab [14] client is a fully automated data mining tool. Given a starting point, it will discover, and execute, every possible BioMOBY service and provide the results in a clickable interface.

External links

- Official BioMOBY website [21]
- Publications about BioMOBY [22] tagged using Connotea

References

[1] http://biomoby.org
[2] http://www.emmalake.usask.ca/
[3] http://www.bioperl.org/wiki/Mark_Wilkinson
[4] http://www.bioperl.org/wiki/Suzi_Lewis
[5] http://geneontology.org
[6] http://genomeprairie.ca
[7] http://genomealberta.ca
[8] http://genomecanada.ca
[9] http://biomoby.org/RESOURCES/MOBY-S/Namespaces
[10] http://biomoby.org/RESOURCES/MOBY-S/Objects
[11] http://biomoby.org/RESOURCES/MOBY-S/Services
[12] http://biomoby.open-bio.org/CVS_CONTENT/moby-live/Docs/MOBY-S_API/CentralRegistry.html
[13] http://mobycentral.icapture.ubc.ca/
[14] http://bioinfo.icapture.ubc.ca/bgood/Ahab.html
[15] http://biomoby.open-bio.org/CVS_CONTENT/moby-live/Docs/MOBY-S_API/DataClassOntology.html
[16] http://biomoby.org/RESOURCES/MOBY-S/ServiceInstances
[17] http://moby.ucalgary.ca/gbrowse_moby
[18] http://www.scfbm.org/content/1/1/4
[19] http://moby.ucalgary.ca/seahawk
[20] http://www.biomedcentral.com/1471-2105/8/208/abstract
[21] http://www.biomoby.org/
[22] http://www.connotea.org/tag/biomoby

BioPAX

BioPAX (Biological Pathway Exchange) is a RDF/OWL-based standard language to represent biological pathways at the molecular and cellular level. Its major use is to facilitate the exchange of pathway data. Pathway data captures our understanding of biological processes, but its rapid growth necessitates development of databases and computational tools to aid interpretation. However, the current fragmentation of pathway information across many databases with incompatible formats presents barriers to its effective use. BioPAX solves this problem by making pathway data substantially easier to collect, index, interpret and share. BioPAX can represent metabolic and signaling pathways, molecular and genetic interactions and gene regulation networks. BioPAX was created through a community process. Through BioPAX, millions of interactions organized into thousands of pathways across many organisms, from a growing number of sources, are available. Thus, large amounts of pathway data are available in a computable form to support visualization, analysis and biological discovery.

It is supported by a variety of online databases (e.g. Reactome) and tools. The latest released version is BioPAX Level 3. There is also an effort to create a version of BioPAX as part of OBO.

Databases with BioPAX Export

Online databases offering BioPAX export include:

- Signaling Gateway Molecule Pages (SGMP) [1]
- Reactome
- BioCyc
- INOH [2]
- BioModels [3]
- Nature/NCI Pathway Interaction Database
- Cancer Cell Map [4]
- Pathway Commons [5]
- Netpath - A curated resource of signal transduction pathways in humans
- ConsensusPathDB - A database integrating human functional interaction networks
- PANTHER [6] (List of Pathways [7])

Software

Software supporting BioPAX include:

- Paxtools [8], a Java API for handling BioPAX files
- Systems Biology Linker (Sybil) [9], an application for visualizing BioPAX and converting BioPAX to SBML, as part of the Virtual Cell [10].
- ChiBE [11] (Chisio BioPAX Editor), an application for visualizing and editing BioPAX.
- BioPAX Validator [12] an application to check rules and best practices (project wiki [13])

External links

- BioPAX homepage [14]

References

[1] http://www.signaling-gateway.org/molecule
[2] http://inoh.org
[3] http://biomodels.org
[4] http://cancer.cellmap.org
[5] http://pathwaycommons.org
[6] http://www.pantherdb.org
[7] http://www.pantherdb.org/pathway/pathwayList.jsp
[8] http://www.biopax.org/paxtools.php
[9] http://vcell.org/biopax
[10] http://vcell.org
[11] http://www.bilkent.edu.tr/~bcbi/chibe.html
[12] http://www.biopax.org/biopax-validator/about.html
[13] http://sf.net/apps/mediawiki/biopax/index.php?title=BioPAXValidator
[14] http://www.biopaxwiki.org

BioPerl

BioPerl

Initial release	11 June 2002
Stable release	1.6.9 / 14 April 2011
Preview release	nightly builds
Development status	Active
Written in	Perl
Platform	Cross-platform
Type	Bioinformatics
License	Artistic License and GPL
Website	bioperl.org [1]

BioPerl [2] is a collection of Perl modules that facilitate the development of Perl scripts for bioinformatics applications. It has played an integral role in the Human Genome Project.[3]

It is an active open source software project supported by the Open Bioinformatics Foundation.

Its history can be traced to a September 1996 mailing list discussion [4]. The first stable release was on 11 June 2002; the most recent stable (in terms of API) release is 1.6.1 from October 2009. There are also developer releases produced periodically. Version 1.6.0 is considered to be the most stable (in terms of bugs) version of BioPerl and is recommended for everyday use, but the nightly builds are also extremely stable, and many BioPerl users stay current with those.

In order to take advantage of BioPerl, the user needs a basic understanding of the Perl programming language including an understanding of how to use Perl references, modules, objects and methods.

Features

BioPerl provides software modules for many of the typical tasks of bioinformatics programming. These include:

- Accessing nucleotide and peptide sequence data from local and remote databases
- Transforming formats of database/ file records
- Manipulating individual sequences
- Searching for similar sequences
- Creating and manipulating sequence alignments
- Searching for genes and other structures on genomic DNA
- Developing machine readable sequence annotations

Usage

In addition to being used directly by end-users, [5] BioPerl has also provided the base for a wide variety of bioinformatic tools, including amongst others [6]:

- SynBrowse [7]
- GeneComber [8]
- TFBS [9]
- MIMOX [10]
- BioParser [11]
- Degenerate primer design [12]
- Querying the public databases [13]
- Current Comparative Table [14]

New tools and algorithms from external developers are often integrated directly into BioPerl itself:

- Dealing with phylogenetic trees and nested taxa [15]
- FPC Web tools [16]

Related Programming Languages

Several related bioinformatics programming languages exist, including:

- BioPython
- BioJava
- BioRuby
- BioPHP
- Bioconductor

References

For a complete, up-to-date list of BioPerl references, please see BioPerl publications [6]

[1] http://bioperl.org/

[2] Stajich J, Block D, Boulez K, Brenner S, Chervitz S, Dagdigian C, Fuellen G, Gilbert J, Korf I, Lapp H, Lehväslaiho H, Matsalla C, Mungall C, Osborne B, Pocock M, Schattner P, Senger M, Stein L, Stupka E, Wilkinson M, Birney E (2002). "The Bioperl Toolkit: Perl Modules for the Life Sciences". *Genome Res* **12** (10): 1611–8. doi:10.1101/gr.361602. PMC 187536. PMID 12368254.

[3] Lincoln Stein (1996). "How Perl saved the human genome project" (http://www.bioperl.org/wiki/How_Perl_saved_human_genome). *The Perl Journal* **1** (2). . Retrieved 2009-02-25 (Bioperl.org).

[4] http://bioperl.org/pipermail/bioperl-l/1996-September/002618.html

[5] Khaja R, MacDonald J, Zhang J, Scherer S (2006). "Methods for identifying and mapping recent segmental and gene duplications in eukaryotic genomes". *Methods Mol Biol* **338**: 9–20. doi:10.1385/1-59745-097-9:9. ISBN 1-59745-097-9. PMID 16888347.

[6] http://www.bioperl.org/wiki/BioPerl_publications

[7] Pan X, Stein L, Brendel V (2005). "SynBrowse: a synteny browser for comparative sequence analysis". *Bioinformatics* **21** (17): 3461–8. doi:10.1093/bioinformatics/bti555. PMID 15994196.

[8] Shah S, McVicker G, Mackworth A, Rogic S, Ouellette B (2003). "GeneComber: combining outputs of gene prediction programs for improved results". *Bioinformatics* **19** (10): 1296–7. doi:10.1093/bioinformatics/btg139. PMID 12835277.

[9] Lenhard B, Wasserman W (2002). "TFBS: Computational framework for transcription factor binding site analysis". *Bioinformatics* **18** (8): 1135–6. doi:10.1093/bioinformatics/18.8.1135. PMID 12176838.

[10] Huang J, Gutteridge A, Honda W, Kanehisa M (2006). "MIMOX: a web tool for phage display based epitope mapping". *BMC Bioinformatics* **7**: 451. doi:10.1186/1471-2105-7-451. PMC 1618411. PMID 17038191.

[11] Catanho M, Mascarenhas D, Degrave W, de Miranda A (2006). "BioParser: a tool for processing of sequence similarity analysis reports". *Appl Bioinformatics* **5** (1): 49–53. doi:10.2165/00822942-200605010-00007. PMID 16539538.

[12] Wei X, Kuhn D, Narasimhan G (2003). "Degenerate primer design via clustering". *Proc IEEE Comput Soc Bioinform Conf* **2**: 75–83. PMID 16452781.

[13] Croce O, Lamarre M, Christen R (2006). "Querying the public databases for sequences using complex keywords contained in the feature lines". *BMC Bioinformatics* **7**: 45. doi:10.1186/1471-2105-7-45. PMC 1403806. PMID 16441875.

[14] Landsteiner B, Olson M, Rutherford R (2005). "Current Comparative Table (CCT) automates customized searches of dynamic biological databases". *Nucleic Acids Res* **33** (Web Server issue): W770–3. doi:10.1093/nar/gki432. PMC 1160193. PMID 15980582.

[15] Llabrés M, Rocha J, Rosselló F, Valiente G (2006). "On the ancestral compatibility of two phylogenetic trees with nested taxa". *J Math Biol* **53** (3): 340–64. doi:10.1007/s00285-006-0011-4. PMID 16823581.

[16] Pampanwar V, Engler F, Hatfield J, Blundy S, Gupta G, Soderlund C (2005). "FPC Web Tools for Rice, Maize, and Distribution". *Plant Physiol* **138** (1): 116–26. doi:10.1104/pp.104.056291. PMC 1104167. PMID 15888684.

External links

- BioPerl.org (http://bioperl.org)
- A tutorial (http://bioperl.org/wiki/Bptutorial.pl) for using BioPerl
- HOWTO (http://bioperl.org/wiki/HOWTOs) documents for using BioPerl
- BioPerl.net (http://bioperl.net)

Biopunk

Biopunk (a portmanteau synthesizing "biotechnology" and "punk") is a term used to describe:

1. A hobbyist who experiments with DNA and other aspects of genetics.[1] [2]
2. A technoprogressive movement advocating open access to genetic information.[3] [4]
3. A science fiction genre that focuses on biotechnology and subversives.[5]

Biohacker

Further information: Synthetic biology

Biopunk is a synonym for **biohacker**, a term used to describe a hobbyist who experiments with DNA and other aspects of genetics.[1] [2] A biohacker (or "wetware hacker") is similar to a computer hacker who creates and modifies computer software or computer hardware as a hobby, but should not be confused with a bioterrorist, whose sole intent is the deliberate release of viruses, bacteria, or other germs used to cause illness or death in people, animals, or plants (in the same way a computer hacker should not be confused with the more popular, yet erroneous, use of the term, describing someone who spreads computer viruses or breaks into computers systems for malicious purposes).[6]

Pat Mooney, executive director of ETC Group, is a critic of biohacking who argues that—using a laptop computer, published gene sequence information, and mail-order synthetic DNA—just about anyone has the potential to construct genes or entire genomes from scratch (including those of the lethal pathogens) in the near-future. He warns that the danger of this development is not just bio-terror, but "bio-error".[7]

Movement

Further information: DIYbio

The **biopunk movement** is a small intellectual and cultural movement, which encompasses a growing number of scientists, artists, and cultural critics who are organizing to create public awareness of how genomic information, produced by bioinformatics, gets used and misused. On the basis of a presumed parallel between genetic and computational code, science journalist Annalee Newitz has called for open-sourcing of genomic databases and declared that "Free our genetic data!" is the rallying cry of the biopunk.[3] [4] Biological Innovation for Open Society is an example of an open-source initiative in biotechnology aiming to apply open license for biological innovation.[8]

Self-described "transgenic artist" Eduardo Kac uses biotechnology and genetics to create provocative works that concomitantly revel in scientific techniques and critique them. In what is likely his most famous work, *Alba*, Kac collaborated with a French laboratory to procure a green-fluorescent rabbit: a rabbit implanted with a green fluorescent protein gene from a type of jellyfish in order for the rabbit to fluoresce green under ultraviolet light.[3] The members of the Critical Art Ensemble have written books and staged multimedia performance interventions around this issue, including *The Flesh Machine* (focusing on in vitro fertilisation, surveillance of the body, and liberal eugenics) and *Cult of the New Eve* (analyzing the pseudoreligious discourse around new reproductive technologies).[9] Contributors to Biotech Hobbyist Magazine have written extensively on the field.[10]

Biologist, speculative-fiction author, and self-described biopunk, Meredith L. Patterson is known for her work on yogurt bacteria within the DIYbio community, as well as being the author of "A Biopunk Manifesto",[11] [12] which she delivered at the UCLA Center for Society and Genetics' symposium, "Outlaw Biology? Public Participation in the Age of Big Bio". This manifesto is modeled after "A Cypherpunk Manifesto" by Eric Hughes, which states the goals of the cypherpunk movement. The influence of the cypherpunks (a cyberpunk derivative like the biopunk subculture) on the biopunk community does not end there; Patterson's husband and long-time collaborator Len Sassaman was a cypherpunk contemporary of Hughes. Patterson and Sassaman have worked together on a number of biohacking projects and heavily promoted the continued legality of citizen science, both on moral and practical grounds.[13] [14]

The biopunk movement is also a political dissident movement to the extent that the arrest and prosecution of some members for their work with harmless microbes, such as artivist Steve Kurtz, has been denounced as political repression by critics who argue the U.S. government has used post-9/11 anti-terrorism powers to intimidate artists and others who use their art to criticize society.[15]

Science fiction

Further information: Cyberpunk derivatives

Biopunk science fiction is a subgenre of cyberpunk fiction that focuses on the near-future unintended consequences of the biotechnology revolution following the discovery of recombinant DNA. Biopunk stories explore the struggles of individuals or groups, often the product of human experimentation, against a backdrop of totalitarian governments and megacorporations which misuse biotechnologies as means of social control and profiteering. Unlike cyberpunk, it builds not on information technology, but on synthetic biology. Like in postcyberpunk fiction, individuals are usually modified and enhanced not with cyberware, but by genetic manipulation.[5] A common feature of biopunk fiction is the "black clinic", which is a laboratory, clinic, or hospital that performs illegal, unregulated, or ethically-dubious biological modification and genetic engineering procedures.[16] Many features of biopunk fiction have their roots in William Gibson's *Neuromancer*, one of the first cyberpunk novels.[17]

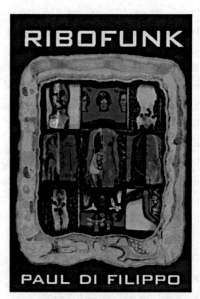

Cover of *Ribofunk* by Paul Di Filippo, a seminal biopunk story collection.

One of the prominent writers in this field is Paul Di Filippo, though he called his collection of such stories **ribofunk**, a portmanteau word synthesizing "ribosome" and "funk".[18] In *RIBOFUNK: The Manifesto*,[19] Di Filippo wrote:

> **Why Ribo?** Cybernetics was a dead science when cyberpunk SF was born, a cul-de-sac without living practitioners. Furthermore, the "cyber" prefix has been irreparably debased by overuse, in vehicles ranging from comic books to bad movies. The tag now stands for nothing in the public mind but computer hacking and fanciful cyborgs such as Robocop. And Weiner's actual texts do not provide enough fruitful metaphors for constructing a systematic worldview. **Why Funk?** Punk was a dead music when cyberpunk SF was born, a

cul-de-sac albeit with living practitioners who just hadn't gotten the message yet. The music's nihilistic, chiliastic worldview had already culminated in its only possible end: self-extinction. **What is Ribofunk then?** Ribofunk is speculative fiction which acknowledges, is informed by and illustrates the tenet that the next revolution--the only one that really matters--will be in the field of biology. To paraphrase Pope, ribofunk holds that: "The proper study of mankind is life." Forget physics and chemistry; they are only tools to probe living matter. Computers? Merely simulators and modelers for life. The cell is King! [19]

Di Filippo argues that precursors of ribofunk fiction include H. G. Wells' *The Island of Doctor Moreau*; Julian Huxley's *The Tissue Culture King*; some of David H. Keller's stories, Damon Knight's *Natural State and Other Stories*; Frederik Pohl and Cyril M. Kornbluth's *Gravy Planet*; novels of T. J. Bass and Varley; Greg Bear's *Blood Music* and Bruce Sterling's *Schismatrix*.[19]

Books

- *Ribofunk* by Paul Di Filippo [5] [20]
- *The Movement of Mountains* and *The Brains of Rats* by Michael Blumlein [21]
- *Clade* and *Crache* by Mark Budz [22]
- *White Devils* by Paul J. McAuley [23] [24]
- The *Xenogenesis* trilogy by Octavia E. Butler [3]
- *The Windup Girl* by Paolo Bacigalupi [25]

Film and television

- *Gattaca* (1997) [26]
- *Dark Angel* (2000) [27]

Computer and video games

- *BioShock* [28]

Comics and manga

- *Doktor Sleepless* comic by Warren Ellis [29]
- *Fluorescent Black* by M.F. Wilson and Nathan Fox[30]

Notes

[1] Katz, J.S.: "Roses are Black, Violets are Green", *New Scientist*, 6 January 1990

[2] Katz, J.S.: "That which is not Forbidden is Mandatory", *BioTech Educ*, 4(1), 1990

[3] Newitz, Annalee (2001). *Biopunk* (http://web.archive.org/web/20021220190353/http://www.sfbg.com/SFLife/tech/71.html). Archived from the original (http://www.sfbg.com/SFLife/tech/71.html) on 2002-12-20. . Retrieved 2007-01-26.

[4] Newitz, Annalee (2002). *Genome Liberation* (http://archive.salon.com/tech/feature/2002/02/26/biopunk/print.html). . Retrieved 2007-01-26.

[5] Quinion, Michael (1997). *World Wide Words: Biopunk* (http://www.worldwidewords.org/turnsofphrase/tp-bio3.htm). . Retrieved 2007-01-26.

[6] Schrage, Michael (1988-01-31). "Playing God in Your Basement". Washington Post.

[7] ETC Group (January 2007) (PDF). *Extreme Genetic Engineering: An Introduction to Synthetic Biology* (http://www.etcgroup.org/upload/publication/602/01/synbioreportweb.pdf). . Retrieved 2007-02-02.

[8] "BiOS" (http://www.bios.net/daisy/bios/home.html). .

[9] "Critical Art Ensemble" (http://www.critical-art.net/). .

[10] "Biotech Hobbyist Magazine" (http://www.nyu.edu/projects/xdesign/biotechhobbyist/). .

[11] A Biopunk Manifesto, 2009 (http://maradydd.livejournal.com/496085.html)

[12] http://www.biopunk.org/maradydd-s-biopunk-manifesto-t336.html

[13] Tyson Anderson. "Darning Genes: Biology for the Homebody" (http://www.hplusmagazine.com/articles/bio/darning-genes-biology-homebody). h+. .

[14] Rise of the Garage Genome Hackers - New Scientist (http://www.newscientist.com/article/mg20126881. 400-genetic-manpulation-now-becoming-a-hobby.html?full=true&print=true)

[15] http://www.firstamendmentcenter.org/news.aspx?id=19246

[16] Pulver, David L. (1998). *GURPS Bio-Tech*. Steve Jackson Games. ISBN 1556343361.

[17] Paul Taylor. "Fleshing Out the Maelstrom: Biopunk and the Violence of Information" (http://journal.media-culture.org.au/0006/biopunk.php). Journal of Media and Culture. .

[18] Fisher, Jeffrey (1996). *Ribofunk* (http://www.wired.com/wired/archive/4.11/ribopunk_pr.html). . Retrieved 2007-01-26.

[19] Di Filippo, Paul (1998). *RIBOFUNK: The Manifesto* (http://www.streettech.com/bcp/BCPtext/Manifestos/Ribofunk.html). . Retrieved 2011-01-05.

[20] "This Just In...News from The Agony Column" (http://www.trashotron.com/agony/news/2005/04-11-05.htm). Trashotron.com. . Retrieved 2008-11-28.

[21] "Locus Online: Review by Claude Lalumière" (http://www.locusmag.com/2002/Reviews/Lalumiere05_WonderAnatomy.html). Locusmag.com. . Retrieved 2008-11-28.

[22] "Science Fiction Book Reviews" (http://www.scifi.com/sfw/issue399/books.html). Scifi.com. . Retrieved 2008-11-28.

[23] Lalumiere BestOf2004.html (http://www.locusmag.com/2005/Features/01)

[24] "White Devils by Paul McAuley - an infinity plus review" (http://www.infinityplus.co.uk/fantasticfiction/whitedevils.htm). Infinityplus.co.uk. . Retrieved 2008-11-28.

[25] Grossman, Lev (8 December 2009). "The Windup Girl by Paulo Bacigalupi" (http://www.time.com/time/specials/packages/article/0,28804,1945379_1943868_1943887,00.html). Time. . Retrieved 29 October 2010.

[26] "NEUROETHICS | The Narrative Perspectives" (http://web.archive.org/web/20080531123956/http://neuroethics.upenn.edu/narrative_perspec.html). Neuroethics.upenn.edu. Archived from the original (http://neuroethics.upenn.edu/narrative_perspec.html) on 2008-05-31. . Retrieved 2008-11-28.

[27] "Science Fiction News of the Week" (http://www.scifi.com/sfw/issue222/news.html). Scifi.com. . Retrieved 2008-11-28.

[28] "BioShock for Xbox 360 Reviews - Xbox 360 BioShock Reviews" (http://www.gamespot.com/xbox360/action/bioshock/player_review.html?id=532056). 2K Games. August 21, 2007. . Retrieved 2008-11-28.

[29] "Warren Ellis: Modify Your Body But Also Worry About the Planet" (http://io9.com/341903/modify-your-body-but-also-worry-about-the-planet). Io9.com. . Retrieved 2008-11-28.

[30] "Genome Alberta Interview" (http://www.genomealberta.ca/blogs/main_08180801.aspx). Genome Alberta. . Retrieved 2008-08-18.

External links

- The Biopunk Directory (http://www.cyberpunked.org/bpkdir/), a comprehensive directory of biopunk resources
- Biopunk.org (http://www.biopunk.org/), a community for bio-hackers
- DIYbio.org (http://www.diybio.org/), a community for DIY biological engineers
- Hackteria.org (http://www.hackteria.org/), a community for bio-artists
- OpenWetWare (http://www.openwetware.org/), an open-source resource for synthetic biology researchers
- OpenPCR (http://www.openpcr.org/), an open-source design for a building a thermal cycler

Biopython

Biopython

Stable release	1.56 / 26 November 2010
Development status	Active
Written in	Python and some C
Platform	Cross-platform
Type	Bioinformatics
License	Biopython License [1]
Website	biopython.org [2]

The **Biopython** Project is an international association of developers of freely available Python tools for computational molecular biology, as well as bioinformatics.

References

- Cock PJ, Antao T, Chang JT, *et al.* (June 2009). "Biopython: freely available Python tools for computational molecular biology and bioinformatics". *Bioinformatics* **25** (11): 1422–3. doi:10.1093/bioinformatics/btp163. PMC 2682512. PMID 19304878.
- refer to the Biopython website for other papers describing Biopython [3], and a list of over one hundred publications using/citing Biopython [4].

External links

- Biopython.org [5]
- Biopython Tutorial and Cookbook [6] (PDF [7])

References

[1] http://www.biopython.org/DIST/LICENSE
[2] http://biopython.org/
[3] http://biopython.org/wiki/Documentation#Papers
[4] http://biopython.org/wiki/Publications
[5] http://biopython.org
[6] http://biopython.org/DIST/docs/tutorial/Tutorial.html
[7] http://biopython.org/DIST/docs/tutorial/Tutorial.pdf

BIOSCI

BIOSCI, also known as **Bionet**, is a set of electronic communication forum used by life scientists around the world. It includes the Bionet Usenet newsgroups and parallel e-mail lists, with public archives since 1992 at www.bio.net [1]. BIOSCI/Bionet provides public, open access biology news and discussion for areas such as molecular biology methods and reagents, bioinformatics software and computational biology, toxicology, and several organism communities including yeast, C.elegans and annelida (worms), the plant arabidopsis, fruitfly, maize (corn), and others.[2]

BIOSCI/Bionet was started as part of the GenBank public biosequence database project by Intelligenetics at Stanford University in the mid 1980s, in collaboration with Martin Bishop and Michael Ashburner in the University of Cambridge.[3] It latter moved to the United Kingdom's MRC Rosalind Franklin Centre for Genomics Research (RFCGR). In 2005, with the closing of RFCGR, BIOSCI/Bionet moved to Indiana University Biology Department's IUBio Archive. As one of the earliest bioinformatics community projects on the Internet, GenBank acquired the bio.net domain and the Usenet hierarchy of Bionet for promoting open access communications among bioscientists, in conjunction with public biology data distribution.

Michael Ashburner, co-founder of BIOSCI with Dave Kristofferson of GenBank (Intelligenetics), writes of its origins

> ... in the early 1980s, Martin Bishop and I ran an email news service for a sequence analysis service that we ran on the Cambridge IBM3084Q mainframe. I was also a user of MOLGEN at Stanford, and there Dave Kristofferson ran an internal bulletin board using ANU News. We combined forces to start the Bulletin boards.

The Usenet hierarchy of **Bionet.*** includes bionet.announce (general biology announcements), and research communities of bionet.microbiology, bionet.molbio.methds-reagnts, bionet.neuroscience, bionet.genome.arabidopsis, bionet.plants.education, bionet.drosophila, bionet.biology.computational plus 50 other active areas of discussion.

References

[1] http://www.bio.net
[2] Gilbert, D.G. (2004). "Software Review: Bioinformatics software resources" (http://bib.oxfordjournals.org/cgi/reprint/5/3/300.pdf). *Briefings in Bioinformatics* **5** (3): 300–304. doi:10.1093/bib/5.3.300. PMID 15383216. .
[3] Benton, D. (1990). "Recent changes in the GenBank On-line Service". *Nucleic Acids Research* **18** (6): 1517–1520. doi:10.1093/nar/18.6.1517. PMC 330520. PMID 2326192.

External links

- BIOSCI/Bionet (http://www.bio.net/)
- IUBio Archive (http://iubio.bio.indiana.edu/)
- Dave Kristofferson on BIOSCI (http://www.bio.net/bionet/mm/bioforum/1991-July/003257.html)
- NIH support of GenBank/BIOSCI (http://www.bio.net/bionet/mm/bioforum/1991-July/001798.html)

bioSearch

Website Information

Website: biosearch
Type : Scientific
Operational since : 2009
Homepage: bioSearch.in [1]

bioSearch is a web application developed to manage marine biodiversity data from Indian waters.

Background

Recent demand for Indian marine biodiversity information has increased manifolds. Owing mainly to realization of marine biodiversity potential in biotechnology, pollution control and energy generation. However until recently, a web based, open access database which could provide comprehensive information on Indian coastal biodiversity was lacking. bioSearch is created to address this need.

Usability

bioSearch enables access to anyone from anywhere and at anytime. Once at the bioSearch search page a user can search information by organism name, location where its presence is recorded, its ecology or its economic importance. The user can then obtain information on organism names, image, description, ecology, economic importance and also referred literature

Requirements

bioSearch being a web-based application, user-end requirements are minimal. Basic requirement includes a computer system with an internet connection and a web browser. bioSearch is designed to enable easy access to organism pages at lowest internet connection speeds. This is particularly important as most parts of the country rely on dial–up (56kbps), internet connections.

Applications

Various applications of bioSearch are anticipated. bioSearch at the most basic level can be used by a fishermen for more information on their fish catch. General public can learn more about marine biodiversity by browsing through name indices. Students and lecturers can use description, lifecycle, reproduction, taxonomic and literature information in their project work and other activities. Conservationist can obtain organism distribution and diversity for a particular area or IUCN Red List status for an organism. Biotechnologist can use bioSearch to know distribution of a biotechnologically important organism, which may help in future specimen collection. More advance applications are anticipated in the fields of pisciculture, remote sensing, geographical information systems (GIS) and ecological modeling.

External links

- bioSearch.in Website [1]
- Bioinformatics Centre, NIO. Website [2]

References

[1] http://www.biosearch.in
[2] http://www.niobioinformatics.in

Biositemap

A **Biositemap** is a way for a biomedical research institution of organisation to show how biological information is distributed throughout their Information Technology systems and networks. This information may be shared with other organisations and researchers.

The Biositemap enables web browsers, crawlers and robots to easily access and process the information to use in other systems, media and computational formats. Biositemaps protocols provide clues for the Biositemap web harvesters, allowing them to find resources and content across the whole interlink of the Biositemap system. This means that human or machine users can access any relevant information on any topic across all organisations throughout the Biositemap system and bring it to their own systems for assimilation or analysis.

File framework

The information is normally stored in a biositemap.rdf or biositemap.xml file which contains lists of information about the data, software, tools material and services provided or held by that organisation. Information is presented in metafields and can be created online through sites such as the biositemaps online editor.[1]

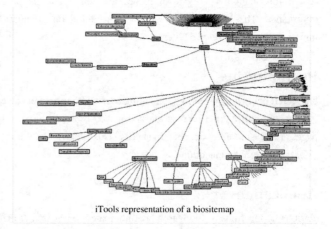

iTools representation of a biositemap

The information is a blend of sitemaps and RSS feeds and is created using the Information Model (IM) and Biomedical Resource Ontology (BRO). The IM is responsible for defining the data held in the metafields and the BRO controls the terminology of the data held in the resource_type field. The BRO is critical in aiding the interactivity of both the other organisations and third parties to search and refine those searches.

Data formats

The Biositemaps Protocol[2] allows scientists, engineers, centers and institutions engaged in modeling, software tool development and analysis of biomedical and informatics data to broadcast and disseminate to the world the information about their latest computational biology resources (data, software tools and web services). The biositemap concept is based on ideas from *Efficient, Automated Web Resource Harvesting*[3] and *Crawler-friendly Web Servers*,[4] and it integrates the features of sitemaps and RSS feeds into a decentralized mechanism for computational biologists and bio-informaticians to openly broadcast and retrieve meta-data about biomedical resources.

These site, institution, or investigator specific *biositemap* descriptions are published in RDF format online and are searched, parsed, monitored and interpreted by web search engines, web applications specific to biositemaps and ontologies, and other applications interested in discovering updated or novel resources for bioinformatics and biomedical research investigations. The biositemap mechanism separates the providers of biomedical resources (investigators or institutions) from the consumers of resource content (researchers, clinicians, news media, funding agencies, educational and research initiatives).

A Biositemap is an RDF file that lists the biomedical and bioinformatics resources for a specific research group or consortium. It allows developers of biomedical resources to describe the functionality and usability of each of their software tools, databases or web-services.[2] [5]

Biositemaps supplement and do not replace the existing frameworks for dissemination of data, tools and services. Using a biositemap does not guarantee that resources will be included in search indexes nor does it influence the way that tools are ranked or perceived by the community. What the Biositemaps protocol will do is provide clues, information and directives to all Biositemap web harvesters that point to the existence and content of biomedical resources at different sites.

Biositemap Information Model

The Biositemap protocol relies on an extensible information model that includes specific properties[6] that are commonly used and necessary for characterizing biomedical resources:

- Name
- Description
- URL
- Stage of development
- Organization
- Resource Ontology Label
- Keywords
- License

Up-to-date documentation on the information model is available at the Biositemaps website.

External links

- Biositemaps website [7]
- Biomedical Resource Ontology [8]
- Biositemaps online editor [9]

References

[1] Biositemaps online editor (http://biositemaps.ncbcs.org/editor/)

[2] Dinov ID, Rubin D, Lorensen W, *et al.* (2008). "iTools: A Framework for Classification, Categorization and Integration of Computational Biology Resources" (http://dx.plos.org/10.1371/journal.pone.0002265). *PLoS ONE* **3** (5): e2265. doi:10.1371/journal.pone.0002265. PMC 2386255. PMID 18509477. .

[3] M.L. Nelson, J.A. Smith, del Campo, H. Van de Sompel, X. Liu (2006). "Efficient, Automated Web Resource Harvesting" (http://public. lanl.gov/herbertv/papers/f140-nelson.pdf). *WIDM'06.* .

[4] Brandman O, Cho J, Garcia-Molina H, Shivakumar N (2000). "Crawler-friendly Web Servers" (http://doi.acm.org/10.1145/362883. 362894). *ACM SIGMETRICS Performance Evaluation Review* **28** (2). doi:10.1145/362883.362894. .

[5] Cannata N, Merelli E, Altman RB (December 2005). "Time to organize the bioinformatics resourceome" (http://dx.plos.org/10.1371/ journal.pcbi.0010076). *PLoS Comput. Biol.* **1** (7): e76. doi:10.1371/journal.pcbi.0010076. PMC 1323464. PMID 16738704. .

[6] Chen YB, Chattopadhyay A, Bergen P, Gadd C, Tannery N (January 2007). "The Online Bioinformatics Resources Collection at the University of Pittsburgh Health Sciences Library System—a one-stop gateway to online bioinformatics databases and software tools" (http:// nar.oxfordjournals.org/cgi/content/full/35/suppl_1/D780). *Nucleic Acids Res.* **35** (Database issue): D780–5. doi:10.1093/nar/gkl781. PMC 1669712. PMID 17108360. .

[7] http://www.biositemaps.org
[8] http://bioportal.bioontology.org/virtual/1104
[9] http://biositemaps.ncbcs.org/editor/

Biostatistics

Biostatistics (a contraction of biology and statistics; sometimes referred to as **biometry** or **biometrics**) is the application of statistics to a wide range of topics in biology. The science of biostatistics encompasses the design of biological experiments, especially in medicine and agriculture; the collection, summarization, and analysis of data from those experiments; and the interpretation of, and inference from, the results.

Biostatistics and the history of biological thought

Biostatistical reasoning and modeling were of critical importance to the foundation theories of modern biology. In the early 1900s, after the rediscovery of Mendel's work, the gaps in understanding between genetics and evolutionary Darwinism led to vigorous debate among biometricians, such as Walter Weldon and Karl Pearson, and Mendelians, such as Charles Davenport, William Bateson and Wilhelm Johannsen. By the 1930s, statisticians and models built on statistical reasoning had helped to resolve these differences and to produce the neo-Darwinian modern evolutionary synthesis.

The leading figures in the establishment of this synthesis all relied on statistics and developed its use in biology.

- Sir Ronald A. Fisher developed several basic statistical methods in support of his work *The Genetical Theory of Natural Selection*
- Sewall G. Wright used statistics in the development of modern population genetics
- J. B. S Haldane's book, *The Causes of Evolution*, reestablished natural selection as the premier mechanism of evolution by explaining it in terms of the mathematical consequences of Mendelian genetics.

These individuals and the work of other biostatisticians, mathematical biologists, and statistically-inclined geneticists helped bring together evolutionary biology and genetics into a consistent, coherent whole that could begin to be quantitatively modeled.

In parallel to this overall development, the pioneering work of D'Arcy Thompson in *On Growth and Form* also helped to add quantitative discipline to biological study.

Despite the fundamental importance and frequent necessity of statistical reasoning, there may nonetheless have been a tendency among biologists to distrust or deprecate results which are not qualitatively apparent. One anecdote describes Thomas Hunt Morgan banning the Friden calculator from his department at Caltech, saying "Well, I am like a guy who is prospecting for gold along the banks of the Sacramento River in 1849. With a little intelligence, I can reach down and pick up big nuggets of gold. And as long as I can do that, I'm not going to let any people in my department waste scarce resources in placer mining."[1] Educators are now adjusting their curricula to focus on more quantitative concepts and tools.[2]

Education and training programs

Almost all educational programmes in biostatistics are at postgraduate level. They are most often found in schools of public health, affiliated with schools of medicine, forestry, or agriculture, or as a focus of application in departments of statistics.

In the United States, where several universities have dedicated biostatistics departments, many other top-tier universities integrate biostatistics faculty into statistics or other departments, such as epidemiology. Thus, departments carrying the name "biostatistics" may exist under quite different structures. For instance, relatively new biostatistics departments have been founded with a focus on bioinformatics and computational biology, whereas older departments, typically affiliated with schools of public health, will have more traditional lines of research involving epidemiological studies and clinical trials as well as bioinformatics. In larger universities where both a statistics and a biostatistics department exist, the degree of integration between the two departments may range from the bare minimum to very close collaboration. In general, the difference between a statistics program and a biostatistics program is twofold: (i) statistics departments will often host theoretical/methodological research which are less common in biostatistics programs and (ii) statistics departments have lines of research that may include biomedical applications but also other areas such as industry (quality control), business and economics and biological areas other than medicine.

Applications of biostatistics

- Public health, including epidemiology, health services research, nutrition, and environmental health
- Design and analysis of clinical trials in medicine
- Population genetics, and statistical genetics in order to link variation in genotype with a variation in phenotype. This has been used in agriculture to improve crops and farm animals (animal breeding). In biomedical research, this work can assist in finding candidates for gene alleles that can cause or influence predisposition to disease in human genetics
- Analysis of genomics data, for example from microarray or proteomics experiments.[3] [4] Often concerning diseases or disease stages.[5]
- Ecology, ecological forecasting
- Biological sequence analysis [6]
- Systems biology for gene network inference or pathways analysis.[7]

Statistical methods are beginning to be integrated into medical informatics, public health informatics, bioinformatics and computational biology.

Biostatistics journals

- *Biometrics*
- *Biometrika*
- *Biostatistics*
- *International Journal of Biostatistics, The*
- *Canadian Journal of Epidemiology and Biostatistics* [8]
- *Journal of Agricultural, Biological, and Environmental Statistics*
- *Journal of Biometrics & Biostatistics*
- *Journal of Biopharmaceutical Statistics*
- *Pharmaceutical Statistics*
- *Statistical Applications in Genetics and Molecular Biology*
- *Statistics in Biopharmaceutical Research*
- *Statistics in Medicine*

- *Turkiye Klinikleri Journal of Biostatistics*

Related fields

Biostatistics shares several methods with quantitative fields such as:

- computational biology
- computer science,
- operations research,
- psychometrics,
- statistics,
- econometrics, and
- mathematical demography

References

[1] Charles T. Munger (2003-10-03). "Academic Economics: Strengths and Faults After Considering Interdisciplinary Needs" (http://www.tilsonfunds.com/MungerUCSBspeech.pdf). .

[2] "Spotlight:application of quantitative concepts and techniques in undergraduate biology" (http://www.reinventioncenter.miami.edu/Spotlights/BioMath.htm). .

[3] Helen Causton, John Quackenbush and Alvis Brazma (2003). "Statistical Analysis of Gene Expression Microarray Data". Wiley-Blackwell.

[4] Terry Speed (2003). "Microarray Gene Expression Data Analysis: A Beginner's Guide". Chapman & Hall/CRC.

[5] Frank Emmert-Streib and Matthias Dehmer (2010). "Medical Biostatistics for Complex Diseases". Wiley-Blackwell. ISBN 3527325859.

[6] Warren J. Ewens and Gregory R. Grant (2004). "Statistical Methods in Bioinformatics: An Introduction". Springer.

[7] Matthias Dehmer, Frank Emmert-Streib, Armin Graber and Armindo Salvador (2011). "Applied Statistics for Network Biology: Methods in Systems Biology". Wiley-Blackwell. ISBN 3527327509.

[8] http://www.cjeb.ca/

External links

- The International Biometric Society (http://www.tibs.org)
- The Collection of Biostatistics Research Archive (http://www.biostatsresearch.com/repository/)
- Guide to Biostatistics (MedPageToday.com) (http://www.medpagetoday.com/Medpage-Guide-to-Biostatistics.pdf)

Journals

- Statistical Applications in Genetics and Molecular Biology (http://www.bepress.com/sagmb/)
- Statistics in Medicine (http://www3.interscience.wiley.com/cgi-bin/jhome/2988)
- The International Journal of Biostatistics (http://www.bepress.com/ijb/)
- Journal of Agricultural, Biological, and Environmental Statistics (http://www.amstat.org/publications/jabes/)
- Journal of Biopharmaceutical Statistics (http://www.tandf.co.uk/journals/titles/10543406.asp)
- Biostatistics (http://www.biostatistics.oxfordjournals.org/)
- Biometrics (http://www.tibs.org/biometrics/)
- Biometrika (http://biomet.oxfordjournals.org/)
- Biometrical Journal (http://www.biometrical-journal.de/)
- Genetics Selection Evolution (http://www.gse-journal.org/)

BISC (database)

BISC

Content	
Description	Protein–protein interaction database linking structural biology with functional genomics
Data types captured	Protein structure and Protein-protein interactions
Contact	
Research center	University of Edinburgh
Primary Citation	PMID 21081561
Release date	2010
Access	
Website	http://bisc.cse.ucsc.edu
Tools	
Miscellaneous	

Binary subcomplexes in proteins database (**BISC**) is a protein–protein interaction database about binary subcomplexes.[1]

References

[1] Juettemann, Thomas; Gerloff Dietlind L (Jan 2011). "BISC: binary subcomplexes in proteins database" (in eng). *Nucleic Acids Res.* (England) **39** (Database issue): D705-11. doi:10.1093/nar/gkq859. PMID 21081561.

External links

- "BISC – Binary Interacting SubComplexes" (http://bisc.cse.ucsc.edu). University of Edinburgh and University of California, Santa Cruz.

BLOSUM

The **BLOSUM** (**BLO**cks of Amino Acid **SU**bstitution **M**atrix) matrix is a substitution matrix used for sequence alignment of proteins. BLOSUM matrices are used to score alignments between evolutionarily divergent protein sequences. They are based on local alignments. BLOSUM matrices were first introduced in a paper by Henikoff and Henikoff.[1] They scanned the BLOCKS database for very conserved regions of protein families (that do not have gaps in the

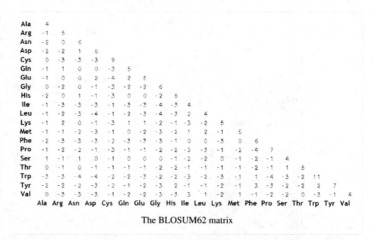

The BLOSUM62 matrix

sequence alignment) and then counted the relative frequencies of amino acids and their substitution probabilities. Then, they calculated a log-odds score for each of the 210 possible substitutions of the 20 standard amino acids. All BLOSUM matrices are based on observed alignments; they are not extrapolated from comparisons of closely related proteins like the PAM Matrices.

Several sets of BLOSUM matrices exist using different alignment databases, named with numbers. BLOSUM matrices with high numbers are designed for comparing closely related sequences, while those with low numbers are designed for comparing distant related sequences. For example, BLOSUM80 is used for less divergent alignments, and BLOSUM45 is used for more divergent alignments. The matrices were created by merging (clustering) all sequences that were more similar than a given percentage into one single sequence and then comparing those sequences (that were all more divergent than the given percentage value) only; thus reducing the contribution of closely related sequences. The percentage used was appended to the name, giving BLOSUM80 for example where sequences that were more than 80% identical were clustered.

Scores within a BLOSUM are log-odds scores that measure, in an alignment, the logarithm for the ratio of the likelihood of two amino acids appearing with a biological sense and the likelihood of the same amino acids appearing by chance.[2] The matrices are based on the minimum percentage identity of the aligned protein sequence used in calculating them.[2] Every possible identity or substitution is assigned a score based on its observed frequences in the alignment of related proteins.[3] A positive score is given to the more likely substitutions while a negative score is given to the less likely substitutions.

To calculate a BLOSUM matrix, the following equation is used:

$$S_{ij} = \left(\frac{1}{\lambda}\right) \log\left(\frac{p_{ij}}{q_i * q_j}\right)$$

Here, p_{ij} is the probability of two amino acids i and j replacing each other in a homologous sequence, and q_i and q_j are the background probabilities of finding the amino acids i and j in any protein sequence at random. The factor λ is a scaling factor, set such that the matrix contains easily computable integer values.

An article in Nature Biotechnology[4] revealed that the BLOSUM62 used for so many years as a standard is not exactly accurate according to the algorithm described by Henikoff and Henikoff.[1] Surprisingly, the miscalculated BLOSUM62 improves search performance.

References

[1] Henikoff, S.; Henikoff, J.G. (1992). "Amino Acid Substitution Matrices from Protein Blocks". *PNAS* **89** (22): 10915–10919.
     doi:10.1073/pnas.89.22.10915. PMC 50453. PMID 1438297.

[2] Albert Y. Zomaya (2006). *Handbook of Nature-Inspired And Innovative Computing* (http://books.google.com/?id=kDFltuQo1dMC&
     pg=PA673&lpg=PA673&dq=blosum+matrix). New York, NY: Springer. ISBN 0387405321. .page 673

[3] NIH "Scoring Systems" (http://www.ncbi.nlm.nih.gov/Education/BLASTinfo/Scoring2.html)

[4] Mark P Styczynski; Kyle L Jensen, Isidore Rigoutsos, Gregory Stephanopoulos (2008). "BLOSUM62 miscalculations improve search
     performance" (http://www.nature.com/nbt/journal/v26/n3/full/nbt0308-274.html). *Nat. Biotech.* **26** (3): 274–275.
     doi:10.1038/nbt0308-274. PMID 18327232. .

External links

- Page on BLOSUM (http://helix.biology.mcmaster.ca/721/distance/node10.html)
- Sean R. Eddy (2004). "Where did the BLOSUM62 alignment score matrix come from?". *Nature Biotechnology* **22** (8): 1035. doi:10.1038/nbt0804-1035. PMID 15286655.
- BLOCKS WWW server (http://blocks.fhcrc.org/)
- Scoring systems for BLAST at NCBI (http://www.ncbi.nlm.nih.gov/Education/BLASTinfo/Scoring2.html)
- Data files of BLOSUM on the NCBI FTP server (ftp://ftp.ncbi.nih.gov/blast/matrices/).

BMC Bioinformatics

BMC Bioinformatics	
Abbreviated title (ISO)	*BMC Bioinformatics*
Discipline	Bioinformatics
Language	English
Publication details	
Publisher	BioMed Central (UK)
Impact factor (2010)	3.03
Indexing	
ISSN	1471-2105 [1]
Links	
• Journal homepage [2]	

BMC Bioinformatics is an online open access scientific journal that publishes original, peer-reviewed research in bioinformatics. The journal is part of a series of BMC journals published by the UK-based publisher BioMed Central.

In 2008 the journal published 606 articles and 1 review. The journals that cited *BMC Bioinformatics* the most were *Nucleic Acids Research*, *Bioinformatics*, *BMC Genomics*, *PLoS Computational Biology* and *Genome Biology*.[3]

External links

• PubMed Central archive [4]

References

[1] http://www.worldcat.org/issn/1471-2105
[2] http://www.biomedcentral.com/bmcbioinformatics/
[3] Journal Citation Reports 2008 Science Edition. ISI Web of Science.
[4] http://www.ncbi.nlm.nih.gov/pmc/journals/13/

Boolean network

A **Boolean network** consists of a set of Boolean variables whose state is determined by other variables in the network. They are a particular case of discrete dynamical networks, where time and states are discrete, i.e. they have a bijection onto an integer series. Boolean and elementary cellular automata are particular cases of Boolean networks, where the state of a variable is determined by its spatial neighbors. In a **random boolean network** the connections are wired randomly and the output of nodes are determined by randomly generated logic functions.

Classical model

The first Boolean networks were proposed by Stuart A. Kauffman in 1969, as random models of genetic regulatory networks (Kauffman 1969, 1993).

Random Boolean networks (RBNs) are known as *NK* networks or Kauffman networks. An RBN is a system of *N* binary-state nodes (representing genes) with *K* inputs to each node representing regulatory mechanisms. The two states (on/off) represent respectively, the status of a gene being

Evolution of a classical random boolean network with *N=40*, *K=2* from a random initial state. Each column represent the state of the network at a time step, beginning from the left. Screenshot from RBNLab[1].

active or inactive. The variable *K* is typically held constant, but it can also be varied across all genes, making it a set of integers instead of a single integer. In the simplest case each gene is assigned, at random, K regulatory inputs from among the N genes, and one of the possible Boolean functions of K inputs. This gives a random sample of the possible ensembles of the *NK* networks. The state of a network at any point in time is given by the current states of all *N* genes. Thus the state space of any such network is 2^N.

Simulation of RBNs is done in discrete time steps. The state of a node at time *t+1* is computed by applying the boolean function associated with the node to the state of its input nodes at time *t*. The behavior of specific RBNs and generalized classes of them has been the subject of much of Kauffman's (and others) research.

Attractors

A Boolean network has 2^N possible states. Sooner or later it will reach a previously visited state, and thus, since the dynamics are deterministic, fall into an attractor. If the attractor has only a single state it is called a *point attractor*, and if the attractor consists of more than one state it is called a *cycle attractor*. The set of states that lead to an attractor is called the *basin* of the attractor. States with no incoming connections are called *garden-of-Eden* states and the dynamics of the network flow from these states towards attractors. The time it takes to reach an attractor is called *transient time*. (Gershenson 2004)

Topologies

- homogeneous
- normal
- scale-free (Aldana, 2003)

Updating Schemes

Classical RBNs (**CRBNs**) use a synchronous updating scheme and a criticism of CRBNs as models of genetic regulatory networks is that genes do not change their states all at the same moment. Harvey and Bossomaier introduced this criticism and defined asynchronous RBNs (**ARBNs**) where a random node is selected at each time step and updated (Harvey and Bossomaier, 1997). Since a random node is updated ARBNs are non-deterministic and does not have the cycle attractors found in CRBNs (Gershenson, 2004).

Deterministic asynchronous RBNs (**DARBNs**) were introduced by Gershenson as a way to have RBNs that do not have asynchronous updating but still are deterministic. In DARBNs each node has two randomly generated parameters P_i and Q_i (P_i, $Q_i \in \square$, $P_i > Q_i$). These parameters remain fixed. A node i will be updated when $t \square Q_i$ (mod P_i) where t is the time step. If more than one node is to be updated at a time step the nodes are updated in a pre-defined order, e.g. from lowest to highest i. Another way to do this is to synchronously update all nodes that fulfill the updating condition. The latter scheme is called deterministic semi-synchronous or deterministic generalized asynchronous RBNs (**DGARBNs**) (Gershenson, 2004).

RBNs where one or more nodes are selected for updating at each time step and the selected nodes are then synchronously updated are called generalized asynchronous RBNs (**GARBNs**). GARBNs are semi-synchronous, but non-deterministic (Gershenson, 2002).

Applications

- genetic regulatory networks

References

- Aldana, M. (2003). *Boolean dynamics of networks with scale-free topology [2]. *Physica D* 185:45–66
- Aldana , M., Coppersmith, S., and Kadanoff, L. P. (2003). Boolean dynamics with random couplings. In Kaplan, E., Marsden, J. E., and Sreenivasan, K. R., editors, *Perspectives and Problems in Nonlinear Science. A Celebratory Volume in Honor of Lawrence Sirovich.* Springer Applied Mathematical Sciences Series.
- Kauffman, S. A. (1969). Metabolic stability and epigenesis in randomly constructed genetic nets. *Journal of Theoretical Biology*, 22:437-467.
- Kauffman, S. A. (1993). *Origins of Order: Self-Organization and Selection in Evolution.* Oxford University Press. Technical monograph. ISBN 0-19-507951-5
- Gershenson, C. (2002). *Classification of random Boolean networks [3]. In Standish, R. K., Bedau, M. A., and Abbass, H. A., editors, *Artificial Life VIII:Proceedings of the Eight International Conference on Artificial Life*, pages 1-8. MIT Press.
- Gershenson, C (2004). *Introduction to Random Boolean Networks [4] Carlos Gershenson, editors M. Bedau and P. Husbands and T. Hutton and S. Kumar and H. Suzuki, "Workshop and Tutorial Proceedings, Ninth International Conference on the Simulation and Synthesis of Living Systems {(ALife} {IX)}", pages 160–173.
- Harvey, I. and Bossomaier, T. (1997). Time out of joint: Attractors in asynchronous random Boolean networks. In Husbands, P. and Harvey, I., editors, *Proceedings of the Fourth European Conference on Artificial Life (ECAL97)*, pages 67-75. MIT Press.
- Wuensche, A. (1998). *Discrete dynamical networks and their attractor basins [5]. In Standish, R., Henry, B., Watt, S., Marks, R., Stocker, R., Green, D., Keen, S., and Bossomaier, T., editors, *Complex Systems'98*,

University of New South Wales, Sydney, Australia.

External links

- DDLab [6]
- Discrete Visualizer of Dynamics [7]
- RBNLab [1]
- NetBuilder Boolean Networks Simulator [8]
- Open Source Boolean Network Simulator [9]
- JavaScript Kauffman Network [10]
- Probabilistic Boolean Networks (PBN) [11]

References

[1] https://sourceforge.net/projects/rbn/

[2] http://www.fis.unam.mx/~max/Spanish/physicad.pdf

[3] http://alife.org/alife8/proceedings/sub67.pdf

[4] http://uk.arxiv.org/abs/nlin.AO/0408006

[5] http://www.complexity.org.au/ci/vol06/wuensche/wuensche.html

[6] http://www.ddlab.com/

[7] http://dvd.vbi.vt.edu/

[8] http://strc.herts.ac.uk/bio/maria/NetBuilder/Tutorial/netbuilder_tutorial09.htm

[9] http://www.rustyspigot.com/software/BooleanNetwork/?url=/software/BooleanNetwork

[10] http://www.beteredingen.nl/?e=179&w=neuroscience

[11] http://personal.systemsbiology.net/ilya/PBN/PBN.htm

Bottom-up proteomics

Bottom-up proteomics is a common method to identify proteins and characterize their amino acid sequences and post-translational modifications by proteolytic digestion of proteins prior to analysis by mass spectrometry.[1] [2] The proteins may first be purified by a method such as gel electrophoresis resulting in one or a few proteins in each proteolytic digest. Alternatively, the crude protein extract is digested directly, followed by one or more dimensions of separation of the peptides by liquid chromatography

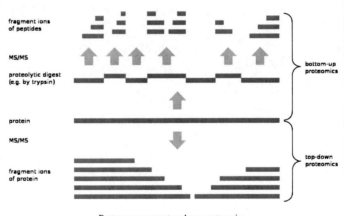

Bottom-up versus top-down proteomics

coupled to mass spectrometry, a technique known as shotgun proteomics.[3] [4] By comparing the masses of the proteolytic peptides or their tandem mass spectra with those predicted from a sequence database or annotated peptide spectral in a peptide spectral library, peptides can be identified and multiple peptide identifications assembled into a protein identification.

References

[1] Aebersold R, Mann M (March 2003). "Mass spectrometry-based proteomics". *Nature* **422** (6928): 198–207. doi:10.1038/nature01511.
     PMID 12634793.

[2] Chait BT (2006). "Chemistry. Mass spectrometry: bottom-up or top-down?". *Science* **314** (5796): 65–6. doi:10.1126/science.1133987.
     PMID 17023639.

[3] Washburn MP, Wolters D, Yates JR (2001). "Large-scale analysis of the yeast proteome by multidimensional protein identification
     technology". *Nat. Biotechnol.* **19** (3): 242–247. doi:10.1038/85686. PMID 11231557.

[4] Wolters DA, Washburn MP, Yates JR (2001). "An automated multidimensional protein identification technology for shotgun proteomics".
     Anal. Chem. **73** (23): 5683–5690. doi:10.1021/ac010617e. PMID 11774908.

Brain mapping

Brain mapping	
Diagnostics	
MeSH	D001931 [1]

Brain mapping is a set of neuroscience techniques predicated on the mapping of (biological) quantities or properties onto spatial representations of the (human or non-human) brain resulting in maps.

Overview

All neuroimaging can be considered part of brain mapping. Brain mapping can be conceived as a higher form of neuroimaging, producing brain images supplemented by the result of additional (imaging or non-imaging) data processing or analysis, such as maps projecting (measures of) behaviour onto brain regions (see fMRI).

Brain Mapping techniques are constantly evolving, and rely on the development and refinement of image acquisition, representation, analysis, visualization and interpretation techniques. Functional and structural neuroimaging are at the core of the mapping aspect of Brain Mapping.

History

In the late 1980s in the United States, the Institute of Medicine of the National Academy of Science was commissioned to establish a panel to investigate the value of integrating neuroscientific information across a variety of techniques.[2]

Of specific interest is using structural and functional magnetic resonance imaging (fMRI), electroencephalography (EEG), positron emission tomography (PET) and other non-invasive scanning techniques to map anatomy, physiology, perfusion, function and phenotypes of the human brain. Both healthy and diseased brains may be mapped to study memory, learning, aging, and drug effects in various populations such as people with schizophrenia, autism, and clinical depression. This led to the establishment of the Human Brain Project.[3]

Following a series of meetings, the International Consortium for Brain Mapping (ICBM) evolved.[4] The ultimate goal is to develop flexible computational brain atlases.

On 5.5.2010 the Supreme Court in India in its historical judgement on several PIL's (Smt. Selvi vs. State of Karnataka) has declared brain mapping,lie detector test and narcoanalysis as unconstitutional as it violates Article 20 (3)of Fundamental Rights.It cannot be conducted forcefully on any individual and requires one's consent for the same.when it is conducted with one's consent the material so obtained will be regarded as evidence during trial of cases according to Section 27 of Evidence Act.

Current atlas tools

- Talairach Atlas, 1988
- Harvard Whole Brain Atlas, 1995[5]
- MNI Template, 1998 (The standard template of SPM and International Consortium for Brain Mapping)

References

[1] http://www.nlm.nih.gov/cgi/mesh/2011/MB_cgi?field=uid&term=D001931
[2] Constance M. Pechura, Joseph B. Martin (1991). *Mapping the Brain and Its Functions: Integrating Enabling Technologies Into Neuroscience Research*. Institute of Medicine (U.S.). Committee on a National Neural Circuitry Database.
[3] Stephen H. Koslow and Michael F. Huerta (1997). *Neuroinformatics: An Overview of the Human Brain Project*.
[4] Mazziotta and Toga, 1995
[5] Harvard Whole Brain Atlas (http://www.med.harvard.edu/AANLIB/home.html)

Further reading

- Rita Carter (1998). *Mapping the Mind*.
- F.J. Chen (2006). *Brain Mapping And Language*.
- F.J. Chen (2006). *Focus on Brain Mapping Research*.
- F.J. Chen (2006). *Trends in Brain Mapping Research*.
- F.J. Chen (2006). *Progress in Brain Mapping Research*.
- Koichi Hirata (2002). *Recent Advances in Human Brain Mapping: Proceedings of the 12th World Congress of the International Society for Brain Electromagnetic Topography (ISBET 2001)*.
- Konrad Maurer and Thomas Dierks (1991). *Atlas of Brain Mapping: Topographic Mapping of Eeg and Evoked Potentials*.
- Konrad Maurer (1989). *Topographic Brain Mapping of Eeg and Evoked Potentials*.
- Arthur W. Toga and John C. Mazziotta (2002). *Brain Mapping: The Methods*.
- Tatsuhiko Yuasa, James Prichard and S. Ogawa (1998). *Current Progress in Functional Brain Mapping: Science and Applications*.

External links

- Epilepsy & Brain Mapping Program (http://www.epilepsyandbrainmapping.com/)
- BrainMapping.org project (http://www.brainmapping.org)
- National Centers for Biomedical Computing (http://www.bisti.nih.gov/ncbc/)
- Mapology.org (http://www.mapology.org)
- Human Brain Mapping (http://www.humanbrainmapping.org)
- National Center for Multi-Scale Study of Cellular Networks (http://magnet.c2b2.columbia.edu/)
- National Center for Biomedical Ontology (http://bioontology.org)
- Physics-based Simulation of Biological Structures (http://cbmc-web.stanford.edu/simbios/)
- National Alliance for Medical Imaging Computing (http://www.na-mic.org/)
- Informatics for Integrating Biology and the Bedside (http://www.partners.org/i2b2)
- National Center for Integrative Biomedical Informatics (http://www.ncibi.org/)
- Elekta Neuromag (http://www.elekta.com/healthcare_us_functional_mapping.php)
- The International Brain Mapping and Intraoperative Surgical Planning Society (IBMISPS) (http://www.ibmisps.org/)
- Annual World Congress for Brain Mapping and Image Guided Therapy (http://www.worldbrainmapping.org/)

Briefings in Bioinformatics

Briefings in Bioinformatics	
Abbreviated title (ISO)	*Brief Bioinform*
Discipline	Bioinformatics
Publication details	
Publisher	Oxford University Press
Impact factor (2010)	7.395
Indexing	
ISSN	1467-5463 [1] (print) 1477-4054 [2] (web)
Links	
• Journal homepage [3]	

Briefings in Bioinformatics is a scientific journal which publishes reviews for the users of databases and analytical tools of contemporary genetics and molecular biology and aims to provide practical help and guidance to the non-specialist. It is published by Oxford University Press.

In 2010 the journal published 43 articles and 6 reviews.[4]

References

[1] http://www.worldcat.org/issn/1467-5463
[2] http://www.worldcat.org/issn/1477-4054
[3] http://bib.oxfordjournals.org/
[4] "ISI Web of Knowledge - Journal Citation Reports" (http://www.isiknowledge.com/jcr). . Retrieved 28th June 2011.

c$^+$-probability

In statistics, a **c$^+$-probability** is the probability that a contrast variable obtains a positive value.[1] Using a replication probability, the c$^+$-probability is defined as follows: if we get a random draw from each group (or factor level) and calculate the sampled value of the contrast variable based on the random draws, then the c$^+$-probability is the chance that the sampled values of the contrast variable are greater than 0 when the random drawing process is repeated infinite times. The c$^+$-probability is a probabilistic index accounting for distributions of compared groups (or factor levels).[2]

The c$^+$-probability and SMCV are two characteristics of a contrast variable. There is a link between SMCV and c$^+$-probability.[1] [2] The SMCV and c$^+$-probability provides a consistent interpretation to the strength of comparisons in contrast analysis.[2] When only two groups are involved in a comparison, the c$^+$-probability becomes d$^+$-probability which is the probability that the difference of values from two groups is positive.[3] To some extent, the d$^+$-probability (especially in the independent situations) is equivalent to the well-established probabilistic index $P(X > Y)$. Historically, the index $P(X > Y)$ has been studied and applied in many areas.[4] [5] [6] [7] [8] The c$^+$-probability and d$^+$-probability have been used for data analysis in high-throughput experiments and biopharmaceutical research.[1] [2]

References

[1] Zhang XHD (2009). "A method for effectively comparing gene effects in multiple conditions in RNAi and expression-profiling research". *Pharmacogenomics* **10**: 345–58. doi:10.2217/14622416.10.3.345.

[2] Zhang XHD (2011). *Optimal High-Throughput Screening: Practical Experimental Design and Data Analysis for Genome-scale RNAi Research*. Cambridge University Press. ISBN 978-0-521-73444-8.

[3] Zhang XHD (2007). "A new method with flexible and balanced control of false negatives and false positives for hit selection in RNA interference high-throughput screening assays". *Journal of Biomolecular Screening* **12**: 645–55. doi:10.1177/1087057107300645.

[4] Owen DB, Graswell KJ, Hanson DL (1964). "Nonparametric upper confidence bounds for Pr($Y < X$) and confidence limits for Pr($Y < X$) when X and Y are normal". *Journal of American Statistical Association* **59**: 906–24.

[5] Church JD, Harris B (1970). "The estimation of reliability from stress-strength relationships". *Technometrics* **12**: 49–54.

[6] Downton F (1973). "The estimation of Pr($Y < X$) in normal case". *Technometrics* **15**: 551–8.

[7] Reiser B, Guttman I (1986). "Statistical inference for of Pr($Y \leq X$) – normal case". *Technometrics* **28**: 253–7.

[8] Acion L, Peterson JJ, Temple S, Arndt S (2006). "Probabilistic index: an intuitive non-parametric approach to measuring the size of treatment effects". *Statistics in Medicine* **25**: 591–602. doi:10.1002/sim.2256.

CaBIG

The cancer Biomedical Informatics Grid (caBIG) is an open source, open access information network with the mission of enabling secure data exchange throughout the cancer community. The initiative was developed by the National Cancer Institute (part of the National Institutes of Health) and is maintained by the Center for Biomedical Informatics and Information Technology (CBIIT).

The caBIG logo

History

The National Cancer Institute (NCI) of the United States funded the cancer Biomedical Informatics Grid (caBIG) initiative in spring 2004, headed by Kenneth Buetow.[1] It goal was to connect US biomedical cancer researchers using technology known as grid computing. The program, led by the Center for Bioinformatics and Information Technology (CBIIT), began with a 3-year pilot phase. The pilot phase concluded in March 2007, and 56 NCI-designated cancer centers started a trial.[2]

In addition to caGrid, the underlying infrastructure for data sharing among organizations, caBIG developed software tools, data sharing policies, and common standards and vocabularies to facilitate data sharing. Many cancer researchers (2,000+ participants representing 700 organizations) are currently trialing caBIG. Software tools targeted:

- Collection, analysis, and management of basic research data
- Clinical trials management, from patient enrollment to adverse event reporting and analysis
- Collection, annotation, sharing, and storage of medical imaging data
- Biospecimen management

Impact

caBIG seeked to provide foundational technology that enables a new approach to biomedicine called a "learning healthcare system."[3] This model of research and care delivery relies on the rapid exchange of information between all sectors of research and care, so that researchers and clinicians are able to collaboratively review and accurately incorporate the latest findings into their work. The ultimate goal is to speed the biomedical research process, leading to improved patient outcomes and more efficient healthcare delivery. This new approach is often called Personalized Medicine where the right patient is given the right drug, at the right time. caBIG technology is powering novel adaptive clinical trials such as the I-SPY2 TRIAL[4] (Investigation of Serial studies to Predict Your Therapeutic Response with Imaging and molecular AnaLysis 2), which are designed to use biomarkers to determine the appropriate therapy for women with advanced breast cancer. By collecting and analyzing clinical data in (nearly) real-time, patients' responses to therapy can be rapidly assessed to measure the effectiveness of a particular treatment, and clinical decisions may be refined to achieve optimal outcomes.

Connections to Health Information Technology

Health Information Technology (HIT) enables comprehensive management and secure exchange of medical information between researchers, health care providers, and consumers. When properly applied, HIT can improve the quality of health care; help prevent medical errors; and reduce redundancy, paperwork and administrative inefficiencies, ultimately leading to improved patient outcomes. caBIG supports national HIT initiatives including:

- **Electronic Health Records** – NCI and the American Society of Clinical Oncology (ASCO) have initiated a collaboration to create an oncology-specific EHR that utilizes caBIG standards for interoperability and that will enable oncologists to manage patient information in an electronic format that accurately captures the specific interventional issues unique to oncology.
- **Family Health History Tool**[5] – CBIIT hosts the Family Health History Tool, a web-based application developed by the U.S. Department of Health and Human Services (HHS) to allow users to easily track and share family health information with healthcare providers so that it may be used to inform decisions about prevention, diagnosis and treatment to improve individual patient outcomes.
- **Nationwide Health Information Network** (NHIN) – An initiative to share patient clinical data across geographically disparate sources and create electronically-linked national health information exchange (HIE).

Collaborations

- **BIG Health Consortium** (BIG Health)[6] – BIG Health was launched as a partnership of previously un-linked healthcare stakeholders who are now connected via caBIG. The Consortium supports personalized medicine by encouraging a collaborative approach to biomedical research and healthcare delivery.
- **Health of Women Study** – In July 2009, caBIG announced a collaboration with the Dr. Susan Love Research Foundation to build an online cohort of women willing to participate in clinical trials.[7] Called the Army of Women, it had a goal of one million in its databse; by December 2009 the site was "launched", and about 30,000 women and men signed up by 2010.[8]
- **The Cancer Genome Atlas (TCGA)** – caBIG forms the information infrastructure of The Cancer Genome Atlas (TCGA), an integrated database of molecular and clinical data. TCGA is a large-scale collaborative effort supported by the National Cancer Institute (NCI) and the National Human Genome Research Institute (NHGRI) to accelerate our understanding of the genetics of cancer using innovative genome analysis technologies. TCGA aims to characterize more than 10,000 tumors across at least 20 cancers by 2015. caBIG provides connectivity, data standards, and tools to collect, organize, share, and analyze the diverse research data from multiple laboratories and among different institutions that populate this database. Through the TCGA Data Portal,[9] researchers and clinicians can easily perform complex queries, allowing unprecedented opportunities to discover and develop a new generation of targeted diagnostics, therapies, and preventive interventions for cancer.
- **National Cancer Research Institute (NCRI)** – Since 2007, NCI has been working with UK cancer research association, NCRI, to foster a partnership that will benefit global cancer research. The two organizations share a variety of technologies developed to enable collaborative research and the secure exchange of research data using caGrid and the NCRI Oncology Information Exchange (ONIX) portal.
- **Duke University**[10] - Duke is leveraging several caBIG clinical trials tools in their collaboration with the Beijing Cancer Hospital of Peking University.
- **Latin American Breast Cancer Study**[11] – The countries that make up the United States-Latin America Cancer Research Network (US-LA CRN) will link their research efforts through caBIG, to allow data- and knowledge-sharing in a recently launched a breast cancer study.

Implementation

Adopt vs. Adapt

Participating institutions may either "adopt" caBIG tools to share data directly through caGrid, or "adapt" commercial or in-house developed software to be caBIG-compatible. The caBIG program developed software development kits (SDKs) that support the creation of interoperable software tools, and detailed instructions on the process of adapting existing tools or developing new applications to be caBIG-compatible.

Programs

- **Cancer Centers Program**[12] – Most of the 65 NCI-designated cancer centers use caBIG technology to report and retrieve data. caBIG was originally developed specifically to connect these centers as a way to enable collaborative research and eliminate data disconnects that slow down the development of personalized medicine.
- **NCI Community Cancer Centers Program**[13] – The NCCCP is a program to test the concept of a national network of community-based cancer centers. Many of the 16 centers in the program are implementing caBIG tools in support of their research and care programs.
- **Enterprise Support Network (ESN)**[14] – The ESN is a diverse collection of organizations that support the caBIG community by providing services, mentoring and expertise. The ESN program includes Knowledge Centers[15] that provide domain-specific expertise to assist users about caBIG tools and their applications, and Support Service Providers,[16] which are third party organizations that provide assistance to end-users and organizations adopting caBIG technology on a contract-for-services basis.

Open source

Since 2004, the caBIG program has established an important new model for open source communities – one that demonstrates a highly successful adaptation of earlier models to a public-private partnership. The caBIG program has produced new software for use in cancer research under contract to software development teams largely within the extramural research community. This has allowed the software to be produced by the teams who know best what the final products should do. Generally, these teams use in-house subject matter experts to define requirements, build functional software, and test the software as part of their own productions in their operations ensuring that it is a good fit across the potential user base. These teams also source the critical software engineering skills in exactly the same way that other government and commercial enterprises do – from the most readily available, best skilled, and most economical sources. The competitive proposal process ensures this engagement of resources and the best value to the American taxpayer for the project dollars expended. It is important to note that sometimes US based sources have not had the capacity or best economic value in these competitive bids.

The above description does apply to virtually any government contracted software development program. In general, the software assets that are produced are the property of the US government and the US taxpayers. Depending on the terms in specific contracts, they might be accessible only by request under the Freedom of Information Act (FOIA). The timeliness of response to such requests might preclude a requester from ever gaining any secondary value from software released under a FOIA request.

The caBIG program placed the all caBIG software in a software repository that is freely accessible to individuals and commercial enterprises for download. Just like any other open source development community, anyone can modify the downloaded software; however, the licensing applied to the downloaded software assets allows far greater flexibility than is typical. An individual or enterprise is allowed to contribute the modified code back to the caBIG program but is not required to do so. Likewise, the modifications can be made available as open source but are not required to be made available as open source. The caBIG licensing even allows the use of the caBIG applications and components, combined with additions and modifications, to be released as commercial products. These aspects of the caBIG program actually encourage commercialization of caBIG technology in a way that is generally atypical of open-source initiatives.

Some private companies claimed benefits from caBIG technology.[17]

Criticism

By 2011, the project had spent an estimated $350 million.[18] Although the goal was considered laudible, much of the software was unevenly adopted after being developed at great expense to compete with commercial offerings. In March 2011, an NCI working group assessment concluded that caBIG "...expanded far beyond those goals to implement an overly complex and ambitious software enterprise of NCI-branded tools, especially in the Clinical Trial Management System (CTMS) space. These have produced limited traction in the cancer community, compete against established commercial vendors, and create financially untenable long-term maintenance and support commitments for the NCL".[2]

References

[1]   Kenneth Buetow (April 1, 2008). "Heading for the BIG Time" (http://classic.the-scientist.com/2008/4/1/60/1/). *The Scientist* **22** (4):
      p. 60. .

[2]   Board of Scientific Advisors Ad Hoc Working Group (March 3, 2011). accessdate= October 4, 2011 "An Assessment of the Impact of the
      NCI Cancer Biomedical Informatics Grid (caBIG®)" (http://deainfo.nci.nih.gov/advisory/bsa/bsa0311/caBIGfinalReport.pdf). National
      Cancer Institute. accessdate= October 4, 2011.

[3]   "A Learning Healthcare System for Cancer Care" (http://www.iom.edu/~/media/Files/Activity Files/Disease/NCPF/2009-OCT-5/
      Clancy-Keynote Address-ALearningHealthcareSystemforCancerCare.ashx). .

[4]   Barker AD, Sigman CC, Kelloff GJ, Hylton NM, Berry DA, Esserman LJ (July 2009). "I-SPY 2: an adaptive breast cancer trial design in the
      setting of neoadjuvant chemotherapy". *Clinical Pharmacology and Therapeutics* **86** (1): 97–100. doi:10.1038/clpt.2009.68. PMID 19440188.

[5]   "Family Health History Tool" (https://familyhistory.hhs.gov/fhh-web/home.action). .

[6]   "BIG Health Consortium" (http://www.bighealthconsortium.org). .

[7]   Edyta Zielinska (July 22, 2009). "NCI tackles trial enrollment" (http://classic.the-scientist.com/blog/display/55833/]). *The Scientist*. .
      Retrieved October 4, 2011.

[8]   "Health of Women study" (http://www.armyofwomen.org/HOW_Study). *Army of Women website*. Archived (http://web.archive.org/
      web/20100530014610/http://www.armyofwomen.org/HOW_Study) from the original on May 30, 2010. . Retrieved October 4, 2011.

[9]   "TCGA Data Portal" (http://cancergenome.nih.gov/dataportal/data/about). .

[10] "Duke University" (http://www.cancer.duke.edu). .

[11] "Latin American Breast Cancer Study" (http://www.cancer.gov/aboutnci/olacpd/page4). .

[12] "Cancer Centers Program" (http://cancercenters.cancer.gov/cancer_centers/cancer-centers-names.html). .

[13] "NCI Community Cancer Centers Program" (http://ncccp.cancer.gov/About/Sites.htm). .

[14] "Enterprise Support Network" (https://cabig.nci.nih.gov/esn). .

[15] "caBIG Knowledge Centers" (https://cabig.nci.nih.gov/esn/knowledge_centers). .

[16] "caBIG Support Service Providers" (https://cabig.nci.nih.gov/esn/service_providers). .

[17] "An Unexpected and Fortuitous Synergy: BIGR® and caBIG®" (http://www.healthcit.com/HCIT/unexpected-synergy-bigr-and-cabig).
      Company website. . Retrieved October 4, 2011.

[18] John Foley (April 8, 2011). "Report Blasts Problem-Plagued Cancer Research Grid" (http://www.informationweek.com/news/
      government/enterprise-architecture/229401221). *Information Week*. . Retrieved October 4, 2011.

Further reading

- Abernethy AP, Coeytauz R, Rowe K, Wheeler JL, Lyerly HK (http://meeting.ascopubs.org/cgi/content/
  abstract/27/15S/6522). Electronic patient-reported data capture as the foundation of a learning health care
  system. JCO. 2009;27:6522.

- Buetow KH. (http://meeting.ascopubs.org/cgi/content/abstract/27/15S/e20712) caBIG: proof of concept for
  personalized cancer care. JCO. 2009:27 Suppl 15S:e20712.

- Holford ME, Rajeevan H, Zhao H, Kidd KK, Cheung KH (2009). "Semantic web-based integration of cancer
  pathways and allele frequency data". *Cancer Informatics* **8**: 19–30. PMC 2664696. PMID 19458791.

- Huang T, Shenoy PJ, Sinha R, Graiser M, Bumpers KW, Flowers CR (2009). "Development of the Lymphoma
  Enterprise Architecture Database: A caBIG(tm) Silver level compliant System". *Cancer Informatics* **8**: 45–64.

PMC 2675136. PMID 19492074.

- Kunz I, Lin MC, Frey L (2009). "Metadata mapping and reuse in caBIG". *BMC Bioinformatics* **10 Suppl 2**: S4. doi:10.1186/1471-2105-10-S2-S4. PMC 2646244. PMID 19208192.

- Novik Y, Escalon L, Rolnitzky L (http://meeting.ascopubs.org/cgi/content/abstract/27/15S/e17576). Academic cancer researchers' perspective on a federally mandated centralized comprehensive database of all cancer clinical trial results. JCO. 2009;27:e17576.

- Ohmann C, Kuchinke W (2009). "Future developments of medical informatics from the viewpoint of networked clinical research. Interoperability and integration" (http://www.schattauer.de/index.php?id=1268&L=1& pii=me09010045&no_cache=1). *Methods of Information in Medicine* **48** (1): 45–54. PMID 19151883.

- Phan JH, Moffitt RA, Stokes TH, *et al.* (June 2009). "Convergence of biomarkers, bioinformatics and nanotechnology for individualized cancer treatment". *Trends in Biotechnology* **27** (6): 350–8. doi:10.1016/j.tibtech.2009.02.010. PMID 19409634.

- Staes CJ, Xu W, LeFevre SD, *et al.* (2009). "A case for using grid architecture for state public health informatics: the Utah perspective". *BMC Medical Informatics and Decision Making* **9**: 32. doi:10.1186/1472-6947-9-32. PMC 2707374. PMID 19545428.

- Tan, Wei; Missier, Paolo; Madduri, Ravi; Foster, Ian (2009). *Building Scientific Workflow with Taverna and BPEL: A Comparative Study in caGrid.* **5472**. pp. 118. doi:10.1007/978-3-642-01247-1_11.

- Peter A. Covitz, Frank Hartel, Carl Schaefer, Sherri De Coronado, Gilberto Fragoso, Himanso Sahni, Scott Gustafson and Kenneth H. Buetow (April 23, 2003). "caCORE: A common infrastructure for cancer informatics". *Bioinformatics* **19** (18): 2404–2412. doi:10.1093/bioinformatics/btg335.

- "Health IT gets personal," (http://www.informationweek.com/news/healthcare/clinical-systems/showArticle. jhtml?articleID=221601549&queryText=health IT gets personal) InformationWeek (11/13/09)

- "Health data in the raw," (http://www.govhealthit.com/Article.aspx?id=72293) Government Health IT (11/6/09)

- "NCI to open research grid to cancer patient 'army'," (http://www.govhealthit.com/newsitem.aspx?tid=74& nid=72190) Government Health IT (10/9/09)

- "GridBriefing: The future of Healthcare - eHealth and Grid Computing," (http://www.gridtalk.org/Documents/ ehealth.pdf) GridTalk (9/09)

- "Collaboration and Sustainability are Front and Center as caBIG Celebrates Fifth Anniversary," (http://www. genomeweb.com/collaboration-and-sustainability-are-front-and-center-cabig-celebrates-fifth-ann?page=show) GenomeWeb/BioInform (7/09)

- "Sharing the Wealth of Data," (http://www.saworldview.com/article/sharing-the-wealth-of-data) Scientific American (5/09)

- "Translational Research Drives Demand for 'Virtual' Biobanks Built on caBIG Tools," (http://www.genomeweb. com/informatics/translational-research-drives-demand-virtual-biobanks-built-cabig-tools) GenomeWeb/BioInfom (4/3/09)

- "Connecting the Cancer Community caBIG Time," (http://www.bio-itworld.com/issues/2008/july-august/ best-practices-cabig.html) Bio-IT World (7/14/08)

- "Heading for the BIG Time," (http://cabig.cancer.gov/objects/pdfs/04_08_caBIG_reprint(FSO)_508.pdf) The Scientist (4/08)

- Cancer research goes open (http://www.bit-tech.net/news/2008/06/23/cancer-research-goes-open/) Bit-Tech (6/23/08)

External links

- caBIG Consumer/User Website (http://cabig.cancer.gov) (non-technical)
- caBIG Community Website (https://cabig.nci.nih.gov) (technical)
- NCI Center for Biomedical Informatics and Information Technology (CBIIT) (http://ncicb.nci.nih.gov)
- BIG Health Consortium (http://bighealthconsortium.org)
- caCORE (http://cabig.nci.nih.gov/tools/concepts/caCORE_overview)

CAFASP

CAFASP, or the Critical Assessment of Fully Automated Structure Prediction, is a large-scale blind experiment in protein structure prediction that studies the performance of automated structure prediction webservers in homology modeling, fold recognition, and *ab initio* prediction of protein tertiary structures based only on amino acid sequence. The experiment runs once every two years in parallel with CASP, which focuses on predictions that incorporate human intervention and expertise. Compared to related benchmarking techniques LiveBench and EVA, which run weekly against newly solved protein structures deposited in the Protein Data Bank, CAFASP generates much less data, but has the advantage of producing predictions that are directly comparable to those produced by human prediction experts. Recently CAFASP has been run essentially integrated into the CASP results rather than as a separate experiment.

External links

- Protein Structure Prediction Center [1]
- CAFASP4 (2004) [2]
- CAFASP5 (2006) [3]

References

[1] http://predictioncenter.org/
[2] http://www.cs.bgu.ac.il/~dfischer/CAFASP4/
[3] http://www.cs.bgu.ac.il/~dfischer/CAFASP5/

caGrid

caGrid

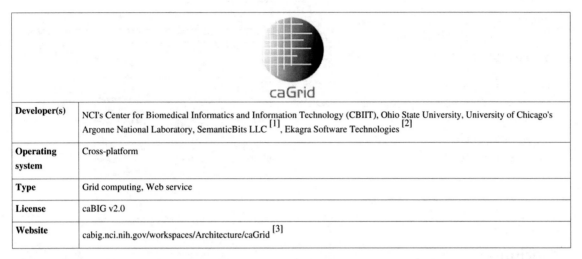

Developer(s)	NCI's Center for Biomedical Informatics and Information Technology (CBIIT), Ohio State University, University of Chicago's Argonne National Laboratory, SemanticBits LLC [1], Ekagra Software Technologies [2]
Operating system	Cross-platform
Type	Grid computing, Web service
License	caBIG v2.0
Website	cabig.nci.nih.gov/workspaces/Architecture/caGrid [3]

The cancer Biomedical Informatics Grid, or caBIG is an initiative of the National Cancer Institute, part of the National Institutes of Health. The **caGrid** computer network and software support caBIG.

caBIG is a voluntary virtual informatics infrastructure that connects data, research tools, scientists, and organizations to leverage their combined strengths and expertise in an open federated environment with widely accepted standards and shared tools. Driven primarily by scientific use cases from the cancer research community, caGrid provides the core enabling infrastructure necessary to compose the Grid of caBIG. It provides the technology that enables collaborating institutions to share information and analytical resources efficiently and securely, while also allowing investigators to easily contribute to and leverage the resources of a national-scale, multi-institutional environment.

caGrid Core Infrastructure

Though caGrid is a suite of products, typically *caGrid* refers to the core Infrastructure.

Globus Toolkit

caGrid uses version 4.03 of the Globus Toolkit, produced by the Globus Alliance.

caGrid Portal

The caGrid Portal [4] is a Web-based application built on Liferay Portal that enables users to discover and interact with the services that are available on the caGrid infrastructure. Portal serves as the primary visualization tool for the caGrid middleware, and provides a standards-based platform for hosting caBIG-related tools. It also serves as a caBIG information source. Through the caGrid Portal, users have instant access to information about caBIG participants, caGrid points of contact (POCs), and caGrid-related news and events.

workflow

caGrid workflow uses:

- Active BPEL
- Taverna

Contributors

- Ohio State University
- University of Chicago, Argonne National Laboratory
- SemanticBits, LLC
- Ekagra Software Technologies

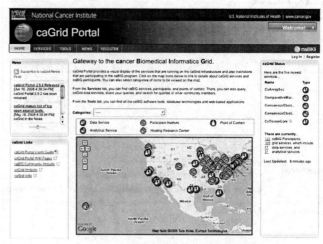

Screenshot of portal

Criticism

In March 2011, the NCI published an extensive review of CaBIG (see [5], [6]), which included a long list of problems with the program, and recommended that most of the software development projects should be discontinued.

References

- "caGrid" [7].
- "caGrid 1.0: An Enterprise Grid Infrastructure for Biomedical Research" [8].
- "Enabling the Provisioning and Management of a Federated Grid Trust Fabric" [9].
- "Introduce: An Open Source Toolkit for Rapid Development of Strongly Typed Grid Services" [10].
- "caGrid: design and implementation of the core architecture of the cancer biomedical informatics grid" [11].
- "Combining the Power of Taverna and caGrid: Scientific Workflows that Enable Web-Scale Collaboration" [12].

External links

- caGrid wiki [13]
- caGrid gforge project [14]
- caGrid Knowledge Center [15]
- caGrid Portal [4]

Components

- Introduce Toolkit [16], also a Globus Incubator Project [17]
- Data Services [18]
- Metadata [19]
- Security
  - Credential Delegation Service (CDS) [20]
  - Dorian [21]
  - GAARDS [22]

- Grid Grouper [23]
- Grid Trust Service (GTS) [24]
- WebSSO [25] - Web Single Sign-on component, based on JASIG CAS [26]

References

[1] http://www.semanticbits.com

[2] http://www.ekagra.com

[3] http://cabig.nci.nih.gov/workspaces/Architecture/caGrid

[4] http://cagrid-portal.nci.nih.gov

[5] http://www.informationweek.com/news/government/enterprise-architecture/229401221

[6] http://deainfo.nci.nih.gov/advisory/bsa/bsa0311/caBIGfinalReport.pdf

[7] https://cabig.nci.nih.gov/workspaces/Architecture/caGrid

[8] http://www.jamia.org/cgi/content/short/15/2/138

[9] http://bmi.osu.edu/publications_more.php?ID=881

[10] http://bmi.osu.edu/publications_more.php?ID=858

[11] http://bmi.osu.edu/publications_more.php?ID=740

[12] http://www.computer.org/portal/web/csdl/doi/10.1109/MIC.2008.120

[13] http://www.cagrid.org

[14] https://gforge.nci.nih.gov/projects/cagrid-1-0/

[15] https://cabig-kc.nci.nih.gov/CaGrid/KC/index.php/Main_Page

[16] http://cagrid.org/display/introduce/Home

[17] http://dev.globus.org/wiki/Incubator/Introduce

[18] http://cagrid.org/display/dataservices/Home

[19] http://cagrid.org/display/metadata/Home

[20] http://cagrid.org/display/cds/Home

[21] http://cagrid.org/display/dorian/Home

[22] http://cagrid.org/display/gaards/Home

[23] http://cagrid.org/display/gridgrouper/Home

[24] http://cagrid.org/display/gts/Home

[25] http://cagrid.org/display/websso/Home

[26] http://www.ja-sig.org/products/cas/

Canadian Bioinformatics Workshops

The Canadian Bioinformatics Workshop

Type	Not for profit workshop delivery
Founded	1999
Headquarters	Toronto, Canada
Area served	Biomedical Research
Key people	Francis Ouellette, Scientific Director
Products	Workshops and Bioinformatics Web resources
Employees	2
Parent	Ontario Institute for Cancer Research
Website	http://bioinformatics.ca/

Canadian Bioinformatics Workshops (CBW) are a series of advanced training workshops in bioinformatics, founded in 1999 in response to an identified need for a skilled bioinformatics workforce in Canada.

1999-2007

The Canadian Bioinformatics Workshops series began offering one and two week short courses in bioinformatics, genomics and proteomics in 1999, in response to an identified need for a skilled bioinformatics workforce in Canada. In partnership with the Canadian Genetics Diseases Network and Human Resources Development Canada, and under the scientific direction of Director, Francis Ouellette, the CBW series was established.

For eight years, the series offered short courses in bioinformatics, genomics and proteomics in various cities across Canada. The courses were taught by top faculty from Canada and the US, and offered small classes and hands-on instruction.

2007-Present

In 2007, the Canadian Bioinformatics Workshops moved to Toronto, where it is now hosted by the Ontario Institute for Cancer Research. A new format and series of workshops were designed in the fall of 2007. It was recognized that with the introduction of new technologies and scientific approaches to research, having the computational biology capacity and skill to deal with this new data has become an even greater asset.

The new series of workshops focuses on training the experts and users of these advanced technologies on the latest approaches being used in computational biology to deal with the new data. The Canadian Bioinformatics Workshops began offering the 2-day advanced topic workshops in 2008.

All workshop material is licensed under a Creative Commons-Share Alike 2.5 license

The CBW is sponsored by the Canadian Institute of Health Research and the Ontario Institute for Cancer Research.

Bioinformatics Links Directory

The Canadian Bioinformatics Workshops also hosts Bioinformatics Links Directory [1] which contains links to molecular resources, tools and databases. The links listed in this directory are from a myriad of sources, selected on the basis of recommendations from bioinformatics experts in the field.

External links

- Canadian Bioinformatics Workshops [2]
- Links Directory [3]
- CBW Alumni on Facebook [4]

As of this edit [5], this article uses content from "About" [2], which is licensed in a way that permits reuse under the Creative Commons Attribution-ShareAlike 3.0 Unported License, but not under the GFDL. All relevant terms must be followed.

References

[1] http://bioinformatics.ca/links_directory/
[2] http://www.bioinformatics.ca/about
[3] http://www.bioinformatics.ca/links_directory
[4] http://www.facebook.com/group.php?gid=19406672644
[5] http://en.wikipedia.org/wiki/Canadian_bioinformatics_workshops?oldid=422886091

CASP

CASP, which stands for **Critical Assessment of Techniques for Protein Structure Prediction**, is a community-wide, worldwide experiment for protein structure prediction taking place every two years since 1994.[1] CASP provides research groups with an opportunity to objectively test their structure prediction methods and delivers an independent assessment of the state of the art in protein structure modeling to the research community and software users. Even though the primary goal of CASP is to help advance the methods of identifying protein three-dimensional structure from its amino acid sequence, many view the experiment more as a "world championship" in this field of science. More than 100 research groups from all over the world participate in CASP on a regular basis and it is not uncommon for the entire groups to suspend their other research for months while they focus on getting their servers ready for the experiment and on performing the detailed predictions.

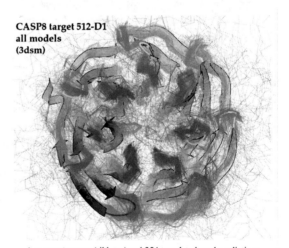

A target structure (ribbons) and 354 template-based predictions superimposed (gray Calpha backbones); from CASP8

Selection of target proteins

In order to ensure that no predictor can have prior information about a protein's structure that would put him/her at an advantage, it is important that the experiment is conducted in a double-blind fashion: Neither predictors nor the organizers and assessors know the structures of the target proteins at the time when predictions are made. Targets for structure prediction are either structures soon-to-be solved by X-ray crystallography or NMR spectroscopy, or structures that have just been solved (mainly by one of the structural genomics centers) and are kept on hold by the Protein Data Bank. If the given sequence is found to be related by common descent to a protein sequence of known structure (called a template), comparative protein modeling may be used to predict the tertiary structure. Templates can be found using sequence alignment methods such as BLAST or FASTA or protein threading methods, which are better in finding distantly related templates. Otherwise, *de novo* protein structure prediction must be applied, which is much less reliable but can sometimes yield models with the correct fold. Truly new folds are becoming quite rare among the targets,[2] [3] making that category smaller than desirable.

Evaluation

The primary method of evaluation[4] is a comparison of the predicted model α-carbon positions with those in the target structure. The comparison is shown visually by cumulative plots of distances between pairs of equivalents α-carbon in the alignment of the model and the structure, such as shown in the figure (a perfect model would stay at zero all the way across), and is assigned a numerical score GDT-TS (Global Distance Test — Total Score) [5] describing percentage of well-modeled residues in the model with respect to the target. Free modeling (template-free, or *de novo*) is also evaluated visually by the assessors, since the numerical scores do not work as well for finding loose resemblances in the most difficult cases.[6]

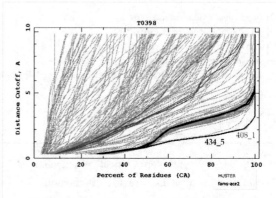

Cumulative plot of α-carbon accuracy, of all predicted models for target T0398 in CASP8, with the two best models labeled

High-accuracy template-based predictions were evaluated in CASP7 by whether they worked for molecular-replacement phasing of the target crystal structure[7] with successes followed up later,[8] and by full-model (not just α-carbon) model quality and full-model match to the target in CASP8.[9]

Evaluation of the results is carried out in the following prediction categories:

- tertiary structure prediction (all CASPs)
- secondary structure prediction (dropped after CASP5)
- prediction of structure complexes (CASP2 only; a separate experiment — CAPRI — carries on this subject)
- residue-residue contact prediction (starting CASP4)
- disordered regions prediction (starting CASP5)
- domain boundary prediction (CASP6–CASP8)
- function prediction (starting CASP6)
- model quality assessment (starting CASP7)
- model refinement (starting CASP7)
- high-accuracy template-based prediction (starting CASP7)

Tertiary structure prediction category was further subdivided into

- homology modeling
- fold recognition (also called protein threading; Note, this is incorrect as threading is a method)

- *de novo* structure prediction, now referred to as 'New Fold' as many methods apply evaluation, or scoring, functions that are biased by knowledge of native protein structures, such as an artificial neural network.

Starting with CASP7, categories have been redefined to reflect developments in methods. The 'Template based modeling' category includes all former comparative modeling, homologous fold based models and some analogous fold based models. The 'Template free modeling' category includes models of proteins with previously unseen folds and hard analogous fold based models.

The CASP results are published in special supplement issues of the scientific journal *Proteins*, all of which are accessible through the CASP website.[10] A lead article in each of these supplements describes specifics of the experiment [11] [12] while a closing article evaluates progress in the field. [13] [14]

Result Ranking

Automated assessments for CASP9 (2010)

- Official ranking for servers only (147 targets) [15]
- Official ranking for humans and servers (78 targets) [16]
- Ranking by Grishin Lab (for server only) [17]
- Ranking by Grishin Lab (for human and servers) [18]
- Ranking by Zhang Lab [19]
- Ranking by Cheng Lab [20]

Automated assessments for CASP8 (2008)

- Official ranking for servers only [21]
- Official ranking for humans and servers [22]
- Ranking by Zhang Lab [23]
- Ranking by Grishin Lab [24]
- Ranking McGuffin Lab [25]
- Ranking by Cheng Lab [26]

Automated assessments for CASP7 (2006)

- Ranking by Livebench [27]
- Ranking by Zhang Lab [28]

References

[1] Moult, J., *et al.* (1995). "A large-scale experiment to assess protein structure prediction methods". *Proteins* **23** (3): ii–iv.

[2] Tress, M., *et al.* (2009). "Target domain definition and classification in CASP8". *Proteins* **77** (Suppl 9): 10–17. doi:10.1002/prot.22497. PMC 2805415. PMID 19603487.

[3] Zhang Y and Skolnick J (2005). "The protein structure prediction problem could be solved using the current PDB library". *Proc Natl Acad Sci USA* **102** (4): 1029–1034. doi:10.1073/pnas.0407152101. PMC 545829. PMID 15653774.

[4] Cozzetto, D., *et al.* (2009). "Evaluation of template-based models in CASP8 with standard measures". *Proteins* **77** (Suppl 9): 18–28. doi:10.1002/prot.22561. PMID 19731382.

[5] Zemla, A. (2003). "LGA: a method for finding 3D similarities in protein structures". *Nucleic Acids Research* **31** (13): 3370–4. doi:10.1093/nar/gkg571. PMC 168977. PMID 12824330.

[6] Ben-David, M., *et al.* (2009). "Assessment of CASP8 structure predictions for template free targets". *Proteins* **77** (Suppl 9): 50–65. doi:10.1002/prot.22591. PMID 19774550.

[7] Read, R.J., Chavali, G. (2007). "Assessment of CASP7 predictions in the high accuracy template-based modeling category". *Proteins: Structure Function Bioinformatics* **69** (Suppl 8): 27–37. doi:10.1002/prot.21662. PMID 17894351.

[8] Qian, B., *et al.* (2007). "High-resolution structure prediction and the crystallographic phase problem". *Nature* **450** (7167): 259–264. doi:10.1038/nature06249. PMC 2504711. PMID 17934447.

[9] Keedy, D.A.; Noivirt-Brik, O; Paz, A; Prilusky, J; Sussman, JL; Levy, Y (2009). "The other 90% of the protein: Assessment beyond the α-carbon for CASP8 template-based and high-accuracy models". *Proteins* **77** (Suppl 9): 50–65. doi:10.1002/prot.22591. PMID 19774550.

[10] "CASP Proceedings" (http://predictioncenter.org/index.cgi?page=proceedings). .

[11] Moult, J., *et al.* (2007). "Critical assessment of methods of protein structure prediction — Round VII". *Proteins* **69** (Suppl 8): 3–9. doi:10.1002/prot.21767. PMC 2653632. PMID 17918729.

[12] Moult, J., *et al.* (2009). "Critical assessment of methods of protein structure prediction — Round VIII". *Proteins* **77** (Suppl 9): 1–4. doi:10.1002/prot.22589. PMID 19774620.

[13] Kryshtafovych, A., *et al.* (2007). "Progress from CASP6 to CASP7". *Proteins: Structure, Function, and Bioinformatics* **69** (Suppl 8): 194–207. doi:10.1002/prot.21769. PMID 17918728.

[14] Kryshtafovych, A., *et al.* (2009). "CASP8 results in context of previous experiments". *Proteins* **77** (Suppl 9): 217–228. doi:10.1002/prot.22562. PMID 19722266.

[15] http://predictioncenter.org/casp9/CD/data/html/groups.2.html

[16] http://predictioncenter.org/casp9/CD/data/html/groups.1.html

[17] http://prodata.swmed.edu/CASP9/serveronly/DomainsAll.First.html

[18] http://prodata.swmed.edu/CASP9/evaluation/DomainsAll.First.html

[19] http://zhanglab.ccmb.med.umich.edu/casp9/

[20] http://sysbio.rnet.missouri.edu/casp9_assess/ts.php

[21] http://predictioncenter.org/casp8/groups_analysis.cgi?target_type=0&gr_type=server&domain_classifications_id=1,2,3,4&field=sum_z_gdt_ts_server_pos

[22] http://predictioncenter.org/casp8/groups_analysis.cgi

[23] http://zhanglab.ccmb.med.umich.edu/casp8/

[24] http://prodata.swmed.edu/CASP8/evaluation/DomainsAll.First.html

[25] http://www.reading.ac.uk/bioinf/CASP8/index.html

[26] http://sysbio.rnet.missouri.edu/casp8_eva/ts.php

[27] http://metav1.bioinfo.pl/results.pl?B=CASP&V=7

[28] http://zhanglab.ccmb.med.umich.edu/casp7/

External links

- CASP experiments home page (http://predictioncenter.org/)
- FORCASP Forum (http://predictioncenter.org/forcasp/)

CAZy

CAZy is a database of Carbohydrate-Active enZYmes.[1] This database contains a classification and associated information about enyzmes involved in the synthesis, metabolism, and transport of carbohydrates. Included in this database are glycoside hydrolases, glycosyltransferases, polysaccharide lyases, carbohydrate esterase and carbohydrate-binding families.

Classification

CAZy identifies evolutionary related families of glycosyl hydrolases using the classification introduced by Bernard Henrissat.[2] [3] As of 2011 CAZy contains 125 families of glycosyl hydrolase families. These families are given a number to identify them, so for example Glycosyl hydrolase family 1 contains enzymes that possess a TIM barrel fold. These families are clustered into 14 different clans that share structural similarity. CAZy contains 94 families of Glycosyl transferase enzymes,[4] 22 families of polysaccharide lysases[5] and 16 families of carbohydrate esterases.

References

[1] Cantarel BL, Coutinho PM, Rancurel C, Bernard T, Lombard V, Henrissat B (January 2009). "The Carbohydrate-Active EnZymes database (CAZy): an expert resource for Glycogenomics". *Nucleic Acids Res.* **37** (Database issue): D233–8. doi:10.1093/nar/gkn663. PMC 2686590. PMID 18838391.

[2] Henrissat, B. (1991). "A classification of glycosyl hydrolases based on amino acid sequence similarities". *The Biochemical journal* **280 (Pt 2)**: 309–316. PMC 1130547. PMID 1747104.

[3] PMID 9345621 (PubMed (http://www.ncbi.nlm.nih.gov/pubmed/9345621))
   Citation will be completed automatically in a few minutes. Jump the queue or expand by hand (http://en.wikipedia.org/w/index. php?preload=Template:Cite_pmid/preload&editintro=Template:Cite_pmid/editintro&action=edit&title=Template:cite_pmid/9345621)

[4] PMID 12691742 (PubMed (http://www.ncbi.nlm.nih.gov/pubmed/12691742))
   Citation will be completed automatically in a few minutes. Jump the queue or expand by hand (http://en.wikipedia.org/w/index. php?preload=Template:Cite_pmid/preload&editintro=Template:Cite_pmid/editintro&action=edit&title=Template:cite_pmid/12691742)

[5] PMID 20925655 (PubMed (http://www.ncbi.nlm.nih.gov/pubmed/20925655))
   Citation will be completed automatically in a few minutes. Jump the queue or expand by hand (http://en.wikipedia.org/w/index. php?preload=Template:Cite_pmid/preload&editintro=Template:Cite_pmid/editintro&action=edit&title=Template:cite_pmid/20925655)

External links

- "CAZy - Carbohydrate-Active enZYmes Database" (http://www.cazy.org/). Architecture et Fonction des Macromolécules Biologiques, CNRS,Université de Provence Université de la Méditerranée.
- "CAZypedia" (http://www.cazypedia.org/). *The Encyclopedia of Carbohydrate-Active Enzymes.*

Cellular model

Creating a **cellular model** has been a particularly challenging task of systems biology and mathematical biology. It involves developing efficient algorithms, data structures, visualization and communication tools to orchestrate the integration of large quantities of biological data with the goal of computer modeling.

It is also directly associated with bioinformatics, computational biology and Artificial life.

It involves the use of computer simulations of the many cellular subsystems such as the networks of metabolites and enzymes which comprise metabolism, signal transduction pathways and gene regulatory networks to both analyze and visualize the complex connections of these cellular processes.

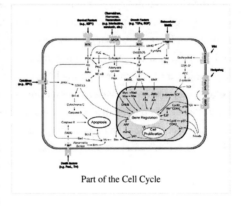

Part of the Cell Cycle

The complex network of biochemical reaction/transport processes and their spatial organization make the development of a predictive model of a living cell a grand challenge for the 21st century.

Overview

The eukaryotic cell cycle is very complex and is one of the most studied topics, since its misregulation leads to cancers. It is possibly a good example of a mathematical model as it deals with simple calculus but gives valid results. Two research groups [1] [2] have produced several models of the cell cycle simulating several organisms. They have recently produced a generic eukaryotic cell cycle model which can represent a particular eukaryote depending on the values of the parameters, demonstrating that the idiosyncrasies of the individual cell cycles are due to different protein concentrations and affinities, while the underlying mechanisms are conserved (Csikasz-Nagy et al., 2006).

By means of a system of ordinary differential equations these models show the change in time (dynamical system) of the protein inside a single typical cell; this type of model is called a deterministic process (whereas a model describing a statistical distribution of protein concentrations in a population of cells is called a stochastic process).

To obtain these equations an iterative series of steps must be done: first the several models and observations are combined to form a consensus diagram and the appropriate kinetic laws are chosen to write the differential equations, such as rate kinetics for stoichiometric reactions, Michaelis-Menten kinetics for enzyme substrate reactions and Goldbeter–Koshland kinetics for ultrasensitive transcription factors, afterwards the parameters of the equations (rate constants, enzyme efficiency coefficients and Michealis constants) must be fitted to match observations; when they cannot be fitted the kinetic equation is revised and when that is not possible the wiring diagram is modified. The parameters are fitted and validated using observations of both wild type and mutants, such as protein half-life and cell size.

In order to fit the parameters the differential equations need to be studied. This can be done either by simulation or by analysis.

In a simulation, given a starting vector (list of the values of the variables), the progression of the system is calculated by solving the equations at each time-frame in small increments.

In analysis, the proprieties of the equations are used to investigate the behavior of the system depending of the values of the parameters and variables. A system of differential equations can be represented as a vector field, where each vector described the change (in concentration of two or more protein) determining where and how fast the trajectory (simulation) is heading. Vector fields can have several special points: a stable point, called a sink, that attracts in all directions (forcing the concentrations to be at a certain value), an unstable point, either a source or a saddle point which repels (forcing the concentrations to change away from a certain value), and a limit cycle, a closed trajectory towards which several trajectories spiral towards (making the concentrations oscillate).

A better representation which can handle the large number of variables and parameters is called a bifurcation diagram (bifurcation theory): the presence of these special steady-state points at certain values of a parameter (e.g. mass) is represented by a point and once the parameter passes a certain value, a qualitative change occurs, called a bifurcation, in which the nature of the space changes, with profound consequences for the protein concentrations: the cell cycle has phases (partially corresponding to G1 and G2) in which mass, via a stable point, controls cyclin levels, and phases (S and M phases) in which the concentrations change independently, but once the phase has changed at a bifurcation event (cell cycle checkpoint), the system cannot go back to the previous levels since at the current mass the vector field is profoundly different and the mass cannot be reversed back through the bifurcation event, making a checkpoint irreversible. In particular the S and M checkpoints are regulated by means of special bifurcations called a Hopf bifurcation and an infinite period bifurcation.

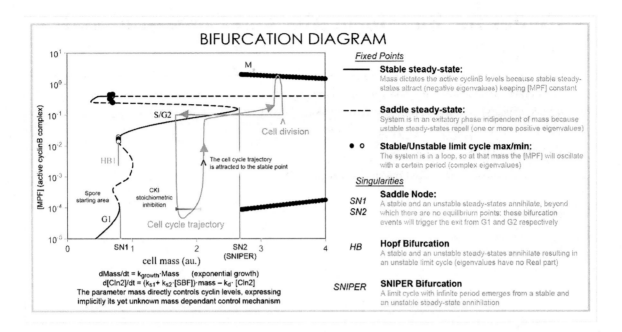

Molecular level simulations

E-Cell Project [3] aims "to make precise whole cell simulation at the molecular level possible".[4]

Projects

Multiple projects are in progress.[5]

- Karyote [6] - Indiana University
- E-Cell Project [3]
- Virtual Cell [7] - University of Connecticut Health Center
- Silicon Cell [8]

References

[1] "The JJ Tyson Lab" (http://mpf.biol.vt.edu/lab_website/). Virginia Tech. . Retrieved 2011-07-20.

[2] "The Molecular Network Dynamics Research Group" (http://www.cellcycle.bme.hu/). Budapest University of Technology and Economics. .

[3] http://www.e-cell.org/ecell/

[4] http://www.e-cell.org/ecell/

[5] http://www.nature.com/naturejobs/2002/020627/full/nj6892-04a.html

[6] http://pubs.acs.org/doi/abs/10.1021/jp0302921

[7] http://nrcam.uchc.edu/

[8] http://www.siliconcell.net/

Center for Bioinformatics and Computational Biology

The **Center for Bioinformatics and Computational Biology** (CBCB) is a University of Maryland, College Park multidisciplinary center dedicated to research on questions arising from the genome revolution.

External links

* Center for Bioinformatics and Computational Biology [1]

References

[1] http://www.cbcb.umd.edu

ChEMBL

ChEMBL

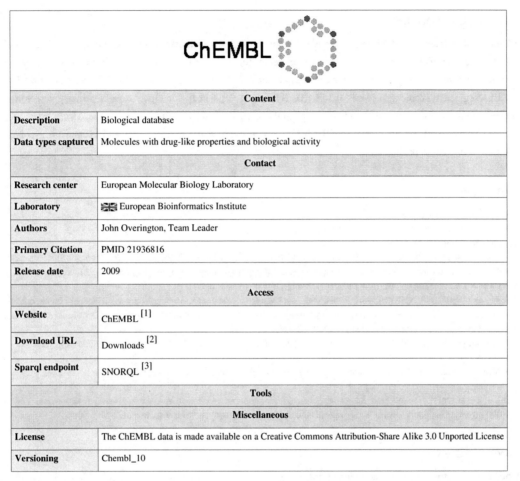

Content	
Description	Biological database
Data types captured	Molecules with drug-like properties and biological activity
Contact	
Research center	European Molecular Biology Laboratory
Laboratory	European Bioinformatics Institute
Authors	John Overington, Team Leader
Primary Citation	PMID 21936816
Release date	2009
Access	
Website	ChEMBL [1]
Download URL	Downloads [2]
Sparql endpoint	SNORQL [3]
Tools	
Miscellaneous	
License	The ChEMBL data is made available on a Creative Commons Attribution-Share Alike 3.0 Unported License
Versioning	Chembl_10

ChEMBL or **ChEMBLdb** is a manually curated chemical database of bioactive molecules with drug-like properties.[4] It is maintained by the European Bioinformatics Institute (EBI), based on the Wellcome Trust Genome Campus, Hinxton, UK. The database, originally known as StARlite, was developed by a pharmaceutical company, Galapagos NV. It was acquired for EMBL in 2008 with an award from The Wellcome Trust, resulting in the creation of the ChEMBL chemogenomics group at EBI, led by John Overington.[5] [6]

Scope and access

ChEMBL version 2 (ChEMBL_02) was launched in January 2010, including 2.4 million bioassay measurements covering 622,824 compounds, including 24,000 natural products. This was obtained from curating over 34,000 publications across twelve medicinal chemistry journals. ChEMBL's coverage of available bioactivity data has grown to become "the most comprehensive ever seen in a public database.".[5] In October 2010 ChEMBL version 8 (ChEMBL_08) was launched, with over 2.97 million bioassay measurements covering 636,269 compounds.[7]

ChEMBL_10 saw the addition of the PubChem confirmatory assays, in order to integrate data that is comparable to the type and class of data contained within ChEMBL.[8]

ChEMBLdb can be accessed via a web interface or downloaded by File Transfer Protocol. It is formated in a manner amenable to computerized data mining, and attempts to standardize activities between different publications, to enable comparative analysis.[4] ChEMBL is also integrated into other large-scale chemistry resources, including PubChem and the ChemSpider system of the Royal Society of Chemistry.

Associated resources

In addition to the database, the ChEMBL group have developed tools and resources for data mining.[9] These include Kinase SARfari, an integrated chemogenomics workbench focussed on kinases. The system incorporates and links sequence, structure, compounds and screening data. GPCR SARfari is a similar workbench focussed on GPCRs and ChEMBL-Neglected Tropical Diseases (ChEMBL-NTD) is a repository for Open Access primary screening and medicinal chemistry data directed at endemic tropical diseases of the developing regions of the Africa, Asia, and the Americas. The primary purpose of ChEMBL-NTD is to provide a freely accessible and permanent archive and distribution centre for deposited data.[5]

References

[1] https://www.ebi.ac.uk/chembldb/

[2] https://www.ebi.ac.uk/chembldb/index.php/downloads/

[3] http://rdf.farmbio.uu.se/chembl/snorql/

[4] Gaulton, A; et al. (2011). "ChEMBL: a large-scale bioactivity database for drug discovery". *Nucleic Acids Research*. doi:10.1093/nar/gkr777.

[5] Bender, A (2010). "Databases: Compound bioactivities go public" (http://www.nature.com/nchembio/journal/v6/n5/full/nchembio.354. html). *Nature Chemical Biology* **309** (6). doi:10.1038/nchembio.354. . Retrieved 2010-11-15.

[6] Overington J (April 2009). "ChEMBL. An interview with John Overington, team leader, chemogenomics at the European Bioinformatics Institute Outstation of the European Molecular Biology Laboratory (EMBL-EBI). Interview by Wendy A. Warr". *J. Comput. Aided Mol. Des.* **23** (4): 195–8. doi:10.1007/s10822-009-9260-9. PMID 19194660.

[7] ChEMBL-og (15 November 2010), *ChEMBL_08 Released* (http://chembl.blogspot.com/2010/11/chembl08-released.html), , retrieved 2010-11-15

[8] ChEMBL-og (6 June 2011), *ChEMBL_10 Released* (http://chembl.blogspot.com/2011/06/chembl-10-released.html), , retrieved 2011-06-09

[9] Bellis, L J; et al. (2011). "Collation and data-mining of literature bioactivity data for drug discovery." (http://www.biochemsoctrans.org/bst/039/bst0391365.htm). *Biochemical Society Transactions* **39**: 1365. doi:10.1042/BST0391365. . Retrieved 2011-24-09.

External links

- ChEMBLdb (https://www.ebi.ac.uk/chembldb)
- Kinase SARfari (https://www.ebi.ac.uk/chembl/sarfari/kinasesarfari)
- ChEMBL-Neglected Tropical Disease Archive (https://www.ebi.ac.uk/chemblntd)
- GPCR SARfari (https://www.ebi.ac.uk/chembl/sarfari/gpcrsarfari)
- The ChEMBL-og (http://chembl.blogspot.com/search/label/Peptide Drugs) Open data and drug discovery blog run by the ChEMBL team.

Chemical library

A **chemical library** or compound library is a collection of stored chemicals usually used ultimately in high-throughput screening or industrial manufacture. The chemical library can consist in simple terms of a series of stored chemicals. Each chemical has associated information stored in some kind of database with information such as the chemical structure, purity, quantity, and physiochemical characteristics of the compound.

Purpose

In drug discovery high-throughput screening, it is desirable to screen a drug target against a selection of chemicals that try to take advantage of as much of the appropriate chemical space as possible. The chemical space of all possible chemical structures is extraordinarily large. Most stored chemical libraries do not typically have a fully represented or sampled chemical space mostly because of storage and cost concerns. However, since many molecular interactions cannot be predicted, the wider the chemical space that is sampled by the chemical library, the better the chance that high-throughput screening will find an "hit" -- a chemical with an appropriate interaction in a biological model that might be developed into a drug.

An example of a chemical library in drug discovery would be a series of chemicals known to inhibit kinases, or in industrial processes, a series of catalysts known to polymerize resins.

Generation of chemical libraries

Chemical libraries are usually generated for a specific goals and larger chemical libraries could be made of several groups of smaller libraries stored in the same location. In the drug discovery process for instance, a wide range of organic chemicals are needed to test against models of disease in high-throughput screening. Therefore, most of the chemical synthesis needed to generate chemical libraries in drug discovery is based on organic chemistry. A company that is interested in screening for kinase inhibitors in cancer may limit their chemical libraries and synthesis to just those types of chemicals known to have affinity for ATP binding sites or allosteric sites.

Generally, however, most chemical libraries focus on large groups of varied organic chemical series where an organic chemist can make many variations on the same molecular scaffold or molecular backbone. Sometimes chemicals can be purchased from outside vendors as well and included into an internal chemical library.

Design and optimization of chemical libraries

Chemical libraries are usually designed by chemists and chemoinformatics scientists and synthesized by organic chemistry and medicinal chemistry. The method of chemical library generation usually depends on the project and there are many factors to consider when using rational methods to select screening compounds.[1] Typically, a range of chemicals is screened against a particular drug target or disease model, and the preliminary "hits", or chemicals that show the desired activity, are re-screened to verify their activity. Once they are qualified as a "hit" by their repeatability and activity, these particular chemicals are registered and analysed. Commonalities among the different chemical groups are studied as they are often reflective of a particular chemical subspace. Additional chemistry work may be needed to further optimize the chemical library in the active portion of the subspace. When it is needed, more synthesis is completed to extend out the chemical library in that particular subspace by generating more compounds that are very similar to the original hits. This new selection of compounds within this narrow range are further screened and then taken on to more sophisticated models for further validation in the Drug Discovery Hit to Lead process.

Storage and management

The "chemical space" of all possible organic chemicals is large and increases exponentially with the size of the molecule. Most chemical libraries do not typically have a fully represented chemical space mostly because of storage and cost concerns.

Because of the expense and effort involved in chemical synthesis, the chemicals must be correctly stored and banked away for later use to prevent early degradation. Each chemical has a particular shelf life and storage requirement and in a good-sized chemical library, there is a timetable by which library chemicals are disposed of and replaced on a regular basis. Some chemicals are fairly unstable, radioactive, volatile or flammable and must be stored under careful conditions in accordance with safety standards such as OSHA.

Most chemical libraries are managed with information technologies such as barcoding and relational databases. Additionally, robotics are necessary to fetch compounds in larger chemical libraries.

Because a chemical library's individual entries can easily reach up into the millions of compounds, the management of even modest-sized chemical libraries can be a full-time endeavor. Compound management is one such field that attempts to manage and upkeep these chemical libraries as well as maximizing safety and effectiveness in their management.

Further reading

- Ian Yates. Compound Management comes of age. Drug Discovery World Spring 2003 p35-43 [2]
- Archer JR. History, evolution, and trends in compound management for high-throughput screening. Assay Drug Dev Technol. 2004 Dec;2(6):675-81 [3]
- Casey R. Designing Chemical Compound Libraries for Drug Discovery. Business Intelligence Network December 1, 2005. [4]
- GLARE - A free open source software for combinatorial library design. [5]
- Examples of Chemical libraries for Drug Discovery [6]

References

[1] Huggins DJ, Venkitaraman AR, Spring DR (January 2011). "Rational Methods for the Selection of Diverse Screening Compounds". *ACS Chem. Biol.* **6** (3): 208–217. doi:10.1021/cb100420r. PMID 21261294.
[2] http://www.rjcoms.com/data/pdfs/compound%20management.pdf
[3] http://www.liebertonline.com/doi/abs/10.1089%2Fadt.2004.2.675
[4] http://www.b-eye-network.com/view/2039
[5] http://glare.sourceforge.net/
[6] http://www.lightbiologicals.com/products.html

Chemistry Development Kit

Chemistry Development Kit

Developer(s)	The CDK Project
Stable release	(July 3, 2011) [+/−] [1]
Preview release	(June 19, 2011) [+/−] [2]
Written in	Java (programming language)
Operating system	Cross-platform
Type	Chemoinformatics/Molecular modelling/Bioinformatics
License	GNU Lesser General Public License
Website	http://cdk.sourceforge.net/

The **Chemistry Development Kit** is an open source Java library for Chemoinformatics and Bioinformatics.[3] It is available for Windows, Unix, and Mac OS. It is distributed under the GNU LGPL.

History

The CDK was created by Christoph Steinbeck, Egon Willighagen and Dan Gezelter, the developers of Jmol and JChemPaint at the time, to provide a common code base, on 27–29 September 2000 at the University of Notre Dame. Since then many people have contributed to the project, leading to a rich set of functionality, as given below.

Library

The CDK itself is a library, instead of a user program. However, it has been integrated into various environments to make its functionality available. CDK is currently used in several applications, among which the R (programming language),[4] CDK-Taverna (a Taverna workbench plugin),[5] Bioclipse, and Cinfony.[6] Additionally, CDK extensions exist for KNIME and Excel (excel-cdk [7]).

In 2008 bits of GPL-licensed code were removed from the library. While those code bits were independent from the main CDK library, and no copylefting was involved, to reduce confusions among users, the ChemoJava [8] project was instantiated.

Major features

Chemoinformatics

- 2D diagram editing and generation
- 3D geometry generation
- substructure search using exact structures and SMARTS-like queries
- QSAR descriptor calculation [9]
- fingerprint calculation
- force field calculations
- many chemical input/output formats
- structure generators

Bioinformatics

- protein active site detection
- cognate ligand detection[10]
- metabolite identification
- pathway databases

General

- Python wrapper
- Ruby wrapper
- active user community

CDK News

CDK News [11] is the project's newsletter and published articles between 2004 and 2007[12]. Due to lack of a steady stream of contributions, this newsletter was put on hold.

References

[1] http://en.wikipedia.org/wiki/Template%3Alatest_stable_software_release%2Fchemistry_development_kit?action=edit& preload=Template:LSR/syntax

[2] http://en.wikipedia.org/wiki/Template%3Alatest_preview_software_release%2Fchemistry_development_kit?action=edit& preload=Template:LSR/syntax

[3] Steinbeck, C.; Han, Y.Q.; Kuhn, S.; Horlacher, O.; Luttmann, E.; Willighagen, E.L. (2003). "The Chemistry Development Kit (CDK): An open-source Java library for chemo- and bioinformatics". *Journal of Chemical Information and Computer Sciences* **43** (2): 493–500. doi:10.1021/ci025584y. PMID 12653513.

[4] Guha, R. (2007). *Journal of Statistical Software* **18**: 1–16.

[5] Kuhn, T.; Willighagen, E.L.; Zielesny, A.; Steinbeck, C. (2010). "CDK-Taverna: an open workflow environment for cheminformatics" (http:/ /www.biomedcentral.com/1471-2105/11/159). *BMC Bioinformatics* **11**: 159. doi:10.1186/1471-2105-11-159. PMC 2862046. PMID 20346188. .

[6] O'Boyle, N.M.; Hutchison, G.R. (2008). *Chemistry Central Journal* **2**.

[7] http://code.google.com/p/excel-cdk/

[8] http://code.google.com/p/chemojava/

[9] Steinbeck, C.; Hoppe, C.; Kuhn, S.; Floris, M.; Guha, R.; Willighagen, E.L. (2006). "Recent developments of the chemistry development kit (CDK) — an open-source java library for chemo- and bioinformatics" (http://www.benthamdirect.org/pages/content.php?CPD/2006/ 00000012/00000017/0005B.SGM). *Curr. Pharm. Des.* **12** (17): 2111–20. doi:10.2174/138161206777585274. PMID 16796559. . Guangli M, Yiyu C (2006). "Predicting Caco-2 permeability using support vector machine and chemistry development kit" (http://www. ualberta.ca/~csps/JPPS9_2/Dr_Guangli/MS_538.htm). *J Pharm Pharm Sci* **9** (2): 210–21. PMID 16959190. .

[10] Bashton, M.; Nobeli, I.; Thornton, J. M. (2006). "Cognate Ligand Domain Mapping for Enzymes". *Journal of Molecular Biology* **364** (4): 836. doi:10.1016/j.jmb.2006.09.041. PMID 17034815.

[11] http://www.cdknews.org/

[12] https://sourceforge.net/projects/cdk/files/CDK%20News/

External links

- CDK Project (http://sourceforge.net/projects/cdk) — the main homepage
- CDK Wiki (http://apps.sourceforge.net/mediawiki/cdk) — the community wiki
- CDK News (http://www.cdknews.org/) — the project journal
- OpenScience.org (http://www.openscience.org/)

ChIP-on-chip

ChIP-on-chip (also known as **ChIP-chip**) is a technique that combines chromatin immunoprecipitation (*"ChIP"*) with microarray technology (*"chip"*). Like regular ChIP, ChIP-on-chip is used to investigate interactions between proteins and DNA *in vivo*. Specifically, it allows the identification of the cistrome, sum of binding sites, for DNA-binding proteins on a genome-wide basis.[1] Whole-genome analysis can be performed to determine

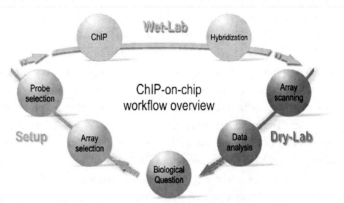

Workflow overview of a ChIP-on-chip experiment.

the locations of binding sites for almost any protein of interest.[1] As the name of the technique suggests, such proteins are generally those operating in the context of chromatin. The most prominent representatives of this class are transcription factors, replication-related proteins, like ORC, histones, their variants, and histone modifications. The goal of ChIP-on-chip is to localize protein binding sites that may help identify functional elements in the genome. For example, in the case of a transcription factor as a protein of interest, one can determine its transcription factor binding sites throughout the genome. Other proteins allow the identification of promoter regions, enhancers, repressors and silencing elements, insulators, boundary elements, and sequences that control DNA replication.[2] If histones are subject of interest, it is believed that the distribution of modifications and their localizations may offer new insights into the mechanisms of regulation. One of the long-term goals ChIP-on-chip was designed for is to establish a catalogue of (selected) organisms that lists all protein-DNA interactions under various physiological conditions. This knowledge would ultimately help in the understanding of the machinery behind gene regulation, cell proliferation, and disease progression. Hence, ChIP-on-chip offers not only huge potential to complement our knowledge about the orchestration of the genome on the nucleotide level, but also on higher levels of information and regulation as it is propagated by research on epigenetics.

Technological platforms

The technical platforms to conduct ChIP-on-chip experiments are DNA microarrays, or *"chips"*. They can be classified and distinguished according to various characteristics:

- *Probe type*: DNA arrays can comprise either mechanically spotted cDNAs or PCR-products, mechanically spotted oligonucleotides, or oligonucleotides that are synthesized *in situ*. The early versions of microarrays were designed to detect RNAs from expressed genomic regions (open reading frames). Although such arrays are perfectly suited to study gene expression profiles, they have limited importance in ChIP experiments since most "interesting" proteins with respect to this technique bind in intergenic regions. Nowadays, even custom-made arrays can be designed and fine-tuned to match the requirements of an experiment. Also, any sequence of nucleotides can be synthesized to cover genic as well as intergenic regions.

- *Probe size*: Early version of cDNA arrays had a probe length of about 200bp. Latest array versions use oligos as short as 70- (Microarrays, Inc.) to 25-mers (Affymetrix). (Feb 2007)

- *Probe composition*: There are tiled and non-tiled DNA arrays. Non-tiled arrays use probes selected according to non-spatial criteria, i.e., the DNA sequences used as probes have no fixed distances in the genome. Tiled arrays, however, select a genomic region (or even a whole genome) and divide it into equal chunks. Such a region is called tiled path. The average distance between each pair of neighboring chunks (measured from the center of each chunk) gives the resolution of the tiled path. A path can be overlapping, end-to-end or spaced.[3]

- *Array size*: The first microarrays used for ChIP-on-Chip contained about 13,000 spotted DNA segments representing all ORFs and intergenic regions from the yeast genome.[2] Nowadays, Affymetrix offers whole-genome tiled yeast arrays with a resolution of 5bp (all in all 3.2 million probes). Tiled arrays for the human genome become more and more powerful, too. Just to name example, Affymetrix offers a set of seven arrays with about 90 million probes, spanning the complete non-repetitive part of the human genome with about 35bp spacing. (Feb 2007)

Besides the actual microarray, other hard- and software equipment is necessary to run ChIP-on-chip experiments. It is generally the case that one company's microarrays can not be analyzed by another company's processing hardware. Hence, buying an array requires also buying the associated workflow equipment. The most important elements are, among others, hybridization ovens, chip scanners, and software packages for subsequent numerical analysis of the raw data.

Workflow of a ChIP-on-chip experiment

Starting with a biological question, a ChIP-on-chip experiment can be divided into three major steps: The first is to set up and design the experiment by selecting the appropriate array and probe type. Second, the actual experiment is performed in the wet-lab. Last, during the dry-lab portion of the cycle, gathered data are analyzed to either answer the initial question or lead to new questions so that the cycle can start again.

Wet-lab portion of the workflow

- In the first step, the protein of interest (POI) is cross-linked with the DNA site it binds to in an *in vivo* environment. Usually this is done by a gentle formaldehyde fixation that is reversible with heat.

- Then, the cells are lysed and the DNA is sheared by sonication or using micrococcal nuclease. This results in double-stranded chunks of DNA fragments, normally 1 kb or less in length. Those that were cross-linked to the POI form a POI-DNA complex.

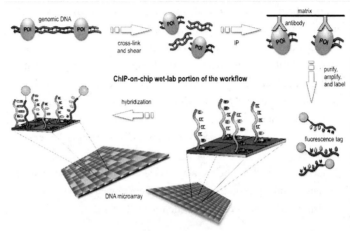

Workflow overview of the wet-lab portion of a ChIP-on-chip experiment.

- In the next step, only these complexes are filtered out of the set of DNA fragments, using an antibody specific to the POI. The antibodies may be attached to a solid surface, may have a magnetic bead, or some other physical property that allow distributing cross-linked complexes and unbound fragments. This procedure is essentially an immunoprecipitation (IP). There are two alternative ways to implement this filtering step:

  - immunoprecipitation of the tagged protein with an antibody against the tag (ex. FLAG, HA, c-myc)
  - affinity purification that does not require antibodies, such as the Tandem Affinity Purification (TAP)
- The cross-linking of POI-DNA complexes is reversed (usually by heating) and the DNA strands are purified. For the rest of the workflow, the POI is no longer necessary.
- After an amplification and denaturation step, the single-stranded DNA fragments are labeled with a fluorescent tag such as Cy5 or Alexa 647.
- Finally, the fragments are poured over the surface of the DNA microarray, which is spotted with short, single-stranded sequences that cover the genomic portion of interest. Whenever a labeled fragment "finds" a complementary fragment on the array, they will hybridize and form again a double-stranded DNA fragment.

Dry-lab portion of the workflow

- After a sufficiently large time frame to allow hybridization, the array is illuminated with fluorescence light. Those probes on the array that are hybridized to one of the labeled fragments emit a light signal that is captured by a camera. This image contains all raw data for the remaining part of the workflow.

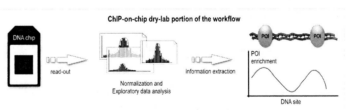

Workflow overview of the dry-lab portion of a ChIP-on-chip experiment.

- This raw data, encoded as false-color image, needs to be converted to numerical values before the actual analysis can be done. The analysis and information extraction of the raw data often remains the most challenging part for ChIP-on-chip experiments. Problems arise throughout this portion of the workflow, ranging from the initial chip read-out, to suitable methods to subtract background noise, and finally to appropriate algorithms that normalize the data and make it available for subsequent statistical analysis, which then hopefully lead to a better understanding of the biological question sought to answer. Furthermore, due to the different array platforms and missing standardization between them, data storage and exchange is a huge problem, too. Generally speaking, the data analysis can be divided into three major steps:

1. During the first step, the captured fluorescence signals from the array are normalized, using control signals derived from the same or a second chip. Such control signals tell which probes on the array were hybridized correctly and which bound nonspecifically.

2. In the second step, numerical and statistical tests are applied to control data and IP fraction data to identify POI-enriched regions along the genome. The following three methods are used widely: Median percentile rank, Single-array error, and Sliding-window. These methods generally differ in a way how low-intensity signals are handled, how much background noise is accepted, and which trait for the data is emphasized during the computation. In the recent past, the sliding-window approach seems to be favored and is often described as most powerful.

3. In the third step, these regions are analyzed further. If, for example, the POI was a transcription factor, such regions would represent its binding sites. Subsequent analysis then may want to infer nucleotide motifs and other patterns to allow functional annotation of the genome.

Strengths and Weaknesses

Using tiled arrays, ChIP-on-chip allows for high resolution of genome-wide maps. These maps can determine the binding sites of many DNA-binding proteins like transcription factors and also chromatin modifications.

Although ChIP-on-chip can be a powerful technique in the area of genomics, it is very expensive. Most published studies using ChIP-on-chip repeat their experiments at least three times to ensure biologically meaningful maps. The cost of the DNA microarrays is often a limiting factor to whether a laboratory should proceed with a ChIP-on-chip experiment. Another limitation is the size of DNA fragments that can be achieved. Most ChIP-on-chip protocols utilize sonication as a method of breaking up DNA into small pieces. However, sonication is limited to a minimal fragment size of 200 bp. For higher resolution maps, this limitation should be overcome to achieve smaller fragments, preferably to single nucleosome resolution. As mentioned previously, the statistical analysis of the huge amount of data generated from arrays is a challenge and normalization procedures should aim to minimize artifacts and determine what is really biologically significant. So far, application to mammalian genomes has been a major limitation, for example, due to a significant percentage of the genome that is occupied by repeats. However, as ChIP-on-chip technology advances, high resolution whole mammalian genome maps should become achievable.

Antibodies used for ChIP-on-chip can be an important limiting factor. ChIP-on-chip requires highly specific antibodies that must recognize its epitope in free solution and also under fixed conditions. If it is demonstrated to successfully immunoprecipitate cross-linked chromatin, it is termed "ChIP-grade". Companies that provide ChIP-grade antibodies include Abcam, Cell Signaling Technology, Santa Cruz, and Upstate. To overcome the problem of specificity, the protein of interest can be fused to a tag like FLAG or HA that are recognized by antibodies. An alternative to ChIP-on-chip that does not require antibodies is DamID.

Also available are antibodies against a specific histone modification like H3 tri methyl K4. As mentioned before, the combination of these antibodies and ChIP-on-chip has become extremely powerful in determining whole genome analysis of histone modification patterns and will contribute tremendously to our understanding of the histone code and epigenetics.

A study demonstrating the non-specific nature of DNA binding proteins has been published in PLoS Biology. This indicates that alternate confirmation of functional relevancy is a necessary step in any ChIP-chip experiment.[4]

History

The ChIP-on-chip technique was first applied successfully in three papers published in 2000 and 2001.[5] [6] [7] The authors identified binding sites for individual transcription factors in the budding yeast *Saccharomyces cerevisiae*. In 2002, Richard Young's group [8] determined the genome-wide positions of 106 transcription factors using a c-Myc tagging system in yeast. Other applications for ChIP-on-chip include DNA replication, recombination, and chromatin structure. Since then, ChIP-on-chip has become a powerful tool in determining genome-wide maps of histone modifications and many more transcription factors. ChIP-on-chip in mammalian systems has been difficult due to the large and repetitive genomes. Thus, many studies in mammalian cells have focused on select promoter regions that are predicted to bind transcription factors and have not analyzed the entire genome. However, whole mammalian genome arrays have recently become commercially available from companies like Nimblegen. In the future, as ChIP-on-chip arrays become more and more advanced, high resolution whole genome maps of DNA-binding proteins and chromatin components for mammals will be analyzed in more detail.

Analysis and Software

[9] CoCAS: a free Analysis software for Agilent ChIP-on-Chip experiments

[10] rMAT: R implementation from MAT program to normalize and analyze tiling arrays and ChIP-chip data.

Software Reference

[11] Touati Benoukraf , Pierre Cauchy , Romain Fenouil , Adrien Jeanniard , Frederic Koch , Sébastien Jaeger , Denis Thieffry , Jean Imbert , Jean-Christophe Andrau , Salvatore Spicuglia , and Pierre Ferrier , CoCAS: a ChIP-on-chip analysis suite, Bioinformatics Advance Access published on April 1, 2009, DOI 10.1093/bioinformatics/btp075, Bioinformatics 25: 954-955.

[12] W. Evan Johnson, Wei Li, Clifford A. Meyer, Raphael Gottardo, Jason S. Carroll, Myles Brown, and X. Shirley Liu. Model-based analysis of tiling-arrays for ChIP-chip. Proc Natl Acad Sci U S A. 2006 Aug 15;103(33):12457-62. Epub 2006 Aug 8.

Alternatives

Chip-Sequencing is a recently developed technology that still uses chromatin immunoprecipitation to crosslink the proteins of interest to the DNA but then instead of using a micro-array, it uses the more accurate, higher throughput method of sequencing to localize interaction points.

DamID is an alternative method that does not require antibodies.

External links

- http://www.genome.gov/10005107 ENCODE project
- http://www.chiponchip.org
- List of ChIP-chip software Wikiomics@OpenWetWare [13]
- Affymetrix Chip-on-Chip Forum [14]
- http://chipanalysis.genomecenter.ucdavis.edu/cgi-bin/tamalpais.cgi Online analysis of NimbleGen ChIP-chip experiments

References

[1] Aparicio, Oscar; Aparicio O, Geisberg JV, Struhl K (2004). "Chromatin immunoprecipitation for determining the association of proteins with
     specific genomic sequences in vivo". *Current Protocols in Cell Biology* (University of Southern California, Los Angeles, California, USA.:
     John Wiley & Sons, Inc.) **Chapter 17** (2004): Unit 17.7. doi:10.1002/0471143030.cb1707s23. ISBN 0471143030. ISSN 1934-2616.
     PMID 18228445.

[2] M.J. Buck, J.D. Lieb, ChIP-chip: considerations for the design, analysis, and application of genome-wide chromatin immunoprecipitation
     experiments, Genomics 83 (2004) 349-360.

[3] Royce TE, Rozowsky JS, Bertone P, Samanta M, Stolc V, Weissman S, Snyder M, Gerstein M. Related Articles. Issues in the analysis of
     oligonucleotide tiling microarrays for transcript mapping. Trends Genet. 2005 Aug;21(8):466-75. Review.

[4] "Transcription Factors Bind Thousands of Active and Inactive Regions in the Drosophila Blastoderm" (http://biology.plosjournals.org/
     perlserv/?request=get-document&doi=10.1371/journal.pbio.0060027). .

[5] J.D. Lieb, X. Liu, D. Botstein, P.O. Brown, Promoter-specific binding of Rap1 revealed by genome-wide maps of protein-DNA association,
     Nat. Genet. 28 (2001) 327-334.

[6] B. Ren, F. Robert, J.J. Wyrick, O. Aparicio, E.G. Jennings, I. Simon, J. Zeitlinger, J. Schreiber, N. Nannett, E. Kanin, T.L. Volkert, C.J.
     Wilson, S.R. Bell, R.A. Young, Genome-wide location and function of DNA binding proteins, Science 290 (2000) 2306-2309.

[7] V.R. Iyer, C.E. Horak, C.S. Scafe, D. Botstein, M. Snyder, P.O. Brown, Genomic binding sites of the yeast cell-cycle transcription factors
     SBF and MBF, Nature 409 (2001) 533-538.

[8] T.I. Lee, N.J. Rinaldi, F. Robert, D.T. Odom, Z. Bar-Joseph, G.K. Gerber, N.M. Hannett, C.T. Harbison, C.M. Thompson, I. Simon, J.
     Zeitlinger, E.G. Jennings, H.L. Murray, D.B. Gordon, B. Ren, J.J. Wyrick, J.B Tagne, T.L. Volkert, E. Fraenkel, D.K. Gifford, R.A Young,
     Transcriptional regulatory networks in Saccharomyces cerevisiae, Science 298 (2002) 799-804.

[9] http://www.ciml.univ-mrs.fr/software/cocas/index.html

[10] http://www.bioconductor.org/packages/2.4/bioc/html/rMAT.html

[11] http://bioinformatics.oxfordjournals.org/cgi/content/abstract/btp075

[12] http://www.pnas.org/content/103/33/12457.abstract

[13] http://openwetware.org/wiki/Wikiomics:ChIP-chip/wiki/ChIP-chip

[14] http://www.chiponchip.net

Chou–Fasman method

The **Chou–Fasman method** are an empirical technique for the prediction of secondary structures in proteins, originally developed in the 1970s.[1] [2] [3] The method is based on analyses of the relative frequencies of each amino acid in alpha helices, beta sheets, and turns based on known protein structures solved with X-ray crystallography. From these frequencies a set of probability parameters were derived for the appearance of each amino acid in each secondary structure type, and these parameters are used to predict the probability that a given sequence of amino acids would form a helix, a beta strand, or a turn in a protein. The method is at most about 50–60% accurate in identifying correct secondary structures,[4] which is significantly less accurate than the modern machine learning–based techniques.[5]

Amino acid propensities

The original Chou–Fasman parameters found some strong tendencies among individual amino acids to prefer one type of secondary structure over others. Alanine, glutamate, leucine, and methionine were identified as helix formers, while proline and glycine, due to the unique conformational properties of their peptide bonds, commonly end a helix. The original Chou–Fasman parameters[6] were derived from a very small and non-representative sample of protein structures due to the small number of such structures that were known at the time of their original work. These original parameters have since been shown to be unreliable[7] and have been updated from a current dataset, along with modifications to the initial algorithm.[8]

The Chou–Fasman method takes into account only the probability that each individual amino acid will appear in a helix, strand, or turn. Unlike the more complex GOR method, it does not reflect the conditional probabilities of an amino acid to form a particular secondary structure given that its neighbors already possess that structure. This lack of cooperativity increases its computational efficiency but decreases its accuracy, since the propensities of individual amino acids are often not strong enough to render a definitive prediction.[5]

Algorithm

The Chou–Fasman method predicts helices and strands in a similar fashion, first searching linearly through the sequence for a "nucleation" region of high helix or strand probability and then extending the region until a subsequent four-residue window carries a probability of less than 1. As originally described, four out of any six contiguous amino acids were sufficient to nucleate helix, and three out of any contiguous five were sufficient for a sheet. The probability thresholds for helix and strand nucleations are constant but not necessarily equal; originally 1.03 was set as the helix cutoff and 1.00 for the strand cutoff.

Turns are also evaluated in four-residue windows, but are calculated using a multi-step procedure because many turn regions contain amino acids that could also appear in helix or sheet regions. Four-residue turns also have their own characteristic amino acids; proline and glycine are both common in turns. A turn is predicted only if the turn probability is greater than the helix or sheet probabilities *and* a probability value based on the positions of particular amino acids in the turn exceeds a predetermined threshold. The turn probability p(t) is determined as:

$$p(t) = p_t(j) \times p_t(j+1) \times p_t(j+2) \times p_t(j+3)$$

where j is the position of the amino acid in the four-residue window. If p(t) exceeds an arbitrary cutoff value (originally 7.5e–3), the mean of the p(j)'s exceeds 1, and p(t) exceeds the alpha helix and beta sheet probabilities for that window, then a turn is predicted. If the first two conditions are met but the probability of a beta sheet p(b) exceeds p(t), then a sheet is predicted instead.

References

[1] Chou PY, Fasman GD (1974). "Prediction of protein conformation". *Biochemistry* **13** (2): 222–245. doi:10.1021/bi00699a002. PMID 4358940.

[2] Chou PY, Fasman GD (1978). "Empirical predictions of protein conformation". *Annu Rev Biochem* **47**: 251–276. doi:10.1146/annurev.bi.47.070178.001343. PMID 354496.

[3] Chou PY, Fasman GD (1978). "Prediction of the secondary structure of proteins from their amino acid sequence". *Adv Enzymol Relat Areas Mol Biol* **47**: 45–148. PMID 364941.

[4] Kabsch W, Sander C (1983). "How good are predictions of protein secondary structure?". *FEBS Lett* **155** (2): 179–82. doi:10.1016/0014-5793(82)80597-8. PMID 6852232.

[5] Mount DM (2004). *Bioinformatics: Sequence and Genome Analysis* (2 ed.). Cold Spring Harbor, NY: Cold Spring Harbor Laboratory Press. ISBN 0-879-69712-1.

[6] Chou PY, Fasman GD (1974). "Conformational parameters for amino acids in helical, beta-sheet, and random coil regions calculated from proteins". *Biochemistry* **13** (2): 211–222. doi:10.1021/bi00699a001. PMID 4358939.

[7] Kyngas J, Valjakka J (1998). "Unreliability of the Chou–Fasman parameters in predicting protein secondary structure". *Protein Eng* **11** (5): 345–348. doi:10.1093/protein/11.5.345. PMID 9681866.

[8] Chen H, Gu F, Huang Z (2006). "Improved Chou–Fasman method for protein secondary structure prediction". *BMC Bioinformatics* **7** (Suppl 4): S14.

External links

- Gerald D. Fasman on the Internet (http://www.wisdomportal.com/Dates/GeraldDFasman.html)

CIT Program Tumor Identity Cards

The **"Cartes d'Identité des Tumeurs (CIT)" program** (or 'Tumor Identity Cards'), launched and financed by the French charity "Ligue Nationale contre le Cancer", aims at characterizing multiple types of tumors through the coupled genomic **analysis of gene expression and chromosomal alterations**.

The CIT Program database contains more than 8,000 cancer samples

Towards personalized treatments

The "Cartes d'Identité des Tumeurs (CIT)" program should benefit each patient by contributing to :

- more accurate diagnosis
- better predictions of the response to treatment and the disease progression
- improved patient follow-up during and after treatment

Collaborations throughout the whole of France

Built with a network of researchers, pathologists, doctors and bioinformaticians, the "Cartes d'Identité des Tumeurs (CIT)" program involves 60 teams and offers one of the largest tumor databases in Europe containing more than 8,000 annotated tumor samples and 10,000 micro-array experiments.

A set of standardized processes and technologies

Curation and standardization of biological and clinical annotations

All the information on the patients is de-identified and sent on by the clinical centers. All the clinical follow-up data, including the results of the various biological and genetic tests carried out on the patients, are included in a database with secure access (Annotator). This CIT program database also contains data generated by each of the technological platforms and the results of the analyses. At each stage of the data integration process, all the information is checked to ensure that it is complete and consistent. The annotations are then recoded in accordance with internal and international standards. This allows for cross-project analyses.

DNA/RNA Extraction and Qualification

The quality of the biological resources constitutes a major element in the reproducibility of the results obtained in the genomic studies. To this end, the CIT program has set up a platform dedicated to the extraction and qualification of RNA and DNA. The extraction of RNA and DNA is carried out from the same tumor sample. The quality of the samples is assessed using agarose gels and electrophoregram profiles in order to evaluate the level of contamination and degradation of these biological resources. All the samples are processed on the same platform, with validated and standardized protocols, to optimize the yield of the platform, to implement precise quality controls, and to improve the performance of the subsequent hybridizations even in case of partial degradation of the tumor samples. Depending on the quality of the surgical procedure, the volume of available biomaterial and the type of pathology, between 0 and 60% (average 25%) of the sample RNAs are filtered out by the platform.

Biochip Experiments

The CIT program chooses commercial technologies and efficient instruments to carry out the hybridizations on biochips (especilly Affymetrix GeneChip arrays to study the expression of genes, and Illumina BeadChip arrays to study allelotypes and DNA modifications). This increases the yield of the platforms and the reproducibility of the results. Standardized protocols are set up at all stages of the process (preparation of the samples, hybridization, scanning, image analysis etc.). A key objective of the CIT program is to process the greatest possible number of samples on the same platform to minimize bias related to the experiments, to optimize the parameters of the different stages and to enable comprehensive quality control checks. Between January 2004 and January 2009, over 9,000 biochip experiments were carried out.

Analysis & Validation

CIT Biostatistical expertise The data processing procedures are based on reference methods from the literature or on innovative internal developments. Implemented with the open source statistical software R, they follow a set of specifications which facilitate collaborative work and tracking.

Pre-processing

The data sent by the hybridization platforms are pre-processed according to a normalization and quality control stage adapted to each technology: background correction, quality control, filtering, aggregation and normalization. For genomic data (CGH, SNPs), an essential segmentation step is added to identify the altered regions along the genome.

Data analysis

The data analysis unfolds into three main stages:

- Class discovery, using unsupervised clustering, enables the identification of the underlying molecular groups. The quality and variety of the supplied annotations are crucial to interpret the resulting classification.
- Class comparison, through a supervised approach, defines a molecular signature, i.e. the set of markers associated with a given phenotype.
- Class prediction, using classification approaches, establishes the smallest combinations of molecular markers to characterize tumor groups and to guide decisions about medical treatments.

Interpretation and Validation

Results are interpreted through additional bioinformatics analysis (pathway analysis, combined genome and transcriptome study), and then validated against independent datasets from the literature or from the CIT program. Finally, a validation of the results is carried out with RT-PCR on a microfluidic platform.

External links

- Official web site [1], from the French National League against Cancer
- Scientific publications [2], from the CIT Program web site
- Network of investigators and collaborators [3], from the CIT Program web site
- Curation and standardization of annotations [4], from the CIT Program web site
- Extraction and qualification of DNA and RNA [5], from the CIT Program web site
- Data analysis and validation in the CIT Program [6], from the CIT Program web site
- Oasys : A graphical viewer for omics data [7], from the CIT Program web site

References

[1] http://cit.ligue-cancer.net/index.php/en

[2] http://cit.ligue-cancer.net/index.php/en/publications

[3] http://cit.ligue-cancer.net/index.php/en/partnerships

[4] http://cit.ligue-cancer.net/images/stories/CIT/pdf/ProcessuCuration_eng_Version1.pdf

[5] http://cit.ligue-cancer.net/images/stories/CIT/pdf/WebSite%20CIT-%20QC%20PF%20Saint-Louis%207%20avril%2009.pdf

[6] http://cit.ligue-cancer.net/images/stories/CIT/pdf/SiteWeb.4AnalysisValidationVersionLongue_v3.0.pdf

[7] http://cit.ligue-cancer.net/oasys

CLC bio

CLC bio

Type	Privately held company
Industry	Bioinformatics
Founded	2005
Headquarters	Aarhus, Denmark
Products	Software, hardware, and consulting
Website	http://www.clcbio.com

CLC bio is a bioinformatics solution provider based in Aarhus, Denmark. CLC bio's software workbenches have more than 75,000 users in more than 100 countries around the globe.

Software

The company started out making a free desktop workbench for basic bioinformatics, CLC Sequence Viewer [1] (originally called CLC Free Workbench), which was released in July 2005. Commercial workbenches for advanced bioinformatics have been added since. CLC bio's software is platform independent and can thus be used for both Mac OS X, Windows, and Linux.

Hardware

The company has also developed high-performance computing solutions, focusing on accelerating scientifically proven algorithms such as HMMER, Smith-Waterman and ClustalW. CLC Bioinformatics Cube [2] and CLC Bioinformatics Cell [3] have garnered considerable positive attention in independent industry publications such as Bio-IT World [4].

External links

- Official website [5]
- CLC Bio exhibiting at Functional Genomics and Disease 2010 [6]

References

[1] http://clcbio.com/viewer
[2] http://clccube.com
[3] http://clccell.com
[4] Bio-IT World (http://www.google.com/search?num=100&hl=en&newwindow=1&safe=off&q=site:bio-itworld.com+"CLC+bio"&
    btnG=Search)
[5] http://clcbio.com/
[6] http://www.esffg2010.org/index.asp

Clone manager

Clone Manager is a commercial bioinformatics software work suite of Sci-Ed, that supports molecular biologists with data management and allows to perform certain *in silico* preanalyis.

External links

- http://www.scied.com Sci-Ed homepage

Clustal

Clustal

Developer(s)	Gibson T. (EMBL), Thompson J. (CNRS), Higgins D. (UCD)
Stable release	2.1 / 17 November 2010
Written in	C++
Operating system	UNIX, Linux, Mac, MS-Windows
Type	Bioinformatics tool
Licence	Free for academic users
Website	Clustal [1]

Clustal is a widely used multiple sequence alignment computer program.[2] The latest version is 2.1.[3] There are two main variations:

- **ClustalW**: command line interface
- **ClustalX**: This version has a graphical user interface.[4] It is available for Windows, Mac OS, and Unix/Linux.

This program is available from the Clustal Homepage [1] or European Bioinformatics Institute ftp server [5].

Input/Output

This program accepts a wide range on input format. Included NBRF/PIR, FASTA, EMBL/Swissprot, Clustal, GCC/MSF, GCG9 RSF, and GDE.

The output format can be one or many of the following: Clustal, NBRF/PIR, GCG/MSF, PHYLIP, GDE, or NEXUS.

Multiple sequence alignment

There are three main steps:

1. Do a pairwise alignment
2. Create a phylogenetic tree (or use a user-defined tree)
3. Use the phylogenetic tree to carry out a multiple alignment

These are done automatically when you select "Do Complete Alignment". Other options are "Do Alignment from guide tree" and "Produce guide tree only".

Setting

Users can align the sequences using the default setting, but occasionally it may be useful to customize one's own parameters.

The main parameters are the gap opening penalty, and the gap extension penalty.

References

[1] http://www.clustal.org

[2] Chenna R, Sugawara H, Koike T, Lopez R, Gibson TJ, Higgins DG, Thompson JD (2003). "Multiple sequence alignment with the Clustal series of programs". *Nucleic Acids Res* **31** (13): 3497–3500. doi:10.1093/nar/gkg500. PMC 168907. PMID 12824352.

[3] Larkin MA, Blackshields G, Brown NP, Chenna R, McGettigan PA, McWilliam H, Valentin F, Wallace IM, Wilm A, Lopez R, Thompson JD, Gibson TJ, Higgins DG (2007). "ClustalW and ClustalX version 2". *Bioinformatics* **23** (21): 2947–2948. doi:10.1093/bioinformatics/btm404. PMID 17846036.

[4] Thompson JD, Gibson TJ, Plewniak F, Jeanmougin F, Higgins DG (1997). "The CLUSTAL_X windows interface: flexible strategies for multiple sequence alignment aided by quality analysis tools". *Nucleic Acids Research* **25** (24): 4876–4882. doi:10.1093/nar/25.24.4876. PMC 147148. PMID 9396791.

[5] ftp://ftp.ebi.ac.uk/pub/software/

External links

- Clustal Homepage (http://www.clustal.org) (free Unix/Linux, Mac, and Windows download)
- ClustalW and ClustalX mirror at the EBI (http://www.ebi.ac.uk/Tools/clustalw2/index.html) (free Unix/Linux, Mac, and Windows download)
- " Accelerating Intensive Applications at 10x-50x Speedup to Remove Bottlenecks in Computational Workflows (http://www.progeniq.com/news/BioBoost White Paper.pdf)" — White Paper by Progeniq Pte Ltd.
- Multiple Sequence Alignment by CLUSTALW (http://align.genome.jp/)

CodonCode Aligner

CodonCode Aligner

Developer(s)	CodonCode Corporation
Stable release	3.0.1 / 30 March 2009
Operating system	Mac OS X, WIndows
Type	Bioinformatics
License	commercial; free for limited use (trace viewing & editing)
Website	[1]

CodonCode Aligner is a commercial application for DNA sequence assembly, sequence alignment, and editing on Mac OS X and Windows.

Features

- Chromatogram editing, end clipping, and vector trimming.
- Sequence assembly and contig editing
- Aligning cDNA against genomic templates
- Sequence alignment and editing.
- Alignment of contigs to each other with ClustalW, MUSCLE, or built-in algorithms.
- Mutation detection, including detection of heterozygous single-nucleotide polymorphism.
- Analysis of heterozygous insertions and deletions.
- Start online BLAST searches.
- Restriction analysis - find and view restriction cut sites.
- Trace sharpening.
- Support for Phred, Phrap, ClustalW, and MUSCLE.

History

The first beta version of CodonCode Aligner was released in April 2003, followed by the first full version in June 2003. Major upgrades were released in 2003, 2004, 2005, 2006, 2007, and 2008.

In April 2009, CodonCode Aligner had been cited in more than 400 scientific publications. Citations cover a wide variety of biomedical research areas, including HIV research,[2] [3] [4], biogeography and environmental biology[5] [6], DNA methylation studies[7], genetic diseases[8] [9] [10], clinical microbiology[11] [12], and evolution research and phylogenetics[13] [14] [15].

References

[1] http://www.codoncode.com/aligner

[2] Bailey JR, Sedaghat AR, Kieffer T, Brennan T, Lee PK, Wind-Rotolo M, Haggerty CM, Kamireddi AR, Liu Y, Lee J, Persaud D, Gallant JE, Cofrancesco J, Quinn TC, Wilke CO, Ray SC, Siliciano JD, Nettles RE, Siliciano RF (2006). "Residual Human Immunodeficiency Virus Type 1 Viremia in Some Patients on Antiretroviral Therapy Is Dominated by a Small Number of Invariant Clones Rarely Found in Circulating CD4+ T Cells,Ä†.". *J Virol* **80** (13): 6441–6457. doi:10.1128/JVI.00591-06. PMC 1488985. PMID 16775332.

[3] Calis JC, Rotteveel HP, van der Kuyl AC, Zorgdrager F, Kachala D, van Hensbroek MB, Cornelissen M (2008). "Severe anaemia is not associated with HIV-1 env gene characteristics in Malawian children.". *BMC Infect Dis* **8**: 26. doi:10.1186/1471-2334-8-26. PMC 2311312. PMID 18312662.

[4] Mild M, Esbjörnsson J, Fenyö EM, Medstrand P (2007). "Frequent Intrapatient Recombination between Human Immunodeficiency Virus Type 1 R5 and X4 Envelopes: Implications for Coreceptor Switch,ñø.". *J Virol* **81** (7): 3369–3376. doi:10.1128/JVI.01295-06. PMC 1866041. PMID 17251288.

[5] Pendley CJ, Becker EA, Karl JA, Blasky AJ, Wiseman RW, Hughes AL, O,O'Connor SL, O,O'Connor DH (2008). "MHC class I characterization of Indonesian cynomolgus macaques.". *Immunogenetics* **60** (7): 339–351. doi:10.1007/s00251-008-0292-4. PMC 2612123. PMID 18504574.

[6] Behnke A, Bunge J, Barger K, Breiner H, Alla V, Stoeck T (2006). "Microeukaryote Community Patterns along an O2/H2S Gradient in a Supersulfidic Anoxic Fjord (Framvaren, Norway),Ä†.". *Appl Environ Microbiol* **72** (5): 3626–3636. doi:10.1128/AEM.72.5.3626-3636.2006. PMC 1472314. PMID 16672511.

[7] Bart A, van Passel MWJ, van Amsterdam K, van der Ende A (2005). "Direct detection of methylation in genomic DNA.". *Nucleic Acids Res* **33** (14): e124. doi:10.1093/nar/gni121. PMC 1184226. PMID 16091626.

[8] Andersson LS, Juras R, Ramsey DT, Eason-Butler J, Ewart S, Cothran G, Lindgren G (2008). "Equine Multiple Congenital Ocular Anomalies maps to a 4.9 megabase interval on horse chromosome 6.". *BMC Genet* **9**: 88. doi:10.1186/1471-2156-9-88. PMC 2653074. PMID 19099555.

[9] Tremblay K, Lemire M, Potvin C, Tremblay A, Hunninghake GM, Raby BA, Hudson TJ, Perez-Iratxeta C, Andrade-Navarro MA, Laprise C (2008). "Genes to Diseases (G2D) Computational Method to Identify Asthma Candidate Genes.". *PLoS ONE* **3**.

[10] McCullough BJ, Adams JC, Shilling DJ, Feeney MP, Sie KCY, Tempel BL (2007). "3p-Syndrome Defines a Hearing Loss Locus in 3p25.3.". *Hear Res* **224** (1-2): 51–60. doi:10.1016/j.heares.2006.11.006. PMC 1995240. PMID 17208398.

[11] Pignone M, Greth KM, Cooper J, Emerson D, Tang J (2006). "Identification of Mycobacteria by Matrix-Assisted Laser Desorption Ionization-Time-of-Flight Mass Spectrometry.". *J Clin Microbiol* **44** (6): 1963–1970. doi:10.1128/JCM.01959-05. PMC 1489414. PMID 16757585.

[12] van Amsterdam K, Bart A, van der Ende A (2005). "A Helicobacter pylori TolC Efflux Pump Confers Resistance to Metronidazole.". *Antimicrob Agents Chemother* **49** (4): 1477–1482. doi:10.1128/AAC.49.4.1477-1482.2005. PMC 1068630. PMID 15793129.

[13] Baxter SW, Papa R, Chamberlain N, Humphray SJ, Joron M, Morrison C, ffrench-Constant RH, McMillan WO, Jiggins CD (2008). "Convergent Evolution in the Genetic Basis of Müllerian Mimicry in Heliconius Butterflies.". *Genetics* **180** (3): 1567–1577. doi:10.1534/genetics.107.082982. PMC 2581958. PMID 18791259.

[14] Siddall ME, Trontelj P, Utevsky SY, Nkamany M, Macdonald KS (2007). "Diverse molecular data demonstrate that commercially available medicinal leeches are not Hirudo medicinalis.". *Proc Biol Sci* **274** (1617): 1481–1487 PMID 17426015. doi:10.1098/rspb.2007.0248. PMC 2176162. PMID 17426015.

[15] Stoeck T, Kasper J, Bunge J, Leslin C, Ilyin V, Epstein S (2007). "Protistan Diversity in the Arctic: A Case of Paleoclimate Shaping Modern Biodiversity?". *PLoS ONE* **2 PMID 17710128**.

External links

- CodonCode Aligner homepage (http://www.codoncode.com/aligner)
- CodonCode Aligner Support Forum (http://www.codoncode.org)

Community Cyberinfrastructure for Advanced Marine Microbial Ecology Research and Analysis

CAMERA

Content	
Description	Community Cyberinfrastructure for Advanced Marine Microbial Ecology Research and Analysis
Contact	
Research center	University of California San Diego
Laboratory	Center for Research on Biological Systems
Primary Citation	PMID 21045053
Release date	2007
Access	
Website	http://camera.calit2.net/
Tools	
Miscellaneous	

CAMERA, or the **Community Cyberinfrastructure for Advanced Marine Microbial Ecology Research and Analysis**, is a microbial ecology research project[1] [2] [3] which was announced in January 2006.[4]

Funding

The project aims to serve the needs of the microbial ecology research community by creating a vast data repository and a bioinformatics tools resource that will address many of the unique challenges of metagenomic analysis. The project is funded by the Gordon and Betty Moore Foundation which awarded a 7-year, $24.5-million research grant to the CAMERA project, beginning in January 2006.[5]

Work

CAMERA is devoted to serving the needs of scientists studying the complexity of organisms as they function in natural ecosystems.[6] The group is managed by:[6]

- Principal Investigator Larry Smarr (UCSD)
- Executive Director Paul Gilna (UCSD)

CAMERA helps scientists access and work with data from the Venter Institute's Global Ocean Sampling Expedition.[7] In 2007, the GOS dataset was the largest ever released in the public domain.[8] The group also places many other datasets for download on its website.[9]

References

[1] Sun, Shulei; Chen Jing, Li Weizhong, Altintas Ilkay, Lin Abel, Peltier Steve, Stocks Karen, Allen Eric E, Ellisman Mark, Grethe Jeffrey, Wooley John (Jan 2011). "Community cyberinfrastructure for Advanced Microbial Ecology Research and Analysis: the CAMERA resource" (in eng). *Nucleic Acids Res.* (England) **39** (Database issue): D546-51. doi:10.1093/nar/gkq1102. PMID 21045053.

[2] PubMed Central: "CAMERA: A Community Resource for Metagenomics" (http://www.pubmedcentral.nih.gov/articlerender. fcgi?artid=1821059)

[3] DOE Microbial Genomics: Microbial Genome Databases (http://microbialgenomics.energy.gov/databases.shtml)

[4] *Gordon and Betty Moore Foundation*: Leading Department of Energy Genome Scientist to Direct Joint Marine Microbial Metagenomics Cyberinfrastructure Initiative (press release) (http://www.moore.org/newsitem.aspx?id=436)

[5] CAMERA: What is CAMERA? (http://www.camera.calit2.net/about-camera/what-is-camera)

[6] CAMERA: Frequently Asked Questions (http://www.camera.calit2.net/faq)

[7] *Anchorage Daily News*: Scientist stalks wily microbes from sailboat (http://dwb.adn.com/news/alaska/story/9155271p-9071801c.html)

[8] *Science Daily*: Millions Of New Genes, Thousands Of New Protein Families Found In Ocean Sampling Expedition (press release) (http://www.sciencedaily.com/releases/2007/03/070314074922.htm)

[9] CAMERA: Full Datasets (http://www.camera.calit2.net/about-camera/full-datasets)

External links

- Official CAMERA Web Site (http://www.camera.calit2.net/)
- UCSD: UCSD Partners with Venter Institute to Build Community Cyberinfrastructure for Advanced Marine Microbial Ecology Research and Analysis (http://www.jacobsschool.ucsd.edu/news/news_releases/release. sfe?id=499)

Complex system biology

Complex systems biology (**CSB**) is a branch or subfield of mathematical and theoretical biology concerned with complexity of both structure and function in biological organisms, as well as the emergence and evolution of organisms and species, with emphasis being placed on the complex interactions of, and within, bionetworks,[1] and on the fundamental relations and relational patterns that are essential to life.[2] [3] [4] [5] [6] **CSB** is thus a field of theoretical sciences aimed at discovering and modeling the relational patterns essential to life that has only a partial overlap with complex systems theory,[7] and also with the systems approach to biology called systems biology; this is because the latter is restricted primarily to simplified models of biological organization and organisms, as well as to only a general consideration of philosophical or semantic questions related to complexity in biology.[8] Moreover, a wide range of abstract theoretical complex systems are studied as a field of applied mathematics, with or without relevance to biology, chemistry or physics.

Complexity of organisms and biosphere

A complete definition of complexity for individual organisms, species, ecosystems, biological evolution and the biosphere has eluded researchers, and still is an ongoing issue[3] [9] .

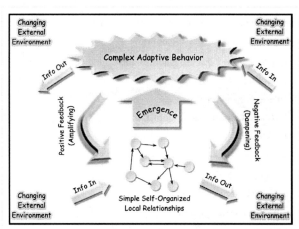

Network Representation of a Complex Adaptive System

Most complex system models are often formulated in terms of concepts drawn from statistical physics, information theory and non-linear dynamics; however, such approaches are not focused on, or do not include, the conceptual part of complexity related to organization and topological attributes or algebraic topology, such as network connectivity of genomes, interactomes and biological organisms that are very important[6] [10] [11] . Recently, the two complementary approaches based both on information theory, network topology/abstract graph theory concepts are being combined for

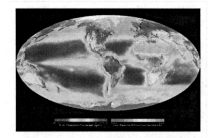

example in the fields of neuroscience and human cognition[12] [7] . It is generally agreed that there is a hierarchy of complexity levels of organization that should be considered as distinct from that of the levels of reality in ontology[13] [14] [15] [7] . The hierarchy of complexity levels of organization in the biosphere is also recognized in modern classifications of taxonomic ranks, such as: biological domain and biosphere, biological kingdom, Phylum, biological class, order, family, genus and species. Because of their dynamic and composition variability, intrinsic "fuzziness", autopoietic attributes, ability to self-reproduce, and so on, organisms do not fit into the 'standard' definition of general systems, and they are therefore 'super-complex' in both their function and structure; organisms can be thus be defined in **CSB** only as 'meta-systems' of simpler dynamic systems[16] [7] Such a meta-system definition of organisms, species, 'ecosystems', and so on, is not equivalent to the definition of a *system of systems* as in Autopoietic Systems Theory,[17] ; it also differs from the definition proposed for example by K.D. Palmer in meta-system engineering[18] , organisms being quite different from machines and automata with fixed input-output transition functions, or a continuous dynamical system with fixed phase space[19] , contrary to the Cartesian philosophical thinking; thus, organisms cannot be defined merely in terms of a quintuple A of *(states, startup state, input and output sets/alphabet, transition function)*[20] , although 'non-deterministic automata', as well as 'fuzzy automata' have also been defined. Tessellation or cellular automata provide however an intuitive, visual/computational insight into the lower levels of complexity, and have therefore become an increasingly popular, discrete model studied in computability theory, applied mathematics, physics, computer science, theoretical biology/systems biology, cancer simulations and microstructure modeling. Evolving cellular automata using genetic algorithms[21] [22] [23] is also an emerging field attempting to bridge the gap between the tessellation automata and the higher level complexity approaches in **CSB**.

Topics in complex systems biology

The following is only a partial list of topics covered in complex systems biology:

- Organisms and species relations and evolution
- Interactions among Species
- Evolution theories and population genetics
  - Population genetics models
  - Epigenetics
  - Molecular evolution theories
- Quantum biocomputation
- Quantum genetics[24]
- Relational biology[25] [26] [27] [28]
- Self-reproduction[29] (also called self-replication in a more general context)
- Computational gene models
  - DNA topology
  - DNA sequencing theory
- Evolutionary developmental biology
- Autopoiesis
- Protein folding
- Telomerase conformations and functions *in vivo*
- Epigenetics
- Interactomics[30] [31]
- Cell signaling
- Signal transduction networks
- Complex neural nets
- Genetic networks
- Morphogenesis
- Digital morphogenesis
- Complex adaptive systems
- Topological models of morphogenesis
- Population dynamics of fisheries
- Epidemiology
- Theoretical ecology

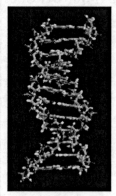

Animated Molecular Model of a DNA double helix

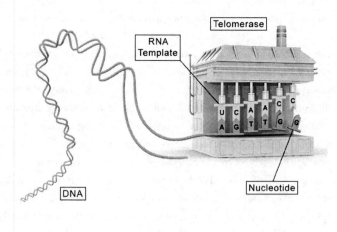

Telomerase structure and function

Related journals

- Acta Biotheoretica [32]
- Bioinformatics [33]
- Biological Theory [34]
- BioSystems [35]
- Bulletin of Mathematical Biology [36]
- Ecological Modelling [37]
- Journal of Mathematical Biology [38]
- Journal of Theoretical Biology [39]
- Mathematical Biosciences [40]
- Medical Hypotheses [41]
- Theoretical and Applied Genetics [42]
- Theoretical Biology and Medical Modelling [43]
- Theoretical Population Biology [44]
- Theory in Biosciences [45] (formerly: Biologisches Zentralblatt)

CBS societies and institutes

- Society for Mathematical Biology
- ESMTB: European Society for Mathematical and Theoretical Biology [46]
- Division of Mathematical Biology at NIMR [47]
- The Israeli Society for Theoretical and Mathematical Biology [48]
- Société Francophone de Biologie Théorique [49]

- International Society for Biosemiotic Studies [50]

Biographies

- Charles Darwin
- D'Arcy Thompson
- William Ross Ashby
- Ludwig von Bertalanffy
- Ronald Brown
- Joseph Fourier
- Brian Goodwin
- George Karreman
- Charles S. Peskin
- Nicolas Rashevsky [51]
- Robert Rosen
- Anatol Rapoport
- Rosalind Franklin
- Francis Crick
- René Thom
- Vito Volterra
- Norbert Wiener

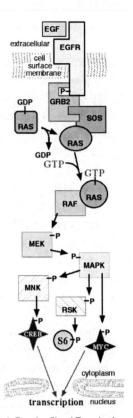

A Complex Signal Transduction Pathway

References cited

- J.D. Murray, *Mathematical Biology*. Springer-Verlag, 3rd ed. in 2 vols.: *Mathematical Biology: I. An Introduction*, 2002 ISBN 0-387-95223-3; *Mathematical Biology: II. Spatial Models and Biomedical Applications*, 2003 ISBN 0-387-95228-4.
- Thompson, D'Arcy W., 1992. *On Growth and Form*. Dover reprint of 1942, 2nd ed. (1st ed., 1917). ISBN 0-486-67135-6
- Nicolas Rashevsky. (1938)., *Mathematical Biophysics*. Chicago: University of Chicago Press.
- Robert Rosen.1970. *Dynamical system theory in biology*. New York, Wiley-Interscience. ISBN 0-471-73550-7
- Israel, G., 2005, "Book on mathematical biology" in Grattan-Guinness, I., ed., *Landmark Writings in Western Mathematics*. Elsevier: 936-44.
- Israel G (1988). "On the contribution of Volterra and Lotka to the development of modern biomathematics". *History and Philosophy of the Life Sciences* **10** (1): 37–49. PMID 3045853.
- Scudo FM (March 1971). "Vito Volterra and theoretical ecology". *Theoretical Population Biology* **2** (1): 1–23. doi:10.1016/0040-5809(71)90002-5. PMID 4950157.
- S.H. Strogatz, *Nonlinear dynamics and Chaos: Applications to Physics, Biology, Chemistry, and Engineering*. Perseus, 2001, ISBN 0-7382-0453-6
- N.G. van Kampen, *Stochastic Processes in Physics and Chemistry*, North Holland., 3rd ed. 2001, ISBN 0-444-89349-0
- I. C. Baianu., Computer Models and Automata Theory in Biology and Medicine., *Monograph*, Ch.11 in M. Witten (Editor), *Mathematical Models in Medicine*, vol. **7**., Vol. **7**: 1513-1577 (1987),Pergamon Press:New York, (updated by Hsiao Chen Lin in 2004 ISBN 0-08-036377-6
- P.G. Drazin, *Nonlinear systems*. C.U.P., 1992. ISBN 0-521-40668-4
- L. Edelstein-Keshet, *Mathematical Models in Biology*. SIAM, 2004. ISBN 0-07-554950-6
- G. Forgacs and S. A. Newman, *Biological Physics of the Developing Embryo*. C.U.P., 2005. ISBN 0-521-78337-2
- E. Renshaw, *Modelling biological populations in space and time*. C.U.P., 1991. ISBN 0-521-44855-7
- Rosen, Robert.1991, *Life Itself: A Comprehensive Inquiry into the Nature, Origin, and Fabrication of Life*, Columbia University Press, published posthumously:
- Rosen, Robert. 2000, *Essays on Life Itself*, Columbia University Press.
- Rosen, Robert. 2003, "*Anticipatory Systems; Philosophical, Mathematical, and Methodolical Foundations*", Rosen Enterprises publs.
- S.I. Rubinow, *Introduction to mathematical biology*. John Wiley, 1975. ISBN 0-471-74446-8
- L.A. Segel, *Modeling dynamic phenomena in molecular and cellular biology*. C.U.P., 1984. ISBN 0-521-27477-X.
- D.W. Jordan and P. Smith, *Nonlinear ordinary differential equations*, 2nd ed. O.U.P., 1987. ISBN 0-19-856562-3
- L. Preziosi, *Cancer Modelling and Simulation*. Chapman Hall/CRC Press, 2003. ISBN 1-58488-361-8.
- Graeme Donald Snooks, "A general theory of complex living systems: Exploring the demand side of dynamics", *Complexity*, vol. 13, no. 6, July/August 2008.
- Tsekeris, Charalambos. "Advances in Understanding Human Complex Systems", *Australian Journal of Basic and Applied Sciences*, vol. 3, no. 4, October/December 2009.
- Bonner, J. T. 1988. *The Evolution of Complexity by Means of Natural Selection*. Princeton: Princeton University Press.

Further reading

- A general list of Theoretical biology/Mathematical biology references, including an updated list of actively contributing authors [52].
- A list of references for applications of category theory in relational biology [53].
- An updated list of publications of theoretical biologist Robert Rosen [54]
- Theory of Biological Anthropology (Documents No. 9 and 10 in English) [55]
- Drawing the Line Between Theoretical and Basic Biology (a forum article by Isidro T. Savillo) [56]
- Semantic Systems Biology [57]
- Synthesis and Analysis of a Biological System [58], by Hiroyuki Kurata, 1999.

Notes

[1] Sprites, P; Glymour, C; Scheines, R (2000). *Causation, Prediction, and Search: Adaptive Computation and Machine Learning* (2nd ed.). MIT Press.

[2] Graeme Donald Snooks, "A general theory of complex living systems: Exploring the demand side of dynamics", Complexity, vol. 13, no. 6, July/August 2008.

[3] Bonner, J. T. 1988. The Evolution of Complexity by Means of Natural Selection. Princeton: Princeton University Press.

[4] Rosen, R.: 1958a, "A Relational Theory of Biological Systems". Bulletin of Mathematical Biophysics 20: 245-260

[5] Baianu, I. C.: 2006, "Robert Rosen's Work and Complex Systems Biology", Axiomathes 16(1-2):25-34

[6] Rosen, R.: 1958b, "The Representation of Biological Systems from the Standpoint of the Theory of Categories.", Bulletin of Mathematical Biophysics 20: 317-341.

[7] http://www.springerlink.com/index/V1RT05876H74V607.pdf I. C. Baianu, R. Brown and J. F. Glazebrook. 2007. Categorical Ontology of Complex Spacetime Structures: The Emergence of Life and Human Consciousness., *Axiomathes*, 17:223–352. doi: 10.1007/s10516-007-9011-2 .

[8] http://www.semantic-systems-biology.org/Semantic Systems Biology Portal

[9] Heylighen, Francis (2008). "Complexity and Self-Organization". In Bates, Marcia J.; Maack, Mary Niles. Encyclopedia of Library and Information Sciences. CRC. ISBN 9780849397127

[10] ^ Heylighen, Francis (2008). "Complexity and Self-Organization". In Bates, Marcia J.; Maack, Mary Niles. Encyclopedia of Library and Information Sciences. CRC. ISBN 9780849397127

[11] "abstract relational biology (ARB)". PlanetPhysics. Retrieved 2010-03-17.

[12] http://hdl.handle.net/10101/npre.2011.6115.1 Wallace, Rodrick. When Spandrels Become Arches: Neural crosstalk and the evolution of consciousness. Available from Nature Precedings (2011)

[13] Poli,R.: 2001a. The Basic Problem of the Theory of Levels of Reality, *Axiomathes*, **12**: 3-4, pp.261-283.

[14] http://philica.com/display_article.php?article_id=256 Baianu, I. and R. Poli.(2011). From Simple to Complex and Ultra-complex Systems: A Paradigm Shift Towards Non-Abelian Systems Dynamics. *philo.philica.com* Article # 256.

[15] Poli, R.: 1998, Levels, *Axiomathes*, **9**, (1-2):197-211

[16] Metasystem Transition Theory (http://pespmc1.vub.ac.be/MST.html), Valentin Turchin, Cliff Joslyn, 1993-1997

[17] Reflexive Autopoietic Systems Theory (http://archonic.net)

[18] Meta-system Engineering (http://archonic.net/incosewg/ppframe.htm), Kent D. Palmer, 1996

[19] Hoff, M.A., Roggia, K.G., Menezes, P.B.:(2004). Composition of Transformations: A Framework for Systems with Dynamic Topology. *International Journal of Computing Anticipatory Systems* **14**:259–270

[20] John E. Hopcroft, Rajeev Motwani, Jeffrey D. Ullman.2000. Introduction to Automata Theory, Languages, and Computation (2nd Edition)Pearson Education. isbn:0-201-44124-1

[21] The Evolutionary Design of Collective Computation in Cellular Automata, James P. Crutchfeld, Melanie Mitchell, Rajarshi Das (In J. P. Crutchfield and P. K. Schuster (editors), Evolutionary Dynamics|Exploring the Interplay of Selection, Neutrality, Accident, and Function. New York: Oxford University Press, 2002.)

[22] Evolving Cellular Automata with Genetic Algorithms: A Review of Recent Work, Melanie Mitchell, James P. Crutchfield, Rajarshi Das (In Proceedings of the First International Conference on Evolutionary Computation and Its Applications (EvCA'96). Moscow, Russia: Russian Academy of Sciences, 1996.)

[23] http://adsabs.harvard.edu/abs/2004PNAS..101..918P Peak, West; Messinger, Mott; Messinger, SM; Mott, KA (2004). "Evidence for complex, collective dynamics and emergent, distributed computation in plants" (http://www.pnas.org/cgi/content/abstract/101/4/918). *Proceedings of the National Academy of Sciences of the USA* **101** (4): 918–922. Bibcode 2004PNAS..101..918P. doi:10.1073/pnas.0307811100. PMC 327117. PMID 14732685. .

[24] Rosen, R. 1960. (1960). "A quantum-theoretic approach to genetic problems". *Bulletin of Mathematical Biophysics* **22** (3): 227–255. doi:10.1007/BF02478347.

[25] Rosen, R.: 1958a, "A Relational Theory of Biological Systems". Bulletin of Mathematical Biophysics 20: 245-260.

[26] Baianu, I. C.: 2006, (2006). "Robert Rosen's Work and Complex Systems Biology". *Axiomathes* **16** (1–2): 25–34. doi:10.1007/s10516-005-4204-z.

[27] Rosen, R.: 1958b, (1958). "The Representation of Biological Systems from the Standpoint of the Theory of Categories". *Bulletin of Mathematical Biophysics* **20** (4): 317–341. doi:10.1007/BF02477890.

[28] http://planetmath.org/?op=getobj&from=objects&id=10921

[29] "PlanetMath" (http://planetmath.org/?method=l2h&from=objects&name=NaturalTransformationsOfOrganismicStructures&op=getobj). PlanetMath. . Retrieved 2010-03-17.

[30] Faith, JJ et al. (2007). "Large-Scale Mapping and Validation of Escherichia coli Transcriptional Regulation from a Compendium of Expression Profiles". *PLoS Biology* **5** (1): 54–66. doi:10.1371/journal.pbio.0050008. PMC 1764438. PMID 17214507.

[31] Hayete, B; Gardner, TS; Collins, JJ (2007). "Size matters: network inference tackles the genome scale". *Molecular Systems Biology* **3** (1): 77. doi:10.1038/msb4100118. PMC 1828748. PMID 17299414.

[32] http://www.springerlink.com/link.asp?id=102835

[33] http://bioinformatics.oupjournals.org/

[34] http://www.mitpressjournals.org/loi/biot/

[35] http://www.elsevier.com/locate/biosystems

[36] http://www.springerlink.com/content/119979/

[37] http://www.elsevier.com/locate/issn/03043800

[38] http://www.springerlink.com/content/100436/

[39] http://www.elsevier.com/locate/issn/0022-5193

[40] http://www.elsevier.com/locate/mbs

[41] http://www.harcourt-international.com/journals/mehy/

[42] http://www.springerlink.com/content/100386/

[43] http://www.tbiomed.com/

[44] http://www.elsevier.com/locate/issn/00405809

[45] http://www.elsevier.com/wps/product/cws_home/701802

[46] http://www.esmtb.org/

[47] http://mathbio.nimr.mrc.ac.uk/wiki/Division_of_Mathematical_Biology_at_NIMR

[48] http://bioinformatics.weizmann.ac.il/istmb/

[49] http://www.necker.fr/sfbt/

[50] http://www.biosemiotics.org/

[51] http://planetphysics.org/encyclopedia/NicolasRashevsky.html

[52] http://www.kli.ac.at/theorylab/index.html

[53] http://planetmath.org/?method=l2h&from=objects&id=10746&op=getobj

[54] http://www.people.vcu.edu/~mikuleck/rosen.htm

[55] http://homepage.uibk.ac.at/~c720126/humanethologie/ws/medicus/block1/inhalt.html

[56] http://www.scientistsolutions.com/t5844-Drawing+the+line+between+Theoretical+and+Basic+Biology.html

[57] http://www.semantic-systems-biology.org

[58] http://www.genome.ad.jp/manuscripts/GIW99/Poster/GIW99P66.pdf

External links

- Center for Complex Systems and Brain Sciences at Florida Atlantic (http://www.ccs.fau.edu/)
- Santa Fe Institute
- Bulletin of Mathematical Biology (http://www.springerlink.com/content/119979/)
- European Society for Mathematical and Theoretical Biology (http://www.esmtb.org/)
- Journal of Mathematical Biology (http://www.springerlink.com/content/100436/)
- Biomathematics Research Centre at University of Canterbury (http://www.math.canterbury.ac.nz/bio/)
- Centre for Mathematical Biology at Oxford University (http://www.maths.ox.ac.uk/cmb/)
- Mathematical Biology at the National Institute for Medical Research (http://mathbio.nimr.mrc.ac.uk/)
- Institute for Medical BioMathematics (http://www.imbm.org/)
- *Mathematical Biology Systems of Differential Equations* (http://eqworld.ipmnet.ru/en/solutions/syspde/spde-toc2.pdf) from EqWorld: The World of Mathematical Equations
- Systems Biology Workbench - a set of tools for modelling biochemical networks (http://sbw.kgi.edu)
- The Collection of Biostatistics Research Archive (http://www.biostatsresearch.com/repository/)
- Statistical Applications in Genetics and Molecular Biology (http://www.bepress.com/sagmb/)

- The International Journal of Biostatistics (http://www.bepress.com/ijb/)
- Theoretical Modeling of Cellular Physiology at Ecole Normale Superieure, Paris (http://www.biologie.ens.fr/bcsmcbs/)
- Theoretical and mathematical biology website (http://www.kli.ac.at/theorylab/index.html)
- Complexity Discussion Group (http://www.complex.vcu.edu/)
- UCLA Biocybernetics Laboratory (http://biocyb.cs.ucla.edu/research.html)
- TUCS Computational Biomodelling Laboratory (http://www.tucs.fi/research/labs/combio.php)
- Nagoya University Division of Biomodeling (http://www.agr.nagoya-u.ac.jp/english/e3senko-1.html)
- Technische Universiteit Biomodeling and Informatics (http://www.bmi2.bmt.tue.nl/Biomedinf/)
- New England Complex Systems Institute
- Northwestern Institute on Complex Systems (NICO) (http://www.northwestern.edu/nico/)
- Complexity Digest (http://comdig.unam.mx/)
- Centro de Ciencias de la Complejidad (http://c3.fisica.unam.mx/), UNAM
- Complexity Complex at the University of Warwick (http://go.warwick.ac.uk/complexity/)
- Southampton Institute for Complex Systems Simulation (http://www.icss.soton.ac.uk)
- Center for the Study of Complex Systems at the University of Michigan (http://www.cscs.umich.edu/)
- ARC Centre for Complex Systems, Australia
- (European) Complex Systems Society (http://cssociety.org)
- (Australian) Complex systems research network. (http://www.complexsystems.net.au/)
- Complex Systems Modeling (http://informatics.indiana.edu/rocha/complex/csm.html) based on Luis M. Rocha, 1999.
- CRM Complex systems research group (http://www.crm.cat/HarmonicAnalysis/defaultHarmonicAnalysis.htm)

Computational biology

Computational biology involves the development and application of data-analytical and theoretical methods, mathematical modeling and computational simulation techniques to the study of biological, behavioral, and social systems.[1] The field is widely defined and includes foundations in computer science, applied mathematics, statistics, biochemistry, chemistry, biophysics, molecular biology, genetics, ecology, evolution, anatomy, neuroscience, and visualization.[2]

Centers/Institutions and leading providers of Computational Biology Resources

- National Center for Biotechnology Information (NCBI)
- European Bioinformatics Institute (EBI)
- European Molecular Biology Laboratory (EMBL)
- Wellcome Trust Sanger Institute (WTSI) or The Sanger
- Broad Institute
- Whitehead Institute
- The Institute for Genomic Research
- Center for Biomolecular Science and Engineering
- Netherlands Bioinformatics Centre
- COSBI - The Centre for Computational and Systems Biology [3]
- T4G Limited - Bioinformatics and Computational Biology Consulting [4]

Professional Societies and Relevant Organizations

- International Society for Computational Biology
- bioinformatics.org [5]

Relevant Journals

- (BMC) Algorithms for Molecular Biology
- Bioinformatics (formerly Computer Applications in the Biosciences)
- BMC Bioinformatics
- BMC Systems Biology
- Genome Biology
- Genomics
- Journal of Computational Biology
- Nucleic Acids Research
- PLoS Computational Biology
- PLoS ONE
- Statistical Applications in Genetics and Molecular Biology

Notable Conferences in Computational Biology

- Intelligent Systems for Molecular Biology (ISMB)
- European Conference on Computational Biology (ECCB)
- Pacific Symposium on Biocomputing (PSB)
- International Conference on Research in Computational Molecular Biology [6] (RECOMB)

Notable Bioinformatics/Computational Biology Databases

- Ensembl
- UCSC Genome Browser
- InterPro
- Pfam
- OMIM
- Superfamily
- CATH
- SCOP
- Protein Data Bank
- DECIPHER

Subfields

Computational biomodeling

Computational biomodeling, a field concerned with building computer models of biological systems.

Computational genomics

Computational genomics, a field within genomics which studies the genomes of cells and organisms. High-throughput genome sequencing produces lots of data, which requires extensive post-processing (sequence assembly) and uses DNA microarray technologies to perform statistical analyses on the genes expressed in individual cell types. This can help find genes of interest for certain diseases or conditions. This field also studies the mathematical foundations of sequencing. Advances in many areas of genomics research are heavily rooted in engineering technology, from the capillary electrophoresis units used in large-scale DNA sequencing projects.

Computational neuroscience

Computational neuroscience is the study of brain function in terms of the information processing properties of the structures that make up the nervous system.

Computational biology vs. Bioinformatics

Bioinformatics and computational biology are rooted in life sciences as well as computer and information sciences and technologies. Both of these interdisciplinary approaches draw from specific disciplines such as mathematics, physics, statistics, computer science and engineering, biology, and behavioral science. Bioinformatics and computational biology each maintain close interactions with life sciences to realize their full potential. Bioinformatics applies principles of information sciences and technologies to make the vast, diverse, and complex life sciences data more understandable and useful. Computational biology uses mathematical and computational approaches to address theoretical and experimental questions in biology. Although bioinformatics and computational biology are distinct, there is also significant overlap and activity at their interface.[1]

References

[1] http://www.bisti.nih.gov/docs/compubiodef.pdf
[2] http://www.brown.edu/Research/CCMB/undergraduate.htm
[3] http://www.cosbi.eu
[4] http://www.T4G.com
[5] http://www.bioinformatics.org
[6] http://recomb.org/

Computational epigenetics

Computational epigenetics[1] [2] uses bioinformatic methods to complement experimental research in epigenetics. Due to the recent explosion of epigenome datasets, computational methods play an increasing role in all areas of epigenetic research.

Definition

Research in computational epigenetics comprises the development and application of bioinformatic methods for solving epigenetic questions, as well as computational data analysis and theoretical modeling in the context of epigenetics.

Current research areas

Epigenetic data processing and analysis

Various experimental techniques have been developed for genome-wide mapping of epigenetic information, the most widely used being ChIP-on-chip, ChIP-seq and bisulfite sequencing. All of these methods generate large amounts of data and require efficient ways of data processing and quality control by bioinformatic methods.

Epigenome prediction

A substantial amount of bioinformatic research has been devoted to the prediction of epigenetic information from characteristics of the genome sequence. Such predictions serve a dual purpose. First, accurate epigenome predictions can substitute for experimental data, to some degree, which is particularly relevant for newly discovered epigenetic mechanisms and for species other than human and mouse. Second, prediction algorithms build statistical models of epigenetic information from training data and can therefore act as a first step toward quantitative modeling of an epigenetic mechanism.

Applications in cancer epigenetics

The important role of epigenetic defects for cancer opens up new opportunities for improved diagnosis and therapy. These active areas of research give rise to two questions that are particularly amenable to bioinformatic analysis. First, given a list of genomic regions exhibiting epigenetic differences between tumor cells and controls (or between different disease subtypes), can we detect common patterns or find evidence of a functional relationship of these regions to cancer? Second, can we use bioinformatic methods in order to improve diagnosis and therapy by detecting and classifying important disease subtypes?

Emerging topics

The first wave of research in the field of computational epigenetics was driven by rapid progress of experimental methods for data generation, which required adequate computational methods for data processing and quality control, prompted epigenome prediction studies as a means of understanding the genomic distribution of epigenetic information, and provided the foundation for initial projects on cancer epigenetics. While these topics will continue to be major areas of research and the mere quantity of epigenetic data arising from epigenome projects poses a significant bioinformatic challenge, several additional topics are currently emerging.

- Epigenetic regulatory circuitry: Reverse engineering the regulatory networks that read, write and execute epigenetic codes.

- Population epigenetics: Distilling regulatory mechanisms from the integration of epigenome data with gene expression profiles and haplotype maps for a large sample from a heterogeneous population.
- Evolutionary epigenetics: Learning about epigenome regulation in human (and its medical consequences) by cross-species comparisons.
- Theoretical modeling: Testing our mechanistic and quantitative understanding of epigenetic mechanisms by in silico simulation.
- Genome browsers: Developing a new blend of web services that enable biologists to perform sophisticated genome and epigenome analysis within an easy-to-use genome browser environment.
- Medical epigenetics: Searching for epigenetic mechanisms that play a role in diseases other than cancer, as there is strong circumstantial evidence for epigenetic regulation being involved in mental disorders, autoimmune diseases and other complex diseases.

Epigenetics Databases

1. MethDB [3] Contains information on 19,905 DNA methylation content data and 5,382 methylation patterns for 48 species, 1,511 individuals, 198 tissues and cell lines and 79 phenotypes.
2. PubMeth [4] Contains over 5,000 records on methylated genes in various cancer types.
3. REBASE [5] Contains over 22,000 DNA methyltransferases genes derived from GenBank.
4. MeInfoText [6] Contains gene methylation information across 205 human cancer types.
5. MethPrimerDB [7] Contains 259 primer sets from human, mouse and rat for DNA methylation analysis.
6. The Histone Database [8] Contains 254 sequences from histone H1, 383 from histone H2, 311 from histone H2B, 1043 from histone H3 and 198 from histone H4, altogether representing at least 857 species.
7. ChromDB [9] Contains 9,341 chromatin-associated proteins, including RNAi-associated proteins, for a broad range of organisms.
8. CREMOFAC [10] Contains 1725 redundant and 720 non-redundant chromatin-remodeling factor sequences in eukaryotes.
9. The Krembil Family Epigenetics Laboratory [11] Contains DNA methylation data of human chromosomes 21, 22, male germ cells and DNA methylation profiles in monozygotic and dizygotic twins.
10. MethyLogiX DNA methylation database [12] Contains DNA methylation data of human chromosomes 21 and 22, male germ cells and late-onset Alzheimer's disease.
11. List of epigenetic databases and computational epigenetic tools online [13] (constantly updated)

Sources and further reading

- The original version of this article was based on a review paper on computational epigenetics that appeared in the January 2008 issue of the Bioinformatics journal: *Bock, C. and Lengauer, T. (2008) Computational epigenetics. Bioinformatics, 24, 1-10* [14]. This review paper provides >100 references to scientific papers and extensive background information. It is published as open access and can be downloaded freely from the publisher's web page: http://dx.doi.org/10.1093/bioinformatics/btm546 [14].

- Additional data has been updated and added, based on a review paper on computational epigenetics that appeared in the January 2010 issue of the Bioinformation [15] journal: *Lim S.J., Tan T.W. and Tong, J.C. (2010) Computational epigenetics: the new scientific paradigm. Bioinformation, 4(7): 331-337* [16]. This review paper provides >129 references to scientific papers. It is published as open access and can be downloaded freely from the publisher's web page: http://bioinformation.net/004/007000042010.pdf [16].

- List of epigenetic databases and computational epigenetic tools online [13]

References

[1] Bock, C; and Lengauer T (2008). "Computational epigenetics". *Bioinformatics* **24** (1): 1–10. doi:10.1093/bioinformatics/btm546. PMID 18024971.

[2] Lim, S J; Tan T W and Tong J C (2010). "Computational epigenetics: the new scientific paradigm" (http://bioinformation.net/004/ 007000042010.pdf) (PDF). *Bioinformation* **4** (7): 331–337. .

[3] http://www.methdb.de

[4] http://www.pubmeth.org/

[5] http://rebase.neb.com/rebase/rebase.html

[6] http://mit.lifescience.ntu.edu.tw/

[7] http://medgen.ugent.be/methprimerdb/

[8] http://genome.nhgri.nih.gov/histones/

[9] http://www.chromdb.org/

[10] http://www.jncasr.ac.in/cremofac/

[11] http://www.epigenomics.ca

[12] http://www.methylogix.com/genetics/database.shtml.htm

[13] http://generegulation.info/index.php?option=com_content&view=category&layout=blog&id=10&Itemid=61

[14] http://dx.doi.org/10.1093/bioinformatics/btm546

[15] http://bioinformation.net/

[16] http://bioinformation.net/004/007000042010.pdf

Computational genomics

Computational genomics refers to the use of computational analysis to decipher biology from genome sequences and related data [1] , including both DNA and RNA sequence as well as other "post-genomic" data (i.e. experimental data obtained with technologies that require the genome sequence, such as genomic DNA microarrays). As such, computational genomics may be regarded as a subset of bioinformatics, but with a focus on using whole genomes (rather than individual genes) to understand the principles of how the DNA of a species controls its biology at the molecular level and beyond. With the current abundance of massive biological datasets, computational studies have become one of the most important means to biological discovery.[2]

History

The roots of computational genomics are shared with those of bioinformatics. During the 1960s, Margaret Dayhoff and others at the National Biomedical Research Foundation assembled databases of homologous protein sequences for evolutionary study.[3] Their research developed a phylogenetic tree that determined the evolutionary changes that were required for a particular protein to change into another protein based on the underlying amino acid sequences. This led them to create a scoring matrix that assessed the likelihood of one protein being related to another.

Beginning in the 1980s, databases of genome sequences began to be recorded, but this presented new challenges in the form of searching and comparing the databases of gene information. Unlike text-searching algorithms that are used on websites such as google or Wikipedia, searching for sections of genetic similarity requires one to find strings that are not simply identical, but similar. This led to the development of the Needleman-Wunsch algorithm, which is a dynamic programming algorithm for comparing sets of amino acid sequences with each other by using scoring matrices derived from the earlier research by Dayhoff. Later, the BLAST algorithm was developed for performing fast, optimized searches of gene sequence databases. BLAST and its derivatives are probably the most widely-used algorithms for this purpose.[4]

The emergence of the phrase "computational genomics" coincides with the availability of complete sequenced genomes in the mid-to-late 1990s. The first meeting of the Annual Conference on Computational Genomics was organized by scientists from The Institute for Genomic Research (TIGR) in 1998, providing a forum for this speciality and effectively distinguishing this area of science from the more general fields of Genomics or Computational Biology.[5] [6] The first use of this term in scientific literature, according to MEDLINE abstracts, was just one year earlier in Nucleic Acids Research.[7] . The final Computational Genomics conference was held in 2006, featuring a keynote talk by Nobel Laureate Barry Marshall, co-discoverer of the link between Helicobacter pylori and stomach ulcers. As of 2010, the leading conferences in the field include Intelligent Systems for Molecular Biology (ISMB), RECOMB, and the Cold Spring Harbor Laboratory and Sanger Institute's meetings titled "Biology of Genomes" and "Genome Informatics".

The development of computer-assisted mathematics (using products such as Mathematica or Matlab) has helped engineers, mathematicians and computer scientists to start operating in this domain, and a public collection of case studies and demonstrations is growing, ranging from whole genome comparisons to gene expression analysis.[8] . This has increased the introduction of different ideas, including concepts from systems and control, information theory, strings analysis and data mining. It is anticipated that computational approaches will become and remain a standard topic for research and teaching, while students fluent in both topics start being formed in the multiple courses created in the past few years.

Contributions of computational genomics research to biology

Contributions of computational genomics research to biology include [2] :

- discovering subtle patterns in genomic sequences
- proposing cellular signalling networks
- proposing mechanisms of genome evolution
- predict precise locations of all human genes using comparative genomics techniques with several mammalian and vertebrate species
- predict conserved genomic regions that are related to early embryonic development
- discover potential links between repeated sequence motifs and tissue-specific gene expression
- measure regions of genomes that have undergone unusually rapid evolution

References

[1]   Koonin EV (2001) Computational Genomics, National Center for Biotechnology Information, National Library of Medicine, NIH (PubMed ID: 11267880)

[2]   Computational Genomics and Proteomics at MIT (http://www.eecs.mit.edu/bioeecs/CompGenProt.html)

[3]   David Mount (2000), *Bioinformatics, Sequence and Genome Analysis,* pp. 2-3, Cold Spring Harbor Laboratory Press, ISBN 0-87969-597-8

[4]   T.A. Brown (1999), *Genomes,* John Wiley & Sons, ISBN 0-471-31618-0

[5]   [backPid]=67&cHash=fd69079f5e The 7th Annual Conference on Computational Genomics (2004) (http://www.jcvi.org/cms/press/ press-releases/full-text/archive/2004//article/computational-genomics-conference-to-attract-leading-scientists/?tx_ttnews)

[6]   The 9th Annual Conference on Computational Genomics (2006) (http://www.cpe.vt.edu/genomics/)

[7]   A. Wagner (1997), A computational genomics approach to the identification of gene networks, *Nucleic Acids Res.,* Sep 15;25(18):3594-604, ISSN 0305-1048

[8]   Cristianini, N. and Hahn, M. *Introduction to Computational Genomics* (http://www.computational-genomics.net/), Cambridge University Press, 2006. (ISBN 9780521671910 I ISBN 0521671914)

External links

- Harvard Extension School Biophysics 101, Genomics and Computational Biology, http://www.courses.fas. harvard.edu/~bphys101/info/syllabus.html
- University of Bristol course in Computational Genomics, http://www.computational-genomics.net/

Computational immunology

In academia, **computational immunology** is a field of science that encompasses high-throughput genomic and bioinformatics approaches to immunology. The field's main aim is to convert immunological data into computational problems, solve these problems using mathematical and computational approaches and then convert these results into immunologically meaningful interpretations.

The explosive growth of bioinformatics techniques and applications in the post-genomics era has radically transformed immunology research. This has led to a comparable growth in the field of computation immunology, or immunoinformatics.

Bibliography

- Getting Started in Computational Immunology [1]

External links

- http://www.immunomics.eu

References

[1] http://www.ploscompbiol.org/article/info%3Adoi%2F10.1371%2Fjournal.pcbi.1000128

Computational Resource for Drug Discovery (CRDD)

Computational Resources for Drug Discovery (CRDD [1]) is one of the important silico modules of Open Source for Drug Discovery (OSDD [2]). The CRDD web portal provides computer resources related to drug discovery on a single platform. Following are major features of CRDD; i) computational resources for researchers in the field of computer-aided drug design, ii) discussion form to discuss their problem with other members, iii) maintain Wikipedia related to drug discovery, iv) developing database related to medicine; v) prediction of inhibitors and vi) prediction of ADME-Tox property of molecules. One of the major objectives of CRDD is to promote open source software in the field of chemoinformatics and pharmacoinformatics. All are welcome to participate in this novel mission. Following are major features of CRDD

Resource compilation

Under CRDD, all the resources related to computer-aided drug design have been collected and compiled. These resources were classify and presented on CRDD so users can got resources from single source.

Target identification

In this category all the resources important for searching drug targets have been saved under following classes, Genome Annotation [3], Proteome Annotation [4], Potential Targets [5], Protein Structure [6]

Virtual screening

In this category all the resources important for virtual screening have been compiled under following classes, QSAR Techniques [7], Docking QSAR [8], Chemoinformatics [9], siRNA/miRNA [10]

Drug design

In this category all the resources important for designing drug inhibitors/molecules have been classify under following classes, Lead Optimization [11], Pharmainformatics [12], ADMET [13], Clinical Informatics [14]

Community contribution

Under this category platform has been developed where community may contribute in the process of drug discovery. Following are major

DrugPedia: A Wikipedia for Drug Discovery

Drugpedia [15] is a Wikipedia created for collecting and compiling information related to computer-aided drug design. The aim of Drugpedia is to provide comprehensive information about drugs. It is developed under the umbrella of Open Source Drug Discovery (OSDD) project. It covers wide range of subjects around drugs like Bioinformatics, Cheminfiormatics, clinical informatics etc.

Indipedia: A Wikipedia for India

Indipedia [16] is a Wikipedia created for collecting and compiling information related to India. The aim of Indipedia is to provide comprehensive information about India created for Indians by Indians. It is developed under the umbrella of Open Source Drug Discovery (OSDD) project.

CRDD Forum

CRDD Forum [17] CRDD forum was launched to discuss the challenge in developing computational resources for drug discovery.

Indigenous Development : Software and Web Services

Beside collecting and compiling resources, CRDD members are actively involved in developing new software and web services. All services developed are free for academic use. CRDD team is working hard to develop the Open Sources software in the field of chemoinformatics/pharmainformatics. CRDD team have dream that in coming years the public will have a platform from where they can contribute in the process of drug discovery. The following are a few major tools developed at CRDD.

Development of Databases

- **HMRBase** [18]: It is a manually curated database of Hormones and their Receptors. It is a compilation of sequence data after extensive manual literature search and from publicly available databases. HMRbase can be searched on the basis of a variety of data types. Owing to the high impact of endocrine research in the biomedical sciences, the Hmrbase could become a leading data portal for researchers. The salient features of Hmrbase are hormone-receptor pair-related information, mapping of peptide stretches on the protein sequences of hormones and receptors, Pfam domain annotations, categorical browsing options, online data submission.[19] This database integrated in drugpedia [20] so public can contribute.
- **BIAdb** [21]: A Database for Benzylisoquinoline Alkaloids. The Benzylisoquinoline Alkaloid Database is an attempt to gather the scattered information related to the BIA's. Many BIA's show therapeutic properties and can be considered as potent drug candidates. This database will also serve researchers working in the field of synthetic biology, as developing medicinally important alkaloids using synthetic process are one of important challenges. This database integrated in drugpedia [22] so public can contribute.[23]
- **AntigenDB** [24]: This database contain more than 500 antigens collected from literature and other immunological resources. These antigens come from 44 important pathogenic species. In AntigenDB, a database entry contains

information regarding the sequence, structure, origin, etc. of an antigen with additional information such as B and T-cell epitopes, MHC binding, function, gene-expression and post translational modifications, where available. AntigenDB also provides links to major internal and external databases.[25]

- **PolysacDB** [26]: The PolysacDB is dedicated to provide comprehensive information about antigenic polysaccharides of microbial origin (bacterial and fungal), antibodies against them, proposed epitopes, structural detail, proposed functions, assay system, cross-reactivity related information and much more. It is a manually curated database where most of data has been collected from PubMed and PubMed Central literature databases.
- TumorHope [27] : TumorHope is a manually curated comprehensive database of experimentally characterized tumor homing peptides. These peptides recoginze tumor tissues and tumor associated micro environment, including tumor metastasis.
- ccPDB [28]: The ccPDB database is designed to provide service to scientific community working in the field of function or structure annoation of proteins. This database of datasets is based on Protein Data Bank (PDB), where all datasets were derived from PDB.
- OSDDchem [29]: OSDDChem chemical database is an open repository of information on synthesised, semi-synthesized, natural and virtually designed molecules from the OSDD [30] community.

Software developed

MycoTB [31]: In order to assist scientific community, we extended flexible system concept for building standalone software MycoTB for Windows Users. MycoTB is one of the computer program developed under OSDD/CRDD programme. This software allow user to built their own flexible system on their personal computers to mange and annotate whole proteome of MycoTB.

Resources created

- CRAG [32]: Computational resources for assembling genomes (CRAG) has been to assist the users in assembling of genomes from short read sequencing (SRS). Following major objective; i) Collection and compilation of computation resources, ii) Brief description of genome assemblers, iii) Maintaing SRS and related data, iv) Service to community to assemble their genomes
- CRIP [33]: Computational resources for predicting protein–macromolecular interactions (CRIP) developed to provide resources related interaction. This site maintain large number of resources on interaction world of proteins that includes, protein–protein, protein–DNA, protein–ligand, protein–RNA.
- BioTherapi [34]: Bioinformatics for Therapeutic Peptides and Proteins (BioTherapi) developed for researchers working in the field of protein/peptide therapeutics. At present there is no single platform that provide this kind of information. This site include all the relevant information about the use of Peptides/Proteins in drug and synthesis of new peptides. It also cover problems, in their formulation, synthesis and delivery process
- HivBio [35]: HIV Bioinformatics (HIVbio) site contains variou types of information on Human Immunodefeciency Virus (HIV) life cycle and Infection.
- GDPbio [36]: GDPbio (Genome based prediction of Diseases and Personal medicines using Bioinformatics) is the project focussed upon providing various resources related to genome analysis particularly for the prediction of disease susceptibility of a particular individual and personalized medicines development, aiming public health improvement.
- AminoFAT [37]: Functional Annotation Tools for Amino Acids (AminoFAT) server is designed to serve the bioinformatics community. Aim is to develop as many as possible tools to understand function of amino acids in proteins based on protein structure in PDB. The broad knowledge of proteins function would help in the identification of noval drug targets.

Web services for Chemoinformatics

First time in the world CRDD team has developed open source platform which allows users to predict inhibitors against novel M. Tuberculosis drug targets and other important properties of drug molecules like ADMET. Following are list of few servers.

- MetaPred [38]: A webserver for the Prediction of Cytochrome P450 Isoform responsible for Metabolizing a Drug Molecule. MetaPred Server predict metabolizing CYP isoform of a drug molecule/substrate, based on SVM models developed using CDK descriptors.This server will be helpful for researcher working in the field of drug discovery.This study demonstrates that it is possible to develop free web servers in the field of chemoinformatics. This will encourage other researchers to develop web server for public use, which may lead to decrease the cost of discovering new drug molecules.[39]
- ToxiPred [40]: A server for prediction of aqueous toxicity of small chemical molecules in T. pyriformis.
- KetoDrug [41]:A web server for binding affinity prediction of ketoxazole derivatives against Fatty Acid Amide Hydrolase (FAAH). It is a user friendly web sever for the prediction of binding affinity of small chemical molecules against FAAH.
- KiDoQ [42]: KiDoQ, a web server has been developed to serve scientific community working in the field of designing inhibitors against Dihydrodipicolinate synthase (DHDPS), a potential drug target enzyme of a unique bacterial DAP/Lysine pathway.[43]
- GDoQ [44]: GDoQ (Prediction of GLMU inhibitors using QSAR and AutoDock) is a open source platform developed for predicting inhibitors against Mycobacterium Tuberculosis (M.Tb) drug target N-acetylglucosamine-1-phosphate uridyltransferase (GLMU) protein. This i a potential drug target involved in bacterial cell wall synthesis. This server uses molecular docking and QSAR strategies to predict inhibitory activity value (IC50) of chemical compounds for GLMU protein.[45]
- ROCR [46]: The ROCR is an R package for evaluating and visualizing classifier performance . It is a flexible tool for creating ROC graphs, sensitivity/specificity curves, area under curve and precision/recall curve. The parametrization can be visualized by coloring the curve according to cutoff.
- WebCDK [47]: A web interface for CDK library, it is a web interface for predicting descriptors of chemicals using CDK library.
- Pharmacokinetics [48]: The Pharmacokinetic data analysis determines the relationship between the dosing regimen and the body's exposure to the drug as measured by the nonlinear concentration time curve. It includes a function, AUC, to calculate area under the curve. It also includes functions for half-life estimation for a biexponential model, and a two phase linear regression

Prediction and analysis of drug targets

- RNApred [49]: Prediction of RNAbinding proteins from ints amino acid sequence.[50]
- ProPrint [51]: Prediction of interaction between proteins from their amino acid sequence.[52]
- DomPrint [53]: Domprint is a domain-domain interaction (DDI) prediction server.
- MycoPrint [54]: MycoPrint is a web interface for exploration of the interactome of Mycobacterium tuberculosis H37Rv (Mtb) predicted by "Domain Interaction Mapping" (DIM) method.
- ATPint [55]: A server for predicting ATP interacting residues in proteins.[56]
- FADpred [57]: Identification of FAD interacting residues in proteins.[58]
- GTPbinder [59]: Prediction of protein GTP interacting residues.[60]
- NADbinder [61]: Prediction of NAD binding residues in proteins.[62]
- PreMier [63]: Designing of Mutants of Antibacterial Peptides.[64]
- DMAP [65]: DMAP: Designing of Mutants of Antibacterial Peptides
- icaars [66]:Prediction and classification of aminoacyl tRNA synthetases using PROSITE domains [67]
- CBtope [68]: Prediction of Conformational B-cell epitope in a sequence from its amino acid sequence.[69]

- DesiRM [70]: Designing of Complementary and Mismatch siRNAs for Silencing a Gene .[71]
- GenomeABC [72] : A server for Benchmarking of Genome Assemblers.

Maintained and Contact

This site is developed and maintained at Institute of Microbial Technology, Chandigarh, by CRDD team under guidance of Gajendra Pal Singh Raghava, for more information contact

- Gajendra P. S. Raghava [73]

News

- OSCAT2012 [74] : 2nd International conference on open source for computer-aided Translational medicine.

References

[1] http://crdd.osdd.net/
[2] http://www.osdd.net
[3] http://crdd.osdd.net/ga.php
[4] http://crdd.osdd.net/pa.php
[5] http://crdd.osdd.net/pmics.php
[6] http://crdd.osdd.net/pstr.php
[7] http://crdd.osdd.net/qsar.php
[8] http://crdd.osdd.net/dqsar.php
[9] http://crdd.osdd.net/chemo.php
[10] http://crdd.osdd.net/rna.php
[11] http://crdd.osdd.net/lopt.php
[12] http://crdd.osdd.net/pharma.php
[13] http://crdd.osdd.net/admet.php
[14] http://crdd.osdd.net/pcllk.php
[15] http://crdd.osdd.net/drugpedia/
[16] http://crdd.osdd.net/indipedia/
[17] http://crdd.osdd.net/forum
[18] http://crdd.osdd.net/raghava/hmrbase/
[19] Rashid, Mamoon; Singla, Deepak; Sharma, Arun; Kumar, Manish; Raghava, Gajendra PS (2009). "Hmrbase: a database of hormones and their receptors". *BMC Genomics* **10**: 307. doi:10.1186/1471-2164-10-307. PMC 2720991. PMID 19589147.
[20] http://crdd.osdd.net/drugpedia/index.php/Category:HMRbase
[21] http://crdd.osdd.net/raghava/biadb/
[22] http://crdd.osdd.net/drugpedia/index.php/Category:BIAdb
[23] Singla, Deepak; Sharma, Arun; Kaur, Jasjit; Panwar, Bharat; Raghava, Gajendra PS (2010). "BIAdb: A curated database of benzylisoquinoline alkaloids". *BMC Pharmacology* **10**: 4. doi:10.1186/1471-2210-10-4. PMC 2844369. PMID 20205728.
[24] http://www.imtech.res.in/raghava/antigendb/
[25] Ansari, H. R.; Flower, D. R.; Raghava, G. P. S. (2009). "AntigenDB: an immunoinformatics database of pathogen antigens". *Nucleic Acids Research* **38** (Database issue): D847. doi:10.1093/nar/gkp830. PMC 2808902. PMID 19820110.
[26] http://crdd.osdd.net/raghava/polysacdb/
[27] http://crdd.osdd.net/raghava/tumorhope/
[28] http://crdd.osdd.net/raghava/ccpdb/
[29] http://crdd.osdd.net/osddchem/
[30] http://www.osdd.net/
[31] http://crdd.osdd.net/raghava/mycotb/
[32] http://imtech.res.in/raghava/crag/
[33] http://www.imtech.res.in/raghava/crip/
[34] http://www.imtech.res.in/raghava/biotherapi/
[35] http://www.imtech.res.in/raghava/hivbio/
[36] http://www.imtech.res.in/raghava/gdpbio/
[37] http://crdd.osdd.net/raghava/aminofat/
[38] http://crdd.osdd.net/raghava/metapred/

[39] Mishra, Nitish K; Agarwal, Sandhya; Raghava, Gajendra PS (2010). "Prediction of cytochrome P450 isoform responsible for metabolizing a drug molecule". *BMC Pharmacology* **10**: 8. doi:10.1186/1471-2210-10-8. PMC 2912882. PMID 20637097.

[40] http://crdd.osdd.net/raghava/toxipred/

[41] http://crdd.osdd.net/raghava/ketodrug/

[42] http://crdd.osdd.net/raghava/kidoq/

[43] Garg, Aarti; Tewari, Rupinder; Raghava, Gajendra PS (2010). "KiDoQ: using docking based energy scores to develop ligand based model for predicting antibacterials". *BMC Bioinformatics* **11**: 125. doi:10.1186/1471-2105-11-125. PMC 2841597. PMID 20222969.

[44] http://crdd.osdd.net/raghava/gdoq/

[45] Singla, Deepak; Anurag, Meenakshi; dash, Debasis; Raghava, Gajendra PS (2011). "A Web Server for Predicting Inhibitors against Bacterial Target GlmU Protein". *BMC Pharmacology* **11**: 5. doi:10.1186/1471-2210-11-5.

[46] http://crdd.osdd.net:8081/Rocr/

[47] http://crdd.osdd.net:8081/webcdk/

[48] http://crdd.osdd.net:8081/Pharmacokinetics/

[49] http://www.imtech.res.in/raghava/rnapred/

[50] Kumar, M; Gromiha, MM; Raghava, GP (2010). "SVM based prediction of RNA-binding proteins using binding residues and evolutionary information". *Journal of molecular recognition : JMR* **24** (2): n/a. doi:10.1002/jmr.1061. PMID 20677174.

[51] http://www.imtech.res.in/raghava/proprint/

[52] Rashid, M. and Raghava, G. P. S. (2010) A simple approach for predicting protein–protein interactions. Current Protein & Peptide Science (In Press).

[53] http://www.imtech.res.in/raghava/domprint/

[54] http://www.imtech.res.in/raghava/mycoprint/

[55] http://www.imtech.res.in/raghava/atpint/

[56] Chauhan, JS; Mishra, NK; Raghava, GP (2009). "Identification of ATP binding residues of a protein from its primary sequence". *BMC bioinformatics* **10**: 434. doi:10.1186/1471-2105-10-434. PMC 2803200. PMID 20021687.

[57] http://www.imtech.res.in/raghava/fadpred/

[58] Mishra, Nitish K.; Raghava, Gajendra P. S. (2010). "Prediction of FAD interacting residues in a protein from its primary sequence using evolutionary information". *BMC bioinformatics* **11**: S48. doi:10.1186/1471-2105-11-S1-S48. PMC 3009520. PMID 20122222.

[59] http://www.imtech.res.in/raghava/gtpbinder/

[60] Chauhan, JS; Mishra, NK; Raghava, GP (2010). "Prediction of GTP interacting residues, dipeptides and tripeptides in a protein from its evolutionary information". *BMC bioinformatics* **11**: 301. doi:10.1186/1471-2105-11-301. PMID 20525281.

[61] http://www.imtech.res.in/raghava/nadbinder

[62] Ansari, HR; Raghava, GP (2010). "Identification of NAD interacting residues in proteins". *BMC bioinformatics* **11**: 160. doi:10.1186/1471-2105-11-160. PMC 2853471. PMID 20353553.

[63] http://www.imtech.res.in/raghava/premier/

[64] Agarwal, et al. (2011). "Identification of Mannose Interacting Residues Using Local Composition". *Plos ONE* **6**: e24039. doi:10.1371/journal.pone.0024039.

[65] http://www.imtech.res.in/raghava/dmap/

[66] http://www.imtech.res.in/raghava/icaars/

[67] Panwar, Bharat; Raghava, Gajendra PS (2010). "Prediction and classification of aminoacyl tRNA synthetases using PROSITE domains". *BMC Genomics* **11**: 507. doi:10.1186/1471-2164-11-507. PMC 2997003. PMID 20860794.

[68] http://www.imtech.res.in/raghava/cbtope/

[69] Ansari, HR; Raghava, Gajendra PS (2010). "Identification of conformational B-cell Epitopes in an antigen from its primary sequence". *Immunome Research* **6**: 6. doi:10.1186/1745-7580-6-6. PMC 2974664. PMID 20961417.

[70] http://www.imtech.res.in/raghava/desirm/

[71] Ahmed, F; Raghava, Gajendra PS (2011). "Designing of Highly Effective Complementary and Mismatch siRNAs for Silencing a Gene". *Plos ONE* **8**: 6. doi:10.1371/journal.pone.0023443. PMID 21853133.

[72] http://crdd.osdd.net/raghava/genomeabc/

[73] http://www.imtech.res.in/raghava/

[74] http://crdd.osdd.net/oscat/

Further reading

- Mishra, Nitish K; Agarwal, Sandhya; Raghava, Gajendra PS (2010). "Prediction of cytochrome P450 isoform responsible for metabolizing a drug molecule". *BMC Pharmacology* **10**: 8. doi:10.1186/1471-2210-10-8. PMC 2912882. PMID 20637097.

Consed

Consed

Developer(s)	David Gordon
Operating system	UNIX, Linux, Mac OS X
Type	Bioinformatics
License	free for academic users
Website	[1]

Consed[2] is a program for viewing, editing, and finishing DNA sequence assemblies. Originally developed for sequence assemblies created with phrap, recent versions also support other sequence assembly programs like Newbler.

History

Consed was originally developed as a contig editing and finishing tool for large-scale cosmid shotgun sequencing in the Human Genome Project. At genome sequencing centers, Consed was used to check assemblies generated by phrap, solve assembly problems like those caused by highly identical repeats, and finishing tasks like primer picking and gap closure. Development of Consed has continued after the completion of the Human Genome Project. Current Consed versions support very large projects with millions of reads, enabling the use with newer sequencing methods like 454 sequencing and Solexa sequencing. Consed also has advanced tools for finishing tasks like automated primer picking [3]

References

[1] http://bozeman.mbt.washington.edu/consed/consed.html

[2] Gordon D, Abajian C, Green P (1998). "Consed: A Graphical Tool for Sequence Finishing". *Genome Research* **8** (3): 195–202. PMID 9521923.

[3] Gordon D, Desmarais C, Green P (2001). "Automated Finishing with Autofinish". *Genome Research* **11** (4): 614–625. doi:10.1101/gr.171401. PMC 311035. PMID 11282977.

External links

* Consed homepage (http://bozeman.mbt.washington.edu/consed/consed.html)

Consensus sequence

In molecular biology and bioinformatics, **consensus sequence** refers to the most common nucleotide or amino acid at a particular position after multiple sequences are aligned. A **consensus sequence** is a way of representing the results of a multiple sequence alignment, where related sequences are compared to each other, and similar functional sequence motifs are found. The consensus sequence shows which residues are most abundant in the alignment at each position.

Developing software for pattern recognition is a major topic in genetics, molecular biology, and bioinformatics. Specific sequence motifs can function as regulatory sequences controlling biosynthesis, or as signal sequences that direct a molecule to a specific site within the cell or regulate its maturation. Since the regulatory function of these sequences is important, they are thought to be conserved across long periods of evolution. In some cases, evolutionary relatedness can be estimated by the amount of conservation of these sites.

The conserved sequence motifs are called **consensus sequences** and they show which residues are conserved and which residues are variable. Consider the following example DNA sequence:

A[CT]N{A}YR

In this notation, A means that an A is always found in that position; [CT] stands for either C or T; N stands for any base; and {A} means any base except A. Y represents any pyrimidine, and R indicates any purine.

In this example, the notation [CT] does not give any indication of the relative frequency of C or T occurring at that position. An alternative method of representing a consensus sequence uses a sequence logo. This is a graphical representation of the consensus sequence, in which the size of a symbol is related to the frequency that a given nucleotide (or amino acid) occurs at a certain position. In sequence logos the more conserved the residue, the larger the symbol for that residue is drawn, the less frequent, the smaller the symbol. Sequence logos can be generated using WebLogo [1], or using the Gestalt Workbench [2], a publicly availablable visualization tool written by Gustavo Glusman at the Institute for Systems Biology [3]. Further discussion on the limitations of consensus sequences is given in a paper 'Consensus Sequence Zen'.[4]

A protein binding site, represented by a consensus sequence, may be a short sequence of nucleotides which is found several times in the genome and is thought to play the same role in its different locations. For example, many transcription factors recognize particular patterns in the promoters of the genes they regulate. In the same way restriction enzymes usually have palindromic consensus sequences, usually corresponding to the site where they cut the DNA. Transposons act in much the same manner in their identification of target sequences for transposition. Finally splice sites (sequences immediately surrounding the exon-intron boundaries) can also be considered as consensus sequences.

Thus a consensus sequence is a model for a putative DNA recognition site: it is obtained by aligning all known examples of a certain recognition site and defined as the idealized sequence that represents the predominant base at each position. All the actual examples shouldn't differ from the consensus by more than a few substitutions, but counting mismatches in this way can lead to inconsistencies.[4]

Any mutation allowing a mutated nucleotide in the core promoter sequence to look more like the consensus sequence is known as an **up mutation**. This kind of mutation will generally make the promoter stronger and thus the RNA polymerase forms a tighter bind to the DNA it wishes to transcribe and transcription is up regulated. On the contrary, mutations that destroy conserved nucleotides in the consensus sequence are known as **down mutations**. These types of mutations down regulate transcription since RNA polymerase can no longer bind as tightly to the core promoter sequence.

References

[1] http://weblogo.berkeley.edu/

[2] http://db.systemsbiology.net/gestalt/

[3] http://www.systemsbiology.org

[4] Schneider TD (2002). "Consensus Sequence Zen". *Appl Bioinformatics* **1** (3): 111–119. PMC 1852464. PMID 15130839.

Conserved sequence

In biology, **conserved sequences** are similar or identical sequences that occur within nucleic acid sequences (such as RNA and DNA sequences), protein sequences, protein structures or polymeric carbohydrates across species (orthologous sequences) or within different molecules produced by the same organism (paralogous sequences). In the case of cross species conservation, this indicates that a particular sequence may have been maintained by evolution despite speciation. The further back up the phylogenetic tree a particular conserved sequence may occur the more highly conserved it is said to be. Since sequence information is normally transmitted from parents to progeny by genes, a conserved sequence implies that there is a **conserved gene**.

It is widely believed that mutation in a "highly conserved" region leads to a non-viable life form, or a form that is eliminated through natural selection.

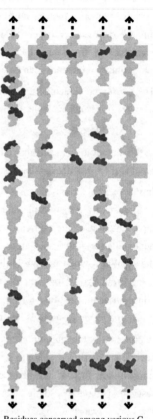

Residues conserved among various G protein coupled receptors are highlighted in green.

Conserved nucleic acid sequences

Highly conserved DNA sequences are thought to have functional value. The role for many of these highly conserved non-coding DNA sequences is not understood. One recent study that eliminated four highly-conserved non-coding DNA sequences in mice yielded viable mice with no significant phenotypic differences; the authors described their findings as "unexpected".[1] .

Many regions of the DNA, including highly conserved DNA sequences, consist of repeated sequence (DNA) elements. One possible explanation of the null hypothesis above is that removal of only one or a subset of a repeated sequence could theoretically preserve phenotypic functioning on the assumption that one such sequence is sufficient and the repetitions are superfluous to essential life processes; it was not specified in the paper whether the eliminated sequences were repeated sequences.

The TATA promoter sequence is an example of a highly conserved DNA sequence, being found in most eukaryotes.

Conserved protein sequences and structures

Highly conserved proteins are often required for basic cellular function, stability or reproduction. Conservation of protein sequences is indicated by the presence of identical amino acid residues at analogous parts of proteins. Conservation of protein structures is indicated by the presence of functionally equivalent, though not necessarily identical, amino acid residues and structures between analogous parts of proteins.

Shown below is an amino acid sequence alignment between two human zinc finger proteins, with GenBank accession numbers AAB24882 [2] and AAB24881 [3]. Alignment was carried out using the clustalw sequence alignment program. Conserved amino acid sequences are marked by strings of * on the third line of the sequence alignment. As can be seen from this alignment, these two proteins contain a number of conserved amino acid sequences (represented by identical letters aligned between the two sequences).

Conserved polymeric carbohydrate sequences

The monosaccharide sequence of the glycosaminoglycan heparin is conserved across a wide range of species.

Biological role of sequence conservation

Sequence similarities serve as evidence for structural and functional conservation, as well as of evolutionary relationships between the sequences. Consequently, comparative analysis is the primary means by which functional elements are identified.

Among the most highly conserved sequences are the active sites of enzymes and the binding sites of a protein receptors.

References

[1] Ahituv N, Zhu Y, Visel A, *et al.* (2007). "Deletion of ultraconserved elements yields viable mice". *PLoS Biol.* **5** (9): e234. doi:10.1371/journal.pbio.0050234. PMC 1964772. PMID 17803355.

[2] http://www.ncbi.nlm.nih.gov/entrez/viewer.fcgi?db=protein&val=263350

[3] http://www.ncbi.nlm.nih.gov/entrez/viewer.fcgi?db=protein&val=263348

- Thompson JD, Gibson TJ, Plewniak F, Jeanmougin F, Higgins DG (1997). The ClustalX windows interface: flexible strategies for multiple sequence alignment aided by quality analysis tools. *Nucleic Acids Research, 25:4876-4882.*

- http://biology.plosjournals.org/perlserv/?request=get-document&doi=10.1371%2Fjournal.pbio.0050253

Contact order

The **contact order** of a protein is a measure of the locality of the inter-amino acid contacts in the protein's native state tertiary structure. It is calculated as the average sequence distance between residues that form native contacts in the folded protein divided by the total length of the protein. Higher contact orders indicate longer folding times,[1] [2] and low contact order has been suggested as a predictor of potential downhill folding, or protein folding that occurs without a free energy barrier.[3] This effect is thought to be due to the lower loss of conformational entropy associated with the formation of local as opposed to nonlocal contacts.[2]

Contact order (CO) is formally defined as:

$$CO = \frac{1}{L \cdot N} \sum^{N} \Delta S_{i,j}$$

where N is the total number of contacts, $\Delta S_{i,j}$ is the sequence separation, in residues, between contacting residues i and j, and L is the total number of residues in the protein[1]. The value of contact order typically ranges from 5% to 25% for single-domain proteins, with lower contact order belonging to mainly helical proteins, and higher contact order belonging to proteins with a high beta-sheet content.

Protein structure prediction methods are more accurate in predicting the structures of proteins with low contact orders. This may be partly because low contact order proteins tend to be small, but is likely to be explained by the smaller number of possible long-range residue-residue interactions to be considered during global optimization procedures that minimize an energy function.[4] Even successful structure prediction methods such as the Rosetta method overproduce low-contact-order structure predictions compared to the distributions observed in experimentally determined protein structures.[2]

The percentage of the natively folded contact order can also be used as a measure of the "nativeness" of folding transition states. Phi value analysis in concert with molecular dynamics has produced transition-state models whose contact order is close to that of the folded state in proteins that are small and fast-folding.[5] Further, contact orders in transition states as well as those in native states are highly correlated with overall folding time.[6]

In addition to their role in structure prediction, contact orders can themselves be predicted based on a sequence alignment, which can be useful in classifying the fold of a novel sequence with some degree of homology to known sequences.[7]

References

[1] Plaxco, K. W., Simons, K. T., and Baker, D. (1998). Contact order, transition state placement, and the refolding rates of single domain proteins. *J. Mol. Biol.* 277, 985-994.

[2] Bonneau R, Ruczinski I, Tsai J, Baker D. (2002). Contact order and ab initio protein structure prediction. *Protein Sci* 11(8):1937-44.

[3] Zuo G, Wang J, Wang W. (2006). Folding with downhill behavior and low cooperativity of proteins. *Proteins* 63(1):165-73.

[4] Mount DM. (2004). *Bioinformatics: Sequence and Genome Analysis* 2nd ed. Cold Spring Harbor Laboratory Press: Cold Spring Harbor, NY.

[5] Pandit AD, Jha A, Freed KF, Sosnick TR. (2006). Small proteins fold through transition states with native-like topologies. *J Mol Biol* 361(4):755-70.

[6] Paci E, Lindorff-Larsen K, Dobson CM, Karplus M, Vendruscolo M. (2005). Transition state contact orders correlate with protein folding rates. *J Mol Biol* 352(3):495-500.

[7] Yi Shi, Jianjun Zhou, David Arndt, David S. Wishart and Guohui Lin (2008). Protein contact order prediction from primary sequences. *BMC Bioinformatics.* 9:255.

CS-BLAST

CS-BLAST

Developer(s)	Andreas Biegert and Johannes Soeding
Stable release	1.03 / April 14, 2009
Preview release	1.1 / April 14, 2009
Written in	C++
Available in	English
Type	Bioinformatics tool
License	Creative Commons Attribution-NonCommercial-3.0
Website	[1]

CS-BLAST (context-specific BLAST), an improved version[2] of BLAST (Basic Local Alignment Search Tool),[3] is a program for protein sequence searching.

Sequence searches are frequently performed by biologists to infer the function of an unknown protein from its sequence. For this purpose, the protein's sequence is compared to the sequences of millions of other protein sequences in public databases. The functions of the protein can often be inferred from the functions of the most similar sequences found in such a search.[4]

Implementation

CS-BLAST is implemented as a wrapper around BLAST. It finds up to twice as many distantly related protein sequences as BLAST at the same speed and error rate.[5] This is achieved by considering the letters that make up protein sequences, the amino acids, in the context of the 12 neighboring amino acids (six on either side). Whereas the probabilities for amino acids to mutate into other types of amino acids in related proteins depend only on the single amino acid in BLAST and other sequence search programs, mutation probabilities in CS-BLAST depend on the local sequence contexts.

An extension of CS-BLAST for iterative search with position-specific scoring matrices is also available. This program (CSI-BLAST) is similar to the popular PSI-BLAST (position-specific iterative BLAST) program.[6] Two search iterations of CS-BLAST are more sensitive than five search iterations of PSI-BLAST.[5]

References

[1] ftp://toolkit.lmb.uni-muenchen.de/csblast/

[2] "Better Sequence Searches Of Genes And Proteins Devised" (http://www.sciencedaily.com/releases/2009/02/090223131125.htm). ScienceDaily. Mar. 7, 2009. . Retrieved 2009-08-14.

[3] Altschul SF, Gish W, Miller W, Myers EW, Lipman DJ (1990). "Basic local alignment search tool.". *J Mol Biol* **215** (3): 403–410. doi:10.1016/S0022-2836(05)80360-2. PMID 2231712.

[4] Davison DB (2002). *3.* "An overview of sequence similarity ("homology") searching". *Curr Protoc Bioinformatics* **Chapter 3**: Unit 3.1. doi:10.1002/0471250953.bi0301s00. PMID 18792936.

[5] Biegert A, Soeding J (2009). "Sequence context-specific profiles for homology searching". *Proc Natl Acad Sci USA* **106** (10): 3770–3775. doi:10.1073/pnas.0810767106. PMC 2645910. PMID 19234132.

[6] Altschul SF, Madden TL, Schäffer AA, Zhang J, Zhang Z, Miller W, Lipman DJ. (1997). "Gapped BLAST and PSI-BLAST: a new generation of protein database search programs.". *Nucleic Acids Res* **25** (17): 3389–3402. doi:10.1093/nar/25.17.3389. PMC 146917. PMID 9254694.

External links

- http://toolkit.lmb.uni-muenchen.de/cs_blast (free server)

CSHALS

The **Conference on Semantics in Healthcare and Life Sciences** (**CSHALS**) is a scientific meeting on the practical applications of semantic technology to pharmaceutical R&D, healthcare, and life sciences. It has been held annually since 2008, and is the premier meeting in this domain.

CSHALS has been held in Cambridge, Massachusetts each year since its inception.

Organization

CSHALS is organized by ISCB (International Society for Computational Biology).

External links

- CSHALS 2011, Cambridge, Mass., USA [1]
- CHALS 2011 FriendFeed Group [2]
- CSHALS 2010, Cambridge, Mass., USA [3]
- CSHALS 2010 FriendFeed Group [4]
- CSHALS 2009, Cambridge, Mass., USA [5]
- CSHALS 2009 FriendFeed Group [6]
- CSHALS 2008, Cambridge, Mass., USA [7]

Notes

evden eve nakliyat [8]

References

[1] http://www.iscb.org/cshals2011
[2] http://friendfeed.com/cshals-2011
[3] http://www.iscb.org/cshals2010-home
[4] http://friendfeed.com/cshals-2010
[5] http://www.iscb.org/cms_addon/conferences/cshals2009/
[6] http://friendfeed.com/cshals-2009
[7] http://www.iscb.org/cms_addon/conferences/cshals2008/index.php
[8] http://www.evdenevenakliyatsec.com

Darwin Core

Darwin Core (often abbreviated to **DwC**) is a body of data standards which function as an extension of Dublin Core for biodiversity informatics applications, establishing a vocabulary of terms to facilitate the discovery, retrieval, and integration of information about organisms, their spatiotemporal occurrence, and supporting evidence housed in biological collections. It is meant to provide a stable standard reference for sharing information on biological diversity.

By providing a well-defined standard core vocabulary, Darwin Core aims to facilitate data sharing in biodiversity research by minimizing the barriers to adoption and maximizing reusability. The terms described in this standard are a part of a larger set of vocabularies and technical specifications under development and maintained by Biodiversity Information Standards (formerly known as the Taxonomic Databases Working Group (TDWG)).

Contents

The Darwin Core is body of standards. It includes a glossary of terms (in other contexts these might be called properties, elements, fields, columns, attributes, or concepts) intended to facilitate the sharing of information about biological diversity by providing reference definitions, examples, and commentaries. The Darwin Core is primarily based on taxa, their occurrence in nature as documented by observations, specimens, and samples, and related information. Included in the standard are documents describing how these terms are managed, how the set of terms can be extended for new purposes, and how the terms can be used. The Simple Darwin Core [1] is a specification for one particular way to use the terms - to share data about taxa and their occurrences in a simply structured way - and is probably what is meant if someone suggests to "format your data according to the Darwin Core".

Each term has a definition and commentaries that are meant to promote the consistent use of the terms across applications and disciplines. Evolving commentaries that discuss, refine, expand, or translate the definitions and examples are referred to through links in the Comments attribute of each term. This means of documentation allows the standard to adapt to new purposes without disrupting existing applications. There is meant to be a clear separation between the terms defined in this standard and the applications that make use of them. For example, though the data types and constraints are not provided in the term definitions, recommendations are made about how to restrict the values where appropriate.

In practice, Darwin Core decouples the definition and semantics of individual terms from application of these terms in different technologies such as XML, RDF or simple CSV text files. Darwin Core provides separate guidelines on how to encode the terms as XML[2] or text files.[3]

History

Darwin Core was originally created as a Z39.50 profile by the Z39.50 Biology Implementers Group (ZBIG), supported by funding from a USA National Science Foundation award.[4] The name "Darwin Core" was first coined by Allen Allison at the first meeting of the ZBIG held at the University of Kansas in 1998 while commenting on the profile's conceptual similarity with Dublin Core. The Darwin Core profile was later expressed as an XML Schema document for use by the Distributed Generic Information Retrieval (DiGIR) protocol. A TDWG task group was created to revise the Darwin Core, and a ratified metadata standard was officially released on 9 October 2009.

Though ratified as a TDWG/Biodiversity Information Standards standard since then, Darwin Core has had numerous previous versions in production usage. The published standard contains a history[5] with details of the versions leading to the current standard.

Darwin Core Versions

Name	Namespace	Number of terms	XML Schema	Date Issued
Darwin Core 1.0	Not Applicable	24	(Z39.50 GRS-1)	1998
Darwin Core 1.2 (Classic)	[6]	46	[7]	2001-09-11
Darwin Core 1.21 (MaNIS/HerpNet/ORNIS/FishNet2)	[6]	63	[8]	2003-03-15
Darwin Core OBIS	http://www.iobis.org/obis	27	[9]	2005-07-10
Darwin Core 1.4 (Draft Standard)	http://rs.tdwg.org/dwc/dwcore/	45	[10]	2005-07-10
Darwin Core Terms (properties)	http://rs.tdwg.org/dwc/terms/	172	[11]	2009-10-09

Key Projects Using Darwin Core

- The Atlas of Living Australia (ALA) [12]
- The Global Biodiversity Information Facility (GBIF) [13]
- The Ocean Biogeographic Information System (OBIS) [14]
- Online Zoological Collections of Australian Museums (OZCAM) [15]
- Mammal Networked Information System (MaNIS) [16]
- Ornithological Information System (ORNIS) [17]
- HerpNet [18]
- FishNet 2 [19]
- VertNet [20]

References

[1] The Simple Darwin Core (http://rs.tdwg.org/dwc/terms/simple/index.htm)

[2] Darwin Core XML Guide (http://rs.tdwg.org/dwc/terms/guides/xml/index.htm)

[3] Darwin Core Text Guide (http://rs.tdwg.org/dwc/terms/guides/text/index.htm)

[4] An Experimental Z39.50 Information Retrieval Protocol Test Bed for Biological Collection and Taxonomic Data, #9811443 (http://nsf.gov/awardsearch/showAward.do?AwardNumber=9811443)

[5] Darwin Core History (http://rs.tdwg.org/dwc/terms/history/index.htm)

[6] http://digir.net/schema/conceptual/darwin/2003/1.0

[7] http://digir.net/schema/conceptual/darwin/2003/1.0/darwin2.xsd

[8] http://digir.net/schema/conceptual/darwin/manis/1.21/darwin2.xsd

[9] http://iobis.org/obis/obis.xsd

[10] http://rs.tdwg.org/dwc/tdwg_dw_core.xsd

[11] http://rs.tdwg.org/dwc/xsd/tdwg_dwcterms.xsd

[12] http://www.ala.org.au/datastandards.htm

[13] "Darwin Core" (http://www.gbif.org/informatics/standards-and-tools/publishing-data/data-standards/darwin-core-archives/). Global Biodiversity Information Facility. . Retrieved April 12, 2011.

[14] "Data Schema and metadata" (http://www.iobis.org/data/schema-and-metadata). Ocean Biogeographic Information System. . Retrieved April 12, 2011.

[15] http://www3.interscience.wiley.com/cgi-bin/fulltext/120713092/PDFSTART

[16] http://manisnet.org

[17] http://ornisnet.org

[18] http://herpnet.org

[19] http://www.fishnet2.net/index.html

[20] http://vertnet.org

External links

- Darwin Core Quick Reference Guide (http://rs.tdwg.org/dwc/terms/index.htm)
- Darwin Core Google Code Development Site (http://code.google.com/p/darwincore/)
- Darwin Core Official Website (http://www.tdwg.org/activities/darwincore/)
- Executive Summary of Darwin Core (http://www.tdwg.org/fileadmin/subgroups/dwc/exec_summary_dwc. doc)

Darwin Core Archive

Darwin Core Archive (DwC-A) is a Biodiversity informatics data standard that makes use of the Darwin Core terms to produce a single, self contained dataset for species occurrence or checklist data. Essentially it is a set of text (CSV) files with a simple descriptor (meta.xml) to inform others how your files are organized. The format is defined in the Darwin Core Text Guidelines.[1] It is the preferred format for publishing data to the GBIF network.

Darwin Core

The Darwin Core standard has been used to mobilise the vast majority of specimen occurrence and observational records within the GBIF network.[2] The Darwin Core standard was originally conceived to facilitate the discovery, retrieval, and integration of information about modern biological specimens, their spatio-temporal occurrence, and their supporting evidence housed in collections (physical or digital).

The Darwin Core today is broader in scope. It aims to provide a stable, standard reference for sharing information on biological diversity. As a glossary of terms, the Darwin Core provides stable semantic definitions with the goal of being maximally reusable in a variety of contexts. This means that Darwin Core may still be used in the same way it has historically been used, but may also serve as the basis for building more complex exchange formats, while still ensuring interoperability through a common set of terms.

Archive Format

The central idea of an archive is that its data files are logically arranged in a star-like manner, with one core data file surrounded by any number of 'extensions'. Each extension record (or 'extension file row') points to a record in the core file; in this way, many extension records can exist for each single core record.

Details about recommended extensions can be found in their respective subsections and will be extensively documented in the GBIF registry, which will catalogue all available extensions.

Sharing entire datasets instead of using pageable web services like DiGIR and TAPIR allows much simpler and more efficient data transfer. For example, retrieving 260,000 records via TAPIR takes about nine hours, issuing 1,300 http requests to transfer 500 MB of XML-formatted data. The exact same dataset, encoded as DwC-A and zipped, becomes a 3 MB file. Therefore, GBIF highly recommends compressing an archive using ZIP or GZIP when generating a DwC-A.

An archive requires stable identifiers for core records, but not for extensions. For any kind of shared data it is therefore necessary to have some sort of local record identifiers. It's good practice to maintain – with the original data – identifiers that are stable over time and are not being reused after the record is deleted. If you can, please provide globally unique identifiers instead of local ones.

Archive Descriptor

To be completed.

Data Files

To be completed.

Dataset Metadata

A Darwin Core Archive should contain a file containing metadata describing the whole dataset. The Ecological Metadata Language (EML) is the most common format for this, but simple Dublin Core files are being used to.

References

[1] Darwin Core Text Guidelines (http://rs.tdwg.org/dwc/terms/guides/text/index.htm)
[2] GBIF, the DwC-A Standard (http://www.gbif.org/informatics/standards-and-tools/publishing-data/data-standards/darwin-core-archives/)

External links

- Darwin Core Quick Reference Guide (http://rs.tdwg.org/dwc/terms/index.htm)
- Biodiversity Information Standards (TDWG)
- Global Biodiversity Information Facility (GBIF)
- Biodiversity informatics

Data curation

In science, **Data curation** is a term used to indicate the process of extraction of important information from scientific texts such as research articles by experts and converting them into an electronic form such as an entry of a biological database.[1]

According to the University of Illinois' Graduate School of Library and Information Science, "Data curation is the active and on-going management of data through its life cycle of interest and usefulness to scholarship, science, and education. Data curation activities enable data discovery and retrieval, maintain its quality, add value, and provide for re-use over time, and this new field includes authentication, archiving, management, preservation, retrieval, and representation."[2] Deep background on data libraries appeared in a 1982 issue of the Illinois journal, *Library Trends.*[3] . For historical background on the data archive movement see "Social Scientific Information Needs for Numeric Data: The Evolution of the International Data Archive Infrastructure." [4] .

In broad terms, curation means a range of activities and processes done to create, manage, maintain, and validate a component.[5]

This term is used in context of biological databases, where specific biological information is firstly obtained from a range of research articles and then stored within a specific category of database. For instance, information about Anti-depressant drugs can be obtained from various sources and after checking whether they are available as a database or not, they are saved under a drug's database's anti-depressive category.

Enterprises are also utilizing data curation within their operational and strategic processes to ensure data quality and accuracy [6] .

The Dissemination Information Packages (DIPS) for Information Reuse (DIPIR) is studying research data produced and used by quantitative social scientists, archaeologists, and zoologists. The intended audiences is researchers who use secondary data and the digital curators, digital repository managers, data center staff, and others who collect, manage, and store digital information. [7]

References

[1] Bio creative Glossary at http://biocreative.sourceforge.net/biocreative_glossary.html

[2] http://www.lis.illinois.edu/academics/programs/ms/datacuration University of Illinois Graduate School of Library and Information
     Science

[3] McCook, Kathleen de la Peña/ Kathleen M. Heim, issue editor,v.30, no. 3 (1982). *Data libraries for the social sciences.*

[4] Kathleen M. Heim, "Social Scientific Information Needs for Numeric Data: The Evolution of the International Data Archive Infrastructure."
     in *Collection Management* 9 (Spring 1987): 1-53.

[5] Pilin Glossary at http://www.pilin.net.au/Project_Documents/Glossary.htm

[6] E. Curry, A. Freitas, and S. O'Riáin, "The Role of Community-Driven Data Curation for Enterprises," (http://3roundstones.com/led_book/
     led-curry-et-al.html) in Linking Enterprise Data, D. Wood, Ed. Boston, MA: Springer US, 2010, pp. 25-47.

[7] http://dipir.org/

External links

* Curation of ecological and environmental data: DataONE (http://www.dataone.org/)

Databases for oncogenomic research

Databases for oncogenomic research are biological databases dedicated to cancer data and oncogenomic research. They can be a primary source of cancer data, offer a certain level of analysis (processed data) or even offer online data mining.

The table below gives an overview of databases for that serve specifically for oncogenomic research. Note that this is not a comprehensive list and does not contain databases that have a generic focus. You may find databases containing cancer data among the List of biological databases or Microarray databases.

Database	Institute / Organization	Alteration Types	Primary Source [1]	Processed Data [2]	Organisms	Cell lines [3]	Public Data [4]	Restricted Data [5]
Catalogue Of Somatic Mutations In Cancer (COSMIC) → [6]	Wellcome Trust Sanger Institute, UK	Mutation	No	Yes	Human	No	Yes	No
International Cancer Genome Consortium → [7]	Worldwide	Copy number, Mutation, Gene Expression	Yes	Yes	Human	No	Yes	Yes
Integrative Oncogenomics Cancer Browser (IntOGen) → [8]	Universitat Pompeu Fabra, Spain	Copy number, Mutation, Gene Expression	No	Yes	Human	No	Yes	No
Mouse Retrovirus Tagged Cancer Gene Database → [9]	Institute of Molecular and Cell Biology, Singapore	Mutations	Yes	Yes	Mouse	No	Yes	No
Mouse Tumor Biology Database → [10][11]	The Jackson Laboratory, USA	Copy number, Mutation, Methylation, Gene Expression	No	No	Mouse	No	No	No

OncoDB.HCC → [12]	Academia Sinica, Taiwan	Copy number, Gene Expression, QTL	No	Yes	Human, Mouse, Rat	No	Yes	No
Oncomine → [13]	Compendia Bioscience, Inc., USA	Gene Expression	No	Yes	Human	Yes	No	Yes
Oncoreveal → [14]	Boğaziçi University, Turkey	Gene Expression	No	Yes	Human	No	Yes	No
Progenetix → [15]	Universität Zürich, Switzerland	Copy number	No	Yes	Human	No	Yes	No
The Cancer Genome Atlas → [16]	National Cancer Institute, USA	Copy number, Mutation, Methylation, Gene Expression, miRNA expression	Yes	Yes	Human	No	Yes	Yes
CancerResource → [17]	University Medicine Berlin, Germany							
Roche Cancer Genome Database (RCGDB) [18]	Roche Diagnostics, Penzberg, Germany							

[1] The database is the publication site for (some of) its cancer raw data

[2] The database contains cancer data at a certain level of analysis (non-raw data)

[3] The database also contains cell line data

[4] The database contains cancer data that is available for everyone

[5] The database contains cancer data that is only available under some restriction

[6] http://www.sanger.ac.uk/genetics/CGP/cosmic/

[7] http://www.icgc.org/

[8] http://www.intogen.org

[9] http://rtcgd.abcc.ncifcrf.gov/

[10] http://tumor.informatics.jax.org/mtbwi/index.do

[11] Only contains *references* to biological data

[12] http://oncodb.hcc.ibms.sinica.edu.tw/index.htm

[13] https://www.oncomine.org/

[14] http://www.oncoreveal.org/

[15] http://www.progenetix.net

[16] http://cancergenome.nih.gov/

[17] http://bioinf-data.charite.de/cancerresource/

[18] http://rcgdb.bioinf.uni-sb.de/MutomeWeb/

DAVID (bioinformatics tool)

DAVID Bioinformatics Resources

Original author(s)	Richard A. Lempicki, Da-Wei Huang, Brad Sherman
Developer(s)	Laboratory of Immunopathogenesis and Bioinformatics
Stable release	6.7 / 27 January 2010
Type	Bioinformatics
Website	[1]

DAVID (the **D**atabase for **A**nnotation, **V**isualization and **I**ntegrated **D**iscovery) is a free online bioinformatics resource developed by the Laboratory of Immunopathogenesis and Bioinformatics (LIB [2]).[3] [4] [5] [6] [7] [8] All tools in the DAVID Bioinformatics Resources aim to provide functional interpretation of large lists of genes derived from genomic studies, e.g. microarray and proteomics studies. DAVID can be found at http://david.niaid.nih.gov or http://david.abcc.ncifcrf.gov

The DAVID Bioinformatics Resources consists of the DAVID Knowledgebase and five integrated, web-based functional annotation tool suites: the DAVID Gene Functional Classification Tool, the DAVID Functional Annotation Tool, the DAVID Gene ID Conversion Tool, the DAVID Gene Name Viewer and the DAVID NIAID Pathogen Genome Browser. The expanded DAVID Knowledgebase now integrates almost all major and well-known public bioinformatics resources centralized by the DAVID Gene Concept, a single-linkage method to agglomerate tens of millions of diverse gene/protein identifiers and annotation terms from a variety of public bioinformatics databases. For any uploaded gene list, the DAVID Resources now provides not only the typical gene-term enrichment analysis, but also new tools and functions that allow users to condense large gene lists into gene functional groups, convert between gene/protein identifiers, visualize many-genes-to-many-terms relationships, cluster redundant and heterogeneous terms into groups, search for interesting and related genes or terms, dynamically view genes from their lists on bio-pathways and more.

Functionality

DAVID provides a comprehensive set of functional annotation tools for investigators to understand biological meaning behind large list of genes. For any given gene list, DAVID tools are able to:

- Identify enriched biological themes, particularly GO terms
- Discover enriched functional-related gene groups
- Cluster redundant annotation terms
- Visualize genes on BioCarta & KEGG pathway maps
- Display related many-genes-to-many-terms on 2-D view.
- Search for other functionally related genes not in the list
- List interacting proteins
- Explore gene names in batch
- Link gene-disease associations
- Highlight protein functional domains and motifs
- Redirect to related literatures
- Convert gene identifiers from one type to another.

External links

- Official website [1]

References

[1] http://david.abcc.ncifcrf.gov/home.jsp

[2] http://david.abcc.ncifcrf.gov/content.jsp?file=about_us.html

[3] Huang DW, Lempicki RA (2009). "Systematic and integrative analysis of large gene lists using DAVID bioinformatics resources.". *Nature Protocols* **4** (1): 44. doi:10.1038/nprot.2008.211. PMID 19131956.

[4] Sherman BT, Huang DW, Tan Q, Guo Y, Bour S, Liu D, Stephens R, Baseler MW, Lane HC, Lempicki RA (2007). "DAVID Knowledgebase: a gene-centered database integrating heterogeneous gene annotation resources to facilitate high-throughput gene functional analysis". *BMC Bioinformatics* **8**: 426. doi:10.1186/1471-2105-8-426. PMC 2186358. PMID 17980028.

[5] Huang DW, Sherman BT, Tan Q, Collins JR, Alvord WG, Roayaei J, Stephens R, Baseler MW, Lane HC, Lempicki RA (2007). "The DAVID Gene Functional Classification Tool: a novel biological module-centric algorithm to functionally analyze large gene lists". *Genome Biol* **8** (9): R183. doi:10.1186/gb-2007-8-9-r183. PMC 2375021. PMID 17784955.

[6] Huang Da, HC; Sherman, BT; Tan, Q; Kir, J; Liu, D; Bryant, D; Guo, Y; Stephens, R et al. (2007). "DAVID Bioinformatics Resources: expanded annotation database and novel algorithms to better extract biology from large gene lists.". *Nucleic Acids Research* **35** (Web Server issue): W169–75. doi:10.1093/nar/gkm415. PMC 1933169. PMID 17576678.

[7] Hosack; Dennis Jr, G; Sherman, BT; Lane, HC; Lempicki, RA (2003). "Identifying biological themes within lists of genes with EASE.". *Genome biology* **4** (10): R70. doi:10.1186/gb-2003-4-10-r70. PMC 328459. PMID 14519205.

[8] Dennis Jr; Sherman, BT; Hosack, DA; Yang, J; Gao, W; Lane, HC; Lempicki, RA (2003). "DAVID: Database for Annotation, Visualization, and Integrated Discovery.". *Genome biology* **4** (5): P3. doi:10.1186/gb-2003-4-5-p3. PMID 12734009.

User:Davidweisss/InSilico DB

'InSilico DB

The InSilico DB: http://insilico.ulb.ac.be.

References

External links

- example.com (http://www.example.com/)

De novo protein structure prediction

In computational biology, *de novo* **protein structure prediction** is the task of estimating a protein's tertiary structure from its sequence alone. The problem is very difficult and has occupied leading scientists for decades. Research has focused in three areas: alternate lower-resolution representations of proteins, accurate energy functions, and efficient sampling methods. At present, the most successful methods have a reasonable probability of predicting the fold of a small protein domain within 5 angstroms. [1]

De novo protein structure prediction methods attempt to predict tertiary structures from sequences based on general principles that govern protein folding energetics and/or statistical tendencies of conformational features that native structures acquire, without the use of explicit templates. A general paradigm for *de novo* prediction involves sampling conformation space, guided by scoring functions and other sequence-dependent biases such that a large set of candidate ("decoy") structures are generated. Native-like conformations are then selected from these decoys using scoring functions as well as conformer clustering. High-resolution refinement is sometimes used as a final step to fine-tune native-like structures. There are two major classes of scoring functions. Physics-based functions are based on mathematical models describing aspects of the known physics of molecular interaction. Knowledge-based functions are formed with statistical models capturing aspects of the properties of native protein conformations [2].

De novo methods tend to require vast computational resources, and have thus only been carried out for relatively small proteins. To predict protein structure *de novo* for larger proteins will require better algorithms and larger computational resources like those afforded by either powerful supercomputers (such as Blue Gene or MDGRAPE-3) or distributed computing projects (such as Folding@home, Rosetta@home, the Human Proteome Folding Project, or Nutritious Rice for the World). Although computational barriers are vast, the potential benefits of structural genomics (by predicted or experimental methods) make *de novo* structure prediction an active research field.

References

[1] Consider Pande, Baker, et.al. Atomistic protein folding simulations on the hundreds of microsecond timescale using worldwide distributed computing. *Kollman Memorial Issue, Biopolymers*, 2002.

[2] Samudrala R, Moult J. An all-atom distance-dependent conditional probability discriminatory function for protein structure prediction. *Journal of Molecular Biology* 275: 893-914, 1998.

- Bradley, P., Malmstrom, L., Qian, B., Schonbrun, J., Chivian, D., Kim, D. E., Meiler, J., Misura, K. M., Baker, D. (2005). Free modeling with Rosetta in CASP6. Proteins 61 Suppl 7:128-34.

- Bonneau, R & Baker, D. (2001). Ab Initio Protein Structure Prediction: Progress and Prospects. Annu. Rev. Biophys. Biomol. Struct. 30, 173-89.

- J. Skolnick, Y. Zhang and A. Kolinski. Ab Initio modeling. Structural genomics and high throughput structural biology. M. Sundsrom, M. Norin and A. Edwards, eds. 2006: 137-162.

[Please expand this set of references]

External links

CASP:

* http://predictioncenter.org/

Folding@Home:

* http://folding.stanford.edu/

HPF project:

* http://www.worldcommunitygrid.org/projects_showcase/viewHpf2Research.do

Foldit:

* http://fold.it/portal/

Debian-Med

The **Debian Med** project is a Debian Pure Blend created to provide a co-ordinated operating system and collection of available free software packages that are well-suited for the requirements for medical practices and research.

Packages

Debian Med includes packages of Free Software in the categories:

* Medical practice and Patient management [1]
* Molecular Biology and Medical Genetics [2]
* Medical imaging [3]
* Drug databases [4]
* Psychology [5]
* and several others

Availability

Debian Med packages have been included in Ubuntu (and derivative) operating system distribution repositories.[6]

References

[1] http://debian-med.alioth.debian.org/tasks/practice
[2] http://debian-med.alioth.debian.org/tasks/bio
[3] http://debian-med.alioth.debian.org/tasks/imaging
[4] http://debian-med.alioth.debian.org/tasks/data
[5] http://debian-med.alioth.debian.org/tasks/psychology
[6] ""debian-med" 1.3ubuntu1 source package in Ubuntu" (https://launchpad.net/ubuntu/+source/debian-med/1.3ubuntu1). Ubuntu. .

External links

- **Debian Med** – Homepage of the Project (http://www.debian.org/devel/debian-med/)
- Debian Med talks (http://people.debian.org/~tille/debian-med/talks/)
- Wiki page (http://wiki.debian.org/DebianMed/) with further information for users and developers.

Related projects

- Ubuntu-Med -- a Kubuntu operating system customization with an EHR and additional software packages incorporated into it
- Project **EU Spirit** (http://www.euspirit.org/) – European portal for open-source based software in medicine
- **Open Med** (http://www.openmed.org/) – Support for free medical software (German)

Demographic and Health Surveys

The MEASURE Demographic and Health Surveys (DHS) Project is responsible for collecting and disseminating accurate, nationally representative data on health and population in developing countries. The project is implemented by Macro International, Inc. and is funded by the United States Agency for International Development (USAID) with contributions from other donors such as UNICEF, UNFPA, WHO, and UNAIDS.

The DHS is highly comparable to the Multiple Indicator Cluster Surveys and the technical teams developing and supporting the surveys are in close collaboration.

Since October 2003 Macro International has been partnering with four internationally experienced organizations to expand access to and use of the DHS data: Johns Hopkins Bloomberg School of Public Health Center for Communication Programs; Program for Appropriate Technology in Health (PATH); Blue Raster; CAMRIS International; and The Futures Institute.

About MEASURE DHS

Since 1984, the MEASURE DHS Project has provided technical assistance to more than 260 demographic and health surveys in over 90 countries - advancing global understanding of health and population trends in developing countries. More specifically, the DHS surveys collect information on fertility and total fertility rate (TFR), reproductive health, maternal health, child health, immunization and survival, HIV/AIDS; maternal mortality, child mortality, malaria, and nutrition among women and children stunted. The strategic objective of MEASURE DHS is to improve and institutionalize the collection and use of data by host countries for program monitoring and evaluation and for policy development decisions.

MEASURE DHS is one of four components of the "Monitoring and Evaluation to Assess and Use Results" (MEASURE) effort begun in 1997. The other three MEASURE partner projects are MEASURE Evaluation, MEASURE U.S. Census Bureau-SCILS, and MEASURE CDC/DRH in cooperation with the CDC.

Surveys

MEASURE DHS supports a range of data collection options:

- Demographic and Health Surveys (DHS): provide data for a wide range of monitoring and impact evaluation indicators in the areas of population, health, and nutrition.
- AIDS Indicator Surveys (AIS): provide countries with a standardized tool to obtain indicators for the effective monitoring of national HIV/AIDS programs.
- Service Provision Assessment (SPA) Surveys: provide information about the characteristics of health and family planning services available in a country.
- Malaria Indicators Surveys (MIS): Provide data on bednet ownership and use, prevention of malaria during pregnancy, and prompt and effective treatment of fever in young children. In some cases, biomarker testing for malaria and anemia are also included.
- Key Indicators Survey (KIS): provide monitoring and evaluation data for population and health activities in small areas—regions, districts, catchment areas—that may be targeted by an individual project, although they can be used in nationally representative surveys as well.
- Other Quantitative Data: include Geographic Data Collection, and Benchmarking Surveys.
- Biomarker Collection: in conjunction with surveys, more than 2 million tests have been conducted for HIV, anemia, malaria, and more than 25 other biomarkers.
- Qualitative Research: provides informed answers to questions that lie outside the purview of standard quantitative approaches.

Data

MEASURE DHS works to put survey data into the hands of program managers, health care providers, policymakers, country leaders, researchers, members of the media, and others who can act to improve public health. MEASURE DHS distributes unrestricted survey data files for legitimate academic research at no cost.

Online databases include: STATcompiler [1], STATmapper [2], HIV/AIDS Survey Indicators Database [3], HIV Spatial Data Repository [4], HIVmapper [5], and Country QuickStats [6].

Publications

MEASURE DHS produces a variety of publications that provide country specific and comparative data on population, health, and nutrition in developing countries. Most publications are available online for download, but if an electronic version of the publication is not available, a hard copy may be available.

Countries

The MEASURE DHS Project has been active in over 90 countries in Africa, Asia, Central Asia; West Asia; and Southeast Asia, Latin America and the Caribbean. A list of the publications for each country is available online at the Measure DHS web site.[7]

The MEASURE DHS Project has been active in the following countries:

A

Afghanistan   Albania   Armenia

Angola   Azerbaijan

B

Bangladesh   Botswana   Burundi

Benin   Brazil

Bolivia   Burkina_Faso

C

Cape Verde   Central African Republic   Chad   Republic of the Congo

Cambodia   Colombia   Democratic Republic of the Congo

Cameroon   Comoros   Cote d'Ivoire

D

Dominican Republic

E

Ecuador   El Salvador   Ethiopia

Egypt   Eritrea

G

Gabon   Guatemala   Guyana

Ghana   Guinea

H

Haiti   Honduras

I

India   Indonesia

J

Jordan

K

Kazakhstan   Kenya   Kyrgyzstan

L

Lesotho   Liberia

M

Madagascar   Mauritania   Morocco

Malawi   Maldives   Mexico   Mozambique

Mali   Republic of Moldova   Myanmar

N

Namibia   Nicaragua   Nigeria

Nepal	Niger		
O			
Ondo State			
P			
Pakistan	Peru		
Paraguay	Philippines		
R			
Rwanda			
S			
Samoa	Sao Tome and Principe	South Africa	Sudan
Senegal	Sierra Leone	Sri Lanka	Swaziland
T			
Tanzania	Trinidad and Tobago	Turkmenistan	
Thailand	Timor-Leste	Tunisia	
Togo	Turkey		
U			
Uganda	Ukraine	Uzbekistan	
V			
Vietnam			
Y			
Yemen			
Z			
Zambia	Zimbabwe		

Special Focus Topics

HIV/AIDS

Since 2001, MEASURE DHS has helped more than 15 countries in Africa, Asia and Latin America and Caribbean conduct population-based HIV testing. By collecting blood for HIV testing from representative samples of the population of men and women in a country, MEASURE DHS can provide nationally representative estimates of HIV rates. The testing protocol provides for anonymous, informed, and voluntary testing of women and men.

The project also collects data on internationally recognized AIDS indicators. Currently, the main sources of HIV/AIDS indicators in the database are the Demographic and Health Surveys (DHS), the Multiple Indicator Cluster Surveys (MICS), the Reproductive Health Surveys (RHS), the Sexual Behavior Surveys (SBS), and Behavioral Surveillance Surveys (BSS).[8] Eventually it will cover all countries for which indicators are available. Finally, the project also collects data on the capacity of health care facilities to deliver HIV prevention and treatment services.

Malaria

Since 2000, DHS (and some AIS) surveys have collected data on ownership and use of mosquito nets, treatment of fever in children, and intermittent preventive treatment of pregnant women. In recent years, additional questions on indoor residual spraying, as well as biomarker testing for anemia and malaria have been conducted.

Gender

The MEASURE DHS program is a major source of gender data, research and training for integrating gender into population, health and nutrition programs and HIV/AIDS-related activities in the developing world. Gender is a fundamental dimension of societal stratification. MEASURE DHS underscores the importance of providing accurate and useful data on gender and emphasizes the need to identify and develop meaningful indicators of gender relations and women's empowerment.

Questions on gender roles and empowerment are integrated into most DHS questionnaires. For countries interested in more in-depth data on gender, modules of questions are available on special topics such as status of women, domestic violence, and female genital cutting.

Youth

MEASURE DHS has interviewed thousands of young people and gathered valuable information about their education, employment, media exposure, nutrition, sexual activity, fertility, unions, and general reproductive health, including HIV prevalence. The Youth Corner in the MEASURE DHS website presents findings about youth and features in-depth profiles of young adults ages 15–24 from more than 30 countries worldwide.[9] The Youth Corner is part of the broader effort by the Interagency Youth Working Group (IYWG) to help program managers, donors, national and local governments, teachers, religious leaders, and nongovernmental organizations (NGOs) plan and implement strong, relevant programs to improve the reproductive health of young adults.[10]

Geographic Information

Geographic location affects peoples' health, nutrition, and access to health care services. The MEASURE DHS project can now analyze the impact of location using DHS data and geographic information systems (GIS). MEASURE DHS routinely collects geographic information in all surveyed countries. Using GIS, researchers can link DHS data with routine health data, health facility locations, local infrastructure such as roads and rivers, and environmental conditions.

MEASURE DHS is a recognized leader in training local interviewers to collect geographic information. The GPS data collection standards and manual prepared by MEASURE DHS are now being used for the World Bank's Living Standards and Measurement studies and the World Health Organization's World Health Surveys. UNICEF has also adapted the DHS manual for their Multiple Indicator Cluster Surveys in the upcoming round of data collection.

Biomarkers

Now, using field-friendly technologies, MEASURE DHS is able to collect biomarker data relating to a wide range of conditions and infections. DHS surveys have tested for anemia (by measuring hemoglobin), HIV infection, sexually transmitted diseases such as syphilis and the herpes simplex virus, serum retinol (Vitamin A), lead exposure, high blood pressure, and immunity from vaccine-preventable diseases like measles and tetanus. Traditionally, much of the data gathered in DHS surveys is self-reported. Biomarkers complement this information by providing an objective profile of a specific disease or health condition in a population. Biomarker data also contribute to the understanding of behavioral risk factors and determinants of different illnesses.

References

[1] http://www.statcompiler.com/

[2] http://macroint.mapsherpa.com/statmapper/

[3] http://www.measuredhs.com/hivdata/

[4] http://www.hivspatialdata.net/

[5] http://www.hivmapper.com/

[6] http://www.measuredhs.com/countries/

[7] Measure DHS Country List (http://www.measuredhs.com/countries/)

[8] FHI.org BSS (http://www.fhi.org/en/topics/bss.htm)

[9] Measure DHS Youth Topics (http://www.measuredhs.com/topics/youth/start.cfm)

[10] Interagency Youth Working Group (http://www.infoforhealth.org/youthwg)

External links

- Official website (http://www.measuredhs.com/)

Dendroscope

Dendroscope

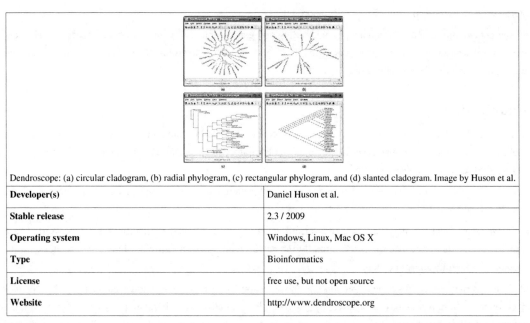

Dendroscope: (a) circular cladogram, (b) radial phylogram, (c) rectangular phylogram, and (d) slanted cladogram. Image by Huson et al.

Developer(s)	Daniel Huson et al.
Stable release	2.3 / 2009
Operating system	Windows, Linux, Mac OS X
Type	Bioinformatics
License	free use, but not open source
Website	http://www.dendroscope.org

Dendroscope is an interactive computer software program written in Java for viewing Phylogenetic trees.[1] This program is designed to view trees of all sizes and is very useful for creating figures. Dendroscope can be used for a variety of analyses of molecular data sets but is particularly designed for metagenomics or analyses of uncultured environmental samples.

It was developed by Daniel Huson and his colleagues at the University of Tübingen in Germany.

References

[1] Huson, Daniel H.; Daniel C. Richter, Christian Rausch, Tobias Dezulian, Markus Franz, and Regula Rupp (2007-11-22). paper "Dendroscope: An interactive viewer for large phylogenetic trees" (http://www.biomedcentral.com/content/pdf/1471-2105-8-460.pdf). *BMC Bioinformatics* (United Kingdom: BioMedCentral) **8:460**: 460. doi:10.1186/1471-2105-8-460. PMC 2216043. PMID 18034891. paper. Retrieved 2008-04-03.

Diseases Database

The **Diseases Database** is a database that underlies a free website that provides information about the relationships between medical conditions, symptoms, and medications. The database is run by Medical Object Oriented Software Enterprises Ltd, a small company based in London, UK.

The site's stated aim is "education, background reading and general interest" with an intended audience "physicians, other clinical healthcare workers and students of these professions". The editor of the site is stated as Malcolm H Duncan, a UK qualified medical doctor.[1]

Organization

The Diseases Database is based around a collection of concepts related to human medicine. These concepts include diseases, drugs, symptoms, physical signs and abnormal laboratory results. These are referred to as 'items'. There are around 8,000 items within the database.[2]

In order to link items to both each other and external information resources three sets of metadata are modelled within the database.

Firstly Diseases Database items are assigned various relationships e.g. diabetes mellitus type 2 is asserted "a risk factor for" ischaemic heart disease. More formally the database employs an entity-attribute-value model with items populating both entity and value slots.

Relationships may be read in either direction e.g. the assertion "myocardial infarction {may cause} chest pain" has the corollary "chest pain {may be caused by} myocardial infarction". Such relationships aggregate within the database and allow lists to be retrieved - e.g. a list of items which may cause chest pain, and a list of items which may be caused by myocardial infarction.

Secondly most Diseases Database items are assigned topic specific hyperlinks to Web resources which include Online Mendelian Inheritance in Man, eMedicine and WikiPedia.

Thirdly most Diseases Database items are mapped to concepts within the Unified Medical Language System (UMLS). UMLS links enable the display of short text definitions and/or Medical Subject Heading (MeSH) scope notes for the majority of items on the database.

The UMLS map also enables links to and from other medical classifications and terminologies e.g. ICD-9 and SNOMED.

Diseases Database content can thus potentially be accessed directly via coded identifiers from multiple medical coding systems e.g. the SNOMED concept code for Myocardial infarction 22298006 finds the equivalent Diseases Database item http:/ / www. diseasesdatabase. com/ code_translate. asp?strCODE=22298006& strSAB=SNOMEDCT as well as a number of other closely related concepts via UMLS supplied relationships.

External links

- Diseases Database [3]

References

[1] http://www.diseasesdatabase.com/money.asp
[2] http://www.diseasesdatabase.com/content_stats.asp
[3] http://www.diseasesdatabase.com/

Distance matrix

In mathematics, computer science and graph theory, a **distance matrix** is a matrix (two-dimensional array) containing the distances, taken pairwise, of a set of points. This matrix will have a size of $N{\times}N$ where N is the number of points, nodes or vertices (often in a graph).

Comparison with related matrices

Comparison with Adjacency matrix

Distance matrices are related to adjacency matrices, with the differences that (a) the latter only provides the information which vertices are connected but does not tell about *costs* or *distances* between the vertices and (b) an entry of a distance matrix is smaller if two elements are closer, while "close" (connected) vertices yield larger entries in an adjacency matrix.

Comparison with Euclidean distance matrix

Unlike a Euclidean distance matrix, the matrix does not need to be symmetric -- that is, the values $x_{i,j}$ do not necessarily equal $x_{j,i}$. Similarly, the matrix values are not restricted to non-negative reals (as they would be in the Euclidean distance matrix) but rather can have negative values, zeros or imaginary numbers depending on the cost metric and specific use. Although it is often the case, distance matrices are not restricted to being hollow -- that is, they can have non-zero entries on the main diagonal.

Examples and uses

For example, suppose these data are to be analyzed, where pixel euclidean distance is the distance metric.

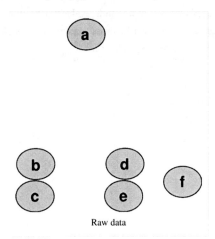

Raw data

The distance matrix would be:

	a	b	c	d	e	f
a	0	184	222	177	216	231
b	184	0	45	123	128	200
c	222	45	0	129	121	203
d	177	123	129	0	46	83
e	216	128	121	46	0	83
f	231	200	203	83	83	0

These data can then be viewed in graphic form as a heat map. In this image, black denotes a distance of 0 and white is maximal distance.

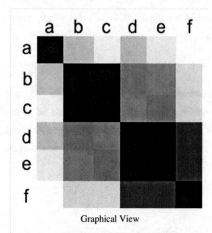

Graphical View

In bioinformatics, distance matrices are used to represent protein structures in a coordinate-independent manner, as well as the pairwise distances between two sequences in sequence space. They are used in structural and sequential alignment, and for the determination of protein structures from NMR or X-ray crystallography.

Sometimes it is more convenient to express data as a similarity matrix.

Distributed Annotation System

The **Distributed Annotation System** (DAS) is used in bioinformatics to share and collate genomic annotation information.[1] [2] [3] It is an open source project.

From the biodas.org [4] web site:

> The distributed annotation system (DAS) is a client-server system in which a single client integrates information from multiple servers. It allows a single machine to gather up genome annotation information from multiple distant web sites, collate the information, and display it to the user in a single view. Little coordination is needed among the various information providers.

Sites and tools currently using DAS

- The DAS registration server [5]
- Ensembl [6] The Ensembl Genome Browser
- UCSC Genome Browser [7]
- WormBase [11]
- FlyBase [8]
- TIGR [9]
- ProServer [10]
- SUPERFAMILY [11]
- InterPro [12]

DAS clients

Name	Description	Links
BioJava DAS Client		
Dasty	A web client for visualizing protein sequence feature information using DAS	[13] [14]
DasView	A server-side Perl application. This tool is mentioned in the original DAS publication, but has subsequently disappeared.	
EnsEMBL	The EnsEMBL Genome Browser. Provides built-in support for DAS	[15]
Geodesic	An stand-alone Java application	[16]
IGB	The Integrated Genome Browser (IGB, pronounced "ig-bee") is an application built upon the GenoViz SDK and Genometry for visualization and exploration of genomes and corresponding annotations from multiple data sources	[17]
Jalview	A multiple sequence alignment editor & viewer	[18]
OmniGene	The user interface is based on the EnsEMBL interface	[19] [20]
SPICE	A browser for the annotations for protein sequences and structures	[21] [22] [23]
STRAP	Underlining sequence features in multiple alignments. Example output: [24]	[25]
TIGR DAS Viewer		[26] ?
WormBase	The WormBase genome Browser. Includes a DAS viewer named DASView	

Edit this table

References

[1] Dowell RD, Jokerst RM, Day A, Eddy SR, Stein L (2001). "The distributed annotation system.". *BMC Bioinformatics* **2**: 7.
     doi:10.1186/1471-2105-2-7. PMC 58584. PMID 11667947.

[2] Finn RD, Stalker JW, Jackson DK, Kulesha E, Clements J, Pettett R (2007). "ProServer: a simple, extensible Perl DAS server.".
     Bioinformatics **23** (12): 1568–70. doi:10.1093/bioinformatics/btl650. PMC 2989875. PMID 17237073.

[3] Jenkinson AM, Albrecht M, Birney E, Blankenburg H, Down T, Finn RD, Hermjakob H, Hubbard TJ, Jimenez RC, Jones P, Kähäri A,
     Kulesha E, Macías JR, Reeves GA, Prlic A (2008). "Integrating biological data - the Distributed Annotation System.". *BMC Bioinformatics*. 9
     Suppl 8: S3. doi:10.1186/1471-2105-9-S8-S3. PMC 2500094. PMID 18673527.

[4] http://www.biodas.org

[5] http://www.dasregistry.org/

[6] http://www.ensembl.org

[7] http://genome.ucsc.edu/

[8] http://www.flybase.org/

[9] http://www.jcvi.org

[10] http://www.sanger.ac.uk/proserver

[11] http://supfam.org/SUPERFAMILY/

[12] http://www.ebi.ac.uk/interpro/

[13] http://www.ebi.ac.uk/dasty/

[14] http://www.ebi.ac.uk/das-srv/uniprot/dasty/index.jsp?id=Q24488

[15] http://www.ensembl.org/

[16] http://www.biodas.org/geodesic/

[17] http://genoviz.sourceforge.net/

[18] http://www.jalview.org/

[19] http://omnigene.sourceforge.net/

[20] http://sourceforge.net/projects/omnigene/

[21] http://www.efamily.org.uk/software/dasclients/spice

[22] http://www.spice-3d.org/

[23] http://www.spice-3d.org/dasobert/

[24] http://www.charite.de/bioinf/strap/exampleOutput.html

[25] http://3d-alignment.eu/

[26] http://www.tigr.org/tdb/DAS/dasview.html

Distributed Annotation System/Clients

This table of client applications for the Distributed Annotation System has been created primarily for inclusion in its parent page. The parent page puts the table in context, and you should go there for more information. The table is provided in a separate page so that it can be transcluded where necessary.

Table follows

Name	Description	Links
BioJava DAS Client		
Dasty	A web client for visualizing protein sequence feature information using DAS	[13] [14]
DasView	A server-side Perl application. This tool is mentioned in the original DAS publication, but has subsequently disappeared.	
EnsEMBL	The EnsEMBL Genome Browser. Provides built-in support for DAS	[15]
Geodesic	An stand-alone Java application	[16]
IGB	The Integrated Genome Browser (IGB, pronounced "ig-bee") is an application built upon the GenoViz SDK and Genometry for visualization and exploration of genomes and corresponding annotations from multiple data sources	[17]
Jalview	A multiple sequence alignment editor & viewer	[18]
OmniGene	The user interface is based on the EnsEMBL interface	[19] [20]
SPICE	A browser for the annotations for protein sequences and structures	[21] [22] [23]
STRAP	Underlining sequence features in multiple alignments. Example output: [24]	[25]
TIGR DAS Viewer		[26] ?
WormBase	The WormBase genome Browser. Includes a DAS viewer named DASView	

DNA barcoding

DNA barcoding is a taxonomic method that uses a short genetic marker in an organism's DNA to identify it as belonging to a particular species. It differs from molecular phylogeny in that the main goal is not to determine classification but to identify an unknown sample in terms of a known classification.[1] Although barcodes are sometimes used in an effort to identify unknown species or assess whether species should be combined or separated,[2] the utility of DNA barcoding for these purposes is subject to debate.[3]

Applications include, for example, identifying plant leaves even when flowers or fruit are not available, identifying insect larvae (which typically have fewer diagnostic characters than adults), identifying the diet of an animal based on stomach contents or faeces,[4] and identifying products in commerce (for example, herbal supplements or wood).[1]

Choice of Locus

A desirable locus for DNA barcoding should be standardized (so that large databases of sequences for that locus can be developed),[5] present in most of the taxa of interest and sequencable without species-specific PCR primers,[5] short enough to be easily sequenced with current technology,[6] and provide a large variation between species yet a relatively small amount of variation within a species.[7]

Although several loci have been suggested, a common set of choices are:

- For animals and many other eukaryotes, the mitochondrial CO1 gene
- For land plants, the concatenation of the rbcL and matK chloroplast genes[5]

Mitochondrial DNA

DNA barcoding is based on a relatively simple concept. Most eukaryote cells contain mitochondria, and mitochondrial DNA (mtDNA) has a relatively fast mutation rate, which results in significant variation in mtDNA sequences between species and, in principle, a comparatively small variance within species. A 658-bp region of the mitochondrial cytochrome c oxidase subunit I (COI) gene was proposed as a potential 'barcode'[8].

However, because all mtDNA genes are maternally inherited (direct evidence for recombination in mtDNA is available in some bivalves such as *Mytilus*[9] but it is suspected that it may be more widespread[10]), any occurrences of hybridization,[11] male-killing microorganisms,[12] cytoplasmic incompatibility-inducing symbionts (e.g., *Wolbachia*[12]), horizontal gene transfer (such as via cellular symbionts[13]), or other "reticulate" evolutionary phenomena in a lineage can lead to misleading results (i.e., it is possible for two different species to share mtDNA,[14] or for one species to have more than one mtDNA sequence exhibited among different individuals).[15][16]

As of 2009, databases of CO1 sequences included at least 620,000 specimens from over 58,000 species of animals.[17]

Identifying flowering plants

Kress *et al.* (2005[11]) suggest that the use of the COI sequence "is not appropriate for most species of plants because of a much slower rate of cytochrome c oxidase I gene evolution in higher plants than in animals". A series of experiments was then conducted to find a more suitable region of the genome for use in the DNA barcoding of flowering plants (or the larger group of land plants).[6] One 2005 proposal was the nuclear internal transcribed spacer region and the plastid trnH-psbA intergenic spacer;[1] other researchers advocated other regions such as matK.[6]

In 2009, a collaboration of a large group of plant DNA barcode researchers proposed two chloroplast genes, rbcL and matK, taken together, as a barcode for plants.[5] Jesse Ausubel, a DNA barcode researcher not involved in that effort, suggested that standardizing on a sequence was the best way to produce a large database of plant sequences, and that time would tell whether this choice would be sufficiently good at distinguishing different plant species.[17]

Vouchered specimens

DNA sequence databases like GenBank contain many sequences that are not tied to vouchered specimens (for example, herbarium specimens, cultured cell lines, or sometimes images). This is problematic in the face of taxonomic issues such as whether several species should be split or combined, or whether past identifications were sound. Therefore, best practice for DNA barcoding is to sequence vouchered specimens.[18] [19]

Origin

The use of nucleotide sequence variations to investigate evolutionary relationships is not a new concept. Carl Woese used sequence differences in ribosomal RNA (rRNA) to discover archaea, which in turn led to the redrawing of the evolutionary tree, and molecular markers (e.g., allozymes, rDNA, and mtDNAvage) have been successfully used in molecular systematics for decades. DNA barcoding provides a standardised method for this process via the use of a short DNA sequence from a particular region of the genome to provide a 'barcode' for identifying species. In 2003, Paul D.N. Hebert from the University of Guelph, Ontario, Canada, proposed the compilation of a public library of DNA barcodes that would be linked to named specimens. This library would "provide a new master key for identifying species, one whose power will rise with increased taxon coverage and with faster, cheaper sequencing".

Case studies

Identification of birds

In an effort to find a correspondence between traditional species boundaries established by taxonomy and those inferred by DNA barcoding, Hebert and co-workers sequenced DNA barcodes of 260 of the 667 bird species that breed in North America (Hebert *et al.* 2004a[20]). They found that every single one of the 260 species had a different COI sequence. 130 species were represented by two or more specimens; in all of these species, COI sequences were either identical or were most similar to sequences of the same species. COI variations between species averaged 7.93%, whereas variation within species averaged 0.43%. In four cases there were deep intraspecific divergences, indicating possible new species. Three out of these four polytypic species are already split into two by some taxonomists. Hebert *et al.*'s (2004a[20]) results reinforce these views and strengthen the case for DNA barcoding. Hebert *et al.* also proposed a standard sequence threshold to define new species, this threshold, the so-called "barcoding gap", was defined as 10 times the mean intraspecific variation for the group under study.

Delimiting cryptic species

The next major study into the efficacy of DNA barcoding was focused on the neotropical skipper butterfly, *Astraptes fulgerator* at the Area Conservacion de Guanacaste (ACG) in north-western Costa Rica. This species was already known as a cryptic species complex, due to subtle morphological differences, as well as an unusually large variety of caterpillar food plants. However, several years would have been required for taxonomists to completely delimit species. Hebert *et al.* (2004b[21]) sequenced the COI gene of 484 specimens from the ACG. This sample included "at least 20 individuals reared from each species of food plant, extremes and intermediates of adult and caterpillar color variation, and representatives" from the three major ecosystems where *Astraptes fulgerator* is found. Hebert *et al.* (2004b[21]) concluded that *Astraptes fulgerator* consists of 10 different species in north-western Costa Rica. These results, however, were subsequently challenged by Brower (2006[22]), who pointed out numerous serious flaws in the analysis, and concluded that the original data could support no more than the possibility of three to seven cryptic taxa rather than ten cryptic species. This highlights that the results of DNA barcoding analyses can be dependent upon the choice of analytical methods used by the investigators, so the process of delimiting cryptic species using

DNA barcodes can be as subjective as any other form of taxonomy.

A more recent example used DNA barcoding for the identification of cryptic species included in the ongoing long-term database of tropical caterpillar life generated by Dan Janzen and Winnie Hallwachs in Costa Rica at the ACG.[23] In 2006 Smith *et al.*[24] examined whether a COI DNA barcode could function as a tool for identification and discovery for the 20 morphospecies of *Belvosia* [25] parasitoid flies (Tachinidae) that have been reared from caterpillars in ACG. Barcoding not only discriminated among all 17 highly host-specific morphospecies of ACG *Belvosia*, but it also suggested that the species count could be as high as 32 by indicating that each of the three generalist species might actually be arrays of highly host-specific cryptic species.

In 2007 Smith *et al.* expanded on these results by barcoding 2,134 flies belonging to what appeared to be the 16 most generalist of the ACG tachinid morphospecies.[26] They encountered 73 mitochondrial lineages separated by an average of 4% sequence divergence and, as these lineages are supported by collateral ecological information, and, where tested, by independent nuclear markers (28S and ITS1), the authors therefore viewed these lineages as provisional species. Each of the 16 initially apparent generalist species were categorized into one of four patterns: (i) a single generalist species, (ii) a pair of morphologically cryptic generalist species, (iii) a complex of specialist species plus a generalist, or (iv) a complex of specialists with no remaining generalist. In sum, there remained 9 generalist species classified among the 73 mitochondrial lineages analyzed.

However, also in 2007, Whitworth *et al.* reported that flies in the related family Calliphoridae could not be discriminated by barcoding.[15] They investigated the performance of barcoding in the fly genus *Protocalliphora*, known to be infected with the endosymbiotic bacteria *Wolbachia*. Assignment of unknown individuals to species was impossible for 60% of the species, and if the technique had been applied, as in the previous study, to identify new species, it would have underestimated the species number in the genus by 75%. They attributed the failure of barcoding to the non-monophyly of many of the species at the mitochondrial level; in one case, individuals from four different species had identical barcodes. The authors went on to state:

> The pattern of *Wolbachia* infection strongly suggests that the lack of within-species monophyly results from introgressive hybridization associated with *Wolbachia* infection. Given that *Wolbachia* is known to infect between 15 and 75% of insect species, we conclude that identification at the species level based on mitochondrial sequence might not be possible for many insects.[15]

Marine biologists have also considered the value of the technique in identifying cryptic and polymorphic species and have suggested that the technique may be helpful when associations with voucher specimens are maintained,[18] though cases of "shared barcodes" (e.g., non-unique) have been documented in cichlid fishes and cowries[16]

Cataloguing ancient life

Lambert *et al.* (2005[27]) examined the possibility of using DNA barcoding to assess the past diversity of the Earth's biota. The COI gene of a group of extinct ratite birds, the moa, were sequenced using 26 subfossil moa bones. As with Hebert's results, each species sequenced had a unique barcode and intraspecific COI sequence variance ranged from 0 to 1.24%. To determine new species, a standard sequence threshold of 2.7% COI sequence difference was set. This value is 10 times the average intraspecies difference of North American birds, which is inconsistent with Hebert's recommendation that the threshold value be based on the group under study. Using this value, the group detected six moa species. In addition, a further standard sequence threshold of 1.24% was also used. This value resulted in 10 moa species which corresponded with the previously known species with one exception. This exception suggested a possible complex of species which was previously unidentified. Given the slow rate of growth and reproduction of moa, it is probable that the interspecies variation is rather low. On the other hand, there is no set value of molecular difference at which populations can be assumed to have irrevocably started to undergo speciation. It is safe to say, however, that the 2.7% COI sequence difference initially used was far too high.

The Moorea Biocode Project

The Moorea Biocode Project [28] is a barcoding initiative to create the first comprehensive inventory of all non-microbial life in a complex tropical ecosystem, the island of Moorea in Tahiti. Supported by a grant from the Gordon and Betty Moore Foundation, the Moorea Biocode Project is a 3-year project that brings together researchers from the Smithsonian Institution, UC Berkeley, France's National Center for Scientific Research (CNRS), and other partners. The outcome of the project is a library of genetic markers and physical identifiers for every species of plant, animal and fungi on the island that will be provided as a publicly available database resource for ecologists and evolutionary biologists around the world.

The software back-end to the Moore Biocode Project is Geneious Pro and two custom-developed plugins from the New Zealand-based company, Biomatters. The Biocode LIMS and Genbank Submission [29] plugins have been made freely available to the public[30] and users of the free Geneious Basic software will be able to access and view the Biocode database upon completion of the project, while a commercial copy of Geneious Pro is required for researchers involved int data creation and analysis.

Criticisms

DNA barcoding has met with spirited reaction from scientists, especially systematists, ranging from enthusiastic endorsement to vociferous opposition.[31] For example, many stress the fact that DNA barcoding does not provide reliable information above the species level, while others indicate that it is inapplicable at the species level, but may still have merit for higher-level groups.[15] Others resent what they see as a gross oversimplification of the science of taxonomy. And, more practically, some suggest that recently diverged species might not be distinguishable on the basis of their COI sequences.[32] Due to various phenomena, Funk & Omland (2003[33]) found that some 23% of animal species are polyphyletic if their mtDNA data are accurate, indicating that using an mtDNA barcode to assign a species name to an animal will be ambiguous or erroneous some 23% of the time (see also Meyer & Paulay, 2005[34]). Studies with insects suggest an equal or even greater error rate, due to the frequent lack of correlation between the mitochondrial genome and the nuclear genome or the lack of a barcoding gap (e.g., Hurst and Jiggins, 2005,[13] Whitworth et al., 2007,[15] Wiemers & Fiedler, 2007[35]). Problems with mtDNA arising from male-killing microorganisms and cytoplasmic incompatibility-inducing symbionts (e.g., Wolbachia)[12] are also particularly common among insects. Given that insects represent over 75% of all known organisms,[36] this suggests that while mtDNA barcoding may work for vertebrates, it may not be effective for the majority of known organisms.

Moritz and Cicero (2004[37]) have questioned the efficacy of DNA barcoding by suggesting that other avian data is inconsistent with Hebert et al.'s interpretation, namely, Johnson and Cicero's (2004[38]) finding that 74% of sister species comparisons fall below the 2.7% threshold suggested by Hebert et al. These criticisms are somewhat misleading considering that, of the 39 species comparisons reported by Johnson and Cicero, only 8 actually use COI data to arrive at their conclusions. Johnson and Cicero (2004[38]) have also claimed to have detected bird species with identical DNA barcodes, however, these 'barcodes' refer to an unpublished 723-bp sequence of ND6 which has never been suggested as a likely candidate for DNA barcoding.

The DNA barcoding debate resembles the phenetics debate of decades gone by. It remains to be seen whether what is now touted as a revolution in taxonomy will eventually go the same way as phenetic approaches, of which was claimed exactly the same decades ago, but which were all but rejected when they failed to live up to overblown expectations.[39] Controversy surrounding DNA barcoding stems not so much from the method itself, but rather from extravagant claims that it will supersede or radically transform traditional taxonomy. Other critics fear a "big science" initiative like barcoding will make funding even more scarce for already underfunded disciplines like taxonomy, but barcoders respond that they compete for funding not with fields like taxonomy, but instead with other big science fields, such as medicine and genomics.[40] Barcoders also maintain that they are being dragged into long-standing debates over the definition of a species and that barcoding is less controversial when viewed primarily as a method of identification, not classification.[1] [19]

The current trend appears to be that DNA barcoding needs to be used alongside traditional taxonomic tools and alternative forms of molecular systematics so that problem cases can be identified and errors detected. Non-cryptic species can generally be resolved by either traditional or molecular taxonomy without ambiguity. However, more difficult cases will only yield to a combination of approaches. And finally, as most of the global biodiversity remains unknown, molecular barcoding can only hint at the existence of new taxa, but not delimit or describe them (DeSalle, 2006;[41] Rubinoff, 2006[42] [43]).

DNA Barcoding Software

Software for DNA barcoding requires integration of a field information management system (FIMS), laboratory information management system (LIMS), sequence analysis tools, workflow tracking to connect field data and laboratory data, database submission tools and pipeline automation for scaling up to eco-system scale projects. Geneious Pro can be used for the sequence analysis components, and the two plugins made freely available through the Moorea Biocode Project, the Biocode LIMS and Genbank Submission [29] plugins handle integration with the FIMS, the LIMS, workflow tracking and database submission.

References

[1] Kress WJ, Wurdack KJ, Zimmer EA, Weigt LA, Janzen DH (June 2005). "Use of DNA barcodes to identify flowering plants". *Proc. Natl. Acad. Sci. U.S.A.* **102** (23): 8369–74. doi:10.1073/pnas.0503123102. PMC 1142120. PMID 15928076. Supporting Information (http://www. pnas.org/cgi/content/full/0503123102/DC1)

[2] Koch, H. 2010. Combining morphology and DNA barcoding resolves the taxonomy of Western Malagasy *Liotrigona* Moure, 1961. *African Invertebrates* **51** (2): 413-421. (http://www.africaninvertebrates.org.za/Koch_2010_51_2_474.aspx) PDF fulltext (http://www.tb1.ethz. ch/PublicationsEO/PDFpapers/Koch_AFRICAN_INVERTEBRATES_2010_51_413-421.pdf)

[3] Seberg O, Petersen G. (2009). Stout, Jane Catherine. ed. "How Many Loci Does it Take to DNA Barcode a Crocus?". *PLoS One* **4** (2): e4598. doi:10.1371/journal.pone.0004598. PMC 2643479. PMID 19240801.

[4] Eeva M Soininen et al. (2009). "Analysing diet of small herbivores: the efficiency of DNA barcoding coupled with high-throughput pyrosequencing for deciphering the composition of complex plant mixtures". *Frontiers in Zoology* **6**: 16. doi:10.1186/1742-9994-6-16. PMC 2736939. PMID 19695081.

[5] CBOL Plant Working Group (August 4, 2009). "A DNA barcode for land plants". *PNAS* **106** (31): 12794–12797. doi:10.1073/pnas.0905845106. PMC 2722355. PMID 19666622.

[6] Kress WJ, Erickson DL (2008). "DNA barcodes: Genes, genomics, and bioinformatics". *PNAS* **105** (8): 2761–2762. doi:10.1073/pnas.0800476105. PMC 2268532. PMID 18287050.

[7] Renaud Lahaye et al. (2008-02-26). "DNA barcoding the floras of biodiversity hotspots". *Proc Natl Acad Sci USA* **105** (8): 2923–2928. doi:10.1073/pnas.0709936105. PMC 2268561. PMID 18258745.

[8] Hebert PDN, Cywinska A, Ball SL, and deWaard JR (7 February 2003). "Biological identifications through DNA barcodes". *Proc. R. Soc. Lond. B* **270** (1512): 313–321. doi:10.1098/rspb.2002.2218. PMC 1691236. PMID 12614582.

[9] Ladoukakis ED, Zouros E (1 July 2001). "Direct evidence for homologous recombination in mussel (*Mytilus galloprovincialis*) mitochondrial DNA" (http://mbe.oxfordjournals.org/cgi/pmidlookup?view=long&pmid=11420358). *Mol. Biol. Evol.* **18** (7): 1168–75. PMID 11420358.

[10] Tsaousis AD, Martin DP, Ladoukakis ED, Posada D, Zouros E (April 2005). "Widespread recombination in published animal mtDNA sequences". *Mol. Biol. Evol.* **22** (4): 925–33. doi:10.1093/molbev/msi084. PMID 15647518.

[11] Melo-Ferreira J, Boursot P, Suchentrunk F, Ferrand N, Alves PC (July 2005). "Invasion from the cold past: extensive introgression of mountain hare (*Lepus timidus*) mitochondrial DNA into three other hare species in northern Iberia". *Mol. Ecol.* **14** (8): 2459–64. doi:10.1111/j.1365-294X.2005.02599.x. PMID 15969727.

[12] Johnstone RA, Hurst GDD (1996). "Maternally inherited male-killing microorganisms may confound interpretation of mitochondrial DNA variability". *Biol. J. Linnaean Soc.* **58** (4): 453–70. doi:10.1111/j.1095-8312.1996.tb01446.x.

[13] Hurst GD, Jiggins FM (August 2005). "Problems with mitochondrial DNA as a marker in population, phylogeographic and phylogenetic studies: the effects of inherited symbionts". *Proc. Biol. Sci.* **272** (1572): 1525–34. doi:10.1098/rspb.2005.3056. PMC 1559843. PMID 16048766.

[14] Croucher PJP, Oxford GS, Searle JB (2004). "Mitochondrial differentiation, introgression and phylogeny of species in the *Tegenaria atrica* group (Araneae: Agelenidae)". *Biological Journal of the Linnean Society* **81**: 79–89. doi:10.1111/j.1095-8312.2004.00280.x.

[15] Whitworth TL, Dawson RD, Magalon H, Baudry E (July 2007). "DNA barcoding cannot reliably identify species of the blowfly genus Protocalliphora (Diptera: Calliphoridae)". *Proc. Biol. Sci.* **274** (1619): 1731–9. doi:10.1098/rspb.2007.0062. PMC 2493573. PMID 17472911.

[16] Meier R (2008). "Ch. 7: DNA sequences in taxonomy: Opportunities and challenges". In Wheeler, Quentin. *The new taxonomy*. Boca Raton: CRC Press. ISBN 0-8493-9088-5.

[17] Jesse H. Ausubel (August 4, 2009). "A botanical macroscope". *Proceedings of the National Academy of Sciences* **106** (31): 12569–70. doi:10.1073/pnas.0906757106. ISSN 00278424. PMC 2722277. PMID 19666620.

[18] Schander C, Willassen E (2005). "What can Biological Barcoding do for Marine Biology?" (http://www.bolinfonet.org/pdf/schander& willassen_2005.pdf) (PDF). *Marine Biology Research* **1** (1): 79–83. doi:10.1080/17451000510018962. .

[19] Scott E. Miller (2007-03-20). "DNA barcoding and the renaissance of taxonomy". *Proc Natl Acad Sci U S A.* **104** (12): 4775–4776. doi:10.1073/pnas.0700466104. PMC 1829212. PMID 17363473.

[20] Hebert PD, Stoeckle MY, Zemlak TS, Francis CM (October 2004). "Identification of Birds through DNA Barcodes". *PLoS Biol.* **2** (10): e312. doi:10.1371/journal.pbio.0020312. PMC 518999. PMID 15455034. Supporting Information (http://biology.plosjournals.org/archive/ 1545-7885/2/10/supinfo/10.1371_journal.pbio.0020312.sg001.pdf)

[21] Hebert PD, Penton EH, Burns JM, Janzen DH, Hallwachs W (October 2004). "Ten species in one: DNA barcoding reveals cryptic species in the neotropical skipper butterfly Astraptes fulgerator". *Proc. Natl. Acad. Sci. U.S.A.* **101** (41): 14812–7. doi:10.1073/pnas.0406166101. PMC 522015. PMID 15465915. Supporting Information (http://www.pnas.org/cgi/content/full/0406166101/DC1)

[22] Brower AVZ (2006). "Problems with DNA barcodes for species delimitation: 'ten species' of *Astraptes fulgerator* reassessed (Lepidoptera: Hesperiidae)". *Systematics and Biodiversity* **4** (2): 127–32. doi:10.1017/S147720000500191X.

[23] "Database homepage for ACG caterpillar (Lepidoptera) rearing databases" (http://janzen.sas.upenn.edu/caterpillars/database.lasso). . Retrieved 2007-08-12.

[24] Smith MA, Woodley NE, Janzen DH, Hallwachs W, Hebert PD (2006). "DNA barcodes reveal cryptic host-specificity within the presumed polyphagous members of a genus of parasitoid flies (Diptera: Tachinidae)". *Proc. Natl. Acad. Sci. U.S.A.* **103** (10): 3657–62. doi:10.1073/pnas.0511318103. PMC 1383497. PMID 16505365.

[25] http://www.itis.gov/servlet/SingleRpt/SingleRpt?search_topic=TSN&search_value=650659

[26] Smith MA, Wood DM, Janzen DH, Hallwachs W, Hebert PD (2007). "DNA barcodes affirm that 16 species of apparently generalist tropical parasitoid flies (Diptera, Tachinidae) are not all generalists". *Proc. Natl. Acad. Sci. U.S.A.* **104** (12): 4967–72. doi:10.1073/pnas.0700050104. PMC 1821123. PMID 17360352.

[27] Lambert DM, Baker A, Huynen L, Haddrath O, Hebert PD, Millar CD (2005). "Is a large-scale DNA-based inventory of ancient life possible?" (http://jhered.oxfordjournals.org/cgi/reprint/96/3/279.pdf) (PDF fulltext). *J. Hered.* **96** (3): 279–84. doi:10.1093/jhered/esi035. PMID 15731217. .

[28] http://www.mooreabiocode.org/

[29] http://software.mooreabiocode.org/index.php?title=Main_Page|Geneious

[30] http://www.bio-itworld.com/2010/11/30/biomatters-moorea-LIMS.html

[31] Rubinoff D, Cameron S, Will K (2006). "A genomic perspective on the shortcomings of mitochondrial DNA for "barcoding" identification". *J. Hered.* **97** (6): 581–94. doi:10.1093/jhered/esl036. PMID 17135463.

[32] Kevin, C.R. Kerr, Mark Y. Stoeckle, Carla J. Dove, Lee A. Weigt, Charles M. Francis & Paul D. N. Hebert. 2006. Comprehensive DNA barcode coverage of North American birds. Molecular Ecology Notes. (OnlineEarly Articles). doi:10.1111/j.1471-8286.2006.01670.x Full text (http://www.blackwell-synergy.com/doi/full/10.1111/j.1471-8286.2006.01670.x)

[33] Funk DJ, Omland KE (2003). "Species-level paraphyly and polyphyly: frequency, causes, and consequences, with insights from animal mitochondrial DNA". *Annu Rev Ecol Syst* **34**: 397–423. doi:10.1146/annurev.ecolsys.34.011802.132421.

[34] Meyer CP, Paulay G (December 2005). "DNA Barcoding: Error Rates Based on Comprehensive Sampling". *PLoS Biol.* **3** (12): e422. doi:10.1371/journal.pbio.0030422. PMC 1287506. PMID 16336051.

[35] Wiemers M, Fiedler K (2007). "Does the DNA barcoding gap exist? – a case study in blue butterflies (Lepidoptera: Lycaenidae)" (http:// www.frontiersinzoology.com/content/4/1/8). *Front. Zool.* **4** (1): 8. doi:10.1186/1742-9994-4-8. PMC 1838910. PMID 17343734. .

[36] (http://www.environment.gov.au/biodiversity/abrs/publications/other/species-numbers/02-exec-summary.html#allspecies)

[37] Moritz C, Cicero C (2004). "DNA Barcoding: Promise and Pitfalls" (http://biology.plosjournals.org/perlserv/?request=get-pdf&file=10. 1371_journal.pbio.0020354-L.pdf) (PDF fulltext). *PLoS Biol.* **2** (10): 1529–31. doi:10.1371/journal.pbio.0020354. PMC 519004. PMID 15486587. .

[38] Johnson NK, Cicero C (May 2004). "New mitochondrial DNA data affirm the importance of Pleistocene speciation in North American birds". *Evolution* **58** (5): 1122–30. PMID 15212392.

[39] Will KW, Mishler BD, Wheeler QD (2005). "The Perils of DNA Barcoding and the Need for Integrative Taxonomy" (http://www.erin. utoronto.ca/~w3bio/bio443/seminar_papers/perils_of_dna_barcoding.pdf) (PDF). *Syst. Biol.* **54** (5): 844–51. doi:10.1080/10635150500354878. PMID 16243769. .

[40] Gregory TR (April 2005). "DNA barcoding does not compete with taxonomy" (http://www.bolinfonet.org/pdf/ DNA_barcoding_does_not_compete_with_taxonomy.pdf) (PDF). *Nature* **434** (7037): 1067. doi:10.1038/4341067b. PMID 15858548. .

[41] Desalle R (October 2006). "Species discovery versus species identification in DNA barcoding efforts: response to Rubinoff". *Conserv. Biol.* **20** (5): 1545–7. doi:10.1111/j.1523-1739.2006.00543.x. PMID 17002772.

[42] Rubinoff D (August 2006). "Utility of mitochondrial DNA barcodes in species conservation". *Conserv. Biol.* **20** (4): 1026–33. doi:10.1111/j.1523-1739.2006.00372.x. PMID 16922219.

[43] Rubinoff D (October 2006). "DNA barcoding evolves into the familiar". *Conserv. Biol.* **20** (5): 1548–9. doi:10.1111/j.1523-1739.2006.00542.x. PMID 17002773.

External links

- Barcode of Life Data Systems (http://www.boldsystems.org/)
- International Barcode of Life (http://www.ibol.org/)
- Consortium for the Barcode of Life (http://www.barcodeoflife.org)
- Fish Barcode of Life Initiative (FISH-BOL) (http://www.fishbol.org)
- All Birds Barcoding Initiative (ABBI) (http://barcoding.si.edu/AllBirds.htm)
- Polar Flora and Fauna Barcoding website (http://www.polarbarcoding.org) (Latest outpost in the Canadian Arctic in the field)
- The Barcode of Life Blog (http://phe.rockefeller.edu/barcode/blog/)
- DNA Barcoding Community Network (http://connect.barcodeoflife.net/)
- Guidelines for non COI gene selection (http://www.barcoding.si.edu/PDF/Guidelines for non-CO1 selection - 4 June.pdf)

DNA binding site

DNA binding sites are a type of binding site found in DNA where other molecules may bind. DNA binding sites are distinct from other binding sites in that (1) they are part of a DNA sequence (e.g. a genome) and (2) they are bound by DNA-binding proteins. DNA binding sites are often associated with specialized proteins known as transcription factors, and are thus linked to transcriptional regulation. The sum of DNA binding sites of a specific transcription factor is referred to as its cistrome. DNA binding sites also encompasses the targets of other proteins, like restriction enzymes, site-specific recombinases (see site-specific recombination) and methyltransferases.[1]

DNA binding sites can be thus defined as short DNA sequences (typically 4 to 30 base pairs long, but up to 200 bp for recombination sites) that are specifically bound by one or more DNA-binding proteins or protein complexes.

Types of DNA binding sites

DNA binding sites can be categorized according to their biological function. Thus, we can distinguish between transcription factor-binding sites, restriction sites and recombination sites. Some authors have proposed that binding sites could also be classified according to their most convenient mode of representation.[2] On the one hand, restriction sites can be generally represented by consensus sequences. This is because they target mostly identical sequences and restriction efficiency decreases abruptly for less similar sequences. On the other hand, DNA binding sites for a given transcription factor are usually all different, with varying degrees of affinity of the transcription factor for the different binding sites. This makes it difficult to accurately represent transcription factor binding sites using consensus sequences, and they are typically represented using position specific frequency matrices (PSFM), which are often graphically depicted using sequence logos. This argument, however, is partly arbitrary. Restriction enzymes, like transcription factors, yield a gradual, though sharp, range of affinities for different sites [3] and are thus also best represented by PSFM. Likewise, site-specific recombinases also show a varied range of affinities for different target sites.[4] [5]

History and main experimental techniques

The existence of something akin to DNA binding sites was suspected from the experiments on the biology of the bacteriophage lambda [6] and the regulation of the Escherichia coli lac operon.[6] DNA binding sites were finally confirmed in both systems [7] [8] [9] with the advent of DNA sequencing techniques. From then on, DNA binding sites for many transcription factors, restriction enzymes and site-specific recombinases have been discovered using a profusion of experimental methods. Historically, the experimental techniques of choice to discover and analyze DNA binding sites have been the DNAse footprinting assay and the Electrophoretic Mobility Shift Assay (EMSA).

However, the development of DNA microarrays and fast sequencing techniques has led to new, massively parallel methods for in-vivo identification of binding sites, such as ChIP-chip and ChIP-Seq.[10] To quantify the binding affinity[11] of proteins and other molecules to specific DNA binding sites the biophysical method Microscale Thermophoresis[12] is used.

Databases

Due to the diverse nature of the experimental techniques used in determining binding sites and to the patchy coverage of most organisms and transcription factors, there is no central database (akin to GenBank at the National Center for Biotechnology Information) for DNA binding sites. Even though NCBI contemplates DNA binding site annotation in its reference sequences (RefSeq), most submissions omit this information. Moreover, due to the limited success of bioinformatics in producing efficient DNA binding site prediction tools (large false positive rates are often associated with in-silico motif discovery / site search methods), there has been no systematic effort to computationally annotate these features in sequenced genomes.

There are, however, several private and public databases devoted to compilation of experimentally reported, and sometimes computationally predicted, binding sites for different transcription factors in different organisms. Below is a non-exhaustive table of available databases:

Name	Organisms	Source	Access	URL
RegTransBase	Prokaryotes	Expert/literature curation	Public	[13]
RegulonDB	Escherichia coli	Expert curation	Public	[14]
PRODORIC	Prokaryotes	Expert curation	Public	[15]
TRANSFAC	Mammals	Expert/literature curation	Private	[16]
TRED	Human, Mouse, Rat	Computer predictions, manual curation	Public	[17]
DBSD	Drosophila species	Literature/Expert curation	Public	[18]

Representation of DNA binding sites

A collection of DNA binding sites, typically referred to as a DNA binding motif, can be represented by a consensus sequence. This representation has the advantage of being compact, but at the expense of disregarding a substantial amount of information.[19] A more accurate way of representing binding sites is through Position Specific Frequency Matrices (PSFM). These matrices give information on the frequency of each base at each position of the DNA binding motif.[2] PSFM are usually conceived with the implicit assumption of positional independence (different positions at the DNA binding site contribute independently to the site function), although this assumption has been disputed for some DNA binding sites.[20] Frequency information in a PSFM can be formally interpreted under the framework of Information Theory,[21] leading to its graphical representation as a sequence logo.

	1	2	3	4	5	6	7	8	9	10	11	12	13	14	15	16
A	1	0	1	5	32	5	35	23	34	14	43	13	34	4	52	3
C	50	1	0	1	5	6	0	4	4	13	3	8	17	51	2	0
G	0	0	54	15	5	5	12	2	7	1	1	3	1	0	1	52
T	5	55	1	35	14	40	9	27	11	28	9	32	4	1	1	1
Sum	56	56	56	56	56	56	56	56	56	56	56	56	56	56	56	56

PSFM for the transcriptional repressor LexA as derived from 56 LexA-binding sites stored in Prodoric. Relative frequencies are obtained by dividing the counts in each cell by the total count (56)

Computational search and discovery of binding sites

In bioinformatics, one can distinguish between two separate problems regarding DNA binding sites: searching for additional members of a known DNA binding motif (the site search problem) and discovering novel DNA binding motifs in collections of functionally related sequences (the sequence motif discovery problem).[22] Many different methods have been proposed to search for binding sites. Most of them rely on the principles of information theory and have available web servers (Yellaboina)(Munch), while other authors have resorted to machine learning methods, such as artificial neural networks.[2] [23] [24] A plethora of algorithms is also available for sequence motif discovery. These methods rely on the hypothesis that a set of sequences share a binding motif for functional reasons. Binding motif discovery methods can be divided roughly into enumerative, deterministic and stochastic.[25] MEME [26] and Consensus [27] are classical examples of deterministic optimization, while the Gibbs sampler [28] is the conventional implementation of a purely stochastic method for DNA binding motif discovery. While enumerative methods often resort to regular expression representation of binding sites, PSFM and their formal treatment under Information Theory methods are the representation of choice for both deterministic and stochastic methods. Recent advances in sequencing have led to the introduction of comparative genomics approaches to DNA binding motif discovery, as exemplified by PhyloGibbs.[29] [30]

More complex methods for binding site search and motif discovery rely on the base stacking and other interactions between DNA bases, but due to the small sample sizes typically available for binding sites in DNA and the need for setting parameters, their efficiency is still questioned. An example of such tool is the ULPB [31][32]

References

[1] Halford E.S, Marko J.F (2004). "How do site-specific DNA-binding proteins find their targets?". *Nucleic Acids Research* **32** (10): 3040–3052. doi:10.1093/nar/gkh624. PMC 434431. PMID 15178741.

[2] Stormo GD (2000). "DNA binding sites: representation and discovery". *Bioinformatics* **16** (1): 16–23. doi:10.1093/bioinformatics/16.1.16. PMID 10812473.

[3] Pingoud A, Jeltsch A (1997). "Recognition and Cleavage of DNA by Type-II Restriction Endonucleases". *European Journal of Biochemistry* **246** (1): 1–22. doi:10.1111/j.1432-1033.1997.t01-6-00001.x. PMID 9210460.

[4] Gyohda A, Komano T (2000). "Purification and characterization of the R64 shufflon-specific recombinase.". *Journal of Bacteriology* **182** (10): 2787–2792. doi:10.1128/JB.182.10.2787-2792.2000. PMC 101987. PMID 10781547.

[5] Birge, E.A (2006). "15: Site Specific Recombination". *Bacterial and Bacteriophage Genetics* (5 ed.). Springer. pp. 463–478. ISBN 978-0-387-23919-4.

[6] Campbell A (1963). "Fine Structure Genetics and its Relation to Function". *Annual Review of Microbiology* **17** (1): 2787–2792. doi:10.1146/annurev.mi.17.100163.000405. PMID 14145311.

[7] Gilbert W, Maxam A (1973). "The nucleotide sequence of the lac operator". *Proceedings of the National Academy of Sciences of the United States of America* **70** (12): 3581–3584. doi:10.1073/pnas.70.12.3581. PMC 427284. PMID 4587255.

[8] Maniatis T, Ptashne M, Barrell BG, Donelson J (1974). "Sequence of a repressor-binding site in the DNA of bacteriophage lambda". *Nature* **250** (465): 394–397. doi:10.1038/250394a0. PMID 4854243.

[9] Nash H. A (1975). "Integrative recombination of bacteriophage lambda DNA in vitro". *Proceedings of the National Academy of Sciences of the United States of America* **72** (3): 1072–1076. doi:10.1073/pnas.72.3.1072. PMC 432468. PMID 1055366.

[10] Elnitski L, Jin VX, Farnham PJ, Jones SJ (2006). "Locating mammalian transcription factor binding sites: a survey of computational and experimental techniques". *Genome Research* **16** (12): 1455–1464. doi:10.1101/gr.4140006. PMID 17053094.

[11] Baaske P, Wienken CJ, Reineck P, Duhr S, Braun D (Feb 2010). "Optical Thermophoresis quantifies Buffer dependence of Aptamer Binding". *Angew. Chem. Int. Ed.* **49** (12): 1–5. doi:10.1002/anie.200903998. PMID 20186894. Lay summary (http://www.physorg.com/news186225693.html) – *Phsyorg.com*.

[12] Wienken CJ et al. (2010). "Protein-binding assays in biological liquids using microscale thermophoresis." (http://www.nature.com/ncomms/journal/v1/n7/full/ncomms1093.html). *Nature Communications* **1** (7): 100. Bibcode 2010NatCo...1E.100W. doi:10.1038/ncomms1093. .

[13] http://regtransbase.lbl.gov/cgi-bin/regtransbase?page=main

[14] http://regulondb.ccg.unam.mx/

[15] http://prodoric.tu-bs.de/

[16] http://www.biobase-international.com/pages/index.php?id=transfac

[17] http://rulai.cshl.edu/cgi-bin/TRED/tred.cgi?process=home

[18] http://rulai.cshl.org/dbsd/index.html

[19] Schneider T.D (2002). "Consensus sequence Zen". *Applied Bioinformatics* **1** (3): 111–119. PMC 1852464. PMID 15130839.

[20] Bulyk M.L, Johnson P.L, Church G.M (2002). "Nucleotides of transcription factor binding sites exert interdependent effects on the binding affinities of transcription factors". *Nucleic Acids Research* **30** (5): 1255–1261. doi:10.1093/nar/30.5.1255. PMC 101241. PMID 11861919.

[21] Schneider TD, Stormo GD, Gold L, Ehrenfeucht A (1986). "Information content of binding sites on nucleotide sequences". *Journal of Molecular Biology* **188** (3): 415–431X. doi:10.1016/0022-2836(86)90165-8. PMID 3525846.

[22] Erill I, O'Neill M.C (2009). "A reexamination of information theory-based methods for DNA-binding site identification". *BMC Bioinformatics* **10** (1): 57. doi:10.1186/1471-2105-10-57. PMC 2680408. PMID 19210776.

[23] Bisant D, Maizel J (1995). "Identification of ribosome binding sites in Escherichia coli using neural network models". *Nucleic Acids Research* **23** (9): 1632–1639. doi:10.1093/nar/23.9.1632. PMC 306908. PMID 7784221.

[24] O'Neill M.C (1991). "Training back-propagation neural networks to define and detect DNA-binding sites". *Nucleic Acids Research* **19** (2): 133–318. doi:10.1093/nar/19.2.313. PMC 333596. PMID 2014171.

[25] Bailey T.L (2008). "Discovering sequence motifs". *Methods in Molecular Biology* **452**: 231–251. doi:10.1007/978-1-60327-159-2_12. PMID 18566768.

[26] Bailey T.L (2002). "Discovering novel sequence motifs with MEME". *Current Protocols in Bioinformatics* **2** (2.4): Unit 2.4. doi:10.1002/0471250953.bi0204s00. PMID 18792935.

[27] Stormo GD, Hartzell GW 3rd (1989). "Identifying protein-binding sites from unaligned DNA fragments". *Proceedings of the National Academy of Sciences of the United States of America* **86** (4): 1183–1187. doi:10.1073/pnas.86.4.1183. PMC 286650. PMID 2919167.

[28] Lawrence CE, Altschul SF, Boguski MS, Liu JS, Neuwald AF, Wootton JC (1993). "Detecting subtle sequence signals: a Gibbs sampling strategy for multiple alignment". *Science* **262** (5131): 208–214. doi:10.1126/science.8211139. PMID 8211139.

[29] Das MK, Dai HK (2007). "A survey of DNA motif finding algorithms". *BMC Bioinformatics* **8** (Suppl 7): S21. doi:10.1186/1471-2105-8-S7-S21. PMC 2099490. PMID 18047721.

[30] Siddharthan R, Siggia ED, van Nimwegen E (2005). "PhyloGibbs: A Gibbs sampling motif finder that incorporates phylogeny". *PLoS Comput Biol* **1** (7): e67. doi:10.1371/journal.pcbi.0010067. PMC 1309704. PMID 16477324.

[31] http://www.ulpb.bham.ac.uk/search.php

[32] Salama RA, Stekel DJ (2010). "Inclusion of neighboring base interdependencies substantially improves genome-wide prokaryotic transcription factor binding site prediction". *Nucleic Acids Research* **38** (12): e135. doi:10.1093/nar/gkq274. PMC 2896541. PMID 20439311.

Further reading

- D'haeseleer P (2006). "What are DNA sequence motifs?". *Nature Biotechnology* **24** (4): 423–425. doi:10.1038/nbt0406-423. PMID 16601727.

- D'haeseleer P (2006). "How does DNA sequence motif discovery work?". *Nature Biotechnology* **24** (8): 959–961. doi:10.1038/nbt0806-959. PMID 16900144.

- Nguyen TT, Androulakis IP (2009). "Recent Advances in the Computational Discovery of Transcription Factor Binding Sites". *Algorithms* **2** (1): 582–605. doi:10.3390/a2010582.

- Merkulova TI, Oshchepkov DY, Ignatieva EV, Ananko EA, Levitsky VG, Vasiliev GV, Klimova NV, Merkulov VM, Kolchanov NA (2007). "Bioinformatical and experimental approaches to investigation of transcription factor binding sites in vertebrate genes". *Biochemistry (Moscow)* **72** (11): 1187–1193. doi:10.1134/S000629790711003X. PMID 18205600.

- Hannenhalli S (2008). "Eukaryotic transcription factor binding sites--modeling and integrative search methods". *Bioinformatics* **24** (11): 1325–1331. doi:10.1093/bioinformatics/btn198. PMID 18426806.

- Bulyk M.L (2003). "Computational prediction of transcription-factor binding site locations". *Genome Biology* **5** (1): 201. doi:10.1186/gb-2003-5-1-201. PMC 395725. PMID 14709165.

- Erill, I., "A gentle introduction to information content in transcription factor binding sites", Eprint (http://research.umbc.edu/~erill/Documents/Introduction_Information_Theory.pdf)

- Schneider, T., "Information Theory Primer", Eprint (http://www.lecb.ncifcrf.gov/~toms/paper/primer)

- Wikiomics:Sequence motifs (http://openwetware.org/wiki/Wikiomics:Sequence_motifs)

- Moss T (2001). *DNA-protein interactions: principles and protocols* (2 ed.). Humana Press. ISBN 9780896036710.

DNA microarray

A **DNA microarray** (also commonly known as gene chip, DNA chip, or biochip) is a collection of microscopic DNA spots attached to a solid surface. Scientists use DNA microarrays to measure the expression levels of large numbers of genes simultaneously or to genotype multiple regions of a genome. Each DNA spot contains picomoles (10^{-12} moles) of a specific DNA sequence, known as *probes* (or *reporters*). These can be a short section of a gene or other DNA element that are used to hybridize a cDNA or cRNA sample (called *target*) under high-stringency conditions. Probe-target hybridization is usually detected and quantified by detection of fluorophore-, silver-, or chemiluminescence-labeled targets to determine relative abundance of nucleic acid sequences in the target. Since an array can contain tens of thousands of probes, a microarray experiment can accomplish many genetic tests in parallel. Therefore arrays have dramatically accelerated many types of investigation.

In standard microarrays, the probes are synthesized and then attached via surface engineering to a solid surface by a covalent bond to a chemical matrix (via epoxy-silane, amino-silane, lysine, polyacrylamide or others). The solid surface can be glass or a silicon chip, in which case they are colloquially known as an *Affy chip* when an Affymetrix chip is used. Other microarray platforms, such as Illumina, use microscopic beads, instead of the large solid support. Alternatively, microarrays can be constructed by the direct synthesis of oligonucleotide probes on solid surfaces. DNA arrays are different from other types of microarray only in that they either measure DNA or use DNA as part of its detection system.

DNA microarrays can be used to measure changes in expression levels, to detect single nucleotide polymorphisms (SNPs), or to genotype or resequence mutant genomes (*see uses and types section*). Microarrays also differ in fabrication, workings, accuracy, efficiency, and cost (*see fabrication section*). Additional factors for microarray experiments are the experimental design and the methods of analyzing the data (*see Bioinformatics section*).

History

Microarray technology evolved from Southern blotting, where fragmented DNA is attached to a substrate and then probed with a known gene or fragment.[1] The first reported use of this approach was the analysis of 378 arrayed lysed bacterial colonies each harboring a different sequence which were assayed in multiple replicas for expression of the genes in multiple normal and tumor tissue.[2] This was expanded to analysis of more than 4000 human sequences with computer driven scanning and image processing for quantitative analysis of the sequences in human colonic tumors and normal tissue [3] and then to comparison of colonic tissues at different genetic risk.[4] The use of a collection of distinct DNAs in arrays for expression profiling was also described in 1987, and the arrayed DNAs were used to identify genes whose expression is modulated by interferon.[5] These early gene arrays were made by spotting cDNAs onto filter paper with a pin-spotting device. The use of miniaturized microarrays for gene expression profiling was first reported in 1995,[6] and a complete eukaryotic genome (*Saccharomyces cerevisiae*) on a microarray was published in 1997.[7]

Principle

The core principle behind microarrays is hybridization between two DNA strands, the property of complementary nucleic acid sequences to specifically pair with each other by forming hydrogen bonds between complementary nucleotide base pairs. A high number of complementary base pairs in a nucleotide sequence means tighter non-covalent bonding between the two strands. After washing off of non-specific bonding sequences, only strongly paired strands will remain hybridized. So fluorescently labeled

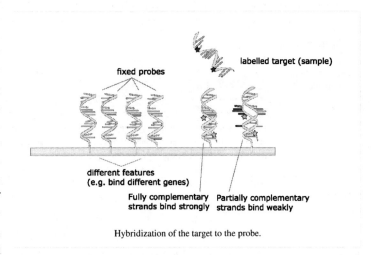

Hybridization of the target to the probe.

target sequences that bind to a probe sequence generate a signal that depends on the strength of the hybridization determined by the number of paired bases, the hybridization conditions (such as temperature), and washing after hybridization. Total strength of the signal, from a spot (feature), depends upon the amount of target sample binding to the probes present on that spot. Microarrays use relative quantization in which the intensity of a feature is compared to the intensity of the same feature under a different condition, and the identity of the feature is known by its position.

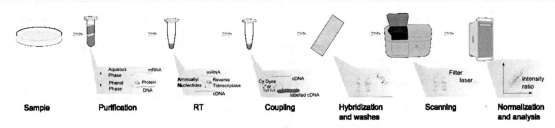

The step required in a microarray experiment.

Uses and types

Many types of array exist and the broadest distinction is whether they are spatially arranged on a surface or on coded beads:

- The traditional solid-phase array is a collection of orderly microscopic "spots", called features, each with a specific probe attached to a solid surface, such as glass, plastic or silicon biochip (commonly known as a *genome chip*, *DNA chip* or *gene array*). Thousands of them can be placed in known locations on a single DNA microarray.

- The alternative bead array is a collection of microscopic polystyrene beads, each with a specific probe and a ratio of two or more dyes, which do not interfere with the fluorescent dyes used on the target sequence.

Two Affymetrix chips. A match is shown at bottom left for size comparison.

DNA microarrays can be used to detect DNA (as in comparative genomic hybridization), or detect RNA (most commonly as cDNA after reverse transcription) that may or may not be translated into proteins. The process of measuring gene expression via cDNA is called expression analysis or expression profiling.

Applications include:

Application or technology	Synopsis
Gene expression profiling	In an mRNA or gene expression profiling experiment the expression levels of thousands of genes are simultaneously monitored to study the effects of certain treatments, diseases, and developmental stages on gene expression. For example, microarray-based gene expression profiling can be used to identify genes whose expression is changed in response to pathogens or other organisms by comparing gene expression in infected to that in uninfected cells or tissues.[8]
Comparative genomic hybridization	Assessing genome content in different cells or closely related organisms.[9] [10]
GeneID	Small microarrays to check IDs of organisms in food and feed (like GMO [11]), mycoplasms in cell culture, or pathogens for disease detection, mostly combining PCR and microarray technology.
Chromatin immunoprecipitation on Chip	DNA sequences bound to a particular protein can be isolated by immunoprecipitating that protein (ChIP), these fragments can be then hybridized to a microarray (such as a tiling array) allowing the determination of protein binding site occupancy throughout the genome. Example protein to immunoprecipitate are histone modifications (H3K27me3, H3K4me2, H3K9me3, etc.), Polycomb-group protein (PRC2:Suz12, PRC1:YY1) and trithorax-group protein (Ash1) to study the epigenetic landscape or RNA Polymerase II to study the transcription landscape.
DamID	Analogously to ChIP, genomic regions bound by a protein of interest can be isolated and used to probe a microarray to determine binding site occupancy. Unlike ChIP, DamID does not require antibodies but makes use of adenine methylation near the protein's binding sites to selectively amplify those regions, introduced by expressing minute amounts of protein of interest fused to bacterial DNA adenine methyltransferase.
SNP detection	Identifying single nucleotide polymorphism among alleles within or between populations.[12] Several applications of microarrays make use of SNP detection, including Genotyping, forensic analysis, measuring predisposition to disease, identifying drug-candidates, evaluating germline mutations in individuals or somatic mutations in cancers, assessing loss of heterozygosity, or genetic linkage analysis.
Alternative splicing detection	An 'exon junction array design uses probes specific to the expected or potential splice sites of predicted exons for a gene. It is of intermediate density, or coverage, to a typical gene expression array (with 1-3 probes per gene) and a genomic tiling array (with hundreds or thousands of probes per gene). It is used to assay the expression of alternative splice forms of a gene. Exon arrays have a different design, employing probes designed to detect each individual exon for known or predicted genes, and can be used for detecting different splicing isoforms.
Fusion genes microarray	A Fusion gene microarray can detect fusion transcripts, e.g. from cancer specimens. The principle behind this is building on the alternative splicing microarrays. The oligo design strategy enables combined measurements of chimeric transcript junctions with exon-wise measurements of individual fusion partners.
Tiling array	Genome tiling arrays consist of overlapping probes designed to densely represent a genomic region of interest, sometimes as large as an entire human chromosome. The purpose is to empirically detect expression of transcripts or alternatively splice forms which may not have been previously known or predicted.

Fabrication

Microarrays can be manufactured in different ways, depending on the number of probes under examination, costs, customization requirements, and the type of scientific question being asked. Arrays may have as few as 10 probes or up to 2.1 million micrometre-scale probes from commercial vendors.

Spotted vs. in situ synthesised arrays

Microarrays can be fabricated using a variety of technologies, including printing with fine-pointed pins onto glass slides, photolithography using pre-made masks, photolithography using dynamic micromirror devices, ink-jet printing,[13] or electrochemistry on microelectrode arrays.

In *spotted microarrays*, the probes are oligonucleotides, cDNA or small fragments of PCR products that correspond to mRNAs. The probes are synthesized prior to deposition on the array surface and are then "spotted" onto glass. A common approach utilizes an array of fine pins or needles controlled by a robotic arm that is dipped into wells containing DNA probes and then depositing each probe at designated locations on the array surface. The resulting "grid" of probes represents the nucleic acid profiles of the prepared probes and is ready to receive complementary cDNA or cRNA "targets" derived from experimental or clinical samples. This technique is used by research scientists around the world to produce "in-house" printed microarrays from their own labs. These arrays may be easily customized for each experiment, because researchers can choose the probes and printing locations on the arrays, synthesize the probes in their own lab (or collaborating facility), and spot the arrays. They can then generate their own labeled samples for hybridization, hybridize the samples to the array, and finally scan the arrays with their own equipment. This provides a relatively low-cost microarray that may be customized for each study, and avoids the costs of purchasing often more expensive commercial arrays that may represent vast numbers of genes that are not of interest to the investigator. Publications exist which indicate in-house spotted microarrays may not provide the same level of sensitivity compared to commercial oligonucleotide arrays,[14] possibly owing to the small batch sizes and reduced printing efficiencies when compared to industrial manufactures of oligo arrays.

In *oligonucleotide microarrays*, the probes are short sequences designed to match parts of the sequence of known or predicted open reading frames. Although oligonucleotide probes are often used in "spotted" microarrays, the term "oligonucleotide array" most often refers to a specific technique of manufacturing. Oligonucleotide arrays are produced by printing short oligonucleotide sequences designed to represent a single gene or family of gene splice-variants by synthesizing this sequence directly onto the array surface instead of depositing intact sequences. Sequences may be longer (60-mer probes such as the Agilent design) or shorter (25-mer probes produced by Affymetrix) depending on the desired purpose; longer probes are more specific to individual target genes, shorter probes may be spotted in higher density across the array and are cheaper to manufacture. One technique used to produce oligonucleotide arrays include photolithographic synthesis (Affymetrix) on a silica substrate where light and light-sensitive masking agents are used to "build" a sequence one nucleotide at a time across the entire array.[15] Each applicable probe is selectively "unmasked" prior to bathing the array in a solution of a single nucleotide, then a masking reaction takes place and the next set of probes are unmasked in preparation for a different nucleotide exposure. After many repetitions, the sequences of every probe become fully constructed. More recently, Maskless Array Synthesis from NimbleGen Systems has combined flexibility with large numbers of probes.[16]

Two-channel vs. one-channel detection

Two-color microarrays or *two-channel microarrays* are typically hybridized with cDNA prepared from two samples to be compared (e.g. diseased tissue versus healthy tissue) and that are labeled with two different fluorophores.[17] Fluorescent dyes commonly used for cDNA labeling include Cy3, which has a fluorescence emission wavelength of 570 nm (corresponding to the green part of the light spectrum), and Cy5 with a fluorescence emission wavelength of 670 nm (corresponding to the red part of the light spectrum). The two Cy-labeled cDNA samples are mixed and hybridized to a single microarray that is then scanned in a microarray scanner to visualize fluorescence of the two fluorophores after excitation with a laser beam of a defined wavelength. Relative intensities of each fluorophore may then be used in ratio-based analysis to identify up-regulated and down-regulated genes.[18]

Oligonucleotide microarrays often carry control probes designed to hybridize with RNA spike-ins. The degree of hybridization between the spike-ins and the control probes is used to normalize the hybridization measurements for the target probes. Although absolute levels of gene expression may be determined in the two-color array in

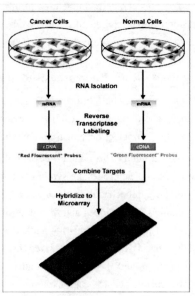

Diagram of typical dual-colour microarray experiment.

rare instances, the relative differences in expression among different spots within a sample and between samples is the preferred method of data analysis for the two-color system. Examples of providers for such microarrays includes Agilent with their Dual-Mode platform, Eppendorf with their DualChip platform for colorimetric Silverquant labeling, and TeleChem International with Arrayit.

In *single-channel microarrays* or *one-color microarrays*, the arrays provide intensity data for each probe or probe set indicating a relative level of hybridization with the labeled target. However, they do not truly indicate abundance levels of a gene but rather relative abundance when compared to other samples or conditions when processed in the same experiment. Each RNA molecule encounters protocol and batch-specific bias during amplification, labeling, and hybridization phases of the experiment making comparisons between genes for the same microarray uninformative. The comparison of two conditions for the same gene requires two separate single-dye hybridizations. Several popular single-channel systems are the Affymetrix "Gene Chip", Illumina "Bead Chip", Agilent single-channel arrays, the Applied Microarrays "CodeLink" arrays, and the Eppendorf "DualChip & Silverquant". One strength of the single-dye system lies in the fact that an aberrant sample cannot affect the raw data derived from other samples, because each array chip is exposed to only one sample (as opposed to a two-color system in which a single low-quality sample may drastically impinge on overall data precision even if the other sample was of high quality). Another benefit is that data are more easily compared to arrays from different experiments so long as batch effects have been accounted for. A drawback to the one-color system is that, when compared to the two-color system, twice as many microarrays are needed to compare samples within an experiment.

Microarrays and bioinformatics

The advent of inexpensive microarray experiments created several specific bioinformatics challenges:

- the multiple levels of replication in experimental design (Experimental design)
- the number of platforms and independent groups and data format (Standardization)
- the treatment of the data (Statistical analysis)
- accuracy and precision (Relation between probe and gene)
- the sheer volume of data and the ability to share it (Data warehousing)

Gene expression values from microarray experiments can be represented as heat maps to visualize the result of data analysis.

Experimental design

Due to the biological complexity of gene expression, the considerations of experimental design that are discussed in the expression profiling article are of critical importance if statistically and biologically valid conclusions are to be drawn from the data.

There are three main elements to consider when designing a microarray experiment. First, replication of the biological samples is essential for drawing conclusions from the experiment. Second, technical replicates (two RNA samples obtained from each experimental unit) help to ensure precision and allow for testing differences within treatment groups. The biological replicates include independent RNA extractions and technical replicates may be two aliquots of the same extraction. Third, spots of each cDNA clone or oligonucleotide are present as replicates (at least duplicates) on the microarray slide, to provide a measure of technical precision in each hybridization. It is critical that information about the sample preparation and handling is discussed, in order to help identify the independent units in the experiment and to avoid inflated estimates of statistical significance.[19]

Standardization

Microarray data is difficult to exchange due to the lack of standardization in platform fabrication, assay protocols, and analysis methods. This presents an interoperability problem in bioinformatics. Various grass-roots open-source projects are trying to ease the exchange and analysis of data produced with non-proprietary chips:

- For example, the "Minimum Information About a Microarray Experiment" (MIAME) checklist helps define the level of detail that should exist and is being adopted by many journals as a requirement for the submission of papers incorporating microarray results. But MIAME does not describe the format for the information, so while many formats can support the MIAME requirements, as of 2007 no format permits verification of complete semantic compliance.
- The "MicroArray Quality Control (MAQC) Project" is being conducted by the US Food and Drug Administration (FDA) to develop standards and quality control metrics which will eventually allow the use of MicroArray data in drug discovery, clinical practice and regulatory decision-making.[20]
- The MGED Society has developed standards for the representation of gene expression experiment results and relevant annotations.

Statistical analysis

Microarray data sets are commonly very large, and analytical precision is influenced by a number of variables. Statistical challenges include taking into account effects of background noise and appropriate normalization of the data. Normalization methods may be suited to specific platforms and, in the case of commercial platforms, the analysis may be proprietary. Algorithms that affect statistical analysis include:

- Image analysis: gridding, spot recognition of the scanned image (segmentation algorithm), removal or marking of poor-quality and low-intensity features (called *flagging*).
- Data processing: background subtraction (based on global or local background), determination of spot intensities and intensity ratios, visualisation of data (e.g. see MA plot), and log-transformation of ratios, global or local normalization of intensity ratios, and segmentation into different copy number regions using step detection algorithms.[21]
- Identification of statistically significant changes: t-test, ANOVA, Bayesian method[22] Mann–Whitney test methods tailored to microarray data sets, which take into account multiple comparisons[23] or cluster analysis.[24] These methods assess statistical power based on the variation present in the data and the number of experimental replicates, and can help minimize Type I and type II errors in the analyses.[25]
- Network-based methods: Statistical methods that take the underlying structure of gene networks into account, representing either associative or causative interactions or dependencies among gene products.[26]

Microarray data may require further processing aimed at reducing the dimensionality of the data to aid comprehension and more focused analysis.[27] Other methods permit analysis of data consisting of a low number of biological or technical replicates; for example, the Local Pooled Error (LPE) test pools standard deviations of genes with similar expression levels in an effort to compensate for insufficient replication.[28]

Relation between probe and gene

The relation between a probe and the mRNA that it is expected to detect is not trivial. Some mRNAs may cross-hybridize probes in the array that are supposed to detect another mRNA. In addition, mRNAs may experience amplification bias that is sequence or molecule-specific. Thirdly, probes that are designed to detect the mRNA of a particular gene may be relying on genomic EST information that is incorrectly associated with that gene.

Data warehousing

Microarray data was found to be more useful when compared to other similar datasets. The sheer volume of data, specialized formats (such as MIAME), and curation efforts associated with the datasets require specialized databases to store the data.

References

[1] Maskos, U; Southern, EM (11 Apr 1992). "Oligonucleotide hybridizations on glass supports: a novel linker for oligonucleotide synthesis and hybridization properties of oligonucleotides synthesised in situ". *Nucleic Acids Res.* (Maskos U, Southern EM.) **20** (7): 1679–84. doi:10.1093/nar/20.7.1679. PMC 312256. PMID 1579459.

[2] Augenlicht LH, Kobrin D (1982). "Cloning and screening of sequences expressed in a mouse colon tumor" (http://cancerres.aacrjournals. org/content/42/3/1088.long). *Cancer Research* **42** (3): 1088–1093. PMID 7059971. .

[3] Augenlicht *et al.*; Wahrman, MZ; Halsey, H; Anderson, L; Taylor, J; Lipkin, M (1987). "Expression of cloned sequences in biopsies of human colonic tissue and in colonic carcinoma cells induced to differentiate in vitro". *Cancer Research* **47** (22): 6017–6021. PMID 3664505.

[4] Augenlicht *et al.* (1991). "Patterns of Gene Expression that Characterize the Colonic Mucosa in Patients at Genetic Risk for Colonic Cancer". *Proceedings National Academy of Sciences* **88** (8): 3286–3289. doi:10.1073/pnas.88.8.3286.

[5] Kulesh DA, Clive DR, Zarlenga DS, Greene JJ (1987). "Identification of interferon-modulated proliferation-related cDNA sequences". *Proc Natl Acad Sci USA* **84** (23): 8453–8457. doi:10.1073/pnas.84.23.8453. PMC 299562. PMID 2446323.

[6] Schena M, Shalon D, Davis RW, Brown PO (1995). "Quantitative monitoring of gene expression patterns with a complementary DNA microarray". *Science* **270** (5235): 467–470. doi:10.1126/science.270.5235.467. PMID 7569999.

[7] Lashkari DA, DeRisi JL, McCusker JH, Namath AF, Gentile C, Hwang SY, Brown PO, Davis RW (1997). "Yeast microarrays for genome wide parallel genetic and gene expression analysis". *Proc Natl Acad Sci USA* **94** (24): 13057–13062. doi:10.1073/pnas.94.24.13057. PMC 24262. PMID 9371799.

[8] Adomas A, Heller G, Olson A, Osborne J, Karlsson M, Nahalkova J, Van Zyl L, Sederoff R, Stenlid J, Finlay R, Asiegbu FO (2008). "Comparative analysis of transcript abundance in Pinus sylvestris after challenge with a saprotrophic, pathogenic or mutualistic fungus". *Tree Physiol.* **28** (6): 885–897. PMID 18381269.

[9] Pollack JR, Perou CM, Alizadeh AA, Eisen MB, Pergamenschikov A, Williams CF, Jeffrey SS, Botstein D, Brown PO (1999). "Genome-wide analysis of DNA copy-number changes using cDNA microarrays". *Nat Genet* **23** (1): 41–46. doi:10.1038/14385. PMID 10471496.

[10] Moran G, Stokes C, Thewes S, Hube B, Coleman DC, Sullivan D (2004). "Comparative genomics using Candida albicans DNA microarrays reveals absence and divergence of virulence-associated genes in Candida dubliniensis". *Microbiology* **150** (Pt 10): 3363–3382. doi:10.1099/mic.0.27221-0. PMID 15470115.

[11] http://bgmo.jrc.ec.europa.eu/home/docs.htm

[12] Hacia JG, Fan JB, Ryder O, Jin L, Edgemon K, Ghandour G, Mayer RA, Sun B, Hsie L, Robbins CM, Brody LC, Wang D, Lander ES, Lipshutz R, Fodor SP, Collins FS (1999). "Determination of ancestral alleles for human single-nucleotide polymorphisms using high-density oligonucleotide arrays". *Nat Genet* **22** (2): 164–167. doi:10.1038/9674. PMID 10369258.

[13] Lausted C et al. (2004). "POSaM: a fast, flexible, open-source, inkjet oligonucleotide synthesizer and microarrayer" (http://genomebiology.com/2004/5/8/R58). *Genome Biology* **5** (8): R58. doi:10.1186/gb-2004-5-8-r58. PMC 507883. PMID 15287980. .

[14] Bammler T, Beyer RP; Consortium, Members of the Toxicogenomics Research; Kerr, X; Jing, LX; Lapidus, S; Lasarev, DA; Paules, RS; Li, JL et al. (2005). "Standardizing global gene expression analysis between laboratories and across platforms". *Nat Methods* **2** (5): 351–356. doi:10.1038/nmeth0605-477a. PMID 15846362.

[15] Pease AC, Solas D, Sullivan EJ, Cronin MT, Holmes CP, Fodor SP. (1994). "Light-generated oligonucleotide arrays for rapid DNA sequence analysis". *PNAS* **91** (11): 5022–5026. doi:10.1073/pnas.91.11.5022. PMC 43922. PMID 8197176.

[16] Nuwaysir EF, Huang W, Albert TJ, Singh J, Nuwaysir K, Pitas A, Richmond T, Gorski T, Berg JP, Ballin J, McCormick M, Norton J, Pollock T, Sumwalt T, Butcher L, Porter D, Molla M, Hall C, Blattner F, Sussman MR, Wallace RL, Cerrina F, Green RD. (2002). "Gene Expression Analysis Using Oligonucleotide Arrays Produced by Maskless Photolithography". *Genome Res* **12** (11): 1749–1755. doi:10.1101/gr.362402. PMC 187555. PMID 12421762.

[17] Shalon D, Smith SJ, Brown PO (1996). "A DNA microarray system for analyzing complex DNA samples using two-color fluorescent probe hybridization". *Genome Res* **6** (7): 639–645. doi:10.1101/gr.6.7.639. PMID 8796352.

[18] Tang T, François N, Glatigny A, Agier N, Mucchielli MH, Aggerbeck L, Delacroix H (2007). "Expression ratio evaluation in two-colour microarray experiments is significantly improved by correcting image misalignment". *Bioinformatics* **23** (20): 2686–2691. doi:10.1093/bioinformatics/btm399. PMID 17698492.

[19] Churchill, GA (2002). "Fundamentals of experimental design for cDNA microarrays" (http://www.vmrf.org/research-websites/gcf/Forms/Churchill.pdf) (– ^Scholar search (http://scholar.google.co.uk/scholar?hl=en&lr=&q=intitle:Fundamentals+of+experimental+design+for+cDNA+microarrays&as_publication=Nature+genetics+suppliment&as_ylo=2002&as_yhi=2002&btnG=Search)). *Nature genetics supplement* **32**: 490–5. doi:10.1038/ng1031. PMID 12454643. .

[20] NCTR Center for Toxicoinformatics - MAQC Project (http://www.fda.gov/nctr/science/centers/toxicoinformatics/maqc/)

[21] Little, M.A.; Jones, N.S. (2011). "Generalized Methods and Solvers for Piecewise Constant Signals: Part I" (http://www.maxlittle.net/publications/pwc_filtering_arxiv.pdf). *Proc. Roy. Soc. A.*. .

[22] Ben-Gal I., Shani A., Gohr A., Grau J., Arviv S., Shmilovici A., Posch S. and Grosse I. (2005), Identification of Transcription Factor Binding Sites with Variable-order Bayesian Networks, Bioinformatics,vol. 21, no. 11, 2657-2666. Available at http://bioinformatics.oxfordjournals.org/content/21/11/2657.full.pdf?keytype=ref&ijkey=KkxNhRdTSfvtvXY

[23] Yuk Fai Leung and Duccio Cavalieri, Fundamentals of cDNA microarray data analysis. TRENDS in Genetics Vol.19 No.11 November 2003

[24] Priness I., Maimon O., Ben-Gal I. (2007). [Available at http://www.biomedcentral.com/1471-2105/8/111 "Evaluation of gene-expression clustering via mutual information distance measure"]. *BMC Bioinformatics* **8** (1): 111. doi:10.1186/1471-2105-8-111. PMC 1858704. PMID 17397530. Available at .

[25] Wei C, Li J, Bumgarner RE. (2004). "Sample size for detecting differentially expressed genes in microarray experiments". *BMC Genomics* **5**: 87. doi:10.1186/1471-2164-5-87. PMC 533874. PMID 15533245.

[26] Emmert-Streib, F. and Dehmer, M. (2008). *Analysis of Microarray Data A Network-Based Approach*. Wiley-VCH. ISBN 3-527-31822-4.

[27] Wouters L, Göhlmann HW, Bijnens L, Kass SU, Molenberghs G, Lewi PJ (2003). "Graphical exploration of gene expression data: a comparative study of three multivariate methods". *Biometrics* **59** (4): 1131–1139. doi:10.1111/j.0006-341X.2003.00130.x. PMID 14969494.

[28] Jain N, Thatte J, Braciale T, Ley K, O'Connell M, Lee JK (2003). "Local-pooled-error test for identifying differentially expressed genes with a small number of replicated microarrays". *Bioinformatics* **19** (15): 1945–1951. doi:10.1093/bioinformatics/btg264. PMID 14555628.

Glossary

- An **Array** or **slide** is a collection of *features* spatially arranged in a two dimensional grid, arranged in columns and rows.
- **Block** or **subarray**: a group of spots, typically made in one print round; several subarrays/blocks form an array.
- **Case/control**: an experimental design paradigm especially suited to the two-colour array system, in which a condition chosen as control (such as healthy tissue or state) is compared to an altered condition (such as a diseased tissue or state).
- **Channel**: the fluorescence output recorded in the scanner for an individual fluorophore and can even be ultraviolet.
- **Dye flip** or **Dye swap** or **Fluor reversal**: reciprocal labelling of DNA targets with the two dyes to account for dye bias in experiments.
- **Scanner**: an instrument used to detect and quantify the intensity of fluorescence of spots on a microarray slide, by selectively exciting fluorophores with a laser and measuring the fluorescence with a filter (optics) photomultiplier system.
- **Spot** or **feature**: a small area on an array slide that contains picomoles of specific DNA samples.
- For other relevant terms see:

    Glossary of gene expression terms

    Protocol (natural sciences)

External links

- Many important links can be found at the Open Directory Project
    - Gene Expression (http://www.dmoz.org/Science/Biology/Biochemistry_and_Molecular_Biology/ Gene_Expression/) at the Open Directory Project
    - Micro Scale Products and Services for Biochemistry and Molecular Biology (http://www.dmoz.org/ Science/Biology/Biochemistry_and_Molecular_Biology/Products_and_Services/Micro_Scale/) at the Open Directory Project
    - Products and Services for Gene Expression (http://www.dmoz.org/Science/Biology/ Biochemistry_and_Molecular_Biology/Gene_Expression/Products_and_Services/) at the Open Directory Project
    - Online Services for Gene Expression Analysis (http://www.dmoz.org/Science/Biology/Bioinformatics/ Online_Services/Gene_Expression_and_Regulation/) at the Open Directory Project
- PLoS Biology Primer: Microarray Analysis (http://biology.plosjournals.org/perlserv/?request=get-document& doi=10.1371/journal.pbio.0000015)
- Rundown of microarray technology (http://www.genome.gov/page.cfm?pageID=10000533)
- ArrayMining.net (http://www.arraymining.net) - a free web-server for online microarray analysis
- CLASSIFI (http://pathcuric1.swmed.edu/pathdb/classifi.html) - Gene Ontology-based gene cluster classification resource
- Microarray - How does it work? (http://www.unsolvedmysteries.oregonstate.edu/microarray_07)
- What Are DNA Microarrays (http://www.bioinformaticstutorials.com/?p=8) - A Non-Biologists Introduction to Microarrays
- Microarray data processing using Self-Organizing Maps tutorial: Part 1 (http://blog.peltarion.com/2007/04/ 10/the-self-organized-gene-part-1) Part 2 (http://blog.peltarion.com/2007/06/13/ the-self-organized-gene-part-2)
- PNAS Commentary: Discovery of Principles of Nature from Mathematical Modeling of DNA Microarray Data (http://www.pnas.org/content/103/44/16063.extract)

DNA microarray experiment

This is an example of a **DNA microarray experiment**, detailing a particular case to better explain DNA microarray experiments, while enumerating possible alternatives.

1. The two samples to be compared (pairwise comparison) are grown/acquired. In this example treated sample (case) and untreated sample (control).

2. The nucleic acid of interest is purified: this can be all RNA for expression profiling, DNA for comparative hybridization, or DNA/RNA bound to a particular protein which is immunoprecipitated (ChIP-on-chip) for epigenetic or regulation studies. In this example total RNA is isolated (total as it is nuclear and cytoplasmic) by Guanidinium thiocyanate-phenol-chloroform extraction (e.g. Trizol) which isolates most RNA (whereas column methods have a cut off of 200 nucleotides) and if done correctly has a better purity.

3. The purified RNA is analysed for quality (by capillary electrophoresis) and quantity (by using a spectrophotometer like NanoPhotometer^{TM} or nanodrop): if enough material (>1μg) is present the experiment can continue.

4. The labelled product is generated via reverse transcription and sometimes with an optional PCR amplification. The RNA is reverse transcribed with either polyT primers which amplify only mRNA or random primers which amplify all RNA which is mostly rRNA, miRNA microarray ligate an oligonucleotide to the purified small RNA (isolated with a fractionator) and then RT and amplified. The

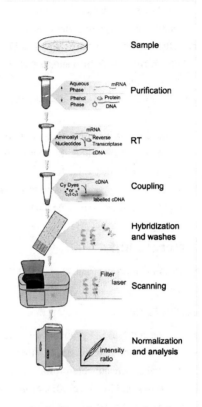

steps involved in a microarray experiment (some steps omitted)

label is added either in the RT step or in an additional step after amplification if present. The sense that is labelled depends on the microarray, which means that if the label is added with the RT mix, the cDNA is on the template strand while the probe is on the sense strand (unless they are negative controls). The label is typically fluorescent; only one machine uses radiolabels. The labelling can be direct (not used) or indirect which requires a coupling stage. The coupling stage can occur before hybridization (two-channel arrays) using aminoallyl-UTP and NHS amino-reactive dyes (like cyanine dyes) or after (single-channel arrays) using biotin and labelled streptavin. The modified nucleotides (typically a 1 aaUTP: 4 TTP mix) are added enzymatically at a lower rate compared to normal nucleotides, typically resulting in 1 every 60 bases. The aaDNA is then purified with a column (using solution containing phosphate buffer as Tris contains amine groups). After purification, labelling efficiency (Frequency of Incorporation (FOI)) of each sample has to be measured with a small volume photometer (like the NanoPhotometer$^{TM[1]}$) to ensure equal amounts of dye incorporation to the samples to be compared. The aminoallyl group is an amine group on a long linker attached to the nucleobase, which reacts with a reactive dye. A dye flip is a type of replicate done to remove any dye effects in two-channel dyes, in one slide one same is labeled with Cy3 the other with Cy5, this is reversed in a different slide. In this example, in the presence of aminoallyl-UTP added in the RT mix.

5. The labeled samples are then mixed with a propriety hybridization solution which may contain SDS, SSC, dextran sulfate, a blocking agent (such as COT1 DNA, salmon sperm DNA, calf thymus DNA, PolyA or PolyT), Denhardt's solution and formamine.

6. This mix is denatured and added to a pin hole in a microarray, which can be a gene chip (holes in the back) or a glass microarray which is bound by a cover, called a mixer, containing two pinholes and sealed with the slide at the perimeter.

7. The holes are sealed and the microarray hybridized, either in a hyb oven, where the microarray is mixed by rotation, or in a mixer, where the microarray is mixed by alternating pressure at the pinholes.

8. After an overnight hybridization, all nonspecific binding is washed off (SDS and SSC).

9. The microarray is dried and scanned in a special machine where a laser excites the dye and a detector measures its emission.

10. The image is gridded with a template and the intensities of the features (several pixels make a feature) are quantified.

11. The raw data is normalized, the simplest way is to subtract the background intensity and then divide the intensities making either the total intensity of the features on each channel equal or the intensities of a reference gene and then the t-value for all the intensities is calculated. More sophisticated methods include z-ratio, loess and lowess regression and RMA (robust multichip analysis) for Affymetrix chips (single-channel, silicon chip, in situ synthesised short oligonucleotides).

External links

- DNA microarray virtual experiment [2]

References

- Gibson and Muse, A primer of genome science etc ISBN 0-87893-232-1
- Chomczynski, P. & Sacchi, N. Single-step method of RNA isolation by acid guanidinium thiocyanate-phenol-chloroform extraction:Twenty-something years on. Nature Prot. 1, 581–585 (2006) [3].
- Sambrook and Russell (2001). Molecular Cloning: A Laboratory Manual, 3rd edition, Cold Spring Harbor Laboratory Press.

Lab protocols found on microarray labs: [4][5] [6][7]

[1] Kartha, R. Spectrophotometric Quantification of Nano- and Standard-Volume Samples, (2008, October 7), American Biotechnology Laboratory, http://www.iscpubs.com/Media/PublishingTitles/b0608kar.pdf
[2] http://learn.genetics.utah.edu/content/labs/microarray/
[3] http://dx.doi.org/10.1038/nprot.2006.83
[4] http://www.microarrays.ca/support/proto.html
[5] http://www.daf.jhmi.edu/microarray/protocols.htm
[6] http://dms.dartmouth.edu/dgml/background/
[7] http://www.hpcgg.org/Microarrays/DNAMicroarray/resources.jsp#A

Peak calling

Peak calling is a computational method used to identify areas in a genome that have been enriched with aligned reads as a consequence of performing a Chip-Sequencing experiment. These areas are those where a protein interacts with DNA.[1] When the protein is a transcription factor, the enriched area is its transcription factor binding site (TFBS).

References

[1] Valouev A, *et al.* (September 2008). "Genome-wide analysis of transcription factor binding sites based on ChIP-Seq data" (http://www. nature.com/nmeth/journal/v6/n11s/full/nmeth.1371.html). *Nature Methods* **6** (5): 829–834. doi:10.1038/nmeth.1246. PMC 2917543. PMID 19160518. .

DNA sequencing theory

DNA sequencing theory is the broad body of work that attempts to lay analytical foundations for DNA sequencing. The practical aspects revolve around designing and optimizing sequencing projects (known as "strategic genomics"), predicting project performance, troubleshooting experimental results, characterizing factors such as sequence bias and the effects of software processing algorithms, and comparing various sequencing methods to one another. In this sense, it could be considered a branch of systems engineering or operations research. The permanent archive of work is primarily mathematical, although numerical calculations are often conducted for particular problems too. DNA sequencing theory addresses *physical processes* related to sequencing DNA and should not be confused with theories of analyzing resultant DNA sequences, e.g. sequence alignment. Publications[1] sometimes do not make a careful distinction, but the latter are primarily concerned with algorithmic issues.

Sequencing as a covering problem

All mainstream methods of DNA sequencing rely on reading small fragments of DNA and subsequently reconstructing these data to infer the original DNA target, either via assembly or alignment to a reference. The abstraction common to these methods is that of a mathematical covering problem.[2] For example, one can imagine a line segment representing the target and a subsequent process where smaller segments are "dropped" onto random locations of the target. The target is considered "sequenced" when adequate coverage accumulates, for example when no gaps remain.

The abstract properties of covering have been studied by mathematicians for over a century.[3] However, direct application of these results has not generally been possible. Closed-form mathematical solutions, especially for probability distributions, often cannot be readily evaluated. That is, they involve inordinately large amounts of computer time for parameters characteristic of DNA sequencing. Stevens' configuration is one such example.[4] Results obtained from the perspective of pure mathematics also do not account for factors that are actually important in sequencing, for instance detectable overlap in sequencing fragments, double-stranding, edge-effects, and target multiplicity. Consequently, development of sequencing theory has proceeded more according to the philosophy of applied mathematics. In particular, it has been problem-focused and makes expedient use of approximations, simulations, etc.

Early uses derived from elementary probability theory

The earliest result was actually borrowed directly from elementary probability theory. If we model the above process and take L and G as the fragment length and target length, respectively, then the probability of "covering" any given location on the target *with one particular fragment* is L/G. Note that this presumes $L \ll G$, which is valid for many, though not all sequencing scenarios. Utilizing concepts from the binomial distribution,[5] it can then be shown that the probability that the location is covered by at least one of N fragments is

$$P = 1 - \left[1 - \frac{L}{G}\right]^N.$$

This equation was first used to characterize plasmid libraries,[6] but is often more useful in a modified form. For most projects $N \gg 1$, so that, to a good degree of approximation

$$\left[1 - \frac{L}{G}\right]^N \sim \exp(-NL/G),$$

where $R = NL/G$ is called the *redundancy*. Note the significance of redundancy as representing the average number of times a position is covered with fragments. Note also that in considering the covering process over all positions in the target, this probability is identical to the expected value of the random variable C, which represents the fraction of the target coverage. The final result,

$$E\langle C \rangle = 1 - e^{-R},$$

remains in widespread use as a "back of the envelope" estimator and predicts that coverage for all projects evolves along a universal curve that is a function only of the redundancy.

Lander-Waterman theory

In 1988, Eric Lander and Michael Waterman published an important paper[7] examining the covering problem from the standpoint of gaps. Although they focused on the so-called mapping problem, the abstraction to sequencing is much the same. They furnished a number of useful results that were adopted as the standard theory from the earliest days of "large-scale" genome sequencing.[8] Their model was also used in designing the Human Genome Project and continues to play an important role in DNA sequencing.

Ultimately, the main goal of a sequencing project is to close all gaps, so the "gap perspective" was a logical basis of developing a sequencing model. One of the more frequently used results from this model is the expected number of contigs, given the number of fragments sequenced. If one neglects the amount of sequence that is essentially "wasted" by having to detect overlaps, their theory yields

$$E\langle contigs \rangle = Ne^{-R}.$$

In 1995, Roach[9] published improvements to this theory, enabling it to be applied to sequencing projects in which the goal was to completely sequence a target genome. Wendl and Waterston[10] confirmed, based on Stevens' method,[4] that both models produced similar results when the number of contigs was substantial, such as in low coverage mapping or sequencing projects. As sequencing projects ramped up in the 1990s, and projects approached completion, low coverage approximations became inadequate, and the exact model of Roach was necessary. However, as the cost of sequencing dropped, parameters of sequencing projects became easier to directly test empirically, and interest and funding for strategic genomics diminished

The basic ideas of Lander-Waterman theory led to a number of additional results for particular variations in mapping techniques.[11] [12] [13] However, technological advancements have rendered mapping theories largely obsolete except in organisms other than highly studied model organisms (e.g., yeast, flies, mice, and humans).

Parking strategy

The parking strategy for sequencing resembles the process of parking cars along a curb. Each car is a sequenced clone, and the curb is the genomic target.[14] Each clone sequenced is screened to ensure that subsequently sequenced clones do not overlap any previously sequenced clone. No sequencing effort is redundant in this strategy. However, much like the gaps between parked cars, unsequenced gaps less than the length of a clone accumulate between sequenced clones. There can be considerable cost to close such gaps.

Pairwise End-sequencing

In 1995, Roach et al.[15] proposed and demonstrated through simulations a generalization of a set of strategies explored earlier by Edwards and Caskey.[16] This whole-genome sequencing method became immensely popular as it was championed by Celera and used to sequenced several model organisms before Celera applied it to the human genome. Today, most sequencing projects employ this strategy, often called paired end sequencing.

Recent advancements

The physical processes and protocols of DNA sequencing have continued to evolve, largely driven by advancements in bio-chemical methods, hardware, and automation techniques. There is now a wide range of problems that DNA sequencing has made in-roads into, including metagenomics and medical (cancer) sequencing. There are important factors in these scenarios that classical theory does not account for. Recent work has begun to focus on resolving the effects of some of these issues. The level of mathematics becomes commensurately more sophisticated.

Multiplicity

Biologists have developed methods to filter highly-repetitive, essentially un-sequenceable regions of genomes. These procedures are important for organisms whose genomes consist mostly of such DNA, for example corn. They yield multitudes of small islands of sequenceable DNA products. Wendl and Barbazuk[17] proposed an extension to Lander-Waterman Theory to account for "gaps" in the target due to filtering and the so-called "edge-effect". The latter is a position-specific sampling bias, for example the terminal base position has only a $1/G$ chance of being covered, as opposed to L/G for interior positions. For $R < 1$, classical Lander-Waterman Theory still gives good predictions, but dynamics change for higher redundancies.

Small versus large fragments

Modern sequencing methods usually sequence both ends of a larger fragment, which provides linking information for *de novo* assembly and improved probabilities for alignment to reference sequence. Researchers generally believe that longer lengths of data (read lengths) enhance performance for very large DNA targets, an idea consistent with predictions from distribution models.[18] However, Wendl[19] showed that smaller fragments provide better coverage on small, linear targets because they reduce the edge effect in linear molecules. These findings have implications for sequencing the products of DNA filtering procedures. Read-pairing and fragment size evidently have negligible influence for large, whole-genome class targets.

Diploid sequencing

Sequencing is emerging as an important tool in medicine, for example in cancer research. Here, the ability to detect heterozygous mutations is important and this can only be done if the sequence of the diploid genome is obtained. In the pioneering efforts to sequence individuals, Levy *et al.*[20] and Wheeler *et al.*,[21] who sequenced Craig Venter and Jim Watson, respectively, outlined models for covering both alleles in a genome. Wendl and Wilson[22] followed with a more general theory that allowed for an arbitrary number of coverings of each allele and arbitrary ploidy. These results point to the general conclusion that the amount of data needed for such projects is significantly higher than for traditional haploid projects.

Limitations

DNA sequencing theories often invoke the assumption that certain random variables in a model are independently and identically distributed. For example, in Lander-Waterman Theory, a sequenced fragment is presumed to have the same probability of covering each region of a genome and all fragments are assumed to be independent of one another. In actuality, sequencing projects are subject to various types of bias, including differences of how well regions can be cloned, sequencing anomalies, biases in the target sequence (which is *not* random), and software-dependent errors and biases. In general, theory will agree well with observation up to the point that enough data have been generated to expose latent biases.[22] The kinds of biases related to the underlying target sequence are particularly difficult to model, since the sequence itself may not be known *a priori*. This presents a type of "chicken and egg" closure problem.

Academic status

Sequencing theory is based on elements of mathematics, biology, and systems engineering, so it is highly interdisciplinary. Although many universities now have programs in computational biology, there does not yet seem to be a strong focus at the graduate level on this topic. Academic contributions have mainly been limited to a small number of PhD dissertations.[23]

References

[1] Waterman, M.S. (1995). *Introduction to Computational Biology*. Chapman and Hall/CRC: Boca Raton. ISBN 0412993910.

[2] Hall, P. (1988). *Introduction to the Theory of Coverage Processes*. Wiley: New York. ISBN 0471857025.

[3] Solomon, H. (1978). *Geometric Probability*. Society for Industrial and Applied Mathematics: Philadelphia. ISBN 0898710251.

[4] Stevens, W.L. (1939). "Solution to a Geometrical Problem in Probability". *Annals of Eugenics* 9: 315–320.

[5] Feller, W. (1968). *Introduction to Probability Theory and Its Applications (3rd Ed.)*. Wiley.

[6] Clarke, L. and Carbon, J. (1976). "A Colony Bank Containing Synthetic Col-El Hybrid Plasmids Representative of the Entire E. coli Genome". *Cell* 9 (1): 91–99. doi:10.1016/0092-8674(76)90055-6. PMID 788919.

[7] Lander, E.S. and Waterman, M.S. (1988). "Genomic Mapping by Fingerprinting Random Clones: A Mathematical Analysis". *Genomics* 2 (3): 231–239. doi:10.1016/0888-7543(88)90007-9. PMID 3294162.

[8] Fleischmann, R.D. et al. (1995). "Whole-Genome Random Sequencing and Assembly of Haemophilus influenzae Rd". *Science* 269 (5223): 496–512. Bibcode 1995Sci...269..496F. doi:10.1126/science.7542800. PMID 7542800.

[9] Roach, J.C. (1995). "Random Subcloning". *Genome Research* 5 (5): 464–473. doi:10.1101/gr.5.5.464. PMID 8808467.

[10] Wendl, M.C. and Waterston, R.H. (2002). "Generalized Gap Model for Bacterial Artificial Chromosome Clone Fingerprint Mapping and Shotgun Sequencing". *Genome Research* 12 (12): 1943–1949. doi:10.1101/gr.655102. PMC 187573. PMID 12466299.

[11] Arratia, R. et al. (1991). "Genomic Mapping by Anchoring Random Clones: A Mathematical Analysis". *Genomics* 11 (4): 806–827. doi:10.1016/0888-7543(91)90004-X. PMID 1783390.

[12] Port, E. et al. (1995). "Genomic Mapping by End-Characterized Random Clones: A Mathematical Analysis". *Genomics* 26 (1): 84–100. doi:10.1016/0888-7543(95)80086-2. PMID 7782090.

[13] Zhang, M.Q. and Marr, T.G. (1993). "Genome Mapping by Nonrandom Anchoring: A Discrete Theoretical Analysis". *Proceedings of the National Academy of Sciences* 90 (2): 600–604. Bibcode 1993PNAS...90..600Z. doi:10.1073/pnas.90.2.600.

[14] Roach, J. C. et al. (2000). "Parking strategies for genome sequencing". *Genome Research* 10 (7): 1020–1030. doi:10.1101/gr.10.7.1020. PMC 310895. PMID 10899151.

[15] Roach, J. C. et al. (1995). "Pairwise end sequencing: a unified approach to genomic mapping and sequencing". *Genomics* 26 (2): 345–353. doi:10.1016/0888-7543(95)80219-C. PMID 7601461.

[16] Edwards, A., and Caskey, T. (1991). *Closure strategies for random DNA sequencing*. 3. A Companion to Methods in Enzymology. pp. 41–47.

[17] Wendl, M.C. and Barbazuk, W.B. (2005). "Extension of Lander-Waterman Theory for Sequencing Filtered DNA Libraries". *BMC Bioinformatics* 6: article 245. doi:10.1186/1471-2105-6-245. PMC 1280921. PMID 16216129.

[18] Wendl, M.C. (2006). "Occupancy Modeling of Coverage Distribution for Whole Genome Shotgun DNA Sequencing". *Bulletin of Mathematical Biology* 68 (1): 179–196. doi:10.1007/s11538-005-9021-4. PMID 16794926.

[19] Wendl, M.C. (2006). "A General Coverage Theory for Shotgun DNA Sequencing". *Journal of Computational Biology* 13 (6): 1177–1196. doi:10.1089/cmb.2006.13.1177. PMID 16901236.

[20] Levy, S. et al. (2007). "The Diploid Genome Sequence of an Individual Human". *PLoS Biology* **5** (10): article e254.
    doi:10.1371/journal.pbio.0050254. PMC 1964779. PMID 17803354.

[21] Wheeler, D.A. et al. (2008). "The Complete Genome of an Individual by Massively Parallel DNA Sequencing". *Nature* **452** (7189):
    872–876. Bibcode 2008Natur.452..872W. doi:10.1038/nature06884. PMID 18421352.

[22] Wendl, M.C. and Wilson, R.K. (2008). "Aspects of Coverage in Medical DNA Sequencing". *BMC Bioinformatics* **9**: article 239.
    doi:10.1186/1471-2105-9-239. PMC 2430974. PMID 18485222.

[23] Roach, J.C. (1998). *Random Subcloning, Pairwise End Sequencing, and the Molecular Evolution of the Vertebrate Trypsinogens*. PhD
    Dissertation, University of Washington.

Docking (molecular)

Docking glossary
• **Receptor** or **host** or **lock** – The "receiving" molecule, most commonly a protein or other biopolymer.
• **Ligand** or **guest** or **key** – The complementary partner molecule which binds to the receptor. Ligands are most often small molecules but could also be another biopolymer.
• **Docking** – Computational simulation of a candidate ligand binding to a receptor.
• **Binding mode** – The orientation of the ligand relative to the receptor as well as the conformation of the ligand and receptor when bound to each other.
• **Pose** – A candidate binding mode.
• **Scoring** – The process of evaluating a particular pose by counting the number of favorable intermolecular interactions such as hydrogen bonds and hydrophobic contacts.
• **Ranking** – The process of classifying which ligands are most likely to interact favorably to a particular receptor based on the predicted free-energy of binding.
[1]

In the field of molecular modeling, **docking** is a method which predicts the preferred orientation of one molecule to a second when bound to each other to form a stable complex.[2] Knowledge of the preferred orientation in turn may be used to predict the strength of association or binding affinity between two molecules using for example scoring functions.

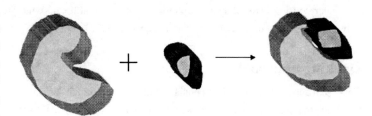

Schematic diagram illustrating the docking of a small molecule ligand (brown) to a protein receptor (green) to produce a complex.

The associations between biologically relevant molecules such as proteins, nucleic acids, carbohydrates, and lipids play a central role in signal transduction. Furthermore, the relative orientation of the two interacting partners may affect the type of signal produced (e.g., agonism vs antagonism). Therefore docking is useful for predicting both the strength and type of signal produced.

Docking is frequently used to predict the binding orientation of small molecule drug candidates to their protein targets in order to in turn predict the affinity and activity of the small molecule. Hence docking plays an important role in the rational design of drugs.[3] Given the biological and pharmaceutical significance of molecular docking, considerable efforts have been directed towards improving the methods used to predict docking .

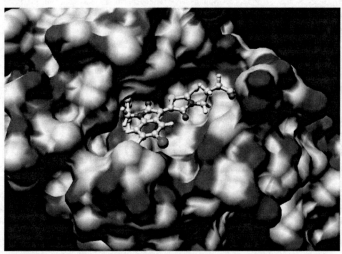

Small molecule docked to a protein.

Definition of problem

Molecular docking can be thought of as a problem of "*lock-and-key*", where one is interested in finding the correct relative orientation of the "*key*" which will open up the "*lock*" (where on the surface of the lock is the key hole, which direction to turn the key after it is inserted, etc.). Here, the protein can be thought of as the "lock" and the ligand can be thought of as a "key". Molecular docking may be defined as an optimization problem, which would describe the "best-fit" orientation of a ligand that binds to a particular protein of interest. However, since both the ligand and the protein are flexible, a "*hand-in-glove*" analogy is more appropriate than "*lock-and-key*".[4] During the course of the process, the ligand and the protein adjust their conformation to achieve an overall "best-fit" and this kind of conformational adjustments resulting in the overall binding is referred to as **"induced-fit"**.[5]

The focus of molecular docking is to computationally simulate the molecular recognition process. The aim of molecular docking is to achieve an optimized conformation for both the protein and ligand and relative orientation between protein and ligand such that the free energy of the overall system is minimized.

Docking approaches

Two approaches are particularly popular within the molecular docking community. One approach uses a matching technique that describes the protein and the ligand as complementary surfaces.[6] [7] The second approach simulates the actual docking process in which the ligand-protein pairwise interaction energies are calculated.[8] Both approaches have significant advantages as well as some limitations. These are outlined below.

Shape complementarity

Geometric matching/ shape complementarity methods describe the protein and ligand as a set of features that make them dockable.[9] These features may include molecular surface/ complementary surface descriptors. In this case, the receptor's molecular surface is described in terms of its solvent-accessible surface area and the ligand's molecular surface is described in terms of its matching surface description. The complementarity between the two surfaces amounts to the shape matching description that may help finding the complementary pose of docking the target and the ligand molecules. Another approach is to describe the hydrophobic features of the protein using turns in the main-chain atoms. Yet another approach is to use a Fourier shape descriptor technique.[10] [11] [12] Whereas the shape complementarity based approaches are typically fast and robust, they cannot usually model the movements or dynamic changes in the ligand/ protein conformations accurately, although recent developments allow these methods to investigate ligand flexibility. Shape complementarity methods can quickly scan through several thousand ligands in a matter of seconds and actually figure out whether they can bind at the protein's active site, and are usually scalable to even protein-protein interactions. They are also much more amenable to pharmacophore based approaches, since they use geometric descriptions of the ligands to find optimal binding.

Simulation

The simulation of the docking process as such is a much more complicated process. In this approach, the protein and the ligand are separated by some physical distance, and the ligand finds its position into the protein's active site after a certain number of "moves" in its conformational space. The moves incorporate rigid body transformations such as translations and rotations, as well as internal changes to the ligand's structure including torsion angle rotations. Each of these moves in the conformation space of the ligand induces a total energetic cost of the system, and hence after every move the total energy of the system is calculated. The obvious advantage of the method is that it is more amenable to incorporate ligand flexibility into its modeling whereas shape complementarity techniques have to use some ingenious methods to incorporate flexibility in ligands. Another advantage is that the process is physically closer to what happens in reality, when the protein and ligand approach each other after molecular recognition. A clear disadvantage of this technique is that it takes longer time to evaluate the optimal pose of binding since they have to explore a rather large energy landscape. However grid-based techniques as well as fast optimization methods have significantly ameliorated these problems.

Mechanics of docking

To perform a docking screen, the first requirement is a structure of the protein of interest. Usually the structure has been determined using a biophysical technique such as x-ray crystallography, or less often, NMR spectroscopy. This protein structure and a database of potential ligands serve as inputs to a docking program. The success of a docking program depends on two components: the search algorithm and the scoring function.

Search algorithm

The search space in theory consists of all possible orientations and conformations of the protein paired with the ligand. However in practice with current computational resources, it is impossible to exhaustively explore the search space—this would involve enumerating all possible distortions of each molecule (molecules are dynamic and exist in an ensemble of conformational states) and all possible rotational and translational orientations of the ligand relative to the protein at a given level of granularity. Most docking programs in use account for a flexible ligand, and several attempt to model a flexible protein receptor. Each "snapshot" of the pair is referred to as a **pose**.

A variety of conformational search strategies have been applied to the ligand and to the receptor. These include:

- systematic or stochastic torsional searches about rotatable bonds
- molecular dynamics simulations
- genetic algorithms to "evolve" new low energy conformations

Ligand flexibility

Conformations of the ligand may be generated in the absence of the receptor and subsequently docked[13] or conformations may be generated on-the-fly in the presence of the receptor binding cavity [14], or with full rotational flexibility of every dihedral angle using fragment based docking [15]. Force field energy evaluation are most often used to select energetically reasonable conformations,[16] but knowledge-based methods have also been used.[17]

Receptor flexibility

Computational capacity has increased dramatically over the last decade making possible the use of more sophisticated and computationally intensive methods in computer-assisted drug design. However, dealing with receptor flexibility in docking methodologies is still a thorny issue. The main reason behind this difficulty is the large number of degrees of freedom that have to be considered in this kind of calculations. Neglecting it, however, leads to poor docking results in terms of binding pose prediction.[18]

Multiple static structures experimentally determined for the same protein in different conformations are often used to emulate receptor flexibility.[19] Alternatively rotamer libraries of amino acid side chains that surround the binding cavity may be searched to generate alternate but energetically reasonable protein conformations.[20] [21]

Scoring function

The scoring function takes a pose as input and returns a number indicating the likelihood that the pose represents a favorable binding interaction.

Most scoring functions are physics-based molecular mechanics force fields that estimate the energy of the pose; a low (negative) energy indicates a stable system and thus a likely binding interaction. An alternative approach is to derive a statistical potential for interactions from a large database of protein-ligand complexes, such as the Protein Data Bank, and evaluate the fit of the pose according to this inferred potential.

There are a large number of structures from X-ray crystallography for complexes between proteins and high affinity ligands, but comparatively fewer for low affinity ligands as the later complexes tend to be less stable and therefore more difficult to crystallize. Scoring functions trained with this data can dock high affinity ligands correctly, but they will also give plausible docked conformations for ligands that do not bind. This gives a large number of false positive hits, i.e., ligands predicted to bind to the protein that actually don't when placed together in a test tube.

One way to reduce the number of false positives is to recalculate the energy of the top scoring poses using (potentially) more accurate but computationally more intensive techniques such as Generalized Born or Poisson-Boltzmann methods.[8]

Applications

A binding interaction between a small molecule ligand and an enzyme protein may result in activation or inhibition of the enzyme. If the protein is a receptor, ligand binding may result in agonism or antagonism. Docking is most commonly used in the field of drug design — most drugs are small organic molecules, and docking may be applied to:

- hit identification – docking combined with a scoring function can be used to quickly screen large databases of potential drugs in silico to identify molecules that are likely to bind to protein target of interest (see virtual screening).
- lead optimization – docking can be used to predict in where and in which relative orientation a ligand binds to a protein (also referred to as the binding mode or pose). This information may in turn be used to design more potent and selective analogs.
- Bioremediation – Protein ligand docking can also be used to predict pollutants that can be degraded by enzymes.[22]

References

[1] http://en.wikipedia.org/wiki/Template:Docking
[2] Lengauer T, Rarey M (1996). "Computational methods for biomolecular docking". *Curr. Opin. Struct. Biol.* **6** (3): 402–6. doi:10.1016/S0959-440X(96)80061-3. PMID 8804827.
[3] Kitchen DB, Decornez H, Furr JR, Bajorath J (2004). "Docking and scoring in virtual screening for drug discovery: methods and applications". *Nature reviews. Drug discovery* **3** (11): 935–49. doi:10.1038/nrd1549. PMID 15520816.
[4] Jorgensen WL (1991). "Rusting of the lock and key model for protein-ligand binding". *Science* **254** (5034): 954–5. doi:10.1126/science.1719636. PMID 1719636.
[5] Wei BQ, Weaver LH, Ferrari AM, Matthews BW, Shoichet BK (2004). "Testing a flexible-receptor docking algorithm in a model binding site". *J. Mol. Biol.* **337** (5): 1161–82. doi:10.1016/j.jmb.2004.02.015. PMID 15046985.
[6] Meng EC, Shoichet BK, Kuntz ID (2004). "Automated docking with grid-based energy evaluation". *Journal of Computational Chemistry* **13** (4): 505–524. doi:10.1002/jcc.540130412.

[7] Morris GM, Goodsell DS, Halliday RS, Huey R, Hart WE, Belew RK, Olson AJ (1998). "Automated docking using a Lamarckian genetic algorithm and an empirical binding free energy function". *Journal of Computational Chemistry* **19** (14): 1639–1662. doi:10.1002/(SICI)1096-987X(19981115)19:14<1639::AID-JCC10>3.0.CO;2-B.

[8] Feig M, Onufriev A, Lee MS, Im W, Case DA, Brooks CL (2004). "Performance comparison of generalized born and Poisson methods in the calculation of electrostatic solvation energies for protein structures". *Journal of Computational Chemistry* **25** (2): 265–84. doi:10.1002/jcc.10378. PMID 14648625.

[9] Shoichet BK, Kuntz ID, Bodian DL (2004). "Molecular docking using shape descriptors". *Journal of Computational Chemistry* **13** (3): 380–397. doi:10.1002/jcc.540130311.

[10] Cai W, Shao X, Maigret B (January 2002). "Protein-ligand recognition using spherical harmonic molecular surfaces: towards a fast and efficient filter for large virtual throughput screening". *J. Mol. Graph. Model.* **20** (4): 313–28. doi:10.1016/S1093-3263(01)00134-6. PMID 11858640.

[11] Morris RJ, Najmanovich RJ, Kahraman A, Thornton JM (May 2005). "Real spherical harmonic expansion coefficients as 3D shape descriptors for protein binding pocket and ligand comparisons". *Bioinformatics* **21** (10): 2347–55. doi:10.1093/bioinformatics/bti337. PMID 15728116.

[12] Kahraman A, Morris RJ, Laskowski RA, Thornton JM (April 2007). "Shape variation in protein binding pockets and their ligands". *J. Mol. Biol.* **368** (1): 283–301. doi:10.1016/j.jmb.2007.01.086. PMID 17337005.

[13] Kearsley SK, Underwood DJ, Sheridan RP, Miller MD (October 1994). "Flexibases: a way to enhance the use of molecular docking methods". *J. Comput. Aided Mol. Des.* **8** (5): 565–82. doi:10.1007/BF00123666. PMID 7876901.

[14] Friesner RA, Banks JL, Murphy RB, Halgren TA, Klicic JJ, Mainz DT, Repasky MP, Knoll EH, Shelley M, Perry JK, Shaw DE, Francis P, Shenkin PS (March 2004). "Glide: a new approach for rapid, accurate docking and scoring. 1. Method and assessment of docking accuracy". *J. Med. Chem.* **47** (7): 1739–49. doi:10.1021/jm0306430. PMID 15027865.

[15] Zsoldos Z, Reid D, Simon A, Sadjad SB, Johnson AP (July 2007). "eHiTS: A new fast, exhaustive flexible ligand docking system". *Journal of Molecular Graphics and Modelling* **26** (1): 198-212. doi:doi:10.1016/j.jmgm.2006.06.002. PMID 16860582.

[16] Wang Q, Pang YP (2007). Romesberg, Floyd. ed. "Preference of small molecules for local minimum conformations when binding to proteins". *PLoS ONE* **2** (9): e820. doi:10.1371/journal.pone.0000820. PMC 1959118. PMID 17786192.

[17] Klebe G, Mietzner T (October 1994). "A fast and efficient method to generate biologically relevant conformations". *J. Comput. Aided Mol. Des.* **8** (5): 583–606. doi:10.1007/BF00123667. PMID 7876902.

[18] Cerqueira NM, Bras NF, Fernandes PA, Ramos MJ (January 2009). "MADAMM: a multistaged docking with an automated molecular modeling protocol". *Proteins* **74** (1): 192–206. doi:10.1002/prot.22146. PMID 18618708.

[19] Totrov M, Abagyan R (April 2008). "Flexible ligand docking to multiple receptor conformations: a practical alternative". *Curr. Opin. Struct. Biol.* **18** (2): 178–84. doi:10.1016/j.sbi.2008.01.004. PMC 2396190. PMID 18302984.

[20] Hartmann C, Antes I, Lengauer T (February 2009). "Docking and scoring with alternative side-chain conformations". *Proteins* **74** (3): 712–26. doi:10.1002/prot.22189. PMID 18704939.

[21] Taylor RD, Jewsbury PJ, Essex JW (October 2003). "FDS: flexible ligand and receptor docking with a continuum solvent model and soft-core energy function". *J Comput Chem* **24** (13): 1637–56. doi:10.1002/jcc.10295. PMID 12926007.

[22] Suresh PS, Kumar A, Kumar R, Singh VP (January 2008). "An in silico [correction of insilico] approach to bioremediation: laccase as a case study". *J. Mol. Graph. Model.* **26** (5): 845–9. doi:10.1016/j.jmgm.2007.05.005. PMID 17606396.

External links

- Bikadi Z, Kovacs S, Demko L, Hazai E. "Molecular Docking Server - Ligand Protein Docking & Molecular Modeling" (http://www.dockingserver.com). Virtua Drug Ltd. Retrieved 2008-07-15. "Internet service that calculates the site, geometry and energy of small molecules interacting with proteins"
- Malinauskas T. "Step by step installation of MGLTools 1.5.2 (AutoDockTools, Python Molecular Viewer and Visual Programming Environment) on Ubuntu Linux 8.04" (http://users.ox.ac.uk/~jesu1458/installation_of_autodock_on_ubuntu_linux/). Retrieved 2008-07-15.
- Malinauskas T. "High-throughput molecular docking using free tools: ZINC 8, AutoDockTools 1.5.2 and Docker 1.0" (http://users.ox.ac.uk/~jesu1458/docker/). Retrieved 2008-07-23.
- AutoDock and MGLTools (http://wiki.debian.org/AutoDock) for Debian
- Docking@GRID (http://dockinggrid.gforge.inria.fr) Project of Conformational Sampling and Docking on Grids : one aim is to deploy some intrinsic distributed docking algorithms on computational Grids, download Docking@GRID open-source Linux version (http://193.49.213.2/Download/FrmDownload.php)
- Docking software (http://www.biomolecular-modeling.com/Software_Docking.html)
- Click2Drug.org (http://www.click2drug.org) - Directory of computational drug design tools.

Dot plot (bioinformatics)

A **dot plot** (a.k.a. **contact plot** or **residue contact map**) is a graphical method that allows the comparison of two biological sequences and identify regions of close similarity between them. It is a kind of recurrence plot.

Introduction

One way to visualize the similarity between two protein or nucleic acid sequences is to use a similarity matrix, known as a dot plot. These were introduced by Philips in the 1970s and are two-dimensional matrices that have the sequences of the proteins being compared along the vertical and horizontal axes. For a simple visual representation of the similarity between two sequences, individual cells in the matrix can be shaded black if residues are identical, so that matching sequence segments appear as runs of diagonal lines across the matrix.

Some idea of the similarity of the two sequences can be gleaned from the number and length of matching segments shown in the matrix. Identical proteins will obviously have a diagonal line in the center of the matrix. Insertions and deletions between sequences give rise to disruptions in this diagonal. Regions of local similarity or repetitive sequences give rise to further diagonal matches in addition to the central diagonal. Because of the limited protein alphabet, many matching sequence segments may simply have arisen by chance. One way of reducing this noise is to only shade runs or 'tuples' of residues, e.g. a tuple of 3 corresponds to three residues in a row. This is effective because the probability of matching three residues in a row by chance is much lower than single-residue matches. It can be seen from Figures 3.3h,c that the number of diagonal runs in the matrix has been considerably reduced by looking for 2-tuples or 3-tuples.

Dot plots are one of the oldest ways of comparing two sequences. They compare two sequences by organizing one sequence on the x-axis, and another on the y-axis, of a plot. When the residues of both sequences match at the same location on the plot, a dot is drawn at the corresponding position. Note, that the sequences can be written backwards or forwards, however the sequences on both axes must be written in the same direction. Also note, that the direction of the sequences on the axes will determine the direction of the line on the dot plot. Once the dots have been plotted, they will combine to form lines. The closeness of the sequences in similarity will determine how close the diagonal line is to what a graph showing a curve demonstrating a direct relationship is. This relationship is affected by certain sequence features such as frame shifts, direct repeats, and inverted repeats. Frame shifts include insertions, deletions, and mutations. The presence of one of these features, or the presence of multiple features, will cause for multiple lines to be plotted in a various possibility of configurations, depending on the features present in the sequences. A feature that will cause a very different result on the dot plot is the presence of low-complexity region/regions. Low-complexity regions are regions in the sequence with only a few amino acids, which in turn, causes redundancy within that small or limited region. These regions are typically found around the diagonal, and may or may not have a square in the middle of the dot plot.

Example

Example of a dot plot for comparing two simple protein sequences:

1. All cells associated with identical residue pairs between the sequences are shaded black;
2. Only those cells associated with identical tuples of two residues are shaded black; and,
3. Only cells associated with tuples of three are shaded and the optimal path through the matrix has been drawn.

This is constrained to be within the window given by the two black lines parallel to the central diagonal. An alternative high-scoring path is also shown.

A DNA dot plot of a human zinc finger transcription factor (GenBank ID NM_002383), showing regional self-similarity. The main diagonal represents the sequence's alignment with itself; lines off the main diagonal represent similar or repetitive patterns within the sequence.

References

- http://www.scribd.com/doc/17727/ complete-notes-on-Bioinformatics

External links

- A tutorial [1]
- Genomdiff [2] — an open source Java Dot Plot program for viruses
- Gepard [3]
- ANACON [4] — Contact analysis of dot plots.
- General introduction to dot plots with example algorithms [5] and a software tool to create small and medium size dot plots. [6]
- Dotlet [7] — provides a program allowing you to construct a dot plot with your own sequences.
- UGENE Dot Plot viewer [8] - a powerful and opensource Dot Plot visualizer

References

[1] http://helix.biology.mcmaster.ca/721/outline2/node38.html
[2] http://sourceforge.net/projects/genomdiff
[3] http://mips.gsf.de/services/analysis/gepard
[4] http://www.csb.yale.edu/userguides/graphics/whatif/html/chap13.html
[5] http://www.code10.info/index.php?option=com_content&view=category&id=52&Itemid=76
[6] http://www.code10.info/index.php?view=article&catid=50%3Acat_coding_software_serolis& id=63%3Aserolis-software-package-for-dot-plot-creation&option=com_content&Itemid=61
[7] http://myhits.isb-sib.ch/cgi-bin/dotlet
[8] http://ugene.unipro.ru/documentation/manual/plugins/dotplot.html

Dry lab

A **dry lab** is a laboratory where computational or applied mathematical analyses are done on a computer-generated model to simulate a phenomenon in the physical realm whether it be a molecule changing quantum states, the event horizon of a black hole or anything that otherwise might be impossible or too dangerous to observe under normal laboratory conditions [1]. This term may also refer to a lab that uses primarily electronic equipment, for example, a robotics lab. A dry lab can also refer to a laboratory space for the storage of dry materials.[2] To dry lab can also refer to supplying fictional (yet plausible) results in lieu of performing an assigned experiment. The term dry lab is also used in the photo printing industry to refer to photo printing systems that do not employ the use of "wet" photographic chemicals.

In silico chemistry

As computing power has grown exponentially this approach to research, often referred to as *in silico* (as opposed to *in vitro*), has amassed more attention especially in the area of bioinformatics. More specifically, within bioinformatics, is the study of proteins or proteomics, which is the elucidation of their unknown structures and folding patterns. The general approach in the elucidation of protein structure has been to first purify a protein, crystallize it and then send X-rays through such a purified protein crystal to observe how these x-rays diffract into specific pattern--a process referred to as X-ray crystallography. However, many proteins, especially those embedded in cellular membranes, are nearly impossible to crystallize due to their hydrophobic nature. Although other techniques exists, such as ramachandran plotting and mass spectrometry, these alone generally do not lead to the full elucidation of protein structure or folding mechanisms.

Distributed computing

As a means of surpassing the limitations of these techniques, projects such as Folding@Home and Rosetta@Home are aimed at resolving this problem using computational analysis, this means of resolving protein structure is referred to as protein structure prediction. Although many labs have a slightly different approach, the main concept is to find, from a myriad of protein conformations, which conformation has the lowest energy or, in the case of Folding@Home, to find relatively low energies of proteins that could cause the protein to misfold and aggregate other proteins to itself -- like in the case of sickle cell anemia. The general scheme in these projects is that a small number of computations are parsed to, or sent to be calculated on, a computer, generally a home computer, and then that computer analyzes the likelihood that a specific protein will take a certain shape or conformation based on the amount of energy required for that protein to stay in that shape, this way of processing data is what is generally referred to as distributed computing. This analysis is done on an extraordinarily large number of different conformations, owing to the support of hundreds of thousands of home-based computers, in hopes to find the conformation of lowest possible energy or set of conformations of lowest possible energy relative to any conformations that are just slightly different. Although doing so is quite difficult, one can, by observing the energy distribution of a large number of conformations, despite the almost infinite number of different protein conformations possible for any given protein (see Levinthal Paradox), with a reasonably large number of protein energy samplings, predict relatively closely what conformation, within a range of conformations, has the expected lowest energy using methods in statistical inference . There are other factors such as salt concentration, pH, ambient temperature or chaperonins, which are proteins that assist in the folding process of other proteins, that can greatly affect how a protein folds. However, if the given protein is shown to fold on its own, especially in vitro, these findings can be further supported. Once we can see how a protein folds then we can see how it works as a catalyst, or in intracellular communication, e.g. neuroreceptor-neurotransmitter interaction. How certain compounds may be used to enhance or prevent the function of these proteins and how an elucidated protein overall plays a role in diseases such as Alzheimer's Disease or Huntington's Disease can also be much better understood [3].

Of course, there are many other avenues of research in which the dry lab approach has been implemented. Other physical phenomena, such as sound, properties of newly discovered or hypothetical compounds and quantum mechanics models have recently received more attention in this area of approach.

References

[1] http://medical.merriam-webster.com/medical/dry%20lab
[2] http://www.wbdg.org/design/lab_dry.php
[3] http://folding.stanford.edu/English/FAQ-Diseases

Dual-flashlight plot

In statistics, a **dual-flashlight plot** is a type of scatter-plot in which the standardized mean (SMCV) is plotted against the mean of a contrast variable representing a comparison of interest .[1] The commonly used dual-flashlight plot is for the difference between two groups in high-throughput experiments such as microarrays and high-throughput screening studies, in which we plot the SSMD versus average log fold-change on the y- and x-axes, respectively, for all genes or compounds (such as siRNAs or small molecules) investigated in an experiment.[1] As a whole, the points in a dual-flashlight plot look like the beams of a flashlight with two heads, hence the name dual-flashlight plot.[1]

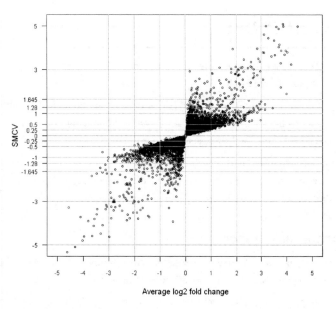

Dual-flashlight plot showing a high-throughput screening dataset.

With the dual-flashlight plot, we can see how the genes or compounds are distributed into each category in effect sizes, as shown in the figure. Meanwhile, we can also see the average fold-change for each gene or compound. The dual-flashlight plot is similar to the volcano plot. In a volcano plot, the p-value (or q-value), instead of SMCV or SSMD, is plotted against average fold-change [2] .[3] The advantage of using SMCV over p-value (or q-value) is that, if there exist any non-zero true effects for a gene or compound, the estimated SMCV goes to its population value whereas the p-value (or q-value) for testing no mean difference (or zero contrast mean) goes to zero when the sample size increases .[4] Hence, the value of SMCV is comparable whereas the value of p-value or q-value is incomparable in experiments with different sample size, especially when many investigated genes or compounds do not have exactly zero effects. The dual-flashlight plot bears the same advantage that the SMCV has, as compared to the volcano plot.

Further reading

- Zhang XHD (2011) "Optimal High-Throughput Screening: Practical Experimental Design and Data Analysis for Genome-scale RNAi Research, Cambridge University Press" [5]

References

[1] Zhang XHD (2010). "Assessing the size of gene or RNAi effects in multifactor high-throughput experiments". *Pharmacogenomics* **11**: 199–213. doi:10.2217/PGS.09.136.

[2] Jin W, Riley RM, Wolfinger RD, White KP, Passador-Gurgel G, Gibson G (2001). "The contributions of sex, genotype and age to transcriptional variance in Drosophila melanogaster". *Nature Genetics* **29**: 389–95. doi:10.1038/ng766.

[3] Cui X, Churchill GA (2003). "Statistical tests for differential expression in cDNA microarray experiments". *Genome Biology* **4**: 210. PMID 1270220.

[4] Zhang XHD (2010). "Strictly standardized mean difference, standardized mean difference and classical t-test for the comparison of two groups". *Statistics in Biopharmaceutical Research* **2**: 292–99. doi:10.1198/sbr.2009.0074.

[5] http://www.cambridge.org/9780521734448

EC number

This article is about the Enzyme Commission codes. For the European Commission system for coding chemicals, see EC-No.

The **Enzyme Commission number** (**EC number**) is a numerical classification scheme for enzymes, based on the chemical reactions they catalyze.[1] As a system of **enzyme nomenclature**, every EC number is associated with a recommended name for the respective enzyme.

Strictly speaking, EC numbers do not specify enzymes, but enzyme-catalyzed reactions. If different enzymes (for instance from different organisms) catalyze the same reaction, then they receive the same EC number.[2] By contrast, UniProt identifiers uniquely specify a protein by its amino acid sequence.[3]

Format of number

Every enzyme code consists of the letters "EC" followed by four numbers separated by periods. Those numbers represent a progressively finer classification of the enzyme.

For example, the tripeptide aminopeptidases have the code "EC 3.4.11.4", whose components indicate the following groups of enzymes:

- *EC 3* enzymes are hydrolases (enzymes that use water to break up some other molecule)
- *EC 3.4* are hydrolases that act on peptide bonds
- *EC 3.4.11* are those hydrolases that cleave off the amino-terminal amino acid from a polypeptide
- *EC 3.4.11.4* are those that cleave off the amino-terminal end from a tripeptide

Top level codes

Top-level EC numbers[4]

Group	Reaction catalyzed	Typical reaction	Enzyme example(s) with trivial name
EC 1 *Oxidoreductases*	To catalyze oxidation/reduction reactions; transfer of H and O atoms or electrons from one substance to another	$AH + B \rightarrow A + BH$ (**reduced**) $A + O \rightarrow AO$ (**oxidized**)	Dehydrogenase, oxidase
EC 2 *Transferases*	Transfer of a functional group from one substance to another. The group may be methyl-, acyl-, amino- or phosphate group	$AB + C \rightarrow A + BC$	Transaminase, kinase
EC 3 *Hydrolases*	Formation of two products from a substrate by hydrolysis	$AB + H_2O \rightarrow AOH + BH$	Lipase, amylase, peptidase
EC 4 *Lyases*	Non-hydrolytic addition or removal of groups from substrates. C-C, C-N, C-O or C-S bonds may be cleaved	$RCOCOOH \rightarrow RCOH + CO_2$ or $[X\text{-}A\text{-}B\text{-}Y] \rightarrow [A{=}B + X\text{-}Y]$	Decarboxylase
EC 5 *Isomerases*	Intramolecule rearrangement, i.e. isomerization changes within a single molecule	$AB \rightarrow BA$	Isomerase, mutase
EC 6 *Ligases*	Join together two molecules by synthesis of new C-O, C-S, C-N or C-C bonds with simultaneous breakdown of ATP	$X + Y + ATP \rightarrow XY + ADP + Pi$	Synthetase

History

The enzyme nomenclature scheme was developed starting in 1955, when the International Congress of Biochemistry in Brussels set up an Enzyme Commission.

The first version was published in 1961.

The current sixth edition, published by the International Union of Biochemistry and Molecular Biology in 1992, contains 3196 different enzymes.

References

[1] Webb, Edwin C. (1992). *Enzyme nomenclature 1992: recommendations of the Nomenclature Committee of the International Union of Biochemistry and Molecular Biology on the nomenclature and classification of enzymes* (http://www.chem.qmul.ac.uk/iubmb/enzyme/). San Diego: Published for the International Union of Biochemistry and Molecular Biology by Academic Press. ISBN 0-12-227164-5. .

[2] "ENZYME (Enzyme nomenclature database)" (http://www.expasy.org/enzyme/). ExPASy. . Retrieved 2006-03-14.

[3] Apweiler R, Bairoch A, Wu CH, Barker WC, Boeckmann B, Ferro S, Gasteiger E, Huang H, Lopez R, Magrane M, Martin MJ, Natale DA, O'Donovan C, Redaschi N, Yeh LS (January 2004). "UniProt: the Universal Protein knowledgebase". *Nucleic Acids Res.* **32** (Database issue): D115–9. doi:10.1093/nar/gkh131. PMC 308865. PMID 14681372.

[4] Moss, G.P.. "Recommendations of the Nomenclature Committee" (http://www.chem.qmul.ac.uk/iubmb/enzyme/). International Union of Biochemistry and Molecular Biology on the Nomenclature and Classification of Enzymes by the Reactions they Catalyse. . Retrieved 2006-03-14.

External links

- Enzyme Nomenclature (http://www.chem.qmul.ac.uk/iubmb/enzyme/)
- Enzyme nomenclature database (http://www.expasy.org/enzyme/) — by ExPASy
- List of all EC numbers (http://www.brenda-enzymes.org/information/all_enzymes.php4) — by BRENDA
- Browse PDB structures by EC number (http://www.pdbe.org/ec)

EMAGE

EMAGE

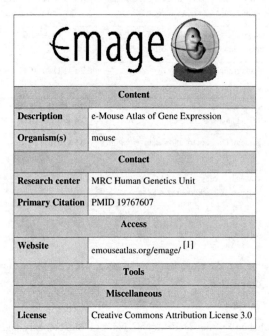

Content	
Description	e-Mouse Atlas of Gene Expression
Organism(s)	mouse
Contact	
Research center	MRC Human Genetics Unit
Primary Citation	PMID 19767607
Access	
Website	emouseatlas.org/emage/ [1]
Tools	
Miscellaneous	
License	Creative Commons Attribution License 3.0

EMAGE (e-Mouse Atlas of Gene Expression[2]) is an online biological database of gene expression data in the developing mouse (*Mus musculus*) embryo.[3] [4] [5] The data held in EMAGE is spatially annotated to a framework of 3D mouse embryo models produced by EMAP [6] (e-Mouse Atlas Project). These spatial annotations allow users to query EMAGE by spatial pattern as well as by gene name, anatomy term or Gene Ontology (GO) term. EMAGE is a freely available web-based resource funded by the Medical Research Council (UK) and based at the MRC Human Genetics Unit in the Institute of Genetics and Molecular Medicine, Edinburgh, UK.

Contents

EMAGE contains *in situ* hybridisation, immunohistochemistry, and *in situ* reporter (e.g. knock-in and gene trap) data. It includes wholemount data, section data and full 3D OPT (Optical Projection Tomography) data. The gene expression patterns are mapped into or onto the standard models by a team of biocurators, using bespoke mapping software. In addition to the spatial annotations, EMAGE data is also text annotated to provide a text based description of the expression patterns. This text annotation is carried out in collaboration with the MGI Gene Expression Database (GXD) [7] using the EMAP mouse anatomy ontology.

EMAGE data comes primarily from peer reviewed, published journal articles, and from large scale screens, but also from direct submissions from researches working in the field. Data does not need to be published to be included in EMAGE, however EMAGE is a curated database. Biocurators check the accuracy of the meta-data included in the database entries and as well as performing the spatial annotations of the data.

EMAGE entries are designed to adhere to the Minimum information specification for in situ hybridization and immunohistochemistry experiments (MISFISHIE)[8] specifications, and as such contain information about the submitter/author publication, detection reagent, assay specimen preparation, and experimental procedures as well as the original data images and the spatial and text annotations. EMAGE entries also contain links to a variety of related resources based on the either the gene being assayed, or the assay itself.

References

[1] http://emouseatlas.org/emage/

[2] Historically, EMAGE was an acronym for Edinburgh Mouse Atlas of Gene Expression.

[3] Richardson L, Venkataraman S, Stevenson P, *et al.* (January 2010). "EMAGE mouse embryo spatial gene expression database: 2010 update". *Nucleic Acids Res.* **38** (Database issue): D703–9. doi:10.1093/nar/gkp763. PMC 2808994. PMID 19767607.

[4] Venkataraman S, Stevenson P, Yang Y, *et al.* (January 2008). "EMAGE--Edinburgh Mouse Atlas of Gene Expression: 2008 update". *Nucleic Acids Res.* **36** (Database issue): D860–5. doi:10.1093/nar/gkm938. PMC 2238921. PMID 18077470.

[5] Christiansen JH, Yang Y, Venkataraman S, *et al.* (January 2006). "EMAGE: a spatial database of gene expression patterns during mouse embryo development". *Nucleic Acids Res.* **34** (Database issue): D637–41. doi:10.1093/nar/gkj006. PMC 1347369. PMID 16381949.

[6] http://www.emouseatlas.org/emap/home.html

[7] http://www.informatics.jax.org/mgihome/GXD/aboutGXD.shtml

[8] Deutsch E W, *et al.* (March 2008). "Minimum information specification for in situ hybridization and immunohistochemistry experiments (MISFISHIE)". *Nature Biotechnology* **26** (3): 305–312. doi:10.1038/nbt1391. PMID 18327244.

Notes

External links

EMAGE resource home page (http://www.emouseatlas.org/emage/)

EMBOSS

EMBOSS is an acronym for **E**uropean **M**olecular **B**iology **O**pen **S**oftware Suite. EMBOSS is a free Open Source software analysis package specially developed for the needs of the molecular biology and bioinformatics user community.[1] The software automatically copes with data in a variety of formats and even allows transparent retrieval of sequence data from the web. Also, as extensive libraries are provided with the package, it is a platform to allow other scientists to develop and release software in true open source spirit. EMBOSS also integrates a range of currently available packages and tools for sequence analysis into a seamless whole.

The EMBOSS package contains a variety of applications for sequence alignment, rapid database searching with sequence patterns, protein motif identification (including domain analysis), and much more.

EMBOSS application groups

Group	Description
Acd	Acd file utilities
Alignment consensus	Merging sequences to make a consensus
Alignment differences	Finding differences between sequences
Alignment dot plots	Dot plot sequence comparisons
Alignment global	Global sequence alignment
Alignment local	Local sequence alignment
Alignment multiple	Multiple sequence alignment
Display	Publication-quality display
Edit	Sequence editing
Enzyme kinetics	Enzyme kinetics calculations
Feature tables	Manipulation and display of sequence annotation
HMM	Hidden markov model analysis
Information	Information and general help for users

Menus	Menu interface(s)
Nucleic 2d structure	Nucleic acid secondary structure
Nucleic codon usage	Codon usage analysis
Nucleic composition	Composition of nucleotide sequences
Nucleic CpG islands	CpG island detection and analysis
Nucleic gene finding	Predictions of genes and other genomic features
Nucleic motifs	Nucleic acid motif searches
Nucleic mutation	Nucleic acid sequence mutation
Nucleic primers	Primer prediction
Nucleic profiles	Nucleic acid profile generation and searching
Nucleic repeats	Nucleic acid repeat detection
Nucleic restriction	Restriction enzyme sites in nucleotide sequences
Nucleic RNA folding	RNA folding methods and analysis
Nucleic transcription	Transcription factors, promoters and terminator prediction
Nucleic translation	Translation of nucleotide sequence to protein sequence
Phylogeny consensus	Phylogenetic consensus methods
Phylogeny continuous characters	Phylogenetic continuous character methods
Phylogeny discrete characters	Phylogenetic discrete character methods
Phylogeny distance matrix	Phylogenetic distance matrix methods
Phylogeny gene frequencies	Phylogenetic gene frequency methods
Phylogeny molecular sequence	Phylogenetic tree drawing methods
Phylogeny tree drawing	Phylogenetic molecular sequence methods
Protein 2d structure	Protein secondary structure
Protein 3d structure	Protein tertiary structure
Protein composition	Composition of protein sequences
Protein motifs	Protein motif searches
Protein mutation	Protein sequence mutation
Protein profiles	Protein profile generation and searching
Test	Testing tools, not for general use
Utils database creation	Database installation
Utils database indexing	Database indexing
Utils misc	Utility tools

References

[1] Rice P, Longden I, Bleasby A (2000). "EMBOSS: The European Molecular Biology Open Software Suite". *Trends in Genetics* **16** (6): 276–277. doi:10.1016/S0168-9525(00)02024-2. PMID 10827456.

External links

- Homepage of EMBOSS (http://emboss.sourceforge.net)
- Homepage of [[EMBnet (http://www.embnet.org)]]
- EMBOSS explorer (http://embossgui.sourceforge.net/) - web-based GUI for EMBOSS

EMBRACE

EMBRACE (A European Model for Bioinformatics Research and Community Education) is a project with the objective of drawing together a wide group of experts throughout Europe who are involved in the use of information technology in the biomolecular sciences. The EMBRACE Network of Excellence will optimise informatics and information exploitation by pure and applied biological scientists in both the academic and commercial sectors.[1] [2]

The EMBRACE network will work to integrate the major databases and software tools in bioinformatics, using existing methods and emerging Grid service technologies. The integration efforts will be driven by an expanding set of test problems representing key issues for bioinformatics service providers and end-user biologists. As a result, groups throughout Europe will be able to use the EMBRACE service interfaces for their own local or proprietary data and tools.

EMBRACE makes many ready-to-go bioinformatics web services freely available to the international research community.

The project is run from the EBI in Hinxton, England. Fred Marcus is its EU project coordinator.

The EMBRACE project is funded by the European Commission within its FP6 Programme, under the thematic area "Life sciences, genomics and biotechnology for health", contract number LHSG-CT-2004-512092.

References

[1] "EMBRACE: European Model for Bioinformatics Research and Community Education" (http://ec.europa.eu/research/health/genomics/newsletter/issue4/article04_en.htm). *EU Genomics News, Newsletter no 4 - July 2005*. EUROPA. . Retrieved 2007-11-06.

[2] Rice, Peter M.; Alan J. Bleasby, Syed A. Haider, Jon C. Ison, Shaun McGlinchey, Mahmut Uludag (December 2006). *EMBRACE: Bioinformatics Data and Analysis Tool Services for e-Science*. Amsterdam: IEEE. 146. doi:10.1109/E-SCIENCE.2006.261079. ISBN 0-7695-2734-5.

External links

- EMBRACE portal (http://www.embracegrid.info/)
- EMBRACE partners (http://www.embracegrid.info/page.php?page=partners)

Ensembl

The Ensembl genome database project.

Content	
Description	**Ensembl**
Contact	
Research center	Wellcome Trust Sanger Institute European Bioinformatics Institute
Primary Citation	Hubbard & al. (2002)[1]
Access	
Website	http://www.ensembl.org/
Tools	
Miscellaneous	

Ensembl is a joint scientific project between the European Bioinformatics Institute and the Wellcome Trust Sanger Institute, which was launched in 1999 in response to the imminent completion of the Human Genome Project.[1] After 10 years in existence,[2] Ensembl's aim remains to provide a centralized resource for geneticists, molecular biologists and other researchers studying the genomes of our own species and other vertebrates and model organisms. Ensembl is one of several well known genome browsers for the retrieval of genomic information.

Similar databases and browsers are found at NCBI and the University of California, Santa Cruz (UCSC).

Background

The human genome consists of three billion base pairs, which code for approximately 20,000–25,000 genes. However the genome alone is of little use, unless the locations and relationships of individual genes can be identified. One option is manual annotation, whereby a team of scientists try to locate genes using experimental data from scientific journals and public databases. However this is a slow, painstaking task. The alternative, known as automated annotation, is to use the power of computers to do the complex pattern-matching of protein to DNA.

In the Ensembl project, sequence data is fed into a software "pipeline" (written in Perl) which creates a set of predicted gene locations and saves them in a MySQL database for subsequent analysis and display. Ensembl makes these data freely accessible to the world research community. All the data and code produced by the Ensembl project is available to download, and there is also a publicly accessible database server allowing remote access. In addition, the Ensembl website provides computer-generated visual displays of much of the data.

Over time the project has expanded to include additional species (including key model organisms such as mouse, fruitfly and zebrafish) as well as a wider range of genomic data, including genetic variations and regulatory features. Since April 2009, a sister project, Ensembl Genomes, has extended the scope of Ensembl into invertebrate metazoa, plants, fungi, bacteria and protists, whilst the original project continues to focus on vertebrates.

Displaying genomic data

Central to the Ensembl concept is the ability to automatically generate graphical views of the alignment of genes and other genomic data against a reference genome. These are shown as data tracks, and individual tracks can be turned on and off, allowing the user to customise the display to suit their research interests. The interface also enables the user to zoom in to a region or move along the genome in either direction.

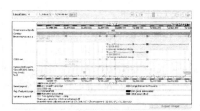

Gene SGCB aligned to the human genome

Other displays show data at varying levels of resolution, from whole karyotypes down to text-based representations of DNA and amino acid sequences, or present other types of display such as trees of similar genes (homologues) across a range of species. The graphics are complemented by tabular displays, and in many cases data can be exported directly from the page in a variety of standard file formats such as FASTA.

Externally produced data can also be added to the display, either via a DAS (Distributed Annotation System) server on the internet, or by uploading a suitable file in one of the supported formats, such as BED or PSL.

Graphics are generated using a suite of custom Perl modules based on GD, the standard Perl graphics display library.

Alternative access methods

In addition its website, Ensembl provides a Perl API (Application Programming Interface) that models biological objects such as genes and proteins, allowing simple scripts to be written to retrieve data of interest. The same API is used internally by the web interface to display the data. It is divided in sections like the core API, the compara API (for comparative genomics data), the variation API (for accessing SNPs, SNVs, CNVs..), etc. The Ensembl website provides extensive information on how to install and use the API [3].

This software can be used to access the public MySQL database, avoiding the need to download enormous datasets. The users could even choose to retrieve data from the MySQL with direct SQL queries, but this requires an extensive knowledge of the current database schema.

Large datasets can be retrieved using the BioMart data-mining tool. It provides a web interface for downloading datasets using complex queries.

Last, there is an FTP server which can be used to download an entire MySQL databases as well some selected data sets in other formats.

Current species

The annotated genomes include most fully sequenced vertebrates and selected model organisms. All of them are eukaryotes, there are no prokaryotes. Currently this includes:

- Chordata
  - Mammalia
    - Primates: Bushbaby, Chimp, Human, Macaque, Mouse Lemur, Orangutan, Tarsier ;
    - Scandentia: Tree shrew ;
    - Glires (= Rodents + Lagomorphs): Guineapig, Kangaroo rat, Mouse, Rat, Ground Squirrel, Pika, Rabbit ;
    - Laurasiatheria: Cow, Dolphin, Alpaca, Pig, Cat, Dog, Horse, Megabat, Microbat, Hedgehog, Shrew ;
    - Afrotheria: Elephant, Hyrax, Tenrec
    - Xenarthra: Armadillo, sloth ;
    - Marsupialia: Opossum, Wallaby ;
    - Monotremes: Platypus ;

- Birds: Chicken, Zebra Finch ;
- Lepidosauria: Anole Lizard (pre) ;
- Lissamphibia: Xenopus tropicalis ;
- Teleost fishes: Takifugu rubripes (Fugu), Tetraodon nigroviridis (Green spotted pufferfish), Danio rerio (Zebrafish), Oryzias latipes (Medaka), Gasterosteus aculeatus (Stickleback) ;
- Cyclostomata: Petromyzon marinus (Sea lamprey) (pre) ;
- Tunicates: Ciona intestinalis, Ciona savignyi ;
- Non-vertebrates
  - Insects: Drosophila melanogaster (Fruitfly), Anopheles gambiae (Mosquito), Aedes aegypti (Mosquito)
  - Worm: Caenorhabditis elegans
- Yeast: Saccharomyces cerevisiae (Baker's yeast)

References

[1] Flicek P, Amode MR, Barrell D, *et al.* (November 2010). "Ensembl 2011". *Nucleic Acids Res* **39** (Database issue): D800–D806. doi:10.1093/nar/gkq1064. PMC 3013672. PMID 21045057.

[2] Flicek P, Aken BL, Ballester B, *et al.* (January 2010). "Ensembl's 10th year". *Nucleic Acids Res.* **38** (Database issue): D557–62. doi:10.1093/nar/gkp972. PMC 2808936. PMID 19906699.

[3] http://www.ensembl.org/info/docs/api/index.html

External links

- Ensembl (http://www.ensembl.org)
- Vega (http://vega.sanger.ac.uk)
- Pre-Ensembl (http://pre.ensembl.org)
- Ensembl genomes (http://www.ensemblgenomes.org)
- UCSC Genome Browser (http://genome.ucsc.edu)
- NCBI (http://www.ncbi.nlm.nih.gov/)

Eukaryotic Linear Motif resource

The **Eukaryotic Linear Motif** (ELM) resource is a computational biology resource (developed at the European Molecular Biology Laboratory (EMBL)) for investigating short linear motifs (SLiMs) in eukaryotic proteins.[1] [2] It is currently the largest collection of linear motif classes with annotated and experimentally validated linear motif instances.

Linear motifs are specified as patterns using regular expression rules. These expressions are used in the ELM prediction pipeline which detects putative motif instances in protein sequences. To improve the predictive power, context-based rules and logical filters are being developed and applied to reduce the amount of false positives matches.

As of 2010 ELM contained 146 different motifs that annotate more than 1300 experimentally determined instances within proteins.[2] The current version of the ELM server provides filtering by cell compartment, phylogeny, globular domain clash (using the SMART/Pfam databases) and structure.[3] In addition, both the known ELM instances and any positionally conserved matches in sequences similar to ELM instance sequences are identified and displayed.

External links

- ELM [4] home page

References

[1] Puntervoll P, Linding R, Gemünd C, *et al.* (July 2003). "ELM server: A new resource for investigating short functional sites in modular eukaryotic proteins". *Nucleic Acids Res.* **31** (13): 3625–30. PMC 168952. PMID 12824381.

[2] Gould CM, Diella F, Via A, *et al.* (January 2010). "ELM: the status of the 2010 eukaryotic linear motif resource". *Nucleic Acids Res.* **38** (Database issue): D167–80. doi:10.1093/nar/gkp1016. PMC 2808914. PMID 19920119.

[3] Via A, Gould CM, Gemünd C, Gibson TJ, Helmer-Citterich M (2009). "A structure filter for the Eukaryotic Linear Motif Resource". *BMC Bioinformatics* **10**: 351. doi:10.1186/1471-2105-10-351. PMC 2774702. PMID 19852836.

[4] http://elm.eu.org/

Eurocarbdb

EuroCarbDB is an EU-funded initiative for the creation of software and standards for the systematic collection of carbohydrate structures and their experimental data. The project includes a database of known carbohydrate structures and experimental data, specifically mass spectrometry, HPLC and NMR data, accessed via a web interface [1] that provides for browsing, searching and contribution of structures and data to the database. The project has also produces a number of associated bioinformatics tools for carbohydrate researchers:

- GlycanBuilder, a Java applet for drawing glycan structures
- GlycoWorkbench, a standalone Java application for semi-automated analysis and annotation of glycan mass spectra
- GlycoPeakfinder, a webapp for calculating glycan compositions from mass data

The online version of EuroCarbDB [1] is hosted by the European Bioinformatics Institute. Eurocarbdb is also an actively developed open source project.

External links

- online version of EuroCarbDB [1]
- Eurocarbdb googlecode project [2]
- Official site for eurocarbdb reports and recommendations [3]

References

[1] http://www.ebi.ac.uk/eurocarb/home.action
[2] http://code.google.com/p/eurocarb/
[3] http://eurocarbdb.org

European Data Format

European Data Format (**EDF**) is a standard file format designed for exchange and storage of medical time series. Being an open and non-proprietary format, EDF(+) is commonly used to archive, exchange and analyse data from commercial devices in a format that is independent of the acquisition system. In this way, the data can be retrieved and analyzed by independent software. EDF(+) software (browsers, checkers, ...) and example files are freely available.

EDF was published in 1992 and stores multichannel data, allowing different sample rates for each signal. Internally it includes a header and one or more data records. The header contains some general information (patient identification, start time...) and technical specs of each signal (calibration, sampling rate, filtering, ...), coded as ASCII characters. The data records contain samples as little-endian 16-bit integers. EDF is a popular format for polysomnography (PSG) recordings.

EDF+ was published in 2003 and is largely compatible to EDF: all existing EDF viewers also show EDF+ signals. But EDF+ files also allow coding discontinuous recordings as well as annotations, stimuli and events in UTF-8 format. EDF+ has applications in PSG, electroencephalography (EEG), electrocardiography (ECG), electromyography (EMG), and Sleep scoring. EDF+ can also be used for nerve conduction studies, evoked potentials and other data acquisition studies.

References

- Kemp B, Värri A, Rosa AC, Nielsen KD, Gade J (May 1992). "A simple format for exchange of digitized polygraphic recordings". *Electroencephalogr Clin Neurophysiol* **82** (5): 391–3. PMID 1374708. — EDF reference.
- Kemp B, Olivan J (September 2003). "European data format 'plus' (EDF+), an EDF alike standard format for the exchange of physiological data" [1]. *Clin Neurophysiol* **114** (9): 1755–61. PMID 12948806.
- EDF specification, examples and tools [2]

External links

- The EDFgroup [3]
- A sample of normal sleep recordings in EDF format [4]

References

[1] http://linkinghub.elsevier.com/retrieve/pii/S1388245703001238
[2] http://www.edfplus.info/
[3] http://tech.groups.yahoo.com/group/EDF
[4] http://www.physionet.org/physiobank/database/sleep-edf/

EVA (benchmark)

EVA is a continuously running benchmark project for assessing the quality of protein structure prediction and secondary structure prediction methods. Methods for predicting both secondary structure and tertiary structure - including homology modeling, protein threading, and contact order prediction - are compared to results from each week's newly solved protein structures deposited in the Protein Data Bank. The project aims to determine the prediction accuracy that would be expected for non-expert users of common, publicly available prediction webservers; this is similar to the related LiveBench project and stands in contrast to the bi-yearly benchmark CASP, which aims to identify the maximum accuracy achievable by prediction experts.

References

- Rost B, Eyrich VA. (2001). EVA: large-scale analysis of secondary structure prediction. *Proteins* Suppl 5:192-9. PMID 11835497
- Eyrich VA, Marti-Renom MA, Przybylski D, Madhusudhan MS, Fiser A, Pazos F, Valencia A, Sali A, Rost B. (2001). EVA: continuous automatic evaluation of protein structure prediction servers. *Bioinformatics* 17(12):1242-3. PMID 11751240
- Koh IY, Eyrich VA, Marti-Renom MA, Przybylski D, Madhusudhan MS, Eswar N, Grana O, Pazos F, Valencia A, Sali A, Rost B. (2003). EVA: Evaluation of protein structure prediction servers. *Nucleic Acids Res* 31(13):3311-5. PMID 12824315

External links

- EVA main site [1]

wow wow blah blah blahblahbalskdjfa;skdfgarkejalkejdf;ladsf

References

[1] http://www.pdg.cnb.uam.es/eva/

Evolution@Home

Evolution@Home is the first parallel computing project for evolutionary biology. The aim of Evolution@Home is to improve understanding of evolutionary processes. This is achieved by simulating individual-based models. The first such model targets the accumulation of mutations in asexual populations and is implemented in Simulator005. The software of Evolution@Home is not the first to simulate this, but previous simulations were hampered by lack of memory (needed for looking at large populations) and lack of computing power (needed for observing long-term evolution and many different parameter combinations). The possibility of parallel computing has allowed Evolution@Home to move the realism of simulated parameter combinations significantly towards observed reality.

Currently the project is operated semi-automatically, which means that a participant has to manually download tasks from the webpage and submit results by email. Development of a fully automated version is under way, but has repeatedly been delayed for a number of reasons. A network connecting the individual systems is required to be truly classified under *distributed computing*

External links

- Project Info Page [1]

References

[1] http://www.evolutionary-research.net/

ExPASy

ExPASy (http://www.expasy.org) is a bioinformatics resource portal operated by the Swiss Institute of Bioinformatics (SIB) and in particular the **SIB Web Team**. It is an extensible and integrative portal accessing many scientific resources, databases and software tools in different areas of life sciences. Scientists can henceforth access seamlessly a wide range of resources in many different domains, such as proteomics, genomics, phylogeny/evolution, systems biology, population genetics, transcriptomics, etc. The individual resources (databases, web-based and downloadable software tools) are hosted in a decentralised way by different groups of the SIB Swiss Institute of Bioinformatics and partner institutions. Specifically, a single web portal provides a common entry point to a wide range of resources developed and operated by many different SIB groups and external institutions. The portal features a search function across selected resources. Internally, the availability and usage of resources are monitored. The portal is aimed for both expert users and for people that are not familiar with a specific domain in life sciences: in particular, the new Web interface provides visual guidance for newcomers to ExPASy.

History

Originally, ExPASy was called **ExPASy** (**Ex**pert **P**rotein **A**nalysis **Sy**stem) and acted as a proteomics server to analyze protein sequences and structures and two-dimensional gel electrophoresis (2-D Page electrophoresis).[1] . Among others, ExPASy references the protein sequence knowledgebase, UniProtKB/Swiss-Prot, and its computer annotated supplement, UniProtKB/Trembl.

As of 5 April 2007, ExPASy has been consulted 1 billion times since its installation on 1 August 1993.[2]

References

[1] Gasteiger, E.; Gattiker, A; Hoogland, C; Ivanyi, I; Appel, RD; Bairoch, A (2003). "ExPASy: The proteomics server for in-depth protein knowledge and analysis". *Nucleic Acids Research* **31** (13): 3784–8. doi:10.1093/nar/gkg563. PMC 168970. PMID 12824418.

[2] ExPASy: SIB Bioinformatics Resource Portal (http://www.expasy.org/)

External links

- ExPASy (http://www.expasy.org/)

Fast statistical alignment

FSA

Developer(s)	Robert Bradley (UC Berkeley), Colin Dewey (UW Madison), Lior Pachter (UC Berkeley)
Stable release	1.5.2
Operating system	UNIX, Linux, Mac
Type	Bioinformatics tool
Licence	Open source

FSA is a multiple sequence alignment program for aligning many proteins or RNAs or long genomic DNA sequences. Along with MUSCLE and MAFFT, FSA is one of the few sequence alignment programs which can align datasets of hundreds or thousands of sequences. FSA uses a different optimization criterion which allows it to more reliably identify non-homologous sequences than these other programs, although this increased accuracy comes at the cost of decreased speed.

FSA is currently being used for projects including sequencing new worm genomes and analyzing *in vivo* transcription factor binding in flies.

Input/Output

This program accepts sequences in FASTA format and outputs alignments in FASTA format or Stockholm format.

References

Bradley RK, Roberts A, Smoot M, Juvekar S, Do J, Dewey C, Holmes I, Pachter L (2009) Fast Statistical Alignment. PLoS Computational Biology. 5:e1000392.

External links

- FSA web server [1]
- FSA source code [2]

References

[1] http://orangutan.math.berkeley.edu/fsa/
[2] http://fsa.sourceforge.net/

FASTA

Developer(s)	Pearson W.R.
Stable release	35
Operating system	UNIX, Linux, Mac, MS-Windows
Type	Bioinformatics tool
Licence	Free for academic users
Website	fasta.bioch.virginia.edu [1]

FASTA is a DNA and protein sequence alignment software package first described (as FASTP) by David J. Lipman and William R. Pearson in 1985.[2] Its legacy is the FASTA format which is now ubiquitous in bioinformatics.

History

The original FASTP program was designed for protein sequence similarity searching. FASTA added the ability to do DNA:DNA searches, translated protein:DNA searches, and also provided a more sophisticated shuffling program for evaluating statistical significance.[3] There are several programs in this package that allow the alignment of protein sequences and DNA sequences.

Usage

FASTA is pronounced "fast A", and stands for "FAST-All", because it works with any alphabet, an extension of "FAST-P" (protein) and "FAST-N" (nucleotide) alignment.

The current FASTA package contains programs for protein:protein, DNA:DNA, protein:translated DNA (with frameshifts), and ordered or unordered peptide searches. Recent versions of the FASTA package include special translated search algorithms that correctly handle frameshift errors (which six-frame-translated searches do not handle very well) when comparing nucleotide to protein sequence data.

In addition to rapid heuristic search methods, the FASTA package provides SSEARCH, an implementation of the optimal Smith-Waterman algorithm.

A major focus of the package is the calculation of accurate similarity statistics, so that biologists can judge whether an alignment is likely to have occurred by chance, or whether it can be used to infer homology. The FASTA package is available from fasta.bioch.virginia.edu [1].

The web-interface [4] to submit sequences for running a search of the European Bioinformatics Institute (EBI)'s online databases is also available using the FASTA programs.

The FASTA file format used as input for this software is now largely used by other sequence database search tools (such as BLAST) and sequence alignment programs (Clustal, T-Coffee, etc.).

Search method

FASTA takes a given nucleotide or amino-acid sequence and searches a corresponding sequence database by using local sequence alignment to find matches of similar database sequences.

The FASTA program follows a largely heuristic method which contributes to the high speed of its execution. It initially observes the pattern of word hits, word-to-word matches of a given length, and marks potential matches before performing a more time-consuming optimized search using a Smith-Waterman type of algorithm.

The size taken for a word, given by the parameter ktup, controls the sensitivity and speed of the program. Increasing the ktup value decreases number of background hits that are found. From the word hits that are returned the program looks for segments that contain a cluster of nearby hits. It then investigates these segments for a possible match.

There are some differences between fastn and fastp relating to the type of sequences used but both use four steps and calculate three scores to describe and format the sequence similarity results. These are:

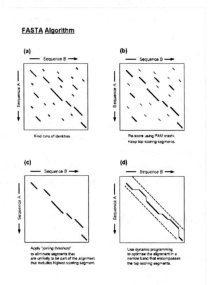

- Identify regions of highest density in each sequence comparison. Taking a ktup to equal 1 or 2.

  In this step all or a group of the identities between two sequences are found using a look up table. The ktup value determines how many consecutive identities are required for a match to be declared. Thus the lesser the ktup value: the more sensitive the search. ktup=2 is frequently taken by users for protein sequences and ktup=4 or 6 for nucleotide sequences. Short oligonucleotides are usually run with ktup = 1. The program then finds all similar **local regions**, represented as diagonals of a certain length in a dot plot, between the two sequences by counting ktup matches and penalizing for intervening mismatches. This way, **local regions** of highest density matches in a diagonal are isolated from background hits. For protein sequences BLOSUM50 values are used for scoring ktup matches. This ensures that groups of identities with high similarity scores contribute more to the local

Diagram from Book *Protein Structure prediction - a practical approach* [5] from chapter *Protein Sequence Alignment and Database Scanning* [6]

diagonal score than to identities with low similarity scores. Nucleotide sequences use the identity matrix for the same purpose. The best 10 local regions selected from all the diagonals put together are then saved.

- Rescan the regions taken using the scoring matrices. trimming the ends of the region to include only those contributing to the highest score.

  Rescan the 10 regions taken. This time use the relevant scoring matrix while rescoring to allow runs of identities shorter than the ktup value. Also while rescoring conservative replacements that contribute to the similarity score are taken. Though protein sequences use the BLOSUM50 matrix, scoring matrices based on the minimum number of base changes required for a specific replacement, on identities alone, or on an alternative measure of similarity such as PAM, can also be used with the program. For each of the diagonal regions rescanned this way, a subregion with the maximum score is identified. The initial scores found in step1 are used to rank the library sequences. The highest score is referred to as *init1* score.

- In an alignment if several initial regions with scores greater than a CUTOFF value are found, check whether the trimmed initial regions can be joined to form an approximate alignment with gaps. Calculate a similarity score that is the sum of the joined regions penalising for each gap 20 points. This initial similarity score (*initn*) is used to rank the library sequences. The score of the single best initial region found in step 2 is reported (*init1*).

  Here the program calculates an optimal alignment of initial regions as a combination of compatible regions with maximal score. This optimal alignment of initial regions can be rapidly calculated using a dynamic programming algorithm. The resulting score initn is used to rank the library sequences.This joining process increases sensitivity but decreases selectivity. A carefully calculated cut-off value is thus used to control where this step is implemented, a value that is approximately one standard deviation above the average score expected from unrelated sequences in the library. A 200-residue query sequence with ktup2 uses a value 28.

- Use a banded Smith-Waterman algorithm to calculate an optimal score for alignment.

    This step uses a banded Smith-Waterman algorithm to create an optimised score (*opt*) for each alignment of query sequence to a database(library) sequence. It takes a band of 32 residues centered on the *init1* region of step2 for calculating the optimal alignment. After all sequences are searched the program plots the initial scores of each database sequence in a histogram, and calculates the statistical significance of the "opt" score. For protein sequences, the final alignment is produced using a full Smith-Waterman alignment. For DNA sequences, a banded alignment is provided.

References

[1] http://fasta.bioch.virginia.edu/

[2] Lipman, DJ; Pearson, WR (1985). "Rapid and sensitive protein similarity searches". *Science* **227** (4693): 1435–41. doi:10.1126/science.2983426. PMID 2983426.

[3] Pearson, WR; Lipman, DJ (1988). "Improved tools for biological sequence comparison". *Proceedings of the National Academy of Sciences of the United States of America* **85** (8): 2444–8. doi:10.1073/pnas.85.8.2444. PMC 280013. PMID 3162770.

[4] http://www.ebi.ac.uk/fasta

[5] http://search.barnesandnoble.com/bookSearch/isbnInquiry.asp?r=1&isbn=0199634963

[6] http://www.compbio.dundee.ac.uk/ftp/preprints/review93/review93.pdf

External links

- FASTA Website (http://fasta.bioch.virginia.edu/fasta_www2/fasta_list2.shtml)
- EBI's FASTA page (http://www.ebi.ac.uk/Tools/fasta) - EBI's page for accessing FASTA services.

FASTA format

In bioinformatics, **FASTA format** is a text-based format for representing either nucleotide sequences or peptide sequences, in which nucleotides or amino acids are represented using single-letter codes. The format also allows for sequence names and comments to precede the sequences. The format originates from the FASTA software package, but has now become a standard in the field of bioinformatics.

The simplicity of FASTA format makes it easy to manipulate and parse sequences using text-processing tools and scripting languages like Python, Ruby, and Perl.

Format

A sequence in FASTA format begins with a single-line description, followed by lines of sequence data. The description line is distinguished from the sequence data by a greater-than (">") symbol in the first column. The word following the ">" symbol is the identifier of the sequence, and the rest of the line is the description (both are optional). There should be no space between the ">" and the first letter of the identifier. It is recommended that all lines of text be shorter than 80 characters. The sequence ends if another line starting with a ">" appears; this indicates the start of another sequence. A simple example of one sequence in FASTA format:

```
>gi|5524211|gb|AAD44166.1| cytochrome b [Elephas maximus maximus]
LCLYTHIGRNIYYGSYLYSETWNTGIMLLLITMATAFMGYVLPWGQMSFWGATVITNLFSAIPYIGTNLV
EWIWGGFSVDKATLNRFFAFHFILPFTMVALAGVHLTFLHETGSNNPLGLTSDSDKIPFHPYYTIKDFLG
LLILILLLLLALLSPDMLGDPDNHMPADPLNTPLHIKPEWYFLFAYAILRSVPNKLGGVLALFLSIVIL
GLMPFLHTSKHRSMMLRPLSQALFWTLTMDLLTLTWIGSQPVEYPYTIIGQMASILYFSIILAFLPIAGX
IENY
```

History

The original FASTA/Pearson format is described in the documentation for the FASTA suite of programs. It can be downloaded with any free distribution of FASTA (see fasta20.doc, fastaVN.doc or fastaVN.me --where VN is the Version Number).

A sequence in FASTA format is represented as a series of lines, which should be no longer than 120 characters and usually do not exceed 80 characters. This probably was because to allow for preallocation of fixed line sizes in software: at the time most users relied on DEC VT (or compatible) terminals which could display 80 or 132 characters per line. Most people preferred the bigger font in 80-character modes and so it became the recommended fashion to use 80 characters or less (often 70) in FASTA lines.

The first line in a FASTA file starts either with a ">" (greater-than) symbol or a ";" (semicolon) and was taken as a comment. Subsequent lines starting with a semicolon would be ignored by software. Since the only comment used was the first, it quickly became used to hold a summary description of the sequence, often starting with a unique library accession number, and with time it has become commonplace use to always use ">" for the first line and to not use ";" comments (which would otherwise be ignored).

Following the initial line (used for a unique description of the sequence) is the actual sequence itself in standard one-letter code. Anything other than a valid code would be ignored (including spaces, tabulators, asterisks, etc...). Originally it was also common to end the sequence with an "*" (asterisk) character (in analogy with use in PIR formatted sequences) and, for the same reason, to leave a blank line between the description and the sequence.

A few sample sequences:

```
;LCBO - Prolactin precursor - Bovine
; a sample sequence in FASTA format
```

```
MDSKGSSQKGSRLLLLLVVSNLLLCQGVVSTPVCPNGPGNCQVSLRDLFDRAVMVSHYIHDLSS
EMFNEFDKRYAQGKGFITMALNSCHTSSLPTPEDKEQAQQTHHEVLMSLILGLLRSWNDPLYHL
VTEVRGMKGAPDAILSRAIEIEEENKRLLEGMEMIFGQVIPGAKETEPYPVWSGLPSLQTKDED
ARYSAFYNLLHCLRRDSSKIDTYLKLLNCRIIYNNNC*

>MCHU - Calmodulin - Human, rabbit, bovine, rat, and chicken
ADQLTEEQIAEFKEAFSLFDKDGDGTITTKELGTVMRSLGQNPTEAELQDMINEVDADGNGTID
FPEFLTMMARKMKDTDSEEEIREAFRVFDKDGNGYISAAELRHVMTNLGEKLTDEEVDEMIREA
DIDGDGQVNYEEFVQMMTAK*

>gi|5524211|gb|AAD44166.1| cytochrome b [Elephas maximus maximus]
LCLYTHIGRNIYYGSYLYSETWNTGIMLLLITMATAFMGYVLPWGQMSFWGATVITNLFSAIPYIGTNLV
EWIWGGFSVDKATLNRFFAFHFILPFTMVALAGVHLTFLHETGSNNPLGLTSDSDKIPFHPYYTIKDFLG
LLILILLLLLALLSPDMLGDPDNHMPADPLNTPLHIKPEWYFLFAYAILRSVPNKLGGVLALFLSIVIL
GLMPFLHTSKHRSMMLRPLSQALFWTLTMDLLTLTWIGSQPVEYPYTIIGQMASILYFSIILAFLPIAGX
IENY
```

A multiple sequence FASTA format would be obtained by concatenating several single sequence FASTA files. This does not imply a contradiction with the format as only the first line in a FASTA file may start with a ";" or ">", hence forcing all subsequent sequences to start with a ">" in order to be taken as different ones (and further forcing the exclusive reservation of ">" for the sequence definition line). Thus, the examples above may as well be taken as a multisequence file if taken together.

Format converters

FASTA files can be batch converted to or from MultiFASTA format using tools, some of which are available as freeware. Tools are also available for batch conversion from [chromatogram] formats (ABI/SCF) to FASTA.

Header line

The header line, which begins with '>', gives a name and/or a unique identifier for the sequence, and often lots of other information too. Many different sequence databases use standardized headers, which helps when automatically extracting information from the header. The header line may contain more than one header, separated by a ^A (Control-A) character.

In the original Pearson FASTA format, one or more comments, distinguished by a semi-colon at the beginning of the line, may occur after the header. Most databases and bioinformatics applications do not recognize these comments and follow the NCBI FASTA specification [1]. An example of a multiple sequence FASTA file follows:

```
>SEQUENCE_1
MTEITAAMVKELRESTGAGMMDCKNALSETNGDFDKAVQLLREKGLGKAAKKADRLAAEG
LVSVKVSDDFTIAAMRPSYLSYEDLDMTFVENEYKALVAELEKENEERRRLKDPNKPEHK
IPQFASRKQLSDAILKEAEEKIKEELKAQGKPEKIWDNIIPGKMNSFIADNSQLDSKLTL
MGQFYVMDDKKTVEQVIAEKEKEFGGKIKIVEFICFEVGEGLEKKTEDFAAEVAAQL
>SEQUENCE_2
SATVSEINSETDFVAKNDQFIALTKDTTAHIQSNSLQSVEELHSSTINGVKFEEYLKSQI
ATIGENLVVRRFATLKAGANGVVNGYIHTNGRVGVVIAAACDSAEVASKSRDLLRQICMH
```

Sequence representation

After the header line and comments, one or more lines may follow describing the sequence: each line of a sequence should have fewer than 80 characters. Sequences may be protein sequences or nucleic acid sequences, and they can contain gaps or alignment characters (see sequence alignment). Sequences are expected to be represented in the standard IUB/IUPAC amino acid and nucleic acid codes, with these exceptions: lower-case letters are accepted and are mapped into upper-case; a single hyphen or dash can be used to represent a gap character; and in amino acid sequences, U and * are acceptable letters (see below). Numerical digits are not allowed but are used in some databases to indicate the position in the sequence.

The nucleic acid codes supported are[2] :

Nucleic Acid Code	Meaning
A	Adenosine
C	Cytosine
G	Guanine
T	Thymidine
U	Uracil
R	G A (puRine)
Y	T U C (pYrimidine)
K	G T U (Ketone)
M	A C (aMino group)
S	G C (Strong interaction)
W	A T U (Weak interaction)
B	G T U C (not A) (B comes after A)
D	G A T U (not C) (D comes after C)
H	A C T U (not G) (H comes after G)
V	G C A (not T, not U) (V comes after U)
N	A G C T U (aNy)
X	masked
-	gap of indeterminate length

The codes supported (24 amino acids and 3 special codes) are:

Amino Acid Code	Meaning
A	Alanine
B	Aspartic acid or Asparagine
C	Cysteine
D	Aspartic acid
E	Glutamic acid
F	Phenylalanine
G	Glycine
H	Histidine
I	Isoleucine

K	Lysine
L	Leucine
M	Methionine
N	Asparagine
O	Pyrrolysine
P	Proline
Q	Glutamine
R	Arginine
S	Serine
T	Threonine
U	Selenocysteine
V	Valine
W	Tryptophan
Y	Tyrosine
Z	Glutamic acid or Glutamine
X	any
*	translation stop
-	gap of indeterminate length

Sequence identifiers

The NCBI defined a standard for the unique identifier used for the sequence (SeqID) in the header line. The formatdb man page has this to say on the subject: "formatdb will automatically parse the SeqID and create indexes, but the database identifiers in the FASTA definition line must follow the conventions of the FASTA Defline Format."

However they do not give a definitive description of the FASTA defline format. An attempt to create such a format is given below (see also "The NCBI Handbook", Chapter 16, The BLAST Sequence Analysis Tool [3].).

```
GenBank                              gi|gi-number|gb|accession|locus
EMBL Data Library                    gi|gi-number|emb|accession|locus
DDBJ, DNA Database of Japan          gi|gi-number|dbj|accession|locus
NBRF PIR                             pir||entry
Protein Research Foundation          prf||name
SWISS-PROT                           sp|accession|name
Brookhaven Protein Data Bank (1)     pdb|entry|chain
Brookhaven Protein Data Bank (2)     entry:chain|PDBID|CHAIN|SEQUENCE
Patents                              pat|country|number
GenInfo Backbone Id                  bbs|number
General database identifier          gnl|database|identifier
NCBI Reference Sequence              ref|accession|locus
Local Sequence identifier            lcl|identifier
```

The vertical bars in the above list are not separators in the sense of the Backus-Naur form, but are part of the format.

File extension

There is no standard file extension for a text file containing FASTA formatted sequences. The table below shows each extension and its respective meaning.

Extension	Meaning	Notes
fasta	generic fasta	Any generic fasta file. Other extensions can be fa, seq, fsa
fna	fasta nucleic acid	For coding regions of a specific genome, use ffn, but otherwise fna is useful for generically specifying nucleic acids.
ffn	FASTA nucleotide coding regions	Contains coding regions for a genome.
faa	fasta amino acid	Contains amino acids. A multiple protein fasta file can have the more specific extension mpfa.
frn	FASTA non-coding RNA	Contains non-coding RNA regions for a genome, in DNA alphabet e.g. tRNA, rRNA

References

[1] http://www.ncbi.nlm.nih.gov/blast/fasta.shtml
[2] "IUPAC code table" (http://www.dna.affrc.go.jp/misc/MPsrch/InfoIUPAC.html). NIAS DNA Bank. .
[3] http://www.ncbi.nlm.nih.gov/books/NBK21097/

External links

- What is FASTA Format? (http://zhanglab.ccmb.med.umich.edu/FASTA/) Explain the FASTA format.
- HUPO-PSI Standard FASTA Format (http://www.proteomecommons.org/data/fasta/hupo_standard.jsp) was describing another FASTA format as put forward by the Human Proteome Organisation's Proteomics Standards Initiative.
- Sequence ID (seqID) Fields in the FASTA Deflines of Sequences from NCBI (http://www.ncbi.nlm.nih.gov/staff/tao/URLAPI/formatdb_fastacmd.html#t1.1) describes the format of FASTA Deflines.
- FASTA File-Format Converter (http://www.bioinformaticsbox.com/tools/sequence_format_converter.php)

FastContact

FastContact is an algorithm for the rapid estimate of contact and binding free energies for protein-protein complex structures. It is based on a statistically determined desolvation contact potential and Coulomb electrostatics with a distance-dependent dielectric constant. The application also reports residue contact free energies that rapidly highlight the hotspots of the interaction.

The programme was written in Fortran 77 by Carlos J. Camacho and Chao Zhang at the Department of Computational Biology, University of Pittsburgh, PA.[1] A web server for running FastContact online or downloading the binary was set up by P. Christoph Champ in July 2005.[2] [3]

References

[1] Camacho CJ, Zhang C (2005). "FastContact: rapid estimate of contact and binding free energies". *Bioinformatics* **21** (10): 2534–2536. doi:10.1093/bioinformatics/bti322. PMID 15713734.

[2] Camacho CJ, Ma H, Champ PC (2006). "Scoring a diverse set of high-quality docked conformations: A metascore based on electrostatic and desolvation interactions". *Proteins* **63** (4): 868–877. doi:10.1002/prot.20932. PMID 16506242.

[3] Champ PC, Camacho CJ (2007). "FastContact: a free energy scoring tool for protein-protein complex structures". *Nucleic Acids Res* **35** (Web addition): W556. doi:10.1093/nar/gkm326. PMC 1933237. PMID 17537824.

External links

- FastContact binaries (http://structure.pitt.edu/software/FastContact) — binaries are freely available for download (with documentation).
- FastContact Server (http://structure.pitt.edu/servers/fastcontact/) — setup by P. Christoph Champ in July 2005.
- FastContact Wiki (http://wiki.christophchamp.com/index.php/FastContact)

FASTQ format

FASTQ format is a text-based format for storing both a biological sequence (usually nucleotide sequence) and its corresponding quality scores. Both the sequence letter and quality score are encoded with a single ASCII character for brevity. It was originally developed at the Wellcome Trust Sanger Institute to bundle a FASTA sequence and its quality data, but has recently become the *de facto* standard for storing the output of high throughput sequencing instruments such as the Illumina Genome Analyzer [1].

Format

A FASTQ file normally uses four lines per sequence. Line 1 begins with a '@' character and is followed by a sequence identifier and an *optional* description (like a FASTA title line). Line 2 is the raw sequence letters. Line 3 begins with a '+' character and is *optionally* followed by the same sequence identifier (and any description) again. Line 4 encodes the quality values for the sequence in Line 2, and must contain the same number of symbols as letters in the sequence.

A minimal FASTQ file might look like this:

```
@SEQ_ID
GATTTGGGGTTCAAAGCAGTATCGATCAAATAGTAAATCCATTTGTTCAACTCACAGTTT
+
!''*((((***+))%%%++)(%%%%).1***-+*''))**55CCF>>>>>>CCCCCCC65
```

The original Sanger FASTQ files also allowed the sequence and quality strings to be wrapped (split over multiple lines), but this is generally discouraged as it can make parsing complicated due to the unfortunate choice of "@" and "+" as markers (these characters can also occur in the quality string).

Illumina sequence identifiers

Sequences from the Illumina software use a systematic identifier:

```
@HWUSI-EAS100R:6:73:941:1973#0/1
```

HWUSI-EAS100R	the unique instrument name
6	flowcell lane
73	tile number within the flowcell lane
941	'x'-coordinate of the cluster within the tile
1973	'y'-coordinate of the cluster within the tile
#0	index number for a multiplexed sample (0 for no indexing)
/1	the member of a pair, /1 or /2 (*paired-end or mate-pair reads only*)

Versions of the Illumina pipeline since 1.4 appear to use **#NNNNNN** instead of **#0** for the multiplex ID, where **NNNNNN** is the sequence of the multiplex tag.

With Casava 1.8 the format of the '@' line has changed:

```
@EAS139:136:FC706VJ:2:2104:15343:197393 1:Y:18:ATCACG
```

EAS139	the unique instrument name
136	the run id
FC706VJ	the flowcell id
2	flowcell lane
2104	tile number within the flowcell lane
15343	'x'-coordinate of the cluster within the tile
197393	'y'-coordinate of the cluster within the tile
1	the member of a pair, 1 or 2 (paired-end or mate-pair reads only)
Y	Y if the read is filtered, N otherwise
18	0 when none of the control bits are on, otherwise it is an even number
ATCACG	index sequence

NCBI Sequence Read Archive

FASTQ files from the NCBI/EBI Sequence Read Archive often include a description, e.g.

```
@SRR001666.1 071112_SLXA-EAS1_s_7:5:1:817:345 length=36
GGGTGATGGCCGCTGCCGATGGCGTCAAATCCCACC
+SRR001666.1 071112_SLXA-EAS1_s_7:5:1:817:345 length=36
IIIIIIIIIIIIIIIIIIIIIIIIIIIIIII9IG9IC
```

In this example there is an NCBI-assigned identifier, and the description holds the original identifier from Solexa/Illumina (as described above) plus the read length.

Also note that the NCBI have converted this FASTQ data from the original Solexa/Illumina encoding to the Sanger standard (see encodings below).

Variations

Quality

A quality value Q is an integer mapping of p (i.e., the probability that the corresponding base call is incorrect). Two different equations have been in use. The first is the standard Sanger variant to assess reliability of a base call, otherwise known as Phred quality score:

$$Q_{\text{sanger}} = -10 \log_{10} p$$

The Solexa pipeline (i.e., the software delivered with the Illumina Genome Analyzer) earlier used a different mapping, encoding the odds $p/(1-p)$ instead of the probability p:

$$Q_{\text{solexa-prior to v.1.3}} = -10 \log_{10} \frac{p}{1-p}$$

Although both mappings are asymptotically identical at higher quality values, they differ at lower quality levels (i.e., approximately $p > 0.05$, or equivalently, $Q < 13$).

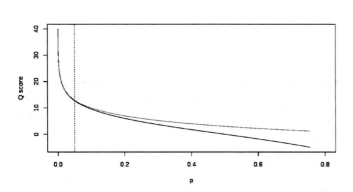

Relationship between Q and p using the Sanger (red) and Solexa (black) equations (described above). The vertical dotted line indicates $p = 0.05$, or equivalently, $Q \approx 13$.

At times there has been disagreement about which mapping Illumina actually uses. The user guide (Appendix B, page 122) for version 1.4 of the Illumina pipeline states that: "The scores are defined as Q=10*log10(p/(1-p)) [*sic*], where p is the probability of a base call corresponding to the base in question"[2]. In retrospect, this entry in the manual appears to have been an error. The user guide (What's New, page 5) for version 1.5 of the Illumina pipeline lists this description instead: "Important Changes in Pipeline v1.3 [*sic*]. The quality scoring scheme has changed to the Phred [i.e., Sanger] scoring scheme, encoded as an ASCII character by adding 64 to the Phred value. A Phred score of a base is: $Q_{phred} = -10 \, log_{10}(e)$, where e is the estimated probability of a base being wrong[3].

Encoding

- Sanger format can encode a Phred quality score from 0 to 93 using ASCII 33 to 126 (although in raw read data the Phred quality score rarely exceeds 60, higher scores are possible in assemblies or read maps). Also used in SAM format[4]. Coming to the end of February 2011, Illumina's newest version (1.8) of their pipeline CASAVA will produce directly fastq in Sanger format, according to the announcement on seqanswers.com forum[5].
- Solexa/Illumina 1.0 format can encode a Solexa/Illumina quality score from -5 to 62 using ASCII 59 to 126 (although in raw read data Solexa scores from -5 to 40 only are expected)
- Illumina 1.3+ format can encode a Phred quality score from 0 to 62 using ASCII 64 to 126 (although in raw read data Phred scores from 0 to 40 only are expected).
- The Phred scores 0 to 2 in Illumina 1.5+ have a slightly different meaning. The values 0 and 1 are no longer used and the value 2, encoded by ASCII 66 "B", is used also at the end of reads as a *Read Segment Quality Control Indicator* [6]. The Illumina manual[7] (page 30) states the following: *If a read ends with a segment of mostly low quality (Q15 or below), then all of the quality values in the segment are replaced with a value of 2 (encoded as the letter B in Illumina's text-based encoding of quality scores)... This Q2 indicator does not predict a specific error rate, but rather indicates that a specific final portion of the read should not be used in further analyses.* Also, the quality score encoded as "B" letter may occur internally within reads at least as late as pipeline version 1.6, as shown in the following example:

```
@HWI-EAS209_0006_FC706VJ:5:58:5894:21141#ATCACG/1

TTAATTGGTAAATAAATCTCCTAATAGCTTAGATNTTACCTTNNNNNNNNNNNTAGTTTCTTGAGATTTGTTGGGGGAGACATTTTTGTGATTGCCTTGAT

+HWI-EAS209_0006_FC706VJ:5:58:5894:21141#ATCACG/1

efcfffffcfeefffcffffffddf`feed]`]_Ba_^__[YBBBBBBBBBBBRTT\]][]dddd`ddd^dddadd^BBBBBBBBBBBBBBBBBBBBBBBBBBB
```

An alternative interpretation of this ASCII encoding has been proposed[8]. Also, in Illumina runs using PhiX controls, the character 'B' was observed to represent an "unknown quality score". The error rate of 'B' reads was roughly 3 phred scores lower the mean observed score of a given run.

For raw reads, the range of scores will depend on the technology and the base caller used, but will typically be up to 40. Recent Illumina chemistry changes have resulted in reported quality scores of 41, which has broken various scripts and tools expecting an upper bound of 40. For aligned sequences and consensuses higher scores are common.

```
SSSSSSSSSSSSSSSSSSSSSSSSSSSSSSSSSSSSSSSSSSSSSSSS.......................................................
......................XXXXXXXXXXXXXXXXXXXXXXXXXXXXXXXXXXXXXXXXXXXXXXXX.................................
...........................IIIIIIIIIIIIIIIIIIIIIIIIIIIIIIIIIIIIIIIIIIIIII.............................
.............................JJJJJJJJJJJJJJJJJJJJJJJJJJJJJJJJJJJJJJJJJJJJJJ............................
!"#$%&'()*+,-./0123456789:;<=>?@ABCDEFGHIJKLMNOPQRSTUVWXYZ[\]^_`abcdefghijklmnopqrstuvwxyz{|}~
 |                          |    |      |                                       |                  |
 33                         59   64     73                                      104                126

S - Sanger, Illumina 1.8+    Phred+33,  raw reads typically (0, 41)
X - Solexa                   Solexa+64, raw reads typically (-5, 40)
I - Illumina 1.3+            Phred+64,  raw reads typically (0, 40)
J - Illumina 1.5+            Phred+64,  raw reads typically (3, 40)
    with 0=unused, 1=unused, 2=Read Segment Quality Control Indicator (bold)
    (Note: See discussion above).
```

Color space

For SOLiD data, the sequence is in color space, except the first position. The quality values are those of the Sanger format. Alignment tools differ in their preferred version of the quality values: some include a quality score (set to 0, i.e. '!') for the leading nucleotide, others do not. The sequence read archive includes this quality score.

File extension

There is no standard file extension for a FASTQ file, but .fq, .fastq, and .txt are commonly used.

Format converters

- Biopython version 1.51 onwards (interconverts Sanger, Solexa and Illumina 1.3+)
- EMBOSS version 6.1.0 patch 1 onwards (interconverts Sanger, Solexa and Illumina 1.3+)
- BioPerl version 1.6.1 onwards (interconverts Sanger, Solexa and Illumina 1.3+)
- BioRuby version 1.4.0 onwards (interconverts Sanger, Solexa and Illumina 1.3+)
- MAQ [9] can convert from Solexa to Sanger (use this patch [10] to support Illumina 1.3+ files).

References

[1] Cock et al (2009) The Sanger FASTQ file format for sequences with quality scores, and the Solexa/Illumina FASTQ variants. Nucleic Acids Research, doi:10.1093/nar/gkp1137 (http://dx.doi.org/10.1093/nar/gkp1137)

[2] Sequencing Analysis Software User Guide: For Pipeline Version 1.4 and CASAVA Version 1.0, dated April 2009 PDF (http://genomecenter.ucdavis.edu/dna_technologies/documents/pipeline_1_4.pdf)

[3] Sequencing Analysis Software User Guide: For Pipeline Version 1.5 and CASAVA Version 1.0, dated August 2009 PDF (http://illumina.ucr.edu/illumina_docs/Pipeline1.5/Pipeline1.5_CASAVA1.0_User_Guide_15006500_A.pdf)

[4] Sequence/Alignment Map format Version 1.0, dated August 2009 PDF (http://samtools.sourceforge.net/SAM1.pdf)

[5] Seqanswer's topic of skruglyak, dated January 2011 website (http://seqanswers.com/forums/showthread.php?s=ba8c7dfba863815f637c0bf45882f14b&t=8895)

[6] Illumina Quality Scores, Tobias Mann, Bioinformatics, San Diego, Illumina (http://seqanswers.com/forums/showthread.php?t=4721)

[7] [Using Genome Analyzer Sequencing Control Software, Version 2.6, Catalog # SY-960-2601, Part # 15009921 Rev. A, November 2009]http://watson.nci.nih.gov/solexa/Using_SCSv2.6_15009921_A.pdf

[8] SolexaQA project website (http://solexaqa.sourceforge.net/questions.htm#illumina)

[9] http://maq.sourceforge.net

[10] http://sourceforge.net/tracker/index.php?func=detail&aid=2824334&group_id=191815&atid=938893

External links

- MAQ (http://maq.sourceforge.net/fastq.shtml) webpage discussing FASTQ variants
- Galaxy fastq tools (http://bitbucket.org/galaxy/galaxy-central/src/tip/tools/fastq/)
- Fastx toolkit (http://hannonlab.cshl.edu/fastx_toolkit/) collection of command line tools for Short-Reads FASTA/FASTQ files preprocessing
- Fastqc (http://www.bioinformatics.bbsrc.ac.uk/projects/fastqc/) quality control tool for high throughput sequence data
- PRINSEQ (http://prinseq.sourceforge.net/) can be used to filter, reformat, or trim your genomic sequence data

FlowJo

FlowJo is a software package for analyzing flow cytometry data. Files produced by modern flow cytometers are written in the Flow Cytometry Standard [1] format with an .fcs file extension. FlowJo will import and analyze cytometry data regardless of which FACS (**F**luorescence **A**ctivated **C**ell **S**orting) machine is used to collect the data.

Operation

In FlowJo, samples are organized in a "Workspace" window, which presents a hierarchical view of all the samples and their analyses (gates and statistics). Viewing an entire experiment in a Workspace permits organizing and managing complex cytometry experiments and produces detailed graphical reports. FlowJo's ability to automate repetitive operations facilitates the production of statistics tables and graphical reports when the experiment involves many samples, parameters and/or operations.

Within a workspace, samples can be grouped or sorted by various attributes such as the panel of antibodies with which they are stained, tissue type, or patient from whom they came. When an operation on a group is initiated, FlowJo can perform the same operation on every sample belonging to that group. Thus, you can apply a gate to a sample, copy it to the group, and that gate will be automatically placed on all samples in the group.

FlowJo provides tools for the creation of:

- Histogram and other plot overlays
- Cell cycle analysis
- Calcium flux analysis
- Proliferation analysis
- Quantitation
- Cluster identification and backgating display

Development

FlowJo became a commercial product in 1996. In 2002, Tree Star released a Windows version. Tree Star is the sponsor of the web portal MyCyte.org [2] a web portal for cytometrists.

External links

- official FlowJo website [3].
- web portal for cytometrists sponsored by Tree Star [4].
- Data File Standard for Flow Cytometry [1]

References

[1] http://www.isac-net.org/content/view/101/150/
[2] http://mycyte.org/
[3] http://www.flowjo.com
[4] http://www.mycyte.org

Flux balance analysis

Flux balance analysis (FBA) is a mathematical method for analysing metabolism. It does not require knowledge of metabolite concentration or details of the enzyme kinetics of the system. The assumption is made that the system being studied is homeostatic and the technique then aims to answer the question: given some known available nutrients, which set of metabolic fluxes maximises the growth rate of an organism while preserving the internal concentration of metabolites?

A notable example of the success of FBA is the ability to accurately predict the growth rate of the prokaryote *E. coli* when cultured in different conditions[1] . More generally, suitable organisms can be cultivated in media with defined concentrations of nutrients, and their

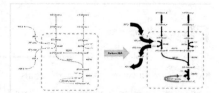

The results of FBA on a prepared metabolic network of the top six reactions of glycolysis. The predicted flux through each reaction is proportional to the width of the line. Objective function in red, constraints on alpha-D-Glucose and beta-D-Glucose import represented as red bars.

growth rates measured, so that the predictions of FBA can be compared with experiments and the underlying metabolic model corrected accordingly.

A good description of the basic concepts of FBA can be found in the freely available supplementary material to Edwards et al. 2001[1] which can be found at the Nature website[2] . Further sources include the book "Systems Biology" by B. Palsson dedicated to the subject[3] and a useful tutorial and paper by J. Orth[4] . Many other sources of information on the technique exist in published scientific literature including Lee et al. 2006[5] and Feist et al. 2008[6] .

Early History

Some of the earliest work in Flux Balance Analysis dates back to the early 1980s. Papoutsakis[7] demonstrated that is was possible to construct flux balance equations using a metabolic map. It was Watson [8] however who first introduced the idea of using linear programming and an objective function to solve for the fluxes in a pathway. The first significant study was subsequently published by Fell and Small [9] who used flux balance analysis together with more elaborate objective functions to study the constraints in fat synthesis.

Model preparation

A comprehensive guide to creating, preparing and analysing a metabolic model using FBA, in addition to other techniques, was published by Thiele and Palsson in 2010[10] . The key parts of model preparation are: creating a metabolic network without holes, adding constraints to the model and finally adding an objective function (often called the Biomass function), usually to simulate the growth of the organism being modelled.

The network

Metabolic networks can vary in scope from those describing the metabolism in a single pathway, up to the cell, tissue or organism. The only requirement of a metabolic network that forms the basis of an FBA-ready network is that it contains no gaps. This typically means that extensive manual curation is required, making the preparation of a metabolic network for flux-balance analysis a process that can take months or years. Software packages such as Pathway Tools [11], Simpheny[12] [13] , CellDesigner[14] and MetNetMaker[15] , exist to speed up the creation of new FBA-ready metabolic networks.

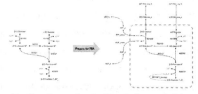

The first six reactions in Glycolysis prepared for FBA through the addition of an objective function (red) and the import and export of nutrients (ATP, ADP, BDG, ADG) across the system boundary (dashed green line)

Generally models are created in BioPAX or SBML format so that further analysis or visualisation can take place in other software although this not a requirement.

Constraints

A key part of FBA is the ability to add constraints to the flux rates of reactions within networks, forcing them to stay within a range of selected values. This lets the model more accurately simulate real metabolism and can be thought of biologically in two subsets; constraints that limit nutrient uptake and excretion and those that limit the flux through reactions within the organism. FBA-ready metabolic models that have had constraints added can be analysed using software such as the COBRA toolbox[16] (requires MATLAB) or SurreyFBA[17] .

Growth media

Organisms, and all other metabolic systems, require some input of nutrients. Typically the rate of uptake of nutrients is dictated by their availability (a nutrient that isn't present cannot be absorbed), their concentration and diffusion constants (higher concentrations of quickly-diffusing metabolites are absorbed more quickly) and the method of absorption (such as active transport or facilitated diffusion versus simple diffusion).

If the rate of absorption (and/or excretion) of certain nutrients can be experimentally measured then this information can be added as a constraint on the flux rate at the edges of a metabolic model. This ensures that nutrients that are not present or not absorbed by the organism do not enter its metabolism (the flux rate is constrained to zero) and also means that known nutrient uptake rates are adhered to by the simulation. This provides a secondary method of making sure that the simulated metabolism has experimentally verified properties rather than just mathematically acceptable ones. In mathematical terms, the application of constraints can be considered to reduce the solution space of the FBA model.

Internal constraints

In addition to constraints applied at the edges of a metabolic network, constraints can be applied to reactions deep within the network. These constraints are usually simple; they may constrain the direction of a reaction due to energy considerations or constrain the maximum speed of a reaction due to the finite speed of all reactions in nature.

Objective function

In FBA there are a large number of mathematically acceptable solutions to the steady-state problem $\left(S\vec{v} = 0\right)$ but the ones that are biologically interesting are those that produce the desired metabolites in the correct proportion. The set of metabolites, in the correct proportions, that an FBA model tries to create is called the objective function. When modelling an organism the objective function is generally the biomass of the organism and simulates growth and reproduction. If the biomass function is defined sensibly, or exactly measured experimentally, it can play an important role in making the results of FBA biologically applicable: by ensuring that the correct proportion of metabolites are produced by metabolism and by predicting exact rates of Biomass production for example.

When modelling smaller networks the objective function can be changed accordingly. An example of this would be in the study of the carbohydrate metabolism pathways where the objective function would probably be defined as a certain proportion of ATP and NADH and thus simulate the production of high energy metabolites by this pathway.

Mathematical description

A metabolic network can be thought of as a set of nodes (compounds) connected by directional edges (reactions) and therefore represented as a matrix. The properties of this matrix are well known and thus a biological problem becomes amenable to computational analysis. A real biological system is extremely complex which in turn leads to problems measuring enough parameters to define the system and in some cases requiring a huge amount of computing time to perform simulations. Flux-balance analysis simplifies the representation of the biological system, requiring fewer parameters (such as enzyme kinetic rates, compound concentrations and diffusion constants) and greatly reduces the computer time required for simulations.

A simple example

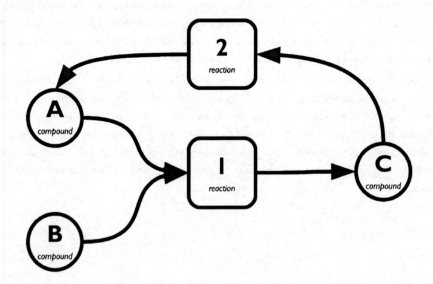

A simple reaction network with two reactions and three compounds

The concentrations of all the metabolites and the fluxes through all the reactions in this simple system can be represented by the following three differential equations.

$$\frac{d[A]}{dt} = \frac{d[C]_1}{dt} = v_2 - v_1$$

$$\frac{d[C]}{dt} = \frac{d[C]_2}{dt} = v_1 - v_2$$

$$\frac{d[B]}{dt} = \frac{d[C]_3}{dt} = -v_1$$

Solving this system of differential equations is not difficult in this case but quickly becomes computationally expensive as the number of differential equations in the system rises. There is a second obstacle to solving this system; the reaction rates, v_1 and v_2 are themselves dependent on a number of factors generally taken from the Michaelis-Menten kinetic theory, including the kinetic parameters of the enzymes catalysing the reactions and the concentration of the metabolites themselves. Isolating enzymes from living organisms and measuring their kinetic parameters is a difficult task, as is measuring the internal concentrations, and diffusion constants, of metabolites within an organism. For this reason the differential equation approach to modelling metabolism becomes extraordinarily difficult and beyond the current scope of science for all but the most studied organisms (link to Heinemann E. Coli paper with all internal fluxes measured and Manchester yeast paper with internal fluxes measured).

The power of homeostasis

Much of the power of flux-balance analysis comes from applying the principle of homeostasis to the problem. Since the internal concentrations of metabolites within a biological system remain more or less the same over time we can apply the homeostatic condition that,

$$\frac{d[C]_1}{dt} = \frac{d[C]_2}{dt} = \frac{d[C]_3}{dt} = 0$$

Or in the general case,

$$\frac{d[C]_i}{dt} = 0$$

And thus simplify the problem to one of simply balancing the fluxes within the system, hence the name flux-balance analysis.

$$v_2 - v_1 = v_1 - v_2 = -v_1$$

This set of equations is now much easier to solve, although in this case the only solution is the null solution $v_1 = v_2 = 0$.

The stoichiometric matrix

The representation of the equations above can be generalised to any similar biological network and represented in a more powerful manner by using matrices. The stoichiometric matrix for the simple set of reactions above is,

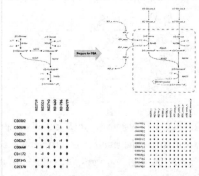

An example stoichiometric matrix for a network representing the top of glycolysis and that same network after being prepared for FBA.

$$\mathbf{S} = \begin{bmatrix} -1 & 1 \\ 1 & -1 \\ -1 & 0 \end{bmatrix}$$

The stoichiometric matrix is also often referred to in chemistry, metabolic control analysis[18] and dynamical systems[19] with the letter $\mathbf{N}$ (meaning number as related to stoichiometry, S is often reserved for species or Entropy) but in FBA it is usually referred to as $\mathbf{S}$. Both letters are exactly equivalent. At this stage it is useful to define a vector $\vec{v}$ where each component of the vector represents the rate (flux through) its respective reaction within the stoichiometric matrix

$$\vec{v} = \begin{bmatrix} v_1 \\ v_2 \end{bmatrix}$$

Multiplying this matrix, $\mathbf{S}$, with $\vec{v}$, is completely equivalent to the equations derived directly from the reaction diagram,

$$\begin{bmatrix} -1 & 1 \\ 1 & -1 \\ -1 & 0 \end{bmatrix} \begin{bmatrix} v_1 \\ v_2 \end{bmatrix} = \begin{bmatrix} -v_1 + v_2 \\ v_1 - v_2 \\ -v_1 \end{bmatrix} = \begin{bmatrix} \frac{d[C]_1}{dt} \\ \frac{d[C]_2}{dt} \\ \frac{d[C]_3}{dt} \end{bmatrix}$$

Applying the homeostatic condition then gives us,

$$\begin{bmatrix} -1 & 1 \\ 1 & -1 \\ -1 & 0 \end{bmatrix} \begin{bmatrix} v_1 \\ v_2 \end{bmatrix} = \begin{bmatrix} -v_1 + v_2 \\ v_1 - v_2 \\ -v_1 \end{bmatrix} = \begin{bmatrix} \frac{d[C]_1}{dt} \\ \frac{d[C]_2}{dt} \\ \frac{d[C]_3}{dt} \end{bmatrix} = \begin{bmatrix} 0 \\ 0 \\ 0 \end{bmatrix}$$

In the general case we can write,

$$\mathbf{S}\,\vec{v} = 0$$

Or often confusingly, given the different nature of the · when referring to the vector dot product, but identically as,

$$\mathbf{S} \cdot \vec{v} = 0$$

With the single $\mathbf{0}$ representing the null vector,

$$0 = \begin{bmatrix} 0 \\ \cdot \\ \cdot \\ \cdot \\ 0 \end{bmatrix}.$$

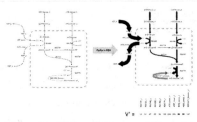

The results of FBA can be represented identically as a vector of fluxes, or by weighting the lines representing the reactions according to the flux they carry.

This general operation is called taking the Null Space of the stoichiometric matrix s and the technique is valid for all stoichiometric matrices, not just the small example here. Since a typical stoichiometric matrix contains many more metabolites than reactions ($m < n$) and the majority of reactions are linearly independent there are many vectors $\vec{v}$ that satisfy the equation and thus span the null space of s.

Application to the biology of the system

The analysis of the null space of matrices is common within linear algebra and many software packages such as Matlab and Octave can help with this process. Nevertheless, knowing the null space of s only tells us all the possible collections of flux vectors (or linear combinations thereof) that balance fluxes within the biological network. Flux-balance analysis has two further aims, to accurately represent the biology limits of the system and to return the flux distribution closest to that naturally occurring within the target system/organism.

Constraints

The stoichiometric matrix is almost always underdetermined meaning that the solution space to $s\vec{v}=0$ is very large. The size of the solution space can be reduced, and made more reflective of the biology of the problem through the application of certain constraints on the solutions.

Thermodynamic

In principle all reactions are reversible however in practise many reactions effectively occur in only one direction. This can be because of a significantly higher concentration of reactants compared to the concentration of the products of the reaction but is more often because the products of a reaction have a much lower free energy than the reactants and therefore the forward direction of a reaction is massively favoured. For ideal reactions,

$$-\infty < v_i < \infty$$

For certain reactions a thermodynamic constraint can be applied implying direction (in this case forward)

$$0 < v_i < \infty$$

Realistically the flux through a reaction cannot be infinite (given that enzymes in the real system are finite) which implies that,

$$0 < v_i < v_{\mathrm{max}}$$

Measured flux rates

Certain flux rates can be measured experimentally ($v_{i,m}$) and the fluxes within a metabolic model can be constrained, within some error (ε), to ensure these known flux rates are accurately reproduced in the simulation.

$$v_{i,m} - \varepsilon < v_i < v_{i,m} + \varepsilon$$

Flux rates are most easily measured for nutrient uptake at the edge of the network but measurements of internal fluxes are possible, generally using radioactively labelled or NMR visible metabolites.

Optimisation (the objective/biomass function)

Even after the application of constraints there is usually a large number of possible solutions to the flux-balance problem. If an optimisation goal is defined, linear programming can be used to find a single optimal solution. The most common biological optimisation goal for a whole organism metabolic network would be to choose the flux vector $\vec{v}$ that maximises the flux through a biomass function composed of the constituent metabolites of the organism placed into the stoichiometric matrix and denoted v_{biomass} or simply v_b

$$\max_{\vec{v}} v_b \quad \text{s.t.} \quad \mathbf{S}\vec{v} = 0$$

In the more general case any reaction be defined and added defined as a biomass function with either the condition that it be maximised or minimised if a single "optimal" solution is desired. Alternatively, and in the most general case, a vector $\vec{c}$ can be defined which defines the weighted set of reactions that the linear programming model should aim to maximise or minimise,

$$\max_{\vec{v}} \vec{v} \cdot \vec{c} \quad \text{s.t.} \quad \mathbf{S}\vec{v} = 0$$

In the case of there being only a single separate biomass function/reaction within the stoichiometric matrix $\vec{c}$ would simplify to all zeroes with a value of 1 (or any non-zero value) in the position corresponding to that biomass function. Where there were multiple separate objective functions $\vec{c}$ would simplify to all zeroes with weighted values in the positions corresponding to all objective functions.

Simulating perturbations

FBA is not computationally intensive, taking on the order of seconds to calculate optimal fluxes for biomass production for a simple organism (around 1000 reactions). This means that the effect of deleting reactions from the network and/or changing flux constraints can be sensibly modelled on a single computer.

Single reaction deletion

A frequently used technique to search a metabolic network for reactions that are particularly critical to the production of biomass. By removing each reaction in a network in turn and measuring the predicted flux through the biomass function, each reaction can be classified as either essential (if the flux through the biomass function is substantially reduced) or non-essential (if the flux through the biomass function is unchanged or only slightly reduced).

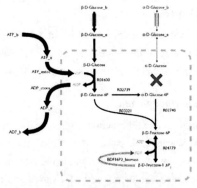

An example of a non lethal gene deletion in a sample metabolic network with fluxes shown by the weight of the reaction lines as calculated by FBA. Here the flux through the objective function is halved but is still present.

Reaction inhibition

The effect of inhibiting a reaction, rather than removing it entirely, can be simulated in FBA by restricting the allowed flux through it. The effect of an inhibition can be classified as lethal or non-lethal by applying the same criteria as in the case of a deletion where a suitable threshold is used to distinguish "substantially reduced" from "slightly reduced". Generally the choice of threshold is arbitrary but a reasonable estimate can be obtained from growth experiments where the simulated inhibitions/deletions are actually performed and growth rate is measured.

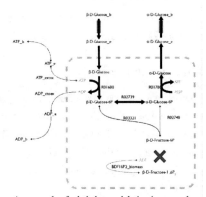

An example of a lethal gene deletion in a sample metabolic network with fluxes shown by the weight of the reaction lines as calculated by FBA. Here there is no flux through the objective function, simulating that the pathway is no longer functional.

Interpreting results

The utility of reaction inhibition and deletion analyses is most clear if a gene-protein-reaction matrix has been assembled for the network being studied with FBA. If this has been done then information on which reactions are essential can be converted into information on which genes are essential (and thus what gene defects may cause a certain disease) or which proteins/enzymes are essential (and thus what enzymes are the most promising drug targets in pathogens).

Reaction deletion in pairs

An extension of single reaction deletions are double reaction deletions where all possible pairs of reactions are deleted. This can be useful when looking for drug targets as it allows the simulation of multi-target treatments, either by a single drug with multiple targets or by drug combinations.

Growth media modification

FBA has also been used to simulate the effect on growth rate of changes in the growth media of the metabolic system being studied. In *E. coli* the predicted growth rates of bacteria in varying media have been shown to correlate well with experimental results[20] as well as to define precise minimal media for the culture of *Salmonella typhimurium*[21].

Extensions of FBA

The success of FBA has led to many extensions aimed at more deeply analysing the system being studied or attempting to mediate the limitations of the technique.

Flux variability analysis

The optimal solution to the flux-balance problem is rarely unique with many possible, and equally optimal, solutions existing. Flux variability analysis (FVA), built-in to both the COBRA toolbox and SurreyFBA, returns the boundaries for the fluxes through each reaction that can, paired with right combination of other fluxes, produce the optimal solution.

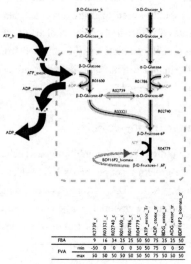

Visual and numerical representation of FVA on complete network.

Reactions which can support a low variability of fluxes through them are likely to be of a higher importance to an organism and FVA is a promising technique for the identification of reactions that are highly important despite being non-essential.

Dynamic FBA

Dynamic FBA attempts to add the ability for models to change over time, thus in some ways avoiding the strict homoeostatic condition of pure FBA. Typically the technique involves running an FBA simulation, changing the model based on the outputs of that simulation, and rerunning the simulation. By repeating this process an element of feedback is achieved over time.

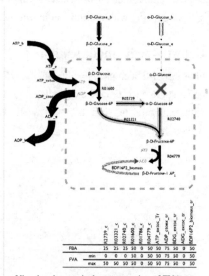

Visual and numerical representation of FVA on network with non-lethal deletion.

Comparison with other techniques

FBA provides a less simplistic analysis than Choke Point Analysis while requiring far less information on reaction rates and a much less complete network reconstruction than a full dynamic simulation would require. In filling this niche, FBA has been shown to be a very useful technique for analysis of the metabolic capabilities of cellular systems.

Choke point analysis

Unlike choke point analysis which only considers points in the network where metabolites are produced but not consumed or vice-versa, FBA is a true form of metabolic network modelling because it considers the metabolic network as a single complete entity (the stoichiometric matrix) at all stages of analysis. This means that network effects, such as chemical reactions in distant pathways affecting each other, can be reproduced in the model. The upside to the inability of choke point analysis to simulate network effects is that it considers each reaction within a network in isolation and thus can suggest important reactions in a network even if a network is highly fragmented and contains many gaps.

Dynamic metabolic simulation

Unlike dynamic metabolic simulation, FBA assumes that the internal concentration of metabolites within a system stays constant over time and thus is unable to provide anything other than steady-state solutions. It is unlikely that FBA could, for example, simulate the functioning of a nerve cell. Since the internal concentration of metabolites is not considered within a model, it is possible that an FBA solution could contain metabolites at a concentration too high to be biologically acceptable. This is a problem that dynamic metabolic simulations would probably avoid. One advantage of the simplicity of FBA over dynamic simulations is that they are far less computationally expensive, allowing the simulation of large numbers of perturbations to the network. A second advantage is that the reconstructed model can be substantially simpler by avoiding the need to consider enzyme rates and the effect of complex interactions on enzyme kinetics.

References

[1] Edwards, J., Ibarra, R. & Palsson, B. In silico predictions of Escherichia coli metabolic capabilities are consistent with experimental data. Nature Biotechnology 19, 125–130(2001).

[2] (http://www.nature.com/nbt/web_extras/supp_info/nbt0201_125/info_frame.html)

[3] Palsson, B.O. Systems Biology: Properties of Reconstructed Networks. 334(Cambridge University Press: 2006).

[4] Orth, J.D., Thiele, I. & Palsson, B.Ø. What is flux balance analysis? Nature Biotechnology 28, 245-248(2010).

[5] Lee, J.M., Gianchandani, E.P. & Papin, J.A. Flux balance analysis in the era of metabolomics. Briefings in bioinformatics 7, 140-50(2006).

[6] Feist, A.M. & Palsson, B.Ø. The growing scope of applications of genome-scale metabolic reconstructions using Escherichia coli. Nature biotechnology 26, 659-67(2008).

[7] Papoutsakis ET, Equations and calculations for fermentations of butyric acid bacteria. Biotech and Bioeng, 26(2), 174-187 (1984)

[8] Watson MR, Metabolic maps for the Apple II. 12, 1093-1094 (1984)

[9] Fell DA and Small JR, Fat synthesis in adipose tissue. An examination of stoichiometric constraints. Biochem J., 238(3), 781-786 (1986)

[10] Thiele, I. & Palsson, B.Ø. A protocol for generating a high-quality genome-scale metabolic reconstruction. Nature protocols 5, 93-121(2010).

[11] http://bioinformatics.ai.sri.com/ptools/

[12] Schilling, C.H. et al. SimPheny: A Computational Infrastructure for Systems Biology. (2008).

[13] http://www.genomatica.com/technology/technologySuite.html

[14] http://www.celldesigner.org

[15] http://www.bioinformatics.leeds.ac.uk/~pytf/metnetmaker

[16] Becker, S.A. et al. Quantitative prediction of cellular metabolism with constraint-based models: the COBRA Toolbox. Nature protocols 2, 727-38(2007).

[17] Gevorgyan A, Bushell ME, Avignone-Rossa C, Kierzek AM. SurreyFBA: a command line tool and graphics user interface for constraint-based modeling of genome-scale metabolic reaction networks. Bioinformatics (Oxford, England). 2011;27(3):433-4. Available at: http://www.ncbi.nlm.nih.gov/pubmed/21148545.

[18] Reder, C (1988) Metabolic control theory: a structural approach. J Theor Biol. 135(2), 175-201. PMID 3267767

[19] Steuer, R and Junker, B H (2008) Computational Models of Metabolism: Stability and Regulation in Metabolic Networks in Advances in Chemical Physics, 142, 105-251

[20] Edwards, J., Ibarra, R. & Palsson, B. In silico predictions of Escherichia coli metabolic capabilities are consistent with experimental data. Nature Biotechnology 19, 125–130(2001).

[21] Raghunathan, A. et al. Constraint-based analysis of metabolic capacity of Salmonella typhimurium during host-pathogen interaction. BMC systems biology 3, 38(2009).

Folding@home

Folding@home

Folding@home distributed computing	
Original author(s)	Vijay Pande
Developer(s)	Stanford University / Pande Group
Initial release	2000-10-01

Stable release	*Windows:*
	   Uniprocessor: 6.23[1]
	   GPU: 6.41[2]
	Mac OS X:
	   x86-64 SMP: 6.29.3[1]
	Linux:
	   SMP: 6.34[1] [2]
	PlayStation 3: 1.4[3]

Preview release	*Windows, Mac, and Linux:* 7.1.38[4] / October 10, 2011[5]
Operating system	Windows, OS-X, Linux
Platform	Cross-platform
Available in	English
Type	Distributed computing
License	Proprietary[6]
Website	[folding.stanford.edu folding.stanford.edu]

Folding@home is a distributed computing project designed to use spare processing power on personal computers to perform simulations of disease-relevant protein folding and other molecular dynamics, and to improve on the methods of doing so. Also referred to as **FAH** or **F@h**, much of its work attempts to determine how proteins reach their final structure, which is of significant academic interest and has implications to both disease research and nanotechnology. To a lesser degree Folding@home also tries to predict that final structure from only the initial amino acid sequence, which has applications in drug design.[7] Folding@home is run by the Pande Group, a non-profit organization within Stanford University's chemistry department, under the supervision of Dr. Vijay Pande.[8] The goal of the project is to "understand protein folding, misfolding, and related diseases".[9] [10]

Folding@home's accurate simulations of protein folding and misfolding enable the scientific community to better understand the development of many diseases, including Alzheimer's disease, Parkinson's disease, cancer, Creutzfeldt–Jakob disease, Huntington's disease, cystic fibrosis, sickle-cell anaemia, HIV, Chagas disease, influenza, osteogenesis imperfecta, autism,[11] and alpha 1-antitrypsin deficiency, among others.[12] More fundamentally, understanding the process of protein folding — how biological molecules assemble themselves into a functional state — is one of the outstanding problems of molecular biology.[13] In addition to producing ninety-five scientific research papers, more than all other major distributing computing projects combined, Folding@home has caused significant paradigm shifts in protein folding theory.[14] [15]

In January 2010 the Folding@home project also successfully simulated protein folding in the 1.5 millisecond range — which is a simulation thousands of times longer than ever previously achieved.[16] Folding@home has pioneered the uses of GPUs, multi-core processors, and Playstation 3s for distributed computing, is one of the world's most powerful computing systems, is more powerful than all distributed computing projects under BOINC combined, and is one of the world's largest projects. Folding@home's distributed simulations remain accurate compared to results from laboratory research.[17] The Pande Group's goal is to refine Folding@home's methods to the level where it will become an essential tool for molecular medical research, and they collaborate with various scientific institutions and laboratories across the world, as well as publicly releasing all of Folding@home's results.[18] [19]

Biomedical significance

Further information: Protein folding

Proteins can act as enzymes, performing biochemical reactions including cell signaling, transportation, cellular regulation, and others; as structural elements they make up much of the body; and as antibodies they help the immune system.[12] Before a protein can take on these roles, it must first fold itself (chemical self-assembly) into a functional three-dimensional shape based on a particular series of steps, (see Levinthal's paradox) which they can do

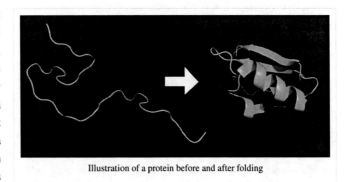

Illustration of a protein before and after folding

spontaneously.[20] [21] Understanding protein folding is thus critical to understanding what a protein does and how it works.[12] Moreover, when proteins do not fold correctly, (fold down the wrong pathway or to the wrong structure) they can aggregate and cause serious and in some cases life-threatening diseases.[22] [23] While the understanding protein folding requires a combination of theories and experiments, creating experimentally comparable simulations of protein folding dynamics is considered a "holy grail" of computational biology.[24] [25] Folding@home's methods allow for unique insights into the complexity of protein folding while quantitative agreeing with experimental data.[24] Folding@home is dedicated to producing significant amounts of results towards protein folding, the diseases that result from protein misfolding, and the novel computational methods for doing so.[12]

While the understanding of protein folding has become increasingly important for disease research, for the last decade simulations of protein molecular dynamics have been severely limited by computational power, forcing the use of simplified native-centric *in silico* molecular models. It has become clear that these models are no longer sufficient for a comprehensive view of protein folding, and that a small number of very long simulations cannot accurately capture detailed information into how a protein misfolds.[24] Instead, Folding@home runs many shorter simulations in parallel, which provide a much more complete description of the protein's energy landscape, conformation space, and equilibrium thermodynamics.[18] [26] While some of these simulations may work themselves into impossible atomic configurations or into the correct native state, others will illustrate how that protein misfolds.[26] Once it is understood why a protein misfolds in a particular way, figuring out the prevention of the misfolding can be the next step. Moreover, preventative treatment can be applied while the protein is misfolding.[23] The Pande Group has used Folding@home to study this for number of years using a variety of different methods.[27]

The Pande Group and other researchers can use Folding@home to study aspects of folding, misfolding, and related diseases that would never be seen experimentally; however, many simulations run on Folding@home are used in conjunction with laboratory experiments.[17] Moreover, the Pande Group are also studying how protein folding in native cells may be different than in environments such as test tubes used during experiments.[28] [29] Results from Rosetta@home, another distributed computing project aimed at protein structure prediction, is in some cases used as a basis for some of Folding@home's projects. While Rosetta@home provides the protein's most likely final structure, it is not definite if that form is natural or actually viable. Folding@home can then be used to verify Rosetta@home's results, but can also provide additional atomic-level information, such as important details into how the molecule changes shape while getting to that structure.[30] [31]

In addition to the diseases listed below, Folding@home is used to study the dynamics of key components of HIV,[32] details of how the influenza virus recognizes and infects cells,[33] as well as malaria, Chagas disease,[12] and the prions which cause Creutzfeldt–Jakob disease.[34] The goal of the first five years of the project was to make significant advances in understanding folding, while the current goal is to understand misfolding and related disease, especially Alzheimer's Disease.[17] [35]

Alzheimer's disease

Alzheimer's disease, a form of dementia which most often affects the elderly, is believed to be caused by specific misfolding and subsequent aggregation of the small amyloid beta (Aβ) peptide.[35] The severity of the disease depends not only depends on amount of Aβ, but also on how it misfolds. Current theory holds that toxic non-plaque Aβ oligomers (aggregates of many monomers) bind to a surface receptor on neurons and change the structure of the synapse, thereby disrupting neuronal communication and cause neuronal cell death which leads to the associated neurodegenerative consequences.[36] [37] Folding@home is currently concentrating on Alzheimer's and is performing full-scale simulations of amyloid beta and its oligomerization.[35] [38] Understanding how and why this peptide misfolds could result in key insights into how to cure Alzheimer's Disease, and will also help the Pande Group prepare for similar aggregation studies.[35] [39] The Pande Group's primary goal is the prediction of the disease's aggregate structure for rational drug design approaches, as well as to gain further insight into how the disease aggregates form, and what methods can be used to prevent it.[12]

Folding@home is also being used to study Aβ fragments of different sizes to determine how various natural enzymes affect the structure and folding of Aβ. These fragments are tied to senile plaques, a pathological marker of Alzheimer's disease in patient's brain. When certain enzymes cleave the amyloid precursor protein, Abeta peptides are produced, while the action of other enzymes can instead produce p3 peptides, much smaller fragments of Aβ. Folding@home is currently simulating one of these smaller peptides in water in an effort determine the structure of p3 compared to regular Aβ.[40]

The Pande Group is also using Folding@home to investigate protein–protein interactions, which occur extensively throughout both benign and disease-related biological activities. Interactions involving the common SH3 protein are also being studied, as it has implications in Alzheimers research. The refinement of these simulations has greatly improved the Pande Group's ability to understand a wide variety of biological interactions.[41]

Huntington's disease

Huntington's disease, an incurable neurodegenerative genetic disorder affecting muscle coordination and leading to dementia, is also associated with protein misfolding. Specifically, it is caused by a mutation in the Huntingtin gene, which causes excessively long repetitive chains of the glutamine amino acid in the Huntingtin protein, a protein that plays important roles in nerve cells.[42] [43] The likelihood of neuronal cell death is primarily affected by the length of the glutamine chain and the neuron's intracellular exposure to the misfolded Huntingtin protein.[44] The defective protein causes Huntington's by aggregating most often in the striatum and frontal cortex of patient's brains. The Pande Group is using Folding@home to study these aggregates, as well as predict how they form.[12] These studies will be useful for drug design approaches against the disease, and will serve as a foundation for methods to stop the aggregation formation in the first place. Additionally, some of the methods used to study Huntington's are also being used for Alzheimer's research.[12]

Cancer

Approximately half of all known cancers involve mutations in p53, a tumor suppressor protein present in every cell which signals for cell death in the event of damage to a cell's DNA. If p53 becomes mutated, breaks down, or fails to fold properly, the cell grows unchecked in ways based on the damaged DNA.[45] Folding@home is used to study specific properties of p53 in order to understand and predict these mutations, and the Pande Group have also expanded their work to other p53-related diseases. Starting in 2007, work is also underway to develop novel inhibitor proteins that deactivate damaged p53.[12]

The Pande Group is also performing research into protein chaperones. These are proteins that assist in the folding of other molecules, assembly of oligomeric structures, the prevention of potential damage caused by protein misfolding, and other functions. They are needed for these purposes by rapidly growing cancerous cells.[46] Using Folding@home and working closely with the Protein Folding Center, they plan to find ways to inhibit chaperones involved in cancer. Using Folding@home for a more comprehensive visualization of their functions, the Pande Group and the Protein Folding Center collectively plan to engineer modified chaperonins to inhibit the folding of particular proteins associated with human diseases such as cancer and Alzheimer's. While this approach has been used before, they believe that this project, if successful, could lead to an interesting new drug against cancer or at least make major advances in that area.[46]

There have been several other additional studies into the onset of cancer. Folding@home is used to study the activation of enzyme src Kinase, mutations of which can be involved in some forms of cancer.[47] The Pande Group also studies folding of forms of the Engrailed Homeodomain, believed to be involved in many diseases including cancer. This protein has a great deal of experimental data for comparison, and is a great model system to understand folding and misfolding.[48]

The small knottin protein EETI has been recently engineered to attach to particular receptors on the surface of cancer cells, which allows these cells to be identified in an imaging scan. The Pande Group uses Folding@home to help understand the dynamics of this protein and how it can be used to bind to other receptors such as imaging agents or drugs.[49]

Some forms of interleukin-2, an important signaling protein for the immune system, have been used as immunotherapy for cancer. The Pande Group hopes that by using Folding@home to understand its dynamics, insights can be gained as to how to design other therapeutics.[50]

Parkinson's disease

Parkinson's disease is a degenerative disorder of the central nervous system, characterized by shaking, rigidity, slowness of movement, and dementia. The Pande Group has performed preliminary studies on the properties of alpha-synuclein, a key natively unfolded protein.[12] Particular mutations of alpha-synuclein can aggregate to form toxic fibrils, and while the mechanism of this aggregation remains largely unknown, it can lead to the Parkinson's disease and other conditions.[51] The Pande Group is also testing how Folding@home's methods apply to this problem, and in 2005 Dr. Pande presented results from FAH at a National Parkinson Foundation conference.[12]

Osteogenesis imperfecta

Osteogenesis imperfecta is a non-curable genetic bone disorder. Those with the disease are unable to successfully make functional connective bone tissue. For many, this is lethal but can also induce a higher rate of miscarriages.[12] The disease is caused by mutations in the Type-1 collagen protein, the most common form of collagen and found abundantly throughout the body. Although some of these mutations of collagen can lead to serious morphological disorders, more benign forms can cause brittle bones and other subtleties.[12] Folding@home has performed simulations of collagen, and has produced a paper on Osteogenesis imperfecta outlining new molecular simulation techniques and revealing new insights into how collagen misfolds. The Pande Group believes these results will be useful for later computational studies of collagen.[52]

Diabetes

Amylin is a misfolded peptide involved in Type II diabetes. While amylin is natively unfolded, it forms an alpha helix structure upon contact with cellular membranes. Moreover, it can aggregate into large deposits on these membranes, inducing cell death of insulin-producing cells, which may be relevant to the development of the disease. Around 95% of patients with Type II diabetes exhibit these aggregate deposits. Folding@home is currently simulating amylin with the goal to understand how this aggregation forms and to design drugs to prevent it.[53]

Antibiotics

The ribosome is a large biological machine that synthesizes proteins from mRNA. It is the target for approximately half of all known antibiotics, which usually kill bacteria by preventing their ribosomes from making new and essential proteins. Folding@home is currently simulating the ribosome in detail using new state-of-the-art calculation methods.[12] Results from these simulations have significantly helped the Pande Group prepare to study more complex biomedical problems. The Pande Group is also using Folding@home to perform antibiotic drug design calculations.[12]

Drug design

The Pande Group is using Folding@home to explore how to model and accurately estimate the binding energy of small molecules to a protein. Accurate prediction of binding affinities have the potential to significantly lower the development cost of new drugs.[54] Additionally, Folding@home is utilized to find prime binding sites on protein surfaces by simulating interactions between ligand binding sites with different molecules. This has a direct application to computational drug design.[55] Folding@home is also performing calculations on beta-lactamase, a protein which plays important roles in drug resistance. The Pande Group hopes that by understanding its dynamics, they may be able to design drugs to deactivate it.[56]

Software

Folding@home software on the user's end consists of three components: a client, work units, and cores.

Client

Contributors to Folding@home install a client program on their personal computer.[17] The client acts as a download and file manager for work units, controls the scientific cores, and is the software with which the user interacts.[57] Through the client, the user may pause the folding process, open an event log, check the work progress, or view personal statistics.[57] Early in the project this client was a screensaver, which would run Folding@home while the computer was not otherwise in use, but this has since replaced by a program that run continuously in the background, using otherwise unused processing power.[1] [57] These clients are designed to run FAH's calculations at an extremely low priority, and will back off to allow other computer programs to have more processing power.[58] [59] Although modern computer chips are designed to be able to operate continuously without degrading,[58] [60] if users wish to reduce power consumption or heat production, the maximum percentage of CPU power used can be adjusted if desired.[57] If interrupted by a computer shutdown or other means, the client will resume work at almost the same point at startup.[61] For users with machines with multiple processor units, multiple clients may be installed on one machine, and users may be credited by clients on multiple machines.[9]

The source code of the client is not publicly available, for security and scientific integrity reasons.[6] [62] The Pande Group works hard to minimize security issues in all of Folding@home's software.[15] [63] For example, clients can be downloaded only from the official Folding@home website or its commercial partners.[6] It will upload and download data only from Stanford's Folding@home data servers, (over port 8080, with 80 as an alternative)[64] and will only interact with FAH computer files.[15] [63] Moreover, it does not normally need computer administrative privileges,[63] so from a security standpoint it behaves similar to but is even more secure than a web browser.[18] [64]

Early Folding@home clients were once tested on the open source BOINC framework; however, this approach became unworkable and was abandoned in June 2006.[65] Both BOINC and Folding@home clients fell short, for neither client type had enough ability to be compatible with the other. BOINC lacked many features that FAH needed, and FAH lacked features that BOINC needed.[66]

V7

The v7 client is the seventh and latest generation of the Folding@home software, currently under heavy development and is available for open beta testing. It is a complete rewrite and unification of the previous clients for Windows, OS-X and Linux operating systems.[67] It uses a new GUI, known as "FAHControl", which has "Novice", "Advanced" and "Expert" user interface modes, and has the ability to monitor, configure and control many remote folding clients from a single computer.[67] "FAHClient" runs behind the scenes, can be controlled and monitored by FAHControl, and manages each

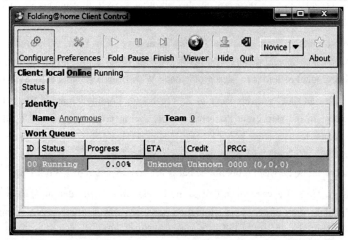

A sample image of the v7 client in Novice mode running under Windows 7. In addition to a variety of controls and user details, v7 also presents Work Unit information, such as its state, calculation progress, ETA, credit points, and identification

"FAHSlot" (or "slot"). Each slot may be of Uniprocessor, SMP, or GPU type, contain the core and data associated with it, and download, process, and upload results independently.[67] [68] The "FAHViewer" function displays a real-time 3D rendering, if available, of the protein currently being processed.[67] FAHViewer is modeled after the PS3 viewer and has a variety of options for displaying the Work Unit animation.[67] [68]

The v7 client is designed to make the installation, start-up, and operation user-friendly for novices, as well as offering greater scientific flexibility than previous clients. The v7 client also supports new cores, including those designed for ATI GPUs.[69] However, all GPUs must be approved and whitelisted before v7 can utilize them.[70] [71] [67] The v7 installer supports Windows 2000, 2003, 2008, XP, Vista, and 7,[67] [72] as well as various 32-bit and 64-bit Linux operating systems, such as Debian, Ubuntu, RedHat, Fedora, and CentOS.[67] [72] V7 also supports 64-bit OS-X, with a 32-bit version under development.[67]

As with previous clients, v7 runs Folding@home in the background at very low priority, which allows other applications to use CPU resources as they need. V7 components also have very little CPU overhead, and FAHViewer protein animation can be disabled to further minimize this.[67]

V7 has been in development since 2009,[73] and Trac is used for the organization of feature requests and bugs.[67] It is the Pande Group's goal to make v7 the recommended client by January 2012 at the latest,[74] and versions of v7 will be frequently released until then.[74]

Work Units

The Work Unit (WU) is the actual data that the client is being asked to process. The client connects to Folding@home servers to retrieve a Work Unit, and returns it upon completion.[75] During transfer, all Work Units are validated through the use of 2048-bit digital signatures.[15] Each WU is identified for its respective protein Project, Run (conformation), Clone (atomic trajectory), and Generation (time steps in the trajectory/simulation).[76] Work Units also have associated deadlines and credit (point) value. If this deadline is is exceeded, the user may not get credit and the unit will be reissued to someone else.[15] As protein folding is serial in nature and each WU is generated from its predecessor, this allows the overall simulation process to proceed normally if a WU is not returned after a certain period of time.[15]

Work units go through several Quality Assurance steps. First, WUs are first tested internally for issues, then they are released to special donors who opt-in for beta WUs, before finally being publicly released across FAH. The goal of this gradual rollout is to keep problematic WUs from becoming fully available.[77]

Unlike BOINC projects such as SETI@home, Folding@home's Work Units are normally processed only once, except in the rare event that errors occur during processing of a WU. If this occurs, the Work Unit will still be reissued to two other users,[78] and if it generates errors for those users as well, at 8am PDT it is automatically marked as "bad" and is pulled from distribution.[79] [80] Topics in the Folding@home forum can be used to differentiate between problematic hardware and an actual bad Work Unit.[81]

Work Units are very much tied to the Pande Group's simulation Markov State Models. These allow for extensive parallelization of very long simulation processes which otherwise seem intrinsically serial.[75] [82] The Pande Group first builds a kinetic model of the protein by dividing the possible dynamics into a series of related conformation states, and create WUs to calculate the rates of transition between these states. When the completed WUs are gathered, the Pande Group then runs sophisticated Bayesian Machine Learning algorithms which calculate the reasonable states and the rates between them.[75] This system is successful even at the millisecond timescale and compares well to traditional simulation methods and experimental results.[16]

Any computer can contribute to Folding@home. However, older and slower machines might not be fast enough to complete a Work Unit before the deadline. The Pande Group states that a Pentium 3 450 MHz CPU with SSE or newer is able to complete WUs before they expire.[15]

Cores

Specialized scientific computer programs, referred to as "cores," perform the calculations on the Work Unit behind the scenes.[83] Folding@home's cores are based on modified and optimized versions of molecular dynamics programs for calculation, including GROMACS, AMBER, TINKER, CPMD, SHARPEN, ProtoMol, BrookGPU and Desmond.[83] [84] [73] These variants are each given an arbitrary identifier (Core xx). While the same core can be used by various versions of the client, separating the core from the client enables the scientific methods to be updated automatically as needed without a client update.[83]

Some of these cores do explicit molecular dynamics calculations, which simulate atoms based on the forces that the atoms exert on each other.[85] These types of calculations reveal how folding happened, not just what the final outcome is, and often tend to be more efficient and optimized than the Monte Carlo methods used to predict particular final properties of a protein.[85] Other cores, such as those designed for the PS3, perform implicit solvation methods, which treat atoms as a mathematical continuum.

Following the Pande Group's pattern of openness, these scientific cores are open-source software or are under similar licenses.[86] [87] During download, the cores are verified by 2048-bit digital signatures.[15] [88] This ensures the tightest possible security with the best software security measures developed to date.[15]

Participation

Interest and participation in the project has grown steadily since its launch.[89] As of October 17, 2011, Folding@home has about 432,000 active CPUs, about 20,000 active GPUs, and about 21,000 active PS3s, for a total of about 4.3 native petaFLOPS, (6.7 x86 petaFLOPS) more computing power than the combined efforts of all distributed computing projects under BOINC.[90] [91] A large majority of this performance comes from the GPU and PS3 clients.[90] Folding@home gains a near linear speedup for every additional processor.[10]

In 2007 Guinness recognized Folding@home as the most powerful distributed computing cluster in the world.[92] Folding@home is also one of the world's largest distributed computing projects.[90] This large and powerful network allows FAH to do work not possible any other way, including through use of supercomputers.[93]

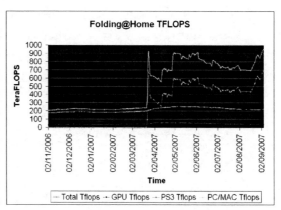

Folding@home computing power shown, by device type, in teraFLOPS as recorded semi-daily from November 2006 until September 2007. Note the large spike in total compute power after March 22, when the PlayStation 3 client was released.

Google collaboration

There used to be cooperation between Folding@home and Google Labs in the form of Google Toolbar.[94] [95] Google Compute started in March 2002,[96] [97] back when Folding@home only had about 10,000 active CPUs, and pushed Folding@home up to about 30,000 active CPUs.[18] The Google Compute clients had certain limits: it could only run the TINKER core and had limited username and team options.[98] Folding@home is no longer supported on Google Toolbar,[99] [100] and even the old Google Toolbar client will not work. Google Compute officially ended in October 2005, and the Google Compute homepage recommends that users wishing to continue contributions to the project download the official Folding@home client instead.[101] [102]

Genome@home

Genome@home was another distributed computing project from the Pande Group Lab, a sister project to Folding@home. The goal of Genome@home was protein design and its applications. The project was officially concluded on March 8, 2004, although data was still collected until April 15.[103] It accumulated a large database of protein sequences, which will be used for important scientific purposes for many years by the Pande Group and many others throughout the world.[103] [104]

Folding@home clients absorbed the remainder of the Genome@home project on March 12, 2004.[104] The work that was started by the Genome@home project has since been completed using the Folding@home network, (as Work Units without deadlines) and no new work is being distributed by this project.[15] All donators were encouraged to download the Folding@home client (the FAH 4.xx client had a Genome@home option), and once the Genome@home work was complete these clients were asked to donate their processing power to the Folding@home project instead.[104]

PetaFLOPS milestones

Native petaFLOPS threshold	Date crossed	Fastest Supercomputer at Date Crossed
1.0	September 16, 2007	0.2806 petaFLOP BlueGene/L[105]
2.0	May 7, 2008	0.4782 petaFLOP BlueGene/L[106]
3.0	August 20, 2008	1.042 petaFLOP Roadrunner[107]
4.0	September 28, 2008	1.042 petaFLOP Roadrunner[107]
5.0	February 18, 2009	1.105 petaFLOP Roadrunner[108]
6.0	March 25, 2011	2.566 petaFLOP Tianhe-1A[109]
7.0	March 28, 2011	2.566 petaFLOP Tianhe-1A[109]

On September 16, 2007, the Folding@home project officially attained a sustained performance level higher than one native petaFLOPS, becoming the first computing system of any kind in the world to do so.[110] [111] [112] [113] In March 2007 Folding@home had, mostly due to about 30,000 PS3s,[114] [115] almost reached a petaFLOP, but then the Pande Group reevaluated the consoles' FLOP performance to about half of the original figure.[114] [116] On May 7, 2008 the project attained a sustained performance level higher than two native petaFLOPS,[117] followed by the three and four native petaFLOPS milestones on August 20 and September 28, 2008 respectively.[118] [119] On February 18, 2009, Folding@home achieved a performance level of just above 5 native petaFLOPS, thereby becoming the first computing system to surpass that performance,[120] [121] just as it was for the other four milestones. In late March 2011 Folding@home briefly peaked above the 7 native petaFLOP barrier.[90]

These supercomputers are expensive to run, and its resources are typically shared.[17] [122] Measurement of the computing speed of these systems is often done using the legacy LINPACK benchmark. However, the FLOP measurement produced is not necessarily a good measure of scientific production,[123] and that the brief benchmarking is not an accurate indication of their prolonged performance over real-world tasks.[124] Folding@home's FLOPs however remain an accurate indication of its sustained performance.[125]

Starting in March 2009, Folding@home began reporting performance in both Native FLOPS and x86 FLOPS.[126] As different hardware can perform the same computations in different ways, "x86 FLOPS" are an estimate of how many FLOPS a given calculation would take on the standard x86 CPU architecture.[127] Despite being conservative in the conversions,[128] [129] "x86" FLOPS are consistently much greater than the "Native" FLOPS.[127] A detailed explanation of the difference between the two figures was given in the Folding@home FLOP FAQ.[127]

Points

Distributed computing projects are often driven by a sense of collegiate competition to compute the most for the project. Folding@home quantitatively assesses this through points. Points are determined by the performance of a each contributor's folding hardware relative to a reference benchmark machine.[130] [131]

One or more Work Units from a project are benchmarked on that machine before any donors can do any work on that project. This generates a fair system of equal pay for equal work.[130] However, certain projects require substantially more computer resources (disk space, network usage, RAM, etc) than others. Contributors can opt in for these projects, and are rewarded with additional bonus points.[130] On some high performance platforms such as the multi-core SMP client, these bonus points can also be rewarded to contributors who reliably and promptly complete Work Units.[130] [131] [132] The goal is to align the points system with the value of the scientific results.[123] The points can foster friendly competition between donors.[131]

Contributors to Folding@home may select user names to track their contributions.[1] Rankings and other statistics for both individuals and teams are posted to the Folding@home website, with third party statistics sites also available.[133]

Passkeys

Passkeys are a unique identifier which securely tie contributions directly to each donor.[134] Passkeys are generated from a case-sensitive hash function based on a donor's email address and username. The passkey is then automatically emailed directly to that donor,[135] [136] creating a secure system in which only the intended donor receives the passkey.[134] A Folding@home contributor can then enter in the passkey into the client. This not only separates them from any policy issues arising from another donor with that same username, but it also allows for bonus points to be awarded for running the SMP high-performance client.[134]

Teams

Users can register their contributions under a team, and teams register the combined score of all their members.[137] A user can start their own team, or they can join an existing team to add the points they receive to a larger collective.[1] By default, each client is configured to donate under Team 0, but this can be changed in the client's configuration screen.[57]

Teams can be used for troubleshooting or recruitment purposes, but can also keep donors motivated.[138] In some cases, team membership also has a sense of camaraderie, and some teams have their own community-driven sources of help such as a forum.[139] [140] In addition, rivalries between teams create friendly competition that benefits the folding community,[141] and members can also have intra-team competitions for top spots.[142] [143] [144] However, regardless of username or team affiliation, all contributions go to the same place and have the same scientific value.[139]

High performance platforms

In order to more rapidly study misfolding and related diseases, not only must many computers participate, but results must also be returned quickly.[145] Currently, some simulations can take many months to complete on a single processor, such as the first Alzheimer's Disease simulations which ran for almost two years straight. High-performance platforms allow for longer trajectories in the same period of time, allowing simulations that would take years to be completed in a few weeks or months.[145] [146]

These high-performance clients often require more computing resources, such as more processing power, more disk space, more network resources, more system memory, etc. Work Units for these clients have a much shorter deadline than those for the uniprocessor client, as a major part of the scientific benefit is dependent on rapid turnaround of simulation units.[145] Bonus points are rewarded to donors who run these clients for their contribution of those resources, for rapidly completing these Work Units, and for contributing to next-generation capabilities.[145] High-performance clients are capable of running types of calculations that would be impractical on the standard uniprocessor architecture - calculations that enhance scientific contributions significantly. The high-performance clients are also responsible for many important projects.[145] By supporting machines with varied functionality, Folding@home has a very rich set of hardware on which to run many different types of calculations, allowing calculations custom-tailored to the hardware to achieve maximum performance.[128]

The Pande Group's goal is to apply this new technology to dramatically advance the capabilities of Folding@home, and to apply simulations to further study of protein folding and related diseases, including Alzheimer's Disease, Huntington's Disease, and certain forms of cancer.[145] With these clients coupled with new simulation methodologies, the Pande Group hopes to address questions previously considered impossible to tackle computationally, and make even greater impacts on knowledge of folding and misfolding-related diseases.[145]

Folding@home was the first project to use GPUs, PS3s, or multi-core processors for distributed computing.[147] [148] [149]

Graphics processing units

GPUs are computer chips used to accelerate 3D graphics, which are most commonly found in video games. GPUs have the possibility to significantly out-perform CPUs in terms of Floating Point OPerations, (FLOPs) at the cost of lower generality.[65] There are only certain types of calculations that are well-suited to GPUs. However, the Pande Group has been able to write highly optimized molecular dynamics code for GPUs, achieving a 20x to 40x speed increase over comparable CPU code for certain types of calculations.[65] GPUs remain the most powerful platform available in terms of FLOPS per client. As of September 23, 2011, GPU clients account for 71% of the entire project's FLOP throughput.[90]

On October 2, 2006, the first generation of Folding@home's Windows GPU client (GPU1) was released to the public as a beta test.[65] At launch, only ATI Radeon X1900 class GPUs were supported, as they were more powerful than their predecessors.[150] The X1900 series proved to perform very well for molecular dynamics; providing Folding@home with a 20-30X speedup for certain calculations over its CPU-based Gromacs counterparts. The Pande Group learned much about GPGPU software and new algorithms that would only be appropriate for GPUs.[150] Citing scientific inaccuracies with DirectX,[150] [151] GPU1 was officially retired on June 6, 2008.[152] [153]

On April 10, 2008, the second generation Windows GPU client (GPU2) was released to open beta testing,[154] using ATI's CAL.[155] Compared to GPU1, GPU2 was significantly easier to use, was more scientifically reliable and productive, and supported more advanced algorithms.[156] [157] GPU2 supported realtime visualization of the protein being processed,[147] [158] as well as simulations of much larger proteins.[159] Although initially supporting only ATI GPUs,[155] on June 17, 2008, a new version of GPU2 for CUDA-enabled Nvidia GPUs was released for public beta testing.[147] [160]

Cores for GPU folding in Linux are being developed.[161] While the GPU client works well in Windows, it can only be run in Linux under WINE for donors with Nvidia graphics cards.[162]

On September 25, 2009, Vijay Pande announced that a new third version of the GPU client (GPU3) was in development.[163] Designed to be backwards compatible to GPU2, GPU3 offers more efficient and stable simulations as well as new scientific capabilities.[163] [164] Publicly released as an open beta on May 25, 2010, the GPU3 client uses OpenCL and the Pande Group's own OpenMM molecular dynamics library.[164] [165] Although initially supporting only Nvidia GPUs,[166] [167] on March 31, 2011, Work Units for the ATI GPUs client were released for testing under the new open beta v7 client.[69]

PlayStation 3

Folding@home can also take advantage of the computing power of PlayStation 3s, to achieve performance previously only possible on supercomputers. Unlike Microsoft's Xbox,[128] the PS3 is well suited for Folding@home simulations. Its main Cell processor delivers a 20x speed increase over PCs for certain calculations,[18] [17] allowing the Pande Group to address problems previously considered impossible to tackle computationally.[128] [168] These additional computational capabilities also allow for greater insights into disease research.[128] The PS3's uniform console

The PlayStation 3's *Life With PlayStation* client displays a 3D animation of the protein being folded

environment makes support easier, as well as making Folding@home user friendly.[17] The PS3 also has the ability to stream data quickly to its GPU, allowing for real-time atomic detail visualizations of the protein dynamics.[65]

The PS3's processor is capable of several different types of molecular dynamics methods. It best performs implicit solvation calculations, like Folding@home's GPUs. However it can also run explicit solvation calculations like FAH's CPUs, although not as rapidly. This makes it more flexible than GPUs, but less so than CPUs. In this manner it takes a middle path between flexibility and speed.[65] Unlike CPUs and GPUs, donors cannot play video games while running Folding@home calculations.[168] Instead, the Pande Group has specifically designed PS3 Work Units to take approximately eight hours so that they can be completed overnight. These WUs have a deadline of two days.[128]

The PS3 client was originally a standalone application, but since September 18, 2008 is now a channel of the application Life with PlayStation, developed in a collaborative effort between Sony and the Pande Group.[128] Both Sony and the Pande Group have acknowledged the PS3 client is safe to use.[128]

Multi-core processing client

The Symmetric MultiProcessing (SMP) client fulfills two purposes: it takes advantage of the high-performance capabilities of recent multiprocessor systems, and it helps develop a simulation architecture that will become one of the dominant FAH computing paradigms as multi-core chips become an industry standard over the next several years.[18] [65] [145] The SMP client is capable of delivering over a 4x calculation speedup over the standard uniprocessor clients.[145]

Folding@home's SMP core handles multi-core CPUs very different from other distributed computing projects, including those under BOINC.[169] Instead of simply doing multiple Work Units simultaneously, single WUs are completed much faster across the multiple CPU cores.[170] This cuts down on the traditional difficulties of scaling a large simulation to many processors. As such, this approach is much more scientifically valuable. The Pande Group notes that some of their papers would not have been possible without the SMP client.[170]

On November 13, 2006, first generation SMP Folding@home clients for x86 Windows, x86-64 Linux, and x86 Mac OS X were released.[145] These clients used Message Passing Interface (MPI) protocols on the localhost,[145] as at the time the Gromacs cores were not designed to be used with multiple threads. This made Folding@home the first to use MPI for distributed computing software, as it had previously been reserved only for supercomputers.[171] The MPI-based clients worked well in Unix-based operating systems such as Linux and Mac's OS-X, but was particularly troublesome in Windows.[171] [170] Despite these difficulties, SMP1 generated significant results that would have been impossible otherwise and which represented a landmark in the simulation of protein folding.[170]

The second generation of the SMP client was released was an open beta on January 24, 2010, marking the beginning of the end of SMP1 client.[172] The SMP2 client replaced the complex MPI for threads, which removed much of the overhead of keeping the cores synced.[73] [172] The SMP2 client also supported a bonus points system, which non-linearly rewarded additional points for quick WU returns. Donors who ran the SMP2 client receive these extra points if they use a passkey and maintained an 80% successful return of Work Units.[172]

SMP2 also supports extra-large Work Units for users with powerful eight-core CPUs or better. While these WUs consume even more RAM and have more network usage than regular SMP WUs, users who run these are rewarded with a 20% increase over SMP2's bonus point system.[173] [174] These powerful computers allow for simulations to be performed on Folding@home that had previously required the use of supercomputing clusters. There is a great scientific need to run these simulations out to long timescales as quickly as possible, so the additional bonus points also serve as an incentive for rapid completions of Work Units. This allows the Pande Group to perform studies of larger molecular systems that would not have been possible anywhere else on Folding@home.[174]

Results

Folding@home has been very successful. To date, the Pande Group has produced 193 scientific papers, although ninety-five peer-reviewed papers have been written using research directly from the Folding@home project.[14] [175] Folding@home researchers have been the recipients of numerous awards and honors for their development of the next generation of molecular dynamics methods and corresponding biomedical research. Several Pande Group members have also been awarded for their talks on Folding@home and its implications.[176]

The Pande Group is a nonprofit institution dedicated to science research and education. They do not sell the results or make any money off of it, and in fact make the data available for others to use.[9] Specifically, analysis of the simulations will be submitted to scientific journals for publication, and these journal articles are then posted on the web page after publication.[9] The raw data from the folding runs is also available for everyone, including other researchers, on the Folding@home website.[9]

Folding@home has produced papers which have been published in top journals such as Science, Nature, PNAS, Nature Structural Biology, and the Journal of Molecular Biology.[15] The Pande Group has noted that it can take quite a while (often as much as a year) to go from a result to a published article.[14]

Folding@home's results compare well with other molecular dynamics systems, such as the Anton supercomputer. Currently Anton and FAH are the two most powerful molecular dynamics systems.[177] Anton has also run simulations out to the millisecond range,[178] [179] although they were proteins that Folding@home folded several years before.[180] Folding@home's statistical assembly of shorter simulations reproduce Anton's long simulations very well, and the Markov State Models can find important new features missing in Anton's traditional analysis.[177] [181] Folding@home is currently running further analysis on one of Anton's simulations, which will better determine how its approaches compare to Anton's more classical methods.[182] Although noting that Anton was in many ways several years behind FAH,[180] Dr. Pande believes that a long-term simulation on Anton followed by more thorough sampling in Folding@home would be very beneficial, and looks forward to see how Anton and FAH can be used together.[177]

In 2006 Folding@home participated in a pharmaceutic drug design challenge set up by OpenEye. Folding@home did well in its predictions and the results were submitted for peer review. The development of new methods for drug design has become a focus for FAH.[183]

Awards

In 2004, Dr. Vijay Pande received a Technovator award in the Biotech/Med/Healthcare category by Global Indus Technovators, a MIT-based group, for their recognition of his work at the "the cutting-edge of technology that may be harnessed for far-reaching applications."[176] In 2006, Pande was also awarded the 2006 Irving Sigal Young Investigator Award from the Protein Society "for his unique approach to employing advances in algorithms that make optimal use of distributed computing, which places his efforts at the cutting edge of simulations. The results have stimulated a re-examination of the meaning of both ensemble and single-molecule measurements, making Dr. Pande's efforts pioneering contributions to simulation methodology." Two years later, he was named a Netxplorateur of 2008 for "seeking to analyze and understand protein folding (assembly), a little understood process that is fundamental to virtually all of biology."[176] Dr. Pande also received the 2012 Michael and Kate Bárány Award for "developing field-defining and field-changing computational methods to produce leading theoretical models for protein and RNA folding."[176]

In March 2010, Greg Bowman was awarded the 2010 Kuhn Paradigm Shift Award from the American Chemical Society for his contributions to major paradigm shifts in the fields of protein folding theory and molecular dynamics simulation methods. Greg Bowman was one of five researchers in the world competing for that year's award.[176] [184]

In February 2004, a paper published in Nature was recognized as one of the "hot papers" of 2003.[176] Then on September 16, 2007, Folding@home became the Guinness World Record's most powerful distributed computing network when it crossed the 1-petaFLOP milestone.[176] [185]

Folding@home researcher Dr. Yu-Shan Lin was awarded the 2010 BioX Postdoctoral Fellowship for her work on Alzheimer's Disease simulation methods.[12] Additionally, FAH researchers Relly Brandman, Vishal Vaidyanathan, Nick Kelley, Guha Jayachandran, Bojan Zagrovic, and Bojan Zagrovic have all won awards for their talks on their biomedical research conducted through Folding@home.[176]

Disease Research

The cause and severity of Alzheimer's Disease seems to be directly tied to the production, misfolding, and aggregations of the 42-residue Abeta peptide. Despite this connection, toxic Abeta aggregations remain so complex that it was not previously possible to simulate it in atomic resolution. A 2011 paper from the Pande Group explored how their Abeta studies using Folding@home could be used as a starting point for a new Alzheimer's therapy. The Pande Group is currently concentrating their research in this direction, and they have produced multiple papers on the disease.[12] [37]

Although simulationing Abeta misfolding and aggregation helps with the understanding of Azheimer's Disease, studying its oligomers, now widely recognized as the primary neurotoxic structures leading to Alzheimer's disease, has been a challenge. *"Simulating oligomerization at experimental concentrations and long timescales: A Markov state model approach"*, published in the Journal of Chemical Physics in 2008, presented novel ways in which to simulate Abeta oligomerization over long timescales.[39] Backed by the power of Folding@home, the Pande Group simulated this process in all-atom detail, the results of which led to specific predictions about the process that are currently being experimentally tested. Such predictions include ways in which to stabilize the protein, hopefully preventing the toxic oligomer formation. This paper has been called the "tip of the iceberg" for Folding@home Alzheimer's studies, for it is quite likely to lead to new drugs and AD therapeutics.[39] [35]

In 2009, Folding@home produced several possible drug leads for Alzheimer's Disease.[12] The following year, working closely with the Nanomedicine Center for Protein Folding, those compounds went from the test tube to testing on living tissue, and continued to be refined based on the results. Significant progress has also been made into using NMR to experimentally test the computational predictions.[12] Additionally, as predicted by FAH's simulations, a stable form of amyloid beta was experimentally verified which the Pande Group believes could be used as a starting point for new Alzheimer's therapy.[35] [39] In 2008, Folding@home produced several small drug candidates to fight Alzheimer's Disease, as they appear to inhibit the toxicity of Abeta.[186] The Pande Group has closely worked with the Nanomedicine Center for Protein Folding on Alzheimer's research,[12] and has also tested and published new ways in which to perform all-atom modeling of particular aspects of relevant proteins.[187]

The Pande Group has also developed a novel method for predicting how mutations affect p53, a tumor suppressor gene, malignant forms of which are involved in over half of all known cancers. This approach was validated by experimental results and has reasonable success in the identification of deleterious mutations such as those linked to cancer.[45] This supplemented work performed in 2005 that studied how mutations affect the folding of p53, and which mutations are relevant to cancer. This study also agreed well with experiments and offered insights that were previously unobtainable.[188]

The Pande Group has also produced work towards Huntington's Disease, believed to be caused by aggregation of the Huntingtin (Htt) protein. How this aggregation occurs and previously remained largely unknown, but a 2009 paper published in the Journal of Molecular Biology investigates possible mechanisms for the aggregation formation, which has implications as to how to prevent it.[43] Folding@home has also produced other papers and several additional results on Huntington's.[12]

In 2010 Folding@home researcher Dr. Veena Thomas proposed a novel therapeutic strategy for HD, which may be funded by the NIH. This strategy could be used to bring the results from Folding@home directly to a therapeutic.[12]

Scientific Computing

Folding@home has produced groundbreaking work in the field of scientific computing. In particular, Folding@home has pioneered the use of a wide variety of hardware architectures for distributed molecular dynamics simulations. Folding@home's first paper, released in 2000, addressed whether distributed computing is itself a fundamental advance, and if so how it could be used to rival supercomputers. A novel algorithm was presented that, using screen savers as a platform, could parallelize molecular dynamics simulations across a large and growing number of personal computers, creating a computing system thousands of times more powerful than any existing supercomputer.[189] The next year, the Pande Group produced *"Mathematical Foundations of ensemble dynamics"*, which discussed how parallel simulations could be coupled to closely approximate larger simulations. Drs. Shirts and Pande demonstrated how this approach gained a near linear speedup over a single simulation or better, which allows previously intractable problems to be within the reach of computing clusters.[190]

In 2002, *"Atomistic protein folding simulations on the submillisecond timescale using worldwide distributed computing"* demonstrated how the Pande Group's algorithms efficiently utilize thousands of highly heterogeneous and loosely coupled PCs to simulated folding of several proteins and polymers. The authors also noted that their distributed computing system is quite capable of reaching the timescales necessary to simulate rapidly folding proteins, and that the interatomic interactions studied strongly correlates with experimental data.[191]

Later in 2002, the Pande Group published *"Folding@home and Genome@home: Using distributed computing to tackle previously intractable problems in computational biology"*, which showed how their novel distributed computing methods can address complex and previously unsolved "grand challenges" in computational biology.[192] The authors also discussed how to efficiently utilize thousands of personal computers, despite their fundamental problem of relatively slow Internet networking, and the implications of using the public for research. Most importantly, this paper introduced several key properties of Folding@home: security, stastical feedback (e.g. "points"), results, and non-interferance with the user. More fundamentally, this paper stated that only through distributed computing can sufficient quantities of protein configurations be explored in a reasonable amount of time, and that only such a system allows for accomplishing both high accuracy and very long simulation timescales.[192]

In 2007 Dr. Pande and Adam Beberg created a distributed storage architecture called Storage@home. This project is designed to store massive amounts of scientific data across thousands of volunteered computers. Storage@home is significant because traditional and expensive methods for storing this data (such as RAID) do not work well in the multi-terabyte scale, which projects like Folding@home generate.[193]

In a collaborative effort between Sony and the Pande Group, the 2008 paper outlined how Folding@home was able to gain a significant speed increase on the PS3 and its implementation details. For certain types of calculations, the PS3's Cell processor was found to be significantly more efficient than in conventional implementations, which for the first time introduced other opportunities for worthwhile optimizations in other area of the simulation code. Moreover, the PS3's streaming processor radically changes the view on the tradeoff between computational efficiency and overall accuracy, allowing for employment of complex mathematical molecular models with even greater accuracy at little extra computational cost.[194]

In 2009, the Pande Group also released a paper which described the implementation details behind the Folding@home GPU clients and how they achieve such a significant speed up compared to CPUs. While scientific computing on GPUs previously remained inefficient and difficult, this paper outlined OpenMM, the Pande Group's own open source molecular dynamics library, and how its optimization take full advantage of the GPU architecture. In fact, the library was shown to be more than 700 times faster than a conventional single-CPU implementations.[195] As an abstraction layer, OpenMM allows molecular dynamics simulations to be efficiently run across a variety of computer architectures and platforms, something previously problematic in scientific software development.[196]

In 2011 the Pande Group released Copernicus, a framework for biomolecular simulations on supercomputer. While it has been exceptionally difficult to scaling a molecular simulation to thousands of tightly-coupled processor cores, Copernicus achieves near-linear scaling up to 5,376 AMD cores. Copernicus delivers parallelization using SIMD, threads, and message-passing, along with kinetic clustering, statistical model building and real-time result monitoring. Its high efficiency significantly outperforms classical simulations even on specialized hardware.[197]

Protein Folding Theory

Distributed computing is an excellent tool for the study of protein folding, and due to the computing power available, reveals important folding properties not seen in previous attempts. For example, in 2001 Folding@home allowed the Pande Group to simulate the C-terminal b-hairpin of protein G for a far longer time than had ever been reported for a peptide of that size, and long-term folding events were observed.[198] While these simulations were consistent with existing experimental data, the study gave additional insights into how that protein forms common secondary structures. This may may lead to answers to many important biological questions as well as indications into how to improve *in silico* methods in general.[198] Several years later, the Pande Group published atomistic detailed results of folding states of several distinct polypeptides.[199] While these states play a great role in the understanding of protein folding, accurately simulating their complexities remains difficult without the use of distributed computing. Their studies using FAH revealed surprising characteristics in the final structures of the ensembless, suggesting important novel implications for the fields of protein folding, structure prediction, and certain protein folding experiments.[199]

In 2002, Folding@home completed detailed folding simulations of a 36-residue a-helical protein from the villin headpiece, starting in its unfolded state with only the amino acid sequence known.[200] The thorough simulation was in excess of 300 microseconds, which is a timescale orders of magnitude greater than any previous simulation for a molecule of that size, and far beyond the capabilities of what a supercomputer could do at that time. The results highlighted the need for averaging multiple molecular ensembles so that meaningful comparison between simulations and experiments can be made. Also noted was how well the results compared to current protein-folding theory.[200] In 2002, the Pande Group revealed computational predictions of specific mutants of the BBA5 protein which strongly agreed with experimental data. This indicated that *in vitro* and *in silico* protein folding can be directly compared. During the study, tens of thousands of independent trajectories were simulated, demonstrating transition states in the folding process.[201]

A 2004 paper addressed some of the unresolved questions regarding the role of water in protein folding, such as whether or not water plays a structural role in the folding process, and whether including it in simulations is crucial to understanding folding mechanisms. Using Folding@home, the Pande Group performed simulations of a model protein in all-atom detail, and observed water-induced effects that are not normally captured in traditional implicit solvation models. This study of the protein's folding process was also in strong agreement with experimental observations.[202]

"Protein folded states are kinetic hubs", published in 2010, presented a set of general properties regarding how proteins fold. Most striking was that the protein's native shape acts as a kinetic hub which can be reached quickly from any of its many states. This was in stark contrast to previous models, and suggested a radical shift in the understanding of protein folding and its applications for diseases.[203] This was then quickly supplemented by *"A simple theory of protein folding kinetics"*, which proposed a new model of protein folding that uses structural information in its equations. This allows for a much more thorough view of folding than was possible in previous theories. Highlighted in the paper was why the kinetic hub was not seen in previous simpler simulation studies.[204]

References

[1] Pande Group (2011-09-19). "Download the Folding@home Software Application" (http://folding.stanford.edu/English/Download). Stanford University. . Retrieved 2011-08-31.

[2] Pande Group. "High Performance Clients" (http://folding.stanford.edu/English/DownloadWinOther). Stanford University. . Retrieved 2011-08-31.

[3] "Folding@home for PlayStation3" (http://www.scei.co.jp/folding/en/update.html). Sony. 2008. . Retrieved 2011-08-31.

[4] "Folding@Home v7 Client Beta Release Page" (https://fah-web.stanford.edu/projects/FAHClient/wiki/BetaRelease). Stanford University. . Retrieved 2011-09-19.

[5] Joseph Coffland (2011-10-10). "FAHClient V7.1.38 released (4th Open-Beta)" (http://foldingforum.org/viewtopic.php?f=67&t=19795). . Retrieved 2011-10-10.

[6] Pande Group. "Folding@home Distributed Computing Client" (http://folding.stanford.edu/English/License). Stanford University. . Retrieved 2010-08-26.

[7] ihaque (Pande Group Member) (2010-08-11). "Re: FAH really doing anything?" (http://foldingforum.org/viewtopic.php?f=17&t=14179#p139017). . Retrieved 2011-08-23.

[8] Pande Group. "Folding@Home Executive summary" (http://www.stanford.edu/group/pandegroup/folding/FoldingFAQ.pdf). Stanford University. . Retrieved 2011-10-04.

[9] Pande Group (2011). "Folding@home - Main" (http://folding.stanford.edu). Stanford University. . Retrieved 2011-10-04.

[10] Pande Group (2009). "The Science Behind Folding@home" (http://folding.stanford.edu/English/Science) (FAQ). Stanford University. . Retrieved 2011-08-15.

[11] Antonella De Jaco, Michael Z. Lin, Noga Dubi, Davide Comoletti, Meghan T. Miller, Shelley Camp, Mark Ellisman, Margaret T. Butko, Roger Y. Tsien, and Palmer Taylor (2010). "Neuroligin Trafficking Deficiencies Arising from Mutations in the α/β-Hydrolase Fold Protein Family". *Journal of Biological Chemistry* **285** (37): 28674–28682. doi:10.1074/jbc.M110.139519. PMC 2937894. PMID 20615874.

[12] Pande Group. "Folding@home Diseases Studied FAQ" (http://folding.stanford.edu/FAQ-diseases.html) (FAQ). Stanford University. . Retrieved 2011-09-23.

[13] Xiche Hu, Dong Xu, Kenneth Hamer, Klaus Schulten, Juergen Koepke, and Hartmut Michel (1991). "Knowledge Based Structure Prediction of the Light-Harvesting Complex II of Rhodospirillum molischianum" (http://www.ks.uiuc.edu/Publications/Papers/PDF/HU96/HU96.pdf). . Retrieved 2011-09-10.

[14] Pande Group (2011-08-05). "Folding@home - Papers" (http://folding.stanford.edu/English/Papers). Stanford University. . Retrieved 2011-10-09.

[15] Pande Group (2011). "Folding@home - Main FAQ" (http://folding.stanford.edu/English/FAQ-main#ntoc7) (FAQ). Stanford University. . Retrieved 2011-08-08.

[16] Vijay Pande (2010-01-17). "Folding@home: Paper #72: Major new result for Folding@home: Simulation of the millisecond timescale" (http://folding.typepad.com/news/2010/01/major-new-result-from-foldinghome-simulation-of-the-millisecond-timescale.html). . Retrieved 2011-09-08.

[17] Pande Group. "Folding@Home Press FAQ" (http://folding.stanford.edu/English/FAQ-Press) (FAQ). Stanford University. . Retrieved 2011-08-31.

[18] "Futures in Biotech 27: Folding@home at 1.3 Petaflops" (http://twit.tv/fib27) (Interview, webcast). 2007-12-28. .

[19] Pande Group (2011). "Folding@home - About" (http://folding.stanford.edu/English/About). Stanford University. . Retrieved 2011-08-31.

[20] Anfinsen, C.B., Haber, E., Sela, M., White Jr., F.H. (1961). "The kinetics of formation of native ribonuclease during oxidation of the reduced polypeptide chain". *Proceedings of the National Academy of Sciences of the United States of America* **45** (1): 1309–1314. ISSN 00278424.

[21] Alberts, Bruce; Alexander Johnson, Julian Lewis, Martin Raff, Keith Roberts, and Peter Walters (2002). "The Shape and Structure of Proteins". *Molecular Biology of the Cell; Fourth Edition*. New York and London: Garland Science. ISBN 0-8153-3218-1.

[22] Uversky, V.N. (2009). "Intrinsic disorder in proteins associated with neurodegenerative diseases". *Frontiers in Bioscience* **14** (14): 5188–5238. doi:10.2741/3594. ISSN 10939946.

[23] "Center for Protein Folding Machinery" (http://www.proteinfoldingcenter.org/). Protein Folding Center. 2011. . Retrieved 2011-09-30.

[24] G. Bowman, V. Volez, and V. S. Pande (2011). "Taming the complexity of protein folding". *Current Opinion in Structural Biology* **21** (1): 4–11. doi:10.1016/j.sbi.2010.10.006. PMC 3042729. PMID 21081274.

[25] "Bio-X Stanford University: Vijay Pande" (http://biox.stanford.edu/clark/pande.html). Bio-X Stanford University. 2011. . Retrieved 2011-10-16.

[26] Vijay Pande (2008-01-23). "Random thoughts on the superbowl and statistics" (http://folding.typepad.com/news/2008/01/random-thoughts.html). . Retrieved 2011-09-11.

[27] Tim Braun (7im) (2011-09-24). "Re: New Invention Unravels Mystery of Protein Folding" (http://foldingforum.org/viewtopic.php?f=17&t=19671#p195980). . Retrieved 2011-09-24.

[28] schwancr (Pande Group Member) (2011-08-15). "Projects 7808 and 7809 to full fah" (http://foldingforum.org/viewtopic.php?f=24&t=19376&start=0#p193378). . Retrieved 2011-10-16.

[29] Vijay Pande (2007-11-16). "Paper highlight: paper #50 & #36" (http://folding.typepad.com/news/2007/11/paper-highlig-1.html). . Retrieved 2011-09-27.

[30] tjlane (Pande Group Member) (2011-06-09). "Re: Course grained Protein folding in under 10 minutes" (http://foldingforum.org/viewtopic.php?p=188496#p188496). . Retrieved 2011-10-15.

[31] jmn (2011-07-29). "Rosetta@home and Folding@home: additional projects" (http://en.fah-addict.net/news/news-0-369+rosetta-home-and-folding-home-additional-projects.php). . Retrieved 2011-09-19.

[32] Pande Group. "Project 10125 Description" (http://fah-web.stanford.edu/cgi-bin/fahproject.overusingIPswillbebanned?p=10125). Stanford University. . Retrieved 2011-09-27.

[33] Pande Group. "Project 2660 Description" (http://fah-web.stanford.edu/cgi-bin/fahproject.overusingIPswillbebanned?p=2660). Stanford University. . Retrieved 2011-09-27.

[34] Pande Group. "Project 6811 Description" (http://fah-web.stanford.edu/cgi-bin/fahproject.overusingIPswillbebanned?p=6811). Stanford University. . Retrieved 2011-09-27.

[35] Vijay Pande (2011-08-05). "Results page updated – new key result published in our work in Alzheimer's Disease" (http://folding.typepad.com/news/2011/08/results-page-updated-new-key-result-published-in-our-work-in-alzheimers-disease.html). . Retrieved 2011-09-10.

[36] Lacor PN,*et al.*; Buniel, MC; Furlow, PW; Clemente, AS; Velasco, PT; Wood, M; Viola, KL; Klein, WL (January 2007). "Aβ Oligomer-Induced Aberrations in Synapse Composition, Shape, and Density Provide a Molecular Basis for Loss of Connectivity in Alzheimer's Disease". *Journal of Neuroscience* **27** (4): 796–807. doi:10.1523/JNEUROSCI.3501-06.2007. PMID 17251419.

[37] P. Novick, J. Rajadas, C.W. Liu, N. W. Kelley, M. Inayathullah, and V. S. Pande (2011). Buehler, Markus J.. ed. "Rationally Designed Turn Promoting Mutation in the Amyloid-β Peptide Sequence Stabilizes Oligomers in Solution". *PLoS ONE* **6** (7): e21776. doi:10.1371/journal.pone.0021776. PMC 3142112. PMID 21799748.

[38] Pande Group. "Project 6802 Description" (http://fah-web.stanford.edu/cgi-bin/fahproject.overusingIPswillbebanned?p=6802). Stanford University. . Retrieved 2011-09-27.

[39] Nicholas W. Kelley, V. Vishal, Grant A. Krafft, and Vijay S. Pande. (2008). "Simulating oligomerization at experimental concentrations and long timescales: A Markov state model approach". *Journal of Chemical Physics* **129** (21): 214707. Bibcode 2008JChPh.129u4707K. doi:10.1063/1.3010881. PMC 2674793. PMID 19063575.

[40] Pande Group. "Project 6871 Description" (http://fah-web.stanford.edu/cgi-bin/fahproject.overusingIPswillbebanned?p=6871). Stanford University. . Retrieved 2011-09-27.

[41] Pande Group. "Project 700 Description" (http://fah-web.stanford.edu/cgi-bin/fahproject.overusingIPswillbebanned?p=700). Stanford University. . Retrieved 2011-09-27.

[42] Walker FO (2007). "Huntington's disease". *Lancet* **369** (9557): 220. doi:10.1016/S0140-6736(07)60111-1. PMID 17240289.

[43] Nicholas W. Kelley, Xuhui Huang, Stephen Tam, Christoph Spiess, Judith Frydman and Vijay S. Pande (2009). "The predicted structure of the headpiece of the Huntingtin protein and its implications on Huntingtin aggregation". *Journal of Molecular Biology* **388** (5): 919–27. doi:10.1016/j.jmb.2009.01.032. PMC 2677131. PMID 19361448.

[44] Orr HT (October 2004). "Neurodegenerative disease: neuron protection agency". *Nature* **431** (7010): 747–8. doi:10.1038/431747a. PMID 15483586.

[45] L.T. Chong, W. C. Swope, J. W. Pitera, and V. S. Pande (2006). "A novel approach for computational alanine scanning: application to the p53 oligomerization domain". *Journal of Molecular Biology* **357** (3): 1039–1049. doi:10.1016/j.jmb.2005.12.083. PMID 16457841.

[46] Vijay Pande (2007-09-28). "Nanomedicine center" (http://folding.typepad.com/news/2007/09/nanomedicine-ce.html). . Retrieved 2011-09-23.

[47] Vijay Pande (2009-12-22). "Release of new Protomol (Core B4) WUs" (http://folding.typepad.com/news/2009/12/release-of-new-protomol-core-b4-wus-.html). . Retrieved 2011-09-23.

[48] Pande Group. "Project 180 Description" (http://fah-web.stanford.edu/cgi-bin/fahproject.overusingIPswillbebanned?p=180). Stanford University. . Retrieved 2011-09-27.

[49] Pande Group. "Project 7600 Description" (http://fah-web.stanford.edu/cgi-bin/fahproject.overusingIPswillbebanned?p=7600). Stanford University. . Retrieved 2011-09-27.

[50] Pande Group. "Project 10113 Description" (http://fah-web.stanford.edu/cgi-bin/fahproject.overusingIPswillbebanned?p=10113). Stanford University. . Retrieved 2011-09-27.

[51] Arima K, Uéda K, Sunohara N, Hirai S, Izumiyama Y, Tonozuka-Uehara H, Kawai M (October 1998). "Immunoelectron-microscopic demonstration of NACP/alpha-synuclein-epitopes on the filamentous component of Lewy bodies in Parkinson's disease and in dementia with Lewy bodies". *Brain Res.* **808** (1): 93–100. doi:10.1016/S0006-8993(98)00734-3. PMID 9795161.

[52] Sanghyun Park, Randall J. Radmer, Teri E. Klein, and Vijay S. Pande (2005). "A New Set of Molecular Mechanics Parameters for Hydroxyproline and Its Use in Molecular Dynamics Simulations of Collagen-Like Peptides". *Journal of Computational Chemistry* **26** (15): 1612–1616. doi:10.1002/jcc.20301. PMID 16170799.

[53] Pande Group. "Project 2974 Description" (http://fah-web.stanford.edu/cgi-bin/fahproject.overusingIPswillbebanned?p=2974). Stanford University. . Retrieved 2011-09-27.

[54] Pande Group. "Project 3855 Description" (http://fah-web.stanford.edu/cgi-bin/fahproject.overusingIPswillbebanned?p=3855). Stanford University. . Retrieved 2011-09-27.

[55] Pande Group. "Project 2450 Description" (http://fah-web.stanford.edu/cgi-bin/fahproject.overusingIPswillbebanned?p=2450). Stanford University. . Retrieved 2011-09-27.

[56] Pande Group. "Project 10115 Description" (http://fah-web.stanford.edu/cgi-bin/fahproject.overusingIPswillbebanned?p=10115). Stanford University. . Retrieved 2011-09-27.

[57] Pande Group (2011-02-10). "Windows Uniprocessor Client Installation Guide" (http://folding.stanford.edu/English/WinUNIGuide). Stanford University. . Retrieved 2011-09-05.

[58] John Naylor (2008-02-09). "Answers to: Reasons for not using F@H" (http://foldingforum.org/viewtopic.php?f=16&t=1164#p9750). . Retrieved 2011-09-05.

[59] Bruce Borden (bruce) (2011-09-11). "Re: F@h Advertisement Techniques" (http://foldingforum.org/viewtopic.php?f=16&t=19555#p195220). . Retrieved 2011-10-18.

[60] Tim Braun (7im) (2008-09-28). "Answers to: Reasons for not using F@H" (http://foldingforum.org/viewtopic.php?f=16&t=1164&start=75#p58696). . Retrieved 2011-09-05.

[61] Bruce Borden (bruce) (2008-07-28). "Re: Answers to: Reasons for not using F@H" (http://foldingforum.org/viewtopic.php?f=16&t=1164&start=75#p43364). . Retrieved 2011-09-05.

[62] Vijay Pande (2009-08-20). "Importance of software and data integrity" (http://folding.typepad.com/news/2009/08/importance-of-software-and-data-integrity.html). . Retrieved 2011-10-19.

[63] Bruce Borden (bruce) (2011-07-18). "Re: Advice for a new user" (http://foldingforum.org/viewtopic.php?f=61&t=19163#p191513). . Retrieved 2011-09-11.

[64] Pande Group (2009-11-19). "Uninstalling Folding@home FAQ" (http://folding.stanford.edu/English/FAQ-Uninstall). Stanford University. . Retrieved 2011-09-21.

[65] Pande Group (2010-05-13). "High Performance FAQ" (http://folding.stanford.edu/English/FAQ-highperformance) (FAQ). Stanford University. . Retrieved 2011-09-05.

[66] Tim Braun (7im) (2010-04-02). "Re: Answers to: Reasons for not using F@H" (http://foldingforum.org/viewtopic.php?f=16&t=1164&start=135#p137893). . Retrieved 2011-09-05.

[67] Vijay Pande (2011-03-29). "Client version 7 now in open beta" (http://folding.typepad.com/news/2011/03/client-version-7-now-in-open-beta.html). . Retrieved 2011-08-14.

[68] Pande Group (2011-09-23). "Windows (FAH V7) Install Guide" (http://folding.stanford.edu/English/WinGuide). Stanford University. . Retrieved 2011-10-09.

[69] Vijay Pande (2011-03-31). "Core 16 for ATI released; also note on NVIDIA GPU support for older boards" (http://folding.typepad.com/news/2011/03/core-16-for-ati-released-also-note-on-nvidia-gpu-support-for-older-boards.html). . Retrieved 2011-09-07.

[70] Bruce Borden (bruce) (2011-06-30). "Re: v7 w. GTX 590..." (http://foldingforum.org/viewtopic.php?f=67&t=19039&p=191521#p190437). . Retrieved 2011-08-14.

[71] MtM (2011-06-12). "Re: Mixing ATI and NVIDIA with V7 Beta" (http://foldingforum.org/viewtopic.php?f=67&t=18866&p=188768#p188768). . Retrieved 2011-09-11.

[72] Pande Group (2011). "Client FAQ" (https://fah-web.stanford.edu/projects/FAHClient/wiki/ClientFAQ) (FAQ). Stanford University. . Retrieved 2011-08-14.

[73] Vijay Pande (2009-06-17). "How does FAH code development and sysadmin get done?" (http://folding.typepad.com/news/2009/06/how-does-fah-code-development-and-sysadmin-get-done.html). . Retrieved 2011-10-14.

[74] Joseph Coffland (2011-09-19). "FAHClient V7.1.33 released (3rd Open-Beta)" (http://foldingforum.org/viewtopic.php?f=67&t=19648#p195686). . Retrieved 2011-09-19.

[75] Vijay Pande (2007-09-22). "How FAH works: Markov State Models" (http://folding.typepad.com/news/2007/09/how-fah-works-m.html). . Retrieved 2011-10-14.

[76] Dan Ensign. "Runs, Clones, and Generations" (http://fahwiki.net/index.php/Runs,_Clones_and_Gens). . Retrieved 2011-08-10.

[77] Vijay Pande (2011-04-05). "More transparency in testing" (http://folding.typepad.com/news/2011/04/more-transparency-in-testing.html). . Retrieved 2011-10-14.

[78] Bruce Borden (bruce) (2011-08-07). "Re: Gromacs Cannot Continue Further" (http://foldingforum.org/viewtopic.php?f=59&t=19315#p192836). . Retrieved 2011-08-07.

[79] Bruce Borden (bruce) (2011-08-09). "Re: Project: 6053 (Run 1, Clone 194, Gen 357)" (http://foldingforum.org/viewtopic.php?f=19&t=19325&p=192927&hilit=8am#p192927). . Retrieved 2011-08-09.

[80] PantherX (2011-10-01). "Re: Project 6803: (Run 4, Clone 66, Gen 255)" (http://foldingforum.org/viewtopic.php?f=19& t=19725#p196444). . Retrieved 2011-10-09.

[81] PantherX (2010-10-31). "Troubleshooting Bad WUs" (http://foldingforum.org/viewtopic.php?f=19&t=16526). . Retrieved 2011-08-07.

[82] Pande Group. "Folding@home project descriptions - Project 10513" (http://fah-web.stanford.edu/cgi-bin/fahproject. overusingIPswillbebanned?p=10513). . Retrieved 2011-08-15.

[83] "Cores - FaHWiki" (http://fahwiki.net/index.php/Cores) (FAQ). . Retrieved 2007-11-06.

[84] Pande Group (2005-10-16). "Folding@home with QMD core FAQ" (http://folding.stanford.edu/QMD.html) (FAQ). Stanford University. . Retrieved 2006-12-03.

[85] Vijay Pande (2007-09-26). "How FAH works: Molecular dynamics" (http://folding.typepad.com/news/2007/09/how-fah-works-1. html). . Retrieved 2011-10-14.

[86] Pande Group (2010-02-03). "Folding@home Open Source FAQ" (http://folding.stanford.edu/English/FAQ-OpenSource) (FAQ). Stanford University. . Retrieved 2011-09-11.

[87] Vijay Pande (2011-09-06). "Re: Utilizing this resource" (http://foldingforum.org/viewtopic.php?f=17&t=19545&p=194838#p194838). . Retrieved 2011-09-11.

[88] Pande Group. "Folding@home Rules and Policies" (http://folding.stanford.edu/English/FAQ-Policies) (FAQ). Stanford University. . Retrieved 2011-09-11.

[89] Pande Group. "Active CPUs" (http://www.stanford.edu/group/pandegroup/images/ActiveCPUs2010.png) (Image). Stanford University. . Retrieved 2011-08-30.

[90] Pande Group (updated automatically). "Client Statistics by OS" (http://fah-web.stanford.edu/cgi-bin/main.py?qtype=osstats). Stanford University. . Retrieved 2011-09-28.

[91] "BOINC Combined Credit Overview" (http://boincstats.com/stats/project_graph.php?pr=bo). . Retrieved 2011-08-08.

[92] Joshua Topolsky (2007-10-31). "Folding@Home recognized by Guinness World Records" (http://www.engadget.com/2007/10/31/ folding-home-recognized-by-guinness-world-records/). . Retrieved 2007-11-05.

[93] Caroline Hadley (2004). "Biologists think bigger" (http://www.nature.com/embor/journal/v5/n3/full/7400108.html). *EMBO reports* **12** (5): 236–238. doi:10.1038/sj.embor.7400108. .

[94] Google (2007). "Your computer's idle time is too precious to waste" (http://toolbar.google.com/dc/offerdc.html/). . Retrieved 2011-09-06.

[95] "Google Toolbar Compute - Folding@Home" (http://www.powder2glass.com/Google_Toolbar_Compute/). . Retrieved 2011-09-06.

[96] Olsen, Stefanie (2003-03-27). "Google tests distributed computing" (http://news.cnet.com/Google-tests-distributed-computing/ 2110-1032_3-994371.html). CNet News. .

[97] Shankland, Stephen (March 22, 2002). "Google takes on supercomputing" (http://news.cnet.com/2100-1001-867091.html). CNet News. .

[98] Tim Braun (7im) (2011-03-28). "Re: Weird issue - Not sure where to post" (http://foldingforum.org/viewtopic.php?f=61&t=18008& p=180435&hilit=google+compute#p180435). . Retrieved 2011-09-06.

[99] Tim Braun (7im) (2008-06-19). "Re: How close do you think we are to end of the project?" (http://foldingforum.org/viewtopic. php?f=16&t=3205&p=31026&hilit=google+compute#p31026). . Retrieved 2011-09-06.

[100] Tim Braun (7im) (2011-08-19). "Re: ChromiumOS Folding integration?" (http://foldingforum.org/viewtopic.php?f=14&t=19388& p=193623&hilit=google+compute#p193637). . Retrieved 2011-09-06.

[101] ChelseaOilman (2005-12-30). "Google is after your CPU cycles" (http://hardforum.com/showpost.php?p=1028770683&postcount=4). . Retrieved 2011-09-06.

[102] "Google is after your CPU cycles" (http://hardforum.com/showthread.php?t=997889). 2005-12-30. . Retrieved 2011-09-06.

[103] "Genome@home Updates" (http://www.stanford.edu/group/pandegroup/genome/new.html). 2002-03-04. . Retrieved 2011-09-05.

[104] Pande Group. "Genome@home FAQ" (http://genomeathome.stanford.edu/faq.html) (FAQ). Stanford University. . Retrieved 2011-09-05.

[105] "BlueGene/L Ranking History" (http://www.top500.org/system/ranking/7747). . Retrieved 2011-08-15.

[106] "BlueGene/L Ranking History" (http://www.top500.org/system/ranking/8968). . Retrieved 2011-08-15.

[107] "Roadrunner Ranking History" (http://www.top500.org/system/ranking/9485). . Retrieved 2011-08-15.

[108] "Roadrunner Ranking History" (http://www.top500.org/system/ranking/9707). . Retrieved 2011-08-15.

[109] "Tianhe-1A Ranking History" (http://www.top500.org/system/ranking/10587). . Retrieved 2011-08-15.

[110] Vijay Pande (2007-09-16). "Crossing the petaFLOPS barrier" (http://folding.typepad.com/news/2007/09/crossing-the-pe.html). . Retrieved 2011-08-28.

[111] David Nagel (2007-09-25). "Folding@home Passes Petaflop Mark" (http://campustechnology.com/articles/2007/09/ foldinghome-passes-petaflop-mark.aspx). . Retrieved 2011-09-06.

[112] David Nagel (2007-09-19). "Folding@home Achieves Petaflop Milestone - PS3 owners help scientists speed up their research" (http:// games.ign.com/articles/821/821350p1.html). . Retrieved 2011-09-06.

[113] Martyn Williams, IDG News (2007-09-20). "Folding@Home Protein Project Hits a Petaflop" (http://www.pcworld.com/article/137396/ foldinghome_protein_project_hits_a_petaflop.html). . Retrieved 2011-09-06.

[114] Mark Wilson (2007-03-25). "PS3 Folding@Home TFLOP Rating Demoted by 50%, PFLOPS Still Possible" (http://gizmodo.com/ 246900/breaking-ps3-foldinghome-tflop-rating-demoted-by-50-pflops-still-possible). . Retrieved 2011-09-14.

[115] Clete (2007-03-24). "Folding@Home Project Nearing 1 Petaflop/sec" (http://clete2.com/2007/03/ foldinghome-project-nearing-1-petaflopsec/). . Retrieved 2011-09-14.

[116] Tim Hanlon (2007-03-09). "Playstation 3 continues to top Folding@Home statistics" (http://www.gizmag.com/go/7086/). . Retrieved 2011-09-14.

[117] "Folding@Home reach 2 Petaflops" (http://n4g.com/news/143113/ps3-andamp-foldingahome-reach-2-petaflops/com). 2008-05-08. . Retrieved 2011-09-23.

[118] "NVIDIA Achieves Monumental Folding@Home Milestone With Cuda" (http://www.nvidia.com/object/io_1219747545128.html). 2008-08-26. . Retrieved 2011-09-06.

[119] "3 PetaFLOP barrier" (http://www.longecity.org/forum/topic/23841-3-petaflop-barrier/). 2008-08-19. . Retrieved 2011-09-23.

[120] Vijay Pande (2009-02-18). "Folding@home Passes the 5 petaFLOP Mark" (http://folding.typepad.com/news/2009/02/ foldinghome-passes-the-5-petaflop-mark.html). . Retrieved 2011-08-31.

[121] "Crossing the 5 petaFLOPS barrier" (http://www.longecity.org/forum/topic/26449-crossing-the-5-petaflops-barrier/). 2009-02-18. . Retrieved 2011-09-23.

[122] "Foldstrong News - What is Folding@home?" (http://site.foldstrong.org/Resources.html). . Retrieved 2011-10-16.

[123] Bruce Borden (bruce) (2010-04-07). "Re: Answers to: Reasons for not using F@H" (http://foldingforum.org/viewtopic.php?f=16& t=1164&start=165#p138646). . Retrieved 2011-09-05.

[124] Vijay Pande (2008-11-09). "Re: ATI and NVIDIA stats vs. PPD numbers" (http://foldingforum.org/viewtopic.php?p=67416#p67416). . Retrieved 2011-09-22.

[125] Tim Braun (7im) (2011-09-19). "Re: Suggested Changes to F@h Website" (http://foldingforum.org/viewtopic.php?f=16& t=19643#p195672). . Retrieved 2011-09-22.

[126] Vijay Pande (2009-03-18). "FLOPS" (http://folding.typepad.com/news/2009/03/flops.html). . Retrieved 2011-10-11.

[127] Pande Group (2009-04-04). "Folding@home FLOP FAQ" (http://folding.stanford.edu/English/FAQ-flops) (FAQ). Stanford University. . Retrieved 2011-08-28.

[128] Pande Group (2009-02-05). "PS3 FAQ" (http://folding.stanford.edu/FAQ-PS3.html) (FAQ). Stanford University. . Retrieved 2011-09-05.

[129] Bruce Borden (bruce) (2011-07-12). "Re: Are my conversion for GPU flops relativly correct? [sic (http://foldingforum.org/viewtopic. php?f=16&t=19118#p191086)"]. . Retrieved 2011-09-08.

[130] Pande Group (2011-02-16). "Folding@home Points FAQ" (http://folding.stanford.edu/English/FAQ-Points) (FAQ). Stanford University. . Retrieved 2011-08-31.

[131] Pande Group (2011-02-16). "Folding@home Points FAQ (New Benchmark Machine -- January 2010)" (http://folding.stanford.edu/ English/FAQ-PointsNew) (FAQ). Stanford University. . Retrieved 2011-08-31.

[132] kasson (Pande Group member) (2010-01-24). "Upcoming Release of SMP2 Cores" (http://foldingforum.org/viewtopic.php?f=24& t=13038). . Retrieved 2011-08-31.

[133] "Third Party Contributions - Stats Pages" (http://fahwiki.net/index.php/Third_Party_Contributions#Stats_Pages). 2011. . Retrieved 2011-08-07.

[134] Pande Group (2011-05-24). "Folding@home Passkey FAQ" (http://folding.stanford.edu/English/FAQ-passkey) (FAQ). Stanford University. . Retrieved 2011-09-06.

[135] Tim Braun (7im) (2011-09-29). "Re: Passkey when changing username" (http://foldingforum.org/viewtopic.php?f=61& t=19712#p196346). . Retrieved 2011-10-02.

[136] Pande Group. "Passkey Form" (http://fah-web.stanford.edu/cgi-bin/getpasskey.py). Stanford University. . Retrieved 2011-09-06.

[137] "Default Team" (http://fah-web.stanford.edu/cgi-bin/main.py?qtype=teampage&teamnum=0). . Retrieved 2011-09-06.

[138] MtM (2009-12-17). "Re: New to F@H need startup info" (http://foldingforum.org/viewtopic.php?f=47&t=12499#p122465). . Retrieved 2011-09-30.

[139] "Re: Why join a team?" (http://foldingforum.org/viewtopic.php?f=16&t=11242&start=0#p109792). 2009-08-28. . Retrieved 2011-09-08.

[140] "Official Extreme Overclocking Folding@Home Team Forum" (http://forums.extremeoverclocking.com/forumdisplay.php?f=45). Extreme Overclocking. . Retrieved 2011-09-08.

[141] Norman Chan (2009-04-06). "Help Maximum PC's Folding Team Win the Next Chimp Challenge!" (http://www.maximumpc.com/ article/news/help_maximum_pcs_folding_team_win_next_chimp_challenge). . Retrieved 2011-09-06.

[142] "Team 24 Folding at Home - March Challenge" (http://forums.overclockers.com.au/showthread.php?t=940743). 2011-02-20. . Retrieved 2011-09-06.

[143] "Announcing the Immortality Institute Folding@Home Prize" (http://www.mprize.org/index.php?ctype=news& pagename=blogdetaildisplay&BID=2008032-20053630&detaildisplay=Y). 2008-03-20. . Retrieved 2011-09-06.

[144] "Announcing the F@H Prize" (http://imminst.org/announcing-foldinghome-prize). Immortality Institute. . Retrieved 2011-09-06.

[145] Pande Group (2010-12-11). "Folding@home SMP FAQ" (http://folding.stanford.edu/English/FAQ-SMP) (FAQ). Stanford University. . Retrieved 2011-08-31.

[146] Tim Braun (7im) (2010-04-02). "Re: Answers to: Reasons for not using F@H" (http://foldingforum.org/viewtopic.php?f=16&t=1164& start=135#p137900). . Retrieved 2011-09-05.

[147] Vijay Pande (2008-05-23). "GPU news (about GPU1, GPU2, & NVIDIA support)" (http://folding.typepad.com/news/2008/05/gpu-news-gpu1-g.html). . Retrieved 2011-09-08.

[148] Travis Desell1, Anthony Waters, Malik Magdon-Ismail, Boleslaw K. Szymanski, Carlos A. Varela, Matthew Newby, Heidi Newberg, Andreas Przystawik, and David Anderson (2009). "Accelerating the MilkyWay@Home volunteer computing project with GPUs" (http://citeseerx.ist.psu.edu/viewdoc/download?doi=10.1.1.158.7614&rep=rep1&type=pdf). *8th International Conference on Parallel Processing and Applied Mathematics (PPAM 2009)*. doi:10.1.1.158.7614. .

[149] M. J. Harvey, G. Giupponi, Vill`a-Freixa, and G. De Fabritiis (2007). "PS3GRID.NET: Building a distributed supercomputer using the PlayStation 3" (http://www.gpugrid.net/pub/ps3grid_chapter.pdf). *Distributed & Grid Computing - Science Made Transparent for EVeryone. Principles, Applications and Supporting Communities*. .

[150] Pande Group (2011-03-18). "ATI FAQ" (http://folding.stanford.edu/English/FAQ-ATI) (FAQ). Stanford University. . Retrieved 2011-08-31.

[151] Vijay Pande (2008-05-27). "More info about the GPU1 to GPU2 transition" (http://folding.typepad.com/news/2008/05/gpu1-to-gpu2-transition-why-does-gpu1-need-to-end.html). . Retrieved 2011-09-07.

[152] Vijay Pande (2008-06-04). "GPU1 retirement: Friday June 6 at 9am pacific time" (http://folding.typepad.com/news/2008/06/gpu1-retirement-friday-june-6-at-9am-pacific-time.html). . Retrieved 2011-09-07.

[153] Vijay Pande (2008-06-06). "GPU1 has been retired, GPU2 for NVIDIA release nearing" (http://folding.typepad.com/news/2008/06/gpu1-has-been-retired-gpu2-for-nvidia-release-nearing.html). . Retrieved 2011-09-07.

[154] Vijay Pande (2008-04-10). "GPU2 open beta" (http://folding.typepad.com/news/2008/04/gpu2-open-beta.html). . Retrieved 2011-09-07.

[155] Vijay Pande (2008-01-25). "Code Development Updates" (http://folding.typepad.com/news/2008/01/code-developmen.html). . Retrieved 2011-09-07.

[156] Vijay Pande (2008-04-15). "Updates to the Download page/GPU2 goes live" (http://folding.typepad.com/news/2008/04/updates-to-the.html). . Retrieved 2011-09-07.

[157] Vijay Pande (2008-04-12). "GPU2 PPD increase" (http://folding.typepad.com/news/2008/06/gpu2-ppd-increase.html). . Retrieved 2011-09-07.

[158] Vijay Pande (2008-04-11). "GPU2 open beta going well" (http://folding.typepad.com/news/2008/04/gpu2-open-bet-1.html). . Retrieved 2011-09-07.

[159] Vijay Pande (2008-04-13). "How the GPU2 core works" (http://folding.typepad.com/news/2008/04/how-the-gpu2-co.html). . Retrieved 2011-09-07.

[160] Vijay Pande (2008-06-17). "Folding@home: GPU2 beta client for NVIDIA now released" (http://folding.typepad.com/news/2008/06/gpu2-beta-client-for-nvidia-now-released.html). . Retrieved 2011-09-07.

[161] Joseph Coffland (2011-10-13). "Re: FAHClient V7.1.38 released (4th Open-Beta)" (http://foldingforum.org/viewtopic.php?f=67&t=19795&start=45#p197198). . Retrieved 2011-10-15.

[162] "NVIDIA GPU3 Linux/Wine Headless Install Guide" (http://foldingforum.org/viewtopic.php?f=54&t=6793). 2008-11-08. . Retrieved 2011-09-05.

[163] Vijay Pande (2009-09-25). "Update on new FAH core and clients" (http://folding.typepad.com/news/2009/09/update-on-new-fah-cores-and-clients.html). . Retrieved 2011-09-10.

[164] Vijay Pande (2010-04-24). "Prepping for the GPU3 rolling: new client and NVIDIA FAH GPU clients will (in the future) need CUDA 2.2 or later" (http://folding.typepad.com/news/2010/04/prepping-for-the-gpu3-rolling-new-client-and-nvidia-fah-gpu-clients-will-need-cuda-22-or-later.html). . Retrieved 2011-09-08.

[165] Vijay Pande (2010-05-25). "Folding@home: Open beta release of the GPU3 client/core" (http://folding.typepad.com/news/2010/05/open-beta-release-of-the-gpu3-clientcore.html). . Retrieved 2011-09-07.

[166] Vijay Pande (2010-05-31). "GPU3 (NVIDIA) open beta test update" (http://folding.typepad.com/news/2010/05/gpu3-nvidia-open-beta-test-update.html). . Retrieved 2011-09-07.

[167] Vijay Pande (2011-01-26). "New GPU3 (version 6.41) client released" (http://folding.typepad.com/news/2011/01/new-gpu3-version-641-client-released.html). . Retrieved 2011-09-07.

[168] David E. Williams (2006-10-20). "PlayStation's serious side: Fighting disease" (http://edition.cnn.com/2006/TECH/fun.games/09/18/playstation.folding/). CNN. . Retrieved 2011-10-16.

[169] Ozzfan (2007-10-01). "Can I have multiple CPUs work on the same task (workunit)?" (http://boincfaq.mundayweb.com/index.php?language=1&view=115&sessionID=f68532da1ffd360def2213188757c695). BOINC. . Retrieved 2011-10-09.

[170] Vijay Pande (2008-06-15). "What does the SMP core do?" (http://folding.typepad.com/news/2008/06/what-does-the-smp-core-do.html). . Retrieved 2011-09-07.

[171] Vijay Pande (2008-03-08). "New Windows client/core development (SMP and classic clients)" (http://folding.typepad.com/news/2008/03/new-windows-cli.html). . Retrieved 2011-09-30.

[172] kasson (Pande Group member) (2010-01-24). "upcoming release of SMP2 cores" (http://foldingforum.org/viewtopic.php?f=24&t=13038#p127406). . Retrieved 2011-09-30.

[173] Vijay Pande (2011-07-02). "Change in the points system for bigadv work units" (http://folding.typepad.com/news/2011/07/change-in-the-points-system-for-bigadv-work-units.html). . Retrieved 2011-10-09.

[174] kasson (Pande Group member) (2009-07-15). "new release: extra-large work units" (http://foldingforum.org/viewtopic.php?t=10697). . Retrieved 2011-10-09.

[175] Pande Group (2011). "Pande Lab Publications" (http://folding.stanford.edu/Pande/Papers). Stanford University. . Retrieved 2011-10-09.

[176] Pande Group (2011). "Folding@home - Awards" (http://folding.stanford.edu/English/Awards). Stanford University. . Retrieved 2011-10-09.

[177] Vijay Pande (2011-10-13). "Comparison between FAH and Anton's approaches" (http://folding.typepad.com/news/2011/10/comparison-between-fah-and-antons-approaches.html). . Retrieved 2011-10-13.

[178] Heidi Ledford (2010-10-14). "Supercomputer sets protein-folding record" (http://www.nature.com/news/2010/101014/full/news.2010.541.html). Nature News. doi:10.1038/news.2010.541. . Retrieved 2011-10-15.

[179] David E. Shaw, Paul Maragakis, Kresten Lindorff-Larsen, Stefano Piana, Ron O. Dror, Michael P. Eastwood, Joseph A. Bank, John M. Jumper, John K. Salmon, Yibing Shan, and Willy Wriggers (2010). "Atomic-Level Characterization of the Structural Dynamics of Proteins". *Science* **330** (6002): 341–346. doi:10.1126/science.1187409. PMID 20947758.

[180] Vijay Pande (2010-10-20). "Re: Supercomputer sets protein-folding record" (http://foldingforum.org/viewtopic.php?f=15&t=16388#p162721). . Retrieved 2011-09-09.

[181] Thomas J. Lane, Gregory R. Bowman, Kyle A Beauchamp, Vincent Alvin Voelz, and Vijay S. Pande (2011). "Markov State Model Reveals Folding and Functional Dynamics in Ultra-Long MD Trajectories". *Journal of the American Chemical Society*. doi:10.1021/ja207470h.

[182] Pande Group (2011). "Project 7610 Description" (http://fah-web.stanford.edu/cgi-bin/fahproject.overusingIPswillbebanned?p=7610). . Retrieved 2011-10-14.

[183] Vijay Pande (2007-09-20). "SAMPL challenge" (http://folding.typepad.com/news/2007/09/sampl-challenge.html). . Retrieved 2011-10-13.

[184] Vijay Pande (2010-03-21). "New award for Folding@home team" (http://folding.typepad.com/news/2010/03/new-award-for-foldinghome-team.html). . Retrieved 2011-08-23.

[185] "Most Powerful Distributed Computing Network: Folding@home" (http://www.guinnessworldrecords.com/records-5000/most-powerful-distributed-computing-network/). Guinness World Records. 2007. . Retrieved 2011-10-09.

[186] Vijay Pande (2008-12-18). "New FAH results on possible new Alzheimer's drug presented" (http://folding.typepad.com/news/2008/12/new-fah-results-on-possible-new-alzheimers-drug-presented.html). . Retrieved 2011-09-23.

[187] Vijay Pande (2008-12-08). "Folding@home Alzheimer's Simulation work published" (http://folding.typepad.com/news/2008/12/foldinghome-alzheimers-simulation-work-published.html). . Retrieved 2011-09-23.

[188] L. T. Chong, C. D. Snow, Y. M. Rhee, and V. S. Pande. (2004). "Dimerization of the p53 Oligomerization Domain: Identification of a Folding Nucleus by Molecular Dynamics Simulations". *Journal of Molecular Biology* **345** (4): 869–878. doi:10.1016/j.jmb.2004.10.083. PMID 15588832.

[189] M. R. Shirts and V. S. Pande. (2000). "Screen Savers of the World, Unite!". *Science* **290** (5498): 1903–1904. doi:10.1126/science.290.5498.1903. PMID 17742054.

[190] Michael R. Shirts and Vijay S. Pande (2001). "Mathematical Foundations of Coupled Parallel Simulations". *Physical Review Letters* **86** (22): 4983–4987. Bibcode 2001PhRvL..86.4983S. doi:10.1103/PhysRevLett.86.4983. PMID 11384401.

[191] Vijay S. Pande, Ian Baker, Jarrod Chapman, Sidney P. Elmer, Siraj Khaliq, Stefan M. Larson, Young Min Rhee, Michael R. Shirts, Christopher D. Snow, Eric J. Sorin, Bojan Zagrovic (2002). "Atomistic protein folding simulations on the submillisecond timescale using worldwide distributed computing". *Biopolymers* **68** (1): 91–109. doi:10.1002/bip.10219. PMID 12579582.

[192] Stefan M. Larson, Christopher D. Snow, Michael R. Shirts, and Vijay S. Pande (2002). "Folding@home and Genome@home: Using distributed computing to tackle previously intractable problems in computational biology" (http://fah-web.stanford.edu/papers/Horizon_Review.pdf). *Computational Genomics*. .

[193] Adam L Beberg and Vijay S. Pande (2007). "Storage@home: Petascale Distributed Storage". *IPDPS*: 1. doi:10.1109/IPDPS.2007.370672. ISBN 1-4244-0909-8.

[194] Edgar Luttmann, Daniel L. Ensign, Vishal Vaidyanathan, Mike Houston, Noam Rimon, Jeppe Øland, Guha Jayachandran, Mark Friedrichs, Vijay S. Pande (2008). "Accelerating Molecular Dynamic Simulation on the Cell processor and PlayStation 3". *Journal of Computational Chemistry* **30** (2): 268–274. doi:10.1002/jcc.21054. PMID 18615421.

[195] M. S. Friedrichs, P. Eastman, V. Vaidyanathan, M. Houston, S. LeGrand, A. L. Beberg, D. L. Ensign, C. M. Bruns, V. S. Pande (2009). "Accelerating Molecular Dynamic Simulation on Graphics Processing Units". *Journal of Computational Chemistry* **30** (6): 864–72. doi:10.1002/jcc.21209. PMC 2724265. PMID 19191337.

[196] P. Eastman and V. S. Pande (2010). "OpenMM: A Hardware Abstraction Layer for Molecular Simulations". *Computing in Science & Engineering* **12** (4): 34–39. doi:10.1109/MCSE.2010.27.

[197] S. Pronk, P. Larson, I. Pouya, G. Bowman, I. Haque, K. Beaucamp, B. Hess, V. S. Pande, P. M. Kasson, E. Lindahl (2011). "Copernicus: A new paradigm for parallel adaptive molecular dynamics" (http://copernicus-computing.org/). *Supercomputing 2011*. .

[198] Bojan Zagrovic, Eric J. Sorin and Vijay Pande (2001). "b-Hairpin Folding Simulations in Atomistic Detail Using an Implicit Solvent Model". *Journal of Molecular Biology* **313** (1): 151–169. doi:10.1006/jmbi.2001.5033. PMID 11601853.

[199] Bojan Zagrovic, Christopher D. Snow, Siraj Khaliq, Michael R. Shirts, and Vijay S. Pande (2002). "Native-like Mean Structure in the Unfolded Ensemble of Small Proteins". *Journal of Molecular Biology* **323** (1): 153–164. doi:10.1016/S0022-2836(02)00888-4.

PMID 12368107.

[200]   Bojan Zagrovic, Christopher D. Snow, Michael R. Shirts, and Vijay S. Pande. (2002). "Simulation of Folding of a Small Alpha-helical Protein in Atomistic Detail using Worldwide distributed Computing". *Journal of Molecular Biology* **323** (5): 927–937. doi:10.1016/S0022-2836(02)00997-X. PMID 12417204.

[201]   Christopher D. Snow, Houbi Ngyen, Vijay S. Pande, and Martin Gruebele (2002). "Absolute comparison of simulated and experimental protein-folding dynamics". *Nature* **420** (6911): 102–106. doi:10.1038/nature01160. PMID 12422224.

[202]   Young Min Rhee, Eric J. Sorin, Guha Jayachandran, Erik Lindahl, & Vijay S Pande (2004). "Simulations of the role of water in the protein-folding mechanism". *Proceedings of the National Academy of Sciences, USA* **101** (17): 6456–6461. Bibcode 2004PNAS..101.6456R. doi:10.1073/pnas.0307898101. PMC 404066. PMID 15090647.

[203]   G. R. Bowman and V. S. Pande (2010). "Protein folded states are kinetic hubs". *Proceedings of the National Academy of Sciences, USA* **107** (24): 10890–10895. Bibcode 2010PNAS..10710890B. doi:10.1073/pnas.1003962107. PMC 2890711. PMID 20534497.

[204]   V. S. Pande (2010). "A simple theory of protein folding kinetics". *Physical Review Letters* **105** (19). Bibcode 2010PhRvL.105s8101P. doi:10.1103/PhysRevLett.105.198101.

External links

- Folding@home homepage (http://folding.stanford.edu/)
- Folding@home official blog (http://folding.typepad.com)
- Folding@home forum (http://foldingforum.org/)
- Folding@home statistics (http://folding.stanford.edu/Stats)
- List of publications from F@h results (http://folding.stanford.edu/Papers)
- Folding@home's policies (http://folding.stanford.edu/English/FAQ-Policies)
- Folding@home Wiki (http://fahwiki.net/index.php/Main_Page)
- "Futures In Biotech" episode (for newcomers) (http://folding.typepad.com/news/2011/08/new-futures-in-biotech-episode-about-foldinghome.html)
- 2009 Interview with Vijay Pande about Folding@home Project (http://www.ustream.tv/recorded/1070617)
- Video of record-breaking 1.5ms protein fold (http://www.youtube.com/watch?v=gFcp2Xpd29I&feature=feedwll)
- Pande Group's OpenMM molecular dynamics library (https://simtk.org/home/openmm)
- Simple multimedia presentation about F@h (http://icrontic.com/files/team93/videos/foldflash2.html)
- Wikipedia Team (http://fah-web.stanford.edu/cgi-bin/main.py?qtype=teampage&teamnum=42223)

Foldit

Foldit

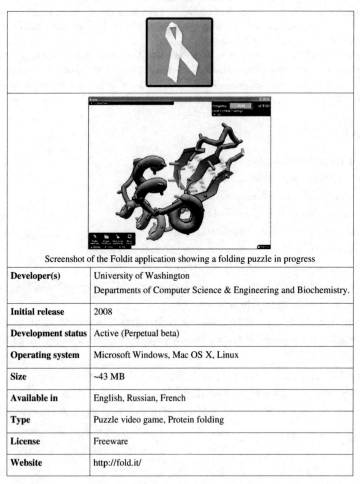

Screenshot of the Foldit application showing a folding puzzle in progress

Developer(s)	University of Washington Departments of Computer Science & Engineering and Biochemistry.
Initial release	2008
Development status	Active (Perpetual beta)
Operating system	Microsoft Windows, Mac OS X, Linux
Size	~43 MB
Available in	English, Russian, French
Type	Puzzle video game, Protein folding
License	Freeware
Website	http://fold.it/

Foldit is an experimental puzzle video game about protein folding, developed as a collaboration between the University of Washington's departments of Computer Science and Engineering and Biochemistry. The objective of the game is to fold the structure of selected proteins to the best of the player's ability, using various tools provided within the game. The best solutions are analysed by researchers, who determine whether or not there is a native structural configuration (or native state) that can be applied to the relevant proteins, in the "real world". Scientists can then use such solutions to solve "real-world" problems, by targeting and eradicating diseases, and creating biological innovations.

History

Many of the same people who created Rosetta@home, worked on the construction of Foldit. The public beta version was released in May 2008.[1]

In 2008, the Foldit project submitted solutions to the CASP protein structure prediction contest. The results were announced in early 2009.

In 2011, players of Foldit helped to decipher the crystal structure of M-PMV retroviral protease, which is linked to an AIDS-like virus. Players produced an accurate 3D model of the enzyme in just ten days. The problem had thwarted scientists for a decade.[2] [3]

Purpose

The process by which living beings create the primary structure of proteins, protein biosynthesis, is reasonably well understood, as is the means by which proteins are encoded as DNA. Determining how the primary structure of a protein turns into a functioning three-dimensional structure—how the molecule "folds"—is more difficult; the general process is known, but predicting protein structures is computationally demanding.

Foldit is an attempt to apply the human brain's natural three-dimensional pattern matching abilities to this problem. Current puzzles are based on well-understood proteins; by analysing the ways in which humans intuitively approach these puzzles, researchers hope to improve the algorithms employed by existing protein-folding software.

Method

Foldit provides a series of tutorials in which the user manipulates simple protein-like structures, and a periodically updated set of puzzles based on real proteins. The application displays a graphical representation of the protein's structure which the user is able to manipulate with the aid of a set of tools.

As the structure is modified, a "score" is calculated based on how well-folded the protein is, and a list of high scores for each puzzle is maintained. Foldit users may create and join groups, and share puzzle solutions with each other; a separate list of group high scores is maintained.

Foldit is a combination of crowdsourcing and distributed computing.

References

[1] Computer Game's High Score Could Earn The Nobel Prize In Medicine [[Science Daily (http://www.sciencedaily.com/releases/2008/05/ 080508122520.htm)], May 9, 2008]

[2] Public Solves Protein Structure [[The Scientist (http://the-scientist.com/2011/09/18/public-solves-protein-structure/)], September 18, 2011]

[3] Khatib, F.; Dimaio, F.; Cooper, S.; Kazmierczyk, M.; Gilski, M.; Krzywda, S.; Zabranska, H.; Pichova, I. et al. (2011). "Crystal structure of a monomeric retroviral protease solved by protein folding game players". *Nature Structural & Molecular Biology*. doi:10.1038/nsmb.2119.

- "Return to the fold" (http://www.economist.com/node/11326188?story_id=11326188). The Economist. 2008-05-08. Retrieved 2008-05-25.

- Hand, E. (2010). "Citizen science: People power". *Nature* **466** (7307): 685–687. doi:10.1038/466685a. PMID 20686547.

- Cooper, S.; Khatib, F.; Treuille, A.; Barbero, J.; Lee, J.; Beenen, M.; Leaver-Fay, A.; Baker, D. et al. (2010). "Predicting protein structures with a multiplayer online game". *Nature* **466** (7307): 756–760. Bibcode 2010Natur.466..756C. doi:10.1038/nature09304. PMC 2956414. PMID 20686574.

- "Gamers Unravel the Secret Life of Protein" (http://www.wired.com/medtech/genetics/magazine/17-05/ ff_protein). Wired. 2010-08-18.

- Andrew McAfee (2010-08-24). "Why Crowdsourcing Works" (http://www.forbes.com/2010/08/23/ science-proteins-foldit-technology-breakthroughs-crowdsourcing.html). Forbes.

External links

- Foldit project homepage (http://fold.it/)
- Official Foldit wiki (http://foldit.wikia.com/wiki/FoldIt_Wiki)
- Computer game's high score could earn the Nobel Prize in medicine (http://www.washington.edu/news/archive/id/41558)
- Biologists Enlist Online Gamers (http://www.technologyreview.com/Biotech/20738/?a=f)
- Online gamers crack AIDS enzyme puzzle (http://games.yahoo.com/blogs/plugged-in/online-gamers-crack-aids-enzyme-puzzle-161920724.html)

FoldX

FoldX is a protein design algorithm that uses an empirical force field. It can determine the energetic effect of point mutations as well as the interaction energy of protein complexes (including Protein-DNA). FoldX can mutate protein and DNA side chains using a probability-based rotamer library, while exploring alternative conformations of the surrounding side chains.

Applications

- Prediction of the effect of point mutations or human SNPs on protein stability or protein complexes
- Protein design to improve stability or modify affinity or specificity
- Homology modeling

The FoldX force field

The energy function includes terms that have been found to be important for protein stability, where the energy of unfolding (ΔG) of a target protein is calculated using the equation:

$$\Delta G = \Delta G_{vdw} + \Delta G_{solvH} + \Delta G_{solvP} + \Delta G_{hbond} + \Delta G_{wb} + \Delta G_{el} + \Delta S_{mc} + \Delta S_{sc}$$

Where ΔG_{vdw} is the sum of the Van der Waals contributions of all atoms with respect to the same interactions with the solvent. ΔG_{solvH} and ΔG_{solvP} is the difference in solvation energy for apolar and polar groups, respectively, when going from the unfolded to the folded state. ΔGhbond is the free energy difference between the formation of an intra-molecular hydrogen-bond compared to inter-molecular hydrogen-bond formation (with solvent). ΔG_{wb} is the extra stabilizing free energy provided by a water molecule making more than one hydrogen-bond to the protein (water bridges) that cannot be taken into account with non-explicit solvent approximations. ΔG_{el} is the electrostatic contribution of charged groups, including the helix dipole. ΔS_{mc} is the entropy cost for fixing the backbone in the folded state. This term is dependent on the intrinsic tendency of a particular amino acid to adopt certain dihedral angles. ΔS_{sc} is the entropic cost of fixing a side chain in a particular conformation. The energy values of ΔG_{vdw}, ΔG_{solvH}, ΔG_{solvP} and ΔG_{hbond} attributed to each atom type have been derived from a set of experimental data, and ΔS_{mc} and ΔS_{mc} have been taken from theoretical estimates. The Van der Waals contributions are derived from vapor to water energy transfer, while in the protein we are going from solvent to protein.

For protein-protein interactions, or protein-DNA interactions FoldX calculates $\Delta\Delta G$ of interaction :

$$\Delta\Delta G_{ab} = \Delta G_{ab} - (\Delta G_a + \Delta G_b) + \Delta G_{kon} + \Delta S_{sc}$$

ΔG_{kon} reflects the effect of electrostatic interactions on the k_{on}. ΔS_{sc} is the loss of translational and rotational entropy upon making the complex.

Key features

- *RepairPDB*: energy minimization of a protein structure
- *BuildModel*: in silico mutagenesis or homology modeling with predicted energy changes
- *AnalyseComplex*: interaction energy calculation
- *Stability*: prediction of free energy changes between alternative structures
- *AlaScan*: in silico alanine scan of a protein structure with predicted energy changes
- *SequenceDetail*: per residue free energy decomposition into separate energy terms (hydrogen bonding, Van der Waals energy, electrostatics, ...)

Graphical interface

Native FoldX is run from the command line. A FoldX plugin for the YASARA molecular graphics program has been developed to access various FoldX tools inside a graphical environment. The results of e.g. in silico mutations or homology modeling with FoldX can be directly analyzed on screen.

Further reading

- Schymkowitz J, Borg J, Stricher F, Nys R, Rousseau F, Serrano L (2005). "The FoldX web server: an online force field.". *Nucl. Acids Res.* **33**: W382-8. doi:10.1093/nar/gki387. PMID 15980494.
- Schymkowitz J, Rousseau F, Martins IC, Ferkinghoff-Borg J, Stricher F, Serrano L (2005). "Prediction of water and metal binding sites and their affinities by using the Fold-X force field.". *Proc Natl Acad Sci USA* **102**: 10147–52. doi:10.1073/pnas.0501980102. PMID 16006526.
- Guerois R, Nielsen JE, Serrano L (2002). "Predicting changes in the stability of proteins and protein complexes: a study of more than 1000 mutations.". *J Mol Biol* **320**: 369–87. doi:10.1016/S0022-2836(02)00442-4. PMID 12079393.

Links

- http://foldx.crg.es [1] FoldX website
- http://foldxyasara.switchlab.org [2] FoldX plugin for YASARA

References

[1] http://foldx.crg.es
[2] http://foldxyasara.switchlab.org

Foundational Model of Anatomy

The **Foundational Model of Anatomy Ontology** or the **FMA**, is a reference ontology for the domain of anatomy. It is a symbolic representation of the canonical, phenotypic structure of an organism; a spatial-structural ontology of anatomical entities and relations which form the physical organization of an organism at all salient levels of granularity.

External links

- The Foundational Model of Anatomy Ontology [1]

References

[1] http://sig.biostr.washington.edu/projects/fm/AboutFM.html

Full genome sequencing

Full genome sequencing (FGS), also known as **whole genome sequencing (WGS)**, **complete genome sequencing**, or **entire genome sequencing**, is a laboratory process that determines the complete DNA sequence of an organism's genome at a single time. This entails sequencing all of an organism's chromosomal DNA as well as DNA contained in the mitochondria and, for plants, in the chloroplast. Almost any biological sample—even a very small amount of DNA or ancient DNA—can provide the genetic material necessary for full genome sequencing. Such samples may include saliva, epithelial cells, bone marrow, hair (as long as the hair contains a hair follicle), seeds, plant leaves, or anything else that has DNA-containing cells. Because the sequence data that

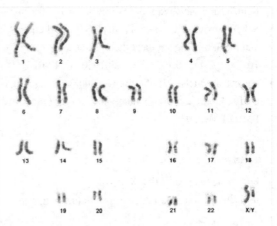

An image of the 46 chromosomes, making up the diploid genome of human male. (The mitochondrial chromosome is not shown.)

is produced can be quite large (for example, there are approximately six billion base pairs in each human diploid genome), genomic data is stored electronically and requires a large amount of computing power and storage capacity. Full genome sequencing would have been nearly impossible before the advent of the microprocessor, computers, and the Information Age.

Unlike full genome sequencing, DNA profiling only determines the likelihood that genetic material came from a particular individual or group; it does not contain additional information on genetic relationships, origin or susceptibility to specific diseases.[1] Also unlike full genome sequencing, SNP genotyping covers less than 0.1% of the genome. Almost all truly complete genomes are of microbes; the term "full genome" is thus sometimes used loosely to mean "greater than 95%". The remainder of this article focuses on nearly complete human genomes.

In general, knowing the complete DNA sequence of an individual's genome does not, on its own, provide useful clinical information, but this may change over time as a large number of scientific studies continue to be published detailing clear associations between specific genetic variants and disease.[2] [3]

The first nearly complete human genomes sequenced were J. Craig Venter's (Caucasian at 7.5-fold average coverage),[4] [5] [6] James Watson's (Caucasian male at 7.4-fold),[7] [8] [9] a Han Chinese (YH at 36-fold),[10] a

Yoruban from Nigeria (at 30-fold),[11] a female leukemia patient (at 33 and 14-fold coverage for tumor and normal tissues),[12] and Seong-Jin Kim (Korean at 29-fold).[13] There are currently over 60 nearly complete human genomes publicly available.[14] Commercialization of full genome sequencing is in an early stage and growing rapidly.

Early Techniques

Sequencing of nearly an entire human genome was first accomplished in 2000 partly through the use of shotgun sequencing technology. While full genome shotgun sequencing for small (4000–7000 base pair) genomes was already in use in 1979,[15] broader application benefited from pairwise end sequencing, known colloquially as *double-barrel shotgun sequencing*. As sequencing projects began to take on longer and more complicated genomes, multiple groups began to realize that useful information could be obtained by sequencing both ends of a fragment of DNA. Although sequencing both ends of the same fragment and keeping track of the paired data was more cumbersome than sequencing a single end of two distinct fragments, the knowledge that the two sequences were oriented in opposite

An ABI PRISM 3100 Genetic Analyzer. Such capillary sequencers automated the early efforts of sequencing genomes.

directions and were about the length of a fragment apart from each other was valuable in reconstructing the sequence of the original target fragment.

The first published description of the use of paired ends was in 1990 as part of the sequencing of the human HPRT locus,[16] although the use of paired ends was limited to closing gaps after the application of a traditional shotgun sequencing approach. The first theoretical description of a pure pairwise end sequencing strategy, assuming fragments of constant length, was in 1991.[17] In 1995 Roach et al. introduced the innovation of using fragments of varying sizes,[18] and demonstrated that a pure pairwise end-sequencing strategy would be possible on large targets. The strategy was subsequently adopted by The Institute for Genomic Research (TIGR) to sequence the entire genome of the bacterium *Haemophilus influenzae* in 1995,[19] and then by Celera Genomics to sequence the entire fruit fly genome in 2000,[20] and subsequently the entire human genome. Applied Biosystems, now called Life Technologies, manufactured the automated capillary sequencers utilized by both Celera Genomics and The Human Genome Project.

While capillary sequencing was the first approach to successfully sequence a nearly full human genome, it is still too expensive and takes too long for commercial purposes. Because of this, shotgun sequencing technology, even though it is still relatively 'new', since 2005 is being displaced by technologies like pyrosequencing, SMRT sequencing, and nanopore technology.[21]

Current Research

One possible way to accomplish the cost-effective high-throughput sequencing necessary to accomplish full genome sequencing is by using nanopore technology, which is a patented technology held by Harvard University and Oxford Nanopore Technologies and licensed to biotechnology companies.[22] To facilitate their full genome sequencing initiatives, Illumina licensed nanopore sequencing technology from Oxford Nanopore Technologies and Sequenom licensed the technology from Harvard University.[23] [24] Another possible way to accomplish cost-effective high-throughput sequencing is by utilizing fluorophore technology. Pacific Biosciences is currently using this approach in their SMRT (single molecule real time) DNA sequencing technology.[25] Complete Genomics has developed DNA Nanoball (DNB) technology that arranges DNA on self-assembling arrays.[26] Complete Genomics' sequencing technology [27] combines its DNB arrays with its proprietary cPAL™ read technology. Pyrosequencing is a method of DNA sequencing based on the sequencing by synthesis principle.[28] The technique was developed by

Pål Nyrén and his student Mostafa Ronaghi at the Royal Institute of Technology in Stockholm in 1996,[29] [30] [31] and is currently being used by 454 Life Sciences in their effort to deliver an affordable, fast and highly accurate full genome sequencing platform.[32]

Commercialization

A number of public and private companies are competing to develop a full genome sequencing platform that is commercially robust for both research and clinical use,[33] including Illumina,[34] Knome,[35] Sequenom,[36] 454 Life Sciences,[37] Pacific Biosciences,[38] Complete Genomics,[39] Intelligent Bio-Systems,[40] Genome Corp.,[41] ION Torrent Systems,[42] Helicos Biosciences,[43] and BioNanomatrix.[44] These companies are heavily financed and backed by venture capitalists, hedge funds, and investment banks.[45] [46]

Incentive

In October 2006, the X Prize Foundation, working in collaboration with the J. Craig Venter Science Foundation, established the Archon X Prize for Genomics,[47] intending to award US$10 million to "the first Team that can build a device and use it to sequence 100 human genomes within 10 days or less, with an accuracy of no more than one error in every 100,000 bases sequenced, with sequences accurately covering at least 98% of the genome, and at a recurring cost of no more than US$10,000 per genome."[48] An error rate of 1 in 100,000 bases, out of a total of six billion bases in the human diploid genome, would mean about 60,000 errors per genome. The error rates required for widespread clinical use, such as Predictive Medicine[49] is currently set by over 1,400 clinical single gene sequencing tests [50] (for example, errors in BRCA1 gene for breast cancer risk analysis). As of July 2011, the Archon X Prize for Genomics remains unclaimed.

2007

In 2007, Applied Biosystems started selling a new type of sequencer called SOLiD System.[51] The technology allowed users to sequence 60 gigabases per run.[52]

2009

In early February 2009, Complete Genomics released a full sequence of a human genome that was sequenced using their service. The data indicates that Complete Genomics' full genome sequencing service accuracy is just under 99.999%, meaning that just one in every one hundred thousand variants was called incorrectly. This means that their full sequence of the human genome will contain approximately 80,000–100,000 false positive errors in each genome. However, this accuracy rate was based on Complete Genomics' sequence that was completed utilizing a 90× depth of coverage (each base in the genome was sequenced 90 times) while their commercialized sequence is reported to be only 40×, so the accuracy may be substantially lower unless they can find some way to improve it before their first service release planned for the summer 2009. This accuracy rate may be acceptable for research purposes, and clinical use would require confirmation by other methods of any reportable alleles.[53] [54] Complete Genomics announced in Dec. 2010 that for the last 500 complete human genomes that it had sequenced, an average of over 98 percent of the genome was read at 10-fold or greater coverage. In addition, its software made high confidence calls of an average of over 95 percent of the genome and over 94 percent of the exome.

In March 2009, it was announced that Complete Genomics has signed a deal with the Broad Institute to sequence cancer patients' genomes and will be sequencing five full genomes to start.[55] In April 2009, Complete Genomics announced that it plans to sequence 1,000 full genomes between June 2009 and the end of the year and that they plan to be able to sequence one million full genomes *per year* by 2013.[56] Complete Genomics sequenced 50 genomes in 2009. Since then, it has significantly increased the throughout in its genome sequencing center and was able to sequence and analyze 300 complete human genomes in Q3 2010. Complete Genomics plans to officially launch in June 2009, although it is unknown if their lab will have received CLIA-certification by that time. Complete

Genomics announced its R&D human genome sequencing service in October 2008 and its commercial sequencing service in May 2010. The company does not produce clinical data and as such its genome center does not require CLIA certification.

In June 2009, Illumina announced that they were launching their own Personal Full Genome Sequencing Service at a depth of 30× for US$48,000 per genome.[57] This is still expensive for widespread consumer use, but the price may decrease substantially over the next few years as they realize economies of scale and given the competition with other companies such as Complete Genomics.[58] [59] Jay Flatley, Illumina's President and CEO, stated that "during the next five years, perhaps markedly sooner," the price point for full genome sequencing will fall from US$48,000 to under US$1,000.[60] Illumina has already signed agreements to supply full genome sequencing services to multiple direct-to-consumer personal genomics companies.

In August 2009, the founder of Helicos Biosciences, Dr. Stephen Quake, stated that using the company's Heliscope Single Molecule Sequencer he sequenced his own full genome for less than US$50,000. He stated that he expects the cost to decrease to the US$1,000 range within the next two to three years.[61]

In August 2009, Pacific Biosciences secured an additional US$68 million in new financing, bringing their total capitalization to US$188 million.[62] Pacific Biosciences said they are going to use this additional investment in order to prepare for the upcoming launch of their full genome sequencing service in 2010.[63] Complete Genomics followed by securing another US$45 million in a fourth round venture funding during the same month.[64] Complete Genomics has also made the claim that it will sequence 10,000 full genomes by the end of 2010.[65] Since then, it has significantly increased the throughout in its genome sequencing center and was able to sequence and analyze 300 complete human genomes in Q3 2010.

GE Global Research is also part of this race to commercialize full genome sequencing as they have been working on creating a service that will deliver a full genome for US$1,000 or less.[66] [67]

In September 2009, the President of Halcyon Molecular announced that they will be able to provide full genome sequencing in under 10 minutes for less than US$100 per genome.[68] This is, to date, the most ambitious promise of any full genome sequencing company.

In October 2009, IBM announced that they were also in the heated race to provide full genome sequencing for under US$1,000, with their ultimate goal being able to provide their service for US$100 per genome.[69] IBM's full genome sequencing technology, which uses nanopores, is known as the "DNA Transistor".[70]

In November 2009, Complete Genomics published a peer-reviewed paper in *Science* demonstrating its ability to sequence a complete human genome for US$1,700.[71] If true, this would mean the cost of full genome sequencing has come down exponentially within just a single year from around US$100,000 to US$50,000 and now to US$1,700. This consumables cost was clearly detailed in the *Science* paper.[72] However, Complete Genomics has previously released statements that it was unable to follow through on. For example, the company stated it would officially launch and release its service during the "summer of 2009", provide a "US$5,000" full genome sequencing service by the "summer of 2009", and "sequence 1,000 genomes between June 2009 and the end of 2009" − all of which, as of November 2009, have not yet occurred.[54] [56] [56] [73] Complete Genomics launched its R&D human genome sequencing service in October 2008 and its commercial service in May 2010. The company sequenced 50 genomes in 2009. Since then, it has significantly increased the throughput of its genome sequencing factory and was able to sequence and analyze 300 genomes in Q3 2010.

Also in November 2009, Complete Genomics announced that it was beginning a large-scale human genome sequencing study of Huntington's disease (up to 100 genomes) with the Institute for Systems Biology.

2010

In March 2010 Researchers from the Medical College of Wisconsin announced the first successful use of Genome Wide sequencing to change the treatment of a patient.[74] This story was later retold in a pulitzer prize winning article [75] and touted as a significant accomplishment in Nature [76] and by the director of the NIH in presentations at congress.

In March 2010, Pacific Biosciences said they have raised more than US$256 million in venture capital money and that they will be shipping their first ten full genome sequencing machines by the end of 2010. The company reported that the market initially will be researchers and academic institutions and then will rapidly turn into clinical applications that will be applicable to every single person in the world. Pacific Biosciences also stated that their second-generation machine, which is scheduled for release in 2015, will be capable of providing a full genome sequence for a person in just 15 minutes for less than US$100. Several other technologies have similar goals. Meanwhile, full genome sequencing might revolutionize medicine at even current prices by providing a clinician with a full genome for each one of his or her patients. However, some critics have stated that even if they are supplied with a full genome sequence of a patient, they would not know how to analyze or make use of that data.[77] Since then, new resources have begun to address this.[78] [79]

Also in March 2010, Complete Genomics' customers began publishing papers describing research breakthroughs that they have made using data it has provided. Examples included the Institute for Systems Biology's project to sequence a family of four and verify the gene responsible for Miller Syndrome, a rare craniofacial disorder[x] and Genentech's work to sequence and compare a patient's primary lung tumor and adjacent normal tissue[y].

In June 2010, Illumina lowered the cost of its individual sequencing service to US$19,500 from US$48,000. The company is offering a discounted price of US$9,500 for people with serious medical conditions who could potentially benefit from having their genomes decoded.

2011

Knome[80] provides full genome (98% genome) sequencing services for US$39,500 for whole genome sequencing and interpretation for consumers. It's US$29,500 for whole genome sequencing and analysis for researchers depending on their requirements.[81] [82]

Complete Genomics charges approximately US$10,000 to sequence a complete human genome and offers discounts for large orders. This service includes sample quality control, library preparation, sequencing, mapping, assembly and data analysis.

Helicos Biosciences, Pacific Biosciences, Complete Genomics, Illumina, Sequenom, ION Torrent Systems, Halcyon Molecular, IBM, and GE Global appear to all be going head to head in the race to commercialize full genome sequencing.[21] [67]

Disruptive technology

Full genome sequencing provides information on a genome that is orders of magnitude larger than that provided by the current leader in genotyping technology, DNA arrays. For humans, DNA arrays currently provide genotypic information on up to one million genetic variants,[83] [84] [85] while full genome sequencing will provide information on all six billion bases in the human genome, or 3,000 times more data. Because of this, full genome sequencing is considered disruptive to the DNA array markets as the accuracy of both range from 99.98% to 99.999% (in non-repetitive DNA regions) and their consumables cost of US$5000 per 6 billion base pairs is competitive (for some applications) with DNA arrays (US$500 per 1 million basepairs).[37] Agilent, another established DNA array manufacturer, is working on targeted (selective region) genome sequencing technologies.[86] It is thought that Affymetrix, the pioneer of array technology in the 1990s, has fallen behind due to significant corporate and stock turbulence and is currently not working on any known full genome sequencing approach.[87] [88] [89] It is unknown what will happen to the DNA array market once full genome sequencing becomes commercially widespread, especially as companies and laboratories providing this disruptive technology start to realize economies of scale. It is postulated, however, that this new technology may significantly diminish the total market size for arrays and any other sequencing technology once it becomes commonplace for individuals and newborns to have their full genomes sequenced.[90]

Sequencing versus analysis

Full genome sequencing provides raw data on all six billion letters in an individual's DNA. However, it does not provide an analysis of what that data means or how that data can be utilized in various clinical applications, such as in medicine to help prevent disease. As of 2010 the companies that are working on providing full genome sequencing provide clinical CLIA certified data (Illumina) and analytical services for the interpretation of the full genome data (Knome) With only one instition offering sequencing and analysis in a clinical setting.[91] Nevertheless there is plenty of room for researchers or companies to improve such analyses and make it useful to physicians and patients.[77] [78] [79]

Societal impact

Further information: Personal genomics — predictive medicine services already available

Inexpensive, time-efficient full genome sequencing will be a major accomplishment not only for the field of Genomics, but for the entire human civilization because, for the first time, individuals will be able to have their entire genome sequenced. Utilizing this information, it is speculated that health care professionals, such as physicians and genetic counselors, will eventually be able to use genomic information to predict what diseases a person may get in the future and attempt to either minimize the impact of that disease or avoid it altogether through the implementation of personalized, preventive medicine. Full genome sequencing will allow health care professionals to analyze the entire human genome of an individual and therefore detect all disease-related genetic variants, regardless of the genetic variant's prevalence or frequency. This will enable the rapidly emerging medical fields of Predictive Medicine and Personalized Medicine and will mark a significant leap forward for the clinical genetic revolution. Full genome sequencing is clearly of great importance for research into the basis of genetic disease and has shown significant benefit to a subset of individuals with rare disease in the clinical setting [92] [93] [94] [95]. Illumina's CEO, Jay Flatley, stated in February 2009 that "A complete DNA read-out for every newborn will be technically feasible and affordable in less than five years, promising a revolution in healthcare" and that "by 2019 it will have become routine to map infants' genes when they are born."[96] This potential use of genome sequencing is highly controversial, as it runs counter to established ethical norms for predictive genetic testing of asymptomatic minors that have been well established in the fields of medical genetics and genetic counseling.[97] [98] [99] [100] The traditional guidelines for genetic testing have been developed over the course of several decades since it first became possible to test for genetic markers associated with disease, prior to the advent of cost-effective, comprehensive genetic screening. It is established that norms, such as in the sciences and the field of genetics, are subject to change and evolve over time.[101] [102] It is unknown whether traditional norms practiced in medical genetics today will be altered by new technological advancements such as full genome sequencing.

Today, parents have the legal authority to obtain testing of any kind for their children. Currently available newborn screening for childhood diseases allows detection of rare disorders that can be prevented or better treated by early detection and intervention. Specific genetic tests are also available to determine an etiology when a child's symptoms appear to have a genetic basis. Full genome sequencing, in addition has the potential to reveal a large amount of information (such as carrier status for autosomal recessive disorders, genetic risk factors for complex adult-onset diseases, and other predictive medical and non-medical information) that is currently not completely understood, may not be clinically useful to the child during childhood, and may not necessarily be wanted by the individual upon reaching adulthood.[103] Despite the benefits of predicting disease risk in childhood, genetic testing also introduces potential harms (such as discovery of non-paternity, genetic discrimination, and psychological impacts). The established ethical guidelines for predictive genetic testing of asymptomatic minors thus has more to do with protecting this vulnerable population and preserving the individual's privacy and autonomy to know or not to know their genetic information, than with the technology that makes this possible. While parents may have legal authority to obtain such testing, the mainstream opinion of professional medical genetics societies is that presymptomatic testing should be offered to minors only when they are competent to understand the relevancy of genetic screening so as to allow them to participate in the decision about whether or not it is appropriate for them.[104] [105]

References

[1] Kijk magazine, 01 January 2009

[2] Wellcome Trust Case Control Consortium; Clayton, David G.; Cardon, Lon R.; Craddock, Nick; Deloukas, Panos; Duncanson, Audrey; Kwiatkowski, Dominic P.; McCarthy, Mark I. et al. (June 2007). "Genome-wide association study of 14,000 cases of seven common diseases and 3,000 shared controls". *Nature* **447** (7145): 661–78. Bibcode 2007Natur.447..661B. doi:10.1038/nature05911. PMC 2719288. PMID 17554300.

[3] Mailman MD, Feolo M, Jin Y, Kimura M, Tryka K, Bagoutdinov R, Hao L, Kiang A, Paschall J, Phan L, Popova N, Pretel S, Ziyabari L, Lee M, Shao Y, Wang ZY, Sirotkin K, Ward M, Kholodov M, Zbicz K, Beck J, Kimelman M, Shevelev S, Preuss D, Yaschenko E, Graeff A, Ostell J, Sherry ST (October 2007). "The NCBI dbGaP database of genotypes and phenotypes". *Nat. Genet.* **39** (10): 1181–6. doi:10.1038/ng1007-1181. PMC 2031016. PMID 17898773.

[4] Wade, Nicholas (September 4, 2007). "In the Genome Race, the Sequel Is Personal" (http://www.nytimes.com/2007/09/04/science/04vent.html). New York Times. . Retrieved February 22, 2009.

[5] Nature. "Access : All about Craig: the first 'full' genome sequence" (http://www.nature.com/nature/journal/v449/n7158/full/449006a.html). Nature. . Retrieved 2009-02-24.

[6] Levy S, Sutton G, Ng PC, Feuk L, Halpern AL, Walenz BP, Axelrod N, Huang J, Kirkness EF, Denisov G, Lin Y, MacDonald JR, Pang AW, Shago M, Stockwell TB, Tsiamouri A, Bafna V, Bansal V, Kravitz SA, Busam DA, Beeson KY, McIntosh TC, Remington KA, Abril JF, Gill J, Borman J, Rogers YH, Frazier ME, Scherer SW, Strausberg RL, Venter JC (September 2007). "The diploid genome sequence of an individual human". *PLoS Biol.* **5** (10): e254. doi:10.1371/journal.pbio.0050254. PMC 1964779. PMID 17803354.

[7] Wade, Wade (June 1, 2007). "DNA pioneer Watson gets own genome map" (http://www.iht.com/articles/2007/06/01/america/dna.php). International Herald Tribune. . Retrieved February 22, 2009.

[8] Wade, Nicholas (May 31, 2007). "Genome of DNA Pioneer Is Deciphered" (http://www.nytimes.com/2007/05/31/science/31cnd-gene.html). New York Times. . Retrieved February 21, 2009.

[9] Wheeler DA, Srinivasan M, Egholm M, Shen Y, Chen L, McGuire A, He W, Chen YJ, Makhijani V, Roth GT, Gomes X, Tartaro K, Niazi F, Turcotte CL, Irzyk GP, Lupski JR, Chinault C, Song XZ, Liu Y, Yuan Y, Nazareth L, Qin X, Muzny DM, Margulies M, Weinstock GM, Gibbs RA, Rothberg JM. (2008). "The complete genome of an individual by massively parallel DNA sequencing". *Nature* **452** (7189): 872–6.. Bibcode 2008Natur.452..872W. doi:10.1038/nature06884. PMID 18421352.

[10] Wang J, et al. (2008). "The diploid genome sequence of an Asian individual". *Nature* **456** (7218): 60–65. Bibcode 2008Natur.456...60W. doi:10.1038/nature07484. PMC 2716080. PMID 18987735.

[11] Bentley DR, Balasubramanian S, et al. (2008). "Accurate whole human genome sequencing using reversible terminator chemistry". *Nature* **456** (7218): 53–9. Bibcode 2008Natur.456...53B. doi:10.1038/nature07517. PMC 2581791. PMID 18987734.

[12] Ley TJ, Mardis ER, Ding L, Fulton B, McLellan MD, Chen K, Dooling D, Dunford-Shore BH, McGrath S, Hickenbotham M, Cook L, Abbott R, Larson DE, Koboldt DC, Pohl C, Smith S, Hawkins A, Abbott S, Locke D, Hillier LW, Miner T, Fulton L, Magrini V, Wylie T, Glasscock J, Conyers J, Sander N, Shi X, Osborne JR, Minx P, Gordon D, Chinwalla A, Zhao Y, Ries RE, Payton JE, Westervelt P, Tomasson MH, Watson M, Baty J, Ivanovich J, Heath S, Shannon WD, Nagarajan R, Walter MJ, Link DC, Graubert TA, DiPersio JF, Wilson RK. (2008). "DNA sequencing of a cytogenetically normal acute myeloid leukaemia genome". *Nature* **456** (7218): 66–72. Bibcode 2008Natur.456...66L. doi:10.1038/nature07485. PMC 2603574. PMID 18987736.

[13] Ahn SM, Kim TH, Lee S, Kim D, Ghang H, Kim D, Kim BC, Kim SY, Kim WY, Kim C, Park D, Lee YS, Kim S, Reja R, Jho S, Kim CG, Cha JY, Kim KH, Lee B, Bhak J, Kim SJ (2009). "The first Korean genome sequence and analysis: Full genome sequencing for a socio-ethnic group". *Genome Research* **19** (9): 1622–9. doi:10.1101/gr.092197.109. PMC 2752128. PMID 19470904.

[14] http://www.completegenomics.com/news-events/press-releases/Complete-Genomics-Adds-29-High-Coverage-Complete-Human-Genome-Sequencing-Datasets-to-its-Public-Genomic-Repository--119298369.html

[15] Staden R (June 1979). "A strategy of DNA sequencing employing computer programs" (http://nar.oxfordjournals.org/cgi/pmidlookup?view=long&pmid=461197). *Nucleic Acids Res.* **6** (7): 2601–10. doi:10.1093/nar/6.7.2601. PMC 327874. PMID 461197. .

[16] Edwards, A; Caskey, T (1991). "Closure strategies for random DNA sequencing". *Methods: A Companion to Methods in Enzymology* **3** (1): 41–47. doi:10.1016/S1046-2023(05)80162-8.

[17] Edwards A, Voss H, Rice P, Civitello A, Stegemann J, Schwager C, Zimmermann J, Erfle H, Caskey CT, Ansorge W (April 1990). "Automated DNA sequencing of the human HPRT locus". *Genomics* **6** (4): 593–608. doi:10.1016/0888-7543(90)90493-E. PMID 2341149.

[18] Roach JC, Boysen C, Wang K, Hood L (March 1995). "Pairwise end sequencing: a unified approach to genomic mapping and sequencing". *Genomics* **26** (2): 345–53. doi:10.1016/0888-7543(95)80219-C. PMID 7601461.

[19] Fleischmann RD, Adams MD, White O, Clayton RA, Kirkness EF, Kerlavage AR, Bult CJ, Tomb JF, Dougherty BA, Merrick JM (July 1995). "Whole-genome random sequencing and assembly of Haemophilus influenzae Rd". *Science* **269** (5223): 496–512. Bibcode 1995Sci...269..496F. doi:10.1126/science.7542800. PMID 7542800.

[20] Adams, MD; et al. (2000). "The genome sequence of Drosophila melanogaster". *Science* **287** (5461): 2185–95. Bibcode 2000Sci...287.2185.. doi:10.1126/science.287.5461.2185. PMID 10731132.

[21] Mukhopadhyay R (February 2009). "DNA sequencers: the next generation". *Anal. Chem.* **81** (5): 1736–40. doi:10.1021/ac802712u. PMID 19193124.

[22] "Harvard University and Oxford Nanopore Technologies Announce Licence Agreement to Advance Nanopore DNA Sequencing and other Applications" (http://www.nanotechwire.com/news.asp?nid=6428). Nanotechwire. August 5, 2008. . Retrieved February 23, 2009.

[23] "Illumina and Oxford Nanopore Enter into Broad Commercialization Agreement" (http://www.reuters.com/article/pressRelease/idUS49869+12-Jan-2009+BW20090112). Reuters. January 12, 2009. . Retrieved February 23, 2009.

[24] (http://www..com/sequenom-licenses-nanopore-technology-harvard-develop-third-generation-sequencer)

[25] "Single Molecule Real Time (SMRT) DNA Sequencing" (http://www.pacificbiosciences.com/index.php?q=technology-introduction). Pacific Biosciences. . Retrieved February 23, 2009.

[26] "Complete Human Genome Sequencing Technology Overview" (http://www.completegenomicsinc.com/pages/materials/CompleteGenomicsTechnologyPaper.pdf). Complete Genomics. 2009. . Retrieved February 23, 2009.

[27] http://www.completegenomics.com/services/technology/

[28] "Definition of pyrosequencing from the Nature Reviews Genetics Glossary" (http://www.nature.com/nrg/journal/v6/n11/glossary/nrg1709_glossary.html). . Retrieved 2008-10-28.

[29] Ronaghi M, Uhlén M, Nyrén P (July 1998). "A sequencing method based on real-time pyrophosphate". *Science* **281** (5375): 363, 365. doi:10.1126/science.281.5375.363. PMID 9705713.

[30] Ronaghi M, Karamohamed S, Pettersson B, Uhlén M, Nyrén P (November 1996). "Real-time DNA sequencing using detection of pyrophosphate release". *Anal. Biochem.* **242** (1): 84–9. doi:10.1006/abio.1996.0432. PMID 8923969.

[31] Nyrén P (2007). "The history of pyrosequencing". *Methods Mol. Biol.* **373**: 1–14. PMID 17185753.

[32] http://files.shareholder.com/downloads/CRGN/0x0x53381/386c4aaa-f36e-4b7a-9ff0-c06e61fad31f/211559.pdf

[33] "Article : Race to Cut Whole Genome Sequencing Costs Genetic Engineering & Biotechnology News — Biotechnology from Bench to Business" (http://www.genengnews.com/articles/chitem.aspx?aid=939&chid=1). Genengnews.com. . Retrieved 2009-02-23.

[34] "Whole Genome Sequencing Costs Continue to Drop" (http://www.eyeondna.com/2008/02/11/whole-genome-sequencing-costs-continue-to-drop/). Eyeondna.com. . Retrieved 2009-02-23.

[35] Harmon, Katherine (2010-06-28). "Genome Sequencing for the Rest of Us" (http://www.scientificamerican.com/article.cfm?id=personal-genome-sequencing&print=true). Scientific American. . Retrieved 2010-08-13.

[36] San Diego/Orange County Technology News. "Sequenom to Develop Third-Generation Nanopore-Based Single Molecule Sequencing Technology" (http://www.freshnews.com/news/biotech-biomedical/article_39927.html). Freshnews.com. . Retrieved 2009-02-24.

[37] "Article : Whole Genome Sequencing in 24 Hours Genetic Engineering & Biotechnology News — Biotechnology from Bench to Business" (http://www.genengnews.com/articles/chitem.aspx?aid=658&chid=2). Genengnews.com. . Retrieved 2009-02-23.

[38] "Pacific Bio lifts the veil on its high-speed genome-sequencing effort" (http://venturebeat.com/2008/02/10/pacific-bio-lifts-the-veil-on-its-high-speed-genome-sequencing-effort/). VentureBeat. . Retrieved 2009-02-23.

[39] "Bio-IT World" (http://www.bio-itworld.com/headlines/2008/oct06/complete-genomics-dna-nanoballs.html). Bio-IT World. 2008-10-06. . Retrieved 2009-02-23.

[40] "Whole genome sequencing costs continue to fall: $300 million in 2003, $1 million 2007, $60,000 now, $5000 by year end" (http://nextbigfuture.com/2008/03/genome-sequencing-costs-continue-to.html). Nextbigfuture.com. 2008-03-25. . Retrieved 2011-01-28.

[41] "Slater Fund invests another $250K in Genome Corp" (http://www.pbn.com/stories/29333.html). *PBN.com*. Providence Business News. 2008-01-22. . Retrieved 2011-01-28.

[42] "Omics! Omics!: CHI Next-Gen Conference, Day 1" (http://omicsomics.blogspot.com/2009/09/chi-next-gen-conference-day-1.html). Omicsomics.blogspot.com. 2009-09-21. . Retrieved 2011-01-28.

[43] "With New Machine, Helicos Brings Personal Genome Sequencing A Step Closer" (http://www.xconomy.com/boston/2008/04/22/with-new-machine-helicos-brings-personal-genome-sequencing-a-step-closer/). Xconomy. 2008-04-22. . Retrieved 2011-01-28.

[44] "Han Cao's nanofluidic chip could cut DNA sequencing costs dramatically" (http://www.technologyreview.com/biomedicine/22112//). Technology Review. .

[45] John Carroll (2008-07-14). "Pacific Biosciences gains $100M for sequencing tech" (http://www.fiercebiotech.com/story/pacific-biosciences-garners-100m-sequencing-tech/2008-07-14). FierceBiotech. . Retrieved 2009-02-23.

[46] Sibley, Lisa (2009-02-08). "Complete Genomics brings radical reduction in cost" (http://sanjose.bizjournals.com/sanjose/stories/2009/02/09/story1.html?b=1234155600^1773923). *Silicon Valley / San Jose Business Journal* (Sanjose.bizjournals.com). . Retrieved 2009-02-23.

[47] Carlson, Rob (2007-01-02). "A Few Thoughts on Rapid Genome Sequencing and The Archon Prize — synthesis" (http://synthesis.cc/2007/01/a-few-thoughts-on-rapid-genome-sequencing-and-the-archon-prize.html). Synthesis.cc. . Retrieved 2009-02-23.

[48] "PRIZE Overview: Archon X PRIZE for Genomics" (http://genomics.xprize.org/genomics/archon-x-prize-for-genomics/prize-overview).

[49] Bentley DR (December 2006). "Whole-genome re-sequencing". *Curr. Opin. Genet. Dev.* **16** (6): 545–52. doi:10.1016/j.gde.2006.10.009. PMID 17055251.

[50] "GeneTests.org" (http://genetests.org). .

[51] "SOLiD System — a next-gen DNA sequencing platform announced" (http://www.gizmag.com/go/8248/). Gizmag.com. 2007-10-27. . Retrieved 2009-02-24.

[52] "The $1000 Genome: Coming Soon?" (http://www.dddmag.com/article-The-1000-Genome-Coming-Soon-41310.aspx). Dddmag.com. 2010-04-01. . Retrieved 2011-01-28.

[53] (http://www.completegenomics.com/dataRelease/sequencingResults.aspx)

[54] "Broad Institute to use Complete Genomics to sequence genomes of cancer patients : Genetic Future" (http://scienceblogs.com/geneticfuture/2009/03/broad_institute_complete_genomics.php). Scienceblogs.com. . Retrieved 2011-01-28.

[55] "Complete Genomics, Broad Institute Forge Cancer Sequencing Collaboration" (http://www.bio-itworld.com/news/03/03/09/complete-genomic-broad-institute-cancer-collaboration.html). Bio-IT World. . Retrieved 2011-01-28.

[56] Walsh, Fergus (2009-04-08). "Era of personalised medicine awaits" (http://news.bbc.co.uk/2/hi/health/7954968.stm). *BBC News*. . Retrieved 2010-05-03.

[57] "Individual genome sequencing — Illumina, Inc" (http://www.everygenome.com). Everygenome.com. . Retrieved 2011-01-28.

[58] "Business news: Financial, stock & investing news online" (http://news.moneycentral.msn.com/provider/providerarticle. aspx?feed=BW&date=20090610&id=9999448). *MSN Money*. News.moneycentral.msn.com. . Retrieved 2011-01-28.

[59] "Illumina launches personal genome sequencing service for $48,000 : Genetic Future" (http://scienceblogs.com/geneticfuture/2009/06/illumina_launches_personal_gen.php). Scienceblogs.com. . Retrieved 2011-01-28.

[60] "Illumina demos concept iPhone app for genetic data sharing" (http://mobihealthnews.com/2658/illumina-demos-concept-iphone-app-for-genetic-data-sharing/). mobihealthnews. 2009-06-10. . Retrieved 2011-01-28.

[61] Wade, Nicholas (2009-08-11). "Cost of Decoding a Genome Is Lowered" (http://www.nytimes.com/2009/08/11/science/11gene. html?_r=1&hp). *The New York Times*. . Retrieved 2010-05-03.

[62] Camille Ricketts (2009-08-13). "Pacific Biosciences takes $68M as genome sequencing becomes more competitive" (http://deals. venturebeat.com/2009/08/13/pacific-biosciences-takes-68m-as-genome-sequencing-becomes-more-competitive/). VentureBeat. . Retrieved 2011-01-28.

[63] "Pacific Biosciences Raises Additional $68 Million in Financing" (http://www.fiercebiotech.com/press-releases/pacific-biosciences-raises-additional-68-million-financing). FierceBiotech. 2009-08-12. . Retrieved 2011-01-28.

[64] "Silicon Valley startup Complete Genomics promises low-cost DNA sequencing" (http://www.mercurynews.com/businessheadlines/ci_13193756?nclick_check=1). *San Jose Mercury News*. Mercurynews.com. . Retrieved 2011-01-28.

[65] "Silicon Valley Startup Complete Genomics Promises Low-Cost DNA Sequencing" (http://www.istockanalyst.com/article/viewiStockNews/articleid/3434217). Istockanalyst.com. 2009-08-24. . Retrieved 2011-01-28.

[66] Jacquin Niles. "Explaining Sequencing | The Daily Scan" (http://www.genomeweb.com//node/922285?emc=el&m=467453&l=4&v=e53aebae7b). GenomeWeb. . Retrieved 2011-01-28.

[67] "NHGRI Awards More than $50M for Low-Cost DNA Sequencing Tech Development" (http://www.genomeweb.com/sequencing/nhgri-awards-more-50m-low-cost-dna-sequencing-tech-development?page=show). *Genome Web*. 2009. .

[68] Leena Rao (2009-09-24). "PayPal Co-Founder And Founders Fund Partner Joins DNA Sequencing Firm Halcyon Molecular" (http://www.techcrunch.com/2009/09/24/paypal-co-founder-and-founders-fund-partner-joins-dna-sequencing-firm-halcyon-molecular/). Techcrunch.com. . Retrieved 2011-01-28.

[69] http://www.nytimes.com/glogin?URI=http://www.nytimes.com/2009/10/06/science/06dna.html&OQ=_rQ3D1&OP=833e743Q2F8bYs8agifEgg.080@@j8P@8@Q7C8fikYTiY8@Q7CaTQ26Ao.-u

[70] Shankland, Stephen (2009-10-06). "IBM Research jumps into genetic sequencing | Deep Tech" (http://news.cnet.com/8301-30685_3-10368045-264.html). *CNET News*. News.cnet.com. . Retrieved 2011-01-28.

[71] (http://abcnews.go.com/Technology/wireStory?id=9010552)

[72] Drmanac R, Sparks AB, Callow MJ et al: Human genome sequencing using unchained base reads on self-assembling DNA nanoarrays. Science 327(5961), 78-81 (2010)

[73] "Five Thousand Bucks for Your Genome" (http://www.technologyreview.com/biomedicine/21466/). Technology Review. 2008-10-20. . Retrieved 2009-02-23.

[74] http://www.jsonline.com/features/health/89340522.html

[75] http://www.jsonline.com/features/health/111224104.html

[76] http://www.nature.com/news/2010/100914/full/news.2010.465.html

[77] *The Wall Street Journal*. http://online.wsj.com/public/page/0_0_WP_3001.html?currentPlayingLocation=82&currentlyPlayingCollection=Small%20Business&currentlyPlayingVideoId={CF4393A6-F71C-4FE2-A2F5-73271E1CA8E7}.

[78] Ashley EA, Butte AJ, Wheeler MT, Chen R, Klein TE, Dewey FE, Dudley JT, Ormond KE, Pavlovic A, Morgan AA, Pushkarev D, Neff NF, Hudgins L, Gong L, Hodges LM, Berlin DS, Thorn CF, Sangkuhl K, Hebert JM, Woon M, Sagreiya H, Whaley R, Knowles JW, Chou MF, Thakuria JV, Rosenbaum AM, Zaranek AW, Church GM, Greely HT, Quake SR, Altman RB. (2010 May). "Clinical assessment incorporating a personal genome.". *Lancet* **375(9725)**: 1525–35.

[79] "Genomes, Environments, Traits (GET) Evidence" (http://evidence.personalgenomes.org). .

[80] "Knome homepage" (http://www.knome.com/). Knome.com. . Retrieved 2011-01-28.

[81] Herper, Matthew (2010-06-03). "Your Genome is Coming" (http://blogs.forbes.com/sciencebiz/2010/06/03/your-genome-is-coming/ ?boxes=businesschannelsections). Forbes. . Retrieved 2010-08-13.

[82] Lauerman, John (2009-02-05). "Complete Genomics Drives Down Cost of Genome Sequence to $5,000" (http://www.bloomberg.com/ apps/news?pid=20601124&sid=aEUlnq6ltPpQ). Bloomberg.com. . Retrieved 2011-01-28.

[83] "Genomics Core" (http://www.gladstone.ucsf.edu/gladstone/site/genomicscore/section/1919). Gladstone.ucsf.edu. . Retrieved 2009-02-23.

[84] Nishida N, Koike A, Tajima A, Ogasawara Y, Ishibashi Y, Uehara Y, Inoue I, Tokunaga K (2008). "Evaluating the performance of Affymetrix SNP Array 6.0 platform with 400 Japanese individuals". *BMC Genomics* **9** (1): 431. doi:10.1186/1471-2164-9-431. PMC 2566316. PMID 18803882.

[85] Petrone, Justin. "Illumina, DeCode Build 1M SNP Chip; Q2 Launch to Coincide with Release of Affy's 6.0 SNP Array | BioArray News | Arrays" (http://www.genomeweb.com/arrays/illumina-decode-build-1m-snp-chip-q2-launch-coincide-release-affys-60-snp-array). GenomeWeb. . Retrieved 2009-02-23.

[86] "Agilent Technologies Announces Licensing Agreement with Broad Institute to Develop Genome-Partitioning Kits to Streamline Next-Generation Sequencing" (http://www.chem.agilent.com/en-US/PressReleases/Pages/PRCA08032.aspx). .

[87] "Affymetrix stock slumps 30% on forecast" (http://sacramento.bizjournals.com/sacramento/stories/2008/07/21/daily52.html). *Sacramento Business Journal* (Sacramento.bizjournals.com). 2008-07-25. . Retrieved 2009-02-23.

[88] Bluis, John (2006-04-24). "Affymetrix Gets Chipped Again" (http://www.fool.com/investing/high-growth/2006/04/24/ affymetrix-gets-chipped-again.aspx). Fool.com. . Retrieved 2009-02-23.

[89] "The chips are down". *Nature* **444** (7117): 256–7. November 2006. Bibcode 2006Natur.444..256.. doi:10.1038/444256a. PMID 17108930.

[90] Coombs A (October 2008). "The sequencing shakeup". *Nat. Biotechnol.* **26** (10): 1109–12. doi:10.1038/nbt1008-1109. PMID 18846083.

[91] http://www.genomeweb.com/sequencing/ following-diagnostic-sequencing-success-mcw-creates-comprehensive-framework-guid?utm_source=feedburner&utm_medium=feed& utm_campaign=Feed%3A+genomeweb+%28GenomeWeb+%C3%9Cberfeed%29

[92] Ng SB, Buckingham KJ, Lee C, *et al.* (January 2010). "Exome sequencing identifies the cause of a mendelian disorder". *Nat. Genet.* **42** (1): 30–5. doi:10.1038/ng.499. PMC 2847889. PMID 19915526.

[93] Hannibal MC, Buckingham KJ, Ng SB, *et al.* (July 2011). "Spectrum of MLL2 (ALR) mutations in 110 cases of Kabuki syndrome". *Am. J. Med. Genet. A* **155A** (7): 1511–6. doi:10.1002/ajmg.a.34074. PMID 21671394.

[94] Worthey EA, Mayer AN, Syverson GD, *et al.* (March 2011). "Making a definitive diagnosis: successful clinical application of whole exome sequencing in a child with intractable inflammatory bowel disease" (http://meta.wkhealth.com/pt/pt-core/template-journal/lwwgateway/ media/landingpage.htm?issn=1098-3600&volume=13&issue=3&spage=255). *Genet. Med.* **13** (3): 255–62. doi:10.1097/GIM.0b013e3182088158. PMID 21173700. .

[95] Goh V, Helbling D, Biank V, Jarzembowski J, Dimmock D (June 2011). "Next Generation Sequencing Facilitates The Diagnosis In A Child With Twinkle Mutations Causing Cholestatic Liver Failure". *J Pediatr Gastroenterol Nutr.* doi:10.1097/MPG.0b013e318227e53c. PMID 21681116.

[96] Henderson, Mark (2009-02-09). "Genetic mapping of babies by 2019 will transform preventive medicine" (http://www.timesonline.co. uk/tol/news/uk/science/article5689052.ece). London: Times Online. . Retrieved 2009-02-23.

[97] McCabe LL, McCabe ER (June 2001). "Postgenomic medicine. Presymptomatic testing for prediction and prevention". *Clin Perinatol* **28** (2): 425–34. doi:10.1016/S0095-5108(05)70094-4. PMID 11499063.

[98] Nelson RM, Botkjin JR, Kodish ED, *et al.* (June 2001). "Ethical issues with genetic testing in pediatrics". *Pediatrics* **107** (6): 1451–5. doi:10.1542/peds.107.6.1451. PMID 11389275.

[99] Borry P, Fryns JP, Schotsmans P, Dierickx K (February 2006). "Carrier testing in minors: a systematic review of guidelines and position papers". *Eur. J. Hum. Genet.* **14** (2): 133–8. doi:10.1038/sj.ejhg.5201509. PMID 16267502.

[100] Borry P, Stultiens L, Nys H, Cassiman JJ, Dierickx K (November 2006). "Presymptomatic and predictive genetic testing in minors: a systematic review of guidelines and position papers". *Clin. Genet.* **70** (5): 374–81. doi:10.1111/j.1399-0004.2006.00692.x. PMID 17026616.

[101] Mesoudi A, Danielson P (August 2008). "Ethics, evolution and culture.". *Theory Biosci.* **127** (3): 229–40. doi:10.1007/s12064-008-0027-y. PMID 18357481.

[102] Ehrlich PR, Levin SA (June 2005). "The evolution of norms.". *PLoS Biol.* **3** (6): e194. doi:10.1371/journal.pbio.0030194. PMC 1149491. PMID 15941355.

[103] Mayer AN, Dimmock DP, Arca MJ, *et al.* (March 2011). "A timely arrival for genomic medicine" (http://meta.wkhealth.com/pt/ pt-core/template-journal/lwwgateway/media/landingpage.htm?issn=1098-3600&volume=13&issue=3&spage=195). *Genet. Med.* **13** (3): 195–6. doi:10.1097/GIM.0b013e3182095089. PMID 21169843. .

[104] Borry, P.; Evers-Kiebooms, G.; Cornel, MC; Clarke, A; Dierickx, K; Public and Professional Policy Committee (PPPC) of the European Society of Human Genetics (ESHG) (2009). "Genetic testing in asymptomatic minors Background considerations towards ESHG Recommendations". *Eur J Hum Genet* **17** (6): 711–9. doi:10.1038/ejhg.2009.25. PMC 2947094. PMID 19277061.

[105] Trott, Amanda A.; Matalon, Reuben (2009). "When Should Children Be Tested for Genetic Diseases?". *Pediatrics* **124** (4): e807–e808. doi:10.1542/peds.2009-1498. PMID 19770173.

External links

- Archon X Prize for Genomics (http://genomics.xprize.org/)
- James Watson's Personal Genome Sequence (http://jimwatsonsequence.cshl.edu/cgi-perl/gbrowse/jwsequence/)
- AAAS/Science: Genome Sequencing Poster (http://www.sciencemag.org/products/posters/SequencingPoster.pdf)
- Genome Sequencing Today — A blog dedicated to the promotion and advancement of full genome sequencing and personalized medicine (http://genomesequence.blogspot.com/)
- Outsmart Your Genes: Book that discusses full genome sequencing and its impact upon health care and society (http://www.outsmartyourgenes.com/)

Gap penalty

Gap penalties are used during sequence alignment. Gap penalties contribute to the overall score of alignments, and therefore, the size of the gap penalty relative to the entries in the similarity matrix affects the alignment that is finally selected. Selecting a higher gap penalty will cause less favourable characters to be aligned, to avoid creating as many gaps.

Constant gap penalty

Constant gap penalties are the simplest type of gap penalty. The only parameter, d, is added to the alignment score when the gap is first opened. This means that any gap receives the same penalty, regardless of its size.

Linear gap penalty

Linear gap penalties have only one parameter, d, which is a penalty per unit length of gap. This is almost always negative, so that the alignment with fewer gaps is favoured over the alignment with more gaps. Under a linear gap penalty, the overall penalty for one large gap is the same as for many small gaps.

Affine gap penalty

Some sequences are more likely to have a large gap, rather than many small gaps. For example, a biological sequence is much more likely to have one big gap of length 10, due to a single insertion or deletion event, than it is to have 10 small gaps of length 1. Affine gap penalties use a gap opening penalty, o, and a gap extension penalty, e. A gap of length l is then given a penalty $o + (l-1)e$. So that gaps are discouraged, o is almost always negative. Because a few large gaps are better than many small gaps, e, though negative, is almost always less negative than o, so as to encourage gap extension, rather than gap introduction.

Further reading

- Taylor WR, Munro RE (1997). "Multiple sequence threading: conditional gap placement". *Fold Des* **2** (4): S33-9.
- Taylor WR (1996). "A non-local gap-penalty for profile alignment". *Bull Math Biol* **58** (1): 1–18. doi:10.1007/BF02458279. PMID 8819751.
- Vingron M, Waterman MS (1994). "Sequence alignment and penalty choice. Review of concepts, case studies and implications". *J Mol Biol* **235** (1): 1–12. doi:10.1016/S0022-2836(05)80006-3. PMID 8289235.
- Panjukov VV (1993). "Finding steady alignments: similarity and distance". *Comput Appl Biosci* **9** (3): 285–90. PMID 8324629.

- Alexandrov NN (1992). "Local multiple alignment by consensus matrix". *Comput Appl Biosci* **8** (4): 339–45. PMID 1498689.
- Hein J (1989). "A new method that simultaneously aligns and reconstructs ancestral sequences for any number of homologous sequences, when the phylogeny is given". *Mol Biol Evol* **6** (6): 649–68. PMID 2488477.
- Henneke CM (1989). "A multiple sequence alignment algorithm for homologous proteins using secondary structure information and optionally keying alignments to functionally important sites". *Comput Appl Biosci* **5** (2): 141–50. PMID 2751764.
- Reich JG, Drabsch H, Daumler A (1984). "On the statistical assessment of similarities in DNA sequences". *Nucleic Acids Res* **12** (13): 5529–43. doi:10.1093/nar/12.13.5529. PMC 318937. PMID 6462914.

Gemini Somatics

Gemini Somatics

Type	Private Corporation
Industry	Biotechnology
Headquarters	Riverside, OR
Key people	Joseph Cavendish: Chairman; Dr. Edward Darmos: Executive Director of Synthetic Somatology;
Products	Somatic synthesis technologies[1] ; Scientific consultancy
Website	www.geminisomatics.com [2]

Gemini Somatics is a biotechnology company located in Riverside, Oregon, working primarily in the field of synthetic somatology, which is an emerging science developed by Dr Edward Darmos.[3] .

Research

Gemini Somatics focuses its efforts on synthetic somatology, which is an adaptation of synthetic biology using pluripotent stem cells and artificially-generated genomes in order to adapt human life to potential future conditions[4] .

Their work is based on the developments surrounding *Mycoplasma mycoides*[5] and *Mycoplasma laboratorium*, as well as taking advantage of technological advancements including the NASA bioreactor and the DARPA REMIND programme[6] .

Gemini Somatics have recently exhibited an interest in sourcing research material from volunteer gamers[7] .

Politics

As a participant in the controversial stem cell and synthetic biology arenas, Gemini Somatics has come under fire from several opponents of synthetic biology and therapeutic cloning[8] .

Company information

Gemini Somatics was founded by Joseph Cavendish and is based in Riverside, Oregon. The company is privately funded, as well as receiving significant private research funding[9] .

References

[1] http://www.pressbox.co.uk/cgi-bin/links/page.cgi?g=detailed%2F574970.html;t=snap;d=ARRAY%280x86921d4%29 "Gemini Somatics Acquires Significant Funding", Press release, Oregon , 12 November 2010, Retrieved on 22 December 2010.

[2] http://www.geminisomatics.com/

[3] Gemini Somatics corporate web site. (http://www.geminisomatics.com)

[4] Darmos, Edward. http://www.scribd.com/doc/43784991/An-Introduction-to-Synthetic-Somatology "An Introduction to Synthetic Somatology".

[5] Henderson, Mark. http://www.timesonline.co.uk/tol/news/science/biology_evolution/article7132299.ece "Scientists create artificial life in laboratory", The Times, London. 21 May 2010.

[6] Golder, D. "The Clone Ranger" (http://www.sfx.co.uk/2010/12/06/the-clone-ranger-2/#ixzz18eCLGR7f), *SFX (magazine)*, 6 December 2010, Retrieved 22 December 2010.

[7] "Gamers are the future" (http://www.ign.com/blogs/Gemini_Somatics/2010/11/25/gamers-are-the-future/) Corporate blog, *IGN*, 25 November 2010.

[8] "Gemini Acquitted" (http://geminisomatics.com/news.php), News article, 11 January 2010.

[9] http://www.pressbox.co.uk/cgi-bin/links/page.cgi?g=detailed%2F574970.html;t=snap;d=ARRAY%280x86921d4%29 "Gemini Somatics Acquires Significant Funding", Press release, Oregon , 12 November 2010, Retrieved on 22 December 2010.

External links

- Corporate web site (http://www.geminisomatics.com)

Gene Designer

Gene Designer

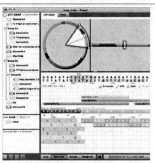

Gene Designer Sequence View enables manipulation of sequence elements, codon choices, and oligonucleotide positions. Rapidly search for sequence motifs, restriction sites and open reading frames.

Developer(s)	DNA2.0 [1]
Stable release	2.0 (Windows/Mac) / May 14, 2010
Operating system	Mac OS X, Windows, Linux
Type	Molecular Biology Toolkit
License	Free
Website	Gene Designer [2]

Gene Designer is a free bioinformatics software package.[3] It is used by Molecular Biologists from academia, government and the pharmaceutical, chemical, agricultural and biotechnology industries to design, clone and validate genetic sequences.

Features

Gene Designer enables Molecular Biologists to capture the entire gene design process in one application, using a range of design tools.

- Algorithms for *in silico* cloning, codon optimization, back translation and Primer Design
- Graphic Molecular View to display, annotate and edit constructs
- Customizable database to store, manage and track genetic elements, Genes and constructs
- Drag-and-Drop interface for moving sequence elements within or between constructs
- Search feature for Sequence motifs, Restriction sites and Open reading frames.
- Codon optimize for recombinant protein expression in any organism using multiple algorithms.
- Remove or add Restriction sites or other Sequence motifs
- Recode Open reading frames
- Check translation frames and fusion junctions
- Design Oligonucleotides for sequencing primers, includes a real time melting point calculator
- Cloning Tool with drag-and-drop ability to cut, combine and clone insert and vector.

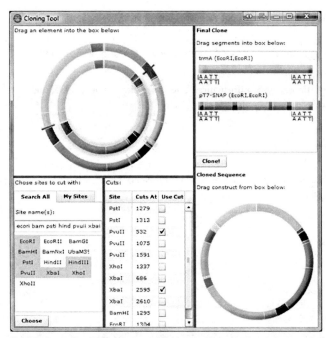

Gene Designer clones with a drag-and-drop feature. Users can drag their vector and insert into the Cloning Tool; cut, combine and clone. Gene Designer assembles a clone that can then be dropped directly into a project.

Educator and Student Use

This free software has been incorporated into Synthetic Biology, Systems Biology, Bioengineering and BioInformatics classroom and lab curricula. Students create and complete projects which capture the entire gene design process in one application, using a range of design tools.

Examples of use in Curricula:

- Synthetic Biophotonics Course; Utah State University, College of Engineering [4]
- Lab Project using Gene Designer 2.0 [5]
- Systems Biology Lesson Overview [6]
- Synthetic Biology Lesson Overview [7]
- Student Projects [8]

References

[1] http://www.dna20.com

[2] http://www.dna20.com/genedesigner2

[3] For a peer-reviewed and detailed description: BMC Bioinformatics 2006 7:285. Gene Designer: a synthetic biology tool for constructing artificial DNA segments. Villalobos, Ness, Gustafsson, Minshull, Govindarajan (http://www.ncbi.nlm.nih.gov/pubmed/16756672?dopt=AbstractPlus)

[4] http://www.engr.usu.edu/wiki/index.php/Synthetic_Biophotonics_2010

[5] http://www.engr.usu.edu/wiki/index.php/Synthetic_Biophotonics_2010_Systems_Biology_Laboratory

[6] http://www.engr.usu.edu/wiki/index.php/Synthetic_Biophotonics_2010_Systems_Biology

[7] http://www.engr.usu.edu/wiki/index.php/Synthetic_Biophotonics_2010_Synthetic_Biology

[8] http://www.engr.usu.edu/wiki/index.php/Synthetic_Biophotonics_2010_Student_Projects

2. Methods Enzymol 2011 498:43-66. Designing genes for successful protein expression. Welch, et al. (http://www.ncbi.nlm.nih.gov/pubmed/21601673)

External links

Description of software

- Gene Designer homepage at DNA2.0 (http://www.dna20.com/genedesigner2)

Tutorials

- BioBrick Video Tutorial using Gene Designer 2.0 from Utah State University (https://tele.engr.usu.edu/biophotonics_2010/Gene Designer/Gene Designer.html)
- Gene Designer User Video (http://www.youtube.com/watch?v=LBAWJCURIEg)
- Cloning Tool User Video (http://www.youtube.com/watch?v=-fKvFK8IypU)
- Gene Designer Help (https://www.dna20.com/gdhelp/doku.php)
- Gene Designer Tutorial from Utah State University (https://www.dna20.com/files/PDF/USU_Gene_Designer_Tutorial.pdf)

Other Software

- ApE - A Multipurpose DNA Engineering Software, Donationware/Freeware (http://www.biology.utah.edu/ jorgensen/wayned/ape/)
- Serial Cloner - A DNA editing and manipulating software for MacOS and Windows, Donationware/Freeware (http://www.serialbasics.com/Serial_Cloner.html)
- QuickGene - DNA analysis software with restriction enzyme information. Useful for cloning. Mac OSX and Windows with a Beta version for Linux coming (http://www.crimsonbase.com/)
- pDRAW32 (http://www.acaclone.com/)
- GENtle (http://gentle.magnusmanske.de/)
- Lasergene (http://www.dnastar.com/)
- Discovery Studio (http://www.csc.fi/english/research/sciences/bioscience/programs/ds)
- CLC Main Workbench (http://www.clcbio.com/main)
- DNADynamo (http://www.bluetractorsoftware.co.uk/)
- Geneious
- UGENE
- Vector NTI
- Clone manager
- MacVector

Gene nomenclature

Gene nomenclature is the scientific naming of genes, the units of heredity in living organisms. An international committee published recommendations for genetic symbols and nomenclature in 1957.[1] The need to develop formal guidelines for human gene names and symbols was recognized in the 1960s and full guidelines were issued in 1979 (Edinburgh Human Genome Meeting).[2] Several other species-specific research communities (e.g., Drosophila, mouse) have adopted nomenclature standards, as well, and have published them on the relevant model organism websites and in scientific journals, including the *Trends in Genetics* Genetic Nomenclature Guide.[3] [4] Scientists familiar with a particular gene family may work together to revise the nomenclature for the entire set of genes when new information becomes available.[5] For many genes and their corresponding proteins, an assortment of alternate names is in use across the scientific literature and public biological databases, posing a challenge to effective organization and exchange of biological information.[6]

Nomenclature guidelines

Species-specific resources

The HUGO Gene Nomenclature Committee is responsible for providing human gene naming guidelines and approving new, unique human gene names and symbols (short form abbreviations). For some non-human species, model organism databases serve as central repositories of guidelines and help resources, including advice from curators and nomenclature committees. In addition to species-specific databases, approved gene names and symbols for many species can be located in the National Center for Biotechnology Information's Entrez Gene [7] database.

Species	Guidelines	Database
Invertebrates		
Fly (*Drosophila melanogaster*)	Genetic nomenclature for *Drosophila melanogaster* [8]	FlyBase [10]
Worm (*Caenorhabditis elegans*)	Genetic Nomenclature for *Caenorhabditis elegans* [9]	WormBase [11]
Plants		
Maize (*Zea mays*)	A Standard For Maize Genetics Nomenclature [10]	MaizeGDB [11]
Thale cress (*Arabidopsis thaliana*)	Arabidopsis Nomenclature [12]	The Arabidopsis Information Resource [13] (TAIR).
Tree		
Flora		
Mustard (*Brassica*)	Standardized gene nomenclature for the Brassica genus (proposed) [14]	
Slime molds		
Dictyostelid (*Dictyostelium discoideum*)	Nomenclature Guidelines [15]	dictyBase [16]
Vertebrates		
Human (*Homo sapiens*)	Guidelines for Human Gene Nomenclature [17]	HUGO Gene Nomenclature Committee [2] (HGNC)
Mouse (*Mus musculus*), rat (*Rattus norvegicus*)	Rules for Nomenclature of Genes, Genetic Markers, Alleles, and Mutations in Mouse and Rat [18]	Mouse Genome Informatics [19] (MGI)
Frog (*Xenopus laevis*, *X. tropicalis*)	Suggested Xenopus Gene Name Guidelines [20]	Xenbase [21]
Zebrafish (*Danio rerio*)	Zebrafish Nomenclature Guidelines [22]	Zebrafish Model Organism Database [23] (ZFIN)
Yeast		
Budding yeast (*Saccharomyces cerevisiae*)	SGD Gene Naming Guidelines [24]	*Saccharomyces* Genome Database [25]
Candida (*Candida albicans*)	*C. albicans* Gene Nomenclature Guide [26]	*Candida* Genome Database [27] (CGD)
Fission yeast (*Schizosaccharomyces pombe*)	Gene Name Registry [28]	*Schizosaccharomyces* pombe GeneDB [29]

Vertebrate gene and protein symbol conventions

Gene and protein symbol conventions ("sonic hedgehog" gene)		
Species	**Gene symbol**	**Protein symbol**
Homo sapiens	*SHH*	SHH
Mus musculus, Rattus norvegicus	*Shh*	SHH
Gallus gallus	*SHH*	SHH
Xenopus laevis, X. tropicalis	*shh*	shh
Danio rerio	*shh*	Shh

The research communities of vertebrate model organisms have adopted guidelines whereby genes in these species are given, whenever possible, the same names as their human orthologs. The use of prefixes on gene symbols to indicate species (e.g., "Z" for zebrafish) is discouraged. The recommended formatting of printed gene and protein symbols varies between species.

Human

Gene symbols generally are italicised, with all letters in uppercase (e.g., *SHH*, for sonic hedgehog). Italics are not necessary in gene catalogs. Protein designations are the same as the gene symbol, but are not italicised; all letters are in uppercase (SHH). mRNAs and cDNAs use the same formatting conventions as the gene symbol.[5]

Mouse and rat

Gene symbols generally are italicised, with only the first letter in uppercase and the remaining letters in lowercase (*Shh*). Italics are not required on web pages. Protein designations are the same as the gene symbol, but are not italicised, all uppercase letters (SHH).[30]

Chicken (Gallus sp.)

Nomenclature generally follows the conventions of human nomenclature. Gene symbols generally are italicised, with all letters in uppercase (e.g., *NLGN1*, for neuroligin1). Protein designations are the same as the gene symbol, but are not italicised; all letters are in uppercase (NLGN1). mRNAs and cDNAs use the same formatting conventions as the gene symbol.[31]

Frog (*Xenopus* sp.)

Gene symbols are italicised and all letters are in lowercase (*shh*). Protein designations are the same as the gene symbol, are not italicised, and all letters are in lowercase (shh).[32]

Zebrafish

Gene symbols are italicised, with all letters in lowercase (*shh*). Protein designations are the same as the gene symbol, but are not italicised; the first letter is in uppercase and the remaining letters are in lowercase (Shh).[33]

See also Bacterial Genetic Nomenclature

Notes and references

[1] Report of the International Committee on Genetic Symbols and Nomenclature (1957). *Union of International Sci Biol Ser B*, Colloquia No. 30.

[2] About the HGNC (http://www.genenames.org/aboutHGNC.html)

[3] Genetic nomenclature guide (1995). *Trends Genet.*

[4] The *Trends In Genetics* Nomenclature Guide (1998). Elsevier, Cambridge.

[5] Guidelines for Human Gene Nomenclature (http://www.genenames.org/guidelines.html)

[6] Fundel and Zimmer (2006). Gene and protein nomenclature in public databases. (http://www.biomedcentral.com/1471-2105/7/372) *BMC Bioinformatics* 7:372.

[7] http://www.ncbi.nlm.nih.gov/sites/entrez?db=gene

[8] http://flybase.bio.indiana.edu/static_pages/docs/nomenclature/nomenclature3.html

[9] http://www.wormbase.org/wiki/index.php/UserGuide:Nomenclature

[10] http://www.maizegdb.org/maize_nomenclature.php

[11] http://www.maizegdb.org/

[12] http://www.arabidopsis.org/portals/nomenclature/guidelines.jsp

[13] http://www.arabidopsis.org/

[14] http://www.plantmethods.com/content/4/1/10

[15] http://dictybase.org/Dicty_Info/nomenclature_guidelines.html

[16] http://dictybase.org/

[17] http://www.genenames.org/guidelines.html

[18] http://www.informatics.jax.org/mgihome/nomen/gene.shtml

[19] http://www.informatics.jax.org/

[20] http://www.xenbase.org/gene/static/geneNomenclature.jsp

[21] http://www.xenbase.org/

[22] http://zfin.org/zf_info/nomen.html

[23] http://zfin.org/

[24] http://www.yeastgenome.org/gene_guidelines.shtml

[25] http://www.yeastgenome.org/

[26] http://www.candidagenome.org/Nomenclature.shtml

[27] http://www.candidagenome.org/

[28] http://www.genedb.org/genedb/pombe/geneRegistry.jsp

[29] http://www.genedb.org/genedb/pombe/index.jsp

[30] Rules for Nomenclature of Genes, Genetic Markers, Alleles, and Mutations in Mouse and Rat (http://www.informatics.jax.org/mgihome/nomen/gene.shtml)

[31] The chicken gene nomenclature committee report (http://www.ncbi.nlm.nih.gov/pubmed/19607656?ordinalpos=1&itool=EntrezSystem2.PEntrez.Pubmed.Pubmed_ResultsPanel.Pubmed_DefaultReportPanel.Pubmed_RVDocSum)

[32] Suggested Xenopus Gene Name Guidelines (http://www.xenbase.org/gene/static/geneNomenclature.jsp)

[33] Zebrafish Nomenclature Guidelines (http://zfin.org/zf_info/nomen.html)

External links

- The Council of Science Editors (CSE) - Resources for Genetic and Cytogenetic Nomenclature (http://www.councilscienceeditors.org/publications/resources.cfm)
- The Protein Naming Utility (http://www.jcvi.org/pn-utility), a rules database for protein nomenclature

Gene Ontology

The **Gene Ontology**, or **GO**, is a major bioinformatics initiative to unify the representation of gene and gene product attributes across all species.[1] More specifically, the project aims to:

1. Maintain and develop its controlled vocabulary of gene and gene product attributes;
2. Annotate genes and gene products, and assimilate and disseminate annotation data;
3. Provide tools for easy access to all aspects of the data provided by the project.

The GO is part of a larger classification effort, the Open Biomedical Ontologies (OBO).

GO terms and ontology

There is no universal standard terminology in biology and related domains, and term usages may be specific to a species, research area or even a particular research group. This makes communication and sharing of data more difficult. The Gene Ontology project provides an ontology of defined terms representing gene product properties. The ontology covers three domains:

- **cellular component**, the parts of a cell or its extracellular environment;
- **molecular function**, the elemental activities of a gene product at the molecular level, such as binding or catalysis;
- **biological process**, operations or sets of molecular events with a defined beginning and end, pertinent to the functioning of integrated living units: cells, tissues, organs, and organisms.

Each GO term within the ontology has a term name, which may be a word or string of words; a unique alphanumeric identifier; a definition with cited sources; and a namespace indicating the domain to which it belongs. Terms may also have synonyms, which are classed as being exactly equivalent to the term name, broader, narrower, or related; references to equivalent concepts in other databases; and comments on term meaning or usage. The GO ontology is structured as a directed acyclic graph, and each term has defined relationships to one or more other terms in the same domain, and sometimes to other domains. The GO vocabulary is designed to be species-neutral, and includes terms applicable to prokaryotes and eukaryotes, single and multicellular organisms.

The GO ontology is not static, and additions, corrections and alterations are suggested by, and solicited from, members of the research and annotation communities, as well as by those directly involved in the GO project. For example, an annotator may request a specific term to represent a metabolic pathway, or a section of the ontology may be revised with the help of community experts (e.g.[2]). Suggested edits are reviewed by the ontology editors, and implemented where appropriate.

The GO ontology file is freely available from the GO website [3] in a number of formats, or can be accessed online using the GO browser AmiGO [4]. The Gene Ontology project also provides downloadable mappings of its terms to other classification systems [5].

Example GO term

```
id:         GO:0000016
name:       lactase activity
namespace:  molecular_function
def:        "Catalysis of the reaction: lactose + H2O = D-glucose + D-galactose." [EC:3.2.1.108]
synonym:    "lactase-phlorizin hydrolase activity" BROAD [EC:3.2.1.108]
synonym:    "lactose galactohydrolase activity" EXACT [EC:3.2.1.108]
xref:       EC:3.2.1.108
xref:       MetaCyc:LACTASE-RXN
xref:       Reactome:20536
is_a:       GO:0004553 ! hydrolase activity, hydrolyzing O-glycosyl compounds
```

Data source:[6]

Annotation

Genome annotation is the practice of capturing data about a gene product, and GO annotations use terms from the GO ontology to do so. The members of the GO Consortium submit their annotation for integration and dissemination on the GO website, where they can be downloaded directly [7] or viewed online using AmiGO [4]. In addition to the gene product identifier and the relevant GO term, GO annotations have the following data:

- The *reference* used to make the annotation (e.g. a journal article)
- An *evidence code* denoting the type of evidence upon which the annotation is based
- The date and the creator of the annotation

The evidence code comes from the Evidence Code Ontology [8], a controlled vocabulary of codes covering both manual and automated annotation methods. For example, *Traceable Author Statement* (TAS) means a curator has read a published scientific paper and the metadata for that annotation bears a citation to that paper; *Inferred from Sequence Similarity* (ISS) means a human curator has reviewed the output from a sequence similarity search and verified that it is biologically meaningful. Annotations from automated processes (for example, remapping annotations created using another annotation vocabulary) are given the code *Inferred from Electronic Annotation* (IEA). As of April 1st, 2010, over 98% of all GO annotations were inferred computationally, not by curators.[9] As these annotations are not checked by a human, the GO Consortium considers them to be less reliable and includes only a subset in the data available online in AmiGO. Full annotation data sets can be downloaded from the GO website [3]. To support the development of annotation, the GO Consortium provides study camps and mentors to new groups of developers.

Example annotation

```
Gene product:    Actin, alpha cardiac muscle 1, UniProtKB:P68032 [10]
GO term:         heart contraction ; GO:0060047 [11] (biological process)
Evidence code:   Inferred from Mutant Phenotype (IMP)
Reference:       PMID 17611253 [12]
Assigned by:     UniProtKB, June 6, 2008
```

Data source:[13]

Tools

There are a large number of tools available both online and to download that use the data provided by the GO project. The vast majority of these come from third parties; the GO Consortium develops and supports two tools, **AmiGO** and **OBO-Edit**.

AmiGO[14] is a web-based application that allows users to query, browse and visualize ontologies and gene product annotation data. In addition, it also has a BLAST tool,[15] tools allowing analysis of larger data sets,[16] [17] and an interface to query the GO database directly.[18] .

AmiGO can be used online at the GO website [4] to access the data provided by the GO Consortium, or can be downloaded and installed for local use on any database employing the GO database schema [19] (e.g. [20]). It is free open source software and is available as part of the go-dev software distribution.[21]

OBO-Edit[22] is an open source, platform-independent ontology editor developed and maintained by the Gene Ontology Consortium. It is implemented in Java, and uses a graph-oriented approach to display and edit ontologies. OBO-Edit includes a comprehensive search and filter interface, with the option to render subsets of terms to make them visually distinct; the user interface can also be customized according to user preferences. OBO-Edit also has a reasoner that can infer links that have not been explicitly stated, based on existing relationships and their properties. Although it was developed for biomedical ontologies, OBO-Edit can be used to view, search and edit any ontology. It is freely available to download.[21]

GO Consortium

The GO Consortium is the set of biological databases and research groups actively involved in the GO project.[23] This includes a number of model organism databases and multi-species protein databases, software development groups, and a dedicated editorial office.

History

The Gene Ontology was originally constructed in 1998 by a consortium of researchers studying the genome of three model organisms: *Drosophila melanogaster* (fruit fly), *Mus musculus* (mouse), and *Saccharomyces cerevisiae* (brewers' or bakers' yeast).[24] Many other model organism databases have joined the Gene Ontology consortium, contributing not only annotation data, but also contributing to the development of the ontologies and tools to view and apply the data. Until now, most of major databases in plant, animal and microorganism make a contribution towards this project. As of January 2008, GO contains over 24,500 terms applicable to a wide variety of biological organisms. There is a significant body of literature on the development and use of GO, and it has become a standard tool in the bioinformatics arsenal. Their objectives have three aspects, building gene ontology, assigning ontology to gene/gene products and develop software and database for first two objects.

References

[1] The Gene Ontology Consortium (Jan 2008). "The Gene Ontology project in 2008.". *Nucleic Acids Research* **36** (Database issue): D440–4. doi:10.1093/nar/gkm883. PMC 2238979. PMID 17984083.

[2] Diehl AD, Lee JA, Scheuermann RH, Blake JA (2007). "Ontology development for biological systems: immunology.". *Bioinformatics* **23** (7): 913–915. doi:10.1093/bioinformatics/btm029. PMID 17267433.

[3] http://www.geneontology.org/

[4] http://amigo.geneontology.org/

[5] http://www.geneontology.org/GO.indices.shtml

[6] The GO Consortium (2009-03-16). "gene_ontology.1_2.obo" (http://www.geneontology.org/ontology/obo_format_1_2/gene_ontology. 1_2.obo) (OBO 1.2 flat file). . Retrieved 2009-03-16.

[7] http://www.geneontology.org/GO.current.annotations.shtml

[8] http://www.obofoundry.org/cgi-bin/detail.cgi?id=evidence_code

[9] "The what, where, how and why of gene ontology—a primer for bioinformaticians — Brief Bioinform". doi:10.1093/bib/bbr002.

[10] http://amigo.geneontology.org/cgi-bin/amigo/gp-details.cgi?gp=UniProtKB:P68032

[11] http://amigo.geneontology.org/cgi-bin/amigo/term-details.cgi?term=GO:0060047

[12] http://www.ncbi.nlm.nih.gov/pubmed/17611253

[13] The GO Consortium (2009-03-16). "AmiGO: P68032 Associations" (http://amigo.geneontology.org/cgi-bin/amigo/gp-assoc. cgi?gp=UniProtKB:P68032). . Retrieved 2009-03-16.

[14] Carbon S, Ireland A, Mungall CJ, Shu S, Marshall B, Lewis S; AmiGO Hub; Web Presence Working Group. (2008). "AmiGO: online access to ontology and annotation data.". *Bioinformatics* **25** (2): 288–9. doi:10.1093/bioinformatics/btn615. PMC 2639003. PMID 19033274.

[15] AmiGO BLAST tool (http://amigo.geneontology.org/cgi-bin/amigo/blast.cgi)

[16] AmiGO Term Enrichment tool (http://amigo.geneontology.org/cgi-bin/amigo/term_enrichment); finds significant shared GO terms in an annotation set

[17] AmiGO Slimmer (http://amigo.geneontology.org/cgi-bin/amigo/slimmer); maps granular annotations up to high-level terms

[18] GOOSE (http://berkeleybop.org/goose), GO Online SQL Environment; allows direct SQL querying of the GO database

[19] http://www.geneontology.org/GO.database.schema.shtml

[20] The Plant Ontology Consortium (2009-03-16). "Plant Ontology Consortium" (http://plantontology.org/amigo/go.cgi). . Retrieved 2009-03-16.

[21] "Gene Ontology downloads at SourceForge" (http://sourceforge.net/project/showfiles.php?group_id=36855). . Retrieved 2009-03-16.

[22] Day-Richter J, Harris MA, Haendel M; Gene Ontology OBO-Edit Working Group, Lewis S. (2007). "OBO-Edit--an ontology editor for biologists.". *Bioinformatics* **23** (16): 2189–200. doi:10.1093/bioinformatics/btm112. PMID 17545183.

[23] "The GO Consortium" (http://www.geneontology.org/GO.consortiumlist.shtml). . Retrieved 2009-03-16.

[24] The Gene Ontology Consortium (2000). "Gene Ontology: tool for the unification of biology". *Nature Genetics* **25** (1): 25–29. doi:10.1038/75556. PMC 3037419. PMID 10802651.

External links

- Gene Ontology Consortium (http://www.geneontology.org/) — Provides access to the ontologies, software tools, annotated gene product lists, and reference documents describing the GO and its uses.
- The OBO Foundry (http://www.nature.com/nbt/journal/v25/n11/pdf/nbt1346.pdf): Coordinated Evolution of Ontologies to Support Biomedical Data Integration, Nature Biotechnology, 25 (11), 2007.
- OBO Foundry library of interoperable gold standard reference ontologies (http://obofoundry.org).
- GONUTS Wiki (http://gowiki.tamu.edu/wiki/index.php/Main_Page) — Third party GO term documentation, including links to GO annotations at many major model organism databases.
- GOCat - An Automatic GO Categorizer/Browser to help Functional Annotation of Biomedical Texts; also useful to functionally characterize protein and gene names lists generated by high-throughput experiments (http://www.geneontology.org/GO.tools.annotation.shtml#gocat)
- Protein Ontology Project (http://proteinontology.org.au/) — Provides access to the Protein Ontology (PO) and reference documents describing the PO and its uses.
- EAGLi - A Terminology-powered (Gene Ontology, Swiss-Prot keywords...) biomedical question answering engine for MEDLINE (http://eagl.unige.ch/EAGLi/)
- PubOnto (http://brainarray.mbni.med.umich.edu/Brainarray/prototype/PubOnto/) Medline Exploration based on Gene Ontology and other ontologies.
- Semantic Systems Biology (http://www.semantic-systems-biology.org)
- National Center for Biomedical Ontology (http://ncbo.us)
- WikiProfessional (http://www.wikiprofessional.org) - Disambiguation, knowledge generation and collaborative intelligence - genes and proteins.

Genenetwork

GeneNetwork

Developer(s)	GeneNetwork Development Team, University of Tennessee
Stable release	1.0 / 15 July 2011 on SourceForge
Operating system	Cross-platform web-based
License	Affero General Public License
Website	http://www.genenetwork.org/

GeneNetwork is a database and open source bioinformatics software resource for systems genetics.[1] This resource is used to study gene regulatory networks that link DNA sequence variants to corresponding differences in gene and protein expression and to differences in traits such as health and disease risk. Data sets in GeneNetwork are typically made up of large collections of genotypes (e.g., SNPs) and phenotypes that are obtained from groups of related individuals, including human families, experimental crosses of strains of mice and rats, and organisms as diverse as Drosophila melanogaster, Arabidopsis thaliana, and barley.[2] The inclusion of genotypes for all individuals makes it practical to carry out web-based gene mapping to discover those regions of the genome that contribute to differences in gene expression, cell function, anatomy, physiology, and behavior among individuals.

History

GeneNetwork was created at the University of Tennessee Health Science Center, Memphis USA in 2000-2001. It was initially developed as a web-adapted version of Kenneth F. Manly's Map Manager [3] QT and QTX programs and was called WebQTL.[4] Gene mapping data were incorporated for several mouse recombinant inbred strains. By early 2003, the first large Affymetrix gene expression data sets (whole mouse brain mRNA and hematopoietic stem cells) were incorporated and the system was renamed.[5] [6] GeneNetwork is now developed by an international group of developers and has mirror and development sites in Europe, Asia, and Australia. The production service is hosted on the Amazon Elastic Compute Cloud.

Organization and Use

GeneNetwork consists of two major components:

- Massive collections of genetic, genomic, and phenotype data for large families
- Sophisticated statistical analysis and gene mapping software that enable analysis of regulatory networks and genotype-to-phenotype relations

Four levels of data are usually obtained for each family or population:

1. DNA sequences and genotypes
2. Gene expression values using microarray, RNA-seq, or proteomic methods (molecular phenotypes)
3. Standard phenotypes of the type that are part of a typical medical record (e.g., blood chemistry, body weight)
4. Annotation files and metadata

The combined data types are housed together in a single relational database, but are conceptually organized and divided by species and family. The system is implemented as a LAMP (software bundle) stack. Code and a simplified version of the MySQL database are available at Sourceforge.net/projects/genenetwork/.

GeneNetwork is primarily used by researchers but has also been adopted successfully for undergraduate courses in genetics (see YouTube example [7]), bioinformatics, physiology, and psychology.[8] Researchers and students typically retrieve sets of genotypes and phenotypes from one or more families and use built-in statistical and mapping functions to explore relations among variables and to assemble networks of associations. Key steps include the analysis of these factors:

1. The range of variation of traits
2. Covariation among traits (scatterplots and correlations)
3. Architecture of larger networks of traits
4. Quantitative trait locus mapping and causal models of the linkage between sequence differences and phenotype differences

Data Sources

Massive expression data sets are submitted by researchers directly or are extracted from repositories such as National Center for Biotechnology Information Gene Expression Omnibus. A wide variety of cells and tissues are included—from single cell populations of the immune system, specific tissues (retina, prefrontal cortex), to entire systems (whole brain, lung, muscle, heart, fat, kidney, flower, even whole plant embryos). A typical data set is often based on hundreds of fully genotyped individuals and may also include biological replicates. Genotypes and phenotypes are taken from peer-reviewed papers. GeneNetwork includes annotation files for several RNA profiling platforms (Affymetrix, Illumina, and Agilent). RNA-seq data are also available for BXD recombinant inbred mice. Content and nomenclature are reviewed and edited by curators. Updates on coverage of species, families, tissues and measurement types are available at this site: [9].

Topics of annotation include the following:

- DNA sequence (SNPs, CNVs, indels)
- transcriptomes (arrays, RNA-seq)
- gene regulatory networks
- phenome

Tools and Features

There are tools on the site for a wide range of functions that range from simple graphical displays of variation in gene expression or other phenotypes, scatter plots of pairs of traits (Pearson or rank order), construction of both simple and complex network graphs, analysis of principal components and synthetic traits, QTL mapping using marker regression, interval mapping, and pair scans for epistatic interactions. Most functions work with up to 100 traits and several functions work with an entire transcriptome.

The database can be browsed and searched at the main search [10] page. An on-line tutorial [11] is available. Users can also download [12] the primary data sets as text files, Excel, or in the case of network graphs, as SBML.

Code

GeneNetwork is an open source project released under the Affero General Public License (AGPLv3). The majority of code is written in Python, but includes modules and other code written in C and JavaScript. GeneNetwork also calls statistical procedures written in the R programming language. The source code [13] and a compact database [13] are available on GeneNetwork sites and at SourceForge [14].

References

[1] Morahan, G; Williams, RW (2007). "Systems genetics: the next generation in genetics research?". *Novartis Foundation symposium* **281**: 181–8; discussion 188–91, 208–9. PMID 17534074.
[2] Druka, A; Druka, I; Centeno, AG; Li, H; Sun, Z; Thomas, WT; Bonar, N; Steffenson, BJ et al. (2008). "Towards systems genetic analyses in barley: Integration of phenotypic, expression and genotype data into GeneNetwork". *BMC genetics* **9**: 73. doi:10.1186/1471-2156-9-73. PMC 2630324. PMID 19017390.
[3] http://mapmanager.org/

[4] Chesler, EJ; Lu, L; Wang, J; Williams, RW; Manly, KF (2004). "WebQTL: rapid exploratory analysis of gene expression and genetic networks for brain and behavior". *Nature neuroscience* **7** (5): 485–6. doi:10.1038/nn0504-485. PMID 15114364.

[5] Chesler, EJ; Lu, L; Shou, S; Qu, Y; Gu, J; Wang, J; Hsu, HC; Mountz, JD et al. (2005). "Complex trait analysis of gene expression uncovers polygenic and pleiotropic networks that modulate nervous system function". *Nature genetics* **37** (3): 233–42. doi:10.1038/ng1518. PMID 15711545.

[6] Bystrykh, L; Weersing, E; Dontje, B; Sutton, S; Pletcher, MT; Wiltshire, T; Su, AI; Vellenga, E et al. (2005). "Uncovering regulatory pathways that affect hematopoietic stem cell function using 'genetical genomics'". *Nature genetics* **37** (3): 225–32. doi:10.1038/ng1497. PMID 15711547.

[7] http://www.youtube.com/watch?v=5UniEc_pzs0

[8] Grisham, W; Schottler, NA; Valli-Marill, J; Beck, L; Beatty, J (2010). "Teaching bioinformatics and neuroinformatics by using free web-based tools". *CBE life sciences education* **9** (2): 98–107. doi:10.1187/cbe.09-11-0079. PMC 2879386. PMID 20516355.

[9] http://www.genenetwork.org/whats_new.html

[10] http://www.genenetwork.org/

[11] http://www.genenetwork.org/tutorial/WebQTLTour/

[12] http://www.genenetwork.org/share/data/

[13] http://www.genenetwork.org/db_webqtl_simplified_1.sql.gz

[14] http://sourceforge.net/projects/genenetwork/files/

External links

- GeneNetwork homepage (http://www.genenetwork.org/)

Related resources

Other systems genetics and network databases

- BioGPS (http://biogps.gnf.org/)
- Sage Bionetworks (http://sagebase.org/)
- AmiGo (http://amigo.geneontology.org/cgi-bin/amigo/go.cgi/)
- WikiPathways (http://www.wikipathways.org)
- Cytoscape (http://www.cytoscape.org/)

General Data Format for Biomedical Signals

The **General Data Format for Biomedical Signals** is a scientific and medical data file format. The aim of GDF is to combine and integrate the best features of all [biosignal file formats] [1] into a single file format. [GDF v1] [2] uses a binary header, and uses an event table. GDF [v2.0] [3] added fields for additional subject-specific information (gender, age, etc), and utilizes several standard codes (for storing physical units and other properties).

GDF is used mostly in Brain-Computer interface research; however GDF provides a superset of features from many different file formats, it could be also used for many other domains.

The free and open source software library [BioSig] [4] provides implementations for reading and writing of GDF in Octave/Matlab and C/C++.

External links

- BioSig [4]
- GDF v2.0 [3]
- GDF v1.x [2]
- More information on the GDF format [5]

References

[1] http://www.dpmi.tu-graz.ac.at/~schloegl/matlab/eeg/
[2] http://hci.tugraz.at/schloegl/matlab/eeg/gdf4/TR_GDF.pdf
[3] http://arxiv.org/abs/cs.DB/0608052
[4] http://biosig.sf.net/
[5] http://www.dpmi.tu-graz.ac.at/~schloegl/matlab/eeg/#GDF

GeneReviews

GeneReviews is an online collection of peer-reviewed articles that describe specific gene-related diseases. Its articles focus on genetic testing and counseling for inherited conditions. Authors are established clinical and research experts, and articles are reviewed by other experts and by editorial staff at the U.S. National Center for Biotechnology Information. Articles are updated every two or three years according to a formal process, and are also revised as needed when research results in changes to clinically relevant information in the articles. Reviews are searchable by author, title, gene, and name of disease or protein.[1]

References

[1] "GeneReviews" (http://www.ncbi.nlm.nih.gov/projects/GeneTests/static/about/content/reviews.shtml). 2009-01-30. . Retrieved 2009-12-04.

External links

- Home page (http://www.ncbi.nlm.nih.gov/sites/GeneTests/review)

GeneRIF

A **GeneRIF** or **Gene Reference Into Function** is a short (255 characters or fewer) statement about the function of a gene. GeneRIFs provide a simple mechanism for allowing scientists to add to the functional annotation of genes described in the Entrez Gene [5] database. In practice, *function* is construed quite broadly. For example, there are GeneRIFs that discuss the role of a gene in a disease, GeneRIFs that point the viewer towards a review article about the gene, and GeneRIFs that discuss the structure of a gene. However, the stated intent is for GeneRIFs to be about gene function. Currently over half a million geneRIFs have been created for genes from almost 1000 different species.[1]

GeneRIFs are always associated with specific entries in the Entrez Gene database. Each GeneRIF has a pointer to the PubMed ID (a type of document identifier) of a scientific publication that provides evidence for the statement made by the GeneRIF. GeneRIFs are often extracted directly from the document that is identified by the PubMed ID, very frequently from its title or from its final sentence.

GeneRIFs are usually produced by NCBI indexers, but anyone may submit a GeneRIF. To be processed, a valid Gene ID must exist for the specific gene, or the Gene staff must have assigned an overall Gene ID to the species. The latter case is implemented via records in Gene with the symbol NEWENTRY. Once the Gene ID is identified, only three types of information are required to complete a submission:

1. a concise phrase describing a function or functions (less than 255 characters in length, preferably more than a restatement of the title of the paper);
2. a published paper describing that function, implemented by supplying the PubMed ID of a citation in PubMed;
3. a valid e-mail address (which will remain confidential).

Example

Here are some GeneRIFs taken from Entrez Gene for GeneID 7157, the human gene TP53. The PubMed document identifiers have been omitted from the examples. Note the wide variability with respect to the presence or absence of punctuation and of sentence-initial capital letters.

- p53 and c-erbB-2 may have independent role in carcinogenesis of gall bladder cancer
- Degradation of endogenous HIPK2 depends on the presence of a functional p53 protein.
- p53 codon 72 alleles influence the response to anticancer drugs in cells from aged people by regulating the cell cycle inhibitor p21WAF1
- Logistic regression analysis showed p53 and COX-2 as dependent predictors in pancreatic carcinogenesis, and a reciprocal relationship to neoplastic progression between p53 and COX-2.

GeneRIFs are an unusual type of textual genre, and they have recently been the subject of a number of articles from the natural language processing community.

External links

- NCBI's web page describing GeneRIFs [2]
- Mitchell JA, Aronson AR, Mork JG, Folk LC, Humphrey SM, Ward JM (2003). "Gene indexing: characterization and analysis of NLM's GeneRIFs". *AMIA Annu Symp Proc*: 460–4. PMC 1480312. PMID 14728215.

References

[1] http://www.ncbi.nlm.nih.gov/projects/GeneRIF/stats/
[2] http://www.ncbi.nlm.nih.gov/projects/GeneRIF/GeneRIFhelp.html

- William Hersh, Ravi Teja Bhupatiraju (2003). "TREC Genomics Track Overview" (http://medir.ohsu.edu/~hersh/trec-03-genomics.pdf). Paper describing a Text Retrieval Conference "shared task" involving automatic prediction of GeneRIFs.
- Lu, Zhiyong; K. Bretonnel Cohen; and Lawrence Hunter (2006). "Finding GeneRIFs via Gene Ontology annotations" (http://helix-web.stanford.edu/psb06/lu.pdf). Proc. Pacific Symposium on Biocomputing 2006. pp. 52–63. Lu et al.'s paper describing a system that automatically suggests GeneRIFs.

GeneSilico

Laboratory of Bioinformatics and Protein Engineering in International Institute of Molecular and Cell Biology in Warsaw, Poland.

Fields of research

- Protein and nucleic acid structure modeling
- Discovery and analysis of enzymes that act on DNA or RNA
- Software development
  - List of protein structure prediction software
  - FileQuirks

External links

- Laboratory main site [1]

References

[1] http://iimcb.genesilico.pl

GenMAPP

GenMAPP

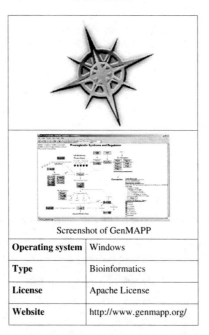

Screenshot of GenMAPP	
Operating system	Windows
Type	Bioinformatics
License	Apache License
Website	http://www.genmapp.org/

GenMAPP (Gene Map Annotator and Pathway Profiler) is a free, open-source bioinformatics software tool designed to visualize and analyze genomic data in the context of pathways (metabolic, signaling), connecting gene-level datasets to biological processes and disease. First created in 2000, GenMAPP is developed by an open-source team based in an academic research laboratory. GenMAPP maintains databases of gene identifiers and collections of pathway maps in addition to visualization and analysis tools. Together with other public resources, GenMAPP aims to provide the research community with tools to gain insight into biology through the integration of data types ranging from genes to proteins to pathways to disease.

History

GenMAPP was first created in 2000 as a prototype software tool in the laboratory of Bruce Conklin [1] at the J. David Gladstone Institutes [2] in San Francisco and continues to be developed in the same non-profit, academic research environment. The first release version of GenMAPP 1.0 was available in 2002 [1], supporting analysis of DNA microarray data from human, mouse, rat and yeast. In 2004, GenMAPP 2.0 was released, combining the previously accessory programs MAPPFinder [2] and MAPPBuilder, and expanding support to additional species. GenMAPP 2.1 was released in 2006 with new visualization features and support for a total of eleven species.

Usage

GenMAPP was developed by biologists and is focused on pathway visualization for bench biologists. Unlike many other computational systems biology tools, GenMAPP is not designed for cell/systems modeling; it focuses on the immediate needs of bench biologists by enabling them to rapidly interpret genomic data with an intuitive, easy-to-use interface. GenMAPP is implemented in Visual Basic 6.0 and is available as a stand-alone application for Microsoft Windows operating systems, including Boot Camp or Parallels Workstation on a Mac. The program is freely available for download [3] and includes an automatic update feature that allows rapid and reliable distribution of updates to the program and documentation.

Content and Features

GenMAPP builds and maintains gene databases for a variety of key model organisms:

- human - *Homo sapiens*
- mouse - *Mus musculus*
- rat - *Rattus norvegicus*
- yeast - *Saccharomyces cerevisiae*
- zebrafish - *Danio rerio*
- worm - *Caenorhabditis elegans*
- fruit fly - *Drosophila melanogaster*
- dog - *Canis familiaris*
- cow - *Bos taurus*
- mosquito - *Anopheles gambiae*
- *E.coli* - *Escherichia coli*

GenMAPP provides tools to create, edit and annotate biological pathway maps.

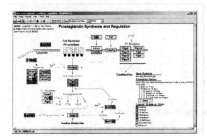

GenMAPP allows users to visualize and analyze their data in the context of pathway collections and the Gene Ontology.

Pathways and associated data can be exported for the web as HTML. See examples:

- IGTC [4]
- GenMAPP archives [5]
- Embryonic Stem Cell Differentiation [6] (dataset from GEO [7]: Andrade Lab, Ottawa Hailesellasse et al. 2005-submitted)

- Mouse Uterine Pregnancy Timecourse [8] (dataset from Salomonis et al. 2005 Genome Biology 6:R12.16)

References

1. http://www.nature.com/cgi-taf/DynaPage.taf?file=/ng/journal/v31/n1/full/ng0502-19.html
2. http://genomebiology.com/2003/4/1/R7

External links

- GenMAPP Website [9]
- GenMAPP – Data Links [10]
- Cytoscape [11]
- PathVisio [12]
- WikiPathways [13]
- GenMAPP [14] on SourceForge.net

Developers

Alexander Pico, Kristina Hanspers, Nathan Salomonis, Kam Dahlquist, Scott Doniger, Jeff Lawlor, Alex Zambon, Lynn Ferrante, Karen Vranizan, Steven C. Lawlor, Bruce Conklin

References

[1] http://www.gladstone.ucsf.edu/gladstone/site/conklin/
[2] http://www.gladstone.ucsf.edu
[3] http://www.genmapp.org/login/loginerror.php?ReferPage=/download-genmapp2.php
[4] http://www.genetrap.org/
[5] http://www.genmapp.org/HTML_MAPPs/Human/MAPPIndex_Hs_Contributed.htm
[6] http://www.genmapp.org/Example_MAPPs/Mm_G1_to_S_cell_cycle_Reactome/Mm_G1_to_S_cell_cycle_Reactome_1.htm
[7] http://www.ncbi.nlm.nih.gov/geo/
[8] http://www.genmapp.org/Example_MAPPs/Mm_Prostaglandin_synthesis_regulation/Mm_Prostaglandin_synthesis_regulation_1.htm
[9] http://www.genmapp.org/
[10] http://www.genmapp.org/links.html
[11] http://www.cytoscape.org/
[12] http://wiki.bigcat.unimaas.nl/pathvisio/
[13] http://www.wikipathways.org
[14] http://sourceforge.net/projects/genmapp

GenoCAD

GenoCAD

Initial release	30 August 2007
Stable release	1.6 / 30 May 2011
Development status	Active
Written in	PHP JavaScript Java Prolog
Type	Computer-Aided Design Bioinformatics
License	Apache v2.0
Website	[genocad.org genocad.org]

GenoCAD [1] is an open source web application to design DNA constructs for genetic engineering using a rule-based methodology. GenoCAD is also considered a Computer Assisted Design (CAD) application for synthetic biology.

Features

The main features of GenoCAD can be organized into three main categories. [2]

- **Management of genetic sequences**: The purpose of this group of features is to help users identify, within large collections of genetic parts, the parts needed for a project and to organize them in project-specific libraries.

  - *Genetic parts*: Parts have a unique identifier, a name and a more general description. They also have a DNA sequence. Parts are associated with a grammar and assigned to a parts category such a promoter, gene, etc.
  - *Parts libraries*: Collections of parts are organized in libraries. In some cases part libraries correspond to parts imported from a single source such as another sequence database. In other cases, libraries correspond to the parts used for a particular design project. Parts can be moved from one library to another through a temporary storage area called the cart (analogous to e-commerce shopping carts).
  - *Searching parts*: Users can search the parts database using the Lucene search engine. Basic and advanced search modes are available. Users can develop complex queries and save them for future reuse.
  - *Importing/Exporting parts*: Parts can be imported and exported individually or as entire libraries using standard file formats (e.g., tab delimited, FASTA).

- **Combining sequences into genetic constructs**: The purpose of this group of features is to streamline the process of combining genetic parts into designs compliant with a specific design strategy.

  - *Point-and-click design tool*: This wizard guides the user through a series of design decisions that determine the design structure and the selection of parts included in the design.
  - *Design management*: Designs can be saved in the user workspace. Design statuses are regularly updated to warn users of the consequences of editing parts on previously saved designs.
  - *Exporting designs*: Designs can be exported using standard file formats (e.g., GenBank, tab delimited, FASTA).

- **User workspace**: Users can personalize their workspace by adding parts to the GenoCAD database, creating specialized libraries corresponding to specific design projects, and saving designs at different stages of development.

Theoretical foundation

GenoCAD is rooted in the theory of formal languages. In particular, the design rules describing how to combine different kinds of parts form context-free grammars. [3]

References

[1] Czar MJ, Cai Y, Peccoud J (2009). "Writing DNA with GenoCAD". *Nucleic Acids Res.* **37** (web server): W40-7. doi:10.1093/nar/gkp361. PMC 2703884. PMID 19429897.

[2] Wilson ML, Hertzberg R, Adam L, Peccoud J. (2011). "A step-by-step introduction to rule-based design of synthetic genetic constructs using GenoCAD.". *Methods Enzymol.* **498**: 173–88. PMID 21601678.

[3] Cai Y, Hartnett B, Gustafsson C, Peccoud J. (2007). "A syntactic model to design and verify synthetic genetic constructs derived from standard biological parts.". *Bioinformatics* **23** (20): 2760–7. doi:10.1093/bioinformatics/btm446. PMID 17804435.

External links

- GenoCAD.org (http://www.genocad.org)
- Project page (http://sourceforge.net/projects/genocad/) on SourceForge.

Genomatix

Genomatix Software GmbH

genomatix	
Type	GmbH
Industry	Bioinformatics
Founded	1997
Headquarters	Munich, Germany
Website	http://www.genomatix.de

Genomatix Software GmbH is a computational biology company headquartered in Munich, Germany, with a seat of business in Ann Arbor, Michigan, U.S.A.

History

Genomatix was founded in 1997 by Dr. Thomas Werner [1] as a spin-off from the Helmholtz Zentrum München (formerly "GSF - National German Research Institute for Environment and Health"). Helmholtz Zentrum Munich is part of the Helmholtz Association of German Research Centres. Genomatix pioneered the analysis and understanding of eukaryotic gene regulation.

Genomatix software tools

Genomatix offers integrated solutions and databases for genome annotation and regulation analysis.

Genomatix product portfolio contains solutions for:

• Literature and pathway mining
• Transcription factor analysis
• Genome annotation integrating a wide variety of transcript sources and a special focus on regulatory regions
• Analysis technology for high throughput genomic technologies (microarrays and next generation sequencing)/>

Literature mining

LitInspector is a literature search tool providing gene and signal transduction pathway mining within NCBI's PubMed database.[2] [3]

Pathway mining
GePS
BiblioSphere

Current research

Personalized medicine developed to a major field for Genomatix.[4] Genomatix is involved in several projects and international conferences e.g. 5th Santorini Conference - "Functional Genomics towards personalized health care" [5]

Since 2008 Genomatix has strongly focused on Next Generation Sequencing data analysis. Because of the large amount of data and the need for high-end computing power, Genomatix deploys its solutions as in-house installations (hardware software bundle)

Two systems are available:

1. The Genomatix Mining Station (GMS) is based on a proprietary genomic pattern recognition paradigm, or GenomeThesaurus, which allows for input of raw sequence reads plus optional quality files from any deep sequencing hardware. It provides ultra fast mapping of sequences of any length (starting from 8bp) with no practical limits on the number of point mutations and/or insertions and deletions that can be taken into account during the mapping process. Depending on the nature of the experiment, the GMS can provide SNP detection and genotyping, copy number analysis, and small RNA analysis. For ChIPseq data, the GMS delivers clustering and peak finding, and performs automated binding pattern identification. For RNAseq experiments, normalized expression values are calculated at the exon and transcript level. A special GenomeThesaurus is also provided for potential splice junctions, which allows for splice junction analysis and identification of new transcriptional units.

For genomic re-sequencing and newly sequenced genomes, a de-novo assembly will be provided.

2. The Genomatix Genome Analyzer (GGA) delivers downstream software tools and databases for the deep biological analysis of data coming from the GMS. It allows for easy integration and visualization in the terabytes of background annotation of the ElDorado genome database. GGA extensively annotates genomic coordinates and surrounding areas derived by the GMS or any other mapping procedure. Clustering and peak finding, analysis for phylogenetic conservation, large scale correlation analysis with annotated genomic elements, meta-analysis of data correlation between different experiments, pathway mining for groups of identified genes, transcription factor binding site (TFBS) analysis (identification, over-representation, binding partner analysis, framework identification, phylogenetic conservation, regulatory SNP effects) and much more are all processes carried out on the GGA.

With the GGA and GMS Genomatix delivers the worldwide first integrative data analysis platform for Next Generation Sequencing analysis with custom workflows tailored towards specific needs.

Further developments will be the link-up of data from clinical sources and medical applications. Pilot projects were already started within Genomatix' consulting platform linking genotype and phenotype information.

External links

- Genomatix Homepage [6]

References

[1] http://www.bioinformatik-muenchen.de/perspektive/perspektive-bioinformatik-werner/

[2] (http://www.ncbi.nlm.nih.gov/pubmed/19417065), Abstract of *Nucleic Acid Research* Article.

[3] (http://www.litinspector.org/) LitInspector start page.

[4] (http://www.genomatix.de/en/forscher.html) Genomatix and personalized medicine.

[5] (http://www.santorini2010.org/) Conference about personalized health care.

[6] http://www.genomatix.de/

Genome survey sequence

In the fields of bioinformatics and computational biology, **Genome Survey Sequences (GSS)** are nucleotide sequences similar to EST's, with the exception that most of them are genomic in origin, rather than mRNA. The name comes from the homonym NCBI GenBank division, which contains (but is not limited to) the following types of data:

- random "single pass read" genome survey sequences
- cosmid/BAC/YAC end sequences
- exon trapped genomic sequences
- Alu PCR sequences
- transposon-tagged sequences

Genome Survey Sequences are typically generated and submitted to NCBI by labs performing genome sequencing and are used, amongst other things, as a framework for the mapping and sequencing of genome size pieces included in the standard GenBank divisions.

References

- The Genome Survey Sequences Database homepage [1]
- GenBank Flat File 96.0 Release Notes [2]

References

[1] http://www.ncbi.nlm.nih.gov/dbGSS
[2] ftp://ftp.ncbi.nih.gov/genbank/release.notes/gb96.release.notes

Genome-Based Peptide Fingerprint Scanning

Genome-based peptide fingerprint scanning (GFS) is a system in bioinformatics analysis that attempts to identify the genomic origin (that is, what species they come from) of sample proteins by scanning their peptide-mass fingerprint against the theoretical translation and proteolytic digest of an entire genome.[1]

References

[1] "Abstract of Genome-based peptide fingerprint scanning" (http://www.pnas.org/cgi/content/abstract/100/1/20). PNAS]. 2003. . Retrieved 2006-10-06.

External links

- GFS Web (http://gfs.unc.edu/cgi-bin/WebObjects/GFSWeb)

Genome@home

Genome@home was a distributed computing project run by Stefan Larson of Stanford University until March 8, 2004. The goal of the project was to design new genes and proteins for the purpose of better understanding how genomes evolve, and how genes and proteins operate. Practical applications of the research included the potential development of new medical treatments.

The project was rolled into the Folding@home project, and is no longer supported.

Surprise shut-down

The long-running project closed down with approximately 2 days' notice, despite recent messages from leaders about 'upcoming work'. This caused some surprise and disappointment among contributors at the time. Reasons appear to be financial. Users were told that results-to-date are available for any scientist who wished to see them.

External links

- Genome@home [1]

References

[1] http://www.stanford.edu/group/pandegroup/genome/

Genostar

Genostar

Genostar	
Type	Privately held company
Industry	Bioinformatics
Founded	2004
Headquarters	Grenoble, France
Products	Software and Database
Website	http://www.genostar.com

Genostar is a bioinformatics solution provider based in Grenoble, France. The company was founded in 2004 following the "Genostar consortium"[1] that was created in 1999 as a public-private consortium by Genome Express, Hybrigenics, INRIA (Institut National de Recherche en Informatique et Automatique / French National Institute for Research in Computer Science and Control)[2] and The Pasteur Institute.

Software

Metabolic Pathway Builder is a bioinformatics environment dedicated to microbial research. This streamlined bioinformatics solution covers sequence assembly, mapping, annotation transfer and identification of protein domains, comparative genomics, structural searches, metabolic pathway analysis, modeling and simulation of biological networks. Genostar's software is platform independent and can thus be used for both Mac OS X, Windows, and Linux.

Sequence assembly

* Mapping of an ensemble of sequences on a reference sequence
  * between a reference sequence and contigs, between two sequences or between two sets of sequences
  * finding of exact matches with minimum length using MUMmer
  * detection of specific regions and SNPs
  * creation of an assembled sequence relative to reference sequences

Genomic annotation

* Gene prediction: ab-initio gene prediction using a Hidden Markov model based method
* BlastX
* Automatic annotation transfer using BlastP

Proteic annotation

Metabolic Pathway Builder integrates several methods dedicated to proteic annotation:

* Pfam domain prediction using HMMER
* Several EMBOSS methods (antigenic, 2D structure prediction)

Expression Data Solution (EDS)

Genostar's Expression Data Solution (EDS) connects microarray data to genes, gene products and biochemical reactions, based on keywords and annotations. This software solution allows to:

- Assign expression values to the gene names and IDs
- Identify co-expressed genes and visually analyze the reactions and metabolic pathways in which they are involved
- Identify and perform analysis on co-regulated genes in terms of genomic localization, functional annotation and metabolism
- Colorize CDSs of interest in genomic maps according to their expression values and highlight the corresponding reactions in interactive metabolic KEGG maps
- Analyze the significance of functional data of a collection or sub-collection of CDSs (GO, KEGG and more): Fisher test
- Collect and visualize all functional data in exportable tables and maps

Database

Genostar's MicroB database is constructed of perfectly integrated and rigorously cross-checked genomic, proteic, biochemical and metabolic data approximately 1100 bacterial and archaeal organisms.

Industrial Partners

- ChemAxon[3]
- Pathway Solutions [4][5]
- KoriLog [6][7]

Academic Partners

- INRIA (Institut National de Recherche en Informatique et Automatique / French National Institute for Research in Computer Science and Control)
- Swiss Institute of Bioinformatics

External links

- Official website [8]
- Genostar Expands Deal with Biopharma Merial To Help Hunt Pathogenic Virulence Factors [9]
- Genostar at Bio 2010 [10]

References

[1] http://www.ercim.eu/publication/Ercim_News/enw51/rechenmann.html
[2] http://www.inria.fr/valorisation/societes/index.fr.html
[3] http://www.chemaxon.com/about/our-partners/integrators/
[4] http://www.pathway.jp/
[5] http://www.pathway.jp/mosaic/index.html#mosaic
[6] http://www.korilog.com/
[7] http://www.korilog.com/index.php/New-Powerful-Pathway-Exploration-Tool.html
[8] http://www.genostar.com/
[9] http://www.genomeweb.com/informatics/genostar-expands-deal-biopharma-merial-help-hunt-pathogenic-virulence-factors
[10] http://bio2010.bdmetrics.com/CDT-6793300/Genostar/Details.aspx

GENSCAN

GENSCAN is an program to identify complete gene structures in genomic DNA. It is a GHMM-based program that can be used to predict the location of genes and their exon-intron boundaries in genomic sequences from a variety of organisms. The GENSCAN Web server can be found at MIT.[1]

GENSCAN was developed by Christopher Burge [2] in the research group of Samuel Karlin [3] [4] Department of Mathematics, Stanford University.

References

[1] http://genes.mit.edu/GENSCAN.html The GENSCAN Web Server at MIT

[2] Burge, C. B. (1998) Modeling dependencies in pre-mRNA splicing signals. In Salzberg, S., Searls, D. and Kasif, S., eds. Computational Methods in Molecular Biology, Elsevier Science, Amsterdam, pp. 127-163. ISBN 9780444502049

[3] Burge, C.; Karlin, S. (1997). "Prediction of complete gene structures in human genomic DNA". *Journal of Molecular Biology* **268** (1): 78–94. doi:10.1006/jmbi.1997.0951. PMID 9149143.

[4] Burge, C.; Karlin, S. (1998). "Finding the genes in genomic DNA". *Current opinion in structural biology* **8** (3): 346–354. PMID 9666331.

GFP-cDNA

The **GFP-cDNA** project documents the localisation of proteins to subcellular compartments of the eukaryotic cell applying fluorescence microscopy. Experimental data are complemented with bioinformatic analyses and published online in a database. A search function allows the finding of proteins containing features or motifs of particular interest. The project is a collaboration of the research groups of Rainer Pepperkok [1] at the European Molecular Biology Laboratory (EMBL) and Stefan Wiemann [2] at the German Cancer Research Centre (DKFZ).

What kinds of experiments are made?

The cDNAs of novel identified Open Reading Frames(ORF) are tagged with Green Fluorescent Protein (GFP) and expressed in eukaryotic cells. Subsequently, the subcellular localisation of the fusion proteins is recorded by fluorescence microscopy.

Steps:

1. Large-scale cloning

Any large-scale manipulation of ORFs requires cloning technologies which are free of restriction enzymes. In this respect those that utilise recombination cloning (Gateway of Invitrogen or Creator of BD Biosciences) have proved to be the most suitable. This cloning technology is based on recombination mechanisms used by phages to integrate their DNA into the host genome. It allows the ORFs to be rapidly and conveniently shuttled between functionally useful vectors without the need for conventional restriction cloning. In the cDNA-GFP project the ORFs are transferred into CFP/YFP expression vectors. For the localisation analysis both N- and C-terminal fusions are generated. This maximises the possibility of correctly ascertaining the localisation, since the presence of GFP may mask targeting signals that may be present at one end of the native protein.

N-Terminal Fluorescent Fusions

Insert your gene of interest into the MCS upstream of the fluorescent protein gene, and express your gene as a fusion to the N-terminus of the fluorescent protein.

C-Terminal Fluorescent Fusions

Insert your gene of interest into the MCS downstream of the fluorescent protein gene, and express your gene as a fusion to the C-terminus of the fluorescent protein.

2. Transfection of eukaryotic cells, Expression

The fusion vectors are transfected in Vero cells (monkey kidney fibroblasts). Particularly interesting ORFs are also screened for localisation in PC12 cells and hippocampal neurons.

3. Protein localisation

At different time points, the subcellular localisation of the fusion proteins is recorded via fluorescence microscopy. At the end of the live cell imaging, the cells can still be fixed and colocalisation experiments made.

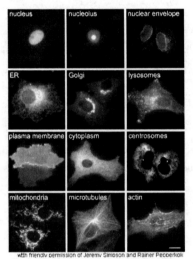

with friendly permission of Jeremy Simpson and Rainer Pepperkok

Examples of subcellular localisations

4. Bioinformatic Analysis

As the sequence of the cDNAs is known, bioinformatics can make predictions regarding the localisation and function of the encoded protein. The bioinformatics analysis is facilitated by the bioinformatic search engine Harvester.

5. Assignment of subcellular localization category

Results from the N- and C-terminal fusions are assessed and in turn these data are compared to the bioinformatic predictions. A final subcellular localisation (from approximately 20 categories) is then assigned for each ORF. Similar localisations with both N- and C-terminal constructs provide a higher degree of reliability of the result. For those ORFs where the two fusions do not give a similar localisation pattern, a series of other criteria, including bioinformatic predictions, are considered. Occasionally a clear cut localisation cannot be assigned.

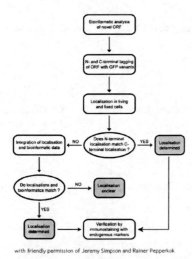

with friendly permission of Jeremy Simpson and Rainer Pepperkok

Flow chart: strategy for the assignment of a
subcellular localisation

Which data is published?

Every data sheet contains the fluorescence images of both N- and C-terminal fusions, the assigned localization, other localizations, comments and the Swissprot ID. For every protein entry, a link is provided to the corresponding Harvester [3] bioinformatics page.

How do I use the GFP-cDNA database?

Images of all localised proteins and their bioinformatic analysis can be viewed via the 'Results Table' or 'Results Images' buttons. In addition, use the search window on the entry site to find proteins containing features or motifs of particular interest to you that have been localised in this project.

External links

- GFP-cDNA database [4]
- FAQ [5]
- Harvester bioinformatic search engine [6]

Sources

- Homepage of the GFP-cDNA project [4]

References

[1] http://www-db.embl.de/jss/EmblGroupsOrg/g_50

[2] http://www.dkfz.de/mga/

[3] http://harvester.embl.de

[4] http://gfp-cdna.embl.de/

[5] http://gfp-cdna.embl.de/html/faqs.html

[6] http://harvester.fzk.de/

GLIMMER

GLIMMER (Gene Locator and Interpolated Markov ModelER) was the first bioinformatics system for finding genes that used the interpolated Markov model formalism. It is very effective at finding genes in bacteria, archaea, and viruses, typically finding 98–99% of all protein-coding genes. The GLIMMER software is open source and can be found at the links below. It is maintained by Steven Salzberg, Art Delcher, and their colleagues at the Center for Bioinformatics and Computational Biology [1] at the University of Maryland, College Park.

Because of its exceptionally high accuracy, Glimmer is the system of choice for genome annotation efforts on a wide range of bacteria, archaeal, and viral species. In a large-scale reannotation effort at the DNA Data Bank of Japan (DDBJ, which mirrors Genbank), Kosuge et al. (Kosuge et al. 2006) examined the gene finding methods used for 183 genomes. They report that of these projects, Glimmer was the gene finder for 49%, followed by Genemark with 12%, with other algorithms used in 3% or fewer of the projects. (They also reported that 33% of genomes used "other" programs, which in many cases meant that they could not identify the method. Excluding those cases, Glimmer was used for 73% of the genomes for which the methods could be unambiguously identified.) Glimmer was used by the DNA Databank of Japan (DDBJ) to re-annotate all bacterial genomes in the International Nucleotide Sequence Databases (Sugawara et al. 2007). It is also being used by this group to annotate viruses (Hirahata et al. 2007). Glimmer is part of the bacterial annotation pipeline at the National Center for Biotechnology Information (NCB)) (http://www.ncbi.nlm.nih.gov/genomes/static/Pipeline.html), which also maintains a web server for Glimmer (http://www.ncbi.nlm.nih.gov/genomes/microbes/glimmer_3.cgi), as do sites in Germany (http://tico.gobics.de/), Canada (http://wishart.biology.ualberta.ca/basys), and elsewhere.

Glimmer is one of the most highly cited bioinformatics systems in the scientific literature. According to Google Scholar, as of early 2011 the original (Salzberg et al., 1998) Glimmer article has been cited 581 times and the Glimmer 2.0 article (Delcher et al., 1999) has been cited 950 times.

References

- S.L. Salzberg, A.L. Delcher, S. Kasif, and O. White. *Microbial gene identification using interpolated Markov models*, Nucleic Acids Research, 26:2 (1998), 544–548. Fulltext [2]
- A.L. Delcher, D. Harmon, S. Kasif, O. White, and S.L. Salzberg. *Improved microbial gene identification with GLIMMER*, Nucleic Acids Research, 27:23 (1999), 4636–4641. Fulltext [3]
- Hirahata, M., T. Abe, et al. (2007). "Genome Information Broker for Viruses (GIB-V): database for comparative analysis of virus genomes." Nucleic Acids Res 35(Database issue): D339-42.
- Kosuge, T., T. Abe, et al. (2006). "Exploration and grading of possible genes from 183 bacterial strains by a common protocol to identification of new genes: Gene Trek in Prokaryote Space (GTPS)." DNA Res 13(6): 245-54.
- Sugawara, H., T. Abe, et al. (2007). "DDBJ working on evaluation and classification of bacterial genes in INSDC." Nucleic Acids Res 35(Database issue): D13-5.

External links

- The Glimmer home page [4], from which the software can be downloaded.

References

[1] http://cbcb.umd.edu
[2] http://nar.oupjournals.org/cgi/content/abstract/26/2/544
[3] http://nar.oupjournals.org/cgi/content/abstract/27/23/4636
[4] http://cbcb.umd.edu/software/glimmer

Global distance test

The **global distance test** or **GDT** (also written as GDT_TS to represent "total score") is a measure of similarity between two protein structures with identical amino acid sequences but different tertiary structures. It is most commonly used to compare the results of protein structure prediction to the experimentally determined structure as measured by X-ray crystallography or protein NMR. The metric is intended as a more accurate measurement than the more common RMSD metric, which is sensitive to outlier regions created by poor modeling of individual loop regions in a structure that is otherwise reasonably accurate. GDT_TS measurements are used as major assessment criteria in the production of results from the Critical Assessment of Structure Prediction (CASP), a large-scale experiment in the structure prediction community dedicated to assessing current modeling techniques and identifying their primary deficiencies.[1] [2] [3]

The GDT score is calculated as the largest set of amino acid residues' alpha carbon atoms in the model structure falling within a defined distance cutoff of their position in the experimental structure. It is typical to calculate the GDT score under several cutoff distances, and scores generally increase with increasing cutoff. A plateau in this increase may indicate an extreme divergence between the experimental and predicted structures, such that no additional atoms are included in any cutoff of a reasonable distance.

The high accuracy version of the GDT measure is called GDT-HA. It uses smaller cut off distances (half the size of GDT_TS) and thus is more rigorous.[4]

References

[1] Zemla A, Venclovas C, Moult J, Fidelis K (1999). "Processing and analysis of CASP3 protein structure predictions". *Proteins* **S3**: 22–29. PMID 10526349.
[2] Zemla A, Venclovas C, Moult J, Fidelis K (2001). "Processing and evaluation of predictions in CASP4". *Proteins* **45** (S5): 13–21. doi:10.1002/prot.10052. PMID 11835478.
[3] Zemla A (2003). "LGA: A method for finding 3D similarities in protein structures". *Nucleic Acids Research* **31** (13): 3370–3374. doi:10.1093/nar/gkg571. PMC 168977. PMID 12824330.
[4] Read, Randy J.; Chavali, Gayatri (2007). "Assessment of CASP7 predictions in the high accuracy template-based modeling category". *Proteins* **69** (S8): 27–37. doi:10.1002/prot.21662. PMID 17894351.

External links

- CASP6 results (http://www2.predictioncenter.org/casp/casp6/public/cgi-bin/results.cgi) plotted by GDT score for each target structure included in the experiment

Global Infectious Disease Epidemiology Network

Global Infectious Diseases Epidemiology Network (GIDEON) is a web-based program for decision support and informatics in the fields of Infectious Diseases and Geographic Medicine. As of 2005, more than 300 generic infectious diseases occur haphazardly in time and space and are challenged by over 250 drugs and vaccines. 1,500 species of pathogenic bacteria, viruses, parasites and fungi have been described. Printed media can no longer follow the dynamics of diseases, outbreaks and epidemics in "real time."

Organization

GIDEON consists of four modules. The first Diagnosis module generates a Bayesian ranked differential diagnosis based on signs, symptoms, laboratory tests, country of origin and incubation period - and can be used for diagnosis support and simulation of all infectious diseases in all countries. Since the program is web-based, this module can also be adapted to disease and bioterror surveillance.

The second module follows the epidemiology of individual diseases, including their global background and status in each of 205 countries and regions. All past and current outbreaks of all diseases, in all countries, are described in detail. The user may also access a list of diseases compatible with any combination of agent, vector, vehicle, reservoir and country (for example, one could list all the mosquito-borne flaviviruses of Brazil which have an avian reservoir). Over 30,000 graphs display all the data, and are updated in "real time." These graphs can be used for preparation of PowerPoint displays, pamphlets, lecture notes, etc. Several thousand high-quality images are also available, including clinical lesions, roentgenograms, Photomicrographs and disease life cycles.

The third module is an interactive encyclopedia which incorporates the pharmacology, usage, testing standards and global trade names of all antiinfective drugs and vaccines.

The fourth module is designed to identify or characterize all species of bacteria, mycobacteria and yeasts. The database includes 50 to 100 taxa which may not appear in standard texts and laboratory databases for several months.

Additional options allow users to add data (in their own font / language) relevant to their own institution, electronic patient charts, material from the internet, important telephone numbers, drug prices, antimicrobial resistance patterns, etc. This form of custom data is particularly useful when running GIDEON on institutional networks. The data in GIDEON are derived from:

- all peer-reviewed journals in the fields of Infectious Diseases, Pediatrics, Internal Medicine, Tropical Medicine, Travel Medicine, Antimicrobial Pharmacology and Clinical Microbiology
- a monthly electronic literature search based on all relevant keywords
- all available health ministry reports (both printed and electronic)
- standard texts
- abstracts of major meetings

Related products

- VIPatients [1] created by the author of GIDEON

External links

- GIDEON description at EBSCO [2]
- GIDEON [3]

References

[1] http://www.vipatients.com
[2] http://www.ebscohost.com/pointOfCare/default.php?id=6
[3] http://www.GIDEONonline.com

Global Public Health Intelligence Network

The **Global Public Health Intelligence Network** (GPHIN) is an electronic public health early warning system developed by Canada's Public Health Agency, and is part of the World Health Organization's (WHO) Global Outbreak and Alert Response Network (GOARN). This system monitors internet media, such as news wires and websites, in seven languages in order to help detect and report potential disease outbreaks around the world.[1]

References

[1] Global Public Health Intelligence Network, *Public Health Agency of Canada*, November 2004 (http://www.phac-aspc.gc.ca/media/nr-rp/
     2004/2004_gphin-rmispbk_e.html)

Glycoinformatics

Glycoinformatics is a relatively new field of bioinformatics that pertains to the study of carbohydrates. It broadly includes (but is not restricted to) database, software, and algorithm development for the study of carbohydrate structures, glycoconjugates, enzymatic carbohydrate synthesis and degradation, as well as carbohydrate interactions. Conventional usage of the term does not currently include the treatment of carbohydrates from the more well-known nutritive aspect.

Complexity

Carbohydrates or "sugars" (this term should not be confused with simple sugars - monosaccharides and disaccharides) as they are generally called,[1] form the third class of biopolymers, other two being proteins and nucleic acids. Unlike proteins and nucleic acids which are linear, carbohydrates are often branched and extremely complex.[2] For instance, just four sugars can be strung together to form more than 5 million different types of carbohydrates[3] or nine different sugars may be assembled into 15 million possible four-sugar-chains.[4] Despite their repetitive nature, carbohydrates are often considered as the "information poor" molecules. Consequently, bioinformatics on glycome is also very poor.[5]

Sequence representation

Owing to the lack of a genetic blue print, carbohydrates do not have a "fixed" sequence. Instead, the sequence is largely determined by the kinetic differences in the enzymes and variations in the biosynthetic micro-environment of the cells.

One of the main constrains in the glycoinformatics is the difficulty of representing sugars in the sequence form especially due to their branching nature.[6]

The sequence of branching information[7] in a carbohydrate molecule is represented in the figure.

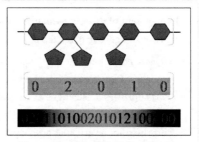

The sequence of branching information in a arabinoxylan molecule.

References

[1] Flitsch SL and Ulijn RV (2003). Nature 421:219-220. http://www.nature.com/nature/journal/v421/n6920/pdf/421219a.pdf

[2] Seeberger PH (2005). Nature 437:1239.

[3] Service RF (2001). Science 291:805-806. http://www.sciencemag.org/cgi/content/full/291/5505/805a

[4] Dove A (2001). Nature Biotechnology 19:913-917. http://www.columbia.edu/cu/biology/courses/w3034/LACpapers/bittersweetNatBiot01.pdf

[5] Kikuchi N, et al. (2005). Bioinformatics 21:1717–1718. http://bioinformatics.oxfordjournals.org/cgi/content/full/21/8/1717

[6] Dove A (2001). Nature Biotechnology 19:913-917. http://www.columbia.edu/cu/biology/courses/w3034/LACpapers/bittersweetNatBiot01.pdf

[7] Dervilly-Pinel G, et al. (2004). Carbohydrate Polymers 55:171–177.

User:GMcArthurIV/GenoCAD

GenoCAD

Initial release	30 August 2007
Stable release	1.6 / 30 May 2011
Development status	Active
Written in	PHP JavaScript Java Prolog
Type	Computer-Aided Design Bioinformatics
License	Apache v2.0
Website	[genocad.org genocad.org]

GenoCAD [1] is an open source web application to design DNA constructs for genetic engineering using a rule-based methodology. GenoCAD is also considered a Computer Assisted Design (CAD) application for synthetic biology.

Features

The main features of GenoCAD can be organized into three main categories. [2]

- **Management of genetic sequences**: The purpose of this group of features is to help users identify, within large collections of genetic parts, the parts needed for a project and to organize them in project-specific libraries.
  - *Genetic parts*: Parts have a unique identifier, a name and a more general description. They also have a DNA sequence. Parts are associated with a grammar and assigned to a parts category such a promoter, gene, etc.
  - *Parts libraries*: Collections of parts are organized in libraries. In some cases part libraries correspond to parts imported from a single source such as another sequence database. In other cases, libraries correspond to the parts used for a particular design project. Parts can be moved from one library to another through a temporary storage area called the cart (analogous to e-commerce shopping carts).
  - *Searching parts*: Users can search the parts database using the Lucene search engine. Basic and advanced search modes are available. Users can develop complex queries and save them for future reuse.
  - *Importing/Exporting parts*: Parts can be imported and exported individually or as entire libraries using standard file formats (e.g., tab delimited, FASTA).
- **Combining sequences into genetic constructs**: The purpose of this group of features is to streamline the process of combining genetic parts into designs compliant with a specific design strategy.
  - *Point-and-click design tool*: This wizard guides the user through a series of design decisions that determine the design structure and the selection of parts included in the design.
  - *Design management*: Designs can be saved in the user workspace. Design statuses are regularly updated to warn users of the consequences of editing parts on previously saved designs.
  - *Exporting designs*: Designs can be exported using standard file formats (e.g., GenBank, tab delimited, FASTA).
- **User workspace**: Users can personalize their workspace by adding parts to the GenoCAD database, creating specialized libraries corresponding to specific design projects, and saving designs at different stages of development.

Theoretical foundation

GenoCAD is rooted in the theory of formal languages. In particular, the design rules describing how to combine different kinds of parts form context-free grammars. [3]

References

[1] Czar MJ, Cai Y, Peccoud J (2009). "Writing DNA with GenoCAD". *Nucleic Acids Res.* **37** (web server): W40-7. PMC PMC2703884. PMID 19429897.
[2] Wilson ML, Hertzberg R, Adam L, Peccoud J. (2011). "A step-by-step introduction to rule-based design of synthetic genetic constructs using GenoCAD.". *Methods Enzymol.* **498**: 173-88. PMID 21601678.
[3] Cai Y, Hartnett B, Gustafsson C, Peccoud J. (2007). "A syntactic model to design and verify synthetic genetic constructs derived from standard biological parts.". *Bioinformatics* **23** (20): 2760-7. PMID 17804435.

External links

- GenoCAD.org (http://www.genocad.org)
- Project page (http://sourceforge.net/projects/genocad/) on SourceForge.

GoPubMed

GoPubMed is a knowledge-based search engine for biomedical texts. The Gene Ontology (GO) and Medical Subject Headings (MeSH) serve as "Table of contents" in order to structure the millions of articles of the MEDLINE database. The search engine allows its users to find relevant search results significantly faster (than what?). **MeshPubMed** was at one point a separate project, but now the two have been merged.

The technologies used in GoPubMed are generic and can in general be applied to any kind of texts and any kind of knowledge bases. GoPubMed is one of the first Web 2.0 semantic search engines. The system was developed at the Technical University of Dresden by Michael Schroeder and his team at Transinsight.

GoPubMed.com, the semantic search engine for the life sciences, has been recognized with the 2009 red dot: best of the best award in the category communication design – graphical user interfaces and interactive tool and the German Industry Prize 2010.

References

- Citations in Pubmed (http://www.gopubmed.org/search?q=gopubmed)
- Citations in Pubmed Central (http://www.ncbi.nlm.nih.gov/sites/entrez?tool=QuerySuggestion& cmd=search&db=pmc&term=gopubmed OR GoGene OR GoWeb OR Go3R)
- Books including GoPubMed's semantic search (http://www.google.de/search?q=gopubmed&um=1& ie=UTF-8&tbo=u&tbs=bks:1&source=og&sa=N&hl=de&tab=wp)
- People about GoPubMed (http://transinsight.com/about-us/?lang=en#People about us)

External links

- GoPubMed (http://www.gopubmed.org)
- Transinsight (http://www.transinsight.com)

GOR method

The **GOR method** (**G**arnier-**O**sguthorpe-**R**obson) is an information theory-based method for the prediction of secondary structures in proteins.[1] It was developed in the late 1970s shortly after the simpler Chou-Fasman method. Like Chou-Fasman, the GOR method is based on probability parameters derived from empirical studies of known protein tertiary structures solved by X-ray crystallography. However, unlike Chou-Fasman, the GOR method takes into account not only the propensities of individual amino acids to form particular secondary structures, but also the conditional probability of the amino acid to form a secondary structure given that its immediate neighbors have already formed that structure. The method is therefore essentially Bayesian in its analysis.[2]

The GOR method analyzes sequences to predict alpha helix, beta sheet, turn, or random coil secondary structure at each position based on 17-amino-acid sequence windows. The original description of the method included four scoring matrices of size 17×20, where the columns correspond to the log-odds score, which reflects the probability of finding a given amino acid at each position in the 17-residue sequence. The four matrices reflect the probabilities of the central, ninth amino acid being in a helical, sheet, turn, or coil conformation. In subsequent revisions to the method, the turn matrix was eliminated due to the high variability of sequences in turn regions (particularly over such a large window). The method was considered as best requiring at least four contiguous residues to score as alpha helices to classify the region as helical, and at least two contiguous residues for a beta sheet.[3]

The mathematics and algorithm of the GOR method were based on an earlier series of studies by Robson and colleagues reported mainly in the *Journal of Molecular Biology* (e.g. [4]) and The Biochemical Journal (e.g. [5]). The latter describes the information theoretic expansions in terms of conditional information measures. The use of the word "simple" in the title of the GOR paper reflected the fact that the above earlier methods provided proofs and techniques somewhat daunting by being rather unfamiliar in protein science in the early 1970s; even Bayes methods were then unfamiliar and controversial. An important feature of these early studies, which survived in the GOR method, was the treatment of the sparse protein sequence data of the early 1970s by expected information measures. That is, expectations on a Bayesian basis considering the distribution of plausible information measure values given the actual frequencies (numbers of observations). The expectation measures resulting from integration over this and similar distributions may now be seen as composed of "incomplete" or extended zeta functions, e.g. $z(s, \text{observed frequency}) - z(s, \text{expected frequency})$ with incomplete zeta function $z(s, n) = 1 + (1/2)^s + (1/3)^s + (1/4)^s + \ldots + (1/n)^s$. The GOR method used s=1. Also, in the GOR method and the earlier methods, the measure for the contrary state to e.g. helix H, i.e. ~H, was subtracted from that for H, and similarly for beta sheet, turns, and coil or loop. Thus the method can be seen as employing a zeta function estimate of log predictive odds. An adjustable decision constant could also be applied, which thus also implies a decision theory approach; the GOR method allowed the option to use decision constants to optimize predictions for different classes of protein. The expected information measure used as a basis for the information expansion was less important by the time of publication of the GOR method because protein sequence data became more plentiful, at least for the terms considered at that time. Then, for s=1, the expression $z(s, \text{observed frequency}) - z(s, \text{expected frequency})$ approaches the natural logarithm of (observed frequency / expected frequency) as frequencies increase. However, this measure (including use of other values of s) remains important in later more general applications with high dimensional data, where data for more complex terms in the information expansion are inevitably sparse (e.g. [6]).

References

[1] Garnier J, Gibrat JF, Robson B. (1996). GOR method for predicting protein secondary structure from amino acid sequence. *Methods Enzymol* 266:540-53 (http://dx.doi.org/10.1016/S0076-6879(96)66034-0).

[2] Garnier J, Osguthorpe DJ, Robson B. (1978). Analysis of the accuracy and implications of simple methods for predicting the secondary structure of globular proteins. *J Mol Biol* 120:97-120 (http://dx.doi.org/10.1016/0022-2836(78)90297-8).

[3] Mount DM (2004). *Bioinformatics: Sequence and Genome Analysis*, 2, Cold Spring Harbor Laboratory Press. ISBN 0879697121.

[4] Robson B, Pain RH. (1971). Analysis of the Code Relating Sequence to Conformation in Globular Proteins: Possible Implications for the Mechanism of Formation of Helical Regions. J. Mol. Biol: 58, 237-256

[5] Robson B. (1974). Analysis of the Code Relating Sequence to Conformation in Globular Proteins: Theory and Application of Expected Information. 141: 853-867

[6] Robson B. (2005). Clinical and Pharmacogenomic Data Mining: 3. Zeta Theory As a General Tactic for Clinical Bioinformatics. J. Proteome Res. (Am. Chem. Soc.) 4(2): 445-455

Haar-like features

Haar-like features are digital image features used in object recognition. They owe their name to their intuitive similarity with Haar wavelets and were used in the first real-time face detector.

Historically, working with only image intensities (i.e., the RGB pixel values at each and every pixel of image) made the task of feature calculation computationally expensive. A publication by Papageorgiou et al.[1] discussed working with an alternate feature set based on Haar wavelets instead of the usual image intensities. Viola and Jones[2] adapted the idea of using Haar wavelets and developed the so called Haar-like features. A Haar-like feature considers adjacent rectangular regions at a specific location in a detection window, sums up the pixel intensities in these regions and calculates the difference between them. This difference is then used to categorize subsections of an image. For example, let us say we have an image database with human faces. It is a common observation that among all faces the region of the eyes is darker than the region of the cheeks. Therefore a common haar feature for face detection is a set of two adjacent rectangles that lie above the eye and the cheek region. The position of these rectangles is defined relative to a detection window that acts like a bounding box to the target object (the face in this case).

In the detection phase of the Viola–Jones object detection framework, a window of the target size is moved over the input image, and for each subsection of the image the Haar-like feature is calculated. This difference is then compared to a learned threshold that separates non-objects from objects. Because such a Haar-like feature is only a weak learner or classifier (its detection quality is slightly better than random guessing) a large number of Haar-like features are necessary to describe an object with sufficient accuracy. In the Viola–Jones object detection framework, the Haar-like features are therefore organized in something called a *classifier cascade* to form a strong learner or classifier.

The key advantage of a Haar-like feature over most other features is its calculation speed. Due to the use of *integral images*, a Haar-like feature of any size can be calculated in constant time (approximately 60 microprocessor instructions for a 2-rectangle feature).

Rectangular Haar-like features

A simple rectangular Haar-like feature can be defined as the difference of the sum of pixels of areas inside the rectangle, which can be at any position and scale within the original image. This modified feature set is called *2-rectangle feature*. Viola and Jones also defined 3-rectangle features and 4-rectangle features. The values indicate certain characteristics of a particular area of the image. Each feature type can indicate the existence (or absence) of certain characteristics in the image, such as edges or changes in texture. For example, a 2-rectangle feature can indicate where the border lies between a dark region and a light region.

Fast computation of Haar-like features

One of the contributions of Viola and Jones was to use summed area tables[3] , which they called *integral images*. Integral images can be defined as two-dimensional lookup tables in the form of a matrix with the same size of the original image. Each element of the integral image contains the sum of all pixels located on the up-left region of the original image (in relation to the element's position). This allows to compute sum of rectangular areas in the image, at any position or scale, using only four lookups:

$$\text{sum} = pt_4 - pt_3 - pt_2 + pt_1.$$

where points pt_n belong to the integral image (include a figure).

Each Haar-like feature may need more than four lookups, depending on how it was defined. Viola and Jones's 2-rectangle features need six lookups, 3-rectangle features need eight lookups, and 4-rectangle features need nine lookups.

Tilted Haar-like features

Lienhart and Maydt[4] introduced the concept of a tilted (45°) Haar-like feature. This was used to increase the dimensionality of the set of features in an attempt to improve the detection of objects in images. This was successful, as some of these features are able to describe the object in a better way. For example, a 2-rectangle tilted Haar-like feature can indicate the existence of an edge at 45°.

Messom and Barczak[5] extended the idea to a generic rotated Haar-like feature. Although the idea sounds mathematically sound, practical problems prevented the use of Haar-like features at any angle. In order to be fast, detection algorithms use low resolution images, causing rounding errors. For this reason, rotated Haar-like features are not commonly used.

References

[1] Papageorgiou, Oren and Poggio, "A general framework for object detection", International Conference on Computer Vision, 1998.

[2] Viola and Jones, "Rapid object detection using boosted cascade of simple features", Computer Vision and Pattern Recognition, 2001

[3] Crow, F, "Summed-area tables for texture mapping", in Proceedings of SIGGRAPH, 18(3):207–212, 1984

[4] Lienhart, R. and Maydt, J., "An extended set of Haar-like features for rapid object detection", ICIP02, pp. I: 900–903, 2002

[5] Messom, C.H. and Barczak, A.L.C., "Fast and Efficient Rotated Haar-like Features Using Rotated Integral Images", Australian Conference on Robotics and Automation (ACRA2006), pp. 1–6, 2006

• Haar A. *Zur Theorie der orthogonalen Funktionensysteme*, Mathematische Annalen, **69**, pp. 331–371, 1910.

HB plot

Knowledge of the relationship between a protein's structure and its dynamic behavior is essential for understanding protein function. The description of a protein three dimensional structure as a network of hydrogen bonding interactions (**HB plot**)[1] was introduced as a tool for exploring protein structure and function. By analyzing the network of tertiary interactions the possible spread of information within a protein can be investigated.

HB plot offers a simple way of analyzing protein secondary structure and tertiary structure. Hydrogen bonds stabilizing secondary structural elements (**secondary hydrogen bonds**) and those formed between distant amino acid residues - defined as **tertiary hydrogen bonds** - can be easily distinguished in HB plot, thus, amino acid residues involved in stabilizing protein structure and function can be identified. By analyzing the network of tertiary interactions the *possible spread of information* within a protein can be investigated as well.

Features

The plot distinguishes between main chain-main chain, main chain-side chain and side chain-side chain hydrogen bonding interactions. Bifurcated hydrogen bonds and multiple hydrogen bonds between amino acid residues; and intra- and interchain hydrogen bonds are also indicated on the plots. Three classes of hydrogen bondings are distinguished by color coding; short (distance smaller than 2.5 Å between donor and acceptor), intermediate (between 2.5 Å and 3.2 Å) and long hydrogen bonds (greater than 3.2 Å).

Secondary structure elements in HB plot

In representations of the HB plot, characteristic patterns of secondary structure elements can be recognised easily, as follows:

1. Helices can be identified as strips directly adjacent to the diagonal.
2. Antiparallel beta sheets appear in HB plot as cross-diagonal.
3. Parallel beta sheets appears in the HB plot as parallel to the diagonal.
4. Loops appear as breaks in the diagonal between the cross-diagonal beta-sheet motifs.

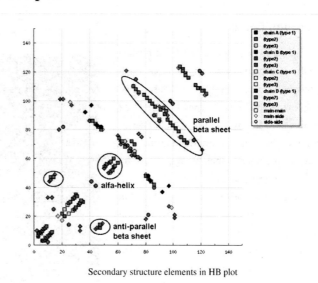

Secondary structure elements in HB plot

Examples of usage

Cytochrome P450s

The cytochrome P450s (P450s) are xenobiotic-metabolizing membrane-bound heme-containing enzymes that use molecular oxygen and electrons from NADPH cytochrome P450 reductase to oxidize their substrates. CYP2B4, a member of the cytochrome P450 family is the only protein within this family, whose X-ray structure in both open 11 and closed form 12 is published. The comparison of the open and closed structures of CYP2B4 structures reveals large-scale conformational rearrangement between the two states, with the greatest conformational change around the residues 215-225, which is widely open in ligand-free state and shut after ligand binding; and the region around loop C near the heme.

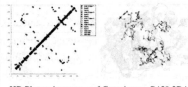

HB Plot and structure of Cytochrome P450 2B4
in closed form

Examining the HB plot of the closed and open state of CYP2B4 revealed that the rearrangement of tertiary hydrogen bonds was in excellent agreement with the current knowledge of the cytochrome P450 catalytic cycle.

The first step in P450 catalytic cycle is identified as substrate binding. Preliminary binding of a ligand near to the entrance breaks hydrogen bonds S212-E474, S207-H172 in the open form of CYP2B4 and hydrogen bonds E218-A102, Q215-L51 are formed that fix the entrance in the closed form as the HB plot reveals.

The second step is the transfer of the first electron from NADPH via an electron transfer chain. For the electron transfer a conformational change occurs that triggers interaction of the P450 with the NADPH cytochrome P450 reductase. Breaking of hydrogen bonds between S128-N287, S128-T291, L124-N287 and forming S96-R434, A116-R434, R125-I435, D82-R400 at the NADPH cytochrome P450 reductase binding site—as seen in HB plot—transform CYP2B4 to a conformation state, where binding of NADPH cytochrome P450 reductase occurs.

In the third step, oxygen enters CYP2B4 in the closed state - the state where newly formed hydrogen bonds S176-T300, H172-S304, N167-R308 open a tunnel which is exactly the size and shape of an oxygen molecule.

Lipocalin family

The **lipocalin family** is a large and diverse family of proteins with functions as small hydrophobic molecule transporters. Beta-lactoglobulin is a typical member of the lipocalin family. Beta-lactoglobulin was found to have a role in the transport of hydrophobic ligands such as retinol or fatty acids. Its crystal structure were determined [e.g. Qin, 1998] with different ligands and in ligand-free form as well. The crystal structures determined so far reveal that the typical lipocalin contains eight-stranded antiparallel-barrel arranged to form a conical central cavity in which the hydrophobic ligand is bound. The structure of beta-lactoglobulin reveals that the barrel-form structure with the central cavity

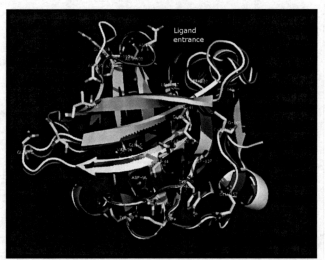

Beta-lactoglobulin in open (white) and ligand-bound (red) form

of the protein has an "entrance" surrounded by five beta-loops with centers around 26, 35, 63, 87, and 111, which undergo a conformational change during the ligand binding and close the cavity.

The overall shape of beta-lactoglobulin is characteristic of the lipocalin family. In the absence of alpha-helices, the main diagonal almost disappears and the cross-diagonals representing the beta-sheets dominate the plot. Relatively low number of tertiary hydrogen bonds can be found in the plot, with three high-density regions, one of which is connected to a loop at the residues around 63, a second is connected to the loop around 87, and a third region which is connected to the regions 26 and 35. The fifth loop around 111 is represented only one tertiary hydrogen bond in the HB plot.

In the three-dimensional structure, tertiary hydrogen bonds are formed (1) near to the entrance, directly involved in conformational rearrangement during ligand binding; and (2) at the bottom of the "barrel". HB plots of the open and closed forms of beta-lactoglobulin are very similar, all unique motifs can be recognized in both forms. Difference in HB plots of open and ligand-bound form show few important individual changes in tertiary hydrogen bonding pattern. Especially, the formation of hydrogen bonds between Y20-E157 and S21-H161 in closed form might be crucial in conformational rearrangement. These hydrogen bonds lie at the bottom of the cavity, which suggests that the closure of the entrance of a lipocalin starts when a ligand reached the bottom of the cavity and broke hydrogen bonds R123-Y99, R123-T18, and V41-Q120. Lipocalins are known to have very low sequence similarity with high structural similarity. The only conserved regions are exactly the region around 20 and 160 with an unknown role.

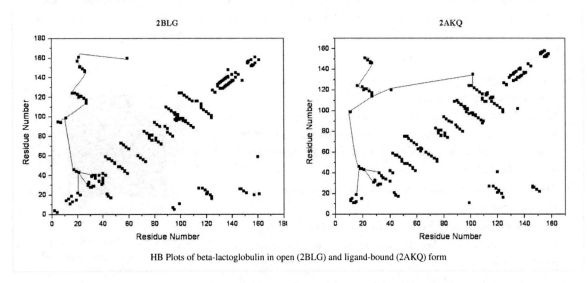

HB Plots of beta-lactoglobulin in open (2BLG) and ligand-bound (2AKQ) form

References

[1] Bikadi Z, Demko L, Hazai E (2007). "Functional and structural characterization of a protein based on analysis of its hydrogen bonding network by hydrogen bonding plot". *Arch Biochem Biophys.* **461** (2): 225–234. doi:10.1016/j.abb.2007.02.020. PMID 17391641.

External links

- HB Plot (http://dept.phy.bme.hu/virtuadrug/hbplot/bin/infopage.php) — a free online HB Plot program

Heat map

A **heat map** is a graphical representation of data where the values taken by a variable in a two-dimensional table are represented as colors. Fractal maps and tree maps both often use a similar system of color-coding to represent the values taken by a variable in a hierarchy. The term is also used to mean its thematic application as a choropleth map.

Heat maps originated in 2D displays of the values in a data matrix. Larger values were represented by small dark gray or black squares (pixels) and smaller values by lighter squares. Sneath (1957) displayed the results of a cluster analysis by permuting the rows and the columns of a matrix to place similar values near each other according to the clustering. Jacques Bertin used a similar representation to display data that conformed to a Guttman scale. The idea for joining cluster trees to the rows and columns of the data matrix originated with Robert Ling in 1973. Ling used overstruck printer characters to represent different shades of gray, one character-width per pixel. Leland Wilkinson developed the first computer program in 1994 (SYSTAT) to produce cluster heat maps with high-resolution color graphics. The Eisen et al. display shown in the figure is a replication of the earlier SYSTAT design.

There are several different kinds of heat map:

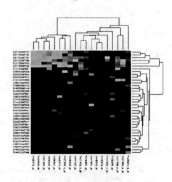

Heat map generated from DNA microarray data reflecting gene expression values in several conditions

- Web heat maps have been used for displaying areas of a Web page most frequently scanned by visitors.
- Biology heat maps are typically used in molecular biology to represent the level of expression of many genes across a number of comparable samples (e.g. cells in different states, samples from different patients) as they are obtained from DNA microarrays.
- The tree map is a 2D hierarchical partitioning of data that visually resembles a heat map.
- A mosaic plot is a tiled heat map for representing a two-way or higher-way table of data. As with treemaps, the rectangular regions in a mosaic plot are hierarchically organized. The means that the regions are rectangles instead of squares. Friendly (1994) surveys the history and usage of this graph.

Software Implementations

Several heat map software implementations are listed here (the list is not complete):

- FusionCharts Heat Map [1], a charting component for visual data, has support for real-time, interactive heat maps [1]
- R Statistics, a free software environment for statistical computing and graphics, contains several functions to trace heat maps [2]
- Gnuplot, a universal and free command-line plotting program, can trace 2D and 3D heat maps [3]
- The Google Docs spreadsheet application includes a Heat Map gadget.
- Qlucore includes a heat map that is dynamically updated when filter parameters are changed.
- The ESPN Gamecast for soccer games uses heat maps to show where certain players have spent time on the field.
- By searching the List of bioinformatics companies more tools for heat maps can be found.
- Microsoft Excel can be used to generate heat maps using the Surface Chart. Though the default color range for Surface Charts in Excel is not conducive to heat maps, the colors can be edited to generate user-friendly and intuitive heat maps.

References

- Bertin, J. (1967). *Sémiologie Graphique. Les diagrammes, les réseaux, les cartes*. Gauthier-Villars.
- Eisen, M.B., Spellman, P.T., Brown, P.O. & Botstein, D. (1998). "Cluster analysis and display of genome-wide expression patterns" [4]. *Proc. Natl. Acad. Sci. USA* **95** (25): 14863–14868. doi:10.1073/pnas.95.25.14863. PMC 24541. PMID 9843981.
- Friendly, M. (1994). "Mosaic displays for multi-way contingency tables" [5]. *Journal of the American Statistical Association* (American Statistical Association) **89** (425): 190–200. doi:10.2307/2291215. JSTOR 2291215.
- Ling, R.F. (1973). "A computer generated aid for cluster analysis". *Communications of the ACM* **16** (6): 355–361. doi:10.1145/362248.362263.
- Sneath, P.H.A. (1957). "The application of computers to taxonomy". *Journal of General Microbiology* **17** (1): 201–226. PMID 13475686.
- Wilkinson, L. (1994). *Advanced Applications: Systat for DOS Version 6*. SYSTAT Inc.. ISBN 9780134472850.

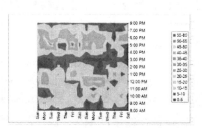

A sample heat map created using a Surface Chart in Microsoft Excel.

External links

- The History of the Cluster Heat Map [6]. Leland Wilkinson and Michael Friendly.
- Heatmap Builder [7]. Heatmap Builder, a program for generating heatmaps developed at the Ashley Labs.
- Matrix2png [8]. Web-based or command-line generation of heat maps.
- [9]. A Map of the Market using a heatmap data visualization and London Stock Exchange data (FTSE 100 Index) from Panopticon Software
- NASDAQ 100 Heatmap [10]. Heatmap visualization of NASDAQ 100 index.
- heatmap.js [11]. Open Source JavaScript library for generating realtime web heatmaps
- heatcanvas [12]. Another open source library for modern web browser.

References

[1] http://www.fusioncharts.com/powercharts/charts/heat-map/
[2] http://www2.warwick.ac.uk/fac/sci/moac/currentstudents/peter_cock/r/heatmap/
[3] http://gnuplot.sourceforge.net/demo_4.4/heatmaps.html
[4] http://www.pnas.org/cgi/content/full/95/25/14863
[5] http://www.math.yorku.ca/SCS/Papers/drew
[6] http://www.cs.uic.edu/~wilkinson/Publications/heatmap.pdf
[7] http://ashleylab.stanford.edu/tools_scripts.html
[8] http://www.bioinformatics.ubc.ca/matrix2png/
[9] http://www.panopticon.com/demo_gallery/view-urls.php?id=104
[10] http://scroli.com/#Nasdaq100-Heatmap
[11] http://www.patrick-wied.at/static/heatmapjs/
[12] https://github.com/sunng87/heatcanvas/

Hidden Markov model

A **hidden Markov model** (HMM) is a statistical Markov model in which the system being modeled is assumed to be a Markov process with unobserved (*hidden*) states. An HMM can be considered as the simplest dynamic Bayesian network.

In a regular Markov model, the state is directly visible to the observer, and therefore the state transition probabilities are the only parameters. In a *hidden* Markov model, the state is not directly visible, but output, dependent on the state, is visible. Each state has a probability distribution over the possible output tokens. Therefore the sequence of tokens generated by an HMM gives some information about the sequence of states. Note that the adjective 'hidden' refers to the state sequence through which the model passes, not to the parameters of the model; even if the model parameters are known exactly, the model is still 'hidden'.

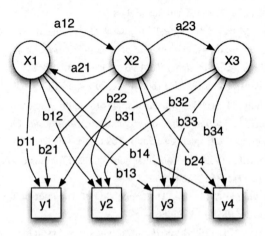

Probabilistic parameters of a hidden Markov model (example)
x — states
y — possible observations
a — state transition probabilities
b — output probabilities

Hidden Markov models are especially known for their application in temporal pattern recognition such as speech, handwriting, gesture recognition, part-of-speech tagging, musical score following, partial discharges and bioinformatics.

A hidden Markov model can be considered a generalization of a mixture model where the hidden variables (or latent variables), which control the mixture component to be selected for each observation, are related through a Markov process rather than independent of each other.

Description in terms of urns

In its discrete form, a hidden Markov process can be visualized as a generalization of the Urn problem. For instance, from Rabiner 1989: A genie is in a room that is not visible to an observer. The genie is drawing balls labeled y1, y2, y3, ... from the urns X1, X2, X3, ... in that room and putting the balls onto a conveyor belt, where the observer can observe the sequence of the balls but not the sequence of urns from which they were drawn. The genie has some procedure to choose urns; the choice of the urn for the *n*-th ball depends upon only a random number and the choice of the urn for the (*n* − 1)-th ball. The choice of urn does not directly depend on the urns further previous, therefore this is called a Markov process. It can be described by the upper part of the diagram at the top of this article.

The Markov process itself cannot be observed, and only the sequence of labeled balls can be observed, thus this arrangement is called a "hidden Markov process". This is illustrated by the lower part of the diagram above, where one can see that balls y1, y2, y3, y4 can be drawn at each state. Even if the observer knows the composition of the urns and has just observed a sequence of three balls, *e.g.* y1, y2 and y3 on the conveyor belt, the observer still cannot be sure which urn (*i.e.*, at which state) the genie has drawn the third ball from. However, the observer can work out other details, such as the identity of the urn the genie is most likely to have drawn the third ball from.

Architecture of a hidden Markov model

The diagram below shows the general architecture of an instantiated HMM. Each oval shape represents a random variable that can adopt any of a number of values. The random variable $x(t)$ is the hidden state at time t (with the model from the above diagram, $x(t) \in \{ x_1, x_2, x_3 \}$). The random variable $y(t)$ is the observation at time t (with $y(t) \in \{ y_1, y_2, y_3, y_4 \}$). The arrows in the diagram (often called a trellis diagram) denote conditional dependencies.

From the diagram, it is clear that the conditional probability distribution of the hidden variable $x(t)$ at time t, given the values of the hidden variable x at all times, depends *only* on the value of the hidden variable $x(t-1)$: the values at time $t-2$ and before have no influence. This is called the Markov property. Similarly, the value of the observed variable $y(t)$ only depends on the value of the hidden variable $x(t)$ (both at time t).

In the standard type of hidden Markov model considered here, the state space of the hidden variables is discrete, while the observations themselves can either be discrete (typically generated from a categorical distribution) or continuous (typically from a Gaussian distribution). The parameters of a hidden Markov model are of two types, *transition probabilities* and *emission probabilities* (also known as *output probabilities*). The transition probabilities control the way the hidden state at time t is chosen given the hidden state at time $t-1$.

The hidden state space is assumed to consist of one of N possible values, modeled as a categorical distribution. (See the section below on extensions for other possibilities.) This means that for each of the N possible states that a hidden variable at time t can be in, there is a transition probability from this state to each of the N possible states of the hidden variable at time $t+1$, for a total of N^2 transition probabilities. (Note, however, that the set of transition probabilities for transitions from any given state must sum to 1, meaning that any one transition probability can be determined once the others are known, leaving a total of $N(N-1)$ transition parameters.)

In addition, for each of the N possible states, there is a set of emission probabilities governing the distribution of the observed variable at a particular time given the state of the hidden variable at that time. The size of this set depends on the nature of the observed variable. For example, if the observed variable is discrete with M possible values, governed by a categorical distribution, there will be $M-1$ separate parameters, for a total of $N(M-1)$ emission parameters over all hidden states. On the other hand, if the observed variable is an M-dimensional vector distributed according to an arbitrary multivariate Gaussian distribution, there will be M parameters controlling the means and $M(M+1)/2$ parameters controlling the covariance matrix, for a total of

$$N(M + \frac{M(M+1)}{2}) = NM(M+3)/2 = O(NM^2)$$ emission parameters. (In such a case, unless the

value of M is small, it may be more practical to restrict the nature of the covariances between individual elements of the observation vector, e.g. by assuming that the elements are independent of each other, or less restrictively, are independent of all but a fixed number of adjacent elements.)

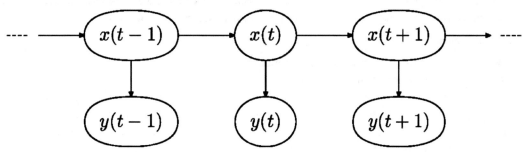

Mathematical description of a hidden Markov model

General description

A basic, non-Bayesian hidden Markov model can be described as follows:

$$
\begin{aligned}
N &= \text{number of states} \\
T &= \text{number of observations} \\
\theta_{i=1...N} &= \text{emission parameter for an observation associated with state } i \\
\phi_{i=1...N, j=1...N} &= \text{probability of transition from state } i \text{ to state } j \\
\phi_{i=1...N} &= N\text{-dimensional vector, composed of } \phi_{i,1...N}; \text{ must sum to 1} \\
x_{t=1...T} &= \text{state of observation at time } t \\
y_{t=1...T} &= \text{observation at time } t \\
F(y|\theta) &= \text{probability distribution of an observation, parametrized on } \theta \\
x_{t=2...T} &\sim \text{Categorical}(\phi_{x_{t-1}}) \\
y_{t=1...T} &\sim F(\theta_{x_t})
\end{aligned}
$$

Note that, in the above model (and also the one below), the prior distribution of the initial state x_1 is not specified. Typical learning models correspond to assuming a discrete uniform distribution over possible states (i.e. no particular prior distribution is assumed).

In a Bayesian setting, all parameters are associated with random variables, as follows:

$$
\begin{aligned}
N, T &= \text{as above} \\
\theta_{i=1...N}, \phi_{i=1...N, j=1...N}, \phi_{i=1...N} &= \text{as above} \\
x_{t=1...T}, y_{t=1...T}, F(y|\theta) &= \text{as above} \\
\alpha &= \text{shared hyperparameter for emission parameters} \\
\beta &= \text{shared hyperparameter for transition parameters} \\
H(\theta|\alpha) &= \text{prior probability distribution of emission parameters, parametrized on } \alpha \\
\theta_{i=1...N} &\sim H(\alpha) \\
\phi_{i=1...N} &\sim \text{Symmetric-Dirichlet}_N(\beta) \\
x_{t=2...T} &\sim \text{Categorical}(\phi_{x_{i-t}}) \\
y_{t=1...T} &\sim F(\theta_{x_t})
\end{aligned}
$$

These characterizations use F and H to describe arbitrary distributions over observations and parameters, respectively. Typically H will be the conjugate prior of F. The two most common choices of F are Gaussian and categorical; see below.

Compared with a simple mixture model

As mentioned above, the distribution of each observation in a hidden Markov model is a mixture density, with the states of the HMM corresponding to mixture components. It is useful to compare the above characterizations for an HMM with the corresponding characterizations, of a mixture model, using the same notation.

A non-Bayesian mixture model:

$$
\begin{aligned}
N &= \text{number of mixture components} \\
T &= \text{number of observations} \\
\theta_{i=1...N} &= \text{parameter of distribution of observation associated with component } i \\
\phi_{i=1...N} &= \text{mixture weight, i.e. prior probability of a particular component } i \\
\phi &= N\text{-dimensional vector composed of all the individual } \phi_{1...N}; \text{ must sum to 1} \\
x_{i=1...T} &= \text{component of observation } i \\
y_{i=1...T} &= \text{observation } i \\
F(y|\theta) &= \text{probability distribution of an observation, parametrized on } \theta \\
x_{i=1...T} &\sim \text{Categorical}(\phi) \\
y_{i=1...T} &\sim F(\theta_{x_i})
\end{aligned}
$$

A Bayesian mixture model:

$$
\begin{array}{lll}
N, T & = & \text{as above} \\
\theta_{i=1...N}, \phi_{i=1...N}, \boldsymbol{\phi} & = & \text{as above} \\
x_{i=1...T}, y_{i=1...T}, F(y|\theta) & = & \text{as above} \\
\alpha & = & \text{shared hyperparameter for component parameters} \\
\beta & = & \text{shared hyperparameter for mixture weights} \\
H(\theta|\alpha) & = & \text{prior probability distribution of component parameters, parametrized on } \alpha \\
\theta_{i=1...N} & \sim & H(\alpha) \\
\boldsymbol{\phi} & \sim & \text{Symmetric-Dirichlet}_N(\beta) \\
x_{i=1...T} & \sim & \text{Categorical}(\boldsymbol{\phi}) \\
y_{i=1...T} & \sim & F(\theta_{x_i})
\end{array}
$$

Examples of HMMs

The following mathematical descriptions are fully written out and explained, for ease of implementation.

A typical non-Bayesian HMM with Gaussian observations looks like this:

$$
\begin{array}{lll}
N & = & \text{number of states} \\
T & = & \text{number of observations} \\
\phi_{i=1...N,j=1...N} & = & \text{probability of transition from state } i \text{ to state } j \\
\boldsymbol{\phi}_{i=1...N} & = & N\text{-dimensional vector, composed of } \phi_{i,1...N}; \text{ must sum to 1} \\
\mu_{i=1...N} & = & \text{mean of observations associated with state } i \\
\sigma^2_{i=1...N} & = & \text{variance of observations associated with state } i \\
x_{t=1...T} & = & \text{state of observation at time } t \\
y_{t=1...T} & = & \text{observation at time } t \\
x_{t=2...T} & \sim & \text{Categorical}(\boldsymbol{\phi}_{x_{t-1}}) \\
y_{t=1...T} & \sim & \mathcal{N}(\mu_{x_t}, \sigma^2_{x_t})
\end{array}
$$

A typical Bayesian HMM with Gaussian observations looks like this:

$$
\begin{array}{lll}
N & = & \text{number of states} \\
T & = & \text{number of observations} \\
\phi_{i=1...N,j=1...N} & = & \text{probability of transition from state } i \text{ to state } j \\
\boldsymbol{\phi}_{i=1...N} & = & N\text{-dimensional vector, composed of } \phi_{i,1...N}; \text{ must sum to 1} \\
\mu_{i=1...N} & = & \text{mean of observations associated with state } i \\
\sigma^2_{i=1...N} & = & \text{variance of observations associated with state } i \\
x_{t=1...T} & = & \text{state of observation at time } t \\
y_{t=1...T} & = & \text{observation at time } t \\
\beta & = & \text{concentration hyperparameter controlling the density of the transition matrix} \\
\mu_0, \lambda & = & \text{shared hyperparameters of the means for each state} \\
\nu, \sigma^2_0 & = & \text{shared hyperparameters of the variances for each state} \\
\boldsymbol{\phi}_{i=1...N} & \sim & \text{Symmetric-Dirichlet}_N(\beta) \\
x_{t=2...T} & \sim & \text{Categorical}(\boldsymbol{\phi}_{x_{t-1}}) \\
\mu_{i=1...N} & \sim & \mathcal{N}(\mu_0, \lambda\sigma^2_i) \\
\sigma^2_{i=1...N} & \sim & \text{Inverse-Gamma}(\nu, \sigma^2_0) \\
y_{t=1...T} & \sim & \mathcal{N}(\mu_{x_t}, \sigma^2_{x_t})
\end{array}
$$

A typical non-Bayesian HMM with categorical observations looks like this:

$$
\begin{aligned}
N &= \text{number of states} \\
T &= \text{number of observations} \\
\phi_{i=1\ldots N, j=1\ldots N} &= \text{probability of transition from state } i \text{ to state } j \\
\boldsymbol{\phi}_{i=1\ldots N} &= N\text{-dimensional vector, composed of } \phi_{i,1\ldots N}; \text{ must sum to 1} \\
V &= \text{dimension of categorical observations, e.g. size of word vocabulary} \\
\theta_{i=1\ldots N, j=1\ldots V} &= \text{probability for state } i \text{ of observing the } j\text{th item} \\
\boldsymbol{\theta}_{i=1\ldots N} &= V\text{-dimensional vector, composed of } \theta_{i,1\ldots V}; \text{ must sum to 1} \\
x_{t=1\ldots T} &= \text{state of observation at time } t \\
y_{t=1\ldots T} &= \text{observation at time } t \\
x_{t=2\ldots T} &\sim \text{Categorical}(\boldsymbol{\phi}_{x_{t-1}}) \\
y_{t=1\ldots T} &\sim \text{Categorical}(\boldsymbol{\theta}_{x_t})
\end{aligned}
$$

A typical Bayesian HMM with categorical observations looks like this:

$$
\begin{aligned}
N &= \text{number of states} \\
T &= \text{number of observations} \\
\phi_{i=1\ldots N, j=1\ldots N} &= \text{probability of transition from state } i \text{ to state } j \\
\boldsymbol{\phi}_{i=1\ldots N} &= N\text{-dimensional vector, composed of } \phi_{i,1\ldots N}; \text{ must sum to 1} \\
V &= \text{dimension of categorical observations, e.g. size of word vocabulary} \\
\theta_{i=1\ldots N, j=1\ldots V} &= \text{probability for state } i \text{ of observing the } j\text{th item} \\
\boldsymbol{\theta}_{i=1\ldots N} &= V\text{-dimensional vector, composed of } \theta_{i,1\ldots V}; \text{ must sum to 1} \\
x_{t=1\ldots T} &= \text{state of observation at time } t \\
y_{t=1\ldots T} &= \text{observation at time } t \\
\alpha &= \text{shared concentration hyperparameter of } \boldsymbol{\theta} \text{ for each state} \\
\beta &= \text{concentration hyperparameter controlling the density of the transition matrix} \\
\boldsymbol{\phi}_{i=1\ldots N} &\sim \text{Symmetric-Dirichlet}_N(\beta) \\
\boldsymbol{\theta}_{1\ldots V} &\sim \text{Symmetric-Dirichlet}_V(\alpha) \\
x_{t=2\ldots T} &\sim \text{Categorical}(\boldsymbol{\phi}_{x_{t-1}}) \\
y_{t=1\ldots T} &\sim \text{Categorical}(\boldsymbol{\theta}_{x_t})
\end{aligned}
$$

Note that in the above Bayesian characterizations, β (a concentration parameter) controls the density of the transition matrix. That is, with a high value of β (significantly above 1), the probabilities controlling the transition out of a particular state will all be similar, meaning there will be a significantly probability of transitioning to any of the other states. In other words, the path followed by the Markov chain of hidden states will be highly random. With a low value of β (significantly below 1), only a small number of the possible transitions out of a given state will have significant probability, meaning that the path followed by the hidden states will be somewhat predictable.

A two-level Bayesian HMM

An alternative for the above two Bayesian examples would be to add another level of prior parameters for the transition matrix. That is, replace the lines

$$
\begin{aligned}
\beta &= \text{concentration hyperparameter controlling the density of the transition matrix} \\
\boldsymbol{\phi}_{i=1\ldots N} &\sim \text{Symmetric-Dirichlet}_N(\beta)
\end{aligned}
$$

with the following:

$$
\begin{aligned}
\gamma &= \text{concentration hyperparameter controlling how many states are intrinsically likely} \\
\beta &= \text{concentration hyperparameter controlling the density of the transition matrix} \\
\boldsymbol{\eta} &= N\text{-dimensional vector of probabilities, specifying the intrinsic probability of a given state} \\
\boldsymbol{\eta} &\sim \text{Symmetric-Dirichlet}_N(\gamma) \\
\boldsymbol{\phi}_{i=1\ldots N} &\sim \text{Dirichlet}_N(\beta N \boldsymbol{\eta})
\end{aligned}
$$

What this means is the following:

1. $\boldsymbol{\eta}$ is a probability distribution over states, specifying which states are inherently likely. The greater the probability of a given state in this vector, the more likely is a transition to that state (regardless of the starting state).

2. γ controls the density of η. Values significantly above 1 cause a dense vector where all states will have similar prior probabilities. Values significantly below 1 cause a sparse vector where only a few states are inherently likely (have prior probabilities significantly above 0).

3. β controls the density of the transition matrix, or more specifically, the density of the N different probability vectors $\phi_{i=1...N}$ specifying the probability of transitions out of state i to any other state.

Imagine that the value of β is significantly above 1. Then the different ϕ vectors will be dense, i.e. the probability mass will be spread out fairly evenly over all states. However, to the extent that this mass is unevenly spread, η controls which states are likely to get more mass than others.

Now, imagine instead that β is significantly below 1. This willl make the ϕ vectors sparse, i.e. almost all the probability mass is distributed over a small number of states, and for the rest, a transition to that state will be very unlikely. Notice that there are different ϕ vectors for each starting state, and so even if all the vectors are sparse, different vectors may distribute the mass to different ending states. However, for all of the vectors, η controls which ending states are likely to get mass assigned to them. For example, if β is 0.1, then each ϕ will be sparse and, for any given starting state i, the set of states $\mathbf{J}_i$ to which transitions are likely to occur will be very small, typically having only one or two members. Now, if the probabilities in η are all the same (or equivalently, one of the above models without η is used), then for different i, there will be different states in the corresponding $\mathbf{J}_i$, so that all states are equally likely to occur in any given $\mathbf{J}_i$. On the other hand, if the values in η are unbalanced, so that one state has a much higher probability than others, almost all $\mathbf{J}_i$ will contain this state; hence, regardless of the starting state, transitions will nearly always occur to this given state.

Hence, a two-level model such as just described allows independent control over (1) the overall density of the transition matrix, and (2) the density of states to which transitions are likely (i.e. the density of the prior distribution of states in any particular hidden variable x_i). In both cases this is done while still assuming ignorance over which particular states are more likely than others. If it is desired to inject this information into the model, the probability vector η can be directly specified; or, if there is less certainty about these relative probabilities, a non-symmetric Dirichlet distribution can be used as the prior distribution over η. That is, instead of using a symmetric Dirichlet distribution with a single parameter γ (or equivalently, a general Dirichlet with a vector all of whose values are equal to γ), use a general Dirichlet with values that are variously greater or less than γ, according to which state is more or less preferred.

Learning

The parameter learning task in HMMs is to find, given an output sequence or a set of such sequences, the best set of state transition and output probabilities. The task is usually to derive the maximum likelihood estimate of the parameters of the HMM given the set of output sequences. No tractable algorithm is known for solving this problem exactly, but a local maximum likelihood can be derived efficiently using the Baum–Welch algorithm or the Baldi–Chauvin algorithm. The Baum–Welch algorithm is an example of a forward-backward algorithm, and is a special case of the expectation-maximization algorithm.

Inference

Several inference problems are associated with hidden Markov models, as outlined below.

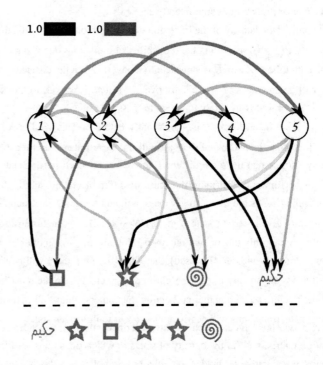

The state transition and output probabilities of an HMM are indicated by the line opacity in the upper part of the diagram. Given that we have observed the output sequence in the lower part of the diagram, we may be interested in the most likely sequence of states that could have produced it. Based on the arrows that are present in the diagram, the following state sequences are candidates: 5 3 2 5 3 2 4 3 2 5 3 2 3 1 2 5 3 2 We can find the most likely sequence by evaluating the joint probability of both the state sequence and the observations for each case (simply by multiplying the probability values, which here correspond to the opacities of the arrows involved). In general, this type of problem (i.e. finding the most likely explanation for an observation sequence) can be solved efficiently using the Viterbi algorithm.

Filtering

The task is to compute, given the model's parameters and a sequence of observations, the distribution over hidden states at the end of the sequence, i.e. to compute $P(x(t) \mid y(1), \ldots, y(t))$. This problem can be handled efficiently using the forward algorithm.

Probability of an observed sequence

The task is to compute, given the parameters of the model, the probability of a particular output sequence. This requires summation over all possible state sequences:

The probability of observing a sequence

$$Y = y(0), y(1), \ldots, y(L-1)$$

of length L is given by

$$P(Y) = \sum_{X} P(Y \mid X) P(X),$$

where the sum runs over all possible hidden-node sequences

$$X = x(0), x(1), \ldots, x(L-1).$$

Applying the principle of dynamic programming, this problem, too, can be handled efficiently using the forward algorithm.

Most likely explanation

The task is to compute, given the parameters of the model and a particular output sequence, the state sequence that is most likely to have generated that output sequence (see illustration on the right). This requires finding a maximum over all possible state sequences, but can similarly be solved efficiently by the Viterbi algorithm.

Smoothing

The task is to compute, given the parameters of the model and a particular output sequence up to time t, the probability distribution over hidden states for a point in time in the past, i.e. to compute $P(x(k) \mid y(1), \ldots, y(t))$ for some $k < t$. The forward-backward algorithm is an efficient method for computing the smoothed values for all hidden state variables.

Statistical significance

For some of the above problems, it may also be interesting to ask about statistical significance. What is the probability that a sequence drawn from some null distribution will have an HMM probability (in the case of the forward algorithm) or a maximum state sequence probability (in the case of the Viterbi algorithm) at least as large as that of a particular output sequence?[1] When an HMM is used to evaluate the relevance of a hypothesis for a particular output sequence, the statistical significance indicates the false positive rate associated with accepting the hypothesis for the output sequence.

A concrete example

Consider two friends, Alice and Bob, who live far apart from each other and who talk together daily over the telephone about what they did that day. Bob is only interested in three activities: walking in the park, shopping, and cleaning his apartment. The choice of what to do is determined exclusively by the weather on a given day. Alice has no definite information about the weather where Bob lives, but she knows general trends. Based on what Bob tells her he did each day, Alice tries to guess what the weather must have been like.

Alice believes that the weather operates as a discrete Markov chain. There are two states, "Rainy" and "Sunny", but she cannot observe them directly, that is, they are *hidden* from her. On each day, there is a certain chance that Bob will perform one of the following activities, depending on the weather: "walk", "shop", or "clean". Since Bob tells Alice about his activities, those are the *observations*. The entire system is that of a hidden Markov model (HMM).

Alice knows the general weather trends in the area, and what Bob likes to do on average. In other words, the parameters of the HMM are known. They can be represented as follows in the Python programming language:

```python
states = ('Rainy', 'Sunny')

observations = ('walk', 'shop', 'clean')

start_probability = {'Rainy': 0.6, 'Sunny': 0.4}

transition_probability = {
    'Rainy' : {'Rainy': 0.7, 'Sunny': 0.3},
    'Sunny' : {'Rainy': 0.4, 'Sunny': 0.6},
```

```
    }

emission_probability = {
    'Rainy' : {'walk': 0.1, 'shop': 0.4, 'clean': 0.5},
    'Sunny' : {'walk': 0.6, 'shop': 0.3, 'clean': 0.1},
    }
```

In this piece of code, `start_probability` represents Alice's belief about which state the HMM is in when Bob first calls her (all she knows is that it tends to be rainy on average). The particular probability distribution used here is not the equilibrium one, which is (given the transition probabilities) approximately {`'Rainy'`: 0.57, `'Sunny'`: 0.43}. The `transition_probability` represents the change of the weather in the underlying Markov chain. In this example, there is only a 30% chance that tomorrow will be sunny if today is rainy. The `emission_probability` represents how likely Bob is to perform a certain activity on each day. If it is rainy, there is a 50% chance that he is cleaning his apartment; if it is sunny, there is a 60% chance that he is outside for a walk.

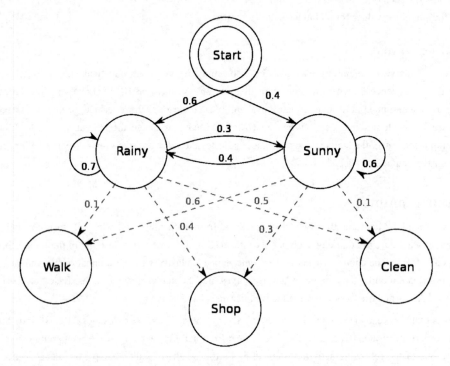

This example is further elaborated in the Viterbi algorithm page.

Applications of hidden Markov models

HMMs can be applied in many fields where the goal is to recover a data sequence that is not immediately observable (but other data that depends on the sequence is). Common applications include:

- Cryptanalysis
- Speech recognition
- Speech synthesis
- Part-of-speech tagging
- Machine translation
- Partial discharge
- Gene prediction

- Alignment of bio-sequences
- Activity recognition
- Protein folding
- Metamorphic Virus Detection[2]

History

Hidden Markov Models were first described in a series of statistical papers by Leonard E. Baum and other authors in the second half of the 1960s. One of the first applications of HMMs was speech recognition, starting in the mid-1970s.[3] [4]

In the second half of the 1980s, HMMs began to be applied to the analysis of biological sequences,[5] in particular DNA. Since then, they have become ubiquitous in the field of bioinformatics.[6]

Types of hidden Markov models

Hidden Markov models can model complex Markov processes where the states emit the observations according to some probability distribution. One such example of distribution is Gaussian distribution, in such a Hidden Markov Model the states output is represented by a Gaussian distribution.

Moreover it could represent even more complex behavior when the output of the states is represented as mixture of two or more Gaussians, in which case the probability of generating an observation is the product of the probability of first selecting one of the Gaussians and the probability of generating that observation from that Gaussian.

Extensions

In the hidden Markov models considered above, the state space of the hidden variables is discrete, while the observations themselves can either be discrete (typically generated from a categorical distribution) or continuous (typically from a Gaussian distribution). Hidden Markov models can also be generalized to allow continuous state spaces. Examples of such models are those where the Markov process over hidden variables is a linear dynamical system, with a linear relationship among related variables and where all hidden and observed variables follow a Gaussian distribution. In simple cases, such as the linear dynamical system just, exact inference is tractable (in this case, using the Kalman filter); however, in general, exact inference in HMMs with continuous latent variables is infeasible, and approximate methods must be used, such as the extended Kalman filter or the particle filter.

Hidden Markov models are generative models, in which the joint distribution of observations and hidden states, or equivalently both the prior distribution of hidden states (the *transition probabilities*) and conditional distribution of observations given states (the *emission probabilities*), is modeled. The above algorithms implicitly assume a uniform prior distribution over the transition probabilities. However, it is also possible to create hidden Markov models with other types of prior distributions. An obvious candidate, given the categorical distribution of the transition probabilities, is the Dirichlet distribution, which is the conjugate prior distribution of the categorical distribution. Typically, a symmetric Dirichlet distribution is chosen, reflecting ignorance about which states are inherently more likely than others. The single parameter of this distribution (termed the *concentration parameter*) controls the relative density or sparseness of the resulting transition matrix. A choice of 1 yields a uniform distribution. Values greater than 1 produce a dense matrix, in which the transition probabilities between pairs of states are likely to be nearly equal. Values less than 1 result in a sparse matrix in which, for each given source state, only a small number of destination states have non-negligible transition probabilities. It is also possible to use a two-level prior Dirichlet distribution, in which one Dirichlet distribution (the upper distribution) governs the parameters of another Dirichlet distribution (the lower distribution), which in turn governs the transition probabilities. The upper distribution governs the overall distribution of states, determining how likely each state is to occur; its concentration parameter determines the density or sparseness of states. Such a two-level prior distribution, where both concentration parameters are set to produce sparse distributions, might be useful for example in unsupervised part-of-speech tagging, where some parts of speech occur much more commonly than others; learning algorithms that assume a uniform prior distribution generally perform poorly on this task. The parameters of models of this sort, with non-uniform prior distributions, can be learned using Gibbs sampling or extended versions of the expectation-maximization algorithm.

An extension of the previously-described hidden Markov models with Dirichlet priors uses a Dirichlet process in place of a Dirichlet distribution. This type of model allows for an unknown and potentially infinite number of states. It is common to use a two-level Dirichlet process, similar to the previously-described model with two levels of Dirichlet distributions. Such a model is called a *hierarchical Dirichlet process hidden Markov model*, or *HDP-HMM* for short.

A different type of extension uses a discriminative model in place of the generative model of standard HMM's. This type of model directly models the conditional distribution of the hidden states given the observations, rather than modeling the joint distribution. An example of this model is the so-called *maximum entropy Markov model* (MEMM), which models the conditional distribution of the states using logistic regression (also known as a "maximum entropy model"). The advantage of this type of model is that arbitrary features (i.e. functions) of the observations can be modeled, allowing domain-specific knowledge of the problem at hand to be injected into the model. Models of this sort are not limited to modeling direct dependencies between a hidden state and its associated observation; rather, features of nearby observations, of combinations of the associated observation and nearby observations, or in fact of arbitrary observations at any distance from a given hidden state can be included in the process used to determine the value of a hidden state. Furthermore, there is no need for these features to be statistically independent of each other, as would be the case if such features were used in a generative model. Finally, arbitrary features over pairs of adjacent hidden states can be used rather than simple transition probabilities. The disadvantages of such models are: (1) The types of prior distributions that can be placed on hidden states are severely limited; (2) It is not possible to predict the probability of seeing an arbitrary observation. This second limitation is often not an issue in practice, since many common usages of HMM's do not require such predictive probabilities.

A variant of the previously described discriminative model is the linear-chain conditional random field. This uses an undirected graphical model (aka Markov random field) rather than the directed graphical models of MEMM's and similar models. The advantage of this type of model is that it does not suffer from the so-called *label bias* problem of MEMM's, and thus may make more accurate predictions. The disadvantage is that training can be slower than for MEMM's.

Yet another variant is the *factorial hidden Markov model*, which allows for a single observation to be conditioned on the corresponding hidden variables of a set of K independent Markov chains, rather than a single Markov chain. Learning in such a model is difficult, as dynamic-programming techniques can no longer be used to find an exact solution ; in practice, approximate techniques must be used.[7]

All of the above models can be extended to allow for more distant dependencies among hidden states, e.g. allowing for a given state to be dependent on the previous two or three states rather than a single previous state; i.e. the transition probabilities are extended to encompass sets of three or four adjacent states (or in general K adjacent states). The disadvantage of such models is that dynamic-programming algorithms for training them have an $O(N^K T)$ running time, for K adjacent states and T total observations (i.e. a length- T Markov chain).

Notes

[1] Newberg (2009)

[2] Wong, Wing; Stamp, Mark (2006). "Hunting for Metamorphic Engines". Journal in Computer Virology , vol. 2, no. 3, pp. 211-229, 2006. doi:10.1007/s11416-006-0028-7

[3] Baker

[4] Jelinek

[5] Bishop and Thompson

[6] Durbin et al.

[7] Ghahramani, Zoubin; Jordan, Michael I. (1997). "Factorial Hidden Markov Models". Machine Learning 29 (2/3): 245–273. doi:10.1023/A:1007425814087.

References

- James K. Baker (1975). "The DRAGON System -- An Overview". *IEEE Transactions on Acoustics Speech and Signal Processing* **23** (1): 24–29. doi:10.1109/TASSP.1975.1162650.

- Frederick Jelinek, Lalit Bahl, Robert Mercer (1975). *IEEE Transactions on Information Theory* **21**.

- Lawrence R. Rabiner (February 1989). "A tutorial on Hidden Markov Models and selected applications in speech recognition" (http://www.ece.ucsb.edu/Faculty/Rabiner/ece259/Reprints/tutorial on hmm and applications. pdf). *Proceedings of the IEEE* **77** (2): 257–286. doi:10.1109/5.18626. (http://www.cs.cornell.edu/courses/ cs481/2004fa/rabiner.pdf)

- Press, WH; Teukolsky, SA; Vetterling, WT; Flannery, BP (2007). "Section 16.3. Markov Models and HIdden Markov Modeling" (http://apps.nrbook.com/empanel/index.html#pg=856). *Numerical Recipes: The Art of Scientific Computing* (3rd ed.). New York: Cambridge University Press. ISBN 978-0-521-88068-8.

- Xuedong Huang, M. Jack, and Y. Ariki (1990). *Hidden Markov Models for Speech Recognition*. Edinburgh University Press. ISBN 0748601627.

- Richard Durbin, Sean R. Eddy, Anders Krogh, Graeme Mitchison (1999). *Biological Sequence Analysis: Probabilistic Models of Proteins and Nucleic Acids*. Cambridge University Press. ISBN 0-521-62971-3.

- M. Bishop and E. Thompson (1986). "Maximum Likelihood Alignment of DNA Sequences". *Journal of Molecular Biology* **190** (2): 159–165. doi:10.1016/0022-2836(86)90289-5. PMID 3641921.

- Xuedong Huang, Alex Acero, and Hsiao-Wuen Hon (2001). *Spoken Language Processing*. Prentice Hall. ISBN 0-13-022616-5.

- Lior Pachter and Bernd Sturmfels (2005). *Algebraic Statistics for Computational Biology*. Cambridge University Press. ISBN 0-521-85700-7.

- Olivier Cappé, Eric Moulines, Tobias Rydén (2005). *Inference in Hidden Markov Models*. Springer. ISBN 0-387-40264-0.

- Kristie Seymore, Andrew McCallum, and Roni Rosenfeld. *Learning Hidden Markov Model Structure for Information Extraction*. AAAI 99 Workshop on Machine Learning for Information Extraction, 1999 *(also at CiteSeer:* (http://citeseer.ist.psu.edu/seymore99learning.html)*).*

- Li J, Najmi A, Gray RM (February 2000). "Image classification by a two dimensional hidden Markov model" (http://www.stat.psu.edu/~jiali). *IEEE Transactions on Signal Processing* **48** (2): 517–533. doi:10.1109/78.823977.

- Ephraim Y, Merhav N (June 2002). "Hidden Markov processes". *IEEE Trans. Inform. Theory* **48** (6): 1518–1569. doi:10.1109/TIT.2002.1003838.

- Newberg LA (July 2009). "Error statistics of hidden Markov model and hidden Boltzmann model results" (http:// www.biomedcentral.com/1471-2105/10/212). *BMC Bioinformatics* **10**: article 212. doi:10.1186/1471-2105-10-212. PMC 2722652. PMID 19589158.

- B. Pardo and W. Birmingham. Modeling Form for On-line Following of Musical Performances (http://www.cs. northwestern.edu/~pardo/publications/pardo-birmingham-aaai-05.pdf). AAAI-05 Proc., July 2005.

- Thad Starner, Alex Pentland. Visual Recognition of American Sign Language Using Hidden Markov (http://citeseer.ist.psu.edu/starner95visual.html). Master's Thesis, MIT, Feb 1995, Program in Media Arts
- Satish L, Gururaj BI (April 2003). " Use of hidden Markov models for partial discharge pattern classification (http://ieeexplore.ieee.org/xpl/freeabs_all.jsp?arnumber=212242)". *IEEE Transactions on Dielectrics and Electrical Insulation.*

The path-counting algorithm, an alternative to the Baum–Welch algorithm:

- Davis RIA, Lovell BC (2000). "Comparing and evaluating HMM ensemble training algorithms using train and test and condition number criteria" (http://citeseer.ist.psu.edu/677948.html). *Journal of Pattern Analysis and Applications* **0** (0): 1–7.

External links

- HMMdotEM (http://www.cs.toronto.edu/~karamano/Code/HMMdotEM.html) General Discrete-State HMM Toolbox (released under 3-clause BSD-like License, *Currently only Matlab*)
- Hidden Markov Model (HMM) Toolbox for Matlab (http://www.cs.ubc.ca/~murphyk/Software/HMM/hmm.html) *(by Kevin Murphy)*
- Hidden Markov Model Toolkit (HTK) (http://htk.eng.cam.ac.uk/) *(a portable toolkit for building and manipulating hidden Markov models)*
- Hidden Markov Model R-Package (http://cran.r-project.org/web/packages/HMM/index.html) to setup, apply and make inference with discrete time and discrete space Hidden Markov Models
- Hidden Markov Models (http://www.cs.brown.edu/research/ai/dynamics/tutorial/Documents/HiddenMarkovModels.html) *(an exposition using basic mathematics)*
- GHMM Library (http://www.ghmm.org) *(home page of the GHMM Library project)*
- CL-HMM Library (http://code.google.com/p/cl-hmm/) *(HMM Library for Common Lisp)*
- Jahmm Java Library (http://jahmm.googlecode.com/) *(general-purpose Java library)*
- A step-by-step tutorial on HMMs (http://www.comp.leeds.ac.uk/roger/HiddenMarkovModels/html_dev/main.html) *(University of Leeds)*
- Hidden Markov Models (http://jedlik.phy.bme.hu/~gerjanos/HMM/node2.html) *(by Narada Warakagoda)*
- HMM and other statistical programs (http://www.kanungo.com/software/software.html) *(Implementation in C by Tapas Kanungo)*
- The hmm package (http://hackage.haskell.org/cgi-bin/hackage-scripts/package/hmm) A Haskell (http://www.haskell.org) library for working with Hidden Markov Models.
- GT2K (http://gt2k.cc.gatech.edu/) Georgia Tech Gesture Toolkit (referred to as GT2K)
- Forward algorithm (http://www.comp.leeds.ac.uk/roger/HiddenMarkovModels/html_dev/forward_algorithm/s1_pg7.html)
- Switching Autoregressive Hidden Markov Model (SAR HMM) (http://www.tristanfletcher.co.uk/SAR HMM.pdf)
- Hidden Markov Models -online calculator for HMM - Viterbi path and probabilities. Examples with perl source code. (http://www.lwebzem.com/cgi-bin/courses/hidden_markov_model_online.cgi)

HMMER

HMMER

Developer(s)	Sean Eddy
Stable release	3.0 / 28 March 2010
Written in	C
Available in	English
Type	Bioinformatics tool
License	GPL
Website	hmmer.janelia.org [1]

HMMER is a free and commonly used software package for sequence analysis written by Sean Eddy.[2] Its general usage is to identify homologous protein or nucleotide sequences. It does this by comparing a profile-HMM to either a single sequence or a database of sequences. Sequences that score significantly better to the profile-HMM compared to a null model are considered to be homologous to the sequences that were used to construct the profile-HMM. Profile-HMMs are constructed from a multiple sequence alignment in the HMMER package using the *hmmbuild* program. The profile-HMM implementation used in the HMMER software was based on the work of Krogh and colleagues.[3] HMMER is a console utility ported to every major operating system, including different versions of Linux, Windows, and Mac OS.

HMMER is the core utility that protein family databases such as Pfam and InterPro are based upon. Some other bioinformatics tools such as UGENE also use HMMER.

HMMER3 is complete rewrite of the earlier HMMER2 package, with the aim of improving the speed of profile-HMM searches. The main performance gain is due to a heuristic filter that finds high-scoring un-gapped matches within database sequences to a query profile. This heuristic results in a computation time comparable to BLAST with little impact on accuracy. Further gains in performance are due to a log-likelihood model that requires no calibration for estimating E-values, and allows the more accurate forward scores to be used for computing the significance of a homologous sequence.[4]

HMMER3 also makes extensive use of vector instructions for increasing computational speed. This work is based upon earlier publication showing a significant acceleration of the Smith-Waterman algorithm for aligning two sequences.[5]

References

[1] http://hmmer.janelia.org/

[2] Durbin, Richard; Sean R. Eddy, Anders Krogh, Graeme Mitchison (1998). *Biological Sequence Analysis: Probabilistic Models of Proteins and Nucleic Acids*. Cambridge University Press. ISBN 0-521-62971-3.

[3] Krogh A, Brown M, Mian IS, Sjölander K, Haussler D (February 1994). "Hidden Markov models in computational biology. Applications to protein modeling". *J. Mol. Biol.* **235** (5): 1501–31. doi:10.1006/jmbi.1994.1104. PMID 8107089.

[4] Eddy SR; Rost, Burkhard (2008). Rost, Burkhard. ed. "A probabilistic model of local sequence alignment that simplifies statistical significance estimation". *PLoS Comput Biol* **4** (5): e1000069. doi:10.1371/journal.pcbi.1000069. PMC 2396288. PMID 18516236.

[5] Farrar M (January 2007). "Striped Smith-Waterman speeds database searches six times over other SIMD implementations". *Bioinformatics* **23** (2): 156–61. doi:10.1093/bioinformatics/btl582. PMID 17110365.

External links

- HMMER homepage (http://hmmer.org/)
- HMMER3 announcement (http://selab.janelia.org/people/eddys/blog/?p=6)
- A blog posting on HMMER policy on trademark, copyright, patents, and licensing (http://selab.janelia.org/people/eddys/blog/?p=127)

HomoloGene

HomoloGene, a tool of the National Center for Biotechnology Information (NCBI), is a system for automated detection of homologs (similarity attributable to descent from a common ancestor) among the annotated genes of several completely sequenced eukaryotic genomes.

The HomoloGene processing consists of the protein analysis from the input organisms. Sequences are compared using blastp[1], then matched up and put into groups, using a taxonomic tree built from sequence similarity, where closer related organisms are matched up first, and then further organisms are added to the tree. The protein alignments are mapped back to their corresponding DNA sequences, and then distance metrics as molecular distances Jukes and Cantor (1969), Ka/Ks ratio can be calculated.

The sequences are matched up by using a heuristic algorithm for maximizing the score globally, rather than locally, in a bipartite matching (see complete bipartite graph). And then it calculates the statistical significance of each match. Cutoffs are made per position and Ks values are set to prevent false "orthologs" from being grouped together. "Paralogs" are identified by finding sequences that are closer within species than other species.

Input organisms

Homo sapiens, Pan troglodytes, Canis lupus familiaris, Bos taurus, Mus musculus, Danio rerio, Rattus norvegicus, Arabidopsis thaliana, Gallus gallus, Oryza sativa, Anopheles gambiae, Drosophila melanogaster, Magnaporthe grisea, Neurospora crassa, Caenorhabditis elegans, Saccharomyces cerevisiae, Kluyveromyces lactis, Eremothecium gossypii, Schizosaccharomyces pombe and *Plasmodium falciparum.*

Interface

The HomoloGene is linked to all Entrez databases and based on homology and phenotype information of these links:

- Mouse Genome Informatics (MGI),
- Zebrafish Information Network (ZFIN),
- Saccharomyces Genome Database (SGD),
- Clusters of Orthologous Groups (COG),
- FlyBase,
- Online Mendelian Inheritance in Man (OMIM)

As a result HomoloGene displays information about Genes, Proteins, Phenotypes, and Conserved Domains.

External links

- HomoloGene [2] at the National Center for Biotechnology Information
- Bioinformatic Harvester [3] - Bioinformatic Harvester, a meta search engine that uses Homologene
- OMIM [9]
- ZFIN [4]
- SGD [25]
- COG [5]
- FlyBase [10]
- MGI [19]
- Rat Genome Database [6]

References

[1] http://www.ncbi.nlm.nih.gov/BLAST/Blast.cgi?CMD=Web&LAYOUT=TwoWindows&AUTO_FORMAT=Semiauto&
     ALIGNMENTS=250&ALIGNMENT_VIEW=Pairwise&CDD_SEARCH=on&CLIENT=web&DATABASE=nr&
     DESCRIPTIONS=500&ENTREZ_QUERY=%28none%29&EXPECT=10&FILTER=L&FORMAT_OBJECT=Alignment&
     FORMAT_TYPE=HTML&I_THRESH=0.005&MATRIX_NAME=BLOSUM62&NCBI_GI=on&PAGE=Proteins&
     PROGRAM=blastp&SERVICE=plain&SET_DEFAULTS.x=41&SET_DEFAULTS.y=5&SHOW_OVERVIEW=on&
     END_OF_HTTPGET=Yes&SHOW_LINKOUT=yes&GET_SEQUENCE=yeslblastp
[2] http://www.ncbi.nlm.nih.gov/sites/entrez?db=homologene
[3] http://harvester.embl.de/
[4] http://zfin.org/cgi-bin/webdriver?MIval=aa-ZDB_home.apg
[5] http://www.ncbi.nlm.nih.gov/COG/
[6] http://rgd.mcw.edu/

Homology modeling

Homology modeling, also known as **comparative modeling** of protein refers to constructing an atomic-resolution model of the "*target*" protein from its amino acid sequence and an experimental three-dimensional structure of a related homologous protein (the "*template*"). Homology modeling relies on the identification of one or more known protein structures likely to resemble the structure of the query sequence, and on the production of an alignment that maps residues in the query sequence to residues in the template sequence. It has been shown that protein structures are more conserved than protein sequences amongst homologues, but sequences falling below a 20% sequence identity can have very different structure.[1]

Evolutionarily related proteins have similar sequences and naturally occurring homologous proteins have similar protein structure. It has been shown that three-dimensional protein structure is evolutionarily more conserved than expected due to sequence conservation. [2]

The sequence alignment and template structure are then used to produce a structural model of the target. Because protein structures are more conserved than DNA sequences, detectable levels of sequence similarity usually imply significant structural similarity.[3]

The quality of the homology model is dependent on the quality of the sequence alignment and template structure. The approach can be complicated by the presence of alignment gaps (commonly called indels) that indicate a structural region present in the target but not in the template, and by structure gaps in the template that arise from poor resolution in the experimental procedure (usually X-ray crystallography) used to solve the structure. Model quality declines with decreasing sequence identity; a typical model has ~1–2 Å root mean square deviation between the matched C^α atoms at 70% sequence identity but only 2–4 Å agreement at 25% sequence identity. However, the errors are significantly higher in the loop regions, where the amino acid sequences of the target and template proteins may be completely different.

Regions of the model that were constructed without a template, usually by loop modeling, are generally much less accurate than the rest of the model. Errors in side chain packing and position also increase with decreasing identity, and variations in these packing configurations have been suggested as a major reason for poor model quality at low identity.[4] Taken together, these various atomic-position errors are significant and impede the use of homology models for purposes that require atomic-resolution data, such as drug design and protein–protein interaction predictions; even the quaternary structure of a protein may be difficult to predict from homology models of its subunit(s). Nevertheless, homology models can be useful in reaching *qualitative* conclusions about the biochemistry of the query sequence, especially in formulating hypotheses about why certain residues are conserved, which may in turn lead to experiments to test those hypotheses. For example, the spatial arrangement of conserved residues may suggest whether a particular residue is conserved to stabilize the folding, to participate in binding some small molecule, or to foster association with another protein or nucleic acid.

Homology modeling can produce high-quality structural models when the target and template are closely related, which has inspired the formation of a structural genomics consortium dedicated to the production of representative experimental structures for all classes of protein folds.[5] The chief inaccuracies in homology modeling, which worsen with lower sequence identity, derive from errors in the initial sequence alignment and from improper template selection.[6] Like other methods of structure prediction, current practice in homology modeling is assessed in a biannual large-scale experiment known as the Critical Assessment of Techniques for Protein Structure Prediction, or CASP.

Motive

The method of homology modeling is based on the observation that protein tertiary structure is better conserved than amino acid sequence.[3] Thus, even proteins that have diverged appreciably in sequence but still share detectable similarity will also share common structural properties, particularly the overall fold. Because it is difficult and time-consuming to obtain experimental structures from methods such as X-ray crystallography and protein NMR for every protein of interest, homology modeling can provide useful structural models for generating hypotheses about a protein's function and directing further experimental work.

There are exceptions to the general rule that proteins sharing significant sequence identity will share a fold. For example, a judiciously chosen set of mutations of less than 50% of a protein can cause the protein to adopt a completely different fold.[7] [8] However, such a massive structural rearrangement is unlikely to occur in evolution, especially since the protein is usually under the constraint that it must fold properly and carry out its function in the cell. Consequently, the roughly folded structure of a protein (its "topology") is conserved longer than its amino-acid sequence and much longer than the corresponding DNA sequence; in other words, two proteins may share a similar fold even if their evolutionary relationship is so distant that it cannot be discerned reliably. For comparison, the function of a protein is conserved much *less* than the protein sequence, since relatively few changes in amino-acid sequence are required to take on a related function.

Steps in model production

The homology modeling procedure can be broken down into four sequential steps: template selection, target-template alignment, model construction, and model assessment.[3] The first two steps are often essentially performed together, as the most common methods of identifying templates rely on the production of sequence alignments; however, these alignments may not be of sufficient quality because database search techniques prioritize speed over alignment quality. These processes can be performed iteratively to improve the quality of the final model, although quality assessments that are not dependent on the true target structure are still under development.

Optimizing the speed and accuracy of these steps for use in large-scale automated structure prediction is a key component of structural genomics initiatives, partly because the resulting volume of data will be too large to process manually and partly because the goal of structural genomics requires providing models of reasonable quality to researchers who are not themselves structure prediction experts.[3]

Template selection and sequence alignment

The critical first step in homology modeling is the identification of the best template structure, if indeed any are available. The simplest method of template identification relies on serial pairwise sequence alignments aided by database search techniques such as FASTA and BLAST. More sensitive methods based on multiple sequence alignment − of which PSI-BLAST is the most common example − iteratively update their position-specific scoring matrix to successively identify more distantly related homologs. This family of methods has been shown to produce a larger number of potential templates and to identify better templates for sequences that have only distant relationships to any solved structure. Protein threading[9] , also known as fold recognition or 3D-1D alignment, can also be used as a search technique for identifying templates to be used in traditional homology modeling methods.[3] When performing a BLAST search, a reliable first approach is to identify hits with a sufficiently low *E*-value, which are considered sufficiently close in evolution to make a reliable homology model. Other factors may tip the balance in marginal cases; for example, the template may have a function similar to that of the query sequence, or it may belong to a homologous operon. However, a template with a poor *E*-value should generally not be chosen, even if it is the only one available, since it may well have a wrong structure, leading to the production of a misguided model. A better approach is to submit the primary sequence to fold-recognition servers or, better still, consensus meta-servers which improve upon individual fold-recognition servers by identifying similarities (consensus) among independent predictions.

Often several candidate template structures are identified by these approaches. Although some methods can generate hybrid models from multiple templates, most methods rely on a single template. Therefore, choosing the best template from among the candidates is a key step, and can affect the final accuracy of the structure significantly. This choice is guided by several factors, such as the similarity of the query and template sequences, of their functions, and of the predicted query and observed template secondary structures. Perhaps most importantly, the *coverage* of the aligned regions: the fraction of the query sequence structure that can be predicted from the template, and the plausibility of the resulting model. Thus, sometimes several homology models are produced for a single query sequence, with the most likely candidate chosen only in the final step.

It is possible to use the sequence alignment generated by the database search technique as the basis for the subsequent model production; however, more sophisticated approaches have also been explored. One proposal generates an ensemble of stochastically defined pairwise alignments between the target sequence and a single identified template as a means of exploring "alignment space" in regions of sequence with low local similarity.[10] "Profile-profile" alignments that first generate a sequence profile of the target and systematically compare it to the sequence profiles of solved structures; the coarse-graining inherent in the profile construction is thought to reduce noise introduced by sequence drift in nonessential regions of the sequence.[11]

Model generation

Given a template and an alignment, the information contained therein must be used to generate a three-dimensional structural model of the target, represented as a set of Cartesian coordinates for each atom in the protein. Three major classes of model generation methods have been proposed.[12] [13]

Fragment assembly

The original method of homology modeling relied on the assembly of a complete model from conserved structural fragments identified in closely related solved structures. For example, a modeling study of serine proteases in mammals identified a sharp distinction between "core" structural regions conserved in all experimental structures in the class, and variable regions typically located in the loops where the majority of the sequence differences were localized. Thus unsolved proteins could be modeled by first constructing the conserved core and then substituting variable regions from other proteins in the set of solved structures.[14] Current implementations of this method differ mainly in the way they deal with regions that are not conserved or that lack a template.[15] The variable regions are often constructed with the help of fragment libraries.

Segment matching

The segment-matching method divides the target into a series of short segments, each of which is matched to its own template fitted from the Protein Data Bank. Thus, sequence alignment is done over segments rather than over the entire protein. Selection of the template for each segment is based on sequence similarity, comparisons of alpha carbon coordinates, and predicted steric conflicts arising from the van der Waals radii of the divergent atoms between target and template. [16]

Satisfaction of spatial restraints

The most common current homology modeling method takes its inspiration from calculations required to construct a three-dimensional structure from data generated by NMR spectroscopy. One or more target-template alignments are used to construct a set of geometrical criteria that are then converted to probability density functions for each restraint. Restraints applied to the main protein internal coordinates – protein backbone distances and dihedral angles – serve as the basis for a global optimization procedure that originally used conjugate gradient energy minimization to iteratively refine the positions of all heavy atoms in the protein.[17]

This method had been dramatically expanded to apply specifically to loop modeling, which can be extremely difficult due to the high flexibility of loops in proteins in aqueous solution.[18] A more recent expansion applies the spatial-restraint model to electron density maps derived from cryoelectron microscopy studies, which provide low-resolution information that is not usually itself sufficient to generate atomic-resolution structural models.[19] To address the problem of inaccuracies in initial target-template sequence alignment, an iterative procedure has also been introduced to refine the alignment on the basis of the initial structural fit.[20] The most commonly used software in spatial restraint-based modeling is MODELLER and a database called ModBase has been established for reliable models generated with it.[21]

Loop modeling

Regions of the target sequence that are not aligned to a template are modeled by loop modeling; they are the most susceptible to major modeling errors and occur with higher frequency when the target and template have low sequence identity. The coordinates of unmatched sections determined by loop modeling programs are generally much less accurate than those obtained from simply copying the coordinates of a known structure, particularly if the loop is longer than 10 residues. The first two sidechain dihedral angles (χ_1 and χ_2) can usually be estimated within 30° for an accurate backbone structure; however, the later dihedral angles found in longer side chains such as lysine and arginine are notoriously difficult to predict. Moreover, small errors in χ_1 (and, to a lesser extent, in χ_2) can cause relatively large errors in the positions of the atoms at the terminus of side chain; such atoms often have a functional importance, particularly when located near the active site.

Model assessment

Assessment of homology models without reference to the true target structure is usually performed with two methods: statistical potentials or physics-based energy calculations. Both methods produce an estimate of the energy (or an energy-like analog) for the model or models being assessed; independent criteria are needed to determine acceptable cutoffs. Neither of the two methods correlates exceptionally well with true structural accuracy, especially on protein types underrepresented in the PDB, such as membrane proteins.

Statistical potentials are empirical methods based on observed residue-residue contact frequencies among proteins of known structure in the PDB. They assign a probability or energy score to each possible pairwise interaction between amino acids and combine these pairwise interaction scores into a single score for the entire model. Some such methods can also produce a residue-by-residue assessment that identifies poorly scoring regions within the model, though the model may have a reasonable score overall.[22] These methods emphasize the hydrophobic core and solvent-exposed polar amino acids often present in globular proteins. Examples of popular statistical potentials include Prosa and DOPE. Statistical potentials are more computationally efficient than energy calculations.[22]

Physics-based energy calculations aim to capture the interatomic interactions that are physically responsible for protein stability in solution, especially van der Waals and electrostatic interactions. These calculations are performed using a molecular mechanics force field; proteins are normally too large even for semi-empirical quantum mechanics-based calculations. The use of these methods is based on the energy landscape hypothesis of protein folding, which predicts that a protein's native state is also its energy minimum. Such methods usually employ implicit solvation, which provides a continuous approximation of a solvent bath for a single protein molecule without necessitating the explicit representation of individual solvent molecules. A force field specifically constructed for model assessment is known as the Effective Force Field (EFF) and is based on atomic parameters from CHARMM.[23]

A very extensive model validation report can be obtained using the Radboud Universiteit Nijmegen [24] *"What Check"* software which is one option of the Radboud Universiteit Nijmegen [25] *"What If"* software package; it produces a many page document with extensive analyses of nearly 200 scientific and administrative aspects of the model. *"What Check"* is available as a free server [26]; it can also be used to validate experimentally determined structures of macromolecules.

One newer method for model assessment relies on machine learning techniques such as neural nets, which may be trained to assess the structure directly or to form a consensus among multiple statistical and energy-based methods. Very recent results using support vector machine regression on a jury of more traditional assessment methods outperformed common statistical, energy-based, and machine learning methods.[27]

Structural comparison methods

The assessment of homology models' accuracy is straightforward when the experimental structure is known. The most common method of comparing two protein structures uses the root-mean-square deviation (RMSD) metric to measure the mean distance between the corresponding atoms in the two structures after they have been superimposed. However, RMSD does underestimate the accuracy of models in which the core is essentially correctly modeled, but some flexible loop regions are inaccurate.[28] A method introduced for the modeling assessment experiment CASP is known as the global distance test (GDT) and measures the total number of atoms whose distance from the model to the experimental structure lies under a certain distance cutoff.[28] Both methods can be used for any subset of atoms in the structure, but are often applied to only the alpha carbon or protein backbone atoms to minimize the noise created by poorly modeled side chain rotameric states, which most modeling methods are not optimized to predict.[29]

Benchmarking

Several large-scale benchmarking efforts have been made to assess the relative quality of various current homology modeling methods. CASP is a community-wide prediction experiment that runs every two years during the summer months and challenges prediction teams to submit structural models for a number of sequences whose structures have recently been solved experimentally but have not yet been published. Its partner CAFASP has run in parallel with CASP but evaluates only models produced via fully automated servers. Continuously running experiments that do not have prediction 'seasons' focus mainly on benchmarking publicly available webservers. LiveBench and EVA run continuously to assess participating servers' performance in prediction of imminently released structures from the PDB. CASP and CAFASP serve mainly as evaluations of the state of the art in modeling, while the continuous assessments seek to evaluate the model quality that would be obtained by a non-expert user employing publicly available tools.

Accuracy

The accuracy of the structures generated by homology modeling is highly dependent on the sequence identity between target and template. Above 50% sequence identity, models tend to be reliable, with only minor errors in side chain packing and rotameric state, and an overall RMSD between the modeled and the experimental structure falling around 1 Å. This error is comparable to the typical resolution of a structure solved by NMR. In the 30–50% identity range, errors can be more severe and are often located in loops. Below 30% identity, serious errors occur, sometimes resulting in the basic fold being mis-predicted.[12] This low-identity region is often referred to as the "twilight zone" within which homology modeling is extremely difficult, and to which it is possibly less suited than fold recognition methods.[30]

At high sequence identities, the primary source of error in homology modeling derives from the choice of the template or templates on which the model is based, while lower identities exhibit serious errors in sequence alignment that inhibit the production of high-quality models.[6] It has been suggested that the major impediment to quality model production is inadequacies in sequence alignment, since "optimal" structural alignments between two proteins of known structure can be used as input to current modeling methods to produce quite accurate reproductions of the original experimental structure.[31]

Attempts have been made to improve the accuracy of homology models built with existing methods by subjecting them to molecular dynamics simulation in an effort to improve their RMSD to the experimental structure. However, current force field parameterizations may not be sufficiently accurate for this task, since homology models used as starting structures for molecular dynamics tend to produce slightly worse structures.[32] Slight improvements have been observed in cases where significant restraints were used during the simulation.[33]

Sources of error

The two most common and large-scale sources of error in homology modeling are poor template selection and inaccuracies in target-template sequence alignment.[6] [34] Controlling for these two factors by using a structural alignment, or a sequence alignment produced on the basis of comparing two solved structures, dramatically reduces the errors in final models; these "gold standard" alignments can be used as input to current modeling methods to produce quite accurate reproductions of the original experimental structure.[31] Results from the most recent CASP experiment suggest that "consensus" methods collecting the results of multiple fold recognition and multiple alignment searches increase the likelihood of identifying the correct template; similarly, the use of multiple templates in the model-building step may be worse than the use of the single correct template but better than the use of a single suboptimal one.[34] Alignment errors may be minimized by the use of a multiple alignment even if only one template is used, and by the iterative refinement of local regions of low similarity.[3] [10] A lesser source of model errors are errors in the template structure. The PDBREPORT [35] database lists several million, mostly very small but occasionally dramatic, errors in experimental (template) structures that have been deposited in the PDB.

Serious local errors can arise in homology models where an insertion or deletion mutation or a gap in a solved structure result in a region of target sequence for which there is no corresponding template. This problem can be minimized by the use of multiple templates, but the method is complicated by the templates' differing local structures around the gap and by the likelihood that a missing region in one experimental structure is also missing in other structures of the same protein family. Missing regions are most common in loops where high local flexibility increases the difficulty of resolving the region by structure-determination methods. Although some guidance is provided even with a single template by the positioning of the ends of the missing region, the longer the gap, the more difficult it is to model. Loops of up to about 9 residues can be modeled with moderate accuracy in some cases if the local alignment is correct.[3] Larger regions are often modeled individually using ab initio structure prediction techniques, although this approach has met with only isolated success.[36]

The rotameric states of side chains and their internal packing arrangement also present difficulties in homology modeling, even in targets for which the backbone structure is relatively easy to predict. This is partly due to the fact that many side chains in crystal structures are not in their "optimal" rotameric state as a result of energetic factors in the hydrophobic core and in the packing of the individual molecules in a protein crystal.[37] One method of addressing this problem requires searching a rotameric library to identify locally low-energy combinations of packing states.[38] It has been suggested that a major reason that homology modeling so difficult when target-template sequence identity lies below 30% is that such proteins have broadly similar folds but widely divergent side chain packing arrangements.[4]

Utility

Uses of the structural models include protein–protein interaction prediction, protein–protein docking, molecular docking, and functional annotation of genes identified in an organism's genome.[39] Even low-accuracy homology models can be useful for these purposes, because their inaccuracies tend to be located in the loops on the protein surface, which are normally more variable even between closely related proteins. The functional regions of the protein, especially its active site, tend to be more highly conserved and thus more accurately modeled.[12]

Homology models can also be used to identify subtle differences between related proteins that have not all been solved structurally. For example, the method was used to identify cation binding sites on the Na^+/K^+ ATPase and to propose hypotheses about different ATPases' binding affinity.[40] Used in conjunction with molecular dynamics simulations, homology models can also generate hypotheses about the kinetics and dynamics of a protein, as in studies of the ion selectivity of a potassium channel.[41] Large-scale automated modeling of all identified protein-coding regions in a genome has been attempted for the yeast *Saccharomyces cerevisiae*, resulting in nearly 1000 quality models for proteins whose structures had not yet been determined at the time of the study, and identifying novel relationships between 236 yeast proteins and other previously solved structures.[42]

References

[1] Chothia C and Lesk AM (1986). The relation between the divergence of sequence and structure in proteins. *EMBO J* 5:823–6.

[2] Kaczanowski S and Zielenkiewicz P (2010). Why similar protein sequences encode similar three-dimensional structures? *Theoretical Chemistry Accounts* 125:543–50

[3] Marti-Renom MA, Stuart AC, Fiser A, Sanchez R, Melo F, Sali A. (2000). Comparative protein structure modeling of genes and genomes. *Annu Rev Biophys Biomol Struct* 29: 291–325.

[4] Chung SY, Subbiah S. (1996.) A structural explanation for the twilight zone of protein sequence homology. *Structure* 4: 1123–27.

[5] Williamson AR. (2000). Creating a structural genomics consortium. *Nat Struct Biol* 7 S1(11s):953.

[6] Venclovas C, Margelevičius M. (2005). Comparative modeling in CASP6 using consensus approach to template selection, sequence-structure alignment, and structure assessment. *Proteins* 61(S7):99–105.

[7] Dalal S, Balasubramanian S, Regan L. (1997). Transmuting alpha helices and beta sheets. *Fold Des* 2(5):R71-9.

[8] Dalal S, Balasubramanian S, Regan L. (1997). Protein alchemy: changing beta-sheet into alpha-helix. *Nat Struct Biol* 4(7):548–52.

[9] Peng, Jian; Jinbo Xu (2011). "RaptorX: Exploiting structure information for protein alignment by statistical inference" (http://onlinelibrary. wiley.com/doi/10.1002/prot.23175/abstract). *PROTEINS*. doi:10.1002/prot.23175. .

[10] Muckstein U, Hofacker IL, Stadler PF. (2002). Stochastic pairwise alignments. *Bioinformatics* 18 Suppl 2:S153-60.

[11] Rychlewski L, Zhang B, Godzik A. (1998). Fold and function predictions for Mycoplasma genitalium proteins. *Fold Des* 3(4):229–38.

[12] Baker D, Sali A. (2001). Protein structure prediction and structural genomics. *Science* 294(5540):93–96.

[13] Zhang Y (2008). "Progress and challenges in protein structure prediction". *Curr Opin Struct Biol* 18 (3): 342–348. doi:10.1016/j.sbi.2008.02.004. PMC 2680823. PMID 18436442.

[14] Greer J. (1981). Comparative model-building of the mammalian serine proteases 153(4):1027–42.

[15] Wallner B, Elofsson A. (2005). All are not equal: A benchmark of different homology modeling programs. *Protein Science* 14:1315–1327.

[16] Levitt M. (1992). Accurate modeling of protein conformation by automatic segment matching. *J Mol Biol* 226(2): 507–33.

[17] Sali A, Blundell TL. (1993). Comparative protein modelling by satisfaction of spatial restraints. *J Mol Biol* 234(3):779–815.

[18] Fiser A, Sali A. (2003). ModLoop: automated modeling of loops in protein structures. *Bioinformatics* 19(18):2500-1.

[19] Topf M, Baker ML, Marti-Renom MA, Chiu W, Sali A. (2006). Refinement of protein structures by iterative comparative modeling and CryoEM density fitting. *J Mol Biol* 357(5):1655–68.

[20] John B, Sali A. (2003). Comparative protein structure modeling by iterative alignment, model building and model assessment. *Nucleic Acids Res* 31(14):3982-92.

[21] Ursula Pieper, Narayanan Eswar, Hannes Braberg, M.S. Madhusudhan, Fred Davis, Ashley C. Stuart, Nebojsa Mirkovic, Andrea Rossi, Marc A. Marti-Renom, Andras Fiser, Ben Webb, Daniel Greenblatt, Conrad Huang, Tom Ferrin, Andrej Sali. MODBASE, a database of annotated comparative protein structure models, and associated resources. *Nucleic Acids Res* 32, D217-D222, 2004.

[22] Sippl MJ. (1993). Recognition of Errors in Three-Dimensional Structures of Proteins. *Proteins* 17:355–62.

[23] Lazaridis T. and Karplus M. 1999a. Discrimination of the native from misfolded protein models with an energy function including implicit solvation. *J. Mol. Biol.* 288: 477–487

[24] http://swift.cmbi.ru.nl/gv/whatcheck/

[25] http://swift.cmbi.ru.nl/whatif/

[26] http://swift.cmbi.ru.nl/

[27] Eramian D, Shen M, Devos D, Melo F, Sali A, Marti-Renom MA. (2006). A composite score for predicting errors in protein structure models. *Protein Science* 15:1653–1666.

[28] Zemla A. (2003). LGA – A Method for Finding 3-D Similarities in Protein Structures. Nucleic Acids Research, 31(13):3370–3374.

[29] Mount DM. (2004). *Bioinformatics: Sequence and Genome Analysis* 2nd ed. Cold Spring Harbor Laboratory Press: Cold Spring Harbor, NY.

[30] Blake JD, Cohen FE. (2001). Pairwise sequence alignment below the twilight zone. *J Mol Biol* 307(2):721–35.

[31] Zhang Y and Skolnick J. (2005). The protein structure prediction problem could be solved using the current PDB library. Proc. Natl. Acad. Sci. USA 102(4):1029–34.

[32] Koehl P, Levitt M. (1999). A brighter future for protein structure prediction. *Nat Struct Biol* 6(2):108–11.

[33] Flohil JA, Vriend G, Berendsen HJ. (2002). Completion and refinement of 3-D homology models with restricted molecular dynamics: application to targets 47, 58, and 111 in the CASP modeling competition and posterior analysis. *Proteins* 48(4):593–604.

[34] Ginalski K. (2006). Comparative modeling for protein structure prediction. *Curr Opin Struct Biol* 16(2):172–7.

[35] http://swift.cmbi.ru.nl/gv/pdbreport/

[36] Kryshtafovych A, Venclovas C, Fidelis K, Moult J. (2005). Progress over the first decade of CASP experiments. *Proteins* 61(S7):225–36.

[37] Vasquez M. (1996). Modeling side-chain conformation. *Curr Opin Struct Biol* 6(2):217–21.

[38] Wilson C, Gregoret LM, Agard DA. (1993). Modeling side-chain conformation for homologous proteins using an energy-based rotamer search. *J Mol Biol* 229(4):996–1006.

[39] Gopal S, Schroeder M, Pieper U, Sczyrba A, Aytekin-Kurban G, Bekiranov S, Fajardo JE, Eswar N, Sanchez R, Sali A, Gaasterland T. (2001). Homology-based annotation yields 1,042 new candidate genes in the Drosophila melanogaster genome. *Nat Genet* 27(3):337–40.

[40] Ogawa H, Toyoshima C. (2002). Homology modeling of the cation binding sites of Na+K+-ATPase. *Proc Natl Acad Sci USA* 99(25):15977-15982

[41] Capener CE, Shrivastava IH, Ranatunga KM, Forrest LR, Smith GR, Sansom MSP. (2000). Homology Modeling and Molecular Dynamics Simulation Studies of an Inward Rectifier Potassium Channel. *Biophys J* 78(6):2929–2942

[42] Sánchez R, Sali A. (1998). Large-scale protein structure modeling of the Saccharomyces cerevisiae genome. *Proc Natl Acad Sci USA* 95(23):13597-13602.

Horizontal correlation

Horizontal correlation is a methodology for gene sequence analysis. Rather than referring to one specific technique, *horizontal correlation* instead encompasses a variety of approaches to sequence analysis that are unified by two specific themes:

- Sequence analysis is performed by making comparisons *horizontally*, along the length of a single genetic sequence; this is in contrast to *vertical* methods that make comparisons across several different genetic sequences.
- The comparisons made generally measure information theoretic quantities such as value of the mutual information function between two regions of the sequence.

The core ideas of the horizontal correlation approach were first presented in a year 2000 paper by Grosse, Herzel, Buldyrev, and Stanley (Grosse, et al. 2000). In this first formulation, Grosse and colleagues sought to characterize a large genetic sequence by dividing the sequence into coding and non-coding regions. Whereas traditional approaches to the coding-vs.-non-coding problem generally relied on sophisticated pattern recognition systems that were first trained on small inputs and then run over the entire sequence (Ohler, et al. 1999), the horizontal correlation approach of Grosse and colleagues worked instead by breaking the sequence into many relatively short sequence fragments, each only 500 base pairs in length. They then sought to characterize each of these fragments as either coding or non-coding. This was accomplished by comparing each size 3 window along the length of a fragment with the first size 3 window in that fragment, then measuring the value of the mutual information function between the two windows. Coding sequences were found to display a stylized pattern of 3-periodicity that non-coding sequences did not. Such a pattern was easy to recognize, and enabled significantly more rapid, more species-independent identification of coding regions (Grosse, et al. 2000).

Since 2000, horizontal correlation methodologies emphasizing the measurement of information theoretic quantities along the length of a gene sequence have been put to widespread use, and have even found application in shotgun sequencing fragment assembly (Otu & Sayood, 2004).

References

- I. Grosse, H. Herzel, S. Buldyrev, H. Stanley: "Species Independence of Mutual Information in Coding and non-Coding DNA," *Physical Review E,* Vol. 61, No. 5 (2000)
- U. Ohler, S. Harbeck, H. Niemann, E. Noth, and M. Reese: "Interpolated Markov Chains for Eukaryotic Promoter Recognition," *Bioinformatics,* Vol. 15, pp. 362-369 (1999)
- H. Otu, K. Sayood: "A Divide and Conquer Approach to Fragment Assembly," *Bioinformatics,* Vol. 19, No. 1 pp. 22-29 (2004)

HubMed

HubMed is an alternative, third-party interface to PubMed, the database of biomedical literature produced by the National Library of Medicine. Features include relevance-ranked search results, web feeds of query updates, direct citation export, tagging and graphical display of related articles.

References

Eaton AD (2006). "HubMed: a web-based biomedical literature search interface.". *Nucleic Acids Res* **34** (Web Server issue): W745–7. doi:10.1093/nar/gkl037. PMC 1538859. PMID 16845111.

External links

- HubMed [1]

References

[1] http://www.hubmed.org

Haplogroup M (mtDNA)

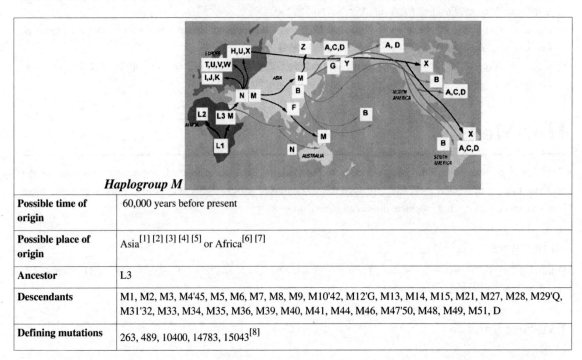

Haplogroup M

Possible time of origin	60,000 years before present
Possible place of origin	Asia[1] [2] [3] [4] [5] or Africa[6] [7]
Ancestor	L3
Descendants	M1, M2, M3, M4'45, M5, M6, M7, M8, M9, M10'42, M12'G, M13, M14, M15, M21, M27, M28, M29'Q, M31'32, M33, M34, M35, M36, M39, M40, M41, M44, M46, M47'50, M48, M49, M51, D
Defining mutations	263, 489, 10400, 14783, 15043[8]

In human mitochondrial genetics, **Haplogroup M** is a human mitochondrial DNA (mtDNA) haplogroup. An enormous haplogroup spanning all the continents, the macro-haplogroup M, like its sibling N, is a descendant of haplogroup L3.

All mtDNA haplogroups considered native outside of Africa are descendants of either haplogroup M or its sibling haplogroup N.[9] The geographical distributions of M and N are associated with discussions concerning out of Africa migrations and the subsequent colonization of the rest of the world. In particular it is often taken to indicate that it is very likely that there was one particularly major prehistoric migration of humans out of Africa, and that both M and N were part of this colonization process.[10]

Origins

There is an ongoing debate concerning geographical origins of Haplogroup M and its sibling haplogroup N. Both these lineages are thought to have been the main surviving lineages involved in the out of Africa migration (or migrations) because all indigenous lineages found outside Africa belong to either haplogroup M or haplogroup N. Yet to be conclusively determined is whether the mutations that define haplogroups M and N occurred in Africa before the exit from Africa or in Asia after the exit from Africa. Determining the origins of haplogroup M is further complicated by the fact that it is found both in Africa and outside of Africa.[3]

It is generally accepted that haplogroup M evolved shortly after the emergence of its parent clade haplogroup L3. Apart from haplogroup M and its sibling haplogroup N, the numerous other subclades of L3 are largely restricted to Africa, which suggests that L3 arose in Africa. In Africa, haplogroup M, specifically its subclade M1, has a fairly restricted distribution, being found mainly in East and North Africa at low to moderate frequencies. The limited distribution of haplogroup M in Africa and its widespread presence outside Africa, suggests that this lineage emerged very close to the time of the Out of Africa migration, either shortly before or shortly after the exit from Africa.

Haplogroup M1

Much of discussion concerning the origins of haplogroup M has been related to its subclade haplogroup M1, which is the only variant of macrohaplogroup M found in Africa.[9] Two possibilities were being considered as potential explanations for the presence of M1 in Africa:

1. M was present in the ancient population which later gave rise to both M1 in Africa, and M more generally found in Eurasia.[11]
2. The presence of M1 in Africa is the result of a back-migration from Asia which occurred sometime after the Out of Africa migration.[4]

Haplogroup M23

In 2009, two independent publications reported a rare, deep-rooted subclade of haplogroup M, referred to as M23, that is present in Madagascar.[12] [13] The contemporary populations of Madagascar were formed in the last 2,000 years by the admixture of African and Southeast Asian (Austronesian) populations. M23 seems to be restricted to Madagascar as it was not detected anywhere else. M23 could have been brought to Madagascar from Asia where most deep rooted subclades of Haplogroup M are found.

Asian origin theory

According to this theory, anatomically modern humans carrying ancestral haplogroup L3 lineages were involved in the Out of Africa migration from East Africa into Asia. Somewhere in Asia, the ancestral L3 lineages gave rise to haplogroups M and N. The ancestral L3 lineages were then lost by genetic drift as they are infrequent outside Africa. The hypothesis of Asia as the place of origin of macrohaplogroup M is supported by the following:

1. The highest frequencies worldwide of macrohaplogroup M are observed in Asia, specifically in India and Bangladesh, where frequencies range from 60%-80%.*[1] [14]
2. With the exception of the African specific M1, India has several M lineages that emerged directly from the root of haplogroup M.[1] [14]
3. Only two subclades of haplogroup M, M1 and M23, are found in Africa, whereas numerous subclades are found outside Africa[1] [3] (with some discussion possible only about sub-clade M1, concerning which see below).

1. Specifically concerning M1

   - Haplogroup M1 has a restricted geographic distribution in Africa, being found mainly in North Africans and East Africa at low or moderate frequencies. If M had originated in Africa around before the Out of Africa migration, it would be expected to have a more widespread distribution [14]
   - According to Gonzalez et al. 2007, M1 appears to have expanded relatively recently. In this study M1 had a younger coalescence age than the Asian-exclusive M lineages.[3]
   - The geographic distribution of M1 in Africa is predominantly North African/supra-equatorial[3] and is largely confined to Afro-Asiatic speakers,[15] which is inconsistent with the Sub-Saharan distribution of sub-clades of haplogroups L3 and L2 that have similar time depths.[9]
   - One of the basal lineages of M1 lineages has been found in Northwest Africa and in the Near East but is abssent in East Africa.[3]
   - M1 is not restricted to Africa. It is relatively common in the Mediterranean, peaking in Iberia. M1 also enjoys a well-established presence in the Middle East, from the South of the Arabian Peninsula to Anatolia and from the Levant to Iran. In addition, M1 haplotypes have occasionally been observed in the Caucasus and the Trans Caucasus, and without any accompanying L lineages.[3] [9] M1 has also been detected in Central Asia, seemingly reaching as far as Tibet.[3]
   - The fact that the M1 sub-clade of macrohaplogroup M has a coalescence age which overlaps with that of haplogroup U6 (a Eurasian haplogroup whose presence in Africa is due to a back-migration from West Asia) and the distribution of U6 in Africa is also restricted to the same North African and Horn African

populations as M1 supports the scenario that M1 and U6 were part of the same population expansion from Asia to Africa.[15]

- The timing of the proposed migration of M1 and U6-carrying peoples from West Asia to Africa (between 40,000 to 45,000 ybp) is also supported by the fact that it coincides with changes in climatic conditions that reduced the desert areas of North Africa, thereby rendering the region more accessible to entry from the Levant. This climatic change also temporally overlaps with the peopling of Europe by populations bearing haplogroup U5, the European sister clade of haplogroup U6.[15]

African origin hypothesis

According to this theory, haplogroups M and N arose from L3 in an East African population that had been isolated from other African populations. Members of this population were involved in the out Africa migration and only carried M and N lineages. With the possible exception of haplogroup M1, all other M and N clades in Africa were lost by genetic drift.[7] [11]

The African origin of Haplogroup M is supported by the following arguments and evidence.

1. L3, the parent clade of haplogroup M, is found throughout Africa, but is rare outside Africa.[11] According to Toomas Kivisild (2003), "the lack of L3 lineages other than M and N in India and among non-African mitochondria in general suggests that the earliest migration(s) of modern humans already carried these two mtDNA ancestors, via a departure route over the Horn of Africa."[7]
2. Ancestral L3 lineages that gave rise to M and N have not been discovered outside Africa.
3. Specifically concerning at least M1:

   - Haplogroup M1 is largely restricted to Africa where the highest frequencies of M1 can be found in East Africa, particularly in Ethiopia. M1 is found in Europe and the Near East but at considerably lower frequencies than in Africa.[16]
   - Early studies once reported the age of haplogroup M1 to be similar to that of haplogroup M. Quintana et al. (1999) suggested that the age of the then-East African specific haplogroup M1, calculated using RFLP data (48,000±15,000), was compatible with that of the Indian-specific haplogroup M lineages (56,000±7,000).[11]

Dispersal

A number of studies have proposed that the ancestors of modern haplogroup M dispersed from Africa through the southern route across the Horn of Africa along the coastal regions of Asia onwards to New Guinea and Australia. These studies suggested that the migrations of haplogroups M and N occurred separately with haplogroup N heading northwards from East Africa to the Levant. However, the results of numerous recent studies indicate that there was only one migration out of Africa and that haplogroups M and N were part of the same migration. This is based on the analysis of a number of relict populations along the proposed beachcombing route from Africa to Australia, all of which possessed both haplogroups N and M.[2] [17]

A 2008 study by Abu-Amero et al., suggests that the Arabian Peninsula may have been the main route out of Africa. However as the region lacks of autochthonous clades of haplogroups M and N the authors suggest that the area has been a more recent receptor of human migrations than an ancient demographic expansion center along the southern coastal route as proposed under the single migration Out-of-Africa scenario of the African origin hypothesis.[5]

Distribution

M is the single most common mtDNA haplogroup in Asia,[18] and peaks in Bangladesh[9] where it represents two thirds of the maternal lineages, and is ubiquitous in India[19] where it has a 60% frequency.[1]

Due to its great age, haplogroup M is an mtDNA lineage which does not correspond well to present-day ethnic groups, as it spans Siberian, Native American, East Asian, Southeast Asian, Central Asian, South Asian, Melanesian populations at a considerable frequency .

Among the descendants of M are C, D, E, G, Q, and Z, with Z and G being observed in North Eurasian populations, C and D being shared between North Eurasian and Native American populations, E being observed in Southeast Asian populations, and Q being observed in Melanesian populations. The lineages M2, M3, M4, M5, M6, M18 and M25 are exclusive to South Asia, with M2 reported to be the oldest lineage on the Indian sub-continent.[1]

Subgroups distribution

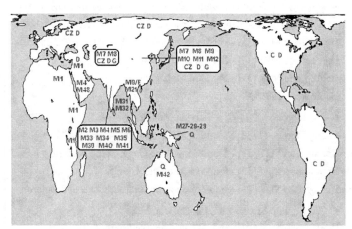

Location of M subclades around the World

- Haplogroup M1 [20] - found in North Africa, Horn of Africa, Mediterranean, and Middle East[1] [3]

- Haplogroup M2 [21] - found in South Asia, with highest concentrations in SE India and Bangladesh;[9] oldest haplogroup M lineage on the Indian sub-continent.[1]

  - M2a - most common in Bangladesh
  - M2b - most common in SE India
- Haplogroup M3 [22] - found mainly in South Asia, with highest concentrations in west and NW India[9]
- M4"45

  - Haplogroup M4 [23] - found mainly in South Asia but some sequences in Eastern Saudi Arabia

    - Haplogroup M4a - found in Gujarat, India[14]
  - Haplogroup M30 - mainly in India, found in Middle East and North Africa.
  - Haplogroup M37

    - Haplogroup M37a - found in Gujarat, India[14]
- Haplogroup M5 [24] - found in South Asia

  - Haplogroup M5a - found in Orissa, India[14]
- Haplogroup M6 [25] - found mainly in South Asia, with highest concentrations in mid-eastern India and Kashmir[9]

  - Haplogroup M6b - found in Kerala, India[14]
- Haplogroup M7 [26] - found in East Asia, especially in Japan
- Haplogroup M8

  - Haplogroup M8a: [27] - found in East Asia, especially in Japan

    - Haplogroup M8a2 - frequently found in indigenous peoples of Kamchatka (Koryaks, Itelmens), with a few examples known from samples of Chukchis, Koreans, and Tuvans[28]
  - Haplogroup CZ

    - Haplogroup C [29] - found especially in Siberia

- Haplogroup C1 [30] - found in Asia and America (Native Americans and Hispanics in particular)
  - Haplogroup C4
  - Haplogroup Z [31] - found among diverse Eurasian populations: Hazara, Finns, Japanese, Sami and some Russians.
- Haplogroup M9 [32] - found in East and Southeast Asia
  - Haplogroup E - a subclade of M9 - found especially in SE Asia
- Haplogroup M10 [33] - small clade found in East Asia, Southeast Asia, Bangladesh, Central Asia, and southern Siberia
- Haplogroup M11 [34] - small clade found especially among the Chinese and some Bangladeshis
- Haplogroup M12'G
  - Haplogroup M12 [34] - small clade found in Japan
  - Haplogroup G [35] - found especially in Japan and in indigenous peoples of Kamchatka (Koryaks, Alyutors, Itelmens) with some isolated instances in diverse places of Asia
- Haplogroup M21 [36] - small clade found in SE Asia and Bangladesh
- Haplogroup M27 [37] - found in Melanesia
- Haplogroup M28 [37] - found in Melanesia
- Haplogroup M29'Q
  - Haplogroup M29 [37] - found in Melanesia
  - Haplogroup Q [38] - found in Melanesia and Australia (Aborigines)
- Haplogroup M31 [39] - found among the Onge, in the Andaman Islands[14]
- Haplogroup M32 [40] - found in Andaman Islands
- Haplogroup M33 [41] - small clade found in South Asia and Belarus
  - Haplogroup M33a - found in Gujarat, India[14]
- Haplogroup M34 [42] - small clade found in South Asia
  - Haplogroup M34a - found in Karnataka, India[14]
- Haplogroup M35 [43] - small clade found in South Asia and Slovakia
- Haplogroup M39 [44] - found in South Asia[14]
- Haplogroup M40 [45] - found in South Asia[14]
- Haplogroup M41 - found in South Asia
  - Haplogroup M41b - found in Andhra Pradesh, India[14]
  - Haplogroup M41c - found in Andrah Pradesh, India[14]
- Haplogroup M42 [46] - found among Australian Abrorigines
- Haplogroup M48 [47] - rare clade found at least in Saudi Arabia
- Haplogroup D - found in Eastern Eurasia, Native Americans, Central Asia[48] and occasionally also in West Asia and Northern Europe.

Subclades

Tree

This phylogenetic tree of haplogroup M subclades is based on the paper by Mannis van Oven and Manfred Kayser *Updated comprehensive phylogenetic tree of global human mitochondrial DNA variation*[8] and subsequent published research.

- **M**
  - **M1**
    - M1a
      - M1a1
        - M1a1a
        - M1a1b
          - M1a1b1
        - M1a1c
        - M1a1d
        - M1a1e
        - M1a1f
      - M1a2
        - M1a2a
        - M1a2b
      - M1a3
        - M1a3a
        - M1a3b
      - M1a4
      - M1a5
    - M1b
      - M1b1
        - M1b1a
      - M1b2
        - M1b2a
  - **M2**
    - M2a
      - M2a1
      - M2a2
      - M2a3
    - M2b
      - M2b1
      - M2b2
  - M3
    - M3a
  - M4"45
    - M4
      - M4a
      - M4b

- M4b1
- M18'38
  - M18
  - M38
- M30
  - M30a
  - M30b
  - M30c
    - M30c1
      - M30c1a
        - M30c1a1
  - M30d
  - M37
    - M37a
  - M43
  - M45
- M5
  - M5a
    - M5a1
      - M5a1a
      - M5a1b
    - M5a2
      - M5a2a
- M6
- **M7**
  - M7a
    - M7a1
      - M7a1a
        - M7a1a1
          - M7a1a1a
        - M7a1a2
        - M7a1a3
        - M7a1a4
          - M7a1a4a
        - M7a1a5
        - M7a1a6
        - M7a1a7
      - M7a1b
    - M7a2
      - M7a2a
      - M7a2b
  - M7b'c'd'e
    - M7b'd

- M7b
  - M7b1'2
    - M7b1
    - M7b2
      - M7b2a
      - M7b2b
      - M7b2c
  - M7b3
    - M7b3a
- M7d
- M7c'e
  - M7c
    - M7c1
      - M7c1a
      - M7c1b
        - M7c1b1
    - M7c2
      - M7c2a
    - M7c3
      - M7c3a
      - M7c3b
      - M7c3c
  - M7e
- **M8**
  - M8a
    - M8a1
    - M8a2
      - M8a2a
      - M8a2b
  - **CZ**
    - **C**
    - **Z**
- **M9**
  - M9a'b'c'd
    - M9a'c'd
      - M9a'd
        - M9a
          - M9a1
          - M9a2
          - M9a3
        - M9d
      - M9c
    - M9b

- **E**
- M10'42
  - M10
    - M10a
      - M10a1
      - M10a2
  - M42
    - M42a
- M11
  - M11a
  - M11b
- M12'G
  - M12
    - M12a
  - **G**
- M13
  - M13a
    - M13a1
- M14
- M15
- M21
  - M21a'b
    - M21a
    - M21b
  - M21c'd
    - M21c
    - M21d
- M22
- M23
- M25
- M27
  - M27a
  - M27b
  - M27c
- M28
  - M28a
  - M28b
- M29'Q
  - M29
    - M29a
    - M29b
  - **Q**
- M31'32
  - M31

- M31a
  - M31a1
    - M31a1a
    - M31a1b
  - M31a2
    - M31a2a
  - M31b
  - M31c
- M32
  - M32a
- M33
  - M33a
  - M33b
  - M33c
- M34
  - M34a
- M35
  - M35a
  - M35b
- M36
  - M36a
- M39
  - M39a
- M40
  - M40a
- M41
- M44'52
  - M44
  - M52
- M46
- M47'50
  - M47
  - M50
- M48
- M49
- M51
- **D**

References

[1] Rajkumar et al. (2005), Phylogeny and antiquity of M macrohaplogroup inferred from complete mt DNA sequence of Indian specific lineages (http://www.biomedcentral.com/1471-2148/5/26), BMC Evolutionary Biology 2005, 5:26 doi:10.1186/1471-2148-5-26

[2] Macaulay et al, V; Hill, C; Achilli, A; Rengo, C; Clarke, D; Meehan, W; Blackburn, J; Semino, O et al. (2005). "Single, Rapid Coastal Settlement of Asia Revealed by Analysis of Complete Mitochondrial Genomes" (http://66.102.1.104/scholar?hl=en&lr=& q=cache:nfrkio5UPzMJ:www4.ncsu.edu/~womcmill/GenomeScience_Papers/Macaulayetal(2005)Science.pdf). *Science* **308** (5724): 1034–6. doi:10.1126/science.1109792. PMID 15890885. .: "Haplogroup L3 (the African clade that gave rise to the two basal non-African clades, haplogroups M and N) is 84,000 years old, and haplogroups M and N themselves are almost identical in age at 63,000 years old, with haplogroup R diverging rapidly within haplogroup N 60,000 years ago."

[3] Gonzalez et al. (2007), Mitochondrial lineage M1 traces an early human backflow to Africa (http://www.pubmedcentral.nih.gov/ articlerender.fcgi?artid=1945034), BMC Genomics 2007, 8:223 doi:10.1186/1471-2164-8-223

[4] Chandrasekar et al. (2007), YAP insertion signature in South Asia (http://www.ncbi.nlm.nih.gov/pubmed/17786594), Ann Hum Biol. 2007 Sep-Oct;34(5):582-6.

[5] Abu-Amero et al., KK; Larruga, JM; Cabrera, VM; González, AM (2008). "Mitochondrial DNA structure in the Arabian Peninsula" (http:// www.biomedcentral.com/1471-2148/8/45). *BMC evolutionary biology* (BMC Evolutionary Biology) **8**: 45. doi:10.1186/1471-2148-8-45. PMC 2268671. PMID 18269758. .

[6] Kivisild, M; Kivisild, T; Metspalu, E; Parik, J; Hudjashov, G; Kaldma, K; Serk, P; Karmin, M et al. (2004). "Most of the extant mtDNA boundaries in South and Southwest Asia were likely shaped during the initial settlement of Eurasia by anatomically modern humans" (http:// www.biomedcentral.com/1471-2156/5/26/ABSTRACT]/ABSTRACT/COMMENTS/ADDITIONAL/COMMENTS/abstract/). *BMC genetics* **5**: 26. doi:10.1186/1471-2156-5-26. PMC 516768. PMID 15339343. .

[7] Kivisild et al., T; Rootsi, S; Metspalu, M; Mastana, S; Kaldma, K; Parik, J; Metspalu, E; Adojaan, M et al. (2003). "The Genetic Heritage of the Earliest Settlers Persists Both in Indian Tribal and Caste Populations". *American journal of human genetics* **72** (2): 313–32. doi:10.1086/346068. PMC 379225. PMID 12536373.

[8] van Oven et al., M; Kayser, M (2009). "Updated comprehensive phylogenetic tree of global human mitochondrial DNA variation". *Human Mutation* **30** (2): E386–E394. doi:10.1002/humu.20921. PMID 18853457.

[9] Metspalu et al., M; Kivisild, T; Metspalu, E; Parik, J; Hudjashov, G; Kaldma, K; Serk, P; Karmin, M et al. (2004). "Most of the extant mtDNA boundaries in South and Southwest Asia were likely shaped during the initial settlement of Eurasia by anatomically modern humans" (http://www.biomedcentral.com/1471-2156/5/26). *BMC genetics* **5**: 26. doi:10.1186/1471-2156-5-26. PMC 516768. PMID 15339343. .

[10] Macaulay et al, V; Hill, C; Achilli, A; Rengo, C; Clarke, D; Meehan, W; Blackburn, J; Semino, O et al. (2005). "Single, Rapid Coastal Settlement of Asia Revealed by Analysis of Complete Mitochondrial Genomes" (http://66.102.1.104/scholar?hl=en&lr=& q=cache:nfrkio5UPzMJ:www4.ncsu.edu/~womcmill/GenomeScience_Papers/Macaulayetal(2005)Science.pdf). *Science* **308** (5724): 1034–6. doi:10.1126/science.1109792. PMID 15890885. .

[11] Quintana et al (1999). *Genetic evidence of an early exit of Homo sapiens sapiens from Africa through eastern Africa* (http://www.clas.ufl. edu/users/krigbaum/proseminar/quintana-murci_naturegenetics_1999.pdf). .

[12] Dubut et al., V; Cartault, F; Payet, C; Thionville, MD; Murail, P (2009). "Complete mitochondrial sequences for haplogroups M23 and M46: insights into the Asian ancestry of the Malagasy population". *Human Biology* **81** (4): 495–500. doi:10.3378/027.081.0407. PMID 20067372.

[13] Ricaut et al., FX; Razafindrazaka, H; Cox, MP; Dugoujon, JM; Guitard, E; Sambo, C; Mormina, M; Mirazon-Lahr, M et al. (2009). "A new deep branch of eurasian mtDNA macrohaplogroup M reveals additional complexity regarding the settlement of Madagascar" (http://www. biomedcentral.com/1471-2164/10/605). *BMC Genomics* **10**: 605. doi:10.1186/1471-2164-10-605. PMC 2808327. PMID 20003445. .

[14] Thangaraj et al. (2006), In situ origin of deep rooting lineages of mitochondrial Macrohaplogroup 'M' in India (http://www.biomedcentral. com/1471-2164/7/151), BMC Genomics 2006, 7:151

[15] Olivieri et al. (2006), The mtDNA legacy of the Levantine early Upper Palaeolithic in Africa (http://www.sciencemag.org/cgi/content/ full/314/5806/1767), Science. 2006 Dec 15;314(5806):1767-70

[16] Gonzalez et al., Mitochondrial lineage M1 traces an early human backflow to Africa (http://www.pubmedcentral.nih.gov/articlerender. fcgi?artid=1945034), BMC Genomics 2007, 8:223 doi:10.1186/1471-2164-8-223

[17] Hudjashov, Kivisild et al., G; Kivisild, T; Underhill, PA; Endicott, P; Sanchez, JJ; Lin, AA; Shen, P; Oefner, P et al. (2007). "Revealing the prehistoric settlement of Australia by Y chromosome and mtDNA analysis" (http://www.pnas.org/content/104/21/8726.full). *Proceedings of the National Academy of Sciences of the United States of America* **104** (21): 8726–30. doi:10.1073/pnas.0702928104. PMC 1885570. PMID 17496137. .

[18] Ghezzi et al. (2005), Mitochondrial DNA haplogroup K is associated with a lower risk of Parkinson's disease in Italians (http://www. nature.com/ejhg/journal/v13/n6/full/5201425a.html), European Journal of Human Genetics (2005) 13, 748–752.

[19] Edwin et al. (2002), Mitochondrial DNA diversity among five tribal populations of southern India (http://www.iisc.ernet.in/currsci/ jul252002/158.pdf), CURRENT SCIENCE, VOL. 83, NO. 2, 25 JULY 2002

[20] http://www.ianlogan.co.uk/discussion/hap_M1.htm

[21] http://www.ianlogan.co.uk/discussion/hap_M2.htm

[22] http://www.ianlogan.co.uk/discussion/hap_M3.htm

[23] http://www.ianlogan.co.uk/discussion/hap_M4.htm

[24] http://www.ianlogan.co.uk/discussion/hap_M5.htm

[25] http://www.ianlogan.co.uk/discussion/hap_M6.htm

[26] http://www.ianlogan.co.uk/discussion/hap_M7.htm

[27] http://www.ianlogan.co.uk/discussion/hap_M8.htm

[28] Masashi Tanaka, Vicente M. Cabrera, Ana M. González *et al.*, "Mitochondrial Genome Variation in Eastern Asia and the Peopling of Japan," *Genome Res.* 2004 October; 14(10a): 1832–1850. doi: 10.1101/gr.2286304

[29] http://www.ianlogan.co.uk/discussion/hap_C.htm

[30] http://www.ianlogan.co.uk/discussion/hap_C1.htm

[31] http://www.ianlogan.co.uk/discussion/hap_Z.htm

[32] http://www.ianlogan.co.uk/discussion/hap_M9.htm

[33] http://www.ianlogan.co.uk/discussion/hap_M10.htm

[34] http://www.ianlogan.co.uk/discussion/hap_M11&12.htm

[35] http://www.ianlogan.co.uk/discussion/hap_G.htm

[36] http://www.ianlogan.co.uk/discussion/hap_M21.htm

[37] http://www.ianlogan.co.uk/discussion/hap_M27-29.htm

[38] http://www.ianlogan.co.uk/discussion/hap_Q.htm

[39] http://www.ianlogan.co.uk/discussion/hap_M31.htm

[40] http://www.ianlogan.co.uk/discussion/hap_M32.htm

[41] http://www.ianlogan.co.uk/discussion/hap_M33.htm

[42] http://www.ianlogan.co.uk/discussion/hap_M34.htm

[43] http://www.ianlogan.co.uk/discussion/hap_M35.htm

[44] http://www.ianlogan.co.uk/discussion/hap_M39.htm

[45] http://www.ianlogan.co.uk/discussion/hap_M40.htm

[46] http://www.ianlogan.co.uk/discussion/hap_M42.htm

[47] http://www.ianlogan.co.uk/discussion/hap_M48.htm

[48] Comas et al. (2004), Admixture, migrations, and dispersals in Central Asia: evidence from maternal DNA lineages (http://www.nature.com/ejhg/journal/v12/n6/full/5201160a.html), European Journal of Human Genetics (2004) 12, 495–504.

External links

- General
  - Ian Logan's Mitochondrial DNA Site (http://www.ianlogan.co.uk/mtDNA.htm)
  - The India DNA (http://www.familytreedna.com/public/india) geographical project at Family Tree DNA
  - The China DNA (http://www.familytreedna.com/public/china) geographical project at Family Tree DNA
- Haplogroup M
  - Mannis van Oven's PhyloTree.org - mtDNA subtree M (http://www.phylotree.org/tree/subtree_M.htm)
  - Spread of Haplogroup M (https://genographic.nationalgeographic.com/genographic/atlas.html?card=mm004), from *National Geographic*
  - Tree of M haplogroup as for 2006 (http://img386.imageshack.us/img386/3619/hapm9ev.jpg)
  - Haplogroup M (mtDNA) (http://www.facebook.com/group.php?gid=6847832518) interest group on Facebook
  - Another tree emphasizing the Andamanese and Nicobarese populations in comparison with other peoples with high M presence (http://img386.imageshack.us/img386/6476/hap1ec.jpg)
  - K.Tharanghaj et al. *In situ origin of deep rooting lineages of mitochondrial Macrohaplogroup M in India* (PDF document) (http://www.biomedcentral.com/content/pdf/1471-2164-7-151.pdf)

Human Proteinpedia

Human Proteinpedia is a portal for sharing and integration of human proteomic data,.[1] [2] It allows research laboratories to contribute and maintain protein annotations. Human Protein Reference Database,[3] [4] (HPRD) integrates data, that is deposited in Human Proteinpedia along with the existing literature curated information at the context of an individual protein. In essence, researchers can add new data to HPRD by registering to Human Proteinpedia. The data deposited in Human Proteinpedia is freely available for download. Emphasizing the importance of proteomics data disposition to public repositories, *Nature Methods* recommends Human Proteinpedia in their editorial.[5] More than 70 labs participate in this effort.

What data can be shared?

Data pertaining to post-translational modifications, protein-protein interactions, tissue expression, expression in cell lines, subcellular localization and enzyme substrate relationships can be submitted to Human Proteinpedia - Proteomics portal

Experimental platforms

Protein annotations present in Human Proteinpedia are derived from a number of platforms such as

1. Co-immunoprecipitation and mass spectrometry-based protein-protein interaction
2. Co-immunoprecipitation and Western blotting based protein-protein interaction
3. Fluorescence based experiments
4. Immunohistochemistry
5. Mass Spectrometric Analysis
6. Protein and peptide microarray
7. Western blotting
8. Yeast two-hybrid based protein-protein interaction

This portal that allows adding of protein information was developed as a collaborative effort between the laboratory of Dr. Akhilesh Pandey [6] at Johns Hopkins University and the Institute of Bioinformatics [7]

FAQs

* What are the criteria for contributing data?

Any investigator who fulfills the following criteria can contribute data:

i) provides experimentally derived data, and,

ii) is willing to share data, and,

iii) is willing to be listed as the 'contributor' of the data

* Can I contribute data anonymously?

Anonymous contributions are not allowed. Contributor details should be clearly presented while contributing data.

* Can bioinformatically predicted data be shared through Human Proteinpedia?

Predictions of any type are not allowed. Contributed data should be derived experimentally and should be accompanied with experimental evidence.

* Is the contributed data subjected to peer review?

The data are not subjected to peer review and the actual experimental data (raw or processed) should be provided.

* What will happen to conflicting results from different laboratories?

In cases where a given entry is documented as erroneous, we will consult with the contributing group(s) about deleting the entry.

External links

- http://www.humanproteinpedia.org
- http://www.hprd.org

References

[1] Kandasamy et al. Human Proteinpedia: a unified discovery resource for proteomics research. Nucleic Acids Research. Advance Access published on October 23, 2008, DOI 10.1093/nar/gkn701.

[2] Mathivanan et al. Human Proteinpedia enables sharing of human protein data. Nat Biotechnology. 2008 Feb;26:164-7

[3] Mishra et al. Human protein reference database--2006 update. Nucleic Acids Res. 2006 Jan;34(Database issue):D411-4

[4] Peri et al. Development of human protein reference database as an initial platform for approaching systems biology in humans. Genome Res. 2003 Oct;13:2363-71.

[5] Editorial. Thou shalt share your data. Nat Mehods. 2008 Mar;5:209

[6] http://pandeylab.igm.jhmi.edu

[7] http://www.ibioinformatics.org

Hypothetical protein

In biochemistry, a **hypothetical protein** is a protein whose existence has been predicted, but for which there is no experimental evidence that it is expressed in vivo.

The usual scenario involving a hypothetical protein is in gene identification during genome analysis. When the bioinformatic tool used for the gene identification finds a large open reading frame without an analog in the protein database, it returns "hypothetical protein" as an annotation remark.

The function of a hypothetical protein can also be predicted by domain homology searches with various confidence levels.

References

- Zarembinski TI, Hung LW, Mueller-Dieckmann HJ, Kim KK, Yokota H, Kim R, Kim SH (December 1998). "Structure-based assignment of the biochemical function of a hypothetical protein: a test case of structural genomics". *Proceedings of the National Academy of Sciences of the United States of America* **95** (26): 15189–93. PMC 28018. PMID 9860944.

- Nan J, Brostromer E, Liu XY, Kristensen O, Su XD (2009). "Bioinformatics and structural characterization of a hypothetical protein from Streptococcus mutans: implication of antibiotic resistance". *Plos One* **4** (10): e7245. doi:10.1371/journal.pone.0007245. PMC 2749211. PMID 19798411.

- Hernández S, Gómez A, Cedano J, Querol E (October 2009). "Bioinformatics annotation of the hypothetical proteins found by omics techniques can help to disclose additional virulence factors". *Current Microbiology* **59** (4): 451–6. doi:10.1007/s00284-009-9459-y. PMID 19636617.

- Dilip Gore (2009). "In silico Prediction of Structure andEnzymatic Activity for Hypothetical Proteins of Shigellaflexneri. Biofrontiers". *Biofrontiers* **1** (2): 1–10.

- Dilip gore, Alankar raut (2009). "Computational Functionand Structural Annotations for Hypothetical proteins ofBacillus anthracis". *Biofrontiers* **1** (1): 27–36.

- Dogra Pranay, Dilip Gore (2010). "Prediction of EnzymaticFunction and Structure of H. influenzae HypotheticalProteins - An In silico Approach". *IJSCB* **1** (in press).

- D G Gore, A P Denge, N M Amrute (2010). "Homology Modeling and Enzyme Function Prediction in the Hypothetical Proteins of Helicobacter pylori - an Insilico Approach". *Biomirror* **1**: 1–5.

External links

- ExPASy [1]

References

[1] http://www.expasy.org/cgi-bin/get-entries?KW=Hypothetical%20protein

Imaging informatics

Introduction

Imaging Informatics, also known as Radiology Informatics or Medical Imaging Informatics, is a subspecialty of Biomedical Informatics that aims to improve the efficiency, accuracy, usability and reliability of medical imaging services within the healthcare enterprise.[1] It is devoted to the study of how information about and contained within medical images is retrieved, analyzed, enhanced, and exchanged throughout the medical enterprise.

As radiology is an inherently data-intensive and technology-driven specialty of medicine, radiologists have become leaders in Imaging Informatics. However, with the proliferation of digitized images across the practice of medicine to include fields such as cardiology, dermatology, surgery, gastroenterology, obstetrics, gynecology and pathology, the advances in Imaging Informatics are also being tested and applied in other areas of medicine. Various industry players and vendors involved with medical imaging, along with IT experts and other biomedical informatics professionals, are contributing and getting involved in this expanding field.

Imaging informatics exists at the intersection of several broad fields:

- biological science - includes bench sciences such as biochemistry, microbiology, physiology and genetics
- clinical services - includes the practice of medicine, bedside research, including outcomes and cost-effectiveness studies, and public health policy
- information science - deals with the acquisition, retrieval, cataloging, and archiving of information
- medical physics / biomedical engineering - entails the use of equipment and technology for a medical purpose
- cognitive science - studying human computer interactions, usability, and information visualization
- computer science - studying the use of computer algorithms for applications such as computer assisted diagnosis and computer vision

Areas of Interest

Key areas relevant to Imaging informatics include:

- Picture Archiving and Communication System (PACS) and Component Systems
- Imaging Informatics for the Enterprise
- Image-Enabled Electronic Medical Records
- Radiology Information Systems (RIS) and Hospital Information Systems (HIS)
- Digital image acquisition
- Image processing and enhancement
- Image data compression
- 3D visualization and multimedia
- Speech recognition

- Computer-aided diagnosis (CAD).
- Imaging facilities design
- Imaging vocabularies and ontologies
- Data mining from medical images databases
- Transforming the Radiological Interpretation Process (TRIP)[2]
- DICOM, HL7 and other standards
- Workflow and process modeling and process simulation
- Quality assurance
- Archive integrity and security
- Teleradiology
- Radiology informatics education
- Digital imaging

Training

Radiologists who wish to pursue sub-specialty training in this field can undergo fellowship training in Imaging Informatics. Medical Imaging Informatics Fellowships are done after completion of Board Certification in Diagnostic Radiology, and may be pursued concurrently with other sub-specialty radiology fellowships.

The American Board of Imaging Informatics (ABII) also administers a certification examination for Imaging Informatics Professionals.

References

[1] Branstetter, B (2007). "Basics of Imaging Informatics". *Radiology* **243** (3): 656–67. doi:10.1148/radiol.2433060243. PMID 17431128.
[2] TRIP - an initiative between the then Society of Computer Applications in Radiology (SCAR), now known as the Society of Imaging Informatics in Medicine (SIIM) (http://www.scarnet.net/trip/html/What_is_TRIP.htm)

External links

- The Society for Imaging Informatics in Medicine (http://www.siimweb.org/)
- American Board of Imaging Informatics (https://www.abii.org/)

Information Hyperlinked over Proteins

Information Hyperlinked over Proteins (or **iHOP**) is an online service that provides a gene-guided network to access PubMed abstracts. By using genes and proteins as hyperlinks between sentences and abstracts, the information in PubMed can be converted into one navigable resource. Navigating across interrelated sentences within this network rather than the use of conventional keyword searches allows for stepwise and controlled acquisition of information. Moreover, this literature network can be superimposed upon experimental interaction data to facilitate the simultaneous analysis of novel and existing knowledge. The network presented in iHOP currently contains 12 million sentences and 80000 genes from over 1,500 organisms, including *Homo sapiens*, *Mus musculus*, *Drosophila melanogaster*, *Caenorhabditis elegans*, *Danio rerio*, *Arabidopsis thaliana*, *Saccharomyces cerevisiae* and *Escherichia coli*.

The system was published in *Nature Genetics* **36**, 664 (2004) as 'A gene network for navigating the literature'.

Source

- Hoffmann R, Valencia A (July 2004). "A gene network for navigating the literature". *Nat. Genet.* **36** (7): 664. doi:10.1038/ng0704-664. PMID 15226743.

External links

- iHOP server [25]

Integrated Genome Browser

Integrated Genome Browser (**IGB**) (pronounced Ig-Bee)[1] is an open source genome browser, a visualization tool used to observe biologically-interesting patterns in genomic data sets, including sequence data, gene models, alignments, and data from DNA microarrays.

Integrated Genome Browser (IGB)

Operating system	UNIX, Linux, Mac, MS-Windows
Type	Bioinformatics tool
License	CPL 1.0
Website	http://igb.bioviz.org

History

Integrated Genome Browser was originally developed at Affymetrix to support visualization of data from the company's tiling array platform and was also partly supported via NIH funding. It was released as open source in 2004. The National Science Foundation later funded further development of the tool as the front end for a companion data repository for plant genomic data sets.

Description

IGB is built on top of the Genoviz SDK [2][3], a Java library that implements key visualization features such as dynamic, real-time zooming and scrolling through a genomic map, a feature of the IGB browser that sets it apart from many similar tools.

IGB is also distinguished by the ease with which individual labs can set up data source servers to share data, notably, via REST-style Web services (Distributed Annotation System) and a simple file-system based approach called QuickLoad.

Supported formats

IGB reads data in dozens of formats, including BAM, BED, Affymetrix CHP, FASTA, GFF, GTF, PSL, SGR, and WIG. The most up-to-date list is available at the BioViz Wiki [4].

IGB can output visualized data in dozens of formats via the FreeHEP library. These include EPS, PostScript, PDF, EMF, SVG, SWF, CGM, GIF, PNG, and PPM.

References

[1] Nicol JW, Helt GA, Blanchard SG Jr, Raja A, Loraine AE. The Integrated Genome Browser: Free software for distribution and exploration of genome-scale data sets. Bioinformatics. 2009 Aug 4 (http://bioinformatics.oxfordjournals.org/cgi/content/full/25/20/2730)

[2] http://genoviz.sourceforge.net

[3] Helt GA, Nicol JW, Erwin E, Blossom E, Blanchard S Jr, Chervitz SA, Harmon C, Loraine AE. The Genoviz Software Development Kit: A Java toolkit for building genomics visualization applications. BMC Bioinformatics. 2009 Aug 25;10(1):266. (http://www.ncbi.nlm.nih.gov/pubmed/19706180?dopt=AbstractPlus)

[4] http://wiki.transvar.org/confluence/display/igbman/File+Formats

External links

- Genoviz SDK at SourceForge (http://genoviz.sourceforge.net)
- IGB Bioviz site (http://www.bioviz.org/igb) at the University of North Carolina at Charlotte
- Affymetrix IGB site (http://www.affymetrix.com/partners_programs/programs/developer/tools/download_igb.affx)
- IGB page (http://bioserver.hci.utah.edu/BioInfo/index.php/Software:IGB) at the Huntsman Cancer Institute

Integrated Microbial Genomes System

The **Integrated Microbial Genomes** (IMG) [1] is a genome browsing and annotation system developed by the DOE-Joint Genome Institute. IMG contains all the draft and complete microbial genomes sequenced by the DOE-JGI integrated with other publicly available genomes (including Archaea, Bacteria, Eukarya, Viruses and Plasmids). IMG provides a set of tools for comparative analysis of genes, genomes and functions.

Users can employee a set of powerful tools for comparative analysis and explore the microbial genomes along its 3 main dimensions (genomes, genes and functions), select them and transfer them in the comparative analysis carts.

Users can also type or upload their own gene annotations (called MyIMG gene annotations) and the IMG system will allow them to generate Genbank or EMBL format files containing these annotations.

For a tutorial on on how to use the system visit OpenHelix [2]

The **Integrated Microbial Genomes with Microbiome Samples** (IMG/M) [3] system is an extension of the IMG system providing a comparative analysis context of metagenomic data with the publicly available isolate genomes.

The **Integrated Microbial Genomes- Expert Review** (IMG/ER) [4] system provides support to individual scientists or group of scientists for functional annotation and curation of their microbial genomes of interest. Users can submit their annotated genomes (or request the IMG automated annotation pipeline to be applied first) into IMG-ER and proceed with manual curation and comparative analysis in the system, through secure (password protected) access.

External links and sources

- IMG home page [1] reference: Nucleic Acids Research, 2006, Vol. 34, Database issue D344-D348 [5]
- IMG/M home page [3] reference: Bioinformatics, 2006, Vol 22(14): e359-e367 [6]
- MicrobesOnline [7]
- NCBI Microbial Genomes [8]
- TIGR Comprehensive Microbial Resource [9]
- The SEED [10]

References

[1] http://img.jgi.doe.gov/
[2] http://www.openhelix.com/downloads/img/img_home.shtml
[3] http://img.jgi.doe.gov/m
[4] http://img.jgi.doe.gov/er
[5] http://nar.oxfordjournals.org/cgi/content/abstract/34/suppl_1/D344
[6] http://bioinformatics.oxfordjournals.org/cgi/content/abstract/22/14/e359?ijkey=mD17gJWYFIfz5x2&keytype=ref
[7] http://MicrobesOnline.org
[8] http://www.ncbi.nlm.nih.gov/genomes/lproks.cgi
[9] http://cmr.jcvi.org
[10] http://theSeed.org

Integrative bioinformatics

Integrative bioinformatics is a discipline of bioinformatics that focuses on problems of data integration for the life sciences.

With the rise of high-throughput (HTP) technologies in the life sciences, particularly in molecular biology, the amount of collected data has grown in an exponential fashion. Furthermore, the data is scattered over a plethora of both public and private repositories, and is stored using a large number of different formats. This situation makes the extraction of new knowledge from the complete set of available data very difficult.

Integrative bioinformatics attempts to tackle this problem by providing unified access to life science data.

Approaches

Data warehousing approaches

In the data warehousing strategy, the data from different sources are extracted and integrated in a single database. For example, various 'omics' datasets may be integrated to provide biological insights into biological systems. Examples include data from genomics, transcriptomics, proteomics, interactomics, metabolomics. Ideally, changes in these sources are regularly synchronized to the integrated database. The data is presented to the users in a common format. One advantage of this approach is that data is available for analysis at a single site, using a uniform schema. Some disadvantages are that the datasets are often huge and are difficult to keep up to date.

References

External links

- Journal of Integrative Bioinformatics (http://journal.imbio.de/)

Intelligent Systems for Molecular Biology

Organized by the International Society for Computational Biology (ISCB), **Intelligent Systems for Molecular Biology (ISMB)** is a scientific meeting on the subjects of bioinformatics and computational biology. Its principal focus is on the development and application of advanced computational methods for biological problems. It has been held annually since 1993 and has grown to the largest and most prestigious meetings in these fields.[1] In recent years, the conference has been attended by between 1,500 and 2,000 delegates.[1] ISMB has been rotating locations mainly between North America and Europe each year. When the meeting is in Europe it has been held jointly with the European Conference of Computational Biology (ECCB). The proceedings of the conference have been published by the journal Bioinformatics.

List of conferences

ISMB 1993 was held in Bethesda, USA, at the National Library of Medicine.[2]

ISMB 1994 was held in Stanford, USA, at Stanford University.[3]

ISMB 1995 was held in Cambridge, UK, at Robinson College.[4]

ISMB 1996 [5] was held in St. Louis, USA, at Washington University in St. Louis.[6]

ISMB 1997 [7] was held in Halkidiki, Greece, at the Sithonia Beach Hotel, Porto Carras.[8]

ISMB 1998 [9] was held in Montreal, Canada, at the Radisson Hotel des Gouverneurs.[10]

ISMB 1999 [11] was held in Heidelberg, Germany, at the Kongresshaus Stadthalle Heidelberg.[12]

ISMB 2000 [13] was held in San Diego, USA, at the University of California, San Diego.[14]

ISMB 2001 [15] was held in Copenhagen, Denmark, at the Tivoli Gardens in the concert hall.

ISMB 2002 [16] was held in Edmonton, Canada, at the Shaw Conference Centre.[17]

ISMB 2003 [18] was held in Brisbane, Australia, at the Brisbane Conference and Exhibition Centre.[19]

ISMB/ECCB 2004 [20] was held in Glasgow, UK, at the Scottish Exhibition and Conference Centre.

ISMB 2005 [21] was held in Detroit, USA, at the Detroit Marriott at the Renaissance Center.

ISMB 2006 [22] was held in Fortaleza, Brazil at the Fortaleza Convention Center.

ISMB/ECCB 2007 [23] was held in Vienna, Austria, at the Austria Center Vienna.

ISMB 2008 [24] was held in Toronto, Canada, at the Toronto Convention Centre.

ISMB/ECCB 2009 [25] was held in Stockholm, Sweden, at the Stockholm International Fairs.[26]

ISMB 2010 [27] was held in Boston, USA, at the John B. Hynes Veterans Memorial Convention Center.[28]

ISMB/ECCB 2011 [29] was held in Vienna, Austria, at the Austria Center Vienna.

ISMB 2012 [30] will be held in Long Beach, California, USA.

References

[1] Linial, M.; Mesirov, J. P.; Morrison Mckay, B. J.; Rost, B. (2008). "ISMB 2008 Toronto". *PLoS Computational Biology* **4** (6): e1000094. doi:10.1371/journal.pcbi.1000094. PMC 2427177. PMID 18584023.

[2] "Proceedings of the 1st International Conference on Intelligent Systems for Molecular Biology. ISMB--93". *Proceedings / ... International Conference on Intelligent Systems for Molecular Biology ; ISMB. International Conference on Intelligent Systems for Molecular Biology* **1**: i–ix, 1–459. 1993. PMID 7584323.

[3] "Proceedings of the 2nd International Conference on Intelligent Systems for Molecular Biology. ISMB--94". *Proceedings / ... International Conference on Intelligent Systems for Molecular Biology ; ISMB. International Conference on Intelligent Systems for Molecular Biology* **2**: 1–384. 1994. PMID 7584376.

[4] "Proceedings of the 3rd International Conference on Intelligent Systems for Molecular Biology. ISMB--95". *Proceedings / ... International Conference on Intelligent Systems for Molecular Biology ; ISMB. International Conference on Intelligent Systems for Molecular Biology* **3**: i–xii, 1–415. 1995. PMID 7584424.

[5] http://www.iscb.org/cms_addon/conferences/ismb1996/ISMB-96%20Home%20Page.htm

[6] "Proceedings of the 4th International Conference on Intelligent Systems for Molecular Biology. ISMB-96". *Proceedings / ... International Conference on Intelligent Systems for Molecular Biology ; ISMB. International Conference on Intelligent Systems for Molecular Biology* **4**: 1–262. 1996. PMID 9005023.

[7] http://www.ebi.ac.uk/ismb97/

[8] "Proceedings of the 5th International Conference on Intelligent Systems for Molecular Biology. Halkidiki, Greece, June 21-26, 1997". *Proceedings / ... International Conference on Intelligent Systems for Molecular Biology ; ISMB. International Conference on Intelligent Systems for Molecular Biology* **5**: 1–371. 1997. PMID 9410501.

[9] http://www-lbit.iro.umontreal.ca/ISMB98/

[10] "Proceedings of the 6th International Conference on Intelligent Systems for Molecular Biology. Montreal, Quebec, Canada. June 28-July 1, 1998". *Proceedings / ... International Conference on Intelligent Systems for Molecular Biology ; ISMB. International Conference on Intelligent Systems for Molecular Biology* **6**: 1–223. 1998. PMID 9867411.

[11] http://bioinf.mpi-inf.mpg.de/conferences/ismb99/WWW/

[12] "ISMB '99. Proceedings of the 7th International Conference on Intelligent Systems for Molecular Biology. Heidelberg, Germany, August 6-10, 1999". *Proceedings / ... International Conference on Intelligent Systems for Molecular Biology ; ISMB. International Conference on Intelligent Systems for Molecular Biology*: 1–307. 1999. PMID 10809579.

[13] http://www.iscb.org/cms_addon/conferences/ismb2000/

[14] "Proceedings of the 8th International Conference on Intelligent Systems for Molecular Biology (ISMB 2000). San Diego, California, USA. August 19-23, 2000". *Proceedings / ... International Conference on Intelligent Systems for Molecular Biology ; ISMB. International Conference on Intelligent Systems for Molecular Biology* **8**: 1–419. 2000. PMID 11221647.

[15] http://ismb01.cbs.dtu.dk/

[16] http://www.iscb.org/cms_addon/conferences/ismb2002/

[17] "Ismb 2002. Proceedings of the 10th International Conference on Intelligent Systems for Molecular Biology. Edmonton, Canada, August 3-7, 2002". *Bioinformatics (Oxford, England)* **18 Suppl 1**: S1–364. 2002. PMID 12169523.

[18] http://www.iscb.org/cms_addon/conferences/ismb2003/

[19] Catherine, A.; Abbott, (2003). "11th Intelligent Systems for Molecular Biology 2003 (ISMB 2003)". *Comparative and Functional Genomics* **4** (6): 654–659. doi:10.1002/cfg.336. PMC 2447307. PMID 18629025.

[20] http://www.iscb.org/cms_addon/conferences/ismbeccb2004/

[21] http://www.iscb.org/cms_addon/conferences/ismb2005/

[22] http://ismb2006.cbi.cnptia.embrapa.br/

[23] http://www.iscb.org/cms_addon/conferences/ismbeccb2007/

[24] http://www.iscb.org/cms_addon/conferences/ismb2008/

[25] http://www.iscb.org/ismbeccb2009/

[26] Lister, A. L.; Datta, R. S.; Hofmann, O.; Krause, R.; Kuhn, M.; Roth, B.; Schneider, R. (2010). Troyanskaya, Olga. ed. "Live Coverage of Intelligent Systems for Molecular Biology/European Conference on Computational Biology (ISMB/ECCB) 2009". *PLoS Computational Biology* **6** (1): e1000640. doi:10.1371/journal.pcbi.1000640. PMC 2813254. PMID 20126524.

[27] http://www.iscb.org/ismb2010

[28] "Proceedings of the ISMB (Intelligent Systems for Molecular Biology) 2010 Conference. July 11-13, 2010. Boston, Massachusetts, USA". *Bioinformatics (Oxford, England)* **26** (12): i7–406. 2010. PMID 20963926.

[29] http://www.iscb.org/ismbeccb2011/

[30] http://www.iscb.org/ismb2012

Interaction network

Interaction network is a network of nodes that are connected by features. If the feature is a physical and molecular, the interaction network is molecular interactions usually found in cells. Interaction network has become a research topic in biology in recent years due to rapid progress in high throughput data production.

External links

- Interactomics.org [1]: Biological interaction research information site.
- BIND database Canada [2]
- VirHostNet [3] - **Vir**us-**Host** protein-protein interaction **Net**works knowledgebase

References

[1] http://interactomics.org
[2] http://www.bind.ca/
[3] http://pbildb1.univ-lyon1.fr/virhostnet

Interactome

Interactome is defined as the whole set of molecular interactions in cells. It is usually displayed as a directed graph. Molecular interactions can occur between molecules belonging to different biochemical families (proteins, nucleic acids, lipids, carbohydrates, etc.) and also within a given family. When spoken in terms of proteomics, interactome refers to protein–protein interaction network (PPI), or protein interaction network (PIN). Another extensively studied type of interactome is the protein–DNA interactome (network

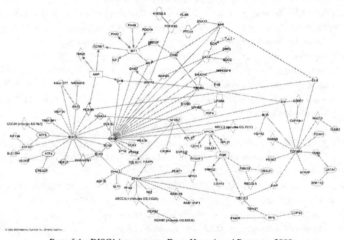

Part of the DISC1 interactome. From Hennah and Porteous, 2009.

formed by transcription factors (and DNA or chromatin regulatory proteins) and their target genes. The word "interactome" was originally coined in 1999 by a group of French scientists headed by Bernard Jacq (see Nucleic acids research 27(1):89-94; PubMed ID: 9847149).

It has been suggested that the size of an organism's interactome correlates better than genome size with the biological complexity of the organism (Stumpf, et al., 2008). Although protein–protein interaction maps containing several thousands of binary interactions are now available for several organisms, none of them is presently complete and the size of interactomes is still a matter of debate. In 2010, the most "complete" gene interactome produced to date was compiled from 54 million two-gene comparisons to describe "the interaction profiles for ~75% of all genes in the Budding yeast," with 170,000 gene interactions.[1]

Although extremely important and useful, the interactome is still being developed and is not complete (as of October 2010). There are various factors that have a role in protein interactions that have yet to be incorporated in the interactome. Many have termed the interactome as a whole as being fuzzy. The binding strength of the various proteins, microenvironmental factors, sensitivity to various procedures, and the physiological state of the cell all affect protein–protein interactions, yet are not accounted for in the interactome. Although the interactome is useful in some ways, it must be analyzed knowing that these factors exist and can affect the protein interactions.[2]

Methods of mapping the interactome

The study of the interactome is called interactomics. The basic unit of protein network is protein–protein interaction (PPI). Because the interactome considers the whole organism, there is a need to collect a massive amount of information.

Experimental methods have been devised to determine PPI, such as affinity purification and yeast two hybrid (Y2H). The former is suited to identify a protein complex, while the latter is suited to explore the binary interactions in mass quantities. The former is considered as a low-throughput method (LTP), while the latter is considered as high-throughput method (HTP).

Using the experimental data as a starting point, the concept of homology transfer has been used to develop algorithms to map the interactome, including ones that produce detailed atomic models of protein protein complexes [3] as well as other protein–molecule interactions.[4]

There have been several efforts to map the eukaryotic interactome through HTP methods. As of 2006, yeast, fly, worm, and human HTP maps have been created. Recently, pathogen-host interactome (Hepatitis C Virus/Human (2008),[5] Epstein Barr virus/Human (2008), Influenza virus/Human (2009)) was also delineated through HTP to identify essential molecular components for pathoghens but also for the host to recognize pathogens and trigger efficient innate immune response.[6]

Using the interactome

Researchers have begun to use preliminary versions of the interactome to gain understanding about the biology and function of the molecules within them. For example, protein interaction networks have been used to produce improved protein functional annotations (or nannotations) for proteins with unknown functions.[7]

Interactome web servers

- Protinfo PPC [8] predicts the atomic 3D structure of protein protein complexes.[9]

Interactome databases

- APID: Agile Protein Interaction DataAnalyzer [10] – an interactive bioinformatic web-tool that integrates and unifies main known experimentally validated protein–protein interactions (Prieto and De Las Rivas, 2006).
- BioGRID [11] database
- ConsensusPathDB includes functional interactions from 12 other databases
- Database of interacting proteins (DIP) (Xenarios et al. 2000).
- MIPS [12] database
- PSIMAP [13] database — the first protein structural interactome DB
- InterPare [14] database — a structural protein interfaceome DB
- Biomolecular Interaction Network Database (BIND) (Bader et al. 2003)
- Online Predicted Human Interaction Database (OPHID) (Brown and Jurisica, 2005)
- Human Protein Reference Database (HPRD [15]) (Peri S et al. 2003)
- HPID: Human Protein Interaction Database [16] (Inha University, Korea)
- MINT: Molecular INTeraction database [17] (Chatr-aryamontri et al. 2006)
- PINdb: Proteins Interacting in the Nucleus Database [18] (Luc PV and Tempst P, 2004)

- IntAct: The Molecular Interaction Database [19]
- VirHostNet [3] — **Vir**us-**Host** protein–protein interaction **Net**works knowledgebase
- Interactome Databases [20] — interactome projects at CCSB.
- TRANSFAC, a database about transcription regulating eukaryotic protein-DNA interactions

References

[1] Costanzo M, Baryshnikova A, Bellay J, *et al.* (2010-01-22). "The genetic landscape of a cell". *Science* **327** (5964): 425–431. doi:10.1126/science.1180823. PMID 20093466.

[2] Welch GR (2008). "The Fuzzy Interactome" (http://200.145.134.134/twiki/pub/Main/Miscelanea/0312081.pdf). Cell Press. .

[3] Kittichotirat W, Guerquin M, Bumgarner RE, Samudrala R. (2009.). "Protinfo PPC: A web server for atomic level prediction of protein complexes.". *Nucleic Acids Research* **37** (Web Server issue): W519–W525. doi:10.1093/nar/gkp306. PMC 2703994. PMID 19420059.

[4] McDermott J, Guerquin M, Frazier Z, Chang AN, Samudrala R. (2005). "BIOVERSE: Enhancements to the framework for structural, functional, and contextual annotations of proteins and proteomes.". *Nucleic Acids Research* **33** (Web Server issue): W324–W325. doi:10.1093/nar/gki401. PMC 1160162. PMID 15980482.

[5] de Chassey B, Navratil V, Tafforeau L, *et al.* (2008-11-04). "Hepatitis C virus infection protein network". *Molecular Systems Biology* **4** (4:230): 230. doi:10.1038/msb.2008.66. PMC 2600670. PMID 18985028.

[6] Navratil V, de Chassey B, *et al.* (2010-11-05). "Systems-level comparison of protein–protein interactions between viruses and the human type I interferon system network.". *Journal of Proteome Research* **9** (7): 3527–36. doi:10.1021/pr100326j. PMID 20459142.

[7] McDermott J, Bumgarner RE, Samudrala R. (2005). "Functional annotation from predicted protein interaction networks.". *Bioinformatics* **21** (15): 3217–3226. doi:10.1093/bioinformatics/bti514. PMID 15919725.

[8] http://protinfo.compbio.washington.edu/ppc/

[9] Kittichotirat W, Guerquin M, Bumgarner R, Samudrala R. (2009). "Protinfo PPC: A web server for atomic level prediction of protein complexes.". *Nucleic Acids Research* **37**: W519-W525.

[10] http://bioinfow.dep.usal.es/apid/

[11] http://www.thebiogrid.org/

[12] http://mips.gsf.de/services/ppi

[13] http://psimap.com

[14] http://interpare.net

[15] http://hprd.org:

[16] http://wilab.inha.ac.kr/hpid/

[17] http://mint.bio.uniroma2.it/mint/Welcome.do

[18] http://pin.mskcc.org

[19] http://www.ebi.ac.uk/intact

[20] http://interactome.dfci.harvard.edu

- De Las Rivas J, Fontanillo C (June 2010). "Protein–Protein Interactions Essentials: Key Concepts to Building and Analyzing Interactome Networks". *PLoS Computational Biology* **6** (6): e1000807. doi:10.1371/journal.pcbi.1000807. PMC 2891586. PMID 20589078..

- Sanchez C, Lachaize C, Janody F, Bellon B, Röder L, Euzenat J, Rechenmann F, Jacq B (1999). "Grasping at molecular interactions and genetic networks in Drosophila melanogaster using FlyNets, an Internet database". *Nucleic Acids Res.* **27** (1): 89–94. doi:10.1093/nar/27.1.89. PMC 148104. PMID 9847149.

- Xenarios I, Rice DW, Salwinski L, Baron MK, Marcotte EM, Eisenberg D (2000). "DIP: the database of interacting proteins". *Nucleic Acids Res.* **28** (1): 289–91. doi:10.1093/nar/28.1.289. PMC 102387. PMID 10592249.

- Park J, Lappe M, Teichmann SA (Mar 2001). "Mapping protein family interactions: intramolecular and intermolecular protein family interaction repertoires in the PDB and yeast". *J Mol Biol.* **307** (3): 929–38. doi:10.1006/jmbi.2001.4526. PMID 11273711.

- Bader GD *et al.* (2003). "BIND: The Biomolecular interaction Network Database". *Nucleic Acids Res.* **31** (1): 248–50. doi:10.1093/nar/gkg056. PMC 165503. PMID 12519993.

- Peri S., Navarro JD, Amanchy R, Kristiansen TZ, Jonnalagadda CK *et al.* (2003). "Development of human protein reference database as an initial platform for approaching systems biology in humans". *Genome Res* **13** (10): 2363–71. doi:10.1101/gr.1680803. PMC 403728. PMID 14525934.

- Brown KR, Jurisica I (2005). "Online Predicted Human Interaction Database". *Bioinformatics* **21** (9): 2076–82. doi:10.1093/bioinformatics/bti273. PMID 15657099.
- Stumpf M, Thorne T *et al.* (2008). "Estimating the size of the human interactome" (http://www.pnas.org/cgi/content/abstract/105/19/6959?etoc). *Proceedings of the National Academy of Sciences* **105** (19): 6959. doi:10.1073/pnas.0708078105. PMC 2383957. PMID 18474861.
- Navratil V. et al. (2009) VirHostNet: a knowledge base for the management and the analysis of proteome-wide virus-host interaction networks. (http://www.ncbi.nlm.nih.gov/pubmed/18984613) *Nucleic Acids Res.* 2009 Jan;37(Database issue):D661-8. Epub 2008 Nov 4.

External links

- PSIbase Database (http://psimap.com/) — a global interactome DB based on PSIMAP.
- Interactome.org (http://interactome.org) — a dedicated interactome web site.

Interactomics

Interactomics is a discipline at the intersection of bioinformatics and biology that deals with studying both the interactions and the consequences of those interactions between and among proteins, and other molecules within a cell.[1] The network of all such interactions is called the Interactome. Interactomics thus aims to compare such networks of interactions (i.e., interactomes) between and within species in order to find how the traits of such networks are either preserved or varied. From a mathematical, or mathematical biology viewpoint an interactome network is a graph or a category representing the most important interactions pertinent to the normal physiological functions of a cell or organism.

Interactomics is an example of "top-down" systems biology, which takes an overhead, as well as overall, view of a biosystem or organism. Large sets of genome-wide and proteomic data are collected, and correlations between different molecules are inferred. From the data new hypotheses are formulated about feedbacks between these molecules. These hypotheses can then be tested by new experiments.[2]

Through the study of the interaction of all of the molecules in a cell the field looks to gain a deeper understanding of genome function and evolution than just examining an individual genome in isolation.[1] Interactomics goes beyond cellular proteomics in that it not only attempts to characterize the interaction between proteins, but between all molecules in the cell.

Methods of interactomics

The study of the interactome requires the collection of large amounts of data by way of high throughput experiments. Through these experiments a large number of data points are collected from a single organism under a small number of perturbations[2] These experiments include:

- Two-hybrid screening
- Tandem Affinity Purification
- X-ray tomography
- Optical fluorescence microscopy

Recent developments

The field of interactomics is currently rapidly expanding and developing. While no biological interactomes have been fully characterized. Over 90% of proteins in *Saccharomyces cerevisiae* have been screened and their interactions characterized, making it the first interactome to be nearly fully specified.[3]

Also there have been recent systematic attempts to explore the human interactome[1] and.

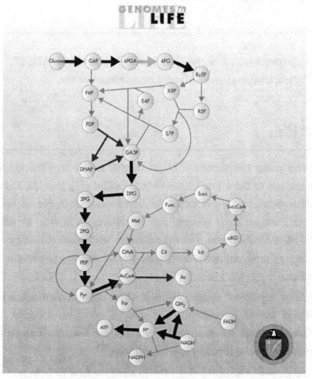

Metabolic Network Model for Escherichia coli.

Other species whose interactomes have been studied in some detail include *Caenorhabditis elegans* and *Drosophila melanogaster*.

Criticisms and concerns

Kiemer and Cesareni[1] raise the following concerns with the current state of the field:

- The experimental procedures associated with the field are error prone leading to "noisy results". This leads to 30% of all reported interactions being artifacts. In fact, two groups using the same techniques on the same organism found less than 30% interactions in common.
- Techniques may be biased, i.e. the technique determines which interactions are found.
- Ineractomes are not nearly complete with perhaps the exception of *S. cerivisiae*.
- While genomes are stable, interactomes may vary between tissues and developmental stages.
- Genomics compares amino acids, and nucleotides which are in a sense unchangeable, but interactomics compares proteins and other molecules which are subject to mutation and evolution.
- It is difficult to match evolutionarily related proteins in distantly related species.

References

[1] Kiemer, L; G Cesareni (2007). "Comparative interactomics: comparing apples and pears?". *TRENDS in Biochemistry* **25** (10): 448–454. doi:10.1016/j.tibtech.2007.08.002. PMID 17825444.

[2] Bruggeman, F J; H V Westerhoff (2006). "The nature of systems biology". *TRENDS in Microbiology* **15** (1): 45–50. doi:10.1016/j.tim.2006.11.003. PMID 17113776.

[3] Krogan, NJ; et al. (2006). "Global landscape of protein complexes in the yeast *Saccharomyeses Cerivisiae* ". *Nature* **440** (7084): 637–643. doi:10.1038/nature04670. PMID 16554755.

External links

- Interactomics.org (http://interactomics.org). A dedicated interactomics web site operated under BioLicense.
- Interactome.org (http://interactome.org). An interactome wiki site.
- PSIbase (http://psibase.kobic.re.kr) Structural Interactome Map of all Proteins.
- Omics.org (http://omics.org). An omics portal site that is openfree (under BioLicense)
- Genomics.org (http://genomics.org). A Genomics wiki site.
- Comparative Interactomics analysis of protein family interaction networks using PSIMAP (protein structural interactome map) (http://bioinformatics.oxfordjournals.org/cgi/content/full/21/15/3234)
- Interaction interfaces in proteins via the Voronoi diagram of atoms (http://www.sciencedirect.com/science?_ob=ArticleURL&_udi=B6TYR-4KXVD30-2&_user=10&_coverDate=11/30/2006&_rdoc=1&_fmt=&_orig=search&_sort=d&view=c&_acct=C000050221&_version=1&_urlVersion=0&_userid=10&md5=8361bf3fe7834b4642cdda3b979de8bb)
- Using convex hulls to extract interaction interfaces from known structures. Panos Dafas, Dan Bolser, Jacek Gomoluch, Jong Park, and Michael Schroeder. Bioinformatics 2004 20: 1486-1490.
- PSIbase: a database of Protein Structural Interactome map (PSIMAP). Sungsam Gong, Giseok Yoon, Insoo Jang Bioinformatics 2005.
- Mapping Protein Family Interactions : Intramolecular and Intermolecular Protein Family Interaction Repertoires in the PDB and Yeast, Jong Park, Michael Lappe & Sarah A. Teichmann,J.M.B (2001).
- Semantic Systems Biology (http://www.semantic-systems-biology.org)

Interferome

INTERFEROME

Content	
Description	database of interferon regulated genes
Organism(s)	Homo sapiens Mus musculus Pan troglodytes
Contact	
Laboratory	Monash Institute of Medical Research University of Cambridge
Primary Citation	Shamith A Samarajiwa & al. (2009)[1]
Release date	2008
Access	
Website	http://www.interferome.org
Tools	
Miscellaneous	

Interferome is an online bioinformatics database of interferon regulated genes (IRGs).[1] These Interferon Regulated Genes are also known as Interferon Stimulated Genes (ISGs). The database contains information on type I (IFN alpha, beta), type II (IFN gamma) and type III (IFN lambda) regulated genes and is regularly updated. It is used by the interferon and cytokine research community [2] both as an analysis tool and an information resource. Interferons were identified as antiviral proteins more than 50 years ago. However, their involvement in immunomodulation, cell proliferation, inflammation and other homeostatic processes has been since identified. These cytokines are used as therapeutics in many diseases such as chronic viral infections, cancer and multiple sclerosis.[3] These interferons regulate the transcription of approximately 2000 genes in an interferon subtype, dose, cell type and stimulus dependent manner. This database of interferon regulated genes is an attempt at integrating information from high-throughput experiments and molecular biology databases to gain a detailed understanding of interferon biology.

Contents

Interferome comprises the following data sets:

- Gene expression data of interferon regulated genes from *Homo sapiens*, *Mus musculus*, and *Pan troglodytes*, manually curated from more than 30 public and inhouse microarray and proteomic datasets.

Tools

Interferome offers many ways of searching and retrieving data from the database:

- Identify interferon regulated gene signatures in microarray data;
- Gene Ontology analysis and annotation;
- Normal tissue expression of interferon regulated genes;
- Regulatory analysis of interferon regulated genes;
- BLAST (Basic Local Alignment Search Tool) analysis and orthologue sequence download;

Interferome Management

Interferome is managed by a team at Monash University :Monash Institute of Medical Research and the University of Cambridge

References

[1] Samarajiwa, Shamith A; Forster Sam, Auchettl Katie, Hertzog Paul J (Jan 2009). "INTERFEROME: the database of interferon regulated genes" (in eng). *Nucleic Acids Res.* (England) **37** (Database issue): D852-7. doi:10.1093/nar/gkn732. PMC 2686605. PMID 18996892.

[2] http://www.isicr.org/

[3] http://www.cancerhelp.org.uk/help/default.asp?page=4009

External links

- INTERFEROME (http://www.interferome.org/)

International Protein Index

The **International Protein Index** (IPI)[1] is database that was created to give the proteomics community a resource that enables

- accession numbers from a variety of bioinformatics databases to be mapped
- a complete set of proteins for a species i.e. a reference set

IPI was launched in 2001 by the European Bioinformatics Institute (EBI) when databases cataloguing human genes varied greatly and had few links between them. Since then much more data has been produced giving a more complete picture and databases have collaborated to synchronize data. Currently many model organisms have a reference set of genes/proteins which are catalogued in Ensembl/UniProt respectively, as well as other species specific databases.

Retirement

Due to advances in data organization the need for IPI is diminishing. The EBI has announced that this service will be closing when appropriate and has advised users of its services to employ UniProtKB accession numbers as their protein identifiers.

References

[1] Kersey PJ, Duarte J, Williams A, Karavidopoulou Y, Birney E, Apweiler R (July 2004). "The International Protein Index: an integrated database for proteomics experiments". *Proteomics* **4** (7): 1985–8. doi:10.1002/pmic.200300721. PMID 15221759.

External links

- IPI @ EBI (http://www.ebi.ac.uk/IPI/IPIhelp.html)
- Ensembl (http://www.ensembl.org/index.html)
- European Bioinformatics Institute (http://www.ebi.ac.uk/)
- UniProt (http://www.uniprot.org/)

Interolog

An **interolog** is a conserved interaction between a pair of proteins which have interacting homologs in another organism. The term was introduced in a 2000 paper by Walhout et al.[1] [2]

Example

Suppose that A and B are two different interacting human proteins, and A' and B' are two different interacting dog proteins. Then the interaction between A and B is an interolog of the interaction between A' and B' if the following conditions all hold:

- A is a homolog of A'. (Protein homologs have similar amino acid sequences and derive from a common ancestral sequence).
- B is a homolog of B'.
- A and B interact.
- A' and B' interact.

Thus, interologs are homologous pairs of protein interactions across different organisms.

References

[1] Walhout, A. J.; Sordella, R.; Lu, X.; Hartley, J. L.; Temple, G. F.; Brasch, M. A.; Thierry-Mieg, N.; Vidal, M. (2000). "Protein Interaction Mapping in C. Elegans Using Proteins Involved in Vulval Development". *Science* **287** (5450): 116–122. doi:10.1126/science.287.5450.116. PMID 10615043.

[2] http://genome.cshlp.org/content/14/6/1107.full#ref-50

- Yu, H.; Luscombe, N. M.; Lu, H. X.; Zhu, X.; Xia, Y.; Han, J. D.; Bertin, N.; Chung, S. et al. (2004). "Annotation Transfer Between Genomes: Protein-Protein Interologs and Protein-DNA Regulogs". *Genome Research* **14** (6): 1107–1118. doi:10.1101/gr.1774904. PMC 419789. PMID 15173116.
- Kemmer, D.; Huang, Y.; Shah, S. P.; Lim, J.; Brumm, J.; Yuen, M. M.; Ling, J.; Xu, T. et al. (2005). "Ulysses - an application for the projection of molecular interactions across species". *Genome Biology* **6** (12): R106. doi:10.1186/gb-2005-6-12-r106. PMC 1414088. PMID 16356269.
- Wiles, A. M.; Doderer, M.; Ruan, J.; Gu, T. T.; Ravi, D.; Blackman, B.; Bishop, A. J. (2010). "Building and analyzing protein interactome networks by cross-species comparisons". *BMC Systems Biology* **4**: 36. doi:10.1186/1752-0509-4-36. PMC 2859380. PMID 20353594.

External links

- Interactome.org (http://interactome.org): Interactome portal site.
- Interactomics.org (http://interactomics.org): Interactomics portal site.
- (http://www.interologfinder.org): Cross-species interaction prediction site.

Ionomics

The **ionome** is the mineral nutrient and trace element composition of an organism, representing the inorganic component of cellular and organismal systems. **Ionomics**, the study of the ionome, requires application of high-throughput elemental analysis technologies, and their integration with bioinformatic and genetic tools. Ionomics has the ability to capture information about the functional state of an organism under different conditions, driven by genetic and developmental differences, and by biotic and abiotic factors. The relatively high throughput and low cost of ionomic analysis means that it has the potential to provide a powerful approach to not only the functional analysis of the genes and gene networks that directly control the ionome, but also to the more extended gene networks controlling developmental and physiological processes that indirectly affect the ionome.

Concepts of the Ionome and Ionomics

The term ionome was defined as all the mineral nutrient (dietary minerals) and trace elements found in an organism, and originally investigated in the plant *Arabidopsis thaliana* (Thale cress)[1]. This definition extended the previously used term metallome [2,3] to include biologically significant nonmetals [4]. The ionome also includes both essential and non essential elements. The concept of the ionome has also been applied to *Saccharomyces cerevisiae* (yeast) where the mineral nutrient and trace element profile of 4,385 mutant strains from the Saccharomyces Genome Deletion collection has been quantified [5]. The ionome can be thought of as the inorganic subset of the metabolome, and the study of the ionome, called ionomics, is defined as the;

Quantitative and simultaneous measurement of the elemental composition of living organisms, and changes in this composition in response to physiological stimuli, developmental state and genetic modifications.

This definition captures and highlights several critical concepts in the study of the ionome. Firstly, the study of the ionome is predicated on the fact that its study should provide a snapshot of the functional status of a complex biological organism, and this information is held in both the quantitative and qualitative patterns of mineral nutrients and trace elements in the organisms various tissues and cells. Such a concept rests heavily on the early work of Pauling and Robinson in which they developed the notion that a quantitative metabolite profile can be indicative of a particular physiological or disease state [6]. To capture this information contained in the ionome the precise and simultaneous quantification of as many of the components of the ionome as possible is necessary. Secondly, the power of ionomics lies in its ability to precisely capture information about the functional state of an organism under different conditions. These conditions may either be driven by genetic differences, developmental differences or by biotic and abiotic factors.

The underlying cause of an alteration in the ionome may either be direct or indirect. For example, alterations in the mineral nutrient levels in the diet or the loss of function of an important ion transporter would be expected to directly affect the ionome. Whereas alterations in cell wall structure or acidification of the apoplast in plants, for example, might be expected to indirectly affect the ionome. Ionomics has the potential to provide a powerful and relatively low cost approach to not only the functional analysis of the genes and gene networks that directly control it, but also to allow analysis of the more extended gene networks controlling developmental and physiological processes that indirectly affect the ionome.

Analytical Technology Required for Ionomics

To achieve the key analytical requirements of ionomics, that is the quantitative and simultaneous measurement of the elemental composition of living organisms, requires choosing specialized instrumentation and sample preparation protocols based on various selection criteria. These criteria include sample throughput, dynamic quantification range, sensitivity, elements to be measured, sample size available, reliability, cost, portability and the need to measure the ionome in either a bulk sample or with either low spatial resolution (1 – 10 mm), or high spatial resolution (10 –

100 µm) in either 2 or 3 dimensions. It is also worth noting that because most ionomic analyses are generally comparative, for example did the ionome change when gene X was deleted, what is important analytically is precision and not accuracy. Precision is critical if you want to establish that an observed alteration in the ionome is due to the perturbation the experimenter applied to the system rather than uncontrolled analytical or environmental error. High accuracy in ionomics is only required if the experimenter wants to make conclusive statements about the absolute concentration of particular elements in the ionome. For example, "the minimal quota for this element is 2 x 10^5 atoms of zinc per cell" [3]. The need for precision, accuracy or both has numerous implications for the analytical methodology chosen to perform ionomics.

Inductively-Coupled Plasma Optical Emission Spectroscopy (ICP-OES) or Inductively-Coupled Plasma Mass Spectrometry (ICP-MS) can both be effectively used for ionomics. ICP-OES has the advantage of lower cost and simplicity, whereas ICP-MS has an edge in sensitivity and the ability to detect different isotopes of the same element. Although ICP-OES is less sensitive than ICP-MS, some of this sensitivity is won back by the robustness of ICP-OES in more concentrated sample matrices. While ICP-MS struggles with sample matrices with greater than about 0.1% solids, ICP-OES can handle up to about 3% dissolved solids. Both ICP-OES and ICP-MS have been used successfully for large-scale ionomics projects, in yeast [5] which used ICP-OES to measure approximately 10,000 samples over 2-years, and Arabidopsis [1,7,8] which used ICP-MS to measure approximately 80,000 samples between 2001–2007.

In the early 90's, before the ionome or ionomics had been defined, Delhaize and coworkers applied X-Ray Fluorescence (XRF) for the successful multi-element screening of over 100,000 mutagenized Arabidopsis seedlings for the identification of mutants with altered ionomes [9]. XRF has also been applied to seed ionomics with the recent use of synchrotron-based microXRF as a rapid screening tool for the possible identification of Arabidopsis seeds with mutant ionomic phenotypes [10].

The use of Neutron activation analysis (NAA) for elemental analysis of biological samples goes back over forty years. NAA has been used to perform multielement quantification on plant samples collected within and across broad phylogenetic groupings, for the identification of trends in mineral nutrient and trace element accumulation in plants across taxa [11], [12]. NAA has also been applied to perform ionomics in the study of breast cancer [13], [14], colorectal cancer [15,16] and brain cancer [17], studies where the ionome was shown to be perturbed in the diseased tissues or organism. However, NAA has not yet been used extensively as a high-throughput elemental analysis tool for ionomics.

Bioinformatics of Ionomics

In any large-scale ionomics project, where many hundreds or thousands of samples are to be analyzed over an extended period of time, it will be critical to implement an information management system to control all aspects of the process. This will include the management of sample acquisition, sample harvesting, sample preparation, elemental analysis and data processing. Such workflow tools will allow, for example, scheduling and tracking of samples for analysis. Critically, workflow tools also provide for the logical organization of the workflow providing a logical framework for the capture of contextual information (metadata, e.g. genotype of sample, culture conditions, date sampled etc) necessary to fully describe the experiment.

The preprocessing of elemental profile, or ionomic data, is a critical step in the ionomic workflow before data can be analyzed for the extraction of knowledge. Because such data preprocessing is best done by the analyst that collected the data, tools to accomplish such data preprocessing need to be incorporated into the work flow at the stage that the analyst interacts with the information management system. For an information management systems to be useful it must also provide tools that allow for the retrieval, display and download of the ionomics data, and associated metadata, which it stores. The Purdue Ionomics Information Management System (PiiMS) is a working example of such an integrated information management system [18]. It stores publicly available ionomic data on over 80,000 Arabidopsis thaliana samples and can be accessed at [1]. Ionomic data on approximately 10,000 yeast samples is also stored at the PlantsT database [19], which can be accessed at [2].

Applications of Ionomics

A central theme of ionomics is the study of changes in the ionome in response to "physiological stimuli, developmental state and genetic modifications". It is in this context that we will discuss the application of ionomics to the discovery of gene function (functional genomics), and its application for the assessment of the physiological status of plants.

Functional Genomics

With genotyping, including sequencing and polymorphisms identification, rapidly becoming routine, it is the identification of phenotypic variation, and its association with genotypic variation, that is limiting the leveraging of genomic information for knowledge generation. As a high-throughput phenotyping platform, ionomics offer the possibility of rapidly generating large ionomics data sets on many thousands of individual samples. Utilization of such a phenotyping platform to screen mapping populations, with available modern genetic tools, provides a very powerful approach for the identification of genes and gene networks that regulate the ionome.

Assessment of physiological status

Given that the ionome of an organism is controlled by a summation of multiple physiological processes, alterations in any of which could potentially affect the ionome. Because of this, the ionome is likely to be very sensitive to the physiological state of an organism, with different ionomic profiles being reflective of different physiological states. Such characteristic ionomic profiles, if they exist, could be useful as biomarkers for the particular physiological condition with which they are associated.

Conclusion

With the $1000 genome sequence a rapidly approaching reality, high-throughput phenotyping platforms are going to be critical for the association of genotype with phenotype, for the process of gene discovery. Here we have discussed the development and application of ionomics as a high-throughput phenotyping platform, with the capacity to analyze approximately 1000 samples/week with a single analytical instrument. Because the ionome is the summation of many biological processes, a high-throughput ionomics platform offers a viable system for probing the multiple physiological and biochemical activities that affect the ionome, in tens of thousands of individuals. Ionomics, in combination with other phenotyping platforms such as transcript profiling (gene array), proteomics and metabolomics, therefore offer the potential to close the growing gap between our knowledge of genotype and the phenotypes it controls.

Literature Cited

1. Lahner B, Gong J, Mahmoudian M, Smith EL, Abid KB, Rogers EE, Guerinot ML, Harper JF, Ward JM, McIntyre L, Schroeder JI, Salt DE (2003) Genomic scale profiling of nutrient and trace elements in *Arabidopsis thaliana*. Nat Biotechnol 21: 1215-1221. [3]

2. Williams RJP (2001) Chemical selection of elements by cells. Coordination Chemistry Reviews 216-217: 583-595.

3. Outten CE, O'Halloran TV (2001) Femtomolar sensitivity of metalloregulatory proteins controlling zinc homeostasis. Science 292: 2488-2492. [4]

4. Salt DE (2004) Update on ionomics. Plant Physiology 136: 2451-2456. [5]

5. Eide DJ, Clark S, Nair TM, Gehl M, Gribskov M, Guerinot ML, Harper JF (2005). Characterization of the yeast ionome: a genome-wide analysis of nutrient mineral and trace element homeostasis in *Saccharomyces cerevisiae*. Genome Biol 6:R77. [6]

6. Robinson AB, Pauling L (1974) Techniques of orthomolecular diagnosis. Clin Chem 20: 961-965. [7]

7. Rus A, Baxter I, Muthukumar B, Gustin J, Lahner B, Yakubova E and Salt DE (2006) Natural variants of AtHKT1 enhance Na+ accumulation in two wild populations of Arabidopsis. PLoS Genet 2(12): e210. [8]

8. Baxter I, Muthukumar B, Park HC, Buchner P, Lahner B, Danku J, Zhao K, Lee J, Hawkesford MJ, Guerinot ML, Salt DE (2008) Variation in Molybdenum Content Across Broadly Distributed Populations of *Arabidopsis thaliana* is Controlled By a Mitochondrial Molybdenum Transporter (MOT1). PLoS Genet 4(2): e1000004. [9]

9. Delhaize E, Randall PJ, Wallace PA, Pinkerton A (1993) Screening Arabidopsis for mutants in mineral nutrition. Plant Soil 155/156: 131-134.

10. Young LW, Westcott ND, Attenkofer K, Reaney MJ (2006). A high-throughput determination of metal concentrations in whole intact *Arabidopsis thaliana* seeds using synchrotron-based X-ray fluorescence spectroscopy. J Synchrotron Radiat 13: 304-313. [10]

11. Ozaki T, Enomoto S, Minai Y, Ambe S, Makide Y (2000). A survey of trace elements in pteridophytes. Biol Trace Elem Res 74: 259-273.

12. Watanabe T, Broadley MR, Jansen S, White PJ, Takada J, Satake K, Takamatsu T, Tuah SJ, Osaki M (2007). Evolutionary control of leaf element composition in plants. New Physiol 174: 516-523. [11]

13. Garg AN, Singh V, Weginwar RG, Sagdeo VN (1994). An elemental correlation study in cancerous and normal breast tissue with successive clinical stages by neutron activation analysis. Biol Trace Elem Res 46: 185-202.

14. Ng KH, Ong SH, Bradley DA, Looi LM (1997). Discriminant analysis of normal and malignant breast tissue based upon INAA investigation of elemental concentration. Appl Radiat Isot 48: 105-109. [12]

15. Shenberg C, Feldstein H, Cornelis R, Mees L, Versieck J, Vanballenberghe L, Cafmeyer J, Maenhaut W (1995). Br, Rb, Zn, Fe, Se and K in blood of colorectal patients by INAA and PIXE. J Trace Elem Med Biol 9: 193-199.

16. Arriola H, Longoria L, Quintero A, Guzman D (1999). INAA of trace elements in colorectal cancer patients. Biol Trace Elem Res 71-72: 563-568.

17. Andrási E, Suhajda M, Sáray I, Bezúr L, Ernyei L, Réffy A (1993). Concentration of elements in human brain: glioblastoma multiforme. Sci Total Environ 139-140: 399-402.

18. Baxter I, Ouzzani M, Orcun S, Kennedy B, Jandhyala SS, Salt DE (2007) Purdue Ionomics Information Management System (PIIMS): An integrated functional genomics platform. Plant Physiol 143: 600-611. [13]

19. Tchieu JH, Fana F, Fink JL, Harper J, Nair TM, Niedner RH, Smith DW, Steube K, Tam TM, Veretnik S, Wang D, Gribskov M (2003) The PlantsP and PlantsT Functional Genomics Databases. Nucleic Acids Red 31: 342-344. [14]

External links

- Purdue Ionomics Information Management System - Purdue University Ionomics for Arabidopsis, Yeast, Rice [15]

References

[1] http://www.purdue.edu/dp/ionomics
[2] http://plantst.genomics.purdue.edu/plantst/html/icp.shtml
[3] http://www.nature.com/nbt/journal/v21/n10/pdf/nbt865.pdf
[4] http://www.sciencemag.org/cgi/reprint/292/5526/2488.pdf
[5] http://www.plantphysiol.org/cgi/reprint/136/1/2451
[6] http://www.pubmedcentral.nih.gov/picrender.fcgi?artid=1242212&blobtype=pdf
[7] http://www.clinchem.org/cgi/reprint/20/8/961
[8] http://www.pubmedcentral.nih.gov/picrender.fcgi?artid=1665649&blobtype=pdf
[9] http://genetics.plosjournals.org/perlserv/?request=get-document&doi=10.1371%2Fjournal.pgen.1000004.eor
[10] http://journals.iucr.org/s/issues/2006/04/00/hi5577/hi5577.pdf
[11] http://www.blackwell-synergy.com/doi/pdf/10.1111/j.1469-8137.2007.02078.x?cookieSet=1
[12] http://www.sciencedirect.com/science?_ob=MImg&_imagekey=B6TJ0-3T5GJ97-K-2&_cdi=5296&_user=29441&_orig=search&
_coverDate=01%2F31%2F1997&_sk=999519998&view=c&wchp=dGLbVzW-zSkWz&md5=4518026bdf3dd2556b557736207f4291&
ie=/sdarticle.pdf
[13] http://www.pubmedcentral.nih.gov/picrender.fcgi?artid=1803751&blobtype=pdf
[14] http://www.pubmedcentral.nih.gov/picrender.fcgi?artid=165472&blobtype=pdf
[15] http://www.ionomicshub.org/home/PiiMS

iTools Resourceome

iTools[1] is a distributed infrastructure for managing, discovery, comparison and integration of computational biology resources. iTools employs Biositemap technology to retrieve and service meta-data about diverse bioinformatics data services, tools, and web-services. iTools is developed by the National Centers for Biomedical Computing as part of the NIH Road Map Initiative [2].

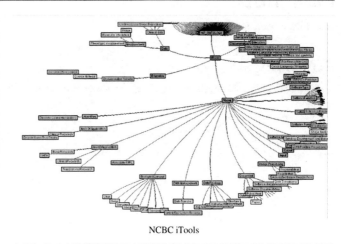

NCBC iTools

References

[1] Dinov ID, Rubin D, Lorensen W, Dugan J, Ma J,
Murphy S, Kirschner B, Bug W, Sherman M, Floratos A, Kennedy D, Jagadish HV, Schmidt J, Athey B, Califano A, Musen M, Altman R, Kikinis R, Kohane I, Delp S, Parker DS, Toga AW (2008). "iTools: A Framework for Classification, Categorization and Integration of Computational Biology Resources" (http://www.plosone.org/article/info:doi/10.1371/journal.pone.0002265). *PLoS ONE 3(5): e2265.* *doi:10.1371/journal.pone.0002265.* .

[2] http://nihroadmap.nih.gov/

External links

• Interactive iTools Server (http://iTools.ccb.ucla.edu)

k-mer

The term *k-mer* (or *x-mer* where *x* can be virtually any consonant of choice) usually refers to a specific n-tuple or n-gram of nucleic acid or amino acid sequences that can be used to identify certain regions within biomolecules like DNA (e.g. for gene prediction) or proteins. Either *k*-mer strings as such can be used for finding regions of interest, or *k*-mer statistics giving discrete probability distributions of a number of possible k-mer combinations (or rather permutations with repetitions) are used. Specific short *k*-mers are called oligomers or "oligos" for short.

Applications

• In algorithms for Sequence assembly
• In algorithms for Sequence alignment

Examples

• A sequence of dimers = AGAGAGAGAGAGAG
• A sequence of trimers = AAGAAGAAGAAG

External links

• Lattice models for protein-DNA binding [1]

References

[1] http://generegulation.info/index.php?option=com_content&view=article&id=47&Itemid=64

KOBIC

KOBIC stands for the Korean Bioinformation Center. It is comparable to the US NCBI in America and EBI in Europe.

The Korean Bioinformation Center (KOBIC) was originally established as NGIC (National Genome Information Center) in 2001 in Korea. In 2006, its function has been extended to include biodiversity and bioresource information management and a new name KOBIC was born. KOBIC is the national research center for bioinformatics which plays a key role in various areas such as genomics, proteomics, systems biology, and personalized medicine.

It has around 50 bioinformatists with various web sites.

LabKey Server

LabKey Server is free, open source software available for scientists to integrate, analyze, and share biomedical research data. The platform provides a secure data repository that allows web-based querying, reporting, and collaborating across a range of data sources. Specific scientific applications and workflows can be added on top of the basic platform and leverage a data processing pipeline.

License

The LabKey Software Foundation licenses LabKey Server and its documentation for free under the Apache License.[1]

Languages and extensibility

The base platform is written in Java. It can be extended through the addition of Java-based modules or simple, file-based modules written in HTML, XML and JavaScript.[2] The platform can also be extended using LabKey Server's Java, JavaScript, R, Python, Perl and SAS client libraries.[3]

History

LabKey Server was spun out of the Computational Proteomics Lab at the Fred Hutchinson Cancer Research Center after contributors realized that the software could be beneficial to the broader scientific community. The software was originally called the Computational Proteomics Analysis System (CPAS).[4] [5] [6]

Features

LabKey Server provides a secure data repository for all types of biomedical data, including mass spectrometry, flow cytometry, microarray, microplate, ELISpot, ELISA, NAb and observational study information. A customizable data processing pipeline allows the upload and processing of the large data files common in biomedical research.

The platform also provides domain-specific support for several areas of research, including:

- **Observational Studies.** Supports management of longitudinal, large-scale studies of participants, subjects or animals over time. Allows the integration of clinical data with assay results.
- **Proteomics.** Allows the processing of high-throughput mass spectrometry data using tools such as the X! Tandem search engine, the Trans-Proteomic Pipeline, Mascot and Sequest. Certified as "Silver-Level Compliant Data Service" with the caBIG standard.

- **Flow Cytometry.** Supports automated quality control, centralized data management and web-based data sharing. Integrates with FlowJo.

Users

Users range from individual labs to large research consortia. Current users include:[7]

- Fred Hutchinson Cancer Research Center
- Statistical Center for HIV/AIDS Research and Prevention (SCHARP)
- Center for HIV-AIDS Vaccine Immunology (CHAVI) at Duke University
- Collaboration for AIDS Vaccine Discovery (CAVD), funded by the Gates Foundation
- Wisconsin National Primate Research Center
- International AIDS Vaccine Initiative (IAVI)
- Infectious Disease Research Institute (IDRI)
- Cedars-Sinai Medical Center
- Harvard Partners
- University of Washington
- University of Michigan
- University of Kentucky
- University of Wisconsin
- Institute of Molecular and Cell Biology (Singapore)

Publications

- Nelson, Elizabeth K; Piehler, Britt; Eckels, Josh; Rauch, Adam; Bellew, Matthew; Hussey, Peter; Ramsay, Sarah; Nathe, Cory et al. (2011). "LabKey Server: An open source platform for scientific data integration, analysis and collaboration". *BMC Bioinformatics* **12**: 71. doi:10.1186/1471-2105-12-71. PMC 3062597. PMID 21385461.
- Rauch, Adam; Bellew, Matthew; Eng, Jimmy; Fitzgibbon, Matthew; Holzman, Ted; Hussey, Peter; Igra, Mark; MacLean, Brendan et al. (2006). "Computational Proteomics Analysis System (CPAS): An Extensible, Open-Source Analytic System for Evaluating and Publishing Proteomic Data and High Throughput Biological Experiments". *Journal of Proteome Research* **5** (1): 112–21. doi:10.1021/pr0503533. PMID 16396501.
- Shulman, Nicholas; Bellew, Matthew; Snelling, George; Carter, Donald; Huang, Yunda; Li, Hongli; Self, Steven G.; McElrath, M. Juliana et al. (2008). "Development of an automated analysis system for data from flow cytometric intracellular cytokine staining assays from clinical vaccine trials". *Cytometry Part A* **73A** (9): 847. doi:10.1002/cyto.a.20600.
- "The Best of Both Worlds: Integrating a Java Web Application with SAS Using the SAS/SHARE Driver for JDBC" [8].

References

[1] "LabKey Frequently Asked Questions: /home" (http://www.labkey.org/wiki/home/page.view?name=HomeFAQ). Labkey.org. . Retrieved 2010-05-29.

[2] "Building Modules: /home/Documentation" (http://www.labkey.org/wiki/home/Documentation/page.view?name=buildingModule). Labkey.org. . Retrieved 2010-05-29.

[3] "LabKey API: /home/Documentation" (http://www.labkey.org/wiki/home/Documentation/page.view?name=viewApis). Labkey.org. . Retrieved 2010-05-29.

[4] "Computational Proteomics Laboratory" (http://proteomics.fhcrc.org/CPL/home.html). Proteomics.fhcrc.org. . Retrieved 2010-05-29.

[5] http://www.fhcrc.org/about/pubs/center_news/2005/mar17/sart1.html

[6] "Center News - 1/5/06 - Center, NCI launch open-source software for proteomics analysis" (http://www.fhcrc.org/about/pubs/center_news/2006/jan5/br4.html). Fhcrc.org. 2006-01-05. . Retrieved 2010-05-29.

[7] "Our Clients | LabKey Software" (http://labkey.com/about/clients.html). Labkey.com. . Retrieved 2010-05-29.

[8] http://labkey.com/resources/publications/Integrating_a_Java_Web_Application_with_SAS.pdf

External links

- LabKey Server (http://www.labkey.org). The official web site for the LabKey Software Foundation includes documentation (http://www.labkey.org/project/home/Documentation/start.view?) and community support forums (http://www.labkey.org/wiki/home/page.view?name=support).
- LabKey Software (http://www.labkey.com). LabKey Software provides professional customization and support for LabKey Server.
- SCHARP (http://www.scharp.org/)
- CHAVI (http://www.chavi.org/)
- CAVD (http://www.cavd.org/)
- IAVI (http://www.iavi.org/)
- IDRI (http://www.idri.org/)

Legume Information System

The **Legume Information System (LIS)**, is legume sciences portal specifically for legume breeders and researchers, established and supported by the Agricultural Research Service of the United States Department of Agriculture. The mission of the Legume Information System is "to facilitate discoveries and crop improvement in the legumes," in particular to improve crop yields, their nutritional value, and our understanding of basic legume science.

Development of the Legume Information System is a joint venture between the National Center for Genome Resources (NCGR) and the USDA-ARS at Iowa State University.

The reference species as a backbone for orphan species research

A fundamental approach taken in LIS is facilitate research in the orphan species by taking advantage of more extensive knowledge developed for the reference species. Use of synteny and local similarity, for instance, provides a basis for trait inference.

Reference species

Note that LIS makes use of the UniProt organism mnemonics for identifying species whenever possible.

The current legume **reference species** (also referred to as model organisms) are the following:

- Glycine max (soybean), GLYMA [1]
- Lotus japonicus, LOTJA [2]
- Medicago truncatula, MEDTR [3]

Orphan species

Orphan species represented at LIS are:

- Arachis hypogaea (peanut), ARAHY [4]
- Cajanus cajan (pigeon pea), CAJCA [5]
- Chamaecrista fasciculata, CHAFS [6]
- Cicer arietinum (chickpea), CICAR [7]
- Lens culinaris (lentil), LENCU [8]
- Lupinus albus (white lupin), LUPAL [9]
- Lupinus angustifolius (blue lupin), LUPAN [10]
- Medicago sativa (alfalfa), MEDSA [11]
- Phaseolus coccineus (scarlet runner bean), PHACN [12]
- Phaseolus vulgaris (common bean), PHAVU [13]
- Pisum sativum (garden pea), PEA [14]
- Trifolium pratense (red clover), TRIPR [15]
- Vicia faba (broad bean), VICFA [16]
- Vigna radiata (mung bean), VIGRA [17]
- Vigna unguiculata (cowpea), VIGUN [18]

External links

- Home page [19] for the Legume Information System.
- Gonzales, MD; Gajendran, K; Farmer, AD; Archuleta, E; Beavis, WD (2007). "Leveraging model legume information to find candidate genes for soybean sudden death syndrome using the legume information system". *Methods in molecular biology* **406**: 245–59. PMID 18287696.
- Gonzales, M. D.; Archuleta, E; Farmer, A; Gajendran, K; Grant, D; Shoemaker, R; Beavis, WD; Waugh, ME (2004). "The Legume Information System (LIS): An integrated information resource for comparative legume biology". *Nucleic Acids Research* **33** (Database issue): D660–5. doi:10.1093/nar/gki128. PMC 540082. PMID 15608283.

References

[1] http://glyma.comparative-legumes.org
[2] http://lotja.comparative-legumes.org
[3] http://medtr.comparative-legumes.org
[4] http://arahy.comparative-legumes.org
[5] http://cajca.comparative-legumes.org
[6] http://chafs.comparative-legumes.org
[7] http://cicar.comparative-legumes.org
[8] http://lencu.comparative-legumes.org
[9] http://lupal.comparative-legumes.org
[10] http://lupan.comparative-legumes.org
[11] http://medsa.comparative-legumes.org
[12] http://phacn.comparative-legumes.org
[13] http://phavu.comparative-legumes.org
[14] http://pea.comparative.legumes.org
[15] http://tripr.comparative-legumes.org
[16] http://vicfa.comparative-legumes.org
[17] http://vigra.comparative-legumes.org
[18] http://vigun.comparative-legumes.org
[19] http://comparative-legumes.org

Arthur M. Lesk

Arthur M. Lesk	
Institutions	Pennsylvania State University
Alma mater	Harvard University, Princeton University, University of Cambridge

Arthur M. Lesk, is an accomplished protein science researcher, who is currently a professor of biochemistry and molecular biology at the Pennsylvania State University, University Park.

Profile

Lesk has made significant contributions to the study of protein evolution. He and Cyrus Chothia, working at the MRC Laboratory of Molecular Biology in Cambridge, United Kingdom, discovered the relationship between changes in amino-acid sequence and changes in protein structure by analyzing the mechanism of evolution in protein families.[1] [2] This discovery has provided the quantitative basis for the most successful and widely used method of structure prediction, known as homology modelling.

Lesk and Chothia also studied the conformations of antigen-binding sites of immunoglobulins. They discovered the "canonical-structure model" for the conformation of the complementarity-determining regions of antibodies, and they applied this model to the analysis of antibody-germ-line genes, including the prediction of the structure of the corresponding proteins. This work has supported the "humanization" of antibodies for therapy in the treatment of cancer. "This approach to cancer therapy is based on the observation of H. Waldmann that rats can raise antibodies against human cancers, but that the rat antibodies lead to immune responses, similar to allergies, in human patients," Lesk explains. "Humanization of these antibodies is the formation of hybrid molecules that are more human than rat, but that retain the therapeutic activity while reducing the patient's immune response."

Lesk's work also involves the detailed comparison of proteins in different structural states as a means for understanding the mechanisms that enable the proteins to change conformation, both as part of their normal activity and in disease. The discovery and analysis of these mechanisms was the key to understanding conformation changes in serine protease inhibitors, also known as serpins, mutations of which are an important cause of several diseases, including emphysema and certain types of inherited mental illness.

Lesk used a systematic analysis of protein-folding patterns to develop a mathematical representation that aids in the recognition and classification of these patterns. He also wrote the first computer program to generate schematic diagrams of proteins using molecular graphics, and he developed many algorithms now used by other researchers to analyze the structures of proteins.

Lesk was formerly chair of the Task Group on Biological Macromolecules for the Committee on Data for Science and Technology (CODATA), which aimed to foster worldwide coordination of databases in molecular biology to enhance their quality and utility. He has given invited lectures and presentations related to his research at universities and professional conferences worldwide.

Lesk is a member of the American Physical Society. He has published 189 scientific articles and 10 books related to his research[3] [4] [5] [6] [7] [8] [9] [10] [11] [12] [13].

Prior to joining Penn State during the fall semester of 2003, Lesk was on the faculty of the clinical school at the University of Cambridge from 1990 to 2003. He was a group leader in the biocomputing program at the European Molecular Biology Laboratory in Heidelberg, Germany, from 1987 to 1990; a visiting scientist at MRC Laboratory of Molecular Biology in Cambridge, United Kingdom, between 1977 and 1990; and a professor of chemistry at Fairleigh Dickinson University in New Jersey from 1971 to 1987. He has held visiting fellowships at the University of Otago in New Zealand and Monash University in Australia. He also is a Life Member of Clare Hall at the

University of Cambridge in the United Kingdom.

Along with Karl D. Hardman, Lesk wrote the first computer program for generating the schematic diagram of protein structure. It is known to produce one of the most effective representations of the protein structures and employs the classification scheme for Ribbon Diagrams created by Jane Richardson. Although these schematic diagrams are less detailed compared to the other representations, such as, picture stimulating wire models or space-filling models, it is more effective in presenting the topological relationships among elements of secondary structure and protein, due to its simplistic structural expression.[14] This was then further improved by creating a program to produce stereoscopic pairs of diagrams. As a result, the viewer's ability to perceive spatial relationship in complex molecules was enhanced.[14]

Lesk received a bachelor's degree, magna cum laude, from Harvard University in 1961. He received his doctoral degree from Princeton University in 1966. He also received a master's degree from the University of Cambridge in the United Kingdom in 1999.

Operation of the program

The basic operation of the program begins with the execution of line drawing. There are four phases involved in this program:[15]

1. The input phase – Program reads the input files. There are two input files. They are the coordinates and the details of the contents and appearance of the picture.
2. Picture generation – Geometric transformation of coordinates are generated by the program into picture elements. For example, a cylinder of appropriate size and orientation about the z-axis represents α-helix; each peptide plane is determined for Ribbon Diagrams and β-sheets; and spline fit is used for curved sheets.
3. Hidden-line removal – This step is only required by the cylinders of α-helices and the arrows of β-sheets, not skeletal models. Picture of these structures are classified by three levels of "optical density" – transparent, translucent, or opaque. If lines are passing behind the transparent object, it is not changed. If it passes behind a translucent object, it is altered into dashed lines. If it is opaque, the lines passing through the object are removed completely. This step can be replaced with an alternative step to create a Colour-Raster Output. The lines are ignored and the windows are painted according to the user.
4. Output – Character strings are extended to sets of line segments through a set of stroke tables. Line segments are placed into the two dimensional space.

Miscellaneous

Arthur Lesk's son, Victor Lesk has followed his father into the field of structural biology and bioinformatics, and currently holds a post-doctoral research position with Michael Sternberg at Imperial College London.[16]

References

[1] Lesk, A.; Chothia, C. (1980). "Solvent accessibility, protein surfaces, and protein folding". *Biophysical Journal* **32** (1): 35–47. Bibcode 1980BpJ....32...35L. doi:10.1016/S0006-3495(80)84914-9. PMC 1327253. PMID 7248454.

[2] Chothia, C.; Lesk, A. (1986). "The relation between the divergence of sequence and structure in proteins". *The EMBO journal* **5** (4): 823–826. PMC 1166865. PMID 3709526.

[3] Lesk, Arthur M. (1982). *Introduction to physical chemistry*. Englewood Cliffs, NJ: Prentice-Hall. ISBN 0-13-492710-9.

[4] Lesk, Arthur M. (1988). *Computational molecular biology: sources and methods for sequence analysis*. Oxford [Oxfordshire]: Oxford University Press. ISBN 0-19-854218-6.

[5] Lesk, Arthur M. (1991). *Protein architecture: a practical approach*. Ithaca, N.Y: IRL Press. ISBN 0-19-963055-0.

[6] Lesk, Arthur M. (2001). *Introduction to protein architecture: the structural biology of proteins*. Oxford [Oxfordshire]: Oxford University Press. ISBN 0-19-850474-8.

[7] Lesk, Arthur M. (2002). *Introduction to bioinformatics*. Oxford [Oxfordshire]: Oxford University Press. ISBN 0-19-925196-7.

[8] Lesk, Arthur M. (2004). *Introduction to symmetry and group theory for chemists*. Boston: Kluwer Academic Publishers. ISBN 1-4020-2150-X.

[9] Lesk, Arthur M. (2004). *Introduction to protein science: architecture, function and genomics*. Oxford [Oxfordshire]: Oxford University Press. ISBN 0-19-926511-9.

[10] Lesk, Arthur M. (2005). *Database annotation in molecular biology*. New York: John Wiley. ISBN 0-470-85681-5.

[11] Lesk, Arthur M.; Anna Tramontano (2006). *Protein Structure Prediction: Concepts and Applications*. Weinheim: Wiley-VCH. ISBN 3-527-31167-X.

[12] Lesk, Arthur M. (2007). *Introduction to genomics*. Oxford [Oxfordshire]: Oxford University Press. ISBN 0-19-929695-2.

[13] Lesk, Arthur M. (2010). *Introduction to Protein Science: Architecture, Function, and Genomics*. Oxford University Press, USA. ISBN 0-19-954130-2.

[14] Lesk, A.; Hardman, K. (1982). "Computer-generated schematic diagrams of protein structures". *Science* **216** (4545): 539–540. Bibcode 1982Sci...216..539L. doi:10.1126/science.7071602. PMID 7071602.

[15] Lesk, A.; Hardman, K. (1985). "Computer-generated pictures of proteins". *Methods in enzymology* **115**: 381–390. PMID 2934605.

[16] Dobbins, S. E.; Lesk, V. I.; Sternberg, M. J. E. (2008). "Insights into protein flexibility: The relationship between normal modes and conformational change upon protein-protein docking". *Proceedings of the National Academy of Sciences* **105** (30): 10390–10395. Bibcode 2008PNAS..10510390D. doi:10.1073/pnas.0802496105. PMC 2475499. PMID 18641126.

List of bioinformatics companies

This is a list of bioinformatics companies.

- Accelrys
- BIOBASE provides biological databases, bioinformatics solutions for expression data, promoter and pathway analysis and KPO services
- Biomatters Ltd. is the New Zealand-based company that creates the Geneious software suite.
- Biomax Informatics AG bioinformatics services and solutions
- CLC Bio free Bioinformatics workbenches.
- DNASTAR provides DNA sequence assembly and analysis, including Sanger and next generation sequence assembly and gene expression analysis.
- Gene Codes Corporation
- Genedata provides software products and services for data analysis and storage in Transcriptomics, Toxicogenomics, High-throughput screening (HTS), Genomics and related disciplines.
- Geneious combines many DNA and protein sequence analysis tools.
- Genomatix offering biology driven analysis pipelines for microarray analysis, ChIP on Chip and Solexa/454 data. Multiple tools and databases for analysis of gene regulation. Comparative genomics and most complete and quality checked genomic annotation for 17 species.
- Genostar provides streamlined bioinformatics solutions: sequence assembly, mapping, annotation transfer and identification of protein domains, comparative genomics, structural searches, metabolic pathway analysis, modeling and simulation of biological networks
- Ingenuity Systems is a provider of information solutions and custom services for life science researchers, computational biologists and bioinformaticists, and life science industry suppliers
- Inte:Ligand
- Invitrogen provides Vector NTI, a desktop bioinformatics suite supporting data record handling and curation, data discovery, reagent design, and experimental validation tool sets.
- Korea Computer Centre Sinhung Company
- MacVector, providing MacVector and Assembler. MacVector is a Macintosh application that provides sequence editing, primer design, internet database searching, protein analysis, sequence confirmation, multiple sequence alignment, phylogenetic reconstruction, coding region analysis, and a wide variety of other functions.
- PREMIER Biosoft International is a bioinformatics company with an expertise in software development, marketing and bioinformatics consultancy for in-silico experiment design. PREMIER Biosoft has authored software for pcr primer & probe design, microarray design, glycan structure identificatin, plasmid map drawing and tissue microarray data analysis.

- Qlucore Qlucore Omics Explorer is a bioinformatics software program.
- Rosetta Biosoftware
- SimBioSys develops the eHITS software for molecular docking (flexible ligand docking & fast pre-docking), pharmacophore modelling, de novo design and retrosynthetic analysis software tools
- Strand Life Sciences offers solutions for micro array gene expression analysis, computational chemistry, data analysis and visualizations.
- VADLO Search engine for bioinformatics software, databases and online tools.

List of bioinformatics journals

This is a **list of bioinformatics journals** containing peer-reviewed scientific journals that focus on bioinformatics.

- *Bioinformatics*
- *BMC Bioinformatics*
- *Cancer Informatics*
- *Computers in Biology and Medicine*
- *International Journal of Functional Informatics and Personalized Medicine*
- *Journal of Bioinformatics and Computational Biology*
- *Journal of Biomedical Informatics*
- *Journal of Computational Biology*
- *Journal of Statistical Software*
- *PLoS Computational Biology*
- *Statistical Applications in Genetics and Molecular Biology*
- *Journal of the American Medical Informatics Association*

List of biological databases

Biological databases are stores of biological information.[1]

Primary sequence databases

The International Nucleotide Sequence Database (INSD) (http://www.insdc.org/) consists of the following databases.

1. DDBJ [2] (DNA Data Bank of Japan)
2. EMBL Nucleotide Sequence DB [3] (European Molecular Biology Laboratory)
3. GenBank [4] (National Center for Biotechnology Information)

The three databases, DDBJ (Japan), GenBank (USA) and EMBL Nucleotide Sequence Database (Europe), are repositories for nucleotide sequence data from all organisms. All three databases accept nucleotide sequence submissions, and then exchange new and updated data on a daily basis to achieve optimal synchronisation between them. These three databases are primary databases, as they house original sequence data.

Metadatabases

Strictly speaking a metadatabase can be considered a database of databases, rather than any one integration project or technology. They collect data from different sources and usually make them available in new and more convenient form, or with an emphasis on a particular disease or organism.

1. Entrez[5] (National Center for Biotechnology Information)
2. euGenes [6] (Indiana University)
3. GeneCards [7] (Weizmann Inst.)
4. SOURCE [8] (Stanford University)
5. mGen [9] containing four of the world biggest databases GenBank, Refseq, EMBL and DDBJ - easy and simple program friendly gene extraction
6. Bioinformatic Harvester[10] (Karlsruhe Institute of Technology) - Integrating 26 major protein/gene resources.
7. MetaBase[11] (KOBIC) - A user contributed database of biological databases.
8. ConsensusPathDB - A molecular functional interaction database, integrating information from 12 other databases.
9. PathogenPortal [12] A repository linking to the Bioinformatics Resource Centers (BRCs) sponsored by the National Institute of Allergy and Infectious Diseases (NIAID)
10. BioGraph [13] (University of Antwerp, Vlaams Instituut voor Biotechnologie) A knowledge discovery service based on the integration of over 20 heterogeneous biomedical knowledge bases

Genome databases

These databases collect organism genome sequences, annotate and analyze them, and provide public access. Some add curation of experimental literature to improve computed annotations. These databases may hold many species genomes, or a single model organism genome.

1. Bioinformatic Harvester
2. SNPedia
3. CAMERA [14] Resource for microbial genomics and metagenomics
4. Corn [11], the Maize Genetics and Genomics Database
5. EcoCyc [15] a database that describes the genome and the biochemical machinery of the model organism *E. coli K-12*
6. Ensembl provides automatic annotation databases for human, mouse, other vertebrate and eukaryote genomes.

7. PATRIC [16], the PathoSystems Resource Integration Center
8. Flybase, genome of the model organism Drosophila melanogaster
9. MGI Mouse Genome [17] (Jackson Lab.)
10. JGI Genomes [18] of the DOE-Joint Genome Institute provides databases of many eukaryote and microbial genomes.
11. National Microbial Pathogen Data Resource [19]. A manually curated database of annotated genome data for the pathogens Campylobacter, Chlamydia, Chlamydophila, Haemophilus, Listeria, Mycoplasma, Neisseria, Staphylococcus, Streptococcus, Treponema, Ureaplasma, and Vibrio.
12. Saccharomyces Genome Database, genome of the yeast model organism.
13. Viral Bioinformatics Resource Center [20] Curated database containing annotated genome data for eleven virus families.
14. The SEED [21] platform for microbial genome analysis includes all complete microbial genomes, and most partial genomes. The platform is used to annotate microbial genomes using subsystems.
15. Xenbase, genome of the model organism Xenopus tropicalis and Xenopus laevis
16. Wormbase, genome of the model organism Caenorhabditis elegans
17. Zebrafish Information Network, genome of this fish model organism.
18. TAIR [22], The Arabidopsis Information Resource.
19. UCSC Malaria Genome Browser, genome of malaria causing species (*Plasmodium falciparumata* and others)
20. RGD [23] Rat Genome Database: Genomic and phenotype data for Rattus norvegicus
21. [24] INTEGRALL: Database dedicated to integrons, bacterial genetic elements involved in the antibiotic resistance
22. Fourmidable ant genome database [25] provides ant genome blast [26] search and sequence download [27].
23. VectorBase [28] The NIAID Bioinformatics Resource Center for Invertebrate Vectors of Human Pathogens

Protein sequence databases

1. UniProt[29] Universal Protein Resource (UniProt Consortium: EBI, Expasy, PIR)
2. PIR [30] Protein Information Resource (Georgetown University Medical Center (GUMC))
3. Swiss-Prot[31] Protein Knowledgebase (Swiss Institute of Bioinformatics)
4. PEDANT [32] Protein Extraction, Description and ANalysis Tool (Forschungszentrum f. Umwelt & Gesundheit)
5. PROSITE [33] Database of Protein Families and Domains
6. DIP [34] Database of Interacting Proteins (Univ. of California)
7. Pfam [35] Protein families database of alignments and HMMs (Sanger Institute)
8. PRINTS [36] PRINTS is a compendium of protein fingerprints (Manchester University)
9. ProDom [37] Comprehensive set of Protein Domain Families (INRA/CNRS)
10. SignalP 3.0 [38] Server for signal peptide prediction (including cleavage site prediction), based on artificial neural networks and HMMs
11. SUPERFAMILY [11] Library of HMMs representing superfamilies and database of (superfamily and family) annotations for all completely sequenced organisms
12. Annotation Clearing House [39] a project from the National Microbial Pathogen Data Resource

Protein structure databases

1. Protein Data Bank[40] (PDB) (Research Collaboratory for Structural Bioinformatics (RCSB))
2. SCOP [41] Structural Classification of Proteins
3. CATH [8] Protein Structure Classification

Protein model databases

1. SWISS-MODEL [42] Server and Repository for Protein Structure Models
2. ModBase [43] Database of Comparative Protein Structure Models (Sali Lab, UCSF)
3. Protein Model Portal[44] (PMP) Meta database that combines several databases of protein structure models (Biozentrum, Basel, Switzerland)

Carbohydrate structure databases

1. EuroCarbDB[45], A repository for both carbohydrate sequences/structures and experimental data.

Protein-protein interactions

1. BioGRID [46] A General Repository for Interaction Datasets (Samuel Lunenfeld Research Institute)
2. STRING: STRING is a database of known and predicted protein-protein interactions. [47] (EMBL)
3. DIP Database of Interacting Proteins [48]
4. BIND Biomolecular Interaction Network Database [2]
5. NetPro [49]

Signal transduction pathway databases

- Cancer Cell Map [4]
- Netpath - A curated resource of signal transduction pathways in humans
- Reactome
- NCI-Nature Pathway Interaction Database
- SignaLink Database [50]
- WikiPathways

Metabolic pathway databases

1. BioCyc Database Collection including EcoCyc and MetaCyc
2. KEGG PATHWAY Database[51] (Univ. of Kyoto)
3. MANET database [52] (University of Illinois)
4. Reactome[53] (Cold Spring Harbor Laboratory, EBI, Gene Ontology Consortium)

Microarray databases

1. ArrayExpress [54] (European Bioinformatics Institute)
2. Gene Expression Omnibus [55] (National Center for Biotechnology Information)
3. GPX [56](Scottish Centre for Genomic Technology and Informatics)
4. maxd [57] (Univ. of Manchester)
5. Stanford Microarray Database (SMD) [58] (Stanford University)

Mathematical model databases

1. Biomodels Database
2. CellML [59]

PCR / real time PCR primer databases

1. PathoOligoDB: A free QPCR oligo database for pathogens [60]

Specialized databases

- Antibody Central [61] Antibody information database and search resource.
- BIOMOVIE [62] (ETH Zurich) movies related to biology and biotechnology
- CGAP Cancer Genes [63] (National Cancer Institute)
- Clone Registry Clone Collections [64] (National Center for Biotechnology Information)
- Connectivity map [65] Transcriptional expression data and correlation tools for drugs
- CTD [66] The Comparative Toxicogenomics Database describes chemical-gene-disease interactions
- DBGET H.sapiens [67] (Univ. of Kyoto)
- DiProDB A database to collect and analyse thermodynamic, structural and other dinucleotide properties.
- Drug2Gene [68] Provides integrated information for identified and reported relations between genes/proteins and drugs/compounds
- Dryad [69] a repository of data underlying scientific publications in evolution, ecology, and related fields
- Edinburgh Mouse Atlas
- GreenPhylDB [70] (A phylogenomic database for plant comparative genomics)
- GDB Hum. Genome Db [71] (Human Genome Organisation)
- HGMD disease-causing mutations [72] (HGMD Human Gene Mutation Database)
- HUGO [73] (Official Human Genome Database: HUGO Gene Nomenclature Committee)
- HvrBase++ [74] Human and primate mitochondrial DNA
- INTERFEROME [75] The Database of Interferon Regulated Genes
- List with SNP-Databases [76]
- NCBI-UniGene [77] (National Center for Biotechnology Information)
- Oncogenomic databases A compilation of databases that serve for cancer research.
- OMIM Inherited Diseases [78] (Online Mendelian Inheritance in Man)
- OrthoMaM [79] (A database of Orthologous Mammalian Markers)
- p53 [80] The p53 Knowledgebase
- PhenCode [81] linking human mutations with phenotype
- PhenomicDB [82] multi-organism database linking genotype to phenotype
- Plasma Proteome Database [83] Human plasma proteins along with their isoforms
- PolygenicPathways [84] Genes and risk factors implicated in Alzheimer's disease, Bipolar disorder, Autism or Schizophrenia, multiple sclerosis and Parkinson's disease
- SHMPD [85] The Singapore Human Mutation and Polymorphism Database
- SciClyc [86] An Open-access database to shared antibodies, cell cultures, and documents for biomedical research.
- SNPSTR database [87] A database of SNPSTRs - compound genetic markers consisting of a microsatellite (STR) and one tightly linked SNP - in human, mouse, rat, dog and chicken.
- TRANSFAC A database about eukaryotic transcription factors, their genomic binding sites and DNA-binding profiles.
- TreeBASE [88] An open-access database of phylogenetic trees and the data behind them
- XTractor [89] Discovering Newer Scientific Relations Across PubMed Abstracts. A tool to obtain manually annotated relationships for Proteins, Diseases, Drugs and Biological Processes as they get published in PubMed.

Wiki-style databases

1. CHDwiki [90]
2. EcoliWiki [91]
3. Gene Wiki
4. GyDB [92]
5. OpenWetWare [93]
6. PDBWiki [94]
7. Proteopedia [95]
8. Topsan [96]
9. WikiGenes [97]
10. WikiPathways [98]
11. WikiProfessional
12. YTPdb [99]

References

[1] Wren JD, Bateman A (2008). "Databases, data tombs and dust in the wind.". *Bioinformatics* **24** (19): 2127–8.
    doi:10.1093/bioinformatics/btn464. PMID 18819940.
[2] http://www.ddbj.nig.ac.jp/Welcome-e.html
[3] http://www.ebi.ac.uk/embl/index.html
[4] http://www.ncbi.nlm.nih.gov/Genbank/index.html
[5] http://www.ncbi.nlm.nih.gov/gquery/gquery.fcgi
[6] http://eugenes.org
[7] http://www.genecards.org
[8] http://smd.stanford.edu/cgi-bin/source/sourceSearch
[9] http://www.cyber-indian.com/bioperl/index.html
[10] http://harvester.fzk.de
[11] http://BioDatabase.Org
[12] http://pathogenportal.org/portal/portal/PathPort/Home
[13] http://biograph.be
[14] http://camera.calit2.net/index.php/
[15] http://ecocyc.org
[16] http://patricbrc.vbi.vt.edu/
[17] http://www.informatics.jax.org
[18] http://genome.jgi.doe.gov/
[19] http://www.nmpdr.org/
[20] http://troy.bioc.uvic.ca/
[21] http://seed-viewer.theseed.org/
[22] http://arabidopsis.org/
[23] http://rgd.mcw.edu
[24] http://integrall.bio.ua.pt
[25] http://www.antgenomes.org
[26] http://www.antgenomes.org/blast
[27] http://www.antgenomes.org/downloads
[28] http://www.vectorbase.org/
[29] http://www.uniprot.org
[30] http://www-nbrf.georgetown.edu/pir/searchdb.html
[31] http://www.expasy.org/sprot/
[32] http://pedant.gsf.de
[33] http://www.expasy.org/prosite/
[34] http://dip.doe-mbi.ucla.edu
[35] http://www.sanger.ac.uk/Software/Pfam
[36] http://www.bioinf.manchester.ac.uk/dbbrowser/PRINTS/index.php
[37] http://protein.foulouse.inra.fr/prodom/current/html/home.php
[38] http://www.cbs.dtu.dk/services/SignalP/

[39] http://clearinghouse.nmpdr.org/aclh.cgi
[40] http://www.rcsb.org/pdb/
[41] http://scop.mrc-lmb.cam.ac.uk/scop/
[42] http://swissmodel.expasy.org//SWISS-MODEL.html
[43] http://salilab.org/modbase
[44] http://proteinmodelportal.org
[45] http://www.ebi.ac.uk/eurocarb
[46] http://www.thebiogrid.org
[47] http://string.embl.de
[48] http://dip.doe-mbi.ucla.edu/
[49] http://www.molecularconnections.com/home/en/home/resources/case-studies/alzheimer-disease-netpro/
[50] http://signalink.org/
[51] http://www.genome.ad.jp/kegg/pathway.html
[52] http://www.manet.uiuc.edu/
[53] http://www.reactome.org
[54] http://www.ebi.ac.uk/arrayexpress
[55] http://www.ncbi.nlm.nih.gov/geo
[56] http://www.gti.ed.ac.uk/GPX
[57] http://www.bioinf.man.ac.uk/microarray/maxd/index.html
[58] http://smd.stanford.edu/
[59] http://www.cellml.org/models
[60] http://www.pathooligodb.com/
[61] http://antibody-central.com
[62] http://biomovie.ethz.ch
[63] http://cgap.nci.nih.gov/Genes/GeneFinder
[64] http://www.ncbi.nlm.nih.gov/genome/clone
[65] http://www.broad.mit.edu/cmap/
[66] http://ctd.mdibl.org/
[67] http://www.genome.ad.jp/dbget-bin/www_bfind?h.sapiens
[68] http://www.drug2gene.com/
[69] http://datadryad.org/repo
[70] http://greenphyl.cirad.fr/v2/cgi-bin/index.cgi
[71] http://www.gdb.org/gdb
[72] http://www.hgmd.cf.ac.uk/
[73] http://www.gene.ucl.ac.uk/nomenclature
[74] http://www.hvrbase.org/
[75] http://www.interferome.org/
[76] http://hgvbase.cgb.ki.se/databases.htm
[77] http://www.ncbi.nlm.nih.gov/entrez/query.fcgi?db=unigene
[78] http://www.ncbi.nlm.nih.gov/Omim
[79] http://www.orthomam.univ-montp2.fr/
[80] http://p53.bii.a-star.edu.sg
[81] http://www.bx.psu.edu/phencode/
[82] http://www.phenomicdb.de/
[83] http://www.plasmaproteomedatabase.org/
[84] http://www.polygenicpathways.co.uk/
[85] http://shmpd.bii.a-star.edu.sg
[86] http://www.SciClyc.com
[87] http://www.sbg.bio.ic.ac.uk/~ino/cgi-bin/SNPSTRdatabase.html
[88] http://www.treebase.org/
[89] http://www.xtractor.in
[90] http://homes.esat.kuleuven.be/~bioiuser/chdwiki/
[91] http://ecoliwiki.net/colipedia
[92] http://gydb.uv.es/index.php/Main_Page
[93] http://openwetware.org/
[94] http://pdbwiki.org/
[95] http://www.proteopedia.org/
[96] http://www.topsan.org/
[97] http://www.wikigenes.org/

[98] http://www.wikipathways.org/
[99] http://homes.esat.kuleuven.be/~sbrohee/ytpdb/

List of molecular graphics systems

This is a list of software systems that are used for visualizing macromolecules [1].

The tables below indicates which types of data can be visualized in each system: **EM** = Electron microscopy; **HM** = Homology modelling; **MD** = Molecular Dynamics; **MM** = Molecular modelling and molecular orbital visualization; **MRI** = Magnetic resonance imaging; **NA** = Nucleic Acids; **NMR** = nuclear magnetic resonance; **Optical** = Optical microscopy; **SMI** = Small molecule interactions; **XRC** = X-ray crystallography data such as electron density.

Stand-alone systems

Name	Data	License	Technology	Citation	Comments
Ascalaph Graphics [2]	MM MD	free	C++	[3]	
Avizo	EM MM MRI Optical XRC	commercial [4]	Windows, Linux, Mac	[5] [6] [7]	
Avogadro [8]	MM XRC MD	free and open-source	C++/Qt, can be extended with Python modules		
BALLView	MM Nucleic Acids XRC SMI	free and open-source, GPL	C++ and Python; Windows, Linux, Solaris, and MacOS X	BALL project [9]	BALLView uses OpenGL and the real time ray tracer RTFact as render backends. For both renderers, BALLView offers stereoscopic visualization in several different modes.
Cn3D		free	stand-alone application	[10] [11]	
CheVi [12]	SMI	free	stand-alone application		
chemkit [13]	MM MD	free and open-source	C++		Software library for cheminformatics, molecular modelling and visualization.
Coot [14]		free		[15]	
Crystal Studio [16]	MM XRC	commercial [17]	Windows	[18]	Various Models: Ball & Stick, Stick, Space Filling, Ribbon etc. Plot XRD and Neutron Powder Patterns
CueMol [19]	MM XRC	free and open-source	Windows, MacOS X, and Linux application based on OpenGL and Mozilla XULRunner.		
Friend [20]	MM SA MSA	free	Win, Linux	[21] [22]	Fast, can work with hundreds of structures and thousands of sequences; millions of atoms. Crosstalk between sequence and structure modules. Sequence module based on Jalview. Accurate Structural alignment by TOPOFIT method. Also available as applet to interface sequence/structure databases.

Gabedit	XRC MM	free and open-source	C		
g0penMol [23]	MD MM	free		[24]	
ICM-Browser		free	Windows,Mac,Linux, fast C++ graphics, free plugin and activeICM for Web delivery	[25]	multiple objects, symmerty, 3D wavefront, alignments, chemistry, tables, plots
Jmol		free and open-source	Java applet or stand-alone application	[26]	Supports advanced capabilities such as loading multiple molecules with independent movement, surfaces and molecular orbitals, cavity visualization, crystal symmetry
MDL Chime		free for noncommercial use, proprietary	C++ browser plugin for Windows only	[27]	Calculates molecular surfaces coloured by electrostatic or hydrophobic potential. Originally based on RasMol.
Molden	MM XRC			[28]	
MOE	MM XRC	commercial		Molecular Operating Environment (MOE)	
Molekel	MM XRC	free and open-source	Java3D applet or stand-alone application		
NOCH		free and open-source		[29]	
O		free for noncommercial use		[30]	see also [31]
Procreate [32]		free	C# stand-alone application	[33]	Currently views SEQ and PDB files. Programmed in pure managed .NET using advanced DirectX rendering and effects
PyMOL	XRC SMI EM	free for noncommercial use, open-source	Python	[34]	According to the author, almost a quarter of all published images of 3D protein structures in the scientific literature were made using PyMOL.
Qmol [35]	MM	free, open-source	C	[36]	Provided by DNASTAR
RasMol		free and open-source	C stand-alone application	[37] [38] [39]	
Sirius		free and open-source	Java3D applet or stand-alone application		
SPARTAN	MM QM	commercial [40]	stand-alone application	[41]	visualize and edit biomolecules, extract bound ligands from PDB files for further computational analysis, full molecular mechanics and quantum chemical calculations package with streamlined graphical user interface.
SRS3D Viewer [42]	HM	free and open-source	Java3D applet or stand-alone application	[43] [44]	Integrates 3D structures with sequence and feature data (domains, SNPs, etc.).

UCSF Chimera	XRC SMI EM MD	free for noncommercial use [45]	Python	[46] [47]	Includes single/multiple sequence viewer, structure-based sequence alignment, automatic sequence-structure crosstalk for integrated analyses.[48]
VMD	EM MD MM	free for noncommercial use [49]	C++	[50] [51]	
WebMol		free	Java applet and stand-alone	[52] [53]	Includes advanced structural analysis features such as packing of secondary structural elements and surface calculations.
WHAT IF	HM XRC	shareware for academics	stand-alone	[54]	Old-fashioned interface; very good software for the experienced bioinformatician; nearly 2000 protein-structure related options; comes with 500 page writeup.
Yasara	HM NMR XRC	commercial; free version for education and elementary structure work	stand-alone	[55]	Very advanced graphics; Best in homology model optimisation in CASP-2008; many drug design options;

Web-based systems

Name	Data	License	Technology	Citation	Comments
Relibase [56]	SMI	partly free (full functionality requires a license)	Java applet integrated into web front-end	[57]	
WebMol		free	Java applet and stand-alone	[52] [53]	Includes advanced structural analysis features such as packing of secondary structural elements and surface calculations.
SRS3D Viewer [42]	HMSMI	free and open-source	Java3D applet or stand-alone application	[43] [44]	Integrates 3D structures with sequence and feature data (domains, SNPs, etc.).
Proteopedia [58]	HMSMI	free	Java applet integrated into web front-end		Integrates 3D structures and different views on those with text descriptions of the structures

References

[1] O'Donoghue, SI; Goodsell, DS; AS, Frangakis; F, Jossinet; Laskowski, M; Nilges, E; Saibil, HR; Schafferhans, A et al. (2010). "Visualization of macromolecular structures". *Nature methods* **7** (3 Suppl): S42–55. doi:10.1038/nmeth.1427. PMID 20195256.

[2] http://www.biomolecular-modeling.com/Ascalaph/Ascalaph_Graphics.html

[3] "Ascalaph Graphics" (http://www.biomolecular-modeling.com/Ascalaph/Ascalaph_Graphics.html). . Retrieved 24 September 2009.

[4] http://www.vsg3d.com

[5] "Avizo, the 3D Visualization and Analysis Software for Scientific and Industrial Data" (http://www.avizo3d.com). . Retrieved August 5, 2010.

[6] "Avizo Official Users' Forum" (http://www.mc3dviz.com/avizo-forum/). . Retrieved August 5, 2010.

[7] "Avizo - Examples of applications (movies)" (http://www.youtube.com/user/Avizo3D). . Retrieved August 5, 2010.

[8] http://avogadro.openmolecules.net

[9] http://www.ball-project.org/Ballview

[10] Wang, Y; Geer, LY; Chappey, C; Kans, JA; Bryant, SH (2000). "Cn3D: sequence and structure views for Entrez". *Trends in biochemical sciences* **25** (6): 300–2. doi:10.1016/S0968-0004(00)01561-9. PMID 10838572.

[11] http://130.14.29.110/Structure/CN3D

[12] http://www.simbiosys.ca/chevi/

[13] http://www.chemkit.org

[14] http://www.ysbl.york.ac.uk/~emsley/coot/

[15] Emsley, P; Cowtan, K (2004). "Coot: model-building tools for molecular graphics". *Acta crystallographica D* **60** (Pt 12 Pt 1): 2126–32. doi:10.1107/S0907444904019158. PMID 15572765.

[16] http://www.crystalsoftcorp.com/

[17] http://www.crystalsoftcorp.com/crystalstudio/order.html

[18] "Crystal Studio" (http://www.crystalsoftcorp.com/). . Retrieved 24 September 2009.

[19] http://www.cuemol.org/

[20] http://ilyinlab.org/

[21] Abyzov, A; Errami, M; Leslin, CM; Ilyin, Valentin (2005). "Friend, an integrated analytical front-end application for bioinformatics". *Bioinformatics* **18** (21): 3677–8. doi:10.1093/bioinformatics/bti602. PMID 16076889.

[22] "Friend - An Integrated front-end Application for Bioinformatics" (http://ilyinlab.org/friend). . Retrieved 24 September 2005.

[23] http://www.csc.fi/english/pages/g0penMol

[24] "g0penMol" (http://www.csc.fi/english/pages/g0penMol). . Retrieved 24 September 2009.

[25] http://www.molsoft.com/icm_browser.html

[26] "Jmol: an open-source Java viewer for chemical structures in 3D" (http://www.jmol.org). . Retrieved 24 September 2009.

[27] "Chime Pro" (http://www.symyx.com/products/software/cheminformatics/chime-pro/index.jsp). Symx. . Retrieved 24 September 2009.

[28] "MOLDEN a visualization program of molecular and electronic structure" (http://www.cmbi.ru.nl/molden/molden.html). .

[29] "NOC Homepage" (http://noch.sourceforge.net/). . Retrieved 24 September 2009.

[30] "O 12 Release Notes" (http://xray.bmc.uu.se/alwyn/Distribution/ov11_12/ov12.html). . Retrieved 24 September 2009.

[31] http://xray.bmc.uu.se/alwyn/O_to_Go/O_to_Go_frameset.html

[32] http://members.iinet.net.au/~lahg/procreate/

[33] "Home Page for Procreate" (http://members.iinet.net.au/~lahg/procreate/). . Retrieved 21 March 2011.

[34] "PyMOL Molecular Viewer - Home Page" (http://www.pymol.org). . Retrieved 24 September 2009.

[35] http://www.dnastar.com/qmol/

[36] "QMOL" (http://www.dnastar.com/qmol/). . Retrieved 24 September 2009.

[37] Sayle, RA; Milner-White, EJ (1995). "RASMOL: biomolecular graphics for all". *Trends in biochemical sciences* **20** (9): 374. doi:10.1016/S0968-0004(00)89080-5. PMID 7482707.

[38] Bernstein, HJ (2000). "Recent changes to RasMol, recombining the variants". *Trends in biochemical sciences* **25** (9): 453–5. doi:10.1016/S0968-0004(00)01606-6. PMID 10973060.

[39] "Home Page for RasMol and OpenRasMol" (http://www.rasmol.org/). . Retrieved 24 September 2009.

[40] http://www.wavefun.com/products/spartan.html

[41] Spartan Tutorial & User's Guide (http://downloads.wavefun.com/Spartan08Manual_New.pdf) ISBN 1-890661-38-4

[42] http://srs3d.org

[43] O'donoghue, SI; Meyer, JE; Schafferhans, A; Fries, K (2004). "The SRS 3D module: integrating structures, sequences and features". *Bioinformatics (Oxford, England)* **20** (15): 2476–8. doi:10.1093/bioinformatics/bth260. PMID 15087318.

[44] "General information about SRS 3D" (http://srs3d.org/About/). . Retrieved 24 September 2009.

[45] http://www.cgl.ucsf.edu/chimera/license.html

[46] Pettersen, EF; Goddard, TD; Huang, CC; Couch, GS; Greenblatt, DM; Meng, EC; Ferrin, TE (2004). "UCSF Chimera--a visualization system for exploratory research and analysis". *Journal of computational chemistry* **25** (13): 1605–12. doi:10.1002/jcc.20084. PMID 15264254.

[47] "UCSF Chimera" (http://www.cgl.ucsf.edu/chimera). . Retrieved 24 September 2009.

[48] Meng, EC; Pettersen, EF; Couch, GS; Huang, CC; Ferrin, TE (2006). "Tools for integrated sequence-structure analysis with UCSF Chimera". *BMC Bioinformatics* **7**: 339. doi:10.1186/1471-2105-7-339. PMC 1570152. PMID 16836757.

[49] http://www.ks.uiuc.edu/Research/vmd/current/LICENSE.html

[50] Humphrey, W; Dalke, A; Schulten, K (1996). "VMD: visual molecular dynamics". *Journal of molecular graphics* **14** (1): 33–8, 27–8. doi:10.1016/0263-7855(96)00018-5. PMID 8744570.

[51] "VMD - Visual Molecular Dynamics" (http://www.ks.uiuc.edu/Research/vmd). . Retrieved 24 September 2009.

[52] Walther, D (1997). "WebMol--a Java-based PDB viewer". *Trends in biochemical sciences* **22** (7): 274–5. doi:10.1016/S0968-0004(97)89047-0. PMID 9255071.

[53] "WebMol Java PDB Viewer" (http://www.cmpharm.ucsf.edu/cgi-bin/webmol.pl). . Retrieved 24 September 2009.

[54] "WHAT IF homepage" (http://swift.cmbi.ru.nl/whatif). . Retrieved 24 September 2009.

[55] "YASARA - Yet Another Scientific Artificial Reality Application" (http://www.yasara.org). . Retrieved 24 September 2009.

[56] http://www.ccdc.cam.ac.uk/free_services/relibase_free

[57] Hendlich, M (1998). "Databases for protein-ligand complexes". *Acta crystallographica. Section D, Biological crystallography* **54** (Pt 6 Pt 1): 1178–82. doi:10.1107/S0907444998007124. PMID 10089494.

[58] http://www.proteopedia.org/wiki/index.php/Main_Page

External links

- Saric, Marc. "Free Molecular Modelling Programs" (http://www.marcsaric.de/index.php/Free_Molecular_Modelling_Programs). A rather detailed, objective, and technical assessment of about 20 tools.
- "PDB list of molecular graphics tools" (http://www.rcsb.org/pdb/static.do?p=software/software_links/molecular_graphics.html).
- "World Index of Molecular Visualization Resources" (http://www.molvisindex.org).
- "Molecular Visualization Resources by Eric Martz" (http://molviz.org).

List of omics topics in biology

Inspired by the terms genome and genomics, other words to describe complete datasets of biological data, mostly sets of biomolecules originating from one organism, have been coined with the suffix *-ome* and *-omics*. Some of these terms are related to each other in a hierarchical fashion. For example, the genome contains the ORFeome, which gives rise to the transcriptome, which is translated to the proteome. Other terms are overlapping and refer to the structure and/or function of a subset of proteins (e.g. glycome, kinome).

List of topics

-ome	Field of study (-omics)	Collection of	Parent subject	Notes
Bibliome	Bibliomics	Scientific bibliographic data		
Connectome	Connectomics	Structural and functional brain connectivity at different spatiotemporal scales	Neuroscience	
Cytome	Cytomics	Cellular systems of an organism	Cytology	
Exposome (2005)	Exposomics	An individual's environmental exposures, including in the prenatal environment	Molecular genetics	A proposed term and field of study of the disease-causing effects of environmental factors (the "nurture" component of "nature vs. nurture").[1]
Exposome (2009)		Composite occupational exposures and occupational health problems	Occupational safety and health	The proposers of this term were aware of the previous term as used above but proposed to apply the term to a new field.[2][3]

Exome	Exomics	Exons in a genome	Molecular Genetics	
Genome	Genomics (Classical genetics)	Genes (DNA sequences/Chromosomes)	Genetics	"Genome" refers to the set of all genes in an organism. However, "genome" was coined decades before it was discovered that most DNA is "non-coding" and not part of a gene; thus, "genome" originally referred to the entire collection of DNA within an organism. Today, both definitions are used, depending on the context.[4]
Glycome	Glycomics	Glycans	Glycobiology	
Interferome	Interferomics	Interferons	Immunology	Also a database of the same name.[75]
Interactome	Interactomics	All interactions		The term "interactomics" is generally not used. Instead, interactomes are considered the study of systems biology.[5] [6]
Ionome	Ionomics	Inorganic biomolecules	Molecular Biology	
Kinome	Kinomics	Kinases	Molecular Biology	Proteins that add a phosphate group
Lipidome	Lipidomics	Lipids	Biochemistry	
Mechanome	Mechanomics	The mechanical systems within an organism		
Metabolome	Metabolomics	Metabolites		All products of a biological reaction (including intermediates)
Metagenome	Metagenomics	Genetic material found in an environmental sample	Molecular Biology	The genetic material is assumed to contain DNA from multiple organisms and therefore multiple genomes, hence the inclusion of the prefix meta-.
Metallome	Metallomics	Metals and metalloids		
ORFeome	ORFeomics	Open reading frames (ORFs)	Molecular Genetics	
Organome	Organomics	Organ interactions	Cell Signaling and Tissue Engineering	The study of crosstalk between organs using physiologically relevant in-vitro models
Pharmacogenome	Pharmacogenomics	SNPs and their effect on pharmacokinetics and pharmacodynamics	Pharmacogenetics Genomics	
Phenome	Phenomics	Phenotypes	Genetics	
Physiome	Physiomics	Physiology of an organism		
Proteome	Proteomics	Proteins	Molecular Biology	
Regulome	Regulomics	Transcription factors and other molecules involved in the regulation of gene expression	Molecular Biology	
Secretome	Secretomics	Secreted proteins	Proteomics	Subset of the proteome consisting of proteins actively exported from cells.[7]
Speechome	Speecheomics	Influences on language acquisition		Coined by the Human Speechome Project[8]
Transcriptome	Transcriptomics	mRNA transcripts	Molecular Biology	

Hierarchy of topics

For the sake of clarity, some topics are listed more than once.

- Bibliome
- Cytome
- Exposome
- Genome
  - Exome
    - ORFeome
      - Transcriptome
        - Proteome
          - Kinome
          - Secretome
  - Pharmacogenome
  - Phenome
  - Regulome
- Interactome
- Metagenome
- Moleculome
  - Glycome
  - Ionome
  - Lipidome
  - Metabolome
  - Metallome
  - Proteome
- Physiome
  - Connectome
  - Mechanome
- Membranome

References

[1] Wild CP (2005). "Complementing the genome with an "exposome": the outstanding challenge of environmental exposure measurement in molecular epidemiology". *Cancer Epidemiol. Biomarkers Prev.* **14** (8): 1847–50. doi:10.1158/1055-9965.EPI-05-0456. PMID 16103423.

[2] Faisandier, Laurie; De Gaudemaris, Régis; Bicout, Dominique J. (2009). "Occupational Health Problem Network : the Exposome". arXiv:0907.3410 [stat.ME].

[3] Faisandier, Laurie; Bonneterre, Vincent; De Gaudemaris, Régis; Bicout, Dominique J. (2009). "A network-based approach for surveillance of occupational health exposures". arXiv:0907.3355 [stat.ME].

[4] "genome, *n.*" (http://dictionary.oed.com/cgi/entry/50093704). *Oxford English Dictionary*. March 2008. .

[5] http://www.the-scientist.com/article/display/14769/

[6] http://interactomics.org/

[7] Dov Greenbaum, Nicholas M. Luscombe, Ronald Jansen et al. (2001). "Interrelating Different Types of Genomic Data, from Proteome to Secretome: 'Oming in on Function" (http://genome.cshlp.org/content/11/9/1463.full.pdf). *Genome Research* **11** (9): 1463–1468. doi:10.1101/gr.207401. PMID 11544189. .

[8] BBC article on the Speechome Project (http://news.bbc.co.uk/2/hi/science/nature/4987880.stm)

External links

- Omics.org (http://omics.org/)

List of open source bioinformatics software

This is a **list of open source bioinformatics software** with articles in Wikipedia.

Software	Description	Resources	Platform	License	Developer
AutoDock	suite of automated docking tools	Website [1]	Platform	License	Developer
Biochemical Algorithms Library (BALL)	C++ library and framework for molecular modeling and visualization designed for rapid prototyping	Website [2] - Articles [3]	Linux, Mac OS X, Windows	LGPL	BALL project team [4]
Bioclipse	Visual platform for chemo- and bioinformatics based on the Eclipse Rich Client Platform (RCP).	Website [3]	Platform	Eclipse Public License	The Bioclipse Project
Bioconductor	R (programming language) language toolkit	Website [2] - Articles [5]	Linux, Mac OS X, Windows	Artistic License 2.0	Fred Hutchinson Cancer Research Center
Bioinformatics Learning Tutorial (BLT) [6]	Educational interactive tutorials and 3D animations for Replication, Transcription, and Translation	Project Home [7] - Download for Windows [8]	Windows (stand-alone), Linux & Mac OS X (source code only with Qt libraries)	Academic Free License	Collaborative project
BioJava	Java (programming language)	Website [9]	Linux, Mac OS X, Windows	LGPL v2.1	Open Bioinformatics Foundation
BioMOBY	registry of web services	Website [21] - Articles [10]	Web	License	Open Bioinformatics Foundation
BioPerl	Perl language toolkit	Website [11]	Cross-platform	Artistic License & GPL	Open Bioinformatics Foundation
BioPHP	PHP language toolkit	Website [12]	Platform	License	Open Bioinformatics Foundation
Biopython	Python language toolkit	Website [2]	Cross-platform	Biopython License [1]	Open Bioinformatics Foundation
BioRails	a data management system designed to support researchers in drug discovery	Website [13]	Platform	License	Developer
BioRuby	Ruby language toolkit	Website [14]	Platform	License	Open Bioinformatics Foundation
caCORE [15]	ontologic representation environment	Website [16] - Articles [17]	Platform	License	National Cancer Institute

caArray [18]	ontologic representation environment	[19] - [20]	Platform	License	National Cancer Institute
EMBOSS	Suite of packages for sequencing, searching, etc.	Website [21]	Platform	General Public Licence (GPL) and Library GPL	Collaborative project
Galaxy	Scientific workflow and data integration system	Website [22]	Unix-like	License [23]	Penn State and Emory University
GMOD	Toolkit for addressing many common challenges at biological databases.	Website [24]	Unix-like (server), Web browser (client)	Varies depending on tool	Collaborative project
GENtle	An equivalent to the proprietary Vector NTI, a tool to analyze and edit DNA sequence files	Website [25]	Platform	GPL	Magnus Manske
Integrated Genome Browser	Java-based desktop genome browser	Website [26]	Linux, Mac OS X, Windows	CPL 1.0	GenoViz [2]
IntAct	molecular interaction database	Website [27] - Articles [28]	Platform	License	European Bioinformatics Institute
Java Treeview	microarray data viewer	Website [29] - Articles [30]	Cross-platform	License	Developer
LabKey Server	platform for integrating, analyzing and sharing data	Website [31]	Linux, Mac OS X, Windows	Apache License	LabKey Software Foundation [31]
OpenClinica	software for capturing and managing data in clinical trials	Website [32]	Linux, Windows	LGPL	OpenClinica [33]
SAM Tools	Data format (SAM) and accompanying tool suite, for storing large nucleotide sequence alignments	Website [34]	Linux	BSD, MIT License	1000 Genomes Project
Taverna workbench	Tool for designing and executing workflows	Website [35]	Linux, Mac OS X, Windows	LGPL	myGrid
UGENE	integrated bioinformatics tools	Website [36] - Podcast [37]	Linux, Mac OS X, Windows	GPL2 License	Unipro [36]

External links

- Bio-Informatics software [38] - SourceForge
- Free Biology Software [39] - Free Software Directory - Free Software Foundation
- Bioinformatics Links Directory [1]

References

[1] http://autodock.scripps.edu
[2] http://www.ball-project.org
[3] http://www.biomedcentral.com/1471-2105/11/531
[4] http://www.ball-project.org/overview/team
[5] http://genomebiology.com/2004/5/10/R80
[6] http://www.cs.transy.edu/nsmith
[7] http://sourceforge.net/projects/biotutorial/
[8] http://www.cs.transy.edu/nsmith/BLT_Windows.zip
[9] http://biojava.org/wiki/Main_Page

[10] http://bib.oxfordjournals.org/cgi/content/abstract/3/4/331

[11] http://www.bioperl.org

[12] http://genephp.sourceforge.net

[13] http://biorails.org/

[14] http://bioruby.org

[15] https://wiki.nci.nih.gov/display/caCORE/

[16] https://cabig.nci.nih.gov/tools/concepts/caCORE_overview

[17] http://bioinformatics.oxfordjournals.org/cgi/content/abstract/19/18/2404

[18] https://cabig.nci.nih.gov/tools/caArray

[19] http://caarray.nci.nih.gov/documentation

[20] https://cabig-kc.nci.nih.gov/Molecular/KC/index.php/CaArray

[21] http://emboss.sourceforge.net

[22] http://galaxyproject.org/

[23] http://galaxyproject.org/wiki/Admin/License

[24] http://gmod.org/

[25] http://gentle.magnusmanske.de/

[26] http://igb.bioviz.org

[27] http://www.ebi.ac.uk/intact/

[28] http://nar.oxfordjournals.org/cgi/content/abstract/35/suppl_1/D561

[29] http://jtreeview.sourceforge.net/

[30] http://bioinformatics.oxfordjournals.org/cgi/content/abstract/20/17/3246

[31] http://www.labkey.org/

[32] https://community.openclinica.com/

[33] https://www.openclinica.com/about

[34] http://samtools.sourceforge.net/

[35] http://www.taverna.org.uk

[36] http://ugene.unipro.ru/

[37] http://youtube.com/uniprougene/

[38] http://sourceforge.net/softwaremap/trove_list.php?form_cat=252

[39] http://directory.fsf.org/category/bio/

List of phylogenetic tree visualization software

This list of **phylogenetic tree viewing software** is a compilation of software tools and web portals used in visualising phylogenetic trees.

Online software

Name	Description	Site	Citation
Archaeopteryx	Java tree viewer and editor (used to be ATV)	[1]	[2]
Hypergeny	visualise large phylogenies with this hyperbolic tree browser	[3]	
InfoViz Tree Tools	the generic Javascript InfoViz toolkit supports hyperbolic, space and icicle trees	[4]	
iTOL - interactive Tree Of Life	annotate trees with various types of data and export to various graphical formats; scriptable through a batch interface	[5]	[6]
TreeVector	scalable, interactive, phylogenetic trees for the web, produces dynamic SVG or PNG output, implemented in Java.	[7]	[8]
jsPhyloSVG	open-source javascript library for rendering highly-extensible, customizable phylogenetic trees.	[9]	[10]
Phylodendron	different tree styles, branch styles and output graphical formats	[11]	
PhyloExplorer	a tool to facilitate assessment and management of phylogenetic tree collections. Given an input collection of rooted trees, PhyloExplorer provides facilities for obtaining statistics describing the collection, correcting invalid taxon names, extracting taxonomically relevant parts of the collection using a dedicated query language, and identifying related trees in the TreeBASE database.	[12]	[13]
Phyloviewer	web-based integrated environment for phylogenomic analysis based on the Bioinformatics Portal System	[14]	
PhyloWidget	view, edit, and publish phylogenetic trees online; interfaces with databases	[15]	[16]
TRED	a tool to visualize and edit phylogenetic trees. Combines a browser-based Javascript client with a Python (web2py) server. Trees are rendered in SVG using Raphael.	[17]	
TreeViz	Java tree viewer that does treemaps as well	[18]	

Applications

Name	Description	OS[1]	Site	Citation
BayesTrees	A program designed to display, analyse and manipulate samples of trees, in particular Bayesian samples.	W	[19]	
Dendroscope	An interactive viewer for large phylogenetic trees and networks	All	[20]	[21]
ETE [22]	A Python Environment for Tree Exploration. This is a programming library to draw and manipulate phylogenetic trees.	All	[22]	[23]
FigTree	Modern treeviewer with coloring and collapsing	All	[24]	
Geneious Pro	All-in-one sequence analysis, phylogenetics and molecular cloning application with modern treeviewer	All	[25]	
MultiDendrograms	Application to calculate and plot phylogenetic trees	All	[26]	[27]

NJplot	Interactive tree plotter, re-roots, exports as PDF	All	[28]	
TreeDyn	Very powerful open-source software for tree manipulation and annotation allowing incorporation of meta information	All	[29]	[30]
TreeGraph 2	Open-source tree editor with numerous editing and formatting operations including combining different phylogenetic analyses	All	[31]	[32]
TreeView	Classic treeviewing software that is very highly cited [33]	All	[34]	[35]
UGENE	An opensource visual interface for Phylip 3.6 package	All	[36]	

[1] "All" refers to Microsoft Windows, Apple OSX and Linux; L=Linux, M=Apple Mac, W=Microsoft Windows

References

[1] http://www.phylosoft.org/archaeopteryx/

[2] Zmasek, CM and Eddy, SR (2001). "TV: display and manipulation of annotated phylogenetic trees". *Bioinformatics* **17** (4): 383–384. doi:10.1093/bioinformatics/17.4.383. PMID 11301314.

[3] http://bioinformatics.psb.ugent.be/hypergeny/home.php

[4] http://thejit.org

[5] http://itol.embl.de

[6] Letunic, I and Bork, P (2007). "Interactive Tree Of Life (iTOL): an online tool for phylogenetic tree display and annotation.". *Bioinformatics* **23** (1): 127–128. doi:10.1093/bioinformatics/btl529. PMID 17050570.

[7] http://supfam.cs.bris.ac.uk/TreeVector/

[8] Pethica, R. and Barker, G. and Kovacs, T. and Gough, J. (2010). "TreeVector: scalable, interactive, phylogenetic trees for the web". *PLoS ONE* **5**: e8934. doi:doi:10.1371/journal.pone.0008934.

[9] http://www.jsphylosvg.com/

[10] Smits, SA and Ouverney, CC (2010). Poon, Art F. Y.. ed. "jsPhyloSVG: A Javascript Library for Visualizing Interactive and Vector-Based Phylogenetic Trees on the Web". *PLoS ONE* **5** (8): e12267. doi:10.1371/journal.pone.0012267. PMC 2923619. PMID 20805892.

[11] http://iubio.bio.indiana.edu/treeapp/treeprint-form.html

[12] http://www.ncbi.orthomam.univ-montp2.fr/phyloexplorer/

[13] Ranwez, V et al., WH (2009). "PhyloExplorer: a web server to validate, explore and query phylogenetic trees". *BMC Evolutionary Biology.* **9 9**: 108. doi:10.1186/1471-2148-9-108.

[14] http://www.phyloviewer.org/intro.php

[15] http://www.phylowidget.org/

[16] Jordan, EG and Piel, WH (2008). "PhyloWidget: web-based visualizations for the tree of life". *Bioinformatics* **24** (14): 1641–1642. doi:10.1093/bioinformatics/btn235. PMID 18487241.

[17] http://code.google.com/p/tred/

[18] http://www.randelshofer.ch/treeviz/

[19] http://www.evolution.rdg.ac.uk/BayesTrees.html

[20] http://www-ab.informatik.uni-tuebingen.de/software/dendroscope/welcome.html

[21] Huson, D. H.; Richter, D. C.; Rausch, C.; Dezulian, T.; Franz, M.; Rupp, R. (2007). "Dendroscope: an interactive viewer for large phylogenetic trees". *BMC Bioinformatics* **8**: 460. doi:10.1186/1471-2105-8-460. PMC 2216043. PMID 18034891.

[22] http://ete.cgenomics.org

[23] Huerta-Cepas, Jaime; Dopazo, Joaquin; Gabaldon, Toni (2010). "ETE: a python Environment for Tree Exploration" (http://www.biomedcentral.com/1471-2105/11/24). *BMC Bioinformatics* **11**: 24. doi:10.1186/1471-2105-11-24. .

[24] http://tree.bio.ed.ac.uk/software/figtree/

[25] http://www.geneious.com

[26] http://deim.urv.cat/~sgomez/multidendrograms.php

[27] Fernández, Alberto; Gómez, Sergio (2008). "Solving Non-uniqueness in Agglomerative Hierarchical Clustering Using Multidendrograms" (http://www.springerlink.com/content/c8795u6232184423/). *Journal of Classification* **25** (1): 43–65. doi:10.1007/s00357-008-9004-x. .

[28] http://pbil.univ-lyon1.fr/software/njplot.html

[29] http://www.treedyn.org/

[30] Chevenet, F. ◆O.; Brun, C.; Bañuls, A. L.; Jacq, B.; Christen, R. (2006). "TreeDyn: towards dynamic graphics and annotations for analyses of trees". *BMC Bioinformatics* **7**: 439. doi:10.1186/1471-2105-7-439. PMC 1615880. PMID 17032440.

[31] http://treegraph.bioinfweb.info/

[32] Stöver, B. C.; Müller, K. F. (2010). "TreeGraph 2: Combining and visualizing evidence from different phylogenetic analyses". *BMC Bioinformatics* **11**: 7. doi:10.1186/1471-2105-11-7. PMC 2806359. PMID 20051126.

[33] http://www.lab-times.org/labtimes/issues/lt2008/lt03/lt_2008_03_34_36.pdf

[34] http://taxonomy.zoology.gla.ac.uk/rod/treeview.html

[35] Page, RDM (1996). "Tree View: An application to display phylogenetic trees on personal computers". *Computer Applications in the Biosciences* **12** (4): 357–358. PMID 8902363.

[36] http://ugene.unipro.ru

External links

- A 'comprehensive list' of Tree Editors (http://bioinfo.unice.fr/biodiv/Tree_editors.html)
- List of Tree Editors (http://www.treedyn.org/Tree_editors.html)

List of phylogenetics software

This **list of phylogenetics software** is a compilation of computational phylogenetics software used to produce phylogenetic trees. Such tools are commonly used in comparative genomics, cladistics, and bioinformatics. Methods for estimating phylogenies include neighbor-joining, maximum parsimony (also simply referred to as parsimony), UPGMA, Bayesian phylogenetic inference, maximum likelihood and distance matrix methods.

Name	Description	Methods	Link	Author
BATWING	Bayesian Analysis of Trees With Internal Node Generation	Bayesian inference, demographic history, population splits	download [1]	I. J. Wilson, Weale, D.Balding
BayesPhylogenies	Bayesian inference of trees using Markov Chain Monte Carlo methods	Bayesian inference, multiple models, mixture model (auto-partitioning)	download [2]	M. Pagel, A. Meade
BayesTraits	Analyses trait evolution among groups of species for which a phylogeny or sample of phylogenies is available	Trait analysis	download [3]	M. Pagel, A. Meade
BEAST	Bayesian Evolutionary Analysis Sampling Trees	Bayesian inference, relaxed molecular clock, demographic history	download [4] or development & download [5]	A. J. Drummond, A. Rambaut
Bosque	Integrated graphical software to perform phylogenetic analyses, from the importing of sequences to the plotting and graphical edition of trees and alignments	Distance and maximum likelihood methods (through phyml, phylip & tree-puzzle)	download [6]	S. Ramirez, E. Rodriguez.
BUCKy	Bayesian concordance of gene trees	Bayesian concordance using modified greedy consensus of unrooted quartets	stat.wisc.edu [7]	C. Ané, B. Larget, D.A. Baum, S.D. Smith, A. Rokas and B. Larget, S.K. Kotha, C.N. Dewey, C. Ané
ClustalW	Progressive multiple sequence alignment	Distance matrix/nearest neighbor	EBI [8] PBIL [9] EMBNet [10] GenomeNet [11]	Thompson et al.
fastDNAml	Optimized maximum likelihood (nucleotides only)	Maximum likelihood	download [12]	G.J. Olsen
Geneious	Geneious provides sophisticated genome and proteome research tools	Neighbor-joining, UPGMA, MrBayes plugin, PHYML plugin	download [13]	A. J. Drummond,M.Suchard,V.Lefort et al.

HyPhy	Hypothesis testing using phylogenies	Maximum likelihood, neighbor-joining, clustering techniques, distance matrices	download [14]	S.L. Kosakovsky Pond, S.D.W. Frost, S.V. Muse
IQPNNI	Iterative ML treesearch with stopping rule	Maximum likelihood, neighbor-joining	download [15]	L.S. Vinh, A. von Haeseler
MEGA	Molecular Evolutionary Genetics Analysis	Distance, Parsimony and Maximum Composite Likelihood Methods	download [16]	Tamura K, Dudley J, Nei M & Kumar S
Mesquite	Mesquite is software for evolutionary biology, designed to help biologists analyze comparative data about organisms. Its emphasis is on phylogenetic analysis, but some of its modules concern population genetics, while others do non-phylogenetic multivariate analysis.	Maximum parsimony, distance matrix, maximum likelihood	Mesquite home page [17]	Wayne Maddison and D. R. Maddison
MOLPHY	Molecular phylogenetics (protein or nucleotide)	Maximum likelihood	server [18]	J. Adachi and M. Hasegawa
MrBayes	Posterior probability estimation	Bayesian inference	download [19]	J. Huelsenbeck, et al.
Network	Free Phylogenetic Network Software	Median Joining, Reduced Median, Steiner Network	download [20]	A. Roehl
Nona	Phylogenetic inference	Maximum parsimony, implied weighting, ratchet	download [21]	P. Goloboff
PAML	Phylogenetic analysis by maximum likelihood	Maximum likelihood and Bayesian inference	download [22]	Z. Yang
PAUP*	Phylogenetic analysis using parsimony (*and other methods)	Maximum parsimony, distance matrix, maximum likelihood	purchase [23]	D. Swofford
PHYLIP	Phylogenetic inference package	Maximum parsimony, distance matrix, maximum likelihood	download [24]	J. Felsenstein
PhyloQuart	Quartet implementation (uses sequences or distances)	Quartet method	download [25]	V. Berry
PyCogent	Software library for genomic biology	Simulating sequences, alignment, controlling third party applications, workflows, querying databases, generating graphics and phylogenetic trees	documentation/download [26]	Knight et al. [27]
QuickTree	Tree construction optimized for efficiency	Neighbor-joining	server [28]	K. Howe, A. Bateman, R. Durbin
RAxML-HPC	Randomized Axelerated Maximum Likelihood for High Performance Computing (nucleotides and aminoacids)	Maximum likelihood, simple Maximum parsimony	download [29]	A. Stamatakis

SEMPHY	Tree reconstruction using the combined strengths of maximum-likelihood (accuracy) and neighbor-joining (speed). SEMPHY has become outdated. The authors now refer users to RAxML, which is superior in both accuracy and speed.	A hybrid maximum-likelihood / neighbor-joining method	SEMPHY [30]	M. Ninio, E. Privman, T. Pupko, N. Friedman
SplitsTree	Tree and network program	Computation, visualization and exploration of phylogenetic trees and networks	SplitsTree [31]	D.H. Huson and D. Bryant
TNT	Phylogenetic inference	Parsimony, weighting, ratchet, tree drift, tree fusing, sectorial searches	download [32]	P. Goloboff et al.
TOPALi	Phylogenetic inference	Phylogenetic model selection, Bayesian analysis and Maximum Likelihood phylogenetic tree estimation, detection of sites under positive selection, and recombination breakpoint location analysis	Main page [33] download [34]	Iain Milne, Dominik Lindner et al.
TreeGen	Tree construction given precomputed distance data	Distance matrix	server [35]	ETH Zurich
TreeAlign	Efficient hybrid method	Distance matrix and approximate parsimony	server [36]	J. Hein
Treefinder	Fast ML tree reconstruction, bootstrap analysis, model selection, hypothesis testing, tree calibration, tree manipulation and visualization, computation of sitewise rates, sequence simulation, many models of evolution (DNA, protein, rRNA, mixed protein, user-definable), GUI and scripting language	Maximum likelihood, distances, and others	download [37]	G. Jobb
TREE-PUZZLE	Maximum likelihood and statistical analysis	Maximum likelihood	download [38]	H.A. Schmidt, K. Strimmer, A. von Haeseler
T-REX	Tree inferring and visualization, Gene transfer detection	Distance, Parsimony and Maximum likelihood	T-REX server [39]	V. Makarenkov, et al.
UGENE	Fast and free multiplatform tree editor	based Phylip 3.6 package algorithms	download [40]	Unipro
Winclada	GUI and tree editor (requires Nona)	Maximum parsimony, ratchet	download [41]	K. Nixon
Xrate	Phylo-grammar engine	Rate estimation, branch length estimation, alignment annotation	homepage [42]	I. Holmes

External links

- Complete list of Institut Pasteur [43] phylogeny webservers
- ExPASy [44] List of phylogenetics programs
- A very comprehensive list [45] of phylogenetic tools (reconstruction, visualization, *etc.*)
- Another list of evolutionary genetics software [46]

References

[1] http://www.mas.ncl.ac.uk/~nijw/

[2] http://www.evolution.rdg.ac.uk/BayesPhy.html

[3] http://www.evolution.rdg.ac.uk/BayesTraits.html

[4] http://beast.bio.ed.ac.uk/

[5] http://code.google.com/p/beast-mcmc/

[6] http://bosque.udec.cl/

[7] http://www.stat.wisc.edu/~ane/bucky/index.html/

[8] http://www.ebi.ac.uk/clustalw/

[9] http://npsa-pbil.ibcp.fr/cgi-bin/npsa_automat.pl?page=npsa_clustalw.html

[10] http://www.ch.embnet.org/software/ClustalW.html

[11] http://align.genome.jp/

[12] ftp://ftp.bio.indiana.edu/molbio/evolve/fastdnaml/fastDNAml.html

[13] http://www.geneious.com/default,28,download.sm

[14] http://www.hyphy.org

[15] http://www.cibiv.at/software/iqpnni

[16] http://www.megasoftware.net/index.html

[17] http://www.mesquiteproject.org/mesquite/mesquite.html

[18] http://bioweb.pasteur.fr/seqanal/interfaces/prot_nucml.html

[19] http://mrbayes.csit.fsu.edu/index.php

[20] http://www.fluxus-engineering.com/sharenet.htm

[21] http://www.cladistics.com/aboutNona.htm

[22] http://abacus.gene.ucl.ac.uk/software/paml.html

[23] http://paup.csit.fsu.edu/

[24] http://evolution.genetics.washington.edu/phylip.html

[25] http://www.lirmm.fr/~vberry/PHYLOQUART/phyloquart.html

[26] http://pycogent.sourceforge.net/

[27] http://genomebiology.com/2007/8/8/R171

[28] http://bioweb.pasteur.fr/seqanal/interfaces/quicktree.html

[29] http://icwww.epfl.ch/~stamatak/

[30] http://compbio.cs.huji.ac.il/semphy/

[31] http://www.splitstree.org

[32] http://www.zmuc.dk/public/phylogeny/TNT/

[33] http://www.topali.org/

[34] http://www.topali.org/download.shtml

[35] http://www.cbrg.ethz.ch/services/TreeGen

[36] http://bioweb.pasteur.fr/seqanal/interfaces/treealign-simple.html

[37] http://www.treefinder.de/

[38] http://www.tree-puzzle.de/

[39] http://www.trex.uqam.ca

[40] http://ugene.unipro.ru/download.html

[41] http://www.cladistics.com/aboutWinc.htm

[42] http://biowiki.org/XRATE

[43] http://bioweb.pasteur.fr/seqanal/phylogeny/intro-uk.html

[44] http://www.expasy.org/tools/#phylo

[45] http://evolution.genetics.washington.edu/phylip/software.html

[46] http://research.amnh.org/users/koloko/softlinks/

List of Y-DNA single-nucleotide polymorphisms

Mutation number	Nucleotide change	Position (base pair)	Total size (base pairs)	Position Forward 5′→3′	Reverse 5′→3′
M1 (YAP)	291bp insertion				
M2	A to G	168	209	aggcactggtcagaatgaag	aatggaaaatacagctcccc
M3					
M4					
M8					
M9					
M15					
M17					
M20					
M33					
M35					
M38					
M40					
M42					
M45					
M52					
M55					
M57					
M60					
M64.1					
M75					
M89					
M91					
M94					
M95					
M96					
M105					
M122					
M124					
M130					
M131					
M132					
M139					
M145					
M168					
M170					

M172					
M173					
M174					
M175					
M176					
M179					
M201					
M203					
M207					
M213					
M214					
M216					
M217					
M231	G to A	110	331	cctattatcctggaaaatgtgg	attccgattcctagtcacttgg
M241	G to A	54	366	aactcttgataaaccgtgctg	tccaatctcaattcatgcctc
M242	C to T	180	366	aactcttgataaaccgtgctg	tccaatctcaattcatgcctc
M253	C to T	283	400	gcaacaatgagggtttttttg	cagctccacctctatgcagttt
M258					
M267	T to G	148	287	ttatcctgagccgttgtccctg	tgtagagacacggttgtaccct
M268					
M269					
M285	G to C	70	287	ttatcctgagccgttgtccctg	tgtagagacacggttgtaccct
M286	G to A	129	287	ttatcctgagccgttgtccctg	tgtagagacacggttgtaccct
M287	A to T	100	287	ttatcctgagccgttgtccctg	tgtagagacacggttgtaccct
M297					
M299					
M304	A to C	421	527	caaagtgctgggattacagg	cttctagcttcatctgcattgt
M306					
M335	T to A	162	417	aagaaatgttgaactgaaagttgat	aggtgtatctggcatccgtta
M339	T to G	285	517	aggcaggacaactgagagca	tgcttgatcctgggaagt
M340	G to C	218	386	ccagtcagcagtacaaaagttg	gcatttctttgattatagaagcaa
M342	C to T	52	173	agagagttttctaacagggcg	tgggaatcacttttgcaact
M343	C to A	402	424	tttaacctcctccagctctgca	acccccacatatctccagg
M347					
M349	G to T	209	493	tgggattaaaggtgctcatg	caaaattggtaagccattagct
M356					
M359	T to C	122	447	cgtctatggccttgaaga	tccgaaaatgcagactt
M365	A to G	246	274	ccttcatttaggctgtagctgc	tgtatctttagttgagatgg
M367	A to G	196	274	ccttcatttaggctgtagctgc	tgtatctttagttgagatgg

M368	A to C	200	274	ccttcatttaggctgtagctgc	tgtatctttagttgagatgg
M369	G to C	45	274	ccttcatttaggctgtagctgc	tgtatctttagttgagatgg
M370	C to G	166	274	ccttcatttaggctgtagctgc	tgtatctttagttgagatgg
M405					

External links

- Sequence information for 218 M series markers published by 2001 [1]
- ISOGG Y-DNA SNP Index - 2007 [2]
- Karafet et al. (2008) Supplemental Research Data [3]

References

[1] http://hpgl.stanford.edu/publications/AHG_2001_218_Y_markers.doc
[2] http://www.isogg.org/tree/ISOGG_YDNA_SNP_Index07.html
[3] http://genome.cshlp.org/cgi/data/gr.7172008/DC1/1

LiveBench

LiveBench is a continuously running benchmark project for assessing the quality of protein structure prediction and secondary structure prediction methods. LiveBench focuses mainly on homology modeling and protein threading but also includes secondary structure prediction, comparing publicly available webserver output to newly deposited protein structures in the Protein Data Bank. Like the EVA project and unlike the related CASP and CAFASP experiments, LiveBench is intended to study the accuracy of predictions that would be obtained by non-expert users of publicly available prediction methods. A major advantage of LiveBench and EVA over CASP projects, which run once every two years is their comparatively large data set.

References

- Bujnicki JM, Elofsson A, Fischer D, Rychlewski L. (2001). LiveBench-1: continuous benchmarking of protein structure prediction servers. *Protein Sci* 10(2):352-61. PMID 11266621
- Rychlewski L, Fischer D. (2005). LiveBench-8: the large-scale, continuous assessment of automated protein structure prediction. *Protein Sci* 14(1):240-5. PMID 15608124

External links

- LiveBench main site [1]

References

[1] http://bioinfo.pl/meta/livebench.pl

Loop modeling

Loop modeling is a problem in protein structure prediction requiring the prediction of the conformations of loop regions in proteins without the use of a structural template. The problem arises often in homology modeling, where the tertiary structure of an amino acid sequence is predicted based on a sequence alignment to a *template*, or a second sequence whose structure is known. Because loops have highly variable sequences even within a given structural motif or protein fold, they often correspond to unaligned regions in sequence alignments; they also tend to be located at the solvent-exposed surface of globular proteins and thus are more conformationally flexible. Consequently, they often cannot be modeled using standard homology modeling techniques. More constrained versions of loop modeling are also used in the data fitting stages of solving a protein structure by X-ray crystallography, because loops can correspond to regions of low electron density and are therefore difficult to resolve.

Regions of a structural model that were predicted by loop modeling tend to be much less accurate than regions that were predicted using template-based techniques. The extent of the inaccuracy increases with the number of amino acids in the loop. The loop amino acids' side chains dihedral angles are often approximated from a rotamer library, but can worsen the inaccuracy of side chain packing in the overall model. Andrej Sali's homology modeling suite MODELLER includes a facility explicitly designed for loop modeling by a satisfaction of spatial restraints method.

Short loops

In general, the most accurate predictions are for loops of fewer than 8 amino acids. Extremely short loops of three residues can be determined from geometry alone, provided that the bond lengths and bond angles are specified. Slightly longer loops are often determined from a "spare parts" approach, in which loops of similar length are taken from known crystal structures and adapted to the geometry of the flanking segments. In some methods, the bond lengths and angles of the loop region are allowed to vary, in order to obtain a better fit; in other cases, the constraints of the flanking segments may be varied to find more "protein-like" loop conformations. The accuracy of such short loops may be almost as accurate as that of the homology model upon which it is based. It should also be considered that the loops in proteins may not be well-structured and therefore have no one conformation that could be predicted; NMR experiments indicate that solvent-exposed loops are "floppy" and adopt many conformations, while the loop conformations seen by X-ray crystallography may merely reflect crystal packing interactions, or the stabilizing influence of crystallization co-solvents.

References

- Mount DM. (2004). Bioinformatics: Sequence and Genome Analysis 2nd ed. Cold Spring Harbor Laboratory Press: Cold Spring Harbor, NY.
- Chung SY, Subbiah S. (1996.) A structural explanation for the twilight zone of protein sequence homology. Structure 4: 1123–27.

External links

- MODLOOP [1], public server for access to MODELLER's loop modeling facility

References

[1] http://modbase.compbio.ucsf.edu/modloop

Louis and Beatrice Laufer Center for Physical and Quantitative Biology

The **Louis and Beatrice Laufer Center for Physical and Quantitative Biology** [1] was founded in 2008 by a gift from Drs. Henry Laufer and Marsha Laufer. The Laufer Center is part of Stony Brook University. The center's current director is Dr. Ken A. Dill. Associate director is Dr. Carlos Simmerling. Dr. David F. Green will head the multi-departmental graduate training program for the center.[2] The center is a multidisciplinary venue where research from such fields as biology, biochemistry, chemistry, computer science, engineering, genetics, mathematics, and physics can come together and target medical and biological problems using both computation and experiment.

References

[1] laufer center webpage (http://www.stonybrook.edu/commcms/laufer/)
[2] happenings press release (http://sb.cc.stonybrook.edu/happenings/?p=33371)

LSID

Life Science Identifiers[1] [2] are a way to name and locate pieces of information on the web. Essentially, an LSID is a unique identifier for some data, and the LSID protocol specifies a standard way to locate the data (as well as a standard way of describing that data). They are a little like DOIs used by many publishers.

An LSID is represented as a Uniform Resource Name (URN) with the following format.

* URN:LSID:<Authority>:<Namespace>:<ObjectID>[:<Version>]

Controversy over the use of LSIDs

There has been a lot of interest in LSIDs in both the bioinformatics and the biodiversity communities. However, more recently, as understanding has increased of how HTTP URIs can perform a similar naming task,[3] [4] the use of LSIDs as identifiers has been criticized[5] as violating the Web Architecture [6] good practice of reusing existing URI schemes.[7] Nevertheless, the explicit separation of data from metadata; specification of a method for discovering multiple locations for data-retrieval; and the ability to discover multiple independent sources of metadata for any identified thing were crucial parts of the LSID and its resolution specification that have not successfully been mimicked by an HTTP-only approach.

The World Wide Web provides a globally distributed communication framework that is essential for almost all scientific collaboration, including bioinformatics. However, several limits and inadequacies were thought to exist, one of which was the inability to programmatically identify locally named objects that may be widely distributed over the network. This perceived shortcoming would have limited our ability to integrate multiple knowledgebases, each of which gives partial information of a shared domain, as is commonly seen in bioinformatics. The Life Science Identifier (LSID) and LSID Resolution System (LSRS) were designed to provide simple and elegant solutions to this problem, consistent with next-generation semantic web and semantic grid, based on the extension of existing internet technologies. However, it has more recently been pointed out that some of these perceived shortcomings are not intrinsic to HTTP URIs, and much (though not all) of the functionality that LSIDs provide can be obtained using properly crafted HTTP URIs.[3]

Notes

[1] Clark T., Martin S., Liefeld T. Briefings in Bioinformatics 5.1:59-70, March 1, 2004.

[2] Technology Report on OMG Life Sciences Identifiers Specification (LSID) (http://xml.coverpages.org/lsid.html)

[3] Booth, David: "Converting New URI Schemes or URN Sub-Schemes to HTTP" (http://dbooth.org/2006/urn2http/#lsid)

[4] Thompson, Henry S.: "A precedent suggesting a compromise for the SWHCLS IG Best Practices", publicly archived email message (http://lists.w3.org/Archives/Public/public-semweb-lifesci/2006Jul/0206.html)

[5] Mendelsohn, Noah: "My conversation with Sean Martin about LSIDs", public email to W3C TAG mailing list 25-Jul-2006 (http://lists.w3.org/Archives/Public/www-tag/2006Jul/0041)

[6] http://www.w3.org/TR/webarch/#pr-reuse-uri-schemes

[7] W3C Architecture of the World Wide Web (http://www.w3.org/TR/webarch/#pr-reuse-uri-schemes)

External links

- Life Sciences Identifiers: OMG Final Available Specification (http://www.omg.org/cgi-bin/doc?dtc/04-10-08)
- LSID Resolution Project (http://lsids.sourceforge.net/)
- LSID best practices (http://www-128.ibm.com/developerworks/opensource/library/os-lsidbp/) from IBM
- LSID Assigning and Resolution Authority (http://www.morphster.org/lsid.html) from The University of Texas at Austin
- Life Science Identifier (http://lsid.biopathways.org/) from BioPathways Consortium
- LSID Tester (http://linnaeus.zoology.gla.ac.uk/~rpage/lsid/tester/)
- A Position on LSIDs (http://www.hyam.net/blog/archives/325) - Reflections from some one involved in implementation and roll out of LSIDs

Macromolecular docking

Macromolecular docking is the computational modelling of the quaternary structure of complexes formed by two or more interacting biological macromolecules. Protein–protein complexes are the most commonly attempted targets of such modelling, followed by protein–nucleic acid complexes.

The ultimate goal of docking is the prediction of the three dimensional structure of the macromolecular complex of interest as it would occur in a living organism. Docking itself only produces plausible candidate structures. These candidates must be ranked using methods such as scoring functions to identify structures that are most likely to occur in nature.

The term "docking" originated in the late 1970s, with a more restricted meaning; then, "docking" meant refining a model of a complex structure by optimizing the separation between the interactors but keeping their relative orientations fixed. Later, the relative orientations of the interacting partners in the modelling was allowed to vary, but the internal geometry of each of the partners was held fixed. This type of modelling is sometimes referred to as "rigid docking". With further increases in computational power, it became possible to model changes in internal geometry of the interacting partners that may occur when a complex is formed. This type of modelling is referred to as "flexible docking".

Background

The biological roles of most proteins, as characterized by which other macromolecules they interact with, are known at best incompletely. Even those proteins that participate in a well-studied biological process (e.g., the Krebs cycle) may have unexpected interaction partners or functions which are unrelated to that process. Moreover, vast numbers of "hypothetical" proteins have been emerging as part of the genomic revolution of the late 1990s, proteins that, apart from their amino acid sequence, are a complete mystery.

In cases of known protein–protein interactions, other questions arise. Genetic diseases (e.g., cystic fibrosis) are known to be caused by misfolded or mutated proteins, and there is a desire to understand what, if any, anomalous protein–protein interactions a given mutation can cause. In the distant future, proteins may be designed to perform biological functions, and a determination of the potential interactions of such proteins will be essential.

For any given set of proteins, the following questions may be of interest, from the point of view of technology or natural history:

- Do these proteins bind *in vivo*?

If they do bind,

- What is the spatial configuration which they adopt in their bound state?
- How strong or weak is their interaction?

If they do not bind,

- Can they be made to bind by inducing a mutation?

Protein–protein docking is ultimately envisaged to address all these issues. Furthermore, since docking methods can be based on purely physical principles, even proteins of unknown function (or which have been studied relatively little) may be docked. The only prerequisite is that their molecular structure has been either determined experimentally, or can be estimated by a protein structure prediction technique.

Protein–nucleic acid interactions feature prominently in the living cell. Transcription factors, which regulate gene expression, and polymerases, which catalyse replication, are composed of proteins, and the genetic material they interact with is composed of nucleic acids. Modeling protein–nucleic acid complexes presents some unique challenges, as described below.

History

In the 1970s, complex modelling revolved around manually identifying features on the surfaces of the interactors, and interpreting the consequences for binding, function and activity; any computer programmes were typically used at the end of the modelling process, to discriminate between the relatively few configurations which remained after all the heuristic constraints had been imposed. The first use of computers was in a study on hemoglobin interaction in sickle-cell fibres.[1] This was followed in 1978 by work on the trypsin-BPTI complex.[2] Computers discriminated between good and bad models using a scoring function which rewarded large interface area, and pairs of molecules in contact but not occupying the same space. The computer used a simplified representation of the interacting proteins, with one interaction centre for each residue. Favorable electrostatic interactions, including hydrogen bonds, were identified by hand.[3]

In the early 1990s, more structures of complexes were determined, and available computational power had increased substantially. With the emergence of bioinformatics, the focus moved towards developing generalized techniques which could be applied to an arbitrary set of complexes at acceptable computational cost. The new methods were envisaged to apply even in the absence of phylogenetic or experimental clues; any specific prior knowledge could still be introduced at the stage of choosing between the highest ranking output models, or be framed as input if the algorithm catered for it. 1992 saw the publication of the correlation method,[4] an algorithm which used the fast Fourier transform to give a vastly improved scalability for evaluating coarse shape complementarity on rigid-body models. This was extended in 1997 to cover coarse electrostatics.[5]

In 1996 the results of the first blind trial were published,[6] in which six research groups attempted to predict the complexed structure of TEM-1 Beta-lactamase with Beta-lactamase inhibitor protein (BLIP). The exercise brought into focus the necessity of accommodating conformational change and the difficulty of discriminating between conformers. It also served as the prototype for the CAPRI assessment series, which debuted in 2001.

Rigid-body docking *vs.* flexible docking

If the bond angles, bond lengths and torsion angles of the components are not modified at any stage of complex generation, it is known as *rigid body docking*. A subject of speculation is whether or not rigid-body docking is sufficiently good for most docking. When substantial conformational change occurs within the components at the time of complex formation, rigid-body docking is inadequate. However, scoring all possible conformational changes is prohibitively expensive in computer time. Docking procedures which permit conformational change, or *flexible docking* procedures, must intelligently select small subset of possible conformational changes for consideration.

Methods

Successful docking requires two criteria:

- Generating a set configurations which reliably includes at least one nearly correct one.
- Reliably distinguishing nearly correct configurations from the others.

For many interactions, the binding site is known on one or more of the proteins to be docked. This is the case for antibodies and for competitive inhibitors. In other cases, a binding site may be strongly suggested by mutagenic or phylogenetic evidence. Configurations where the proteins interpenetrate severely may also be ruled out *a priori*.

After making exclusions based on prior knowledge or stereochemical clash, the remaining space of possible complexed structures must be sampled exhaustively, evenly and with a sufficient coverage to guarantee a near hit. Each configuration must be scored with a measure that is capable of ranking a nearly correct structure above at least 100,000 alternatives. This is a computationally intensive task, and a variety of strategies have been developed.

Reciprocal space methods

Each of the proteins may be represented as a simple cubic lattice. Then, for the class of scores which are discrete convolutions, configurations related to each other by translation of one protein by an exact lattice vector can all be scored almost simultaneously by applying the convolution theorem.[4] It is possible to construct reasonable, if approximate, convolution-like scoring functions representing both stereochemical and electrostatic fitness.

Reciprocal space methods have been used extensively for their ability to evaluate enormous numbers of configurations. They lose their speed advantage if torsional changes are introduced. Another drawback is that it is impossible to make efficient use of prior knowledge. The question also remains whether convolutions are too limited a class of scoring function to identify the best complex reliably.

Monte Carlo methods

In Monte Carlo, an initial configuration is refined by taking random steps which are accepted or rejected based on their induced improvement in score (see the Metropolis criterion), until a certain number of steps have been tried. The assumption is that convergence to the best structure should occur from a large class of initial configurations, only one of which needs to be considered. Initial configurations may be sampled coarsely, and much computation time can be saved. Because of the difficulty of finding a scoring function which is both highly discriminating for the correct configuration and also converges to the correct configuration from a distance, the use of two levels of refinement, with different scoring functions, has been proposed.[7] Torsion can be introduced naturally to Monte Carlo as an additional property of each random move.

Monte Carlo methods are not guaranteed to search exhaustively, so that the best configuration may be missed even using a scoring function which would in theory identify it. How severe a problem this is for docking has not been firmly established.

Evaluation

Scoring functions

To find a score which forms a consistent basis for selecting the best configuration, studies are carried out on a standard benchmark (see below) of protein–protein interaction cases. Scoring functions are assessed on the rank they assign to the best structure (ideally the best structure should be ranked 1), and on their coverage (the proportion of the benchmark cases for which they achieve an acceptable result). Types of scores studied include:

- Heuristic scores based on residue contacts.
- Shape complementarity of molecular surfaces ("stereochemistry").
- Free energies, estimated using parameters from molecular mechanics force fields such as CHARMM or AMBER.
- Phylogenetic desirability of the interacting regions.
- Clustering coefficients.

It is usual to create hybrid scores by combining one or more categories above in a weighted sum whose weights are optimized on cases from the benchmark. To avoid bias, the benchmark cases used to optimize the weights must not overlap with the cases used to make the final test of the score.

The ultimate goal in protein–protein docking is to select the ideal ranking solution according to a scoring scheme that would also give an insight into the affinity of the complex. Such a development would drive *in silico* protein engineering, computer-aided drug design and/or high-throughput annotation of which proteins bind or not (annotation of interactome). Several scoring functions have been proposed for binding affinity / free energy prediction.[7] [8] [9] [10] However the correlation between experimentally determined binding affinities and the predictions of nine commonly used scoring functions have been found to be nearly orthogonal ($R^2 \sim 0$).[11] [12] It was also observed that some components of the scoring algorithms may display better correlation to the experimental binding energies than the full score, suggesting that a significantly better performance might be obtained by combining the appropriate contributions from different scoring algorithms. Experimental methods for the determination of binding affinities are: surface plasmon resonance (SPR), Förster resonance energy transfer, radioligand-based techniques, isothermal titration calorimetry (ITC), Microscale Thermophoresis (MST) or spectroscopic measurements and other fluorescence techniques.

Benchmarks

A benchmark of 84 protein–protein interactions with known complexed structures has been developed for testing docking methods.[13] The set is chosen to cover a wide range of interaction types, and to avoid repeated features, such as the profile of interactors' structural families according to the SCOP database. Benchmark elements are classified into three levels of difficulty (the most difficult containing the largest change in backbone conformation). The protein–protein docking benchmark contains examples of enzyme-inhibitor, antigen-antibody and homomultimeric complexes.

A binding affinity benchmark has been based on the protein–protein docking benchmark.[11] 81 protein–protein complexes with known experimental affinities are included; these complexes span over 11 orders of magnitude in terms of affinity. Each entry of the benchmark includes several biochemical parameters associated with the experimental data, along with the method used to determine the affinity. This benchmark was used to assess the extent to which scoring functions could also predict affinities of macromolecular complexes.

This Benchmark was post-peer reviewed and significantly expanded.[14] The new set is diverse in terms of the biological functions it represents, with complexes that involve G-proteins and receptor extracellular domains, as well as antigen/antibody, enzyme/inhibitor, and enzyme/substrate complexes. It is also diverse in terms of the partners' affinity for each other, with K_d ranging between 10^{-5} and 10^{-14} M. Nine pairs of entries represent closely related complexes that have a similar structure, but a very different affinity, each pair comprising a cognate and a noncognate assembly. The unbound structures of the component proteins being available, conformation changes can be assessed. They are significant in most of the complexes, and large movements or disorder-to-order transitions are frequently observed. The set may be used to benchmark biophysical models aiming to relate affinity to structure in protein–protein interactions, taking into account the reactants and the conformation changes that accompany the association reaction, instead of just the final product.[14]

The CAPRI assessment

The Critical Assessment of PRediction of Interactions[15] is an ongoing series of events in which researchers throughout the community try to dock the same proteins, as provided by the assessors. Rounds take place approximately every 6 months. Each round contains between one and six target protein–protein complexes whose structures have been recently determined experimentally. The coordinates and are held privately by the assessors, with the cooperation of the structural biologists who determined them. The assessment of submissions is double blind.

CAPRI attracts a high level of participation (37 groups participated worldwide in round seven) and a high level of interest from the biological community in general. Although CAPRI results are of little statistical significance owing to the small number of targets in each round, the role of CAPRI in stimulating discourse is significant. (The CASP assessment is a similar exercise in the field of protein structure prediction).

References

[1] Levinthal C, Wodak SJ, Kahn P, Dadivanian AK (1975). "Hemoglobin Interactions in Sickle Cell Fibers: I. Theoretical Approaches to the Molecular Contacts". *Proceedings of the National Academy of Sciences* **72** (4): 1330–1334. doi:10.1073/pnas.72.4.1330. PMC 432527. PMID 1055409.

[2] Wodak SJ, Janin J (1978). "Computer Analysis of Protein-Protein Interactions". *Journal of Molecular Biology* **124** (2): 323–342. doi:10.1016/0022-2836(78)90302-9. PMID 712840.

[3] Wodak SJ, De Crombrugghe M, Janin J (1987). "Computer Studies of Interactions between Macromolecules". *Progress in Biophysics and Molecular Biology* **49** (1): 29–63. doi:10.1016/0079-6107(87)90008-3. PMID 3310103.

[4] Katchalski-Katzir E, Shariv I, Eisenstein M, Friesem AA, Aflalo C, Vakser IA (1992). "Molecular surface recognition: determination of geometric fit between proteins and their ligands by correlation techniques". *Proc. Natl. Acad. Sci. U.S.A.* **89** (6): 2195–2199. doi:10.1073/pnas.89.6.2195. PMC 48623. PMID 1549581.

[5] Gabb HA, Jackson RM, Sternberg MJ (September 1997). "Modelling protein docking using shape complementarity, electrostatics and biochemical information". *J. Mol. Biol.* **272** (1): 106–120. doi:10.1006/jmbi.1997.1203. PMID 9299341.

[6] Strynadka NC, Eisenstein M, Katchalski-Katzir E, Shoichet BK, Kuntz ID, Abagyan R, Totrov M, Janin J, Cherfils J, Zimmerman F, Olson A, Duncan B, Rao M, Jackson R, Sternberg M, James MN (1996). "Molecular Docking Programs Successfully Predict the Binding of a Beta-lactamase Inhibitory Protein to TEM-1 Beta-Lactamase". *Nature Structural Biology* **3** (3): 233–239. doi:10.1038/nsb0396-233. PMID 8605624.

[7] Gray JJ, Moughon S, Wang C, Schueler-Furman O, Kuhlman B, Rohl CA, Baker D (2003). "Protein-protein docking with simultaneous optimization of rigid-body displacement and side-chain conformations". *J. Mol. Biol.* **331** (1): 281–299. doi:10.1016/S0022-2836(03)00670-3. PMID 12875852.

[8] Camacho CJ, Vajda S (2008). "Protein docking along smooth association pathways". *Proceedings of the National Academy of Sciences* **98** (19): 10636–10641. doi:10.1073/pnas.181147798. PMC 58518. PMID 11517309.

[9] Camacho CJ, Vajda S (2007). "In silico screening of mutational effects on enzyme-proteic inhibitor affinity: a docking-based approach". *BMC structural biology* **7**: 37. doi:10.1186/1472-6807-7-37. PMC 1913526. PMID 17559675.

[10] Zhang C, Liu S, Zhu Q, Zhou Y. (2005). "A knowledge-based energy function for protein-ligand, protein-protein, and protein-DNA complexes". *Journal of Medicinal chemistry* **7** (48): 2325–2335. doi:10.1021/jm049314d. PMID 15801826.

[11] Kastritis PL, Bonvin AM (May 2010). "Are scoring functions in protein-protein docking ready to predict interactomes? Clues from a novel binding affinity benchmark". *J. Proteome Res.* **9** (5): 2216–2225. doi:10.1021/pr9009854. PMID 20329755.

[12] Rosato A, Fuentes G, Verma C (2010). "Faculty of 1000 Biology: evaluations for Kastritis PL & Bonvin AM J Proteome Res 2010 May 7 9 (5) :2216-25" (http://f1000biology.com/article/id/3437978/evaluation). *Faculty of 1000 Biology.* .

[13] Mintseris J, Wiehe K, Pierce B, Anderson R, Chen R, Janin J, Weng Z (2005). "Protein-Protein Docking Benchmark 2.0: an update". *Proteins* **60** (2): 214–216. doi:10.1002/prot.20560. PMID 15981264.

[14] Kastritis PL, Moal IH, Hwang H, Weng Z, Bates PA, Bonvin AM, Janin J (March 2011). "A structure-based benchmark for protein-protein binding affinity". *Protein Science* **20** (3): 482–491. doi:10.1002/pro.580. PMC 3064828. PMID 21213247.

[15] Janin J, Henrick K, Moult J, Eyck LT, Sternberg MJ, Vajda S, Vakser I, Wodak SJ (2003). "CAPRI: a Critical Assessment of PRedicted Interactions". *Proteins* **52** (1): 2–9. doi:10.1002/prot.10381. PMID 12784359.

MacVector

MacVector

Developer(s)	MacVector, Inc.
Stable release	12.0.5 / 20th July, 2011
Operating system	Mac OS X
Platform	Xcode
Type	Bioinformatics
License	commercial
Website	http://www.macvector.com

MacVector is a commercial sequence analysis application for Apple Macintosh computers running Mac OS X. It is intended to be used by Molecular Biologists to help analyze, design, research and document their experiments in the laboratory.

Features

MacVector is a collection of sequence analysis algorithms linked to various sequence editors, including a single sequence editor, a multiple sequence alignment editor and a contig editor. MacVector tries to use a minimum of windows and steps to access all the functionality. Functions include:

- Sequence alignment (ClustalW) and editing.
- Subsequence search and open reading frames (ORFs) analysis.
- Phylogenetic tree construction UPGMA, Neighbour joining with bootstrapping and consensus trees
- Online Database searching - Search public databases at the NCBI such as Genbank, PubMed, and UniProt.
- Perform online BLAST searches.
- Protein analysis.
- Contig assembly and chromatogram editing
- Aligning cDNA against genomic templates
- Creating dot plots of DNA to DNA, Protein to Protein and DNA to protein.
- Restriction analysis - find and view restriction cut sites. Uses digested fragments to clone genes into vectors.
- PCR Primer design - easy primer design and testing. Also uses primer3

MacVector has a contig assembly plugin called Assembler that uses phred, phrap and cross match.

History

MacVector was originally developed by IBI in 1994 [1] . It was acquired by Kodak, and subsequently Oxford Molecular [2] . Oxford Molecular was merged into Accelrys in 2001[3] . It was acquired by MacVector, Inc on the 1st of January, 2007 [4] .

References

[1] MacVector: an integrated sequence analysis program for the Macintosh.Olson SA. Methods Mol Biol. (1994) 25,195-201.

[2] http://findarticles.com/p/articles/mi_hb197/is_/ai_n5566980#

[3] http://accelrys.com/company/

[4] http://accelrys.com/products/macvector/

External links

- MacVector homepage (http://www.macvector.com)
- MacVector Forums (http://www.macvector.com/phpbb)

Other Software

- Gene Designer - A free gene design software suite with a range of design and cloning tools
- Geneious http://www.geneious.com
- QuickGene - Actively developed, intuitive DNA analysis software with extensive restriction enzyme information. Particularly useful for cloning. Mac OSX and Windows with a Beta version for Linux coming (http://www. crimsonbase.com/)
- ApE -A Powerful Multipurpose DNA Engineering Software (http://www.biology.utah.edu/jorgensen/ wayned/ape/)
- Serial Cloner - A DNA editing and manipulating software for MacOS and Windows (http://www.serialbasics. com/Serial_Cloner.html)
- Vector NTI
- Discovery Studio (http://www.csc.fi/english/research/sciences/bioscience/programs/ds)
- CLC Main Workbench (http://www.clcbio.com/main)
- UGENE

MAGMA (Molecular Animation, Graphics and Modeling Application framework)

MAGMA

Developer(s)	Advanced Molecular Software
Stable release	0.0.6.0 / February 6, 2008
Operating system	Microsoft Windows
Type	Bioinformatics/Cheminformatics/Molecular modelling
License	GNU Lesser General Public License2.1
Website	[1]

MAGMA (*Molecular Animation, Graphics and Modeling Application framework*) is a rapid application development (RAD) system in the field of molecular modelling, computational chemistry and computational biology. It is an extension dynamic-link library (DLL) for The Microsoft Foundation Class Library (MFC) written completely in C++ that acts as a framework for developing molecular graphics and modelling applications under all generations of Microsoft Windows operating systems. It is distributed under the GNU Lesser General Public License (LGPL). MAGMA has been developed in Armin Madadkar Sobhani Research Group at Bioinformatics Department of Institute of Biochemistry and Biophysics (IBB), University of Tehran.

Major features

- It supports all major versions of Microsoft Windows and Visual C++.
- Easy installation and deployment using automated installation file.
- Easy generation of new applications in few steps using a specially designed Custom Application Wizard.
- A comprehensive online help which is automatically integrated into MSDN during setup and provides context sensitive help during programming in IDE.
- Support for plugin technology at the library level instead of application level.
- Easy development and installation of new plugins using a specially designed Custom Plugin Wizard.
- Support for loading/saving molecules, models and workspaces in compressed binary file format suitable for exchanging information between all applications developed using MAGMA. In addition, each application can have proprietary compressed binary format of its own.
- OpenGL was used for displaying molecular structures.
- Ability to Print and Print preview of molecular graphics.
- Ability to save molecular views in more than 16 different graphical file formats.
- Support for exclusive full screen mode suitable for 3D shutter glasses.

- Support for cube map texture backgrounds.
- SIMD extensions (i.e. 3DNow!, 3DNow! Extended, SSE, and SSE2) are used for matrix and vector calculations for supported platforms.

External links

- MAGMA Home Page [1]
- Armin Madadkar Sobhani Research Group [2]

References

[1] http://ams.ut.ac.ir/magma
[2] http://bioinformatics.ut.ac.ir/armin

MaMF

MaMF, or Mammalian Motif Finder, is an algorithm for identifying motifs to which transcription factors bind.

The algorithm takes as input a set of promoter sequences, and a motif width(w), and as output, produces a ranked list of 30 predicted motifs(each motif is defined by a set of N sequences, where N is a parameter).

The algorithm firstly indexes each sub-sequence of length n, where n is a parameter around 4-6 base pairs, in each promoter, so they can be looked up efficiently. This index is then used to build a list of all pairs of sequences of length w, such that each sequence shares an n-mer, and each sequence forms an ungapped alignment with a substring of length w from the string of length 2w around the match, with a score exceeding a cut-off.

The pairs of sequences are then scored. The scoring function favours pairs which are very similar, but disfavours sequences which are very common in the target genome. The 1000 highest scoring pairs are kept, and the others are discarded. Each of these 1000 'seed' motifs are then used to search iteratively search for further sequences of length which maximise the score(a greedy algorithm), until N sequences for that motif are reached.

Very similar motifs are discarded, and the 30 highest scoring motifs are returned as output.

References

- Lawrence S Hon and Ajay N Jain: "A deterministic motif finding algorithm with application to the human genome". Bioinformatics 2006 22(9):1047-1054

MANET database

The **Molecular Ancestry Network (MANET)** database is a bioinformatics database that maps evolutionary relationships of protein architectures directly onto biological networks.[2] It was originally developed by Hee Shin Kim, Jay E. Mittenthal and Gustavo Caetano-Anolles in the Department of Crop Sciences of the University of Illinois at Urbana-Champaign.[1]

MANET traces for example the ancestry of individual metabolic enzymes in metabolism with bioinformatic, phylogenetic, and statistical methods. MANET currently links information in the Structural Classification of Proteins (SCOP) database, the metabolic pathways database of the Kyoto Encyclopedia of Genes and Genomes (KEGG), and phylogenetic reconstructions describing the evolution of protein fold architecture at a universal level.[3] MANET literally "paints" the ancestries of enzymes derived from rooted phylogenetic trees directly onto over one hundred metabolic pathways representations, paying homage to one of the fathers of impressionism. It also provides numerous

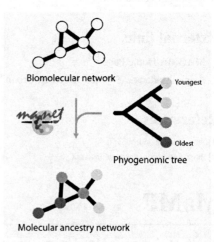

MANET paints ancestries derived from phylogenetic trees onto proteins in biological networks. Figure modified from Kim et al.[1]

functionalities that enable searching specific protein folds with defined ancestry values, displaying the distribution of enzymes that are painted, and exploring quantitative details describing individual protein folds. This permits the study of global and local metabolic network architectures, and the extraction of evolutionary patterns at global and local levels.

A statistical analysis of the data in MANET showed for example a patchy distribution of ancestry values assigned to protein folds in each subnetwork, indicating that evolution of metabolism occurred globally by widespread recruitment of enzymes.[1] MANET was used recently to sort out enzymatic recruitment processes in metabolic networks and propose that modern metabolism originated in the purine nucleotide metabolic subnetwork.[4] The database is useful for the study of metabolic evolution.

External links

- Molecular Ancestry Network (MANET) database [52]

References

[1] Kim HS, Mittenthal JE, Caetano-Anolles G, (2006). "MANET:tracing evolution of protein architecture in metabolic networks". *BMC Bioinformatics* **7**: 351. doi:10.1186/1471-2105-7-351. PMC 1559654. PMID 16854231.

[2] http://www.manet.uiuc.edu

[3] Caetano-Anolles G, Caetano-Anolles D (2003). "An evolutionarily structured universe of protein architecture". *Genome Res* **13** (7): 1563–71. doi:10.1101/gr.1161903. PMC 403752. PMID 12840035.

[4] Caetano-Anolles G, Kim HS, Mittenthal JE (2007). "The origin of modern metabolic networks inferred from phylogenomic analysis of protein architecture". *Proc Natl Acad Sci USA* **104** (22): 9358–63. doi:10.1073/pnas.0701214104. PMC 1890499. PMID 17517598.

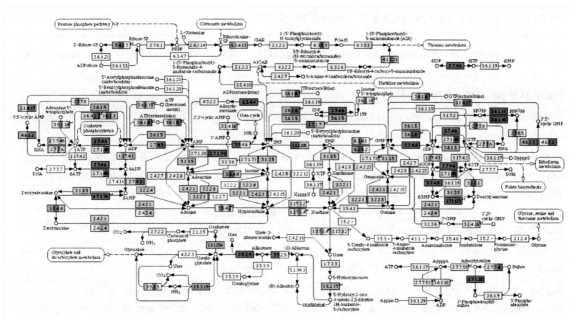

Molecular ancestries of enzymes in purine metabolism.

Manhattan plot

A **Manhattan plot** is a type of scatter plot, usually used to display data with a large number of data-points - many of non-zero amplitude, and with a distribution of higher-magnitude values, for instance in genome-wide association studies (GWAS).[1] In GWAS Manhattan plots, genomic coordinates are displayed along the X-axis, with the negative logarithm of the association P-value for each single nucleotide polymorphism displayed on the Y-axis. Because the strongest associations have the smallest P-values (e.g., 10^{-15}), their negative logarithms will be the greatest (e.g., 15).

It gains its name from the similarity of such a plot to the Manhattan skyline: a profile of skyscrapers towering above the lower level "buildings" which vary around a lower height.

References

[1] Gibson, Greg (2010). "Hints of hidden heritability in GWAS.". *Nature Genetics* **42** (7): 558–560. doi:10.1038/ng0710-558. PMID 20581876.

Mass spectrometry software

Mass spectrometry software is software used for data acquisition, analysis, or representation in mass spectrometry.

MS/MS peptide identification

Within the field of protein mass spectrometry, tandem mass spectrometry (also known as MS/MS or MS^2) experiments are used for protein/peptide identification.

In these experiments, sample proteins are broken up into short peptides using an enzyme like trypsin and separated in time using liquid chromatography. They are then sent through one mass spectrometer to separate them by mass. Peptide having a specific mass are then typically fragmented using collision-induced dissociation and sent through a second mass spectrometer, which will generate a set of fragment peaks from which the amino acid sequence of the peptide may often be inferred. Peptide identification software is used to try to reliably make these inferences.[1]

A typical experiment involves several hours of mass spectrometer time, and recent instruments may produce hundreds of thousands of MS/MS spectra, which must then be interpreted.

Peptide identification algorithms fall into two broad classes: database search and *de novo* search. The former search takes place against a database containing all amino acid sequences assumed to be present in the analyzed sample, whereas the latter infers peptide sequences without knowledge of genomic data. At present, database search is more popular and considered to produce higher quality results for most uses. With increasing instrument precision, however, *de novo* search may become increasingly attractive.

Database search algorithms

SEQUEST

SEQUEST is a proprietary tandem mass spectrometry data analysis program developed by John Yates and Jimmy Eng in 1994.[2] The algorithm used by this program is covered by several US and European software patents.

SEQUEST identifies collections of tandem mass spectra to peptide sequences that have been generated from databases of protein sequences. It was one of the first, if not the first, database search program.

SEQUEST, like many engines, identifies each tandem mass spectrum individually. The software evaluates protein sequences from a database to compute the list of peptides that could result from each. The peptide's intact mass is known from the mass spectrum, and SEQUEST uses this information to determine the set of candidate peptides sequences that could meaningfully be compared to the spectrum by including only those which are near the mass of the observed peptide ion. For each candidate peptide, SEQUEST projects a theoretical tandem mass spectrum, and SEQUEST compares these theoretical spectra to the observed tandem mass spectrum by the use of cross correlation. The candidate sequence with the best matching theoretical tandem mass spectrum is reported as the best identification for this spectrum.

While very successful in terms of sensitivity, it is quite slow to process data and there are concerns against specificity, especially if multiple posttranslational modifications (PTMs) are present.

Mascot

Mascot [3] is a proprietary identification program available from Matrix Science. It performs mass spectrometry data analysis through a statistical evaluation of matches between observed and projected peptide fragments rather than cross correlation. As of version 2.2, support for peptide quantitation methods is provided in addition to the identification features.

PEAKS

PEAKS DB is a proprietary proteomic mass spectrometry database search engine, developed by Bioinformatics Solutions Inc. In addition to providing an independent database search, results can be incorporated as part of the software's multi-engine (Sequest, Mascot, X!Tandem, OMSSA, PEAKS DB) consensus reporting tool, inChorus.[4] In addition to reporting database sequences, it also provides a list of sequences identified exclusively by de novo sequencing. The approach of considering de novo sequence results with those of database searching increases the efficiency of the search process, maintains speed and ultimately maintains a low false discovery rate (FDR).[5]

X!Tandem

X!Tandem[6] is open source software that can match tandem mass spectra with peptide sequences, in a process that has come to be known as protein identification.

This software has a simple, XML-based input file format.[7] This format is used for all of the X! series search engines, as well as the GPM and GPMDB.

Unlike some earlier generation search engines, all of the X! Series search engines calculate statistical confidence (expectation values) for all of the individual spectrum-to-sequence assignments. They also reassemble all of the peptide assignments in a data set onto the known protein sequences and assign the statistical confidence that this assembly and alignment is non-random (i.e., did not occur by chance).[8] Therefore, separate assembly and statistical analysis software (e.g. PeptideProphet and ProteinProphet) are not needed.

This approach is good in terms of speed but poor with regard to false negatives and sensitivity.

X!!Tandem

X!!Tandem [9] is a parallel, high performance version of X!Tandem that has been parallelized via MPI to run on clusters or other non-shared memory multiprocessors running Linux. In X!!Tandem the search is parallelized by splitting the input spectra into as many subsets as there are processors, and processing each subset independently. Both compute-intensive stages of the processing (initial and refinement) are parallelized, and overall speedups in excess of 20-fold have been observed on real datasets.

With the exception of the details related to MPI launch, it is run exactly as X!Tandem, and produces exactly the same results using the same input and configuration files. It differs from Parallel Tandem[10] in that the parallelism is handled internally, rather than as an external driver/wrapper.

Phenyx

Phenyx is developed by Geneva Bioinformatics (GeneBio) in collaboration with the Swiss Institute of Bioinformatics (SIB). Phenyx incorporates OLAV, a family of statistical scoring models, to generate and optimize scoring schemes that can be tailored for all kinds of instruments, instrumental set-ups and general sample treatments. Although, not RAW, unprocessed data. [11] Phenyx computes a score to evaluate the quality of a match between a theoretical and experimental peak list (i.e. mass spectrum). A match is thus a collection of observations deduced from this comparison. The basic peptide score is ultimately transformed into a normalized z-Score and a p-Value. A basic peptide score is the sum of raw scores for up to twelve physico-chemical properties.

In addition to regular peptide and protein identification features, Phenyx proposes a number of additional functionalities, such as: a result comparison interface to visualise side-by-side multiple results; an import functionality to incorporate results from other search engines; a manual validation feature to manually accept/reject identifications and dynamically recalculates protein scores.

OMSSA

OMSSA[12] is an open source database search program developed at NCBI.[13]

MyriMatch

MyriMatch[14] is an open source database search program developed at the Vanderbilt Medical Center.[15]

greylag

Greylag is an open source database search program developed at the Stowers Institute for Medical Research.[16] Its scoring algorithm is based on that of MyriMatch, but it includes a novel FDR (false discovery rate) validation algorithm as well. It is designed to perform large searches on computational clusters having hundreds of nodes. Notably, it is largely implemented in an interpreted language, Python, with only the CPU-intensive routines written in a compiled language (C++).

ByOnic

ByOnic is a database search program with a public web interface.[17] developed at PARC.[18] ByOnic works together with ComByne,[19] which combines peptide identifications to produce a protein score.

InsPecT

A MS-alignment search engine available at the Center for Computational Mass Spectrometry at the University of California, San Diego [20]

SIMS

SIMS (Sequential Interval Motif Search)[21] is a software tool design to perform unrestrictive PTM search over tandem mass spectra. In other words, users do not have to characterize the potential PTMs. Instead, users only need to specify the range of modification mass for each individual amino acid.[22]

MassWiz

MassWiz[23] is a free, open source search algorithm developed at Institute of Genomics and Integrative Biology. It is available as a windows commandline tool [24] and also as a webserver.[25]

De novo sequencing algorithms

De novo peptide sequencing algorithms are based, in general, on the approach proposed in.[26]

DeNoS

DeNoS is part of the software tool Proteinmatching Analysis Software (PAS) which in turn is part of the software package Medicwave Bioinformatics Suite (MBS).[27] [28]

Task: DeNoS performs complete or almost complete sequencing of peptides with reliability (>95%). DeNoS uses all information from CAD and ECD spectra. It is a hierarchal algorithm. In the first step fragments that are confirmed in both CAD and ECD (so called Golden Complementary Pairs) along with fragments that are only found in CAD (so called Complementary Pairs) are used. After that, step-by-step fragments with low reliability are used. In the last step, if the peptide is still not fully sequenced, the software uses a trivial application from the graf theory to sequence the remaining peptide parts with "unreliable" fragments.

Advantage: DeNoS is the first algorithm ever to be able to sequence peptides with >95% reliability. 13% percent of all MS/MS spectra are almost completely sequenced (in typical experiments you usually only identify about 10% of all MS/MS spectra using a search engine, so 13% in this case is very good).

Input: DTA files, where each file contains data from a mass spectrum, either ECD or CAD.

Output: Complete or almost complete peptide sequences.

PEAKS

PEAKS de novo automatically provides a complete sequence for each peptide, confidence scores on individual amino acid assignments, simple reporting for high-throughput analysis, and greater knowledge for scientifically sensitive, in-depth investigations.[29] A de novo, manually-assisted mode, is available for users who wish to tweak/optimize their results further. According to published reports, PEAKS is currently the fastest, most accurate auto de novo algorithm available. Automated de novo sequencing on an entire LC run processed data faster than 1 spectra per second.[30] The results went unmatched in accuracy; PEAKS determines at least 3 times as many completely correct sequences as the next best de novo software.[31] Accurate mass capabilities mean de novo at 97% accuracy is possible.[32]

Lutefisk

Lutefisk is software for the de novo interpretation of peptide CID spectra.[33]

Homology Seaching Algorithms

SPIDER

For the identification of proteins using MS/MS, *de novo* sequencing software computes one or several possible amino acid sequences (called sequence tags) for each MS/MS spectrum.[34] [35] Those tags are then used to match, accounting amino acid mutations, the sequences in a protein database. If the *de novo* sequencing gives correct tags, the homologs of the proteins can be identified by this approach and software such as MS-BLAST is available for the matching. The most common error is that a segment of amino acids is replaced by another segment with approximately the same masses. The SPIDER algorithm matches sequence tags with errors to database sequences for the purpose of protein and peptide identification.[36] BLAST (and similar) homology approaches can fail when confronted with common sequence substitutions such as I/L, N/GG, SAT/TAS. SPIDER is designed to avoid these problems. SPIDER can be used in conjunction with PEAKS mass spectrometry data analysis software.

Other Software

AnalyzerPro

AnalyzerPro is a proprietary software by SpectralWorks Limited. It is a vendor independent software application for processing mass spectrometry data.Using proprietory algorithms, AnalyzerPro can analyze both GC-MS and LC-MS using both qualitative and quantitative data processing. It is widely used for metabolomics data processing using MatrixAnalyzer for the comparison of multiple data sets.

RemoteAnalyzer

RemoteAnalyzer is a proprietary software by SpectralWorks Limited. It is a vendor independent 'Open Access' client/server based solution to provide a walk-up and use LC-MS and GC-MS data system. Instrument control and data processing support for multiple vendors' hardware is provided.

ESIprot 1.0

Electrospray ionization (ESI) mass spectrometry (MS) devices with relatively low resolution are widely used for proteomics and metabolomics. Ion trap devices like the Agilent MSD/XCT ultra or the Bruker HCT ultra are typical representatives. However, even if ESI-MS data of most of the naturally occurring proteins can be measured, the availability of data evaluation software for such ESI protein spectra with low resolution is quite limited.

ESIprot 1.0 enables the charge state determination and molecular weight calculation for low resolution electrospray ionization (ESI) mass spectrometry (MS) data of proteins.[37] [38]

Medicwave Bioinformatics Suite

Medicwave Bioinformatics Suite (MBS) is a flexible Microsoft Windows based software package that provides bioinformatics data analysis tools for different mass spectrometers.

MBS focuses on finding protein biomarkers and detecting protein deviations. MBS is compatible with most mass spectrometers, i.e. TANDEM MS (MS/MS), MALDI-TOF MS and SELDI-TOF MS. The software ensures high quality of analysis, while allowing high flexibility for special requirements and reduces time needed for each analysis. MBS is a software package that contains several other software tools where each of them focuses on analyzing data from a certain mass spectrometry technology, i.e. TANDEM MS (MS/MS), MALDI-TOF MS and SELDI-TOF MS.[39]

PROTRAWLER

ProTrawler is an LC/MS data reduction application that reads raw mass spectrometry vendor data (from a variety of well-known instrument companies) and creates lists of {mass, retention time, integrated signal intensity} triplets summarizing the LC/MS chromatogram. The measurements are reported with errors, which are essential for performing dynamic binning for comparisons between data sets. ProTrawler operates in two modes: a highly visual hands-on (expert) mode for the development of parameters used in data reduction and a fully automated mode for moving through many chromatograms in an automated fashion. ProTrawler's data reduction work flow includes background elimination, noise estimation, peak shape estimation, shape deconvolution, and isotopic and charge-state list deconvolution (factoring in errors and signal noise) to give a list features. Typically, ProTrawler reduces 1 GB of raw data to 10 Kb of processed results with a detection sensitivity of three orders of magnitude in 25% of the data acquisition time. No formal Bayesian methods are used, but sophisticated statistical inference is employed throughout. ProTrawler has been used for bacterial protein biomarker discovery efforts as well as for IPEx-related applications.

REGATTA

Regatta is an LC/MS list comparison application that works hand-in-hand with ProTrawler (but accepts input in Excel/CSV form) to provide an environment for LC/MS results list filtering and normalization {mass, retention time, integrated intensity} lists. To accomplish this, Regatta solves the famous Transitive Property of Equality problem that arises in the comparison of analytical list data, viz., if Peak A in Sample A overlaps Peak B in Sample B, and Peak B overlaps Peak C in Sample C, but Peak A does not overlap Peak C, then can we say that we've measured the same analyte in all three samples or not? Regatta also implements multivariate analysis, e.g., hierarchical cluster analysis, principal component analysis, as well as statistical tests, e.g., coefficients of variation. Input is not necessarily restricted to output from ProTrawler. Regatta has been used for successfully for biomarker discovery.

OmicsHub Proteomics

OmicsHub® Proteomics combines a LIMS for mass spec information management with data analysis functionalities on one platform. The software allows the user to import data files from multiple instruments, and conduct protein peak detection, filtering, protein identification, annotation and exportation of formatted reports. It is a single server platform with a web interface for multiuser access and is proprietary software of Integromics.

VIPER and Decon2LS

The "Proteomics Research Resource for Integrative Biology" distributes software tools (VIPER,[40] Decon2LS, and others) that can be used to perform analysis of accurate mass and chromatography retention time analysis of LC-MS features. Sometimes referred to as the Accurate Mass and Time tag approach (AMT tag approach) generally these tools are used for Proteomics.

OpenMS / TOPP

OpenMS is a software C++ library for LC/MS data management and analysis.[41] It offers an infrastructure for the development of mass spectrometry related software. OpenMS is free software available under the LGPL.

TOPP - The OpenMS Proteomics Pipeline - is a set of small applications that can be chained to create analysis pipelines tailored for a specific problem. TOPP is developed using the datastructures and algorithms provided by OpenMS. TOPP is free software available under the LGPL. TOPP provides ready-to-use applications for peak picking, the finding of peptides features, their quantitation and interfaces for most of the database search engines.

OpenMS and TOPP are a joint project of the Algorithmic Bioinformatics group at the Free University of Berlin, the Applied Bioinformatics group at Tübingen University and the Junior Research Group for Protein-Protein Interactions and Computational Proteomics at Saarland University.

Mass Frontier

Mass Frontier is a software tool for interpretation and management of mass spectra of small molecules. Computer methods for interpretation of mass spectral data in Mass Frontier centre on three fundamental methodologies: library search techniques, expert system procedures and classification methods. Mass Frontier uses automated generation of possible fragments at an expert level, including complete fragmentation and rearrangement mechanisms, starting from a user-supplied chemical structure. This software contains an expert system that automatically extracts a decomposition mechanism for each fragmentation reaction in the fragmentation library and determines the compound class range that the mechanism can be applied to. The expert system applies database mechanisms to a user provided structure and automatically predicts the fragmentation reactions for a given compound. The knowleadge base uses around 30,000 fragmentation schemes that contain around 100,000 reactions collected from mass spectrometry literature.

Mass Frontier also incorporates an automated system for detecting chromatographic components in complex GC/MS, LC/MS or MS^n runs and extracting mass spectral signals from closely coeluting components (deconvolution).

Classification methods include principal component analysis, neural networks and fuzzy clustering.

massXpert

The program massXpert [42] is a graphical user interface-based (GUI) software for simulating and analyzing mass spectrometric data obtained on known bio-polymer sequences.[43] The software runs in an identical manner on MS-Windows, Mac OS X and GNU/Linux/Unix platforms. massXpert is not for identifying proteins, but is useful when characterizing biopolymer sequences (post-translational modifications, intra-molecular cross-links...). It comprises four modules, all available in the same program interface: XpertDef will let the user define any aspect of the polymer chemistry at hand (atoms/isotopes, monomers, modifications, cleavage agents, fragmentation patterns, cross-links, default ionization...) ; XpertCalc is a desktop calculator with which anything mass is calculatable (the calculation is polymer chemistry definition-aware and is fully programmable; m/z ratios are computable with automatic replacement of the ionization agent ; isotopic patterns are computable starting from an elemental composition, with the possibility to specify the resolution of the mass spectrometer) ; XpertEdit is the central part of the software suite. In it reside all the simulation/analysis functionalities, like polymer sequence editing, sequence/monomer chemical modifications, cleavages, fragmentations, elemental/monomeric composition determinations, pI/net charge calculations, arbitrary mass searches in the polymer sequence; XpertMiner is a rather recently developed module (still experimental) in which it is possible to import lists of (m/z, z) pairs to submit them to any kind of calculation. Typically this module will be used to apply a formula to all the pairs in a single strike, or to perform matches between two lists, one from a simulation and another from the mass spectrometric data actually gotten from the mass spectrometer. All the simulations' results can be exported in the form of text either to the clipboard or to text files.

mMass

mMass[44] presents open source multi-platform package of tools for precise mass spectrometric data analysis and interpretation. It is written in Python language, so it is portable to different computer platforms, and released under GNU General Public License, so it can be modified or extended by modules for specific needs.

ProteoIQ

ProteoIQ is commercial software for the post-analysis of Mascot, SEQUEST, or X!Tandem database search results. The software provides the means to combine tandem mass spectrometry database search results derived from different instruments/platforms. Since the primary goal of many proteomics projects is to determine thresholds which identify as many real proteins as possible while encountering a minimal number of false positive protein identifications, ProteoIQ incorporates the two most common methods for statistical validation of large proteome datasets: the false discovery rate and protein probability approaches.[45] [46] [47] For false discovery rate calculations, ProteoIQ incorporates proprietary Protein Validation Technology (ProValT) algorithms licensed from the University of Georgia Research Foundation. Protein and peptide probabilities are generated by independent implementations of the Peptide Prophet and Protein Prophet algorithms. In ProteoIQ, protein relative quantitation is performed via spectral counting, standard deviations are automatically calculated across replicates, and spectral count abundances are normalized between samples. Integrated comparison functions allow user to quickly compare proteomic results across biological samples.

PatternLab for proteomics

PatternLab is a free software for post-analysis of SEQUEST or ProLuCID database search results filtered by DTASelect or Census. It offers several tools that combine false discovery rates with statistical tests and protein fold changes to pinpoint differentially expressed proteins, find trend of proteins having similar expression profiles in time course experiments, generate area proportional Venn diagrams, and even deconvolute mass spectra to enable analysis of top-down / middle-down proteomic data (YADA module). Results can also be analyzed using its Gene Ontology Explorer module.[48]

MolAna

MolAna was developed by Phenomenom Discoveries Inc, (PDI) for use in IONICS Mass Spectrometry Group's 3Q Molecular Analyzer, Triple quadrupole mass spectrometer

Xcalibur

Xcalibur is a proprietary software by Thermo Fisher Scientific used with mass spectrometry instruments.

MassCenter

MassCenter is a proprietary software by JEOL used with mass spectrometry instruments like The JMS AccuTOF T100LC.

MassLynx

MassLynx is a proprietary software by Waters Corporation.

TurboMass

TurboMass is proprietary GC/MS software by PerkinElmer.

MSight

MSight is a free software for mass spectrometry imaging developed by the Swiss Institute of Bioinformatics.[49]

Spectromania

Spectromania is a commercial software for analysis and visualization of mass spectrometric data.[50]

Peacock

Peacock is an open source Mac OS X application developed by Johan Kool that can be used to interpret gas-chromatography/mass-spectrometry (GC/MS) data files.[51]

MSGraph

MSGraph is an open source mass spectrometry software working in MS-DOS.[52]

OpenChrom

OpenChrom is an open source chromatography and mass spectrometry software. It can be extended using plug-ins and is available for several operating systems (Microsoft Windows, Linux, Unix, Mac OS X) and processor architectures (x86, x86_64, ppc).[53] A free of charge read only converter for Agilents ChemStation (*.D) files is also available.[54]

File formats

- Mass spectrometry data format: for a list of mass spectrometry data viewers and format converters.

References

[1] Changjiang Xu, Bin Ma, Software for Computational Peptide Identification from MS-MS data (http://www.csd.uwo.ca/~bma/pub/ msreview.pdf) Drug Discovery Today, Volume 11, Numbers 13/14, July 2006, p 595-600.

[2] Jimmy K. Eng, Ashley L. McCormack, and John R. Yates, III (1994). "An Approach to Correlate Tandem Mass Spectral Data of Peptides with Amino Acid Sequences in a Protein Database". *J Am Soc Mass Spectrom* **5** (11): 976–989. doi:10.1016/1044-0305(94)80016-2.

[3] Perkins, David N.; Pappin, Darryl J. C.; Creasy, David M.; Cottrell, John S. (1999). "Probability-based protein identification by searching sequence databases using mass spectrometry data". *Electrophoresis* **20** (18): 3551–67. doi:10.1002/(SICI)1522-2683(19991201)20:18<3551::AID-ELPS3551>3.0.CO;2-2. PMID 10612281.

[4] Liang, C; Smith, JC; Hendrie, Christopher (2003). *A Comparative Study of Peptide Sequencing Software Tools for MS/MS.*

[5] Xin, Lei (2010). "1" (http://gateway.proquest.com/openurl?url_ver=Z39.88-2004&res_dat=xri:pqdiss&rft_val_fmt=info:ofi/ fmt:kev:mtx:dissertation&rft_dat=xri:pqdiss:NR73567). *Probability Scoring System for De Novo And Protein Identification with Tandem Mass Spectrometry* (Computer Science thesis). University of Western Ontario. OCLC DAI-B 72/07. Docket NR73567. .

[6] "X! Tandem Project" (http://www.thegpm.org/TANDEM/index.html). *The Global Proteome Machine Organization.* . Retrieved 2009-10-21.

[7] "X! series search engine file format" (http://www.thegpm.org/docs/X_series_output_form.pdf) (PDF). *GPM Documents.*

[8] "Calculation of protein expectation value from peptide expectation values in X! Tandem" (http://www.thegpm.org/docs/ peptide_protein_expect.pdf) (PDF). *GPM Documents.*

[9] "X!!Tandem" (http://wiki.thegpm.org/wiki/X!!Tandem). . Retrieved 2009-11-16.

[10] Dexter Duncan and Andrew Link, Vanderbilt University School of Medicine. "Parallel Tandem Project" (http://www.thegpm.org/ parallel/). The Global Proteome Machine Organization. . Retrieved 2009-11-16.

[11] Colinge, Jacques; Masselot, Alexandre; Giron, Marc; Dessingy, Thierry; Magnin, Jérôme (2003). "OLAV: Towards high-throughput tandem mass spectrometry data identification". *Proteomics* **3** (8): 1454–63. doi:10.1002/pmic.200300485. PMID 12923771.

[12] "OMSSA ms/ms search engine" (http://pubchem.ncbi.nlm.nih.gov/omssa/). Pubchem.ncbi.nlm.nih.gov. . Retrieved 2011-09-27.

[13] Geer, Lewis Y.; Markey, Sanford P.; Kowalak, Jeffrey A.; Wagner, Lukas; Xu, Ming; Maynard, Dawn M.; Yang, Xiaoyu; Shi, Wenyao et al. (2004). "Open Mass Spectrometry Search Algorithm". *Journal of Proteome Research* **3** (5): 958–64. doi:10.1021/pr0499491. PMID 15473683.

[14] "Software from the Tabb Lab" (http://fenchurch.mc.vanderbilt.edu/lab/software.php). Fenchurch.mc.vanderbilt.edu. . Retrieved 2011-09-27.

[15] Tabb, David L.; Fernando, Christopher G.; Chambers, Matthew C. (2007). "MyriMatch: Highly Accurate Tandem Mass Spectral Peptide Identification by Multivariate Hypergeometric Analysis". *Journal of Proteome Research* **6** (2): 654–61. doi:10.1021/pr0604054. PMC 2525619. PMID 17269722.

[16] "greylag: software for tandem mass spectrum peptide identification" (http://greylag.org/). . Retrieved 2009-11-16.

[17] "PARC Automated Mass Spec" (http://bio.parc.xerox.com/). Palo Alto Research Center Incorporated. . Retrieved 2009-11-16.

[18] Bern, Marshall; Cai, Yuhan; Goldberg, David (2007). "Lookup Peaks: A Hybrid of de Novo Sequencing and Database Search for Protein Identification by Tandem Mass Spectrometry". *Analytical Chemistry* **79** (4): 1393–1400. doi:10.1021/ac0617013. PMID 17243770.

[19] Bern, Marshall; Goldberg, David (2008). "Improved Ranking Functions for Protein and Modification-Site Identifications". *Journal of Computational Biology* **15** (7): 705–719. doi:10.1089/cmb.2007.0119. PMID 18651800.

[20] "Inspect and MS-Alignment" (http://proteomics.ucsd.edu/Software/Inspect.html). . Retrieved 2009-11-16.

[21] Liu, Jian; Erassov, Alexandre; Halina, Patrick; Canete, Myra; Vo, Nguyen Dinh; Chung, Clement; Cagney, Gerard; Ignatchenko, Alexandr et al. (2008). "Sequential Interval Motif Search: Unrestricted Database Surveys of Global MS/MS Data Sets for Detection of Putative Post-Translational Modifications". *Analytical Chemistry* **80** (20): 7846–54. doi:10.1021/ac8009017. PMID 18788753.

[22] "EMILILAB TOOLS" (http://emililab.med.utoronto.ca/http://emililab.med.utoronto.ca/). . Retrieved 2009-11-16.

[23] "Amit Kumar Yadav, Dhirendra Kumar, and Debasis Dash. MassWiz: A Novel Scoring Algorithm with Target-Decoy Based Analysis Pipeline for Tandem Mass Spectrometry. J. Proteome Res., 2011, 10 (5), pp 2154–2160DOI: 10.1021/pr200031z" (http://pubs.acs.org/doi/ abs/10.1021/pr200031z). Pubs.acs.org. . Retrieved 2011-09-27.

[24] "MassWiz Project at Sourceforge" (http://sourceforge.net/projects/masswiz). Sourceforge.net. . Retrieved 2011-09-27.

[25] "MassWiz Webserver" (http://masswiz.igib.res.in/). Masswiz.igib.res.in. . Retrieved 2011-09-27.

[26] Bartels, Christian (31 May 1990). "Fast algorithm for peptide sequencing by mass spectroscopy". *Biological Mass Spectrometry* **19** (6): 363–368. doi:10.1002/bms.1200190607.

[27] Savitski, Mikhail M.; Nielsen, Michael L.; Kjeldsen, Frank; Zubarev, Roman A. (2005). "Proteomics-Grade de Novo Sequencing Approach". *Journal of Proteome Research* **4** (6): 2348–54. doi:10.1021/pr050288x. PMID 16335984.

[28] MedicWave PAS (http://www.medicwave.com/pas.php)

[29] Ma, Bin; Zhang, Kaizhong; Hendrie, Christopher; Liang, Chengzhi; Li, Ming; Doherty-Kirby, Amanda; Lajoie, Gilles (2003). "PEAKS: powerful software for peptidede novo sequencing by tandem mass spectrometry". *Rapid Communications in Mass Spectrometry* **17** (20): 2337–42. doi:10.1002/rcm.1196. PMID 14558135.

[30] Tannu, Nilesh S; Hemby, Scott E (2007). "De novo protein sequence analysis of Macaca mulatta". *BMC Genomics* **8**: 270. doi:10.1186/1471-2164-8-270. PMC 1965481. PMID 17686166.

[31] Chengzhi Liang, Jeffrey C. Smith, Christopher Hendrie, Ming Li, K. W. Michael Siu. A Comparative Study of Peptide Sequencing Software Tools for MS/MS. ASMS 2003.

[32] Lee, Su Seong; Lim, Jaehong; Tan, Sylvia; Cha, Junhoe; Yeo, Shi Yun; Agnew, Heather D.; Heath, James R. (2010). "Accurate MALDI-TOF/TOF Sequencing of One-Bead–One-Compound Peptide Libraries with Application to the Identification of Multiligand Protein Affinity Agents Using in Situ Click Chemistry Screening". *Analytical Chemistry* **82** (2): 672–9. doi:10.1021/ac902195y. PMC 2829877. PMID 20000699.

[33] "Lutefisk - de novo MS/MS Sequencing" (http://www.hairyfatguy.com/Lutefisk/). J. Alex Taylor. . Retrieved 2009-11-16.

[34] Yonghua Han; Bin Ma; Kaizhong Zhang (2004). "SPIDER: software for protein identification from sequence tags with de novo sequencing error". *Proceedings. 2004 IEEE Computational Systems Bioinformatics Conference, 2004. CSB 2004.* pp. 206–15. doi:10.1109/CSB.2004.1332434. ISBN 0-7695-2194-0.

[35] Ma, Bin (2007). "Search for the Undiscovered Peptide; Using de novo sequencing and sequence tag homology search to improve protein characterization". *Biotechniques Journal* **42** (5).

[36] PEAKS: SPIDER (Sequence Homology Search Tool) (http://www.bioinfor.com/products/peaks/spider.php)

[37] Robert Winkler. "ESIprot Homepage" (http://www.bioprocess.org/esiprot/). Bioprocess.org. . Retrieved 2011-09-27.

[38] Winkler, Robert (2010). "ESIprot: a universal tool for charge state determination and molecular weight calculation of proteins from electrospray ionization mass spectrometry data". *Rapid Communications in Mass Spectrometry* **24** (3): 285–94. doi:10.1002/rcm.4384. PMID 20049890.

[39] "Medicwave Bioinformatics Suite (MBS)" (http://www.medicwave.com/mbs.php). Medicwave.com. . Retrieved 2011-09-27.

[40] Monroe, M. E.; Tolic, N.; Jaitly, N.; Shaw, J. L.; Adkins, J. N.; Smith, R. D. (2007). "VIPER: an advanced software package to support high-throughput LC-MS peptide identification". *Bioinformatics* **23** (15): 2021–3. doi:10.1093/bioinformatics/btm281. PMID 17545182.

[41] "OpenMSt" (http://www.openms.de). . Retrieved 2009-11-16.

[42] Filippo Rusconi, Ph.D., ed. "http://massxpert.org/userman/pdf/massxpert.pdf" (PDF). *massXpert version 2.0.2 User Manual*

[43] Rusconi, F. (2009). "massXpert 2: a cross-platform software environment for polymer chemistry modelling and simulation/analysis of mass spectrometric data". *Bioinformatics* **25** (20): 2741–2. doi:10.1093/bioinformatics/btp504. PMID 19740912.

[44] "Open Source Mass Spectrometry Tool" (http://www.mmass.org). mMass. . Retrieved 2011-09-27.

[45] Weatherly, D. B.; Atwood Ja, 3rd; Minning, TA; Cavola, C; Tarleton, RL; Orlando, R (2005). "A Heuristic Method for Assigning a False-discovery Rate for Protein Identifications from Mascot Database Search Results". *Molecular & Cellular Proteomics* **4** (6): 762–72. doi:10.1074/mcp.M400215-MCP200. PMID 15703444.

[46] Keller, Andrew; Nesvizhskii, Alexey I.; Kolker, Eugene; Aebersold, Ruedi (2002). "Empirical Statistical Model To Estimate the Accuracy of Peptide Identifications Made by MS/MS and Database Search". *Analytical Chemistry* **74** (20): 5383–92. doi:10.1021/ac025747h. PMID 12403597.

[47] Nesvizhskii, AI; Keller, A; Kolker, E; Aebersold, R (2003). "A statistical model for identifying proteins by tandem mass spectrometry". *Analytical chemistry* **75** (17): 4646–58. doi:10.1021/ac0341261. PMID 14632076.

[48] Carvalho, Paulo C; Fischer, Juliana SG; Chen, Emily I; Yates, John R; Barbosa, Valmir C (2008). "PatternLab for proteomics: a tool for differential shotgun proteomics". *BMC Bioinformatics* **9**: 316. doi:10.1186/1471-2105-9-316. PMC 2488363. PMID 18644148.

[49] Palagi, Patricia M.; Walther, Daniel; Quadroni, Manfredo; Catherinet, SéBastien; Burgess, Jennifer; Zimmermann-Ivol, Catherine G.; Sanchez, Jean-Charles; Binz, Pierre-Alain et al. (2005). "MSight: An image analysis software for liquid chromatography-mass spectrometry". *Proteomics* **5** (9): 2381–4. doi:10.1002/pmic.200401244. PMID 15880814.

[50] Zucht, Hans-Dieter; Lamerz, Jens; Khamenia, Valery; Schiller, Carsten; Appel, Annette; Tammen, Harald; Crameri, Reto; Selle, Hartmut (2005). "Datamining Methodology for LC-MALDI-MS Based Peptide Profiling". *Combinatorial Chemistry & High Throughput Screening* **8** (8): 717–23. doi:10.2174/138620705774962481.

[51] "Peacock on Google Code" (http://code.google.com/p/peacock-gcms/). Code.google.com. . Retrieved 2011-09-27.

[52] "MSGraph on sourceforge.net" (http://msgraph.sourceforge.net/). . Retrieved 2011-09-27.

[53] "OpenChrom on SourceForge" (http://sourceforge.net/projects/openchrom). Sourceforge.net. . Retrieved 2011-09-27.

[54] "Agilent ChemStation plug-in on www.openchrom.net" (http://www.openchrom.net/plugins/converter/agilent). . Retrieved 2011-09-27.

External links

Mass Spectrometry Software (http:/ / www. dmoz. org/ Science/ Chemistry/ Analytical/ Mass_Spectrometry/ Software/) at the Open Directory Project

Matthews correlation coefficient

The **Matthews correlation coefficient** is used in machine learning as a measure of the quality of binary (two-class) classifications. It takes into account true and false positives and negatives and is generally regarded as a balanced measure which can be used even if the classes are of very different sizes. The MCC is in essence a correlation coefficient between the observed and predicted binary classifications; it returns a value between −1 and +1. A coefficient of +1 represents a perfect prediction, 0 an average random prediction and −1 an inverse prediction. The statistic is also known as the phi coefficient. MCC is related to the chi-square statistic for a 2×2 contingency table

$$|\mathrm{MCC}| = \sqrt{\frac{\chi^2}{n}}$$

where n is the total number of observations.

While there is no perfect way of describing the confusion matrix of true and false positives and negatives by a single number, the Matthews correlation coefficient is generally regarded as being one of the best such measures. Other measures, such as the proportion of correct predictions (also termed accuracy), are not useful when the two classes are of very different sizes. For example, assigning every object to the larger set achieves a high proportion of correct predictions, but is not generally a useful classification.

The MCC can be calculated directly from the confusion matrix using the formula:

$$\mathrm{MCC} = \frac{TP \times TN - FP \times FN}{\sqrt{(TP+FP)(TP+FN)(TN+FP)(TN+FN)}}$$

In this equation, TP is the number of true positives, TN the number of true negatives, FP the number of false positives and FN the number of false negatives. If any of the four sums in the denominator is zero, the denominator can be arbitrarily set to one; this results in a Matthews correlation coefficient of zero, which can be shown to be the correct limiting value.

See Also

- Phi coefficient
- F1 score
- Cramér's V, a similar measure of association between nominal variables.

References

- Baldi, P.; Brunak, S.; Chauvin, Y.; Andersen, C. A. F.; Nielsen, H. Assessing the accuracy of prediction algorithms for classification: an overview. Bioinformatics 2000, 16, 412–424. [1]
- Matthews, B.W., Comparison of the predicted and observed secondary structure of T4 phage lysozyme. Biochim. Biophys. Acta 1975, 405, 442–451
- Carugo, O., Detailed estimation of bioinformatics prediction reliability through the Fragmented Prediction Performance Plots. BMC Bioinformatics 2007. [2]

References

[1] http://bioinformatics.oxfordjournals.org/cgi/content/abstract/16/5/412
[2] http://www.ncbi.nlm.nih.gov/pmc/articles/PMC2148069/

MAVID

MAVID

Developer(s)	Nicolas Bray (UC Berkeley), Lior Pachter (UC Berkeley)
Stable release	2.0.4
Operating system	UNIX, Linux, Mac
Type	Bioinformatics tool
Licence	Open source
Website	MAVID download [1]

MAVID is a multiple sequence alignment program suitable for the alignment of large numbers of DNA sequences. The sequences can be small mitochondrial genomes or large genomic regions up to megabases long. The latest version is 2.0.4.

The program can be used through the MAVID web server [2] or as a standalone program which can be installed with the source code [1].

Input/Output

This program accepts sequences in FASTA format.

The output format includes: FASTA format, Clustal, PHYLIP.

References

[1] http://bio.math.berkeley.edu/mavid/download/
[2] http://baboon.math.berkeley.edu/mavid/

N. Bray and L. Pachter, MAVID: Constrained ancestral alignment of multiple sequences, Genome Research 14 (2004), p 693--699.

External links

- MAVID web server (http://baboon.math.berkeley.edu/mavid/)

Medical library

A **health or medical library** is designed to assist physicians, health professionals, students, patients, consumers and medical researchers in finding health and scientific information to improve, update, assess or evaluate health care. Medical libraries are typically found in hospitals, medical schools, private industry and in medical or health associations. A typical health or medical library has access to MEDLINE, a range of electronic resources, print and digital journal collections and print reference books. The influence of open access (OA) and free searching via Google and PubMed has a major impact on the way medical libraries operate.

To become accredited, every American and Canadian college of medicine, nursing, dentistry, pharmacy, veterinary medicine or public health is required to have a health or medical library appropriate to the needs of the school, as specified by an accrediting body, such as the Liaison Committee on Medical Education (LCME)'s standards [1]. These accreditation standards include having qualified library staff on hand to answer reference questions, and provide training in using electronic resources. Some academic medical libraries are located in the same building as the general undergraduate library but most are located near or in the medical college or faculty.

The United States National Library of Medicine (NLM) is the largest biomedical library in the world, and collects and provides access to some of the best health information in the world (due to its linkage to the National Institutes of Health). The NLM maintains numerous medical and genomic databases, searchable via its Entrez search system, including MEDLINE (PubMed) and OMIM (a genetic traits database).

In support of open access to the journal literature, the U.S. NLM established an online library of digital journal articles, PubMed Central (PMC), which will soon be supplemented by a UK version. NLM works with the National Network of Libraries of Medicine (NN/LM [2]) to provide regional medical library support in the United States, while its consumer health information service MEDLINEplus offers free access to health information, images and interactive tutorials. Many countries like Australia, Canada and the United Kingdom have well-developed medical libraries, though nothing quite as evolved as the U.S. NLM.

Associations

The Medical Library Association (MLA) is a Chicago-based advocate for library professionals and health sciences libraries - primarily in the United States. MLA maintains an online list of ALA-accredited library school programs [3] for those who would like to pursue a master's degree in library and information studies in the US and Canada(MLIS). It furthermore administers the U.S credentialing organization for medical librarians, the Academy of Health Information Professionals(AHIP).

The Special Libraries Association has a Medical Section of the Biomedical and Life Science Division [4], which serves as a forum for Division members who are engaged or interested in the exchange of information in the biomedical and health sciences, and the acquisition, organization, dissemination, and use of such information in all formats.

In Canada and Australia, health librarians and libraries are represented by the [[Canadian Health Libraries Association [5]]] and the Health Libraries Australia Group of the Australian Library and Information Association [6]. A list of health libraries in Australia may by found on the website of the National Library of Australia [7].

In the United Kingdom medical (or health) librarians are represented by the Health Libraries Group of the Chartered Institute of Library and Information Professionals. CILIP. Health Libraries Group. [8] The medical and health libraries of the German speaking countries Germany, Austria and Switzerland are represented by the Medical Libraries Association Arbeitsgemeinschaft fuer Medizinisches Bibliothekswesen (AGMB) e.V. [9]. There are similar, if smaller, national groups in many European countries and these groups and individual health librarians and libraries are represented by the European Association for Health Information and Libraries (EAHIL) [10] since 1987.

The International Federation of Library Associations and Institutions (IFLA) has a Health and Biosciences Libraries Section [11]. The last International Congress on Medical Librarianship (ICML) [12] was in Brisbane in 2009, the next ICML will be in Baltimore, 2013.

External links

- Canadian Health Libraries Association [5]
- Health Libraries Group, CILIP [8]
- Medical Library Association (US) [13]
- Academy of Health Information Professionals (US) [14]
- Arbeitsgemeinschaft fuer Medizinisches Bibliothekswesen (AGMB) e.V. [9]
- Liaison Committee of Medical Education (LCME) [15]
- National Library of Medicine [16] (US)
- National Network of Libraries of Medicine [2](NNLM)(US)
- PubMed Central [17]
- MeSH: Libraries, Medical [18]
- PubMed search [19]: *"Libraries, Medical"[MAJR:noexp] AND English[Lang]*
- UBC HealthLib-Wiki — A Knowledge-Base for Health Librarians [20]

References

[1] http://www.lcme.org/functionslist.htm#information%20resources

[2] http://nnlm.gov/

[3] http://www.mlanet.org/education/libschools/index.html

[4] http://www.sla.org/content/community/units/divs/division.cfm

[5] http://www.chla-absc.ca/

[6] http://www.alia.org.au/groups/healthnat/

[7] http://www.nla.gov.au/apps/libraries

[8] http://www.cilip.org.uk/specialinterestgroups/bysubject/health/

[9] http://www.agmb.de/

[10] http://www.eahil.net/

[11] http://www.ifla.org/VII/s28/

[12] http://www.icml.org/

[13] http://www.mlanet.org

[14] http://mlanet.org/academy/

[15] http://www.lcme.org/

[16] http://www.nlm.nih.gov/

[17] http://www.pubmedcentral.nih.gov/

[18] http://www.ncbi.nlm.nih.gov/entrez/query.fcgi?cmd=Retrieve&db=mesh&list_uids=68007993&dopt=Full

[19] http://www.ncbi.nlm.nih.gov/entrez/query.fcgi?cmd=PureSearch&db=pubmed&
       details_term=%22Libraries%2C%20Medical%22%5BMAJR%3Anoexp%5D%20AND%20English%5BLang%5D

[20] http://hlwiki.slais.ubc.ca/

Medical literature retrieval

Medical literature retrieval or **medical document retrieval** is an activity that uses professional methods for medical research papers retrieval, report and other data to improve medicine research and practice.

Medical Search engine

Professional medical search engine

- Pubmed
- GoPubMed[1]
- Pubget
- eTBLAST
- Cochrane Reviews, The Cochrane Library

Meta-search tools

- TRIP Database
- NLM Gateway
- Entrez, NLM's cross-database search
- SUMSearch

Consumer health search engine

- MedlinePlus by the U.S. NLM
- Healthfinder by the U.S. HHS
- Mednar
- Healthline
- Medstory
- Healia

Reference

[1] http://www.transinsight.com/peopleAbout

External links

- MEDLINE/PubMed (http://www.pubmed.gov/)
- William R. Hersh. Information Retrieval: A Health and Biomedical Perspective (http://medir.ohsu.edu/~hersh/ irbook/). 2003, Springer-Verlag. ISBN 0387955224
- The Top Five Medical Search Engines on the Web (http://websearch.about.com/od/enginesanddirectories/tp/ medical.htm?terms=Medical+search engine) at About.com by Wendy Boswell

Medical Subject Headings

Medical subject headings.

Content	
Description	Medical subject headings.
Data types captured	controlled vocabulary
Contact	
Research center	United States National Library of Medicine National Center for Biotechnology Information
Laboratory	United States National Library of Medicine
Authors	F B ROGERS
Primary Citation	PMID 13982385[1]
Access	
Tools	
Miscellaneous	

Medical Subject Headings (**MeSH**) is a comprehensive controlled vocabulary for the purpose of indexing journal articles and books in the life sciences; it can also serve as a thesaurus that facilitates searching. Created and updated by the United States National Library of Medicine (NLM), it is used by the MEDLINE/PubMed article database and by NLM's catalog of book holdings.

MeSH can be browsed and downloaded free of charge on the Internet through PubMed. The yearly printed version was discontinued in 2007 and MeSH is now available online only.[2] Originally in English, MeSH has been translated into numerous other languages and allows retrieval of documents from different languages.

Structure of MeSH

The 2009 version of MeSH contains a total of 25,186 *subject headings*, also known as *descriptors*.[3] Most of these are accompanied by a short description or definition, links to related descriptors, and a list of synonyms or very similar terms (known as *entry terms*). Because of these synonym lists, MeSH can also be viewed as a thesaurus.[4]

Descriptor hierarchy

The *descriptors* or *subject headings* are arranged in a hierarchy. A given descriptor may appear at several places in the hierarchical tree. The tree locations carry systematic labels known as *tree numbers*, and consequently one descriptor can carry several tree numbers. For example, the descriptor "Digestive System Neoplasms" has the tree numbers C06.301 and C04.588.274; C stands for Diseases, C06 for Digestive System Diseases and C06.301 for Digestive System Neoplasms; C04 for Neoplasms, C04.588 for Neoplasms By Site, and C04.588.274 also for Digestive System Neoplasms. The tree numbers of a given descriptor are subject to change as MeSH is updated. Every descriptor also carries a unique alphanumerical ID that will not change.

Descriptions

Most subject headings come with a short description or definition. See the MeSH description for diabetes type 2 [5] as an example. The explanatory text is written by the MeSH team based on their standard sources if not otherwise stated. References are mostly encyclopaedias and standard textbooks of the subject areas. References for specific statements in the descriptions are not given, instead readers are referred to the bibliography [6].

Qualifiers

In addition to the descriptor hierarchy, MeSH contains a small number of standard *qualifiers* (also known as *subheadings*), which can be added to descriptors to narrow down the topic.[7] For example, "Measles" is a descriptor and "epidemiology" is a qualifier; "Measles/epidemiology" describes the subheading of epidemiological articles about Measles. The "epidemiology" qualifier can be added to all other disease descriptors. Not all descriptor/qualifier combinations are allowed since some of them may be meaningless. In all there are 83 different qualifiers.

Supplements

In addition to the descriptors, MeSH also contains some 139,000 *Supplementary Concept Records*. These do not belong to the controlled vocabulary as such and are not used for indexing MEDLINE articles; instead they enlarge the thesaurus and contain links to the closest fitting descriptor to be used in a MEDLINE search. Many of these records describe chemical substances.

Use in Medline/PubMed

In MEDLINE/PubMed, every journal article is indexed with some 10-15 headings and subheadings, with some of them designated as *major* and marked with an asterisk. When performing a MEDLINE search via PubMed, entry terms are automatically translated into (= 'mapped to) the corresponding descriptors with a good degree of reliability; it is recommended to check the *Details tab* in PubMed to see how a search formulation was 'translated'. By default a search will include all the descriptors that are located below the given one in the hierarchy.

Categories

The top-level categories in the MeSH descriptor hierarchy are:

- Anatomy [A]
- Organisms [B]
- Diseases [C]
- Chemicals and Drugs [D]
- Analytical, Diagnostic and Therapeutic Techniques and Equipment [E]
- Psychiatry and Psychology [F]
- Biological Sciences [G]
- Physical Sciences [H]
- Anthropology, Education, Sociology and Social Phenomena [I]
- Technology and Food and Beverages [J]
- Humanities [K]
- Information Science [L]
- Persons [M]
- Health Care [N]
- Publication Characteristics [V]
- Geographic Locations [Z]

For the full hierarchy, see List of MeSH codes.

References

[1] ROGERS, F B (Jan 1963). "Medical subject headings" (in eng). *Bull Med Libr Assoc* (Not Available) **51**: 114-6. ISSN 0025-7338. PMC PMC197951. PMID 13982385.

[2] "Medical Subject Headings (MeSH) Fact sheet" (http://www.nlm.nih.gov/pubs/factsheets/mesh.html). National Library of Medicine. 2005-05-27. . Retrieved 2007-05-31.

[3] Fact Sheet MeSH (http://www.nlm.nih.gov/pubs/factsheets/mesh.html)

[4] Introduction to MeSH - 2010 (http://www.nlm.nih.gov/mesh/introduction.html)

[5] http://www.ncbi.nlm.nih.gov/sites/entrez?Db=mesh&Cmd=ShowDetailView&TermToSearch=68003924&ordinalpos=3& itool=EntrezSystem2.PEntrez.Mesh.Mesh_ResultsPanel.Mesh_RVDocSum

[6] http://www.nlm.nih.gov/mesh/intro_biblio2007.html

[7] List of qualifiers - MeSH 2009 (http://www.nlm.nih.gov/mesh/2009/introduction/topsubscope.html)

External links

- Medical Subject Heading Home (http://www.nlm.nih.gov/mesh/) provided by National Library of Medicine, National Institutes of Health (U.S.)
- MeSH database tutorials (http://www.ncbi.nlm.nih.gov/entrez/query.fcgi?db=mesh)
- Automatic Term Mapping (http://www.nlm.nih.gov/bsd/disted/pubmedtutorial/020_040.html)
- Browsing MeSH:
  - Entrez (http://www.ncbi.nlm.nih.gov/entrez/query.fcgi?db=mesh)
  - MeSH Browser (http://www.nlm.nih.gov/mesh/MBrowser.html)
  - Visual MeSH Browser (http://www.curehunter.com/public/dictionary.do) mapping drug-disease relationships in research
    - Reference.MD (http://www.reference.md/)
    - MeSHine (http://www.meshine.info/)
- List of qualifiers - 2009 (http://www.nlm.nih.gov/mesh/2009/introduction/topsubscope.html)

List of MeSH codes

The following is a list of the codes for MeSH. It is a product of the United States National Library of Medicine. Click on the prefixes (A01 etc.) in the list below to see detailed codes.

Source for content is 2006 MeSH Trees [1].

- A - Anatomy
    - A01 --- body regions (74 articles)
    - A02 --- musculoskeletal system (213 articles)
    - A03 --- digestive system (98 articles)
    - A04 --- respiratory system (46 articles)
    - A05 --- urogenital system (87 articles)
    - A06 --- endocrine system
    - A07 --- cardiovascular system
    - A08 --- nervous system
    - A09 --- sense organs
    - A10 --- tissues
    - A11 --- cells
    - A12 --- fluids and secretions
    - A13 --- animal structures
    - A14 --- stomatognathic system
    - A15 --- hemic and immune systems
    - A16 --- embryonic structures
    - A17 --- integumentary system
- B - Organisms
    - B01 --- animals
    - B02 --- algae
    - B03 --- bacteria
    - B04 --- viruses
    - B05 --- fungi
    - B06 --- plants
    - B07 --- archaea
    - B08 --- mesomycetozoea
- C - Diseases
    - C01 --- bacterial infections and mycoses
    - C02 --- virus diseases
    - C03 --- parasitic diseases
    - C04 --- neoplasms
    - C05 --- musculoskeletal diseases
    - C06 --- digestive system diseases
    - C07 --- stomatognathic diseases
    - C08 --- respiratory tract diseases
    - C09 --- otorhinolaryngologic diseases
    - C10 --- nervous system diseases
    - C11 --- eye diseases
    - C12 --- urologic and male genital diseases

- C13 --- female genital diseases and pregnancy complications
- C14 --- cardiovascular diseases
- C15 --- hemic and lymphatic diseases
- C16 --- congenital, hereditary, and neonatal diseases and abnormalities
- C17 --- skin and connective tissue diseases
- C18 --- nutritional and metabolic diseases
- C19 --- endocrine system diseases
- C20 --- immune system diseases
- C21 --- disorders of environmental origin
- C22 --- animal diseases
- C23 --- pathological conditions, signs and symptoms
- D - Chemicals and Drugs
  - D01 --- inorganic chemicals
  - D02 --- organic chemicals
  - D03 --- heterocyclic compounds
  - D04 --- polycyclic compounds
  - D05 --- macromolecular substances
  - D06 --- hormones, hormone substitutes, and hormone antagonists
  - D07 --- none (enzymes and coenzymes)
  - D08 --- enzymes and coenzymes (carbohydrates)
  - D09 --- carbohydrates (lipids)
  - D10 --- lipids (amino acids, peptides, and proteins)
  - D11 --- none (nucleic acids, nucleotides, and nucleosides)
  - D12/20 --- amino acids, peptides, and proteins (complex mixtures)
  - D13/23 --- nucleic acids, nucleotides, and nucleosides (biological factors)
  - D14/25 --- biomedical and dental materials
  - D15/26 --- pharmaceutical preparations
  - D16/27 --- chemical actions and uses
  - D20 --- complex mixtures
  - D23 --- biological factors
- E - Analytical, Diagnostic and Therapeutic Techniques and Equipment
  - E01 --- diagnosis
  - E02 --- therapeutics
  - E03 --- anesthesia and analgesia
  - E04 --- surgical procedures, operative
  - E05 --- investigative techniques
  - E06 --- dentistry
  - E07 --- equipment and supplies
- F - Psychiatry and Psychology
  - F01 --- behavior and behavior mechanisms
  - F02 --- psychological phenomena and processes
  - F03 --- mental disorders
  - F04 --- behavioral disciplines and activities
- G - Biological Sciences
  - G01 --- biological sciences
  - G02 --- health occupations

- G03 --- environment and public health
- G04 --- biological phenomena, cell phenomena, and immunity
- G05 --- genetic processes
- G06 --- biochemical phenomena, metabolism, and nutrition
- G07 --- physiological processes
- G08 --- reproductive and urinary physiology
- G09 --- circulatory and respiratory physiology
- G10 --- digestive, oral, and skin physiology
- G11 --- musculoskeletal, neural, and ocular physiology
- G12 --- chemical and pharmacologic phenomena
- G13 --- genetic phenomena
- G14 --- genetic structures

- H - Physical Sciences
  - H01 --- natural sciences

- I - Anthropology, Education, Sociology and Social Phenomena
  - I01 --- social sciences
  - I02 --- education
  - I03 --- human activities

- J - Technology and Food and Beverages
  - J01 --- technology, industry, and agriculture
  - J02 --- food and beverages

- K - Humanities
  - K01 --- humanities

- L - Information Science
  - L01 --- information science

- M - Persons
  - M01 --- persons

- N - Health Care
  - N01 --- population characteristics
  - N02 --- health care facilities, manpower, and services
  - N03 --- health care economics and organizations
  - N04 --- health services administration
  - N05 --- health care quality, access, and evaluation

- V - Publication Characteristics
  - V01 --- publication components (publication type)
  - V02 --- publication formats (publication type)
  - V03 --- study characteristics (publication type)
  - V04 --- support of research

- Z - Geographic Locations
  - Z01 --- geographic locations

References

[1] http://www.nlm.nih.gov/mesh/filelist.html

Metabolic network modelling

Metabolic network reconstruction and simulation allows for an in depth insight into comprehending the molecular mechanisms of a particular organism, especially correlating the genome with molecular physiology (Francke, Siezen, and Teusink 2005). A reconstruction breaks down metabolic pathways into their respective reactions and enzymes, and analyzes them within the perspective of the entire network. Examples of various metabolic pathways include glycolysis, Krebs cycle, pentose phosphate pathway. In simplified terms, a reconstruction involves collecting all of the relevant metabolic information of an organism and then compiling it in a way that makes sense for various types of analyses to be performed. The correlation between the genome and metabolism is made by searching gene databases, such as KEGG [1], GeneDB [2], for particular genes by inputting enzyme or protein names. For example, a search can be conducted based on the protein name or the EC number (a number that represents the catalytic function of the enzyme of interest) in order to find the associated gene (Francke *et al.* 2005).

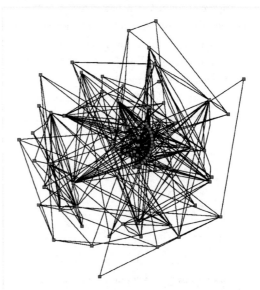

Metabolic network showing interactions between enzymes and metabolites in the *Arabidopsis thaliana* citric acid cycle. Enzymes and metabolites are the red dots and interactions between them are the lines.

Beginning steps of a reconstruction

Resources

Below is more detailed description of a few gene/enzyme/reaction/pathway databases that are crucial to a metabolic reconstruction:

- **Kyoto Encyclopedia of Genes and Genomes (KEGG)**: This is a bioinformatics database containing information on genes, proteins, reactions, and pathways. The 'KEGG Organisms' section, which is divided into eukaryotes and prokaryotes, encompasses many organisms for which gene and DNA information can be searched by typing in the enzyme of choice. This resource can be extremely useful when building the association between metabolism enzymes, reactions and genes.

- **BioCyc, EcoCyc, and MetaCyc**: BioCyc is a collection of 1,000 pathway/genome databases (as of Oct 2010), with each database dedicated to one organism. For example, EcoCyc is a highly detailed bioinformatics database on the genome and metabolic reconstruction of *Escherichia coli*, including thorough descriptions of *E. coli* signaling pathways and regulatory network. The EcoCyc database can serve as a paradigm and model for any reconstruction. Additionally, MetaCyc, an encyclopedia of experimentally defined metabolic pathways and enzymes, contains 1,500 metabolic pathways and 8,700 metabolic reactions (Oct 2010).

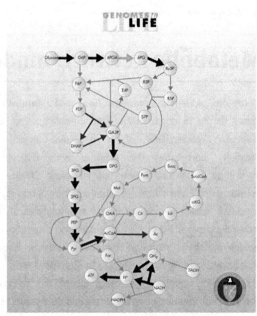

Metabolic Network Model for Escherichia coli.

- **Pathway Tools** [11]: A bioinformatics software package that assists in the construction of pathway/genome databases such as EcoCyc (Karp 2010). Developed by Peter Karp and associates at the SRI International Bioinformatics Group, Pathway Tools comprises several separate units. First, PathoLogic takes an annotated genome for an organism and infers probable metabolic pathways to produce a new pathway/genome database. This can be followed by application of the Pathway Hole Filler, which predicts likely genes to fill "holes" (missing steps) in predicted pathways. Afterward, the Pathway Tools Navigator and Editor functions let users visualize, analyze, access and update the database. Thus, using PathoLogic and encyclopedias like MetaCyc, an initial fast reconstruction can be developed automatically, and then using the other units of Pathway Tools, a very detailed manual update, curation and verification step can be carried out (SRI 2005).

- **ERGO**: ERGO [3] integrates data from every level including genomic, biochemical data, literature, and high-throughput analysis into a comprehensive user friendly network of metabolic and nonmetabolic pathways.

- **metaTIGER** [4]: is a collection of metabolic profiles and phylogenomic information on a taxonomically diverse range of eukaryotes. Phylogenomic information is provided by 2,257 large phylogenetic trees which can be interactively explored. High-throughput tree analysis can also be carried out to identify trees of interest, e.g. trees containing horizontal gene transfers. metaTIGER also provides novel facilities for viewing and comparing the metabolic profiles.

- **ENZYME**: This is an enzyme nomenclature database (part of the ExPASY [3] proteonomics server of the Swiss Institute of Bioinformatics). After searching for a particular enzyme on the database, this resource gives you the reaction that is catalyzed. Additionally, ENZYME has direct links to various other gene/enzyme/medical literature databases such as KEGG, BRENDA, PUBMED, and PUMA2 to name a few.

- **BRENDA**: A comprehensive enzyme database, BRENDA, allows you to search for an enzyme by name or EC number. You can also search for an organism and find all the relevant enzyme information. Moreover, when an enzyme search is carried out, BRENDA provides a list of all organisms containing the particular enzyme of interest.

- **PUBMED**: This is an online library developed by the National Center for Biotechnology Information, which contains a massive collection of medical journals. Using the link provided by ENZYME, the search can be directed towards the organism of interest, thus recovering literature on the enzyme and its use inside of the organism.

- **Model SEED** [5]: This is an online resource for the analysis, comparison, reconstruction, and curation of genome-scale metabolic models (Henry et al. 2010). Users can submit genome sequences to the RAST annotation system, and the resulting annotation can be automatically piped into the Model SEED to produce a draft metabolic model. The Model SEED automatically constructs a network of metabolic reactions, gene-protein-reaction associations for each reaction, and a biomass composition reaction for each genome to produce a model of microbial metabolism that can be simulated using Flux Balance Analysis.

Next steps of the reconstruction

After the initial stages of the reconstruction, a systematic verification is made in order to make sure no inconsistencies are present and that all the entries listed are correct and accurate (Francke *et al.* 2005). Furthermore, previous literature can be researched in order to support any information obtained from one of the many metabolic reaction and genome databases. This provides an added level of assurance for the reconstruction that the enzyme and the reaction it catalyzes do actually occur in the organism.

Any new reactions not present in the databases need to be added to the reconstruction. The presence or absence of certain reactions of the metabolism will affect the amount of reactants/products that are present for other reactions within the particular pathway. This is because products in one reaction go on to become the reactants for another reaction, i.e. products of one reaction can combine with other proteins or compounds to form new proteins/compounds in the presence of different enzymes or catalysts (Francke *et al.* 2005).

Francke *et al.* (2005) provide an excellent example as to why the verification step of the project needs to be performed in significant detail. During a metabolic network reconstruction of *Lactobacillus plantarum*, the model showed that succinyl-CoA was one of the reactants for a reaction that was a part of the biosynthesis of methionine. However, an understanding of the physiology of the organism would have revealed that due to an incomplete tricarboxylic acid pathway, *Lactobacillus plantarum* does not actually produce succinyl-CoA, and the correct reactant for that part of the reaction was acetyl-CoA.

Therefore, systematic verification of the initial reconstruction will bring to light several inconsistencies that can adversely affect the final interpretation of the reconstruction, which is to accurately comprehend the molecular mechanisms of the organism. Furthermore, the simulation step also ensures that all the reactions present in the reconstruction are properly balanced. To sum up, a reconstruction that is fully accurate can lead to greater insight about understanding the functioning of the organism of interest (Francke *et al.* 2005).

Advantages of a reconstruction

- Several inconsistencies exist between gene, enzyme, and reaction databases and published literature sources regarding the metabolic information of an organism. A reconstruction is a systematic verification and compilation of data from various sources that takes into account all of the discrepancies.
- A reconstruction combines the relevant metabolic and genomic information of an organism.
- A reconstruction also allows for metabolic comparisons to be performed between various organisms of the same species as well as between different organisms.

Metabolic network simulation

A metabolic network can be broken down into a stoichiometric matrix where the rows represent the compounds of the reactions, while the columns of the matrix correspond to the reactions themselves. Stoichiometry is a quantitative relationship between substrates of a chemical reaction (Merriam 2002). In order to deduce what the metabolic network suggests, recent research has centered on two approaches; namely extreme pathways and elementary mode analysis (Papin, Stelling, Price, Klamt, Schuster, and Palsson 2004).

Extreme Pathways

Price, Reed, Papin, Wiback and Palsson (2003) use a method of singular value decomposition (SVD) of extreme pathways in order to understand regulation of a human red blood cell metabolism. Extreme pathways are convex basis vectors that consist of steady state functions of a metabolic network (Papin, Price, and Palsson 2002). For any particular metabolic network, there is always a unique set of extreme pathways available (Papin *et al.* 2004). Furthermore, Price *et al.* (2003) define a constraint-based approach, where through the help of constraints like mass balance and maximum reaction rates, it is possible to develop a 'solution space' where all the feasible options fall within. Then, using a kinetic model approach, a single solution that falls within the extreme pathway solution space can be determined (Price *et al.* 2003). Therefore, in their study, Price *et al.* (2003) use both constraint and kinetic approaches to understand the human red blood cell metabolism. In conclusion, using extreme pathways, the regulatory mechanisms of a metabolic network can be studied in further detail.

Elementary mode analysis

Elementary mode analysis closely matches the approach used by extreme pathways. Similar to extreme pathways, there is always a unique set of elementary modes available for a particular metabolic network (Papin *et al.* 2004). These are the smallest sub-networks that allow a metabolic reconstruction network to function in steady state (Schuster, Fell, and Dandekar 2000; Stelling, Klamt, Bettenbrock, Schuster, and Gilles 2002). According to Stelling *et al.* (2002), elementary modes can be used to understand cellular objectives for the overall metabolic network. Furthermore, elementary mode analysis takes into account stoichiometrics and thermodynamics when evaluating whether a particular metabolic route or network is feasible and likely for a set of proteins/enzymes (Schuster *et al.* 2000).

Minimal metabolic behaviors (MMBs)

Recently, Larhlimi and Bockmayr (2009) presented a new approach called "minimal metabolic behaviors" for the analysis of metabolic networks. Like elementary modes or extreme pathways, these are uniquely determined by the network, and yield a complete description of the flux cone. However, the new description is much more compact. In contrast with elementary modes and extreme pathways, which use an inner description based on generating vectors of the flux cone, MMBs are using an outer description of the flux cone. This approach is based on sets of non-negativity constraints. These can be identified with irreversible reactions, and thus have a direct biochemical interpretation. One can characterize a metabolic network by MMBs and the reversible metabolic space.

Flux balance analysis

A different technique to simulate the metabolic network is to perform flux balance analysis. This method uses linear programming, but in contrast to elementary mode analysis and extreme pathways, only a single solution results in the end. Linear programming is usually used to obtain the maximum potential of the objective function that you are looking at, and therefore, when using flux balance analysis, a single solution is found to the optimization problem (Stelling *et al.* 2002). In a flux balance analysis approach, exchange fluxes are assigned to those metabolites that enter or leave the particular network only. Those metabolites that are consumed within the network are not assigned any exchange flux value. Also, the exchange fluxes along with the enzymes can have constraints ranging from a negative to positive value (ex: -10 to 10).

Furthermore, this particular approach can accurately define if the reaction stoichiometry is in line with predictions by providing fluxes for the balanced reactions. Also, flux balance analysis can highlight the most effective and efficient pathway through the network in order to achieve a particular objective function. In addition, gene knockout studies can be performed using flux balance analysis. The enzyme that correlates to the gene that needs to be removed is given a constraint value of 0. Then, the reaction that the particular enzyme catalyzes is completely removed from the analysis.

Dynamic simulation and parameter estimation

In order to perform a dynamic simulation with such a network it is necessary to construct an ordinary differential equation system that describes the rates of change in each metabolite's concentration or amount. To this end, a rate law, i.e., a kinetic equation is required for each reaction. Often these rate laws contain kinetic parameters with uncertain values. In many cases it is desired to estimate these parameter values with respect to given time-series data of metabolite concentrations. The system is then supposed to reproduce the given data. For this purpose the distance between the given data set and the result of the simulation, i.e., the numerically or in few cases analytically obtained solution of the differential equation system is computed. The values of the parameters are then estimated to minimize this distance (Dräger et al. 2009). One step further, it may be desired to estimate the mathematical structure of the differential equation system because the real rate laws are not known for the reactions within the system under study. To this end, the program SBMLsqueezer [6] allows automatic creation of appropriate rate laws for all reactions with the network.

Conclusion

In conclusion, metabolic network reconstruction and simulation can be effectively used to understand how an organism or parasite functions inside of the host cell. For example, if the parasite serves to compromise the immune system by lysing macrophages, then the goal of metabolic reconstruction/simulation would be to determine the metabolites that are essential to the organism's proliferation inside of macrophages. If the proliferation cycle is inhibited, then the parasite would not continue to evade the host's immune system. A reconstruction model serves as a first step to deciphering the complicated mechanisms surrounding disease. The next step would be to use the predictions and postulates generated from a reconstruction model and apply it to drug delivery and drug-engineering techniques.

Currently, many tropical diseases affecting third world nations are very inadequately characterized, and thus poorly understood. Therefore, a metabolic reconstruction and simulation of the parasites that cause the tropical diseases would aid in developing new and innovative cures and treatments.

References

1. Dräger, A, Kronfeld, M, Ziller, M. J., Supper, J., Planatscher, H., Magnus, J. B., Oldiges, M., Kohlbacher, O., and Zell, A. (2009). Modeling metabolic networks in C. glutamicum: a comparison of rate laws in combination with various parameter optimization strategies. BMC Systems Biology, 3(5). doi:10.1186/1752-0509-3-5

2. Francke, C., Siezen, R. J. and Teusink, B. (2005). Reconstructing the metabolic network of a bacterium from its genome. Trends in Microbiology. 13(11): 550-558.

3. Merriam Webster's Medical Dictionary. (2002). http://dictionary.reference.com/medical/

4. Papin, J.A., Price, N.D., and Palsson, B.O. (2002). Extreme Pathway Lengths and Reaction Participation in Genome-Scale Metabolic Networks. Genome Research. 12: 1889–1900.

5. Papin, J.A., Stelling, J., Price, N.D., Klamt, S., Schuster, S., and Palsson, B.O. (2004). Comparison of network-based pathway analysis methods. Trends in Biotechnology. 22(8): 400-405.

6. Price, N.D., Reed, J.L., Papin, J.A., Wiback, S.J., and Palsson, B.O. (2003). Network-based analysis of metabolic regulation in the human red blood cell. Journal of Theoretical Biology. 225: 185-194.

7. Schuster, S., Fell, D.A. and Dandekar, T. (2000). A general definition of metabolic pathways useful for systematic organization and analysis of complex metabolic networks. Nature Biotechnology. 18: 326-332.

8. SRI International. (2005). Pathway Tools Information Site. http://bioinformatics.ai.sri.com/ptools/

9. Stelling, J., Klamt, S., Bettenbrock, K., Schuster, S. and Gilles, E.D. (2002). Metabolic network structure determines key aspects of functionality and regulation. Nature. 420: 190-193.

10. Larhlimi, A., Bockmayr, A. (2009) A new constraint-based description of the steady-state flux cone of metabolic networks. Discrete Applied Mathematics. 157: 2257–2266. doi:10.1016/j.dam.2008.06.039

11. Overbeek R, Larsen N, Walunas T, D'Souza M, Pusch G, Selkov Jr, Liolios K, Joukov V, Kaznadzey D, Anderson I, Bhattacharyya A, Burd H, Gardner W, Hanke P, Kapatral V, Mikhailova N, Vasieva O, Osterman A, Vonstein V, Fonstein M, Ivanova N, Kyrpides N. (2003) The ERGO genome analysis and discovery system. Nucleic Acids Res. 31(1):164-71

12. Whitaker, J.W., Letunic, I., McConkey, G.A. and Westhead, D.R. metaTIGER: a metabolic evolution resource. Nucleic Acids Res. 2009 37: D531-8.

13. Karp, P.D., *et al.,* Pathway Tools version 13.0: Integrated Software for Pathway/Genome Informatics and Systems Biology. Briefings in Bioinformatics. 2010 11:40-79.

14. Henry, C.S., DeJongh, M., Best, A.B., Frybarger, P.M., Linsay, B., and R.L. Stevens. High-throughput Generation and Optimization of Genome-scale Metabolic Models. Nature Biotechnology. 2010. doi:10.1038/nbt.1672

External links

- ERGO [7]
- GeneDB [8]
- KEGG [9]
- PathCase [10] Case Western Reserve University
- BRENDA [11]
- BioCyc [12] and Cyclone [13] - provides an open source Java API to the pathway tool BioCyc to extract Metabolic graphs.
- EcoCyc [14]
- MetaCyc [15]
- SEED [16]
- Model SEED [5]
- ENZYME [17]
- SBRI Bioinformatics Tools and Software [18]
- TIGR [9]
- Pathway Tools [11]
- metaTIGER [4]
- Stanford Genomic Resources [19]
- Pathway Hunter Tool [20]
- IMG [1] The Integrated Microbial Genomes system, for genome analysis by the DOE-JGI.
- Systems Analysis, Modelling and Prediction Group [21] at the University of Oxford, Biochemical reaction pathway inference techniques.
- EFMtool provided by Marco Terzer [22]
- SBMLsqueezer [6]
- Cellnet analyzer from Klamt and von Kamp [23]
- Copasi [24]

References

[1] http://www.genome.ad.jp

[2] http://www.genedb.org

[3] http://ergo.integratedgenomics.com

[4] http://www.bioinformatics.leeds.ac.uk/metatiger/

[5] http://www.theseed.org/models/

[6] http://www.ra.cs.uni-tuebingen.de/software/SBMLsqueezer

[7] http://ergo.integratedgenomics.com/

[8] http://www.genedb.org/

[9] http://www.genome.ad.jp/

[10] http://nashua.case.edu/pathwaysweb

[11] http://www.brenda.uni-koeln.de/

[12] http://www.biocyc.org/

[13] http://nemo-cyclone.sourceforge.net

[14] http://ecocyc.org/

[15] http://metacyc.org/

[16] http://pubseed.theseed.org/

[17] http://www.expasy.org/enzyme/

[18] http://apps.sbri.org/Genome/Link/Bioinformatics_Tools_Software.aspx/

[19] http://genome-www.stanford.edu/

[20] http://pht.tu-bs.de/

[21] http://www.eng.ox.ac.uk/samp

[22] http://www.csb.ethz.ch/tools/efmtool/

[23] http://www.mpi-magdeburg.mpg.de/projects/cna/cna.html/

[24] http://www.copasi.org/tiki-index.php?page=homepage/

Metabolome

Metabolome[FirstUse] refers to the complete set of small-molecule metabolites (such as metabolic intermediates, hormones and other signalling molecules, and secondary metabolites) to be found within a biological sample, such as a single organism. The word was coined in analogy with transcriptomics and proteomics; like the transcriptome and the proteome, the metabolome is dynamic, changing from second to second. Although the metabolome can be defined readily enough, it is not currently possible to analyse the entire range of metabolites by a single analytical method (see metabolomics). In January 2007 scientists at the University of Alberta and the University of Calgary finished a draft of the human metabolome. They have catalogued and characterized 2,500 metabolites, 1,200 drugs and 3,500 food components that can be found in the human body.

External links

- Proteome.org [1]
- Metabolomics journal [2]
- Bioinformatics Journal [33]
- The Human Metabolome Project [3]
- The Human Metabolome Database [4]
- The Human Metabolite Library [5]
- The Human Serum Metabolome Project (HUSERMET) [6]
- PDF of Reporting Standards for Metabolomic Studies [7]
- Scientists complete human metabalome [8]

References

[1] http://proteome.org

[2] http://www.springer.com/life+sciences/biochemistry+%26+biophysics/journal/11306

[3] http://www.metabolomics.ca/

[4] http://www.hmdb.ca/

[5] http://www.metabolibrary.ca/

[6] http://www.husermet.org/

[7] http://www.liebertonline.com/doi/pdf/10.1089/omi.2006.10.158

[8] http://www.sciencedaily.com/upi/index.php?feed=Science&article=UPI-1-20070124-15033700-bc-canada-metabalome.xml

1. First use of the term "metabolome" in the literature — Oliver SG, Winson MK, Kell DB, Baganz F (September 1998). "Systematic functional analysis of the yeast genome" (http://linkinghub.elsevier.com/retrieve/pii/S0167-7799(98)01214-1). *Trends Biotechnol.* **16** (9): 373–8. doi:10.1016/S0167-7799(98)01214-1. PMID 9744112.

2. First book on metabolomics — Harrigan, G. G. & Goodacre, R. (eds) (2003). *Metabolic Profiling: Its Role in Biomarker Discovery and Gene Function Analysis.* Kluwer Academic Publishers (Boston). ISBN 1-4020-7370-4.

3. Fiehn O, Kloska S, Altmann T (February 2001). "Integrated studies on plant biology using multiparallel techniques" (http://linkinghub.elsevier.com/retrieve/pii/S0958-1669(00)00165-8). *Curr. Opin. Biotechnol.* **12** (1): 82–6. doi:10.1016/S0958-1669(00)00165-8. PMID 11167078.

4. Fiehn O (2001). "Combining Genomics, Metabolome Analysis, and Biochemical Modelling to Understand Metabolic Networks". *Comp. Funct. Genomics* **2** (3): 155–68. doi:10.1002/cfg.82. PMC 2447208. PMID 18628911.

- Weckwerth W (2003). "Metabolomics in systems biology". *Annu Rev Plant Biol* **54**: 669–89. doi:10.1146/annurev.arplant.54.031902.135014. PMID 14503007.

- Goodacre R, Vaidyanathan S, Dunn WB, Harrigan GG, Kell DB (May 2004). "Metabolomics by numbers: acquiring and understanding global metabolite data". *Trends Biotechnol.* **22** (5): 245–52. doi:10.1016/j.tibtech.2004.03.007. PMID 15109811.

- Wishart DS, Tzur D, Knox C, Eisner R, Guo AC, Young N, Cheng D, Jewell K, Arndt D, Sawhney S, Fung C, Nikolai L, Lewis M, Coutouly M-A, Forsythe I, Tang P, Shrivastava S, Jeroncic K, Stothard P, Amegbey G, Block D, Hau DD, Wagner J, Miniaci J, Clements M, Gebremedhin M, Guo N, Zhang Y, Duggan GE, MacInnis GD, Weljie AM, Dowlatabadi R, Bamforth F, Clive D, Greiner R, Li L, Marrie T, Sykes BD, Vogel HJ, Querengesser L (January 2007). "HMDB: the Human Metabolome Database". *Nucleic Acids Research* **35 (Database issue)** (Database issue): D521–6. doi:10.1093/nar/gkl923. PMC 1899095. PMID 17202168.

- Wishart DS, Knox C, Guo AC, Eisner R, Young N, Gautam B, Hau DD, Psychogios N, Dong E, Bouatra S, Mandal R, Sinelnikov I, Xia J, Jia L, Cruz JA, Lim E, Sobsey CA, Shrivastava S, Huang P, Liu P, Fang L, Peng J, Fradette R, Cheng D, Tzur D, Clements M, Lewis A, De Souza A, Zuniga A, Dawe M, Xiong Y, Clive D, Greiner R, Nazyrova A, Shaykhutdinov R, Li L, Vogel HJ, Forsythe I (January 2009). "HMDB: a knowledgebase for the human metabolome". *Nucleic Acids Research* **37 (Database issue)** (Database issue): D603–10. doi:10.1093/nar/gkn810. PMC 2686599. PMID 18953024.

- Nicholson JK, Holmes E, Lindon JC, Wilson ID (October 2004). "The challenges of modeling mammalian biocomplexity". *Nat. Biotechnol.* **22** (10): 1268–74. doi:10.1038/nbt1015. PMID 15470467.. Stresses the role of intestinal microorganisms in contributing to the human metabolome.

- van der Greef J, Stroobant P, van der Heijden R (October 2004). "The role of analytical sciences in medical systems biology". *Curr Opin Chem Biol* **8** (5): 559–65. doi:10.1016/j.cbpa.2004.08.013. PMID 15450501.

  - The importance of analytical sciences to omics and systems biology.

- Kell DB (June 2004). "Metabolomics and systems biology: making sense of the soup". *Curr. Opin. Microbiol.* **7** (3): 296–307. doi:10.1016/j.mib.2004.04.012. PMID 15196499.

- Dunn W.B., Ellis D.I. (2005). "Metabolomics: current analytical platforms and methodologies". *Trends in Analytical Chemistry* **24** (4): 285–294. doi:10.1016/j.trac.2004.11.021.

- Ellis DI, Goodacre R (August 2006). "Metabolic fingerprinting in disease diagnosis: biomedical applications of infrared and Raman spectroscopy". *Analyst* **131** (8): 875–85. doi:10.1039/b602376m. PMID 17028718.
  - Metabolomic data as an input to systems biology models.

Metabolomics

Metabolomics is the scientific study of chemical processes involving metabolites. Specifically, metabolomics is the "systematic study of the unique chemical fingerprints that specific cellular processes leave behind", the study of their small-molecule metabolite profiles.[1] The metabolome represents the collection of all metabolites in a biological cell, tissue, organ or organism, which are the end products of cellular processes.[2] Thus, while mRNA gene expression data and proteomic analyses do not tell the whole story of what might be happening in a cell, metabolic profiling can give an instantaneous snapshot of the physiology of that cell. One of the challenges of systems biology and functional genomics is to integrate proteomic, transcriptomic, and metabolomic information to give a more complete picture of living organisms.

Origins

The idea that biological fluids reflect the health of an individual has existed for a long time. Ancient Chinese doctors used ants for the evaluation of urine of patients to detect whether the urine contained high levels of glucose, and hence detect diabetes.[3] In the Middle Ages, "urine charts" were used to link the colours, tastes and smells of urine to various medical conditions, which are metabolic in origin.[4]

The concept that individuals might have a "metabolic profile" that could be reflected in the makeup of their biological fluids was introduced by Roger Williams in the late 1940s,[5] who used paper chromatography to suggest characteristic metabolic patterns in urine and saliva were associated with diseases such as schizophrenia. However, it was only through technological advancements in the 1960s and 1970s that it became feasible to quantitatively (as opposed to qualitatively) measure metabolic profiles.[6] The term "metabolic profile" was introduced by Horning, *et al.* in 1971 after they demonstrated that gas chromatography-mass spectrometry (GC-MS) could be used to measure compounds present in human urine and tissue extracts.[3] [7] The Horning group, along with that of Linus Pauling and Arthur Robinson led the development of GC-MS methods to monitor the metabolites present in urine through the 1970s.[8]

Concurrently, NMR spectroscopy, which was discovered in the 1940s, was also undergoing rapid advances. In 1974, Seeley et al. demonstrated the utility of using NMR to detect metabolites in unmodified biological samples.[9] This first study on muscle highlighted the value of NMR in that it was determined that 90% of cellular ATP is complexed with magnesium. As sensitivity has improved with the evolution of higher magnetic field strengths and magic-angle spinning, NMR continues to be a leading analytical tool to investigate metabolism.[3] [4] Recent efforts to utilize NMR for metabolomics have been largely driven by the laboratory of Dr. Jeremy Nicholson at Birkbeck College, University of London and later at Imperial College London. In 1984, Nicholson showed ^{1}H NMR spectroscopy could potentially be used to diagnose and treat diabetes mellitus, and later pioneered the application of pattern recognition methods to NMR spectroscopic data.[10] [11]

In 2005, the first metabolomics web database, METLIN,[12] for characterizing human metabolites was developed in the Siuzdak laboratory at The Scripps Research Institute and contained over 5,000 metabolites and tandem mass spectral data. As of 2011, METLIN contains over 40,000 metabolites as well as the largest repository of tandem mass spectrometry data in metabolomics.

On 23 January 2007, the Human Metabolome Project, led by Dr. David Wishart of the University of Alberta, Canada, completed the first draft of the human metabolome, consisting of a database of approximately 2500 metabolites, 1200 drugs and 3500 food components.[13] [14] Similar projects have been underway in several plant species, most notably *Medicago truncatula* and *Arabidopsis thaliana* for several years.

As late as mid-2010, metabolomics was still considered an "emerging field".[15] Further, it was noted that further progress in the field depended in large part, through addressing otherwise "irresolvable technical challenges", by technical evolution of mass spectrometry instrumentation.[15]

Metabolome

Metabolome refers to the complete set of small-molecule metabolites (such as metabolic intermediates, hormones and other signaling molecules, and secondary metabolites) to be found within a biological sample, such as a single organism.[16] [17] The word was coined in analogy with transcriptomics and proteomics; like the transcriptome and the proteome, the metabolome is dynamic, changing from second to second. Although the metabolome can be defined readily enough, it is not currently possible to analyse the entire range of metabolites by a single analytical method. The first metabolite database(called METLIN) for searching m/z values from mass spectrometry data was developed by scientists at The Scripps Research Institute in 2005.[12] In January 2007, scientists at the University of Alberta and the University of Calgary completed the first draft of the human metabolome. They catalogued approximately 2500 metabolites, 1200 drugs and 3500 food components that can be found in the human body, as reported in the literature.[13] This information, available at the Human Metabolome Database (www.hmdb.ca) and based on analysis of information available in the current scientific literature, is far from complete.[18] In contrast, much more is known about the metabolomes of other organisms. For example, over 50,000 metabolites have been characterized from the plant kingdom, and many thousands of metabolites have been identified and/or characterized from single plants.[19] [20]

Metabolites

Metabolites are the intermediates and products of metabolism. Within the context of metabolomics, a metabolite is usually defined as any molecule less than 1 kDa in size.[21] However, there are exceptions to this depending on the sample and detection method. For example, macromolecules such as lipoproteins and albumin are reliably detected in NMR-based metabolomics studies of blood plasma.[22] In plant-based metabolomics, it is common to refer to "primary" and "secondary" metabolites. A primary metabolite is directly involved in the normal growth, development, and reproduction. A secondary metabolite is not directly involved in those processes, but usually has important ecological function. Examples include antibiotics and pigments.[23] By contrast, in human-based metabolomics, it is more common to describe metabolites as being either endogenous (produced by the host organism) or exogenous.[24] Metabolites of foreign substances such as drugs are termed xenometabolites.[25]

The metabolome forms a large network of metabolic reactions, where outputs from one enzymatic chemical reaction are inputs to other chemical reactions. Such systems have been described as hypercycles.

Metabonomics

Metabonomics is defined as "the quantitative measurement of the dynamic multiparametric metabolic response of living systems to pathophysiological stimuli or genetic modification". The word origin is from the Greek *meta* meaning change and *nomos* meaning a rule set or set of laws.[26] This approach was pioneered by Jeremy Nicholson at Imperial College London and has been used in toxicology, disease diagnosis and a number of other fields. Historically, the metabonomics approach was one of the first methods to apply the scope of systems biology to studies of metabolism.[27] [28] [29]

There has been some disagreement over the exact differences between 'metabolomics' and 'metabonomics'. The difference between the two terms is not related to choice of analytical platform: although metabonomics is more associated with NMR spectroscopy and metabolomics with mass spectrometry-based techniques, this is simply because of usages amongst different groups that have popularized the different terms. While there is still no absolute agreement, there is a growing consensus that 'metabolomics' places a greater emphasis on metabolic profiling at a cellular or organ level and is primarily concerned with normal endogenous metabolism. 'Metabonomics' extends metabolic profiling to include information about perturbations of metabolism caused by environmental factors (including diet and toxins), disease processes, and the involvement of extragenomic influences, such as gut microflora. This is not a trivial difference; metabolomic studies should, by definition, exclude metabolic contributions from extragenomic sources, because these are external to the system being studied. However, in practice, within the field of human disease research there is still a large degree of overlap in the way both terms are used, and they are often in effect synonymous.[30]

Analytical technologies

Separation methods

- Gas chromatography, especially when interfaced with mass spectrometry (GC-MS), is one of the most widely used and powerful methods. It offers very high chromatographic resolution, but requires chemical derivatization for many biomolecules: only volatile chemicals can be analysed without derivatization. (Some modern instruments allow '2D' chromatography, using a short polar column after the main analytical column, which increases the resolution still further.) Some large and polar metabolites cannot be analysed by GC.[31]

- High performance liquid chromatography (HPLC). Compared to GC, HPLC has lower chromatographic resolution, but it does have the advantage that a much wider range of analytes can potentially be measured.[32]

- Capillary electrophoresis (CE). CE has a higher theoretical separation efficiency than HPLC, and is suitable for use with a wider range of metabolite classes than is GC. As for all electrophoretic techniques, it is most appropriate for charged analytes.[33]

Detection methods

- Mass spectrometry (MS) is used to identify and to quantify metabolites after separation by GC, HPLC (LC-MS), or CE. GC-MS is the most 'natural' combination of the three, and was the first to be developed. In addition, mass spectral fingerprint libraries exist or can be developed that allow identification of a metabolite according to its fragmentation pattern. MS is both sensitive (although, particularly for HPLC-MS, sensitivity is more of an issue as it is affected by the charge on the metabolite, and can be subject to ion suppression artifacts) and can be very specific. There are also a number of studies which use MS as a stand-alone technology: the sample is infused directly into the mass spectrometer with no prior separation, and the MS serves to both separate and to detect metabolites.

- Surface-based mass analysis has seen a resurgence in the past decade, with new MS technologies focused on increasing sensitivity, minimizing background, and reducing sample preparation. The ability to analyze metabolites directly from biofluids and tissues continues to challenge current MS technology, largely because of the limits imposed by the complexity of these samples, which contain thousands to tens of thousands of metabolites. Among the technologies being developed to address this challenge is Nanostructure-Initiator MS (NIMS),[34] [35] a desorption/ ionization approach that does not require the application of matrix and thereby facilitates small-molecule (i.e., metabolite) identification. MALDI is also used however, the application of a MALDI matrix can add significant background at <1000 Da that complicates analysis of the low-mass range (i.e., metabolites). In addition, the size of the resulting matrix crystals limits the spatial resolution that can be achieved in tissue imaging. Because of these limitations, several other matrix-free desorption/ionization approaches have been applied to the analysis of biofluids and tissues. Secondary ion mass spectrometry (SIMS) was one of the first matrix-free desorption/ionization approaches used to analyze metabolites from biological samples. SIMS uses a high-energy primary ion beam to desorb and generate secondary ions from a surface. The primary advantage of SIMS is its high spatial resolution (as small as 50 nm), a powerful characteristic for tissue imaging with MS.

However, SIMS has yet to be readily applied to the analysis of biofluids and tissues because of its limited sensitivity at >500 Da and analyte fragmentation generated by the high-energy primary ion beam. Desorption electrospray ionization (DESI) is a matrix-free technique for analyzing biological samples that uses a charged solvent spray to desorb ions from a surface. Advantages of DESI are that no special surface is required and the analysis is performed at ambient pressure with full access to the sample during acquisition. A limitation of DESI is spatial resolution because "focusing" the charged solvent spray is difficult. However, a recent development termed laser ablation ESI (LAESI) is a promising approach to circumvent this limitation.

- Nuclear magnetic resonance (NMR) spectroscopy. NMR is the only detection technique which does not rely on separation of the analytes, and the sample can thus be recovered for further analyses. All kinds of small molecule metabolites can be measured simultaneously - in this sense, NMR is close to being a universal detector. The main advantages of NMR are high analytical reproducibility and simplicity of sample preparation. Practically, however, it is relatively insensitive compared to mass spectrometry-based techniques.[36] [37]

- Although NMR and MS are the most widely used techniques, other methods of detection that have been used include ion-mobility spectrometry, electrochemical detection (coupled to HPLC) and radiolabel (when combined with thin-layer chromatography).

Statistical methods

The data generated in metabolomics usually consist of measurements performed on subjects under various conditions. These measurements may be digitized spectra, or a list of metabolite levels. In its simplest form this generates a matrix with rows corresponding to subjects and columns corresponding to metabolite levels.[3] Several statistical programs are currently available for analysis of both NMR and mass spectrometry data. For mass spectrometry data, software is available that identifies molecules that vary in subject groups on the basis of mass and sometimes retention time depending on the experimental design. The first comprehensive software to analyze global mass spectrometry-based metabolomics datasets was developed by the Siuzdak laboratory at The Scripps Research Institute in 2006. This software, called XCMS, is freely available, has over 20,000 downloads since its inception in 2006,[38] and is one of the most widely cited mass spectrometry-based metabolomics software programs in scientific literature. Other popular metabolomics programs for mass spectral analysis are MZmine,[39] MetAlign,[40] MathDAMP,[41] which also compensate for retention time deviation during sample analysis. LCMStats[42] is another R package for detailed analysis of liquid chromatography mass spectrometry(LCMS)data and is helpful in identification of co-eluting ions especially isotopologues from a complicated metabolic profile. It combines xcms package functions and can be used to apply many statistical functions for correcting detector saturation using coates correction and creating heat plots. Metabolomics data may also be analyzed by statistical projection (chemometrics) methods such as principal components analysis and partial least squares regression.[43]

Key applications

- Toxicity assessment/toxicology. Metabolic profiling (especially of urine or blood plasma samples) can be used to detect the physiological changes caused by toxic insult of a chemical (or mixture of chemicals). In many cases, the observed changes can be related to specific syndromes, e.g. a specific lesion in liver or kidney. This is of particular relevance to pharmaceutical companies wanting to test the toxicity of potential drug candidates: if a compound can be eliminated before it reaches clinical trials on the grounds of adverse toxicity, it saves the enormous expense of the trials.[30]

- Functional genomics. Metabolomics can be an excellent tool for determining the phenotype caused by a genetic manipulation, such as gene deletion or insertion. Sometimes this can be a sufficient goal in itself—for instance, to detect any phenotypic changes in a genetically-modified plant intended for human or animal consumption. More exciting is the prospect of predicting the function of unknown genes by comparison with the metabolic perturbations caused by deletion/insertion of known genes. Such advances are most likely to come from model organisms such as *Saccharomyces cerevisiae* and *Arabidopsis thaliana*. The Cravatt laboratory at The Scripps Research Institute has recently applied this technology to mammalian systems, identifying the *N*-acyltaurines as previously uncharacterized endogenous substrates for the enzyme fatty acid amide hydrolase (FAAH) and the monoalkylglycerol ethers (MAGEs) as endogenous substrates for the uncharacterized hydrolase KIAA1363.[44] [45]

• Nutrigenomics is a generalised term which links genomics, transcriptomics, proteomics and metabolomics to human nutrition. In general a metabolome in a given body fluid is influenced by endogenous factors such as age, sex, body composition and genetics as well as underlying pathologies. The large bowel microflora are also a very significant potential confounder of metabolic profiles and could be classified as either an endogenous or exogenous factor. The main exogenous factors are diet and drugs. Diet can then be broken down to nutrients and non- nutrients. Metabolomics is one means to determine a biological endpoint, or metabolic fingerprint, which reflects the balance of all these forces on an individual's metabolism.[46]

Sources and notes

[1] Daviss, Bennett (April 2005). "Growing pains for metabolomics" (http://www.the-scientist.com/article/display/15427/). *The Scientist* **19** (8): 25–28. .

[2] Jordan KW, Nordenstam J, Lauwers GY, Rothenberger DA, Alavi K, Garwood M, Cheng LL (March 2009). "Metabolomic characterization of human rectal adenocarcinoma with intact tissue magnetic resonance spectroscopy". *Diseases of the Colon & Rectum* **52** (3): 520–5. doi:10.1007/DCR.0b013e31819c9a2c. PMC 2720561. PMID 19333056.

[3] Van der greef and Smilde, J Chemomet, (2005) 19:376-386

[4] Nicholson JK, Lindon JC (October 2008). "Systems biology: Metabonomics". *Nature* **455** (7216): 1054–6. doi:10.1038/4551054a. PMID 18948945.

[5] Gates and Sweeley, Clin Chem (1978) 24(10):1663-73

[6] Preti, George. "Metabolomics comes of age?" *The Scientist*, 19[11]:8, June 6, 2005.

[7] Novotny et al J Chromatog B (2008) 866:26-47

[8] Griffiths, W.J. and Wang, Y. (2009) Chem Soc Rev 38:1882-96

[9] Hoult DI, Busby SJ, Gadian DG, Radda GK, Richards RE, Seeley PJ (November 1974). "Observation of tissue metabolites using 31P nuclear magnetic resonance". *Nature* **252** (5481): 285–7. Bibcode 1974Natur.252..285H. doi:10.1038/252285a0. PMID 4431445.

[10] Holmes E and Antti H (2002) Analyst 127:1549-57

[11] Lenz EM and Wilson ID (2007) J Proteome Res 6(2):443-58

[12] Smith CA, I'Maille G, Want EJ, Qin C, Trauger SA, Brandon TR, Custodio DE, Abagyan R, Siuzdak G (December 2005). "METLIN: a metabolite mass spectral database" (http://masspec.scripps.edu/publications/public_pdf/107_art.pdf). *Ther Drug Monit* **27** (6): 747–51. PMID 16404815. .

[13] Wishart DS, Tzur D, Knox C, *et al.* (January 2007). "HMDB: the Human Metabolome Database". *Nucleic Acids Research* **35** (Database issue): D521–6. doi:10.1093/nar/gkl923. PMC 1899095. PMID 17202168.

[14] Wishart DS, Knox C, Guo AC, Eisner R, Young N, Gautam B, Hau DD, Psychogios N, Dong E, Bouatra S, Mandal R, Sinelnikov I, Xia J, Jia L, Cruz JA, Lim E, Sobsey CA, Shrivastava S, Huang P, Liu P, Fang L, Peng J, Fradette R, Cheng D, Tzur D, Clements M, Lewis A, De Souza A, Zuniga A, Dawe M, Xiong Y, Clive D, Greiner R, Nazyrova A, Shaykhutdinov R, Li L, Vogel HJ, Forsythe I (2009). "HMDB: a knowledgebase for the human metabolome". *Nucleic Acids Research* **37** (Database issue): D603. doi:10.1093/nar/gkn810. PMC 2686599. PMID 18953024.

[15] Morrow Jr., Ph.D., K. John (1 April 2010). "Mass Spec Central to Metabolomics" (http://www.webcitation.org/5qp39ElGM). *Genetic Engineering & Biotechnology News* **30** (7): p. 1. Archived from the original (http://www.genengnews.com/gen-articles/ mass-spec-central-to-metabolomics/3229/) on 28 June 2010. . Retrieved 28 June 2010

[16] Oliver SG, Winson MK, Kell DB, Baganz F (September 1998). "Systematic functional analysis of the yeast genome". *Trends in Biotechnology* **16** (9): 373–8. doi:10.1016/S0167-7799(98)01214-1. PMID 9744112.

[17] Griffin JL, Vidal-Puig A (June 2008). "Current challenges in metabolomics for diabetes research: a vital functional genomic tool or just a ploy for gaining funding?". *Physiol. Genomics* **34** (1): 1–5. doi:10.1152/physiolgenomics.00009.2008. PMID 18413782.

[18] Pearson H (March 2007). "Meet the human metabolome". *Nature* **446** (7131): 8. doi:10.1038/446008a. PMID 17330009.

[19] De Luca V, St Pierre B (April 2000). "The cell and developmental biology of alkaloid biosynthesis". *Trends Plant Sci.* **5** (4): 168–73. doi:10.1016/S1360-1385(00)01575-2. PMID 10740298.

[20] Griffin JL, Shockcor JP (July 2004). "Metabolic profiles of cancer cells". *Nat. Rev. Cancer* **4** (7): 551–61. doi:10.1038/nrc1390. PMID 15229480.

[21] Samuelsson LM, Larsson DG (October 2008). "Contributions from metabolomics to fish research". *Mol Biosyst* **4** (10): 974–9. doi:10.1039/b804196b. PMID 19082135.

[22] Nicholson JK, Foxall PJ, Spraul M, Farrant RD, Lindon JC (March 1995). "750 MHz 1H and 1H-13C NMR spectroscopy of human blood plasma". *Anal. Chem.* **67** (5): 793–811. doi:10.1021/ac00101a004. PMID 7762816.

[23] Bentley R (1999). "Secondary metabolite biosynthesis: the first century". *Crit. Rev. Biotechnol.* **19** (1): 1–40. doi:10.1080/0738-859991229189. PMID 10230052.

[24] Nordström A, O'Maille G, Qin C, Siuzdak G (May 2006). "Nonlinear data alignment for UPLC-MS and HPLC-MS based metabolomics: quantitative analysis of endogenous and exogenous metabolites in human serum". *Anal. Chem.* **78** (10): 3289–95. doi:10.1021/ac060245f. PMID 16689529.

[25] Crockford DJ, Maher AD, Ahmadi KR, *et al.* (September 2008). "1H NMR and UPLC-MS(E) statistical heterospectroscopy: characterization of drug metabolites (xenometabolome) in epidemiological studies". *Anal. Chem.* **80** (18): 6835–44. doi:10.1021/ac801075m. PMID 18700783.

[26] Nicholson JK (2006). "Global systems biology, personalized medicine and molecular epidemiology". *Mol. Syst. Biol.* **2** (1): 52. doi:10.1038/msb4100095. PMC 1682018. PMID 17016518.

[27] Nicholson JK, Lindon JC, Holmes E (November 1999). "'Metabonomics': understanding the metabolic responses of living systems to pathophysiological stimuli via multivariate statistical analysis of biological NMR spectroscopic data". *Xenobiotica* **29** (11): 1181–9. doi:10.1080/004982599238047. PMID 10598751.

[28] Nicholson JK, Connelly J, Lindon JC, Holmes E (February 2002). "Metabonomics: a platform for studying drug toxicity and gene function". *Nat Rev Drug Discov* **1** (2): 153–61. doi:10.1038/nrd728. PMID 12120097.

[29] Holmes E, Wilson ID, Nicholson JK (September 2008). "Metabolic phenotyping in health and disease". *Cell* **134** (5): 714–7. doi:10.1016/j.cell.2008.08.026. PMID 18775301.

[30] Robertson DG (June 2005). "Metabonomics in toxicology: a review". *Toxicol. Sci.* **85** (2): 809–22. doi:10.1093/toxsci/kfi102. PMID 15689416.

[31] Schauer N, Steinhauser D, Strelkov S, *et al.* (February 2005). "GC-MS libraries for the rapid identification of metabolites in complex biological samples". *FEBS Lett.* **579** (6): 1332–7. doi:10.1016/j.febslet.2005.01.029. PMID 15733837.

[32] Gika HG, Theodoridis GA, Wingate JE, Wilson ID (August 2007). "Within-day reproducibility of an LC-MS-based method for metabonomic analysis: application to human urine". *J. Proteome Res.* **6** (8): 3291–303. doi:10.1021/pr070183p. PMID 17625818.

[33] Soga T, Ohashi Y, Ueno Y (September 2003). "Quantitative metabolome analysis using capillary electrophoresis mass spectrometry". *J. Proteome Res.* **2** (5): 488–494. doi:10.1021/pr034020m. PMID 14582645.

[34] Northen T.R, Yanes O, Northen M, Marrinucci D, Uritboonthai W, Apon J, Golledge S, Nordstrom A, Siuzdak G (October 2007). "Clathrate nanostructures for mass spectrometry". *Nature* **449** (7165): 1033–6. doi:10.1038/nature06195. PMID 17960240.

[35] Woo H, Northern TR, Yanes O, Siuzdak G (July 2008). "Nanostructure-initiator mass spectrometry: a protocol for preparing and applying NIMS surfaces for high-sensitivity mass analysis". *Nature protocols* **3** (8): 1341–9. doi:10.1038/nprot.2008.110. PMID 18714302.

[36] Griffin JL (October 2003). "Metabonomics: NMR spectroscopy and pattern recognition analysis of body fluids and tissues for characterisation of xenobiotic toxicity and disease diagnosis". *Curr Opin Chem Biol* **7** (5): 648–54. doi:10.1016/j.cbpa.2003.08.008. PMID 14580571.

[37] Beckonert O, Keun HC, Ebbels TM, *et al.* (2007). "Metabolic profiling, metabolomic and metabonomic procedures for NMR spectroscopy of urine, plasma, serum and tissue extracts". *Nat Protoc* **2** (11): 2692–703. doi:10.1038/nprot.2007.376. PMID 18007604.

[38] Smith CA, Want EJ, O'Maille G, Abagyan R, Siuzdak G (February 2006). "XCMS: processing mass spectrometry data for metabolite profiling using nonlinear peak alignment, matching, and identification". *Anal Chem* **78** (3): 779–87. doi:10.1021/ac051437y. PMID 16448051.

[39] Katajamaa M, Miettinen J, Oresic M (March 2006). "MZmine: toolbox for processing and visualization of mass spectrometry based molecular profile data" (http://mzmine.sourceforge.net/download.shtml). *Bioinformatics* **22** (5): 634–36. doi:10.1093/bioinformatics/btk039. PMID 16403790. .

[40] Lommen A (April 2009). "MetAlign: interface-driven, versatile metabolomics tool for hyphenated full-scan mass spectrometry data processing" (http://www.metalign.wur.nl/UK/Download+and+publications/). *Anal Chem* **81** (8): 3079–86. doi:10.1021/ac900036d. PMID 19301908. .

[41] Baran R, Kochi H, Saito N, Suematsu M, Soga T, Nishioka T, Robert M, Tomita M (December 2006). "MathDAMP: a package for differential analysis of metabolite profiles" (http://mathdamp.iab.keio.ac.jp/). *BMC Bioinformatics* **7**: 530. doi:10.1186/1471-2105-7-530. PMC 1764210. PMID 17166258. .

[42] Singh S, *LCMStats: an R package for detailed analysis of LCMS data* (http://sourceforge.net/projects/lcmstats/),

[43] Trygg J, Holmes E, Lundstedt T (February 2007). "Chemometrics in metabonomics". *J. Proteome Res.* **6** (2): 469–79. doi:10.1021/pr060594q. PMID 17269704.

[44] Saghatelian A, Trauger SA, Want EJ, Hawkins EG, Siuzdak G, Cravatt BF (November 2004). "Assignment of endogenous substrates to enzymes by global metabolite profiling". *Biochemistry* **43** (45): 14332–9. doi:10.1021/bi0480335. PMID 15533037.

[45] Chiang KP, Niessen S, Saghatelian A, Cravatt BF (October 2006). "An enzyme that regulates ether lipid signaling pathways in cancer annotated by multidimensional profiling". *Chem. Biol.* **13** (10): 1041–50. doi:10.1016/j.chembiol.2006.08.008. PMID 17052608.

[46] Gibney MJ, Walsh M, Brennan L, Roche HM, German B, van Ommen B (September 2005). "Metabolomics in human nutrition: opportunities and challenges". *Am. J. Clin. Nutr.* **82** (3): 497–503. PMID 16155259.

• Tomita M., Nishioka T. (2005), Metabolomics: The Frontier of Systems Biology, Springer, ISBN 4-431-25121-9

- Wolfram Weckwerth W. (2006), Metabolomics: Methods And Protocols (Methods in Molecular Biology), Humana Press, ISBN 1-58829-561-3
- Dunn, W.B. and Ellis, D.I. (2005), Metabolomics: current analytical platforms and methodologies. Trends in Analytical Chemistry 24(4), 285-294.
- Ellis D.I., Goodacre R. (2006). "Metabolic fingerprinting in disease diagnosis: biomedical applications of infrared and Raman spectroscopy". *Analyst* **131** (8): 875–885. doi:10.1039/b602376m. PMID 17028718.

http://dbkgroup.org/dave_files/AnalystMetabolicFingerprinting2006.pdf

- Claudino, W.M., Quatronne, A., Pestrim, M., Biganzoli, L., Bertini and Di Leo, A.(2007) Metabolomics: Available Results, Current Research Projects in Breast Cancer, and Future *Applications. J Clin Oncol May 14; [Epub ahead of print]. http://lab.bcb.iastate.edu/projects/plantmetabolomics/
- Ellis, D.I., Dunn, W.B., Griffin, J.L., Allwood, J.W. and Goodacre, R. (2007) Metabolic Fingerprinting as a Diagnostic Tool. Pharmacogenomics, 8(9), 1243-1266. http://dbkgroup.org/dave_files/Pharmacogenomics.pdf

External links

- Metabolism (http://www.dmoz.org/Science/Biology/Biochemistry_and_Molecular_Biology/Metabolism/) at the Open Directory Project
- HMDB (http://www.hmdb.ca)
- METLIN (http://metlin.scripps.edu)
- XCMS (http://metlin.scripps.edu/xcms/)
- LCMStats (http://sourceforge.net/projects/lcmstats/)

Metagenomics

Metagenomics is the study of **metagenomes**, genetic material recovered directly from environmental samples. The broad field may also be referred to as **environmental genomics**, **ecogenomics** or **community genomics**. Traditional microbiology and microbial genome sequencing rely upon cultivated clonal cultures. This relatively new field of genetic research enables studies of organisms that are not easily cultured in a laboratory as well as studies of organisms in their natural environment.[1] [2]

Early environmental gene sequencing cloned specific genes (often the 16S rRNA gene) to produce a profile of diversity in a natural sample. Such work revealed that the vast majority of microbial biodiversity had been missed by cultivation-based methods.[3] Recent studies use "shotgun" Sanger sequencing or massively parallel pyrosequencing to get largely unbiased samples of all genes from all the members of the sampled communities.[4]

History

Origin of the term

The term "metagenomics" was first used by Jo Handelsman, Jon Clardy, Robert M. Goodman, and others, and first appeared in publication in 1998.[5] The term metagenome referenced the idea that a collection of genes sequenced from the environment could be analyzed in a way analogous to the study of a single genome. The exploding interest in environmental genetics, along with the buzzword-like nature of the term, has resulted in the broader use of metagenomics to describe any sequencing of genetic material from environmental (i.e. uncultured) samples, even work that focuses on one organism or gene. Recently, Kevin Chen and Lior Pachter (researchers at the University of California, Berkeley) defined metagenomics as "the application of modern genomics techniques to the study of communities of microbial organisms directly in their natural environments, bypassing the need for isolation and lab cultivation of individual species."[6]

Environmental gene surveys

Conventional sequencing begins with a culture of identical cells as a source of DNA. However, early metagenomic studies revealed that there are probably large groups of microorganisms in many environments that cannot be cultured and thus cannot be sequenced. These early studies focused on 16S ribosomal RNA sequences which are relatively short, often conserved within a species, and generally different between species. Many 16S rRNA sequences have been found which do not belong to any known cultured species, indicating that there are numerous non-isolated organisms out there.

Early molecular work in the field was conducted by Norman R. Pace and colleagues, who used PCR to explore the diversity of ribosomal RNA sequences.[7] The insights gained from these breakthrough studies led Pace to propose the idea of cloning DNA directly from environmental samples as early as 1985.[8] This led to the first report of isolating and cloning bulk DNA from an environmental sample, published by Pace and colleagues in 1991[9] while Pace was in the Department of Biology at Indiana University. Considerable efforts ensured that these were not PCR false positives and supported the existence of a complex community of unexplored species. Although this methodology was limited to exploring highly conserved, non-protein coding genes, it did support early microbial morphology-based observations that diversity was far more complex than was known by culturing methods.

Soon after that, Healy reported the metagenomic isolation of functional genes from "zoolibraries" constructed from a complex culture of environmental organisms grown in the laboratory on dried grasses in 1995.[10] After leaving the Pace laboratory, Ed DeLong continued in the field and has published work that has largely laid the groundwork for environmental phylogenies based on signature 16S sequences, beginning with his group's construction of libraries from marine samples.[11]

Longer sequences from environmental samples

Recovery of DNA sequences longer than a few thousand base pairs from environmental samples was very difficult until recent advances in molecular biological techniques, particularly related to constructing libraries in bacterial artificial chromosomes (BACs), provided better vectors for molecular cloning.[12]

Shotgun metagenomics

Advances in bioinformatics, refinements of DNA amplification, and proliferation of computational power have greatly aided the analysis of DNA sequences recovered from environmental samples. These advances have enabled the adaptation of shotgun sequencing to metagenomic samples. The approach, used to sequence many cultured microorganisms as well as the human genome, randomly shears DNA, sequences many short sequences, and reconstructs them into a consensus sequence.

In 2002, Mya Breitbart, Forest Rohwer, and colleagues used environmental shotgun sequencing to show that 200 liters of seawater contains over 5000 different viruses.[13] Subsequent studies showed that there are >1000 viral species in human stool and possibly a million different viruses per kilogram of marine sediment, including many bacteriophages. Essentially all of the viruses in these studies were new species. In 2004, Gene Tyson, Jill Banfield, and colleagues at the University of California, Berkeley and the Joint Genome Institute sequenced DNA extracted from an acid mine drainage system.[14] This effort resulted in the complete, or nearly complete, genomes for a handful of bacteria and archaea that had previously resisted attempts to culture them. It was now possible to study entire genomes without the biases associated with laboratory cultures.[15]

Global Ocean Sampling Expedition

Beginning in 2003, Craig Venter, leader of the privately-funded parallel of the Human Genome Project, has led the Global Ocean Sampling Expedition, circumnavigating the globe and collecting metagenomic samples throughout. All of these samples are sequenced using shotgun sequencing, in hopes that new genomes (and therefore new organisms) would be identified. The pilot project, conducted in the Sargasso Sea, found DNA from nearly 2000 different species, including 148 types of bacteria never before seen.[16] As of 2009, Venter has circumnavigated the globe and thoroughly explored the West Coast of the United States, and is currently in the midst of a two-year expedition to explore the Baltic, Mediterranian and Black Seas.

Pyrosequencing

In 2006 Robert Edwards, Forest Rohwer, and colleagues at San Diego State University published the first sequences of environmental samples generated with so-called next generation sequencing, in this case chip-based pyrosequencing developed by 454 Life Sciences.[17] This technique for sequencing DNA generates shorter fragments than conventional techniques, however this limitation is compensated for by the very large number of sequences generated. In addition, this technique does not require cloning the DNA before sequencing, removing one of the main biases in metagenomics.

Software

A major problem with metagenomes is binning. Binning is the process of identifying from what organism a particular sequence has originated. Traditionally, BLAST is a method used to rapidly search for similar sequences in existing public databases. More advanced methods have been employed to bin sequences. Big successes have been achieved for a family of methods using intrinsic features of the sequence, such as oligonucleotide frequencies. These methods include TETRA (Teeling et al., 2004),[18] Phylopythia (McHardy et al., 2007), TACOA (Diaz et al., 2009), PCAHIER (Zheng and Wu, 2010),[19] , DiScRIBinATE (Ghosh et al., 2010) [20] , SPHINX (Mohammed et al., 2011)[21] , and Parallel-META (Su et al., 2011)[22] . In 2007, Daniel Huson and Stephan Schuster developed and published the first stand-alone metagenome analysis tool, MEGAN, which can be used to perform a first analysis of a metagenomic shotgun dataset. This tool was originally developed to analyse the metagenome of a mammoth sample.[23] However in a recent study by Monzoorul et al. 2009,[24] it was shown that adopting the LCA approach (of MEGAN) solely based on bit-score of the alignment leads to a number of false positive assignments especially in the context of metagenomic sequences originating from new organisms. This study proposed a new approach called SOrt-ITEMS which used several alignment parameters to increase the accuracy of assignments.

MG-RAST

In 2007, Folker Meyer and Robert Edwards and a team at Argonne National Laboratory and the University of Chicago released the Metagenomics RAST server [25] (MG-RAST) a community resource for metagenome data set analysis.[26] As of October 2011 3.7 Terabases (10^{12} bases) of DNA have been analyzed by MG-RAST, more than 4300 public data sets are freely available for comparison within MG-RAST. Over 7000 users now have submitted a total of 38,000 metagenomes to MG-RAST. The server also acts as the de-fact repository for metagenomics data.

Applications

Metagenomics can improve strategies for monitoring the impact of pollutants on ecosystems and for cleaning up contaminated environments. Increased understanding of how microbial communities cope with pollutants is helping assess the potential of contaminated sites to recover from pollution and increase the chances of bioaugmentation or biostimulation trials to succeed.[27]

Recent progress in mining the rich genetic resource of non-culturable microbes has led to the discovery of new genes, enzymes, and natural products. The impact of metagenomics is witnessed in the development of commodity and fine chemicals, agrochemicals and pharmaceuticals where the benefit of enzyme-catalyzed chiral synthesis is increasingly recognized.[28]

Metagenomic sequencing is being used to characterize the microbial communities from 15-18 body sites from at least 250 individuals. This is part of the Human Microbiome initiative with primary goals to determine if there is a core human microbiome, to understand the changes in the human microbiome that can be correlated with human health, and to develop new technological and bioinformatics tools to support these goals.[29]

It is well known that the vast majority of microbes have not been cultivated. Functional metagenomics strategies are being used to explore the interactions between plants and microbes through cultivation-independent study of the microbial communities.[30]

Microbial diversity

Much of the interest in metagenomics comes from the discovery that the vast majority of microorganisms had previously gone unnoticed. Traditional microbiological methods relied upon laboratory cultures of organisms. Surveys of ribosomal RNA (rRNA) genes taken directly from the environment revealed that cultivation based methods find less than 1% of the bacteria and archaea species in a sample.[3]

Gene surveys

Shotgun sequencing and screens of clone libraries reveal genes present in environmental samples. This provides information both on which organisms are present and what metabolic processes are possible in the community. This can be helpful in understanding the ecology of a community, particularly if multiple samples are compared to each other.[31]

Environmental genomes

Shotgun metagenomics also is capable of sequencing nearly complete microbial genomes directly from the environment.[14] Because the collection of DNA from an environment is largely uncontrolled, the most abundant organisms in an environmental sample are most highly represented in the resulting sequence data. To achieve the high coverage needed to fully resolve the genomes of underrepresented community members, large samples, often prohibitively so, are needed. On the other hand, the random nature of shotgun sequencing ensures that many of these organisms will be represented by at least some small sequence segments. Due to the limitations of microbial isolation methods, the vast majority of these organisms would go unnoticed using traditional culturing techniques.

Community metabolism

Many bacterial communities show significant division of labor in metabolism. Waste products of some organisms are metabolites for others. Working together they turn raw resources into fully metabolized waste. Using comparative gene studies and expression experiments with microarrays or proteomics researchers can piece together a metabolic network that goes beyond species boundaries. Such studies require detailed knowledge about which versions of which proteins are coded by which species and even by which strains of which species. Therefore, community genomic information is another fundamental tool (with metabolomics and proteomics) in the quest to determine how metabolites are transferred and transformed by a community.[32]

References

[1] Marco, D, ed (2010). *Metagenomics: Theory, Methods and Applications*. Caister Academic Press. ISBN 978-1-904455-54-7.

[2] Marco, D (editor) (2011). *Metagenomics: Current Innovations and Future Trends*. Caister Academic Press. ISBN 978-1-904455-87-5.

[3] Hugenholz, P; Goebel BM, Pace NR (1 September 1998). "Impact of culture-independent studies on the emerging phylogenetic view of bacterial diversity". *J. Bacteriol* **180** (18): 4765–74. PMC 107498. PMID 9733676.

[4] Eisen, JA (2007). "Environmental shotgun sequencing: its potential and challenges for studying the hidden world of microbes.". *PLoS Biology* **5** (3): e82. doi:10.1371/journal.pbio.0050082. PMC 1821061. PMID 17355177.

[5] Handelsman, J; Rondon MR, Brady SF, Clardy J, Goodman RM (1998). "Molecular biological access to the chemistry of unknown soil microbes: a new frontier for natural products". *Chemistry & Biology* **5**: 245–249. doi:10.1016/S1074-5521(98)90108-9..

[6] Chen, K; Pachter L (2005). "Bioinformatics for whole-genome shotgun sequencing of microbial communities". *PLoS Comp Biol* **1** (2): 24. Bibcode 2005PLSCB...1...24C. doi:10.1371/journal.pcbi.0010024. PMC 1185649. PMID 16110337..

[7] Lane, DJ; Pace B, Olsen GJ, Stahl DA, Sogin ML, Pace NR (1985). "Rapid determination of 16S ribosomal RNA sequences for phylogenetic analyses". *Proceedings of the National Academy of Sciences* **82** (20): 6955–9. Bibcode 1985PNAS...82.6955L. doi:10.1073/pnas.82.20.6955. PMC 391288. PMID 2413450..

[8] Pace, NR; DA Stahl, DJ Lane, GJ Olsen (1985). "Analyzing natural microbial populations by rRNA sequences" (http://md1.csa.com/partners/viewrecord.php?requester=gs&collection=ENV&recid=913954&q=Analyzing+natural+microbial+populations+by+rRNA+sequences&uid=790164755&setcookie=yes). *ASM News* **51**: 4–12. ..

[9] Pace, NR; Delong, EF; Pace, NR (1991). "Analysis of a marine picoplankton community by 16S rRNA gene cloning and sequencing". *Journal of Bacteriology* **173** (14): 4371–4378. PMC 208098. PMID 2066334..

[10] Healy, FG; RM Ray, HC Aldrich, AC Wilkie, LO Ingram, KT Shanmugam (1995). "Direct isolation of functional genes encoding cellulases from the microbial consortia in a thermophilic, anaerobic digester maintained on lignocellulose". *Appl. Microbiol Biotechnol.* **43** (4): 667–74. doi:10.1007/BF00164771. PMID 7546604..

[11] Stein, JL; TL Marsh, KY Wu, H Shizuya, EF DeLong (1996). "Characterization of uncultivated prokaryotes: isolation and analysis of a 40-kilobase-pair genome fragment from a planktonic marine archaeon". *Journal of Bacteriology* **178** (3): 591–599. PMC 177699. PMID 8550487.

[12] Beja, O.; Suzuki, MT; Koonin, EV; Aravind, L; Hadd, A; Nguyen, LP; Villacorta, R; Amjadi, M et al. (2000). "Construction and analysis of bacterial artificial chromosome libraries from a marine microbial assemblage". *Environmental Microbiology* **2** (5): 516–29. doi:10.1046/j.1462-2920.2000.00133.x. PMID 11233160.

[13] Breitbart, M; Salamon P, Andresen B, Mahaffy JM, Segall AM, Mead D, Azam F, Rohwer F (2002). "Genomic analysis of uncultured marine viral communities". *Proceedings of the National Academy USA* **99** (22): 14250–14255. Bibcode 2002PNAS...9914250B. doi:10.1073/pnas.202488399. PMC 137870. PMID 12384570..

[14] Tyson, GW; Chapman J, Hugenholtz P, Allen EE, Ram RJ, Richardson PM, Solovyev VV, Rubin EM, Rokhsar DS, Banfield JF (2004). "Insights into community structure and metabolism by reconstruction of microbial genomes from the environment" (http://www.nature.com/nature/journal/v428/n6978/full/nature02340.html). *Nature* **428** (6978): 37–43. doi:10.1038/nature02340. PMID 14961025. ..

[15] Hugenholz, P (2002). "Exploring prokaryotic diversity in the genomic era". *Genome Biology* **3**: 1–8. doi:10.1186/gb-2002-3-2-reviews0003. PMC 139013. PMID 11864374..

[16] Venter, JC; Remington K, Heidelberg JF, Halpern AL, Rusch D, Eisen JA, Wu D, Paulsen I, Nelson KE, Nelson W, Fouts DE, Levy S, Knap AH, Lomas MW, Nealson K, White O, Peterson J, Hoffman J, Parsons R, Baden-Tillson H, Pfannkoch C, Rogers Y, Smith HO (2004). "Environmental Genome Shotgun Sequencing of the Sargasso Sea". *Science* **304** (5667): 66–74. Bibcode 2004Sci...304...66V. doi:10.1126/science.1093857. PMID 15001713..

[17] Edwards, RA; Rodriguez-Brito B, Wegley L, Haynes M, Breitbart M, Peterson DM, Saar MO, Alexander S, Alexander EC, Rohwer F (2006). "Using pyrosequencing to shed light on deep mine microbial ecology". *BMC Genomics* **7**: 57. doi:10.1186/1471-2164-7-57. PMC 1483832. PMID 16549033..

[18] Teeling, Hanno; Waldmann, Jost; Lombardot, Thierry; Bauer, Margarete; Oliver, Frank (2004). "TETRA: a web-service and a stand-alone program for the analysis and comparison of tetranucleotide usage patterns in DNA sequences". *BMC Bioinformatics* **5** (163). doi:10.1186/1471-2105-5-163.

[19] Zheng, Hao; Wu, Hongwei (2010). "Short prokaryotic DNA fragment binning using a hierarchical classifier based on linear discriminant analysis and principal component analysis.". *J Bioinform Comput Biol.* **8** (6): 995–1011. PMID 21121023.

[20] Ghosh T S, Monzoorul HM, Mande S S (October 2010). "DiScRIBinATE: a rapid method for accurate taxonomic classification of metagenomic sequences". *BMC Bioinformatics* **25** (Suppl 7 : S14). doi:http://dx.crossref.org/10.1186%2F1471-2105-11-S7-S14. PMID 21106121.

[21] Mohammed MH, Ghosh TS, Dinakar K, Mande SS (October 2010). "SPHINX—an algorithm for taxonomic binning of metagenomic sequences". *Bioinformatics* **27** (1): 22–30. doi:10.1093/bioinformatics/btq608. PMID 21030462.

[22] http://computationalbioenergy.org/parallel-meta.html

[23] Poinar, HN; Schwarz, C; Qi, J; Shapiro, B; MacPhee, RD; Buigues, B; Tikhonov, A; Huson, DH et al. (2006). "Metagenomics to paleogenomics: large-scale sequencing of mammoth DNA.". *Science* **311** (5759): 392–4. Bibcode 2006Sci...311..392P. doi:10.1126/science.1123360. PMID 16368896.

[24] Monzoorul HM, Tarini S, Dinakar K, Sharmila S M (May 2009). "SOrt-ITEMS : Sequence Orthology based approach for Improved Taxonomic Estimation of Metagenomic Sequences". *Bioinformatics* **25** (14): 1722–30. doi:10.1093/bioinformatics/btp317. PMID 19439565.

[25] http://metagenomics.anl.gov

[26] Meyer, F; Paarmann D, D'Souza M, Olson R, Glass EM, Kubal M, Paczian T, Rodriguez A, Stevens R, Wilke A, Wilkening J, Edwards RA (2008). "The metagenomics RAST server - a public resource for the automatic phylogenetic and functional analysis of metagenomes". *BMC Bioinformatics* **9**: 0. doi:10.1186/1471-2105-9-386. PMC 2563014. PMID 18803844.

[27] George I et al. (2010). "Application of Metagenomics to Bioremediation". *Metagenomics: Theory, Methods and Applications*. Caister Academic Press. ISBN 978-1-904455-54-7.

[28] Wong D (2010). "Applications of Metagenomics for Industrial Bioproducts". *Metagenomics: Theory, Methods and Applications*. Caister Academic Press. ISBN 978-1-904455-54-7.

[29] Nelson KE and White BA (2010). "Metagenomics and Its Applications to the Study of the Human Microbiome". *Metagenomics: Theory, Methods and Applications*. Caister Academic Press. ISBN 978-1-904455-54-7.

[30] CharlesT (2010). "The Potential for Investigation of Plant-microbe Interactions Using Metagenomics Methods". *Metagenomics: Theory, Methods and Applications*. Caister Academic Press. ISBN 978-1-904455-54-7.

[31] Allen, EE; Banfield, JF (2005). "Community genomics in microbial ecology and evolution". *Nature Reviews Microbiology* **3** (6): 489–498. doi:10.1038/nrmicro1157. PMID 15931167.

[32] Klitgord, N.; Segrè, D. (2011). "Ecosystems biology of microbial metabolism". *Current Opinion in Biotechnology* **22** (4): 541–546. doi:10.1016/j.copbio.2011.04.018. PMID 21592777.

Further reading

Review articles

- Edwards RA, Rohwer F (June 2005). "Viral metagenomics". *Nat. Rev. Microbiol.* **3** (6): 504–10. doi:10.1038/nrmicro1163. PMID 15886693.

- Eisen, Jonathan A. (2007). "Environmental Shotgun Sequencing: Its Potential and Challenges for Studying the Hidden World of Microbes". *PLoS Biology* **5** (3): e82. doi:10.1371/journal.pbio.0050082. PMC 1821061. PMID 17355177.

- Green, BD; Keller, M (2006). "Capturing the uncultivated majority.". *Current opinion in biotechnology* **17** (3): 236–40. doi:10.1016/j.copbio.2006.05.004. PMID 16701994.

- Handelsman J. (2004). "Metagenomics: application of genomics to uncultured microorganisms". *Microbiology and Molecular Biology Reviews* **68** (4): 669–685. doi:10.1128/MMBR.68.4.669-685.2004. PMC 539003. PMID 15590779.

- Junca H. (2010). "Metabolic networks, microbial ecology and 'omics' technologies: towards understanding in situ biodegradation processes.". *Environmental Microbiology* **12** (12): 3089-30104. doi:10.1111/j.1462-2920.2010.02340.x. PMID 20860734.

- Keller, M.; Sengler, K. (2004). "Tapping into microbial diversity". *Nature Reviews Microbiology* **2** (2): 141–150. doi:10.1038/nrmicro819. PMID 15040261.

- Riesenfeld, C. S.; Schloss, PD; Handelsman, J (2004). "Metagenomics: genomic analysis of microbial communities". *Annu Rev Genet* **38**: 525–52. doi:10.1146/annurev.genet.38.072902.091216. PMID 15568985.

- Rodriguez Valera, F. (2002). "Approaches to prokaryotic biodiversity: a population genetics perspective". *Environmental Microbiology* **4** (11): 628–33. doi:10.1046/j.1462-2920.2002.00354.x. PMID 12460270.

- Rodriguez-Valera F (2004). "Environmental genomics, the big picture?.". *FEMS Microbiology Letters* **231** (2): 153–158. doi:10.1016/S0378-1097(04)00006-0. PMID 15027428.

- Torsvik, V.; Ovreas, L. (2002). "Microbial diversity and function in soil: from genes to ecosystems". *Current opinion in Microbiology* **5** (3): 240–5. doi:10.1016/S1369-5274(02)00324-7. PMID 12057676.

- Whitaker, R. J.; Banfield, J. F. (2006). "Population genomics in natural microbial communities". *Trends in Ecology & Evolution* **21**: 508–16. doi:10.1016/j.tree.2006.07.001.

- Worden, A. Z.; Cuvelier, ML; Bartlett, DH (2006). "In-depth analyses of marine microbial community genomics". *Trends in Microbiology* **14** (8): 331–6. doi:10.1016/j.tim.2006.06.008. PMID 16820296.
- Xu, J. P. (2006). "Microbial ecology in the age of genomics and metagenomics: concepts, tools, and recent advances". *Molecular Ecology* **15** (7): 1713–31. doi:10.1111/j.1365-294X.2006.02882.x. PMID 16689892.

Methods

- Beja, O.; Suzuki, MT; Koonin, EV; Aravind, L; Hadd, A; Nguyen, LP; Villacorta, R; Amjadi, M et al. (2000). "Construction and analysis of bacterial artificial chromosome libraries from a marine microbial assemblage". *Environmental Microbiology* **2** (5): 516–29. doi:10.1046/j.1462-2920.2000.00133.x. PMID 11233160.
- Sebat, J. L.; Colwell, FS; Crawford, RL (2003). "Metagenomic profiling: Microarray analysis of an environmental genomic library". *Applied and Environmental Microbiology* **69** (8): 4927–34. doi:10.1128/AEM.69.8.4927-4934.2003. PMC 169101. PMID 12902288.
- Suzuki, M. T.; Preston, CM; Béjà, O; De La Torre, JR; Steward, GF; Delong, EF (2004). "Phylogenetic screening of ribosomal RNA gene-containing clones in bacterial artificial chromosome (BAC) libraries from different depths in Monterey Bay". *Microbial Ecology* **48** (4): 473–88. doi:10.1007/s00248-004-0213-5. PMID 15696381.
- Zhu, W.; Lomsadze, A.; Borodovsky, M. (2010). "Ab initio gene identification in metagenomic sequences". *Nucleic Acids Research* **38** (12): e132. doi:10.1093/nar/gkq275.

Bioinformatics

- Krause, L.; Diaz, N. N.; Goesmann, A.; Kelley, S.; Nattkemper, T. W.; Rohwer, F.; Edwards, R. A.; Stoye, J. (2008). "Phylogenetic classification of short environmental DNA fragments". *Nucleic Acids Research* **36** (7): 2230–9. doi:10.1093/nar/gkn038. PMC 2367736. PMID 18285365.
- Huson, D. H.; Auch, A. F.; Qi, J.; Schuster, S. C. (2007). "MEGAN analysis of metagenomic data". *Genome Research* **17** (3): 377–86. doi:10.1101/gr.5969107. PMC 1800929. PMID 17255551.
- Krause L, Diaz NN, Bartels D, *et al.* (July 2006). "Finding novel genes in bacterial communities isolated from the environment" (http://bioinformatics.oxfordjournals.org/cgi/pmidlookup?view=long&pmid=16873483). *Bioinformatics* **22** (14): e281–9. doi:10.1093/bioinformatics/btl247. PMID 16873483.
- Rodriguez-Brito B, Rohwer F, Edwards RA (2006). "An application of statistics to comparative metagenomics" (http://www.biomedcentral.com/1471-2105/7/162). *BMC Bioinformatics* **7**: 162. doi:10.1186/1471-2105-7-162. PMC 1473205. PMID 16549025.
- Raes J, Foerstner KU, Bork P (October 2007). "Get the most out of your metagenome: computational analysis of environmental sequence data" (http://linkinghub.elsevier.com/retrieve/pii/S1369-5274(07)00123-3). *Curr. Opin. Microbiol.* **10** (5): 490–8. doi:10.1016/j.mib.2007.09.001. PMID 17936679.
- Harrington ED, Singh AH, Doerks T, *et al.* (August 2007). "Quantitative assessment of protein function prediction from metagenomics shotgun sequences" (http://www.pnas.org/cgi/pmidlookup?view=long&pmid=17717083). *Proc. Natl. Acad. Sci. U.S.A.* **104** (35): 13913–8. Bibcode 2007PNAS..10413913H. doi:10.1073/pnas.0702636104. PMC 1955820. PMID 17717083.
- Tress, ML; Cozzetto, D; Tramontano, A; Valencia, A (2006). "An analysis of the Sargasso Sea resource and the consequences for database composition.". *BMC bioinformatics* **7**: 213. doi:10.1186/1471-2105-7-213. PMC 1513258. PMID 16623953.
- Foerstner KU, von Mering C, Hooper SD, Bork P (2005). "Environments shape the nucleotide composition of genomes". *EMBO Rep.* **6** (12): 1208–13. doi:10.1038/sj.embor.7400538. PMC 1369203. PMID 16200051.
- Raes, J; Korbel, JO; Lercher, MJ; Von Mering, C; Bork, P (2007). "Prediction of effective genome size in metagenomic samples.". *Genome biology* **8** (1): R10. doi:10.1186/gb-2007-8-1-r10. PMC 1839125. PMID 17224063.
- Von Mering, C; Hugenholtz, P; Raes, J; Tringe, SG; Doerks, T; Jensen, LJ; Ward, N; Bork, P (2007). "Quantitative phylogenetic assessment of microbial communities in diverse environments.". *Science* **315** (5815):

1126–30. Bibcode 2007Sci...315.1126V. doi:10.1126/science.1133420. PMID 17272687.

- Mavromatis K, Ivanova N, Barry K, *et al.* (June 2007). "Use of simulated data sets to evaluate the fidelity of metagenomic processing methods". *Nat. Methods* **4** (6): 495–500. doi:10.1038/nmeth1043. PMID 17468765.

- Markowitz VM, Ivanova N, Palaniappan K, *et al.* (July 2006). "An experimental metagenome data management and analysis system" (http://bioinformatics.oxfordjournals.org/cgi/pmidlookup?view=long& pmid=16873494). *Bioinformatics* **22** (14): e359–67. doi:10.1093/bioinformatics/btl217. PMID 16873494.

- Markowitz, VM; Ivanova, NN; Szeto, E; Palaniappan, K; Chu, K; Dalevi, D; Chen, IM; Grechkin, Y et al. (2008). "IMG/M: a data management and analysis system for metagenomes.". *Nucleic Acids Research* **36** (Database issue): D534–8. doi:10.1093/nar/gkm869. PMC 2238950. PMID 17932063.

- Pushker, R.; D'Auria, G.; Alba-Casado, J.C.; Rodríguez-Valera, F. (2005). "Micro-Mar: a database for dynamic representation of marine microbial biodiversity" (http://www.biomedcentral.com/1471-2105/6/222). *BMC Bioinformatics* **6**: 222. doi:10.1186/1471-2105-6-222.

- Meyer, F; Paarmann, D; D'souza, M; Olson, R; Glass, EM; Kubal, M; Paczian, T; Rodriguez, A et al. (2008). "The metagenomics RAST server - a public resource for the automatic phylogenetic and functional analysis of metagenomes.". *BMC bioinformatics* **9**: 386. doi:10.1186/1471-2105-9-386. PMC 2563014. PMID 18803844.

- Hingamp P, Brochier C, Talla E, Gautheret D, Thieffry D, Herrmann Carl (2008). "Metagenome Annotation Using a Distributed Grid of Undergraduate Students" (http://biology.plosjournals.org/perlserv/ ?request=get-document&doi=10.1371/journal.pbio.0060296). *PLoS Biol* **6** (11): e296. doi:10.1371/journal.pbio.0060296.

- Sun, Y.; Cai, Y.; Liu, L.; Yu, F.; Farrell, M. L.; McKendree, W.; Farmerie, W. (2009). "ESPRIT: estimating species richness using large collections of 16S rRNA pyrosequences". *Nucleic Acids Research* **37** (10): e76. doi:10.1093/nar/gkp285. PMC 2691849. PMID 19417062.

Marine ecosystems

- Angly, F. E.; Felts, Ben; Breitbart, Mya; Salamon, Peter; Edwards, Robert A.; Carlson, Craig; Chan, Amy M.; Haynes, Matthew et al. (2006). "The marine viromes of four oceanic regions" (http://biology.plosjournals.org/ perlserv/?request=get-document&doi=10.1371/journal.pbio.0040368). *PLoS Biology* **4**: 2121–31. doi:10.1371/journal.pbio.0040368.

- Beja, O.; Aravind, L; Koonin, EV; Suzuki, MT; Hadd, A; Nguyen, LP; Jovanovich, SB; Gates, CM et al. (2000). "Bacterial rhodopsin: Evidence for a new type of phototrophy in the sea". *Science* **289** (5486): 1902–6. Bibcode 2000Sci...289.1902B. doi:10.1126/science.289.5486.1902. PMID 10988064.

- Beja, O.; Spudich, EN; Spudich, JL; Leclerc, M; Delong, EF (2001). "Proteorhodopsin phototrophy in the ocean". *Nature* **411** (6839): 786–9. doi:10.1038/35081051. PMID 11459054.

- Beja, O.; Suzuki, MT; Heidelberg, JF; Nelson, WC; Preston, CM; Hamada, T; Eisen, JA; Fraser, CM et al. (2002). "Unsuspected diversity among marine aerobic anoxygenic phototrophs". *Nature* **415** (6872): 630–3. doi:10.1038/415630a. PMID 11832943.

- Culley, A. I.; Lang, AS; Suttle, CA (2006). "Metagenomic analysis of coastal RNA virus communities". *Science* **312** (5781): 1795–8. Bibcode 2006Sci...312.1795C. doi:10.1126/science.1127404. PMID 16794078.

- DeLong, E. F.; Preston, CM; Mincer, T; Rich, V; Hallam, SJ; Frigaard, NU; Martinez, A; Sullivan, MB et al. (2006). "Community genomics among stratified microbial assemblages in the ocean's interior". *Science* **311** (5760): 496–503. Bibcode 2006Sci...311..496D. doi:10.1126/science.1120250. PMID 16439655.

- Hallam, S. J.; Konstantinidis, KT; Putnam, N; Schleper, C; Watanabe, Y; Sugahara, J; Preston, C; De La Torre, J et al. (2006). "Genomic analysis of the uncultivated marine crenarchaeote Cenarchaeum symbiosum". *Proceedings of the National Academy of Sciences of the United States of America* **103** (48): 18296–301. Bibcode 2006PNAS..10318296H. doi:10.1073/pnas.0608549103. PMC 1643844. PMID 17114289.

- John, D. E.; Wawrik, B; Tabita, FR; Paul, JH (2006). "Gene diversity and organization in rbcL-containing genome fragments from uncultivated *Synechococcus* in the Gulf of Mexico". *Marine Ecology-Progress Series*

316: 23–33. doi:10.3354/meps316023.

- Kannan, Natarajan; Taylor, Susan S.; Zhai, Yufeng; Venter, J. Craig; Manning, Gerard (2007). "Structural and Functional Diversity of the Microbial Kinome". *PLoS Biology* **5**: 467–478. doi:10.1371/journal.pbio.0050017. PMC 1821047. PMID 17355172.
- Rusch, Douglas B.; Halpern, Aaron L.; Sutton, Granger; Heidelberg, Karla B.; Williamson, Shannon; Yooseph, Shibu; Wu, Dongying; Eisen, Jonathan A. et al. (2007). "The Sorcerer II Global Ocean Sampling Expedition: Northwest Atlantic through Eastern Tropical Pacific". *PLoS Biology* **5**: 398–431. doi:10.1371/journal.pbio.0050077. PMC 1821060. PMID 17355176.
- Tringe SG, von Mering C, Kobayashi A, *et al.* (April 2005). "Comparative metagenomics of microbial communities" (http://www.sciencemag.org/cgi/pmidlookup?view=long&pmid=15845853). *Science* **308** (5721): 554–7. Bibcode 2005Sci...308..554T. doi:10.1126/science.1107851. PMID 15845853.
- Woyke, T.; Teeling, H; Ivanova, NN; Huntemann, M; Richter, M; Gloeckner, FO; Boffelli, D; Anderson, IJ et al. (2006). "Symbiosis insights through metagenomic analysis of a microbial consortium". *Nature* **443** (7114): 950–5. Bibcode 2006Natur.443..950W. doi:10.1038/nature05192. PMID 16980956.
- Yooseph, Shibu; Sutton, Granger; Rusch, Douglas B.; Halpern, Aaron L.; Williamson, Shannon J.; Remington, Karin; Eisen, Jonathan A.; Heidelberg, Karla B. et al. (2007). "The Sorcerer II Global Ocean Sampling Expedition: Expanding the Universe of Protein Families". *PLoS Biology* **5**: 432–466. doi:10.1371/journal.pbio.0050016. PMC 1821046. PMID 17355171.
- Yutin, N.; Beja, O. (2005). "Putative novel photosynthetic reaction centre organizations in marine aerobic anoxygenic photosynthetic bacteria: insights from metagenomics and environmental genomics". *Environmental Microbiology* **7** (12): 2027–33. doi:10.1111/j.1462-2920.2005.00843.x. PMID 16309398.
- Mussmann, M; Richter, M; Lombardot, T; Meyerdierks, A; Kuever, J; Kube, M; Glöckner, FO; Amann, R (2005). "Clustered genes related to sulfate respiration in uncultured prokaryotes support the theory of their concomitant horizontal transfer.". *Journal of bacteriology* **187** (20): 7126–37. doi:10.1128/JB.187.20.7126-7137.2005. PMC 1251608. PMID 16199583.

Sediments

- Abulencia, CB; Wyborski, DL; Garcia, JA; Podar, M; Chen, W; Chang, SH; Chang, HW; Watson, D et al. (2006). "Environmental whole-genome amplification to access microbial populations in contaminated sediments.". *Applied and Environmental Microbiology* **72** (5): 3291–3301. doi:10.1128/AEM.72.5.3291-3301.2006. PMC 1472342. PMID 16672469.
- Breitbart M, Felts B, Kelley S, Mahaffy JM, Nulton J, Salamon P, Rohwer F (2004). "Diversity and population structure of a nearshore marine sediment viral community". *Proceedings of the Royal Society B* **271** (1539): 565–574. doi:10.1098/rspb.2003.2628. PMC 1691639. PMID 15156913.

Extreme environments

- Baker, B. J.; Tyson, GW; Webb, RI; Flanagan, J; Hugenholtz, P; Allen, EE; Banfield, JF (2006). "Lineages of acidophilic archaea revealed by community genomic analysis". *Science* **314** (5807): 1933–5. Bibcode 2006Sci...314.1933B. doi:10.1126/science.1132690. PMID 17185602.
- Schoenfeld, T.; Patterson, M; Richardson, PM; Wommack, KE; Young, M; Mead, D (2008). "Assembly of Viral Metagenomes from Yellowstone Hot Springs". *AEM* **74** (13): 4166–74. doi:10.1128/AEM.02598-07. PMC 2446518. PMID 18441115.

Medical sciences and biotechnological applications

- Arumugam M, Raes J, Peletier E, Le Paslier D, Yamada T, Mende DR, Fernandes GR, Tap J *et al.* (2011). "Enterotypes of the human gut microbiome" (http://www.nature.com/nature/journal/vaop/ncurrent/full/ nature09944.html). *Nature* **473** (7346): 174–80. Bibcode 2011Natur.473..174.. doi:10.1038/nature09944. PMID 21508958.
- Breitbart M, Hewson I, Felts B, Mahaffy JM, Nulton J, Salamon P, Rohwer F (2003). "Metagenomic analyses of an uncultured viral community from human feces". *Journal of Bacteriology* **185** (20): 6220–6223. doi:10.1128/JB.185.20.6220-6223.2003. PMC 225035. PMID 14526037.
- Schloss, P. D.; Handelsman, J. (2003). "Biotechnological prospects from metagenomics". *Current Opinion in Biotechnology* **14** (3): 303–310. doi:10.1016/S0958-1669(03)00067-3. PMID 12849784.
- Brennerova, M; Josefiova, J; Brenner, V; Pieper, DH; Junca, H (2010). "Metagenomics reveals diversity and abundance of meta-cleavage pathways in microbial communities from soil highly contaminated with jet fuel under air-sparging bioremediation.". *Environmental Microbiology* **11** (9): 2216–2227. doi:10.1111/j.1462-2920.2009.01943.x. PMC 2784041. PMID 19575758.
- Breitbart, M.; Rohwer, F. (2005). "Method for discovering novel DNA viruses in blood using viral particle selection and shotgun sequencing". *BioTechniques* **39** (5): 729–736. doi:10.2144/000112019. PMID 16312220.
- Mathur, E.; Toledo, G.; Green, B. D.; Podar, M.; Richardson, T. H.; Kulwiec, Michael; Chang, Hwai W. (2005). "A biodiversity-based approach to development of performance enzymes: Applied metagenomics and directed evolution". *Industrial Biotechnology* **1**: 283–287. doi:10.1089/ind.2005.1.283.
- Zengler, Karsten; Paradkar, Ashish; Keller, Martin (2005). *New Methods to Access Microbial Diversity for Small Molecule Discovery*. pp. 275–293. doi:10.1007/978-1-59259-976-9_12.
- Zhang, T.; Breitbart, M.; Lee, W.H.; Run, J.Q.; Wei, C.L.; Soh, S.W.; Hibberd, M.L.; Liu, E.T. et al. (2006). "RNA viral community in human feces: prevalence of plant pathogenic viruses". *PLoS biology* **4** (1): e3. doi:10.1371/journal.pbio.0040003. PMC 1310650. PMID 16336043.
- Gill, S. R.; Pop, M; Deboy, RT; Eckburg, PB; Turnbaugh, PJ; Samuel, BS; Gordon, JI; Relman, DA et al. (2006). "Metagenomic analysis of the human distal gut microbiome". *Science* **312** (5778): 1355–1359. Bibcode 2006Sci...312.1355G. doi:10.1126/science.1124234. PMID 16741115.
- Kurokawa, K.; Itoh, T; Kuwahara, T; Oshima, K; Toh, H; Toyoda, A; Takami, H; Morita, H et al. (2007). "Comparative metagenomics revealed commonly enriched gene sets in human gut microbiomes". *DNA Res.* **14** (4): 169–181. doi:10.1093/dnares/dsm018. PMC 2533590. PMID 17916580.

Ancient DNA

- Poinar, H. N.; Schwarz, C.; Qi, Ji; Shapiro, B.; MacPhee, R. D. E.; Buigues, B.; Tikhonov, A.; Huson, D. H. et al. (2006). "Metagenomics to Paleogenomics: Large-Scale Sequencing of Mammoth DNA" (http://www.sciencemag.org/cgi/content/abstract/1123360v1?maxtoshow=&HITS=10&hits=10&RESULTFORMAT=& fulltext=wooly+mammoth&searchid=1135358119618_7589&FIRSTINDEX=0&journalcode=sci). *Science* **311** (5759): 392–394. Bibcode 2006Sci...311..392P. doi:10.1126/science.1123360. PMID 16368896.

External links

- Wooley JC, Godzik A, Friedberg I (2010). "A primer on metagenomics" (http://dx.plos.org/10.1371/journal. pcbi.1000667). *PLoS Comput. Biol.* **6** (2): e1000667. Bibcode 2010PLSCB...610006W. doi:10.1371/journal.pcbi.1000667. PMC 2829047. PMID 20195499.
- MEGAN (http://www-ab.informatik.uni-tuebingen.de/software/megan/) MEtaGenome ANalyzer. A stand-alone metagenome analysis tool.
- Metagenomics and Our Microbial Planet (http://dels.nas.edu/metagenomics/) A website on metagenomics and the vital role of microbes on Earth from the National Academies. (http://nationalacademies.org)
- The New Science of Metagenomics: Revealing the Secrets of Our Microbial Planet (http://books.nap.edu/ catalog.php?record_id=11902) A report released by the National Research Council in March 2007. Also, see the Report In Brief. (http://dels.nas.edu/dels/rpt_briefs/metagenomics_brief_final.pdf)
- IMG/M (http://img.jgi.doe.gov/m) The Integrated Microbial Genomes system, for metagenome analysis by the DOE-JGI.
- CAMERA (http://camera.calit2.net/index.php) Cyberinfrastructure for Metagenomics, data repository and tools for metagenomics research.
- A good overview of metagenomics from the Science Creative Quarterly (http://www.scq.ubc.ca/?p=509)
- list of Metagenome Projects from genomesonline.org (http://www.genomesonline.org/gold. cgi?want=Metagenomes)
- MG-RAST (http://metagenomics.nmpdr.org) publicly available, free, metagenomics annotation pipeline and repository for pyrosequences, Sanger sequences, and other sequence approaches.
- METAREP (http://www.jcvi.org/metarep): JCVI Metagenomics Reports - an open source (http://github.com/ jcvi/METAREP) tool for high-performance comparative metagenomics
- Human microbiome project
- MetaHIT (http://www.metahit.eu/) official website for the EU-funded project : Metagenomics of the Human Intestinal Tract
- Annotathon (http://annotathon.univ-mrs.fr/) Bioinformatics Training Through Metagenomic Sequence Annotation
- Metagenomics (http://www.highveld.com/pages/metagenomics.html) Metagenomics research and applications.
- Metagenomics: Sequences from the Environment (http://www.ncbi.nlm.nih.gov/books/NBK6858) free ebook from NCBI Bookshelf.

Metallome

The term **metallome** has been introduced by R.J.P. Williams by analogy with proteome as distribution of free metal ions in every one of cellular compartments. Subsequently, the term **metallomics** has been coined as the study of metallome. Szpunar (2005) defined metallomics as "comprehensive analysis of the entirety of metal and metalloid species within a cell or tissue type". Therefore, metallomics can be considered a branch of metabolomics, even though the metals are not typically considered as metabolites.

Hiroki Haraguchi gave an alternative definition of "metallomes" as metalloproteins or any other metal-containing biomolecules, and "metallomics" as a study of such biomolecules. In the study of metallomes the transcriptome, proteome and the metabolome will constitute the whole metallome. A study of the metallome is done to arrive at the metallointeractome

The metallotranscriptome (word introduced by Shanker et al 2009) by can be ideally defined as the map of the entire transcriptome in the presence of biologically or environmentally relevant concentrations of an essential or toxic metal, respectively metallometabolome would constitute the complete pool of small metabolites in a cell at any given time and this would give rise to the whole metallointeractome and knowledge of this would be of paramount importance in comparative metallomics dealing with toxicity and drug discovery. (Shanker et al 2009)

External links

* Metallomics, the journal covering the research fields related to biometals [1]

References

* Mounicou, S., Szpunar, J. and Lobinski, R. (2009). "Metallomics: the concept and methodology". *Chemical Society Reviews* **38** (4): 1119–1138. doi:10.1039/b713633c. PMID 19421584.
* Williams, R.J.P. (2001). "Chemical selection of elements by cells". *Coordination Chemistry Reviews* **216–217**: 583–595.
* Szpunar, J. (2005). "Advances in analytical methodology for bioinorganic speciation analysis: metallomics, metalloproteomics and heteroatom-tagged proteomics and metabolomics". *The Analyst* **130** (4): 442–465. doi:10.1039/b418265k. PMID 15776152.
* Haraguchi, H. (2004). "Metallomics as integrated biometal science". *Journal of Analytical Atomic Spectrometry* **19**: 5–14. doi:10.1039/b308213j.
* Wackett, L.P., Dodge, A.G. and Ellis, L.B.M. (2004). "Microbial genomics and the periodic table". *Applied and Environmental Microbiology* **70** (2): 647–655. doi:10.1128/AEM.70.2.647-655.2004. PMC 348800. PMID 14766537.
* Shanker, A.K., Djanaguiraman, M. and Venkateswarlu, B. (2009). "Chromium interactions in plants: current status and future strategiesw". *Metallomics* **1** (5): 375–383. doi:10.1039/b904571f.

References

[1] http://www.rsc.org/metallomics/

MicrobesOnline

The **MicrobesOnline** website is a resource for comparative and functional genomics that serves the scientific community for the analysis of microbial genes and genomes. The website, created by the Virtual Institute for Microbial Stress and Survival (VIMSS) a Department of Energy Genomics: GTL project was originally developed to aid analysis of the Environmental Stress Pathway Project (ESPP) but has been open to the public since 2003 due to is broader utility to the scientific community.

MicrobesOnline offers:

- Homologs, PDBs, domains & families, metabolic maps and operon predictions
- Tree-based browser with pre-computed phylogenies for all gene families
- Build your own sequence alignments and phylogenetic trees from "Gene Carts"
- Microarray data: up-regulated genes and operons, and overlays on metabolism

External links

- MicrobesOnline home page [1] reference:

The MicrobesOnline Web site for comparative genomics [2]

- IMG home page [1] reference: Nucleic Acids Research, 2006, Vol. 34, Database issue D344-D348 [5]

References

[1] http://microbesonline.org
[2] http://www.genome.org/cgi/content/abstract/15/7/1015

MicroRNA and microRNA target database

This **microRNA database and microRNA targets database** is a compilation of databases and web portals and servers used for microRNAs and their targets. MicroRNAs (miRNAs) represent an important class of small non-coding RNAs (ncRNAs) that regulate gene expression by targeting messenger RNAs[1] .

microRNA target gene databases

Name	Description	type	Link	References
targetScan	targetScan is Search for predicted microRNA targets in animals	database,webserver	website [2]	[3]
StarBase	starBase is a database for exploring **microRNA-target** interaction maps from **Argonaute (Ago)** CLIP-Seq (HITS-CLIP) and degradome sequencing (Degradome-Seq, PARE) data.	database	website [4]	[5]
TarBase	A comprehensive database of experimentally supported animal microRNA targets	database	website [6]	[7]
Diana-microT	DIANA-microT 3.0 is an algorithm based on several parameters calculated individually for each microRNA and it combines conserved and non-conserved microRNA recognition elements into a final prediction score.	webserver	webserver [8]	[9]

miRecords	an integrated resource for microRNA-target interactions.	database	website [10]	[11]
PicTar	PicTar is Combinatorial microRNA target predictions.	database,webserver,predictions	website [12]	[13]
PITA	PITA, incorporates the role of target-site accessibility, as determined by base-pairing interactions within the mRNA, in microRNA target recognition.	webserver,predictions	predictions [14]	[15]
RepTar	A database of inverse miRNA target predictions, based on the RepTar algorithm that is independent of evolutionary conservation considerations and is not limited to seed pairing sites.	database	website [16]	[17]
RNA22	First finds putative microRNA binding sites in the sequence of interest, then identifies the targeted microRNA.	webserver,predictions	webserver [18]	[19]
.				

microRNA database

Name	Description	type	Link	References
miRBase	miRBase database is a searchable database of published miRNA sequences and annotation.	database	website [20]	[21]
deepBase	deepBase is a database for annotating and discovering small and long ncRNAs (microRNAs, siRNAs, piRNAs...) from high-throughput deep sequencing data.	database	website [22]	[23]
microRNA.org	microRNA.org is a ddatabase for Experimentally observed microRNA expression patterns and predicted microRNA targets & target downregulation scores.	database	website [24]	[25]
miRGen 2.0	miRGen 2.0: a database of microRNA genomic information and regulation	database	website [26]	[27]
miRNAMap	miRNAMap: genomic maps of microRNA genes and their target genes in mammalian genomes	database	website [28]	[29]
PMRD	PMRD: plant microRNA database	database	website [30]	[31]
.				

References

[1] Bartel, D. P. (2009). "MicroRNAs: target recognition and regulatory functions". *Cell* **136** (2): 215–233. doi:10.1016/j.cell.2009.01.002. PMID 19167326.

[2] http://www.targetscan.org/

[3] Lewis BP, Burge CB, Bartel DP. (2005). "Conserved seed pairing, often flanked by adenosines, indicates that thousands of human genes are microRNA targets.". *Cell* **120** (1): 15–20. doi:10.1016/j.cell.2004.12.035. PMID 15652477.

[4] http://starbase.sysu.edu.cn/

[5] Yang JH, Li JH, Shao P, Zhou H, Chen YQ, Qu LH. (2011). "starBase: a database for exploring microRNA–mRNA interaction maps from Argonaute CLIP-Seq and Degradome-Seq data.". *Nucl. Acids Res.* **39** (Database issue): 1–8. doi:10.1093/nar/gkq1056. PMC 3013664. PMID 21037263.

[6] http://diana.cslab.ece.ntua.gr/tarbase/

[7] Sethupathy P, Corda B, Hatzigeorgiou AG. (2006). "TarBase: A comprehensive database of experimentally supported animal microRNA targets.". *RNA.* **12** (2): 192–197. doi:10.1261/rna.2239606. PMID 16373484.

[8] http://diana.cslab.ece.ntua.gr/microT/

[9] Maragkakis M, Alexiou P, Papadopoulos GL, Reczko M, Dalamagas T, Giannopoulos G, Goumas G, Koukis E, Kourtis K, Simossis VA, Sethupathy P, Vergoulis T, Koziris N, Sellis T, Tsanakas P, Hatzigeorgiou AG (2009). "Accurate microRNA target prediction correlates with protein repression levels.". *BMC Bioinformatics* **10**: 295. doi:10.1186/1471-2105-10-295. PMC 2752464. PMID 19765283.

[10] http://mirecords.biolead.org/

[11] Xiao F, Zuo Z, Cai G, Kang S, Gao X, Li T. (2009). "miRecords: an integrated resource for microRNA-target interactions.". *Nucl. Acids Res.* **37** (Database issue): D105-110. doi:10.1093/nar/gkn851. PMID 18996891.

[12] http://pictar.bio.nyu.edu

[13] Krek A, Grün D, Poy MN, Wolf R, Rosenberg L, Epstein EJ, MacMenamin P, da Piedade I, Gunsalus KC, Stoffel M, Rajewsky N (2005). "Combinatorial microRNA target predictions.". *Nat Genet* **37** (5): 495–500. doi:10.1038/ng1536. PMID 15806104.

[14] http://genie.weizmann.ac.il/pubs/mir07/mir07_data.html

[15] Kertesz M, Iovino N, Unnerstall U, Gaul U, Segal E (2007). "The role of site accessibility in microRNA target recognition.". *Nat Genet* **39** (10): 1278–84. doi:10.1038/ng2135. PMID 17893677.

[16] http://reptar.ekmd.huji.ac.il/

[17] Elefant, Naama; Berger Amnon, Shein Harel, Hofree Matan, Margalit Hanah, Altuvia Yael (Jan 2011). "RepTar: a database of predicted cellular targets of host and viral miRNAs" (in eng). *Nucleic Acids Res.* (England) **39** (Database issue): D188-94. doi:10.1093/nar/gkq1233. PMC 3013742. PMID 21149264.

[18] http://cbcsrv.watson.ibm.com/rna22.html

[19] Miranda KC, Huynh T, Tay Y, Ang YS, Tam WL, Thomson AM, Lim B, Rigoutsos I (2006). "A pattern-based method for the identification of MicroRNA binding sites and their corresponding heteroduplexes.". *Cell* **126** (6): 1203–17. doi:10.1016/j.cell.2006.07.031. PMID 16990141.

[20] http://www.mirbase.org/

[21] Griffiths-Jones S, Saini HK, van Dongen S, Enright AJ. (2008). "miRBase: tools for microRNA genomics.". *Nucl. Acids Res.* **36**: D154-D158. doi:10.1093/nar/gkm952. PMC 2238936. PMID 17991681.

[22] http://deepbase.sysu.edu.cn/

[23] Yang JH, Shao P, Zhou H, Chen YQ, Qu LH. (2010). "deepBase: a database for deeply annotating and mining deep sequencing data.". *Nucl. Acids Res.* **38** (Database issue): D123-130. doi:10.1093/nar/gkp943. PMC 2808990. PMID 19966272.

[24] http://www.microrna.org/microrna/getExprForm.do

[25] Betel D, Wilson M, Gabow A, Marks DS, Sander C. (2007). "The microRNA.org resource: targets and expression.". *Nucl. Acids Res.* **36** (Database issue): D149-153. doi:10.1093/nar/gkm995. PMC 2238905. PMID 18158296.

[26] http://www.microrna.gr/mirgen/

[27] Alexiou P, Vergoulis T, Gleditzsch M, Prekas G, Dalamagas T, Megraw M, Grosse I, Sellis T, Hatzigeorgiou AG. (2010). "miRGen 2.0: a database of microRNA genomic information and regulation.". *Nucl. Acids Res.* **38** (Database issue): D137-41. doi:10.1093/nar/gkp888. PMC 2808909. PMID 19850714.

[28] http://mirnamap.mbc.nctu.edu.tw/

[29] Hsu PW, Huang HD, Hsu SD, Lin LZ, Tsou AP, Tseng CP, Stadler PF, Washietl S, Hofacker IL. (2006). "miRNAMap: genomic maps of microRNA genes and their target genes in mammalian genomes.". *Nucl. Acids Res.* **34** (Database issue): D135-139. doi:10.1093/nar/gkj135. PMC 1347497. PMID 16381831.

[30] http://bioinformatics.cau.edu.cn/PMRD/

[31] Zhang Z, Yu J, Li D, Zhang Z, Liu F, Zhou X, Wang T, Ling Y, Su Z. (2010). "PMRD: plant microRNA database.". *Nucl. Acids Res.* **38** (Database issue): D806-813. doi:10.1093/nar/gkp818. PMC 2808885. PMID 19808935.

Further reading

- Lee, RC; Ambros V (2001). "An extensive class of small RNAs in Caenorhabditis elegans". *Science* **294** (5543): 862–864. doi:10.1126/science.1065329. PMID 11679672.
- Ambros, V (2001). "microRNAs: tiny regulators with great potential". *Cell* **107** (7): 823–826. doi:10.1016/S0092-8674(01)00616-X. PMID 11779458.

External links

- miRBase database (http://www.mirbase.org/)
- deepBase database (http://deepbase.sysu.edu.cn/)
- targetScan (http://www.targetscan.org/)
- starBase database (http://starbase.sysu.edu.cn/)
- picTar (http://pictar.bio.nyu.edu)
- miRecords database (http://mirecords.biolead.org/)

- TarBase database (http://diana.cslab.ece.ntua.gr/tarbase/)

Minimotif Miner

Minimotif Miner is a program and database designed to identify minimotifs in any protein.[1] [2] Minimotifs are short contiguous peptide sequences that are known to have a function in at least one protein. Minimotifs are also called sequence motifs or short linear motifs or SLiMs. These are generally restricted to one secondary structure element and are less than 15 amino acids in length. Functions can be binding motifs that bind another macromolecule or small compound, that induce a covalent modification of minimotif, or are involved in protein trafficking of the protein containing the minimotif. The basic premise of Minimotif Miner is that is a short peptide sequence is known to have a function in one protein, may have a similar function in another query protein. The current release of the MnM database has ~5300 minimotifs and can be searched at the website.

There are two workflows that are of interest to scientists that use Minimotif Miner 1) Entering any query protein into Minimotif Miner returns a table with a list of minimotif sequence and functions that have a sequence pattern match with the protein query sequence. These provide potential new functions in the protein query. 2) By using the view Single Nucleotide Polymorphism (SNP) function, SNPs from dbSNP are mapped in the sequence window. A user can select any set of the SNPs and then identify any minimotif that is introduced or eliminated by the SNP or mutation. This helps to identify minimotifs involved in generating organism diversity or those that may be associated with a disease.

External links

- MinimotifMiner.org [3] (does not work)
- Minimotif Miner query engine [4]

References

[1] Schiller, Martin R. (2007). "Minimotif Miner: A Computational Tool to Investigate Protein Function, Disease, and Genetic Diversity". *Current Protocols in Protein Science* **48**: 2.12.1–2.12.14. doi:10.1002/0471140864.ps0212s48. ISBN 0471140864. PMID 18429315.

[2] Rajasekaran, Sanguthevar; Balla, Sudha; Gradie, Patrick; Gryk, Michael R.; Kadaveru, Krishna; Kundeti, Vamsi; MacIejewski, Mark W.; Mi, Tian et al. (2009). "Minimotif miner 2nd release: a database and web system for motif search". *Nucleic Acids Research* **37** (Database issue): D185–90. doi:10.1093/nar/gkn865. PMC 2686579. PMID 18978024.

[3] http://www.minimotifminer.org/

[4] http://bio-toolkit.com/MnMQueryEngine/project

Further reading

- Vyas, Jay; Nowling, Ronald J.; MacIejewski, Mark W.; Rajasekaran, Sanguthevar; Gryk, Michael R.; Schiller, Martin R. (2009). "A proposed syntax for Minimotif Semantics, version 1". *BMC Genomics* **10**: 360. doi:10.1186/1471-2164-10-360. PMC 2733157. PMID 19656396.
- Vyas, Jay; Nowling, Ronald J.; Meusburger, Thomas; Sargeant, David; Kadaveru, Krishna; Gryk, Michael R.; Kundeti, Vamsi; Rajasekaran, Sanguthevar et al. (2010). "MimoSA: a system for minimotif annotation". *BMC Bioinformatics* **11**: 328. doi:10.1186/1471-2105-11-328. PMC 2905367. PMID 20565705.
- Kadaveru, Krishna; Vyas, Jay; Schiller, Martin R. (2008). "Viral infection and human disease - insights from minimotifs". *Frontiers in Bioscience* **13**: 6455–71. PMC 2628544. PMID 18508672.

Minimum Information Standards

Minimum Information (MI) standards or reporting guidelines specify the minimum amount of meta data (information) and data required to meet a specific aim or aims. Usually the aim is to provide enough meta data and data to enable the unambiguous reproduction and interpretation of an experiment. MI guidelines are normally informal human readable specifications that inform the development of formal data models (e.g. XML or UML), data exchange formats (e.g. FuGE [1], MAGE-ML, MAGE-TAB) or knowledge models such as an ontology (e.g. OBI, MGED-Ontology).

MI standards are developed by working bodies of practitioners working in a particular scientific domain. The MI standards listed below are all from the life sciences, largely driven by the development of high throughput experimental technologies.

These MI standards groups have been brought together in 2007 to form the "Minimum Information about a Biomedical or Biological Investigation" (MIBBI) umbrella community. More information about the MIBBI initiative and the MIBBI Foundry can be found below and on the MIBBI homepage [2]

MI Standards

MIAME, gene expression microarray

Minimum Information About a Microarray Experiment (MIAME) describes the Minimum Information About a Microarray Experiment that is needed to enable the interpretation of the results of the experiment unambiguously and potentially to reproduce the experiment and is aimed at facilitating the dissemination of data from microarray experiments.

MIAME contains a number of extensions to cover specific biological domains

MINI: Minimum Information about a Neuroscience Investigation

MINI: Electrophysiology

Electrophysiology is a technology used to study the electrical properties of biological cells and tissues. Electrophysiology typically involves the measurements of voltage change or electrical current flow on a wide variety of scales from single ion channel proteins to whole tissues. This document is a single module, as part of the Minimum Information about a Neuroscience investigation (MINI) family of reporting guideline documents, produced by community consultation and continually available for public comment. A MINI module represents the minimum information that should be reported about a dataset to facilitate computational access and analysis to allow a reader to interpret and critically evaluate the processes performed and the conclusions reached, and to support their experimental corroboration. In practice a MINI module comprises a checklist of information that should be provided (for example about the protocols employed) when a data set is described for publication. The full specification of the MINI module can be found here.[3]

MIARE, RNAi experiment

Minimum Information About an RNAi Experiment (MIARE) is a data reporting guideline which describes the minimum information that should be reported about an RNAi experiment to enable the unambiguous interpretation and reproduction of the results.

MIACA, cell based assay

Advances in genomics and functional genomics have enabled large-scale analyses of gene and protein function by means of high-throughput cell biological analyses. Thereby, cells in culture can be perturbed in vitro and the induced effects recorded and analyzed. Perturbations can be triggered in several ways, for instance with molecules (siRNAs, expression constructs, small chemical compounds, ligands for receptors, etc.), through environmental stresses (such as temperature shift, serum starvation, oxygen deprivation, etc.), or combinations thereof. The cellular responses to such perturbations are analyzed in order to identify molecular events in the biological processes addressed and understand biological principles. We propose the Minimum Information About a Cellular Assay (MIACA) for reporting a cellular assay, and CA-OM, the modular cellular assay object model, to facilitate exchange of data and accompanying information, and to compare and integrate data that originate from different, albeit complementary approaches, and to elucidate higher order principles. Documents describing MIACA [4] are available and provide further information as well as the checklist of terms that should be reported.

MIAPE, proteomic experiments

The Minimum Information About a Proteomic Experiment documents describe information which should be given along with a proteomic experiment. The parent document describes the processes and principles underpinning the development of a series of domain specific documents which now cover all aspects of a MS-based proteomics workflow.

MIMIx, molecular interactions

This document has been developed and maintained by the Molecular Interaction worktrack of the HUPO-PSI (www.psidev.info) and describes the Minimum Information about a Molecular Interaction experiment.

MIAPAR, protein affinity reagents

The Minimum Information About a Protein Affinity Reagent has been developed and maintained by the Molecular Interaction worktrack of the HUPO-PSI (www.psidev.info)in conjunction with the HUPO Antibody Initiative and a European consortium of binder producers and seeks to encourage users to improve their description of binding reagents, such as antibodies, used in the process of protein identification.

MIABE, bioactive entities

The Minimum Information About a Bioactive Entity was produced by representatives from both large pharma and academia who are looking to improve the description of usually small molecules which bind to, and potentially modulate the activity of, specific targets in a living organism. This document encompasses drug-like molecules as well as hebicides, pesticides and food additives. It is primarily maintained through the EMBL-EBI Industry program (www.ebi.ac.uk/industry).

MIGS/MIMS, genome/metagenome sequences

This specification is being developed by the Genomic Standards Consortium

MIFlowCyt, flow cytometry

Minimum Information about a Flow Cytometry Experiment

The fundamental tenet of any scientific research is that the published results of any study have to be open to independent validation or refutation. The Minimum Information about a Flow Cytometry Experiment (MIFlowCyt) establishes the criteria to record information about the experimental overview, samples, instrumentation and data analysis. It promotes consistent annotation of clinical, biological and technical issues surrounding a flow cytometry experiment by specifying the requirements for data content and by providing a structured framework for capturing information.

More information can be found at:

- The Flow Informatics and Computational Cytometry Society (FICCS) MIFlowCyt wiki [5] page.
- The Bioinformatics Standards for Flow Cytometry MIFlowCyt web [6] page.

MIRIAM, Minimum Information Required in the Annotation of Models

The Minimal Information Required In the Annotation of Models (MIRIAM), is a set of rules for the curation and annotation of quantitative models of biological systems.

MIASE, Minimum Information About a Simulation Experiment

The Minimum Information About a Simulation Experiment (MIASE) is an effort to standardize the description of simulation experiments in the field of systems biology.

External links

MIBBI [7] Minimum Information for Biological and Biomedical Investigations

A 'one-stop shop' for exploring the range of extant projects, foster collaborative development and ultimately promote gradual integration.

FGED Society [8]

FGED Society is an international organisation of biologists, computer scientists, and data analysts that aims to facilitate the sharing of data generated by functional genomics experiments using DNA microarray and other genome-scale technologies.

HUPO-PSI [9] HUPO Protein Standards Initiative

The HUPO Proteomics Standards Initiative (PSI) defines community standards for data representation in proteomics to facilitate data comparison, exchange and verification.

FuGE [10] Functional Genomics Experiment

FuGE provides a model of common components in functional genomics investigations. It can be extended to develop modular data formats and provides a consistent framework to capture complete lab workflows.

MSI [11] The Metabolomics Standards Initiative

MSI has be appointed by the Metabolomics Society to monitor, coordinate and review the efforts of working groups in specialist areas that will examine standardization and make recommendations.

MIACA [12], Minimum Information About a Cellular Assay

Minimum Information About a Cellular Assay (MIACA) is a data reporting guideline which describes the minimum information that should be reported about a Cellular Assay Experiment to enable the interpretation of results, and the exchange and integration of data and information.

MIARE [13], Minimum Information About an RNAi Experiment

Minimum Information About an RNAi Experiment (MIARE) is a data reporting guideline which describes the minimum information that should be reported about an RNAi experiment to enable the unambiguous interpretation and reproduction of the results.

MIFlowCyt [14], Minimum Information about a Flow Cytometry Experiment

Minimum Information about a Flow Cytometry Experiment (MIFlowCyt) is a data reporting guideline which describes the minimum information that should be reported about a flow cytometry experiment to enable the interpretation of the results.

Nature Community Consultation [15]

Standards papers under consideration for publication in Nature Biotechnology.

References

[1] http://fuge.sourceforge.net/

[2] http://www.mibbi.org/index.php/Main_Page

[3] Gibson, Frank, Overton, Paul, Smulders, Tom, Schultz, Simon, Eglen, Stephen, Ingram, Colin, Panzeri, Stefano, Bream, Phil, Sernagor, Evelyne, Cunningham, Mark, Adams, Christopher, Echtermeyer, Christoph, Simonotto, Jennifer, Kaiser, Marcus, Swan, Daniel, Fletcher, Marty, and Lord, Phillip. Minimum Information about a Neuroscience Investigation (MINI) Electrophysiology. Available from Nature Precedings <http://hdl.handle.net/10101/npre.2008.1720.1> (2008)

[4] http://sourceforge.net/project/showfiles.php?group_id=158121

[5] http://wiki.ficcs.org/ficcs/MIFlowCyt

[6] http://flowcyt.sourceforge.net/miflowcyt/

[7] http://mibbi.sourceforge.net/

[8] http://www.fged.org

[9] http://psidev.info/

[10] http://fuge.sourceforge.net

[11] http://msi-workgroups.sourceforge.net/

[12] http://miaca.sf.net

[13] http://www.miare.org

[14] http://flowcyt.sf.net

[15] http://www.nature.com/nbt/consult/index.html

MiRBase

miRBase

Content	
Description	microRNA annotation and deep-sequencing data.
Contact	
Research center	University of Manchester
Laboratory	Faculty of Life Sciences
Authors	Ana Kozomara
Primary Citation	Kozomara & al. (2011)[1]
Release date	2010
Access	
Website	http://www.mirbase.org/
Tools	
Miscellaneous	

The **miRBase** database is an archive of microRNA sequences.[1] [2] [3] [4] [5] As of September 2010 it contained information about 15,172 microRNAs.[1] The miRBase registry provides a centralised system for assigning new names to microRNA genes.

miRBase grew from the microRNA registry resource set up by Sam Griffiths-Jones in 2003.[6]

References

[1] Kozomara, A.; Griffiths-Jones, S. (2010). "MiRBase: integrating microRNA annotation and deep-sequencing data". *Nucleic Acids Research* **39** (Database issue): D152–7. doi:10.1093/nar/gkq1027. PMC 3013655. PMID 21037258.

[2] Griffiths-Jones, Sam (2010). *MiRBase: microRNA Sequences and Annotation*. pp. Unit 12.9.1–10. doi:10.1002/0471250953.bi1209s29.

[3] Griffiths-Jones, S.; Saini, H. K.; Van Dongen, S.; Enright, A. J. (2007). "MiRBase: tools for microRNA genomics". *Nucleic Acids Research* **36** (Database issue): D154–8. doi:10.1093/nar/gkm952. PMC 2238936. PMID 17991681.

[4] Griffiths-Jones, Sam (2006). *MiRBase: the MicroRNA Sequence Database*. **342**. pp. 129–38. doi:10.1385/1-59745-123-1:129.

[5] Griffiths-Jones, S.; Grocock, RJ; Van Dongen, S; Bateman, A; Enright, AJ (2006). "MiRBase: microRNA sequences, targets and gene nomenclature". *Nucleic Acids Research* **34** (Database issue): D140–4. doi:10.1093/nar/gkj112. PMC 1347474. PMID 16381832.

[6] Griffiths-Jones S (January 2004). "The microRNA Registry". *Nucleic Acids Res*. **32** (Database issue): D109–11. doi:10.1093/nar/gkh023. PMC 308757. PMID 14681370.

External links

- miRBase (http://www.mirbase.org)

Mobile Patient Diary

Mobile Patient Diaries are the next generation Patient Diaries that can use mobile phones during clinical and behavioral trials or a disease treatment and management, to measure treatment compliance and capture patient related information.

Patient Diaries have predominantly been using paper as the medium for capturing patient information, however with the fast moving mobile phone and communication revolution, patient data capture using mobile phones has come up as a new facet to the Clinical Trials and Healthcare sector. Mobile phones can be used for capturing Quality Of Life, Health Related Quality Of Life and other assessments during clinical trials and research studies.

Mobile phone (Cell phones) applications, which are built while being compliant with International guidelines such as CFR 21 Part 11, FDA, HIPAA etc, can be used as an innovative solution that allows the clinical and research fraternity to get access to patient information in real time and thereby make important decisions with respect to the ongoing trial. Using mobile phones as patient diaries could play an important role to ensure that the patients enrolled in a clinical trial are compliant to their assessment filling regimens, by sending timely and scheduled alerts and follow ups for filling up their assessments. Mobile technology also enables multiple languages and real time data capture to be inbuilt in the devices to cater to the growing global patient populations that participate in clinical and behavioral trials.

References

ePRO Guidance for Industry [1]

References

[1] http://www.fda.gov/downloads/Drugs/GuidanceComplianceRegulatoryInformation/Guidances/UCM193282.pdf

MochiView

MochiView (*Mo*tif and *Ch*/*P Viewer*) [1] is software that integrates a genome browser and tools for data and Sequence motif visualization and analysis. The software uses the Java language, contains a fully integrated JavaDB database, is platform-independent, and is freely available.

Description

MochiView was originally designed as a platform for rapidly browsing, visualizing, and extracting Sequence motifs from ChIP-chip and ChIP-Seq data. The software uses a generalized data format that serves other purposes as well, such as the visualization and analysis of RNA-Seq data or the import, maintenance, exploration, and analysis of Sequence motif libraries. The MochiView website [2] contains a detailed feature list [3] and demo videos [4] of the software showing smooth panning/zooming, data/gene/sequence/coordinate browsers, and plot interactivity. The software was created by Oliver Homann in the laboratory of Alexander Johnson at the University of California at San Francisco.

References

[1] Homann OR and Johnson AD. MochiView: versatile software for genome browsing and DNA Motif analysis. BMC Biology. 2010, 8:49 (http://www.biomedcentral.com/1741-7007/8/49)

[2] MochiView website: main page (http://johnsonlab.ucsf.edu/sj/mochiview-start/)

[3] MochiView website: feature list (http://johnsonlab.ucsf.edu/sj/mochiview-features/)

[4] MochiView website: sample videos (http://johnsonlab.ucsf.edu/sj/mochiview-screenshots/)

External links

- MochiView website (http://johnsonlab.ucsf.edu/sj/mochiview-start/)

Modelling biological systems

Modeling biological systems is a significant task of systems biology and mathematical biology. Computational systems biology aims to develop and use efficient algorithms, data structures, visualization and communication tools with the goal of computer modeling of biological systems. It involves the use of computer simulations of biological systems, like cellular subsystems (such as the networks of metabolites and enzymes which comprise metabolism, signal transduction pathways and gene regulatory networks) to both analyze and visualize the complex connections of these cellular processes.

Artificial life or virtual evolution attempts to understand evolutionary processes via the computer simulation of simple (artificial) life forms.

Overview

It is understood that an unexpected emergent property of a complex system is a result of the interplay of the cause-and-effect among simpler, integrated parts (see biological organisation). Biological systems manifest many important examples of emergent properties in the complex interplay of components. Traditional study of biological systems requires reductive methods in which quantities of data are gathered by category, such as concentration over time in response to a certain stimulus. Computers are critical to analysis and modeling of these data. The goal is to create accurate real-time models of a system's response to environmental and internal stimuli, such as a model of a cancer cell in order to find weaknesses in its signaling pathways, or modeling of ion channel mutations to see effects on cardiomyocytes and in turn, the function of a beating heart.

A monograph on this topic summarizes an extensive amount of published research in this area up to 1987,[1] including subsections in the following areas: computer modeling in biology and medicine, arterial system models, neuron models, biochemical and oscillation networks, quantum automata [2], quantum computers in molecular biology and genetics, cancer modeling, neural nets, genetic networks, abstract relational biology, metabolic-replication systems, category theory[3] applications in biology and medicine,[4] automata theory, cellular automata, tessallation models[5] [6] and complete self-reproduction [7], chaotic systems in organisms, relational biology and organismic theories.[8] [9] This published report also includes 390 references to peer-reviewed articles by a large number of authors.[10] [11] [12]

Standards

By far the most widely accepted standard format for storing and exchanging models in the field is the Systems Biology Markup Language (SBML)[13] The SBML.org [14] website includes a guide to many important software packages used in computational systems biology. Other markup languages with different emphases include BioPAX and CellML.

Particular tasks

Cellular model

Creating a cellular model has been a particularly challenging task of systems biology and mathematical biology. It involves the use of computer simulations of the many cellular subsystems such as the networks of metabolites and enzymes which comprise metabolism, signal transduction pathways and gene regulatory networks to both analyze and visualize the complex connections of these cellular processes.

The complex network of biochemical reaction/transport processes and their spatial organization make the development of a predictive model of a living cell a grand challenge for the 21st century.

In 2006, the National Science Foundation (NSF) put forward a grand challenge for systems biology in the 21st century to build a mathematical model of the whole cell.[15] E-Cell Project [3] aims "to make precise whole cell simulation at the molecular level possible".[16] CytoSolve developed by V. A. Shiva Ayyadurai and C. Forbes Dewey, Jr. of Department of Biological Engineering at the Massachusetts Institute of Technology, provided a method to model the whole cell by dynamically integrating multiple molecular pathway models.[17] [18]

Membrane computing is the task of modeling specifically a cell membrane.

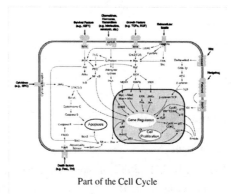

Part of the Cell Cycle

Summerhayes and Elton's 1923 food web of Bear Island (*Arrows represent an organism being consumed by another organism*).

Protein folding

Protein structure prediction is the prediction of the three-dimensional structure of a protein from its amino acid sequence—that is, the prediction of a protein's tertiary structure from its primary structure. It is one of the most important goals pursued by bioinformatics and theoretical chemistry. Protein structure prediction is of high importance in medicine (for example, in drug design) and biotechnology (for example, in the design of novel enzymes).

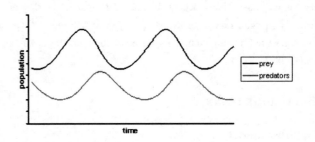

A sample time-series of the Lotka-Volterra model. Note that the two populations exhibit cyclic behaviour.

Every two years, the performance of current methods is assessed in the CASP experiment.

Human biological systems

Brain model

The Blue Brain Project is an attempt to create a synthetic brain by reverse-engineering the mammalian brain down to the molecular level. The aim of the project, founded in May 2005 by the Brain and Mind Institute of the *École Polytechnique* in Lausanne, Switzerland, is to study the brain's architectural and functional principles. The project is headed by the Institute's director, Henry Markram. Using a Blue Gene supercomputer running Michael Hines's NEURON software, the simulation does not consist simply of an artificial neural network, but involves a partially biologically realistic model of neurons.[19] [20] It is hoped by its proponents that it will eventually shed light on the nature of consciousness. There are a number of sub-projects, including the Cajal Blue Brain, coordinated by the Supercomputing and Visualization Center of Madrid (CeSViMa), and others run by universities and independent laboratories in the UK, U.S., and Israel.

Model of the immune system

The last decade has seen the emergence of a growing number of simulations of the immune system.[21] [22]

Tree model

Electronic trees (e-trees) usually use L-systems to simulate growth. L-systems are very important in the field of complexity science and A-life. A universally accepted system for describing changes in plant morphology at the cellular or modular level has yet to be devised.[23] The most widely implemented tree generating algorithms are described in the papers "Creation and Rendering of Realistic Trees" [24], and Real-Time Tree Rendering [25]

Ecological models

Ecosystem models are mathematical representations of ecosystems. Typically they simplify complex foodwebs down to their major components or trophic levels, and quantify these as either numbers of organisms, biomass or the inventory/concentration of some pertinent chemical element (for instance, carbon or a nutrient species such as nitrogen or phosphorus).

Modeling of infectious disease

It is possible to model the progress of most infectious diseases mathematically to discover the likely outcome of an epidemic or to help manage them by vaccination. This field tries to find parameters for various infectious diseases and to use those parameters to make useful calculations about the effects of a mass vaccination programme.

Notes

[1] http://en.scientificcommons.org/1857371
[2] http://planetphysics.org/encyclopedia/QuantumAutomaton.html
[3] http://planetphysics.org/encyclopedia/BibliographyForCategoryTheoryAndAlgebraicTopologyApplicationsInTheoreticalPhysics.html
[4] http://planetphysics.org/encyclopedia/BibliographyForMathematicalBiophysicsAndMathematicalMedicine.html
[5] *Modern Cellular Automata* by Kendall Preston and M. J. B. Duff http://books.google.co.uk/books?id=l0_0q_e-u_UC&dq=cellular+automata+and+tessalation&pg=PP1&ots=ciXYCF3AYm&source=citation&sig=CtaUDhisM7MalS7rZfXvp689y-8&hl=en&sa=X&oi=book_result&resnum=12&ct=result
[6] http://mathworld.wolfram.com/DualTessellation.html
[7] http://planetphysics.org/encyclopedia/ETACAxioms.html
[8] Baianu, I. C. 1987, Computer Models and Automata Theory in Biology and Medicine., in M. Witten (ed.),*Mathematical Models in Medicine*, vol. 7., Ch.11 Pergamon Press, New York, 1513-1577. http://cogprints.org/3687/
[9] http://www.kli.ac.at/theorylab/EditedVol/W/WittenM1987a.html
[10] http://www.springerlink.com/content/w2733h7280521632/
[11] Currently available for download as an updated PDF: http://cogprints.ecs.soton.ac.uk/archive/00003718/01/COMPUTER_SIMULATIONCOMPUTABILITYBIOSYSTEMSrefnew.pdf
[12] http://planetphysics.org/encyclopedia/BibliographyForMathematicalBiophysics.html
[13] Klipp, Liebermeister, Helbig, Kowald and Schaber. (2007). "Systems biology standards—the community speaks" (2007), Nature Biotechnology 25(4):390–391.
[14] http://sbml.org
[15] American Association for the Advancement of Science (http://www.sciencemag.org/content/314/5806/1696.full)
[16] http://www.e-cell.org/ecell/
[17] National Center for Biotechnology Information [2. http://www.ncbi.nlm.nih.gov/pmc/articles/PMC3032229/]
[18] Massachusetts Institute of Technology (http://cytosolve.mit.edu/)
[19] Graham-Rowe, Duncan. "Mission to build a simulated brain begins" (http://www.newscientist.com/article/dn7470--mission-to-build-a-simulated-brain-begins.html), *NewScientist*, June 2005.
[20] Palmer, Jason. Simulated brain closer to thought (http://news.bbc.co.uk/2/hi/science/nature/8012496.stm), BBC News.
[21] (http://www.springerlink.com/content/5qn66fvhu6cvlyvc/)
[22] "Computer Simulation Captures Immune Response To Flu" (http://www.sciencedaily.com/releases/2009/05/090518111729.htm). . Retrieved 2009-08-19.
[23] "Simulating plant growth" (http://www.acm.org/crossroads/xrds8-2/plantsim.html). . Retrieved 2009-10-18.
[24] http://portal.acm.org/citation.cfm?id=218427
[25] http://www.springerlink.com/content/n0nacdyjpyvxnnef/

References

Barab, A. -L.; Oltvai, Z. (2004). "Network biology: understanding the cell's functional organization". *Nature reviews. Genetics* **5** (2): 101–113. doi:10.1038/nrg1272. PMID 14735121.

Covert; Schilling, C.; Palsson, B. (2001). "Regulation of gene expression in flux balance models of metabolism". *Journal of theoretical biology* **213** (1): 73–88. doi:10.1006/jtbi.2001.2405. PMID 11708855.

Covert, M. W.; Palsson, B. . (2002). "Transcriptional regulation in constraints-based metabolic models of Escherichia coli". *The Journal of biological chemistry* **277** (31): 28058–28064. doi:10.1074/jbc.M201691200. PMID 12006566.

Edwards; Palsson, B. (2000). "The Escherichia coli MG1655 in silico metabolic genotype: its definition, characteristics, and capabilities". *Proceedings of the National Academy of Sciences of the United States of America* **97** (10): 5528–5533. Bibcode 2000PNAS...97.5528E. doi:10.1073/pnas.97.10.5528. PMC 25862. PMID 10805808.

Bonneau, R. (2008). "Learning biological networks: from modules to dynamics". *Nature chemical biology* **4** (11): 658–664. doi:10.1038/nchembio.122. PMID 18936750.

Edwards, J. S.; Ibarra, R. U.; Palsson, B. O. (2001). "In silico predictions of Escherichia coli metabolic capabilities are consistent with experimental data". *Nature biotechnology* **19** (2): 125–130. doi:10.1038/84379. PMID 11175725.

Fell, D. A. (1998). "Increasing the flux in metabolic pathways: A metabolic control analysis perspective". *Biotechnology and Bioengineering* **58** (2–3): 121–124. doi:10.1002/(SICI)1097-0290(19980420)58:2/3<121::AID-BIT2>3.0.CO;2-N. PMID 10191380.

Hartwell, L. H.; Hopfield, J. J.; Leibler, S.; Murray, A. W. (1999). "From molecular to modular cell biology". *Nature* **402** (6761 Suppl): C47–C52. doi:10.1038/35011540. PMID 10591225.

Ideker; Galitski, T.; Hood, L. (2001). "A new approach to decoding life: systems biology". *Annual review of genomics and human genetics* **2** (1): 343–372. doi:10.1146/annurev.genom.2.1.343. PMID 11701654.

Kitano, H. (2002). "Computational systems biology". *Nature* **420** (6912): 206–210. Bibcode 2002Natur.420..206K. doi:10.1038/nature01254. PMID 12432404.

Kitano, H. (2002). "Systems biology: a brief overview". *Science* **295** (5560): 1662–1664. Bibcode 2002Sci...295.1662K. doi:10.1126/science.1069492. PMID 11872829.

Kitano (2002). "Looking beyond the details: a rise in system-oriented approaches in genetics and molecular biology". *Current genetics* **41** (1): 1–10. doi:10.1007/s00294-002-0285-z. PMID 12073094.

Gilman, A. G.; Simon, M. I.; Bourne, H. R.; Harris, B. A.; Long, R.; Ross, E. M.; Stull, J. T.; Taussig, R. et al. (2002). "Overview of the Alliance for Cellular Signaling". *Nature* **420** (6916): 703–706. doi:10.1038/nature01304. PMID 12478301.

Palsson, Bernhard (2006). *Systems biology: properties of reconstructed networks*. Cambridge: Cambridge University Press. ISBN 978-0-521-85903-5.

Kauffman; Prakash, P.; Edwards, J. S. (2003). "Advances in flux balance analysis". *Current opinion in biotechnology* **14** (5): 491–496. doi:10.1016/j.copbio.2003.08.001. PMID 14580578.

Segrè, D.; Vitkup, D.; Church, G. M. (2002). "Analysis of optimality in natural and perturbed metabolic networks". *Proceedings of the National Academy of Sciences of the United States of America* **99** (23): 15112–15117. Bibcode 2002PNAS...9915112S. doi:10.1073/pnas.232349399. PMC 137552. PMID 12415116.

Wildermuth, MC (2000). "Metabolic control analysis: biological applications and insights.". *Genome biology* **1** (6): REVIEWS1031. PMC 138895. PMID 11178271.

Further reading

- Antmann, S. S.; Marsden, J. E.; Sirovich, L., eds (2009). *Mathematical Physiology* (2nd ed.). New York, New York: Springer. ISBN 9780387758466.
- Barnes, D.J.; Chu, D. (2010), *Introduction to Modelling for Biosciences* (http://www.cs.kent.ac.uk/projects/ imb/), Springer Verlag

External links

- Semantic Systems Biology (http://www.semantic-systems-biology.org).
- The Center for Modeling Immunity to Enteric Pathogens (MIEP) (http://www.modelingimmunity.org)

Models of DNA evolution

A number of different Markov **models of DNA sequence evolution** have been proposed. These substitution models differ in terms of the parameters used to describe the rates at which one nucleotide replaces another during evolution. These models are frequently used in molecular phylogenetic analyses. In particular, they are used during the calculation of likelihood of a tree (in Bayesian and maximum likelihood approaches to tree estimation) and they are used to estimate the evolutionary distance between sequences from the observed differences between the sequences.

Introduction

These models are phenomenological descriptions of the evolution of DNA as a string of four discrete states. These Markov models do **not** explicitly depict the mechanism of mutation nor the action of natural selection. Rather they describe the relative rates of different changes. For example, mutational biases and purifying selection favoring conservative changes are probably both responsible for the relatively high rate of transitions compared to transversions in evolving sequences. However, the Kimura (K80) model described below merely attempts to capture the effect of both forces in a parameter that reflects the relative rate of transitions to transversions.

Evolutionary analyses of sequences are conducted on a wide variety of time scales. Thus, it is convenient to express these models in terms of the instantaneous rates of change between different states (the Q matrices below). If we are given a starting (ancestral) state at one position, the model's Q matrix and a branch length expressing the expected number of changes to have occurred since the ancestor, then we can derive the probability of the descendant sequence having each of the four states. The mathematical details of this transformation from rate-matrix to probability matrix are described in the mathematics of substitution models section of the substitution model page. By expressing models in terms of the instantaneous rates of change we can avoid estimating a large numbers of parameters for each branch on a phylogenetic tree (or each comparison if the analysis involves many pairwise sequence comparisons).

The models described on this page describe the evolution of a single site within a sequences. They are often used for analyzing the evolution of an entire locus by making the simplifying assumption that different sites evolve independently and are identically distributed. This assumption may be justifiable if the sites can be assumed to be evolving neutrally. If the primary effect of natural selection on the evolution of the sequences is to constrain some sites, then models of among-site rate-heterogeneity can be used. This approaches allows one to estimate only one matrix of relative rates of substitution, and another set of parameters describing the variance in the total rate of substitution across sites.

DNA evolution as a continuous-time Markov chain

Continuous-time Markov chains

Continuous-time Markov chains have the usual transition matrices which are, in addition, parameterized by time, t. Specifically, if $E_1, \ldots, E_4$ are the states, then the transition matrix

$P(t) = (P_{ij}(t))$ where each individual entry, $P_{ij}(t)$ refers to the probability that state E_i will change to state E_j in time t.

Example: We would like to model the substitution process in DNA sequences (*i.e.* Jukes–Cantor, Kimura, *etc.*) in a continuous-time fashion. The corresponding transition matrices will look like:

$$P(t) = \begin{pmatrix} p_{AA}(t) & p_{GA}(t) & p_{CA}(t) & p_{TA}(t) \\ p_{AG}(t) & p_{GG}(t) & p_{CG}(t) & p_{TG}(t) \\ p_{AC}(t) & p_{GC}(t) & p_{CC}(t) & p_{TC}(t) \\ p_{AT}(t) & p_{GT}(t) & p_{CT}(t) & p_{TT}(t) \end{pmatrix}$$

where the top-left and bottom-right 2×2 blocks correspond to *transition probabilities* and the top-right and bottom-left 2×2 blocks corresponds to *transversion probabilities*.

Assumption: If at some time t_0, the Markov chain is in state E_i, then the probability that at time $t_0 + t$, it will be in state E_j depends only upon i, j and t. This then allows us to write that probability as $p_{ij}(t)$.

Theorem: Continuous-time transition matrices satisfy:

$$P(t + \tau) = P(t)P(\tau)$$

Deriving the dynamics of substitution

Consider a DNA sequence of fixed length m evolving in time by base replacement. Assume that the processes followed by the m sites are Markovian independent, identically distributed and constant in time. For a fixed site, let

$$\mathbf{P}(t) = (p_A(t), \ p_G(t), \ p_C(t), \ p_T(t))^T$$

be the column vector of probabilities of states A, G, C, and T at time t. Let

$$\mathcal{E} = \{A, \ G, \ C, \ T\}$$

be the state-space. For two distinct

$$x, y \in \mathcal{E}, \text{ let } \mu_{xy}$$

be the transition rate from state x to state y. Similarly, for any x, let:

$$\mu_x = \sum_{y \neq x} \mu_{xy}$$

The changes in the probability distribution $p_A(t)$ for small increments of time Δt are given by:

$$p_A(t + \Delta t) = p_A(t) - p_A(t)\mu_A \Delta t + \sum_{x \neq A} p_x(t)\mu_{xA}\Delta t$$

In other words (in frequentist language), the frequency of A's at time $t + \Delta t$ is equal to the frequency at time t minus the frequency of the *lost* A's plus the frequency of the *newly created* A's.

Similarly for the probabilities $p_G(t)$, $p_C(t)$, and $p_T(t)$. We can write these compactly as:

$$\mathbf{P}(t + \Delta t) = \mathbf{P}(t) + Q\mathbf{P}(t)\Delta t$$

where,

$$Q = \begin{pmatrix} -\mu_A & \mu_{GA} & \mu_{CA} & \mu_{TA} \\ \mu_{AG} & -\mu_G & \mu_{CG} & \mu_{TG} \\ \mu_{AC} & \mu_{GC} & -\mu_C & \mu_{TC} \\ \mu_{AT} & \mu_{GT} & \mu_{CT} & -\mu_T \end{pmatrix}$$

or, alternately:

$$\mathbf{P}'(t) = Q\mathbf{P}(t)$$

where, Q is the *rate* matrix. Note that by definition, the columns of Q sum to zero.

Ergodicity

If all the transition probabilities, μ_{xy} are positive, *i.e.* if all states $x, y \in \mathcal{E}$ *communicate*, then the Markov chain has a *stationary* distribution $\Pi = \{\pi_x, \; x \in \mathcal{E}\}$ where each π_x is the proportion of time spent in state x after the Markov chain has run for infinite time, and this probability does not depend upon the initial state of the process. Such a Markov chain is called, ***ergodic***. In DNA evolution, under the assumption of a common process for each site, the stationary frequencies, $\pi_A, \pi_G, \pi_C, \pi_T$ correspond to equilibrium base compositions.

Definition A Markov process is *stationary* if its current distribution is the stationary distribution, *i.e.* $\mathbf{P}(t) = \Pi$

Thus, by using the differential equation above,

$$\frac{d\Pi}{dt} = Q\Pi = 0$$

Time reversibility

Definition: A stationary Markov process is *time reversible* if (in the steady state) the amount of change from state x to y is equal to the amount of change from y to x, (although the two states may occur with different frequencies). This means that:

$$\pi_x \mu_{xy} = \pi_y \mu_{yx}$$

Not all stationary processes are reversible, however, almost all DNA evolution models assume time reversibility, which is considered to be a reasonable assumption.

Under the time reversibility assumption, let $s_{xy} = \mu_{xy}/\pi_y$, then it is easy to see that:

$$s_{xy} = s_{yx}$$

Definition The symmetric term s_{xy} is called the *exchangeability* between states x and y. In other words, s_{xy} is the fraction of the frequency of state x that results as a result of transitions from state y to state x.

Corollary The 12 off-diagonal entries of the rate matrix, Q (note the off-diagonal entries determine the diagonal entries, since the rows of Q sum to zero) can be completely determined by 9 numbers; these are: 6 exchangeability terms and 3 stationary frequencies π_x, (since the stationary frequencies sum to 1).

Scaling of branch lengths

By comparing extant sequences, one can determine the amount of sequence divergence. This raw measurement of divergence provides information about the number of changes that have occurred along the path separating the sequences. The simple count of differences (the Hamming distance) between sequences will often underestimate the number of substitution because of multiple hits (see homoplasy). Trying to estimate the exact number of changes that have occurred is difficult, and usually not necessary. Instead, branch lengths (and path lengths) in phylogenetic analyses are usually expressed in the expected number of changes per site. The path length is the product of the duration of the path in time and the mean rate of substitutions. While their product can be estimated, the rate and time are not identifiable from sequence divergence.

The descriptions of rate matrices on this page accurately reflect the relative magnitude of different substitutions, but these rate matrices are **not** scaled such that a branch length of 1 yields one expected change. This scaling can be accomplished by multiplying every element of the matrix by the same factor, or simply by scaling the branch lengths. If we use the β to denote the scaling factor, and v to denote the branch length measured in the expected number of substitutions per site then βv is used the transition probability formulae below in place of μt. Note that v is a parameter to be estimated from data, and is referred to as the branch length, while β is simply a number that can be calculated from the rate matrix (it is not a separate free parameter).

The value of β can be found by forcing the expected rate of flux of states to 1. The diagonal entries of the rate-matrix (the Q matrix) represent -1 times the rate of leaving each state. For time-reversible models, we know the equilibrium state frequencies (these are simply the π_i parameter value for state i). Thus we can find the expected rate of change by calculating the sum of flux out of each state weighted by the proportion of sites that are expected to be in that class. Setting β to be the reciprocal of this sum will guarantee that scaled process has an expected flux of 1:

$$\beta = 1/\left(-\sum_i \pi_i \mu_{ii}\right)$$

For example, in the Jukes-Cantor, the scaling factor would be *4/(3μ)' because the rate of leaving each state is* 3μ/4.

Most common models of DNA evolution

JC69 model (Jukes and Cantor, 1969)[1]

JC69 is the simplest substitution model. There are several assumptions. It assumes equal base frequencies $\left(\pi_A = \pi_G = \pi_C = \pi_T = \dfrac{1}{4}\right)$ and equal mutation rates. The only parameter of this model is therefore μ, the overall substitution rate. As previously mentioned, this variable becomes a constant when we normalize to the mean-rate to 1.

$$Q = \begin{pmatrix} * & \frac{\mu}{4} & \frac{\mu}{4} & \frac{\mu}{4} \\ \frac{\mu}{4} & * & \frac{\mu}{4} & \frac{\mu}{4} \\ \frac{\mu}{4} & \frac{\mu}{4} & * & \frac{\mu}{4} \\ \frac{\mu}{4} & \frac{\mu}{4} & \frac{\mu}{4} & * \end{pmatrix}$$

$$P = \begin{pmatrix} \frac{1}{4} + \frac{3}{4}e^{-t\mu} & \frac{1}{4} - \frac{1}{4}e^{-t\mu} & \frac{1}{4} - \frac{1}{4}e^{-t\mu} & \frac{1}{4} - \frac{1}{4}e^{-t\mu} \\ \frac{1}{4} - \frac{1}{4}e^{-t\mu} & \frac{1}{4} + \frac{3}{4}e^{-t\mu} & \frac{1}{4} - \frac{1}{4}e^{-t\mu} & \frac{1}{4} - \frac{1}{4}e^{-t\mu} \\ \frac{1}{4} - \frac{1}{4}e^{-t\mu} & \frac{1}{4} - \frac{1}{4}e^{-t\mu} & \frac{1}{4} + \frac{3}{4}e^{-t\mu} & \frac{1}{4} - \frac{1}{4}e^{-t\mu} \\ \frac{1}{4} - \frac{1}{4}e^{-t\mu} & \frac{1}{4} - \frac{1}{4}e^{-t\mu} & \frac{1}{4} - \frac{1}{4}e^{-t\mu} & \frac{1}{4} + \frac{3}{4}e^{-t\mu} \end{pmatrix}$$

When branch length, ν, is measured in the expected number of changes per site then:

$$P_{ij}(\nu) = \begin{cases} \frac{1}{4} + \frac{3}{4}e^{-4\nu/3} & \text{if } i = j \\ \frac{1}{4} - \frac{1}{4}e^{-4\nu/3} & \text{if } i \neq j \end{cases}$$

The Jukes-Cantor estimate of the evolutionary distance (in terms of the expected number of changes) between two sequences is given by

$$\hat{d} = -\frac{3}{4}\ln\left(1 - \frac{4}{3}p\right)$$

where p is the proportion of sites that differ between the two sequences. The p in this formula is frequently referred to as the p-distance. It is a sufficient statistic for calculated the Jukes-Cantor distance correction, but is not sufficient for the calculation of the evolutionary distance under the more complex models that follow (also note that p used in subsequent formulae is not identical to the " p-distance").

K80 model (Kimura, 1980)[2]

The K80 model distinguishes between transitions (A <-> G, i.e. from purine to purine, or C <-> T, i.e. from pyrimidine to pyrimidine) and transversions (from purine to pyrimidine or vice versa). In Kimura's original description of the model the α and β were used denote the rates of these types of substitutions, but it is more now common to set the rate of transversions to 1 and use κ to denote the transition/transversion rate ratio (as is done below). The K80 model assumes that all of the bases are equally frequent ($\pi_T = \pi_C = \pi_A = \pi_G = 0.25$).

$$\text{Rate matrix } Q = \begin{pmatrix} * & \kappa & 1 & 1 \\ \kappa & * & 1 & 1 \\ 1 & 1 & * & \kappa \\ 1 & 1 & \kappa & * \end{pmatrix}$$

The Kimura two-parameter distance is given by:

$$\hat{d} = -\frac{1}{2}\ln(1 - 2p - q) - \frac{1}{4}\ln(1 - 2q)$$

where p is the proportion of sites that show transitional differences and q is the proportion of sites that show transversional differences.

F81 model (Felsenstein 1981)[3]

Felsenstein's 1981 model is an extension of the JC69 model in which base frequencies are allowed to vary from 0.25 ($\pi_T \neq \pi_C \neq \pi_A \neq \pi_G$)

Rate matrix:

$$Q = \begin{pmatrix} * & \pi_C & \pi_A & \pi_G \\ \pi_T & * & \pi_A & \pi_G \\ \pi_T & \pi_C & * & \pi_G \\ \pi_T & \pi_C & \pi_A & * \end{pmatrix}$$

When branch length, ν, is measured in the expected number of changes per site then:

$$\beta = 1/(1 - \pi_A^2 - \pi_C^2 - \pi_G^2 - \pi_T^2)$$

$$P_{ij}(\nu) = \begin{cases} \pi_i + (1 - \pi_i)\,e^{-\beta\nu} & \text{if } i = j \\ \pi_j\left(1 - e^{-\beta\nu}\right) & \text{if } i \neq j \end{cases}$$

HKY85 model (Hasegawa, Kishino and Yano 1985)[4]

The HKY85 model can be thought of as combining the extensions made in the Kimura80 and Felsenstein81 models. Namely, it distinguishes between the rate of transitions and transversions (using the κ parameter), and it allows unequal base frequencies ($\pi_T \neq \pi_C \neq \pi_A \neq \pi_G$). Felsenstein described an equivalent model in 1984 using a different parameterization[5]; thus, the model is sometimes referred to as the F84 model[6].

$$\text{Rate matrix } Q = \begin{pmatrix} * & \kappa\pi_C & \pi_A & \pi_G \\ \kappa\pi_T & * & \pi_A & \pi_G \\ \pi_T & \pi_C & * & \kappa\pi_G \\ \pi_T & \pi_C & \kappa\pi_A & * \end{pmatrix}$$

If we express the branch length, ν in terms of the expected number of changes per site then:

$$\beta = \frac{1}{2(\pi_A + \pi_G)(\pi_C + \pi_T) + 2\kappa[(\pi_A\pi_G) + (\pi_C\pi_T)]}$$

$$P_{AA}(\nu, \kappa, \pi) = \left[\pi_A\left(\pi_A + \pi_G + (\pi_C + \pi_T)e^{-\beta\nu}\right) + \pi_G e^{-(1+(\pi_A+\pi_G)(\kappa-1.0))\beta\nu}\right]/(\pi_A + \pi_G)$$

$$P_{AC}(\nu, \kappa, \pi) = \pi_C\left(1.0 - e^{-\beta\nu}\right)$$

$$P_{AG}(\nu, \kappa, \pi) = \left[\pi_G \left(\pi_A + \pi_G + (\pi_C + \pi_T)e^{-\beta\nu} \right) - \pi_G e^{-(1+(\pi_A+\pi_G)(\kappa-1.0))\beta\nu} \right] / (\pi_A + \pi_G)$$

$$P_{AT}(\nu, \kappa, \pi) = \pi_T \left(1.0 - e^{-\beta\nu} \right)$$

and formula for the other combinations of states can be obtained by substituting in the appropriate base frequencies.

T92 model (Tamura 1992)[7]

T92 is a simple mathematical method developed to estimate the number of nucleotide substitutions per site between two DNA sequences, by extending Kimura's (1980) two-parameter method to the case where a G+C-content bias exists. This method will be useful when there are strong transition-transversion and G+C-content biases, as in the case of Drosophila mitochondrial DNA. (Tamura 1992)

One frequency only π_{GC}

$$\pi_G = \pi_C = \frac{\pi_{GC}}{2}$$

$$\pi_A = \pi_T = \frac{(1 - \pi_{GC})}{2}$$

Rate matrix $Q = \begin{pmatrix} * & \kappa(1-\pi_{GC})/2 & (1-\pi_{GC})/2 & (1-\pi_{GC})/2 \\ \kappa\pi_{GC}/2 & * & \pi_{GC}/2 & \pi_{GC}/2 \\ (1-\pi_{GC})/2 & (1-\pi_{GC})/2 & * & \kappa(1-\pi_{GC})/2 \\ \pi_{GC}/2 & \pi_{GC}/2 & \kappa\pi_{GC}/2 & * \end{pmatrix}$

The evolutionary distance between two noncoding sequences according to this model is given by

$$d = -h\ln(1 - \frac{p}{h} - q) - \frac{1}{2}(1 - h)\ln(1 - 2q)$$

where $h = 2\theta(1 - \theta)$ where $\theta \in (0, 1)$ is the GC content.

TN93 model (Tamura and Nei 1993)[8]

The TN93 model distinguishes between the two different types of transition - i.e. (A <-> G) is allowed to have a different rate to (C<->T). Transversions are all assumed to occur at the same rate, but that rate is allowed to be different from both of the rates for transitions.

TN93 also allows unequal base frequencies ($\pi_T \neq \pi_C \neq \pi_A \neq \pi_G$).

Rate matrix $Q = \begin{pmatrix} * & \kappa_1\pi_C & \pi_A & \pi_G \\ \kappa_1\pi_T & * & \pi_A & \pi_G \\ \pi_T & \pi_C & * & \kappa_2\pi_G \\ \pi_T & \pi_C & \kappa_2\pi_A & * \end{pmatrix}$

GTR: Generalised time-reversible (Tavaré 1986) [9]

GTR is the most general neutral, independent, finite-sites, time-reversible model possible. It was first described in a general form by Simon Tavaré in 1986.[9]

The GTR parameters consist of an equilibrium base frequency vector, $\Pi = (\pi_1, \pi_2, \pi_3, \pi_4)$, giving the frequency at which each base occurs at each site, and the rate matrix

$$Q = \begin{pmatrix} -(x_1 + x_2 + x_3) & \frac{\pi_1 x_1}{\pi_2} & \frac{\pi_1 x_2}{\pi_3} & \frac{\pi_1 x_3}{\pi_4} \\ x_1 & -\left(\frac{\pi_1 x_1}{\pi_2} + x_4 + x_5\right) & \frac{\pi_2 x_4}{\pi_3} & \frac{\pi_2 x_5}{\pi_4} \\ x_2 & x_4 & -\left(\frac{\pi_1 x_2}{\pi_3} + \frac{\pi_2 x_4}{\pi_3} + x_6\right) & \frac{\pi_3 x_6}{\pi_4} \\ x_3 & x_5 & x_6 & -\left(\frac{\pi_1 x_3}{\pi_4} + \frac{\pi_2 x_5}{\pi_4} + \frac{\pi_3 x_6}{\pi_4}\right) \end{pmatrix}$$

Therefore, GTR (for four characters, as is often the case in phylogenetics) requires 6 substitution rate parameters, as well as 4 equilibrium base frequency parameters. However, this is usually eliminated down to 9 parameters plus μ, the overall number of substitutions per unit time. When measuring time in substitutions (μ =1) only 9 free parameters remain.

In general, to compute the number of parameters, one must count the number of entries above the diagonal in the matrix, i.e. for n trait values per site $\dfrac{n^2 - n}{2}$, and then add n for the equilibrium base frequencies, and subtract 1 because μ is fixed. One gets

$$\frac{n^2 - n}{2} + n - 1 = \frac{1}{2}n^2 + \frac{1}{2}n - 1.$$

For example, for an amino acid sequence (there are 20 "standard" amino acids that make up proteins), one would find there are 209 parameters. However, when studying coding regions of the genome, it is more common to work with a codon substitution model (a codon is three bases and codes for one amino acid in a protein). There are $4^3 = 64$ codons, but the rates for transitions between codons which differ by more than one base is assumed to be zero. Hence, there are $\dfrac{20 \times 19 \times 3}{2} + 64 - 1 = 633$ parameters.

References

[1] Jukes TH and Cantor CR (1969). *Evolution of Protein Molecules*. New York: Academic Press. pp. 21–132.

[2] Kimura M (1980). "A simple method for estimating evolutionary rates of base substitutions through comparative studies of nucleotide sequences". *Journal of Molecular Evolution* **16**: 111–120. doi:10.1007/BF01731581. PMID 7463489.

[3] Felsenstein J (1981). "Evolutionary trees from DNA sequences: a maximum likelihood approach". *Journal of Molecular Evolution* **17**: 368–376. doi:10.1007/BF01734359.

[4] Hasegawa M, Kishino H, Yano T (1985). "Dating of human-ape splitting by a molecular clock of mitochondrial DNA". *Journal of Molecular Evolution* **22**: 160–174. doi:10.1007/BF02101694.

[5] Kishino H, Hasegawa M (1989). "Evaluation of the maximum likelihood estimate of the evolutionary tree topologies from DNA sequence data, and the branching order in hominoidea". *Journal of Molecular Evolution* **29** (2): 170–179. doi:10.1007/BF02100115.

[6] Felsenstein J, Churchill GA (1996). "A Hidden Markov Model approach to variation among sites in rate of evolution, and the branching order in hominoidea." (http://mbe.oxfordjournals.org/cgi/content/abstract/13/1/93). *Molecular Biology and Evolution* **13** (1): 93–104. .

[7] Tamura K (1992). "Estimation of the number of nucleotide substitutions when there are strong transition-transversion and G+C content biases" (http://mbe.oxfordjournals.org/cgi/content/abstract/9/4/678). *Molecular Biology and Evolution* **9** (4): 678–687. .

[8] Tamura K, Nei M (1993). "Estimation of the number of nucleotide substitutions in the control region of mitochondrial DNA in humans and chimpanzees" (http://mbe.oxfordjournals.org/cgi/content/abstract/10/3/512). *Molecular Biology and Evolution* **10** (3): 512–526. .

[9] Tavaré S (1986). "Some Probabilistic and Statistical Problems in the Analysis of DNA Sequences" (http://www.cmb.usc.edu/people/stavare/STpapers-pdf/T86.pdf). *Lectures on Mathematics in the Life Sciences* (American Mathematical Society) **17**: 57–86. .

Further reading

- Gu X, Li W (1992). "Higher rates of amino acid substitution in rodents than in man". *Molecular Phylogenetics and Evolution* **1**: 211–214. doi:10.1016/1055-7903(92)90017-B. PMID 1342937.

- Li W-H, Ellsworth DL, Krushkal J, Chang BH-J, Hewett-Emmett D (1996). "Rates of nucleotide substitution in primates and rodents and the generation-time effect hypothesis". *Molecular Phylogenetics and Evolution* **5**: 182–187. doi:10.1006/mpev.1996.0012. PMID 8673286.

External links

- DAWG: DNA Assembly With Gaps (http://scit.us/projects/dawg) — free software for simulating sequence evolution

Molecular modelling

Molecular modelling encompasses all theoretical methods and computational techniques used to model or mimic the behaviour of molecules. The techniques are used in the fields of computational chemistry, computational biology and materials science for studying molecular systems ranging from small chemical systems to large biological molecules and material assemblies. The simplest calculations can be performed by hand, but inevitably computers are required to perform molecular modelling of any reasonably sized system. The common feature of molecular modelling techniques is the atomistic level description of the molecular systems; the lowest level of information is individual atoms (or a small group of atoms). This is in contrast to quantum chemistry (also known as electronic structure calculations) where electrons are considered explicitly. The benefit of molecular modelling is that it reduces the complexity of the system, allowing many more particles (atoms) to be considered during simulations.

Molecular mechanics

Molecular mechanics is one aspect of molecular modelling, as it refers to the use of classical mechanics/Newtonian mechanics to describe the physical basis behind the models. Molecular models typically describe atoms (nucleus and electrons collectively) as point charges with an associated mass. The interactions between neighbouring atoms are described by spring-like interactions (representing chemical bonds) and van der Waals forces. The Lennard-Jones potential is commonly used to describe van der Waals forces. The electrostatic interactions are computed based on Coulomb's law. Atoms are assigned coordinates in Cartesian space or in internal coordinates, and can also be assigned velocities in dynamical simulations. The atomic velocities are related to the temperature of the system, a macroscopic quantity. The collective mathematical expression is known as a potential function and is related to the system internal energy (U), a thermodynamic quantity equal to the sum of potential and kinetic energies. Methods which minimize the potential energy are known as energy minimization techniques (e.g., steepest descent and conjugate gradient), while methods that model the behaviour of the system with propagation of time are known as molecular dynamics.

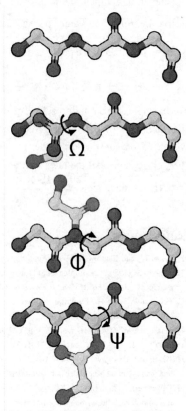

The backbone dihedral angles are included in the molecular model of a protein.

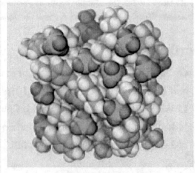

Modelling of ionic liquid

$$E = E_\text{bonds} + E_\text{angle} + E_\text{dihedral} + E_\text{non-bonded}$$

$$E_\text{non-bonded} = E_\text{electrostatic} + E_\text{van der Waals}$$

This function, referred to as a potential function, computes the molecular potential energy as a sum of energy terms that describe the deviation of bond lengths, bond angles and torsion angles away from equilibrium values, plus terms for non-bonded pairs of atoms describing van der Waals and electrostatic interactions. The set of parameters consisting of equilibrium bond lengths, bond angles, partial charge values, force constants and van der Waals parameters are collectively known as a force field. Different implementations of molecular mechanics use different mathematical expressions and different parameters for the potential function. The common force fields in use today have been developed by using high level quantum calculations and/or fitting to experimental data. The technique known as energy minimization is used to find positions of zero gradient for all atoms, in other words, a local energy minimum. Lower energy states are more stable and are commonly investigated because of their role in chemical and biological processes. A molecular dynamics simulation, on the other hand, computes the behaviour of a system as a function of time. It involves solving Newton's laws of motion, principally the second law, $\mathbf{F} = m\mathbf{a}$. Integration of Newton's laws of motion, using different integration algorithms, leads to atomic trajectories in space and time. The force on an atom is defined as the negative gradient of the potential energy function. The energy minimization technique is useful for obtaining a static picture for comparing between states of similar systems, while molecular dynamics provides information about the dynamic processes with the intrinsic inclusion of temperature effects.

Variables

Molecules can be modelled either in vacuum or in the presence of a solvent such as water. Simulations of systems in vacuum are referred to as *gas-phase* simulations, while those that include the presence of solvent molecules are referred to as *explicit solvent* simulations. In another type of simulation, the effect of solvent is estimated using an empirical mathematical expression; these are known as *implicit solvation* simulations.

Applications

Molecular modelling methods are now routinely used to investigate the structure, dynamics, surface properties and thermodynamics of inorganic, biological and polymeric systems. The types of biological activity that have been investigated using molecular modelling include protein folding, enzyme catalysis, protein stability, conformational changes associated with biomolecular function, and molecular recognition of proteins, DNA, and membrane complexes.

Popular software for molecular modelling

- Abalone classical
- ADF quantum
- AMBER classical
- Ascalaph Designer[1] classical & quantum
- AutoDock,
- AutoDock Vina,
- BALLView
- Biskit
- BOSS classical
- Cerius2
- CHARMM classical
- Chimera
- Coot[2]
- COSMOS (software)[3]
- CP2K quantum
- CPMD quantum
- Culgi
- Discovery Studio [4] classical and quantum
- DOCK classical

- eHiTS [5] docking and virtual screening package
- Firefly quantum
- FoldX
- GAMESS (UK) quantum
- GAMESS (US) quantum
- GAUSSIAN quantum
- Ghemical
- GPIUTMD classical
- Gorgon[6]
- GROMACS classical
- GROMOS classical
- InsightII classical & quantum
- LAMMPS classical
- Lead Finder [7] classical
- LigandScout
- MacroModel classical
- MADAMM.[8] [9]
- MarvinSpace[10]
- Materials and Processes Simulations[11]
- Materials Studio [12] classical & quantum
- MDynaMix classical
- MMTK
- Molecular Docking Server
- Molecular Operating Environment (MOE) classical & quantum
- MolIDE [13] homology modelling
- Molsoft ICM[14]
- MOPAC quantum
- NAMD classical
- NOCH
- Oscail X
- PyMOL visualization
- Q-Chem quantum
- ReaxFF
- ROSETTA
- SCWRL [15] side-chain prediction
- Sirius
- Spartan (software)[16] quantum
- StruMM3D (STR3DI32)[17]
- Sybyl (software)[18]
- MCCCS Towhee[19] classical
- TURBOMOLE quantum
- VMD visualization
- VLifeMDS Integrated molecular modelling & simulation
- WHAT IF[20]
- xeo[21]
- XPLOR-NIH[22]
- YASARA[23]

- Zodiac (software)[24]

References

[1] *Agile Molecule* (http://www.biomolecular-modeling.com/index.html)

[2] *York Structural Biology Laboratory* (http://www.ysbl.york.ac.uk/~emsley/coot/)

[3] COSMOS (http://www.cosmos-software.de/ce_intro.html) - Computer Simulation of Molecular Structures

[4] *Accelrys Inc* (http://accelrys.com)

[5] *SimBioSys Inc* (http://www.simbiosys.com)

[6] *Gorgon-An interactive molecular modeling system* (http://gorgon.wustl.edu)

[7] *MolTech Lead Finder* (http://www.moltech.ru)

[8] *MADAMM* (http://www.fc.up.pt/pessoas/nscerque/MADAMM.html)

[9] Cerqueira NM, Fernandes PA, Eriksson LA, Ramos MJ (July 2009). "MADAMM: A multistaged docking with an automated molecular modeling protocol". *Proteins: Structure, Function, and Bioinformatics* **74** (1): 192–206. doi:10.1002/prot.22146. PMID 18618708.

[10] *ChemAxon* (http://www.chemaxon.com/product/mspace.html)

[11] *MAPS* (http://www.scienomics.com/index.php)

[12] *Accelrys Inc* (http://accelrys.com)

[13] *MolIDE* (http://dunbrack.fccc.edu/molide)

[14] *Molsoft* (http://www.molsoft.com/)

[15] *SCWRL4* (http://dunbrack.fccc.edu/scwrl4)

[16] *Wavefunction, Inc.* (http://www.wavefun.com/)

[17] *Exorga, Inc.* (http://www.exorga.com/)

[18] *Tipos* (http://www.tripos.com/sybyl/)

[19] *MCCCS Towhee* (http://towhee.sourceforge.net/) - Monte Carlo for Complex Chemical Systems

[20] *CMBI* (http://swift.cmbi.ru.nl/whatif/)

[21] *xeo* (http://sourceforge.net/projects/xeo)

[22] *[http://nmr.cit.nih.gov/xplor-nih xplor'*

[23] *YASARA* (http://www.yasara.org/)

[24] *ZedeN* (http://www.zeden.org)

- C.D. Schwieters, J.J. Kuszewski, N. Tjandra and G.M. Clore, "The Xplor-NIH NMR Molecular Structure Determination Package," J. Magn. Res., 160, 66-74 (2003).

- C.D. Schwieters, J.J. Kuszewski, and G.M. Clore, "Using Xplor-NIH for NMR molecular structure determination," Progr. NMR Spectroscopy 48, 47-62 (2006).

- M. P. Allen, D. J. Tildesley, *Computer simulation of liquids*, 1989, Oxford University Press, ISBN 0-19-855645-4.

- A. R. Leach, *Molecular Modelling: Principles and Applications*, 2001, ISBN 0-582-38210-6

- D. Frenkel, B. Smit, *Understanding Molecular Simulation: From Algorithms to Applications*, 1996, ISBN 0-12-267370-0

- D. C. Rapaport, *The Art of Molecular Dynamics Simulation*, 2004, ISBN 0-521-82586-7

- R. J. Sadus, *Molecular Simulation of Fluids: Theory, Algorithms and Object-Orientation*, 2002, ISBN 0-444-51082-6

- K.I.Ramachandran, G Deepa and Krishnan Namboori. P.K. *Computational Chemistry and Molecular Modeling Principles and Applications* 2008 (http://www.amrita.edu/cen/ccmm) ISBN 978-3-540-77302-3 Springer-Verlag GmbH

- Baeurle, S.A. (2009). "Multiscale modeling of polymer materials using field-theoretic methodologies: a survey about recent developments" (http://www.springerlink.com/content/xl057580272w8703/). *J. Math. Chem.* **46**: 363–426. doi:10.1007/s10910-008-9467-3.

External links

- Center for Molecular Modeling at the National Institutes of Health (NIH) (http://cmm.info.nih.gov/modeling/) (U.S. Government Agency)
- Molecular Simulation (http://www.tandf.co.uk/journals/titles/08927022.asp), details for the Molecular Simulation journal, ISSN: 0892-7022 (print), 1029-0435 (online)
- The eCheminfo (http://www.echeminfo.com/) Network and Community of Practice in Informatics and Modeling

Homepage

Morphometrics

Morphometrics[1] Morphometrics refers to the quantitative analysis of *form*, a concept that encompasses size and shape. Morphometric analyses are commonly performed on organisms, and are useful in analyzing their fossil record, the impact of mutations on shape, developmental changes in form, covariances between ecological factors and shape, as well for estimating quantitative-genetic parameters of shape. Morphometrics can be used to quantify a trait of evolutionary significance, and by detecting changes in the shape, deduce something of their ontogeny, function or evolutionary relationships. A major objective of morphometrics is to statistically test hypotheses about the factors that affect shape.

"Morphometrics", in the broader sense of the term, is also used to precisely locate certain areas of featureless organs such as the brain, and is used in describing the shapes of other things.

Forms of morphometrics

Three general approaches to form are usually distinguished: traditional morphometrics, landmark-based morphometrics and outline-based morphometrics.

"Traditional" morphometrics

Traditional morphometrics analyzes lengths, widths, masses, angles, ratios and areas (image [1]).[2] In general, traditional morphometric data are measurements of size. A drawback of using many measurements of size is that most will be highly correlated; as a result, there are few independent variables despite the many measurements. For instance, tibia length will vary femur length and also with humerus and ulna length and even with measurements of the head. Traditional morphometric data are nonetheless useful when either absolute or relative sizes are of particular interest, such as in studies of growth. These data are also useful when size measurements are of theoretical importance such as body mass and limb cross-sectional area and length in studies of functional morphology. However, these measurements have one important limitation: they contain little information about the spatial distribution of shape changes across the organism.

Landmark-based geometric morphometrics

In landmark-based geometric morphometrics that spatial information is contained in the data because the data are coordinates of "landmarks": discrete anatomical loci that are arguably homologous in all individuals in the analysis. For example, where sutures intersect is a landmark as are intersections between veins on an insect wing or leaf. So are foramina, small holes through which veins and blood vessels pass. These points can be regarded as the "same" point in all specimens in the study. Landmark-based studies have traditionally analyzed 2D data, but with the increasing availability of 3D imaging techniques, 3D analysis are becoming more feasible even for small structures such as teeth.[3] Finding enough landmarks to provide a comprehensive description of shape can be difficult when working with fossils or easily damaged specimens. That is because all landmarks must be present in all specimens, although coordinates of missing landmarks can be estimated. The data for each individual consists of a *configuration* of landmarks.

There are three recognized categories of landmarks ([4]). Type 1 landmarks are locally defined, meaning that they are defined in terms of structures close to that point; for example, an intersection between three sutures, or intersections between veins on an insect wing are locally defined and surrounded by tissue on all sides. Type 3 landmarks, in contrast, are defined in terms of points far away from the landmark, and are often defined in terms of a point "furthest away" from another point. Type 2 landmarks are intermediate; this category includes points such as the tip structure, or local minima and maxima of curvature. They are defined in terms of local features, but they are not surrounded on all sides. In addition to landmarks, there are "semilandmarks," points along a curve. Their position along the curve is arbitrary but these points provide information about curvature in two [5] or three dimensions [6]

Procrustes-based geometric morphometrics

Shape analysis begins by removing the information that is not about shape. By definition, shape is not altered by translation, scaling or rotation.[7] Thus, to compare shapes, the non-shape information is removed from the coordinates of landmarks. There is more than one way to do these three operations. One method is to fix the coordinates of two points to (0,0) and (0,1), which are the two ends of a baseline. In one step, the shapes are translated to the same position (the same two coordinates are fixed to those values), the shapes are scaled (to unit baseline length) and the shapes are rotated[4]. An alternative, and preferred method, is **Procrustes superimposition**. This method translates the centroid of the shapes to (0,0); the x centroid of the centroid is the average of the x coordinates of the landmarks of an individual, and the y coordinate of the centroid is the average of the y-coordinates. Shapes are scaled to unit centroid size, which is the square root of the summed squared distances of each landmark to the centroid. The configuration is rotated to minimize the deviation between it and a reference, typically the mean shape. In the case of semi-landmarks, variation in position along the curve is also removed. Because shape space is curved, analyses are done by projecting shapes onto a space tangent to shape space. Within the tangent space, conventional multivariate statistical methods such as multivariate analysis of variance and multivariate regression, can be used to test statistical hypotheses about shape.

Procrustes-based analyses have some limitations. One is that the Procrustes superimposition uses a least-squares criterion to find the optimal rotation; consequently, variation that is localized to a single landmark will be smeared out across many. This is called the ""Pinocchio Effect." Another is that the superimposition may itself impose a pattern of covariation on the landmarks.[8] [9] Additionally, any information that cannot be captured by landmarks and semilandmarks cannot be analyzed, including classical measurements like "greatest skull breadth." Moreover, there are criticisms of Procrustes-based methods that motivate an alternative approach to analyzing landmark data.

Outline analysis

Outline analysis is another approach to analyzing shape. What distinguishes outline analysis is that coefficients of mathematical functions are fitted to points sampled along the outline. There are a number of ways of quantifying an outline. Older techniques such as the "fit to a polynomial curve" [10] and Principal components quantitative analysis [11] have been superseded by the two main modern approaches: eigenshape analysis,[12] and elliptical fourier analysis (EFA),[13] using hand- or computer-traced outlines. The former involves fitting a preset number of semilandmarks at equal intervals around the outline of a shape, recording the deviation of each step from semilandmark to semilandmark from what the angle of that step would be were the object a simple circle.[14] The latter defines the outline as the sum of the minimum number of ellipses required to mimic the shape.[15]

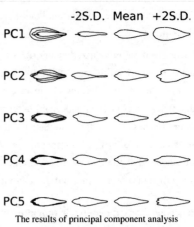

The results of principal component analysis performed on an outline analysis of some thelodont denticles.

Both methods have their weaknesses; the most dangerous (and easily overcome) is their susceptibility to noise in the outline.[16] Likewise, neither compares homologous points, and global change is always given more weight than local variation (which may have large biological consequences). Eigenshape analysis requires an equivalent starting point to be set for each specimen, which can be a source of error EFA also suffers from redundancy in that not all variables are independent.[16] On the other hand, it is possible to apply them to complex curves without having to define a centroid; this makes removing the effect of location, size and rotation much simpler.[16] The perceived failings of outline morphometrics are that it doesn't compare points of a homologous origin, and that it oversimplifies complex shapes by restricting itself to considering the outline and not internal changes. Also, since it works by approximating the outline by a series of ellipses, it deals poorly with pointed shapes.[17]

One criticism of outline-based methods is that they disregard homology – a famous example of this disregard being the ability of outline-based methods to compare a scapula to a potato chip.[18] Such a comparison which would not be possible if the data were restricted to biologically homologous points. An argument against that critique is that, if landmark approaches to morphometrics can be used to test biological hypotheses in the absence of homology data, it is inappropriate to fault outline-based approaches for enabling the same types of studies [19]

Analyzing data

To display the differences in shape, the data need to be reduced to a comprehensible (low-dimensional) form. Principal component analysis (PCA) is the most commonly employed tool to do this. Simply put, the technique projects as much of the overall variation as possible into a few dimensions. See the figure (upload imminent) for an example. Each axis on a PCA plot is an eigenvector of the covariance matrix of shape variables. The first axis accounts for maximum variation in the sample, with further axes representing further ways in which the samples vary. The pattern of clustering of samples in this morphospace represents similarities and differences in shapes, which can reflect phylogenetic relationships. As well as exploring patterns of variation, Multivariate statistical methods can be used to test statistical hypotheses about factors that affect shape and to visualize their effects.

Landmark data allow the difference between population means, or the deviation an individual from its population mean, to be visualized in at least two ways. One depicts vectors at landmarks that show the magnitude and direction in which that landmark is displaced relative to the others. The second depicts the difference via the thin plate splines, an interpolation function that models change *between* landmarks from the data of changes in coordinates *of* landmarks. This function produces what look like deformed grids; where regions that relatively elongated, the grid will look stretched and where those regions are relatively shortened, the grid will look compressed.

Applications

Neuroimaging

In neuroimaging, the most common variants are voxel-based morphometry, deformation-based morphometry and surface-based morphometry of the brain.

Bone histomorphometry

Histomorphometry of bone involves obtaining a bone biopsy specimen and processing of bone specimens in the laboratory, obtaining estimates of the proportional volumes and surfaces occupied by different components of bone.[20] Obtaining a bone biopsy is accomplished by using a bone biopsy trephine.[21]

Other applications

The application of morphometrics is not restricted to biological uses. It can also be applied to terrain in the form of geomorphometrics. It also has a host of other applications.

Notes

1 from Greek: "morph," meaning shape or form, and "metron", measurement

External links

Discussion

- Dickinson, T.A. (2001). "Morphometric methods" [22]. Retrieved 2008-03-10.

Software

- PAST [23]
- SHAPE [24] – Elliptic Fourier Descriptors
- Morphometric software [25] – Archive of many different types of software for use in morphometrics - especially geometric morphometrics.

Bibliography

- Adams, Dean C.; Michael L. Collyer (2009). "A general framework for the analysis of phenotypic trajectories in evolutionary studies". *Evolution* **63** (5): 1143–1154. doi:10.1111/j.1558-5646.2009.00649.x. PMID 19210539.

- Bookstein, Fred (1991). *Morphometric Tools for Landmark Data: Geometry and Biology*. Cambridge: Cambridge University Press. ISBN 0521585988.

- Cadrin, Steven X. (2000). "Advances in morphometric identification of fishery stocks". *Reviews in Fish Biology and Fisheries* **10**: 91–112. doi:10.1023/A:1008939104413.

- Elewa, A.M.T., editor (2004). *Morphometrics: Applications In Biology And Paleontology*. Berlin: Springer. ISBN 3–540–21429–1.

- Klingenberg, C.P.; N. A. Gidaszewski (2010). "Testing and quantifying phylogenetic signals and homoplasy in morphometric data". *Systematic Biology* **59** (39): 4245–261.

- McLellan, Tracy; John A. Endler (June 1998). "The Relative Success of Some Methods for Measuring and Describing the Shape of Complex Objects" [26]. *Systematic Biology* (Society of Systematic Biologists) **47** (2):

264–281. doi:10.1080/106351598260914. Retrieved 2007-03-22.

• Rohlf, F.J.; D. Slice (1990). "Extensions of the Procrustes method for the optimal superimposition of landmarks". *Systematic Zoology* **10** (39): 40–59.

References

[1] http://www.botany.utoronto.ca/faculty/dickinson/leaf1tiny.jpg

[2] Marcus, L. F. (1990). Chapter 4. Traditional morphometrics. In Proceedings of the Michigan Morphometric Workshop. Special Publication No. 2. F. J. Rohlf and F. L. Bookstein. Ann Arbor MI, The University of Michigan Museum of Zoology: 77–122.

[3] Singleton, M.; Rosenberger, A. L., Robinson, C., O'Neill, R. (2011). "Allometric and metameric shape variation in *Pan* mandibular molars: A digital morphometric analysis". *Anatomical Record-Advances in Integrative Anatomy and Evolutionary Biology* **294** (2): 322–334. doi:10.1002/ar.21315.

[4] Bookstein, F. L. (1991). *Morphometric Tools for Landmark Data: Geometry and Biology.* Cambridge: Cambridge University Press.

[5] Zelditch, M.; Wood, A. R.. Bonnet, R. M., Swiderski, D. L. (2008). "Modularity of the rodent mandible: Integrating muscles, bones and teeth". *Evolution & Development* **10** (6): 756–768. doi:10.1111/j.1525-142X.2008.00290.x.

[6] Mitteroecker, P; Bookstein, F.L. (2008). "The evolutionary role of modularity and integration in the hominoid cranium". *Evolution* **62** (4): 943–958. doi:10.1111/j.1558-5646.2008.00321.x. PMID 18194472.

[7] Kendall, D.G. (1977). "The diffusion of shape". *Advances in Applied Probability* **9** (3): 428–430. doi:10.2307/1426091.

[8] Rohlf, F. J.; Slice, D. (1990). "Extensions of the Procrustes method for the optimal superimposition of landmarks". *Systematic Zoology* **39** (1): 40–59. doi:10.2307/2992207.

[9] Walker, J. (2000). "The ability of geometric morphometric methods to estimate a known covariance matrix". *Systematic Biology* **49** (4): 686–696. doi:10.1080/106351500750049770. PMID 12116434.

[10] Rogers, Margaret (1982). "A description of the generating curve of bivalves with straight hingess". *Palaeontology* **25**: 109–117.

[11] Glassburn, T.A. (1995). "A new palaeontological technique describing temporal shape variation in Miocene bivalves". *Palaeontology* **38**: 133–151.

[12] Lohmann, G.P. (1983). "Eigenshape analysis of microfossils: A general morphometric procedure for describing changes in shape" (http://www.springerlink.com/index/Q09U01G648273374.pdf) (PDF). *Mathematical Geology* **15** (6): 659–672. doi:10.1007/BF01033230. . Retrieved 2008-03-10.

[13] Ferson, S.; Rohlf, F.J.; Koehn, R.K. (1985). "Measuring Shape Variation of Two-Dimensional Outlines". *Systematic Zoology* **34** (1): 59–68. doi:10.2307/2413345. JSTOR 2413345.

[14] For an example "in use", see MacLeod, N.; Rose, K.D. (January 1, 1993). "Inferring locomotor behavior in Paleogene mammals via eigenshape analysis" (http://www.ajsonline.org/cgi/content/abstract/293/A/300) (abstract). *American Journal of Science* **293** (A): 300. doi:10.2475/ajs.293.A.300. . Retrieved 2008-03-10.

[15] e.g. Schmittbuhl, M.; Rieger, J.; Le Minor, J.M.; Schaaf, A.; Guy, F. (2007). "Variations of the mandibular shape in extant hominoids: Generic, specific, and subspecific quantification using elliptical fourier analysis in lateral view". *American Journal of Physical Anthropology* **132** (1): 119. doi:10.1002/ajpa.20476. PMID 17063462.

[16] Haines, A.J.; Crampton, J.S. (2000). "Improvements To The Method Of Fourier Shape Analysis As Applied In Morphometric Studies". *Palaeontology* **43** (4): 765–783. doi:10.1111/1475-4983.00148.

[17] Zelditch, M.L,; Swiderski,D.L., Sheets,H.D., Fink,W.L. (2004). *Geometric Morphometrics for Biologists: A Primer.* San Diego: Elsevier Academic Press.

[18] Zelditch, M.; Fink, W. L, Swiderski, D. L (1995). "Morphometrics, homology, and phylogenetics - Quantified characters as synapomorphies". *Systematic Biology* **44** (2): 179–189.

[19] MacLeod, N. (1999). "Generalizing and Extending the Eigenshape Method of Shape Space Visualization and Analysis" (http://links.jstor.org/sici?sici=0094–8373(199924)25:1<107:GAETEM>2.0.CO;2–2). *Paleobiology* **25** (1): 107–138. . Retrieved 2008-03-10.

[20] Revell PA (December 1983). "Histomorphometry of bone". *J. Clin. Pathol.* **36** (12): 1323–31. doi:10.1136/jcp.36.12.1323. PMC 498562. PMID 6361070.

[21] Hodgson SF; Johnson, KA; Muhs, JM; Lufkin, EG; McCarthy, JT (January 1986). "Outpatient percutaneous biopsy of the iliac crest: methods, morbidity, and patient acceptance". *Mayo Clin Proc* **61** (1): 28–33. PMID 3941566.

[22] http://www.botany.utoronto.ca/faculty/dickinson/MorphometricMethods.HTML

[23] http://folk.uio.no/ohammer/past/

[24] http://cse.naro.affrc.go.jp/iwatah/shape/

[25] http://life.bio.sunysb.edu/morph/

[26] http://links.jstor.org/sici?sici=1063–5157%28199806%2947%3A2%3C264%3ATRSOSM%3E2.0.CO%3B2-S

MOWSE

MOWSE (for **MOlecular Weight SEarch**) is a method for identification of proteins from the molecular weight of peptides created by proteolytic digestion and measured with mass spectrometry.[1] The **MOWSE** algorithm was developed by Darryl Pappin and David Perkins at the Imperial Cancer Research Fund, and licensed from Cancer Research Technology. The probability-based **MOWSE** score formed the basis of development of **Mascot**, a proprietary software for protein identification from mass spectrometry data. It is documented here [2]

References

[1] Pappin DJ, Hojrup P, Bleasby AJ (June 1993). "Rapid identification of proteins by peptide-mass fingerprinting" (http://linkinghub.elsevier.
      com/retrieve/pii/0960-9822(93)90195-T). *Curr. Biol.* **3** (6): 327–32. doi:10.1016/0960-9822(93)90195-T. PMID 15335725. .
[2] http://www.matrixscience.com/help/scoring_help.html

Multiple displacement amplification

Multiple displacement amplification (MDA) is a non-PCR based DNA amplification technique. This method can rapidly amplify minute amount of DNA samples to reasonable quantity for genomic analysis. The reaction starts by annealing random hexamer primers to the template and DNA synthesis is carried out by high fidelity enzyme, preferentially *Φ29* at a constant temperature. Comparing with the conventional PCR amplification techniques, MDA generates larger sized products with lower error frequency. This method has been currently actively used in whole genome amplification (WGA) and has become a promising method to be applied in single cell genome sequencing and sequencing based genetic studies.

Background

Many biological and forensic cases involving genetic analysis require sequencing of minute amounts of samples, such as DNA from uncultured single cells or trace amounts of tissues collected from crime scenes. Conventional Polymerase Chain Reaction (PCR)-based DNA amplification methods are usually carried out on at least nanograms of DNA samples from cultured cells by using *Taq* polymerase and primers. However, the amount of DNA from uncultured single cells, which could be as little as a few femtograms, is not enough to start PCR reactions. Sufficient amount of DNA sample is crucial in sequencing based DNA analysis. Therefore, a more efficient method to amplify minute amounts of DNA is necessary, especially in single cell genomic studies.

Materials

Phi 29 DNA polymerase

Bacteriophage *Φ29* DNA polymerase is a high processivity enzyme that can produce DNA product of 7kb to 10kb long. Its high fidelity and 3'–5'proofreading activity reduces the amplification error rate to 1 in 10^6–10^7 bases compared to conventional *Taq* polymerase. The reaction can be carried out at a moderate isothermal condition of 30 °C and therefore exempts the needs of the Thermocycler. It has been actively used in cell-free cloning, which is the enzymatic method of amplifying DNA in vitro without cell culturing and DNA extraction. The large fragment of *Bst* DNA polymerase is also used in MDA, but *Φ29* is generally preferred due to its sufficient product yield and proofreading activity.[1]

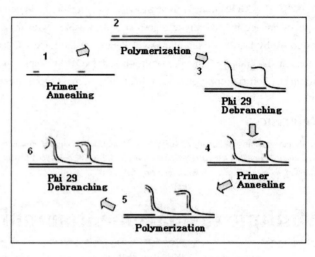

MDA reaction steps.JPG.

Hexamer primers

Hexamer primers are sequences composed of six random nucleotides. The sequences are thiophosphate-modified at their 3' end and therefore resistant to 3'–5' exonuclease activity by *Φ29* DNA polymerase. MDA reaction starts with the annealing of random hexamer primers to the DNA template and then continues with the chain elongation phi29. Increasing number of primer annealing events happens along the amplification reaction.

Reaction

The amplification reaction initiates when multiple primer hexamers anneal to the template. When DNA synthesis proceeds to the next starting site, the polymerase displaces the newly produced DNA strand and continues its strand elongation. The strand displacement generates newly synthesized single stranded DNA template for more primers to anneal. Further primer annealing and strand displacement on the newly synthesized template results in a hyper-branched DNA network. The sequence debranching during amplification results in high yield of the products. To separate the DNA branching network, S1 nucleases is used to cleave the fragments at displacement sites. The nicks on the resulting DNA fragments are repaired by DNA polymerase I. The generated DNA fragments can be directly used for analysis or be ligated to generate genomic libraries for further sequencing analysis.[2]

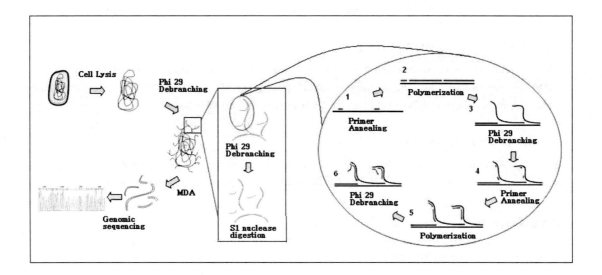

Product quality

MDA can generate 1–2 µg of DNA from single cell with genome coverage of up to 99%. Products also have lower error rate and larger sizes compared to PCR based *Taq* amplification.

General work flow of MDA:[3]

1. *Sample preparation*: Samples are collected and diluted in the appropriate reaction buffer(Ca^{2+} and Mg^{2+} free). Cells are lysed with alkaline buffer.
2. *Condition*: The MDA reaction with *Φ29* polymerase is carried out at 30 ℃. The reaction usually takes about 2.5–3 hours.
3. *End of reaction*: Inactivate enzymes at 65 ℃ before collection of the amplified DNA products
4. DNA products can be purified with commercial purification kit.

Advantages

MDA generates sufficient yield of DNA products. It is a powerful tool of amplifying DNA molecules from samples, such as uncultured microorganism or single cells to the amount that would be sufficient for sequencing studies. The large size of MDA amplified DNA products also provide desirable sample quality for identifying the size of polymorphic repeat alleles. Its high fidelity also makes it reliable to be used in the single-nucleotide polymorphism (SNP) allele detection. Due to its strand displacement during amplification, the amplified DNA has sufficient coverage of the source DNA molecules, which provides high quality product for genomic analysis. The products of displaced strands can be subsequently cloned into vectors to construct library for subsequent sequencing reactions.

Limitations

Allelic dropout (ADO)

ADO is defined as the random non-amplification of one of the alleles present in a heterozygous sample. Some studies have reported the ADO rate of the MDA products to be 0–60%. This drawback decreases the accuracy of genotyping of single sample and misdiagnosis in other MDA involved applications. ADO appears to be independent of the fragment sizes and has been reported to have similar rate in other single-cell techniques. Possible solutions are to use a different lysing conditions or to carry out multiple rounds of amplifications from the diluted MDA products since PCR mediated amplification from cultured cells has been reported to give lower ADO rates.

Preferential amplification

'Preferential amplification' is over-amplification of one of the alleles in comparison to the other. Most studies on MDA have reported this issue. The amplification bias is currently observed to be random. It might affect the analysis of small stretches of genomic DNA in identifying Short Tandem Repeats (STR) alleles.

Primer-primer interactions

Endogenous template-independent primer-primer interaction is due to the random design of hexmer primers. One possible solution is to design constrained-randomized hexanucleotide primers that do not cross-hybridize.

Applications

Single cell genome sequencing

Genome sequencing of single sperm cell have been reported and successfully amplified in Preimplantation Genetic Diagnosis (PGD) or parental diagnosis. This ensures that an oocyte or early-stage embryo has no symptoms of disease before implantation.[4]

Sequencing genome of single uncultured cell bacteria cell, such as *Prochlorococcus*, and single spore of fungi has been reported.[5] The success of more MDA based genome sequencing from a single cell provides a powerful tool of studying diseases that have heterogeneous property, such as Cancer.

The MDA products from a single cell has also been successfully used in array comparative genomics hybridization(CGH) experiments, which usually requires relatively large amount of amplified DNA.

Forensic analysis

Trace amount of samples collected from crime scenes can be amplified by MDA to the quantity that is enough for forensic DNA analysis, which is popularly used to in identifying victims and suspects.

References

[1] Hutchison, C. A. (2005). "Cell-free cloning using 29 DNA polymerase". *Proceedings of the National Academy of Sciences* **102** (48): 17332–6. doi:10.1073/pnas.0508809102. PMC 1283157. PMID 16286637.

[2] Shoaib; Baconnais, S; Mechold, U; Le Cam, E; Lipinski, M; Ogryzko, V (2008). "Multiple displacement amplification for complex mixtures of DNA fragments". *BMC genomics* **9**: 415. doi:10.1186/1471-2164-9-415. PMC 2553422. PMID 18793430.

[3] Spits; Le Caignec, C; De Rycke, M; Van Haute, L; Van Steirteghem, A; Liebaers, I; Sermon, K (2006). "Whole-genome multiple displacement amplification from single cells". *Nature protocols* **1** (4): 1965–70. doi:10.1038/nprot.2006.326. PMID 17487184.

[4] Coskun; Alsmadi, O (2007). "Whole genome amplification from a single cell: a new era for preimplantation genetic diagnosis". *Prenatal diagnosis* **27** (4): 297–302. doi:10.1002/pd.1667. PMID 17278176.

[5] Zhang; Martiny, AC; Reppas, NB; Barry, KW; Malek, J; Chisholm, SW; Church, GM (2006). "Sequencing genomes from single cells by polymerase cloning". *Nature biotechnology* **24** (6): 680–6. doi:10.1038/nbt1214. PMID 16732271.

Multiple EM for Motif Elicitation

Multiple EM for Motif Elicitation or **MEME** is a tool for discovering motifs in a group of related DNA or protein sequences.[1]

A motif is a sequence pattern that occurs repeatedly in a group of related protein or DNA sequences. MEME represents motifs as position-dependent letter-probability matrices which describe the probability of each possible letter at each position in the pattern. Individual MEME motifs do not contain gaps. Patterns with variable-length gaps are split by MEME into two or more separate motifs.

MEME takes as input a group of DNA or protein sequences (the training set) and outputs as many motifs as requested. It uses statistical modeling techniques to automatically choose the best width, number of occurrences, and description for each motif.

Definition

What the MEME algorithms actually does can be understood from two different perspectives. From a biological point of view, MEME identifies and characterizes shared motifs in a set of unaligned sequences. From the computer science aspect, MEME finds a set of non-overlapping, approximately matching substrings given a starting set of strings.

Use

With MEME one can find similar biological functions and structures in different sequences. One has to take into account that the sequences variation can be significant and that the motifs are sometimes very small. It is also useful to take into account that the binding sites for proteins are very specific. This makes it easier to reduce wet-lab experiments (reduces costs and time). Indeed to better discover the motifs relevant for a biological point of view one has to carefully choose:

- The best width of motifs.
- The number of occurrences in each sequence.
- The composition of each motif.

Algorithm Components

The algorithm uses several types of well know functions:

- Expectation maximization (EM).
- EM based heuristic for choosing the EM starting point.
- Maximum likelihood ratio based (LRT-based). Heuristic for determining the best number of model-free parameters.
- Multi-start for searching over possible motif widths.
- Greedy search for finding multiple motifs.

However, one often doesn't know where the starting position is. Several possibilities exist:

- Exactly one motif per sequence.
- One or zero motif per sequence.
- Any number of motifs per sequence.

Example

In the following example, one has a weight matrix of 3 different sequences, without gaps.

| 1: C G G G T A A G T |
| 2: A A G G T A T G C |
| 3: C A G G T G A G G |

Now one counts the number of nucleotides contained in all sequences:

A: 1 2 0 0 0 2 2 0 0	7
C: 2 0 0 0 0 0 0 0 1	3
G: 0 1 3 3 0 1 0 3 1	12
T: 0 0 0 0 3 0 1 0 1	5

Now one needs to sum up the total: 7+3+12+5 = 27; this gives us a "dividing factor" for each base, or the equivalent probability of each nucleotides.

A: 7/27 = 0.26

C: 3/27 = 0.11

G: 12/27 = 0.44

T: 5/27 = 0.19

Now one can "redo" the weight matrix (WM) by dividing it by the total number of sequences (in our case 3):

A: 0.33 0.66 0.00 0.00 0.00 0.66 0.66 0.00 0.00

C: 0.66 0.00 0.00 0.00 0.00 0.00 0.00 0.00 0.33

G: 0.00 0.33 1.00 1.00 0.00 0.33 0.00 1.00 0.33

T: 0.00 0.00 0.00 0.00 1.00 0.00 0.33 0.00 0.33

Next, one divides the entries of the WM at position x_i with the probability of the base x.

A: 1.27 2.30 0.00 0.00 0.00 2.30 2.30 0.00 0.00

C: 6.00 0.00 0.00 0.00 0.00 0.00 0.00 0.00 3.00

G: 0.00 0.75 2.27 2.27 0.00 0.75 0.00 2.27 0.75

T: 0.00 0.00 0.00 0.00 5.26 0.00 1.74 0.00 1.74

In general one would now multiply the probabilities. In our case one would have zero for every one. Due to this we take the logarithm and define log(0)=(-10):

| A: 0.10 0.36 -10 -10 -10 0.36 0.36 -10 -10 |
| C: 0.78 -10 -10 -10 -10 -10 -10 -10 0.48 |
| G: -10 -0.1 0.36 0.36 -10 -0.1 -10 0.36 |
| T: -10 -10 -10 -10 0.72 -10 0.24 -10 0.24 |

This is our new weight matrix (WM). One is ready to use an example of a promoter sequence to determine its score. To do this, one has to add the numbers found at the position x_i of the logarithmic WM. For instance, if one takes the AGGCTGATC promoter:

0.10 - 0.1 + 0.36 - 10 + 0.72 - 0.1 + 0.36 - 10 + 0.48 = -18.18

This is then divided by the number of entries (in our case 9) yielding a score of -2.02.

Shortcomings

The MEME algorithms has several drawbacks including:

- Allowance for gaps/substitutions/insertions not included.
- Ability to test significance often not included.
- Erased input data each time a new motif is discovered (the algorithm assumes the new motif is correct).
- Limitation to two component case.
- Time complexity is high.
- Very pessimistic about alignment (which might lead to missed signals).

References

[1] Bailey TL, Williams N, Misleh C, Li WW (2006). "MEME: discovering and analyzing DNA and protein sequence motifs". *Nucleic Acids Res* **34** (Web Server issue): W369-373. doi:10.1093/nar/gkl198. PMC 1538909. PMID 16845028.

External links

- The MEME Suite (http://meme.sdsc.edu/meme/intro.html) — Motif-based sequence analysis tools

Multiple sequence alignment

A **multiple sequence alignment (MSA)** is a sequence alignment of three or more biological sequences, generally protein, DNA, or RNA. In many cases, the input set of query sequences are assumed to have an evolutionary relationship by which they share a lineage and are descended from a common ancestor. From the resulting MSA, sequence homology can be inferred and phylogenetic analysis can be conducted to assess the sequences' shared evolutionary origins. Visual depictions of the alignment as in the image at right illustrate mutation events such as point mutations (single amino acid or nucleotide changes) that appear as differing characters in a single alignment column, and insertion or deletion mutations (indels or gaps) that appear as hyphens in one or more of the sequences in the alignment. Multiple sequence alignment is often used to assess sequence conservation of protein domains, tertiary and secondary structures, and even individual amino acids or nucleotides.

Multiple sequence alignment also refers to the process of aligning such a sequence set. Because three or more sequences of biologically relevant length can be difficult and are almost always time-consuming to align by hand, computational algorithms are used to produce and analyze the alignments. MSAs require more sophisticated methodologies than pairwise alignment because they are more computationally complex. Most multiple sequence alignment programs use heuristic methods rather than

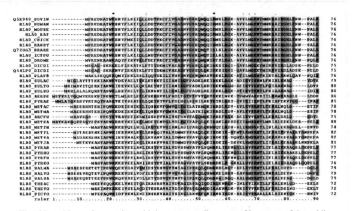

First 90 positions of a protein multiple sequence alignment of instances of the acidic ribosomal protein P0 (L10E) from several organisms. Generated with ClustalX.

global optimization because identifying the optimal alignment between more than a few sequences of moderate length is prohibitively computationally expensive.

Dynamic programming and computational complexity

A direct method for producing an MSA uses the dynamic programming technique to identify the globally optimal alignment solution. For proteins, this method usually involves two sets of parameters: a gap penalty and a substitution matrix assigning scores or probabilities to the alignment of each possible pair of amino acids based on the similarity of the amino acids' chemical properties and the evolutionary probability of the mutation. For nucleotide sequences a similar gap penalty is used, but a much simpler substitution matrix, wherein only identical matches and mismatches are considered, is typical. The scores in the substitution matrix may be either all positive or a mix of positive and negative in the case of a global alignment, but must be both positive and negative, in the case of a local alignment.[1]

For n individual sequences, the naive method requires constructing the n-dimensional equivalent of the matrix formed in standard pairwise sequence alignment. The search space thus increases exponentially with increasing n and is also strongly dependent on sequence length. Expressed with the big O notation commonly used to measure computational complexity, a naïve MSA takes $O(Length^{Nseqs})$ time to produce. To find the global optimum for n sequences this way has been shown to be an NP-complete problem.[2] [3] [4] In 1989, based on Carrillo-Lipman Algorithm,[5] Altschul introduced a practical method that uses pairwise alignments to constrain the n-dimensional search space.[6] In this approach pairwise dynamic programming alignments are performed on each pair of sequences in the query set, and only the space near the n-dimensional intersection of these alignments is searched for the n-way alignment. The MSA program optimizes the sum of all of the pairs of characters at each position in the alignment (the so-called *sum of pair* score) and has been implemented in a software program for constructing multiple sequence alignments.[7]

Progressive alignment construction

The most widely used approach to multiple sequence alignments uses a heuristic search known as progressive technique (also known as the hierarchical or tree method), that builds up a final MSA by combining pairwise alignments beginning with the most similar pair and progressing to the most distantly related. All progressive alignment methods require two stages: a first stage in which the relationships between the sequences are represented as a tree, called a *guide tree*, and a second step in which the MSA is built by adding the sequences sequentially to the growing MSA according to the guide tree. The initial *guide tree* is determined by an efficient clustering method such as neighbor-joining or UPGMA, and may use distances based on the number of identical two letter sub-sequences (as in FASTA rather than a dynamic programming alignment).[8]

Progressive alignments are not guaranteed to be globally optimal. The primary problem is that when errors are made at any stage in growing the MSA, these errors are then propagated through to the final result. Performance is also particularly bad when all of the sequences in the set are rather distantly related. Most modern progressive methods modify their scoring function with a secondary weighting function that assigns scaling factors to individual members of the query set in a nonlinear fashion based on their phylogenetic distance from their nearest neighbors. This corrects for non-random selection of the sequences given to the alignment program.[8]

Progressive alignment methods are efficient enough to implement on a large scale for many (100s to 1000s) sequences. Progressive alignment services are commonly available on publicly accessible web servers so users need not locally install the applications of interest. The most popular progressive alignment method has been the Clustal family,[9] especially the weighted variant ClustalW[10] to which access is provided by a large number of web portals including GenomeNet [11], EBI [11], and EMBNet [10]. Different portals or implementations can vary in user interface and make different parameters accessible to the user. ClustalW is used extensively for phylogenetic tree construction, in spite of the author's explicit warnings that unedited alignments should not be used in such studies and as input for protein structure prediction by homology modeling.

Another common progressive alignment method called T-Coffee[12] is slower than Clustal and its derivatives but generally produces more accurate alignments for distantly related sequence sets. T-Coffee calculates pairwise alignments by combining the direct alignment of the pair with indirect alignments that aligns each sequence of the pair to a third sequence. It uses the output from Clustal as well as another local alignment program LALIGN, which finds multiple regions of local alignment between two sequences. The resulting alignment and phylogenetic tree are used as a guide to produce new and more accurate weighting factors.

Because progressive methods are heuristics that are not guaranteed to converge to a global optimum, alignment quality can be difficult to evaluate and their true biological significance can be obscure. A semi-progressive method that improves alignment quality and does not use a lossy heuristic while still running in polynomial time has been implemented in the program PSAlign [13],[14]

Iterative methods

A set of methods to produce MSAs while reducing the errors inherent in progressive methods are classified as "iterative" because they work similarly to progressive methods but repeatedly realign the initial sequences as well as adding new sequences to the growing MSA. One reason progressive methods are so strongly dependent on a high-quality initial alignment is the fact that these alignments are always incorporated into the final result - that is, once a sequence has been aligned into the MSA, its alignment is not considered further. This approximation improves efficiency at the cost of accuracy. By contrast, iterative methods can return to previously calculated pairwise alignments or sub-MSAs incorporating subsets of the query sequence as a means of optimizing a general objective function such as finding a high-quality alignment score.[8]

A variety of subtly different iteration methods have been implemented and made available in software packages; reviews and comparisons have been useful but generally refrain from choosing a "best" technique.[15] The software package PRRN/PRRP [16] uses a hill-climbing algorithm to optimize its MSA alignment score[17] and iteratively corrects both alignment weights and locally divergent or "gappy" regions of the growing MSA.[8] PRRP performs best when refining an alignment previously constructed by a faster method.[8]

Another iterative program, DIALIGN, takes an unusual approach of focusing narrowly on local alignments between sub-segments or sequence motifs without introducing a gap penalty.[18] The alignment of individual motifs is then achieved with a matrix representation similar to a dot-matrix plot in a pairwise alignment. An alternative method that uses fast local alignments as anchor points or "seeds" for a slower global-alignment procedure is implemented in the CHAOS/DIALIGN [19] suite.[18]

A third popular iteration-based method called MUSCLE (multiple sequence alignment by log-expectation) improves on progressive methods with a more accurate distance measure to assess the relatedness of two sequences.[20] The distance measure is updated between iteration stages (although, in its original form, MUSCLE contained only 2-3 iterations depending on whether refinement was enabled).

Hidden Markov models

Hidden Markov models are probabilistic models that can assign likelihoods to all possible combinations of gaps, matches, and mismatches to determine the most likely MSA or set of possible MSAs. HMMs can produce a single highest-scoring output but can also generate a family of possible alignments that can then be evaluated for biological significance. HMMs can produce both global and local alignments. Although HMM-based methods have been developed relatively recently, they offer significant improvements in computational speed, especially for sequences that contain overlapping regions.[8]

Typical HMM-based methods work by representing an MSA as a form of directed acyclic graph known as a partial-order graph, which consists of a series of nodes representing possible entries in the columns of an MSA. In this representation a column that is absolutely conserved (that is, that all the sequences in the MSA share a particular character at a particular position) is coded as a single node with as many outgoing connections as there are possible characters in the next column of the alignment. In the terms of a typical hidden Markov model, the observed states are the individual alignment columns and the "hidden" states represent the presumed ancestral sequence from which the sequences in the query set are hypothesized to have descended. An efficient search variant of the dynamic programming method, known as the Viterbi algorithm, is generally used to successively align the growing MSA to the next sequence in the query set to produce a new MSA.[21] This is distinct from progressive alignment methods because the alignment of prior sequences is updated at each new sequence addition. However, like progressive methods, this technique can be influenced by the order in which the sequences in the query set are integrated into the alignment, especially when the sequences are distantly related.[8]

Several software programs are available in which variants of HMM-based methods have been implemented and which are noted for their scalability and efficiency, although properly using an HMM method is more complex than using more common progressive methods. The simplest is POA [22] (Partial-Order Alignment);[23] a similar but more generalized method is implemented in the packages SAM [24] (Sequence Alignment and Modeling System).[21] and HMMER.[25] SAM has been used as a source of alignments for protein structure prediction to participate in the CASP structure prediction experiment and to develop a database of predicted proteins in the yeast species *S. cerevisiae*. HHsearch[26] is a software package for the detection of remotely related protein sequences based on the pairwise comparison of HMMs. A server running HHsearch (HHpred) was by far the fastest of the 10 best automatic structure prediction servers in the CASP7 and CASP8 structure prediction competitions.[27]

Genetic algorithms and simulated annealing

Standard optimization techniques in computer science - both of which were inspired by, but do not directly reproduce, physical processes - have also been used in an attempt to more efficiently produce quality MSAs. One such technique, genetic algorithms, has been used for MSA production in an attempt to broadly simulate the hypothesized evolutionary process that gave rise to the divergence in the query set. The method works by breaking a series of possible MSAs into fragments and repeatedly rearranging those fragments with the introduction of gaps at varying positions. A general objective function is optimized during the simulation, most generally the "sum of pairs" maximization function introduced in dynamic programming-based MSA methods. A technique for protein sequences has been implemented in the software program SAGA (Sequence Alignment by Genetic Algorithm)[28] and its equivalent in RNA is called RAGA.[29]

The technique of simulated annealing, by which an existing MSA produced by another method is refined by a series of rearrangements designed to find better regions of alignment space than the one the input alignment already occupies. Like the genetic algorithm method, simulated annealing maximizes an objective function like the sum-of-pairs function. Simulated annealing uses a metaphorical "temperature factor" that determines the rate at which rearrangements proceed and the likelihood of each rearrangement; typical usage alternates periods of high rearrangement rates with relatively low likelihood (to explore more distant regions of alignment space) with periods of lower rates and higher likelihoods to more thoroughly explore local minima near the newly "colonized" regions. This approach has been implemented in the program MSASA (Multiple Sequence Alignment by Simulated Annealing).[30]

Motif finding

Motif finding, also known as profile analysis, is a method of locating sequence motifs in global MSAs that is both a means of producing a better MSA and a means of producing a scoring matrix for use in searching other sequences for similar motifs. A variety of methods for isolating the

Alignment of the seven Drosophila caspases colored by motifs as identified by MEME. When motif positions and sequence alignments are generated independently, they often correlate well but not perfectly, as in this example.

motifs have been developed, but all are based on identifying short highly conserved patterns within the larger alignment and constructing a matrix similar to a substitution matrix that reflects the amino acid or nucleotide composition of each position in the putative motif. The alignment can then be refined using these matrices. In standard profile analysis, the matrix includes entries for each possible character as well as entries for gaps.[8] Alternatively, statistical pattern-finding algorithms can identify motifs as a precursor to an MSA rather than as a derivation. In many cases when the query set contains only a small number of sequences or contains only highly related sequences, pseudocounts are added to normalize the distribution reflected in the scoring matrix. In particular, this corrects zero-probability entries in the matrix to values that are small but nonzero.

Blocks analysis is a method of motif finding that restricts motifs to ungapped regions in the alignment. Blocks can be generated from an MSA or they can be extracted from unaligned sequences using a precalculated set of common motifs previously generated from known gene families.[31] Block scoring generally relies on the spacing of high-frequency characters rather than on the calculation of an explicit substitution matrix. The BLOCKS [32] server provides an interactive method to locate such motifs in unaligned sequences.

Statistical pattern-matching has been implemented using both the expectation-maximization algorithm and the Gibbs sampler. One of the most common motif-finding tools, known as MEME, uses expectation maximization and hidden Markov methods to generate motifs that are then used as search tools by its companion MAST in the combined suite MEME/MAST [33],[34] [35]

Visualization and editing tools

The necessary use of heuristics for multiple alignment means that for an arbitrary set of proteins, there is always a good chance that an alignment will contain errors. These can arise because of unique insertions into one or more regions of sequences, or through some more complex evolutionary process leading to proteins that do not align easily by sequence alone. Multiple sequence alignment viewers enable alignments to be visually verified, often by inspecting the quality of alignment for annotated functional sites on two or more sequences. Many also enable the alignment to be edited to correct these (usually minor) errors, in order to obtain an optimal 'curated' alignment suitable for use in phylogenetic analysis or comparative modeling.[36]

Use in phylogenetics

Multiple sequence alignments can be used to create a phylogenetic tree.[37] This is made possible by two reasons. The first is because functional domains that are known in annotated sequences can be used for alignment in non-annotated sequences. The other is that conserved regions known to be functionally important can be found. This makes it possible for multiple sequence alignments to be used to analyze and find evolutionary relationships through homology between sequences. Point mutations and insertion or deletion events (called indels) can be detected.

Multiple sequence alignments can also be used to identify functionally important sites, such as binding sites, active sites, or sites corresponding to other key functions, by locating conserved domains. When looking at multiple sequence alignments, it is useful to consider different aspects of the sequences when comparing sequences. These aspects include identity, similarity, and homology. Identity means that the sequences have identical residues at their respective positions. On the other hand, similarity has to do with the sequences being compared having similar residues quantitatively. For example, in terms of nucleotide sequences, pyrimidines are considered similar to each other, as are purines. Similarity ultimately leads to homology, in that the more similar sequences are, the closer they are to being homologous. This homology in sequences, can then go on to help find common ancestry.[37]

References

[1] "Help with matrices used in sequence comparison tools" (http://www.ebi.ac.uk/help/matrix.html). European Bioinformatics Institute. . Retrieved March 3, 2010.

[2] Wang L, Jiang T (1994). "On the complexity of multiple sequence alignment". *J Comput Biol* **1** (4): 337–348. doi:10.1089/cmb.1994.1.337. PMID 8790475.

[3] Just W (2001). "Computational complexity of multiple sequence alignment with SP-score". *J Comput Biol* **8** (6): 615–23. doi:10.1089/106652701753307511. PMID 11747615.

[4] Elias, Isaac (2006). "Settling the intractability of multiple alignment" (http://www.liebertonline.com/doi/abs/10.1089/cmb.2006.13. 1323). *J Comput Biol* **13** (7): 1323–1339. doi:10.1089/cmb.2006.13.1323. PMID 17037961. .

[5] Carrillo H, Lipman DJ,(1988) The Multiple Sequence Alignment Problem in Biology. SIAM Journal of Applied Mathematics, Vol.48, No. 5, 1073-1082

[6] Lipman DJ, Altschul SF, Kececioglu JD (1989). "A tool for multiple sequence alignment". *Proc Natl Acad Sci U S A* **86** (12): 4412–4415. doi:10.1073/pnas.86.12.4412. PMC 287279. PMID 2734293.

[7] "Genetic analysis software" (http://www.ncbi.nlm.nih.gov/CBBresearch/Schaffer/msa.html). National Center for Biotechnology Information. . Retrieved March 3, 2010.

[8] Mount DM. (2004). Bioinformatics: Sequence and Genome Analysis 2nd ed. Cold Spring Harbor Laboratory Press: Cold Spring Harbor, NY.

[9] Higgins DG, Sharp PM (1988). "CLUSTAL: a package for performing multiple sequence alignment on a microcomputer". *Gene* **73** (1): 237–244. doi:10.1016/0378-1119(88)90330-7. PMID 3243435.

[10] Thompson JD, Higgins DG, Gibson TJ (1994). "CLUSTAL W: improving the sensitivity of progressive multiple sequence alignment through sequence weighting, position-specific gap penalties and weight matrix choice". *Nucleic Acids Res* **22** (22): 4673–4680. doi:10.1093/nar/22.22.4673. PMC 308517. PMID 7984417.

[11] http://www.ebi.ac.uk/Tools/clustalw2/index.html

[12] Notredame C, Higgins DG, Heringa J (2000). "T-Coffee: A novel method for fast and accurate multiple sequence alignment". *J Mol Biol* **302** (1): 205–217. doi:10.1006/jmbi.2000.4042. PMID 10964570.

[13] http://faculty.cs.tamu.edu/shsze/psalign/

[14] Sze SH, Lu Y, Yang Q (2006). "A polynomial time solvable formulation of multiple sequence alignment". *J Comput Biol* **13** (2): 309–319. doi:10.1089/cmb.2006.13.309. PMID 16597242.

[15] Hirosawa M, Totoki Y, Hoshida M, Ishikawa M (1995). "Comprehensive study on iterative algorithms of multiple sequence alignment". *Comput Appl Biosci* **11** (1): 13–18. doi:10.1093/bioinformatics/11.1.13. PMID 7796270.

[16] http://web.archive.org/web/20080703101054/http://prrn.hgc.jp/

[17] Gotoh O (1996). "Significant improvement in accuracy of multiple protein sequence alignments by iterative refinement as assessed by reference to structural alignments". *J Mol Biol* **264** (4): 823–38. doi:10.1006/jmbi.1996.0679. PMID 8980688.

[18] Brudno M, Chapman M, Göttgens B, Batzoglou S, Morgenstern B (2003). "Fast and sensitive multiple alignment of large genomic sequences". *BMC Bioinformatics* **4**: 66.

[19] http://dialign.gobics.de/chaos-dialign-submission

[20] Edgar RC (2004). "MUSCLE: multiple sequence alignment with high accuracy and high throughput". *Nucleic Acids Research* **32** (5): 1792–97. doi:10.1093/nar/gkh340. PMC 390337. PMID 15034147.

[21] Hughey R, Krogh A (1996). "Hidden Markov models for sequence analysis: extension and analysis of the basic method". *CABIOS* **12** (2): 95–107. PMID 8744772.

[22] http://sourceforge.net/projects/poamsa/files/

[23] Grasso C, Lee C (2004). "Combining partial order alignment and progressive multiple sequence alignment increases alignment speed and scalability to very large alignment problems". *Bioinformatics* **20** (10): 1546–56. doi:10.1093/bioinformatics/bth126. PMID 14962922.

[24] http://compbio.soe.ucsc.edu/sam.html

[25] Durbin R, Eddy S, Krogh A, Mitchison G. (1998). Biological sequence analysis: probabilistic models of proteins and nucleic acids, Cambridge University Press, 1998.

[26] Söding J (2005). "Protein homology detection by HMM-HMM comparison". *Bioinformatics* **21** (7): 951–960. doi:10.1093/bioinformatics/bti125. PMID 15531603.

[27] Battey JN, Kopp J, Bordoli L, Read RJ, Clarke ND, Schwede T (2007). "Automated server predictions in CASP7". *Proteins* **69** (Suppl 8): 68–82. doi:10.1002/prot.21761. PMID 17894354.

[28] Notredame C, Higgins DG (1996). "SAGA: sequence alignment by genetic algorithm". *Nucleic Acids Res* **24** (8): 1515–24. doi:10.1093/nar/24.8.1515. PMC 145823. PMID 8628686.

[29] Notredame C, O'Brien EA, Higgins DG (1997). "RAGA: RNA sequence alignment by genetic algorithm". *Nucleic Acids Res* **25** (22): 4570–80. doi:10.1093/nar/25.22.4570. PMC 147093. PMID 9358168.

[30] Kim J, Pramanik S, Chung MJ (1994). "Multiple sequence alignment using simulated annealing". *Comput Appl Biosci* **10** (4): 419–26. PMID 7804875.

[31] Henikoff S, Henikoff JG (1991). "Automated assembly of protein blocks for database searching". *Nucleic Acids Res* **19** (23): 6565–6572. doi:10.1093/nar/19.23.6565. PMC 329220. PMID 1754394.

[32] http://blocks.fhcrc.org/

[33] http://meme.sdsc.edu/meme/intro.html

[34] Bailey TL, Elkan C (1994). "Fitting a mixture model by expectation maximization to discover motifs in biopolymers". *Proceedings of the Second International Conference on Intelligent Systems for Molecular Biology*. Menlo Park, California: AAAI Press. pp. 28–36.

[35] Bailey TL, Gribskov M (1998). "Combining evidence using p-values: application to sequence homology searches". *Bioinformatics* **14** (1): 48–54. doi:10.1093/bioinformatics/14.1.48. PMID 9520501.

[36] "Manual editing and adjustment of MSAs" (http://www.embl.de/~seqanal/MSAcambridgeGenetics2007/MSAmanualAdjustments/MSAmanualAdjustments.html). European Molecular Biology Laboratory. 2007. . Retrieved March 7, 2010.

[37] Budd, Aidan (10 February 2009). "Multiple sequence alignment exercises and demonstrations" (http://www.embl.de/~seqanal/courses/commonCourseContent/commonMsaExercises.html). European Molecular Biology Laboratory. . Retrieved June 30, 2010.

Survey articles

- Duret, L.; S. Abdeddaim (2000). "Multiple alignment for structural functional or phylogenetic analyses of homologous sequences". In D. Higgins and W. Taylor. *Bioinformatics sequence structure and databanks*. Oxford: Oxford University Press.

- Notredame, C. (2002). "Recent progresses in multiple sequence alignment: a survey". *Pharmacogenomics* **31** (1): 131–144. doi:10.1517/14622416.3.1.131. PMID 11966409.

- Thompson, J. D.; F. Plewniak and O. Poch (1999). "A comprehensive comparison of multiple sequence alignment programs". *Nucleic Acids Research* **27** (13): 12682–2690. doi:10.1093/nar/27.13.2682. PMC 148477. PMID 10373585.

- Wallace, I.M.; Blackshields G and Higgins DG. (2005). "Multiple sequence alignments". *Curr Opin Struct Biol* **15** (3): 261–266. doi:10.1016/j.sbi.2005.04.002. PMID 15963889.

- Notredame, C (2007). "Recent Evolutions of Multiple Sequence Alignment Algorithms". *PLOS Computational Biology* **8** (3): e123. doi:10.1371/journal.pcbi.0030123. PMC 1963500. PMID 17784778.

External links

- ExPASy sequence alignment tools (http://www.expasy.org/tools/#align)
- Multiple Alignment Resource Page (http://www.techfak.uni-bielefeld.de/bcd/Curric/MulAli/welcome.html) — from the Virtual School of Natural Sciences
- Tools for Multiple Alignments (http://pbil.univ-lyon1.fr/alignment.html) — from Pôle Bioinformatique Lyonnais
- An entry point to clustal servers and information (http://www.clustal.org/)
- An entry point to the main T-Coffee servers (http://www.tcoffee.org/)
- European Bioinformatics Institute servers:

  - ClustalW2 (http://www.ebi.ac.uk/Tools/clustalw2/) — general purpose multiple sequence alignment program for DNA or proteins.
  - Muscle (http://www.ebi.ac.uk/Tools/muscle/) — MUltiple Sequence Comparison by Log-Expectation
  - T-coffee (http://www.ebi.ac.uk/Tools/t-coffee/) — multiple sequence alignment.
  - MAFFT (http://www.ebi.ac.uk/Tools/mafft/) — Multiple Alignment using Fast Fourier Transform
  - KALIGN (http://www.ebi.ac.uk/Tools/kalign/) — a fast and accurate multiple sequence alignment algorithm.

Lecture notes, tutorials, and courses

*   Multiple sequence alignment lectures (http://cmb.molgen.mpg.de/) — from the Max Planck Institute for Molecular Genetics
*   notes and practical exercises (http://www.embl.de/~seqanal/courses/tuebingenMpiPhyloMsaFeb2009/MsaExercises.html/Lecture) on multiple sequences alignments at the EMBL
*   Molecular Bioinformatics Lecture Notes (http://www.avatar.se/molbioinfo2001/index.html)
*   Molecular Evolution and Bioinformatics Lecture Notes (http://bioinf.may.ie/school02/notes.html)

Multiscale Electrophysiology Format

Multiscale Electrophysiology Format (MEF) was developed to handle the large amounts of data produced by large-scale electrophysiology in human and animal subjects. MEF can store any time series data up to 24 bits in length, and employs lossless range encoded difference compression. Subject identifying information in the file header can be encrypted using 128-bit AES encryption in order to comply with HIPAA requirements for patient privacy when transmitting data across an open network.

Compressed data is stored in independent blocks to allow direct access to the data, facilitate parallel processing and limit the effects of potential damage to files. Data fidelity is ensured by a 32-bit cyclic redundancy check in each compressed data block using the Koopman polynomial (0xEB31D82E), which has a Hamming distance of from 4 to 114 kbits.

A formal specification can be found here [1],[2]

References

[1] http://mayoresearch.mayo.edu/mayo/research/msel/upload/mef%20_format.pdf
[2] Source code (http://mayoresearch.mayo.edu/mayo/research/msel/example_code.cfm)

Sources

*   Martin, GNN. Range encoding: an algorithm for removing redundancy from a digitised message. Video & Data Recoding Conference, Southampton, 1979.
*   Koopman, P. 32-Bit Cyclic Redundancy Codes for Internet Applications. The International Conference on Dependable Systems and Networks (June 2002). 459.
*   Brinkmann, BH et al. Large-scale electrophysiology: acquisition, compression, encryption, and storage of big data. Journal of Neuroscience Methods 180 (2009) 185–192.

External links

*   Source code: http://mayoresearch.mayo.edu/mayo/research/msel/example_code.cfm

myGrid

The **myGrid** consortium is a multi-institutional, multi-disciplinary internationally leading research group focussing on the challenges of eScience. The consortium specialises in data and knowledge-intensive e-Laboratories.

The consortium is led by Professor Carole Goble of the School of Computer Science at the University of Manchester, UK.

Phase 1

The consortium was formed in 2001, bringing together collaborators at the Universities of Manchester, Southampton, Newcastle, Nottingham and Sheffield, The European Molecular Biology Laboratory-European Bioinformatics Institute (EMBL-EBI) in Cambridge, and industrial partners GlaxoSmithKline, Merck KGaA, AstraZeneca, Sun Microsystems, IBM, GeneticXchange, Epistemics and Cerebra , (formerly Network Inference). The UK Engineering and Physical Sciences Research Council funded the first phase of the project with £3.5 million.

Phase 2

In phase 2, from 2006 to 2009, the consortium is funded for £2 million as part of the Open Middleware Infrastructure Institute. The membership of the consortium was concentrated in the University of Manchester and EMBL-EBI.

Phase 3

In December 2008, the UK's Engineering and Physical Sciences Research Council approved the team's renewal grant proposal. The grant is for £1.15m and runs from January 2009 to January 2014. The members of the myGrid team for Phase 3 are the University of Manchester and the University of Southampton. The project is organised around 4 themes: Knowledge Management for e-Science, Metadata management in e-Laboratories, Scientific Workflow Design, Management and Enactment, and Social Computing for e-Scientists. The Social Computing theme is oriented around the myExperiment Virtual Research Environment for the social curation and sharing of scientific research objects.

Overview from grant proposal in 2001

To date, Grid development has focused on the basic issues of storage, computation and resource management needed to make a global scientific community's information and tools accessible in a high performance environment. However, from an e-Science viewpoint, the purpose of the Grid is to deliver a collaborative and supportive environment that allows geographically distributed scientists to achieve research goals more effectively. MyGrid will design, develop and demonstrate higher level functionalities over an existing Grid infrastructure that support scientists in making use of complex distributed resources.

The project has developed an e-Science workbench called Taverna that supports:

- the scientific process of experimental investigation, evidence accumulation and result assimilation;
- the scientist's use of the community's information; and
- scientific collaboration, allowing dynamic groupings to tackle emergent research problems.

The workbench will support individual scientists by providing personalisation facilities relating to resource selection, data management and process enactment. The design and development activity will be informed by and evaluated using problems in bioinformatics, which is characterised by a highly distributed community, with many shared tools resources. myGrid will develop two application environments, one that supports individual scientists in the analysis of functional genomic data, and another that supports the annotation of a pattern database. Both of these tasks require explicit representation and enactment of scientific processes, and have challenging performance requirements.

External links

- Official myGrid website mygrid.org.uk [1]
- myGrid@EBI [2] description from the European Bioinformatics Institute
- myGrid phase one funding from EPSRC: grant reference GR/R67743/01 value £3.5 million (2001-2005) [3]
- myGrid phase two funding from EPSRC: grant reference EP/D044324/ value £2 million (2006-2009) [4]
- myGrid phase three funding from EPSRC: grant reference EP/G026238/1 value £1.15 million (2009-20014) [5]
- myGrid: personalised bioinformatics on the information grid [6]
- Exploring Williams-Beuren syndrome using myGrid [7]
- Peer reviewed publications about myGrid [8] on PubMed
- Publications about myGrid [9] tagged using Connotea
- Publications about myGrid [10] tagged using Citeulike
- Taverna Scientific Workflow Workbench [11]
- The myExperiment web site [12]

References

[1] http://www.mygrid.org.uk/
[2] http://www.ebi.ac.uk/mygrid/
[3] http://gow.epsrc.ac.uk/ViewGrant.aspx?GrantRef=GR/R67743/01
[4] http://gow.epsrc.ac.uk/ViewGrant.aspx?GrantRef=EP/D044324/1
[5] http://gow.epsrc.ac.uk/ViewGrant.aspx?GrantRef=EP/G026238/1
[6] http://dx.doi.org/10.1093/bioinformatics/btg1041
[7] http://dx.doi.org/10.1093/bioinformatics/bth944
[8] http://www.ncbi.nlm.nih.gov/entrez/query.fcgi?db=pubmed&cmd=search&term=mygrid
[9] http://www.connotea.org/tag/mygrid
[10] http://www.citeulike.org/tag/mygrid
[11] http://www.taverna.org.uk//
[12] http://myexperiment.org//

N50 statistic

In Computational Biology, the **N50 statistic** is a measure of the average length of a set of sequences, with greater weight given to longer sequences. It is used widely in genome assembly, especially in reference to contig lengths within a draft assembly. Given a set of sequences of varying lengths, the N50 length is defined as the length N for which 50% of all bases in the sequences are in a sequence of length $L < N$.

N50 may also be defined as the contig length such that using equal or longer contigs produces half the bases of the genome. The N50 size is computed by sorting all contigs from largest to smallest and by determining the minimum set of contigs whose sizes total 50% of the entire genome. For example, for a genome of 600Mb, if the assembled sequences add up to 500Mb, the N50 would the calculated by sorting the contigs from largest to smallest and finding the length of the contig where the cumulative size is 250Mb. Thus, N50 is calculated in the context of the assembly size rather than the genome size. The NG50 statistic is the same as the N50 except that the genome size is used rather than the assembly size.

N50 can be found mathematically as follows: Take a list L of positive integers. Create another list L' , which is identical to L, except that every element n in L has been replaced with n copies of itself. Then the median of L' is the N50 of L. For example: If L = {2, 2, 2, 3, 3, 4, 8, 8}, then L' consists of six 2's, six 3's, four 4's, and sixteen 8's (e.g. We replaced every 2 in L with 2, 2, so in L' there are six 2s in L') ; the N50 of L is the median of L' , which is the average of the 16th element 4 and 17th element 8, so it is (4+8)/2 = 6.

Contradictory definitions

There has been identified some contradictions in the definition(s) of the N50 value, as discussed in a thread [1] on the SEQ Answers forum.

References

- Broad institute wiki "http://www.broad.harvard.edu/crd/wiki/index.php/N50"
- "Assembly algorithms for next-generation sequencing data", Miller JR, Koren S, Sutton G ("http://www.ncbi. nlm.nih.gov/pubmed/20211242")

References

[1] http://seqanswers.com/forums/showthread.php?p=41420

National Center for Genome Resources

The National Center for Genome Resources (NCGR) [1] is a nonprofit research organization in Santa Fe, New Mexico founded in 1994 focusing on life sciences research, bioinformatics technologies, and leading-edge molecular data production including sequencing, genotyping, and gene expression.

External links

NCGR home page [1].

References

[1] http://www.ncgr.org

National Institute for Mathematical and Biological Synthesis

The **National Institute for Mathematical and Biological Synthesis** is a research institute focused on the science of mathematics and biology. Known by its acronym NIMBioS (pronounced NIM-bus), the Institute opened in September 2008, arising from a collaborative agreement between the National Science Foundation, the U.S. Department of Homeland Security, and the U.S. Department of Agriculture, with additional support from The University of Tennessee (UT), Knoxville.[1] [2] NIMBioS hosts more than 600 scientists each year at its facility located on the UT campus.

Primary goals of NIMBios are:

- to address key biological questions using cross-disciplinary approaches in mathematical biology
- to foster the development of a cadre of researchers who are capable of conceiving and engaging in creative and collaborative connections across disciplines.

To achieve its goals, NIMBioS advances a wide variety of research and outreach/education activities designed to facilitate interaction between mathematicians and biologists to arrive at innovative solutions to environmental problems. Two primary mechanisms for research are Working Groups and Investigative Workshops. Working Groups are composed of 10-15 invited participants focusing on specific questions related to mathematical biology. Each group typically meets at the Institute two to three times over the course of two years. Investigative workshops may include 30-40 participants with some invited by organizers and others accepted through an open application process. Workshops are more general in focus and may lead to working group formation. NIMBioS also provides support for post-doctoral and sabbatical fellows, short-term visitors, graduate research assistants, and faculty collaborators at UT.

Research activities have investigated intragenomic conflict, multi-scale simulation of cellular processes, human origins, natural system dynamics, and infectious diseases in systems with wildlife hosts.[3]

NIMBioS encourages multidisciplinary participation in all its activities. Participants at NIMBioS have included behavioral biologists, ecologists, evolutionary biologists, computational scientists, anthropologists, geneticists, psychologists, bioinformaticians, mathematicians, statisticians, veterinarians, epidemiologists, and wildlife biologists.

NIMBioS has an active Education and Outreach program with events and activities for everyone from elementary school students through college professors and the general public. At the college level, NIMBioS organizes a Research Experience for Undergraduates and a Research Experience for Veterinary Students program for seven weeks each summer. Veterinary students and undergraduates majoring in math, biology, and related fields live on campus and work in teams with UT professors on innovative research projects. High school teachers can also participate in the program.

For teachers, NIMBioS offers the Teacher Collaboration Program in which teachers with interest in mathematics and biology are paired with active researchers in the math biology community. Collaboration activities range from teaching projects and classroom visits to curriculum design and after school activities.

NIMBioS provides varying levels of tutorial workshops designed to enlighten biologists about key quantitative methods, such as optimal control and optimization or high performance computing methods for analyzing biological problems involving large data sets, spatial information, and dynamics.

NIMBioS' director is Louis Gross, Professor of Ecology and Evolutionary Biology and Mathematics at the University of Tennessee, Knoxville. NIMBioS leadership team also includes four associate directors and a deputy director. NIMBioS has an external Board of Advisors consisting of 23 members from academic institutions from around the world. In addition, NIMBioS has a group of seven senior personnel consisting of UT faculty and Oak Ridge National Laboratory (ORNL) scientists, and a group of 39 additional associated faculty and staff collaborators from UT and ORNL.

NIMBioS collaborates with the Great Smoky Mountains National Park to develop methods of particular interest for natural area management that are transferable to numerous U.S. locations. Other partners in NIMBioS include IBM and ESRI.

The need for the Institute arose out of the significant growth of the field of mathematical biology over the last decade with research becoming more closely linked to observation and experiment. Rather than starting from mathematical abstractions, it is now common for researchers to 1) begin with observations; 2) use those to suggest promising methods, tools and models; and 3) proceed to analysis, simulation, evaluation and application. Across the spectrum of the life sciences in which mathematics has been contributing new insights, data are increasingly used to focus conceptual models as the first step in problem formulation.

The NIMBioS website includes descriptions of working groups, investigative workshops, post-doctoral fellowships, sabbaticals, short-term visits, graduate assistantships, and faculty positions and information on how to submit requests for support. The web site also describes education and outreach opportunities for undergraduates, teachers, and K-12 students.

References

[1] http://www.nsf.gov/news/news_summ.jsp?cntn_id=112167&org=NSF&from=news.html
[2] http://www.nature.com/news/2008/080903/full/455011a.html
[3] http://quest.utk.edu/2009/nimbios/

External links

- National Institute for Mathematical and Biological Synthesis: www.nimbios.org official website (http://www.nimbios.org)

Shamkant Navathe

Shamkant B. Navathe	
Fields	Databases, Bioinformatics
Institutions	Georgia Tech College of Computing
Alma mater	University of Michigan, Ohio State University, Indian Institute of Science, University of Pune
Doctoral advisor	Alan G. Merten

Shamkant B. Navathe is a noted researcher in the field of databases with more than 150 publications on different topics in the area of databases.[1] [2] [3] [4] [5]

He is presently a Professor in the College of Computing at Georgia Institute of Technology and founded the Research Group in Database Systems [6] at the College of Computing at Georgia Institute of Technology (popularly called Georgia Tech). He has been at Georgia Tech since 1990. He has been teaching in the database area since 1975 and his textbook: "Fundamentals of Database Systems [7]" (with R. Elmasri, published by Addison Wesley, Edition 5, 2007) has been a leading textbook in the database area worldwide for the last 19 years.[8] It is now in its 6th edition and is used as a standard textbook in India, Europe, South America, Australia and South-east Asia. The book has been translated into Spanish, German, French, Italian, Portuguese, Chinese, Korean, Greek, and most recently in Arabic. His research is presently in the area of bioinformatics[9] Navathe is also working in advisory roles with Indian companies like Tata Consultancy Services (TCS), and Persistent Systems. He is also consultant for companies in information systems and software products design area and is an independent director of GTL Limited, a Mumbai based telecommunications company.[10]

Education

Navathe completed his S.S.C. [11] from Modern High School, Pune in 1961 and F.Y.Bsc (Inter Science) in 1963 and at B.Sc. (Physics) in 1965. He obtained his B.E. degree in Electrical Communications Engineering at the Indian Institute of Science where he was a gold medalist. Navathe came to the U.S. in Fall of 1969. He was working as a System Engineer for IBM [12] and Electronic Data Systems in Calcutta when he left India. He received an M.S. degree in Computer and Information Science in 1970 from Ohio State University. He then received a Ph.D. from University of Michigan Industrial and Operations Engineering in 1976. His doctoral thesis was on "A Methodology for Generalized Database Restructuring".[10]

Career

Navathe taught as an Assistant Professor in the Computer Applications and Information Systems Department at the Graduate School of Business Administration New York University and at the Computer and Information Sciences Department at University of Florida before joining Georgia Institute Of Technology in 1990. He has been a Professor at the College of Computing at Georgia Tech since 1990 and is a faculty Member in the Bioengineering [13], Bioinformatics [14] and the Health Sciences Institute [15] programs at Georgia Tech.

He was the Program Co-Chair at the SIGMOD 1985 [16] ACM Annual Conference of the Special Interest Group on Management of Data, Austin, TX, and also at the PARBASE 1990 [17] First International Conference on Databases, Parallel Architectures and their Applications, Miami, FL., March 6–9, 1990, IEEE Computer Society. He was the General Chairman at the IFIP WG 2.6 Working Conference on Database Application Semantics (DS-6) [18], Stone Mountain, GA, May 31-June 2. He was the Conference Chair at VLDB 1996 [19] Very Large Database Conference, Mumbai, India, Sept. 3-6, 1996.

He has been a member of international steering committees like PDIS (Parallel and Distributed Information Systems) International Conference [20](est 1991), http:// www. informatik. uni-trier. de/ ~ley/ db/ conf/ er/ index. html Conceptual Modeling (Object Oriented and ER modeling) International Conference] (est 1993), International Federation on Cooperative Information Systems (IFCIS), (est 1994), IPIC (Information and Process Integration in enterprises Conference) (est 1996).

He has been the Associate Editor of ACM Computing Surveys [21], September 1986 - December 1997, IEEE Transactions on Knowledge and Data Engineering [22], Sept. '94. - Dec. '98, Data and Knowledge Engineering, a North Holland Elsevier Journal [23], (since June 1985), Journal of Data Semantics [24] (since 2005).

He has also been a member of editorial board for Information Systems, a journal published by Pergamon Press [25], since 1987, Parallel and Distributed Database Systems, a journal published by Kluwer Academic Press, (since 1992), Information Technology and Management, a journal by Chapman and Hall, (since 1999), The World Wide Web Journal, Kluwer Academic Press, (since 2001)

He is the Editor of the Series on "Database Systems and Applications," Benjamin Cummings Publishing Co., Redwood City, California (est 1985), and the Series on Emerging Directions in Database Systems and Applications, CRC Press [26]; which was launched in 2008.

[10]

Bibliography

Books written by Navathe:[10]

- Elmasri, R.; Navathe, S.B. (2010). *Fundamentals of Database Systems, Sixth Edition*. Pearson. pp. 1200 pp.
- Bussler, C.; Castellanos, M.; Navathe, S.B. (2007). *Business Intelligence for the Real-Time Enterprises, First International Workshop BIRTE 2006*. Seoul, Korea: Springer LNCS 4365. pp. 156pp.
- Elmasri, R.; Navathe, S.B. (2007). *Fundamentals of Database Systems, Fifth Edition*. Addison Wesley. pp. 1040 pp.
- Elmasri, R.; Navathe, S.B. (2004). *Fundamentals of Database Systems, Fourth Edition*. Addison Wesley. pp. 1015 pp.
- Elmasri, R.; Navathe, S.B. (2000). *Fundamentals of Database Systems, Third Edition*. Addison Wesley. pp. 955 pp.(Translated into German, Italian, French, Spanish, Portuguese, Chinese, Greek, Korean)
- Wakayama, T.; Kannapan, S.; Khoong, C.M.; Navathe, S.B.; Yates, Yates (1998). *Information and Process Integration in Enterprises: Rethinking Documents*. Kluwer Academic Publishers.
- Elmasri, R.; Navathe, S.B. (1994). *Fundamentals of Database Systems, Second Edition*. Addison Wesley. pp. 873 pp.(Translated into Spanish, Korean, Greek and Chinese in 1997)
- Batini, C.; Navathe, S.B. (August 1991). *Conceptual Database Design: An Entity Relationship Approach*. Benjamin Cummings. pp. 470 pp.
- Rishe, N.; Navathe, S.B.; Tal, D. (1991). *Databases: Theory, Design and Applications, IEEE Computer Society Press*.
- Rishe, N.; Navathe, S.B.; Tal, D. (1991). *Parallel Architectures, IEEE Computer Society Press*.
- Elmasri, R.; Navathe, S.B. (February 1989). *Fundamentals of Database Systems, First Edition*. Benjamin Cummings. pp. 802 pp.

References

[1] "DBLP Computer Science Bibliography for Shamkant B. Navathe showing 156 publications from 1975 to 2009" (http://www.informatik. uni-trier.de/~ley/db/indices/a-tree/n/Navathe:Shamkant_B=.html). .

[2] "IEEE Bibliography for Shamkant B. Navathe" (http://www.ieee.org/web/web/search/results. html?cx=006539740418318249752:f2h38l7gvis&cof=FORID:11&q=Shamkant+B.+Navathe&qp=&ie=UTF-8&oe=UTF-8& qt=Shamkant+B.+Navathe&sa.x=0&sa.y=0#1052). .

[3] "ACM Bibliography for Shamkant B. Navathe" (http://www.acm.org/search?SearchableText=Shamkant+B.+Navathe). Association for Computing Machinery (ACM). .

[4] "Google Scholar results for Shamkant B. Navathe" (http://scholar.google.com/scholar?q=Shamkant+Navathe&hl=en&btnG=Search). Google. .

[5] "Scientific Commons Bibliography for Shamkant B. Navathe showing 50 publications from 1989- 2008" (http://en.scientificcommons.org/ shamkant_b_navathe). .

[6] http://www.cc.gatech.edu/computing/Database/

[7] http://www.amazon.com/dp/0321369572

[8] Elmasri, R.; Navathe, S. B.. *Fundamentals of Database Systems, Fifth Edition, 2007*. Addison Wesley.

[9] "Pubmed Bibliography for Shamkant B. Navathe" (http://www.ncbi.nlm.nih.gov/sites/entrez). .

[10] "Prof Sham Navathe's Resume on College of Computing, Georgia Tech website" (http://www.cc.gatech.edu/~sham/). College of Computing, Georgia Institute Of Technology. .

[11] http://msbshse.ac.in/

[12] http://www.ibm.com

[13] http://www.bioengineering.gatech.edu/

[14] http://www.biology.gatech.edu/graduate-programs/bioinformatics/

[15] http://www.hsi.gatech.edu/

[16] http://portal.acm.org/citation.cfm?id=318898&coll=portal&dl=ACM

[17] http://www.informatik.uni-trier.de/~ley/db/conf/parbase/index.html

[18] http://www.informatik.uni-trier.de/~ley/db/conf/ds/index.html

[19] http://www.almaden.ibm.com/cs/vldb/

[20] http://www.informatik.uni-trier.de/~ley/db/conf/pdis/index.html

[21] http://csur.acm.org/

[22] http://www2.computer.org/portal/web/tkde

[23] http://www.elsevier.com/wps/find/homepage.cws_home

[24] http://lbdwww.epfl.ch/e/Springer/

[25] http://www.elsevier.com/wps/find/journaldescription.cws_home/236/description#description

[26] http://www.crcpress.com/

External links

- Link to Sham Navathe's GT webpage (http://www.cc.gatech.edu/~sham)

Netherlands Bioinformatics for Proteomics Platform

The **Netherlands Bioinformatics for Proteomics Platform** (for short **NBPP**) is joint initiative of the **Netherlands Bioinformatics Centre (NBIC)** and the **Netherlands Proteomics Centre (NPC)**.

Its main goal is to provide user friendly, high-througput data processing services to analyse proteomics LC-MS data based on open source tools or tools developed and available within the platform members. And build an infrastructure that will make possible for non-experts i.e. wet lab scientist to run a typical proteomics analysis fix pipeline/workflow, and for experts to experiment with different variations of the analysis.

References

External links

- Official site: http://www.nbpp.nl/

NeuroLex

NeuroLex

Content	
Description	Dynamic lexicon of neuroscience terms in a Semantic wiki
Data types captured	Neuroscience
Contact	
Authors	Maryann Martone, Stephen Larson and others
Access	
Website	http://neurolex.org/wiki/
Tools	
Miscellaneous	

NeuroLex is a dynamic lexicon of neuroscience concepts.[1] It is a structured as a semantic wiki, using Semantic MediaWiki. NeuroLex is supported by the Neuroscience Information Framework project.

Overview

The NeuroLex is intended to help improve the way that neuroscientists communicate about their data (http://neurolex.org/wiki/Category:Data_object), so that information systems like the NIF can find data more easily and provide more powerful means of integrating data that occur across distributed resources. One of the big roadblocks to data integration in neuroscience is the inconsistent use of terminology in databases and other resources (http://neurolex. org/ wiki/ Category:Structured_knowledge_resource) like the literature (http:/ / neurolex. org/ wiki/ Category:Literature_corpus). When one uses the same terms to mean different things, one cannot easily ask questions that span across multiple resources. For example, if three databases have information about what genes are expressed in cortex, but they all use different definitions of cerebral cortex (http:/ / neurolex. org/ wiki/ Category:Cerebral_cortex), then one cannot compare them easily.

Utilization within the Neuroscience Information Framework

The NIF enables discovery and access to public research data and tools worldwide through an open source, networked environment. Funded by the NIH Blueprint for Neuroscience Research,[2] the NIF enables scientists and students to discover global neuroscience web resources that cut across traditional boundaries − from experimental, clinical and translational neuroscience databases, to knowledge bases, atlases, and genetic/genomic resources.

Unlike general search engines, NIF provides deeper access to a more focused set of resources that are relevant to neuroscience, search strategies tailored to neuroscience, and access to content that is traditionally "hidden" from web search engines. The Framework is a dynamic inventory of neuroscience databases, annotated and integrated with a unified system of biomedical terminology (i.e. NeuroLex [3]). NIF supports concept-based queries across multiple scales of biological structure and multiple levels of biological function, making it easier to search for and understand the results.

As part of the NIF, a simple search interface [4] to many different sources of neuroscience information and data is provided. To make this search more effective, the NIF is constructing ontologies [5] to help organize neuroscience concepts into category hierarchies, e.g. stating that a neuron is a cell. This helps users to perform more effective searches and also to organize and understand the information that is returned. But an important adjunct to this activity is to clearly define all of the terms that are used to describe data, e.g., anatomical terms, techniques, organism names.

Content

The initial entries in the NeuroLex were built from the NIFSTD ontologies [6] which subsumed an earlier vocabulary BIRNLex. It currently contains concepts that span gross anatomy, cells of the nervous system (http://neurolex.org/wiki/ Category:Nervous_system), subcellular structures (http:/ / neurolex. org/ wiki/ Subcellular_Hierarchy), diseases (http://neurolex.org/wiki/Category:Disease), functions and techniques. NIF is soliciting community input to add more content and correct what is there.

Notes and references

[1] Initial content for this article was adapted from the NeuroLex project which is licensed under a Creative Commons Attribution License (http:/ /creativecommons.org/licenses/by/3.0/).

[2] The NIH Blueprint for Neuroscience Research (http://neuroscienceblueprint.nih.gov) is a cooperative effort among the 16 NIH Institutes, Centers and Offices that support neuroscience research. By pooling resources and expertise, the Blueprint supports the development of new tools, training opportunities, and other resources to assist neuroscientists in both basic and clinical research. Read more about the Blueprint (http://neuroscienceblueprint.nih.gov/blueprint_basics/about_blueprint.htm).

[3] http://neurolex.org

[4] http://www.neuinfo.org/nif/nifBasic.html

[5] https://wiki.neuinfo.org/xwiki/bin/view/Main/NIFSTDoverview

[6] http://neuinfo.org/about/vocabularies.shtml

Further reading

NIF was featured in the volume 6 number 3 issue in the journal Neuroinformatics in September 2008:

1. Bug WJ, Ascoli GA, Grethe JS, Gupta A, Fennema-Notestine C, Laird AR, Larson SD, Rubin D, Shepherd GM, Turner JA, Martone ME (September 2008). "The NIFSTD and BIRNLex vocabularies: building comprehensive ontologies for neuroscience" (http://www.neuinfo.org/about/vocabularies.shtml). *Neuroinformatics* **6** (3): 175–94. doi:10.1007/s12021-008-9032-z. PMC 2743139. PMID 18975148.

2. Gardner D, Akil H, Ascoli GA, Bowden DM, Bug W, Donohue DE, Goldberg DH, Grafstein B, Grethe JS, Gupta A, Halavi M, Kennedy DN, Marenco L, Martone ME, Miller PL, Müller HM, Robert A, Shepherd GM, Sternberg PW, Van Essen DC, Williams RW. (September 2008). "The neuroscience information framework: a data and knowledge environment for neuroscience". *Neuroinformatics* **6** (3): 149–60. doi:10.1007/s12021-008-9024-z. PMC 2661130. PMID 18946742.

3. Gardner D, Goldberg DH, Grafstein B, Robert A, Gardner EP (September 2008). "Terminology for neuroscience data discovery: multi-tree syntax and investigator-derived semantics". *Neuroinformatics* **6** (3): 161–74. doi:10.1007/s12021-008-9029-7. PMC 2663521. PMID 18958630.

4. Gupta A, Bug W, Marenco L, Qian X, Condit C, Rangarajan A, Müller HM, Miller PL, Sanders B, Grethe JS, Astakhov V, Shepherd G, Sternberg PW, Martone ME (September 2008). "Federated access to heterogeneous information resources in the Neuroscience Information Framework (NIF)". *Neuroinformatics* **6** (3): 205–17. doi:10.1007/s12021-008-9033-y. PMC 2689790. PMID 18958629.

5. Halavi M, Polavaram S, Donohue DE, Hamilton G, Hoyt J, Smith KP, Ascoli GA (September 2008). "NeuroMorpho.Org implementation of digital neuroscience: dense coverage and integration with the NIF". *Neuroinformatics* **6** (3): 241–52. doi:10.1007/s12021-008-9030-1. PMC 2655120. PMID 18949582.

6. Marenco L, Ascoli GA, Martone ME, Shepherd GM, Miller PL (September 2008). "The NIF LinkOut broker: a web resource to facilitate federated data integration using NCBI identifiers". *Neuroinformatics* **6** (3): 219–27. doi:10.1007/s12021-008-9025-y. PMC 2704600. PMID 18975149.

7. Marenco L, Li Y, Martone ME, Sternberg PW, Shepherd GM, Miller PL (September 2008). "Issues in the design of a pilot concept-based query interface for the neuroinformatics information framework". *Neuroinformatics* **6** (3): 229–39. doi:10.1007/s12021-008-9035-9. PMC 2664632. PMID 18953674.

8. Müller HM, Rangarajan A, Teal TK, Sternberg PW (September 2008). "Textpresso for neuroscience: searching the full text of thousands of neuroscience research papers". *Neuroinformatics* **6** (3): 195–204. doi:10.1007/s12021-008-9031-0. PMC 2666735. PMID 18949581.

More information on related publications can be found on the NIF publications page (http://www.neuinfo.org/publications/index.shtml).

External links

- NeuroLex site (http://neurolex.org)
- Neuroscience Information Framework (NIF) website (http://www.neuinfo.org)
- National Institutes of Health NIF website (http://nif.nih.gov)
- Bioinformatics resources in NeuroLex (http://neurolex.org/wiki/Category:Resource)

Newbler

Newbler

Developer(s)	454 Life Sciences
Stable release	v2.5.3 / January 5, 2011
Operating system	Linux i386/x86_64
Type	Bioinformatics
License	Commercial

Newbler is a software package for *de novo* DNA sequence assembly. It is designed specifically for assembling sequence data generated by the 454 GS-series of pyrosequencing platforms sold by 454 Life Sciences, a Roche Diagnostics company.

Usage

Newbler can run via a Java GUI (gsAssembler) or the command line (runAssembly). It works natively with the .SFF data output by the sequencer, but is also able to accept FASTA files with or without quality information. It will utilise older Sanger sequence data if appropriately formatted to aid in assembly and scaffolding.

External links

- 454 Sequencing home page [1]

References

[1] http://www.454.com/

Nextbio

NextBio

NEXTBIO ›™	
Type	Private
Founded	California, USA (2004)
Founder(s)	Saeid Akhtari Ilya Kupershmidt Mostafa Ronaghi
Headquarters	Cupertino, California, US
Area served	Worldwide
Key people	Saeid Akhtari (President & CEO) Ilya Kupershmidt (VP of Product Management) Dr. Satnam Alag (VP of Engineering)
Employees	75
Website	www.nextbio.com [1]

NextBio is a privately owned software company that provides a platform for drug companies and life science researchers to search, discover, and share knowledge across public and proprietary data. It was co-founded by Saeid Akhtari, Ilya Kupershmidt and Mostafa Ronaghi in 2004 and based in Cupertino, California, USA.

The NextBio Platform is an ontology-based semantic framework that connects highly heterogeneous data and textual information. The semantic framework is based on gene, tissue, disease and compound ontologies. This framework contains information from different organisms, platforms, data types and research areas that is integrated into and correlated within a single searchable environment using proprietary algorithms. It provides a unified interface for researchers to formulate and test new hypotheses across vast collections of experimental data. [2] [3]

According to the company, the enterprise version of the NextBio platform is being used in life science research and development and drug development by researchers and clinicians at: Merck Pharmaceutical, Johnson & Johnson Pharmaceutical Research & Development, L.L.C., Celgene, Genzyme, Eli Lilly and Company, and Regeneron Pharmaceuticals.[4] This enterprise version allows internal, proprietary data to be uploaded and integrated into the NextBio database of publicly-available data. [5] According to the company, scientists are using NextBio to improve their ability to identify relevant prognostic and predictive molecular signatures which are significant in their research.[6]

NextBio was a receiver of the Frost & Sullivan North American Life Sciences Customer Value Enhancement Award in 2008.[7]

Articles

- Business Wire, March 2007 [8]
- Venture Beat, February 2007 [9]
- Scientific Computing, May 2008 [10]

References

[1] http://www.nextbio.com/

[2] stanford.edu | 2008 Release: What is NextBio? (http://lane.stanford.edu/howto/index.html?id=_3391)

[3] bio-itworld.com | 2007 Release: NextBio Life Science Search Engine Advances Systems Biology Approach to Research (http://www. bio-itworld.com/issues/2006/dec-jan/nextbio/)

[4] businesswire.com | 2008 Release: NextBio Announces Public Launch of Its Life Science Search Engine (http://findarticles.com/p/articles/ mi_m0EIN/is_2008_April_28/ai_n25359106)

[5] nextbio.com | 2008 Release: NextBio FAQ (http://www.nextbio.com/b/corp/faq.nb#ent_howorg)

[6] nextbio.com | 2008 Release: NextBio Testimonials (http://www.nextbio.com/b/corp/user.nb)

[7] businesswire.com | 2008 Release: NextBio Awarded the 2008 Frost & Sullivan North American Life Sciences "Customer Value Enhancement Award" for Innovative Life Science Search Engine (http://findarticles.com/p/articles/mi_m0EIN/is_2008_June_24/ ai_n27505358?tag=content;col1)

[8] http://findarticles.com/p/articles/mi_m0EIN/is_2007_March_6/ai_n27287287

[9] http://venturebeat.com/2007/02/21/nextbio-is-latest-search-engine-for-healthcare-research-community/

[10] http://www.scientific-computing.com/products/product_details.php?product_id=344

NeXtProt

neXtProt

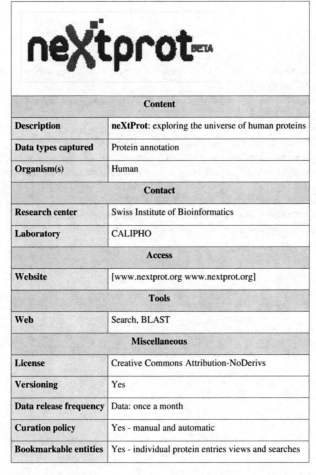

Content	
Description	**neXtProt**: exploring the universe of human proteins
Data types captured	Protein annotation
Organism(s)	Human
Contact	
Research center	Swiss Institute of Bioinformatics
Laboratory	CALIPHO
Access	
Website	[www.nextprot.org www.nextprot.org]
Tools	
Web	Search, BLAST
Miscellaneous	
License	Creative Commons Attribution-NoDerivs
Versioning	Yes
Data release frequency	Data: once a month
Curation policy	Yes - manual and automatic
Bookmarkable entities	Yes - individual protein entries views and searches

neXtProt is an on-line knowledge platform on human proteins. It strives to be a comprehensive resource that provides a variety of types of information on human proteins, such as their function, subcellular location, expression, interactions and role in diseases. Currently, the major part of the information in neXtProt[1] is obtained from the UniProt Swiss-Prot database but is gradually being complemented by data originating from high-throughput studies. It is developed jointly by the CALIPHO group[2] directed by Amos Bairoch and Lydie Lane of the Swiss Institute of Bioinformatics (SIB) and by GeneBio SA.

References

[1] Abstract of a recent conference (http://bip.weizmann.ac.il/conferences/sibwis2011/abstract/AmosBairoch.html), on the web site of the WIS

[2] CALIPHO group (http://www.isb-sib.ch/groups/geneva/calipho-bairoch.html), on the web site of the SIB

External links

- neXtProt (http://www.nextprot.org/) - Exploring the universe of human proteins
- UniProt (http://www.uniprot.org/) - The Universal protein resource
- SIB (http://www.isb-sib.ch/) - The Swiss Institute of Bioinformatics
- GeneBio (http://www.genebio.com/) - Geneva Bioinformatics SA

Nexus file

Nexus file format[1] is widely used in Bioinformatics. Several popular phylogenetic programs such as Paup*,[2] MrBayes,[3] Mesquite, and MacClade[4] use this format.

Syntax

Command inside square brackets [and] are ignored (comment). Each block starts with **BEGIN block_name;** and finishes with **END;** [5]

An example for a simple DNA alignment would be:

```
#NEXUS
Begin data;
Dimensions ntax=4 nchar=15;
Format datatype=dna symbols="ACTG" missing=? gap=-;
Matrix
Species1    atgctagctagctcg
Species2    atgcta??tag-tag
Species3    atgttagctag-tgg
Species4    atgttagctag-tag
;
End;
```

Basic blocks

TAXA block

    The TAXA block contains information about taxa.

CHARACTER block

    The CHARACTER block contains information about the data matrix.

DATA block

    The DATA block contains the data matrix (e.g. sequence alignment).

TREES block

    The TREES block contains phylogenetic trees described using the Newick format, e.g. ((A,B),C);

Paup

ASSUMPTIONS block

SETS block;

TREES block

CODONS block

DISTANCES block

PAUP block

> This block contains all the commands used by Paup*. (refer to Command Reference Document - Second Draft [6] for detail describtion of each command.)

References

[1] Maddison DR, Swofford DL, Maddison WP (1997). "NEXUS: An extensible file format for systematic information". *Systematic Biology* **46** (4): 590–621. doi:10.1093/sysbio/46.4.590. PMID 11975335.

[2] PAUP* (http://paup.csit.fsu.edu/index.html) — Phylogenetic Analysis Using Parsimony *and other methods

[3] MyBayes (http://mrbayes.csit.fsu.edu/)

[4] MacClade (http://macclade.org/index.html)

[5] Detailed NEXUS specification (https://www.nescent.org/wg_phyloinformatics/NEXUS_Specification)

[6] http://paup.csit.fsu.edu/Cmd_ref_v2.pdf

External links

- NEXUS file format (http://wiki.christophchamp.com/index.php/NEXUS_file_format) — detailed explanation with lots of examples
- Nexus to phyloXML converter (http://phylosoft.org/forester/applications/phyloxml_converter/)
- NeXML (http://nexml.org)
- Nexus to Fasta converter (http://www.bugaco.com/bioinf/)

NIAID ChemDB

The **NIAID ChemDB** is a database maintained by the National Institute of Allergy and Infectious Diseases containing preclinical data on drugs with potential therapeutic applications against HIV/AIDS and related opportunistic infections.[1]

References

[1] "Division of AIDS Anti-HIV/OI/TB Therapeutics Database" (http://chemdb.niaid.nih.gov/AboutChemDB.aspx). National Institutes of Health, U.S. Department of Health and Human Services. . Retrieved 2011-09-21.

NoeClone

NoeClone

Developer(s)	NoeGen Inc.
Stable release	2.01 / 2009
Operating system	Windows, Linux, Mac OS X, Solaris
Type	bioinformatics
License	commercial
Website	http://www.noegen.com

NoeClone is a bioinformatics software which can run in multiple operating systems (Windows, Mac OS, Unix/Linux) with the same interface.

Main features

NoeClone provides a knowledge-enhanced and comprehensive solution for virtual cloning, gel simulation, plasmid map drawing and sequence analysis.

- Sequence comparison and sequence view
- Plasmid map drawing
- Motif search and ORF
- Gel simulation
- Restriction enzyme analysis
- PCR design
- High-throughput cloning
- Support advanced TOPO clone and Gateway clone

References

Relevant software

- NoePrimer
- SeqCorator
- Vector NTI
- Gbench (http://www.ncbi.nlm.nih.gov/projects/gbench/)

External links

- NoeGen Official website (http://www.noegen.com/)
- List of phylogeny software (http://evolution.genetics.washington.edu/phylip/software.html), hosted at the University of Washington

NoePrimer

NoePrimer

Developer(s)	NoeGen Inc.
Stable release	2.01 / 2009
Operating system	Windows, Linux, Mac OS X, Solaris
Type	bioinformatics
License	commercial
Website	http://www.noegen.com

NoePrimer is a bioinformatics software which can run in multiple operating systems (windows, Mac OS, Unix/Linux) with the same interface.

Main features

NoePrimer provides an easy, simple and graphics-enhanced sequence view for primer design. In addition to supporting conventional applications for PCR, hybridization and sequencing, NoePrimer provides advanced capabilities for multiplex PCR and high-throughput primer search and analysis.

- Direct visualization of PCR products, hairpins, self-dimers and false-priming
- Support multiple PCR primer analysis
- High-throughput primer search
- Tracking and saving primers to primer library
- Direct visualization of feature on temple sequence while you can edit, create and annotate new sequence feature

References

External links

- NoeGen Official Website (http://www.noegen.com/)
- List of phylogeny software (http://evolution.genetics.washington.edu/phylip/software.html), hosted at the University of Washington

Nuclear Receptor Signaling Atlas

The **Nuclear Receptor Signaling Atlas** (**NURSA**) is a United States National Institutes of Health-funded research consortium focussed on nuclear receptors and nuclear receptor coregulators.[1] [2] Its co-principal investigators are Bert O'Malley of Baylor College of Medicine and Ron Evans of the Salk Institute.

References

[1] Margolis RN, Evans RM, O'Malley BW (October 2005). "The Nuclear Receptor Signaling Atlas: development of a functional atlas of nuclear receptors". *Mol. Endocrinol.* **19** (10): 2433–6. doi:10.1210/me.2004-0461. PMID 16051673.

[2] Lanz RB, Jericevic Z, Zuercher WJ, Watkins C, Steffen DL, Margolis R, McKenna NJ (January 2006). "Nuclear Receptor Signaling Atlas (): hyperlinking the nuclear receptor signaling community". *Nucleic Acids Res.* **34** (Database issue): D221–6. doi:10.1093/nar/gkj029. PMC 1347392. PMID 16381851.

External links

- "NURSA (Nuclear Receptor Signaling Atlas)" (http://www.nursa.org/). Retrieved 2008-08-27. "Receptors, Coactivators, Corepressors and Ligands"

Ontology engineering

Ontology engineering in computer science and information science is a new field, which studies the methods and methodologies for building ontologies: formal representations of a set of concepts within a domain and the relationships between those concepts. A large scale representation of abstract concepts such as actions, time, physical objects and beliefs would be an example of ontological engineering.

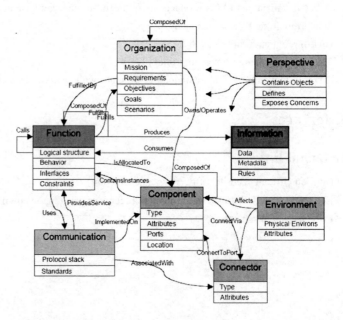

Example of a constructed MBED Top Level Ontology based on the Nominal set of views.[1]

Overview

[Ontology engineering] aims at making explicit the knowledge contained within software applications, and within enterprises and business procedures for a particular domain. Ontology engineering offers a direction towards solving the inter-operability problems brought about by semantic obstacles, i.e. the obstacles related to the definitions of business terms and software classes. Ontology engineering is a set of tasks related to the development of ontologies for a particular domain.

— Line Pouchard, Nenad Ivezic and Craig Schlenoff, Ontology Engineering for Distributed Collaboration in Manufacturing[2]

Ontologies provide a common vocabulary of an area and define, with different levels of formality, the meaning of the terms and the relationships between them. During the last decade, increasing attention has been focused on ontologies. Ontologies are now widely used in knowledge engineering, artificial intelligence and computer science; in applications related to areas such as knowledge management, natural language processing, e-commerce, intelligent information integration, bio-informatics, education; and in new emerging fields like the semantic web. Ontological engineering is a new field of study concerning the ontology development process, the ontology life cycle, the methods and methodologies for building ontologies,[3] [4] and the tool suites and languages that support them.

Ontology languages

Further information: ontology language

An ontology language is a formal language used to encode the ontology. There are a number of such languages for ontologies, both proprietary and standards-based:

- Common logic is ISO standard 24707, a specification for a family of ontology languages that can be accurately translated into each other.
- The Cyc project has its own ontology language called CycL, based on first-order predicate calculus with some higher-order extensions.
- The Gellish language includes rules for its own extension and thus integrates an ontology with an ontology language.
- IDEF5 is a software engineering method to develop and maintain usable, accurate, domain ontologies.
- KIF is a syntax for first-order logic that is based on S-expressions.
- Rule Interchange Format (RIF) and F-Logic combine ontologies and rules.
- OWL is a language for making ontological statements, developed as a follow-on from RDF and RDFS, as well as earlier ontology language projects including OIL, DAML and DAML+OIL. OWL is intended to be used over the World Wide Web, and all its elements (classes, properties and individuals) are defined as RDF resources, and identified by URIs.
- XBRL (Extensible Business Reporting Language) is a syntax for expressing business semantics.

Ontology Engineering In Life Sciences

Life sciences is flourishing with ontologies that biologists use to make sense of their experiments. For inferring correct conclusions from experiments, ontologies have to be structured optimally against the knowledge base they represent. The structure of an ontology needs to be changed continuously so that it is an accurate representation of the underlying domain.

Recently, an automated method was introduced for engineering ontologies in life sciences such as Gene Ontology (GO),[5] one of the most successful and widely used biomedical ontology.[6] Based on information theory, it restructures ontologies so that the levels represent the desired specificity of the concepts. Similar information theoretic approaches have also been used for optimal partition of Gene Ontology.[7] Given the mathematical nature of such engineering algorithms, these optimizations can be automated to produce a principled and scalable architecture to restructure ontologies such as GO.

Open Biomedical Ontologies (OBO), a 2006 initiative of the U.S. National Center for Biomedical Ontology, that provides a common 'foundry' for various ontology initiatives, amongst which are:

- The Generic Model Organism Project (GMOD)
- Gene Ontology Consortium
- Sequence Ontology
- Ontology Lookup Service

- The Plant Ontology Consortium
- Standards and Ontologies for Functional Genomics

and more

Tools for ontology engineering

- DOGMA
- DogmaModeler
- KAON
- OntoClean
- OnToContent
- HOZO
- Protégé (software)

References

Ⓔ *This article incorporates public domain material from websites or documents* [8] *of the National Institute of Standards and Technology.*

[1] Peter Shames, Joseph Skipper. "Toward a Framework for Modeling Space Systems Architectures" (http://trs-new.jpl.nasa.gov/dspace/bitstream/2014/39851/1/06-0876.pdf). NASA, JPL.

[2] Line Pouchard, Nenad Ivezic and Craig Schlenoff (2000) "Ontology Engineering for Distributed Collaboration in Manufacturing" (http://www.mel.nist.gov/msidlibrary/doc/AISfinal2.pdf). In *Proceedings of the AIS2000 conference*, March 2000.

[3] Asunción Gómez-Pérez, Mariano Fernández-López, Oscar Corcho (2004). *Ontological Engineering: With Examples from the Areas of Knowledge Management, E-commerce and the Semantic Web*. Springer, 2004.

[4] Denicola, A; Missikoff, M; Navigli, R (2009). "A software engineering approach to ontology building" (http://www.dsi.uniroma1.it/~navigli/pubs/De_Nicola_Missikoff_Navigli_2009.pdf). *Information Systems* 34 (2): 258. doi:10.1016/j.is.2008.07.002. .

[5] Alterovitz, G; Xiang, M; Hill, DP; Lomax, J; Liu, J; Cherkassky, M; Dreyfuss, J; Mungall, C et al. (2010). "Ontology engineering". *Nature biotechnology* 28 (2): 128–30. doi:10.1038/nbt0210-128. PMID 20139945.

[6] Botstein, David; Cherry, J. Michael; Ashburner, Michael; Ball, Catherine A.; Blake, Judith A.; Butler, Heather; Davis, Allan P.; Dolinski, Kara et al. (2000). "Gene ontology: Tool for the unification of biology. The Gene Ontology Consortium" (http://www.geneontology.org/GO_nature_genetics_2000.pdf). *Nature Genetics* 25 (1): 25–9. doi:10.1038/75556. PMC 3037419. PMID 10802651. .

[7] Alterovitz, G.; Xiang, M.; Mohan, M.; Ramoni, M. F. (2007). "GO PaD: The Gene Ontology Partition Database". *Nucleic Acids Research* 35 (Database issue): D322–7. doi:10.1093/nar/gkl799. PMC 1669720. PMID 17098937.

[8] http://www.nist.gov

Further reading

- John Davies (Ed.) (2006). *Larger ImageSemantic Web Technologies: Trends and Research in Ontology-based Systems*. Wiley. ISBN 978-0-470-02596-3

- Asunción Gómez-Pérez, Mariano Fernández-López, Oscar Corcho (2004). *Ontological Engineering: With Examples from the Areas of Knowledge Management, E-commerce and the Semantic Web*. Springer, 2004.

- Jarrar, Mustafa (2006). "Position paper" (http://www.jarrar.info/publications/J06.pdf.htm). *Proceedings of the 15th international conference on World Wide Web - WWW '06*. pp. 497. doi:10.1145/1135777.1135850. ISBN 1595933239.

- Mustafa Jarrar and Robert Meersman (2008). "Ontology Engineering -The DOGMA Approach" (http://www.jarrar.info/publications/JM08.pdf.htm). Book Chapter (Chapter 3). In Advances in Web Semantics I. Volume LNCS 4891, Springer.

- Riichiro Mizoguchi (2004). "Tutorial on ontological engineering: part 3: Advanced course of ontological engineering" (http://www.ei.sanken.osaka-u.ac.jp/pub/miz/Part3V3.pdf). In: *New Generation Computing*. Ohmsha & Springer-Verlag, 22(2):198-220.

- Elena Paslaru Bontas Simperl and Christoph Tempich (2006). " Ontology Engineering: A Reality Check (http:// ontocom.ag-nbi.de/docs/odbase2006.pdf)"
- Devedzić, Vladan (2002). "Understanding ontological engineering". *Communications of the ACM* **45** (4): 136. doi:10.1145/505248.506002.

External links

- Metadata? Thesauri? Taxonomies? Topic Maps! (http://www.ontopia.net/topicmaps/materials/tm-vs-thesauri. html).

Ontology for Biomedical Investigations

The **Ontology for Biomedical Investigations (OBI)** is an open access, integrated ontology for the description of biological and clinical investigations. OBI provides a model for the design of an investigation, the protocols and instrumentation used, the materials used, the data generated and the type of analysis performed on it. The project is being developed as part of the OBO Foundry and as such adheres to all the principles therein such as orthogonal coverage (i.e. clear delineation from other foundry member ontologies) and the use of a common formal language. In OBI the common formal language used is the Web Ontology Language (OWL). As of March 2008, a pre-release version of the ontology was made available at the project's SVN repository[1]

Ontology for Biomedical Investigations

The OBI Consortium logo.

Scope of the Ontology

The Ontology for Biomedical Investigations (OBI) addresses the need for controlled vocabularies to support integration and joint ("cross-omics") analysis of experimental data, a need originally identified in the transcriptomics domain by the FGED Society, which developed the MGED Ontology as an annotation resource for microarray data.[2] OBI uses the Basic Formal Ontology[3] upper level ontology as a means of describing general entities that do not belong to a specific problem domain. As such, all OBI classes are a subclass of some BFO class.

The ontology has the scope of modeling all biomedical investigations and as such contains ontology terms for aspects such as:

- biological material - for example blood plasma
- instrument (and parts of an instrument therein) - for example DNA microarray, centrifuge
- information content - such as an image or a digital information entity such as an electronic medical record
- design and execution of an investigation (and individual experiments therein) - for example study design, electrophoresis material separaition
- data transformation (incorporating aspects such as data normalization and data analysis) - for example principal components analysis dimensionality reduction, mean calculation

Less 'concrete' aspects such as the role a given entity may play in a particular scenario (for example the role of a chemical compound in an experiment) and the function of an entity (for example the digestive function of the stomach to nutriate the body) are also covered in the ontology.

OBI Consortium

The MGED Ontology was originally identified in the transcriptomics domain by the FGED Society and was developed to address the needs of data integration. Following a mutual decision to collaborate, this effort later became a wider collaboration between groups such as FGED, PSI and MSI in response to the needs of areas such as transcriptomics, proteomics and metabolomics and the FuGO (Functional Genomics Investigation Ontology)[4] was created. This later became the OBI covering the wider scope of all biomedical investigations.

As an international, cross-domain initiative, the OBI consortium draws upon a pool of experts from a variety of fields, not limited to biology. The current list of OBI consortium members is available at the OBI consortium website. [5] The consortium is made up of a coordinating committee which is a combination of two subgroups, the Community Representative (those representing a particular biomedical community) and the Core Developers (ontology developers who may or may not be members of any single community). Separate to the coordinating committee is the Developers Working Group which consists of developers within the communities collaborating in the development of OBI at the discretion of current OBI Consortium members.

References

[1] Ontology for Biomedical Investigations (OBI) | Home (http://purl.obofoundry.org/obo/obi/)

[2] Smith *et al.* (2007) Nature Biotechnology 25, 1251 - 1255 (2007)

[3] Basic Formal Ontology (BFO) | Home (http://www.ifomis.org/bfo)

[4] Whetzel, PL et al. Development of FuGO: an ontology for functional genomics investigations. OMICS 10, 199–204

[5] http://obi-ontology.org/page/Consortium

External links

- The OBI Consortium project homepage http://obi-ontology.org/
- The OBI Consortium SVN Repository homepage http://obi.svn.sourceforge.net/viewvc/obi/
- The OBI Consortium mailing list homepage http://obi-ontology.org/page/Mailing_lists

Open Biomedical Ontologies

Open Biomedical Ontologies (abbreviated **OBO**; formerly Open Biological Ontologies) is an effort to create controlled vocabularies for shared use across different biological and medical domains. As of 2006, OBO forms part of the resources of the U.S. National Center for Biomedical Ontology, where it will form a central element of the NCBO's BioPortal.

OBO Foundry

The OBO Ontology library forms the basis of the OBO Foundry[1] , a collaborative experiment involving a group of ontology developers who have agreed in advance to the adoption of a growing set of principles specifying best practices in ontology development. These principles are designed to foster interoperability of ontologies within the broader OBO framework, and also to ensure a gradual improvement of quality and formal rigor in ontologies, in ways designed to meet the increasing needs of data and information integration in the biomedical domain.

Related Projects

Ontology Lookup Service

The Ontology Lookup Service [2] is a spin-off of the PRIDE project, which required a centralized query interface for ontology and controlled vocabulary lookup. While many of the ontologies queriable by the OLS are available online, each has its own query interface and output format. The OLS provides a web service interface to query multiple ontologies from a single location with a unified output format.

Gene Ontology Consortium

The goal of the Gene ontology (GO) consortium is to produce a controlled vocabulary that can be applied to all organisms even as knowledge of gene and protein roles in cells is accumulating and changing. GO provides three structured networks of defined terms to describe gene product attributes.

Sequence Ontology

The Sequence Ontology [3] (SO) is a part of the Gene Ontology project and the aim is to develop an ontology suitable for describing biological sequences. It is a joint effort by genome annotation centres, including WormBase, the Berkeley Drosophila Genome Project, FlyBase, the Mouse Genome Informatics group, and the Sanger Institute.

Generic Model Organism Databases

The Generic Model Organism Project (GMOD) is a joint effort by the model organism system databases WormBase, FlyBase, MGI, SGD, Gramene, Rat Genome Database, EcoCyc, and TAIR to develop reusable components suitable for creating new community databases of biology.

Standards and Ontologies for Functional Genomics

SOFG [4] is both a meeting and a website; it aims to bring together biologists, bioinformaticians, and computer scientists who are developing and using standards and ontologies with an emphasis on describing high-throughput functional genomics experiments.

FGED

The Functional Genomics Data (FGED) Society is an international organisation of biologists, computer scientists, and data analysts that aims to facilitate the sharing of microarray data generated by functional genomics experiments.

Ontology for Biomedical Investigations

The Ontology for Biomedical Investigations (OBI) is an open access, integrated ontology for the description of biological and clinical investigations. OBI provides a model for the design of an investigation, the protocols and instrumentation used, the materials used, the data generated and the type of analysis performed on it. The project is being developed as part of the OBO Foundry and as such adheres to all the principles therein such as orthogonal coverage (i.e. clear delineation from other foundry member ontologies) and the use of a common formal language. In OBI the common formal language used is the Web Ontology Language (OWL).

Plant ontology

The Plant Ontology Consortium [5] (POC) aims to develop, curate and share structured controlled vocabularies (ontologies) that describe plant structures and growth/developmental stages. Through this effort, the project aims to facilitate cross database querying by fostering consistent use of these vocabularies in the annotation of tissue and/or growth stage specific expression of genes, proteins and phenotypes.

Phenoscape

Phenoscape [6] is a project to develop a database of phenotype data for species across the Osteriophysi, a large group of Teleost fish. The data is captured using annotations that combine terms from an Anatomy Ontology [7], an accompanying Taxonomic Ontology [8], and quality terms from the PATO ontology of phenotype qualities [9]. Several other OBO ontologies are also used. The anatomy ontology was developed from the zebrafish anatomy ontology developed by the Zebrafish Information Network [10].

OBO and Semantic Web

OBO & OWL Roundtrip Transformations

As a community effort, a standard common mapping has been created for lossless roundtrip transformations between Open Biomedical Ontologies (OBO) format and OWL. The research contains methodical examination of each of the constructs of OBO and a layer cake for OBO, similar to the Semantic Web stack. Project Page [11] Morphster Project [12]

References

[1] Smith, B.; Ashburner, M.; Rosse, C.; Bard, J.; Bug, W.; Ceusters, W.; Goldberg, L. J.; Eilbeck, K. et al. (2007). "The OBO Foundry: Coordinated evolution of ontologies to support biomedical data integration". *Nature Biotechnology* **25** (11): 1251–1255. doi:10.1038/nbt1346. PMC 2814061. PMID 17989687.

[2] http://www.ebi.ac.uk/ontology-lookup/

[3] http://song.sourceforge.net/

[4] http://www.sofg.org/

[5] http://www.plantontology.org/

[6] http://phenoscape.org/

[7] http://bioportal.bioontology.org/ontologies/39892/

[8] http://bioportal.bioontology.org/ontologies/39905/

[9] http://bioportal.bioontology.org/ontologies/39886/

[10] http://www.zfin.org/

[11] http://www.cs.utexas.edu/~hamid/oboowl.html

[12] http://www.morphster.org/

External links

- Open Biomedical Ontologies (OBO) (http://obofoundry.org)
- Ontology browser for most of the Open Biological Ontologies at BRENDA website (http://www.brenda-enzymes.info/index.php4?page=ontology/)
- PubOnto: OBO-based literature search tool (http://brainarray.mbni.med.umich.edu/Brainarray/prototype/PubOnto/)

Open Regulatory Annotation Database

The **Open Regulatory Annotation Database** (also known as **ORegAnno**) is designed to promote community-based curation of regulatory information. Specifically, the database contains information about regulatory regions, transcription factor binding sites, regulatory variants, and haplotypes.

Overview

Data Management

For each entry, cross-references are maintained to EnsEMBL [6], dbSNP [1],Entrez Gene [2], the NCBI Taxonomy database [3] and PubMed [4]. The information within ORegAnno is regularly mapped and provided as a UCSC Genome Browser [5] track. Furthermore, each entry is associated with its experimental evidence, embedded as an Evidence Ontology [6] within ORegAnno. This allows the researcher to analyze regulatory data using their own conditions as to the suitability of the supporting evidence.

Software and data access

The project is open source - all data and all software that is produced in the project can be freely accessed and used.

Database contents

As of December 20 2006, ORegAnno contained 4220 regulatory sequences (excluding deprecated records) for 2190 transcription factor binding sites, 1853 regulatory regions (enhancers, promoters, etc), 170 regulatory polymorphisms, and 7 regulatory haplotypes for 17 different organisms (predominantly Drosophila melanogaster, Homo sapiens, Mus musculus, Caenorhabditis elegans, and Rattus norvegicus in that order). These records were obtained by manual curation of 828 publications by 45 ORegAnno users from the gene regulation community. The ORegAnno publication queue contained 4215 publications of which 858 were closed, 34 were in progress (open status), and 3321 were awaiting annotation (pending status). ORegAnno is continually updated and therefore current database contents should be obtained from www.oreganno.org [7].

RegCreative Jamboree 2006

The RegCreative jamboree was stimulated by a community initiative to curate in perpetuity the genomic sequences which have been experimentally determined to control gene expression. This objective is of fundamental importance to evolutionary analysis and translational research as regulatory mechanisms are widely-implicated in species-specific adaptation and the etiology of disease. This initiative culminated in the formation of an international consortium of like-minded scientists dedicated to accomplishing this task. The RegCreative jamboree was the first opportunity for these groups to meet to be able to accurately assess the current state of knowledge in gene regulation and to begin to develop standards by which to curate regulatory information.

In total, 44 researchers attended the workshop from 9 different countries and 23 institutions. Funding was also obtained from ENFIN, the BioSapiens Network, FWO Research Foundation, Genome Canada and Genome British Columbia.

The specific outcomes of the RegCreative meeting to date are:

- Prior to the RegCreative Jamboree, attendees were asked to participate in an interannotator agreement assessment. Two ORegAnno mirrors were established with identical sets of publications to be annotated in their queue. In total, 33 redundant annotations from 18 publications were collected. (79 annotations for 31 papers and 60 annotations for 21 papers were collected on servers 1 and 2, respectively.) This effort was used as a baseline from which to establish annotator efficiency.

- Hands-on annotation activities occurred during the first 2 days of the 3-day workshop. In total, 39 researchers contributed 184 TFBS and 317 Regulatory Regions from 96 papers. Many of these researchers were also trained on the ORegAnno system, significantly increasing its experienced-user community. The contribution of these annotations to individual species was 339 annotations in Homo sapiens, 42 annotations in Mus musculus, 72 annotations in Drosophila melanogaster, 24 annotations in Ciona intestinalis, 14 annotations in Rattus norvegicus, 6 annotations in Halocynthia roretzi, 2 annotations in Ciona savignyi and 2 annotations in HIV. Within these annotations, one new dataset was added to ORegAnno; 274 human enhancers were programmatically annotated by Maximillian Haessler, Institute Alfred Fessard, from Visel et al., Nucleic Acids Research, 2006. In total, 130 scientific studies were examined in depth. The annotated papers were pre-selected from expert-curated publications in the ORegAnno queue that had full-text available through HighWire Press.

- There exists an immediate need for improved data standardization and development of associated ontologies. Specifically, this should include the open access development and integration of transcription factor naming conventions and sequence, cell type, cell line, tissue, and evidence ontologies. The groundwork for addressing and prioritizing these needs was accomplished in several ways during the meeting:

  - Transcription factor naming issues were addressed through discussion of integration of transcription factor prediction pipelines, such as DBD or flyTF, which have been supplemented with manual curation versus solely manual curated implementations like TFcat.
  - Marc Halfon [8], University at Buffalo, led a breakout session to improve the Sequence Ontology [3] from existing ORegAnno and REDfly database conventions within the framework being developed as part of the Open Biomedical Ontologies. A preliminary version of these improvements can be found on the ORegAnno wiki [9].
  - Learning-based ontology development was widely regarded as an essential feature of the annotation process. Such that, annotators are not restricted from annotating based on the limitations of the controlled vocabulary and that these exceptions can be used to further develop the backbone ontologies.
  - Ontology development should be decentralized from the ORegAnno annotation framework. Specifically, it is planned that the ORegAnno evidence ontology will be removed and made available to broader community development.
  - Renewed focus on integrating species-specific resources with annotation framework.

- A specific focus of the workshop was addressing the role of text-mining in facilitating regulatory annotation. Sessions were led by Dr. Lynette Hirschman, MITRE, and Dr. Martin Krallinger, CNIO, to formulate where text-mining can help. A short term object of text-mining based analyses was formulated around both populating the ORegAnno queue and using the expert-curated portion of the ORegAnno queue to validate text-mining-based publication acquisition. The latter objectives are being led by Dr. Stein Aerts, University of Leuven.

References

- Montgomery SB, Griffith OL, Sleumer MC, Bergman CM, Bilenky M, Pleasance ED, Prychyna Y, Zhang X, Jones SJ. (2006). "ORegAnno: an open access database and curation system for literature-derived promoters, transcription factor binding sites and regulatory variation.". *Bioinformatics* **22** (5): 637–40. doi:10.1093/bioinformatics/btk027. PMID 16397004.
- Griffith OL, Montgomery SB, Bernier B, Chu B, Kasaian K, Aerts S, Mahony S, Sleumer MC, Bilenky M, Haeussler M, Griffith M, Gallo SM, Giardine B, Hooghe B, Van Loo P, Blanco E, Ticoll A, Lithwick S, Portales-Casamar E, Donaldson IJ, Robertson G, Wadelius C, De Bleser P, Vlieghe D, Halfon MS, Wasserman W, Hardison R, Bergman CM, Jones SJ; Open Regulatory Annotation Consortium. (2008). "ORegAnno: an open-access community-driven resource for regulatory annotation.". *Nucleic Acids Research* **36** (Database issue): D107–13. doi:10.1093/nar/gkm967. PMC 2239002. PMID 18006570.

External links

- ORegAnno [7]
- RegCreative Jamboree 2006 [10]

References

[1] http://www.ncbi.nlm.nih.gov/projects/SNP/
[2] http://www.ncbi.nlm.nih.gov/entrez/query.fcgi?DB=gene
[3] http://www.ncbi.nlm.nih.gov/entrez/query.fcgi?CMD=search&DB=taxonomy
[4] http://www.pubmed.com
[5] http://genome.ucsc.edu/cgi-bin/hgTrackUi?org=Human&g=oreganno
[6] http://www.oreganno.org/oregano/evidenceview.action
[7] http://www.oreganno.org
[8] http://www.ccr.buffalo.edu/halfon
[9] http://www.bcgsc.ca/wiki/display/oreganno/SeqOntology
[10] http://www.dmbr.ugent.be/bioit/contents/regcreative/

OpenMS

OpenMS is an open-source C++ library for LC/MS data management and analyses. It offers an infrastructure for the development of mass spectrometry related software. OpenMS is free software available under the LGPL. OpenMS is intended to offer a rich functionality while keeping in mind the design goals of ease-of-use, robustness, extensibility and portability.

OpenMS covers a wide range of functionalities needed to develop software for the analysis of high throghput protein separation and mass spectrometry related data. Among others algorithms for signal processing, feature finding, visualization, map mapping and peptide identification.

OpenMS will be compatible with the upcoming Proteomics Standard Initiative (PSI) formats for MS data.

OpenMS is developed in the groups of Prof. Knut Reinert [1] at the Free University of Berlin and in the group of Prof. Kohlbacher [2] at the University of Tübingen.

Please see the OpenMS [3] website for the most up-to-date information, including download information.

OpenMS has been successfully used for the implementation of The OpenMS Proteomics Pipeline(TOPP). TOPP is a set of computational tools that can be chained together to tailor problem-specific analysis pipelines for HPLC-MS data. It transforms most of the OpenMS functionality into small command line tools that are the building blocks for more complex analysis pipelines.

References

- Sturm M, Bertsch A, Groepl C, Hildebrandt A, Hussong R, Lange E, Pfeifer N, Schulz-Trieglaff O, Zerck A, Reinert K, Kohlbacher O: **OpenMS – An open-source software framework for mass spectrometry.** *BMC Bioinformatics* 2008, **9:**163.(fulltext [4])
- Kohlbacher O, Reinert K, Gröpl C, Lange E, Pfeifer N, Schulz-Trieglaff O, Sturm M: **TOPP - the OpenMS proteomics pipeline.** *Bioinformatics* 2007, **23(2):**e191-7. (fulltext [5])

References

[1] http://www.inf.fu-berlin.de/inst/ag-bio/

[2] http://www-bs.informatik.uni-tuebingen.de/

[3] http://open-ms.sourceforge.net/

[4] http://www.biomedcentral.com/1471-2105/9/163

[5] http://bioinformatics.oxfordjournals.org/cgi/content/full/23/2/e191

The OpenMS Proteomics Pipeline

The OpenMS Proteomics Pipeline (TOPP) is a set of computational tools that can be chained together to tailor problem-specific analysis pipelines for HPLC-MS data. It transforms most of the OpenMS functionality into small command line tools that are the building blocks for more complex analysis pipelines. The functionality of the tools ranges from data preprocessing (file format conversion, baseline reduction, noise reduction, peak picking, map alignment,...) over quantitation (isotope-labeled and label-free) to identification (wrapper tools for Mascot, Sequest, InsPecT and OMSSA).

TOPP is developed in the groups of Prof. Knut Reinert [1] at the Free University of Berlin and in the group of Prof. Kohlbacher [2] at the University of Tübingen.

For more detailed information about the TOPP tools, see the TOPP documentation [1] of the latest release and the TOPP publication in the references.

References

- Sturm M, Bertsch A, Groepl C, Hildebrandt A, Hussong R, Lange E, Pfeifer N, Schulz-Trieglaff O, Zerck A, Reinert K, Kohlbacher O: **OpenMS – An open-source software framework for mass spectrometry.** *BMC Bioinformatics* 2008, **9:**163.(fulltext [4])

- Kohlbacher O, Reinert K, Gröpl C, Lange E, Pfeifer N, Schulz-Trieglaff O, Sturm M: **TOPP - the OpenMS proteomics pipeline.** *Bioinformatics* 2007, **23(2):**e191-7. (fulltext [5])

References

[1] http://www-bs2.informatik.uni-tuebingen.de/services/OpenMS-release/

Overton Prize

The **Overton Prize** is an annual prize is awarded for outstanding accomplishment to a scientist in the early to mid stage of his or her career who has already made a significant contribution to the field of computational biology either through research, education, service, or a combination of the three. The prize was established by the International Society for Computational Biology in memory of G. Christian Overton[1] , a major contributor to the field of bioinformatics and member of the ISCB Board of Directors who died unexpectedly in 2000. [2] . The Overton Prize is traditionally awarded a the Intelligent Systems for Molecular Biology (ISMB) conference.

Laureates

- 2011 - Olga Troyanskaya[3]
- 2010 - Steven E. Brenner[4]
- 2009 - Trey Ideker[5]
- 2008 - Aviv Regev[6]
- 2007 - Eran Segal[7]
- 2006 - Mathieu Blanchette[8]
- 2005 - Ewan Birney[9]
- 2004 - Uri Alon[10]
- 2003 - Jim Kent[2]
- 2002 - David Baker[2]
- 2001 - Christopher Burge[2]

Sources

[1] http://www.bioinfo.de/isb/2000/01/0021/Chris-Overton.html Dr. G. Christian Overton

[2] Overton Prize (http://www.iscb.org/iscb-awards/overton-prize)

[3] Mullins, J.; Morrison Mckay, B. (2011). "International Society for Computational Biology Honors Michael Ashburner and Olga Troyanskaya with Top Bioinformatics/Computational Biology Awards for 2011". *PLoS Computational Biology* **7** (6): e1002081. doi:10.1371/journal.pcbi.1002081. PMC 3107244. PMID 21673867.

[4] McKay, B. M.; Sansom, C. (2010). "2010 ISCB Overton Prize Awarded to Steven E. Brenner". *PLoS Computational Biology* **6** (6): e1000831. doi:10.1371/journal.pcbi.1000831. PMC 2891695. PMID 20585610.

[5] Morrison Mckay, B. J.; Sansom, C. (2009). "Webb Miller and Trey Ideker to Receive Top International Bioinformatics Awards for 2009 from the International Society for Computational Biology". *PLoS Computational Biology* **5** (4): e1000375. doi:10.1371/journal.pcbi.1000375. PMC 2666155. PMID 19390599.

[6] Sansom, C.; Morrison Mckay, B. J. (2008). Bourne, Philip E.. ed. "ISCB Honors David Haussler and Aviv Regev". *PLoS Computational Biology* **4** (7): e1000101. doi:10.1371/journal.pcbi.1000101. PMC 2536508. PMID 18795145.

[7] Maisel, M. (2007). "ISCB Honors Temple F. Smith and Eran Segal". *PLoS Computational Biology* **3** (6): e128. Bibcode 2007PLSCB...3..128M. doi:10.1371/journal.pcbi.0030128. PMC 1904388. PMID 17604447.

[8] Maisel, M. (2006). "ISCB Honors Michael S. Waterman and Mathieu Blanchette". *PLoS Computational Biology* **2** (8): e105. Bibcode 2006PLSCB...2..105M. doi:10.1371/journal.pcbi.0020105. PMC 1526462.

[9] http://www.iscb.org/images/stories/newsletter/newsletter8-2/birney.html ISCB Newsletter 8-2 Dr. Ewan Birney Named as the 2005 Overton Prize Winner!

[10] http://www.iscb.org/images/stories/newsletter/newsletter7-3/overton.html ISCB Newsletter 7-3 Dr. Uri Alon Named as ISCB 2004 Overton Prize Winner

Ovid Technologies

Ovid Technologies, Inc. (or just **Ovid** for short), part of the Wolters Kluwer group of companies, provides access to online bibliographic databases, journals and other products, chiefly in the area of health sciences. The National Library of Medicine's MEDLINE database was once its chief product but now that this is freely available through PubMed, Ovid has diversified into a wide range of other databases and other products. Ovid has its global headquarters in New York City.[1]

Ovid was founded by Mark Nelson who developed his first interface to MEDLINE in 1984.[2] He formed the company in New York in 1988[2] and called it **Online Research Systems**.[3] [4] The company's first Microsoft Windows interface to MEDLINE was named Ovid and released in 1992.[2] In 1994 the company changed its name to **CD Plus**,[4] took over BRS Online[2] [3] and shortly after listed on NASDAQ.[2] It then changed to its present name in 1995, reflecting the importance of its Ovid product.[2] Wolters Kluwer took the company over in 1998. In 2001 Wolters Kluwer purchased the rival SilverPlatter company and merged it into Ovid during 2001 and early 2002.[5]

Ovid introduced a new database search interface called **OvidSP** in 2007. This has replaced the Ovid Gateway interface, which was retired in February 2008, and the SilverPlatter interface, which was retired in January 2009.

References

[1] " Contacts and locations (http://www.ovid.com/site/contacts/index.jsp?top=47)", Ovid Technologies, Inc.
[2] " Ovid: A narrative chronology (http://www.nicsolution.com/partners/ovid/ovid.htm)", NIC Corporation
[3] Quint, Barbara. " Ovid Technologies bought by Wolters Kluwer for $200 million (http://newsbreaks.infotoday.com/nbreader.asp?ArticleID=17998)". *Information Today* October 5, 1998
[4] " Ovid Technologies, Inc. (http://investing.businessweek.com/research/stocks/private/snapshot.asp?privcapId=334364)", BusinessWeek
[5] " Company history (http://www.ovid.com/site/about/history.jsp?top=42&mid=43)", Ovid Technologies, Inc.

External links

- Ovid website (http://www.ovid.com)
- OvidSP page (http://www.ovid.com/site/products/tools/ovid/ovidsp_access.jsp) at Ovid website
- Wolters Kluwer Health - OvidSP (http://www.iwr.co.uk/2216015) — a review of OvidSP by Davey Winder in *Information World Review*

Paola Sebastiani

Paola Sebastiani is a biostatistician and a Professor at Boston University working in the field of genetic epidemiology, building prognostic models that can be used for the dissection of complex traits. Her most important contribution is a model based on a Bayesian network that integrates more than 60 single-nucleotide polymorphisms (SNPs) and other biomarkers to compute the risk for stroke in patients with sickle cell anemia. This model was shown to have high sensitivity and specificity and demonstrated, for the first time, how an accurate risk prediction model of a complex genetic trait that is modulated by several interacting genes can be built using Bayesian networks.[1]

Sebastiani obtained a first degree in Mathematics from the University of Perugia, Italy (1987), an M.Sc. in Statistics from University College London (1990), and a Ph.D. in Statistics from the University of Rome (1992). Her research interests include Bayesian modeling of biomedical data, particularly genetic and genomic data. She came to Boston University in 2003, after previously having been an Assistant Professor in the Department of Mathematics and Statistics at the University of Massachusetts Amherst.[2]

Publications

She has published several peer-reviewed papers. According to Scopus the most cited ones are:

- Ramoni, M.F., Sebastiani, P., Kohane, I.S., "Cluster analysis of gene expression dynamics" (2002) *Proceedings of the National Academy of Sciences of the United States of America*, 99 (14), pp. 9121–9126.

- Sebastiani, P., Ramoni, M.F., Nolan, V., Baldwin, C.T., Steinberg, M.H., "Genetic dissection and prognostic modeling of overt stroke in sickle cell anemia" (2005) *Nature Genetics*, 37 (4), pp. 435–440.

- Mandl, K.D., Overhage, J.M., Wagner, M.M., Lober, W.B., Sebastiani, P., Mostashari, F., Pavlin, J.A., Gesteland, P.H., Treadwell, T., Koski, E., Hutwagner, L., Buckeridge, D.L., Aller, R.D., Grannis, S., "Implementing syndromic surveillance: A practical guide informed by the early experience" (2004) *Journal of the American Medical Informatics Association*, 11 (2), pp. 141–150.

- Sebastiani, P., Gussoni, E., Kohane, I.S., Ramoni, M.F., Baker, H.V., "Statistical challenges in functional genomics" (2003) *Statistical Science*, 18 (1), pp. 33–70.

References

[1] Sebastiani P, Ramoni MF, Nolan V, Baldwin CT, Steinberg MH (April 2005). "Genetic dissection and prognostic modeling of overt stroke in sickle cell anemia". *Nature Genetics* **37** (4): 435–40. doi:10.1038/ng1533. PMC 2896308. PMID 15778708.
[2] "BU Homepage for Paola Sebastiani" (http://sph.bu.edu/index.php?option=com_sphdir&id=239&Itemid=340&INDEX=11326). . Retrieved 2009-02-03.

Patrocladogram

Patrocladograms are graphs that assert hypotheses of similarity.

Further reading

- Stuessy, Tod F.; König, Christiane (May 2008), "Patrocladistic classification", *Taxon* **57** (2): 594–601
- Wiley, E.O. (February 2009), "Patrocladistics, nothing new", *Taxon* **58** (1): 2–6
- Stuessy, Tod F. (February 2009), "Paradigms in biological classification (1707-2007): Has anything really changed?", *Taxon* **58** (1): 68–76
- Hörandl, Elvira (April 2010), "Beyond cladistics: Extending evolutionary classifications into deeper time levels", *Taxon* **59** (2): 345–350
- Hörandl, Elvira; Stuessy, Tod F. (December 2010), "Paraphyletic groups as natural units of biological classification", *Taxon* **59** (6): 1641–1653

Peptide sequence

Peptide sequence or **amino acid sequence** is the order in which amino acid residues, connected by peptide bonds, lie in the chain in **peptides** and **proteins**. The sequence is generally reported from the N-terminal end containing free amino group to the C-terminal end containing free carboxyl group. Peptide sequence is often called **protein sequence** if it represents the primary structure of a protein.

Sequence notation and applications

Many peptide sequences have been in sequence databases. These databases may use various notations to describe the peptide sequence. The full names of the amino acids are rarely given; instead, 3-letter or 1-letter abbreviations are usually recorded for conciseness.

Several deductions can be made from the sequence itself. Long stretches of hydrophobic residues may indicate transmembrane helices. These helices may indicate the peptide is a cell receptor. Certain residues indicate a beta sheet area. If full-length protein sequence is available, it is possible to estimate the isoelectric point of the protein. Methods for determining the peptide sequence include deduction from DNA sequence, Edman degradation, and mass spectrometry.

Techniques in sequence analysis can be applied to learn more about the peptide. These techniques generally consist of comparing the sequence to other sequences from sequence databases. Other sequences may have already been studied and determined to be significant. Findings about these sequences may be applicable to the sequence under investigation.

External links

- A bibliography on features, patterns, correlations in DNA and protein texts [1]

References

[1] http://www.nslij-genetics.org/dnacorr/

Peptide-mass fingerprint

In bio-informatics, a **peptide-mass fingerprint** or **peptide-mass map** is a mass spectrum of a mixture of peptides that comes from a digested protein being analyzed. The mass spectrum serves as a fingerprint in the sense that it is a pattern that can serve to identify the protein.[1]

References

[1] Mass spectrometry in the biological sciences (http://books.google.com/books?id=JHJJpZ26ocMC&pg=PA151)

Personal genomics

Personal genomics is a branch of genomics where individual genomes are genotyped and analyzed using bioinformatics tools. It is also related to traditional population genetics. The genotyping stage can have many different experimental approaches including single-nucleotide polymorphism (SNP) chips (typically 0.02% of the genome), or partial or full genome sequencing. Once the genotypes are known, there are many bioinformatics analysis tools that can compare individual genomes and find disease association of the genes and loci. The most important aspect of personal genomics is that it may eventually lead to personalized medicine, where patients can take genotype specific drugs for medical treatments.

Personal genomics is not a single individual's vision or invention. Many researchers for decades anticipated this biological branch will eventually arrive with minimum cost of genotyping. Due to the advent of cheap and fast sequencers, full genome personal genomics is becoming a reality. However, there have been active early proponents of personal genomics projects such as George Church in Harvard Medical School.

Genomics used to mean academic research on consensus genomes which have been assembled from many different individuals of a particular species. The personal genomics changes this into customized bioinformatic discovery on individuals.

Use of personal genomics in predictive medicine

Predictive medicine is the use of the information produced by personal genomics techniques when deciding what medical treatments are appropriate for a particular individual.

An example of the use of predictive medicine is pharmacogenomics, in which genetic information can be used to select the most appropriate drug to prescribe to a patient. The drug should be chosen to maximize the probability of obtaining the desired result in the patient and minimize the probability that the patient will experience side effects. It is hoped that genetic information will allow physicians to tailor therapy to a given patient, in order to increase drug efficacy and minimize side effects. There are only a few examples in which this information is currently useful in clinical practice, but it is anticipated that tailored therapy will emerge rapidly as researchers validate the clinical utility of different pharmacogenomic markers.

Another area in which there is great interest is disease risk prediction based on genetic markers. Researchers in this area have generated a great deal of information through the use of genome-wide association studies. While there is hope that risk information will be useful in providing predictive medicine, most common medical conditions are multifactorial and the actual risk to the individual depends on both genetic and environmental components, both of which are not completely understood at present. Therefore, the clinical utility of personal genomic information is currently limited. It is hoped that with further research, an accurate risk profile might enable individuals to take steps to prevent diseases for which they are at increased risk based on genetics.

Cost of sequencing an individual's genome

There is currently great interest in personal genomics. This is being fuelled by the rapid drop in the cost of sequencing a human genome. This drop in cost is due to the continual development of new, faster, cheaper DNA sequencing technologies such as "next generation DNA sequencing" that may provide access to full genome sequencing so that the entire genetic code of an individual can be deduced all at once.

The National Human Genome Research Institute, part of the U.S. National Institute of Health has set a target to be able to sequence a human-sized genome for US$100,000 by 2009 and US$1,000 by 2014.[1] There is a widespread belief that within 10 years the cost of sequencing a human genome will fall to $1,000.

There are 6 billion base pairs in the diploid human genome. Statistical analysis reveals that a coverage of approximately ten times is required to get coverage of both alleles in 90% human genome from 25 base-pair reads with shotgun sequencing.[2] This means a total of 60 billion base pairs that must be sequenced. An Applied Biosystems SOLiD, Illumina or Helicos[3] sequencing machine can sequence 2 to 10 billion base pairs in each $8,000 to $18,000 run. The purchase cost, personnel costs and data processing costs must also be taken into account. Sequencing a human genome therefore costs approximately $300,000 in 2008.

In 2009, Complete Genomics of Mountain View announced that it would provide full genome sequencing for $5,000, from June 2009.[4] This will only be available to institutions, not individuals.[5]

This cost is still too high for governments to introduce programs into health services to sequence the genomes of all individuals in a country. However, it may be viable when it falls below $1,000, and the cost of sequencing a human genome is dropping rapidly. For example, approximately 1 million babies are born in Canada each year. To sequence all of their genomes would cost approximately $1 billion per year, or just 1% of Canada's total healthcare budget. Given the ethical concerns about presymptomatic genetic testing of minors,[6] [7] [8] [9] it is likely that personal genomics will first be applied to adults who can provide consent to undergo such testing.

In June 2009, Illumina announced that they were launching their own Personal Full Genome Sequencing Service at a depth of 30X for $48,000 per genome.[10] Only one year later, in 2010, they cut the price 60% to $19,500.[11] Still too expensive for true commercialization, prices are expected to drop further over the next few years as they realize economies of scale and given the competition with other companies such as Complete Genomics.[12] [13]

Knome's whole genome sequencing approach[14] aims, instead, to read every site in the whole euchromatic portion of a person's genome (roughly 3 billion sites). While significantly more expensive than SNP chip-based genotyping, this approach yields significantly more data, identifying both novel (never-before-seen) and known sequence variants, some of which may be particularly relevant in efforts to understand personal health, as well as ancestry.[15]

Timeline of personal genomes sequenced

Year	Cost	Personal genomes sequenced	Company	Source
2003	$3,000,000,000	1	Various	
2009	$48,000	100	Illumina	[10]
2010	$19,500	?	Illumina	[11]
2011	$9,500	?	Illumina	[10]

Comparative genomics

Comparative genomics analysis is concerned with characterising the differences and similarities between whole genomes. It may be applied to both genomes from individuals from different species or individuals from the same species, generally at lower cost than sequencing from scratch. In personal genomics and personalized medicine, we are concerned with comparing the genomes of different humans. It is likely that many of the techniques which are developed in comparative genomic analysis will be useful in personal genomics and personalized medicine. This includes rare and common single-nucleotide polymorphisms (consisting substituting one base pair by another, for example CATGCCGG to CATGACGG), as well as insertion or deletion of one or many base pairs.

Predictive medicine services already available

At least four companies which offer genome-wide personal genomics services already have gone to market and are selling their services direct to consumer. They are likely to be the first of many. However, the validity of individual risk predictions based on SNPs and the clinical utility of this information is currently questionable.

- deCODEme.com[16] charges $1100 to carry out genotyping of approximately 1 million SNPs and provides risk estimates for 47 diseases as well as ancestry analyses.

- Existence Genetics[17] provides genetic testing services through healthcare providers and health and wellness organizations, with prices starting at $350. This company provides testing for over 700 different diseases and traits, including a large number of diseases not covered by any other personal genomics company, such as preventable sudden cardiac death, malignant hyperthermia, and screening for hundreds of rare diseases and syndromes.[18] They also state that their service provides a much more comprehensive analysis of markers involved in disease risk. Existence Genetics uses a custom-built DNA genotyping array called the 'Nexus DNA Chip,' which was custom-configured by the company's founder and physician/geneticist, Brandon Colby, MD, manufactured by Illumina and is run in a CLIA-certified laboratory.[19] [20] [21] The company offers testing as discrete panels, which are sets of diseases and/or traits, and uses patent-pending analysis and reporting technologies such as the disease matrix and reflex analysis.[22] As opposed to online reporting, Existence Genetics provide their clients with printed and bound genetic reports that include substantial information about prevention.[23] Current services offered include a range of adult screening, newborn screening, childhood screening, preconception screening for couples, and egg and sperm donor screening.[24]

- Navigenics,[25] began offering SNP-based genomic risk assessments as of April 2008. Navigenics is medically focused and emphasizes a clinician's and genetic counselor's role in interpreting results. The Health Compass comprehensive genetic test for $999 analyzes your genetic predispositions for a variety of health conditions that meet stringent scientific criteria. Navigenics uses Affymetrix Genome-Wide Human SNP Array 6.0 , which genotypes 900,000 SNPs.[26]

- Pathway Genomics[27] analyzes over 100 genetic markers to identify genetic risk for common health conditions such as melanoma, prostate cancer and rheumatoid arthritis.

- 23andMe sells mail order kits for SNP genotyping.[28] The $99 kit, with $9.00/month subscription, or $399 without a subscription contains everything a consumer needs to take their own saliva sample. The consumer then mails the sample to 23andMe who carry out microarray analysis on it. This provides genotype information for approximately 1,000,000 SNPs. This information is used to estimate the genetic risk of the consumer for 178 diseases and conditions, as well as ancestry analysis. 23andMe utilizes a DNA array manufactured by Illumina.

- SNPedia is a wiki that collects and shares information about the consequences of DNA variations, and through the associated program Promethease [29], anyone who has obtained DNA data about themselves (from any company) can get a free, independent report containing risk assessments and related information.

- Bioresolve describes a similar service to that of 23andMe; however, the Better Business Bureau gave them an "F" reliability rating.[30]

- Knome[31] provides full genome (98% genome) sequencing services for $4,998 for whole genome sequencing and interpretation for consumers.[32] It's $29,500 for whole genome sequencing and analysis for researchers depending on their requirements.[5] [33] [34] [35]

- HelloGene and HelloGenome personal genome information services describe genotyping and full genome sequencing launched by Theragen in Korea. HelloGenome is the first commercial whole genome sequencing service in Asia while HelloGene is the first in Korea. HelloGene uses Affymetrix SNP chips while HelloGenome uses Solexa machines.

- Illumina, Oxford Nanopore Technologies, Sequenom, Pacific Biosciences, Complete Genomics and 454 Life Sciences are companies focused on commercializing full genome sequencing but are not involved in the predictive medicine (interpretative) side.[36] [37] [38] [39] [40]

Ethical issues

While personalized medicine will certainly be a great asset to healthcare, it opens up several ethical issues which will need to be thought about carefully. No doubt there will be a huge amount of debate concerning the ethics of personalised medicine in the coming years.

Genetic discrimination is discriminating on the grounds of information obtained from an individual's genome. Genetic non-discrimination laws have been enacted in most US states and, at the federal level, by the Genetic Information Nondiscrimination Act (GINA). The GINA legislation prevents discrimination by health insurers and employers but does not apply to life insurance or long-term care insurance.

The likelihood of an individual developing breast cancer is affected by which alleles they have of particular genes. Screening can reveal breast cancer in the early stages, allowing it to be successfully treated. 50% of breast cancers occur in the 12% of the population who are at greatest risk. This poses a very difficult question for health services: Is it ethical to deny somebody free screening for a disease if they are genetically at low (but non-zero) risk of developing that disease?

Other issues

Medical genetics will confront the fact that full sequencing of the genome identifies many polymorphisms that are neutral or harmless. This prospect will create uncertainty in the analysis of individual genomes, particularly in the context of clinical care. Czech medical geneticist Eva Macháčková writes: "In some cases it is difficult to distinguish if the detected sequence variant is a causal mutation or a neutral (polymorphic) variation without any effect on phenotype. The interpretation of rare sequence variants of unknown significance detected in disease-causing genes becomes an increasingly important problem."[41]

References

[1] "Coming Soon: Your Personal DNA Map?" (http://news.nationalgeographic.com/news/2006/03/0307_060307_dna.html). News.nationalgeographic.com. 28 October 2010. . Retrieved 19 October 2011.

[2] "Microsoft Word - JDW-genome-supp-mat-march-proof.doc" (http://www.nature.com/nature/journal/v452/n7189/extref/ nature06884-s1.pdf) (PDF). . Retrieved 19 October 2011.

[3] "True Single Molecule Sequencing (tSMS): Helicos BioSciences" (http://www.helicosbio.com/Technology/ TrueSingleMoleculeSequencingtrade/tabid/64/Default.aspx). Helicosbio.com. . Retrieved 19 October 2011.

[4] Karow, Julia. "Complete Genomics to Offer $5,000 Human Genome as a Service Business in Q2 2009 I In Sequence I Sequencing" (http:// www.genomeweb.com/sequencing/complete-genomics-offer-5000-human-genome-service-business-q2-2009-0). GenomeWeb. . Retrieved 19 October 2011.

[5] Lauerman, John (5 February 2009). "Complete Genomics Drives Down Cost of Genome Sequence to $5,000" (http://www.bloomberg. com/apps/news?pid=20601124&sid=aEUlnq6ltPpQ). Bloomberg. . Retrieved 19 October 2011.

[6] McCabe LL, McCabe ER (June 2001). "Postgenomic medicine. Presymptomatic testing for prediction and prevention". *Clin Perinatol* **28** (2): 425–34. doi:10.1016/S0095-5108(05)70094-4. PMID 11499063.

[7] Nelson RM, Botkjin JR, Kodish ED, *et al.* (June 2001). "Ethical issues with genetic testing in pediatrics". *Pediatrics* **107** (6): 1451–5. doi:10.1542/peds.107.6.1451. PMID 11389275.

[8] Borry P, Fryns JP, Schotsmans P, Dierickx K (February 2006). "Carrier testing in minors: a systematic review of guidelines and position papers". *Eur. J. Hum. Genet.* **14** (2): 133–8. doi:10.1038/sj.ejhg.5201509. PMID 16267502.

[9] Borry P, Stultiens L, Nys H, Cassiman JJ, Dierickx K (November 2006). "Presymptomatic and predictive genetic testing in minors: a systematic review of guidelines and position papers". *Clin. Genet.* **70** (5): 374–81. doi:10.1111/j.1399-0004.2006.00692.x. PMID 17026616.

[10] "Individual genome sequencing – Illumina, Inc" (http://www.everygenome.com). Everygenome.com. . Retrieved 19 October 2011.

[11] "Illumina Cutting Personal Genome Sequencing Price by 60% | GPlus.com" (http://www.glgroup.com/News/Illumina-Cutting-Personal-Genome-Sequencing-Price-by-60-48777.html). Glgroup.com. 4 June 2010. . Retrieved 19 October 2011.

[12] (http://news.moneycentral.msn.com/provider/providerarticle.aspx?feed=BW&date=20090610&id=9999448)

[13] "Illumina launches personal genome sequencing service for $48,000 : Genetic Future" (http://scienceblogs.com/geneticfuture/2009/06/illumina_launches_personal_gen.php). Scienceblogs.com. . Retrieved 19 October 2011.

[14] Karow, Julia (2009-05-19). "Knome Adds Exome Sequencing, Starts Offering Services to Researchers" (http://www.genomeweb.com/sequencing/knome-adds-exome-sequencing-starts-offering-services-researchers). GenomeWeb. . Retrieved 2010-02-24.

[15] Harmon, Katherine (2010-06-28). "Genome Sequencing for the Rest of Us" (http://www.scientificamerican.com/article.cfm?id=personal-genome-sequencing&print=true). Scientific American. . Retrieved 2010-08-13.

[16] Amy Doneen, Nurse Practitioner read our customer stories (15 October 2011). "deCODEme, unlock your DNA" (http://www.decodeme.com/). Decodeme.com. . Retrieved 19 October 2011.

[17] http://www.existencegenetics.com

[18] "Panels | Predictive Medicine" (http://www.existencegenetics.com/swf_panel.html). Existence Genetics. . Retrieved 19 October 2011.

[19] "Nexus DNA Chip | Predictive Medicine" (http://www.existencegenetics.com/genechip.html). Existence Genetics. . Retrieved 19 October 2011.

[20] "Reputable CLIA Certified Laboratory | Predictive Medicine" (http://www.existencegenetics.com/certifiedlab.html). Existence Genetics. . Retrieved 19 October 2011.

[21] "About Dr. Brandon Colby | Predictive Medicine" (http://outsmartyourgenes.com/author.php). Outsmart Your Genes. . Retrieved 19 October 2011.

[22] "Nexus DNA Chip | Predictive Medicine" (http://www.existencegenetics.com/nexus.html). Existence Genetics. . Retrieved 19 October 2011.

[23] "Next-Generation Genetic Reports | Predictive Medicine" (http://www.existencegenetics.com/geneticreports.html). Existence Genetics. . Retrieved 19 October 2011.

[24] "Panels | Predictive Medicine" (http://www.existencegenetics.com/swf_panel.html). Existence Genetics. . Retrieved 19 October 2011.

[25] "Personalized genetic health services" (http://www.navigenics.com/). Navigenics. . Retrieved 19 October 2011.

[26] Aaron, Internet entrepreneur. "Navigenics – How it works" (http://www.navigenics.com/healthcompass/HowProcessWorks/). Navigenics.com. . Retrieved 19 October 2011.

[27] "Genetic DNA Reports | Pathway Genomics" (http://www.pathway.com/). Pathway.com. . Retrieved 19 October 2011.

[28] 23andMe – Our Service: How the Process Works (https://www.23andme.com/ourservice/process/)

[29] http://www.Promethease.com/

[30] "BioResolve Business Review in Gatineau, QC – Eastern and Northern Ontario and the Outaouais BBB" (http://www.bbb.org/ottawa/business-reviews/medical-record-service/bioresolve-in-ottawa-on-35925). Bbb.org. . Retrieved 19 October 2011.

[31] "Knome homepage" (http://www.knome.com/). Knome.com. . Retrieved 19 October 2011.

[32] "Knome Special Pricing" (http://knome.com/sherlock-special-pricing/). Knome.com. 5 October 2011. . Retrieved 19 October 2011.

[33] Herper, Matthew (2010-06-03). "Your Genome is Coming" (http://blogs.forbes.com/sciencebiz/2010/06/03/your-genome-is-coming/?boxes=businesschannelsections). *Forbes*. . Retrieved 2010-08-13.

[34] Knome FAQ (http://www.knome.com/FAQ/tabid/51818/Default.aspx)

[35] Harmon, Amy (4 March 2008). "The DNA Age: Gene Map Becomes a Luxury Item, New York Times, March 2008" (http://www.nytimes.com/2008/03/04/health/research/04geno.html?_r=1&adxnnl=1&oref=slogin&adxnnlx=1217772475-+MgNWGgVZmU6mG58Fc5HJQ). *The New York Times*. . Retrieved 19 October 2011.

[36] "Illumina and Oxford Nanopore Enter into Broad Commercialization Agreement" (http://www.reuters.com/article/pressRelease/idUS49869+12-Jan-2009+BW20090112). Reuters. 12 January 2009. . Retrieved 23 February 2009.

[37] http://www..com/sequenom-licenses-nanopore-technology-harvard-develop-third-generation-sequencer

[38] "Single Molecule Real Time (SMRT) DNA Sequencing" (http://www.pacificbiosciences.com/index.php?q=technology-introduction). Pacific Biosciences. . Retrieved 23 February 2009.

[39] "Complete Human Genome Sequencing Technology Overview" (http://www.completegenomicsinc.com/pages/materials/CompleteGenomicsTechnologyPaper.pdf). Complete Genomics. 2009. . Retrieved 23 February 2009.

[40] http://files.shareholder.com/downloads/CRGN/0x0x53381/386c4aaa-f36e-4b7a-9ff0-c06e61fad31f/211559.pdf

[41] Macháčková, Eva (2003). "Disease-causing mutations versus neutral polymorphism: Use of bioinformatics and DNA diagnosis". *Cas Lek Cesk* (Czech Republic: Ceskoslovenska Lekarska Spolecnost) **142** (3): 150–153. PMID 12756842

External links

- Personalgenome.org (http://personalgenome.org)
- Personalgenome.net (http://personalgenome.net)
- Genomics.org (http://genomics.org)
- DNATest.org (http://www.dnatest.org)
- Personal Genomics Blog (http://www.personomics.wordpress.com)
- SNPedia (http://www.snpedia.com)
- BioResolve Complaints (http://www.bioresolvescam.com)
- Personal Genomics Institute (PGI) (http://personalgenomicsinstitute.org)
- National Geographic Genographic Project (https://genographic.nationalgeographic.com/genographic/participate.html)

Pfam

Pfam

Content	
Description	The Pfam database provides alignments and hidden Markov models for protein domains.
Data types captured	Protein families
Organism(s)	all
Contact	
Research center	WTSI
Primary Citation	PMID 19920124
Access	
Data format	Stockholm format
Website	Pfam (UK) [1] Pfam (USA) [2] Pfam (Sweden) [3]
Download URL	Pfam ftp [4]
Tools	
Miscellaneous	
License	GNU Lesser General Public License
Bookmarkable entities	yes

Pfam is a database of protein families that includes their annotations and multiple sequence alignments generated using hidden Markov models.[5] [6] [7]

Features

For each family in Pfam one can:

- Look at multiple alignments
- View protein domain architectures
- Examine species distribution
- Follow links to other databases
- View known protein structures

The descriptions of Pfam families are managed by the general public using Wikipedia.

74% of protein sequences have at least one match to Pfam. This number is called the sequence coverage.

The Pfam database contains information about protein domains and families. Pfam-A is the manually curated portion of the database that contains over 10,000 entries. For each entry a protein sequence alignment and a hidden Markov model is stored. These hidden Markov models can be used to search sequence databases with the HMMER package written by Sean Eddy. Because the entries in Pfam-A do not cover all known proteins, an automatically generated supplement is provided called Pfam-B. Pfam-B contains a large number of small families derived from clusters produced by an algorithm called ADDA.[8] Although of lower quality, Pfam-B families can be useful when no Pfam-A families are found.

The database **iPfam**[9] builds on the domain description of Pfam. It investigates if different proteins described together in the protein structure database PDB are close enough to potentially interact.

The current release of Pfam is "Pfam 25.0" (March 2011; 12,273 families).[10]

References

[1] http://pfam.sanger.ac.uk
[2] http://pfam.janelia.org
[3] http://pfam.sbc.su.se/
[4] ftp://ftp.sanger.ac.uk/pub/databases/Pfam/
[5] Finn RD, Tate J, Mistry J, Coggill PC, Sammut SJ, Hotz HR, Ceric G, Forslund K, Eddy SR, Sonnhammer EL, Bateman A (2008). "The Pfam protein families database". *Nucleic Acids Res* **36** (Database issue): D281–8. doi:10.1093/nar/gkm960. PMC 2238907. PMID 18039703.
[6] Finn, D.; Mistry, J.; Schuster-Böckler, B.; Griffiths-Jones, S.; Hollich, V.; Lassmann, T.; Moxon, S.; Marshall, M. et al. (Jan 2006). "Pfam: clans, web tools and services" (http://nar.oxfordjournals.org/cgi/pmidlookup?view=long&pmid=16381856) (Free full text). *Nucleic Acids Research* **34** (Database issue): D247–D251. doi:10.1093/nar/gkj149. ISSN 0305-1048. PMC 1347511. PMID 16381856. .
[7] Bateman, A.; Coin, L.; Durbin, R.; Finn, D.; Hollich, V.; Griffiths-Jones, S.; Khanna, A.; Marshall, M. et al. (Jan 2004). "The Pfam protein families database" (http://nar.oxfordjournals.org/cgi/pmidlookup?view=long&pmid=14681378) (Free full text). *Nucleic Acids Research* **32** (Database issue): 138D–1141. doi:10.1093/nar/gkh121. ISSN 0305-1048. PMC 308855. PMID 14681378. .
[8] Heger, A.; Wilton, A.; Sivakumar, A.; Holm, L. (Jan 2005). "ADDA: a domain database with global coverage of the protein universe" (http://nar.oxfordjournals.org/cgi/pmidlookup?view=long&pmid=15608174) (Free full text). *Nucleic Acids Research* **33** (Database issue): D188–D191. doi:10.1093/nar/gki096. ISSN 0305-1048. PMC 540050. PMID 15608174. .
[9] Finn, D.; Marshall, M.; Bateman, A. (Feb 2005). "IPfam: visualization of protein-protein interactions in PDB at domain and amino acid resolutions" (http://bioinformatics.oxfordjournals.org/cgi/pmidlookup?view=long&pmid=15353450) (Free full text). *Bioinformatics (Oxford, England)* **21** (3): 410–412. doi:10.1093/bioinformatics/bti011. ISSN 1367-4803. PMID 15353450. .
[10] "Pfam release notes" (ftp://ftp.sanger.ac.uk/pub/databases/Pfam/current_release/relnotes.txt). Sanger. . Retrieved 2011-05-23.

External links

- Pfam (http://pfam.sanger.ac.uk) - Protein family database at Sanger Institute UK
- Pfam (http://pfam.janelia.org/) - Protein family database at Janelia Farm Research Campus USA
- Pfam (http://pfam.sbc.su.se/) - Protein family database at Stockholm Bioinformatics Centre Sweden
- iPfam (http://www.sanger.ac.uk/Software/Pfam/iPfam/) - Interactions of Pfam domains in PDB

Phenome

A **phenome** is the set of all phenotypes expressed by a cell, tissue, organ, organism, or species.

Just as the genome and proteome signify all of an organism's genes and proteins, the phenome represents the sum total of its phenotypic traits. Examples of human phenotypic traits are skin color, eye color, body height, or specific personality characteristics. Although any phenotype of any organism has a basis in its genotype, phenotypic expression may be influenced by environmental influences, mutation, and genetic variation such as single nucleotide polymorphisms (SNPs), or a combination of these factors.

Phenomics is the study of the phenome and how it is determined, particularly when studied in relation to the set of all genes (genomics) or all proteins (proteomics).

Origin and usage

The term was first used by Davis in 1949, "We here propose the name *phenome* for the sum total of extragenic, non-autoreproductive portions of the cell, whether cytoplasmic or nuclear. The phenome would be the material basis of the phenotype, just as the genome is the material basis of the genotype."[1]

Although phenome has been in use for many years, the distinction between the use of phenome and phenotype is problematical. A proposed definition for both terms as the "physical totality of all traits of an organism or of one of its subsystems" was put forth by Mahner and Kary in 1997, who argue that although scientists tend to intuitively use these and related terms in a manner that does not impede research, the terms are not well defined and usage of the terms is not consistent.[2]

Some usages of the term suggest that the phenome of a given organism is best understood as a kind of matrix of data representing physical manifestation of phenotype. For example, discussions led by A.Varki among those who had used the term up to 2003 suggested the following definition: "The body of information describing an organism's phenotypes, under the influences of genetic and environmental factors".[3] Another team of researchers characterize "the human phenome [as] a multidimensional search space with several neurobiological levels, spanning the proteome, cellular systems (e.g., signaling pathways), neural systems and cognitive and behavioural phenotypes."[4]

References

[1] Davis BD (January 1949). "The Isolation of Biochemically Deficient Mutants of Bacteria by Means of Penicillin". *Proceedings of the National Academy of Sciences of the United States of America* **35** (1): 1–10. doi:10.1073/pnas.35.1.1. PMC 1062948. PMID 16588845.

[2] Loeffler M, Bratke T, Paulus U, Li YQ, Potten CS (May 1997). "Clonality and life cycles of intestinal crypts explained by a state dependent stochastic model of epithelial stem cell organization" (http://linkinghub.elsevier.com/retrieve/pii/S0022-5193(96)90340-9). *Journal of Theoretical Biology* **186** (1): 41–54. doi:10.1006/jtbi.1996.0340. PMID 9176636. .

[3] Varki A, Altheide TK (December 2005). "Comparing the human and chimpanzee genomes: searching for needles in a haystack" (http://www.genome.org/cgi/pmidlookup?view=long&pmid=16339373). *Genome Research* **15** (12): 1746–58. doi:10.1101/gr.3737405. PMID 16339373. .

[4] Siebner HR, Callicott JH, Sommer T, Mattay VS (November 2009). "From the genome to the phenome and back: linking genes with human brain function and structure using genetically informed neuroimaging" (http://linkinghub.elsevier.com/retrieve/pii/S0306-4522(09)01484-5). *Neuroscience* **164** (1): 1–6. doi:10.1016/j.neuroscience.2009.09.009. PMC 3013363. PMID 19751805. .

External links

- Mouse Phenome Project (http://phenome.jax.org/pub-cgi/phenome/mpdcgi?rtn=docs/home) at the Jackson Laboratory

Phrap

Phrap is a widely used program for DNA sequence assembly. It is part of the Phred-Phrap-Consed package.

History

Phrap was originally developed by Prof. Phil Green for the assembly of cosmids in large-scale cosmid shotgun sequencing within the Human Genome Project. Phrap has been widely used for many different sequence assembly projects, including bacterial genome assemblies and EST assemblies.

Phrap was written as a command line program for easy integration into automated data workflows in genome sequencing centers. For users who want to use Phrap from a graphical interface, the commercial programs MacVector (for Mac OS X only) and CodonCode Aligner (for Mac OS X and Microsoft Windows) are available.

Methods

A detailed (albeit partially outdated) description of the Phrap algorithms can be found in the Phrap documentation [1]. A recurring thread within the Phrap algorithms is the use of Phred quality scores. Phrap used quality scores to mitigate a problem that other assembly programs had struggled with at the beginning of the Human Genome Project: correctly assembling frequent imperfect repeats, in particular Alu sequences. Phrap uses quality scores to tell if any observed differences in repeated regions are likely to be due to random ambiguities in the sequencing process, or more likely to be due to the sequences being from different copies of the Alu repeat. Typically, Phrap had no problems differentiating between the different Alu copies in a cosmid, and to correctly assemble the cosmids (or, later, BACs). The logic is simple: a base call with a high probability of being correct should never be aligned with another high quality but different base. However, Phrap does not rule out such alignments entirely, and the cross_match alignment gap and alignment penalties used while looking for local alignments are not always optimal for typical sequencing errors and a search for overlapping (contiguous) sequences. (Affine gaps are helpful for homology searches but not usually for sequencing error alignment). Phrap attempts to classify chimeras, vector sequences and low quality end regions all in a single alignment and will sometimes make mistakes. Furthermore, Phrap has more than one round of assembly building internally and later rounds are less stringent - Greedy algorithm.

These design choices were helpful in the 1990s when the program was originally written (at Washington University in Saint Louis, USA) but are less so now. Phrap appears error prone in comparison with newer assemblers like Euler and cannot use mate-pair information directly to guide assembly and assemble past perfect repeats. Phrap is not free software so it has not been extended and enhanced like less restricted open-source software Sequence assembly.

Quality based consensus sequences

Another use of Phred quality scores by Phrap that contributed to the program's success was the determination of consensus sequences using sequence qualities. In effect, Phrap automated a step that was a major bottleneck in the early phases of the Human Genome Project: to determine the correct consensus sequence at all positions where the assembled sequences had discrepant bases. This approach had been suggested by Bonfield and Staden in 1995,[2] and was implemented and further optimized in Phrap. Basically, at any consensus position with discrepant bases, Phrap examines the quality scores of the aligned sequences to find the highest quality sequence. In the process, Phrap takes confirmation of local sequence by other reads into account, after considering direction and sequencing chemistry.

The mathematics of this approach were rather simple, since Phred quality scores are logarithmically linked to error probabilities. This means that the quality scores of confirming reads can simply be added, as long as the error distributions are sufficiently independent. To satisfy this independence criterion, reads must typically be in different direction, since peak patterns that cause base calling errors are often identical when a region is sequenced several times in the same direction.

If a consensus base is covered by both high-quality sequence and (discrepant) low-quality sequence, Phrap's selection of the higher quality sequence will in most cases be correct. Phrap then assigns the confirmed base quality to the consensus sequence base. This makes it easy to (a) find consensus regions that are not covered by high quality sequence (which will also have low quality), and (b) to quickly calculate a reasonably accurate estimate of the error rate of the consensus sequence. This information can then be used to direct finishing efforts, for example re-sequencing of problem regions.

The combination of accurate, base-specific quality scores and a quality-based consensus sequence was a critical element in the success of the Human Genome Project. Phred and Phrap, and similar programs who picked up on the ideas pioneered by these two programs, enabled the assembly of large parts of the human genome (and many other genomes) at an accuracy that was substantially higher (less than 1 error in 10,000 bases) than the typical accuracy of carefully hand-edited sequences that had been submitted to the GenBank database before.[3]

References

[1] http://www.phrap.org/phredphrap/phrap.html
[2] Bonfield JK, Staden R (1995): The application of numerical estimates of base calling accuracy to DNA sequencing projects. Nucleic Acids Res. 1995 Apr 25;23(8):1406-10. PMID 7753633
[3] Krawetz SA (1989): Sequence errors described in GenBank: a means to determine the accuracy of DNA sequence interpretation. Nucleic Acids Res. 1989 May 25;17(10):3951-7

External links

- Phrap homepage (http://www.phrap.org/phredphrapconsed.html#block_phrap)

Other Software

- Phred
- Consed
- DNA Baser Command Line Tool

Phylogenetic profiling

Phylogenetic profiling is an important and elegant bioinformatics technique in which the joint presence or joint absence of two traits across a similar distribution of species is used to infer a meaningful biological connection, such as involvement of two different proteins in the same biological pathway. Along with examination of conserved synteny, conserved operon structure, or "Rosetta Stone" domain fusions, comparing phylogenetic profiles is designated a "post-homology" technique, in that the computation essential to the method begins after it is determined which proteins are homologous to which. A number of these techniques were developed by David Eisenberg and colleagues; phylogenetic profile comparison was introduced in 1999 by Pellegrini, *et al.* [1]

Method

Over 2000 organisms[2] of Bacteria, Archaea, and Eukaryotes now are represented by complete DNA genome sequences. Typically, each gene in a genome encodes a protein that can be assigned to a particular protein family on the basis of homology. For a given protein family, its presence or absence in each genome (in the original formulation) is represented by 1 (present) or 0 (absent). Consequently, the phylogenetic distribution of the protein family can be represented by a long binary number with a digit for each genome; such binary representations are readily compared with each other to show correlated phylogenetic distributions. The large number of complete genomes makes these profiles rich in information. The advantage of using only complete genomes is that the 0 values, representing the absence of a trait, tend to be reliable. Presence or absence of a protein is usually determined by sequence similarity.

Theory

Closely related species should be expected to have very similar sets of genes. However, changes accumulate between more distantly related species by processes that include horizontal gene transfer and gene loss. Individual proteins have specific molecular functions, such as carrying out a single enzymatic reaction or serving as one subunit of a larger protein complex. A biological process such as photosynthesis, methanogenesis, or histidine biosynthesis may require the concerted action of many proteins. If some protein critical to such a process were lost, other proteins dedicated to that process would become useless; natural selection makes it unlikely they will be retained over evolutionary time. Therefore, should two different protein families tend always to be either both present or both absent, a likely hypothesis is that the two proteins cooperate in some biological process.

Advances and Challenges

Phylogenetic profiling has led to numerous discoveries in biology, including previously unknown enzymes in metabolic pathways, transcription factors that bind to conserved regulatory sites, and explanations for roles of certain mutations in human disease [3]. Improving the method itself is an active area of research because the method itself faces several limitations. First, co-occurrence of two protein families often represents recent common ancestry of two species rather than a conserved functional relationship; disambiguating these two sources of correlation may require improved statistical methods. Second, proteins grouped as homologs may differ in function, or proteins conserved in function may fail to register as homologs; improved methods for tailoring the size of each protein family to reflect functional conservation will lead to improved results.

Notes

[1] Pellegrini M, Marcotte EM, Thompson MJ, Eisenberg D, Yeates TO. Proc Natl Acad Sci U S A. 1999 Apr 13;96(8):4285-8: "Assigning protein functions by comparative genome analysis: protein phylogenetic profiles." (http://www.ncbi.nlm.nih.gov/pubmed/10200254)

[2] http://www.ebi.ac.uk/integr8/

[3] Kensche PR, van Noort V, Dutilh BE, Huynen MA. J R Soc Interface. 2008 Feb 6;5(19):151-70.

Phyloscan

Phyloscan

Developer(s)	Wadsworth Center, New York State Department of Health
Initial release	March 14, 2005
Stable release	2.2 / January 28, 2010
Platform	web service
Available in	English
Type	Bioinformatics tool
Website	[1]

Phyloscan[2] [3] is a web service for DNA sequence analysis that is free and open to all users (without login requirement). For locating matches to a user-specified sequence motif for a regulatory binding site, Phyloscan provides a statistically sensitive scan of user-supplied mixed aligned and unaligned DNA sequence data. Phyloscan's strength is that it brings together

- the Staden method[4] for computing statistical significance,
- the "phylogenetic motif model" scanning functionality of the MONKEY software[5] that models evolutionary relationships among aligned sequences,
- the use of the Bailey & Gribskov method[6] for combining statistics across non-aligned sequence data, and
- the Neuwald & Green technique[7] for combining statistics across multiple binding sites found within a single gene promoter region.

References

[1] http://bayesweb.wadsworth.org/phyloscan/

[2] Palumbo, MJ; Newberg, LA (July 1 2010). "Phyloscan: locating transcription-regulating binding sites in mixed aligned and unaligned sequence data" (http://nar.oxfordjournals.org/cgi/content/abstract/38/suppl_2/W268). *Nucleic Acids Research* **38** (Web server issue): W268–W274. doi:10.1093/nar/gkq330. PMC 2896078. PMID 20435683. .

[3] Carmack, CS; McCue, LA; Newberg, LA; Lawrence, CE (January 23 2007). "PhyloScan: identification of transcription factor binding sites using cross-species evidence" (http://www.almob.org/content/2/1/1). *Algorithms for Molecular Biology* **2** (1): article 1. doi:10.1186/1748-7188-2-1. PMC 1794230. PMID 17244358. .

[4] Staden, R (April 1989). "Methods for calculating the probabilities of finding patterns in sequences" (http://bioinformatics.oxfordjournals.org/cgi/content/abstract/5/2/89). *Computer Applications in the Biosciences* **5** (2): 89–96. doi:10.1093/bioinformatics/5.2.89. PMID 2720468. .

[5] Moses, AM; Chiang, DY; Pollard, DA; Iyer, VN; Eisen, MB (November 30 2004). "MONKEY: identifying conserved transcription-factor binding sites in multiple alignments using a binding site-specific evolutionary model" (http://genomebiology.com/2004/5/12/R98). *Genome Biology* **5** (12): R98. doi:10.1186/gb-2004-5-12-r98. PMC 545801. PMID 15575972. .

[6] Bailey, TL; Gribskov, M (Summer 1998). "Methods and statistics for combining motif match scores" (http://www.liebertonline.com/doi/abs/10.1089/cmb.1998.5.211). *Journal of Computational Biology* **5** (2): 211–221. doi:10.1089/cmb.1998.5.211. PMID 9672829. .

[7] Neuwald, AF; Green, P (June 24 1994). "Detecting patterns in protein sequences" (http://www.sciencedirect.com/science/article/B6WK7-45NSJRT-BC/2/21eaf0a0831a83996e53fd380cd03c61). *Journal of Molecular Biology* **239** (5): 698–712. doi:10.1006/jmbi.1994.1407. PMID 8014990. .

External links

- Phyloscan homepage (http://bayesweb.wadsworth.org/phyloscan/)

PhyloXML

PhyloXML is an XML language for the analysis, exchange, and storage of phylogenetic trees (or networks) and associated data.[1] The structure of phyloXML is described by XML Schema Definition (XSD) language.

A shortcoming of current formats for describing phylogenetic trees (such as Nexus and Newick/New Hampshire) is a lack of a standardized means to annotate tree nodes and branches with distinct data fields (which in the case of a basic species tree might be: species names, branch lengths, and possibly multiple support values). Data storage and exchange is even more cumbersome in studies in which trees are the result of a reconciliation of some kind:

- gene-function studies (requires annotation of nodes with taxonomic information as well as gene names, and possibly gene-duplication data)
- evolution of host-parasite interactions (requires annotation of tree nodes with taxonomic information for both host and parasite)
- phylogeographic studies (requires annotation of tree nodes with taxonomic and geographic information)

To alleviate this, a variety of ad-hoc, special purpose formats have come into use (such as the NHX format, which focuses on the needs of gene-function and phylogenomic studies).

A well defined XML format addresses these problems in a general and extensible manner and allows for interoperability between specialized and general purpose software.

An example of a program for visualizing phyloXML is Archaeopteryx.

Basic phyloXML example

```
<phyloxml xmlns:xsi="http://www.w3.org/2001/XMLSchema-instance"
  xsi:schemaLocation="http://www.phyloxml.org http://www.phyloxml.org/1.10/phyloxml.xsd"
  xmlns="http://www.phyloxml.org">
  <phylogeny rooted="true">
    <name>example from Prof. Joe Felsenstein's book "Inferring Phylogenies"</name>
    <description>MrBayes based on MAFFT alignment</description>
    <clade>
      <clade branch_length="0.06">
        <confidence type="probability">0.88</confidence>
        <clade branch_length="0.102">
          <name>A</name>
        </clade>
        <clade branch_length="0.23">
          <name>B</name>
        </clade>
      </clade>
      <clade branch_length="0.4">
        <name>C</name>
      </clade>
    </clade>
  </phylogeny>
```

```
</phyloxml>
```

References

[1] Han, Mira V.; Zmasek, Christian M. (2009). "phyloXML: XML for evolutionary biology and comparative genomics" (http://www.biomedcentral.com/1471-2105/10/356). *BMC Bioinformatics* (United Kingdom: BioMed Central) **10**: 356. doi:10.1186/1471-2105-10-356. PMC 2774328. PMID 19860910. .

External links

- www.phyloxml.org (http://www.phyloxml.org)
- Archaeopteryx (http://phylosoft.org/archaeopteryx/)

Point accepted mutation

Point accepted mutation (PAM) or **percent accepted mutation**, is a set of matrices used to score sequence alignments. The PAM matrices were introduced by Margaret Dayhoff in 1978 based on 1572 observed mutations in 71 families of closely related proteins.[1] Each matrix has the twenty standard amino acids in its twenty rows and columns; the value in a given cell represents the probability of a substitution of one amino acid for another. This type of matrix is commonly known as a substitution matrix.

This matrix is used to derive a scoring matrix, used in bioinformatics to assess the similarity of two aligned sequences. For example, an 18% probability of replacing arginine with lysine (in the substitution matrix) is turned into a score of 3 in the scoring matrix. The calculation uses the ratio of the probability value and the frequency of the original amino acid (arginine) in known sequences.[2]

The PAM matrices imply a Markov chain model of protein mutation.[3] [4] The PAM matrices are normalized so that, for instance, the PAM1 matrix gives substitution probabilities for sequences that have experienced one point mutation for every hundred amino acids. The mutations may overlap so that the sequences reflected in the PAM250 matrix have experienced 250 mutation events for every 100 amino acids, yet only 80 out of every 100 amino acids have been affected.

References

[1] Dayhoff, M.O., Schwartz, R. and Orcutt, B.C. (1978). "A model of Evolutionary Change in Proteins". *Atlas of protein sequence and structure* (volume 5, supplement 3 ed.). Nat. Biomed. Res. Found.. pp. 345–358. ISBN 0912466073

[2] Pevsner J (2009). "Pairwise Sequence Alignment". *Bioinformatics and Functional Genomics* (2nd ed.). Wiley-Blackwell. pp. 58–63. ISBN 978-0-470-08585-1.

[3] Kosiol C, Goldman N. (2005). "Different versions of the Dayhoff rate matrix." (http://mbe.oxfordjournals.org/cgi/content/full/22/2/193). *Molecular biology and evolution.* **22** (2): 193–9. doi:10.1093/molbev/msi005. PMID 15483331. .

[4] Liò P, Goldman N. (1998). "Models of molecular evolution and phylogeny." (http://pixfunlobdot.59.to/content/8/12/1233.full). *Genome research.* **8** (12): 1233–44. doi:10.1101/gr.8.12.1233. PMID 9872979. .

External links

- http://www.inf.ethz.ch/personal/gonnet/DarwinManual/node148.html

Position-specific scoring matrix

A **position weight matrix (PWM)**, also called **position-specific weight matrix (PSWM)** or **position-specific scoring matrix (PSSM)**, is a commonly used representation of motifs (patterns) in biological sequences.[1]

A PWM is a matrix of score values that gives a weighted match to any given substring of fixed length. It has one row for each symbol of the alphabet, and one column for each position in the pattern. The score assigned by a PWM to a substring $s = \left(s_j\right)_{j=1}^{N}$ is defined as $\sum_{j=1}^{N} m_{s_j,j}$, where j represents position in the substring, s_j is the symbol at position j in the substring, and $m_{\alpha,j}$ is the score in row α, column j of the matrix. In other words, a PWM score is the sum of position-specific scores for each symbol in the substring.

Basic PWM with log-likelihoods

A PWM assumes independence between positions in the pattern, as it calculates scores at each position independently from the symbols at other positions. The score of a substring aligned with a PWM can be interpreted as the log-likelihood of the substring under a product multinomial distribution. Since each column defines log-likelihoods for each of the different symbols, where the sum of likelihoods in a column equals one, the PWM corresponds to a Multinomial distribution. A PWM's score is the sum of log-likelihoods, which corresponds to the product of likelihoods, meaning that the score of a PWM is then a product-multinomial distribution. The PWM scores can also be interpreted in a physical framework as the sum of binding energies for all nucleotides (symbols of the substring) aligned with the PWM.

Incorporating background distribution

Instead of using log-likelihood values in the PWM, as described in the previous paragraph, several methods uses log-odds scores in the PWMs. An element in a PWM is then calculated as $m_{i,j} = log(p_{i,j}/b_i)$, where $p_{i,j}$ is the probability of observing symbol i at position j of the motif, and b_i is the probability of observing the symbol i in a background model. The PWM score then corresponds to the log-odds of the substring being generated by the motif versus being generated by the background, in a generative model of the sequence.

Information content of a PWM

The information content (IC) of a PWM is sometimes of interest, as it says something about how different a given PWM is from a uniform distribution.

The self-information of observing a particular symbol at a particular position of the motif is:

$$- \log(p_{i,j})$$

The expected (average) self-information of a particular element in the PWM is then:

$$-p_{i,j} \cdot \log(p_{i,j})$$

Finally, the IC of the PWM is then the sum of the expected self-information of every element:

$$- \sum_{i,j} p_{i,j} \cdot \log(p_{i,j})$$

Often, it is more useful to calculate the information content with the background letter frequencies of the sequences you are studying rather than assuming equal probabilities of each letter (e.g., the GC-content of DNA of thermophilic bacteria range from 65.3 to 70.8[2], thus a motif of ATAT would contain much more information than a motif of CCGG). The equation for information content thus becomes

$$- \sum_{i,j} p_{i,j} \cdot \log(p_{i,j}/p_b)$$

where p_b is the background frequency for that letter. This corresponds to the Kullback-Leibler divergence or relative entropy. However, it has been shown that when using PSSM to search genomic sequences (see below) this uniform correction can lead to overestimation of the importance of the different bases in a motif, due to the uneven distribution of n-mers in real genomes, leading to a significantly larger number of false positives [3].

Using PWMs

There are various algorithms to scan for hits of PWMs in sequences. One example is the MATCH™ algorithm [4] which has been implemented in the ModuleMaster[5]. More sophisticated algorithms for fast database searching with nucleotide as well as amino acid PWMs/PSSMs are implemented in the possumsearch software and are described in [6].

References

[1] Ben-Gal I, Shani A, Gohr A, Grau J, Arviv S, Shmilovici A, Posch S, Grosse I (2005). "Identification of Transcription Factor Binding Sites with Variable-order Bayesian Networks" (http://bioinformatics.oxfordjournals.org/cgi/reprint/bti410?ijkey=KkxNhRdTSfvtvXY& keytype=ref). *Bioinformatics* **21** (11): 2657–2666. doi:10.1093/bioinformatics/bti410. PMID 15797905. .

[2] Aleksandrushkina NI, Egorova LA (1978). "Nucleotide makeup of the DNA of thermophilic bacteria of the genus Thermus". *Mikrobiologiia* **47** (2): 250–2. PMID 661633.

[3] Erill I, O'Neill MC (2009). "A reexamination of information theory-based methods for DNA-binding site identification". *BMC Bioinformatics* **10**: 57. doi:10.1186/1471-2105-10-57. PMC 2680408. PMID 19210776.

[4] Kel, A. E. et. al. (2003). "MATCHTM: a tool for searching transcription factor binding sites in DNA sequences". *Nucleic Acids Research* **31** (13): 3576–3579. doi:10.1093/nar/gkg585. PMC 169193. PMID 12824369.

[5] Wrzodek, Clemens; Schröder, Adrian; Dräger, Andreas; Wanke, Dierk; Berendzen, Kenneth W.; Kronfeld, Marcel; Harter, Klaus; Zell, Andreas (9 October 2009). "ModuleMaster: A new tool to decipher transcriptional regulatory networks". *Biosystems* (Ireland: Elsevier) **99** (1): 79–81. doi:10.1016/j.biosystems.2009.09.005. ISSN 0303-2647. PMID 19819296.

[6] Beckstette, M. et al. (2006). "Fast index based algorithms and software for matching position specific scoring matrices". *BMC Bioinformatics* **7**: 389. doi:10.1186/1471-2105-7-389. PMC 1635428. PMID 16930469.

External links

- JASPAR (http://jaspar.genereg.net/)
- 3PFDB - A database of Best Representative PSSM Profiles (BRPs) of Protein Families generated using a novel data mining approach (http://www.biodatamining.org/content/2/1/8)
- UGENE (http://ugene.unipro.ru/) - PSS matrices design, integrated interface to JASPAR, Uniprobe and SITECON databases

Power graph analysis

In computational biology, **power graph analysis** is a method for the analysis and representation of complex networks. Power graph analysis is the computation, analysis and visual representation of a power graph from a graphs (networks).

Power graph analysis can be thought of as a lossless compression algorithm for graphs. It extends graph syntax with representations of cliques, bicliques and stars. Compression levels of up to 95% have been obtained for complex biological networks.

Hypergraphs are a generalization of graphs in which edges are not just couples of nodes but arbitrary n-tuples. Power Graphs are not another generalization of graphs, but instead a novel representation of graphs that proposes a shift from the "node and edge" language to an using cliques, bicliques and stars as primitives.

Power graphs

Graphical representation

Graphs are drawn with circles or points that represent **nodes** and lines connecting pairs of nodes that represent **edges**. Power graphs extend the syntax of graphs with **power nodes**, which are drawn as a circle enclosing nodes or *other power nodes*, and **power edges**, which are lines between power nodes.

Bicliques are two sets of nodes with an edge between every member of one set and every member of the other set. In a power graph, a biclique is represented as an edge between two power nodes.

Cliques are a set of nodes with an edge between every pair of nodes. In a power graph, a clique is represented by a power node with a loop.

Stars are a set of nodes with an edge between every member of that set and a single node outside the set. In a power graph, a star is represented by a power edge between a regular node and a power node.

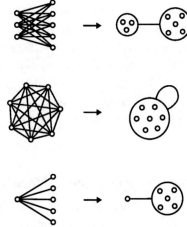

The primitive motifs of used for power graph analysis and their corresponding diagrammatic representation: biclique, clique and star.

Formal definition

Given a graph $G = (V, E)$ where $V = \{v_0, \ldots, v_n\}$ is the set of nodes and $E \subseteq V \times V$ is the set of edges, a **power graph** $G' = (V', E')$ is a graph defined on the power set $V' \subseteq \mathcal{P}(V)$ of **power nodes** connected to each other by **power edges**: $E' \subseteq V' \times V'$. Hence power graphs are defined on the power set of nodes as well as on the power set of edges of the graph G.

The semantics of power graphs are as follows: if two power nodes are connected by a power edge, this means that all nodes of the first power node are connected to all nodes of the second power node. Similarly, if a power node is connected to itself by a power edge, this signifies that all nodes in the power node are connected to each other by edges.

The following two conditions are required:

- Power node hierarchy condition: Any two power nodes are either disjoint, or one is included in the other.
- Power edge disjointness condition: There is an onto mapping from edges of the original graph to power edges.

Analogy to Fourier analysis

The Fourier analysis of a function can be seen as a rewriting of the function in terms of harmonic functions instead of $t->x$ pairs. This transformation changes the point of view from **time domain** to **frequency domain** and enables many interesting applications in signal analysis, data compression, and filtering. Similarly, Power Graph Analysis is a rewriting or decomposition of a network using bicliques, cliques and stars as primitive elements (just as harmonic functions for Fourier analysis). It can be used to analyze, compress and filter networks. There are, however, several key differences. First, in Fourier analysis the two spaces (time and frequency domains) are the same function space - but stricto sensu, power graphs are not graphs. Second, there is not a unique power graph representing a given graph. Yet a very interesting class of power graphs are **minimal power graphs** which have the least number of power edges and power nodes necessary to represent a given graph.

Minimal power graphs

In general, there is no unique minimal power graph for a given graph. In this example (right) a graph of four nodes and five edges admits two minimal power graphs of two power edges each. The main difference between these two minimal power graphs is the higher nesting level of the second power graph as well as a loss of symmetry with respect to the underlying graph. Loss of symmetry is only a problem in small toy examples since complex networks rarely exhibit such symmetries in the first place. Additionally, one can minimize the nesting level but even then, there is in general not a unique minimal power graph of minimal nesting level.

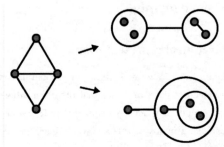

Two different power graphs that represent the same graph.

Power graph greedy algorithm

The power graph greedy algorithm relies on two simple steps to perform the decomposition:

The **first step** identifies candidate power nodes through a hierarchical clustering of the nodes in the network based on the similarity of their neighboring nodes. The similarity of two sets of neighbors is taken as the Jaccard index of the two sets.

The **second step** performs a greedy search for possible power edges between candidate power nodes. Power edges abstracting the most edges in the original network are added first to the power graph. Thus bicliques, cliques and stars are incrementally replaced with power edges, until all remaining single edges are also added. Candidate power nodes that are not the end point of any power edge are ignored.

Modular decomposition

Modular decomposition can be used to compute a power graph by using the strong modules of the modular decomposition. Modules in modular decomposition are groups of nodes in a graph that have identical neighbors. A Strong Module is a module that does not overlap with another module. However, in complex networks strong modules are more the exception than the rule. Therefore the power graphs obtained through modular decomposition are far from minimality. The main difference between modular decomposition and power graph analysis is the emphasis of power graph analysis in decomposing graphs not only using modules of nodes but also modules of edges (cliques, bicliques). Indeed, power graph analysis can be seen as a loss-less simultaneous clustering of both nodes and edges.

Applications

Power Graph Analysis has been showed to be useful for the analysis of several types of biological networks such as Protein-protein interaction networks, domain-peptide binding motifs, Gene regulatory networks and Homology/Paralogy networks.

References

Loic Royer, Matthias Reimann; Bill Andreopoulos, and Michael Schroeder (2008-07-11). Berg, Johannes. ed. "Unraveling Protein Networks with Power Graph Analysis" [1] (PDF). *PLoS Computational Biology* **4** (7): e1000108. doi:10.1371/journal.pcbi.1000108. PMC 2424176. PMID 18617988.

External links

- [2] Power Graph Analysis tools and example applications
- [1] Power graph Analysis paper published in PLoS Computational Biology

References

[1] http://www.ploscompbiol.org/doi/pcbi.1000108
[2] http://www.biotec.tu-dresden.de/schroeder/group/powergraphs

Precision and recall

In pattern recognition and information retrieval, **precision** is the fraction of retrieved instances that are relevant, while **recall** is the fraction of relevant instances that are retrieved. Both precision and recall are therefore based on an understanding and measure of relevance. When a program for recognizing the dogs in a scene correctly identifies four of the nine dogs but mistakes three cats for dogs, its precision is 4/7 while its recall is 4/9. When a search engine returns 30 pages only 20 of which were relevant while failing to return 40 relevant pages, its precision is 20/30 = 2/3 while its recall is 20/60 = 1/3.

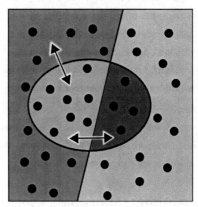

In this figure the relevant items are to the left of the straight line while the retrieved items are within the oval. The red regions represent errors. On the left these are the relevant items not retrieved (false negatives), while on the right they are the retrieved items that are not relevant (false positives). Precision and recall are the quotient of the left green region by respectively the oval (horizontal arrow) and the left region (diagonal arrow).

In statistics, if the null hypothesis is that all and only the relevant items are retrieved, absence of type I and type II errors corresponds respectively to maximum precision (no false positives) and maximum recall (no false negatives). The above pattern recognition example contained 7 − 4 = 3 type I errors and 9 − 4 = 5 type II errors. Precision can be seen as a measure of exactness or *quality*, whereas recall is a measure of completeness or *quantity*.

In even simpler terms, a high **recall** means you haven't missed anything but you may have a lot of useless results to sift through (which would imply low **precision**). High **precision** means that everything returned was a relevant result, but you might not have found all the relevant items (which would imply low **recall**).

Introduction

As an example, in an information retrieval scenario, the instances are documents and the task is to return a set of relevant documents given a search term; or equivalently, to assign each document to one of two categories, "relevant" and "not relevant". In this case, the "relevant" documents are simply those that belong to the "relevant" category. Recall is defined as the *number of relevant documents* retrieved by a search *divided by the total number of existing relevant documents*, while precision is defined as the *number of relevant documents* retrieved by a search *divided by the total number of documents retrieved* by that search.

In a classification task, the precision for a class is the *number of **true positives*** (i.e. the *number of items correctly labeled as belonging to the positive class*) *divided by the total number of elements labeled as belonging to the positive class* (i.e. the sum of true positives and **false positives**, which are items incorrectly labeled as belonging to the class). Recall in this context is defined as the *number of true positives divided by the total number of elements that actually belong to the positive class* (i.e. the sum of true positives and **false negatives**, which are items which were not labeled as belonging to the positive class but should have been).

In information retrieval, a perfect precision score of 1.0 means that every result retrieved by a search was relevant (but says nothing about whether all relevant documents were retrieved) whereas a perfect recall score of 1.0 means that all relevant documents were retrieved by the search (but says nothing about how many irrelevant documents were also retrieved).

In a classification task, a precision score of 1.0 for a class C means that every item labeled as belonging to class C does indeed belong to class C (but says nothing about the number of items from class C that were not labeled correctly) whereas a recall of 1.0 means that every item from class C was labeled as belonging to class C (but says nothing about how many other items were incorrectly also labeled as belonging to class C).

Often, there is an inverse relationship between precision and recall, where it is possible to increase one at the cost of reducing the other. For example, an information retrieval system (such as a search engine) can often increase its recall by retrieving more documents, at the cost of increasing number of irrelevant documents retrieved (decreasing precision). Similarly, a classification system for deciding whether or not, say, a fruit is an orange, can achieve high precision by only classifying fruits with the exact right shape and color as oranges, but at the cost of low recall due to the number of *false negatives* from oranges that did not quite match the specification.

Usually, precision and recall scores are not discussed in isolation. Instead, either values for one measure are compared for a fixed level at the other measure (e.g. *precision at a recall level of 0.75*) or both are combined into a single measure, such as the **F-measure**, which is the *weighted harmonic mean of precision and recall* (see below), or the Matthews correlation coefficient.

Definition (information retrieval context)

In information retrieval contexts, precision and recall are defined in terms of a set of **retrieved documents** (e.g. the list of documents produced by a web search engine for a query) and a set of **relevant documents** (e.g. the list of all documents on the internet that are relevant for a certain topic), cf. relevance.

Precision

In the field of information retrieval, **precision** is the fraction of retrieved documents that are relevant to the search:

$$\text{precision} = \frac{|\{\text{relevant documents}\} \cap \{\text{retrieved documents}\}|}{|\{\text{retrieved documents}\}|}$$

Precision takes all retrieved documents into account, but it can also be evaluated at a given cut-off rank, considering only the topmost results returned by the system. This measure is called **precision at n** or **P@n**.

For example for a text search on a set of documents precision is the number of correct results divided by the number of all returned results.

Precision is also used with recall, the percent of *all* relevant documents that is returned by the search. The two measures are sometimes used together in the F1 Score (or f-measure) to provide a single measurement for a system.

Note that the meaning and usage of "precision" in the field of Information Retrieval differs from the definition of accuracy and precision within other branches of science and technology.

Recall

Recall in information retrieval is the fraction of the documents that are relevant to the query that are successfully retrieved.

$$\text{recall} = \frac{|\{\text{relevant documents}\} \cap \{\text{retrieved documents}\}|}{|\{\text{relevant documents}\}|}$$

For example for text search on a set of documents recall is the number of correct results divided by the number of results that should have been returned

In binary classification, recall is called sensitivity. So it can be looked at as the probability that a relevant document is retrieved by the query.

It is trivial to achieve recall of 100% by returning all documents in response to any query. Therefore, recall alone is not enough but one needs to measure the number of non-relevant documents also, for example by computing the precision.

Definition (classification context)

For classification tasks, the terms **true positives**, **true negatives**, **false positives**, and **false negatives** (see also Type I and type II errors) compare the results of the classifier under test with trusted external judgments. The terms *positive* and *negative* refer to the classifier's prediction (sometimes known as the *observation*), and the terms *true* and *false* refer to whether that prediction corresponds to the external judgment (sometimes known as the *expectation*). This is illustrated by the table below:

	actual class (expectation)	
predicted class (observation)	**tp** (true positive) Correct result	**fp** (false positive) Unexpected result
	fn (false negative) Missing result	+

|+

Precision and recall are then defined as:[1]

$$\text{Precision} = \frac{tp}{tp + fp}$$

$$\text{Recall} = \frac{tp}{tp + fn}$$

Recall in this context is also referred to as the True Positive Rate, other related measures used in classification include True Negative Rate and Accuracy:[1] . True Negative Rate is also called Specificity.

$$\text{True negative rate} = \frac{tn}{tn + fp}$$

$$\text{Accuracy} = \frac{tp + tn}{tp + tn + fp + fn}$$

Probabilistic interpretation

It is possible to interpret precision and recall not as ratios but as probabilities:

- **Precision** is the probability that a (randomly selected) retrieved document is relevant.

- **Recall** is the probability that a (randomly selected) relevant document is retrieved in a search.

Note that the random selection refers to a uniform distribution over the appropriate pool of documents; i.e. by **randomly selected retrieved document**, we mean selecting a document from the set of retrieved documents in a random fashion. The random selection should be such that all documents in the set are equally likely to be selected.

Note that, in a typical classification system, the probability that a retrieved document is relevant depends on the document. The above interpretation extends to that scenario also (needs explanation).

Another interpretation for precision and recall is as follows. Precision is the average probability of relevant retrieval. Recall is the average probability of complete retrieval. Here we average over multiple retrieval queries.

F-measure

A measure that combines precision and recall is the harmonic mean of precision and recall, the traditional F-measure or balanced F-score:

$$F = 2 \cdot \frac{\text{precision} \cdot \text{recall}}{\text{precision} + \text{recall}}$$

This is also known as the F_1 measure, because recall and precision are evenly weighted.

It is a special case of the general F_β measure (for non-negative real values of β):

$$F_\beta = (1 + \beta^2) \cdot \frac{\text{precision} \cdot \text{recall}}{\beta^2 \cdot \text{precision} + \text{recall}}$$

Two other commonly used F measures are the F_2 measure, which weights recall higher than precision, and the $F_{0.5}$ measure, which puts more emphasis on precision than recall.

The F-measure was derived by van Rijsbergen (1979) so that F_β "measures the effectiveness of retrieval with respect to a user who attaches β times as much importance to recall as precision". It is based on van Rijsbergen's effectiveness measure $E = 1 - \frac{1}{\frac{\alpha}{P} + \frac{1-\alpha}{R}}$. Their relationship is $F_\beta = 1 - E$ where $\alpha = \frac{1}{1 + \beta^2}$.

Limitations as goals

There are other parameters and strategies for performance metric of information retrieval system. In particular, for web document retrieval, if the user's objectives are not clear, the precision and recall can't be optimized. As summarized by D. Lopresti,

> "*Browsing is a comfortable and powerful paradigm (the serendipity effect).*

- *Search results don't have to be very good.*
- *Recall? Not important (as long as you get at least some good hits).*
- *Precision? Not important (as long as at least some of the hits on the first page you return are good).*

"[2]

Sources

[1] Olson, David L.; Delen, Dursun "Advanced Data Mining Techniques" Springer; 1 edition (February 1, 2008), page 138, ISBN 3540769161

[2] Daniel Lopresti 2001, WDA 2001 panel (http://www.csc.liv.ac.uk/~wda2001/Panel_Presentations/Lopresti/Lopresti_files/v3_document.htm)

- Baeza-Yates, R.; Ribeiro-Neto, B. (1999). *Modern Information Retrieval*. New York: ACM Press, Addison-Wesley. Seiten 75 ff. ISBN 0-201-39829-X

- Hjørland, Birger (2010). The foundation of the concept of relevance. Journal of the American Society for Information Science and Technology, 61(2), 217-237.

- Makhoul, John; Francis Kubala; Richard Schwartz; Ralph Weischedel: *Performance measures for information extraction*. (http://citeseerx.ist.psu.edu/viewdoc/summary?doi=10.1.1.27.4637) In: *Proceedings of DARPA Broadcast News Workshop, Herndon, VA, February 1999*.

- van Rijsbergen, C.V.: *Information Retrieval*. London; Boston. Butterworth, 2nd Edition 1979. ISBN 0-408-70929-4

External links

- Information Retrieval – C. J. van Rijsbergen 1979 (http://www.dcs.gla.ac.uk/Keith/Preface.html)

PRINTS

In molecular biology, the **PRINTS** database is a collection of so-called "fingerprints": it provides both a detailed annotation resource for protein families, and a diagnostic tool for newly-determined sequences. A fingerprint is a group of conserved motifs taken from a multiple sequence alignment - together, the motifs form a characteristic signature for the aligned protein family. The motifs themselves are not necessarily contiguous in sequence, but may come together in 3D space to define molecular binding sites or interaction surfaces. The particular diagnostic strength of fingerprints lies in their ability to distinguish sequence differences at the clan, superfamily, family and subfamily levels. This allows fine-grained functional diagnoses of uncharacterised sequences, allowing, for example, discrimination between family members on the basis of the ligands they bind or the proteins with which they interact, and highlighting potential oligomerisation or allosteric sites.

PRINTS is a founding partner of the integrated resource, InterPro, a widely used database of protein families, domains and functional sites.

External links

- PRINTS Database [1] (University of Manchester Bioinformatics Education and Research)

References

- Attwood, T.K., Bradley, P., Flower, D.R., Gaulton, A., Maudling, N., Mitchell, A.L., Moulton, G., Nordle, A., Paine, K., Taylor, P. and Uddin, A. (2003). "PRINTS and its automatic supplement, prePRINTS". *Nucleic Acids Res.* **31** (1): 400–402. doi:10.1093/nar/gkg030. PMC 165477. PMID 12520033.

- Scordis, P., Flower, D.R. and Attwood, T.K. (1999). "FingerPRINTScan: Intelligent searching of the PRINTS motif database". *Bioinformatics* **15** (10): 799–806. doi:10.1093/bioinformatics/15.10.799. PMID 10705433.

References

[1] http://www.bioinf.manchester.ac.uk/dbbrowser/PRINTS/

ProbCons

ProbCons is an open source probabilistic consistency-based multiple alignment of amino acid sequences. It is an efficient protein multiple sequence alignment program, which has demonstrated a statistically significant improvement in accuracy compared to several leading alignment tools.[1]

References

[1] Do CB, Mahabhashyam MSP, Brudno M, Batzoglou S (2005). "PROBCONS: Probabilistic Consistency-based Multiple Sequence Alignment". *Genome Research* **15** (2): 330–340. doi:10.1101/gr.2821705. PMC 546535. PMID 15687296.

External links

- Official website (http://probcons.stanford.edu/)

PROSITE

PROSITE

Content	
Description	PROSITE, a protein domain database for functional characterization and annotation.
Contact	
Research center	Swiss Institute of Bioinformatics
Laboratory	Structural Biology and Bioinformatics Department
Primary Citation	PMID 19858104
Release date	1988
Access	
Website	http://www.expasy.org/prosite/PROSITE
Tools	
Miscellaneous	

PROSITE is a protein database.[1] [2] It consists of entries describing the protein families, domains and functional sites as well as amino acid patterns, signatures, and profiles in them. These are manually curated by a team of the Swiss Institute of Bioinformatics and tightly integrated into Swiss-Prot protein annotation. PROSITE was created in 1988 by Amos Bairoch, who directed the group for more than 20 years. Since July 2009 the director of the PROSITE, Swiss-Prot and Vital-IT groups is Ioannis Xenarios.

PROSITE's uses include identifying possible functions of newly discovered proteins and analysis of known proteins for previously undetermined activity. Properties from well-studied genes can be propagated to biologically related organisms, and for different or poorly known genes biochemical functions can be predicted from similarities. PROSITE offers tools for protein sequence analysis and motif detection (see sequence motif, PROSITE patterns). It is part of the ExPASy proteomics analysis servers.

The database **ProRule** builds on the domain descriptions of PROSITE.[3] It provides additional information about functionally or structurally critical amino acids. The rules contain information about biologically meaningful residues, like active sites, substrate- or co-factor-binding sites, posttranslational modification sites or disulfide bonds, to help function determination. These can automatically generate annotation based on PROSITE motifs.

References

[1] De Castro E, Sigrist CJA, Gattiker A, Bulliard V, Langendijk-Genevaux PS, Gasteiger E, Bairoch A, Hulo N (2006). "ScanProsite: detection of PROSITE signature matches and ProRule-associated functional and structural residues in proteins" (http://nar.oxfordjournals.org/cgi/ screenpdf/34/suppl_2/W362). *Nucleic Acids Res.* **34** (Web Server issue): W362–365. doi:10.1093/nar/gkl124. PMC 1538847. PMID 16845026. .

[2] Hulo N, Bairoch A, Bulliard V, Cerutti L, Cuche B, De Castro E, Lachaize C, Langendijk-Genevaux PS, Sigrist CJA (2007). "The 20 years of PROSITE" (http://nar.oxfordjournals.org/cgi/screenpdf/gkm977v1). *Nucleic Acids Res.* **36** (Database issue): D245–9. doi:10.1093/nar/gkm977. PMC 2238851. PMID 18003654. .

[3] Sigrist CJ, De Castro E, Langendijk-Genevaux PS, Le Saux V, Bairoch A, Hulo N (2005). "ProRule: a new database containing functional and structural information on PROSITE profiles" (http://bioinformatics.oxfordjournals.org/cgi/reprint/21/21/4060). *Bioinformatics.* **21** (21): 4060–4066. doi:10.1093/bioinformatics/bti614. PMID 16091411. .

External links

- PROSITE (http://www.expasy.org/prosite/) — official website
- ProRule (http://www.expasy.org/prosite/prorule.html) — database of rules based on PROSITE predictors

ProtCID

ProtCID

Content	
Description	Similar interactions of homologous proteins in multiple crystal forms
Contact	
Research center	Fox Chase Cancer Center
Laboratory	Institute for Cancer Research
Authors	Qifang Xu, Roland Dunbrack
Primary Citation	Xu & Dunbrack (2011)[1]
Release date	2010
Access	
Website	[2]
Tools	
Miscellaneous	

The **Protein Common Interface Database (ProtCID)** is a database of similar protein-protein interfaces in crystal structures of homologous proteins.[1]

Its main goal is to identify and cluster homodimeric and heterodimeric interfaces observed in multiple crystal forms of homologous proteins. Such interfaces, especially of non-identical proteins or protein complexes, have been associated with biologically relevant interactions.[3]

A common interface in ProtCID indicates chain-chain interactions that occur in different crystal forms. All protein sequences of known structure in the Protein Data Bank (PDB) are assigned a "Pfam chain architecture", which denotes the ordered Pfam assignments for that sequence, e.g. (Pkinase) or (Cyclin_N)_(Cyclin_C). Homodimeric interfaces in all crystals that contain a particular architecture are compared, regardless of whether there are other protein types in the crystals. All interfaces between two different Pfam architectures in all PDB entries that contain them are also compared (e.g., (Pkinase) and

Example of cluster of similar interfaces of homologous proteins identified by ProtCID -- similar homodimers of ERBB kinases (EGFR, ERBB2, ERBB4) associated with kinase activation. Each monomer is colored from blue to red from N to C terminus. ProtCID provides PyMol scripts for each cluster to produce similar images.

(Cyclin_N)_(Cyclin_C)). For both homodimers and heterodimers, the interfaces are clustered into common interfaces based on a similarity score.

ProtCID reports the number of crystal forms that contain a common interface, the number of PDB entries, the number of PDB and PISA biological assembly annotations that contain the same interface, the average surface area, and the minimum sequence identity of proteins that contain the interface. ProtCID provides an independent check on publicly available annotations of biological interactions for PDB entries.

References

[1] Xu, Q.; Dunbrack, R. L. (2010). "The protein common interface database (ProtCID)—a comprehensive database of interactions of homologous proteins in multiple crystal forms". *Nucleic Acids Research* **39** (Database issue): D761–70. doi:10.1093/nar/gkq1059. PMC 3013667. PMID 21036862.

[2] http://dunbrack2.fccc.edu/protcid

[3] Xu, Qifang; Canutescu, Adrian A.; Wang, Guoli; Shapovalov, Maxim; Obradovic, Zoran; Dunbrack, Roland L. (2008). "Statistical Analysis of Interface Similarity in Crystals of Homologous Proteins". *Journal of Molecular Biology* **381** (2): 487–507. doi:10.1016/j.jmb.2008.06.002. PMC 2573399. PMID 18599072.

External links

• http://dunbrack2.fccc.edu/protcid

Protein family

A **protein family** is a group of evolutionarily-related proteins, and is often nearly synonymous with gene family. The term *protein family* should not be confused with *family* as it is used in taxonomy.

Proteins in a family descend from a common ancestor (see homology) and typically have similar three-dimensional structures, functions, and significant sequence similarity. While it is difficult to evaluate the significance of functional or structural similarity, there is a fairly well developed framework for evaluating the significance of similarity between a group of sequences using sequence alignment methods. Proteins that do not share a common ancestor are very unlikely to show statistically significant sequence similarity, making sequence alignment a powerful tool for identifying the members of protein families.

Currently, over 60,000 protein families have been defined,[1] although ambiguity in the definition of *protein family* leads different researchers to wildly varying numbers.

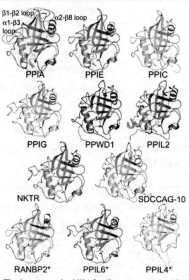

The human cyclophilin family, as represented by the structures of the isomerase domains of some of its members.

Terminology and usage

As with many biological terms, the use of *protein family* is somewhat context dependent; it may indicate large groups of proteins with the lowest possible level of detectable sequence similarity, or very narrow groups of proteins with almost identical sequence, function, and three-dimensional structure, or any kind of group in-between. To distinguish between these situations, Dayhoff introduced the concept of a protein superfamily.[2] [3] [4] Other terms such as *protein class*, *protein group*, and *protein sub-family* have been coined over the years, but all suffer similar ambiguities of usage. A common usage is superfamily > family > sub-family. In the end, *caveat emptor*, it is up to a reader to discern exactly how these terms are being used in a particular context.

Protein domains and motifs

The concept of *protein family* was conceived at a time when very few protein structures or sequences were known; at that time, primarily small, single-domain proteins such as myoglobin, hemoglobin, and cytochrome c. Since that time, it was found that many proteins comprise multiple independent structural and functional units or *domains*. Due to evolutionary shuffling, different domains in a protein have evolved independently. This has led, in recent years, to a focus on families of protein domains. A number of online resources are devoted to identifying and cataloging such domains (see list of links at the end of this article).

Regions of each protein have differing functional constraints (features critical to the structure and function of the protein). For example, the active site of an enzyme requires certain amino acid residues to be precisely oriented in three dimensions. On the other hand, a protein–protein binding interface may consist of a large surface with constraints on the hydrophobicity or polarity of the amino acid residues. Functionally constrained regions of proteins evolve more slowly than unconstrained regions such as surface loops, giving rise to discernible blocks of conserved sequence when the sequences of a protein family are compared (see multiple sequence alignment). These blocks are most commonly referred to as *motifs*, although many other terms are used (blocks, signatures, fingerprints, etc.). Again, a large number of online resources are devoted to identifying and cataloging protein motifs (see list at end of article).

Evolution of protein families

According to current dogma, protein families arise in two ways. Firstly, the separation of a parent species into two genetically isolated descendent species allows a gene/protein to independently accumulate variations (mutations) in these two lineages. This results in a family of orthologous proteins, usually with conserved sequence motifs. Secondly, a gene duplication may create a second copy of a gene (termed a paralog). Because the original gene is still able to perform its function, the duplicated gene is free to diverge and may acquire new functions (by random mutation). Certain gene/protein families, especially in eukaryotes, undergo extreme expansions and contractions in the course of evolution, sometimes in concert with whole genome duplications. This expansion and contraction of protein families is one of the salient features of genome evolution, but its importance and ramifications are currently unclear.

Use and importance of protein families

As the total number of sequenced proteins increases and interest expands in proteome analysis, there is an ongoing effort to organize proteins into families and to describe their component domains and motifs. Reliable identification of protein families is critical to phylogenetic analysis, functional annotation, and the exploration of diversity of protein function in a given phylogenetic branch.

The algorithmic means for establishing protein families on a large scale are based on a notion of similarity. Most of the time the only similarity we have access to is sequence similarity.

External links

- Pfam [5] - Protein families database of alignments and HMMs
- PROSITE [33] - Database of protein domains, families and functional sites
- PIRSF [6] - SuperFamily Classification System
- PASS2 [7] - Protein Alignment as Structural Superfamilies v2 - PASS2@NCBS
- SUPERFAMILY [8] - Library of HMMs representing superfamilies and database of (superfamily and family) annotations for all completely sequenced organisms

References

[1] V.Kunin, I. Cases, A.J. Enrigh, V. de Lorenzo, C.A. Ouzounis, 'Myriads of protein families, and still counting', Genome Biology 4, 401, 2003. (http://genomebiology.com/2003/4/2/401)

[2] Dayhoff, M.O., Computer analysis of protein sequences, Fed. Proc. 33, 2314-2316, 1974.

[3] Dayhoff, M.O., McLaughlin, P.J., Barker, W.C., and Hunt, L.T., Evolution of sequences within protein superfamilies,Naturwissenschaften 62, 154-161, 1975.

[4] Dayhoff, M.O., The origin and evolution of protein superfamilies, Fed. Proc. 35, 2132-2138, 1976.

[5] http://www.sanger.ac.uk/Software/Pfam/index.shtml

[6] http://pir.georgetown.edu/pirsf/

[7] http://caps.ncbs.res.in/campass/pass2.html

[8] http://supfam.org/SUPERFAMILY

Protein fragment library

Protein backbone fragment libraries have been used successfully in a variety of structural biology applications, including homology modeling,[1] de novo structure prediction,[2] [3] [4] and structure determination.[5] By reducing the complexity of the search space, these fragment libraries enable more rapid search of conformational space, leading to more efficient and accurate models.

Motivation

Proteins can adopt an exponential number of states when modeled discretely. Typically, a protein's conformations are represented as sets of dihedral angles, bond lengths, and bond angles between all connected atoms. The most common simplification is to assume ideal bond lengths and bond angles. However, this still leaves the phi-psi angles of the backbone, and up to four dihedral angles for each side chain, leading to a worst case complexity of k^{6*n} possible states of the protein, where n is the number of residues and k is the number of discrete states modeled for each dihedral angle. In order to reduce the conformational space, one can use protein fragment libraries rather than explicitly model every phi-psi angle.

Fragments are short segments of the peptide backbone, typically from 5 to 15 residues long, and do not include the side chains. They may specify the location of just the C-alpha atoms if it is a reduced atom representation, or all the backbone heavy atoms (N, C-alpha, C carbonyl, O). Note that side chains are typically not modeled using the fragment library approach. To model discrete states of a side chain, one could use a rotamer library approach.[6]

This approach operates under the assumption that local interactions play a large role in stabilizing the overall protein conformation. In any short sequence, the molecular forces constrain the structure, leading to only a small number of possible conformations, which can be modeled by fragments. Indeed, according to Levinthal's paradox, a protein could not possibly sample all possible conformations within a biologically reasonable amount of time. Locally stabilized structures would reduce the search space and allow proteins to fold on the order of milliseconds.

Construction

Libraries of these fragments are constructed from an analysis of the Protein Data Bank (PDB). First, a representative subset of the PDB is chosen which should cover a diverse array of structures, preferably at a good resolution. Then, for each structure, every set of n consecutive residues is taken as a sample fragment. The samples are then clustered into k groups, based upon how similar they are to each other in spatial configuration, using algorithms such as k-means clustering. The parameters n and k are chosen according to the application (see discussion on complexity below). The centroids of the clusters are then taken to represent the fragment. Further optimization can be performed to ensure that the centroid possesses ideal bond geometry, as it was derived by averaging other geometries. [7]

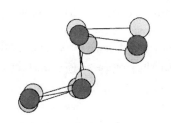

Clustering of similar fragments. Centroid is shown in blue.

Because the fragments are derived from structures that exist in nature, the segment of backbone they represent will have realistic bonding geometries. This helps avoid having to explore the full space of conformation angles, much of which would lead to unrealistic geometries.

The clustering above can be performed without regard to the identities of the residues, or it can be residue-specific.[2] That is, for any given input sequence of amino acids, a clustering can be derived using only samples found in the PDB with the same sequence in the k-mer fragment. This requires more computational work than deriving a sequence-independent fragment library but can potentially produce more accurate models. Conversely, a larger sample set is required, and one may not achieve full coverage.

Example use: loop modeling

In homology modeling, a common application of fragment libraries is to model the loops of the structure. Typically, the alpha helices and beta sheets are threaded against a template structure, but the loops in between are not specified and need to be predicted. Finding the loop with the optimal configuration is NP-hard. To reduce the conformational space that needs to be explored, one can model the loop as a series of overlapping fragments. The space can then be sampled, or if the space is now small enough, exhaustively enumerated.

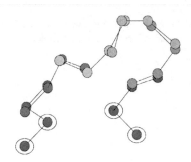

Loop of length 10 constructed using 6 fragments, each of length 4. Only overlaps of 2 were used in this 2D model. Anchor points are circled.

One approach for exhaustive enumeration goes as follows.[1] Loop construction begins by aligning all possible fragments to overlap with the three residues at the N terminus of the loop (the anchor point).

Then all possible choices for a second fragment are aligned to (all possible choices of) the first fragment, ensuring that the last three residues of the first fragment overlap with the first three residues of the second fragment. This ensures that the fragment chain forms realistic angles both within the fragment and between fragments. This is then repeated until a loop with the correct length of residues is constructed.

The loop must both begin at the anchor on the N side and end at the anchor on the C side. Each loop must therefore be tested to see if its last few residues overlap with the C terminal anchor. Very few of these exponential numbers of candidate loops will close the loop. After filtering out loops that don't close, one must then determine which loop has the optimal configuration, as determined by having the lowest energy using some molecular mechanics force field.

Complexity

The complexity of the state space is still exponential in the number of residues, even after using fragment libraries. However, the degree of the exponent is reduced. For a library of F-mer fragments, with L fragments in the library, and to model a chain of N residues overlapping each fragment by 3, there will be $L^{[N/(F-3)]+1}$ possible chains. [7] This is much less than the K^N possibilities if explicitly modeling the phi-psi angles as K possible combinations, as the complexity grows at a degree smaller than N.

The complexity increases in L, the size of the fragment library. However, libraries with more fragments will capture a greater diversity of fragment structures, so there is a trade off in the accuracy of the model vs the speed of exploring the search space. This choice governs what K is used when performing the clustering.

Additionally, for any fixed L, the diversity of structures capable of being modeled decreases as the length of the fragments increases. Shorter fragments are more capable of covering the diverse array of structures found in the PDB than longer ones. Recently, it was shown that libraries of up to length 15 are capable of modeling 91% of the fragments in the PDB to within 2.0 angstroms. [8]

References

[1] Kolodny, R., Guibas, L., Levitt, M., and Koehl, P. (2005, March). Inverse Kinematics in Biology: The Protein Loop Closure Problem. The International Journal of Robotics Research 24(2-3), 151-163.

[2] Simons, K., Kooperberg, C., Huang, E., and Baker, D. (1997). Assembly of Protein Tertiary Structures from Fragments with Similar Local Sequences using Simulated Annealing and Bayesian Scoring Functions. J Mol Biol 268, 209-225.

[3] Bujnicki, J. (2006) Protein Structure Prediction by Recombination of Fragments. ChemBioChem. 7, 19-27.

[4] Li, S. et al. (2008) Fragment-HMM: A New Approach to Protein Structure Prediction. Protein Science. 17, 1925-1934.

[5] DiMaio, F., Shavlik, J., Phillips, G. A probabilistic approach to protein backbone tracing in electron density maps (2006). Bioinformatics 22(14), 81-89.

[6] Canutescu, A., Shelenkov, A., and Dunbrack, R. (2003). A graph theory algorithm for protein side-chain prediction. Protein Sci. 12, 2001-2014.

[7] Kolodny, R., Koehl, P., Guibas, L., and Levitt, M. (2005). Small Libraries of Protein Fragments Model Native Protein Structures Accurately. J Mol Biol 323, 297-307.

[8] Du, P., Andrec, M., and Levy, R. Have We Seen All Structures Corresponding to Short Protein Fragments in the Protein Data Bank? An Update. Protein Engineering. 2003, 16(6) 407-414.

Protein function prediction

Protein function prediction involves the computational prediction of Proteins. Source information may come from homologous sequences, protein structures, or text mining of publications. Because of the strong link between a protein's structure and function, protein function prediction is similar to Protein structure prediction, with a key difference being that protein function prediction methods may use structural information about the target. One example of a simple protein function prediction method is, given the target protein sequence, do a BLAST search to find the protein with highest sequence similarity with functional annotation, and then transfer that annotation to the target protein.

Protein Information Resource

The **Protein Information Resource** (PIR), located at Georgetown University Medical Center (GUMC), is an integrated public bioinformatics resource to support genomic and proteomic research, and scientific studies[1] [2] [3] [4] [5] [6] [7]

History

PIR was established in 1984 by the National Biomedical Research Foundation (NBRF) as a resource to assist researchers in the identification and interpretation of protein sequence information. Prior to that, the NBRF compiled the first comprehensive collection of macromolecular sequences in the Atlas of Protein Sequence and Structure, published from 1965-1978 under the editorship of Margaret Dayhoff. Dr. Dayhoff and her research group pioneered in the development of computer methods for the comparison of protein sequences, for the detection of distantly related sequences and duplications within sequences, and for the inference of evolutionary histories from alignments of protein sequences.

Dr. Winona Barker and Dr. Robert Ledley assumed leadership of the project after the untimely death of Dr. Dayhoff in 1983. In 1999, Dr. Cathy H. Wu joined NBRF, and later on GUMC, to head the bioinformatics efforts of PIR, and has served first as Principal Investigator and, since 2001, as Director.

For four decades, PIR has provided many protein databases and analysis tools freely accessible to the scientific community, including the Protein Sequence Database (PSD), the first international database (see PIR-International), which grew out of Atlas of Protein Sequence and Structure.

In 2002, PIR along with its international partners, EBI (European Bioinformatics Institute) and SIB (Swiss Institute of Bioinformatics), were awarded a grant from NIH to create UniProt, a single worldwide database of protein sequence and function, by unifying the PIR-PSD, Swiss-Prot, and TrEMBL databases.

Present

As of 2010, PIR offers a wide variety of resources mainly oriented to assist the propagation and standardization of protein annotation: PIRSF[8] , iProClass, iProLINK

References

[1] http://pir.georgetown.edu/Official website of PIR at Georgetown University.

[2] Wu, C.; Nebert, D. W. (2004). "Update on genome completion and annotations: Protein Information Resource". *Human genomics* **1** (3): 229–233. PMID 15588483.

[3] Wu, C. H.; Yeh, L. S.; Huang, H.; Arminski, L.; Castro-Alvear, J.; Chen, Y.; Hu, Z.; Kourtesis, P. et al. (2003). "The Protein Information Resource". *Nucleic Acids Research* **31** (1): 345–347. doi:10.1093/nar/gkg040. PMC 165487. PMID 12520019.

[4] Wu, C. H.; Huang, H.; Arminski, L.; Castro-Alvear, J.; Chen, Y.; Hu, Z. Z.; Ledley, R. S.; Lewis, K. C. et al. (2002). "The Protein Information Resource: An integrated public resource of functional annotation of proteins". *Nucleic Acids Research* **30** (1): 35–37. doi:10.1093/nar/30.1.35. PMC 99125. PMID 11752247.

[5] Barker, W. C.; Garavelli, J. S.; Hou, Z.; Huang, H.; Ledley, R. S.; McGarvey, P. B.; Mewes, H. W.; Orcutt, B. C. et al. (2001). "Protein Information Resource: A community resource for expert annotation of protein data". *Nucleic Acids Research* **29** (1): 29–32. doi:10.1093/nar/29.1.29. PMC 29802. PMID 11125041.

[6] Barker, W. C.; Garavelli, J. S.; Huang, H.; McGarvey, P. B.; Orcutt, B. C.; Srinivasarao, G. Y.; Xiao, C.; Yeh, L. S. et al. (2000). "The protein information resource (PIR)". *Nucleic Acids Research* **28** (1): 41–44. PMC 102418. PMID 10592177.

[7] George, D. G.; Dodson, R. J.; Garavelli, J. S.; Haft, D. H.; Hunt, L. T.; Marzec, C. R.; Orcutt, B. C.; Sidman, K. E. et al. (1997). "The Protein Information Resource (PIR) and the PIR-International Protein Sequence Database". *Nucleic Acids Research* **25** (1): 24–28. doi:10.1093/nar/25.1.24. PMC 146415. PMID 9016497.

[8] Wu, C. H.; Nikolskaya, A.; Huang, H.; Yeh, L. S.; Natale, D. A.; Vinayaka, C. R.; Hu, Z. Z.; Mazumder, R. et al. (2004). "PIRSF: Family classification system at the Protein Information Resource". *Nucleic Acids Research* **32** (90001): 112D–1114. doi:10.1093/nar/gkh097. PMC 308831. PMID 14681371.

Protein structure prediction

Protein structure prediction is the prediction of the three-dimensional structure of a protein from its amino acid sequence — that is, the prediction of its secondary, tertiary, and quaternary structure from its primary structure. Structure prediction is fundamentally different from the inverse problem of protein design. Protein structure prediction is one of the most important goals pursued by bioinformatics and theoretical chemistry; it is highly important in medicine (for example, in drug design) and biotechnology (for example, in the design of novel enzymes). Every two years, the performance of current methods is assessed in the CASP experiment (Critical Assessment of Techniques for Protein Structure Prediction).

Secondary structure

Secondary structure prediction is a set of techniques in bioinformatics that aim to predict the local secondary structures of proteins and RNA sequences based only on knowledge of their primary structure — amino acid or nucleotide sequence, respectively. For proteins, a prediction consists of assigning regions of the amino acid sequence as likely alpha helices, beta strands (often noted as "extended" conformations), or turns. The success of a prediction is determined by comparing it to the results of the DSSP algorithm applied to the crystal structure of the protein; for nucleic acids, it may be determined from the hydrogen bonding pattern. Specialized algorithms have been developed for the detection of specific well-defined patterns such as transmembrane helices and coiled coils in proteins, or canonical microRNA structures in RNA.[1]

The best modern methods of secondary structure prediction in proteins reach about 80% accuracy; this high accuracy allows the use of the predictions in fold recognition and ab initio protein structure prediction, classification of structural motifs, and refinement of sequence alignments. The accuracy of current protein secondary structure prediction methods is assessed in weekly benchmarks such as LiveBench and EVA.

Background

Early methods of secondary structure prediction, introduced in the 1960s and early 1970s,[2] focused on identifying likely alpha helices and were based mainly on helix-coil transition models.[3] Significantly more accurate predictions that included beta sheets were introduced in the 1970s and relied on statistical assessments based on probability parameters derived from known solved structures. These methods, applied to a single sequence, are typically at most about 60-65% accurate, and often underpredict beta sheets.[1] The evolutionary conservation of secondary structures can be exploited by simultaneously assessing many homologous sequences in a multiple sequence alignment, by calculating the net secondary structure propensity of an aligned column of amino acids. In concert with larger databases of known protein structures and modern machine learning methods such as neural nets and support vector machines, these methods can achieve up 80% overall accuracy in globular proteins.[4] The theoretical upper limit of accuracy is around 90%,[4] partly due to idiosyncrasies in DSSP assignment near the ends of secondary structures, where local conformations vary under native conditions but may be forced to assume a single conformation in crystals due to packing constraints. Limitations are also imposed by secondary structure prediction's inability to account for tertiary structure; for example, a sequence predicted as a likely helix may still be able to adopt a beta-strand conformation if it is located within a beta-sheet region of the protein and its side chains pack well with their neighbors. Dramatic conformational changes related to the protein's function or environment can also alter local secondary structure.

Chou-Fasman method

The Chou-Fasman method was among the first secondary structure prediction algorithms developed and relies predominantly on probability parameters determined from relative frequencies of each amino acid's appearance in each type of secondary structure.[5] The original Chou-Fasman parameters, determined from the small sample of structures solved in the mid-1970s, produce poor results compared to modern methods, though the parameterization has been updated since it was first published. The Chou-Fasman method is roughly 50-60% accurate in predicting secondary structures.[1]

GOR method

The GOR method, named for the three scientists who developed it — *G*arnier, *O*sguthorpe, and *R*obson — is an information theory-based method developed not long after Chou-Fasman. It uses a more powerful probabilistic techniques of Bayesian inference.[6] The method is a specific optimized application of mathematics and algorithms developed in a series of papers by Robson and colleagues, eg.[7] and [8]). The GOR method is capable of continued extension by such principles, and has gone through several versions. The GOR method takes into account not only the probability of each amino acid having a particular secondary structure, but also the conditional probability of the amino acid assuming each structure given the contributions of its neighbors (it does not assume that the neighbors have that same structure). The approach is both more sensitive and more accurate than that of Chou and Fasman because amino acid structural propensities are only strong for a small number of amino acids such as proline and glycine. Weak contributions from each of many neighbors can add up to strong effect overall. The original GOR method was roughly 65% accurate and is dramatically more successful in predicting alpha helices than beta sheets, which it frequently mispredicted as loops or disorganized regions.[1] Later GOR methods considered also pairs of amino acids, significantly improving performance. The major difference from the following technique is perhaps that the weights in an implied network of contributing terms are assigned *a priori*, from statistical analysis of proteins of known structure, not by feedback to optimize agreement with a training set of such.

Machine learning

Neural network methods use training sets of solved structures to identify common sequence motifs associated with particular arrangements of secondary structures. These methods are over 70% accurate in their predictions, although beta strands are still often underpredicted due to the lack of three-dimensional structural information that would allow assessment of hydrogen bonding patterns that can promote formation of the extended conformation required for the presence of a complete beta sheet.[1]

Support vector machines have proven particularly useful for predicting the locations of turns, which are difficult to identify with statistical methods.[9] The requirement of relatively small training sets has also been cited as an advantage to avoid overfitting to existing structural data.[10]

Extensions of machine learning techniques attempt to predict more fine-grained local properties of proteins, such as backbone dihedral angles in unassigned regions. Both SVMs[11] and neural networks[12] have been applied to this problem.[9]

Other improvements

It is reported that in addition to the protein sequence, secondary structure formation depends on other factors. For example, it is reported that secondary structure tendencies depend also on local environment,[13] solvent accessibility of residues,[14] protein structural class,[15] and even the organism from which the proteins are obtained.[16] Based on such observations, some studies have shown that secondary structure prediction can be improved by addition of information about protein structural class,[17] residue accessible surface area[18] [19] and also contact number information.[20]

Sequence covariation methods rely on the existence of a data set composed of multiple homologous RNA sequences with related but dissimilar sequences. These methods analyze the covariation of individual base sites in evolution; maintenance at two widely separated sites of a pair of base-pairing nucleotides indicates the presence of a structurally required hydrogen bond between those positions. The general problem of pseudoknot prediction has been shown to be NP-complete.[21]

Tertiary structure

The practical role of protein structure prediction is now more important than ever. Massive amounts of protein sequence data are produced by modern large-scale DNA sequencing efforts such as the Human Genome Project. Despite community-wide efforts in structural genomics, the output of experimentally determined protein structures—typically by time-consuming and relatively expensive X-ray crystallography or NMR spectroscopy—is lagging far behind the output of protein sequences.

The protein structure prediction remains an extremely difficult and unresolved undertaking. The two main problems are calculation of protein free energy and finding the global minimum of this energy. A protein structure prediction method must explore the space of possible protein structures which is astronomically large. These problems can be partially bypassed in "comparative" or homology modeling and fold recognition methods, in which the search space is pruned by the assumption that the protein in question adopts a structure that is close to the experimentally determined structure of another homologous protein. On the other hand, the *de novo* or ab initio protein structure prediction methods must explicitly resolve these problems. The progress and challenges in protein structure prediction has been reviewed in Zhang 2008.[22]

Ab initio protein modelling

Ab initio- or *de novo-* protein modelling methods seek to build three-dimensional protein models "from scratch", i.e., based on physical principles rather than (directly) on previously solved structures. There are many possible procedures that either attempt to mimic protein folding or apply some stochastic method to search possible solutions (i.e., global optimization of a suitable energy function). These procedures tend to require vast computational resources, and have thus only been carried out for tiny proteins. To predict protein structure *de novo* for larger proteins will require better algorithms and larger computational resources like those afforded by either powerful supercomputers (such as Blue Gene or MDGRAPE-3) or distributed computing (such as Folding@home, the Human Proteome Folding Project and Rosetta@Home). Although these computational barriers are vast, the potential benefits of structural genomics (by predicted or experimental methods) make *ab initio* structure prediction an active research field.[22]

As an intermediate step towards predicted protein structures, contact map predictions have been proposed.

Comparative protein modelling

Comparative protein modelling uses previously solved structures as starting points, or templates. This is effective because it appears that although the number of actual proteins is vast, there is a limited set of tertiary structural motifs to which most proteins belong. It has been suggested that there are only around 2,000 distinct protein folds in nature, though there are many millions of different proteins.

These methods may also be split into two groups [22] :

Homology modeling

> is based on the reasonable assumption that two homologous proteins will share very similar structures. Because a protein's fold is more evolutionarily conserved than its amino acid sequence, a target sequence can be modeled with reasonable accuracy on a very distantly related template, provided that the relationship between target and template can be discerned through sequence alignment. It has been suggested that the primary bottleneck in comparative modelling arises from difficulties in alignment rather than from errors in structure prediction given a known-good alignment.[23] Unsurprisingly, homology modelling is most accurate when the target and template have similar sequences.

Protein threading[24]

> scans the amino acid sequence of an unknown structure against a database of solved structures. In each case, a scoring function is used to assess the compatibility of the sequence to the structure, thus yielding possible three-dimensional models. This type of method is also known as **3D-1D fold recognition** due to its compatibility analysis between three-dimensional structures and linear protein sequences. This method has also given rise to methods performing an **inverse folding search** by evaluating the compatibility of a given structure with a large database of sequences, thus predicting which sequences have the potential to produce a given fold.

Side-chain geometry prediction

Accurate packing of the amino acid side chains represents a separate problem in protein structure prediction. Methods that specifically address the problem of predicting side-chain geometry include dead-end elimination and the self-consistent mean field methods. The side chain conformations with low energy are usually determined on the rigid polypeptide backbone and using a set of discrete side chain conformations known as "rotamers." The methods attempt to identify the set of rotamers that minimize the model's overall energy.

These methods use rotamer libraries, which are collections of favorable conformations for each residue type in proteins. Rotamer libraries may contain information about the conformation, its frequency, and the standard deviations about mean dihedral angles, which can be used in sampling.[25] Rotamer libraries are derived from structural bioinformatics or other statistical analysis of side-chain conformations in known experimental structures of proteins, such as by clustering the observed conformations for tetrahedral carbons near the staggered (60°, 180°, -60°) values.

Rotamer libraries can be backbone-independent, secondary-structure-dependent, or backbone-dependent. Backbone-independent rotamer libraries make no reference to backbone conformation, and are calculated from all available side chains of a certain type (for instance, the first example of a rotamer library, done by Ponder and Richards at Yale in 1987).[26] Secondary-structure-dependent libraries present different dihedral angles and/or rotamer frequencies for α-helix, β-sheet, or coil secondary structures.[27] [28] Backbone-dependent rotamer libraries present conformations and/or frequencies dependent on the local backbone conformation as defined by the backbone dihedral angles ϕ and ψ, regardless of secondary structure.[29]

The modern versions of these libraries as used in most software are presented as multidimensional distributions of probability or frequency, where the peaks correspond to the dihedral-angle conformations considered as individual rotamers in the lists. Some versions are based on very carefully curated data and are used primarily for structure validation,[30] while others emphasize relative frequencies in much larger data sets and are the form used primarily for structure prediction, such as the Dunbrack rotamer libraries.[31]

Side-chain packing methods are most useful for analyzing the protein's hydrophobic core, where side chains are more closely packed; they have more difficulty addressing the looser constraints and higher flexibility of surface residues, which often occupy multiple rotamer conformations rather than just one.[32] [33]

Prediction of structural classes

Statistical methods have been developed for predicting structural classes of proteins based on their amino acid composition,[34] pseudo amino acid composition[35] [36] [37] [38] and functional domain composition.[39]

Quaternary structure

In the case of complexes of two or more proteins, where the structures of the proteins are known or can be predicted with high accuracy, protein–protein docking methods can be used to predict the structure of the complex. Information of the effect of mutations at specific sites on the affinity of the complex helps to understand the complex structure and to guide docking methods.

Software

I-TASSER [40] is the best server for protein structure prediction according to the 2006-2010 CASP experiments [41] (CASP7 [42], CASP8 [43] and CASP9 [44]).

RaptorX excels at aligning hard targets according to the 2010 CASP9 [44] experiments. RaptorX generates the significantly better alignments for the hardest 50 CASP9 template-based modeling targets than other servers including those using consensus and refinement methods. The RaptorX server is available at server [45]

MODELLER is a popular software tool for producing homology models using methodology derived from NMR spectroscopy data processing. SwissModel [42] provides an automated web server for basic homology modeling.

HHpred, bioinfo.pl [46] and Robetta [47] widely used servers for protein structure prediction. HHsearch is a free software package for protein threading and remote homology detection.

SPARKSx [48] is one of the top performing servers in the CASP focused on the remote fold recognition.[49]

PEP-FOLD [50] is a *de novo* approach aimed at predicting peptide structures from amino acid sequences, based on a HMM structural alphabet.[51] [52]

Phyre and Phyre2 are amongst the top performing servers in the CASP international blind trials of structure prediction in homology modelling and remote fold recognition, and are designed with an emphasis on ease of use for non-experts.

RAPTOR (software) is a protein threading software that is based on integer programming. The basic algorithm for threading is described in[24] and is fairly straightforward to implement.

QUARK [53] is an on-line server suitable for *ab initio* protein structure modeling.

Abalone [54] is a Molecular Dynamics program for folding simulations with explicit or implicit water models.

TIP [55] is a knowledgebase of STRUCTFAST[56] models and precomputed similarity relationships between sequences, structures, and binding sites. Several distributed computing projects concerning protein structure prediction have also been implemented, such as the Folding@home, Rosetta@home, Human Proteome Folding Project, Predictor@home, and TANPAKU.

The Foldit program seeks to investigate the pattern-recognition and puzzle-solving abilities inherent to the human mind in order to create more successful computer protein structure prediction software.

Computational approaches provide a fast alternative route to antibody structure prediction. Recently developed antibody F_v region high resolution structure prediction algorithms, like RosettaAntibody [57], have been shown to generate high resolution homology models which have been used for successful docking.[58]

Reviews of software for structure prediction can be found at[59].

Automatic structure prediction servers

CASP, which stands for Critical Assessment of Techniques for Protein Structure Prediction, is a community-wide experiment for protein structure prediction taking place every two years since 1994. CASP provides users and research groups with an opportunity to assess the quality of available methods and automatic servers for protein structure prediction. Official results for automatic structure prediction servers in the CASP7 benchmark (2006) are discussed by Battey *et al.*.[60] Official CASP8 results are available for automatic servers [21] and for human and server predictors [22]. Unofficial results for automatic servers of the 2008 CASP8 benchmark are summarized on several lab websites and ranked according to slightly varying criteria: Zhang lab [61], Grishin lab [24], McGuffin lab [25], Baker lab [62], and Cheng lab [63].

References

[1] Mount DM (2004). *Bioinformatics: Sequence and Genome Analysis*. **2**. Cold Spring Harbor Laboratory Press. ISBN 0879697121.

[2] Guzzo, AV (1965). "Influence of Amino-Acid Sequence on Protein Structure". *Biophys. J.* **5** (6): 809–822. Bibcode 1965BpJ.....5..809G. doi:10.1016/S0006-3495(65)86753-4. PMC 1367904. PMID 5884309.
Prothero, JW (1966). "Correlation between Distribution of Amino Acids and Alpha Helices". *Biophys. J.* **6** (3): 367–370. Bibcode 1966BpJ.....6..367P. doi:10.1016/S0006-3495(66)86662-6. PMC 1367951. PMID 5962284.
Schiffer, M; Edmundson AB (1967). "Use of Helical Wheels to Represent Structures of Proteins and to Identify Segments with Helical Potential". *Biophys. J.* **7** (2): 121–35. Bibcode 1967BpJ.....7..121S. doi:10.1016/S0006-3495(67)86579-2. PMC 1368002. PMID 6048867.
Kotelchuck, D; Scheraga HA (1969). "The Influence of Short-Range Interactions on Protein Conformation, II. A Model for Predicting the α-Helical Regions of Proteins". *Proc Natl Acad Sci USA* **62** (1): 14–21. doi:10.1073/pnas.62.1.14. PMC 285948. PMID 5253650.
Lewis, PN; Gō N, Gō M, Kotelchuck D, Scheraga HA (1970). "Helix Probability Profiles of Denatured Proteins and Their Correlation with Native Structures". *Proc Natl Acad Sci USA* **65** (4): 810–5. doi:10.1073/pnas.65.4.810. PMC 282987. PMID 5266152.

[3] Froimowitz M, Fasman GD (1974). "Prediction of the secondary structure of proteins using the helix-coil transition theory". *Macromolecules* **7** (5): 583–9. doi:10.1021/ma60041a009. PMID 4371089.

[4] Dor O, Zhou Y (2006). "Achieving 80% tenfold cross-validated accuracy for secondary structure prediction by large-scale training". *Proteins* **66** (4): 838–45. doi:10.1002/prot.21298. PMID 17177203.

[5] Chou PY, Fasman GD (1974). "Prediction of protein conformation". *Biochemistry* **13** (2): 222–245. doi:10.1021/bi00699a002. PMID 4358940.

[6] Garnier J, Osguthorpe DJ, Robson B (1978). "Analysis of the accuracy and implications of simple methods for predicting the secondary structure of globular proteins". *J Mol Biol* **120** (1): 97–120. doi:10.1016/0022-2836(78)90297-8. PMID 642007.

[7] Robson B, Pain RH (May 1971). "Analysis of the code relating sequence to conformation in proteins: possible implications for the mechanism of formation of helical regions" (http://linkinghub.elsevier.com/retrieve/pii/0022-2836(71)90243-9). *J. Mol. Biol.* **58** (1): 237–59. doi:10.1016/0022-2836(71)90243-9. PMID 5088928. .

[8]   Robson B (September 1974). "Analysis of code relating sequences to conformation in globular proteins. Theory and application of expected information". *Biochem. J.* **141** (3): 853–67. PMC 1168191. PMID 4463965.

[9]   Pham TH, Satou K, Ho TB (2005). "Support vector machines for prediction and analysis of beta and gamma-turns in proteins". *J Bioinform Comput Biol* **3** (2): 343–358. doi:10.1142/S0219720005001089. PMID 15852509.

[10] Zhang Q, Yoon S, Welsh WJ (2005). "Improved method for predicting beta-turn using support vector machine". *Bioinformatics* **21** (10): 2370–4. doi:10.1093/bioinformatics/bti358. PMID 15797917.

[11] Zimmermann O, Hansmann UH (2006). "Support vector machines for prediction of dihedral angle regions". *Bioinformatics* **22** (24): 3009–15. doi:10.1093/bioinformatics/btl489. PMID 17005536.

[12] Kuang R, Leslie CS, Yang AS (2004). "Protein backbone angle prediction with machine learning approaches". *Bioinformatics* **20** (10): 1612–21. doi:10.1093/bioinformatics/bth136. PMID 14988121.

[13] Zhong L, Johnson WC Jr (1992). "Environment affects amino acid preference for secondary structure". *Proc Natl Acad Sci USA* **89** (10): 4462–5. doi:10.1073/pnas.89.10.4462. PMC 49102. PMID 1584778.

[14] Macdonald JR, Johnson WC Jr (2001). "Environmental features are important in determining protein secondary structure". *Protein Sci.* **10** (6): 1172–7. doi:10.1110/ps.420101. PMC 2374018. PMID 11369855.

[15] Costantini S, Colonna G, Facchiano AM (2006). "Amino acid propensities for secondary structures are influenced by the protein structural class". *Biochem Biophys Res Commun.* **342** (2): 441–451. doi:10.1016/j.bbrc.2006.01.159. PMID 16487481.

[16] Marashi SA, *et al.* (2007). "Adaptation of proteins to different environments: a comparison of proteome structural properties in *Bacillus subtilis* and *Escherichia coli*". *J Theor Biol* **244** (1): 127–132. doi:10.1016/j.jtbi.2006.07.021. PMID 16945389.

[17] Costantini S, Colonna G, Facchiano AM (2007). "PreSSAPro: a software for the prediction of secondary structure by amino acid properties". *Comput Biol Chem* **31** (5-6): 389–392. doi:10.1016/j.compbiolchem.2007.08.010. PMID 17888742.

[18] Momen-Roknabadi A, *et al.* (2008). "Impact of residue accessible surface area on the prediction of protein secondary structures". *BMC Bioinformatics* **9**: 357. doi:10.1186/1471-2105-9-357. PMC 2553345. PMID 18759992.

[19] Adamczak R, Porollo A, Meller J (2005). "Combining prediction of secondary structure and solvent accessibility in proteins". *Proteins* **59** (3): 467–475. doi:10.1002/prot.20441. PMID 15768403.

[20] Lakizadeh A, Marashi SA (2009). "Addition of contact number information can improve protein secondary structure prediction by neural networks" (http://www.excli.de/vol8/lakizadeh_03_2009/lakizadeh_250309a_proof.pdf). *Excli J.* **8**: 66–73. .

[21] Lyngsø RB, Pedersen CN (2000). "RNA pseudoknot prediction in energy-based models". *J Comput Biol* **7** (3-4): 409–427. doi:10.1089/106652700750050862. PMID 11108471.

[22] Zhang Y (2008). "Progress and challenges in protein structure prediction". *Curr Opin Struct Biol* **18** (3): 342–8. doi:10.1016/j.sbi.2008.02.004. PMC 2680823. PMID 18436442.

[23] Zhang Y and Skolnick J (2005). "The protein structure prediction problem could be solved using the current PDB library". *Proc Natl Acad Sci USA* **102** (4): 1029–34. doi:10.1073/pnas.0407152101. PMC 545829. PMID 15653774.

[24] Bowie JU, Luthy R, Eisenberg D (1991). "A method to identify protein sequences that fold into a known three-dimensional structure". *Science* **253** (5016): 164–170. doi:10.1126/science.1853201. PMID 1853201.

[25] Dunbrack, RL (2002). "Rotamer Libraries in the 21st Century". *Curr. Opin. Struct. Biol.* **12** (4): 431–440. doi:10.1016/S0959-440X(02)00344-5. PMID 12163064.

[26] Ponder JW, Richards FM (1987). "Tertiary templates for proteins: use of packing criteria in the enumeration of allowed sequences for different structural classes". *J. Mol. Biol.* **193** (4): 775–791. doi:10.1016/0022-2836(87)90358-5. PMID 2441069.

[27] Lovell SC, Word JM, Richardson JS, Richardson DC (2000). "The penultimate rotamer library". *Proteins: Struc. Func. Genet.* **40**: 389–408. doi:10.1002/1097-0134(20000815)40:3<389::AID-PROT50>3.0.CO;2-2.

[28] Richardson Rotamer Libraries (http://kinemage.biochem.duke.edu/databases/rotamer.php)

[29] Shapovalov MV, Dunbrack, RL (2011). "A smoothed backbone-dependent rotamer library for proteins derived from adaptive kernel density estimates and regressions". *Structure (Cell Press)* **19** (6): 844–858. doi:10.1016/j.str.2011.03.019. PMC PMC3118414. PMID 21645855.

[30] MolProbity (http://molprobity.biochem.duke.edu/)

[31] Dunbrack Rotamer Libraries (http://dunbrack.fccc.edu/bbdep2010)

[32] Voigt CA, Gordon DB, Mayo SL (2000). "Trading accuracy for speed: A quantitative comparison of search algorithms in protein sequence design". *J Mol Biol* **299** (3): 789–803. doi:10.1006/jmbi.2000.3758. PMID 10835284.

[33] Krivov GG, Shapovalov MV, Dunbrack, RL (2009). "Improved prediction of protein side-chain conformations with SCWRL4". *Proteins* **77** (3): 778–795. doi:10.1002/prot.22488. PMC PMC2885146. PMID 19603484.

[34] Chou KC, Zhang CT (1995). "Prediction of protein structural classes". *Crit. Rev. Biochem. Mol. Biol.* **30** (4): 275–349. doi:10.3109/10409239509083488. PMID 7587280.

[35] Chen C, Zhou X, Tian Y, Zou X, Cai P (October 2006). "Predicting protein structural class with pseudo-amino acid composition and support vector machine fusion network". *Anal. Biochem.* **357** (1): 116–21. doi:10.1016/j.ab.2006.07.022. PMID 16920060.

[36] Chen C, Tian YX, Zou XY, Cai PX, Mo JY (December 2006). "Using pseudo-amino acid composition and support vector machine to predict protein structural class". *J. Theor. Biol.* **243** (3): 444–8. doi:10.1016/j.jtbi.2006.06.025. PMID 16908032.

[37] Lin H, Li QZ (July 2007). "Using pseudo amino acid composition to predict protein structural class: approached by incorporating 400 dipeptide components". *J Comput Chem* **28** (9): 1463–6. doi:10.1002/jcc.20554. PMID 17330882.

[38] Xiao X, Wang P, Chou KC (October 2008). "Predicting protein structural classes with pseudo amino acid composition: an approach using geometric moments of cellular automaton image". *J. Theor. Biol.* **254** (3): 691–6. doi:10.1016/j.jtbi.2008.06.016. PMID 18634802.

[39] Chou KC, Cai YD (September 2004). "Predicting protein structural class by functional domain composition". *Biochem. Biophys. Res. Commun.* **321** (4): 1007–9. doi:10.1016/j.bbrc.2004.07.059. PMID 15358128.

[40] http://zhanglab.ccmb.med.umich.edu/I-TASSER

[41] http://predictioncenter.org

[42] http://www.predictioncenter.org/casp7/Casp7.html

[43] http://www.predictioncenter.org/casp8/index.cgi

[44] http://www.predictioncenter.org/casp9

[45] http://raptorx.uchicago.edu

[46] http://meta.bioinfo.pl/submit_wizard.pl

[47] http://robetta.bakerlab.org/

[48] http://sparks.informatics.iupui.edu/yueyang/sparks-x/

[49] Yang, Yuedong; Eshel Faraggi, Huiying Zhao, Yaoqi Zhou (2011). "Improving protein fold recognition and template-based modeling by employing probabilistic-based matching between predicted one-dimensional structural properties of the query and corresponding native properties of templates" (http://bioinformatics.oxfordjournals.org/content/27/15/2076.long). *Bioinformatics* **27**: 2076-82. .

[50] http://bioserv.rpbs.univ-paris-diderot.fr/PEP-FOLD/

[51] Maupetit J, Derreumaux P, Tuffery P (2009). "A fast and accurate method for large-scale de novo peptide structure prediction.". *J Comput Chem.*: In press..

[52] Maupetit J, Derreumaux P, Tuffery P (2009). "PEP-FOLD: an online resource for de novo peptide structure prediction.". *Nucleic Acids Res.* **37** (Web Server issue): W498–503. doi:10.1093/nar/gkp323. PMC 2703897. PMID 19433514.

[53] http://zhanglab.ccmb.med.umich.edu/QUARK

[54] http://www.biomolecular-modeling.com/Abalone/index.html

[55] http://www.eidogen-sertanty.com/products_tip_content.html

[56] Debe DA, Danzer JF, Goddard WA, Poleksic A (2006). "STRUCTFAST: Protein sequence remote homology detection and alignment using novel dynamic programming and profile-profile scoring". *Proteins* **64** (4): 960–7. doi:10.1002/prot.21049. PMID 16786595.

[57] http://antibody.graylab.jhu.edu

[58] Sivasubramanian A, Sircar A, Chaudhury S, Gray J J (2009). "Toward high-resolution homology modeling of antibody Fv regions and application to antibody–antigen docking". *Proteins* **74** (2): 497–514. doi:10.1002/prot.22309. PMC 2909601. PMID 19062174.

[59] Nayeem A, Sitkoff D, Krystek S Jr (2006). "A comparative study of available software for high-accuracy homology modeling: From sequence alignments to structural models". *Protein Sci* **15** (4): 808–824. doi:10.1110/ps.051892906. PMC 2242473. PMID 16600967.

[60] Battey JN, Kopp J, Bordoli L, Read RJ, Clarke ND, Schwede T (2007). "Automated server predictions in CASP7". *Proteins* **69** (Suppl 8): 68–82. doi:10.1002/prot.21761. PMID 17894354.

[61] http://zhang.bioinformatics.ku.edu/casp8/index.html

[62] http://robetta.bakerlab.org/CASP8_eval_domains/

[63] http://sysbio.rnet.missouri.edu/casp8_eva/

Samudrala R, Moult J (February 1998). "An all-atom distance-dependent conditional probability discriminatory function for protein structure prediction" (http://linkinghub.elsevier.com/retrieve/pii/S0022-2836(97)91479-0). *J. Mol. Biol.* **275** (5): 895–916. doi:10.1006/jmbi.1997.1479. PMID 9480776.

External links

- NetSurfP — Secondary Structure and Surface Accessibility predictor (http://www.cbs.dtu.dk/services/NetSurfP/)
- CASP experiments home page (http://predictioncenter.org/)
- Structure Prediction Flowchart (http://www.russell.embl-heidelberg.de/gtsp/flowchart2.html) (a clickable map)
- ExPASy Proteomics tools (http://www.expasy.ch/tools/) — list of prediction tools and servers
- DomPred (http://bioinf.cs.ucl.ac.uk/dompred/) — London's Global University
- DOMpro (http://www.ics.uci.edu/~baldig/dompro.html) — University of California Irvine
- DomainSplit (http://structure.pitt.edu/servers/domainsplit/) — University of Pittsburgh
- Meta-DP (http://meta-dp.cse.buffalo.edu/) — University at Buffalo
- DOMAC (http://www.bioinfotool.org/domac.html) — University of Missouri Columbia
- PredictProtein (http://www.predictprotein.org/)
- Protinfo (http://protinfo.compbio.washington.edu) — comparative and de novo protein structure and complex modelling server

- SCRATCH (http://scratch.proteomics.ics.uci.edu/) Protein structure prediction suite that includes SSpro

Protein subcellular localization prediction

Protein subcellular localization prediction involves the computational prediction of where a protein resides in a cell. Prediction of protein subcellular localization is an important component of bioinformatics-based prediction of protein function and genome annotation, and it can aid the identification of drug targets.

Most eukaryotic proteins are encoded in the nuclear genome and synthesized in the cytosol, but many need to be further sorted before they reach their final destination. For prokaryotes, proteins are synthesized in the cytoplasm and some must be targeted to other locations such as to a cell membrane or the extracellular environment. Proteins must be localized at their appropriate subcellular compartment to perform their desired function.

Experimentally determining the subcellular localization of a protein is a laborious and time consuming task. Through the development of new approaches in computer science, coupled with an increased dataset of proteins of known localization, computational tools can now provide fast and accurate localization predictions for many organisms. This has resulted in subcellular localization prediction becoming one of the challenges being successfully aided by bioinformatics. Many protein subcellular localization prediction methods now exceed the accuracy of some high-throughput laboratory methods for the identification of protein subcellular localization.[1]

Particularly, some predictors developed recently[2] can be used to deal with proteins that may simultaneously exist, or move between, two or more different subcellular locations.

Methods

Several computational tools for predicting the subcellular localization of a protein are publicly available, a few of which are listed below. The development of protein subcellular location prediction has been summarized in two comprehensive review articles. [3] [4]

Also, the predictors were specialized for proteins in different organisms. Some was specialized for eukaryotic proteins, [5] some for human proteins,[6] and some for plant proteins.[7] Methods for the prediction of bacterial localization predictors, and their accuracy, have been recently reviewed.[8]

- Cell-PLoc [9]: A package of web-servers for predicting subcellular localization of proteins in various organisms.[2]
- BaCelLo [10]: Prediction of eukaryotic protein subcellular localization. Unlike other methods, the predictions are balanced among different classes and all the localizations that are predicted are considered as equiprobable, to avoid mispredictions.[11]
- CELLO [12]: CELLO uses a two-level Support Vector Machine system to assign localizations to both prokaryotic and eukaryotic proteins.[13] [14]
- Euk-mPLoc 2.0 [15]: Predicting the subcellular localization of eukaryotic proteins with both single and multiple sites.[16]
- CoBaltDB [17]: CoBaltDB is a novel powerful platform that provides easy access to the results of multiple localization tools and support for predicting prokaryotic protein localizations.[18]
- HSLpred [19]: This method allow to predict subcellular localization of human proteins. This method combines power of composition based SVM models and similarity search techniques PSI-BLAST.[20]
- LOCtree [21]: Prediction based on mimicking the cellular sorting mechanism using a hierarchical implementation of support vector machines. LOCtree is a comprehensive predictor incorporating predictions based on PROSITE/PFAM signatures as well as SwissProt keywords.[22]
- MultiLoc [23]: An SVM-based prediction engine for a wide range of subcellular locations.[24]
- PSORT [25]: The first widely used method for protein subcellular localization prediction, developed under the leadership of Kenta Nakai.[26] Now researchers are also encouraged to use other PSORT programs such as WoLF

PSORT and PSORTb for making predictions for certain types of organisms (see below). PSORT prediction performances are lower than those of recently developed predictors.

- PSORTb [27]: Prediction of bacterial protein localization.[28] [29]
- PredictNLS [30]: Prediction of nuclear localization signals.[31]
- Proteome Analyst [32]: Prediction of protein localization for both prokaryotes and eukaryotes using a text mining approach.[33]
- SecretomeP [34]: Prediction of eukaryotic proteins that are secreted via a non-traditional secretory mechanism.[35]
- SherLoc [36]: An SVM-based predictor combining MultiLoc with text-based features derived from PubMed abstracts.[37]
- TargetP [38]: Prediction of N-terminal sorting signals.[39]
- WoLF PSORT [40]: An updated version of PSORT/PSORT II for the prediction of eukaryotic sequences.[41]

Application

Determining subcellular localization is important for understanding protein function and is a critical step in genome annotation.

Knowledge of the subcellular localization of a protein can significantly improve target identification during the drug discovery process. For example, secreted proteins and plasma membrane proteins are easily accessible by drug molecules due to their localization in the extracellular space or on the cell surface.

Bacterial cell surface and secreted proteins are also of interest for their potential as vaccine candidates or as diagnostic targets.

Aberrant subcellular localization of proteins has been observed in the cells of several diseases, such as cancer and Alzheimer's disease.

Secreted proteins from some archaea that can survive in unusual environments have industrially important applications.

References

[1] Rey S, Gardy JL, Brinkman FS (2005). "Assessing the precision of high-throughput computational and laboratory approaches for the genome-wide identification of protein subcellular localization in bacteria". BMC Genomics 6: 162. doi:10.1186/1471-2164-6-162. PMC 1314894. PMID 16288665.
[2] Chou KC, Shen HB (2008). "Cell-PLoc: a package of Web servers for predicting subcellular localization of proteins in various organisms (updated version: Cell-PLoc 2.0: An improved package of web-servers for predicting subcellular localization of proteins in various organisms, Natural Science, 2010, 2, 1090-1103)". Nat Protoc 3 (2): 153–62. doi:10.1038/nprot.2007.494. PMID 18274516.
[3] Nakai, K. Protein sorting signals and prediction of subcellular localization. Adv. Protein Chem., 2000, 54, 277-344.
[4] Chou, K. C.; Shen, H. B. Review: Recent progresses in protein subcellular location prediction. Anal. Biochem., 2007, 370, 1-16.
[5] Chou, K. C.; Wu, Z. C.; Xiao, X. iLoc-Euk: A Multi-Label Classifier for Predicting the Subcellular Localization of Singleplex and Multiplex Eukaryotic Proteins, PLoS One, 2011, 6, e18258.
[6] Shen HB, Chou KC (November 2009). "A top-down approach to enhance the power of predicting human protein subcellular localization: Hum-mPLoc 2.0". Anal. Biochem. 394 (2): 269–74. doi:10.1016/j.ab.2009.07.046. PMID 19651102.
[7] Chou KC, Shen HB (2010). "Plant-mPLoc: a top-down strategy to augment the power for predicting plant protein subcellular localization". PLoS ONE 5 (6): e11335. doi:10.1371/journal.pone.0011335. PMC 2893129. PMID 20596258.
[8] Gardy JL, Brinkman FS (October 2006). "Methods for predicting bacterial protein subcellular localization". Nat. Rev. Microbiol. 4 (10): 741–51. doi:10.1038/nrmicro1494. PMID 16964270.
[9] http://www.csbio.sjtu.edu.cn/bioinf/Cell-PLoc/
[10] http://gpcr.biocomp.unibo.it/bacello/
[11] Pierleoni A, Martelli PL, Fariselli P, Casadio R (July 2006). "BaCelLo: a balanced subcellular localization predictor". Bioinformatics 22 (14): e408–16. doi:10.1093/bioinformatics/btl222. PMID 16873501.
[12] http://cello.life.nctu.edu.tw/
[13] Yu CS, Lin CJ, Hwang JK (May 2004). "Predicting subcellular localization of proteins for Gram-negative bacteria by support vector machines based on n-peptide compositions". Protein Sci. 13 (5): 1402–6. doi:10.1110/ps.03479604. PMC 2286765. PMID 15096640.

[14] Yu CS, Chen YC, Lu CH, Hwang JK (August 2006). "Prediction of protein subcellular localization". *Proteins* **64** (3): 643–51.
doi:10.1002/prot.21018. PMID 16752418.

[15] http://www.csbio.sjtu.edu.cn/bioinf/euk-multi-2/

[16] Chou KC, Shen HB (2010). "A new method for predicting the subcellular localization of eukaryotic proteins with both single and multiple
sites: Euk-mPLoc 2.0". *PLoS ONE* **5** (4): e9931. doi:10.1371/journal.pone.0009931. PMC 2848569. PMID 20368981.

[17] http://www.umr6026.univ-rennes1.fr/english/home/research/basic/software/cobalten

[18] Goudenège D, Avner S, Lucchetti-Miganeh C, Barloy-Hubler F (2010). "CoBaltDB: Complete bacterial and archaeal orfeomes subcellular
localization database and associated resources". *BMC Microbiol.* **10**: 88. doi:10.1186/1471-2180-10-88. PMC 2850352. PMID 20331850.

[19] http://www.imtech.res.in/raghava/hslpred/

[20] Garg A, Bhasin M, Raghava GP (April 2005). "Support vector machine-based method for subcellular localization of human proteins using
amino acid compositions, their order, and similarity search". *J. Biol. Chem.* **280** (15): 14427–32. doi:10.1074/jbc.M411789200.
PMID 15647269.

[21] http://rostlab.org/services/LOCtree/

[22] Nair R, Rost B (April 2005). "Mimicking cellular sorting improves prediction of subcellular localization". *J. Mol. Biol.* **348** (1): 85–100.
doi:10.1016/j.jmb.2005.02.025. PMID 15808855.

[23] http://www-bs.informatik.uni-tuebingen.de/Services/MultiLoc

[24] Höglund A, Dönnes P, Blum T, Adolph HW, Kohlbacher O (May 2006). "MultiLoc: prediction of protein subcellular localization using
N-terminal targeting sequences, sequence motifs and amino acid composition". *Bioinformatics* **22** (10): 1158–65.
doi:10.1093/bioinformatics/btl002. PMID 16428265.

[25] http://psort.nibb.ac.jp/

[26] Nakai K, Kanehisa M (1991). "Expert system for predicting protein localization sites in gram-negative bacteria". *Proteins* **11** (2): 95–110.
doi:10.1002/prot.340110203. PMID 1946347.

[27] http://www.psort.org/psortb/

[28] Gardy JL, Spencer C, Wang K, Ester M, Tusnády GE, Simon I, Hua S, deFays K, Lambert C, Nakai K, Brinkman FS (July 2003).
"PSORT-B: Improving protein subcellular localization prediction for Gram-negative bacteria". *Nucleic Acids Res.* **31** (13): 3613–7.
doi:10.1093/nar/gkg602. PMC 169008. PMID 12824378.

[29] Gardy JL, Laird MR, Chen F, Rey S, Walsh CJ, Ester M, Brinkman FS (March 2005). "PSORTb v.2.0: expanded prediction of bacterial
protein subcellular localization and insights gained from comparative proteome analysis". *Bioinformatics* **21** (5): 617–23.
doi:10.1093/bioinformatics/bti057. PMID 15501914.

[30] http://rostlab.org/predictNLS/

[31] Nair R, Carter P, Rost B (January 2003). "NLSdb: database of nuclear localization signals". *Nucleic Acids Res.* **31** (1): 397–9.
doi:10.1093/nar/gkg001. PMC 165448. PMID 12520032.

[32] http://www.cs.ualberta.ca/%7Ebioinfo/PA/Sub/index.html

[33] Lu Z, Szafron D, Greiner R, Lu P, Wishart DS, Poulin B, Anvik J, Macdonell C, Eisner R (March 2004). "Predicting subcellular localization
of proteins using machine-learned classifiers". *Bioinformatics* **20** (4): 547–56. doi:10.1093/bioinformatics/bth026. PMID 14990451.

[34] http://www.cbs.dtu.dk/services/SecretomeP

[35] Bendtsen JD, Jensen LJ, Blom N, Von Heijne G, Brunak S (April 2004). "Feature-based prediction of non-classical and leaderless protein
secretion". *Protein Eng. Des. Sel.* **17** (4): 349–56. doi:10.1093/protein/gzh037. PMID 15115854.

[36] http://www-bs.informatik.uni-tuebingen.de/Services/SherLoc

[37] Shatkay H, Höglund A, Brady S, Blum T, Dönnes P, Kohlbacher O (June 2007). "SherLoc: high-accuracy prediction of protein subcellular
localization by integrating text and protein sequence data". *Bioinformatics* **23** (11): 1410–7. doi:10.1093/bioinformatics/btm115.
PMID 17392328.

[38] http://www.cbs.dtu.dk/services/TargetP/

[39] Emanuelsson O, Nielsen H, Brunak S, von Heijne G (July 2000). "Predicting subcellular localization of proteins based on their N-terminal
amino acid sequence". *J. Mol. Biol.* **300** (4): 1005–16. doi:10.1006/jmbi.2000.3903. PMID 10891285.

[40] http://wolfpsort.org/

[41] Horton P, Park KJ, Obayashi T, Fujita N, Harada H, Adams-Collier CJ, Nakai K (July 2007). "WoLF PSORT: protein localization
predictor". *Nucleic Acids Res.* **35** (Web Server issue): W585–7. doi:10.1093/nar/gkm259. PMC 1933216. PMID 17517783.

Further reading

- Bork P, Dandekar T, Diaz-Lazcoz Y, Eisenhaber F, Huynen M, Yuan Y (November 1998). "Predicting function: from genes to genomes and back". *J. Mol. Biol.* **283** (4): 707–25. doi:10.1006/jmbi.1998.2144. PMID 9790834.
- Nakai K (2000). "Protein sorting signals and prediction of subcellular localization". *Adv. Protein Chem.* **54**: 277–344. PMID 10829231.
- Emanuelsson O (December 2002). "Predicting protein subcellular localisation from amino acid sequence information". *Brief. Bioinformatics* **3** (4): 361–76. PMID 12511065.
- Schneider G, Fechner U (June 2004). "Advances in the prediction of protein targeting signals". *Proteomics* **4** (6): 1571–80. doi:10.1002/pmic.200300786. PMID 15174127.
- Gardy JL, Brinkman FS (October 2006). "Methods for predicting bacterial protein subcellular localization". *Nat. Rev. Microbiol.* **4** (10): 741–51. doi:10.1038/nrmicro1494. PMID 16964270.
- Chou KC, Shen HB (November 2007). "Recent progress in protein subcellular location prediction". *Anal. Biochem.* **370** (1): 1–16. doi:10.1016/j.ab.2007.07.006. PMID 17698024.

External links

- Cell Centered Database - Protein subcellular localization data (http://ccdb.ucsd.edu/sand/main?typeid=2&event=showMPByType&start=1)
- Cell-PLoc 2.0 (http://www.csbio.sjtu.edu.cn/bioinf/Cell-PLoc-2/) - A recently updated version of Cell-PLoc
- BaCelLo (http://gpcr.biocomp.unibo.it/) - Balanced subCellular Localization predictor
- CELLO (http://cello.life.nctu.edu.tw/) - subCELlular LOcalization predictor for prokaryotes and eukaryotes
- CoBaltDB (http://www.umr6026.univ-rennes1.fr/english/home/research/basic/software/cobalten) - Complete bacterial and archaeal orfeomes subcellular localization database and associated resources
- LOCtree (http://rostlab.org/services/LOCtree/) - prediction webserver for prokaryotes and eukaryotes]:
- MultiLoc (http://www-bs.informatik.uni-tuebingen.de/Services/MultiLoc) - MultiLoc prediction webserver
- Protein Analysis Subcellular Localization Prediction
- PSORT.org (http://www.psort.org/) - A portal for protein subcellular localization predictors
- SherLoc (http://www-bs.informatik.uni-tuebingen.de/Services/SherLoc) - SherLoc prediction webserver

Protein-DNA interaction

Protein–DNA interactions are when a protein binds a molecule of DNA, often to regulate the biological function of DNA, usually the expression of a gene. Among the proteins that bind to DNA are transcription factors that activate or repress gene expression by binding to DNA motifs and histones that form part of the structure of DNA and bind to it less specifically.

In general, proteins bind to DNA in the major groove, however there are exceptions.[1]

References

[1] Bewley CA, Gronenborn AM, Clore GM (1998). "Minor groove-binding architectural proteins: structure, function, and DNA recognition". *Annu Rev Biophys Biomol Struct* **27**: 105–31. doi:10.1146/annurev.biophys.27.1.105. PMID 9646864.

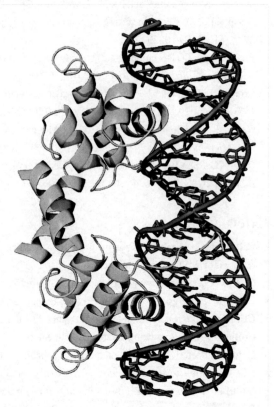

The lambda repressor protein interacting with the lambda operator DNA.

Protein–protein interaction

Protein–protein interactions occur when two or more proteins bind together, often to carry out their biological function. Many of the most important molecular processes in the cell such as DNA replication are carried out by large molecular machines that are built from a large number of protein components organised by their protein–protein interactions. Protein interactions have been studied from the perspectives of biochemistry, quantum chemistry, molecular dynamics, chemical biology, signal transduction and other metabolic or genetic/epigenetic networks. Indeed, protein–protein interactions are at the core of the entire interactomics system of any living cell.

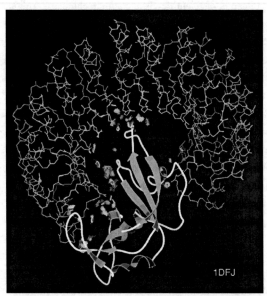

The horseshoe shaped ribonuclease inhibitor (shown as wireframe) forms a protein–protein interaction with the ribonuclease protein. The contacts between the two proteins are shown as coloured patches.

Interactions between proteins are important for the majority of biological functions. For example, signals from the exterior of a cell are mediated to the inside of that cell by protein–protein interactions of the signaling molecules. This process, called signal transduction, plays a fundamental role in many biological processes and in many diseases (e.g. cancers). Proteins might interact for a long time to form part of a protein complex, a protein may be carrying another protein (for example, from cytoplasm to nucleus or vice versa in the case of the nuclear pore importins), or a protein may interact briefly with another protein just to modify it (for example, a protein kinase will add a phosphate to a target protein). This modification of proteins can itself change protein–protein interactions. For example, some proteins with SH2 domains only bind to other proteins when they are phosphorylated on the amino acid tyrosine while bromodomains specifically recognise acetylated lysines. In conclusion, protein–protein interactions are of central importance for virtually every process in a living cell. Information about these interactions improves our understanding of diseases and can provide the basis for new therapeutic approaches.

Methods to investigate protein–protein interactions

As protein–protein interactions are so important there are a multitude of methods to detect them. Each of the approaches has its own strengths and weaknesses, especially with regard to the sensitivity and specificity of the method. A high sensitivity means that many of the interactions that occur in reality are detected by the screen. A high specificity indicates that most of the interactions detected by the screen are also occurring in reality. Methods such as yeast two-hybrid screening can be used to detect novel protein–protein interactions. There are also many biophysical methods for investigating the nature and properties of interactions. At the theoretical level, large scale experimental data on interactions is often modelled by graph theoretic methods.[1]

Visualization of networks

Visualization of protein–protein interaction networks is a popular application of scientific visualization techniques. Although protein interaction diagrams are common in textbooks, diagrams of whole cell protein interaction networks were not as common since the level of complexity made them difficult to generate. One example of a manually produced molecular interaction map is Kurt Kohn's 1999 map of cell cycle control.[2] Drawing on Kohn's map, in 2000 Schwikowski, Uetz, and Fields published a paper on protein–protein interactions in yeast, linking together 1,548 interacting proteins determined by two-hybrid testing. They used a layered graph drawing method to find an initial placement of the nodes and then improved the layout using a force-based algorithm.[3] [4] [5] The Cytoscape software is a widely used application to visualise protein-protein interaction networks.

Network visualisation of the human interactome where each point represents a protein and each blue line between them is an interaction.

Database collections

Methods for identifying interacting proteins have defined hundreds of thousands of interactions. These interactions are collected together in specialised biological databases that allow the interactions to be assembled and studied further. The first of these databases was DIP, the database of interacting proteins.[6] Since that time a large number of further database collections have been created such as BioGRID and STRING.

References

[1] Mashaghi A et al. Investigation of a protein complex network EUROPEAN PHYSICAL JOURNAL B 41(1) 113–121 (2004)

[2] Kurt W. Kohn (August 1, 1999). "Molecular Interaction Map of the Mammalian Cell Cycle Control and DNA Repair Systems". *Molecular Biology of the Cell* **10** (8): 2703–2734. PMC 25504. PMID 10436023.

[3] Benno Schwikowski1, Peter Uetz, and Stanley Fields (2000). "A network of protein–protein interactions in yeast" (http://www.nature.com/nbt/journal/v18/n12/full/nbt1200_1257.html). *Nature Biotechnology* **18** (12): 1257–1261. doi:10.1038/82360. PMID 11101803. .

[4] Rigaut G, Shevchenko A, Rutz B, Wilm M, Mann M, Seraphin B (1999) A generic protein purification method for protein complex characterization and proteome exploration. Nat Biotechnol. 17:1030-2. Rigaut, G; Shevchenko, A; Rutz, B; Wilm, M; Mann, M; Séraphin, B (1999). "A generic protein purification method for protein complex characterization and proteome exploration.". *Nature biotechnology* **17** (10): 1030–2. doi:10.1038/13732. PMID 10504710.

[5] Prieto C, De Las Rivas J (2006). APID: Agile Protein Interaction DataAnalyzer. Nucleic Acids Res. 34:W298-302. Prieto, C; De Las Rivas, J (2006). "APID: Agile Protein Interaction DataAnalyzer.". *Nucleic Acids Research* **34** (Web Server issue): W298–302. doi:10.1093/nar/gkl128. PMC 1538863. PMID 16845013.

[6] Xenarios I, Rice DW, Salwinski L, Baron MK, Marcotte EM, Eisenberg D (January 2000). "DIP: the database of interacting proteins". *Nucleic Acids Res.* **28** (1): 289–91. doi:10.1093/nar/28.1.289. PMC 102387. PMID 10592249.

Further reading

1. De Las Rivas J, Fontanillo C (2010). Lewitter, Fran. ed. "Protein-protein interactions essentials: key concepts to building and analyzing interactome networks". *PLoS Comput Biol* **6** (6): e1000807. doi:10.1371/journal.pcbi.1000807. PMC 2891586. PMID 20589078.

2. Phizicky EM, Fields S (1995). "Protein-protein interactions: methods for detection and analysis". *Microbiol. Rev.*: 94–123. PMC 239356. PMID 7708014.

External links

- Proteins and Enzymes (http://www.dmoz.org/Science/Biology/Biochemistry_and_Molecular_Biology/ Biomolecules/Proteins_and_Enzymes/) at the Open Directory Project

Protein–protein interaction prediction

Protein–protein interaction prediction is a field combining bioinformatics and structural biology in an attempt to identify and catalog physical interactions between pairs or groups of proteins. Understanding protein–protein interactions is important for the investigation of intracellular signaling pathways, modelling of protein complex structures and for gaining insights into various biochemical processes. Experimentally, physical interactions between pairs of proteins can be inferred from a variety of experimental techniques, including yeast two-hybrid systems, protein-fragment complementation assays (PCA), affinity purification/mass spectrometry, protein microarrays, fluorescence resonance energy transfer (FRET), and Microscale Thermophoresis (MST). Efforts to experimentally determine the interactome of numerous species are ongoing, and a number of computational methods for interaction prediction have been developed in recent years.

Methods

Proteins that interact are more likely to co-evolve,[DandekarEnrightMarcottePazos] therefore, it is possible to make inferences about interactions between pairs of proteins based on their phylogenetic distances. It has also been observed in some cases that pairs of interacting proteins have fused orthologues in other organisms. In addition, a number of bound protein complexes have been structurally solved and can be used to identify the residues that mediate the interaction so that similar motifs can be located in other organisms.

Phylogenetic profiling

Phylogenetic profiling[Pellegrini] finds pairs of protein families with similar patterns of presence or absence across large numbers of species. This method identifies pairs likely to act in the same biological process, but does not necessarily imply physical interaction.

Prediction of co-evolved protein pairs based on similar phylogenetic trees

This method[Tan] involves using a sequence search tool such as BLAST for finding homologues of a pair of proteins, then building multiple sequence alignments with alignment tools such as Clustal. From these multiple sequence alignments, phylogenetic distance matrices are calculated for each protein in the hypothesized interacting pair. If the matrices are sufficiently similar (as measured by their Pearson correlation coefficient) they are deemed likely to interact.

Identification of homologous interacting pairs

This method[Aloy] consists of searching whether the two sequences have homologues which form a complex in a database of known structures of complexes. The identification of the domains is done by sequence searches against domain databases such as Pfam using BLAST. If more than one complex of Pfam domains is identified, then the query sequences are aligned using a hidden Markov tool called HMMER to the closest identified homologues, whose structures are known. Then the alignments are analysed to check whether the contact residues of the known complex are conserved in the alignment.

Identification of structural patterns

This method[AytunaOgmen] builds a library of known protein–protein interfaces from the PDB, where the interfaces are defined as pairs of polypeptide fragments that are below a threshold slightly larger than the Van der Waals radius of the atoms involved. The sequences in the library are then clustered based on structural alignment and redundant sequences are eliminated. The residues that have a high (generally >50%) level of frequency for a given position are considered hotspots.[Keskin] This library is then used to identify potential interactions between pairs of targets, providing that they have a known structure (i.e. present in the PDB).

Bayesian network modelling

Bayesian methods[Jansen] integrate data from a wide variety of sources, including both experimental results and prior computational predictions, and use these features to assess the likelihood that a particular potential protein interaction is a true positive result. These methods are useful because experimental procedures, particularly the yeast two-hybrid experiments, are extremely noisy and produce many false positives, while the previously mentioned computational methods can only provide circumstantial evidence that a particular pair of proteins might interact.

3D template-based protein complex modelling

This method[AloyChenFukuharaKittichotirat] makes use of known protein complex structures to predict as well as structurally model interactions between query protein sequences. The prediction process generally starts by employing a sequence based method (e.g Interolog) to search for protein complex structures that are homologous to the query sequences. These known complex structures are then used as templates to structurally model the interaction between query sequences. This method has the advantage of not only inferring protein interactions but also suggests models of how proteins interact structurally, which can provide some insights into the atomic level mechanism of that interaction. On the other hand, the ability for this method to makes a prediction is limited to a relatively small number of known protein complex structures.

Supervised learning problem

The problem of PPI prediction can be framed as a supervised learning problem. In this paradigm the known protein interactions supervise the estimation of a function that can predict whether an interaction exists or not between two proteins given data about the proteins (e.g., expression levels of each gene in different experimental conditions, location information, phylogenetic profile, etc.).

Relationship to docking methods

The field of protein–protein interaction prediction is closely related to the field of protein–protein docking, which attempts to use geometric and steric considerations to fit two proteins of known structure into a bound complex. This is a useful mode of inquiry in cases where both proteins in the pair have known structures and are known (or at least strongly suspected) to interact, but since so many proteins do not have experimentally determined structures, sequence-based interaction prediction methods are especially useful in conjunction with experimental studies of an organism's interactome.

Servers

- 3D-Partner [1]
- APID [10]
- APID2NET [2]
- cons-PPISP [3]
- FastContact
- GeneMANIA [4]
- HOMCOS [5]
- Human Protein-Protein Interaction Prediction (PIPs) [6]
- InterPreTS [7]
- InterProSurf [8]
- metaPPI (combining the power of cons-PPISP, PINUP, Promate, SPPIDER and PPI_PRED [9]
- PatchDock [10]
- PIP [11]
- PRISM [12]
- Protinfo PPC [8]
- SCOPPI [13]
- SPPIDER [14]
- STRING [15]
- [[ProtCID [2]]: the Protein Common Interface Database]
- VORFFIP [16]

References

1. Dandekar T., Snel B.,Huynen M. and Bork P. (1998) "Conservation of gene order: a fingerprint of proteins that physically interact." *Trends Biochem. Sci.* (23),324-328

2. Enright A.J.,Iliopoulos I.,Kyripides N.C. and Ouzounis C.A. (1999) "Protein interaction maps for complete genomes based on gene fusion events." *Nature* (402), 86-90

3. Marcotte E.M., Pellegrini M., Ng H.L., Rice D.W., Yeates T.O., Eisenberg D. (1999) "Detecting protein function and protein-protein interactions from genome sequences." *Science* (285), 751-753

4. Pazos F., Valencia A. (2001). "Similarity of phylogenetic trees as indicator of protein-protein interaction." *Protein Engineering*, 9 (14), 609-614

5. Pellegrini M, Marcotte EM, Thompson MJ, Eisenberg D, Yeates TO. (1999) "Assigning protein functions by comparative genome analysis: protein phylogenetic profiles." *Proc Natl Acad Sci U S A.*, **96**, 4285-8

6. Tan S.H., Zhang Z., Ng S.K. (2004) "ADVICE: Automated Detection and Validation of Interaction by Co-Evolution." *Nucl. Ac. Res.*, **32** (Web Server issue):W69-72.

7. Aloy P.,Russell R.B. "InterPreTS: Protein Interaction Prediction through Tertiary Structure." *Bioinformatics*, **19** (1), 161-162

8. Aytuna A. S., Keskin O., Gursoy A. (2005) "Prediction of protein-protein interactions by combining structure and sequence conservation in protein interfaces." *Bioinformatics*, **21** (12), 2850-2855

9. Ogmen U., Keskin O., Aytuna A.S., Nussinov R. and Gursoy A. (2005) "PRISM: protein interactions by structural matching." *Nucl. Ac. Res.*,**33** (Web Server issue):W331-336

10. Keskin O., Ma B. and Nussinov R. (2004) "Hot regions int protein-protein interactions: The organization and contribution of structurally conserved hot spot residues" *J. Mol. Biol.*, (345),1281-1294

11. Jansen R, Yu H, Greenbaum D, Kluger Y, Krogan NJ, Chung S, Emili A, Snyder M, Greenblatt JF, Gerstein M. (2003) A Bayesian networks approach for predicting protein-protein interactions from genomic data." *Science*, 302(5644):449-53.

12. Aloy P., and R. B. Russell. (2003) "InterPreTS: protein Interaction Prediction through Tertiary Structure". *Bioinformatics*, **19** (1), 161-162.

13. Chen YC, YS Lo, WC Hsu, and JM Yang. (2007). "3D-partner: a web server to infer interacting partners and binding models". *Nucleic Acids Research*, **35** (Web Server issue): 561-7.

14. Fukuhara, Naoshi, and Takeshi Kawabata. (2008) "HOMCOS: a server to predict interacting protein pairs and interacting sites by homology modeling of complex structures" *Nucleic Acids Research*, **36** (S2): 185-.

15. Kittichotirat W, M Guerquin, RE Bumgarner, and R Samudrala (2009) "Protinfo PPC: a web server for atomic level prediction of protein complexes" *Nucleic Acids Research*, **37** (Web Server issue): 519-25.

References

[1] http://3d-partner.life.nctu.edu.tw/vers-pub/index.php
[2] http://bioinfow.dep.usal.es/apid/apid2net.html
[3] http://pipe.scs.fsu.edu/
[4] http://www.genemania.org
[5] http://biunit.naist.jp/homcos/
[6] http://www.compbio.dundee.ac.uk/www-pips
[7] http://www.russell.embl.de/interprets
[8] http://curie.utmb.edu/prosurf.html
[9] http://scoppi.biotec.tu-dresden.de/metappi/
[10] http://bioinfo3d.cs.tau.ac.il/PatchDock/
[11] http://bmm.cancerresearchuk.org/~pip/
[12] http://gordion.hpc.eng.ku.edu.tr/prism
[13] http://www.scoppi.org
[14] http://sppider.cchmc.org
[15] http://string-db.org
[16] http://www.bioinsilico.org/cgi-bin/VORFFIP/htmlVORFFI/home

Protein–protein interaction screening

The **screening of protein–protein interactions** refers to the identification of protein interactions with high-throughput screening methods such as computer- and/or robot-assisted plate reading, flow cytometry analyzing.

The interactions between proteins are central to virtually every process in a living cell. Information about these interactions improves understanding of diseases and can provide the basis for new therapeutic approaches.

Methods to screen protein–protein interactions

Though there are many methods to detect protein–protein interactions, the majority of these methods—such as Co-immunoprecipitation, Fluorescence resonance energy transfer (FRET) and dual polarisation interferometry—are not screening approaches.

Ex vivo or *in vivo* **methods**

Methods that screen protein–protein interactions in the living cells.

- Bimolecular Fluorescence Complementation (BiFC) is a new technique for observing the interactions of proteins. Combining it with other new techniques DERB can enable the screening of protein–protein interactions and their modulators.[1]

- The yeast two-hybrid screen investigates the interaction between artificial fusion proteins inside the nucleus of yeast. This approach can identify the binding partners of a protein without bias. However, the method has a notoriously high false-positive rate, which makes it necessary to verify the identified interactions by co-immunoprecipitation.[2]

In-vitro **methods**

- The Tandem affinity purification (TAP) method allows the high-throughput identification of proteins interactions. In contrast with the Y2H approach, the accuracy of the method can be compared to those of small-scale experiments (Collins et al., 2007) and the interactions are detected within the correct cellular environment as by co-immunoprecipitation. However, the TAP tag method requires two successive steps of protein purification, and thus can not readily detect transient protein–protein interactions. Recent genome-wide TAP experiments were performed by Krogan et al., 2006 and Gavin et al., 2006, providing updated protein interaction data for yeast organisms.

- Chemical crosslinking is often used to "fix" protein interactions in place before trying to isolate/identify interacting proteins. Common crosslinkers for this application include the non-cleavable [NHS-ester] crosslinker, [*bis*-sulfosuccinimidyl suberate] (BS3); a cleavable version of BS3, [dithiobis(sulfosuccinimidyl propionate)](DTSSP); and the [imidoester] crosslinker [dimethyl dithiobispropionimidate] (DTBP) that is popular for fixing interactions in ChIP assays.[3]

References

[1] Lu JP, Beatty LK, Pinthus JH (2008). "Dual expression recombinase based (DERB) single vector system for high throughput screening and verification of protein interactions in living cells". *Nature Precedings*. doi:10101/npre.2008.1550.2.

[2] Fields S (2005). "High-throughput two-hybrid analysis: The promise and the peril". *FEBS Journal* **272** (21): 5391–5399. doi:10.1111/j.1742-4658.2005.04973.x. PMID 16262681.

[3] Chen CS, Zhu H (2006). "Protein microarrays". *Biotechniques* **40** (4): 423, 425, 427. doi:10.2144/06404TE01. PMID 16629388.

External links

Protein–protein interaction databases

- HPRD Human Protein Reference Database (http://hprd.org), a (manually) curated database of human protein information with visualization tools
- IntAct Interaction Database (http://www.ebi.ac.uk/intact), a public repository for manually curated molecular interaction data from the literature
- DIP Database of Interacting Proteins (http://dip.doe-mbi.ucla.edu/), a manual and automatic catalog of experimentally determined interactions between proteins
- MINT Molecular INTeraction Database (http://mint.bio.uniroma2.it/mint/), a tool that focuses on experimentally verified protein interactions mined from the literature by curators
- MIPS Mammalian Protein–Protein Interaction Database (http://mips.gsf.de/proj/ppi/), the MIPS mammalian protein–protein interaction database
- BioGRID (http://www.thebiogrid.org/)

Proteogenomics

Proteogenomics is an emerging field of biological research at the intersection of proteomics and genomics. While this intersection is large and can be defined in multiple ways, the term proteogenomics commonly refers to studies that use proteomic information, often derived from mass spectrometry, to improve gene annotations. [1] [2]

Practical applications

Proteogenomics has been applied to improve the gene annotations of various organisms. The term proteogenomics was first used in this context by a Harvard team in 2004,[3] although the research in this field had been building up in the previous decade. [4] Since then, the approach has been extended to other species including *Arabidopsis thaliana*,[5] humans,[6] multiple species of *Shewanella* bacteria, [1] [7] chicken,[8] among many others.

Besides improving gene annotations, proteogenomic studies can also provide valuable information about the presence of programmed frameshifts, N-terminal methionine excision, signal peptides, proteolysis and other posttranslational modifications. [1] [7]

Methodology

The main idea behind the proteogenomic approach is to identify peptides in a biological sample using mass spectrometry by searching the six-frame translation of the genome sequence, as opposed to searching the protein database. This enables identification of protein regions that are absent from or incorrectly represented in current gene annotations, and thus allows improvement of the gene annotations.

Comparative proteogenomics is a branch of proteogenomics that compares proteomic data from multiple related species concurrently and exploits the homology between their proteins to improve annotations with higher statistical confidence. [7] [9]

References

[1] Gupta N., Tanner S., Jaitly N., Adkins J.N., Lipton M., Edwards R., Romine M., Osterman A., Bafna V., Smith R.D., et al. Whole proteome analysis of post-translational modifications: Applications of mass-spectrometry for proteogenomic annotation. Genome Res. 2007;17:1362–1377.

[2] . Ansong C., Purvine S. O., Adkins J. N., Lipton M. S., Smith R. D. (2008) Proteogenomics: needs and roles to be filled by proteomics in genome annotation. Brief. Funct. Genomics Proteomics 7, 50– 62.

[3] Jaffe J.D., Berg H.C., Church G.M. Proteogenomic mapping as a complementary method to perform genome annotation. Proteomics. 2004a;4:59–77.

[4] Shevchenko A., Jensen O. N., Podtelejnikov A. V., Sagliocco F., Wilm M., Vorm O., Mortensen P., Shevchenko A., Boucherie H., Mann M. (1996) Linking genome and proteome by mass spectrometry: large-scale identification of yeast proteins from two dimensional gels. Proc. Natl. Acad. Sci. U.S.A 93, 14440– 14445.

[5] Castellana N. E., Payne S. H., Shen Z., Stanke M., Bafna V., Briggs S. P. (2008) Discovery and revision of Arabidopsis genes by proteogenomics. Proc. Natl. Acad. Sci. U.S.A 105, 21034– 21038.

[6] Tanner S., Shen Z., Ng J., Florea L., Guigo R., Briggs S.P., Bafna V. Improving gene annotation using peptide mass spectrometry. Genome Res. 2007;17:231–239.

[7] Gupta N., Benhamida J., Bhargava V., Goodman D., Kain E., Kerman I., Nguyen N., Ollikainen N., Rodriguez J., Wang J., et al. Comparative proteogenomics: Combining mass spectrometry and comparative genomics to analyze multiple genomes. Genome Res. 2008;18:1133–1142.

[8] McCarthy FM, Cooksey AM, Wang N, Bridges SM, Pharr GT, Burgess SC. (2006) Modeling a whole organ using proteomics: the avian bursa of Fabricius. Proteomics 6(9):2759-71.

[9] Gallien S., Perrodou E., Carapito C., Deshayes C., Reyrat J. M., Van Dorsselaer A., Poch O., Schaeffer C., Lecompte O. (2009) Ortho-proteogenomics: multiple proteomes investigation through orthology and a new MS-based protocol. Genome Res 19, 128– 135.

External links

- Prof. Vineet Bafna (University of California San Diego) presents his research on proteogenomics. (http://www. scivee.tv/node/6578)

Proteome

The **proteome** is the entire set of proteins expressed by a genome, cell, tissue or organism. More specifically, it is the set of expressed proteins in a given type of cells or an organism at a given time under defined conditions. The term is a portmanteau of *proteins* and *genome*.

The term has been applied to several different types of biological systems. A **cellular proteome** is the collection of proteins found in a particular cell type under a particular set of environmental conditions such as exposure to hormone stimulation. It can also be useful to consider an organism's **complete proteome**, which can be conceptualized as the complete set of proteins from all of the various cellular proteomes. This is very roughly the protein equivalent of the genome. The term "proteome" has also been used to refer to the collection of proteins in certain sub-cellular biological systems. For example, all of the proteins in a virus can be called a viral proteome.

The proteome is larger than the genome, especially in eukaryotes, in the sense that there are more proteins than genes. This is due to alternative splicing of genes and post-translational modifications like glycosylation or phosphorylation.

Moreover the proteome has at least two levels of complexity lacking in the genome. While the genome is defined by the sequence of nucleotides, the proteome cannot be limited to the sum of the sequences of the proteins present. Knowledge of the proteome requires knowledge of (1) the structure of the proteins in the proteome and (2) the functional interaction between the proteins.

Proteomics, the study of the proteome, has largely been practiced through the separation of proteins by two dimensional gel electrophoresis. In the first dimension, the proteins are separated by isoelectric focusing, which resolves proteins on the basis of charge. In the second dimension, proteins are separated by molecular weight using SDS-PAGE. The gel is dyed with Coomassie Brilliant Blue or silver to visualize the proteins. Spots on the gel are proteins that have migrated to specific locations.

The mass spectrometer has augmented proteomics. Peptide mass fingerprinting identifies a protein by cleaving it into short peptides and then deduces the protein's identity by matching the observed peptide masses against a sequence database. Tandem mass spectrometry, on the other hand, can get sequence information from individual peptides by isolating them, colliding them with a non-reactive gas, and then cataloguing the fragment ions produced.

History

The term was coined by Marc Wilkins[1] in 1994 in the symposium: "2D Electrophoresis: from protein maps to genomes" in Siena, Italy, and was subsequently published in 1995,[2] which was part of his PhD thesis. Wilkins used it to describe the entire complement of proteins expressed by a genome, cell, tissue or organism.

References

[1] Wilkins, Marc (Dec. 2009). "Proteomics data mining". *Expert review of proteomics* (England) **6** (6): 599–603. doi:10.1586/epr.09.81. PMID 19929606.

[2] Wasinger VC, Cordwell SJ, Cerpa-Poljak A, Yan JX, Gooley AA, Wilkins MR, Duncan MW, Harris R, Williams KL, Humphery-Smith I. (1995). "Progress with gene-product mapping of the Mollicutes: Mycoplasma genitalium". *Electrophoresis* **7** (7): 1090–94. doi:10.1002/elps.11501601185. PMID 7498152.

External links

- Bioinformatics Journal (http://bioinformatics.oupjournals.org/)
- Grid Computing of the Human Proteome (http://www.grid.org/content/about-us) Dead link
- Databases: PIR I Swissprot I Pfam

Proteomics

Proteomics is the large-scale study of proteins, particularly their structures and functions.[1] [2] Proteins are vital parts of living organisms, as they are the main components of the physiological metabolic pathways of cells. The term "proteomics" was first coined in 1997[3] to make an analogy with genomics, the study of the genes. The word "proteome" is a blend of "**prote**in" and "gen**ome**", and was coined by Marc Wilkins in 1994 while working on the concept as a PhD student.[4] [5] The proteome is the entire complement of proteins,[4] including the modifications made to a particular set of proteins, produced by an organism or system. This

Robotic preparation of MALDI mass spectrometry samples on a sample carrier.

will vary with time and distinct requirements, or stresses, that a cell or organism undergoes.

Complexity of the problem

After genomics, proteomics is considered the next step in the study of biological systems. It is much more complicated than genomics mostly because while an organism's genome is more or less constant, the proteome differs from cell to cell and from time to time. This is because distinct genes are expressed in distinct cell types. This means that even the basic set of proteins which are produced in a cell needs to be determined.

In the past this was done by mRNA analysis, but this was found not to correlate with protein content.[6] [7] It is now known that mRNA is not always translated into protein,[8] and the amount of protein produced for a given amount of mRNA depends on the gene it is transcribed from and on the current physiological state of the cell. Proteomics confirms the presence of the protein and provides a direct measure of the quantity present.

Post-translational modifications

Not only does the translation from mRNA cause differences, many proteins are also subjected to a wide variety of chemical modifications after translation. Many of these post-translational modifications are critical to the protein's function.

Phosphorylation

One such modification is phosphorylation, which happens to many enzymes and structural proteins in the process of cell signaling. The addition of a phosphate to particular amino acids—most commonly serine and threonine[9] mediated by serine/threonine kinases, or more rarely tyrosine mediated by tyrosine kinases—causes a protein to become a target for binding or interacting with a distinct set of other proteins that recognize the phosphorylated domain.

Because protein phosphorylation is one of the most-studied protein modifications, many "proteomic" efforts are geared to determining the set of phosphorylated proteins in a particular cell or tissue-type under particular circumstances. This alerts the scientist to the signaling pathways that may be active in that instance.

Ubiquitination

Ubiquitin is a small protein that can be affixed to certain protein substrates by enzymes called E3 ubiquitin ligases. Determining which proteins are poly-ubiquitinated can be helpful in understanding how protein pathways are regulated. This is therefore an additional legitimate "proteomic" study. Similarly, once it is determined what substrates are ubiquitinated by each ligase, determining the set of ligases expressed in a particular cell type will be helpful.

Additional modifications

Listing all the protein modifications that might be studied in a "Proteomics" project would require a discussion of most of biochemistry; therefore, a short list will serve here to illustrate the complexity of the problem. In addition to phosphorylation and ubiquitination, proteins can be subjected to (among others) methylation, acetylation, glycosylation, oxidation and nitrosylation. Some proteins undergo ALL of these modifications, often in time-dependent combinations, aptly illustrating the potential complexity one has to deal with when studying protein structure and function.

Distinct proteins are made under distinct settings

Even if one is studying a particular cell type, that cell may make different sets of proteins at different times, or under different conditions. Furthermore, as mentioned, any one protein can undergo a wide range of post-translational modifications.

Therefore a "proteomics" study can become quite complex very quickly, even if the object of the study is very restricted. In more ambitious settings, such as when a biomarker for a tumor is sought – when the proteomics scientist is obliged to study sera samples from multiple cancer patients – the amount of complexity that must be dealt with is as great as in any modern biological project.

Limitations to genomic study

Scientists are very interested in proteomics because it gives a much better understanding of an organism than genomics. First, the level of transcription of a gene gives only a rough estimate of its level of expression into a protein. An mRNA produced in abundance may be degraded rapidly or translated inefficiently, resulting in a small amount of protein. Second, as mentioned above many proteins experience post-translational modifications that profoundly affect their activities; for example some proteins are not active until they become phosphorylated. Methods such as phosphoproteomics and glycoproteomics are used to study post-translational modifications. Third, many transcripts give rise to more than one protein, through alternative splicing or alternative post-translational modifications. Fourth, many proteins form complexes with other proteins or RNA molecules, and only function in the presence of these other molecules. Finally, protein degradation rate plays an important role in protein content.[10]

Methods of studying proteins

Determining proteins which are post-translationally modified

One way in which a particular protein can be studied is to develop an antibody which is specific to that modification. For example, there are antibodies which only recognize certain proteins when they are tyrosine-phosphorylated, known as phospho-specific antibodies; also, there are antibodies specific to other modifications. These can be used to determine the set of proteins that have undergone the modification of interest.

For sugar modifications, such as glycosylation of proteins, certain lectins have been discovered which bind sugars. These too can be used.

A more common way to determine post-translational modification of interest is to subject a complex mixture of proteins to electrophoresis in "two-dimensions", which simply means that the proteins are electrophoresed first in one direction, and then in another, which allows small differences in a protein to be visualized by separating a modified protein from its unmodified form. This methodology is known as "two-dimensional gel electrophoresis".[11]

Recently, another approach has been developed called PROTOMAP which combines SDS-PAGE with shotgun proteomics to enable detection of changes in gel-migration such as those caused by proteolysis or post translational modification.

Determining the existence of proteins in complex mixtures

Classically, antibodies to particular proteins or to their modified forms have been used in biochemistry and cell biology studies. These are among the most common tools used by practicing biologists today.

For more quantitative determinations of protein amounts, techniques such as ELISAs can be used.

For proteomic study, more recent techniques such as matrix-assisted laser desorption/ionization (MALDI)[11] have been employed for rapid determination of proteins in particular mixtures and increasingly electrospray ionization (ESI).

Computational methods in studying protein biomarkers

Computational predictive models[12] have shown that extensive and diverse feto-maternal protein trafficking occurs during pregnancy and can be readily detected non-invasively in maternal whole blood. This computational approach circumvented a major limitation, the abundance of maternal proteins interfering with the detection of fetal proteins, to fetal proteomic analysis of maternal blood. Computational models can use fetal gene transcripts previously identified in maternal whole blood to create a comprehensive proteomic network of the term neonate. Such work shows that the fetal proteins detected in pregnant woman's blood originate from a diverse group of tissues and organs from the developing fetus. The proteomic networks contain many biomarkers that are proxies for development and illustrate the potential clinical application of this technology as a way to monitor normal and abnormal fetal development.

An information theoretic framework has also been introduced for biomarker discovery, integrating biofluid and tissue information.[13] This new approach takes advantage of functional synergy between certain biofluids and tissues with the potential for clinically significant findings not possible if tissues and biofluids were considered individually. By conceptualizing tissue-biofluid as information channels, significant biofluid proxies can be identified and then used for guided development of clinical diagnostics. Candidate biomarkers are then predicted based on information transfer criteria across the tissue-biofluid channels. Significant biofluid-tissue relationships can be used to prioritize clinical validation of biomarkers.

Establishing protein–protein interactions

Most proteins function in collaboration with other proteins, and one goal of proteomics is to identify which proteins interact. This is especially useful in determining potential partners in cell signaling cascades.

Several methods are available to probe protein–protein interactions. The traditional method is yeast two-hybrid analysis. New methods include protein microarrays, immunoaffinity chromatography followed by mass spectrometry, dual polarisation interferometry, Microscale Thermophoresis and experimental methods such as phage display and computational methods

Practical applications of proteomics

One of the most promising developments to come from the study of human genes and proteins has been the identification of potential new drugs for the treatment of disease. This relies on genome and proteome information to identify proteins associated with a disease, which computer software can then use as targets for new drugs. For example, if a certain protein is implicated in a disease, its 3D structure provides the information to design drugs to interfere with the action of the protein. A molecule that fits the active site of an enzyme, but cannot be released by the enzyme, will inactivate the enzyme. This is the basis of new drug-discovery tools, which aim to find new drugs to inactivate proteins involved in disease. As genetic differences among individuals are found, researchers expect to use these techniques to develop personalized drugs that are more effective for the individual.

Biomarkers

The FDA defines a biomarker as, "A characteristic that is objectively measured and evaluated as an indicator of normal biologic processes, pathogenic processes, or pharmacologic responses to a therapeutic intervention".

Understanding the proteome, the structure and function of each protein and the complexities of protein–protein interactions will be critical for developing the most effective diagnostic techniques and disease treatments in the future.

An interesting use of proteomics is using specific protein biomarkers to diagnose disease. A number of techniques allow to test for proteins produced during a particular disease, which helps to diagnose the disease quickly. Techniques include western blot, immunohistochemical staining, enzyme linked immunosorbent assay (ELISA) or mass spectrometry.[11] [14]

Proteogenomics

In what is now commonly referred to as proteogenomics, proteomic technologies such as mass spectrometry are used for improving gene annotations. Parallel analysis of the genome and the proteome facilitates discovery of post-translational modifications and proteolytic events [15], especially when comparing multiple species (comparative proteogenomics). [16]

Current research methodologies

Fluorescence two-dimensional differential gel electrophoresis (2-D DIGE)[17] can be used to quantify variation in the 2-D DIGE process and establish statistically valid thresholds for assigning quantitative changes between samples.[18]

Comparative proteomic analysis can reveal the role of proteins in complex biological systems, including reproduction. For example, treatment with the insecticide triazophos causes an increase in the content of brown planthopper (*Nilaparvata lugens* (Stål)) male accessory gland proteins (Acps) that can be transferred to females via mating, causing an increase in fecundity (i.e. birth rate) of females.[19] To identify changes in the types of accessory gland proteins (Acps) and reproductive proteins that mated female planthoppers received from male planthoppers, researchers conducted a comparative proteomic analysis of mated *N. lugens* females.[20] The results indicated that these proteins participate in the reproductive process of *N. lugens* adult females and males.[21]

Proteome analysis of *Arabidopsis peroxisomes*[22] has been established as the major unbiased approach for identifying new peroxisomal proteins on a large scale.[23]

There are many approaches to characterizing the human proteome, which is estimated to contain between 20,000 and 25,000 non-redundant proteins. The number of unique protein species likely increase by between 50,000 and 500,000 due to RNA splicing and proteolysis events, and when post-translational modification are also considered, the total number of unique human proteins is estimated to range in the low millions.[24] [25]

In addition, first promising attempts to decipher the proteome of animal tumors have recently been reported.[11]

References

[1] Anderson NL, Anderson NG (1998). "Proteome and proteomics: new technologies, new concepts, and new words". *Electrophoresis* **19** (11): 1853–61. doi:10.1002/elps.1150191103. PMID 9740045.

[2] Blackstock WP, Weir MP (1999). "Proteomics: quantitative and physical mapping of cellular proteins". *Trends Biotechnol.* **17** (3): 121–7. doi:10.1016/S0167-7799(98)01245-1. PMID 10189717.

[3] P. James (1997). "Protein identification in the post-genome era: the rapid rise of proteomics.". *Quarterly reviews of biophysics* **30** (4): 279–331. doi:10.1017/S0033583597003399. PMID 9634650.

[4] Marc R. Wilkins, Christian Pasquali, Ron D. Appel, Keli Ou, Olivier Golaz, Jean-Charles Sanchez, Jun X. Yan, Andrew. A. Gooley, Graham Hughes, Ian Humphery-Smith, Keith L. Williams & Denis F. Hochstrasser (1996). "From Proteins to Proteomes: Large Scale Protein Identification by Two-Dimensional Electrophoresis and Amino Acid Analysis". *Nature Biotechnology* **14** (1): 61–65. doi:10.1038/nbt0196-61. PMID 9636313.

[5] UNSW Staff Bio: Professor Marc Wilkins (http://www.babs.unsw.edu.au/directory.php?personnelID=12)

[6] Simon Rogers, Mark Girolami, Walter Kolch, Katrina M. Waters, Tao Liu, Brian Thrall and H. Steven Wiley (2008). "Investigating the correspondence between transcriptomic and proteomic expression profiles using coupled cluster models". *Bioinformatics* **24** (24): 2894–2900. doi:10.1093/bioinformatics/btn553. PMID 18974169.

[7] Vikas Dhingraa, Mukta Gupta, Tracy Andacht and Zhen F. Fu (2005). "New frontiers in proteomics research: A perspective". *International Journal of Pharmaceutics* **299** (1–2): 1–18. doi:10.1016/j.ijpharm.2005.04.010. PMID 15979831.

[8] Buckingham, Steven (May 2003). "The major world of microRNAs" (http://www.nature.com/horizon/rna/background/micrornas.html). . Retrieved 2009-01-14.

[9] Olsen JV, Blagoev B, Gnad F, Macek B, Kumar C, Mortensen P, Mann M. (2006). "Global, in vivo, and site-specific phosphorylation dynamics in signaling networks". *Cell* **127** (3): 635–648. doi:10.1016/j.cell.2006.09.026. PMID 17081983.

[10] Archana Belle, Amos Tanay, Ledion Bitincka, Ron Shamir and Erin K. O'Shea (2006). "Quantification of protein half-lives in the budding yeast proteome". *PNAS* **103** (35): 13004–13009. doi:10.1073/pnas.0605420103. PMC 1550773. PMID 16916930.

[11] Klopfleisch R, Klose P, Weise C, Bondzio A, Multhaup G, Einspanier R, Gruber AD. (2010). "Proteome of metastatic canine mammary carcinomas: similarities to and differences from human breast cancer.". *J Proteome Res* **9** (12): 6380–91. doi:10.1021/pr100671c. PMID 20932060.

[12] J.L. Maron , G. Alterovitz, M.F. Ramoni, K.L. Johnson, D.W. Bianchi. "High-throughput Discovery and Characterization of Fetal Protein Trafficking in the Blood of Pregnant Women" (http://www.ncbi.nlm.nih.gov/pubmed/20186258), *Proteomics Clinical Applications*, 2009; **3**(12): 1389–1396, pmid=20186258.

[13] G. Alterovitz, M. Xiang, J. Liu, A. Chang, M.F. Ramoni. "System-Wide Peripheral Biomarker Discovery Using Information Theory" (http://psb.stanford.edu/psb-online/proceedings/psb08/alterovitz.pdf), *Pacific Symposium on Biocomputing*, 2008; 231–242, "pmid=18229689" (http://www.ncbi.nlm.nih.gov/pubmed).

[14] Klopfleisch R, Gruber AD. (2009). "Increased expression of BRCA2 and RAD51 in lymph node metastases of canine mammary adenocarcinomas.". *Veterinary Pathology* **46** (3): 416–22. doi:10.1354/vp.08-VP-0212-K-FL. PMID 19176491.

[15] Gupta N., Tanner S., Jaitly N., Adkins J.N., Lipton M., Edwards R., Romine M., Osterman A., Bafna V., Smith R.D., et al. Whole proteome analysis of post-translational modifications: Applications of mass-spectrometry for proteogenomic annotation. Genome Res. 2007;17:1362–1377.

[16] Gupta N., Benhamida J., Bhargava V., Goodman D., Kain E., Kerman I., Nguyen N., Ollikainen N., Rodriguez J., Wang J., et al. Comparative proteogenomics: Combining mass spectrometry and comparative genomics to analyze multiple genomes. Genome Res. 2008;18:1133–1142.

[17] http://onlinelibrary.wiley.com/doi/10.1002/1615-9861%28200103%291:3%3C377::AID-PROT377%3E3.0.CO;2-6/abstract

[18] Tonge, R., Shaw, J., Middleton, B., Rowlinson, R., Rayner, S., Young, J., Pognan, F., Hawkins, E., Currie, I. and Davison, M. (2001), Validation and development of fluorescence two-dimensional differential gel electrophoresis proteomics technology. PROTEOMICS, 1: 377–396 (http://onlinelibrary.wiley.com/doi/10.1002/1615-9861(200103)1:3<377::AID-PROT377>3.0.CO;2-6/abstract). doi:

10.1002/1615-9861(200103)1:3<377::AID-PROT377>3.0.CO;2-6

[19] Wang, LP, Jun Shen, Lin-Quan Ge, Jin-Cai Wu, Guo-Qin Yang, Gary C. Jahn. 2010. Insecticide-induced increase in the protein content of male accessory glands and its effect on the fecundity of females in the brown planthopper, Nilaparvata lugens Stål (Hemiptera: Delphacidae). Crop Protection 29:1280-1285 (http://www.sciencedirect.com/science/article/pii/S0261219410002061).

[20] [http://pubs.acs.org/doi/pdfplus/10.1021/pr200414g

[21] Ge, Lin-Quan, Yao Chen , Jin-Cai Wu , and Gary C. Jahn. 2011. Proteomic analysis of insecticide triazophos-induced mating–responsive proteins of Nilaparvata lugens Stål (Hemiptera:Delphacidae). J. Proteome Res., DOI: 10.1021/pr200414g (http://pubs.acs.org/doi/pdfplus/10.1021/pr200414g), Publication Date (Web): August 1, 2011.

[22] http://onlinelibrary.wiley.com/doi/10.1002/pmic.201000681/full

[23] Reumann, S. (2011), Toward a definition of the complete proteome of plant peroxisomes: Where experimental proteomics must be complemented by bioinformatics. PROTEOMICS, 11: 1764–1779 (http://onlinelibrary.wiley.com/doi/10.1002/pmic.201000681/full). doi: 10.1002/pmic.201000681

[24] Mathial Uhlen and Fredrik Ponten (2005). "Antibody-based Proteomics for Human Tissue Profiling". *Mollecular & Cellular Proteomics* **4** (4): 384-393. doi:10.1074/mcp.R500009-MCP200.

[25] Ole Nørregaard Jensen (2004). "Modification-specific proteomics: characterization of post-translational modifications by mass spectrometry". *Current Opinion in Chemical Biology* **8** (1): 33-41. doi:10.1016/j.cbpa.2003.12.009.

Bibliography

- Belhajjame, K. et al. Proteome Data Integration: Characteristics and Challenges (http://www.allhands.org.uk/2005/proceedings/papers/525.pdf). Proceedings of the UK e-Science All Hands Meeting, ISBN 1-904425-53-4, September 2005, Nottingham, UK.
- Twyman RM (2004). *Principles Of Proteomics (Advanced Text Series)*. Oxford, UK: BIOS Scientific Publishers. ISBN 1-85996-273-4. (covers almost all branches of proteomics)
- Naven T, Westermeier R (2002). *Proteomics in Practice: A Laboratory Manual of Proteome Analysis*. Weinheim: Wiley-VCH. ISBN 3-527-30354-5. (focused on 2D-gels, good on detail)
- Liebler DC (2002). *Introduction to proteomics: tools for the new biology*. Totowa, NJ: Humana Press. ISBN 0-89603-992-7. ISBN 0-585-41879-9 (electronic, on Netlibrary?), ISBN 0-89603-991-9 hbk
- Wilkins MR, Williams KL, Appel RD, Hochstrasser DF (1997). *Proteome Research: New Frontiers in Functional Genomics (Principles and Practice)*. Berlin: Springer. ISBN 3-540-62753-7.
- Arora PS, Yamagiwa H, Srivastava A, Bolander ME, Sarkar G (2005). "Comparative evaluation of two two-dimensional gel electrophoresis image analysis software applications using synovial fluids from patients with joint disease" (http://www.springerlink.com/openurl.asp?genre=article&doi=10.1007/s00776-004-0878-0). *J Orthop Sci* **10** (2): 160–6. doi:10.1007/s00776-004-0878-0. PMID 15815863.
- Rediscovering Biology Online Textbook. Unit 2 Proteins and Proteomics. 1997–2006.
- Weaver RF (2005). *Molecular biology* (3rd ed.). New York: McGraw-Hill. pp. 840–9. ISBN 0-07-284611-9.
- Reece J, Campbell N (2002). *Biology* (6th ed.). San Francisco: Benjamin Cummings. pp. 392–3. ISBN 0-8053-6624-5.
- Hye A, Lynham S, Thambisetty M, *et al.* (November 2006). "Proteome-based plasma biomarkers for Alzheimer's disease". *Brain* **129** (Pt 11): 3042–50. doi:10.1093/brain/awl279. PMID 17071923.
- Perroud B, Lee J, Valkova N, *et al.* (2006). "Pathway analysis of kidney cancer using proteomics and metabolic profiling". *Mol Cancer* **5**: 64. doi:10.1186/1476-4598-5-64. PMC 1665458. PMID 17123452.
- Yohannes E, Chang J, Christ GJ, Davies KP, Chance MR (July 2008). "Proteomics analysis identifies molecular targets related to diabetes mellitus-associated bladder dysfunction". *Mol. Cell Proteomics* **7** (7): 1270–85. doi:10.1074/mcp.M700563-MCP200. PMC 2493381. PMID 18337374..
- Macaulay IC, Carr P, Gusnanto A, Ouwehand WH, Fitzgerald D, Watkins NA (December 2005). "Platelet genomics and proteomics in human health and disease". *J Clin Invest.* **115** (12): 3370–7. doi:10.1172/JCI26885. PMC 1297260. PMID 16322782.
- Rogers MA, Clarke P, Noble J, *et al.* (15 October 2003). "Proteomic profiling of urinary proteins in renal cancer by surface enhanced laser desorption ionization and neural-network analysis: identification of key issues affecting potential clinical utility" (http://cancerres.aacrjournals.org/cgi/pmidlookup?view=long&pmid=14583499).

Cancer Res. **63** (20): 6971–83. PMID 14583499.

- Vasan RS (May 2006). "Biomarkers of cardiovascular disease: molecular basis and practical considerations". *Circulation* **113** (19): 2335–62. doi:10.1161/CIRCULATIONAHA.104.482570. PMID 16702488.

- "Myocardial Infarction" (http://medlib.med.utah.edu/WebPath/TUTORIAL/MYOCARD/MYOCARD. html). (Retrieved 29 November 2006)

- Introduction to Antibodies – Enzyme-Linked Immunosorbent Assay (ELISA) (http://www.chemicon.com/ resource/ANT101/a2C.asp). (Retrieved 29 November 2006)

- Decramer S, Wittke S, Mischak H, *et al.* (April 2006). "Predicting the clinical outcome of congenital unilateral ureteropelvic junction obstruction in newborn by urinary proteome analysis" (http://www.nature.com/nm/ journal/v12/n4/abs/nm1384.html). *Nat Med.* **12** (4): 398–400. doi:10.1038/nm1384. PMID 16550189.

- Mayer U (January 2008). "Protein Information Crawler (PIC): extensive spidering of multiple protein information resources for large protein sets". *Proteomics* **8** (1): 42–4. doi:10.1002/pmic.200700865. PMID 18095364.

- Jörg von Hagen, VCH-Wiley 2008 *Proteomics Sample Preparation. ISBN 978-3-527-31796-7*

External links

- Proteomics (http://www.dmoz.org//Science/Biology/Biochemistry_and_Molecular_Biology/Biomolecules/ Proteins_and_Enzymes/Proteomics/) at the Open Directory Project

Protomap (proteomics)

PROTOMAP is a recently developed proteomic technology for identifying changes to proteins that manifest in altered migration by one-dimensional SDS-PAGE. It is similar, conceptually, to two-dimensional gel electrophoresis and difference gel electrophoresis in that it enables global identification of proteins that undergo altered electrophoretic migration resulting from, for example, proteolysis or post-translational modification. However, it is unique in that all proteins are sequenced using mass spectrometry which provides information on the sequence coverage detected in each isoform of each protein thereby facilitating interpretation of proteolytic events. [1]

PROTOMAP is performed by resolving control and experimental samples in separate lanes of a 1D SDS-PAGE gel. Each lane is cut into evenly spaced bands (usually 15-30 bands) and proteins in these bands are sequenced using shotgun proteomics. Sequence information from all of these bands are bioinformatically integrated into a visual format called a **peptograph** which plots gel-migration in the vertical dimension (high- to low-molecular weight, top to bottom) and sequence coverage in the horizontal dimension (N- to C-terminus, left to right). A peptograph is generated for each protein the sample (thousands of peptographs are generated from a single experiment) and this data format enables rapid identification of proteins undergoing proteolytic cleavage by making evident changes in gel-migration that are accompanied by altered topography.

PROTOMAP stands for **PRotein TOpography and Migration Analysis Platform** and was invented and developed by Ben Cravatt and colleagues at The Scripps Research Institute.[2]

External links

- The PROTOMAP website [3] - provides access to publicly available PROTOMAP data as well as software and protocols for running PROTOMAP experiments.
- PROTOMAP Description [4] - on the Cravatt Lab website

References

[1] Johnson CE, Kornbluth S (September 2008). "Caspase cleavage is not for everyone" (http://openurl.ebscohost.com/linksvc/linking. aspx?genre=article&sid=PubMed&issn=0092-8674&title=Cell&volume=134&issue=5&spage=720&atitle=Caspase cleavage is not for everyone.&aulast=Johnson&date=2008). *Cell* **134** (5): 720–1. doi:10.1016/j.cell.2008.08.019. PMID 18775303. .

[2] Dix MM, Simon GM, Cravatt BF (August 2008). "Global mapping of the topography and magnitude of proteolytic events in apoptosis" (http://www.cell.com/retrieve/pii/S0092867408008258). *Cell* **134** (4): 679–91. doi:10.1016/j.cell.2008.06.038. PMC 2597167. PMID 18724940. .

[3] http://www.scripps.edu/chemphys/cravatt/protomap

[4] http://www.scripps.edu/chemphys/cravatt/research.html#protomap

PubGene

PubGene Inc.

Type	Privately held
Industry	Bio-informatics
Founded	2001
Headquarters	Boston, USA
Area served	Global
Key people	Eirik Næss-Ulseth (CEO)
Services	Bioinformatics
Website	pubgene.com [1]

PubGene AS is located in Oslo, Norway and is the daughter company of PubGene Inc.

In 2001, PubGene founders demonstrated one of the first[2] applications of text mining to research in biomedicine (i.e., biomedical text mining). They went on to create the PubGene public search engine [3], exemplifying the approach they pioneered by presenting biomedical terms as graphical networks based on their co-occurrence in MEDLINE texts. Co-occurrence networks provide a visual overview of possible relationships between terms and facilitate medical literature retrieval for relevant sets of articles implied by the network display. Commercial applications of the technology are available[4].

Original development of PubGene technologies was undertaken in collaboration between the Norwegian Cancer Hospital (Radiumhospitalet) and the Norwegian University of Science and Technology. The work is supported by the Research Council of Norway and commercialization assisted by Innovation Norway.

References

[1] http://www.pubgene.com
[2] Tor-Kristian Jenssen, Astrid Lægreid, Jan Komorowski & Eivind Hovig (May 2001). "A literature network of human genes for high-throughput analysis of gene expression". *Nature Genetics* **28** (1): 21–28. doi:10.1038/ng0501-21. PMID 11326270.
[3] Browse literature or sequence neighbours (http://www.pubgene.org)
[4] PubGene - Find connections, speed discovery (http://www.pubgene.com)

Pubget

Pubget

Founded	Cambridge, MA, USA (2007)
Headquarters	Boston, MA, USA
Key people	Ramy Arnaout, Ian Connor, Ryan Jones
Website	www.pubget.com [1]

Pubget, Inc. is a private American company that develops cloud-based search and content access tools for scientists. It provides advertising services, enterprise search services, and a public search engine.[2] The company was founded in 2007 by Beth Israel Hospital clinical pathologist, Ramy Arnaout, out of his own need to find papers.[3] [4] [5] Pubget moved its headquarters from Cambridge, Massachusetts to Boston's Innovation District in 2011.[6] [7]

Pubget.com is a free service for non-profit institutions and their libraries and researchers. The site provides direct access to full-text content from 450 libraries around the world. The company is privately funded and profitable.[8]

Products and Services

Search Engine

Pubget's search engine retrieves article citations and full text PDFs from PubMed, ArXiv, JSTOR, IEEE, RSS feeds, XML from publishers, and Open Archive sources.[9] The company's search engine contains over 28 million scientific documents and adds 10,000 papers each day. Pubget creates a link directly from the article citation to the paper itself via a continuously updated database of links.[10] Because of this database, users are directly linked from a citation to the full-text paper.

Access to closed full-text PDFs is granted through the institution's subscriptions. Pubget does not bypass copyright laws and will display only the abstract of restricted papers if the end user does not have institutional access.

PaperStats

Pubget PaperStats is a usage and spend analysis tool for libraries. PaperStats automatically harvests serials usage statistics delivering consolidated usage, cost, and other reports directly from publishers. Content performance can be assessed through cost-per-view analysis. Upon introduction, PaperStats was beta tested with the USC Norris Medical Library and yielded positive results for Pubget, USC and the library community.[11] [12]

PaperStore

The Pubget PaperStore provides Pubget.com users the option of purchasing full text papers from thousands of journals on the search engine results page. Content rights and delivery is provided by document delivery vendor, Reprints Desk [13]. [14]

Advertising

Pubget provides several advertising solutions. Customers include Bio-Rad, Agilent, and other scientific brands. Ads are matched with paper content via contextual targeting. For example, manufacturers of a piece of scientific equipment will pay to advertise alongside a paper that mentions using said product.[15] [16] Pubget, however, does not reveal data on individual users and their searches.[17]

Textmining

Pubget's textmining technology allows research and development teams to uncover specific text strings across large groups of papers.[18]

PaperStream

PaperStream is a web app that allows lab teams to share, store, and find documents all in one place.[19] PaperStream organizes companies' subscriptions, purchased papers, and internal documents into an automated library database.[20] [21]

API

Pubget's API provides access to its search and linking technology from third-party websites or applications such as SharePoint.[22] [23]

References

[1] http://www.pubget.com/

[2] "Pubget Everywhere" (http://corporate.pubget.com/about/where_you_are). *Pubget.*. Retrieved 17 June 2011.

[3] Kevin Davies (June 10, 2009). "Got PubMed? Pubget Searches and Delivers Scientific PDFs" (http://www.bio-itworld.com/news/06/10/09/pubget-full-text-PDF-search.html). Bio-IT World. . Retrieved 17 June 2011.

[4] "Founder's Friday: Pubget" (http://greenhornconnect.com/blog/founders-friday-pubget). Greenhorn Connect. (January 7, 2011). . Retrieved 21 June 2011.

[5] Goodison, Donna (28 May 2011). "Southie Firm Speeds Up Access to Research Papers" (http://bostonherald.com/jobfind/news/technology/view.bg?articleid=1341114). *Boston Herald.*. Retrieved 21 June 2011.

[6] "Welcome home, Pubget" (http://www.innovationdistrict.org/2011/05/13/welcome-pubget/). Innovation District. (May 13, 2011). . Retrieved 16 June 2011.

[7] Goodison, Donna (28 May 2011). "Southie Firm Speeds Up Access to Research Papers" (http://bostonherald.com/jobfind/news/technology/view.bg?articleid=1341114). *Boston Herald.*. Retrieved 21 June 2011.

[8] Goodison, Donna (28 May 2011). "Southie Firm Speeds Up Access to Research Papers" (http://bostonherald.com/jobfind/news/technology/view.bg?articleid=1341114). *Boston Herald.*. Retrieved 21 June 2011.

[9] Featherstone, Robin; Denise Hersey (October 4, 2010). "The quest for full text: an in-depth examination of Pubget for medical searchers." (http://www.tandfonline.com/doi/abs/10.1080/02763869.2010.518911). *Medical Reference Services Quarterly (Routledge)* **29** (4): 307–319. doi:10.1080/02763869.2010.518911. PMID 21058175. . Retrieved 30 June 2011.

[10] Murray, P.E. (August 4, 2009). "Analysis of Pubget - An Expedited Fulltext Service for Life Science Journal Articles" (http://dltj.org/article/analysis-of-pubget-an-expedited-fulltext-service-for-life-science-journal-articles/). Disruptive Library Technology Jester. . Retrieved 21 June 2011.

[11] Curran, Megan (March 2, 2011). "Debating Beta: Considerations for Libraries". *Journal of Electronic Resources in Medical Libraries* **8** (2): 117–125. doi:10.1080/15424065.2011.576604.

[12] Featherstone, Robin; Denise Hersey (October 4, 2010). "The quest for full text: an in-depth examination of Pubget for medical searchers." (http://www.tandfonline.com/doi/abs/10.1080/02763869.2010.518911). *Medical Reference Services Quarterly (Routledge)* **29** (4): 307–319. doi:10.1080/02763869.2010.518911. PMID 21058175. . Retrieved 30 June 2011.

[13] http://www2.reprintsdesk.com/

[14] Featherstone, Robin; Denise Hersey (October 4, 2010). "The quest for full text: an in-depth examination of Pubget for medical searchers." (http://www.tandfonline.com/doi/abs/10.1080/02763869.2010.518911). *Medical Reference Services Quarterly (Routledge)* **29** (4): 307–319. doi:10.1080/02763869.2010.518911. PMID 21058175. . Retrieved 21 June 2011.

[15] "Media Kit: Pubget Ads" (http://corporate.pubget.com/pdfs/mediakit_glossy.pdf). Pubget, Inc.. . Retrieved 24 June 2011.

[16] Kevin Davies (June 10, 2009). "Got PubMed? Pubget Searches and Delivers Scientific PDFs" (http://www.bio-itworld.com/news/06/10/09/pubget-full-text-PDF-search.html). Bio-IT World. . Retrieved 17 June 2011.

[17] Kevin Davies (June 10, 2009). "Got PubMed? Pubget Searches and Delivers Scientific PDFs" (http://www.bio-itworld.com/news/06/10/09/pubget-full-text-PDF-search.html). Bio-IT World. . Retrieved 17 June 2011.

[18] "Textmining Fact Sheet" (http://corporate.pubget.com/pdfs/Pubget_Textmine_2010.pdf). Pubget, Inc.. . Retrieved 15 June 2011.

[19] "Pubget PaperStream" (http://pubget.com/paperstream). Pubget, Inc.. . Retrieved 24 June 2011.

[20] "Pubget PaperStream For Companies" (http://pubget.com/paperstream/forcompanies). Pubget, Inc.. . Retrieved 24 June 2011.

[21] "Pubget PaperStream For Researchers" (http://pubget.com/paperstream/forresearchers). Pubget, Inc.. . Retrieved 24 June 2011.

[22] "PubgetCloud" (http://corporate.pubget.com/pdfs/Pubget_API_2010.pdf). Pubget, Inc.. . Retrieved 16 June 2011.

[23] Munger, Dave (June 10, 2009). "Pubget - Useful, Growing Resource for Anyone Interested in Research" (http://researchblogging.org/news/?p=126). Researchblogging News. . Retrieved 29 June 2011.

External links

- PubMed (http://www.pubmed.com)
- Pubget (http://pubget.com/site/contact/about)
- Got PubMed? Pubget Searches and Delivers Scientific PDFs (http://www.bio-itworld.com/news/06/10/09/pubget-full-text-PDF-search.html)
- UCSF Pubget page (http://www.library.ucsf.edu/node/1836)
- PubMed Portuguese (http://www.pubmed.com.br)
- Pubget Speeds Up Science Journal Searches, Provides Marketing Tools (http://www.xconomy.com/boston/2009/06/23/pubget-speeds-up-science-journal-searches-provides-marketing-tools/)
- Pubget RSS and Firefox Download Extension (http://davidrothman.net/2009/03/05/pubget-rss-and-firefox-download-extension/)
- Reprints Desk (http://www2.reprintsdesk.com/)

PubMed Annual Reload Tester

Every December, the United States National Library of Medicine - the operators of PubMed - re-upload all the PubMed records which they already uploaded during that calendar year.[1] Last year, it was on December 19, with a much smaller number of additional abstracts being re-uploaded on December 20 (2009).

For the 11 other days that month on which abstracts were uploaded, the number of uploads (in the databases we queried using Dialog Classic) ranged from 210 to 2,620 per day. During the 19th and 20 December, 330,012 abstracts were uploaded.

This year's annual PubMed re-upload is supposed to occur on or about Monday 13 December.

Rationale

The annual reload can cause problems for anyone running searches spanning the re-upload date(s). If you use "added since" in Dialog Datastar Web, for example, you will encounter this problem, and your searches will return an improbably high number of hits. You may also encounter the problem when using Ovid, and you definitely will encounter the problem if you are searching directly on PubMed.

One way to avoid capturing a large number of re-uploaded (duplicate) records is to know when the re-upload occurred, and then ignore abstracts added during that period.

Reload tests

With the below encapsulated and clickable searches, you can check to see if the upload has occurred, and on which day(s) (during December 2010).

Results values can fluctuate slightly over time.

Date (2010)	PubMed "jumpstart"	PubMed results
1 December	\<Ctrl\> + click [2]	3,180
2 December	\<Ctrl\> + click [3]	3,554
3 December	\<Ctrl\> + click [4]	4,412
4 December	\<Ctrl\> + click [5]	2,382
5 December	\<Ctrl\> + click [6]	
6 December	\<Ctrl\> + click [7]	
7 December	\<Ctrl\> + click [8]	
8 December	\<Ctrl\> + click [9]	
9 December	\<Ctrl\> + click [10]	
10 December	\<Ctrl\> + click [11]	
11 December	\<Ctrl\> + click [12]	
12 December	\<Ctrl\> + click [13]	
13 December	\<Ctrl\> + click [14]	

References

[1] 2011 DTD and XML Changes; Enhanced Character Set; *Forthcoming 2011 Baseline and Update Files*; Schedule Changes; Continuing to
     Lease NLM Data in 2011 (http://www.nlm.nih.gov/bsd/licensee/announce/2010.html#d08_16)
[2] http://www.ncbi.nlm.nih.gov/sites/entrez?cmd=Search&db=PubMed&
     amp;term=%28%222010%2F12%2F01%22%5BCreate%20Date%5D%20%3A%20%222010%2F12%2F01%22%5BCreate%20Date%5D%29%20AND%20%22
[3] http://www.ncbi.nlm.nih.gov/sites/entrez?cmd=Search&db=PubMed&
     amp;term=%28%222010%2F12%2F02%22%5BCreate%20Date%5D%20%3A%20%222010%2F12%2F02%22%5BCreate%20Date%5D%29%20AND%20%22
[4] http://www.ncbi.nlm.nih.gov/sites/entrez?cmd=Search&db=PubMed&term=(%222010/12/
     03%22%5BCreate%20Date%5D%20:%20%222010/12/
     03%22%5BCreate%20Date%5D)%20AND%20%220%22%5BCreate%20Date%5D%20:%20%223000%22%5BCreate%20Date%5D
[5] http://www.ncbi.nlm.nih.gov/sites/entrez?cmd=Search&db=PubMed&
     amp;term=%28%222010%2F12%2F04%22%5BCreate%20Date%5D%20%3A%20%222010%2F12%2F04%22%5BCreate%20Date%5D%29%20AND%20%22
[6] http://www.ncbi.nlm.nih.gov/sites/entrez?cmd=Search&db=PubMed&
     amp;term=%28%222010%2F12%2F05%22%5BCreate%20Date%5D%20%3A%20%222010%2F12%2F05%22%5BCreate%20Date%5D%29%20AND%20%22
[7] http://www.ncbi.nlm.nih.gov/sites/entrez?cmd=Search&db=PubMed&
     amp;term=%28%222010%2F12%2F06%22%5BCreate%20Date%5D%20%3A%20%222010%2F12%2F06%22%5BCreate%20Date%5D%29%20AND%20%22
[8] http://www.ncbi.nlm.nih.gov/sites/entrez?cmd=Search&db=PubMed&
     amp;term=%28%222010%2F12%2F07%22%5BCreate%20Date%5D%20%3A%20%222010%2F12%2F07%22%5BCreate%20Date%5D%29%20AND%20%22
[9] http://www.ncbi.nlm.nih.gov/sites/entrez?cmd=Search&db=PubMed&
     amp;term=%28%222010%2F12%2F08%22%5BCreate%20Date%5D%20%3A%20%222010%2F12%2F08%22%5BCreate%20Date%5D%29%20AND%20%22
[10] http://www.ncbi.nlm.nih.gov/sites/entrez?cmd=Search&db=PubMed&
     amp;term=%28%222010%2F12%2F09%22%5BCreate%20Date%5D%20%3A%20%222010%2F12%2F09%22%5BCreate%20Date%5D%29%20AND%20%22
[11] http://www.ncbi.nlm.nih.gov/sites/entrez?cmd=Search&db=PubMed&
     amp;term=%28%222010%2F12%2F10%22%5BCreate%20Date%5D%20%3A%20%222010%2F12%2F10%22%5BCreate%20Date%5D%29%20AND%20%22
[12] http://www.ncbi.nlm.nih.gov/sites/entrez?cmd=Search&db=PubMed&
     amp;term=%28%222010%2F12%2F11%22%5BCreate%20Date%5D%20%3A%20%222010%2F12%2F11%22%5BCreate%20Date%5D%29%20AND%20%22
[13] http://www.ncbi.nlm.nih.gov/sites/entrez?cmd=Search&db=PubMed&
     amp;term=%28%222010%2F12%2F12%22%5BCreate%20Date%5D%20%3A%20%222010%2F12%2F12%22%5BCreate%20Date%5D%29%20AND%20%22
[14] http://www.ncbi.nlm.nih.gov/sites/entrez?cmd=Search&db=PubMed&
     amp;term=%28%222010%2F12%2F13%22%5BCreate%20Date%5D%20%3A%20%222010%2F12%2F13%22%5BCreate%20Date%5D%29%20AND%20%22

John Quackenbush

John Quackenbush	
Born	January 4, 1962 Kingston, Pennsylvania, United States
Institutions	Harvard University Dana-Farber Cancer Institute Institute for Molecular Bioscience, (University of Queensland)
Alma mater	California Institute of Technology (B.S.) University of California, Los Angeles (Ph.D.)
Known for	bioinformatics, computational biology, microarray analysis, genomics, functional genomics

John Quackenbush (born January 4, 1962) is an American computational biologist and genome scientist. He is the Professor of Biostatistics and Computational Biology, Professor of Cancer Biology at the Dana-Farber Cancer Institute (DFCI), as well as the director of its Center for Cancer Computational Biology (CCCB). Quackenbush also holds an appointment as Professor of Computational Biology and Bioinformatics in the Department of Biostatistics at the Harvard School of Public Health (HSPH).

Biography

A native of Mountain Top, Pennsylvania, Quackenbush attended Bishop Hoban High School in Wilkes Barre, graduating in 1979, after which he attended the California Institute of Technology, where he earned a bachelor's degree in physics. He went on to earn a doctorate in theoretical particle physics from the University of California, Los Angeles (UCLA) in 1990.

After working two years as a postdoctoral fellow in physics, Quackenbush was awarded a Special Emphasis Research Career Award from the National Center for Human Genome Research (the predecessor of the National Human Genome Research Institute), and subsequently spent the next two years at the Salk Institute working on physical maps of human chromosome 11, followed by another two years at Stanford University developing new laboratory and computational strategies for sequencing the human genome.

In 1997, Quackenbush joined the faculty of The Institute for Genomic Research (TIGR) in Rockville, Maryland, where his focus began to shift to post-genomic applications, with an emphasis on microarray analysis. Using a combination of laboratory and computational approaches, Quackenbush and his group developed analytical methods based on the integration of data across domains to derive biological meaning from high-dimensional data.

In 2005, Quackenbush was appointed to his current positions at the Dana-Farber Cancer Institute (DFCI) and the Harvard School of Public Health. Four years later, he launched the DFCI's Center for Cancer Computational Biology (CCCB),[1] which he directs and which provides broad-based bioinformatics and computational biology support to the research community through a collaborative consulting model, and which also performs and analyzes large-scale second-generation DNA sequencing.[2]

A leader in the fields of genomics and computational biology, Quackenbush's current research focuses on the analysis of human cancer using systems biology-based approaches to understanding and modeling the biological networks that underlie disease. This has led him and his colleagues to make fundamental discoveries about the role that variation in gene expression plays in defining biological phenotypes.

In 2010, Quackenbush and his colleagues at DFCI's CCCB, together with investigators at National Jewish Health's Center for Genes, Environment and Health, University of Pittsburgh's, Dorothy P. and Richard P. Simmons Center for Interstitial Lung Disease, Boston University's, Section for Computational Biomedicine and the Pulmonary Center, and the University of Colorado Denver, Genomics Core Facility received an $11 million grant under the American Recovery and Reinvestment Act of 2009 to launch the Lung Genomics Research Consortium.[3] This project, funded by the National Heart Lung and Blood Institute (NHLBI), will add genetic, genomic, and epigenetic data to a collection of clinical biological samples developed by the NHLBI's Lung Tissue Research Consortium. The consortium aims to use genomic technologies and advanced data-analysis tools on available patient lung-tissue samples to gain new insights into pulmonary disease and thus develop more effective, personalized treatments.

In 2011, Quackenbush published *The Human Genome: Book of Essential Knowledge* (Imagine Publishing, U.S.), which outlines the history, science, and implications behind the Human Genome Project. He was also awarded with a $4 million-dollar fellowship bestowed by Australia's National Health and Medical Research Council to study chemotherapy resistant ovarian cancers in collaboration with colleagues at the University of Queensland's Institute for Molecular Bioscience.[4]

Quackenbush currently serves on the editorial boards of five major journals and is editor-in-chief at *Genomics*. He has served on several committees at the National Academies and the Institute of Medicine, including the Panel on Emerging Issues in Toxicogenomics, the Panel on Collecting, Storing, and Distributing Biodata linked to Social Science Surveys, and the Committee Review of Omics-Based Predictive Tests. He is currently a member of scientific advisory boards at St. Jude Children's Research Hospital, at the Lovelace Respiratory Research Institute, The Hope Funds for Cancer Research. and for the National Institute for Health's Roadmap Epigenomics Project. Quackenbush is also a member of the scientific advisory boards of a number of biotech start-up companies, including Exosome Diagnostics, Karyopharm Therapeutics, and NABsys.

Awards and Honors

- Jun John Sakurai Scholarship, 24th International School of Subnuclear Physics, Ettore Majorana Foundation and Centre for Scientific Culture, Erice, Italy, 1986
- Prize for Best Student and Prize for Best Scientific Secretary, 25th International School of Subnuclear Physics, Ettore Majorana Foundation and Centre for Scientific Culture, Erice, Italy, 1987
- SERCA Fellow, National Human Genome Research Institute, 1992
- Myra Samuels Memorial Lecture, Perdue University, Lafayette, Indiana USA, 2002
- George D. Wilbanks Lectureship in Gynecological Oncology, University of South Florida College of Medicine, Tampa, Florida, USA, 2006
- President's Distinguished Lectureship, American Society of Reproductive Medicine, 2007
- Leopold G. Koss Lectureship, Universität Bern, Switzerland, 2007
- Distinguished Lecture in Computer Science, Wayne State University, Detroit, Michigan, USA, 2008
- Institute for Personalized, Medicine, Distinguished Lecture, Mount Sinai Medical School, New York, New York, USA, 2010
- The Ian Lawson Van Toch Memorial Seminar in Computational Biology, Ontario Cancer Institute, Toronto, Ontario, Canada, 2010
- Harvard-Australia Foundation Fellowship, 2010
- Bancroft Fellow-in-Residence, Queensland Institute of Medical Research, Queensland, Australia, 2010

- Jackson Memorial Fellowship, Griffith University, Queensland, Australia, 2010
- National Health and Medical Research Council (NHMRC), Australia Fellowship 2011

Publications

Books

- Author, *The Human Genome: Book of Essential Knowledge* (Imagine Publishing, U.S., 2011)
- Contributor, *Bioinformatics: A Practical Guide to the Analysis of Genes and Proteins* (Wiley Interscience, 2004)
- Coauthor, *Microarray Gene Expression Data Analysis: A Beginner's Guide* (Wiley-Blackwell, 2003)

Select Papers

- Mar, J. C.; Wells, C. A.; Quackenbush, J. (2011). "Defining an informativeness metric for clustering gene expression data". *Bioinformatics* **27** (8): 1094–1100. doi:10.1093/bioinformatics/btr074. PMC 3072547. PMID 21330289.
- Culhane, A. C.; Schwarzl, T.; Sultana, R.; Picard, K. C.; Picard, S. C.; Lu, T. H.; Franklin, K. R.; French, S. J. et al. (2009). "GeneSigDB--a curated database of gene expression signatures". *Nucleic Acids Research* **38** (Database issue): D716–D725. doi:10.1093/nar/gkp1015. PMC 2808880. PMID 19934259.
- Mar, J. C.; Quackenbush, J. (2009). Papin, Jason A.. ed. "Decomposition of Gene Expression State Space Trajectories". *PLoS Computational Biology* **5** (12): e1000626. doi:10.1371/journal.pcbi.1000626. PMC 2791157. PMID 20041215.
- Djebbari, A.; Quackenbush, J. (2008). "Seeded Bayesian Networks: Constructing genetic networks from microarray data". *BMC Systems Biology* **2**: 57. doi:10.1186/1752-0509-2-57. PMC 2474592. PMID 18601736.
- Mar, J. C.; Rubio, R.; Quackenbush, J. (2006). "Inferring steady state single-cell gene expression distributions from analysis of mesoscopic samples". *Genome Biology* **7** (12): R119. doi:10.1186/gb-2006-7-12-r119. PMC 1794432. PMID 17169148.
- Larkin, J. E.; Frank, B. C.; Gavras, H.; Sultana, R.; Quackenbush, J. (2005). "Independence and reproducibility across microarray platforms". *Nature Methods* **2** (5): 337–344. doi:10.1038/nmeth757. PMID 15846360.
- Eschrich, S.; Yang, I.; Bloom, G.; Kwong, K.; Boulware, D.; Cantor, A.; Coppola, D.; Kruhøffer, M. et al. (2005). "Molecular Staging for Survival Prediction of Colorectal Cancer Patients". *Journal of Clinical Oncology* **23** (15): 3526–3535. doi:10.1200/JCO.2005.00.695. PMID 15908663.
- Whitelaw, C. A.; Barbazuk, W.; Pertea, G.; Chan, A.; Cheung, F.; Lee, Y.; Zheng, L.; Van Heeringen, S. et al. (2003). "Enrichment of Gene-Coding Sequences in Maize by Genome Filtration". *Science* **302** (5653): 2118–2120. doi:10.1126/science.1090047. PMID 14684821.
- Saeed, A.; Sharov, V.; White, J.; Li, J.; Liang, W.; Bhagabati, N.; Braisted, J.; Klapa, M. et al. (2003). "TM4: A free, open-source system for microarray data management and analysis". *BioTechniques* **34** (2): 374–378. PMID 12613259.
- Brazma, A.; Hingamp, P.; Quackenbush, J.; Sherlock, G.; Spellman, P.; Stoeckert, C.; Aach, J.; Ansorge, W. et al. (2001). "Minimum information about a microarray experiment (MIAME)-toward standards for microarray data". *Nature Genetics* **29** (4): 365–371. doi:10.1038/ng1201-365. PMID 11726920.

References

1. Dublin, Matthew (1 June 2009), "Dana Farber, Quackenbush Launch Analysis Consultancy Center" [5], *GenomeWeb*, retrieved 18 May 2011

[1] http://www.genomeweb.com/informatics/dana-farber-quackenbush-launch-analysis-consultancy-center

[2] http://www.bio-itworld.com/issues/2009/mar-apr/quackenbush-cover-story.html

[3] http://2429-genomeweb.voxcdn.com/informatics/
    dana-farber-builds-data-collection-and-analysis-infrastructure-lung-disease-geno?page=show

[4] http://www.biotechnologynews.net/storyview.asp?storyid=2382745

[5] http://www.genomeweb.com/informatics/dana-farber-quackenbush-launch-analysis-consultancy-center

External links

- Harvard School of Public Health Bio (http://www.hsph.harvard.edu/faculty/john-quackenbush/)
- Dana-Farber Cancer Institute Bio (http://physicians.dana-farber.org/directory/profile.asp?dbase=main&setsize=10&display=Y&nxtfmt=pc&gs=adf&picture_id=0000440&lookup=Y&pict_id=0000440)
- Center for Cancer Computational Biology, Dana-Farber Cancer Institute (http://cccb.dfci.harvard.edu/cccb)
- Lung Genomics Research Consortium Investigator Bio (http://www.lung-genomics.org/lgrc/whoweare/team/quackenbush)

Quertle

Quertle

Type	Privately Held
Industry	Life, Chemical, and Biomedical Science Search Engine
Founded	Colorado, USA (2008)
Headquarters	Henderson, Nevada, US
Area served	Worldwide
Key people	Jeffrey D. Saffer (President) Vicki L. Burnett(Executive VP)
Website	www.quertle.info [1]

Quertle is a semantic search engine for life and chemical science literature and information.[2] [3] [4] [5] It covers a wide variety of information sources.

How Quertle Works

Quertle uses semantic-based linguistics to automatically extract subject–verb–object relationships asserted by the author(s) of each document. The identification of these assertions uses several methods including natural language processing.[6] [7] For full-text documents, Quertle includes only the main content, not, for example, the references.

The subject–verb–object relationships are stored in a metadatabase and the user's query is matched against that metadata. This identifies documents based on meaning and context and generally provides fewer, but more relevant, hits than a traditional keyword search. Thus, Quertle is fundamentally different from search sites such as PubMed. Nonetheless, Quertle does simultaneously search a keyword index to find documents based on inclusion of the search terms. These are presented on a separate tab in the results.

An ontology covering genes, proteins, chemicals, diseases, cell types, and other life, chemical, and biomedical science nomenclature is used to automatically search for all variants of a term in the user's query. For example, a search for "aspirin" will find asserted relationships that mention "acetylsalicylic acid". The ontology also is used to find members of a class of entities, such as "neurotransmitters".[8]

Content

Quertle indexes MEDLINE, full-text articles from BioMed Central[9] and PubMed Central (open access subset), NIH grants, the US National Library of Medicine TOXNET database, and biomedical news.[10]

Criticism

It has been suggested that details of how Quertle works 'are not clearly described to the public'.[8]

References

[1] http://www.quertle.info/

[2] Coppernoll-Blach P (April 2011). "Quertle: The Conceptual Relationships Alternative Search Engine for PubMed". *J Med Libr Assoc* **99** (2): 176–177. doi:10.3163/1536-5050.99.2.017. PMC 3066589.

[3] University of Colorado-Denver Health Science Library l Quertle Biomedical Search Engine (http://hslibrary.ucdenver.edu/newsletter/archives/appendixOCT10.html#5)

[4] Science Intelligence and InfoPros I Quertle: A new semantic search for Medline (http://scienceintelligence.wordpress.com/2010/10/08/
     quertle-a-great-new-semantic-search-for-medline/)

[5] BioJob Blog I Quertle: A Powerful, New Search Engine (http://www.biojobblog.com/2010/10/articles/biotraining/
     quertle-a-powerful-new-search-engine-that-make-biomedical-literature-searches-smarter-easier-and-less-timeconsuming/)

[6] Novichkova S, Egorov S, Daraselia N (September 2003). "MedScan, a natural language processing engine for MEDLINE abstracts".
     Bioinformatics **19** (13): 1699–1706. doi:10.1093/bioinformatics/btg207. PMID 12967967.

[7] Daraselia N, Yuryev A, Egorov S, Novichkova S, Nikitin A, Mazo I (March 2004). "Extracting human protein interactions from MEDLINE
     using a full-sentence parser". *Bioinformatics* **20** (5): 604–611. doi:10.1093/bioinformatics/btg452. PMID 15033866.

[8] Lu Z (17 January 2011). "PubMed and beyond: a survey of web tools for searching biomedical literature". *Database* **baq036**.
     doi:10.1093/database/baq036. PMC 3025693. PMID 21245076.

[9] Business Wire 2009 I Quertle Announces Full-Text Searching and Partnership with BioMed Central (http://www.businesswire.com/news/
     home/20091119006407/en/Quertle-Announces-Full-Text-Searching-Partnership-BioMed-Central)

[10] Business Wire 2010 I Quertle Announces Content Expansion and Partnership with FierceMarkets (http://www.businesswire.com/news/
     home/20100121007009/en/Quertle-Announces-Content-Expansion-Partnership-FierceMarkets)

Regulome

Regulome refers to the whole set of regulation components in a cell. Those components can be genes, mRNAs, proteins, and metabolites. The description includes the interplay of regulatory effects between these components, and their dependence on variables such as subcellular localization, tissue, developmental stage, and pathological state.

Components

One of the major players in cellular regulation are transcription factors, proteins that regulate the expression of genes. Other proteins that bind to transcription factors to form transcriptional complexes might modify the activity of transcription factors, for example blocking their capacity to bind to a promoter.

Signaling pathways are groups of proteins that produce an effect in a chain that transmit a signal from one part of the cell to another part, for example, linking the presence of substance at the exterior of the cell to the activation of the expression of a gene.

Measuring

High-throughput technologies for the analysis of biological samples (for example, DNA microarrays, proteomics analysis) allow the measurement of thousands of biological components such as mRNAs, proteins, or metabolites. Chromatin immunoprecipitation of transcription factors can be used to map transcription factor binding sites in the genome.

Such techniques allow researchers to study the effects of particular substances and/or situations on a cellular sample at a genomic level (for example, by addition of a drug, or by placing cells in a situation of stress). The information obtained allows parts of the regulome to be inferred.

Modeling

One of the objectives of systems biology is the modelization of biological processes using mathematics and computer simulation. The production of data from techniques of genomic analysis is not always amenable to interpretation mainly due to the complexity of the data and the large amount of data points. Modelization can handle the data and allow to test a hypothesis (for example, gene A is regulated by protein B) that can be verified experimentally.

Applications

The complete knowledge of the regulome will allow researchers to model cell behaviour entirely. This will facilitate the design of drugs for therapy, the control of stem cell differentiation, and the prognosis of disease.

External links

- Bioinformatics Journal [33]

Representative sequences

Protein sequences can provide data about the biological function and evolution of proteins and protein domains. Grouping and interrelating protein sequences can therefore provide information about both human biological processes, and the historical development of biological processes on earth.

Such Sequence clusters allow the effective coverage of sequence space.

Sequence clusters can reduce a large database of sequences to a smaller set of "sequence representatives", each of which should "represent" its cluster at the sequence level.

Sequence representatives allow the effective coverage of the original database with fewer sequences. The database of sequence representatives is called "non-redundant", as similar (or redundant) sequences have been removed at a certain similarity threshold.

RNA integrity number

The **RNA integrity number** (RIN) is an algorithm for assigning integrity values to RNA measurements.

The integrity of RNA is a major concern for gene expression studies and traditionally has been evaluated using the 28S to 18S rRNA ratio, a method that has been shown to be inconsistent. The RIN algorithm was devised to overcome this issue. The RIN algorithm is applied to electrophoretic RNA measurements and based on a combination of different features that contribute information about the RNA integrity to provide a more robust universal measure.

External links

- RIN information from Agilent Technologies [1]
- RIN article in BMC Molecular Biology [2]
- More info here => http://RNA-integrity.gene-quantification.info [3]

References

[1] http://www.agilent.com/about/newsroom/lsca/background/rna_integrity.pdf
[2] http://www.biomedcentral.com/1471-2199/7/3
[3] http://RNA-integrity.gene-quantification.info/

Rosetta@home

Rosetta@home

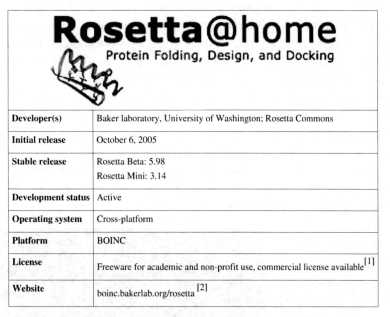

Developer(s)	Baker laboratory, University of Washington; Rosetta Commons
Initial release	October 6, 2005
Stable release	Rosetta Beta: 5.98 Rosetta Mini: 3.14
Development status	Active
Operating system	Cross-platform
Platform	BOINC
License	Freeware for academic and non-profit use, commercial license available[1]
Website	boinc.bakerlab.org/rosetta [2]

Rosetta@home is a distributed computing project for protein structure prediction on the Berkeley Open Infrastructure for Network Computing (BOINC) platform, run by the Baker laboratory at the University of Washington. Rosetta@home aims to predict protein–protein docking and design new proteins with the help of about sixty thousand active volunteered computers processing at 62 teraFLOPS on average as of October 18, 2011.[3] Foldit, a Rosetta@Home videogame, aims to reach these goals with a crowdsourcing approach. Though much of the project is oriented towards basic research on improving the accuracy and robustness of the proteomics methods, Rosetta@home also does applied research on malaria, Alzheimer's disease and other pathologies.[4]

Like all BOINC projects, Rosetta@home uses idle computer processing resources from volunteers' computers to perform calculations on individual workunits. Completed results are sent to a central project server where they are validated and assimilated into project databases. The project is cross-platform, and runs on a wide variety of hardware configurations. Users can view the progress of their individual protein structure prediction on the Rosetta@home screensaver.

In addition to disease-related research, the Rosetta@home network serves as a testing framework for new methods in structural bioinformatics. These new methods are then used in other Rosetta-based applications, like RosettaDock and the Human Proteome Folding Project, after being sufficiently developed and proven stable on Rosetta@home's large and diverse collection of volunteer computers. Two particularly important tests for the new methods developed in Rosetta@home are the Critical Assessment of Techniques for Protein Structure Prediction (CASP) and Critical Assessment of Prediction of Interactions (CAPRI) experiments, biannual experiments which evaluate the state of the art in protein structure prediction and protein–protein docking prediction, respectively. Rosetta@home consistently ranks among the foremost docking predictors, and is one of the best tertiary structure predictors available.[5]

Computing platform

Both the Rosetta@home application and the BOINC distributed computing platform are available for the Microsoft Windows, Linux and Macintosh platforms (BOINC also runs on several other platforms, e.g. FreeBSD).[6] Participation in Rosetta@home requires a central processing unit (CPU) with a clock speed of at least 500 MHz, 200 megabytes of free disk space, 512 megabytes of physical memory, and Internet connectivity.[7] As of May 4, 2010, the current version of the Rosetta application is 5.98, and the current version of the Rosetta Mini application is 2.14.[8] The current recommended BOINC program version is 6.2.19.[6] Standard HTTP (port 80) is used for communication between the user's BOINC client and the Rosetta@home servers at the University of Washington; HTTPS (port 443) is used during password exchange. Remote and local control of the BOINC client use port 31416 and port 1043, which might need to be specifically unblocked if they are behind a firewall.[9] Workunits containing data on individual proteins are distributed from servers located in the Baker lab at the University of Washington to volunteers' computers, which then calculate a structure prediction for the assigned protein. To avoid duplicate structure predictions on a given protein, each workunit is initialized with a random number seed. This gives each prediction a unique trajectory of descent along the protein's energy landscape.[10] Protein structure predictions from Rosetta@home are approximations of a global minimum in a given protein's energy landscape. That global minimum represents the most energetically favorable conformation of the protein, i.e. its native state.

A primary feature of the Rosetta@home graphical user interface (GUI) is a screensaver which shows a current workunit's progress during the simulated protein folding process. In the upper-left of the current screensaver, the target protein is shown adopting different shapes (conformations) in its search for the lowest energy structure. Depicted immediately to the right is the structure of the most recently accepted. On the upper right the lowest energy conformation of the current decoy is shown; below that is the true, or native, structure of the protein if it has already been determined. Three graphs are

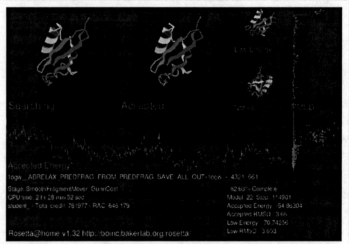

Rosetta@home screensaver, showing the progress of a structure prediction for a synthetic ubiquitin protein (PDB ID: 1ogw)

included in the screensaver. Near the middle, a graph for the accept model's free energy is displayed, which fluctuates as the accepted model changes. A graph of the accepted model's root mean square deviation (RMSD), which measures how structurally similar the accepted model is to the native model, is shown far right. On the right of the accepted energy graph and below the RMSD graph, the results from these two functions are used to produce an energy vs. RMSD plot as the model is progressively refined.[11]

Like all BOINC projects, Rosetta@home runs in the background of the user's computer using idle computer power, either at or before logging in to an account on the host operating system. Rosetta@home frees resources from the CPU as they are required by other applications so that normal computer usage is unaffected. To minimize power consumption or heat production from a computer running at sustained capacity, the maximum percentage of CPU resources that Rosetta@home is allowed to use can be specified through a user's account preferences. The times of day during which Rosetta@home is allowed to do work can also be adjusted, along with many other preferences, through a user's account settings.

Rosetta, the software that runs on the Rosetta@home network, was rewritten in C++ to allow easier development than that offered by its original version, which was written in Fortran. This new version is object-oriented, and was released on February 8, 2008.[8] [12] Development of the Rosetta code is done by Rosetta Commons.[13] The software is freely licensed to the academic community and available to pharmaceutical companies for a fee.[13]

Project significance

Further information: Protein structure prediction, Protein docking, Protein design

With the proliferation of genome sequencing projects, scientists can infer the amino acid sequence, or primary structure, of many proteins that carry out functions within the cell. To better understand a protein's function and aid in rational drug design, scientists need to know the protein's three-dimensional tertiary structure.

CASP6 target T0281, the first *ab initio* protein structure prediction to approach atomic-level resolution. Rosetta produced a model for T0281 (superpositioned in magenta) 1.5 Å RMSD from the crystal structure (blue).

Protein 3D structures are currently determined experimentally through X-ray crystallography or nuclear magnetic resonance (NMR) spectroscopy. The process is slow (it can take weeks or even months to figure out how to crystallize a protein for the first time) and comes at high cost (around $100,000 USD per protein).[14] Unfortunately, the rate at which new sequences are discovered far exceeds the rate of structure determination − out of more than 7,400,000 protein sequences available in the NCBI non-redundant (nr) protein database, fewer than 52,000 proteins' 3D structures have been solved and deposited in the Protein Data Bank, the main repository for structural information on proteins.[15] One of the main goals of Rosetta@home is to predict protein structures with the same accuracy as existing methods, but in a way that requires significantly less time and money. Rosetta@home also develops methods to determine the structure and docking of membrane proteins (e.g., GPCRs),[16] which are exceptionally difficult to analyze with traditional techniques like X-ray crystallography and NMR spectroscopy, yet represent the majority of targets for modern drugs.

Progress in protein structure prediction is evaluated in the biannual Critical Assessment of Techniques for Protein Structure Prediction (CASP) experiment, in which researchers from around the world attempt to derive a protein's structure from the protein's amino acid sequence. High scoring groups in this sometimes competitive experiment are considered the *de facto* standard-bearers for what is the state of the art in protein structure prediction. Rosetta, the program on which Rosetta@home is based, has been used since CASP5 in 2002. In the 2004 CASP6 experiment, Rosetta made history by being the first to produce a close to atomic-level resolution, *ab initio* protein structure prediction in its submitted model for CASP target T0281.[17] *Ab initio* modeling is considered an especially difficult category of protein structure prediction, as it does not use information from structural homology and must rely on information from sequence homology and modeling physical interactions within the protein. Rosetta@home has been used in CASP since 2006, where it was among the top predictors in every category of structure prediction in CASP7.[18] [19] [20] These high quality predictions were enabled by the computing power made available by Rosetta@home volunteers.[21] Increasing computational power allows Rosetta@home to sample more regions of conformation space (the possible shapes a protein can assume), which, according to Levinthal's paradox, is predicted to increase exponentially with protein length.

Rosetta@home is also used in protein docking prediction, which determines the structure of multiple complexed proteins, or quaternary structure. This type of protein interaction affects many cellular functions, including antigen–antibody and enzyme–inhibitor binding and cellular import and export. Determining these interactions is critical for drug design. Rosetta is used in the Critical Assessment of Prediction of Interactions (CAPRI) experiment, which evaluates the state of the protein docking field similar to how CASP gauges progress in protein structure prediction. The computing power made available by Rosetta@home's project volunteers has been cited as a major factor in Rosetta's performance in CAPRI, where its docking predictions have been among the most accurate and complete.[22]

In early 2008, Rosetta was used to computationally design a protein with a function never before observed in nature.[23] This was inspired in part by the retraction of a high-profile paper from 2004 which originally described the computational design of a protein with improved enzymatic activity compared to its natural form.[24] The 2008 research paper from David Baker's group describing how the protein was made, which cited Rosetta@home for the computational resources it made available, represented an important proof of concept for this protein design method.[23] This type of protein design could have future applications in drug discovery, green chemistry, and bioremediation.[23]

Disease-related research

In addition to basic research in predicting protein structure, docking and design, Rosetta@home is also used in immediate disease-related research.[25] Numerous minor research projects are described in David Baker's Rosetta@home journal.[26]

Alzheimer's disease

A component of the Rosetta software suite, RosettaDesign, was used to accurately predict which regions of amyloidogenic proteins were most likely to make amyloid-like fibrils.[27] By taking hexapeptides (six amino acid-long fragments) of a protein of interest and selecting the lowest energy match to a structure similar to that of a known fibril forming hexapeptide, RosettaDesign was able to identify peptides twice as likely to form fibrils as are random proteins.[28] Rosetta@home was used in the same study to predict structures for amyloid beta, a fibril-forming protein that has been postulated to cause Alzheimer's disease.[29] Preliminary but as yet unpublished results have been produced on Rosetta-designed proteins that may prevent fibrils from forming, although it is unknown whether it can prevent the disease.[30]

Anthrax

Another component of Rosetta, RosettaDock,[31] [32] [33] was used in conjunction with experimental methods to model interactions between three proteins—lethal factor (LF), edema factor (EF) and protective antigen (PA)—that make up anthrax toxin. The computational model accurately predicted docking between LF and PA, helping to establish which domains of the respective proteins are involved in the LF–PA complex. This insight was eventually used in research resulting in improved anthrax vaccines.[34] [35]

Herpes simplex virus 1

RosettaDock was used to model docking between an antibody (immunoglobulin G) and a surface protein expressed by herpes simplex virus 1 (HSV-1) which serves to degrade the antiviral antibody. The protein complex predicted by RosettaDock closely agreed with the particularly difficult-to-obtain experimental models, leading researchers to conclude that the docking method has potential in addressing some of the problems that X-ray crystallography has with modeling protein–protein interfaces.[36]

HIV

As part of research funded by a $19.4 million dollar grant by the Bill and Melinda Gates Foundation,[37] Rosetta@home has been used in designing multiple possible vaccines for human immunodeficiency virus (HIV).[38] [39]

Malaria

In research involved with the Grand Challenges in Global Health initiative,[40] Rosetta has been used to computationally design novel homing endonuclease proteins, which could eradicate *Anopheles gambiae* or otherwise render the mosquito unable to transmit malaria.[41] Being able to model and alter protein–DNA interactions specifically, like those of homing endonucleases, gives computational protein design methods like Rosetta an important role in gene therapy (which includes possible cancer treatments).[25] [42]

Development history and branches

Originally introduced by the Baker laboratory in 1998 as an *ab initio* approach to structure prediction,[43] Rosetta has since branched into several development streams and distinct services. The Rosetta platform derives its name from the Rosetta Stone, as it attempts to decipher the structural "meaning" of proteins' amino acid sequences.[44] More than seven years after Rosetta's first appearance, the Rosetta@home project was released (i.e. announced as no longer beta) on October 6, 2005.[8] Many of the graduate students and other researchers involved in Rosetta's initial development have since moved to other universities and research institutions, and subsequently enhanced different parts of the Rosetta project.

RosettaDesign

RosettaDesign, a computational approach to protein design based on Rosetta, began in 2000 with a study in redesigning the folding pathway of Protein G.[45] In 2002 RosettaDesign was used to design Top7, a 93-amino acid long α/β protein that had an overall fold never before recorded in nature. This new conformation was predicted by Rosetta to within 1.2 Å RMSD of the structure determined by X-ray crystallography, representing an unusually accurate structure prediction.[46] Rosetta and RosettaDesign earned widespread recognition by being the first to design and accurately predict the structure of a novel protein of such length, as reflected by the 2002 paper describing the dual approach prompting two positive letters in the journal *Science*,[47] [48] and being cited by more than 240 other scientific articles.[49] The visible product of that research, Top7, was featured as the Protein Data Bank's 'Molecule of the Month' in October

Superposition of Rosetta-designed model (red) for Top7 onto its X-ray crystal structure (blue, PDB ID: 1QYS)

2006;[50] a superposition of the respective cores (residues 60–79) of its predicted and X-ray crystal structures are featured in the Rosetta@home logo.[17]

Brian Kuhlman, a former postdoctoral associate in David Baker's lab and now an associate professor at the University of North Carolina, Chapel Hill,[51] offers RosettaDesign as an online service.[52]

RosettaDock

RosettaDock was added to the Rosetta software suite during the first CAPRI experiment in 2002 as the Baker laboratory's algorithm for protein–protein docking prediction.[53] In that experiment, RosettaDock made a high-accuracy prediction for the docking between streptococcal pyogenic exotoxin A and a T cell-receptor β-chain, and a medium accuracy prediction for a complex between porcine α-amylase and a camelid antibody. While the RosettaDock method only made two acceptably accurate predictions out of seven possible, this was enough to rank it seventh out of nineteen prediction methods in the first CAPRI assessment.[53]

Development of RosettaDock diverged into two branches for subsequent CAPRI rounds as Jeffrey Gray, who laid the groundwork for RosettaDock while at the University of Washington, continued working on the method in his new position at Johns Hopkins University. Members of the Baker laboratory further developed RosettaDock in Gray's absence. The two versions differed slightly in side-chain modeling, decoy selection and other areas.[33] [54] Despite these differences, both the Baker and Gray methods performed well in the second CAPRI assessment, placing fifth and seventh respectively out of 30 predictor groups.[55] Jeffrey Gray's RosettaDock server is available as a free docking prediction service for non-commercial use.[56]

In October 2006, RosettaDock was integrated into Rosetta@home. The method used a fast, crude docking model phase using only the protein backbone. This was followed by a slow full-atom refinement phase in which the orientation of the two interacting proteins relative to each other, and side-chain interactions at the protein–protein interface, were simultaneously optimized to find the lowest energy conformation.[57] The vastly increased computational power afforded by the Rosetta@home network, in combination with revised "fold-tree" representations for backbone flexibility and loop modeling, made RosettaDock sixth out of 63 prediction groups in the third CAPRI assessment.[5] [22]

Robetta

The Robetta server is an automated protein structure prediction service offered by the Baker laboratory for non-commercial *ab initio* and comparative modeling.[58] It has participated as an automated prediction server in the biannual CASP experiments since CASP5 in 2002, performing among the best in the automated server prediction category.[59] Robetta has since competed in CASP6 and 7, where it did better than average among both automated server and human predictor groups.[20] [60] [61]

In modeling protein structure as of CASP6, Robetta first searches for structural homologs using BLAST, PSI-BLAST, and 3D-Jury, then parses the target sequence into its individual domains, or independently folding units of proteins, by matching the sequence to structural families in the Pfam database. Domains with structural homologs then follow a "template-based model" (i.e., homology modeling) protocol. Here, the Baker laboratory's in-house alignment program, K*sync, produces a group of sequence homologs, and each of these is modeled by the Rosetta *de novo* method to produce a decoy (possible structure). The final structure prediction is selected by taking the lowest energy model as determined by a low-resolution Rosetta energy function. For domains that have no detected structural homologs, a *de novo* protocol is followed in which the lowest energy model from a set of generated decoys is selected as the final prediction. These domain predictions are then connected together to investigate inter-domain, tertiary-level interactions within the protein. Finally, side-chain contributions are modeled using a protocol for Monte Carlo conformational search.[62]

In CASP8, Robetta was augmented to use Rosetta's high resolution all-atom refinement method,[63] the absence of which was cited as the main cause for Robetta being less accurate than the Rosetta@home network in CASP7.[21]

Foldit

On May 9, 2008, after Rosetta@home users suggested an interactive version of the distributed computing program, the Baker lab publicly released Foldit, an online protein structure prediction game based on the Rosetta platform.[64] As of September 25, 2008, Foldit has over 59,000 registered users.[65] The game gives users a set of controls (e.g. "shake", "wiggle", "rebuild") to manipulate the backbone and amino acid side chains of the target protein into more energetically favorable conformations. Users can work on solutions individually as "soloists" or collectively as "evolvers", accruing points under either category as they improve their structure predictions.[66] Users can also individually compete with other users through a "duel" feature, in which the player with the lowest energy structure after 20 moves wins.

Comparison to similar distributed computing projects

There are several distributed computed projects which have study areas similar to those of Rosetta@home, but differ in their research approach:

Folding@home

Of all the major distributed computing projects involved in protein research, Folding@home is the only one not to use the BOINC platform.[67] [68] [69] Both Rosetta@home and Folding@home study protein misfolding diseases such as Alzheimer's disease, but Folding@home does so much more exclusively.[70] [71] Folding@home almost exclusively uses all-atom molecular dynamics models to understand how and why proteins fold (or potentially misfold, and subsequently aggregate to cause diseases).[72] [73] In other words, Folding@home's strength is modeling the process of protein folding, while Rosetta@home's strength is computational protein design and prediction of protein structure and docking.

Some of Rosetta@home's results are used as the basis for some Folding@home projects. Rosetta provides the most likely structure, but it is not definite if that is the form the molecule takes or whether or not it is viable. Folding@home can then be used to verify Rosetta@home's results, but can also provide additional atomic-level information, as well as details into how the molecule changes shape.[73] [74]

The two projects also differ significantly in their computing power and host diversity. Averaging about 6,650 teraFLOPS from a host base of CPUs, GPUs and PS3s,[75] Folding@home has nearly 108 times more computing power than Rosetta@home.[3]

World Community Grid

Both Phase I and Phase II of the Human Proteome Folding Project (HPF), a subproject of World Community Grid, have used the Rosetta program to make structural and functional annotations of various genomes.[76] [77] Although he now uses it to create databases for biologists, Richard Bonneau, head scientist of the Human Proteome Folding Project, was active in the original development of Rosetta at David Baker's laboratory while obtaining his PhD.[78] More information on the relationship between the HPF1, HPF2 and Rosetta@home can be found on Richard Bonneau's website.[79]

Predictor@home

Like Rosetta@home, Predictor@home specializes in protein structure prediction. Predictor@home plans to develop new areas for its distributed computing platform in protein design and docking (using the CHARMM package for molecular dynamics),[80] further likening it to Rosetta@home. While Rosetta@home uses the Rosetta program for its structure prediction, Predictor@home uses the dTASSER methodology.[81]

Other protein related distributed computing projects on BOINC include QMC@home, Docking@home, POEM@home, SIMAP, and TANPAKU. RALPH@home, the Rosetta@home alpha project which tests new application versions, work units, and updates before they move on to Rosetta@home, runs on BOINC as well.[82]

Volunteer contributions

Rosetta@home depends on computing power donated by individual project members for its research. As of October 18, 2011, about 40,000 users from 150 countries were active members of Rosetta@home, together contributing idle processor time from about 60,000 computers for a combined average performance of over 62 teraFLOPS.[3]

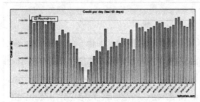

Bar chart showing cumulative credit per day for Rosetta@home over a 60-day period, indicating its computational power during the CASP8 experiment

Users are granted BOINC credits as a measure of their contribution. The credit granted for each workunit is the number of decoys produced for that workunit multiplied by the average claimed credit for the decoys submitted by all computer hosts for that workunit. This custom system was designed to address significant differences between credit granted to users with the standard BOINC client and an optimized BOINC client, and credit differences between users running Rosetta@home on Windows and Linux operating systems.[83] The amount of credit granted per second of CPU work is lower for Rosetta@home than most other BOINC projects.[84] Despite this disadvantage to BOINC users competing for rank, Rosetta@home is fifth out of over 40 BOINC projects in terms of total credit.[85]

Rosetta@home users who predict protein structures submitted for the CASP experiment are acknowledged in scientific publications regarding their results.[21] Users who predict the lowest energy structure for a given workunit are featured on the Rosetta@home homepage as 'Predictor of the Day', along with any team of which they are a member.[86] A 'User of the Day' is chosen at random each day to be on the homepage as well from users who have made a Rosetta@home profile.[87]

References

[1] "Portfolio Highlight: Rosetta++ Software Suite" (http://depts.washington.edu/ventures/UW_Technology/Express_Licenses/rosetta.php). UW TechTransfer – Digital Ventures. . Retrieved September 7, 2008.

[2] http://boinc.bakerlab.org/rosetta

[3] de Zutter W. "Rosetta@home: Credit overview" (http://boincstats.com/stats/project_graph.php?pr=rosetta). boincstats.com. . Retrieved 2011-10-18.

[4] "What is Rosetta@home?" (http://boinc.bakerlab.org/rosetta/rah_about.php). *Rosetta@home forums*. University of Washington. . Retrieved September 7, 2008.

[5] Lensink MF, Méndez R, Wodak SJ (December 2007). "Docking and scoring protein complexes: CAPRI 3rd Edition". *Proteins* **69** (4): 704–18. doi:10.1002/prot.21804. PMID 17918726.

[6] "Download BOINC client software" (http://boinc.berkeley.edu/download_all.php). *BOINC*. University of California. 2008. . Retrieved December 1, 2008.

[7] "Rosetta@home: Recommended System Requirements" (http://boinc.bakerlab.org/rosetta/rah_requirements.php). *Rosetta@home*. University of Washington. 2008. . Retrieved October 7, 2008.

[8] "Rosetta@home: News archive" (http://boinc.bakerlab.org/rosetta/old_news.php). *Rosetta@home*. University of Washington. 2010. . Retrieved May 4, 2010.

[9] "Rosetta@home: FAQ (work in progress) (message 10910)" (http://boinc.bakerlab.org/rosetta/forum_thread.php?id=669& nowrap=true#10910). *Rosetta@home forums*. University of Washington. 2006. . Retrieved October 7, 2008.

[10] Kim DE (2005). "Rosetta@home: Random Seed (message 3155)" (http://boinc.bakerlab.org/rosetta/forum_thread.php?id=391& nowrap=true#3155). *Rosetta@home forums*. University of Washington. . Retrieved October 7, 2008.

[11] "Rosetta@home: Quick guide to Rosetta and its graphics" (http://boinc.bakerlab.org/rosetta/rah_graphics.php). *Rosetta@home*. University of Washington. 2007. . Retrieved October 7, 2008.

[12] Kim DE (2008). "Rosetta@home: Problems with minirosetta version 1.+ (Message 51199)" (http://boinc.bakerlab.org/rosetta/ forum_thread.php?id=3934&nowrap=true#51199). *Rosetta@home forums*. University of Washington. . Retrieved September 7, 2008.

[13] "Rosetta Commons" (http://www.rosettacommons.org/main.html). RosettaCommons.org. 2008. . Retrieved October 7, 2008.

[14] Bourne PE, Helge W, ed (2003). *Structural Bioinformatics*. Hoboken, NJ: Wiley-Liss. ISBN 978-0471201991. OCLC 50199108.

[15] "Yearly Growth of Protein Structures" (http://www.pdb.org/pdb/statistics/contentGrowthChart.do?content=molType-protein& seqid=100). RCSB Protein Data Bank. 2008. . Retrieved November 30, 2008.

[16] Baker D (2008). "Rosetta@home: David Baker's Rosetta@home journal (message 55893)" (http://boinc.bakerlab.org/rosetta/ forum_thread.php?id=1177&nowrap=true#55893). *Rosetta@home forums*. University of Washington. . Retrieved October 7, 2008.

[17] "Rosetta@home: Research Overview" (http://boinc.bakerlab.org/rosetta/rah_research.php). *Rosetta@home*. University of Washington. 2007. . Retrieved October 7, 2008.

[18] Kopp J, Bordoli L, Battey JN, Kiefer F, Schwede T (2007). "Assessment of CASP7 predictions for template-based modeling targets". *Proteins* **69 Suppl 8**: 38–56. doi:10.1002/prot.21753. PMID 17894352.

[19] Read RJ, Chavali G (2007). "Assessment of CASP7 predictions in the high accuracy template-based modeling category". *Proteins* **69 Suppl 8**: 27–37. doi:10.1002/prot.21662. PMID 17894351.

[20] Jauch R, Yeo HC, Kolatkar PR, Clarke ND (2007). "Assessment of CASP7 structure predictions for template free targets". *Proteins* **69 Suppl 8**: 57–67. doi:10.1002/prot.21771. PMID 17894330.

[21] Das R, Qian B, Raman S, *et al.* (2007). "Structure prediction for CASP7 targets using extensive all-atom refinement with Rosetta@home". *Proteins* **69 Suppl 8**: 118–28. doi:10.1002/prot.21636. PMID 17894356.

[22] Wang C, Schueler-Furman O, Andre I, *et al.* (December 2007). "RosettaDock in CAPRI rounds 6–12". *Proteins* **69** (4): 758–63. doi:10.1002/prot.21684. PMID 17671979.

[23] Jiang L, Althoff EA, Clemente FR, *et al.* (March 2008). "De novo computational design of retro-aldol enzymes". *Science* **319** (5868): 1387–91. doi:10.1126/science.1152692. PMID 18323453.

[24] Hayden EC (February 13, 2008). "Protein prize up for grabs after retraction". *Nature*. doi:10.1038/news.2008.569.

[25] "Disease Related Research" (http://boinc.bakerlab.org/rosetta/rah_medical_relevance.php). *Rosetta@home*. University of Washington. 2008. . Retrieved October 8, 2008.

[26] Baker D (2008). "Rosetta@home: David Baker's Rosetta@home journal" (http://boinc.bakerlab.org/rosetta/forum_thread.php?id=1177). *Rosetta@home forums*. University of Washington. . Retrieved September 7, 2008.

[27] Kuhlman B, Baker D (September 2000). "Native protein sequences are close to optimal for their structures". *Proceedings of the National Academy of Sciences of the United States of America* **97** (19): 10383–8. doi:10.1073/pnas.97.19.10383. PMC 27033. PMID 10984534.

[28] Thompson MJ, Sievers SA, Karanicolas J, Ivanova MI, Baker D, Eisenberg D (March 2006). "The 3D profile method for identifying fibril-forming segments of proteins". *Proceedings of the National Academy of Sciences of the United States of America* **103** (11): 4074–8. doi:10.1073/pnas.0511295103. PMC 1449648. PMID 16537487.

[29] Bradley P. "Rosetta@home forum: Amyloid fibril structure prediction" (http://boinc.bakerlab.org/rosetta/forum_thread.php?id=2583& sort=6). *Rosetta@home forums*. University of Washington. . Retrieved September 7, 2008.

[30] Baker D. "Rosetta@home forum: Publications on R@H's Alzheimer's work? (message 54681)" (http://boinc.bakerlab.org/rosetta/ forum_thread.php?id=4263&nowrap=true#54681). *Rosetta@home forums*. University of Washington. . Retrieved October 8, 2008.

[31] Wang C, Schueler-Furman O, Baker D (May 2005). "Improved side-chain modeling for protein–protein docking". *Protein science : a publication of the Protein Society* **14** (5): 1328–39. doi:10.1110/ps.041222905. PMC 2253276. PMID 15802647.

[32] Gray JJ, Moughon S, Wang C, *et al.* (August 2003). "Protein–protein docking with simultaneous optimization of rigid-body displacement and side-chain conformations". *Journal of molecular biology* **331** (1): 281–99. doi:10.1016/S0022-2836(03)00670-3. PMID 12875852.

[33] Schueler-Furman O, Wang C, Baker D (August 2005). "Progress in protein-protein docking: atomic resolution predictions in the CAPRI experiment using RosettaDock with an improved treatment of side-chain flexibility". *Proteins* **60** (2): 187–94. doi:10.1002/prot.20556. PMID 15981249.

[34] Lacy DB, Lin HC, Melnyk RA, *et al.* (November 2005). "A model of anthrax toxin lethal factor bound to protective antigen". *Proceedings of the National Academy of Sciences of the United States of America* **102** (45): 16409–14. doi:10.1073/pnas.0508259102. PMC 1283467. PMID 16251269.

[35] Albrecht MT, Li H, Williamson ED, *et al.* (November 2007). "Human monoclonal antibodies against anthrax lethal factor and protective antigen act independently to protect against Bacillus anthracis infection and enhance endogenous immunity to anthrax". *Infection and immunity* **75** (11): 5425–33. doi:10.1128/IAI.00261-07. PMC 2168292. PMID 17646360.

[36] Sprague ER, Wang C, Baker D, Bjorkman PJ (June 2006). "Crystal structure of the HSV-1 Fc receptor bound to Fc reveals a mechanism for antibody bipolar bridging". *PLoS biology* **4** (6): e148. doi:10.1371/journal.pbio.0040148. PMC 1450327. PMID 16646632.

[37] Paulson, Tom (July 19, 2006). "Gates Foundation awards $287 million for HIV vaccine research" (http://www.seattlepi.com/local/ 278100_aidsvaccine19ww.html). *Seattle Post-Intelligencer*. . Retrieved September 7, 2008.

[38] Liu Y et al. (2007). "Development of IgG1 b12 scaffolds and HIV-1 env-based outer domain immunogens capable of eliciting and detecting IgG1 b12-like antibodies" (http://www.hivvaccineenterprise.org/_dwn/Oral_Sessions.pdf) (PDF). Global HIV Vaccine Enterprise. . Retrieved September 28, 2008.

[39] Baker D. "David Baker's Rosetta@home journal archives (message 40756)" (http://boinc.bakerlab.org/rosetta/forum_thread. php?id=2431&nowrap=true#40756). *Rosetta@home forums*. University of Washington. . Retrieved September 7, 2008.

[40] "Homing Endonuclease Genes: New Tools for Mosquito Population Engineering and Control" (http://www.gcgh.org/ControlInsect/ Challenges/GeneticStrategy/Pages/EndonucleaseGenes.aspx). Grand Challenges in Global Health. . Retrieved September 7, 2008.

[41] Windbichler N, Papathanos PA, Catteruccia F, Ranson H, Burt A, Crisanti A (2007). "Homing endonuclease mediated gene targeting in Anopheles gambiae cells and embryos". *Nucleic Acids Research* **35** (17): 5922–33. doi:10.1093/nar/gkm632. PMC 2034484. PMID 17726053.

[42] Ashworth J, Havranek JJ, Duarte CM, *et al.* (June 2006). "Computational redesign of endonuclease DNA binding and cleavage specificity". *Nature* **441** (7093): 656–9. doi:10.1038/nature04818. PMC 2999987. PMID 16738662.

[43] Simons KT, Bonneau R, Ruczinski I, Baker D (1999). "Ab initio protein structure prediction of CASP III targets using ROSETTA". *Proteins* **Suppl 3**: 171–6. doi:10.1002/(SICI)1097-0134(1999)37:3+<171::AID-PROT21>3.0.CO;2-Z. PMID 10526365.

[44] "Interview with David Baker" (http://www.teampicard.com/profiles/Interview.php?id=4). Team Picard Distributed Computing. 2006. . Retrieved December 23, 2008.

[45] Nauli S, Kuhlman B, Baker D (July 2001). "Computer-based redesign of a protein folding pathway". *Nature structural biology* **8** (7): 602–5. doi:10.1038/89638. PMID 11427890.

[46] Kuhlman B, Dantas G, Ireton GC, Varani G, Stoddard BL, Baker D (November 2003). "Design of a novel globular protein fold with atomic-level accuracy". *Science* **302** (5649): 1364–8. Bibcode 2003Sci...302.1364K. doi:10.1126/science.1089427. PMID 14631033.

[47] Jones DT (November 2003). "Structural biology. Learning to speak the language of proteins". *Science* **302** (5649): 1347–8. doi:10.1126/science.1092492. PMID 14631028.

[48] von Grotthuss M, Wyrwicz LS, Pas J, Rychlewski L (June 2004). "Predicting protein structures accurately". *Science* **304** (5677): 1597–9; author reply 1597–9. doi:10.1126/science.304.5677.1597b. PMID 15192202.

[49] "Articles citing: Kuhlman et al. (2003) 'Design of a novel globular protein fold with atomic-level accuracy'" (http://www.sciencemag.org/ cgi/external_ref?access_num=sci;302/5649/1364&link_type=ISI_Citing). ISI Web of Science. . Retrieved July 10, 2008.

[50] "October 2005 molecule of the month: Designer proteins" (http://www.pdb.org/pdb/static.do?p=education_discussion/ molecule_of_the_month/pdb70_1.html). RCSB Protein Data Bank. . Retrieved September 7, 2008.

[51] "Kuhlman laboratory homepage" (http://www.unc.edu/kuhlmanpg/index.htm). *Kuhlman Laboratory*. University of North Carolina. . Retrieved September 7, 2008.

[52] "RosettaDesign web server" (http://rosettadesign.med.unc.edu/). *Kuhlman Laboratory*. University of North Carolina. . Retrieved September 7, 2008.

[53] Gray JJ, Moughon SE, Kortemme T, *et al.* (July 2003). "Protein-protein docking predictions for the CAPRI experiment". *Proteins* **52** (1): 118–22. doi:10.1002/prot.10384. PMID 12784377.

[54] Daily MD, Masica D, Sivasubramanian A, Somarouthu S, Gray JJ (2005). "CAPRI rounds 3–5 reveal promising successes and future challenges for RosettaDock" (http://www3.interscience.wiley.com/cgi-bin/fulltext/110548131/HTMLSTART). *Proteins* **60** (2): 181–86. doi:10.1002/prot.20555. PMID 15981262. .

[55] Méndez R, Leplae R, Lensink MF, Wodak SJ (2005). "Assessment of CAPRI predictions in rounds 3–5 shows progress in docking procedures" (http://www3.interscience.wiley.com/cgi-bin/fulltext/110548130/HTMLSTART). *Proteins* **60** (2): 150–69. doi:10.1002/prot.20551. PMID 15981261. .

[56] "RosettaDock server" (http://rosettadock.graylab.jhu.edu/). *Gray laboratory*. Johns Hopkins University. . Retrieved September 7, 2008.

[57] "Protein-protein docking at Rosetta@home" (http://boinc.bakerlab.org/rosetta/forum_thread.php?id=2395). *Rosetta@home forums*. University of Washington. . Retrieved September 7, 2008.

[58] "Robetta web server" (http://robetta.bakerlab.org/). *Baker laboratory*. University of Washington. . Retrieved September 7, 2008.

[59] Aloy P, Stark A, Hadley C, Russell RB (2003). "Predictions without templates: new folds, secondary structure, and contacts in CASP5". *Proteins* **53 Suppl 6**: 436–56. doi:10.1002/prot.10546. PMID 14579333.

[60] Tress M, Ezkurdia I, Graña O, López G, Valencia A (2005). "Assessment of predictions submitted for the CASP6 comparative modeling category". *Proteins* **61 Suppl 7**: 27–45. doi:10.1002/prot.20720. PMID 16187345.

[61] Battey JN, Kopp J, Bordoli L, Read RJ, Clarke ND, Schwede T (2007). "Automated server predictions in CASP7". *Proteins* **69 Suppl 8**: 68–82. doi:10.1002/prot.21761. PMID 17894354.

[62] Chivian D, Kim DE, Malmström L, Schonbrun J, Rohl CA, Baker D (2005). "Prediction of CASP6 structures using automated Robetta protocols". *Proteins* **61 Suppl 7**: 157–66. doi:10.1002/prot.20733. PMID 16187358.

[63] Baker D. "David Baker's Rosetta@home journal, message 52902" (http://boinc.bakerlab.org/rosetta/forum_thread.php?id=1177& nowrap=true#52902). *Rosetta@home forums*. University of Washington. . Retrieved September 7, 2008.

[64] Baker D. "David Baker's Rosetta@home journal (message 52963)" (http://boinc.bakerlab.org/rosetta/forum_thread.php?id=1177& nowrap=true#52963). *Rosetta@home forums*. University of Washington. . Retrieved September 16, 2008.

[65] "Foldit forums: How many users does Foldit have? Etc. (message 2)" (http://fold.it/portal/node/444975). University of Washington. . Retrieved September 27, 2008.

[66] "Foldit: Frequently Asked Questions" (http://fold.it/portal/info/faq). *fold.it*. University of Washington. . Retrieved September 19, 2008.

[67] "Project list – BOINC" (http://boinc.berkeley.edu/wiki/Project_list). University of California. . Retrieved September 8, 2008.

[68] Pande Group (2010). "High Performance FAQ" (http://folding.stanford.edu/English/FAQ-highperformance) (FAQ). Stanford University. . Retrieved 2011-09-19.

[69] 7im (2010-04-02). "Re: Answers to: Reasons for not using F@H" (http://foldingforum.org/viewtopic.php?f=16&t=1164& start=135#p137893). . Retrieved 2011-09-19.

[70] Vijay Pande (2011-08-05). "Results page updated – new key result published in our work in Alzheimer's Disease" (http://folding.typepad. com/news/2011/08/results-page-updated-new-key-result-published-in-our-work-in-alzheimers-disease.html). . Retrieved 2011-09-19.

[71] Pande Group. "Folding@home Diseases Studied FAQ" (http://folding.stanford.edu/FAQ-diseases.html) (FAQ). Stanford University. . Retrieved 2011-09-12.

[72] Vijay Pande (2007-09-26). "How FAH works: Molecular dynamics" (http://folding.typepad.com/news/2007/09/how-fah-works-1. html). . Retrieved 2011-09-10.

[73] tjlane (2011-06-09). "Re: Course grained Protein folding in under 10 minutes" (http://foldingforum.org/viewtopic. php?p=188496#p188392). . Retrieved 2011-09-19.

[74] jmn (2011-07-29). "Rosetta@home and Folding@home: additional projects" (http://en.fah-addict.net/news/news-0-369+ rosetta-home-and-folding-home-additional-projects.php). . Retrieved 2011-09-19.

[75] Pande Group (updated automatically). "Client Statistics by OS" (http://fah-web.stanford.edu/cgi-bin/main.py?qtype=osstats). Stanford University. . Retrieved 2011-10-18.

[76] Malmström L, Riffle M, Strauss CE, *et al.* (April 2007). "Superfamily assignments for the yeast proteome through integration of structure prediction with the gene ontology". *PLoS biology* **5** (4): e76. doi:10.1371/journal.pbio.0050076. PMC 1828141. PMID 17373854.

[77] Bonneau R (2006). "World Community Grid Message Board Posts: HPF -> HPF2 transition" (http://homepages.nyu.edu/~rb133/wcg/ thread_7398.html). Bonneau Lab, New York University. . Retrieved September 7, 2008.

[78] "List of Richard Bonneau's publications" (http://homepages.nyu.edu/~rb133/papers.html). Bonneau Lab, New York University. . Retrieved September 7, 2008.

[79] Bonneau R. "World Community Grid Message Board Posts" (http://homepages.nyu.edu/~rb133/wcg/rbonneau_posts.html). Bonneau Lab, New York University. . Retrieved September 7, 2008.

[80] "Predictor@home: Developing new application areas for P@H" (http://predictor.chem.lsa.umich.edu/scientific_update_cp.php#dpath). The Brooks Research Group. . Retrieved September 7, 2008.

[81] Carrillo-Tripp M (2007). "dTASSER" (http://web.archive.org/web/20070706073650/http://www.scripps.edu/~trippm/dtasser/). The Scripps Research Institute. Archived from the original (http://www.scripps.edu/~trippm/dtasser/) on July 6, 2007. . Retrieved September 7, 2008.

[82] "RALPH@home website" (http://ralph.bakerlab.org/). *RALPH@home forums*. University of Washington. . Retrieved September 7, 2008.

[83] "Rosetta@home: The new credit system explained" (http://boinc.bakerlab.org/rosetta/forum_thread.php?id=2194). *Rosetta@home forums*. University of Washington. 2006. . Retrieved October 8, 2008.

[84] "BOINCstats: Project Credit Comparison" (http://boincstats.com/stats/project_cpcs.php). boincstats.com. 2008. . Retrieved October 8, 2008.

[85] "Credit divided over projects" (http://boincstats.com/charts/chart_uk_bo_project_pie3dcredits.gif). boincstats.com. . Retrieved November 30, 2008.

[86] "Rosetta@home: Predictor of the day archive" (http://boinc.bakerlab.org/rosetta/rah_old_potd.php). *Rosetta@home*. University of Washington. 2008. . Retrieved October 8, 2008.

[87] "Rosetta@home: Protein Folding, Design, and Docking" (http://boinc.bakerlab.org/rosetta). *Rosetta@home*. University of Washington. 2008. . Retrieved October 8, 2008.

External links

- Rosetta@home (http://boinc.bakerlab.org/rosetta/) Project website
- Baker Lab (http://depts.washington.edu/bakerpg/drupal/) Baker Lab website
- David Baker's Rosetta@home journal (http://boinc.bakerlab.org/rosetta/forum_thread.php?id=1177&sort=5)
- BOINC (http://boinc.berkeley.edu/) Includes platform overview, as well as a guide for installing BOINC and attaching to Rosetta@home
- BOINCstats – Rosetta@home (http://boincstats.com/stats/project_graph.php?pr=rosetta) Detailed contribution statistics
- RALPH@home (http://ralph.bakerlab.org/) Website for Rosetta@home alpha testing project
- Rosetta@home video on YouTube (http://www.youtube.com/watch?v=GzATbET3g54) Overview of Rosetta@home given by David Baker and lab members
- Rosetta Commons (http://www.rosettacommons.org/) Academic collaborative for development of the Rosetta platform

- (http://sites.google.com/site/kuhlmanlabwebpage/) Kuhlman lab webpage, home of RosettaDesign

Online Rosetta services

- Robetta (http://robetta.bakerlab.org/) Protein structure prediction server
- RosettaDesign (http://rosettadesign.med.unc.edu/) Protein design server
- RosettaDock (http://rosettadock.graylab.jhu.edu/) Protein–protein docking server

SCHEMA (bioinformatics)

SCHEMA is a computational algorithm used in protein engineering to identify fragments of proteins (called *schemas*) that can be recombined without disturbing the integrity of the proteins' three-dimensional structure.[1] The algorithm calculates the interactions between a protein's different amino acid residues to determine which interactions may be disrupted by swapping structural domains of the protein. By minimizing these disruptions, SCHEMA can be used to engineer chimeric proteins that stably fold and may have altered function relative to their parent proteins.[2]

References

[1] Voigt, CA et al; Martinez, C; Wang, ZG; Mayo, SL; Arnold, FH (June 2002). "Protein building blocks preserved by recombination". *Nature Structural Biology* **9** (7): 553–558. doi:10.1038/nsb805. PMID 12042875.

[2] Otey, CR; Landwehr, M; Endelman, JB; Hiraga, K; Bloom, JD; Arnold, FH (May 2006). "Structure-guided recombination creates an artificial family of cytochromes P450". *PLoS Biology* **4** (5): e112. doi:10.1371/journal.pbio.0040112. PMC 1431580. PMID 16594730.

Scoring functions for docking

Docking glossary
• **Receptor** or **host** or **lock** – The "receiving" molecule, most commonly a protein or other biopolymer.
• **Ligand** or **guest** or **key** – The complementary partner molecule which binds to the receptor. Ligands are most often small molecules but could also be another biopolymer.
• **Docking** – Computational simulation of a candidate ligand binding to a receptor.
• **Binding mode** – The orientation of the ligand relative to the receptor as well as the conformation of the ligand and receptor when bound to each other.
• **Pose** – A candidate binding mode.
• **Scoring** – The process of evaluating a particular pose by counting the number of favorable intermolecular interactions such as hydrogen bonds and hydrophobic contacts.
• **Ranking** – The process of classifying which ligands are most likely to interact favorably to a particular receptor based on the predicted free-energy of binding.
[1]

In the fields of computational chemistry and molecular modelling, **scoring functions** are fast approximate mathematical methods used to predict the strength of the non-covalent interaction (also referred to as binding affinity) between two molecules after they have been docked. Most commonly one of the molecules is a small organic compound such as a drug and the second is the drug's biological target such as a protein receptor.[1] Scoring functions have also been developed to predict the strength of other types of intermolecular interactions, for example between two proteins[2] or between protein and DNA.[3]

Utility

Scoring functions are widely used in drug discovery and other molecular modelling applications. These include:[4]

- **Virtual screening** of small molecule databases of candidate ligands to identify novel small molecules that bind to a protein target of interest and therefore are useful starting points for drug discovery[5]
- **De novo design** (design "from scratch") of novel small molecules that bind to a protein target[6]
- **Lead optimization** of screening hits to optimize their affinity and selectivity[7]

A potentially more reliable but much more computationally demanding alternative to scoring functions are free energy perturbation calculations.[8]

Prerequisites

Scoring functions are normally parameterized (or trained) against a data set consisting of experimentally determined binding affinities between molecular species similar to the species that one wishes to predict.

For currently used methods aiming to predict affinities of ligands for proteins the following must first be known or predicted:

- **Protein tertiary structure** – arrangement of the protein atoms in three dimensional space. Protein structures may be determined by experimental techniques such as X-ray crystallography or solution phase NMR methods or predicted by homology modelling.
- **Ligand active conformation** – three dimensional shape of the ligand when bound to the protein
- **Binding-mode** – orientation of the two binding partners relative to each other in the complex

The above information yields the three dimensional structure of the complex. Based on this structure, the scoring function can then estimate the strength of the association between the two molecules in the complex using one of the methods outlined below. Finally the scoring function itself may be used to help predict both the binding mode and the active conformation of the small molecule in the complex, or alternatively a simpler and computationally faster function may be utilised within the docking run.

Classes

There are three general classes of scoring functions:

- **Force field** – affinities are estimated by summing the strength of intermolecular van der Waals and electrostatic interactions between all atoms of the two molecules in the complex. The intramolecular energies (also referred to as strain energy) of the two binding partners are also frequently included. Finally since the binding normally takes place in the presence of water, the desolvation energies of the ligand and of the protein are sometimes taken into account using implicit solvation methods such as GBSA or PBSA.
- **Empirical** – based on counting the number of various types of interactions between the two binding partners.[6] Counting may be based on the number of ligand and receptor atoms in contact with each other or by calculating the change in solvent accessible surface area (ΔSASA) in the complex compared to the uncomplexed ligand and protein. The coefficients of the scoring function are usually fit using multiple linear regression methods. These interactions terms of the function may include for example:
  - hydrophobic — hydrophobic contacts (favorable),
  - hydrophobic — hydrophilic contacts (unfavorable),
  - hydrophilic — hydrophilic contacts (no contribution to affinity except for the following special cases):
    - number of hydrogen bonds (favorable electrostatic contribution to affinity, especially if shielded from solvent, if solvent exposed no contribution),
    - number of hydrogen bond "mismatches" or other types of electrostatic repulsion (very unfavorable and rarely seen in stable complexes),

- number of rotatable bonds immobilized in complex formation (unfavorable entropic contribution).
- **Knowledge-based** – based on statistical observations of intermolecular close contacts in large 3D databases (such as the Cambridge Structural Database or Protein Data Bank) which are used to derive "potentials of mean force". This method is founded on the assumption that close intermolecular interactions between certain types of atoms or functional groups that occur more frequently than one would expect by a random distribution are likely to be energetically favorable and therefore contribute favorably to binding affinity.[9]

Finally hybrid scoring functions have also been developed in which the components from two or more of the above scoring functions are combined into one function.

Evaluation

A 2009 paper suggested that, since different scoring functions are relatively co-linear, consensus scoring functions may not improve accuracy significantly.[10] This claim went somewhat against the prevailing view in the field, since previous studies had suggested that consensus scoring was beneficial.[11]

References

[1] Jain AN (2006). "Scoring functions for protein-ligand docking". *Curr. Protein Pept. Sci.* **7** (5): 407–20. doi:10.2174/138920306778559395. PMID 17073693.

[2] Lensink MF, Méndez R, Wodak SJ (2007). "Docking and scoring protein complexes: CAPRI 3rd Edition". *Proteins Structure Function and Bioinformatics* **69** (4): 704. doi:10.1002/prot.21804. PMID 17918726.

[3] Robertson TA, Varani G (2007). "An all-atom, distance-dependent scoring function for the prediction of protein-DNA interactions from structure". *Proteins* **66** (2): 359–74. doi:10.1002/prot.21162. PMID 17078093.

[4] Rajamani R, Good AC (2007). "Ranking poses in structure-based lead discovery and optimization: current trends in scoring function development". *Current opinion in drug discovery & development* **10** (3): 308–15. PMID 17554857.

[5] Seifert MH, Kraus J, Kramer B (2007). "Virtual high-throughput screening of molecular databases". *Current opinion in drug discovery & development* **10** (3): 298–307. PMID 17554856.

[6] Böhm HJ (July 1998). "Prediction of binding constants of protein ligands: a fast method for the prioritization of hits obtained from de novo design or 3D database search programs". *J. Comput. Aided Mol. Des.* **12** (4): 309–23. doi:10.1023/A:1007999920146. PMID 9777490.

[7] Joseph-McCarthy D, Baber JC, Feyfant E, Thompson DC, Humblet C (2007). "Lead optimization via high-throughput molecular docking". *Current opinion in drug discovery & development* **10** (3): 264–74. PMID 17554852.

[8] Foloppe N, Hubbard R (2006). "Towards predictive ligand design with free-energy based computational methods?". *Curr. Med. Chem.* **13** (29): 3583–608. doi:10.2174/092986706779026165. PMID 17168725.

[9] Muegge I (2006). "PMF scoring revisited". *J. Med. Chem.* **49** (20): 5895–902. doi:10.1021/jm050038s. PMID 17004705.

[10] Englebienne P, Moitessier N (2009). "Docking Ligands into Flexible and Solvated Macromolecules. 4. Are Popular Scoring Functions Accurate for this Class of Proteins?" (http://pubs.acs.org/doi/abs/10.1021/ci8004308). *J Chem Inf Model* **49** (6): 1568–1580. doi:10.1021/ci8004308. PMID 19445499. .

[11] Oda A, Tsuchida K, Takakura T, Yamaotsu N, Hirono S (2006). "Comparison of consensus scoring strategies for evaluating computational models of protein-ligand complexes" (http://pubs.acs.org/doi/abs/10.1021/ci050283k). *J Chem Inf Model* **46** (1): 380–391. doi:10.1021/ci050283k. PMID 16426072. .

Searching the conformational space for docking

In molecular modelling, **docking** is a method which predicts the preferred orientation of one molecule to another when bound together in a stable complex. In the case of protein docking, the **search space** consists of all possible orientations of the protein with respect to the ligand. Flexible docking in addition considers all possible conformations of the protein paired with all possible conformations of the ligand.[1]

With present computing resources, it is impossible to exhaustively explore these search spaces; instead, there are many strategies which attempt to sample the search space with optimal efficiency. Most docking programs in use account for a flexible ligand, and several attempt to model a flexible protein receptor. Each "snapshot" of the pair is referred to as a pose.

Molecular dynamics (MD) simulations

In this approach, proteins are typically held rigid, and the ligand is allowed to freely explore their conformational space. The generated conformations are then docked successively into the protein, and an MD simulation consisting of a simulated annealing protocol is performed. This is usually supplemented with short MD energy minimization steps, and the energies determined from the MD runs are used for ranking the overall scoring. Although this is a computer-expensive method (involving potentially hundreds of MD runs), it has some advantages: for example, no specialized energy/scoring functions are required. MD force-fields can typically be used to find poses that are reasonable and can be compared with experimental structures.

The Distance Constrained Essential Dynamics method (DCED) has been used to generate multiple structures for docking, called eigenstructures. This approach, although avoiding most of the costly MD calculations, can capture the essential motions involved in a flexible receptor, representing a form of coarse-grained dynamics.[2]

Shape-complementarity methods

The most common technique used in many docking programs, shape-complementarity methods focus on the match between the receptor and the ligand in order to find an optimal pose. Programs include DOCK,[3] FRED,[4] GLIDE,[5] SURFLEX,[6] eHiTS[7] and many more. Most methods describe the molecules in terms of a finite number of descriptors that include structural complementarity and binding complementarity. Structural complementarity is mostly a geometric description of the molecules, including solvent-accessible surface area, overall shape and geometric constraints between atoms in the protein and ligand. Binding complementarity takes into account features like hydrogen bonding interactions, hydrophobic contacts and van der Waals interactions to describe how well a particular ligand will bind to the protein. Both kinds of descriptors are conveniently represented in the form of structural templates which are then used to quickly match potential compounds (either from a database or from the user-given inputs) that will bind well at the active site of the protein. Compared to the all-atom molecular dynamics approaches, these methods are very efficient in finding optimal binding poses for the protein and ligand.

Genetic algorithms

Two of the most used docking programs belong to this class: GOLD[8] and AutoDock.[9] Genetic algorithms allow the exploration of a large conformational space − which is basically spanned by the protein and ligand jointly in this case − by representing each spatial arrangement of the pair as a "gene" with a particular energy. The entire genome thus represents the complete energy landscape which is to be explored. The simulation of the evolution of the genome is carried out by cross-over techniques similar to biological evolution, where random pairs of individuals (conformations) are "mated" with the possibility for a random mutation in the offspring. These methods have proven very useful in sampling the vast state-space while maintaining closeness to the actual process involved.

Although genetic algorithms are quite successful in sampling the large conformational space, many docking programs require the protein to remain fixed, while allowing only the ligand to flex and adjust to the active site of the protein. Genetic algorithms also require multiple runs to obtain reliable answers regarding ligands that may bind to the protein. The time it takes to typically run a genetic algorithm in order to allow a proper pose may be longer, hence these methods may not be as efficient as shape complementarity-based approaches in screening large databases of compounds. Recent improvements in using grid-based evaluation of energies, limiting the exploration of the conformational changes at only local areas (active sites) of interest, and improved tabling methods have significantly enhanced the performance of genetic algorithms and made them suitable for virtual screening applications.

References

[1] Halperin I, Ma B, Wolfson H, Nussinov R (June 2002). "Principles of docking: An overview of search algorithms and a guide to scoring functions". *Proteins* **47** (4): 409–443. doi:10.1002/prot.10115. PMID 12001221.

[2] Mustard D, Ritchie DW (August 2005). "Docking essential dynamics eigenstructures". *Proteins* **60** (2): 269–274. doi:10.1002/prot.20569. PMID 15981272.

[3] Shoichet BK, Stroud RM, Santi DV, Kuntz ID, Perry KM (March 1993). "Structure-based discovery of inhibitors of thymidylate synthase". *Science* **259** (5100): 1445–50. doi:10.1126/science.8451640. PMID 8451640.

[4] McGann MR, Almond HR, Nicholls A, Grant JA, Brown FK (January 2003). "Gaussian docking functions". *Biopolymers* **68** (1): 76–90. doi:10.1002/bip.10207. PMID 12579581.

[5] Friesner RA, Banks JL, Murphy RB, Halgren TA, Klicic JJ, Mainz DT, Repasky MP, Knoll EH, Shelley M, Perry JK, Shaw DE, Francis P, Shenkin PS (March 2004). "Glide: a new approach for rapid, accurate docking and scoring. 1. Method and assessment of docking accuracy". *J. Med. Chem.* **47** (7): 1739–1749. doi:10.1021/jm0306430. PMID 15027865.

[6] Jain AN (February 2003). "Surflex: fully automatic flexible molecular docking using a molecular similarity-based search engine". *J. Med. Chem.* **46** (4): 499–511. doi:10.1021/jm020406h. PMID 12570372.

[7] Zsoldos Z, Reid D, Simon A, Sadjad SB, Johnson AP (July 2007). "eHiTS: a new fast, exhaustive flexible ligand docking system". *J. Mol. Graph. Model.* **26** (1): 198–212. doi:10.1016/j.jmgm.2006.06.002. PMID 16860582.

[8] Jones G, Willett P, Glen RC, Leach AR, Taylor R (April 1997). "Development and validation of a genetic algorithm for flexible docking". *J. Mol. Biol.* **267** (3): 727–748. doi:10.1006/jmbi.1996.0897. PMID 9126849.

[9] Goodsell DS, Morris GM, Olson AJ (1996). "Automated docking of flexible ligands: applications of AutoDock". *J. Mol. Recognit.* **9** (1): 1–5. doi:10.1002/(SICI)1099-1352(199601)9:1<1::AID-JMR241>3.0.CO;2-6. PMID 8723313.

Semantic integration

Semantic integration is the process of interrelating information from diverse sources, for example calendars and to do lists; email archives; physical, psychological, and social presence information; documents of all sorts; contacts (including social graphs); search results; and advertising and marketing relevance derived from them. In this regard, semantics focuses on the organization of and action upon information by acting as a mediary between heterogeneous data sources which may conflict not only by structure but also context or value.

In Enterprise Application Integration, semantic integration will facilitate or potentially automate the communication between computer systems using metadata publishing. Metadata publishing potentially offers the ability to automatically link ontologies. One approach to (semi-)automated ontology mapping requires the definition of a semantic distance or its inverse, semantic similarity and appropriate rules. Other approaches include so-called *lexical methods,* as well as methodologies that rely on exploiting the structures of the ontologies. For explicitly stating similarity/equality, there exist special properties or relationships in most ontology languages. OWL, for example has "sameIndividualAs" or "same-ClassAs". Eventually systems design may see the advent of composable architectures where published semantic-based interfaces are joined together in new and meaningful capabilities. These will be predominately described through design-time declarative specifications, that could ultimately be rendered and executed at run-time.

Semantic integration can also be used to facilitate design-time activities of interface design and mapping. In this model, semantics are only explicitly applied to design and the run-time systems work at the syntax level. This "early semantic binding" approach can improve overall system performance while retaining the benefits of semantic driven design.

The Pacific Symposium on Biocomputing has been a venue for the popularization of the ontology mapping task in the biomedical domain, and a number of papers on the subject can be found in its proceedings.

References

External links

- Semantic Integration: Loosely Coupling the Meaning of Data (http://www.zapthink.com/report. html?id=ZapFlash-08082003)
- Concept of Semantic Constraints on Service Composition (http://swese2007.fzi.de/papers/08. Service_Domain_Spaces.doc)
- http://www.srdc.metu.edu.tr/webpage/seminars/Ontology/Ontology%20Mapping%20Survey.ppt
- http://www.aifb.uni-karlsruhe.de/WBS/ysu/publications/2004_mapping_TR.pdf
- http://drops.dagstuhl.de/opus/volltexte/2005/40/
- http://www.cyc.com/doc/white_papers/kimas2003.pdf
- OpenPSI the (OpenPSI project (http://www.openpsi.org))is a community effort to create UK government linked data service that supports research. It is a collaboration between the University of Southampton and the UK government, led by OPSI at the National Archive and is supported by JISC funding.
- A historical perspective on developing foundations for privacy-friendly client cloud computing: The Paradigm Shift from "Inconsistency Denial" to "Semantic Integration" (http://arxiv.org/abs/0901.4934)
- Mitchell Ummel (Editor), The Rise of the Semantic Enterprise (http://www.cutter.com/offers/ semanticenterprise.html), Cutter Consortium, 2009.
- A historical perspective on developing foundations for privacy-friendly client cloud computing: The Paradigm Shift from "Inconsistency Denial" to "Practical Semantic Integration" (http://arxiv.org/abs/0901.4934) ArXiv 0901.4934.

- Semantic MediaWiki Plus (http://smwforum.ontoprise.com), Semantic MediaWiki from Ontoprise
- Semantic MediaWiki Plus User Forum (http://smwforum.ontoprise.com/smwboard)

Sensitivity and specificity

Sensitivity and **specificity** are statistical measures of the performance of a binary classification test, also known in statistics as classification function. **Sensitivity** (also called **recall rate** in some fields) measures the proportion of actual positives which are correctly identified as such (e.g. the percentage of sick people who are correctly identified as having the condition). **Specificity** measures the proportion of negatives which are correctly identified (e.g. the percentage of healthy people who are correctly identified as not having the condition). These two measures are closely related to the concepts of type I and type II errors. A theoretical, optimal prediction aims to achieve 100% sensitivity (i.e. predict all people from the sick group as sick) and 100% specificity (i.e. not predict anyone from the healthy group as sick), however theoretically any predictor will possess a minimum error bound known as the Bayes error rate.

For any test, there is usually a trade-off between the measures. For example: in an airport security setting in which one is testing for potential threats to safety, scanners may be set to trigger on low-risk items like belt buckles and keys (low specificity), in order to reduce the risk of missing objects that do pose a threat to the aircraft and those aboard (high sensitivity). This trade-off can be represented graphically as an ROC curve.

Definitions

Imagine a study evaluating a new test that screens people for a disease. Each person taking the test either has or does not have the disease. The test outcome can be positive (predicting that the person has the disease) or negative (predicting that the person does not have the disease). The test results for each subject may or may not match the subject's actual status. In that setting:

- True positive: Sick people correctly diagnosed as sick
- False positive: Healthy people incorrectly identified as sick
- True negative: Healthy people correctly identified as healthy
- False negative: Sick people incorrectly identified as healthy.

Sensitivity

Sensitivity relates to the test's ability to identify positive results.

Again, consider the example of the medical test used to identify a disease. The sensitivity of a test is the proportion of people who have the disease who test positive for it. This can also be written as:

$$\text{sensitivity} = \frac{\text{number of true positives}}{\text{number of true positives} + \text{number of false negatives}}$$

If a test has high sensitivity then a negative result would suggest the absence of disease.[1] For example, a sensitivity of 100% means that the test recognizes all actual positives – i.e. all sick people are recognized as being ill. Thus, in contrast to a high specificity test, *negative results* in a *high sensitivity test* are used to *rule out* the disease.[1]

From a theoretical point of view, a 'bogus' test kit which always indicates positive, regardless of the disease status of the patient, will achieve 100% sensitivity. Therefore the sensitivity alone cannot be used to determine whether a test is useful in practice.

Sensitivity is not the same as the precision or positive predictive value (ratio of true positives to combined true and false positives), which is as much a statement about the proportion of actual positives in the population being tested as it is about the test.

The calculation of sensitivity does not take into account indeterminate test results. If a test cannot be repeated, the options are to exclude indeterminate samples from analysis (but the number of exclusions should be stated when quoting sensitivity), or, alternatively, indeterminate samples can be treated as false negatives (which gives the worst-case value for sensitivity and may therefore underestimate it).

A test with a high sensitivity has a low type II error rate.

Specificity

Specificity relates to the ability of the test to identify negative results.

Consider the example of the medical test used to identify a disease. The specificity of a test is defined as the proportion of patients who do not have the disease who will test negative for it. This can also be written as:

$$\text{specificity} = \frac{\text{number of true negatives}}{\text{number of true negatives} + \text{number of false positives}}$$

If a test has high specificity, a positive result from the test means a high probability of the presence of disease.[1]

From a theoretical point of view, a 'bogus' test kit which always indicates negative, regardless of the disease status of the patient, will achieve 100% specificity. Therefore the specificity alone cannot be used to determine whether a test is useful in practice.

A test with a high specificity has a low type I error rate.

Graphical illustration

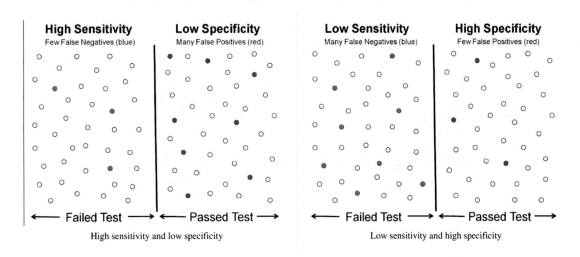

High sensitivity and low specificity   Low sensitivity and high specificity

Medical examples

In medical diagnostics, test sensitivity is the ability of a test to correctly identify those with the disease (true +ve rate), whereas test specificity is the ability of the test to correctly identify those without the disease (true -ve rate).[2]

If 100 patients known to have a disease were tested, and 43 test positive, then the test has 43% sensitivity. If 100 with no disease are tested and 96 return a negative result, then the test has 96% specificity.

A highly specific test is unlikely to give a false positive result: a positive result should thus be regarded as a true positive. A sign or symptom with very high specificity is often termed *pathognomonic*. An example of such a test is the inspection for erythema chronicum migrans to diagnose lyme disease.[3] In contrast, a sensitive test rarely misses a condition, so a negative result should be reassuring (the disease tested for is absent). A sign or symptom with very high sensitivity is often termed *sine qua non*. An example of such test is a genetic test to find an underlying mutation in certain types of hereditary colon cancer.[4] [5]

SPIN and SNOUT are commonly used mnemonics which says: A highly SPecific test, when Positive, rules IN disease (SP-P-IN), and a highly 'SeNsitive' test, when Negative rules OUT disease (SN-N-OUT).

Worked example

Relationships among terms

		Condition (as determined by "Gold standard")		
		Positive	*Negative*	
Test outcome	*Positive*	True Positive	False Positive (Type I error)	→ Positive predictive value $= \dfrac{\Sigma \text{ True Positive}}{\Sigma \text{ Test outcome Positive}}$
	Negative	False Negative (Type II error)	True Negative	→ Negative predictive value $= \dfrac{\Sigma \text{ True Negative}}{\Sigma \text{ Test outcome Negative}}$
		↓ Sensitivity $= \dfrac{\Sigma \text{ True Positive}}{\Sigma \text{ Condition Positive}}$	↓ Specificity $= \dfrac{\Sigma \text{ True Negative}}{\Sigma \text{ Condition Negative}}$	

A worked example

The fecal occult blood (FOB) screen test was used in 2030 people to look for bowel cancer:

		Patients with bowel cancer (as confirmed on endoscopy)		
		Positive	*Negative*	
Fecal occult blood screen test outcome	*Positive*	True Positive (TP) = 20	False Positive (FP) = 180	→ Positive predictive value = TP / (TP + FP) = 20 / (20 + 180) = 20 / 200 = **10%**
	Negative	False Negative (FN) = 10	True Negative (TN) = 1820	→ Negative predictive value = TN / (FN + TN) = 1820 / (10 + 1820) = 1820 / 1830 ≈ **99.5%**
		↓ Sensitivity = TP / (TP + FN) = 20 / (20 + 10) = 20 / 30 ≈ **66.67%**	↓ Specificity = TN / (FP + TN) = 1820 / (180 + 1820) = 1820 / 2000 = **91%**	

Related calculations

- False positive rate (α) = FP / (FP + TN) = 180 / (180 + 1820) = 9% = 1 − specificity
- False negative rate (β) = FN / (TP + FN) = 10 / (20 + 10) = 33% = 1 − sensitivity
- Power = sensitivity = 1 − β
- Likelihood ratio positive = sensitivity / (1 − specificity) = 66.67% / (1 − 91%) = 7.4
- Likelihood ratio negative = (1 − sensitivity) / specificity = (1 − 66.67%) / 91% = 0.37

Hence with large numbers of false positives and few false negatives, a positive FOB screen test is in itself poor at confirming cancer (PPV = 10%) and further investigations must be undertaken; it did, however, correctly identify 66.7% of all cancers (the sensitivity). However as a screening test, a negative result is very good at reassuring that a patient does not have cancer (NPV = 99.5%) and at this initial screen correctly identifies 91% of those who do not have cancer (the specificity).

Terminology in information retrieval

In information retrieval positive predictive value is called **precision**, and sensitivity is called **recall**.

The F-measure can be used as a single measure of performance of the test. The F-measure is the harmonic mean of precision and recall:

$$F = 2 \times \frac{\text{precision} \times \text{recall}}{\text{precision} + \text{recall}}$$

In the traditional language of statistical hypothesis testing, the sensitivity of a test is called the statistical power of the test, although the word *power* in that context has a more general usage that is not applicable in the present context. A sensitive test will have fewer Type II errors.

Further reading

- Altman DG, Bland JM (1994). "Diagnostic tests. 1: Sensitivity and specificity" [6]. *BMJ* **308** (6943): 1552. PMC 2540489. PMID 8019315.

External links

- Calculators:
  - Vassar College's Sensitivity/Specificity Calculator [7]
  - OpenEpi software program

References

[1] http://www.cebm.net/index.aspx?o=1042
[2] MedStats.Org (http://medstats.org/sens-spec)
[3] Ogden NH, Lindsay LR, Morshed M, Sockett PN, Artsob H (January 2008). "The rising challenge of Lyme borreliosis in Canada" (http:// www.phac-aspc.gc.ca/publicat/ccdr-rmtc/08vol34/dr-rm3401a-eng.php). *Can. Commun. Dis. Rep.* **34** (1): 1–19. PMID 18290267. .
[4] Lynch, H. T.; Lynch, J. F.; Lynch, P. M.; Attard, T. (2007). "Hereditary colorectal cancer syndromes: Molecular genetics, genetic counseling, diagnosis and management". *Familial Cancer* **7** (1): 27–39. doi:10.1007/s10689-007-9165-5. PMID 17999161.
[5] Lynch, H. T.; Lanspa, S. J. (2010). "Colorectal Cancer Survival Advantage in MUTYH-Associated Polyposis and Lynch Syndrome Families". *JNCI Journal of the National Cancer Institute* **102** (22): 1687. doi:10.1093/jnci/djq439.
[6] http://www.bmj.com/cgi/content/full/308/6943/1552
[7] http://faculty.vassar.edu/lowry/clin1.html

SeqCorator

SeqCorator

Developer(s)	NoeGen Inc.
Stable release	2.01 / 2009
Operating system	Windows, Linux, Mac OS X, Solaris
Type	bioinformatics
License	commercial
Website	http://www.noegen.com

SeqCorator is a bioinformatics software which can run in multiple operating systems (Windows, Mac OS, Unix/Linux) with the same interface.

Main features

SeqCorator brings advanced graphics to the world of sequence analysis and illustration, creating an environment akin to a combination of Word and PowerPoint that understands sequence data. The integration of graphic drawing and styled text editing enables innovative ways for designing experiments, annotating sequences and features, and creating eye-catching presentations.

- Graphic sequence editing and decoration with complete flexibility and total control
- Graphical features display and it also can record in the feature list
- Enzyme site analysis
- Find ORF
- Translation and find motif
- Allow setup mismatch parameter to search or match sub-sequence

References

relevant software

- NoeClone
- NoePrimer
- Vector NTI
- Gbench (http://www.ncbi.nlm.nih.gov/projects/gbench/)

External links

- NoeGen Official website (http://www.noegen.com/)
- List of phylogeny software (http://evolution.genetics.washington.edu/phylip/software.html), hosted at the University of Washington

Sequence alignment

In bioinformatics, a **sequence alignment** is a way of arranging the sequences of DNA, RNA, or protein to identify regions of similarity that may be a consequence of functional, structural, or evolutionary relationships between the sequences.[1] Aligned sequences of nucleotide or amino acid residues are typically represented as rows within a matrix. Gaps are inserted between the residues so that identical or similar characters are aligned in successive columns.

A sequence alignment, produced by ClustalW, of two human zinc finger proteins, identified on the left by GenBank accession number. Key: Single letters: amino acids. Red: small, hydrophobic, aromatic, not Y. Blue: acidic. Magenta: basic. Green: hydroxyl, amine, amide, basic. Gray: others. "*": identical. ":": conserved substitutions (same colour group). ".": semi-conserved substitution (similar shapes).[2]

Sequence alignments are also used for non-biological sequences, such as those present in natural language or in financial data.

Interpretation

If two sequences in an alignment share a common ancestor, mismatches can be interpreted as point mutations and gaps as indels (that is, insertion or deletion mutations) introduced in one or both lineages in the time since they diverged from one another. In sequence alignments of proteins, the degree of similarity between amino acids occupying a particular position in the sequence can be interpreted as a rough measure of how conserved a particular region or sequence motif is among lineages. The absence of substitutions, or the presence of only very conservative substitutions (that is, the substitution of amino acids whose side chains have similar biochemical properties) in a particular region of the sequence, suggest [3] that this region has structural or functional importance. Although DNA and RNA nucleotide bases are more similar to each other than are amino acids, the conservation of base pairs can indicate a similar functional or structural role.

Alignment methods

Very short or very similar sequences can be aligned by hand. However, most interesting problems require the alignment of lengthy, highly variable or extremely numerous sequences that cannot be aligned solely by human effort. Instead, human knowledge is applied in constructing algorithms to produce high-quality sequence alignments, and occasionally in adjusting the final results to reflect patterns that are difficult to represent algorithmically (especially in the case of nucleotide sequences). Computational approaches to sequence alignment generally fall into two categories: *global alignments* and *local alignments*. Calculating a global alignment is a form of global optimization that "forces" the alignment to span the entire length of all query sequences. By contrast, local alignments identify regions of similarity within long sequences that are often widely divergent overall. Local alignments are often preferable, but can be more difficult to calculate because of the additional challenge of identifying the regions of similarity. A variety of computational algorithms have been applied to the sequence alignment problem, including slow but formally correct methods like dynamic programming, and efficient, heuristic algorithms or probabilistic methods that do not guarantee to find best matches designed for large-scale database search.

Representations

Alignments are commonly represented both graphically and in text format. In almost all sequence alignment representations, sequences are written in rows arranged so that aligned residues appear in successive columns. In text formats, aligned columns containing identical or similar characters are indicated with a system of conservation symbols. As in the image above, an asterisk or pipe symbol is used to show identity between two columns; other less common symbols include a colon for conservative substitutions and a period for semiconservative substitutions. Many sequence visualization programs also use color to display information about the properties of the individual sequence elements; in DNA and RNA sequences, this equates to assigning each nucleotide its own color. In protein alignments, such as the one in the image above, color is often used to indicate amino acid properties to aid in judging the conservation of a given amino acid substitution. For multiple sequences the last row in each column is often the consensus sequence determined by the alignment; the consensus sequence is also often represented in graphical format with a sequence logo in which the size of each nucleotide or amino acid letter corresponds to its degree of conservation.[4]

Sequence alignments can be stored in a wide variety of text-based file formats, many of which were originally developed in conjunction with a specific alignment program or implementation. Most web-based tools allow a limited number of input and output formats, such as FASTA format and GenBank format and the output is not easily editable. Several conversion programs are available, READSEQ [5] or EMBOSS having a graphical interfaces or command line interfaces, while several programming packages like BioPerl, BioRuby provide functions to do this.

Global and local alignments

Global alignments, which attempt to align every residue in every sequence, are most useful when the sequences in the query set are similar and of roughly equal size. (This does not mean global alignments cannot end in gaps.) A general global alignment technique is the Needleman–Wunsch algorithm, which is based on dynamic programming. Local alignments are more useful for dissimilar sequences that are suspected to contain regions of similarity or similar sequence motifs within their larger sequence context. The Smith–Waterman algorithm is a general local alignment method also based on dynamic programming. With sufficiently similar sequences, there is no difference between local and global alignments.

```
Global  FTFTALILLAVAV
        F--TAL-LLA-AV

Local   FTFTALILL-AVAV
        --FTAL-LLAAV--
```

Illustration of global and local alignments demonstrating the 'gappy' quality of global alignments that can occur if sequences are insufficiently similar

Hybrid methods, known as semiglobal or "glocal" (short for global-local) methods, attempt to find the best possible alignment that includes the start and end of one or the other sequence. This can be especially useful when the downstream part of one sequence overlaps with the upstream part of the other sequence. In this case, neither global nor local alignment is entirely appropriate: a global alignment would attempt to force the alignment to extend beyond the region of overlap, while a local alignment might not fully cover the region of overlap.[6]

Pairwise alignment

Pairwise sequence alignment methods are used to find the best-matching piecewise (local) or global alignments of two query sequences. Pairwise alignments can only be used between two sequences at a time, but they are efficient to calculate and are often used for methods that do not require extreme precision (such as searching a database for sequences with high similarity to a query). The three primary methods of producing pairwise alignments are dot-matrix methods, dynamic programming, and word methods;[1] however, multiple sequence alignment techniques can also align pairs of sequences. Although each method has its individual strengths and weaknesses, all three pairwise methods have difficulty with highly repetitive sequences of low information content - especially where the number of repetitions differ in the two sequences to be aligned. One way of quantifying the utility of a given pairwise alignment is the 'maximum unique match' (MUM), or the longest subsequence that occurs in both query sequence. Longer MUM sequences typically reflect closer relatedness.

Dot-matrix methods

The dot-matrix approach, which implicitly produces a family of alignments for individual sequence regions, is qualitative and conceptually simple, though time-consuming to analyze on a large scale. In the absence of noise, it can be easy to visually identify certain sequence features—such as insertions, deletions, repeats, or inverted repeats—from a dot-matrix plot. To construct a dot-matrix plot, the two sequences are written along the top row and leftmost column of a two-dimensional matrix and a dot is placed at any point where the characters in the appropriate columns match—this is a typical recurrence plot. Some implementations vary the size or intensity of the dot depending on the degree of similarity of the two characters, to accommodate conservative substitutions. The dot plots of very closely related sequences will appear as a single line along the matrix's main diagonal.

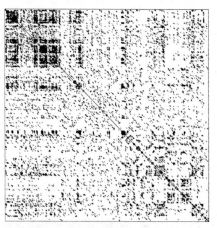

A DNA dot plot of a human zinc finger transcription factor (GenBank ID NM_002383), showing regional self-similarity. The main diagonal represents the sequence's alignment with itself; lines off the main diagonal represent similar or repetitive patterns within the sequence. This is a typical example of a recurrence plot.

Problems with dot plots as an information display technique include: noise, lack of clarity, non-intuitiveness, difficulty extracting match summary statistics and match positions on the two sequences. There is also much wasted space where the match data is inherently duplicated across the diagonal and most of the actual area of the plot is taken up by either empty space or noise, and, finally, dot-plots are limited to two sequences. None of these limitations apply to Miropeats alignment diagrams but they have their own particular flaws.

Dot plots can also be used to assess repetitiveness in a single sequence. A sequence can be plotted against itself and regions that share significant similarities will appear as lines off the main diagonal. This effect can occur when a protein consists of multiple similar structural domains.

Dynamic programming

The technique of dynamic programming can be applied to produce global alignments via the Needleman-Wunsch algorithm, and local alignments via the Smith-Waterman algorithm. In typical usage, protein alignments use a substitution matrix to assign scores to amino-acid matches or mismatches, and a gap penalty for matching an amino acid in one sequence to a gap in the other. DNA and RNA alignments may use a scoring matrix, but in practice often simply assign a positive match score, a negative mismatch score, and a negative gap penalty. (In standard dynamic programming, the score of each amino acid position is independent of the identity of its neighbors, and therefore base stacking effects are not taken into account. However, it is possible to account for such effects by modifying the algorithm.) A common extension to standard linear gap costs, is the usage of two different gap penalties for opening a gap and for extending a gap. Typically the former is much larger than the latter, e.g. -10 for gap open and -2 for gap extension. Thus, the number of gaps in an alignment is usually reduced and residues and gaps are kept together, which typically makes more biological sense. The Gotoh algorithm implements affine gap costs by using three matrices.

Dynamic programming can be useful in aligning nucleotide to protein sequences, a task complicated by the need to take into account frameshift mutations (usually insertions or deletions). The framesearch method produces a series of global or local pairwise alignments between a query nucleotide sequence and a search set of protein sequences, or vice versa. Its ability to evaluate frameshifts offset by an arbitrary number of nucleotides makes the method useful for sequences containing large numbers of indels, which can be very difficult to align with more efficient heuristic methods. In practice, the method requires large amounts of computing power or a system whose architecture is specialized for dynamic programming. The BLAST and EMBOSS suites provide basic tools for creating translated alignments (though some of these approaches take advantage of side-effects of sequence searching capabilities of the tools). More general methods are available from both commercial sources, such as *FrameSearch*, distributed as part of the Accelrys GCG package, and Open Source software such as Genewise [7].

The dynamic programming method is guaranteed to find an optimal alignment given a particular scoring function; however, identifying a good scoring function is often an empirical rather than a theoretical matter. Although dynamic programming is extensible to more than two sequences, it is prohibitively slow for large numbers of or extremely long sequences.

Word methods

Word methods, also known as *k*-tuple methods, are heuristic methods that are not guaranteed to find an optimal alignment solution, but are significantly more efficient than dynamic programming. These methods are especially useful in large-scale database searches where it is understood that a large proportion of the candidate sequences will have essentially no significant match with the query sequence. Word methods are best known for their implementation in the database search tools FASTA and the BLAST family.[1] Word methods identify a series of short, nonoverlapping subsequences ("words") in the query sequence that are then matched to candidate database sequences. The relative positions of the word in the two sequences being compared are subtracted to obtain an offset; this will indicate a region of alignment if multiple distinct words produce the same offset. Only if this region is detected do these methods apply more sensitive alignment criteria; thus, many unnecessary comparisons with sequences of no appreciable similarity are eliminated.

In the FASTA method, the user defines a value *k* to use as the word length with which to search the database. The method is slower but more sensitive at lower values of *k*, which are also preferred for searches involving a very short query sequence. The BLAST family of search methods provides a number of algorithms optimized for particular types of queries, such as searching for distantly related sequence matches. BLAST was developed to provide a faster alternative to FASTA without sacrificing much accuracy; like FASTA, BLAST uses a word search of length *k*, but evaluates only the most significant word matches, rather than every word match as does FASTA. Most BLAST implementations use a fixed default word length that is optimized for the query and database type, and that is changed only under special circumstances, such as when searching with repetitive or very short query sequences. Implementations can be found via a number of web portals, such as EMBL FASTA [8] and NCBI BLAST [9].

Multiple sequence alignment

Multiple sequence alignment is an extension of pairwise alignment to incorporate more than two sequences at a time. Multiple alignment methods try to align all of the sequences in a given query set. Multiple alignments are often used in identifying conserved sequence regions across a group of sequences hypothesized to be evolutionarily related. Such conserved sequence motifs can be used in conjunction with structural and mechanistic information to locate the catalytic active sites of enzymes. Alignments are also used to aid in establishing evolutionary relationships by constructing phylogenetic trees. Multiple sequence alignments are computationally difficult to produce and most formulations of the problem lead to NP-complete combinatorial optimization problems.[10] [11] Nevertheless, the utility of these alignments in bioinformatics has led to the development of a variety of methods suitable for aligning three or more sequences.

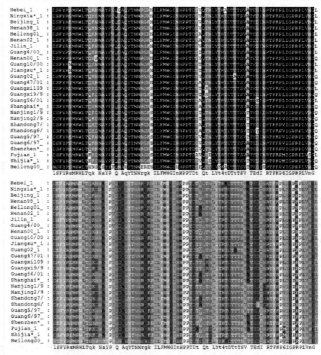

Alignment of 27 avian influenza hemagglutinin protein sequences colored by residue conservation (top) and residue properties (bottom)

Dynamic programming

The technique of dynamic programming is theoretically applicable to any number of sequences; however, because it is computationally expensive in both time and memory, it is rarely used for more than three or four sequences in its most basic form. This method requires constructing the *n*-dimensional equivalent of the sequence matrix formed from two sequences, where *n* is the number of sequences in the query. Standard dynamic programming is first used on all pairs of query sequences and then the "alignment space" is filled in by considering possible matches or gaps at intermediate positions, eventually constructing an alignment essentially between each two-sequence alignment. Although this technique is computationally expensive, its guarantee of a global optimum solution is useful in cases where only a few sequences need to be aligned accurately. One method for reducing the computational demands of dynamic programming, which relies on the "sum of pairs" objective function, has been implemented in the MSA [12] software package.[13]

Progressive methods

Progressive, hierarchical, or tree methods generate a multiple sequence alignment by first aligning the most similar sequences and then adding successively less related sequences or groups to the alignment until the entire query set has been incorporated into the solution. The initial tree describing the sequence relatedness is based on pairwise comparisons that may include heuristic pairwise alignment methods similar to FASTA. Progressive alignment results are dependent on the choice of "most related" sequences and thus can be sensitive to inaccuracies in the initial pairwise alignments. Most progressive multiple sequence alignment methods additionally weight the sequences in the query set according to their relatedness, which reduces the likelihood of making a poor choice of initial sequences and thus improves alignment accuracy.

Many variations of the Clustal progressive implementation[14] [15] [16] are used for multiple sequence alignment, phylogenetic tree construction, and as input for protein structure prediction. A slower but more accurate variant of the progressive method is known as T-Coffee.[17]

Iterative methods

Iterative methods attempt to improve on the weak point of the progressive methods, the heavy dependence on the accuracy of the initial pairwise alignments. Iterative methods optimize an objective function based on a selected alignment scoring method by assigning an initial global alignment and then realigning sequence subsets. The realigned subsets are then themselves aligned to produce the next iteration's multiple sequence alignment. Various ways of selecting the sequence subgroups and objective function are reviewed in.[18]

Motif finding

Motif finding, also known as profile analysis, constructs global multiple sequence alignments that attempt to align short conserved sequence motifs among the sequences in the query set. This is usually done by first constructing a general global multiple sequence alignment, after which the highly conserved regions are isolated and used to construct a set of profile matrices. The profile matrix for each conserved region is arranged like a scoring matrix but its frequency counts for each amino acid or nucleotide at each position are derived from the conserved region's character distribution rather than from a more general empirical distribution. The profile matrices are then used to search other sequences for occurrences of the motif they characterize. In cases where the original data set contained a small number of sequences, or only highly related sequences, pseudocounts are added to normalize the character distributions represented in the motif.

Techniques inspired by computer science

A variety of general optimization algorithms commonly used in computer science have also been applied to the multiple sequence alignment problem. Hidden Markov models have been used to produce probability scores for a family of possible multiple sequence alignments for a given query set; although early HMM-based methods produced underwhelming performance, later applications have found them especially effective in detecting remotely related sequences because they are less susceptible to noise created by conservative or semiconservative substitutions.[19] Genetic algorithms and simulated annealing have also been used in optimizing multiple sequence alignment scores as judged by a scoring function like the sum-of-pairs method. More complete details and software packages can be found in the main article multiple sequence alignment.

Structural alignment

Structural alignments, which are usually specific to protein and sometimes RNA sequences, use information about the secondary and tertiary structure of the protein or RNA molecule to aid in aligning the sequences. These methods can be used for two or more sequences and typically produce local alignments; however, because they depend on the availability of structural information, they can only be used for sequences whose corresponding structures are known (usually through X-ray crystallography or NMR spectroscopy). Because both protein and RNA structure is more evolutionarily conserved than sequence,[20] structural alignments can be more reliable between sequences that are very distantly related and that have diverged so extensively that sequence comparison cannot reliably detect their similarity.

Structural alignments are used as the "gold standard" in evaluating alignments for homology-based protein structure prediction[21] because they explicitly align regions of the protein sequence that are structurally similar rather than relying exclusively on sequence information. However, clearly structural alignments cannot be used in structure prediction because at least one sequence in the query set is the target to be modeled, for which the structure is not known. It has been shown that, given the structural alignment between a target and a template sequence, highly accurate models of the target protein sequence can be produced; a major stumbling block in homology-based structure prediction is the production of structurally accurate alignments given only sequence information.[21]

DALI

The DALI method, or distance matrix alignment, is a fragment-based method for constructing structural alignments based on contact similarity patterns between successive hexapeptides in the query sequences.[22] It can generate pairwise or multiple alignments and identify a query sequence's structural neighbors in the Protein Data Bank (PDB). It has been used to construct the FSSP structural alignment database (Fold classification based on Structure-Structure alignment of Proteins, or Families of Structurally Similar Proteins). A DALI webserver can be accessed at EBI DALI [23] and the FSSP is located at The Dali Database [24].

SSAP

SSAP (sequential structure alignment program) is a dynamic programming-based method of structural alignment that uses atom-to-atom vectors in structure space as comparison points. It has been extended since its original description to include multiple as well as pairwise alignments,[25] and has been used in the construction of the CATH (Class, Architecture, Topology, Homology) hierarchical database classification of protein folds.[26] The CATH database can be accessed at CATH Protein Structure Classification [8].

Combinatorial extension

The combinatorial extension method of structural alignment generates a pairwise structural alignment by using local geometry to align short fragments of the two proteins being analyzed and then assembles these fragments into a larger alignment.[27] Based on measures such as rigid-body root mean square distance, residue distances, local secondary structure, and surrounding environmental features such as residue neighbor hydrophobicity, local alignments called "aligned fragment pairs" are generated and used to build a similarity matrix representing all possible structural alignments within predefined cutoff criteria. A path from one protein structure state to the other is then traced through the matrix by extending the growing alignment one fragment at a time. The optimal such path defines the combinatorial-extension alignment. A web-based server implementing the method and providing a database of pairwise alignments of structures in the Protein Data Bank is located at the Combinatorial Extension [28] website.

Phylogenetic analysis

Phylogenetics and sequence alignment are closely related fields due to the shared necessity of evaluating sequence relatedness.[29] The field of phylogenetics makes extensive use of sequence alignments in the construction and interpretation of phylogenetic trees, which are used to classify the evolutionary relationships between homologous genes represented in the genomes of divergent species. The degree to which sequences in a query set differ is qualitatively related to the sequences' evolutionary distance from one another. Roughly speaking, high sequence identity suggests that the sequences in question have a comparatively young most recent common ancestor, while low identity suggests that the divergence is more ancient. This approximation, which reflects the "molecular clock" hypothesis that a roughly constant rate of evolutionary change can be used to extrapolate the elapsed time since two genes first diverged (that is, the coalescence time), assumes that the effects of mutation and selection are constant across sequence lineages. Therefore it does not account for possible difference among organisms or species in the rates of DNA repair or the possible functional conservation of specific regions in a sequence. (In the case of nucleotide sequences, the molecular clock hypothesis in its most basic form also discounts the difference in acceptance rates between silent mutations that do not alter the meaning of a given codon and other mutations that result in a different amino acid being incorporated into the protein.) More statistically accurate methods allow the evolutionary rate on each branch of the phylogenetic tree to vary, thus producing better estimates of coalescence times for genes.

Progressive multiple alignment techniques produce a phylogenetic tree by necessity because they incorporate sequences into the growing alignment in order of relatedness. Other techniques that assemble multiple sequence alignments and phylogenetic trees score and sort trees first and calculate a multiple sequence alignment from the highest-scoring tree. Commonly used methods of phylogenetic tree construction are mainly heuristic because the problem of selecting the optimal tree, like the problem of selecting the optimal multiple sequence alignment, is NP-hard.[30]

Assessment of significance

Sequence alignments are useful in bioinformatics for identifying sequence similarity, producing phylogenetic trees, and developing homology models of protein structures. However, the biological relevance of sequence alignments is not always clear. Alignments are often assumed to reflect a degree of evolutionary change between sequences descended from a common ancestor; however, it is formally possible that convergent evolution can occur to produce apparent similarity between proteins that are evolutionarily unrelated but perform similar functions and have similar structures.

In database searches such as BLAST, statistical methods can determine the likelihood of a particular alignment between sequences or sequence regions arising by chance given the size and composition of the database being searched. These values can vary significantly depending on the search space. In particular, the likelihood of finding a given alignment by chance increases if the database consists only of sequences from the same organism as the query sequence. Repetitive sequences in the database or query can also distort both the search results and the assessment of statistical significance; BLAST automatically filters such repetitive sequences in the query to avoid apparent hits that are statistical artifacts.

Methods of statistical significance estimation for gapped sequence alignments are available in the literature.[29] [31] [32] [33]

Assessment of credibility

Statistical significance indicates the probability that an alignment of a given quality could arise by chance, but does not indicate how much superior a given alignment is to alternative alignments of the same sequences. Measures of alignment credibility indicate the extent to which the best scoring alignments for a given pair of sequences are substantially similar. Methods of alignment credibility estimation for gapped sequence alignments are available in the literature.[34]

Scoring functions

The choice of a scoring function that reflects biological or statistical observations about known sequences is important to producing good alignments. Protein sequences are frequently aligned using substitution matrices that reflect the probabilities of given character-to-character substitutions. A series of matrices called PAM matrices (Point Accepted Mutation matrices, originally defined by Margaret Dayhoff and sometimes referred to as "Dayhoff matrices") explicitly encode evolutionary approximations regarding the rates and probabilities of particular amino acid mutations. Another common series of scoring matrices, known as BLOSUM (Blocks Substitution Matrix), encodes empirically derived substitution probabilities. Variants of both types of matrices are used to detect sequences with differing levels of divergence, thus allowing users of BLAST or FASTA to restrict searches to more closely related matches or expand to detect more divergent sequences. Gap penalties account for the introduction of a gap - on the evolutionary model, an insertion or deletion mutation - in both nucleotide and protein sequences, and therefore the penalty values should be proportional to the expected rate of such mutations. The quality of the alignments produced therefore depends on the quality of the scoring function.

It can be very useful and instructive to try the same alignment several times with different choices for scoring matrix and/or gap penalty values and compare the results. Regions where the solution is weak or non-unique can often be identified by observing which regions of the alignment are robust to variations in alignment parameters.

Other biological uses

Sequenced RNA, such as expressed sequence tags and full-length mRNAs, can be aligned to a sequenced genome to find where there are genes and get information about alternative splicing[35] and RNA editing.[36] Sequence alignment is also a part of genome assembly, where sequences are aligned to find overlap so that *contigs* (long stretches of sequence) can be formed.[37] Another use is SNP analysis, where sequences from different individuals are aligned to find single basepairs that are often different in a population.[38]

Non-biological uses

The methods used for biological sequence alignment have also found applications in other fields, most notably in natural language processing and in social sciences.[39] Techniques that generate the set of elements from which words will be selected in natural-language generation algorithms have borrowed multiple sequence alignment techniques from bioinformatics to produce linguistic versions of computer-generated mathematical proofs.[40] In the field of historical and comparative linguistics, sequence alignment has been used to partially automate the comparative method by which linguists traditionally reconstruct languages.[41] Business and marketing research has also applied multiple sequence alignment techniques in analyzing series of purchases over time.[42]

Software

A more complete list of available software categorized by algorithm and alignment type is available at sequence alignment software, but common software tools used for general sequence alignment tasks include ClustalW [43] and T-coffee [44] for alignment, and BLAST [45] and FASTA3x [46] for database searching.

Alignment algorithms and software can be directly compared to one another using a standardized set of benchmark reference multiple sequence alignments known as BAliBASE.[47] The data set consists of structural alignments, which can be considered a standard against which purely sequence-based methods are compared. The relative performance of many common alignment methods on frequently encountered alignment problems has been tabulated and selected results published online at BAliBASE [48].[49] A comprehensive list of BAliBASE scores for many (currently 12) different alignment tools can be computed within the protein workbench STRAP [25].

References

[1] Mount DM. (2004). *Bioinformatics: Sequence and Genome Analysis* (2nd ed.). Cold Spring Harbor Laboratory Press: Cold Spring Harbor, NY.. ISBN 0-87969-608-7.

[2] ClustalW2 FAQs http://www.ebi.ac.uk/Tools/clustalw2/help.html#color

[3] Ng PC, Henikoff S. Predicting deleterious amino acid substitutions. Genome Res. 2001 May;11(5):863-74. (http://www.ncbi.nlm.nih.gov/pubmed/11337480)

[4] Schneider TD, Stephens RM (1990). "Sequence logos: a new way to display consensus sequences" (http://nar.oxfordjournals.org/cgi/pmidlookup?view=long&pmid=2172928). *Nucleic Acids Res* 18 (20): 6097–6100. doi:10.1093/nar/18.20.6097. PMC 332411. PMID 2172928. .

[5] http://bioweb.pasteur.fr/seqanal/interfaces/readseq.html

[6] Brudno M, Malde S, Poliakov A, Do CB, Couronne O, Dubchak I, Batzoglou S (2003). "Glocal alignment: finding rearrangements during alignment" (http://bioinformatics.oxfordjournals.org/cgi/pmidlookup?view=long&pmid=12855437). *Bioinformatics*. 19 **Suppl 1** (90001): i54–62. doi:10.1093/bioinformatics/btg1005. PMID 12855437. .

[7] http://www.ebi.ac.uk/Wise2

[8] http://www.ebi.ac.uk/fasta33/

[9] http://www.ncbi.nlm.nih.gov/BLAST/

[10] Wang L, Jiang T. (1994). "On the complexity of multiple sequence alignment" (http://www.liebertonline.com/doi/abs/10.1089/cmb. 1994.1.337). *J Comput Biol* **1** (4): 337–48. doi:10.1089/cmb.1994.1.337. PMID 8790475. .

[11] Elias, Isaac (2006). "Settling the intractability of multiple alignment" (http://www.liebertonline.com/doi/abs/10.1089/cmb.2006.13. 1323). *J Comput Biol* **13** (7): 1323–1339. doi:10.1089/cmb.2006.13.1323. PMID 17037961. .

[12] http://www.ncbi.nlm.nih.gov/CBBresearch/Schaffer/msa.html

[13] Lipman DJ, Altschul SF, Kececioglu JD (1989). "A tool for multiple sequence alignment" (http://www.pnas.org/cgi/ pmidlookup?view=long&pmid=2734293). *Proc Natl Acad Sci USA* **86** (12): 4412–5. doi:10.1073/pnas.86.12.4412. PMC 287279. PMID 2734293. .

[14] Higgins DG, Sharp PM (1988). "CLUSTAL: a package for performing multiple sequence alignment on a microcomputer" (http:// linkinghub.elsevier.com/retrieve/pii/0378-1119(88)90330-7). *Gene* **73** (1): 237–44. doi:10.1016/0378-1119(88)90330-7. PMID 3243435. .

[15] Thompson JD, Higgins DG, Gibson TJ. (1994). "CLUSTAL W: improving the sensitivity of progressive multiple sequence alignment through sequence weighting, position-specific gap penalties and weight matrix choice" (http://nar.oxfordjournals.org/cgi/ pmidlookup?view=long&pmid=7984417). *Nucleic Acids Res* **22** (22): 4673–80. doi:10.1093/nar/22.22.4673. PMC 308517. PMID 7984417. .

[16] Chenna R, Sugawara H, Koike T, Lopez R, Gibson TJ, Higgins DG, Thompson JD. (2003). "Multiple sequence alignment with the Clustal series of programs" (http://nar.oxfordjournals.org/cgi/pmidlookup?view=long&pmid=12824352). *Nucleic Acids Res* **31** (13): 3497–500. doi:10.1093/nar/gkg500. PMC 168907. PMID 12824352. .

[17] Notredame C, Higgins DG, Heringa J. (2000). "T-Coffee: A novel method for fast and accurate multiple sequence alignment" (http:// linkinghub.elsevier.com/retrieve/pii/S0022-2836(00)94042-7). *J Mol Biol* **302** (1): 205–17. doi:10.1006/jmbi.2000.4042. PMID 10964570. .

[18] Hirosawa M, Totoki Y, Hoshida M, Ishikawa M. (1995). "Comprehensive study on iterative algorithms of multiple sequence alignment" (http://bioinformatics.oxfordjournals.org/cgi/content/abstract/11/1/13). *Comput Appl Biosci* **11** (1): 13–8. doi:10.1093/bioinformatics/11.1.13. PMID 7796270. .

[19] Karplus K, Barrett C, Hughey R. (1998). "Hidden Markov models for detecting remote protein homologies" (http://bioinformatics. oxfordjournals.org/cgi/pmidlookup?view=long&pmid=9927713). *Bioinformatics* **14** (10): 846–856. doi:10.1093/bioinformatics/14.10.846. PMID 9927713. .

[20] Chothia C, Lesk AM. (April 1986). "The relation between the divergence of sequence and structure in proteins". *EMBO J* **5** (4): 823–6. PMC 1166865. PMID 3709526.

[21] Zhang Y, Skolnick J. (2005). "The protein structure prediction problem could be solved using the current PDB library" (http://www.pnas. org/cgi/pmidlookup?view=long&pmid=15653774). *Proc Natl Acad Sci USA* **102** (4): 1029–34. doi:10.1073/pnas.0407152101. PMC 545829. PMID 15653774. .

[22] Holm L, Sander C (1996). "Mapping the protein universe" (http://www.sciencemag.org/cgi/pmidlookup?view=long&pmid=8662544). *Science* **273** (5275): 595–603. doi:10.1126/science.273.5275.595. PMID 8662544. .

[23] http://www.ebi.ac.uk/dali/

[24] http://ekhidna.biocenter.helsinki.fi/dali/start

[25] Taylor WR, Flores TP, Orengo CA. (1994). "Multiple protein structure alignment" (http://www.proteinscience.org/cgi/ pmidlookup?view=long&pmid=7849601). *Protein Sci* **3** (10): 1858–70. doi:10.1002/pro.5560031025. PMC 2142613. PMID 7849601. .

[26] Orengo CA, Michie AD, Jones S, Jones DT, Swindells MB, Thornton JM (1997). "CATH--a hierarchic classification of protein domain structures". *Structure* **5** (8): 1093–108. doi:10.1016/S0969-2126(97)00260-8. PMID 9309224.

[27] Shindyalov IN, Bourne PE. (1998). "Protein structure alignment by incremental combinatorial extension (CE) of the optimal path" (http:// peds.oxfordjournals.org/cgi/pmidlookup?view=long&pmid=9796821). *Protein Eng* **11** (9): 739–47. doi:10.1093/protein/11.9.739. PMID 9796821. .

[28] http://web.archive.org/web/cl.sdsc.edu/

[29] Ortet P, Bastien O (2010). "Where Does the Alignment Score Distribution Shape Come from?" (http://www.la-press.com/ where-does-the-alignment-score-distribution-shape-come-from-article-a2393). *Evolutionary Bioinformatics* **6**: 159–187. doi:10.4137/EBO.S5875. PMID 21258650. .

[30] Felsenstein J. (2004). *Inferring Phylogenies*. Sinauer Associates: Sunderland, MA. ISBN 0-87893-177-5.

[31] Newberg LA (2008). "Significance of gapped sequence alignments". *J Comput Biolo* **15** (9): 1187–1194. doi:10.1089/cmb.2008.0125. PMC 2737730. PMID 18973434.

[32] Eddy SR; Rost, Burkhard (2008). Rost, Burkhard. ed. "A probabilistic model of local sequence alignment that simplifies statistical significance estimation". *PLoS Comput Biol* **4** (5): e1000069. doi:10.1371/journal.pcbi.1000069. PMC 2396288. PMID 18516236.

[33] Bastien O, Aude JC, Roy S, Marechal E (2004). "Fundamentals of massive automatic pairwise alignments of protein sequences: theoretical significance of Z-value statistics" (http://bioinformatics.oxfordjournals.org/content/20/4/534.long). *Bioinformatics* **20** (4): 534–537. doi:10.1093/bioinformatics/btg440. PMID 14990449. .

[34] Newberg LA, Lawrence CE (2009). "Exact Calculation of Distributions on Integers, with Application to Sequence Alignment". *J Comput Biolo* **16** (1): 1–18. doi:10.1089/cmb.2008.0137. PMC 2858568. PMID 19119992.

[35] Kim N, Lee C (2008). "Bioinformatics detection of alternative splicing". *Methods Mol. Biol.* **452**: 179–97. doi:10.1007/978-1-60327-159-2_9. PMID 18566765.

[36] Li JB, Levanon EY, Yoon JK, *et al.* (May 2009). "Genome-wide identification of human RNA editing sites by parallel DNA capturing and sequencing". *Science* **324** (5931): 1210–3. doi:10.1126/science.1170995. PMID 19478186.

[37] Blazewicz J, Bryja M, Figlerowicz M, *et al.* (June 2009). "Whole genome assembly from 454 sequencing output via modified DNA graph concept". *Comput Biol Chem* **33** (3): 224–30. doi:10.1016/j.compbiolchem.2009.04.005. PMID 19477687.

[38] Duran C, Appleby N, Vardy M, Imelfort M, Edwards D, Batley J (May 2009). "Single nucleotide polymorphism discovery in barley using autoSNPdb". *Plant Biotechnol. J.* **7** (4): 326–33. doi:10.1111/j.1467-7652.2009.00407.x. PMID 19386041.

[39] Abbott A., Tsay A. (2000). "Sequence Analysis and Optimal Matching Methods in Sociology, Review and Prospect". *Sociological Methods and Research* **29** (1): 3–33. doi:10.1177/0049124100029001001.

[40] Barzilay R, Lee L. (2002). "Bootstrapping Lexical Choice via Multiple-Sequence Alignment" (http://www.cs.cornell.edu/home/llee/papers/gen-msa.pdf) (PDF). *Proceedings of the Conference on Empirical Methods in Natural Language Processing (EMNLP)* **10**: 164–171. doi:10.3115/1118693.1118715. .

[41] Kondrak, Grzegorz (2002) (PDF). *Algorithms for Language Reconstruction* (http://www.cs.ualberta.ca/~kondrak/papers/thesis.pdf). University of Toronto, Ontario. . Retrieved 2007-01-21.

[42] Prinzie A., D. Van den Poel (2006). "Incorporating sequential information into traditional classification models by using an element/position-sensitive SAM" (http://econpapers.repec.org/paper/rugrugwps/05_2F292.htm). *Decision Support Systems* **42** (2): 508–526. doi:10.1016/j.dss.2005.02.004. . See also Prinzie and Van den Poel's paper Prinzie, A; Vandenpoel, D (2007). "Predicting home-appliance acquisition sequences: Markov/Markov for Discrimination and survival analysis for modeling sequential information in NPTB models" (http://econpapers.repec.org/paper/rugrugwps/07_2F442.htm). *Decision Support Systems* **44** (1): 28–45. doi:10.1016/j.dss.2007.02.008. .

[43] http://www2.ebi.ac.uk/clustalw/

[44] http://tcoffee.vital-it.ch/cgi-bin/Tcoffee/tcoffee_cgi/index.cgi

[45] http://ncbi.nih.gov/BLAST/

[46] http://fasta.bioch.virginia.edu/fasta_www2/fasta_list2.shtml

[47] Thompson JD, Plewniak F, Poch O (1999). "BAliBASE: a benchmark alignment database for the evaluation of multiple alignment programs" (http://bioinformatics.oxfordjournals.org/cgi/pmidlookup?view=long&pmid=10068696). *Bioinformatics* **15** (1): 87–8. doi:10.1093/bioinformatics/15.1.87. PMID 10068696. .

[48] http://bips.u-strasbg.fr/fr/Products/Databases/BAliBASE/prog_scores.html

[49] Thompson JD, Plewniak F, Poch O. (1999). "A comprehensive comparison of multiple sequence alignment programs" (http://nar.oxfordjournals.org/cgi/pmidlookup?view=long&pmid=10373585). *Nucleic Acids Res* **27** (13): 2682–90. doi:10.1093/nar/27.13.2682. PMC 148477. PMID 10373585. .

Sequence analysis

In biology, the term **sequence analysis** refers to the process of subjecting a DNA, RNA or peptide sequence to any of a wide range of analytical methods to understand its features, function, structure or evolution. Methodologies used includes sequence alignment, searches against biological databases,[1] or other bioinformatics methods.

Since the development of methods of high-throughput production of gene and protein sequences, the rate of addition of new sequences to the databases increased exponentially. Such a collection of sequences does not, by itself, increase the scientist's understanding of the biology of organisms. However, comparing these new sequences to those with known functions is a key way of understanding the biology of an organism from which the new sequence comes. Thus, sequence analysis can be used to assign function to genes and proteins by the study of the similarities between the compared sequences. Nowadays there are many tools and techniques that provide the sequence comparisons (sequence alignment) and analyze the alignment product to understand its biology.

Sequence analysis in molecular biology includes a very wide range of relevant topics:

1. The comparison of sequences in order to find similarity often to infer if they are related (homologous)
2. Identification of intrinsic features of the sequence such as active sites, post translational modification sites, gene-structures, reading frames, distributions of introns and exons and regulatory elements
3. Identification of sequence differences and variations such as point mutations and single nucleotide polymorphism (SNP) in order to get the genetic marker.
4. Revealing the evolution and genetic diversity of sequences and organisms
5. Identification of molecular structure from sequence alone

In chemistry, sequence analysis comprises techniques used to do determine the sequence of a polymer formed of several monomers. In molecular biology and genetics, the same process is called simply "sequencing".

In marketing, sequence analysis is often used in analytical customer relationship management applications, such as NPTB models (Next Product to Buy).

History

Since the very first sequences of the insulin protein was characterised by Fred Sanger in 1951 biologists have been trying to use this knowledge to understand the function of molecules.[2] [3]

Sequence Alignment

```
A5ASC3.1  14 SIKLWPPSQTTRLLLVERMANNLST..PSIFTRK..YGSLSKEEARENAKQIEEVACSTANQ.....HYEKEPDGDGGSAVQLYAKECSKLILEVLK 101
B4F917.1  13 SIKLWPPSESTRIMLVDRMTNNLST..ESIFSRK..YRLLGKQEAHENAKTIEELCFALADE.....HFREEPDGDGSSAVQLYAKETSKMMLEVLK 100
A9S1V2.1  23 VFKLWPPSQGTREAVRQKMALKLSS..ACFESQS..FARIELADAQEHARAIEEVAFGAAQE......ADSGGDKTGSAVVMVYAKHASKLHLETLR 109
B9GSN7.1  13 SVKLWPPGQSTRLMLVERMTKNFIT..PSFISRK..YGLLSKEEAEEDAKKIEEVAFAAANQ.....HYEKQPDGDGSSAVQIYAKESSRLMLEVLK 100
Q8H056.1  30 SFSIWPPTQRTRDAVVRRLVDTLGG..DTILCKR..YGAVPAADAEPAARGIEAEAFDAAAA..SGEAAATASVEEGIKALQLYSKEVSRRLLDFVK 120
Q0D4Z3.2  44 SLSIWPPSQRTRDAVVRRLVQTLVA..PSILSQR..YGAVPEAEAGRAAAAVEAEAYAAVTES.SSAAAAPASVEDGIEVLQAYSKEVSRRLLELAK 135
B9MVW8.1  56 SFSIWPPTQRTRDAIISRLIETLST..TSVLSKR..YGTIPKEEASEASRRIEEEAFSGAST.......VASSEKDGLEVLQLYSKEISKRMLETVK 141
Q0IYC5.1  29 SFAVWPPTRRTRDAVVRRLVAVLSGDTTTALRKRYRYGAVPAADAERAARAVEAQAFDAASA....SSSSSSSVEDGIETLQLYSREVSNRLLAFVR 121
A9NWJ46.1 13 SIKLWPPSESTRLMLVERMTDNLSS..VSFFSRK..YGLLSKEEAAENAKRIEETAFLAAND.....HEAKEPNLDDSSVVQFYAREASKLMLEALK 100
Q9C500.1  57 SLRIWPPTQKTRDAVLNRLIETLST..ESILSKR..YGTLKSDDATTVAKLIEEEAYGVASN.......AVSSDDDGIKILELYSKEISKRMLESVK 142
Q2HRI7.1  25 NYSIWPPKQRTRDAVKNRLIETLST..PSVLTKR..YGTMSADEASAAAIQIEDEAFSVANA......SSSTSNDNVTILEVYSKEISKRMIETVK 110
Q9M7N3.1  28 SFKIWPPTQRTREAVVRRLVETLTS..QSVLSKR..YGVIPEEDATSAARIIEEEAFSVASV.ASAASTGGRPEDEWIEVLHIYSQEIXQRVVESAK 119
Q9M7N6.1  25 SFSIWPPTQRTRDAVINRLIESLST..PSILSKR..YGTLPQDEASETARLIEEEAFAAAGS.......TASDADDGIEILQVYSKEISKRMIDTVK 110
Q9LE82.1  14 SVKMWPPSKSTRLMLVERMTKNITT..PSIFSRK..YGLLSVEEAEQDAKRIEDLAFATANK.....HFQNEPDGDGTSAVHVYAKESSKLMLDVIK 101
Q9M651.2  13 SIKLWPPSLPTRKALIERITNNFSS..KTIFTEK..YGSLTKDQATENAKRIEDIAFSTANQ.....QFEREPDGDGGSAVQLYAKECSKLILEVLK 100
B9R748.1  48 SLSIWPPTQRTRDAVITRLIETLSS..PSVLSKR..YGTISHDEAESAARRIEDEAFGVANT.......ATSAEDDGLEILQLYSKEISRRMLDTVK 133
```

Example multiple sequence alignment

There are millions of protein and nucleotide sequences known. These sequences fall into many groups of related sequences known as protein families or gene families. Relationships between these sequences are usually discovered by aligning them together and assigning this alignment a score. There are two main types of sequence alignment. Pair-wise sequence alignment only compares two sequences at a time and multiple sequence alignment compares many sequences in one go. Two important algorithms for aligning pairs of sequences are the Needleman-Wunsch algorithm and the Smith-Waterman algorithm. Popular tools for sequence alignment include:

- Pair-wise alignment - BLAST
- Multiple alignment - ClustalW, PROBCONS, MUSCLE, MAFFT, and T-Coffee.

A common use for pairwise sequence alignment is to take a sequence of interest and compare it to all known sequences in a database to identify homologous sequences. In general the matches in the database are ordered to show the most closely related sequences first followed by sequences with diminishing similarity. These matches are usually reported with a measure of statistical significance such as an Expectation value.

Profile comparison

In 1987 Michael Gribskov, Andrew McLachlan and David Eisenberg introduced the method of profile comparison for identifying distant similarities between proteins.[4] Rather than using a single sequence profile methods use a multiple sequence alignment to encode a profile which contains information about the conservation level of each residue. Profiles are also known as Position Specific Scoring Matrices (PSSMs). In 1993 a probabilistic interpretation of profiles was introduced by David Haussler and colleagues using hidden Markov models.[5] [6]

Sequence assembly

Sequence assembly refers to the reconstruction of a DNA sequence by aligning and merging small DNA fragments. It is an integral part of modern DNA sequencing. Since presently-available DNA sequencing technologies are ill-suited for reading long sequences, large pieces of DNA (such as genomes) are often sequenced by (1) cutting the DNA into small pieces, (2) reading the small fragments, and (3) reconstituting the original DNA by merging the information on various fragment.

Gene prediction

Gene prediction or gene finding refers to the process of identifying the regions of genomic DNA that encode genes. This includes protein-coding genes as well as RNA genes, but may also include prediction of other functional elements such as regulatory regions. Gene finding is one of the first and most important steps in understanding the genome of a species once it has been sequenced. In general the prediction of bacterial genes is significantly simpler and more accurate than the prediction of genes in eukaryotic species that usually have complex intron/exon patterns.

Protein Structure Prediction

The 3D structures of molecules are of great importance to their functions in nature. Since structural prediction of large molecules at an atomic level is largely intractable problem, some biologists introduced ways to predict 3D structure at a primary sequence level. This includes biochemical or statistical analysis of amino acid residues in local regions and structural inference from homologs (or other potentially related proteins) with known 3D structures.

There have been a large number of diverse approaches to solve the structure prediction problem. In order to determine which methods were most effective a structure prediction competition was founded called CASP (Critical Assessment of Structure Prediction).

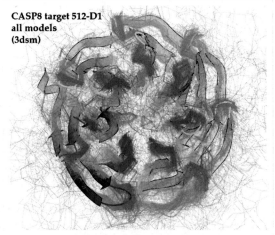

Target protein structure (3dsm, shown in ribbons), with Calpha backbones (in gray) of 354 predicted models for it submitted in the CASP8 structure-prediction experiment.

Methodology

The tasks that lie in the space of sequence analysis are often non-trivial to resolve and require the use of relatively complex approaches. Of the many types of methods used in practice, the most popular include:

- Artificial Neural Network,
- Hidden Markov Model
- Support Vector Machine
- Clustering
- Bayesian Network
- Regression Analysis

References

[1] Durbin, Richard (1998). *Biological sequence analysis: probalistic models of proteins and nucleic acids*. Cambridge, UK: Cambridge University Press. ISBN 0-521-62971-3.

[2] SANGER F, TUPPY H (September 1951). "The amino-acid sequence in the phenylalanyl chain of insulin. I. The identification of lower peptides from partial hydrolysates". *Biochem. J.* **49** (4): 463–81. PMC 1197535. PMID 14886310.

[3] SANGER F, TUPPY H (September 1951). "The amino-acid sequence in the phenylalanyl chain of insulin. 2. The investigation of peptides from enzymic hydrolysates". *Biochem. J.* **49** (4): 481–90. PMC 1197536. PMID 14886311.

[4] Gribskov M, McLachlan AD, Eisenberg D (July 1987). "Profile analysis: detection of distantly related proteins". *Proc. Natl. Acad. Sci. U.S.A.* **84** (13): 4355–8. doi:10.1073/pnas.84.13.4355. PMC 305087. PMID 3474607.

[5] Brown M, Hughey R, Krogh A, Mian IS, Sjölander K, Haussler D (1993). "Using Dirichlet mixture priors to derive hidden Markov models for protein families". *Proc Int Conf Intell Syst Mol Biol* **1**: 47–55. PMID 7584370.

[6] Krogh A, Brown M, Mian IS, Sjölander K, Haussler D (February 1994). "Hidden Markov models in computational biology. Applications to protein modeling". *J. Mol. Biol.* **235** (5): 1501–31. doi:10.1006/jmbi.1994.1104. PMID 8107089.

Sequence assembly

In bioinformatics, **sequence assembly** refers to aligning and merging fragments of a much longer DNA sequence in order to reconstruct the original sequence. This is needed as DNA sequencing technology cannot read whole genomes in one go, but rather reads small pieces of between 20 and 1000 bases, depending on the technology used. Typically the short fragments, called reads, result from shotgun sequencing genomic DNA, or gene transcript (ESTs).

The problem of sequence assembly can be compared to taking many copies of a book, passing them all through a shredder, and piecing a copy of the book back together from only shredded pieces. Besides the confusion introduced by shredding the book, the original may have many repeated paragraphs, and some shreds may be modified during shredding to have typos. Excerpts from another book may also be added in, and some shreds may be completely unrecognizable.

Genome assemblers

The first sequence assemblers began to appear in the late 1980s and early 1990s as variants of simpler sequence alignment programs to piece together vast quantities of fragments generated by automated sequencing instruments called DNA sequencers. As the sequenced organisms grew in size and complexity (from small viruses over plasmids to bacteria and finally eukaryotes), the assembly programs used in these genome projects needed to increasingly employ more and more sophisticated strategies to handle:

- terabytes of sequencing data which need processing on computing clusters;
- identical and nearly identical sequences (known as *repeats*) which can, in the worst case, increase the time and space complexity of algorithms exponentially;
- and errors in the fragments from the sequencing instruments, which can confound assembly.

Faced with the challenge of assembling the first larger eukaryotic genomes, the fruit fly Drosophila melanogaster, in 2000 and the human genome just a year later, scientists developed assemblers like Celera Assembler[1] and Arachne[2] able to handle genomes of 100-300 million base pairs. Subsequent to these efforts, several other groups, mostly at the major genome sequencing centers, built large-scale assemblers, and an open source effort known as AMOS[3] was launched to bring together all the innovations in genome assembly technology under the open source framework.

EST assemblers

EST assembly differs from genome assembly in several ways. The sequences for EST assembly are the transcribed mRNA of a cell and represent only a subset of the whole genome. At a first glance, underlying algorithmical problems differ between genome and EST assembly. For instance, genomes often have large amounts of repetitive sequences, mainly in the inter-genic parts. Since ESTs represent gene transcripts, they will not contain these repeats. On the other hand, cells tend to have a certain number of genes that are constantly expressed in very high amounts (housekeeping genes), which again leads to the problem of similar sequences present in high amounts in the data set to be assembled.

Furthermore, genes sometimes overlap in the genome (sense-antisense transcription), and should ideally still be assembled separately. EST assembly is also complicated by features like (cis-) alternative splicing, trans-splicing, single-nucleotide polymorphism, recoding, and post-transcriptional modification.

De-novo vs. mapping assembly

In sequence assembly, two different types can be distinguished:

1. de-novo: assembling reads together so that they form a new, previously unknown sequence
2. mapping: assembling reads against an existing backbone sequence, building a sequence that is similar but not necessarily identical to the backbone sequence

In terms of complexity and time requirements, de-novo assemblies are orders of magnitude slower and more memory intensive than mapping assemblies. This is mostly due to the fact that the assembly algorithm need to compare every read with every other read (an operation that has a complexity of $O(n^2)$ but can be reduced to $O(n \ \log(n))$. Referring to the comparison drawn to shredded books in the introduction: while for mapping assemblies one would have a very similar book as template (perhaps with the names of the main characters and a few locations changed), the de-novo assemblies are more hardcore in a sense as one would not know beforehand whether this would become a science book, or a novel, or a catalogue etc.

Influence of technological changes

The complexity of sequence assembly is driven by two major factors: the number of fragments and their lengths. While more and longer fragments allow better identification of sequence overlaps, they also pose problems as the underlying algorithms show quadratic or even exponential complexity behaviour to both number of fragments and their length. And while shorter sequences are faster to align, they also complicate the layout phase of an assembly as shorter reads are more difficult to use with repeats or near identical repeats.

In the earliest days of DNA sequencing, scientists could only gain a few sequences of short length (some dozen bases) after weeks of work in laboratories. Hence, these sequences could be aligned in a few minutes by hand.

In 1975, the Dideoxy termination method (also known as *Sanger sequencing*) was invented and until shortly after 2000, the technology was improved up to a point were fully automated machines could churn out sequences in a highly parallelised mode 24 hours a day. Large genome centers around the world housed complete farms of these sequencing machines, which in turn led to the necessity of assemblers to be optimised for sequences from whole-genome shotgun sequencing projects where the reads

- are about 800–900 bases long
- contain sequencing artifacts like sequencing and cloning vectors
- have error rates between 0.5 and 10%

With the Sanger technology, bacterial projects with 20,000 to 200,000 reads could easily be assembled on one computer. Larger ones like the human genome with approximately 35 million reads needed already large computing farms and distributed computing.

By 2004 / 2005, pyrosequencing had been brought to commercial viability by 454 Life Sciences. This new sequencing methods generated reads much shorter than from Sanger sequencing: initially about 100 bases, now 400-500 bases. However, due to the much higher throughput and lower cost than Sanger sequencing, the adoption of this technology by genome centers pushed development of sequence assemblers to deal with this new type of sequences. The sheer amount of data coupled with technology specific error patterns in the reads delayed development of assemblers, at the beginning in 2004 only the Newbler assembler from 454 was available. Presented in mid 2007,[4] the hybrid version of the MIRA assembler by Chevreux et al. was the first freely available assembler who could assemble 454 reads and mixtures of 454 reads and Sanger reads; using sequences from different sequencing technologies was subsequently coined *hybrid assembly*.

Since 2006, the Illumina (previously Solexa) technology is available and able to generate about 100 million reads per run on a single sequencing machine. Compare this to the 35 million reads of the human genome project which needed several years to be produced on hundreds of sequencing machines. Illumina initially was limited to a length of only 36 bases, making it less suitable for de novo assembly, but newer iterations of the technology achieve read lengths above 100 bases from both ends of a 3-400bp clone. Presented by the end of 2007, the SHARCGS assembler[5] by Dohm et al. was the first published assembler that was used for an assembly with Solexa reads, quickly followed by a number of others.

Later, new technologies like SOLiD from Applied Biosystems are released, and new technologies (e.g. IonTorrent, PacBio) continue to emerge at a rapid rate.

Greedy algorithm

Given a set of sequence fragments the object is to find the Shortest common supersequence.

1. calculate pairwise alignments of all fragments
2. choose two fragments with the largest overlap
3. merge chosen fragments
4. repeat step 2. and 3. until only one fragment is left

The result is a suboptimal solution to the problem.

Available assemblers

The following table lists assemblers that have a de-novo assembly capability on at least one of the supported technologies.[6]

Name	Type	Technologies	Author	Presented / Last updated	Licence*	Homepage
ABySS	(large) genomes	Solexa, SOLiD	Simpson, J. et al.	2008 / 2011	OS	link [7]
ALLPATHS-LG	(large) genomes	Solexa, SOLiD	Gnerre, S. et al.	2011	OS	link [8]
AMOS	genomes	Sanger, 454	Salzberg, S. et al.	2002? / 2008?	OS	link [9]
Celera WGA Assembler / CABOG	(large) genomes	Sanger, 454, Solexa	Myers, G. et al.; Miller G. et al.	2004 / 2010	OS	link [10]
CLC Genomics Workbench	genomes	Sanger, 454, Solexa, SOLiD	CLC bio	2008 / 2010	C	link [11]
Cortex	genomes	Solexa, SOLiD	Iqbal, Z. *et al.*	2011	OS	link [12]
DNA Dragon	genomes	Illumina, SOLiD, Complete Genomics, 454, Sanger	SequentiX	2011	C	link [13]
DNAnexus	genomes	Illumina, SOLiD, Complete Genomics	DNAnexus	2011	C	link [14]
Edena	genomes	Solexa	D. Hernandez, P. François, L. Farinelli, M. Osteras, and J. Schrenzel.	2008	C	link [15]
Euler	genomes	Sanger, 454 (,Solexa ?)	Pevzner, P. et al.	2001 / 2006?	(C / NC-A?)	link [16]
Euler-sr	genomes	454, Solexa	Chaisson, MJ. et al.	2008	NC-A	link [17]
Forge	(large) genomes, EST, metagenomes	454, Solexa , SOLID, Sanger	Platt, DM, Evers, D.	2010	OS	link [18]
Geneious	genomes	Sanger, 454, Solexa	Biomatters Ltd	2009 / 2010	C	link [19]

Graph Constructor	(large) genomes	Sanger, 454, Solexa, SOLiD	Convey Computer Corporation	2011	C	link [20]
IDBA (Iterative De Bruijn graph short read Assembler)	(large) genomes	Sanger,454,Solexa	Yu Peng, Henry C. M. Leung, Siu-Ming Yiu, Francis Y. L. Chin	2010	(C / NC-A?)	link [21]
MIRA (Mimicking Intelligent Read Assembly)	genomes, ESTs	Sanger, 454, Solexa	Chevreux, B.	1998 / 2011	OS	link [22]
NextGENe	(small genomes?)	454, Solexa, SOLiD	Softgenetics	2008	C	link [23]
Newbler	genomes, ESTs	454, Sanger	454/Roche	2009	C	link [1]
PASHA	(large) genomes	Illumina	Liu, Schmidt, Maskell	2011	OS	link [24]
Phrap	genomes	Sanger, 454	Green, P.	2002 / 2003 / 2008	C / NC-A	link [25]
TIGR Assembler	genomic	Sanger	-	1995 / 2003	OS	link [26]
Ray [27]	genomes	Illumina, mix of Illumina and 454, paired or not	Sébastien Boisvert, François Laviolette & Jacques Corbeil.	2010	OS [GNU General Public License]	link [28]
Sequencher	genomes	traditional and next generation sequence data	Gene Codes Corporation	1991 / 2009 / 2011	C	link [29]
SeqMan NGen	(large) genomes, exomes, transcriptomes, metagenomes, ESTs	Illumina, ABI SOLiD, Roche 454, Ion Torrent, Solexa, Sanger	DNASTAR	2007 / 2011	C	link [30]
SHARCGS	(small) genomes	Solexa	Dohm et al.	2007 / 2007	OS	link [31]
SOPRA	genomes	Illumina, SOLiD, Sanger, 454	Dayarian, A. et al.	2010 / 2011	OS	link [32]
SSAKE	(small) genomes	Solexa (SOLiD? Helicos?)	Warren, R. et al.	2007 / 2007	OS	link [33]
SOAPdenovo	genomes	Solexa	Li, R. et al.	2009 / 2009	Closed	link [34]
Staden gap4 package	BACs (, small genomes?)	Sanger	Staden et al.	1991 / 2008	OS	link [35]
Taipan	(small) genomes	Illumina	Schmidt, B. et al.	2009	OS	link [36]
VCAKE	(small) genomes	Solexa (SOLiD?, Helicos?)	Jeck, W. et al.	2007 / 2007	OS	link [37]
Phusion assembler	(large) genomes	Sanger	Mullikin JC, et al.	2003	OS	link [38]
Quality Value Guided SRA (QSRA)	genomes	Sanger, Solexa	Bryant DW, et al.	2009	OS	link [39]
Velvet	(small) genomes	Sanger, 454, Solexa, SOLiD	Zerbino, D. et al.	2007 / 2009	OS	link [40]

*Licences: OS = Open Source; C = Commercial; C / NC-A = Commercial but free for non-commercial and academics; Brackets = unclear, but most likely C / NC-A

References

[1] Myers EW, Sutton GG, Delcher AL, *et al.* (March 2000). "A whole-genome assembly of Drosophila" (http://www.sciencemag.org/cgi/pmidlookup?view=long&pmid=10731133). *Science* **287** (5461): 2196–204. doi:10.1126/science.287.5461.2196. PMID 10731133. .

[2] Batzoglou S, Jaffe DB, Stanley K, *et al.* (January 2002). "ARACHNE: a whole-genome shotgun assembler" (http://www.genome.org/cgi/pmidlookup?view=long&pmid=11779843). *Genome Res.* **12** (1): 177–89. doi:10.1101/gr.208902. PMC 155255. PMID 11779843. .

[3] AMOS page (http://amos.sourceforge.net/) with links to various papers

[4] Copy in Google groups of the post announcing MIRA 2.9.8 hybrid version (http://groups.google.com/group/bionet.software/browse_thread/thread/b34b348011d04f0e?fwc=1) in the bionet.software Usenet group

[5] Dohm JC, Lottaz C, Borodina T, Himmelbauer H (November 2007). "SHARCGS, a fast and highly accurate short-read assembly algorithm for de novo genomic sequencing" (http://www.genome.org/cgi/pmidlookup?view=long&pmid=17908823). *Genome Res.* **17** (11): 1697–706. doi:10.1101/gr.6435207. PMC 2045152. PMID 17908823. .

[6] list of software including mapping assemblers in the SeqAnswers discussion forum. (http://seqanswers.com/forums/showthread.php?t=43)

[7] http://www.bcgsc.ca/platform/bioinfo/software/abyss

[8] http://www.broadinstitute.org/science/programs/genome-biology/crd

[9] http://sourceforge.net/apps/mediawiki/amos/index.php?title=AMOS

[10] http://www.jcvi.org/cms/research/projects/celera-assembler/overview/

[11] http://www.clcbio.com/index.php?id=575

[12] http://cortexassembler.sourceforge.net/

[13] https://www.dna-dragon.com/

[14] https://dnanexus.com/

[15] http://www.genomic.ch/edena.php

[16] http://nbcr.sdsc.edu/euler/

[17] http://euler-assembler.ucsd.edu/portal/

[18] http://combiol.org/forge/

[19] http://geneious.com/

[20] http://www.conveycomputer.com/lifesciences/

[21] http://www.cs.hku.hk/~alse/idba/

[22] http://sourceforge.net/apps/mediawiki/mira-assembler/

[23] http://softgenetics.com/NextGENe.html

[24] http://sites.google.com/site/yongchaosoftware/pasha

[25] http://www.phrap.org/

[26] ftp://ftp.jcvi.org/pub/software/assembler/

[27] Boisvert S, Laviolette F, Corbeil J. (October 2010). "Ray: simultaneous assembly of reads from a mix of high-throughput sequencing technologies." (http://www.liebertonline.com/doi/abs/10.1089/cmb.2009.0238). *J Comput Biol.* **17** (11): 1519–33. doi:10.1089/cmb.2009.0238. PMID 20958248. .

[28] http://denovoassembler.sf.net/

[29] http://www.genecodes.com/

[30] http://www.dnastar.com/t-products-seqman-ngen.aspx

[31] http://sharcgs.molgen.mpg.de/

[32] http://www.physics.rutgers.edu/~anirvans/SOPRA/

[33] http://www.bcgsc.ca/platform/bioinfo/software/ssake

[34] http://soap.genomics.org.cn/soapdenovo.html

[35] http://staden.sourceforge.net/

[36] http://sourceforge.net/projects/taipan/

[37] http://sourceforge.net/projects/vcake

[38] http://www.sanger.ac.uk/Software/production/phusion/

[39] http://qsra.cgrb.oregonstate.edu/

[40] http://www.ebi.ac.uk/~zerbino/velvet/

Sequence clustering

In bioinformatics, **sequence clustering** algorithms attempt to group sequences that are somehow related. The sequences can be either of genomic, "transcriptomic" (ESTs) or protein origin. For proteins, homologous sequences are typically grouped into families. For EST data, clustering is important to group sequences originating from the same gene before the ESTs are assembled to reconstruct the original mRNA.

Some clustering algorithms use single-linkage clustering, constructing a transitive closure of sequences with a similarity over a particular threshold. UCLUST and CD-HIT use a greedy algorithm that identifies a representative sequence for each cluster and assigns a new sequence to that cluster if it is sufficiently similar to the representative; if a sequence is not matched then it becomes the representative sequence for a new cluster. The similarity score is often based on sequence alignment. Sequence clustering is often used to make a non-redundant set of representative sequences.

Sequence clusters are often synonymous with (but not identical to) protein families. Determining a representative tertiary structure for each *sequence cluster* is the aim of many structural genomics initiatives.

External links

Sequence clustering packages

- UCLUST: An exceptionally fast sequence clustering program for nucleotide and protein sequences [1]
- RDB90 and nrdb90.pl: a nonredundant sequence database [2]
- TribeMCL: a method for clustering proteins into related groups
- BAG: a graph theoretic sequence clustering algorithm [3]
- CD-HIT: a ultra-fast method for clustering protein and nucleotide sequences, with many new applications in next generation sequencing (NGS) data [4]
- JESAM: Open source parallel scalable DNA alignment engine with optional clustering software component [5]
- RSDB: Representative Sequences DataBase project [6]
- UICluster: Parallel Clustering of EST (Gene) Sequences [7]
- BLASTClust single-linkage clustering with BLAST [8]
- Clusterer: extendable java application for sequence grouping and cluster analyses [9]
- PATDB: a program for rapidly identifying perfect substrings
- nrdb: a program for merging trivially redundant (identical) sequences [10]
- CluSTr: A single-linkage protein sequence clustering database from Smith-Waterman sequence similarities; covers over 7 mln sequences including UniProt and IPI [11]
- ICAtools - original (ancient) DNA clustering package with many algorithms useful for artifact discovery or EST clustering [12]
- Virus Orthologous Clusters: A viral protein sequence clustering database; contains all predicted genes from eleven virus families organized into ortholog groups by BLASTP similarity [13]

Non-redundant sequence databases

- PISCES: A Protein Sequence Culling Server [14]
- RDB90 and nrdb90.pl: a nonredundant sequence database [2]
- UniRef: A non-redundant UniProt sequence database [15]

References

[1] http://www.drive5.com/uclust
[2] http://www.ebi.ac.uk/~holm/nrdb90
[3] http://bio.informatics.indiana.edu/sunkim/BAG/
[4] http://cd-hit.org
[5] http://www.littlest.co.uk/software/bioinf/old_packages/jesam/jesam_paper.html
[6] http://skyrah.bio.cc/RSDB/
[7] http://ratest.eng.uiowa.edu/pubsoft/clustering/
[8] http://www.ncbi.nlm.nih.gov/Web/Newsltr/Spring04/blastlab.html
[9] http://web.mit.edu/polz/clusterer
[10] http://web.archive.org/web/20080101032917/http://blast.wustl.edu/pub/nrdb/
[11] http://www.ebi.ac.uk/clustr/
[12] http://www.littlest.co.uk/software/bioinf/old_packages/icatools/
[13] http://athena.bioc.uvic.ca/tools/VOCS
[14] http://dunbrack.fccc.edu/pisces/
[15] http://www.uniprot.org/database/DBDescription.shtml#uniref

Sequence database

In the field of bioinformatics, a **sequence database** is a large collection of computerized ("digital") nucleic acid sequences, protein sequences, or other sequences stored on a computer. A database can include sequences from only one organism (e.g., a database for all proteins in Saccharomyces cerevisiae), or it can include sequences from all organisms whose DNA has been sequenced.

Search issues

Sequence databases can be searched using a variety of methods. The most common is probably searching for a sequence similar to a certain target protein or gene whose sequence is already known to the user. The BLAST program is a method of this type.

Many inputs create inconsistencies

A major problem with all the large genetic sequence databases is that records are deposited in them from a wide range of sources, from individual researchers to large genome sequencing centers. As a result, the sequences themselves, and especially the biological annotations attached to these sequences, vary tremendously in quality. Also there is much redundancy, as multiple labs often submit numerous sequences that are identical, or nearly identical, to others in the databases.

Many annotations are based not on laboratory experiments, but on the results of sequence similarity searches for previously-annotated sequences. Of course, once a sequence has been annotated based on similarity to others, and itself deposited in the database, it can also become the basis for future annotations. This leads to the *transitive annotation problem* because there may be several such annotation transfers by sequence similarity between a particular database record and actual wet lab experimental information. Therefore, one must always regard the biological annotations in major sequence databases with a considerable degree of skepticism, unless they can be verified by reference to published papers describing high-quality experimental data, or at least by reference to a human-curated sequence database.

External links

Major bioinformatics databases

- European Bioinformatics Institute databases [1]
- NCBI completely sequenced genomes [2]
- Stanford Saccharomyces Genome Database [25]
- Protein [3], the NIH protein database, a collection of sequences from several sources, including translations from annotated coding regions in GenBank, RefSeq and TPA, as well as records from SwissProt, PIR, PRF, and PDB

References

[1] http://www.ebi.ac.uk/Databases/
[2] http://www.ncbi.nlm.nih.gov/entrez/query.fcgi?db=Genome
[3] http://www.ncbi.nlm.nih.gov/protein

Sequence logo

In bioinformatics, a **sequence logo** is a graphical representation of the sequence conservation of nucleotides (in a strand of DNA/RNA) or amino acids (in protein sequences).[1]

Logo creation

To create sequence logos, related DNA, RNA or protein sequences, or DNA sequences that have common conserved binding sites, are aligned so that the most conserved parts create good alignments. A sequence logo can then be created from the conserved multiple sequence alignment. The sequence logo will show how well residues are conserved at each position: the fewer the number of residues, the higher the letters will be, because the better the conservation is at that position. Different residues at the same position are scaled according to their frequency. The height of the entire stack of residues is the information measured in bits. Sequence logos can be used to represent conserved DNA binding sites, where transcription factors bind.

A sequence logo showing the most conserved bases around the initiation codon from all human mRNAs. Note that the initiation codon is not drawn to scale, or the letters AUG would each have a height of 2 bits.

The information content (y-axis) of position i is given by:

for amino acids, $R_i = \log_2(20) - (H_i + e_n)$

for nucleic acids, $R_i = 2 - (H_i + e_n)$

where H_i is the uncertainty (sometimes called the Shannon entropy) of position i

$$H_i = -\sum f_{a,i} * \log_2 f_{a,i}$$

Here, $f_{a,i}$ is the relative frequency of base or amino acid a at position i , and e_n is the small-sample correction for an alignment of n letters. The height of letter a in column i is given by

$$\text{height} = f_{a,i} * R_i$$

The approximation for the small-sample correction, e_n , is given by:

$$e_n = \frac{s-1}{2 * \ln(2) * n}$$

where s is 4 for nucleotides, 20 for amino acids, and n is the number of sequences in the alignment.

References

[1] Schneider TD, Stephens RM (1990). "Sequence Logos: A New Way to Display Consensus Sequences" (http://alum.mit.edu/www/toms/papers/logopaper). *Nucleic Acids Res* **18** (20): 6097–6100. doi:10.1093/nar/18.20.6097. PMC 332411. PMID 2172928. .

External links

- How to read sequence logos (http://alum.mit.edu/www/toms/how.to.read.sequence.logos/).
- Recommendations for Making Sequence Logos (http://alum.mit.edu/www/toms/logorecommendations. html).
- WebLogo: A Sequence Logo Generator (http://www.genome.org/cgi/content/abstract/14/6/1188) (Publication with full-text access).
- MoRAine (http://moraine.cebitec.uni-bielefeld.de/files/moraine_ib08.pdf) (A web server for sequence logo generation and computational transcription factor binding motif re-annotation - Publication with full-text access).
- Erill, I., "A gentle introduction to information content in transcription factor binding sites", Eprint (http://research.umbc.edu/~erill/Documents/Introduction_Information_Theory.pdf)
- What is (in) a sequence logo? (http://userpages.umbc.edu/~erill/Documents/Sequence_logo.pdf)

Tools for creating sequence logos

- WebLogo Python Code (http://code.google.com/p/weblogo/) Python Code (BSD license, somewhat difficult to use)
- WebLogo 3.0 (http://weblogo.threeplusone.com) (Online)
- MoRAine (http://moraine.cebitec.uni-bielefeld.de) (Online application with integrated binding site re-annotation)
- GENIO (http://biogenio.com/logo/) (Online)
- LogoBar (http://www.bionut.ki.se/groups/tbu/logobar/) (Java application)
- CorreLogo (http://alum.mit.edu/www/toms/papers/correlogo/) An online server for 3D sequence logos of RNA and DNA alignments

Sequence mining

Sequence mining is concerned with finding statistically relevant patterns between data examples where the values are delivered in a sequence. It is usually presumed that the values are discrete, and thus Time series mining is closely related, but usually considered a different activity. Sequence mining is a special case of structured data mining.

There are two different kinds of sequence mining: *string mining* and *itemset mining*. String mining is widely used in biology, to examine gene and protein sequences, and is primarily concerned with sequences with a single member at each position. There exist a variety of prominent algorithms to perform alignment of a query sequence with those existing in databases. The kind of alignment could either involve matching a query with one subject e.g. BLAST or matching multiple query sets with each other e.g. ClustalW. Itemset mining is used more often in marketing and CRM applications, and is concerned with multiple-symbols at each position. Itemset mining is also a popular approach to text mining.

There are several key problems within this field. These include building efficient databases and indexes for sequence information, extracting the frequently occurring patterns, comparing sequences for similarity, and recovering missing sequence members.

Two common techniques that are applied to sequence databases for frequent itemset mining are the influential apriori algorithm and the more-recent FP-Growth technique. However, there is nothing in these techniques that restricts them to sequences, per se.

Sequence motif

In genetics, a **sequence motif** is a nucleotide or amino-acid sequence pattern that is widespread and has, or is conjectured to have, a biological significance. For proteins, a sequence motif is distinguished from a structural motif, a motif formed by the three dimensional arrangement of amino acids, which may not be adjacent.

An example is the *N*-glycosylation site motif:

> *Asn, followed by anything but Pro, followed by either Ser or Thr, followed by anything but Pro*

where the three-letter abbreviations are the conventional designations for amino acids (see genetic code).

Overview

When a sequence motif appears in the exon of a gene, it may encode the "structural motif" of a protein; that is a stereotypical element of the overall structure of the protein. Nevertheless, motifs need not be associated with a distinctive secondary structure. "Noncoding" sequences are not translated into proteins, and nucleic acids with such motifs need not deviate from the typical shape (e.g. the "B-form" DNA double helix).

Outside of gene exons, there exist **regulatory sequence motifs** and motifs within the "junk," such as satellite DNA. Some of these are believed to affect the shape of nucleic acids (see for example RNA self-splicing), but this is only sometimes the case. For example, many DNA binding proteins that have affinities for specific motifs only bind DNA in its double-helical form. They are able to recognize motifs through contact with the double helix's major or minor groove.

Short coding motifs, which appear to lack secondary structure, include those that label proteins for delivery to particular parts of a cell, or mark them for phosphorylation.

Within a sequence or database of sequences, researchers search and find motifs using computer-based techniques of sequence analysis, such as BLAST. Such techniques belong to the discipline of bioinformatics.

See also consensus sequence.

Motif bioinformatics

Consider the *N*-glycosylation site motif mentioned above:

Asn, followed by anything but Pro, followed by either Ser or Thr, followed by anything but Pro

This pattern may be written as **N{P}[ST]{P}** where N = Asn, P = Pro, S = Ser, T = Thr; {X} means any amino acid except X; and [XY] means either X or Y.

The notation [XY] does not give any indication of the probability of X or Y occurring in the pattern. Observed probabilities can be graphically represented using sequence_logos. Sometimes patterns are defined in terms of a probabilistic model such as a hidden Markov model.

Motifs and consensus sequences

The notation [XYZ] means X or Y or Z, but does not indicate the likelihood of any particular match. For this reason, two or more patterns are often associated with a single motif: the defining pattern, and various typical patterns.

For example, the defining sequence for the IQ motif may be taken to be:

```
[FILV]Qxxx[RK]Gxxx[RK]xx[FILVWY]
```

where x signifies any amino acid, and the square brackets indicate an alternative (see below for further details about notation).

Usually, however, the first letter is I, and both [RK] choices resolve to R. Since the last choice is so wide, the pattern IQxxxRGxxxR is sometimes equated with the IQ motif itself, but a more accurate description would be a *consensus sequence for the IQ motif.*

De novo computational discovery of motifs

There are software programs which, given multiple input sequences, attempt to identify one or more candidate motifs. One example is MEME, which generates statistical information for each candidate. Other algorithms include AlignAce, Amadeus, CisModule, FIRE, Gibbs Motif Sampler, PhyloGibbs, and Weeder. SCOPE [1] is an ensemble motif finder that uses several algorithms simultaneously. There currently exist more than 100 publications with similar algorithms without a comprehensive benchmark so selecting one is not straightforward.

Discovery through evolutionary conservation

Motifs have been discovered by studying similar genes in different species. For example, by aligning the amino acid sequences specified by the GCM (*glial cells missing*) gene in man, mouse and *D. melanogaster*, Akiyama[2] and others discovered a pattern which they called the GCM motif. It spans about 150 amino acid residues, and begins as follows:

```
WDIND*.*P..*...D.F.*W***.**.IYS**...A.*H*S*WAMRNTNNHN
```

Here each . signifies a single amino acid or a gap, and each * indicates one member of a closely-related family of amino acids.

The authors were able to show that the motif has DNA binding activity. PhyloGibbs [3][4] [5] and the Gibbs Motif Sampler[6] [7] are motif discovery algorithms that consider phylogenetic conservation.

Pattern description notations

Several notations for describing motifs are in use but most of them are variants of standard notations for regular expressions and use these conventions:

- there is an alphabet of single characters, each denoting a specific amino acid or a set of amino acids;
- a string of characters drawn from the alphabet denotes a sequence of the corresponding amino acids;
- any string of characters drawn from the alphabet enclosed in square brackets matches any one of the corresponding amino acids; e.g. [abc] matches any of the amino acids represented by a or b or c.

The fundamental idea behind all these notations is the matching principle, which assigns a meaning to a sequence of elements of the pattern notation:

> *a sequence of elements of the pattern notation matches a sequence of amino acids if and only if the latter sequence can be partitioned into subsequences in such a way that each pattern element matches the corresponding subsequence in turn.*

Thus the pattern [AB] [CDE] F matches the six amino acid sequences corresponding to ACF, ADF, AEF, BCF, BDF, and BEF.

Different pattern description notations have other ways of forming pattern elements. One of these notations is the PROSITE notation, described in the following subsection.

PROSITE pattern notation

The PROSITE notation uses the IUPAC one-letter codes and conforms to the above description with the exception that a concatenation symbol, '-', is used between pattern elements, but it is often dropped between letters of the pattern alphabet.

PROSITE allows the following pattern elements in addition to those described previously:

- The lower case letter 'x' can be used as a pattern element to denote any amino acid.
- A string of characters drawn from the alphabet and enclosed in braces (curly brackets) denotes any amino acid except for those in the string. For example, {ST} denotes any amino acid other than S or T.
- If a pattern is restricted to the N-terminal of a sequence, the pattern is prefixed with '<'.
- If a pattern is restricted to the C-terminal of a sequence, the pattern is suffixed with '>'.
- The character '>' can also occur inside a terminating square bracket pattern, so that S[T>] matches both "ST" and "S>".
- If e is a pattern element, and m and n are two decimal integers with m <= n, then:
  - e(m) is equivalent to the repetition of e exactly m times;
  - e(m,n) is equivalent to the repetition of e exactly k times for any integer k satisfying: m <= k <= n.

Some examples:

- x(3) is equivalent to x-x-x.
- x(2,4) matches any sequence that matches x-x or x-x-x or x-x-x-x.

The signature of the C2H2-type *zinc finger* domain is:

- C-x(2,4)-C-x(3)-[LIVMFYWC]-x(8)-H-x(3,5)-H

Matrices

A matrix of numbers containing scores for each residue or nucleotide at each position of a fixed-length motif. There are two types of weight matrices.

- A position frequency matrix (PFM) records the position-dependent frequency of each residue or nucleotide. PFMs can be experimentally determined from SELEX experiments or computationally discovered by tools such as MEME using hidden Markov models.
- A position weight matrix (PWM) contains log odds weights for computing a match score. A cutoff is needed to specify whether an input sequence matches the motif or not. PWMs are calculated from PFMs.

An example of a PFM from the TRANSFAC database for the transcription factor AP-1:

Pos	A	C	G	T	IUPAC
01	6	2	8	1	R
02	3	5	9	0	S
03	0	0	0	17	T
04	0	0	17	0	G
05	17	0	0	0	A
06	0	16	0	1	C
07	3	2	3	9	T
08	4	7	2	4	N
09	9	6	1	1	M
10	4	3	7	3	N
11	6	3	1	7	W

The first column specifies the position, the second column contains the number of occurrences of A at that position, the third column contains the number of occurrences of C at that position, the fourth column contains the number of occurrences of G at that position, the fifth column contains the number of occurrences of T at that position, and the last column contains the IUPAC notation for that position. Note that the sums of occurrences for A, C, G, and T for each row should be equal because the PFM is derived from aggregating several consensus sequences.

Another scheme

The following example comes from the paper by Matsuda, *et al.* 1997.[8]

The *E. coli* lactose operon repressor LacI (PDB 1lcc [9] chain A) and *E. coli* catabolite gene activator (PDB 3gap [10] chain A) both have a *helix-turn-helix* motif, but their amino acid sequences do not show much similarity, as shown in the table below.

Matsuda, *et al.*[8] devised a code they called the "three-dimensional chain code" for representing a protein structure as a string of letters. This encoding scheme reveals the similarity between the proteins much more clearly than the amino acid sequence:

	3D chain code	Amino acid sequence
1lccA	TWWWWWWWKCLKWWWWWWG	LYDVAEYAGVSYQTVSRVV
3gapA	KWWWWWWGKCFKWWWWWWW	RQEIGQIVGCSRETVGRIL

where "W" corresponds to an α-helix, and "E" and "D" correspond to a β-strand.

References

[1] http://genie.dartmouth.edu/scope/

[2] Akiyama Y, Hosoya T, Poole AM, Hotta Y (1996). "The gcm-motif: a novel DNA-binding motif conserved in Drosophila and mammals". *Proc Natl Acad Sci USA* **93** (25): 14912–14916. doi:10.1073/pnas.93.25.14912. PMC 26236. PMID 8962155.

[3] http://www.imsc.res.in/~rsidd/phylogibbs/

[4] Siddharthan R, van Nimwegen E, Siggia ED (2004). "PhyloGibbs: A Gibbs sampler incorporating phylogenetic information". *In Eskin E, Workman C (eds), RECOMB 2004 Satellite Workshop on Regulatory Genomics, LNBI 3318, 3041 (Springer-Verlag Berlin Heidelberg 2005).*

[5] Siddharthan R, Siggia ED, van Nimwegen E (2005). "PhyloGibbs: A Gibbs sampling motif finder that incorporates phylogeny". *PLoS Comput Biol* **1** (7): e67. doi:10.1371/journal.pcbi.0010067. PMC 1309704. PMID 16477324.

[6] Lawrence, Charles E.; Altschul, Stephen F.; Boguski, Mark S.; Liu, Jun S.; Neuwald, Andrew F.; Wootton, John C. (October 8 1993). "Detecting subtle sequence signals: a Gibbs sampling strategy for multiple alignment" (http://www.sciencemag.org/content/262/5131/208). *Science* **262** (5131): 208–214. doi:10.1126/science.8211139. PMID 8211139. .

[7] Newberg, Lee A.; Thompson, William A.; Conlan, Sean; Smith, Thomas M.; McCue, Lee Ann; Lawrence, Charles E. (July 15 2007). "A phylogenetic Gibbs sampler that yields centroid solutions for cis regulatory site prediction" (http://bioinformatics.oxfordjournals.org/content/23/14/1718). *Bioinformatics* **23** (14): 1718–1727. doi:10.1093/bioinformatics/btm241. PMC 2268014. PMID 17488758. .

[8] Matsuda H, Taniguchi F, Hashimoto A (1997). "An approach to detection of protein structural motifs using an encoding scheme of backbone conformations" (http://helix-web.stanford.edu/psb97/matsuda.pdf). *Proc. of 2nd Pacific Symposium on Biocomputing*: 280–291. .

[9] http://www.rcsb.org/pdb/explore/explore.do?structureId=1lcc

[10] http://www.rcsb.org/pdb/explore/explore.do?structureId=3gap

Further reading

- Stormo GD (2000). "DNA binding sites: representation and discovery". *Bioinformatics* **16** (1): 16–23. doi:10.1093/bioinformatics/16.1.16. PMID 10812473.

- Balla S, Thapar V, Verma S, Luong T, Faghri T, Huang CH, Rajasekaran S, del Campo JJ, Shinn JH, Mohler WA, Maciejewski MW, Gryk MR, Piccirillo B, Schiller SR, Schiller MR (2006). "Minimotif Miner: a tool for investigating protein function". *Nature Methods* **3** (3): 175–177. doi:10.1038/nmeth856. PMID 16489333.

- Schiller MR (2007). "Minimotif miner: a computational tool to investigate protein function, disease, and genetic diversity". *Curr Protoc Protein Sci* **chapter 2** (unit 2.12): Unit 2.12. doi:10.1002/0471140864.ps0212s48. PMID 18429315.

- Kadaveru K, Vyas J, Schiller MR (2008). "Viral infection and human disease--insights from minimotifs". *Front Biosci* **13**: 6455–6471. PMC 2628544. PMID 18508672.

External links

Motif-finding methods

- Minimotif Miner (http://mnm.engr.uconn.edu/MNM/SMSSearchServlet) — for discovery of short contiguous motifs of known function (from University of Nevada Las Vegas and University of Connecticut)
- Amadeus and Allegro motif finding platforms (http://acgt.cs.tau.ac.il/allegro/) (from Tel-Aviv University)
- PROSITE (http://us.expasy.org/prosite) — database of protein families and domains
- Database and Analysis Suite for Quadruplex forming motifs in Nucleotide Sequences (http://202.54.26.221/quadfinder)
- MEME Suite of motif-based sequence analysis tools (http://meme.nbcr.net)

- TRANSFAC (http://www.gene-regulation.com/pub/databases.html) — a commercial (limited public access) database for transcription factor motifs
- eMotif (http://dna.stanford.edu/emotif) (from Stanford University)
- Bioprospector (http://bioprospector.stanford.edu) (from Stanford University)
- FIRE motif discovery approach (http://tavazoielab.princeton.edu/FIRE/) (from the Tavazoie lab at Princeton)
- Cis-analysis (http://bioinformatics.caltech.edu/cis-analysis.txt) — list of and comments on other programs useful for discovering cis-regulatory element motifs
- NCBI Home Page (http://www.ncbi.nlm.nih.gov/) — NIH's National Library of Medicine NCBI (National Center for Biotechnology Information) link to a tremendous number of resources including sequence analysis and motif discovery.
- Transcriptional Regulation Wiki (http://www.stud.uni-potsdam.de/~haussler/wiki/index.php/Main_Page)
- Wikiomic Sequence motifs page (http://openwetware.org/wiki/Wikiomics:Sequence_motifs)

Motif-finding Web applications

- BLOCK-maker (http://blocks.fhcrc.org/blocks/blockmkr/make_blocks.html) — finds conserved blocks in a group of two or more unaligned protein sequences
- ELM (http://elm.eu.org) — functional site prediction of short linear motifs
- FIRE (https://iget.princeton.edu) — finds DNA and RNA motifs from expression data using the mutual information
- Gibbs Motif Sampler (http://bayesweb.wadsworth.org/gibbs/gibbs.html) — discovers overrepresented conserved motifs in an aligned set of orthologous sequences
- GIMSAN (http://www.cs.cornell.edu/~ppn3/gimsan/) — motif-finder with biologically realistic and reliable statistical significance analysis
- Improbizer (http://www.soe.ucsc.edu/~kent/improbizer/improbizer.html) — searches for motifs in DNA or RNA sequences that occur with improbable frequency
- MEME Suite (http://meme.nbcr.net) — discover motifs (highly conserved regions) in groups of related DNA or protein sequences
- Minimotif Miner (http://mnm.engr.uconn.edu/) — public interface to the minimotif miner database which correlates short sequence amino acids to their biological function
- ModuleMaster (http://www.ra.cs.uni-tuebingen.de/software/ModuleMaster/) — allows to search for motifs by pre-defined or custom PWMs
- MotifVoter (http://defiant.i2r.a-star.edu.sg/~ewijaya/MotifVoter2/) — variance based ensemble method for discovery of binding sites
- PhyloGibbs (http://www.phylogibbs.unibas.ch/cgi-bin/phylogibbs.pl) — discovers overrepresented conserved motifs in an aligned set of orthologous sequences
- PLACE (http://www.dna.affrc.go.jp/PLACE/signalscan.html) — database of plant cis-acting regulatory DNA elements
- SCOPE (http://genie.dartmouth.edu/scope/) — an ensemble of programs aimed at identifying novel cis-regulatory elements from groups of upstream sequences
- TEIRESIS (http://cbcsrv.watson.ibm.com/Tspd.html) — search for short sequence motifs in Proteins
- WebMotifs (http://fraenkel.mit.edu/webmotifs/form.html) — use different programs to search for DNA-sequence motifs, and to easily combine and evaluate the results

Motif visualization and browsing

- MochiView (http://johnsonlab.ucsf.edu/sj/mochiview-start/) — a genome browser supporting import of motif libraries and containing tools for motif discovery, visualization, and analysis

Sequence Ontology

SO

Content		
Description	Biological sequence ontology	
Contact		
Research center	WormBase, FlyBase, the Mouse Genome Informatics group, and the Sanger Institute	
Access		
Website	[1]	
Tools		
Miscellaneous		

The **Sequence Ontology**, or **SO**, is an ontology suitable for describing biological sequences.[2]

References

[1] http://www.sequenceontology.org/

[2] Mungall CJ, Batchelor C, Eilbeck K (February 2011). "Evolution of the Sequence Ontology terms and relationships". *J Biomed Inform* **44** (1): 87–93. doi:10.1016/j.jbi.2010.03.002. PMID 20226267.

External links

- "The Sequence Ontology" (http://www.sequenceontology.org/). Sequence Ontology. Retrieved 2011-09-19.

Sequence profiling tool

A **sequence profiling tool** in bioinformatics is a type of software that presents information related to a genetic sequence, gene name, or keyword input. Such tools generally take a query such as a DNA, RNA, or protein sequence or 'keyword' and search one or more databases for information related to that sequence. Summaries and aggregate results are provided in standardized format describing the information that would otherwise have required visits to many smaller sites or direct literature searches to compile. Many sequence profiling tools are software portals or gateways that simplify the process of finding information about a query in the large and growing number of bioinformatics databases. The access to these kinds of tools is either web based or locally downloadable executables.

Introduction and usage

The "post-genomics" era has given rise to a range of web-based tools and software to compile, organize, and deliver large amounts of primary sequence information, as well as protein structures, gene annotations, sequence alignments, and other common bioinformatics tasks.

In general, there exist three types of databases and service providers. The first one includes the popular public-domain or open-access databases supported by funding and grants such as NCBI, ExPASy, Ensembl, and PDB. The second one includes smaller or more specific databases organized and compiled by individual research groups Examples include Yeast Genome Database [25], RNA database [1]. The third and final one includes private corporate or institutional databases that require payment or institutional affiliation to access. Such examples rare given the globalization of the public databases unless the purported service is 'in-development' or the end point of the analysis is of commercial value.

Typical scenarios of a profiling approach become relevant, particularly, in the cases of the first two groups, where researchers commonly wish to combine information derived from several sources about a single query or target sequence. For example, users might use the sequence alignment and search tool BLAST to identify homologs of their gene of interest in other species, and then use these results to locate a solved protein structure for one of the homologs. Similarly, they might also want to know the likely secondary structure of the mRNA encoding the gene of interest, or whether a company sells a DNA construct containing the gene. Sequence profiling tools serve to automate and integrate the process of seeking such disparate information by rendering the process of searching several different external databases transparent to the user.

Many public databases are already extensively linked so that complementary information in another database is easily accessible; for example, Genbank and the PDB are closely intertwined. However, specialized tools organized and hosted by specific research groups can be difficult to integrate into this linkage effort because they are narrowly focused, are frequently modified, or use custom versions of common file formats. Advantages of sequence profiling tools include the ability to use multiple of these specialized tools in a single query and present the output with a common interface, the ability to direct the output of one set of tools or database searches into the input of another, and the capacity to disseminate hosting and compilation obligations to a network of research groups and institutions rather than a single centralized repository.

Keyword based profilers

Most of the profiling tools available on the web today fall into this category. The user, upon visiting the site/tool, enters any relevant information like a keyword e.g. dystrophy, diabetes etc., or GenBank accession numbers, PDB ID. All the relevant hits by the search are presented in a format unique to each tool's main focus. Profiling tools based on keyword searches are essentially search engines that are highly specialized for bioinformatics work, thereby eliminating a clutter of irrelevant or non-scholarly hits that might occur with a traditional search engine like Google. Most keyword-based profiling tools allow flexible types of keyword input, accession numbers from indexed databases as well as traditional keyword descriptors.

The network of Bioinformatic Harvester [10]

Each profiling tool has its own focus and area of interest. For example, the NCBI search engine Entrez segregates its hits by category, so that users looking for protein structure information can screen out sequences with no corresponding structure, while users interested in perusing the literature on a subject can view abstracts of papers published in scholarly journals without distraction from gene or sequence results. The Pubmed biosciences literature database is a popular tool for literature searches, though this service is nearly equaled with the more general Google Scholar.

Keyword-based data aggregation services like the Bioinformatic Harvester performs provide reports from a variety of third-party servers in an *as-is* format so that users need not visit the website or install the software for each individual component service. This is particularly invaluable given the rapid emergence of various sites providing different sequence analysis and manipulation tools. Another aggregative web portal, the Human Protein Reference Database (Hprd), contains manually annotated and curated entries for human proteins. The information provided is thus both selective and comprehensive, and the query format is flexible and intuitive. The pros of developing manually curated databases include presentation of proofread material and the concept of 'molecule authorities' to undertake the responsibility of specific proteins. However, the cons are that they are typically slower to update and may not contain very new or disputed data.

Sequence data based profilers

A typical sequence profiling tool carries this further by using an actual DNA, RNA, or protein sequence as an input and allows the user to visit different web-based analysis tools to obtain the information desired. Such tools are also commonly supplied with commercial laboratory equipment like gene sequencers or sometimes sold as software applications for molecular biology. In another public-database example, the BLAST sequence search report from NCBI provides a link from its alignment report to other relevant information in its own databases, if such specific information exists.

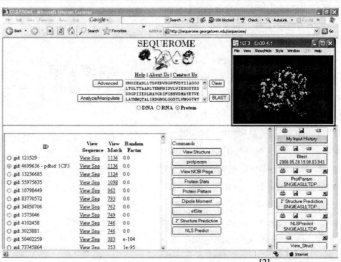

Display of sequence profiling features on a SEQUEROME [2] browser

For example, a retrieved record that contains a human sequence will carry a separate link that connects to its location on a human genome map; a record that contains a sequence for which a 3-D structure has been solved would carry a link that connects it to its structure database. Sequerome, a public service tool, links the entire BLAST report to many third party servers/sites that provide highly specific services in sequence manipulations such as restriction enzyme maps, open reading frame analyses for nucleotide sequences, and secondary structure prediction. The tool provides added advantage of maintaining a research log of the operations performed by the user, which can be then conveniently archived using 'mail', 'print' or 'save' functionality. Thus an entire operation of researching on a sequence using different research tools and thus carrying a project to its completion can be completed within one browser interface. Consequently, future generation of sequence profiling tools would include ability to collaborate online with researchers to share project logs and research tools, annotate results of sequence analysis or lab work, customize and automate the processing of sets of sequence data etc. InstaSeq [3] is a Google powered search tool that allows the user to directly enter a sequence and search the entire World Wide Web. This unique search engine, which is the only one of its kind, is in contrast to searching specific databases e.g. GenBank.

As a result the user can end up with a privately hosted document or a page from a lesser known database from just about anywhere in the world. Though the presence of sequence based profilers are far and few in the present scenario, their key role will become evident when huge amounts of sequence data need to be cross processed across portals and domains.

Future growth and directions

The proliferation of bioinformatics tools for genetic analysis aids researchers in identifying and categorizing genes and gene sets of interest in their work; however, the large variety of tools that perform substantially similar aggregative and analytical functions can also confuse and frustrate new users. The decentralization encouraged by aggregative tools allows individual research groups to maintain specialized servers dedicated to specific types of data analysis in the expectation that their output will be collected into a larger report on a gene or protein of interest to other researchers.

Data produced by microarray experiments, two-hybrid screening, and other high-throughput biological experiments is voluminous and difficult to analyze by hand; the efforts of structural genomics collaborations that are aimed at quickly solving large numbers of highly varied protein structures also increase the need for integration between sequence and structure databases and portals. This impetus toward developing more comprehensive and more user-friendly methods of sequence profiling makes this an active area of research among current genomics researchers.

References

- Peri S, Navarro JD, Kristiansen TZ, *et al.* (January 2004). "Human protein reference database as a discovery resource for proteomics" [4]. *Nucleic Acids Res.* **32** (Database issue): D497–501. doi:10.1093/nar/gkh070. PMC 308804. PMID 14681466.
- Liebel U, Kindler B, Pepperkok R (August 2004). "'Harvester': a fast meta search engine of human protein resources" [3]. *Bioinformatics* **20** (12): 1962–3. doi:10.1093/bioinformatics/bth146. PMID 14988114.
- Ganesan N, Bennett NF, Velauthapillai M, Pattabiraman N, Squier R, Kalyanasundaram B (August 2005). "Web-based interface facilitating sequence-to-structure analysis of BLAST alignment reports". *BioTechniques* **39** (2): 186, 188. doi:10.2144/05392BM05. PMID 16116790.}}
- Beaton J, Smith C (November 2005). "Google versus PubMed" [5]. *Ann R Coll Surg Engl* **87** (6): 491–2. doi:10.1308/003588405X71207. PMC 1964102. PMID 16263030.
- Hunter L, Cohen KB (March 2006). "Biomedical language processing: what's beyond PubMed?" [6]. *Mol. Cell* **21** (5): 589–94. doi:10.1016/j.molcel.2006.02.012. PMC 1702322. PMID 16507357.
- Ganesan N, Kalyanasundaram B, Velauthapillai M (March 2007). "Bioinformatics data profiling tools: a prelude to metabolic profiling". *Pac.Symp. Biocomput.*: 127–32. PMID 17990486.

References

[1] http://www.rnabase.org/
[2] http://www.sequerome.org
[3] http://bioinformatics.georgetown.edu/InstaSeq.htm
[4] http://nar.oxfordjournals.org/cgi/pmidlookup?view=long&pmid=14681466
[5] http://openurl.ingenta.com/content/nlm?genre=article&issn=0035-8843&volume=87&issue=6&spage=491&aulast=Beaton
[6] http://linkinghub.elsevier.com/retrieve/pii/S1097-2765(06)00114-6

Sequence Read Archive

Sequence Read Archive

Content	
Description	FASTQ Sequences
Contact	
Research center	European Bioinformatics Institute
Access	
Website	http://www.ebi.ac.uk/ena/
Tools	
Miscellaneous	

The **Sequence Read Archive** or **Short Read Archive** is an important bioinformatics database hosted at the European Bioinformatics Institute. It provides a public repository for the 'short reads' generated by second generation sequencing technologies.

The 'short reads' are typically less than 1000bp of DNA sequence and associated quality information collected from a genomic, environmental or transcriptomic (reverse transcribed) sample.

The NCBI mirror of the SRA was closed in 2010 due to funding cuts.

Deposition of data in the SRA is a mandatory requirement of some funding agencies and open access journals.

External links

- European Nucleotide Archive [1], page for search in SRA
- SRA homepage [2] at the NCBI.
- SRA 'homepage' [3] in typical EBI style.

References

- A SEQanswers thread on the topic [4]

References

[1] http://www.ebi.ac.uk/ena/
[2] http://www.ncbi.nlm.nih.gov/sra
[3] http://www.ebi.ac.uk/ena/about/sra_submissions
[4] http://seqanswers.com/forums/showthread.php?t=9431

Sequential structure alignment program

The **SSAP** (**Sequential Structure Alignment Program**) method uses double dynamic programming to produce a structural alignment based on atom-to-atom vectors in structure space. Instead of the alpha carbons typically used in structural alignment, SSAP constructs its vectors from the beta carbons for all residues except glycine, a method which thus takes into account the rotameric state of each residue as well as its location along the backbone. SSAP works by first constructing a series of inter-residue distance vectors between each residue and its nearest non-contiguous neighbors on each protein. A series of matrices are then constructed containing the vector differences between neighbors for each pair of residues for which vectors were constructed. Dynamic programming applied to each resulting matrix determines a series of optimal local alignments which are then summed into a "summary" matrix to which dynamic programming is applied again to determine the overall structural alignment.

SSAP originally produced only pairwise alignments but has since been extended to multiple alignments as well.[1] It has been applied in an all-to-all fashion to produce a hierarchical fold classification scheme known as CATH (Class, Architecture, Topology, Homology),[2] which has been used to construct the CATH Protein Structure Classification [3] database.

Generally, SSAP scores above 80 are associated with highly similar structures. Scores between 70 and 80 indicate a similar fold with minor variations. Structures yielding a score between 60 and 70 do not generally contain the same fold, but usually belong to the same protein class with common structural motifs[4].

References

[1] Taylor WR, Flores TP, Orengo CA. (1994). Multiple protein structure alignment. *Protein Sci* 3(10):1858-70.

[2] Orengo CA, Michie AD, Jones S, Jones DT, Swindells MB, Thornton JM. (1997) CATH: A hierarchical classification of protein domain structures. *Structure* 5(8): 1093-1108.

[3] http://www.cathdb.info/latest/index.html

[4] Porwal G, Jain S, Babu SD, Singh D, Nanavati H, Noronha S. (2007) Protein Structure Prediction Aided by Geometrical and Probabilistic Constraints. *J. Comput. Chem.* 28(12): 1943-1952.

External links

- SSAP Server (http://www.cathdb.info/cgi-bin/SsapServer.pl) for pairwise structural comparison

Sequerome

Stable release	NA
Operating system	Linux, Mac, MS-Windows
Type	Bioinformatics - Sequence profiling tool
Licence	Freeware
Website	http://www.sequerome.org

Sequerome is a web-based Sequence profiling tool for integrating the results of a BLAST sequence-alignment report with external research tools and servers that perform advanced sequence manipulations, and allowing the user to record the steps of such an analysis. Sequerome is a web based Java tool that acts as a front-end to BLAST queries and provides simplified access to web-distributed resources for protein and nucleic acid analysis.

Since its inception in 2005, the tool has been featured in *Science*[1] and officially linked to many bioinformatics portals around the globe.

Description

Sequerome has the following features: profiling Sequence alignment reports from BLAST by linking the results page to a panel of third party services, tabbed browsing allowing user to come back earlier operations, visit third party services to perform customized sequence manipulations, one-box any-format sequence input and alternate options for sequence input including visiting third party sites, cached storage of input sequences and retrieval, a three pane browsing environment allowing simultaneous input and analysis of multiple sequences, and archival options on top of each icon, for results from each pane

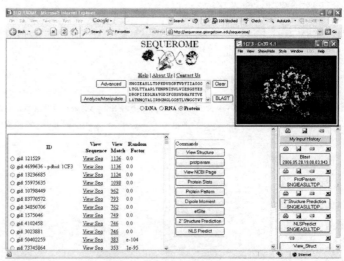

Display of profiling features on a browser

The software application can be accessed directly. The homepage shows three panels: Query pane, Results pane and the Search History pane. The user may resize these panes to perform parallel actions in any of these panes. In a single browser it is possible to run parallel BLAST searches on different sequences, analyzing them or viewing the restriction digests for each document of a BLAST result

Query Pane

Each browser session can be initiated perform without asking too many questions at the outset. The user has to just dump in the sequence in the Query pane, and BLAST the sequence right away under standard parameters. Experienced users have a choice to perform further special operations under the Advanced options. Some of features include selection of specific databases to BLAST from, *upload* facility to work with FASTA files stored in individual computers, sequence retrieval using NCBI IDs and visit any user-defined URL to *drag-N-drop* the sequences. Alternatively the user can also perform a variety of other actions including Sequence manipulation, analysis, and alignment using existing tools available in the web. The One-box any-sequence, takes input in any format (FASTA, with or without spaces/numbers...). Alerts also exist to warn wrong selection of choices (DNA/RNA/Protein). Results obtained from 'sequence manipulation' e.g. translation, can be further carried on to do further BLAST analysis while preserving the history of the earlier search.

Results Pane

Sequerome directly queries the input sequence against a variety of databases/tools ('popular public domains' and 'privately hosted services') including BLAST, PDB, REBASE and others, and generates outputs that are intuitive and easily comprehensible. Access to various analysis tools, (including viewing a 3D structure-viewer from a PDBid), is provided as separate command buttons to analyze every record from a BLAST report before making a final selection. In case of results from a protein BLAST, PDBids are displayed prominently in appropriate cases next to the BLAST record, so that the structure of the molecule with a match can be viewed directly (with an already downloaded version of molecular structure viewer e.g. Cn3D, 'Rasmol'.... Once the BLAST report is displayed on the Results pane, the user can to directly perform an analysis on any of the BLAST hits using a series of command buttons that are linked to the respective servers/ sites. Most of the results from third party servers can be viewed directly in the Results pane without opening up as many browsers e.g. ORF prediction, Protparam.

Search History Pane

One of the key features of a profiling an input sequence data is to store, retrieve and effectively combine and re-use the older inputs. These can be further enhanced if there is retrieval options for each of the operations performed. The bottom right panel in the browser does this while also storing all the input sequences entered earlier. Thus the browser lends an environment to carry out tabbed browsing.. For each of the icons linking to the stored results, the user has a choice of archiving them, including print, save and mail options. These can be seen as small colored pictures on top of each icon.

Implementation

Sequerome has a three-tiered architecture that uses Java servlet and Server Page technologies with Java database connectivity (JDBC), making it both server and platform-independent. Sequerome is compatible with essentially all Java-enabled, graphical browsers but is better accessed using Internet Explorer and can be run on most operating systems equipped with a Java Virtual Machine (JVM) and Jakarta Tomcat server. End-users have to download plugins for viewing structure of molecules from PDB e.g. Cn3D, Rasmol, SwissPDB etc.

Further directions

The "post-genomics" era has given rise to a range of web based tools and software to compile, organize, and deliver large amounts of primary sequence information, as well as protein structures, gene annotations, sequence alignments, and other common bioinformatics tasks. A simple web-search returns any number of such services and software tools.

References

[1] "A Bigger BLAST", NetWatch, Science (http://www.sciencemag.org/) VOL 309, 23 Sep 2005, p-1971 [DOI: 10.1126/science.309.5743.1971b],"Seq and Find"

• "A Bigger BLAST", NetWatch, Science (http://www.sciencemag.org/) VOL 309, 23 Sep 2005, p-1971 [DOI: 10.1126/science.309.5743.1971b]

• "Seq and Find", WebWatch feature, Biotechniques (http://www.biotechniques.com/), Volume 39, Number 5: pp 629

• "A web based interface facilitating sequence to structure analysis of BLAST alignment reports", Biotechniques (http://www.biotechniques.com/) Volume 39, Number 2: pp 186–188

Short Oligonucleotide Analysis Package

Short Oligonucleotide Analysis Package (SOAP) is a bioinformatics package used for the assembly and analysis of DNA sequences. SOAP is particularly well-suited for Illumina next generation sequences. There are 5 members in this package :

• SOAPaligner: A new alignment tool from SOAP v1.
• SOAPdenovo: A short reads do novo assembler.
• SOAPsnp: An accurate consensus sequence builder.
• SOAPsv: A structural variation scanner.
• SOAPindel: A tool to find insertion and deletion specially for re-sequence technology.

All programs in the SOAP package may be used free of charge.

SOAPdenovo, a program in the SOAP package, was used to assemble the Panda genome entirely from short Illumina next generation sequences [1].

SOAP v1

SOAP v1 is the previous version of SOAPaligner, and it is only a sequence alignment tool while SOAP (SOAP v2) is a program package that contains 5 members as above .

External links

• http://soap.genomics.org.cn
• http://soap.genomics.org.cn/soap1
• http://bioinformatics.genomics.org.cn
• http://seqanswers.com/forums/showthread.php?t=43

Reference

- SOAP2: an improved ultrafast tool for short read alignment [2]
- The sequence and de novo assembly of the giant panda genome [1]

References

[1] http://www.nature.com/nature/journal/v463/n7279/full/nature08696.html
[2] http://bioinformatics.oxfordjournals.org/cgi/content/abstract/btp336

Shotgun proteomics

Shotgun proteomics is a method of identifying proteins in complex mixtures using a combination of high performance liquid chromatography combined with mass spectrometry.[1] [2] [3] [4] [5] The name is derived from shotgun sequencing of DNA which is itself named by analogy with the rapidly-expanding, quasi-random firing pattern of a shotgun. In shotgun proteomics, the proteins in the mixture are digested and the resulting peptides are separated by liquid chromatography. Tandem mass spectrometry is then used to identify the peptides.

References

[1] Washburn MP, Wolters D, Yates JR (2001). "Large-scale analysis of the yeast proteome by multidimensional protein identification technology". *Nat. Biotechnol.* **19** (3): 242–247. doi:10.1038/85686. PMID 11231557.
[2] Wolters DA, Washburn MP, Yates JR (2001). "An automated multidimensional protein identification technology for shotgun proteomics". *Anal. Chem.* **73** (23): 5683–5690. doi:10.1021/ac010617e. PMID 11774908.
[3] Hu L, Ye M, Jiang X, Feng S, Zou H (2007). "Advances in hyphenated analytical techniques for shotgun proteome and peptidome analysis--a review". *Anal. Chim. Acta* **598** (2): 193–204. doi:10.1016/j.aca.2007.07.046. PMID 17719892.
[4] Fournier ML, Gilmore JM, Martin-Brown SA, Washburn MP (2007). "Multidimensional separations-based shotgun proteomics". *Chem. Rev.* **107** (8): 3654–86. doi:10.1021/cr068279a. PMID 17649983.
[5] Nesvizhskii AI (2007). "Protein identification by tandem mass spectrometry and sequence database searching". *Methods Mol. Biol.* **367**: 87–119. doi:10.1385/1-59745-275-0:87. PMID 17185772.

Bibliography

- Marcotte EM (2007). "How do shotgun proteomics algorithms identify proteins?" (http://www.nature.com/nbt/journal/v25/n7/full/nbt0707-755.html). *Nat. Biotechnol.* **25** (7): 755–7. doi:10.1038/nbt0707-755. PMID 17621303.
- Veenstra, Timothy D.; Yates, John R. (2006). *Proteomics for Biological Discovery*. New York: Wiley-Liss. ISBN 0-471-16005-9.

Shredding (disassembling genomic data)

Shredding refers to the process in bioinformatics of taking assembled sequences and disassembling them into short sequences of usually 500 to 750 base pairs (bp). This is generally done for the purpose of taking the short *shredded* sequences and reapplying various analysis and bioinformatic techniques.

Human Genome Project

The process of shredding was used successfully several times during the analysis phase of the human genome project.[1]

References

[1] Venter, C. The sequence of the human genome. Science. Vol 291.16 Feb, 2001.

Silverquant

Silverquant is a labeling and detection method for DNA microarrays or protein microarrays. A synonym is <colorimetric> detection. In contrast to the classical signal detection on microarrays by using fluorescence, the colorimetric detection is more sensitive and ozone-stable.

Chemical reaction

The probe to be detected is labeled with some biotin-molecules. After incubation with a gold-coupled anti-biotin conjugate, silver nitrate and a reducing agent are added. The reaction starts whereas the gold particle serves as a starting point for the silver precipitation. The reaction needs to be stopped after a specific time. The constant reaction time is essential to obtain comparable results.

Detection

The silver-stained spots on the microarray are clearly visible. By using a transmission microarray scanner, the signals are transformed into digital values which are finally available as an image file.

References

Alexandre I et al. Anal Biochem. 2001 Aug 1;295(1):1-8.

Sim4

Sim4 is a nucleotide sequence alignment program akin to BLAST but specifically tailored to DNA to cDNA/EST (Expressed Sequence Tag) alignment (as opposed to DNA-DNA or protein-protein alignment). It was written by Florea et al.

External links

- A Computer Program for Aligning a cDNA Sequence with a Genomic DNA Sequence [1]
- Download [2]

References

[1] http://www.genome.org/cgi/content/full/8/9/967
[2] http://sibsim4.sourceforge.net/

Similarity matrix

A **similarity matrix** is a matrix of scores which express the similarity between two data points. Similarity matrices are strongly related to their counterparts, distance matrices and substitution matrices.

Use in sequence alignment

Similarity matrices are used in sequence alignment. Higher scores are given to more-similar characters, and lower or negative scores for dissimilar characters.

Nucleotide similarity matrices are used to align nucleic acid sequences. Because there are only four nucleotides commonly found in DNA (Adenine (A), Cytosine (C), Guanine (G) and Thymine (T)), nucleotide similarity matrices are much simpler than protein similarity matrices. For example, a simple matrix will assign identical bases a score of +1 and non-identical bases a score of −1. A more complicated matrix would give a higher score to transitions (changes from a pyrimidine such as C or T to another pyrimidine, or from a purine such as A or G to another purine) than to transversions (from a pyrimidine to a purine or vice versa). The match/mismatch ratio of the matrix sets the target evolutionary distance.[1] [2] The +1/−3 DNA matrix used by BLASTN is best suited for finding matches between sequences that are 99% identical; a +1/−1 (or +4/−4) matrix is much more suited to sequences with about 70% similarity. Matrices for lower similarity sequences require longer sequence alignments.

Amino acid similarity matrices are more complicated, because there are 20 amino acids coded for by the genetic code. Therefore, the similarity matrix for amino acids contains 400 entries (although it is usually symmetric). The first approach scored all amino acid changes equally. A later refinement was to determine amino acid similarities based on how many base changes were required to change a codon to code for that amino acid. This model is better, but it doesn't take into account the selective pressure of amino acid changes. Better models took into account the chemical properties of amino acids.

One approach has been to empirically generate the similarity matrices. The Dayhoff method used phylogenetic trees and sequences taken from species on the tree. This approach has given rise to the PAM series of matrices. PAM matrices are labelled based on how many nucleotide changes have occurred, per 100 amino acids. While the PAM matrices benefit from having a well understood evolutionary model, they are most useful at short evolutionary distances (PAM10 - PAM120). At long evolutionary distances, for example PAM250 or 20% identity, it has been shown that the BLOSUM matrices are much more effective.

The BLOSUM series were generated by comparing a number of divergent sequences. The BLOSUM series are labeled based on how much entropy remains unmutated between all sequences, so a lower BLOSUM number corresponds to a higher PAM number.

Notes and references

[1] States, D; Gish, W; Altschul, S (1991). "Improved sensitivity of nucleic acid database searches using application-specific scoring matrices". *Methods: a companion to methods in enzymology* **3** (1): 66. doi:10.1016/S1046-2023(05)80165-3.

[2] Sean R. Eddy (2004). "Where did the BLOSUM62 alignment score matrix come from?" (http://informatics.umdnj.edu/bioinformatics/ courses/5020/notes/BLOSUM62 primer.pdf). *Nature Biotechnology* **22** (8): 1035. doi:10.1038/nbt0804-1035. PMID 15286655. .

Simulated growth of plants

The **simulated growth of plants** is a significant task in of systems biology and mathematical biology, which seeks to reproduce plant morphology with computer software. Electronic trees (e-trees) usually use L-systems to simulate growth. L-systems are very important in the field of complexity science and A-life. A universally accepted system for describing changes in plant morphology at the cellular or modular level has yet to be devised. [1] The most widely implemented tree-generating algorithms are described in the papers "Creation and Rendering of Realistic Trees" [24], and Real-Time Tree Rendering [25]

The realistic modeling of plant growth is of high value to biology, but also for computer games.

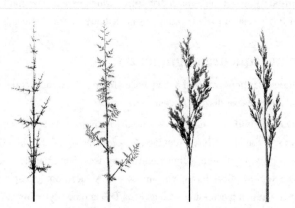

'Weeds', generated using an L-system in 3D.

Theory + Algorithms

A biologist, Aristid Lindenmayer (1925–1989) worked with yeast and filamentous fungi and studied the growth patterns of various types of algae, such as the blue/green bacteria *Anabaena catenula*. Originally the L-systems were devised to provide a formal description of the development of such simple multicellular organisms, and to illustrate the neighbourhood relationships between plant cells. Later on, this system was extended to describe higher plants and complex branching structures. Central to L-systems, is the notion of rewriting, where the basic idea is to define complex objects by successively replacing parts of a simple object using a set of rewriting rules or productions. The rewriting can be carried out recursively. L-Systems are also closely related to Koch curves.

Environmental interaction

A challenge for plant simulations is to consistently integrate environmental factors, such as surrounding plants, obstructions, water and mineral availability, and lighting conditions. is to build virtual/environments with as many parameters as computationally feasible, thereby, not only simulating the growth of the plant, but also the environment it is growing within, and, in fact, whole ecosystems. Changes in resource availability influence plant growth, which in turn results in a change of resource availability. Powerful models and powerful hardware will be necessary to effectively simulate these recursive interactions of recursive structures.

Software

- Branching: L-system Tree [2] A Java applet and its source code (open source) of the botanical tree growth simulation using the L-system.
- Arbaro [3]- opensource
- Treal [4]- opensource
- L-arbor [5]
- AMAP Genesis 3.0 - from CIRDAD
- ONETREE [6] -Accompanying the CDROM is a CO2 meter that plugs into your local serial port. It is this that controls the growth rate of the trees. It is the actual carbon dioxide level right at your computer that controls the growth rate of these virtual trees.
- Powerplant [7]

see Comparison of tree generators [8] *and A Survey of Modeling and Rendering Trees* [9]

External links

- David J. Wright's article on L-systems [10]
- Algorithmic Botany at the University of Calgary [11]
- The Algorithmic Beauty of Plants [12]

References

[1] "Simulating plant growth" (http://www.acm.org/crossroads/xrds8-2/plantsim.html). . Retrieved 2009-10-18.

[2] http://www.mizuno.org/applet/branching/

[3] http://arbaro.sourceforge.net/

[4] http://members.chello.nl/~l.vandenheuvel2/TReal/

[5] http://web.archive.org/web/20091024205412/http://geocities.com/grubertm/id34.htm

[6] http://www.nyu.edu/projects/xdesign/onetrees/atrees/

[7] http://sourceforge.net/projects/pplant/files/

[8] http://www.treegenerator.com/compare.htm

[9] http://www.springerlink.com/content/d047j770587w7411/

[10] http://www.math.okstate.edu/mathdept/dynamics/lecnotes/node12.html#SECTION00040000000000000000

[11] http://algorithmicbotany.org/

[12] http://algorithmicbotany.org/papers/#abop

Single molecule real time sequencing

Single molecule real time sequencing (also known as SMRT) is a parallelized single molecule DNA sequencing by synthesis technology developed by Pacific Biosciences. Single molecule real time sequencing utilizes the zero-mode waveguide (ZMW), developed in the laboratories of Harold G. Craighead and Watt W. Webb[1] at Cornell University. A single DNA polymerase enzyme is affixed at the bottom of a ZMW with a single molecule of DNA as a template. The ZMW is a structure that creates an illuminated observation volume that is small enough to observe only a single nucleotide of DNA (also known as a base) being incorporated by DNA polymerase. Each of the four DNA bases is attached to one of four different fluorescent dyes. When a nucleotide is incorporated by the DNA polymerase, the fluorescent tag is cleaved off and diffuses out of the observation area of the ZMW where its fluorescence is no longer observable. A detector detects the fluorescent signal of the nucleotide incorporation, and the base call is made according to the corresponding fluorescence of the dye.

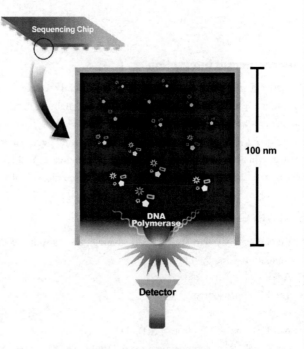

Overview of Single Molecule Real Time Sequencing

Technology

The DNA sequencing is done on a chip that contains many ZMWs. Inside each ZMW, a single active DNA polymerase with a single molecule of single stranded DNA template is immobilized to the bottom through which light can penetrate and create a visualization chamber that allows monitoring of the activity of the DNA polymerase at a single molecule level. The signal from a phospho-linked nucleotide incorporated by the DNA polymerase is detected as the DNA synthesis proceeds which results in the DNA sequencing in real time.

Phospholinked nucleotide

For each of the nucleotide bases, there are four corresponding fluorescent dye molecules that enable the detector to identify the base being incorporated by the DNA polymerase as it performs the DNA synthesis. The fluorescent dye molecule is attached to the phosphate chain of the nucleotide. When the nucleotide is incorporated by the DNA polymerase, the fluorescent dye is cleaved off with the phosphate chain as a part of a natural DNA synthesis process during which a phosphodiester bond is created to elongate the DNA chain. The cleaved fluorescent dye molecule then diffuses out of the detection volume so that the fluorescent signal is no longer detected. [2]

Zero-mode waveguide

The zero-mode waveguide (ZMW) is a nanophotonic confinement structure that consists of a circular hole in an aluminum cladding film deposited on a clear silica substrate.[3] The ZMW holes are ~70 nm in diameter and ~100 nm in depth. Due to the behavior of light when it travels through a small aperture, the optical field decays exponentially inside the chamber.[4] The observation volume within an illuminated ZMW is ~20 zeptoliters (20 X 10^{-21} liters). Within this volume, the activity of DNA polymerase incorporating a single nucleotide can be readily detected.

Sequencing performance

Pacific Biosciences expects to commercialize SMRT sequencing in 2010 or 2011. The prototype of the SMRT chip contains ~3000 ZMW holes that allow parallelized DNA sequencing. Each of the ZMW holes produces approximately 1,500 bp (base pair) read lengths at a speed of 10 bp per second.

Application

Single molecule real time sequencing will be applicable for a broad range of genomics research, namely:

- *De novo* **genome sequencing**: The read length from the single molecule real time sequencing is currently comparable to that from the Sanger sequencing method based on dideoxynucleotide chain termination. The longer read length allows *de novo* genome sequencing and easier genome assemblies.[5]
- **Individual whole genome sequencing**: Individual genome sequencing may utilize the single molecule real time sequencing method for personalized medicine.
- **Resequencing**: A same DNA molecule can be resequenced independently by creating the circular DNA template and utilizing a strand displacing enzyme that separates the newly synthesized DNA strand from the template.[2]
- **Methylation detection**: the dynamics of polymerase can indicate whether a base is methylated.[6]

References

[1] M.J. Levene, J. Korlach, S.W. Turner, M. Foquet, H.G. Craighead, W.W. Webb, Zero-Mode Waveguides for Single-Molecule Analysis at high concentrations. Science. 299 (2003) 682-686

[2] Pacific Biosciences Technology Backgrounder (http://www.pacificbiosciences.com/assets/files/pacbio_technology_backgrounder.pdf) from Pacific Biosciences (http://www.pacificbiosciences.com/index.php)

[3] J. Korlach, P.J. Marks, R.L. Cicero, J.J. Gray, D.L. Murphy, D.B. Roitman, T.T. Pham, G.A. otto, M. Foquet, S.W. Turner, Selective aluminum passivation for targeted immobilization of single DNA polymerase molecules in zero-mode waveguide nanostructures. PNAS. 105(2008) 1176-1181

[4] M. Foquet, K.T. Samiee, X. Kong, B.P. Chauduri, P.M. Lundquist, S.W. Turner, J. Freudenthal, d.B. Roitman, Improved fabrication of zero-mode waveguides for single-molecule detection. Journal of Applied Physics. 103 (2008) 034301-1-034301-9

[5] http://www.sciencemag.org/content/323/5910/133.short

[6] http://www.nature.com/nmeth/journal/v7/n6/full/nmeth.1459.html

External links

- Report from the BioIT World.com (http://www.bio-itworld.com/BioIT_Content.aspx?id=71746)
- Report from Genome Web (http://www.genomeweb.com/issues/news/144976-1.html)
- Report from New York Times (http://www.nytimes.com/2008/02/09/business/09genomebar.html?_r=1& ref=business&oref=slogin)

Snagger

Snagger[1] is a bioinformatics software program for selecting tag SNPs using pairwise r^2 linkage disequilibrium. It is implemented as extension to the popular software, Haploview[2] , and is freely available under the MIT License. Snagger distinguishes itself from existing single nucleotide polymorphism (SNP) selection algorithms, including Tagger[3] , by providing user options that allow for:

(1) **Prioritization of tagSNPs** based on certain characteristics, including platform-specific design scores, functionality (i.e. coding status), and chromosomal position

(2) Efficient selection of SNPs across **multiple populations**

(3) Selection of tagSNPs **outside defined genomic regions** to improve coverage and genotyping success

(4) Picking of **surrogate tagSNPs** that serve as backups for tagSNPs whose failure would result in a significant loss of data

Haploview with Snagger has been developed and is maintained at the Genomics Center at the University of Southern California.

References

[1] Edlund CK, Lee WH, Li D, Van Den Berg DJ, Conti DV. " Snagger: A user-friendly program for incorporating additional information for tag SNP selection (http://www.biomedcentral.com/1471-2105/9/174)". BMC Bioinformatics. 2008 Mar 27; 9(1):174

[2] Barrett J.C., Fry B., Maller J., Daly M.J. (2005). " Haploview: analysis and visualization of LD and haplotype maps (http://bioinformatics. oxfordjournals.org/cgi/reprint/21/2/263?maxtoshow=&HITS=10&hits=10&RESULTFORMAT=&fulltext=haploview&searchid=1& FIRSTINDEX=0&resourcetype=HWCIT)". Bioinformatics 21: 263-265.

[3] de Bakker P. I., Yelensky R., Pe'er I., Gabriel S. B., Daly M. J., Altshuler D. (2005). " Efficiency and power in genetic association studies (http://www.nature.com/ng/journal/v37/n11/pdf/ng1669.pdf).". Nature Genetics 37: 1217-1223.

External links

- Snagger Homepage (http://snagger.sourceforge.net/)
- Haploview Homepage (http://www.broad.mit.edu/mpg/haploview/)
- Tagger Homepage (http://www.broad.mit.edu/mpg/tagger/)

SNP array

In molecular biology and bioinformatics, a **SNP array** is a type of DNA microarray which is used to detect polymorphisms within a population. A single nucleotide polymorphism (SNP), a variation at a single site in DNA, is the most frequent type of variation in the genome. For example, there are around 10 million SNPs that have been identified in the human genome[1]. As SNPs are highly conserved throughout evolution and within a population, the map of SNPs serves as an excellent genotypic marker for research.

Principles

The basic principles of SNP array are the same as the DNA microarray. These are the convergence of DNA hybridization, fluorescence microscopy, and solid surface DNA capture. The three mandatory components of the SNP arrays are:

1. The array that contains immobilized nucleic acid sequences or target;
2. One or more labeled allele-specific oligonucleotide (ASO) probes;
3. A detection system that records and interprets the hybridization signal.

To achieve relative concentration independence and minimal cross-hybridization, raw sequences and SNPs of multiple databases are scanned to design the probes. Each SNP on the array is interrogated with different probes. Depending on the purpose of experiments, the amount of SNPs present on an array is considered.

Applications

A SNP array is a useful tool to study the whole genome. The most important application of SNP array is in determining disease susceptibility and consequently, in pharmacogenomics by measuring the efficacy of drug therapies specifically for the individual. As each individual has many single nucleotide polymorphisms that together create a unique DNA sequence, SNP-based genetic linkage analysis could be performed to map disease loci, and hence determine disease susceptibility genes for an individual. The combination of SNP maps and high density SNP array allows the use of SNPs as the markers for Mendelian diseases with complex traits efficiently. For example, whole-genome genetic linkage analysis shows significant linkage for many diseases such as rheumatoid arthritis, prostate cancer, and neonatal diabetes. As a result, drugs can be personally designed to efficiently act on a group of individuals who share a common allele - or even a single individual. A SNP array can also be used to generate a virtual karyotype using software to determine the copy number of each SNP on the array and then align the SNPs in chromosomal order.

In addition, SNP array can be used for studying the loss of heterozygosity (LOH). LOH is a form of allelic imbalance that can result from the complete loss of an allele or from an increase in copy number of one allele relative to the other. While other chip-based methods (e.g. comparative genomic hybridization) can detect only genomic gains or deletions, SNP array has the additional advantage of detecting copy number neutral LOH due to uniparental disomy (UPD). In UPD, one allele or whole chromosome from one parent are missing leading to reduplication of the other parental allele (uni-parental = from one parent, disomy = duplicated). In a disease setting this occurrence may be pathological when the wildtype allele (e.g. from the mother) is missing and instead two copies of the mutant allele (e.g. from the father) are present. Using high density SNP array to detect LOH allows identification of pattern of allelic imbalance with potential prognostic and diagnostic utilities. This usage of SNP array has a huge potential in cancer diagnostics as LOH is a prominent characteristic of most human cancers. Recent studies based on the SNP array technology have shown that not only solid tumors (gastric cancer, liver cancer etc.) but also hematologic malignancies (ALL, MDS, CML etc.) have a high rate of LOH due to genomic deletions or UPD and genomic gains. The results of these studies may help to gain insights into mechanisms of these diseases and to create targeted drugs.

References

[1] Sherry ST, Ward MH, Kholodov M, Baker J, Phan L, Smigielski EM, Sirotkin K. dbSNP: the NCBI database of genetic variation. Nucleic Acids Res. 2001;29:308–311. doi: 10.1093/nar/29.1.308. [PubMed] Link: http://www.ncbi.nlm.nih.gov/pubmed/11125122

Further reading

- Barnes, M.R. (2003) Chapter 3: Human Genetic Variation: Databases and Concepts, *Bioinformatics for geneticists*, edited by Barnes, M.R. and Gray, I.C., John Wiley and Sons, Ltd.
- Hehir-Kwa, J., Egmont-Petersen, M., Janssen,I., Smeets, D., Geurts van Kessel, A., Veltman, J. (2007) "Genome-wide copy number profiling on high-density BAC, SNP and oligonucleotide microarrays: a platform comparison based on statistical power analysis" *DNA Research*. 14:1-11. Link: http://dnaresearch.oxfordjournals.org/cgi/content/full/14/1/1
- John, S., Shephard, N., Liu, G., Zeggini, E., Cao, M., Chen, W., Vasavda, N., Mills, T., Barton, A., Hinks, A., Eyre, S., Johes, K.W., Ollier, W., Silman, A., Gibson, N., Worthington, J., and Kennedy, G.C. (2004) "Whole-Genome scan, in a complex disease, using 11,245 single-nucleotide polymorphism: comparison with microsatellites." *American Journal of Human Genetics*. 75(1):54-64. PMID 15154113
- Mei, R., Galipeau, P.C., Prass, C., Berno, A., Ghandour, G., Patil, N., Wolff, R.K., Chee, M.S., Reid, B.J., and Lockhart, D.J. (2000) "Genome-wide detection of allelic imbalance using human SNPs and high-density DNA arrays." *Genome Research*. 10:1126-1137. PMID 10958631
- Schaid, D.J., Guenther, J.C., Christensen, G.B., Hebbring, S., Rosenow, C., Hilker, C.A., McDonnell, S.K., Cunningham, J.M., Slager, S.L., Blute, M.L., and Thibodeau, S.N. (2004) "Comparison of Microsatellites Versus Single Nucleotide Polymorphisms by a Genome Linkage Screen for Prostate Cancer Susceptibility Loci", *American Journal of Human Genetics*. 75 (6): 948-65. PMID 15514889
- Sellick GS, Longman C, Tolmie J, Newbury-Ecob R, Geenhalgh L, Hughes S, Whiteford M, Garrett C, Houlston RS., "Genome-wide linkage searches for Mendelian disease loci can be efficiently conducted using high-density SNP genotyping arrays." *Nucleic Acids Research*. 32(20):e164. PMID 15561999
- Sheils, O., Finn, S. and O'Leary J. (2003) "Nucleic acid microarray: an overview." *Current Diagnostic Pathology*. 9:155-158.

Society for Mathematical Biology

The Society for Mathematical Biology (SMB) is an international association co-founded in 1972 in USA by Drs.George Karreman, Herbert Daniel Landahl and (initially chaired) by Anthony Bartholomay for the furtherance of joint scientific activities between Mathematics and Biology research communities[1],[2] . SMB publishes the "*Bulletin of Mathematical Biology*" [3] (ISSN 1522–9602)[4][5] , as well as the SMB annual newsletter[6] .

History of The Society for Mathematical Biology

The Society for Mathematical Biology emerged and grew from the earlier school of mathematical biophysics, initiated and supported by the Founder of Mathematical Biology, Nicolas Rashevsky[7][8] . Thus, the roots of SMB go back to the publication in 1939 of the first international journal of mathematical biology, previously entitled "The Bulletin of Mathematical Biophysics [9]"-- which was founded by Nicolas Rashevsky, and which is currently published by SMB under the name of "*Bulletin of Mathematical Biology*"[10] . Professor Rashevsky also founded in 1969 the non-profit organization "*Mathematical Biology, Incorporated*"--the precursor of SMB. Another notable member of the University of Chicago school of mathematical biology was Anatol Rapoport whose major interests were in developing basic concepts in the related area of mathematical sociology, who cofounded the Society for General Systems Research and became a president of the latter society in 1965. Herbert D. Landahl was initially also a member of Rashevsky's school of mathematical biology, and became the second president of SMB in the 1980s; both Herbert Landahl and Robert Rosen from Rashevsky's research group were focused on dynamical systems approaches to complex systems biology, with the latter researcher becoming in 1980 the president of the Society for General Systems Research.

Research and educational activities

In addition to its research and news publications, The Society for Mathematical Biology supports education in: mathematical biology, mathematical biophysics, complex systems biology and theoretical biology through sponsorship of several topic-focused graduate and postdoctoral courses. To encourage and stimulate young researchers in this relatively new and rapidly developing field of mathematical biology *The Society for Mathematical Biology* awards several prizes, as well as lists regularly new open international opportunities for researchers and students in this field[11] .

References

[1] Conrad, Michael (September 1996). "SMB – "Childhood, Boyhood, Youth."" (http://www.smb.org/governance/smb_history.shtml). Society for Mathematical Biology Newsletter. . Retrieved 2009-06-25.

[2] http://www.smb.org/governance/history.shtml History of SMB

[3] http://www.springer.com/math/biology/journal/11538

[4] "Bulletin of Mathematical Biology" (http://www.springer.com/math/biology/journal/11538). Springer New York. . Retrieved 2009-06-25.

[5] http://people.maths.ox.ac.uk/maini/PKM%20publications/170.pdf "Bulletin of Mathematical Biology—Facts, Figures and Comparisons.", by Philip K. Maini, Santiago Schnell and Sara Jolliffee., *Bulletin of Mathematical Biology* (2004) 66, 595–603,DOI:10.1016/j.bulm.2004.03.003

[6] http://www.smb.org/publications/index.shtml SMB Publications

[7] Rosen, Robert. 1972. "*Tribute to Nicolas Rashevsky*" 1899-1972. *Progress in Theoretical Biology* **2**.

[8] Conrad, Michael (September 1996). "SMB – CHILDHOOD, BOYHOOD, YOUTH" (http://www.smb.org/governance/smb_history. shtml). Society for Mathematical Biology Newsletter. . Retrieved 2009-06-25.

[9] http://www.springerlink.com/content/x513p402w52w1128/

[10] The Bulletin of Mathematical Biophysics (http://www.springerlink.com/content/x513p402w52w1128/)

[11] http://www.smb.org/prizes/index.shtml SMB Mathematical Biology Prize Awards

Further reading

- Nicolas Rashevsky. 1965. The Representation of Organisms in Terms of Predicates, *Bulletin of Mathematical Biophysics* **27**: 477–491.
- Nicolas Rashevsky. 1969, Outline of a Unified Approach to Physics, Biology and Sociology., *Bulletin of Mathematical Biophysics* **31**: 159–198.
- Elsasser, M.W.: 1981, A Form of Logic Suited for Biology., In: Robert, Rosen, ed., *Progress in Theoretical Biology*, Volume **6**, Academic Press, New York and London, pp. 23–62.
- Rosen, R. 1958a, A Relational Theory of Biological Systems., *Bulletin of Mathematical Biophysics* **20**: 245–260.
- Rosen, R. 1958b, The Representation of Biological Systems from the Standpoint of the Theory of Categories., *Bulletin of Mathematical Biophysics* **20**: 317–341.
- Warren McCulloch and Walter Pitts, "A Logical Calculus of Ideas Immanent in Nervous Activity", 1943, *Bulletin of Mathematical Biophysics* 5:115-133.
- Warren McCulloch and Walter Pitts, "On how we know universals: The perception of auditory and visual forms", 1947, *Bulletin of Mathematical Biophysics* 9:127-147.
- Santiago Schnell, Ramon Grima and Philip K. Maini. 2007. Multiscale modeling in biology (http://eprints. maths.ox.ac.uk/567/1/224.pdf). *American Scientist* **95**: 134-142.

External links

- *The Society for Mathematical Biology* (http://www.smb.org)
- Bulletin of Mathematical Biology (http://www.springerlink.com/content/x513p402w52w1128/)
- "In Memory of George Karreman." (http://www.smb.org/governance/karreman.shtml)—the first SMB President, by Paul De Weer.
- SMB home page (http://www.smb.org)
- IFSR Home page (http://www.ifsr.org/) of "The International Federation for Systems Research" (IFSR)
- European Society for Mathematical and Theoretical Biology (ESMTB) (http://www.esmtb.org/news/news. htm)
- The Centre for Mathematical Biology (CMB) at the [[University of Oxford (http://www2.maths.ox.ac.uk/ cmb/)]]

Software for protein model error verification

This **list of software for protein model error verification** is a compilation of bioinformatics software frequently employed to check experimental and theoretical models of protein structures for errors.

NAME	Description	Methods	Link	Author
ANOLEA			ANOLEA [1]	
NQ-Flipper			NQ-Flipper [2]	
Prosa			ProSA [3]	
QMEAN			QMEAN [4]	
Verify3D			Verify3D [5]	
WHAT_CHECK			WHAT_CHECK [24]	Gert Vriend

References

[1] http://www.swissmodel.unibas.ch/anolea/

[2] https://flipper.services.came.sbg.ac.at/

[3] http://www.came.sbg.ac.at/typo3/index.php?id=prosa

[4] http://swissmodel.expasy.org/qmean/

[5] http://www.doe-mbi.ucla.edu/Services/Verify_3D/

Software for protein structure visualization

This **list of software for protein structure visualization** is a compilation of bioinformatics software used to view protein structures. Such tools are commonly used in molecular biology, and bioinformatics.

NAME	Link	Author
BioBlender	BioBlender official web site [1]	SciVis team
Visual_Molecular_Dynamics	VMD official website [2]	
Jmol	Jmol official web site [3]	Jmol development team
Geneious Pro (implemented Jmol viewer as part of an all-in-one sequence analysis software package)	Geneious homepage [25]	Geneious development team
PyMOL	PyMOL Wiki [4]	Warren Lyford DeLano
RasMol	Official website [5]	Roger Sayle
UCSF Chimera	Official website [6]	UCSF RBVI
STING	STAR STING [7]	
Friend	[8]	Valentin Ilyin
VisProt3DS [9] (3D Stereoscopic view: anaglyth, side by side, hardware)	Official website [9]	Nick Vtyurin

Polyview-3D [10] (Web-based high resolution static views and animations using Pymol or Rasmol)	Official website [10]	Aleksey Porollo & Jarek Meller

References

[1] http://www.bioblender.eu/
[2] http://www.ks.uiuc.edu/Research/vmd/
[3] http://www.jmol.org/
[4] http://www.pymolwiki.org/index.php/Main_Page
[5] http://www.rasmol.org/
[6] http://www.rbvi.ucsf.edu/chimera/
[7] http://www.cbi.cnptia.embrapa.br/SMS
[8] http://ilyinlab.org/friend
[9] http://www.molsystems.com/vp3ds.html
[10] http://polyview.cchmc.org/polyview3d.html

SOSUI

SOSUI is a free online tool that predicts a part of the secondary structure of proteins from a given amino acid sequence (AAS). The main objective is to determine whether the protein in question is a soluble or a transmembrane protein.

History

SOSUI's algorithm was developed in 1996 at Tokyo University. The name means as much as "hydrophobic", an allusion to its molecular "clients".

How SOSUI works

First of all, SOSUI looks for α helices that are relatively easy to predict, taking into account the known helical potentials of the given amino acid sequence(AAS). The much more difficult task is to differentiate between the α helices in soluble proteins and the ones in transmembrane proteins, the α helix being a very common secondary structure pattern in proteins. SOSUI uses 4 characteristics of the AAS in its prediction:

1. "hydropathy index" (Kyte und Doolittle 1982)
2. weighted presence of amphiphilic amino acids (AA) and their localization: "amphiphilicity index"
3. the AA's charge
4. the length of the AAS

An important improvement compared to Kyte und Doolittle's "hydropathy index", which relies entirely on one characteristic, is the introduction of the so-called "amphiphilicity index". It is calculated by giving every AA with an amphiphilic residue a certain value which is derived from the AA's molecular structure. To meet SOSUI's criteria for amphiphilicity, the polar, hydrophilic residue may not be linked directly to the beta-carbon; there must be at least one apolar carbon interposed (therefore only lysine, arginine, histidine, glutamic acid, glutamine, tryptophan and tyrosine are relevant). SOSUI then looks for accumulations of amphiphilic AAs at the ends of α helices, which seems to be typical for transmembrane α helices (it makes the transmembrane position the energetically best one for these α helices by placing amphiphilic AAs at the lipid-water boundary and is thus co-responsible for the protein's correct localization). The AA's charge is also taken into consideration; the length is important because biological lipid membranes have a certain thickness determining the length of membrane-spanning proteins. According to a study published by SOSUI's developers it successfully differentiated 99% of a chosen group of proteins with known structure [1]. However, another study that had several prediction tools perform on the AAS's of 122 known proteins claimed that SOSUI was correct about the number of α helices in only about 60% of the cases [2]. But even if the number of transmembrane domains is not always exact, the differentiation between soluble and transmembrane proteins often works, as it is only necessary to find out if a protein has such a domain at all. Of course, membrane proteins which don't have transmembrane α helices (e.g. porins) or which are fixed with a covalent bond cannot be found by SOSUI.

Results

The result page first shows general information (length, average hydrophobicity). If the protein in question is a transmembrane protein, the number of transmembrane domains and their localization is noted. A "hydropathy-profile" with colored accentation of hydrophobic parts; the helical wheel diagrams of potential transmembrane domains are shown as well. The last image shows a schematic overview of the transmembrane protein's location.

Sources

1. Hirokawa, Boon-Chieng, Mitaku, *SOSUI: Classification and secondary structure prediction for membrane proteins*, Bioinformatics Vol.14 S.378-379 (1998) [1]
2. Masami Ikeda, Masafumi Arai, Toshio Shimizu, *Evaluation of transmembrane topology prediction methods by using an experimentally characterized topology dataset*, Genome Informatics 11: 426–427 (2000) [2]

External links

- SOSUI-homepage [3]

References

[1] http://bioinformatics.oxfordjournals.org/cgi/reprint/14/4/378
[2] http://www.jsbi.org/journal/GIW00/GIW00P094.pdf
[3] http://bp.nuap.nagoya-u.ac.jp/sosui/

Staden Package

Staden Package

Developer(s)	James Bonfield, Rodger Staden, *et al.*
Operating system	UNIX, Linux, Windows, Mac OS X
Type	Bioinformatics
License	open source
Website	http://staden.sourceforge.net/

The **Staden Package** is a set of open source tools for DNA sequence assembly, editing, and sequence analysis.

Package Components

The Staden package consists of a number of different programs. The main components are:

- pregap4 - base calling with Phred, end clipping, and vector trimming.
- trev - trace viewing and editing
- gap4 - sequence assembly, contig editing, and finishing
- Spin - DNA and protein sequence analysis

History

The Staden Package was developed by Rodger Staden's group at the MRC Cambridge in England since 1977.[1] [2] [3] The Staden package was available free to academic users, with 2500 licenses issued in 2003 and an estimated 10,000 users, when funding for further development was cut.[4] The Staden Package was converted to open source in 2004, and new versions were released in 2004, 2005, and 2009.

During the years of active development, the Staden group published a number of widely used file formats and ideas, including the SCF file format,[5] the use of sequence quality scores to generate accurate consensus sequences,[6] and the ZTR file format.[7]

References

[1] Staden R (1979). "A strategy of DNA sequencing employing computer programs.". *Nucleic Acids Res* **6** (7): 2601–2610PMID461197. doi:10.1093/nar/6.7.2601. PMC 327874. PMID 461197.

[2] Staden R (1984). "Computer methods to aid the determination and analysis of DNA sequences.". *Biochem Soc Trans* **12**: 1005–1008PMID6397374. PMID 6397374.

[3] Staden R, Beal KF, Bonfield JK (2000). "The Staden package, 1998.". *Methods Mol Biol* **132**: 115–130PMID10547834. PMID 10547834.

[4] http://www.genomeweb.com/informatics/uk-s-mrc-ends-support-staden-package-first-sign-post-hgp-funding-priority-shift

[5] Dear S, Staden R (1992). "A standard file format for data from DNA sequencing instruments.". *DNA Seq* **3**: 107–110PMID1457811. PMID 1457811.

[6] Bonfield JK, Staden R (1995). "The application of numerical estimates of base calling accuracy to DNA sequencing projects.". *Nucleic Acids Res* **23**: 1406–1410. doi:10.1093/nar/23.8.1406. PMC 306869. PMID 7753633.

[7] Bonfield JK, Staden R (2002). "ZTR: a new format for DNA sequence trace data.". *Bioinformatics* **18**: 3–10PMID11836205. doi:10.1093/bioinformatics/18.1.3.

External links

- Staden Package home at the Sanger Center (http://www.sanger.ac.uk/Software/production/staden/)

Statistical coupling analysis

Statistical coupling analysis or SCA is a technique used in bioinformatics to measure covariation between pairs of amino acids in a protein multiple sequence alignment (MSA). More specifically, it quantifies how much the amino acid distribution at some position i changes upon a perturbation of the amino acid distribution at another position j. The resulting **statistical coupling energy** indicates the degree of evolutionary dependence between the residues, with higher coupling energy corresponding to increased dependence.[1]

Definition of statistical coupling energy

Statistical coupling energy measures how a perturbation of amino acid distribution at one site in an MSA effects the amino acid distribution at another site. For example, consider a multiple sequence alignment with sites (or columns) a through z, where each site has some distribution of amino acids. At position i, 60% of the sequences have a valine and the remaining 40% of sequences have a leucine, at position j the distribution is 40% isoleucine, 40% histidine and 20% methionine, k has an average distribution (the 20 amino acids are present at roughly the same frequencies seen in all proteins), and l has 80% histidine, 20% valine. Since positions i, j and l have an amino acid distribution different from the mean distribution observed in all proteins, they are said to have some degree of **conservation**.

In statistical coupling analysis, the conservation (ΔG^{stat}) at each site (i) is defined as: $\Delta G_i^{stat} = \sqrt{\sum_x (ln P_i^x)^2}$

[2]

Here, P_i^x describes the probability of finding amino acid x at position i, and is defined by a function in binomial form as follows:

$$P_i^x = \frac{N!}{n_x!(N - n_x)!} p_x^{n_x} (1 - p_x)^{N - n_x},$$

where N is 100, n_x is the percentage of sequences with residue x (e.g. methionine) at position i, and p_x corresponds to the approximate distribution of amino acid x in all positions among all sequenced proteins. The summation runs over all 20 amino acids. After ΔG_i^{stat} is computed, the conservation for position i in a subalignment produced after a perturbation of amino acid distribution at j ($\Delta G_{i \mid \delta j}^{stat}$) is taken. Statistical coupling energy, denoted $\Delta \Delta G_{i,j}^{stat}$, is simply the difference between these two values. That is:

$$\Delta \Delta G_{i,j}^{stat} = \Delta G_{i|\delta j}^{stat} - \Delta G_i^{stat} \text{, or, more commonly, } \Delta \Delta G_{i,j}^{stat} = \sqrt{\sum_x (ln P_{i|\delta j}^x - ln P_i^x)^2}$$

Statistical coupling energy is often systematically calculated between a fixed, perturbated position, and all other positions in an MSA. Continuing with the example MSA from the beginning of the section, consider a perturbation at position j where the amino distribution changes from 40% I, 40% H, 20% M to 100% I. If, in a subsequent subalignment, this changes the distribution at i from 60% V, 40% L to 90% V , 10% L, but does not change the distribution at position l, then there would be some amount of statistical coupling energy between i and j but none between l and j.

Applications

Ranganathan and Lockless originally developed SCA to examine thermodynamic (energetic) coupling of residue pairs in proteins.[3] Using the PDZ domain family, they were able to identify a small network of residues that were energetically coupled to a binding site residue. The network consisted of both residues spatially close to the binding site in the tertiary fold, called contact pairs, and more distant residues that participate in longer-range energetic interactions. Later applications of SCA by the Ranganathan group [4] on the GPCR, serine protease and hemoglobin families also showed energetic coupling in sparse networks of residues that cooperate in allosteric communication.[5]

Statistical coupling analysis has also been used as a basis for computational protein design. In 2005, Russ et al.[6] used an SCA for the WW domain to create artificial proteins with similar thermodynamic stability and structure to natural WW domains. The fact that 12 out of the 43 designed proteins with the same SCA profile as natural WW domains properly folded provided strong evidence that little information—only coupling information—was required for specifying the protein fold. This support for the SCA hypothesis was made more compelling considering that a) the successfully folded proteins had only 36% average sequence identity to natural WW folds, and b) none of the artificial proteins designed without coupling information folded properly. An accompanying study showed that the artificial WW domains were functionally similar to natural WW domains in ligand binding affinity and specificity.[7]

In *de novo* protein structure prediction, it has been shown that, when combined with a simple residue-residue distance metric, SCA-based scoring can fairly accurately distinguish native from non-native protein folds.[8]

External links

- What is a WW domain? [9]
- Ranganathan lecture on statistical coupling analysis (audio included) [10]
- Protein folding — a step closer? [11] - A summary of the Ranganathan lab's SCA-based design of artificial yet functional WW domains.

References

[1] "Supplementary Material for 'Evolutionarily conserved networks of residues mediate allosteric communication in proteins.'" (http://www.hhmi.swmed.edu/Labs/rr/SCA.html). .

[2] Dekker et al.; Fodor, A; Aldrich, RW; Yellen, G (2004). "A perturbation-based method for calculating explicit likelihood of evolutionary co-variance in multiple sequence alignments" (http://bioinformatics.oxfordjournals.org/cgi/reprint/20/10/1565). *Bioinformatics* **20** (10): 1565–1572. doi:10.1093/bioinformatics/bth128. PMID 14962924. .

[3] Lockless SW, Ranaganathan R (1999). "Evolutionarily conserved pathways of energetic connectivity in protein families" (http://www.sciencemag.org/cgi/content/full/286/5438/295). *Science* **286** (5438): 295–299. doi:10.1126/science.286.5438.295. PMID 10514373. .

[4] http://www.hhmi.swmed.edu/Labs/rr/world/people.html

[5] Suel et al.; Lockless, SW; Wall, MA; Ranganathan, R (2003). "Evolutionarily conserved networks of residues mediate allosteric communication in proteins." (http://www.nature.com/nsmb/journal/v10/n1/full/nsb881.html). *Nature Structural Biology* **10** (1): 59–69. doi:10.1038/nsb881. PMID 12483203. .

[6] Socolich et al.; Lockless, SW; Russ, WP; Lee, H; Gardner, KH; Ranganathan, R (2005). "Evolutionary information for specifying a protein fold" (http://www.nature.com/nature/journal/v437/n7058/full/nature03991.html). *Nature* **437** (7058): 512–518. doi:10.1038/nature03991. PMID 16177782. .

[7] Russ et al.; Lowery, DM; Mishra, P; Yaffe, MB; Ranganathan, R (2005). "Natural-like function in artificial WW domains" (http://www.nature.com/nature/journal/v437/n7058/full/nature03990.html). *Nature* **437** (7058): 579–583. doi:10.1038/nature03990. PMID 16177795.

[8] Bartlett GJ, Taylor WR (2008). "Using scores derived from statistical coupling analysis to distinguish correct and incorrect folds in de-novo protein structure prediction." (http://www3.interscience.wiley.com/cgi-bin/fulltext/116842426/HTMLSTART). *Proteins* **71** (1): 950–959. doi:10.1002/prot.21779. PMID 18004776. .

[9] http://www.bork.embl-heidelberg.de/Modules/ww_summary.html

[10] http://esmane.physics.lsa.umich.edu/wl/external/ICSB/2005/20051021-umwlap001-02-ranganathan-movies/realaudio/f001.htm

[11] http://www.pandasthumb.org/archives/2005/10/protein-folding.html

Statistical potential

In protein structure prediction, a **statistical potential** or **knowledge-based potential** is an energy function derived from an analysis of known protein structures in the Protein Data Bank.

Many methods exist to obtain such potentials; two notable method are the *quasi-chemical approximation* (due to Miyazawa and Jernigan [1]) and the *potential of mean force* (due to Sippl [2]). Although the obtained energies are often considered as approximations of the free energy, this physical interpretation is highly disputed. [3] [4] Nonetheless, they have been applied with great success, and do have a rigorous probabilistic justification. [5]

Assigning an energy

Possible features to which an energy can be assigned include torsion angles (such as the ϕ, ψ angles of the Ramachandran plot), solvent exposure or hydrogen bond geometry. The classic application of such potentials is however pairwise amino acid contacts or distances. For pairwise amino acid contacts, a statistical potential is formulated as an interaction matrix that assigns a weight or energy value to each possible pair of standard amino acids. The energy of a particular structural model is then the combined energy of all pairwise contacts (defined as two amino acids within a certain distance of each other) in the structure. The energies are determined using statistics on amino acid contacts in a database of known protein structures (obtained from the Protein Data Bank).

Sippl's potential of mean force

Overview

Many textbooks present the potentials of mean force (PMFs) as proposed by Sippl [2] as a simple consequence of the Boltzmann distribution, as applied to pairwise distances between amino acids. This is incorrect, but a useful start to introduce the construction of the potential in practice. The Boltzmann distribution applied to a specific pair of amino acids, is given by:

$$P(r) = \frac{1}{Z} e^{-\frac{F(r)}{kT}}$$

where r is the distance, k is the Boltzmann constant, T is the temperature and Z is the partition function, with

$$Z = \int e^{-\frac{F(r)}{kT}} dr$$

The quantity $F(r)$ is the free energy assigned to the pairwise system. Simple rearrangement results in the *inverse Boltzmann formula*, which expresses the free energy $F(r)$ as a function of $P(r)$:

$$F(r) = -kT \ln P(r) - kT \ln Z$$

To construct a PMF, one then introduces a so-called *reference* state *with a corresponding distribution* Q_R *and partition function* Z_R, and calculates the following free energy difference:

$$\Delta F(r) = -kT \ln \frac{P(r)}{Q_R(r)} - kT \ln \frac{Z}{Z_R}$$

The reference state typically results from a hypothetical system in which the specific interactions between the amino acids are absent. The second term involving Z and Z_R can be ignored, as it is a constant.

In practice, $P(r)$ is estimated from the database of known protein structures, while $Q_R(r)$ typically results from calculations or simulations. For example, $P(r)$ could be the conditional probability of finding the $C\beta$ atoms of a valine and a serine at a given distance r from each other, giving rise to the free energy difference ΔF. The total free energy difference of a protein, ΔF_T, is then claimed to be the sum of all the pairwise free energies:

$$\Delta F_{\mathrm{T}} = \sum_{i<j} \Delta F(r_{ij} \mid a_i, a_j) = -kT \sum_{i<j} \ln \frac{P(r_{ij} \mid a_i, a_j)}{Q_R(r_{ij} \mid a_i, a_j)}$$

where the sum runs over all amino acid pairs a_i, a_j (with $i < j$) and r_{ij} is their corresponding distance. It should be noted that in many studies Q_R does not depend on the amino acid sequence [6].

Intuitively, it is clear that a low value for ΔF_{T} indicates that the set of distances in a structure is more likely in proteins than in the reference state. However, the physical meaning of these PMFs have been widely disputed since their introduction. [3] [4] [7] [8] The main issues are the interpretation of this "potential" as a true, physically valid potential of mean force, the nature of the reference state and its optimal formulation, and the validity of generalizations beyond pairwise distances.

Justification

Analogy with liquid systems

The first, qualitative justification of PMFs is due to Sippl, and based on an analogy with the statistical physics of liquids. [9] For liquids [10], the potential of mean force is related to the radial distribution function $g(r)$, which is given by:

$$g(r) = \frac{P(r)}{Q_R(r)}$$

where $P(r)$ and $Q_R(r)$ are the respective probabilities of finding two particles at a distance r from each other in the liquid and in the reference state. For liquids, the reference state is clearly defined; it corresponds to the ideal gas, consisting of non-interacting particles. The two-particle potential of mean force $W(r)$ is related to $g(r)$ by:

$$W(r) = -kT \log g(r) = -kT \log \frac{P(r)}{Q_R(r)}$$

According to the reversible work theorem, the two-particle potential of mean force $W(r)$ is the reversible work required to bring two particles in the liquid from infinite separation to a distance r from each other. [10]

Sippl justified the use of PMFs - a few years after he introduced them for use in protein structure prediction [9] - by appealing to the analogy with the reversible work theorem for liquids. For liquids, $g(r)$ can be experimentally measured using small angle X-ray scattering; for proteins, $P(r)$ is obtained from the set of known protein structures, as explained in the previous section. However, as Ben-Naim writes in a publication on the subject [4]:

> [...]the quantities, referred to as `statistical potentials,' `structure based potentials,' or `pair potentials of mean force', as derived from the protein data bank, are neither `potentials' nor `potentials of mean force,' in the ordinary sense as used in the literature on liquids and solutions.

Another issue is that the analogy does not specify a suitable reference state for proteins.

Analogy with likelihood

Baker and co-workers [11] justified PMFs from a Bayesian point of view and used these insights in the construction of the coarse grained ROSETTA energy function. According to Bayesian probability calculus, the conditional probability $P(X \mid A)$ of a structure X, given the amino acid sequence A, can be written as:

$$P(X \mid A) = \frac{P(A \mid X) P(X)}{P(A)} \propto P(A \mid X) P(X)$$

$P(X \mid A)$ is proportional to the product of the likelihood $P(A \mid X)$ times the prior $P(X)$. By assuming that the likelihood can be approximated as a product of pairwise probabilities, and applying Bayes' theorem, the likelihood can be written as:

$$P(A \mid X) \approx \prod_{i<j} P(a_i, a_j \mid r_{ij}) \propto \prod_{i<j} \frac{P(r_{ij} \mid a_i, a_j)}{P(r_{ij})}$$

where the product runs over all amino acid pairs a_i, a_j (with $i < j$), and r_{ij} is the distance between amino acids i and j. Obviously, the negative of the logarithm of the expression has the same functional form as the classic pairwise distance PMFs, with the denominator playing the role of the reference state. This explanation has two shortcomings: it is purely qualitative, and relies on the unfounded assumption the likelihood can be expressed as a product of pairwise probabilities.

Reference ratio explanation

Expressions that resemble PMFs naturally result from the application of probability theory to solve a fundamental problem that arises in protein structure prediction: how to improve an imperfect probability distribution $Q(X)$ over a first variable X using a probability distribution $P(Y)$ over a second variable Y, with $Y = f(X)$. [5] Typically, X and Y are fine and coarse grained variables, respectively. For example, $Q(X)$ could concern the local structure of the protein, while $P(Y)$ could concern the pairwise distances between the amino acids. In that case, X could for example be a vector of dihedral angles that specifies all atom positions (assuming ideal bond lengths and angles). In order to combine the two distributions, such that the local structure will be distributed according to $Q(X)$,

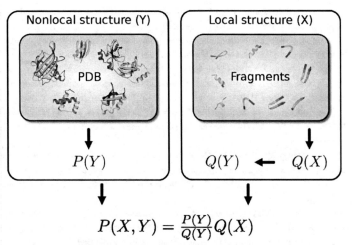

The reference ratio method. $Q(X)$ is a probability distribution that describes the structure of proteins on a local length scale (right). Typically, $Q(X)$ is embodied in a fragment library, but other possibilities are an energy function or a graphical model. In order to obtain a complete description of protein structure, one also needs a probability distribution $P(Y)$ that describes nonlocal aspects, such as hydrogen bonding.

$P(Y)$ is typically obtained from a set of solved protein structures from the Protein data bank (PDB, left). In order to combine $Q(X)$ with $P(Y)$ in a meaningful way, one needs the reference ratio expression (bottom), which takes the signal in $Q(X)$ with respect to Y into account.

while the pairwise distances will be distributed according to $P(Y)$, the following expression is needed:

$$P(X, Y) = \frac{P(Y)}{Q(Y)} Q(X)$$

where $Q(Y)$ is the distribution over Y implied by $Q(X)$. The ratio in the expression corresponds to the PMF. Typically, $Q(X)$ is brought in by sampling (typically from a fragment library), and not explicitly evaluated; the ratio, which in contrast is explicitly evaluated, corresponds to Sippl's potential of mean force. This explanation is quantitive, and allows the generalization of PMFs from pairwise distances to arbitrary coarse grained variables. It also provides a rigorous definition of the reference state, which is implied by $Q(X)$. Conventional applications of pairwise distance PMFs usually lack two necessary features to make them fully rigorous: the use of a proper probability distribution over pairwise distances in proteins, and the recognition that the reference state is rigorously defined by $Q(X)$.

Applications

Statistical potentials are used as energy functions in the assessment of an ensemble of structural models produced by homology modeling or protein threading - predictions for the tertiary structure assumed by a particular amino acid sequence made on the basis of comparisons to one or more homologous proteins with known structure. Many differently parameterized statistical potentials have been shown to successfully identify the native state structure from an ensemble of "decoy" or non-native structures.[12] [13] [14] [15] [16] [17] Statistical potentials are not only used for protein structure prediction, but also for modelling the protein folding pathway [18] .

References

[1] Miyazawa S, Jernigan R (1985) Estimation of effective interresidue contact energies from protein crystal structures: quasi-chemical approximation. Macromolecules 18: 534–552.

[2] Sippl MJ (1990) Calculation of conformational ensembles from potentials of mean force. An approach to the knowledge-based prediction of local structures in globular proteins. J Mol Biol 213: 859–883.

[3] Thomas PD, Dill KA (1996) Statistical potentials extracted from protein structures: how accurate are they? J Mol Biol 257: 457–469.

[4] Ben-Naim A (1997) Statistical potentials extracted from protein structures: Are these meaningful potentials? J Chem Phys 107: 3698–3706.

[5] Hamelryck T, Borg M, Paluszewski M, et al. (2010). Flower, Darren R.. ed. "Potentials of mean force for protein structure prediction vindicated, formalized and generalized". PLoS ONE 5 (11): e13714. doi:10.1371/journal.pone.0013714. PMC 2978081. PMID 21103041.

[6] Rooman M, Wodak S (1995) Are database-derived potentials valid for scoring both forward and inverted protein folding? Protein Eng 8: 849–858.

[7] Koppensteiner WA, Sippl MJ (1998) Knowledge-based potentials–back to the roots. Biochemistry Mosc 63: 247–252.

[8] Shortle D (2003) Propensities, probabilities, and the Boltzmann hypothesis. Protein Sci 12: 1298–1302.

[9] Sippl MJ, Ortner M, Jaritz M, Lackner P, Flockner H (1996) Helmholtz free energies of atom pair interactions in proteins. Fold Des 1: 289–98.

[10] Chandler D (1987) Introduction to Modern Statistical Mechanics. New York: Oxford University Press, USA.

[11] Simons KT, Kooperberg C, Huang E, Baker D (1997) Assembly of protein tertiary structures from fragments with similar local sequences using simulated annealing and Bayesian scoring functions. J Mol Biol 268: 209–225.

[12] Miyazawa S. & Jernigan RL. (1996). Residue–Residue Potentials with a Favorable Contact Pair Term and an Unfavorable High Packing Density Term, for Simulation and Threading. J Mol Biol 256:623–644.

[13] Tobi D & Elber R. (2000). Distance Dependent, Pair Potential for Protein Folding: Results from Linear Optimization. Proteins 41:40-46.

[14] Shen MY & Sali A. (2006). Statistical potential for assessment and prediction of protein structures. Protein Sci 15:2507-2524.

[15] Narang P, Bhushan K, Bose S, Jayaram B. (2006). Protein structure evaluation using an all-atom energy based empirical scoring function. J Biomol Struct Dyn 23(4):385-406.

[16] Sippl MJ. (1993). Recognition of Errors in Three-Dimensional Structures of Proteins. Proteins 17:355-62.

[17] Bryant SH, Lawrence CE. (1993). An empirical energy function for threading protein sequence through the folding motif. Proteins 16(1):92-112.

[18] Kmiecik S and Kolinski A (2007). "Characterization of protein-folding pathways by reduced-space modeling" (http://www.pnas.org/cgi/content/abstract/104/30/12330). Proc. Natl. Acad. Sci. U.S.A. 104 (30): 12330–12335. doi:10.1073/pnas.0702265104. PMC 1941469. PMID 17636132. .

Stochastic context-free grammar

A **stochastic context-free grammar** (**SCFG**; also **probabilistic context-free grammar**, **PCFG**) is a context-free grammar in which each production is augmented with a probability. The probability of a derivation (parse) is then the product of the probabilities of the productions used in that derivation; thus some derivations are more consistent with the stochastic grammar than others. SCFGs extend context-free grammars in the same way that hidden Markov models extend regular grammars. SCFGs have application in areas as diverse as Natural language processing to the study of RNA molecules. SCFGs are a specialized form of weighted context-free grammars.

Techniques

A variant of the CYK algorithm finds the Viterbi parse of a sequence for a given SCFG. The Viterbi parse is the most likely derivation (parse) of the sequence by the given SCFG.

The Inside-Outside algorithm is an analogue of the Forward-Backward algorithm, and can be used to compute the total probability of all derivations that are consistent with a given sequence, based on some SCFG. This is equivalent to the probability of the SCFG generating the sequence, and is intuitively a measure of how consistent the sequence is with the given grammar.

The Inside/Outside algorithms can also be used to compute the probabilities that a given production will be used in a random derivation of a sequence. This is used as part of an Expectation-maximization algorithm to learn the maximum likelihood probabilities for an SCFG based on a set of training sequences that the SCFG should model. [1] The algorithm is analogous to that used by hidden Markov models.

Applications

Natural language processing

Context-free grammars were originally conceived in an attempt to model natural languages, i.e. those normally spoken by humans.[2] Such grammars were originally conceived as sets of rules (productions), typically specified in a syntax such as Backus-Naur Form, where the rules are absolute; such grammars are still appropriate for numerous situations (notably, the design of programming languages). Probabilistic CFGs are an attempt to deal with difficulties encountered when attempting to extend CFGs to deal with the complexities of natural languages. Specifically, one often finds that more than one production rule may apply to a sequence of words, thus resulting in a conflict: an ambiguous parse. This happens for several reasons, such as homographs - identically spelled words with multiple meanings - so that the same word sequence can have more than one interpretation. A pun is an example of an ambiguous parse used deliberately to humorous effect, such as in the newspaper headline "Iraqi Head Seeks Arms".

One strategy of dealing with ambiguous parses (originating with grammarians as early as Pāṇini) is to add yet more rules, or prioritize them so that one rule takes precedence over others. This, however, has the drawback of proliferating the rules, often to the point where they become hard to manage. Another difficulty is overgeneration, where unlicensed structures are also generated. Probabilistic grammars circumvent these problems by using the frequency of various productions to order them, resulting in a "most likely" (winner-take-all) interpretation. As usage patterns are altered in diachronic shifts, these probabilistic rules can be re-learned, thus upgrading the grammar.

One may construct a probabilistic grammar from a traditional formal syntax by assigning each non-terminal a probability taken from some distribution, to be eventually estimated from usage data. On most samples of broad language, probabilistic grammars that tune these probabilities from data typically outperform hand-crafted grammars (although some rule-based grammars are now approaching the accuracies of PCFG).

Here is a tiny example of a 2-rule PCFG grammar. Each rule is preceded by a probability that reflects the relative frequency with which it occurs.

0.7 VP → V NP

0.3 VP → V NP NP

Given this grammar, we can now say that the number of NPs expected while deriving VPs is 0.7 x 1 + 0.3 x 2 = 1.3.

The probabilities are typically computed by machine learning programs that operate (learn or "train") on large volumes of annotated text ("corpora"), such as the Penn TreeBank [3], which contains a large collection of articles from the Wall Street Journal. As such, a probabilistic grammar's validity is constrained by context of the text used to train it; the definition of "most likely" is likely to vary with the context of discourse.

An example of a probabilistic CFG parser that has been trained using the Penn Treebank is the Stanford Statistical Parser of Klein and Manning[4] , downloadable at http://nlp.stanford.edu/software/lex-parser.shtml

In particular, some speech recognition systems use SCFGs to improve their probability estimate and thereby their performance.[5]

RNA

Context-free grammars are adept at modeling the secondary structure of RNA[6] [7] Secondary structure involves nucleotides within a single-stranded RNA molecule that are complementary to each other, and therefore base pair. This base pairing is biologically important to the proper function of the RNA molecule. Much of this base pairing can be represented in a context-free grammar (the major exception being pseudoknots).

For example, consider the following grammar, where a,c,g,u represents nucleotides and S is the start symbol (and only non-terminal):

S → aSu | cSg | gSc | uSa

This simple CFG represents an RNA molecule consisting entirely of two wholly complementary regions, in which only canonical complementary pairs are allowed (i.e. A-U and C-G).

By attaching probabilities to more sophisticated CFGs, it is possible to model bases or base pairings that are more or less consistent with an expected RNA molecule pattern. SCFGs are used to model the patterns in RNA gene families in the Rfam Database, and search genome sequences for likely additional members of these families. SCFGs have also been used to find RNA genes using comparative genomics. In this work, homologs of a potential RNA gene in two related organisms were inspected using SCFG techniques to see if their secondary structure is conserved. If it is, the sequence is likely to be an RNA gene, and the secondary structure is presumed to be conserved because of the functional needs of that RNA gene. It has been shown that SCFGs could predict the secondary structure of an RNA molecule similarly to existing techniques: such SCFGs are used, for example, by the Stemloc program.

Linguistics and Psycholinguistics

With the publication of Gold's Theorem[8] 1967 it was claimed that grammars for natural languages governed by deterministic rules could not be learned based on positive instances alone. This was part of the argument from the poverty of stimulus, presented in 1980[9] and implicit since the early works by Chomsky of the 1950s. Among other arguments, this led to the nativist (but still unproven) view, that a form of grammar, including a complete conceptual lexicon in certain versions, were hardwired from birth. However, Gold's learnability result can easily be circumvented, if we either assume the learner learns a near-perfect approximation to the correct language or that the learner learns from typical input rather than arbitrarily devious input. In fact, it has been proved that simply receiving input from a speaker who produces positive instances randomly rather than according to a pre-specified devious plan leads to identifiability in the limit with probability 1.[10] [11]

Recently, probabilistic grammars appear to have gained some cognitive plausibility. It is well known that there are degrees of difficulty in accessing different syntactic structures (e.g. the Accessibility Hierarchy for relative clauses). Probabilistic versions of Minimalist Grammars have been used to compute information-theoretic entropy values which appear to correlate well with psycholinguistic data on understandability and production difficulty.[12]

References

[1] Aycinena, M.A., (2005,) (PhD thesis). *Probabilistic geometric grammars for object recognition,* (Thesis).

[2] Noam Chomsky: Syntactic Structures. Mouton & Co. Publishers, Den Haag, Netherlands, 1957

[3] http://www.cis.upenn.edu/~treebank/

[4] Klein, Daniel; Manning, Christopher (2003). "Accurate Unlexicalized Parsing" (http://nlp.stanford.edu/~manning/papers/ unlexicalized-parsing.pdf). *Proceedings of the 41st Meeting of the Association for Computational Linguistics:* 423–430.. .

[5] Beutler, R; Kaufman, T; Pfister, B. (2005). "Integrating a non-probabilistic grammar into large vocabulary continuous speech recognition" (http://ieeexplore.ieee.org/xpl/freeabs_all.jsp?arnumber=1566496). *IEEE Workshop on Automated Speech recognition and Understanding:* 104–109. .

[6] R. Durbin, S. Eddy, A. Krogh, G. Mitchinson, ed (1998). *Biological sequence analysis : probabilistic models of proteins and nucleic acids* (http://books.google.com/books?id=R5P2GlJvigQC). Cambridge University Press. ISBN 9780521629713. . This bioinformatics textbook includes an accessible introduction to the use of SCFGs for modelling RNA, as well as the history of this application to 1998.

[7] Eddy SR, Durbin R (June 1994). "RNA sequence analysis using covariance models" (http://nar.oxfordjournals.org/cgi/ pmidlookup?view=long&pmid=8029015). *Nucleic Acids Res.* **22** (11): 2079–88. doi:10.1093/nar/22.11.2079. PMC 308124. PMID 8029015.

[8] Gold, E. (1967). "Language identification in the limit". *Information and Control* **10** (5): 447–474. doi:10.1016/S0019-9958(67)91165-5.

[9] Chomsky, N. (1980). *Rules and representations.* Oxford: Basil Blackwell.

[10] Clark, A. (2001). "Unsupervised Language Acquisition: Theory and Practice" (PhD thesis). arXiv:cs.CL/0212024 [cs.CL].

[11] Horning, J.J. (1969). *A study of grammatical inference* (Ph.D. thesis). Computer Science Department, Stanford University.

[12] John Hale (2006). "Uncertainty About the Rest of the Sentence". *Cognitive Science* **30** (4): 643–672. doi:10.1207/s15516709cog0000_64.

Further reading

- Rivas E, Eddy SR (2001). "Noncoding RNA gene detection using comparative sequence analysis" (http://www. biomedcentral.com/1471-2105/2/8). *BMC Bioinformatics* **2**: 8. doi:10.1186/1471-2105-2-8. PMC 64605. PMID 11801179.

External links

- Rfam Database (http://rfam.janelia.org/)

Stockholm format

Stockholm format is a Multiple sequence alignment format used by Pfam and Rfam to disseminate protein and RNA sequence alignments [1] [2] . The alignment editors Ralee [3] [4] and Belvu [5] support Stockholm format as do the probabilistic database search tools, Infernal [6] and HMMER, and the phylogenetic analysis tool Xrate. A simple example of an Rfam alignment (UPSK RNA) with a pseudoknot in Stockholm format is shown below:[7]

```
# STOCKHOLM 1.0
#=GF ID    UPSK
#=GF SE    Predicted; Infernal
#=GF SS    Published; PMID:9223489
#=GF RN    [1]
#=GF RM    9223489
#=GF RT    The role of the pseudoknot at the 3' end of turnip yellow mosaic
#=GF RT    virus RNA in minus-strand synthesis by the viral RNA-dependent RNA
#=GF RT    polymerase.
#=GF RA    Deiman BA, Kortlever RM, Pleij CW;
#=GF RL    J Virol 1997;71:5990-5996.


AF035635.1/619-641         UGAGUUCUCGAUCUCUAAAAUCG
M24804.1/82-104            UGAGUUCUCUAUCUCUAAAAUCG
J04373.1/6212-6234         UAAGUUCUCGAUCUUUAAAAUCG
M24803.1/1-23              UAAGUUCUCGAUCUCUAAAAUCG
#=GC SS_cons               .AAA....<<<<aaa....>>>>
//
```

Here is a slightly more complex example showing the Pfam CBS domain:

```
# STOCKHOLM 1.0
#=GF ID CBS
#=GF AC PF00571
#=GF DE CBS domain
#=GF AU Bateman A
#=GF CC CBS domains are small intracellular modules mostly found
#=GF CC in 2 or four copies within a protein.
#=GF SQ 5
#=GS O31698/18-71 AC O31698
#=GS O83071/192-246 AC O83071
#=GS O83071/259-312 AC O83071
#=GS O31698/88-139 AC O31698
#=GS O31698/88-139 OS Bacillus subtilis
O83071/192-246             MTCRAQLIAVPRASSLAEAIACAQKMRVSRVPVYERS
#=GR O83071/192-246 SA     999887756453524252551525253646377477
O83071/259-312             MQHVSAPVFVFECTRLAYVQHKLRAHSRAVAIVLDEY
#=GR O83071/259-312 SS     CCCCCHHHHHHHHHHHHHHEEEEEEEEEEEEEEEEEE
O31698/18-71               MIEADKVAHVQVGNNLEHALLVLTKTGYTAIPVLDPS
#=GR O31698/18-71 SS       CCCHHHHHHHHHHHHHHHEEEEEEEEEEEEEEEEHHH
O31698/88-139              EVMLTDIPRLHINDPIMKGFGMVINN..GFVCVENDE
```

```
#=GR O31698/88-139 SS     CCCCCCCHHHHHHHHHHHHHHEEEEEEEEEEEEEEEEEH
#=GC SS_cons              CCCCCHHHHHHHHHHHHHHHEEEEEEEEEEEEEEEEEEH
O31699/88-139             EVMLTDIPRLHINDPIMKGFGMVINN..GFVCVENDE
#=GR O31699/88-139 AS     _____*_____
#=GR O31699/88-139 IN     _____1_____2_____0_____
//
```

A minimal well formed Stockholm files should contain the **header** which states the format and version identifier, currently '# STOCKHOLM 1.0'. Followed by the sequences and corresponding unique sequence names:

```
<seqname> <aligned sequence>
<seqname> <aligned sequence>
<seqname> <aligned sequence>
```

'<seqname>' stands for "sequence name", typically in the form "name/start-end" or just "name". Finally, the "//" line indicates the end of the alignment. Sequence letters may include any characters except whitespace. Gaps may be indicated by "." or "-".

The alignment mark-up

Mark-up lines may include any characters except whitespace. Use underscore ("_") instead of space.

```
#=GF <feature> <Generic per-File annotation, free text>
#=GC <feature> <Generic per-Column annotation, exactly 1 char per column>
#=GS <seqname> <feature> <Generic per-Sequence annotation, free text>
#=GR <seqname> <feature> <Generic per-Sequence AND per-Column markup, exactly 1 char per column>
```

Recommended features

#=GF

(See the Pfam [8] and the Rfam [9] documentation under "Description of fields")

Pfam and Rfam may use the following tags:

```
Compulsory fields:
-------------------

AC   Accession number:        Accession number in form PFxxxxx (Pfam) or RFxxxxx (Rfam).

ID   Identification:          One word name for family.

DE   Definition:              Short description of family.

AU   Author:                  Authors of the entry.

SE   Source of seed:          The source suggesting the seed members belong to one family.

SS   Source of structure:     The source (prediction or publication) of the consensus RNA secondary structure used by Rfam.

BM   Build method:            Command line used to generate the model

SM   Search method:           Command line used to perform the search

GA   Gathering method:        Search threshold to build the full alignment.

TC   Trusted Cutoff:          Lowest sequence score (and domain score for Pfam) of match in the full alignment.

NC   Noise Cutoff:            Highest sequence score (and domain score for Pfam) of match not in full alignment.

TP   Type:                    Type of family -- presently Family, Domain, Motif or Repeat for Pfam.

                                       -- a tree with roots Gene, Intron or Cis-reg for Rfam.

SQ   Sequence:                Number of sequences in alignment.
```

```
Optional fields:

----------------

DC   Database Comment:          Comment about database reference.

DR   Database Reference:        Reference to external database.

RC   Reference Comment:         Comment about literature reference.

RN   Reference Number:          Reference Number.

RM   Reference Medline:         Eight digit medline UI number.

RT   Reference Title:           Reference Title.

RA   Reference Author:          Reference Author

RL   Reference Location:        Journal location.

PI   Previous identifier:       Record of all previous ID lines.

KW   Keywords:                  Keywords.

CC   Comment:                   Comments.

NE   Pfam accession:              Indicates a nested domain.

NL   Location:                  Location of nested domains - sequence ID, start and end of insert.

WK   Wikipedia link:            Wikipedia page

CL   Clan:                      Clan accession

MB   Membership:                Used for listing Clan membership


For embedding trees:

----------------

NH   New Hampshire              A tree in New Hampshire eXtended format.

TN   Tree ID                    A unique identifier for the next tree.
```

- Notes: A tree may be stored on multiple #=GF NH lines.
- If multiple trees are stored in the same file, each tree must be preceded by a #=GF TN line with a unique tree identifier. If only one tree is included, the #=GF TN line may be omitted.

#=GS

Rfam and Pfam may use these features:

```
Feature                        Description

----------------------         -----------

AC <accession>                 ACcession number

DE <freetext>                  DEscription

DR <db>; <accession>;          Database Reference

OS <organism>                  OrganiSm (species)

OC <clade>                     Organism Classification (clade, etc.)

LO <look>                      Look (Color, etc.)
```

#=GR

```
Feature   Description          Markup letters

-------   -----------          --------------

SS        Secondary Structure  For RNA [.,;<>(){}[]AaBb...],

                               For protein [HGIEBTSCX]

SA        Surface Accessibility [0-9X]

             (0=0%-10%; ...; 9=90%-100%)

TM        TransMembrane        [Mio]

PP        Posterior Probability [0-9*]
```

```
            (0=0.00-0.05; 1=0.05-0.15; *=0.95-1.00)

  LI       LIgand binding        [*]

  AS       Active Site           [*]

  pAS      AS - Pfam predicted   [*]

  sAS      AS - from SwissProt   [*]

  IN       INtron (in or after)  [0-2]

  RF       ReFerence annotation  Often the consensus RNA or protein sequence is used as a reference

                                 Any non-gap character (eg. x's) can indicate consensus/conserved/match columns

                                 .'s or -'s indicate insert columns

                                 ~'s indicate unaligned insertions

                                 Upper and lower case can be used to discriminate strong and weakly conserved

                                 residues respectively
```

#=GC

The same features as for #=GR with "_cons" appended, meaning "consensus". Example: "SS_cons".

Notes

- Do not use multiple lines with the same #=GR label. Only one unique feature assignment can be made for each sequence.
- "X" in SA and SS means "residue with unknown structure".
- The protein SS letters are taken from DSSP: H=alpha-helix, G=3/10-helix, I=p-helix, E=extended strand, B=residue in isolated b-bridge, T=turn, S=bend, C=coil/loop.)
- The RNA SS letters are taken from WUSS (Washington University Secondary Structure) notation. Matching nested parentheses characters <>, (), [], or { } indicate a basepair. The symbols '.', ',' and ';' indicate unpaired regions. Matched upper and lower case characters from the English alphabet indicate pseudoknot interactions. The 5' nucleotide within the knot should be in uppercase and the 3' nucleotide lowercase.

Recommended placements

- #=GF Above the alignment
- #=GC Below the alignment
- #=GS Above the alignment or just below the corresponding sequence
- #=GR Just below the corresponding sequence

Size limits

- There are no explicit size limits on any field. However, a simple parser that uses fixed field sizes should work safely on Pfam and Rfam alignments with these limits:
  - Line length: 10000.
  - <seqname>: 255.
  - <feature>: 255.

References

[1] Gardner PP, Daub J, Tate JG, *et al.* (January 2009). "Rfam: updates to the RNA families database" (http://nar.oxfordjournals.org/cgi/
pmidlookup?view=long&pmid=18953034). *Nucleic Acids Res.* **37** (Database issue): D136–40. doi:10.1093/nar/gkn766. PMC 2686503.
PMID 18953034. .

[2] Finn RD, Tate J, Mistry J, Coggill PC, Sammut SJ, Hotz HR, Ceric G, Forslund K, Eddy SR, Sonnhammer EL, Bateman A (2008). "The
Pfam protein families database.". *Nucleic Acids Res* **36** (Database issue): D281–8. doi:10.1093/nar/gkm960. PMC 2238907. PMID 18039703.

[3] http://personalpages.manchester.ac.uk/staff/sam.griffiths-jones/software/ralee/

[4] Griffiths-Jones S (January 2005). "RALEE--RNA ALignment editor in Emacs" (http://bioinformatics.oxfordjournals.org/cgi/
pmidlookup?view=long&pmid=15377506). *Bioinformatics* **21** (2): 257–9. doi:10.1093/bioinformatics/bth489. PMID 15377506. .

[5] ftp://ftp.cgb.ki.se/pub/prog/belvu

[6] http://infernal.janelia.org/

[7] Deiman BA, Kortlever RM, Pleij CW (August 1997). "The role of the pseudoknot at the 3' end of turnip yellow mosaic virus RNA in
minus-strand synthesis by the viral RNA-dependent RNA polymerase" (http://jvi.asm.org/cgi/pmidlookup?view=long&pmid=9223489).
J. Virol. **71** (8): 5990–6. PMC 191855. PMID 9223489. .

[8] ftp://ftp.sanger.ac.uk/pub/databases/Pfam/current_release/userman.txt

[9] ftp://ftp.sanger.ac.uk/pub/databases/Rfam/CURRENT/USERMAN

External links

- Erik Sonnhammers' definition of Stockholm format (http://sonnhammer.sbc.su.se/Stockholm.html)

Structural bioinformatics

Structural bioinformatics is the branch of bioinformatics which is related to the analysis and prediction of the three-dimensional structure of biological macromolecules such as proteins, RNA, and DNA. It deals with generalizations about macromolecular 3D structure such as comparisons of overall folds and local motifs, principles of molecular folding, evolution, and binding interactions, and structure/function relationships, working both from experimentally solved structures and from computational models. The term *structural* has the same meaning as in structural biology, and structural bioinformatics can be seen as computational structural biology.

References

Books

- Bourne, P.E., and Gu, J. (2009) *Structural Bioinformatics* (2nd edition), John Wiley & Sons, New York, ISBN
978-0-470-18105-8
- Bourne, P.E., and Weissig, H. (2003) *Structural Bioinformatics*, Wiley ISBN 0-471-20199-5
- Leach, Andrew (2001) *Molecular Modelling: Principles and Applications* (2nd edition), Prentice Hall, ISBN
978-0582382107

Hallmark publications

- Leontis NB, Westhof E. (2001). "Geometric nomenclature and classification of RNA base pairs". *RNA* **7** (4): 499–512. doi:10.1017/S1355838201002515. PMC 1370104. PMID 11345429.
- Richardson JS. (1981). "The anatomy and taxonomy of protein structure" [1]. *Adv Protein Chem*. Advances in Protein Chemistry **34**: 167–339. doi:10.1016/S0065-3233(08)60520-3. ISBN 9780120342341. PMID 7020376.
- Ramachandran GN, Sasisekharan V. (1968). "Conformation of polypeptides and proteins". *Adv Protein Chem*. Advances in Protein Chemistry **23**: 283–438. doi:10.1016/S0065-3233(08)60402-7. ISBN 9780120342235. PMID 4882249.
- Ramachandran GN, Ramakrishnan C, Sasisekharan V. (1963). "Stereochemistry of polypeptide chain configurations". *J Mol Biol* **7**: 95–9. doi:10.1016/S0022-2836(63)80023-6. PMID 13990617.

External links

Databases

- MMDB [2]
- Protein Data Bank (PDB) [3]
- Nucleic acid Data Base (NDB) [4]
- Structural Classification of Proteins (SCOP) [41]
- TOPOFIT-DB [5]
- Electron Density Server (EDS) [6]
- CASP Prediction Center [7]
- PISCES server for creating non-redundant lists of proteins [8]
- The Structural Biology Knowledgebase [9]
- ProtCID: The Protein Common Interface Database [2]

Software

- BALLView [9] molecular modeling and visualization
- FRIEND [10] visualization and analysis
- STING [7] visualization and analysis
- PyMOL [111] viewer and modeling
- VMD [2] viewer, molecular dynamics
- KiNG [12], an open-source Java kinemage viewer
- MolMol [13] viewer, NMR
- SPDBV DeepView [14] viewer
- STRIDE [15] determination of secondary structure from coordinates
- MolProbity [16] structure-validation web server
- PROCHECK [17], a structure-validation web service
- MolTalk [18], structural bioinformatics software
- Jmol [3], a molecular viewer Java applet with rasmol-like scripting capabilities and Javascript interaction
- PROPKA [19], rapid prediction of protein pKa values based on empirical structure/function relationships
- CARA [20] – Computer Aided Resonance Assignment
- Docking Server [21], a molecular docking web server
- StarBiochem [22], a java protein viewer, features direct search of protein databank
- Biskit, a python platform for structural bioinformatics
- SPADE [23] the structural proteomics application development environment
- UGENE, an opensource multiplatform viewer for PDB and MMDB files

- PocketSuite [24], a web portal for various web-servers for binding site level analysis

References

[1] http://kinemage.biochem.duke.edu/teaching/anatax/index.html

[2] http://www.ncbi.nlm.nih.gov/Structure/MMDB/mmdb.shtml

[3] http://www.pdb.org/

[4] http://ndbserver.rutgers.edu/

[5] http://mozart.bio.neu.edu/topofit/index.php

[6] http://eds.bmc.uu.se/eds/

[7] http://www.predictioncenter.org/

[8] http://dunbrack.fccc.edu/PISCES.php

[9] http://sbkb.org

[10] http://ilyinlab.org/friend/

[11] http://www.pymol.org/

[12] http://kinemage.biochem.duke.edu/software/

[13] http://www.mol.biol.ethz.ch/wuthrich/software/molmol/

[14] http://www.expasy.org/spdbv/

[15] http://www.embl-heidelberg.de/argos/stride/stride_info.html

[16] http://molprobity.biochem.duke.edu/

[17] http://www.biochem.ucl.ac.uk/~roman/procheck/procheck.html

[18] http://www.moltalk.org/

[19] http://propka.ki.ku.dk,

[20] http://cara.nmr.ch/

[21] http://www.dockingserver.com/

[22] http://web.mit.edu/star/biochem

[23] http://www.spadeweb.org/

[24] http://proline.physics.iisc.ernet.in/pocketsuite/

Substitution matrix

In bioinformatics and evolutionary biology, a **substitution matrix** describes the rate at which one character in a sequence changes to other character states over time. Substitution matrices are usually seen in the context of amino acid or DNA sequence alignments, where the similarity between sequences depends on their divergence time and the substitution rates as represented in the matrix.

Background

In the process of evolution, from one generation to the next the amino acid sequences of an organism's proteins are gradually altered through the action of DNA mutations. For example, the sequence

```
ALEIRYLRD
```

could mutate into the sequence

```
ALEINYLRD
```

in one step, and possibly

```
AQEINYQRD
```

over a longer period of evolutionary time. Each amino acid is more or less likely to mutate into various other amino acids. For instance, a hydrophilic residue such as arginine is more likely to be replaced another hydrophilic residue such as glutamine, than it is to be mutated into a hydrophobic residue such as leucine. This is primarily due to redundancy in the genetic code, which translates similar codons into similar amino acids. Furthermore, mutating an amino acid to a residue with significantly different properties could affect the folding and/or activity of the protein. There is therefore usually strong selective pressure to remove such mutations quickly from a population.

If we have two amino acid sequences in front of us, we should be able to say something about how likely they are to be derived from a common ancestor, or homologous. If we can line up the two sequences using a sequence alignment algorithm such that the mutations required to transform a hypothetical ancestor sequence into both of the current sequences would be evolutionarily plausible, then we'd like to assign a high score to the comparison of the sequences.

To this end, we will construct a 20x20 matrix where the (i, j) th entry is equal to the probability of the i th amino acid being transformed into the j th amino acid in a certain amount of evolutionary time. There are many different ways to construct such a matrix, called a **substitution matrix**. Here are the most commonly used ones:

Identity matrix

The simplest possible substitution matrix would be one in which each amino acid is considered maximally similar to itself, but not able to transform into any other amino acid. This matrix would look like:

$$\begin{bmatrix} 1 & 0 & \cdots & 0 & 0 \\ 0 & 1 & & 0 & 0 \\ \vdots & & \ddots & & \vdots \\ 0 & 0 & & 1 & 0 \\ 0 & 0 & \cdots & 0 & 1 \end{bmatrix}$$

This identity matrix will succeed in the alignment of very similar amino acid sequences but will be miserable at aligning two distantly related sequences. We need to figure out all the probabilities in a more rigorous fashion. It turns out that an empirical examination of previously aligned sequences works best.

Log-odds matrices

We express the probabilities of transformation in what are called log-odds scores. The scores matrix S is defined as

$$S_{i,j} = \log \frac{p_i \cdot M_{i,j}}{p_i \cdot p_j} = \log \frac{M_{i,j}}{p_j} = \log \frac{observed\ frequency}{expected\ frequency}$$

where $M_{i,j}$ is the probability that amino acid i transforms into amino acid j and p_i is the frequency of amino acid i. The base of the logarithm is not important, and you will often see the same substitution matrix expressed in different bases.

PAM

One of the first amino acid substitution matrices, the PAM *(Point Accepted Mutation)* matrix was developed by Margaret Dayhoff in the 1970s. This matrix is calculated by observing the differences in closely related proteins. The PAM1 matrix estimates what rate of substitution would be expected if 1% of the amino acids had changed. The PAM1 matrix is used as the basis for calculating other matrices by assuming that repeated mutations would follow the same pattern as those in the PAM1 matrix, and multiple substitutions can occur at the same site. Using this logic, Dayhoff derived matrices as high as PAM250. Usually the PAM 30 and the PAM70 are used.

A matrix for divergent sequences can be calculated from a matrix for closely related sequences by taking the second matrix to a power. For instance, we can roughly approximate the WIKI2 matrix from the WIKI1 matrix by saying $W_2 = W_1^2$ where W_1 is WIKI1 and W_2 is WIKI2. This is how the PAM250 matrix is calculated.

BLOSUM

Dayhoff's methodology of comparing closely related species turned out not to work very well for aligning evolutionarily divergent sequences. Sequence changes over long evolutionary time scales are not well approximated by compounding small changes that occur over short time scales. The BLOSUM *(BLOck SUbstitution Matrix)* series of matrices rectifies this problem. Henikoff and Henikoff constructed these matrices using multiple alignments of evolutionarily divergent proteins. The probabilities used in the matrix calculation are computed by looking at "blocks" of conserved sequences found in multiple protein alignments. These conserved sequences are assumed to be of functional importance within related proteins. To reduce bias from closely related sequences, segments in a block with a sequence identity above a certain threshold were clustered giving weight to each such cluster (Henikoff and Henikoff). For the BLOSUM62 matrix, this threshold was set at 62%. Pairs frequencies were then counted between clusters, hence pairs were only counted between segments less than 62% identical. One would use a higher numbered BLOSUM matrix for aligning two closely related sequences and a lower number for more divergent sequences.

It turns out that the BLOSUM62 matrix does an excellent job detecting similarities in distant sequences, and this is the matrix used by default in most recent alignment applications such as BLAST.

Differences between PAM and BLOSUM

1. PAM matrices are based on an explicit evolutionary model (i.e. replacements are counted on the branches of a phylogenetic tree), whereas the BLOSUM matrices are based on an implicit model of evolution.
2. The PAM matrices are based on mutations observed throughout a global alignment, this includes both highly conserved and highly mutable regions. The BLOSUM matrices are based only on highly conserved regions in series of alignments forbidden to contain gaps.
3. The method used to count the replacements is different: unlike the PAM matrix, the BLOSUM procedure uses groups of sequences within which not all mutations are counted the same.
4. Higher numbers in the PAM matrix naming scheme denote larger evolutionary distance, while larger numbers in the BLOSUM matrix naming scheme denote higher sequence similarity and therefore smaller evolutionary distance. Example: PAM150 is used for more distant sequences than PAM100; BLOSUM62 is used for closer sequences than Blosum50.

Extensions and improvements

Many specialized substitution matrices have been developed that describe the amino acid substitution rates in specific structural or sequence contexts, such as in transmembrane alpha helices,[1] for combinations of secondary structure states and solvent accessibility states,[2] [3] [4] or for local sequence-structure contexts.[5] These context-specific substitution matrices lead to generally improved alignment quality at some cost of speed but are not yet widely used. Recently, sequence context-specific amino acid similarities have been derived that do not need substitution matrices but that rely on a library of sequence contexts instead. Using this idea, a context-specific extension of the popular BLAST program has been demonstrated to achieve a twofold sensitivity improvement for remotely related sequences over BLAST at similar speeds (CS-BLAST).

Terminology

Although "transition matrix" is often used interchangeably with "substitution matrix" in fields other than bioinformatics, the former term is problematic in bioinformatics. With regards to nucleotide substitutions, "transition" is also used to indicate those substitutions that are between the two-ring purines (A → G and G → A) or are between the one-ring pyrimidines (C → T and T → C). Because these substitutions do not require a change in the number of rings, they occur more frequently than the other substitutions. "Transversion" is the term used to indicate the slower-rate substitutions that change a purine to a pyrimidine or vice versa (A ↔ C, A ↔ T, G ↔ C, and G ↔ T).

References

[1] Müller, T; Rahmann, S; Rehmsmeier, M (2001). "Non-symmetric score matrices and the detection of homologous transmembrane proteins". *Bioinformatics (Oxford, England)* **17 Suppl 1**: S182–9. PMID 11473008.

[2] Rice, DW; Eisenberg, D (1997). "A 3D-1D substitution matrix for protein fold recognition that includes predicted secondary structure of the sequence". *Journal of molecular biology* **267** (4): 1026–38. doi:10.1006/jmbi.1997.0924. PMID 9135128.

[3] Gong, Sungsam; Blundell, Tom L. (2008). Levitt, Michael. ed. "Discarding functional residues from the substitution table improves predictions of active sites within three-dimensional structures". *PLoS Computational Biology* **4** (10): e1000179. doi:10.1371/journal.pcbi.1000179. PMC 2527532. PMID 18833291.

[4] Goonesekere, NC; Lee, B (2008). "Context-specific amino acid substitution matrices and their use in the detection of protein homologs". *Proteins* **71** (2): 910–9. doi:10.1002/prot.21775. PMID 18004781.

[5] Huang, YM; Bystroff, C (2006). "Improved pairwise alignments of proteins in the Twilight Zone using local structure predictions". *Bioinformatics* **22** (4): 413–22. doi:10.1093/bioinformatics/bti828. PMID 16352653.

Further reading

- Altschul, SF (1991). "Amino acid substitution matrices from an information theoretic perspective". *Journal of molecular biology* **219** (3): 555–65. doi:10.1016/0022-2836(91)90193-A. PMID 2051488.

- Dayhoff, M. O.; Schwartz, R. M.; Orcutt, B. C. (1978). "A model of evolutionary change in proteins". *Atlas of Protein Sequence and Structure* **5** (3): 345–352.

- Henikoff, S; Henikoff, JG (1992). "Amino acid substitution matrices from protein blocks". *Proceedings of the National Academy of Sciences of the United States of America* **89** (22): 10915–9. doi:10.1073/pnas.89.22.10915. PMC 50453. PMID 1438297.

- Eddy, SR (2004). "Where did the BLOSUM62 alignment score matrix come from?". *Nature biotechnology* **22** (8): 1035–6. doi:10.1038/nbt0804-1035. PMID 15286655.

- Henikoff, S; Henikoff, JG (1992). "Amino acid substitution matrices from protein blocks" (http://www.pnas.org/cgi/reprint/89/22/10915). *Proceedings of the National Academy of Sciences of the United States of America* **89** (22): 10915–9. doi:10.1073/pnas.89.22.10915. PMC 50453. PMID 1438297.

External links

- PAM Matrix calculator (http://www.bioinformatics.nl/tools/pam.html)

Substitution model

In biology, a **substitution model** describes the process from which a sequence of characters changes into another set of traits. For example, in cladistics, each position in the sequence might correspond to a property of a species which can either be present or absent. The alphabet could then consist of "0" for absence and "1" for presence. Then the sequence 00110 could mean, for example, that a species does not have feathers or lay eggs, does have fur, is warm-blooded, and cannot breathe underwater. Another sequence 11010 would mean that a species has feathers, lays eggs, does not have fur, is warm-blooded, and cannot breathe underwater. In phylogenetics, sequences are often obtained by firstly obtaining a nucleotide or protein sequence alignment, and then taking the bases or amino acids at corresponding positions in the alignment as the characters. Sequences achieved by this might look like AGCGGAGCTTA and GCCGTAGACGC.

Substitution models are used for a number of things:

1. Constructing evolutionary trees in phylogenetics or cladistics.
2. Simulating sequences to test other methods and algorithms.

Neutral, independent, finite sites models

Most substitution models used to date are neutral, independent, finite sites models.

Neutral

> Selection does not operate on the substitutions, and so they are unconstrained.

Independent

> Changes in one site do not affect the probability of changes in another site.

Finite Sites

> There are finitely many sites, and so over evolution, a single site can be changed multiple times. This means that, for example, if a character has value 0 at time 0 and at time t, it could be that no changes occurred, or that it changed to a 1 and back to a 0, or that it changed to a 1 and back to a 0 and then to a 1 and then back to a 0, and so on.

The molecular clock and the units of time

Typically, a branch length of a phylogenetic tree is expressed as the expected number of substitutions per site; if the evolutionary model indicates that each site within an ancestral sequence will typically experience x substitutions by the time it evolves to a particular descendant's sequence then the ancestor and descendant are considered to be separated by branch length x.

Sometimes a branch length is measured in terms of geological years. For example, a fossil record may make it possible to determine the number of years between an ancestral species and a descendant species. Because some species evolve at faster rates than others, these two measures of branch length are not always in direct proportion. The expected number of substitutions per site per year is often indicated with the Greek letter mu (μ).

A model is said to have a molecular clock if the expected number of substitutions per year μ is constant regardless of which species' evolution is being examined. An important implication of a molecular clock is that the number of expected substitutions between an ancestral species and any of its present-day descendants must be independent of which descendant species is examined.

Note that the assumption of a molecular clock is often unrealistic, especially across long periods of evolution. For example, even though rodents are genetically very similar to primates, they have undergone a much higher number of substitutions in the estimated time since divergence in some regions of the genome.[1] This could be due to their shorter generation time,[2] higher metabolic rate, increased population structuring, increased rate of speciation, or smaller body size.[3] [4] When studying ancient events like the Cambrian explosion under a molecular clock assumption, poor concurrence between cladistic and phylogenetic data is often observed. There has been some work on models allowing variable rate of evolution (see for example [5] and [6]).

Time-reversible and stationary models

Many useful substitution models are time-reversible; in terms of the mathematics, the model does not care which sequence is the ancestor and which is the descendant so long as all other parameters (such as the number of substitutions per site that is expected between the two sequences) are held constant.

When an analysis of real biological data is performed, there is generally no access to the sequences of ancestral species, only to the present-day species. However, when a model is time-reversible, which species was the ancestral species is irrelevant. Instead, the phylogenetic tree can be rooted using any of the species, re-rooted later based on new knowledge, or left unrooted. This is because there is no 'special' species, all species will eventually derive from one another with the same probability.

A model is time reversible if and only if it satisfies the property

$$\pi_i Q_{ij} = \pi_j Q_{ji}$$

or, equivalently, the detailed balance property,

$$\pi_i P(t)_{ij} = \pi_j P(t)_{ji}$$

for every i, j, and t. The notation is explained below.

Time-reversibility should not be confused with stationarity. A model is **stationary** if Q does not change with time. The analysis below assumes a stationary model.

The mathematics of substitution models

Stationary, neutral, independent, finite sites models (assuming a constant rate of evolution) have two parameters, π, an **equilibrium vector** of base (or character) frequencies and a **rate matrix**, Q, which describes the rate at which bases of one type change into bases of another type; element Q_{ij} for $i \neq j$ is the rate at which base i goes to base j.

The diagonals of the Q matrix are chosen so that the rows sum to zero:

$$Q_{ii} = - \sum_{\{j | j \neq i\}} Q_{ij} ,$$

The equilibrium row vector π must be annihilated by the rate matrix Q:

$$\pi Q = 0 .$$

The transition matrix function is a function from the branch lengths (in some units of time, possibly in substitutions), to a matrix of conditional probabilities. It is denoted $P(t)$. The entry in the ith column and the jth row, $P_{ij}(t)$, is the probability, after time t, that there is a base j at a given position, conditional on there being a base i in that position at time 0. When the model is time reversible, this can be performed between any two sequences, even if one is not the ancestor of the other, if you know the total branch length between them.

The asymptotic properties of $P_{ij}(t)$ are such that $P_{ij}(0) = \delta_{ij}$, where δ_{ij} is the Kronecker delta function. That is, there is no change in base composition between a sequence and itself. At the other extreme, $\lim_{t \to \infty} P_{ij}(t) = \pi_j$,or, in other words, as time goes to infinity the probability of finding base j at a position given there was a base i at that position originally goes to the equilibrium probability that there is base j at that position, regardless of the original base. Furthermore, it follows that $\pi P(t) = \pi$ for all t.

The transition matrix can be computed from the rate matrix via matrix exponentiation:

$$P(t) = e^{Qt} = \sum_{n=0}^{\infty} Q^n \frac{t^n}{n!},$$

where Q^n is the matrix Q multiplied by itself enough times to give its nth power.

If Q is diagonalizable, the matrix exponential can be computed directly: let $Q = U^{-1} \Lambda U$ be a diagonalization of Q, with

$$\Lambda = \begin{pmatrix} \lambda_1 & \cdots & 0 \\ \vdots & \ddots & \vdots \\ 0 & \cdots & \lambda_4 \end{pmatrix},$$

where Λ is a diagonal matrix and where $\{\lambda_i\}$ are the eigenvalues of Q, each repeated according to its multiplicity. Then

$$P(t) = e^{Qt} = e^{U^{-1}(\Lambda t)U} = U^{-1} e^{\Lambda t} U,$$

where the diagonal matrix $e^{\Lambda t}$ is given by

$$e^{\Lambda t} = \begin{pmatrix} e^{\lambda_1 t} & \cdots & 0 \\ \vdots & \ddots & \vdots \\ 0 & \cdots & e^{\lambda_4 t} \end{pmatrix}.$$

GTR: Generalised time reversible

GTR is the most general neutral, independent, finite-sites, time-reversible model possible. It was first described in a general form by Simon Tavaré in 1986.[7]

The GTR parameters for nucleotides consist of an equilibrium base frequency vector, $\vec{\pi} = (\pi_1, \pi_2, \pi_3, \pi_4)$, giving the frequency at which each base occurs at each site, and the rate matrix

$$Q = \begin{pmatrix} -(x_1 + x_2 + x_3) & x_1 & x_2 & x_3 \\ \frac{\pi_1 x_1}{\pi_2} & -\left(\frac{\pi_1 x_1}{\pi_2} + x_4 + x_5\right) & x_4 & x_5 \\ \frac{\pi_1 x_2}{\pi_3} & \frac{\pi_2 x_4}{\pi_3} & -\left(\frac{\pi_1 x_2}{\pi_3} + \frac{\pi_2 x_4}{\pi_3} + x_6\right) & x_6 \\ \frac{\pi_1 x_3}{\pi_4} & \frac{\pi_2 x_5}{\pi_4} & \frac{\pi_3 x_6}{\pi_4} & -\left(\frac{\pi_1 x_3}{\pi_4} + \frac{\pi_2 x_5}{\pi_4} + \frac{\pi_3 x_6}{\pi_4}\right) \end{pmatrix}$$

Because the model must be time reversible and must approach the equilibrium nucleotide (base) frequencies at long times, each rate below the diagonal equals the reciprocal rate above the diagonal multiplied by the equlibrium ratio of the two bases. As such, the nucleotide GTR requires 6 substitution rate parameters and 4 equilibrium base frequency parameters. Since the 4 frequency parameters must sum to 1, there are only 3 free frequency parameters. The total of nine free parameters is often further reduced to 8 parameters plus μ, the overall number of substitutions per unit time. When measuring time in substitutions ($\mu = 1$) only 8 free parameters remain.

In general, to compute the number of parameters, you count the number of entries above the diagonal in the matrix, i.e. for n trait values per site $\dfrac{n^2 - n}{2}$, and then add $n-1$ for the equilibrium frequencies, and subtract 1 because μ is fixed. You get

$$\frac{n^2 - n}{2} + (n - 1) - 1 = \frac{1}{2}n^2 + \frac{1}{2}n - 2.$$

For example, for an amino acid sequence (there are 20 "standard" amino acids that make up proteins), you would find there are 208 parameters. However, when studying coding regions of the genome, it is more common to work with a codon substitution model (a codon is three bases and codes for one amino acid in a protein). There are $4^3 = 64$ codons, resulting in 2078 free parameters, but when the rates for transitions between codons which differ by more than one base are assumed to be zero, then there are only $\dfrac{20 \times 19 \times 3}{2} + 63 - 1 = 632$ parameters.

Mechanistic vs. empirical models

A main difference in evolutionary models is how many parameters are estimated every time for the data set under consideration and how many of them are estimated once on a large data set. Mechanistic models describe all substitution as a function of a number of parameters which are estimated for every data set analyzed, preferably using maximum likelihood. This has the advantage that the model can be adjusted to the particularities of a specific data set (e.g. different composition biases in DNA). Problems can arise when too many parameters are used, particularly if they can compensate for each other. Then it is often the case that the data set is too small to yield enough information to estimate all parameters accurately.

Empirical models are created by estimating many parameters (typically all entries of the rate matrix and the character frequencies, see the GTR model above) from a large data set. These parameters are then fixed and will be reused for every data set. This has the advantage that those parameters can be estimated more accurately. Normally, it is not possible to estimate all entries of the substitution matrix from the current data set only. On the downside, the estimated parameters might be too generic and do not fit a particular data set well enough.

With the large-scale genome sequencing still producing very large amounts of DNA and protein sequences, there is enough data available to create empirical models with any number of parameters. Because of the problems mentioned above, the two approaches are often combined, by estimating most of the parameters once on large-scale data, while a few remaining parameters are then adjusted to the data set under consideration. The following sections give an overview of the different approaches taken for DNA, protein or codon-based models.

Models of DNA substitution

See main article: **Models of DNA evolution** for more formal descriptions of the DNA models.

Models of DNA evolution were first proposed in 1969 by Jukes and Cantor,[8] assuming equal transition rates as well as equal equilibrium frequencies for all bases. In 1980 Kimura[9] introduced a model with two parameters: one for the transition and one for the transversion rate and in 1981, Felsenstein[10] made a model in which the substitution rate corresponds to the equilibrium frequency of the target nucleotide. Hasegawa, Kishino and Yano (HKY)[11] unified the two last models to a six parameter model. In the 1990s, models similar to HKY were developed and refined by several researchers.[12] [13] [14]

For DNA substitution models, mainly mechanistic models (as described above) are employed. The small number of parameters to estimate makes this feasible, but also DNA is often highly optimized for specific purposes (e.g. fast expression or stability) depending on the organism and the type of gene, making it necessary to adjust the model to these circumstances.

Models of amino acid substitutions

For many analyses, particularly for longer evolutionary distances, the evolution is modeled on the amino acid level. Since not all DNA substitution also alter the encoded amino acid, information is lost when looking at amino acids instead of nucleotide bases. However, several advantages speak in favor of using the amino acid information: DNA is much more inclined to show compositional bias than amino acids, not all positions in the DNA evolve at the same speed (non-synonymous mutations are more likely to become fixed in the population than synonymous ones), but probably most important, because of those fast evolving positions and the limited alphabet size (only four possible states), the DNA suffers much more from back substitutions, making it difficult to accurately estimate longer distances.

Unlike the DNA models, amino acid models traditionally are empirical models. They were pioneered in the 1970s by Dayhoff and co-workers ,[15] by estimating replacement rates from protein alignments with at least 85% identity. This minimized the chances of observing multiple substitutions at a site. From the estimated rate matrix, a series of replacement probability matrices were derived, known under names such as PAM250. The Dayhoff model was used to assess the significance of homology search results, but also for phylogenetic analyses. The Dayhoff PAM matrices were based on relatively few alignments (since not more were available at that time), but in the 1990s, new matrices were estimated using almost the same methodology, but based on the large protein databases available then (,[16] [17] the latter being known as "JTT" matrices).

References

[1] Gu X, Li WH (September 1992). "Higher rates of amino acid substitution in rodents than in humans" (http://linkinghub.elsevier.com/retrieve/pii/1055-7903(92)90017-B). *Mol. Phylogenet. Evol.* **1** (3): 211–4. doi:10.1016/1055-7903(92)90017-B. PMID 1342937. .

[2] Li WH, Ellsworth DL, Krushkal J, Chang BH, Hewett-Emmett D (February 1996). "Rates of nucleotide substitution in primates and rodents and the generation-time effect hypothesis" (http://linkinghub.elsevier.com/retrieve/pii/S1055-7903(96)90012-3). *Mol. Phylogenet. Evol.* **5** (1): 182–7. doi:10.1006/mpev.1996.0012. PMID 8673286. .

[3] Martin AP, Palumbi SR (May 1993). "Body size, metabolic rate, generation time, and the molecular clock" (http://www.pnas.org/cgi/pmidlookup?view=long&pmid=8483925). *Proc. Natl. Acad. Sci. U.S.A.* **90** (9): 4087–91. doi:10.1073/pnas.90.9.4087. PMC 46451. PMID 8483925. .

[4] Yang Z, Nielsen R (April 1998). "Synonymous and nonsynonymous rate variation in nuclear genes of mammals" (http://link.springer-ny.com/link/service/journals/00239/bibs/46n4p409.html). *J. Mol. Evol.* **46** (4): 409–18. doi:10.1007/PL00006320. PMID 9541535. .

[5] Kishino H, Thorne JL, Bruno WJ (March 2001). "Performance of a divergence time estimation method under a probabilistic model of rate evolution" (http://mbe.oxfordjournals.org/cgi/pmidlookup?view=long&pmid=11230536). *Mol. Biol. Evol.* **18** (3): 352–61. PMID 11230536. .

[6] Thorne JL, Kishino H, Painter IS (December 1998). "Estimating the rate of evolution of the rate of molecular evolution" (http://mbe.oxfordjournals.org/cgi/pmidlookup?view=long&pmid=9866200). *Mol. Biol. Evol.* **15** (12): 1647–57. PMID 9866200. .

[7] Tavaré S. "Some Probabilistic and Statistical Problems in the Analysis of DNA Sequences" (http://www.cmb.usc.edu/people/stavare/STpapers-pdf/T86.pdf). *Lectures on Mathematics in the Life Sciences* (American Mathematical Society) **17**: 57–86. .

[8] Jukes, T.H., Cantor, C.R. (1969). "Evolution of protein molecules". In Munro, H.N.. *Mammalian protein metabolism*. New York: Academic Press. pp. 21–123.

[9] Kimura M (December 1980). "A simple method for estimating evolutionary rates of base substitutions through comparative studies of nucleotide sequences". *J. Mol. Evol.* **16** (2): 111–20. doi:10.1007/BF01731581. PMID 7463489.

[10] Felsenstein J (1981). "Evolutionary trees from DNA sequences: a maximum likelihood approach". *J. Mol. Evol.* **17** (6): 368–76. doi:10.1007/BF01734359. PMID 7288891.

[11] Hasegawa M, Kishino H, Yano T (1985). "Dating of the human-ape splitting by a molecular clock of mitochondrial DNA". *J. Mol. Evol.* **22** (2): 160–74. doi:10.1007/BF02101694. PMID 3934395.

[12] Tamura K (July 1992). "Estimation of the number of nucleotide substitutions when there are strong transition-transversion and G+C-content biases" (http://mbe.oxfordjournals.org/cgi/pmidlookup?view=long&pmid=1630306). *Mol. Biol. Evol.* **9** (4): 678–87. PMID 1630306. .

[13] Tamura K, Nei M (May 1993). "Estimation of the number of nucleotide substitutions in the control region of mitochondrial DNA in humans and chimpanzees" (http://mbe.oxfordjournals.org/cgi/pmidlookup?view=long&pmid=8336541). *Mol. Biol. Evol.* **10** (3): 512–26. PMID 8336541. .

[14] Halpern, AL; Bruno, WJ (July 1998). "Evolutionary distances for protein-coding sequences: modeling site-specific residue frequencies". *Mol. Biol. Evol.* **15** (7): 910–7. PMID 9656490.

[15] Dayhoff MO, Schwartz RM, Orcutt BC (1978). "A model for evolutionary change in proteins". *Atlas of Protein Sequence and Structure* **5**: 345–352.

[16] Gonnet GH, Cohen MA, Benner SA (1992). "Exhaustive matching of the entire protein sequence database". *Science* **256** (5062): 1443–5. doi:10.1126/science.1604319. PMID 1604319.

[17] Jones DT, Taylor WR, Thornton JM (1992). "The rapid generation of mutation data matrices from protein sequences". *Comput Applic Biosci* **8**: 275–282.

Sulston score

The **Sulston Score** is an equation used in DNA mapping to numerically assess the likelihood that a given "fingerprint" similarity between two DNA clones is merely a result of chance. Used as such, it is a test of statistical significance. That is, low values imply that similarity is *significant*, suggesting that two DNA clones overlap one another and that the given similarity is not just a chance event. The name is an eponym that refers to John Sulston by virtue of his being the lead author of the paper that first proposed the equation's use[1].

The Overlap Problem in Mapping

Each clone in a DNA mapping project has a "fingerprint", *i.e.* a set of DNA fragment lengths inferred from (1) enzymatically digesting the clone, (2) separating these fragments on a gel, and (3) estimating their lengths based on gel location. For each pairwise clone comparison, one can establish how many lengths from each set match-up. Cases having at least 1 match indicate that the clones *might* overlap because matches *may* represent the same DNA. However, the underlying sequences for each match are not known. Consequently, two fragments whose lengths match may still represent different sequences. In other words, matches do not conclusively indicate overlaps. The problem is instead one of using matches to probabilistically classify overlap status.

Mathematical Scores in Overlap Assessment

Biologists have used a variety of means (often in combination) to discern clone overlaps in DNA mapping projects. While many are biological, *i.e.* looking for shared markers, others are basically mathematical, usually adopting probabilistic and/or statistical approaches.

Sulston Score Exposition

The Sulston Score is rooted in the concepts of Bernoulli and Binomial processes, as follows. Consider two clones, α and β, having m and n measured fragment lengths, respectively, where $m \geq n$. That is, clone α has at least as many fragments as clone β, but usually more. The Sulston score is the probability that at least h fragment lengths on clone β will be matched by any combination of lengths on α. Intuitively, we see that, at most, there can be n matches. Thus, for a given comparison between two clones, one can measure the statistical significance of a match of h fragments, *i.e.* how likely it is that this match occurred simply as a result of random chance. Very low values would indicate a significant match that is highly unlikely to have arisen by pure chance, while higher values would suggest that the given match could be just a coincidence.

Derivation of the Sulston Score

One of the basic assumptions is that fragments are uniformly distributed on a gel, *i.e.* a fragment has an equal likelihood of appearing anywhere on the gel. Since gel position is an indicator of fragment length, this assumption is equivalent to presuming that the fragment lengths are uniformly distributed. The measured location of any fragment x, has an associated error tolerance of $\pm t$, so that its true location is only known to lie within the segment $x \pm t$.

In what follows, let us refer to individual fragment lengths simply as *lengths*. Consider a specific length j on clone β and a specific length i on clone α. These two lengths are arbitrarily selected from their respective sets $i \in \{1, 2, \ldots, m\}$ and $j \in \{1, 2, \ldots, n\}$. We assume that the gel location of fragment j has been determined and we want the probability of the event E_{ij} that the location of fragment i will match that of j. Geometrically, i will be declared to match j if it falls inside the window of size $2t$ around j. Since fragment i could occur anywhere in the gel of length G, we have $P\langle E_{ij}\rangle = 2t/G$. The probability that i *does not* match j is simply the complement, i.e. $P\langle E_{i,j}^{C}\rangle = 1 - 2t/G$, since it must either match or not match.

Now, let us expand this to compute the probability that no length on clone α matches the single particular length j on clone β. This is simply the intersection of all individual trials $i \in \{1, 2, \ldots, m\}$ where the event $E_{i,j}^C$ occurs, *i.e.* $P\langle E_{1,j}^C \cap E_{2,j}^C \cap \cdots \cap E_{m,j}^C \rangle$. This can be restated verbally as: length 1 on clone α does not match length j on clone β *and* length 2 does not match length j *and* length 3 does not match, etc. Since each of these trials is assumed to be independent, the probability is simply

$$P\langle E_{1,j}^C \rangle \times P\langle E_{2,j}^C \rangle \times \cdots \times P\langle E_{m,j}^C \rangle = (1 - 2t/G)^m .$$

Of course, the actual event of interest is the complement: *i.e.* there is *not* "no matches". In other words, the probability of one or more matches is $p = 1 - (1 - 2t/G)^m$. Formally, p is the probability that at least one band on clone α matches band j on clone β .

This event is taken as a Bernoulli trial having a "success" (matching) probability of p for band j . However, we want to describe the process over *all* the bands on clone β . Since p is constant, the number of matches is distributed binomially. Given h observed matches, the Sulston score S is simply the probability of obtaining *at least* h matches by chance according to

$$S = \sum_{j=h}^{n} C_{n,j} p^j (1 - p)^{n-j},$$

where $C_{n,j}$ are binomial coefficients.

Mathematical Refinement

In a 2005 paper[2] , Michael Wendl gave an example showing that the assumption of independent trials is not valid. So, although the traditional Sulston score does indeed represent a Probability distribution, it is not actually the distribution characteristic of the fingerprint problem. Wendl went on to give the general solution for this problem in terms of the Bell polynomials, showing the traditional score overpredicts P-values by orders of magnitude. (P-values are very small in this problem, so we are talking, for example, about probabilities on the order of 10e-14 versus 10e-12, the latter Sulston value being 2 orders of magnitude too high.) This solution provides a basis for determining when a problem has sufficient information content to be treated by the probabilistic approach and is also a general solution to the birthday problem of 2 types.

A disadvantage of the exact solution is that its evaluation is computationally intensive and, in fact, is not feasible for comparing large clones[2] . Some fast approximations for this problem have been proposed[3] .

References

[1] Sulston J, Mallett F, Staden R, Durbin R, Horsnell T, Coulson A (Mar 1988). "Software for genome mapping by fingerprinting techniques". *Comput Appl Biosci.* **4** (1): 125–32. PMID 2838135.

[2] Wendl MC (Apr 2005). "Probabilistic assessment of clone overlaps in DNA fingerprint mapping via a priori models". *J Comput Biol.* **12** (3): 283–97. doi:10.1089/cmb.2005.12.283. PMID 15857243.

[3] Wendl MC (2007). "Algebraic correction methods for computational assessment of clone overlaps in DNA fingerprint mapping". *BMC Bioinformatics* **8**: 127. doi:10.1186/1471-2105-8-127. PMC 1868038. PMID 17442113.

Suspension array technology

Suspension Array Technology (or **SAT**) is a high throughput, large-scale, and multiplexed screening platform used in molecular biology. SAT has been widely applied to genomic and proteomic research, such as single nucleotide polymorphism (SNP) genotyping, genetic disease screening, gene expression profiling, screening drug discovery and clinical diagnosis[1] [2] [3] . SAT uses microsphere beads (5.6 um in diameter) to prepare arrays. SAT allows for the simultaneous testing of multiple gene variants through the use of these microshpere beads as each type of microsphere bead has a unique identification based on variations in optical properties, most common is fluorescent colour. As each colour and intensity of colour has a unique wavelength, beads can easily be differentiated based on their wavelength intensity. Microspheres are readily suspendable in solution and exhibit favorable kinetics during an assay. Similar to flat microarrays (e.g. DNA microarray), an appropriate receptor molecule, such as DNA oligonucleotide probes, antibodies, or other proteins, attach themselves to the differently labeled microspheres. This produces thousands of microsphere array elements. Probe-target hybridization is usually detected by optically labeled targets, which determines the relative abundance of each target in the sample[4] .

Overview of SAT using DNA hybridization

DNA is extracted from cells used to create test fragments. These test fragments are added to a solution containing a variety of microsphere beads. Each type of microsphere bead contains a known DNA probe with a unique fluorescent identity. Test fragments and probes on the microsphere beads are allowed to hybridize to each other. Once hybridized, the microsphere beads are sorted, usually using flow cytometry. This allows for the detection of each of the gene variants from the original sample. The resulting data collected will indicate the relative abundance of each hybridized sample to the microsphere.

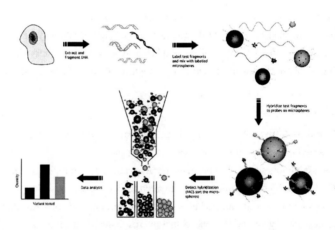

Overview of the suspension array technology procedures, using DNA hybridization as a model.

Multiplexing

Since microsphere beads are easily suspended in solution and each microsphere retains its identity when hybridized to the test sample, a typical suspension array experiment can analyze wide range of biological analysis in a single reaction, called "multiplexing". In general, each type of microsphere used in an array is individually prepared in bulk. For example, the commercially available microsphere arrays from Luminex xMAP[TM] technology uses 10X10 element array. This array involves beads with red and infrared dyes, each with ten different intensities, to give a 100-element array[4] . Thus, the array size would increase exponentially if multiple dyes are used. For example, five different dyes with 10 different intensities per dye will give rise to 10,000 different array elements.

Procedure

Sample targeting

When using different types of microspheres, SAT is capable of simultaneously testing multiple variables, such as DNA and proteins, in a given sample. This allows SAT to analyze variety of molecular targets during a single reaction. The common nucleic acid detection method includes direct DNA hybridization. The direct DNA hybridization approach is the simplest suspension array assay whereby 15 to 20 bp DNA oligonucleotides attached to microspheres are amplified using PCR. This is the optimized probe length as it minimizes the melting temperature variation among different probes during probe-target hybridization[1] . After amplifying one DNA oligoprobe of interest, it can be used to create 100 different probes on 100 different sets of microspheres, each with the capability of capturing 100 potential targets (if using a 100-plex array). Similarly, target DNA samples are usually PCR amplified and labeled[4] . Hybridization between the capture probe and the target DNA is achieved by melting and annealing complementary target DNA sequence to their capture probes located on the microspheres. After washing to remove non-specific binding between sequences, only strongly paired probe-target will remain hybridized[1] .

Sorting and detection with flow cytometry

For more details on this topic, see flow cytometry

Since the optical identity of each microsphere is known, the quantification of target samples hybridized to the microspheres can be achieved by comparing the relative intensity of target markers in one set of microspheres to target markers in another set of microspheres using flow cytometry. Microspheres can be sorted based using both their unique optical properties and level of hybridization to the target sequence.

Strengths

- **Rapid/high throughput:** In multiplex analysis, a 100-plex assay can be analyzed in every 30 seconds. The recent reported high-throughput flow cytometry can sample a 96-well plate in 1 minute, and theoretically, the 100-plex assay with this system can be analyzed in less than 1 second, or potentially deliver 12 million samples per day[4] .
- **High array density/multiplex:** Compared to flat microarrays, SAT allows one to perform parallel measurements. A few microliters of microspheres could contain thousands of array elements and each array element is represented by hundreds of individual microspheres. Thus, the measurement by flow cytometry represents a replicate analysis of each array element[4] .
- **Effective gathering of information:** One of the benefits of using SAT is that it allows you to take one sample from a patient or research organism and simultaneously test for multiple gene variants. Thus, from a single sample you can determine which virus from a series of viruses a patient has, or which base pair mutation is present in the organism with a unique phenotype[3] .
- **Cost-effective:** Currently, commercially available suspension array kits costs $0.10-$0.25 per sequence tested[1] .

Weaknesses

- **Relatively low array size**: Although it has the potential to use an increased amount of dyes to generate millions of different array elements, the current generation of commercially available microsphere arrays (from Luminex xMAP[TM] technology) only uses two sets of dyes and therefore can only detect ~100 targets per experiment[4] .
- Hybridization between different sets of probes and target sequences requires a **specific annealing temperature**, which is affected by length and sequence of the oligonucleotide probe. Therefore, for every experiment, only one possible annealing temperature can be used. Thus, all probes used in given experiment must be designed to hybridize to the target at the same temperature. Although introducing base pair mismatch in some sets of the probes could minimize annealing temperature difference between each sets of probes, the hybridization problem

is still significant if more than 10-20 targets are tested in one reaction[1].

References

[1] Dunbar, Sherry A. (2006). "Applications of Luminex xMAP technology for rapid, high-throughput multiplexed nucleic acid detection". *Clinica Chimica Acta* **363**: 71–82. doi:10.1016/j.cccn.2005.06.023.

[2] Seideman, Jonathan; Peritt, David (2002). "A novel monoclonal antibody screening method using Luminex-100 microsphere system". *Journal of Immunological Methods* **267**: 165–171.

[3] Dunbar, Sherry A.; Vander Zee, James W.; Oliver, Kerry G.; Karem; Jacobson (2003). "Quantitative, multiplexed detection of bacterial pathogens: DNA and protein applications of the Luminex LabMAP system". *Journal of Microbiological Methods* **53**: 245–252. doi:10.1016/S0167-7012(03)00028-9.

[4] Nolan, John P.; Sklar, Larry A. (2002). "Suspension array technology: evolution of the flat-array paradigm". *TRENDS in Biotechnology* **20** (1): 9–12.

External links

- Luminex products (http://www.luminexcorp.com/)

Synteny

In classical genetics, **synteny** describes the physical co-localization of genetic loci on the same chromosome within an individual or species. The concept is related to genetic linkage: Linkage between two loci is established by the observation of lower-than-expected recombination frequencies between them. In contrast, any loci on the same chromosome are by definition syntenic, even if their recombination frequency cannot be distinguished from unlinked loci by practical experiments. Thus, in theory, all linked loci are syntenic, but not all syntenic loci are necessarily linked. Similarly, in genomics, the genetic loci on a chromosome are syntenic regardless of whether this relationship can be established by experimental methods such as DNA sequencing/assembly, genome walking, physical localization or hap-mapping.

Students of genetics employ the term synteny to describe the situation in which two genetic loci have been assigned to the same chromosome but still may be separated by a large enough distance in map units that genetic linkage has not been demonstrated.

The Encyclopædia Britannica gives the following description of synteny[1]:

> Genomic sequencing and mapping have enabled comparison of the general structures of genomes of many different species. The general finding is that organisms of relatively recent divergence show similar blocks of genes in the same relative positions in the genome. This situation is called synteny, translated roughly as possessing common chromosome sequences. For example, many of the genes of humans are syntenic with those of other mammals—not only apes but also cows, mice, and so on. Study of synteny can show how the genome is cut and pasted in the course of evolution.

Shared synteny

Shared synteny (also known as conserved synteny) describes preserved co-localization of genes on chromosomes of different species. During evolution, rearrangements to the genome such as chromosome translocations may separate two loci apart, resulting in the loss of synteny between them. Conversely, translocations can also join two previously separate pieces of chromosomes together, resulting in a gain of synteny between loci. Stronger-than-expected shared synteny can reflect selection for functional relationships between syntenic genes, such as combinations of alleles that are advantageous when inherited together, or shared regulatory mechanisms.[2]

The term is sometimes also used to describe preservation of the precise order of genes on a chromosome passed down from a common ancestor,[3] [4] [5] [6] although many geneticists reject this use of the term.[7] The analysis of synteny in the gene order sense has several applications in genomics. Shared synteny is one of the most reliable criteria for establishing the orthology of genomic regions in different species. Additionally, exceptional conservation of synteny can reflect important functional relationships between genes. For example, the order of genes in the "Hox cluster", which are key determinants of the animal body plan and which interact with each other in critical ways, is essentially preserved throughout the animal kingdom. Patterns of shared synteny or synteny breaks can also be used as characters to infer the phylogenetic relationships among several species, and even to infer the genome organization of extinct ancestral species. A qualitative distinction is sometimes drawn between **macrosynteny**, preservation of synteny in large portions of a chromosome, and **microsynteny**, preservation of synteny for only a few genes at a time.

Etymology

Synteny is a neologism meaning "on the same ribbon"; Greek: σύν, *syn* = along with + ταινία, *tainiā* = band.

References

[1] http://www.britannica.com/EBchecked/topic/262934/heredity/262018/Synteny?anchor=ref944552

[2] Moreno-Hagelsieb G, Treviño V, Pérez-Rueda E, Smith TF, Collado-Vides J (2001). "Transcription unit conservation in the three domains of life: a perspective from *Escherichia coli*". *Trends in Genetics* **17** (4): 175–177. doi:10.1016/S0168-9525(01)02241-7. PMID 11275307.

[3] Engström PG, Ho Sui SJ, Drivenes O, Becker TS, Lenhard B (2007). "Genomic regulatory blocks underlie extensive microsynteny conservation in insects". *Genome Res.* **17** (12): 1898–908. doi:10.1101/gr.6669607. PMC 2099597. PMID 17989259.

[4] Heger A, Ponting CP (2007). "Evolutionary rate analyses of orthologs and paralogs from 12 Drosophila genomes". *Genome Res.* **17** (12): 1837–49. doi:10.1101/gr.6249707. PMC 2099592. PMID 17989258.

[5] Poyatos JF, Hurst LD (2007). "The determinants of gene order conservation in yeasts". *Genome Biol* **8** (11): R233. doi:10.1186/gb-2007-8-11-r233. PMC 2258174. PMID 17983469.

[6] Dawson DA, Akesson M, Burke T, Pemberton JM, Slate J, Hansson B (2007). "Gene order and recombination rate in homologous chromosome regions of the chicken and a passerine bird". *Mol. Biol. Evol.* **24** (7): 1537–52. doi:10.1093/molbev/msm071. PMID 17434902.

[7] Passarge, E., B. Horsthemke & R. A. Farber (1999). "Incorrect use of the term synteny". *Nature Genetics* **23** (4): 387. doi:10.1038/70486.

External links

- Synteny server (http://cinteny.cchmc.org/) Server for Synteny Identification and Analysis of Genome Rearrangement—the Identification of synteny and calculating reversal distances.
- Comparative Maps (http://www.ncbi.nlm.nih.gov/projects/homology/maps/) NIH's National Library of Medicine NCBI link to Gene Homology resources, and Comparative Chromosome Maps of the Human, Mouse, and Rat.
- NCBI Home Page (http://www.ncbi.nlm.nih.gov/) NIH's National Library of Medicine NCBI (National Center for Biotechnology Information) link to a tremendous number of resources.
- ACT (Artemis Comparison Tool) (http://www.sanger.ac.uk/Software/ACT/) — Probably the most used synteny software program used in comparative genomics.

Synthetic biology

Synthetic biology is a new area of biological research that combines science and engineering. It encompasses a variety of different approaches, methodologies, and disciplines with a variety of definitions. What they all have in common, however, is that they see synthetic biology as the design and construction of new biological functions and systems not found in nature.

History

The term "synthetic biology" has a history spanning the twentieth century.[2] The first use was in Stéphane Leducs's publication of « Théorie physico-chimique de la vie et générations spontanées » (1910) [3] and « La Biologie Synthétique » (1912).[4] In 1974, the Polish geneticist Waclaw Szybalski used the term "synthetic biology",[5] writing:

A light programmable biofilm made by the UT Austin / UCSF team during the 2004 Synthetic Biology competition [1], displaying "Hello World"

> Let me now comment on the question "what next". Up to now we are working on the descriptive phase of molecular biology. ... But the real challenge will start when we enter the synthetic biology phase of research in our field. We will then devise new control elements and add these new modules to the existing genomes or build up wholly new genomes. This would be a field with the unlimited expansion potential and hardly any limitations to building "new better control circuits" and ..... finally other "synthetic" organisms, like a "new better mouse". ... I am not concerned that we will run out of exciting and novel ideas, ... in the synthetic biology, in general.

When in 1978 the Nobel Prize in Physiology or Medicine was awarded to Arber, Nathans and Smith for the discovery of restriction enzymes, Waclaw Szybalski wrote in an editorial comment in the journal *Gene*:

> The work on restriction nucleases not only permits us easily to construct recombinant DNA molecules and to analyze individual genes, but also has led us into the new era of synthetic biology where not only existing genes are described and analyzed but also new gene arrangements can be constructed and evaluated.[6]

Perspectives

Biology

Biologists are interested in learning more about how natural living systems work. One simple, direct way to test our current understanding of a natural living system is to build an instance (or version) of the system in accordance with our current understanding of the system. Michael Elowitz's [7] early work on the Repressilator[8] is one good example of such work. Elowitz had a model for how gene expression should work inside living cells. To test his model, he built a piece of DNA in accordance with his model, placed the DNA inside living cells, and watched what happened. Slight differences between observation and expectation highlight new science that may be well worth doing. Work of this sort often makes good use of mathematics to predict and study the dynamics of the biological system before experimentally constructing it. A wide variety of mathematical descriptions have been used with varying accuracy, including graph theory, Boolean networks, ordinary differential equations, stochastic differential equations, and Master equations (in order of increasing accuracy). Good examples include the work of Adam Arkin [9], Jim Collins [10] and Alexander van Oudenaarden [11]. See also the PBS Nova special on artificial life [12].

Chemistry

Biological systems are physical systems that are made up of chemicals. Around the turn of the 20th century, the science of chemistry went through a transition from studying natural chemicals to trying to design and build new chemicals. This transition led to the field of synthetic chemistry. In the same tradition, some aspects of synthetic biology can be viewed as an extension and application of synthetic chemistry to biology, and include work ranging from the creation of useful new biochemicals to studying the origins of life. Eric Kool's [13] group at Stanford, the Foundation for Applied Molecular Evolution, Carlos Bustamante's [14] group at Berkeley, Jack Szostak's [15] group at Harvard, and David McMillen's group at University of Toronto are good examples of this tradition. Much of the improved economics and versatility of synthetic biology is driven by ongoing improvements in gene synthesis.

Engineering

Engineers view biology as a *technology* - the *systems biotechnology* or *systems biological engineering*[16] . Synthetic Biology includes the broad redefinition and expansion of biotechnology, with the ultimate goals of being able to design and build engineered biological systems that process information, manipulate chemicals, fabricate materials and structures, produce energy, provide food, and maintain and enhance human health and our environment.[17] A good example of these technologies include the work of Chris Voigt, who redesigned the Type III secretion system used by *Salmonella typhimurium* to secrete spider silk proteins, a strong elastic biomaterial, instead of its own natural infectious proteins. One aspect of Synthetic Biology which distinguishes it from conventional genetic engineering is a heavy emphasis on developing foundational technologies that make the engineering of biology easier and more reliable. Good examples of engineering in synthetic biology include the pioneering work of Tim Gardner and Jim Collins on an engineered genetic toggle switch,[18] a riboregulator, the Registry of Standard Biological Parts [19], and the International Genetically Engineered Machine competition (iGEM) [20].

Studies in synthetic biology can be subdivided into broad classifications according to the approach they take to the problem at hand: photocell design, biomolecular engineering, genome engineering, and biomolecular-design. The photocell approach includes projects to make self-replicating systems from entirely synthetic components. Biomolecular engineering includes approaches which aim to create a toolkit of functional units that can be introduced to present new orthogonal functions in living cells. Genome engineering includes approaches to construct synthetic chromosomes for whole or minimal organisms. Biomolecular-design approach refers to the general idea of the de novo design and combination of biomolecular components. The task of each of these approaches is similar: To create a more synthetic entry at a higher level of complexity by manipulating a part of the proceeding level.[21]

Re-writing

Re-writers are Synthetic Biologists who are interested in testing the idea that since natural biological systems are so complicated, we would be better off re-building the natural systems that we care about, from the ground up, in order to provide engineered surrogates that are easier to understand and interact with. Re-writers draw inspiration from refactoring, a process sometimes used to improve computer software. Drew Endy and his group [22] have done some preliminary work on re-writing (e.g., Refactoring Bacteriophage T7 [23]). Oligonucleotides harvested from a photolithographic or inkjet manufactured DNA chip combined with DNA mismatch error-correction allows inexpensive large-scale changes of codons in genetic systems to improve gene expression or incorporate novel amino-acids (see George Church's and Anthony Forster's synthetic cell projects [24],[25] As in the T7 example above, this favors a synthesis-from-scratch approach.

Key enabling technologies

There are several key enabling technologies that are critical to the growth of synthetic biology. The key concepts include standardization of biological parts and hierarchical abstraction to permit using those parts in increasingly complex synthetic systems.[26] Achieving this is greatly aided by basic technologies of reading and writing of DNA (sequencing and fabrication), which are improving in price/performance exponentially (Kurzweil 2001) [27]. Measurements under a variety of conditions are needed for accurate modeling and computer-aided-design (CAD).

DNA sequencing

DNA sequencing is determining the order of the nucleotide bases in a molecule of DNA. Synthetic biologists make use of DNA sequencing in their work in several ways. First, large-scale genome sequencing efforts continue to provide a wealth of information on naturally occurring organisms. This information provides a rich substrate from which synthetic biologists can construct parts and devices. Second, synthetic biologists use sequencing to verify that they fabricated their engineered system as intended. Third, fast, cheap and reliable sequencing can also facilitate rapid detection and identification of synthetic systems and organisms.

Fabrication

A critical limitation in synthetic biology today is the time and effort expended during fabrication of engineered genetic sequences. To speed up the cycle of design, fabrication, testing and redesign, synthetic biology requires more rapid and reliable *de novo* DNA synthesis and assembly of fragments of DNA, in a process commonly referred to as gene synthesis.

In 2000, researchers at Washington University, mentioned synthesis of the 9.6 kbp Hepatitis C virus genome from chemically synthesized 60 to 80-mers.[28] In 2002 researchers at SUNY Stony Brook succeeded in synthesizing the 7741 base poliovirus genome from its published sequence, producing the second synthetic genome. This took about two years of painstaking work.[29] In 2003 the 5386 bp genome of the bacteriophage Phi X 174 was assembled in about two weeks.[30] In 2006, the same team, at the J. Craig Venter Institute, has constructed and patented a synthetic genome of a novel minimal bacterium, *Mycoplasma laboratorium* and is working on getting it functioning in a living cell.[31] [32]

In 2007 it was reported that several companies were offering the synthesis of genetic sequences up to 2000 bp long, for a price of about $1 per base pair and a turnaround time of less than two weeks.[33] By September 2009, the price had dropped to less than $0.50 per base pair with some improvement in turn around time. Not only is the price judged lower than the cost of conventional cDNA cloning, the economics make it practical for researchers to design and purchase multiple variants of the same sequence to identify genes or proteins with optimized performance.

In 2010, Venter's group announced they had been able to assemble a complete genome of millions of base pairs, insert it into a cell, and cause that cell to start replicating.[34]

Modeling

Models inform the design of engineered biological systems by allowing synthetic biologists to better predict system behavior prior to fabrication. Synthetic biology will benefit from better models of how biological molecules bind substrates and catalyze reactions, how DNA encodes the information needed to specify the cell and how multi-component integrated systems behave. Recently, multiscale models of gene regulatory networks have been developed that focus on synthetic biology applications. Simulations have been used that model all biomolecular interactions in transcription, translation, regulation, and induction of gene regulatory networks, guiding the design of synthetic systems.[35]

Measurement

Precise and accurate quantitative measurements of biological systems are crucial to improving understanding of biology. Such measurements often help to elucidate how biological systems work and provide the basis for model construction and validation. Differences between predicted and measured system behavior can identify gaps in understanding and explain why synthetic systems don't always behave as intended. Technologies which allow many parallel and time-dependent measurements will be especially useful in synthetic biology. Microscopy and flow cytometry are examples of useful measurement technologies.

Examples

Molecular cloning is a method used frequently by geneticists to obtain large quantities of a particular strand of DNA. It involves shaping a selected piece of DNA and inserting it into the DNA of a bacterium called a plasmid. Once the alien DNA is inserted the bacteria is allowed to replicate thus replicating the DNA that it contains. After replication is completed the copies of foreign DNA are separated from the plasmid. In this sense the bacteria becomes a cyborg because a foreign element is introduced and interacts with the bacteria.

The Sleeping Beauty transposon system is an example of an engineered enzyme for inserting precise DNA sequences into genomes of vertebrate animals. The SB transposon is a synthetic sequence that was created based on deriving a consensus sequence of extinct Tc1/mariner-type transposons that are found as evolutionary relics in the genomes of most, if not all, vertebrates. This enzyme took about a year to engineer[36] and since its creation has been used for gene transfer, gene discovery, and gene therapy applications[37] [38] [39]

Biosensor technology is another example of cyborg bacteria. One such sensor created in Oak Ridge National Laboratory and named "critter on a chip" used a coating of bioluminescent bacteria on a light sensitive computer chip to detect certain petroleum pollutants. When the bacteria sense the pollutant, it lights up and is then processed or amplified.[40] In Australia, biosensors have been created to detect viruses, bacteria, hormones, drugs, and DNA sequences. In the future scientists hope to create chips that can sense toxins such as environmental estrogens and warfare agents. Even more recently chemists at the University of Nebraska created a humidity gauge by using gold plated bacteria on a silicon chip. With a decrease in humidity there was an increase in the circuit flow. One unique feature that separates the chip from the bioluminescent ones is that that after it has been assimilated the bacteria no longer needs to be kept alive for the humidity gauge to work.[41]

Nanotechnology also has made advances by using cyborgs. Researchers at the École polytechnique de Montréal in Canada have attached a microscopic bead to swimming bacteria. Using a magnetic resonance imaging machine (MRI) the researchers have been able to use the magnetic properties of the bacteria to direct it to certain locations. The bead has no purpose at the moment but researchers hope store drugs or other viral fighting agents inside so that it may be released at the directed location.[42]

Challenges

Opposition to Synthetic Biology

Opposition by civil society groups to Synthetic Biology has been led by the ETC Group who have called for a global moratorium on developments in the field and for no synthetic organisms to be released from the lab. In 2006 38 civil society organizations authored an open letter opposing voluntary regulation of the field and in 2008 ETC Group released the first critical report on the societal impacts of synthetic biology which they dubbed "Extreme Genetic Engineering".[43]

Safety and Security

In addition to numerous scientific and technical challenges, synthetic biology raises questions for ethics, biosecurity, biosafety, involvement of stakeholders and intellectual property.[44] [45] To date, key stakeholders (especially in the US) have focused primarily on the biosecurity issues, especially the so-called dual-use challenge. For example, while the study of synthetic biology may lead to more efficient ways to produce medical treatments (e.g. against malaria), it may also lead to synthesis or redesign of harmful pathogens (e.g., smallpox) by malicious actors.[46] Proposals for licensing and monitoring [47] the various phases of gene and genome synthesis began to appear in 2004. A 2007 study [48] compared several policy options for governing the security risks associated with synthetic biology. Other initiatives, such as OpenWetWare [93], diybio [49], biopunk [50], biohack [51], and possibly others, have attempted to integrate self-regulation in their proliferation of open source synthetic biology projects. However the distributed and diffuse nature of open-source biotechnology may make it more difficult to track, regulate, or mitigate potential biosafety and biosecurity concerns.[52]

An initiative for self-regulation has been proposed by the International Association Synthetic Biology[53] that suggests some specific measures to be implemented by the synthetic biology industry, especially DNA synthesis companies. Some scientists, however, argue for a more radical and forward looking approaches to improve safety and security issues. They suggest to use not only physical containment as safety measures, but also trophic and semantic containment. Trophic containment includes for example the design of new and more robust forms of auxotrophy, while semantic containment means the design and construction of completely novel orthogonal life-forms.[54]

Social and Ethical

Online discussion of "societal issues" took place at the SYNBIOSAFE forum [55] on issues regarding ethics, safety, security, IPR, governance, and public perception (summary paper) [56]. On July 9–10, 2009, the National Academies' Committee of Science, Technology & Law convened a symposium on "Opportunities and Challenges in the Emerging Field of Synthetic Biology" [57] (transcripts, audio, and presentations available).

Some efforts have been made to engage social issues "upstream" focus on the integral and mutually formative relations among scientific and other human practices. These approaches attempt to invent ongoing and regular forms of collaboration among synthetic biologists, ethicists, political analysts, funders, human scientists and civil society activists. These collaborations have consisted either of intensive, short term meetings, aimed at producing guidelines or regulations, or standing committees whose purpose is limited to protocol review or rule enforcement. Such work has proven valuable in identifying the ways in which synthetic biology intensifies already-known challenges in rDNA technologies. However, these forms are not suited to identifying new challenges as they emerge,[58] and critics worry about uncritical complicity.[43]

An example of efforts to develop ongoing collaboration is the "Human Practices" [59] component of the Synthetic Biology Engineering Research Center [60] in the US and the SYNBIOSAFE [61] project in Europe, coordinated by IDC,[62] that investigated the biosafety, biosecurity and ethical aspects of synthetic biology. A report from the Woodrow Wilson Center and the Hastings Center, a prestigious bioethics research institute, found that ethical concerns in synthetic biology have received scant attention.[63]

In January 2009, the Alfred P. Sloan Foundation funded the Woodrow Wilson Center, the Hastings Center, and the J. Craig Venter Institute to examine the public perception, ethics, and policy implications of synthetic biology.[64] Public perception and communication of synthetic biology is the main focus of COSY: Communicating Synthetic Biology [65], that showed that in the general public synthetic biology is not seen as too different from 'traditional' genetic engineering.[66] [67] To better communicate synthetic biology and its societal ramifications to a broader public, COSY and SYNBIOSAFE published a 38 min. documentary film in October 2009 [68].

After a series of meetings in the fall of 2010, the Presidential Commission for the study of Bioethical Issues released a report, on December 16, to the President calling for enhanced Federal oversight in the emerging field of sythetic biology. The panel that facilitated the production of the report, composed of 13 scientists, ethicists, and public policy experts, said that the very newness of the science, which involves the design and construction of laboratory-made biological parts, gives regulators, ethicists and others time to identify problems early on and craft solutions that can harness the technology for the public good.

> "We comprehensively reviewed the developing field of synthetic biology to understand both its potential rewards and risks," said Dr. Amy Gutmann, the Commission Chair and President of the University of Pennsylvania. "We considered an array of approaches to regulation—from allowing unfettered freedom with minimal oversight and another to prohibiting experiments until they can be ruled completely safe beyond a reasonable doubt. We chose a middle course to maximize public benefits while also safeguarding against risks."

Dr. Gutmann said the Commission's approach recognizes the great potential of synthetic biology, including life saving medicines, and the generally distant risks posed by the field's current capacity. "Prudent vigilance suggests that federal oversight is needed and can be exercised in a way that is consistent with scientific progress," she said.[69]

References

[1] http://parts.mit.edu/r/parts/htdocs/SBC04/index.cgi

[2] Luis Campos, "That Was the Synthetic Biology That Was" in M. Schmidt, A. Kelle, A. Ganguli-Mitra and H. Vriend, eds., *Synthetic Biology: The Technoscience and Its Societal Consequences.* Springer Academic Publishing, 2010

[3] Théorie physico-chimique de la vie et générations spontanées, S. Leduc,1910 (http://openlibrary.org/books/OL23348076M/ Théorie_physico-chimique_de_la_vie_et_générations_spontanées)

[4] Leduc, Stéphane (1912). Poinat, A.. ed. *La biologie synthétique, étude de biophysique* (http://www.peiresc.org/bstitre.htm). .

[5] Waclaw Szybalski, *In Vivo and in Vitro Initiation of Transcription*, Page 405. In: A. Kohn and A. Shatkay (Eds.), Control of Gene Expression, pp. 23–4, and Discussion pp. 404–5 (Szybalski's concept of Synthetic Biology), 411–2, 415–7. New York: Plenum Press, 1974

[6] Szybalski, W; Skalka, A (November-1978). "Nobel prizes and restriction enzymes" (http://www.sciencedirect.com/ science?_ob=IssueURL&_tockey=#TOC#4941#1978#999959996#383739#FLP#&_auth=y&view=c&_acct=C000050221&_version=1& _urlVersion=0&_userid=10&md5=cf7bbc6f0e4d37c1de98c80fc9b50a3e). *Gene* **4** (3): 181–2. doi:10.1016/0378-1119(78)90016-1. PMID 744485. .

[7] http://www.elowitz.caltech.edu/

[8] Elowitz MB, Leibler S (January 2000). "A synthetic oscillatory network of transcriptional regulators". *Nature* **403** (6767): 335–8. doi:10.1038/35002125. PMID 10659856.

[9] http://genomics.lbl.gov

[10] http://www.bu.edu/abl

[11] http://web.mit.edu/biophysics/

[12] http://www.pbs.org/wgbh/nova/sciencenow/3214/01.html

[13] http://www.stanford.edu/group/kool/

[14] http://alice.berkeley.edu/

[15] http://genetics.mgh.harvard.edu/szostakweb/

[16] Zeng BJ., On the concept of systems biological engineering, The Communications on Transgenic Animals, CAS, Nov. 1994.

[17] Chopra, Paras; Akhil Kamma. "Engineering life through Synthetic Biology" (http://www.bioinfo.de/isb/2006/06/0038/). *In Silico Biology* **6**. . Retrieved 2008-06-09.

[18] Gardner TS, Cantor CR, Collins JJ (January 2000). "Construction of a genetic toggle switch in Escherichia coli". *Nature* **403** (6767): 339–42. doi:10.1038/35002131. PMID 10659857.

[19] http://partsregistry.org/

[20] http://igem.org

[21] Channon, Kevin; Bromley, Elizabeth HC; Woolfson, Derek N (August 2008). "Synthetic Biology through Biomolecular Design and Engineering". *Current Opinion in Structural Biology* **18** (4): 491–8. doi:10.1016/j.sbi.2008.06.006. PMID 18644449.

[22] http://mit.edu/endy/

[23] http://www.nature.com/msb/journal/v1/n1/full/msb4100025.html

[24] http://arep.med.harvard.edu/SBP

[25] Forster, AC; Church GM. (2006-08-22). "Towards synthesis of a minimal cell". *Mol Syst Biol.* **2** (1): 45. doi:10.1038/msb4100090. PMC 1681520. PMID 16924266.

[26] Group, Bio FAB; Baker D, Church G, Collins J, Endy D, Jacobson J, Keasling J, Modrich P, Smolke C, Weiss R (June-2006). "Engineering life: building a fab for biology". *Scientific American* **294** (6): 44–51. doi:10.1038/scientificamerican0606-44. PMID 16711359.

[27] http://www.kurzweilai.net/articles/art0134.html

[28] Blight KJ, Kolykhalov AA, Rice CM. (2000-12-08). "Efficient initiation of HCV RNA replication in cell culture". *Science* **290** (5498): 1972–4. doi:10.1126/science.290.5498.1972. PMID 11110665.

[29] Couzin J (2002). "Virology. Active poliovirus baked from scratch". *Science* **297** (5579): 174–5. doi:10.1126/science.297.5579.174b. PMID 12114601.

[30] Smith, Hamilton O.; Clyde A. Hutchison, Cynthia Pfannkoch, J. Craig Venter (2003-12-23). "Generating a synthetic genome by whole genome assembly: {phi}X174 bacteriophage from synthetic oligonucleotides" (http://www.pnas.org/cgi/content/abstract/100/26/15440). *Proc. Natl. Acad. Sci. U.S.A.* **100** (26): 15440–5. doi:10.1073/pnas.2237126100. PMID 14657399. .

[31] Wade, Nicholas (2007-06-29). "Scientists Transplant Genome of Bacteria" (http://www.nytimes.com/2007/06/29/science/29cells.html). *The New York Times*. ISSN 0362-4331. . Retrieved 2007-12-28.

[32] Gibson, DG; Benders GA, Andrews-Pfannkoch C, Denisova EA, Baden-Tillson H, Zaveri J, Stockwell TB, Brownley A, Thomas DW, Algire MA, Merryman C, Young L, Noskov VN, Glass JI, Venter JC, Hutchison CA 3rd, Smith HO. (2008-01-24). "Complete chemical synthesis, assembly, and cloning of a *Mycoplasma genitalium* genome". *Science* **319** (5867): 1215–20. doi:10.1126/science.1151721. PMID 18218864.

[33] Pollack, Andrew (2007-09-12). "How Do You Like Your Genes? Biofabs Take Orders" (http://www.nytimes.com/2007/09/12/technology/techspecial/12gene.html?pagewanted=2&_r=1). *The New York Times*. ISSN 0362-4331. . Retrieved 2007-12-28.

[34] "Scientists Reach Milestone On Way To Artificial Life" (http://www.npr.org/templates/transcript/transcript.php?storyId=127010591). 2010-05-20. . Retrieved 2010-06-09.

[35] Kaznessis YN (2007). "Models for Synthetic Biology" (http://www.biomedcentral.com/1752-0509/1/47). *BMC Systems Biology* **1**: 47. doi:10.1186/1752-0509-1-47. PMC 2194732. PMID 17986347. .

[36] Ivics Z., Hackett P.B., Plasterk R.H., Izsvak Z. (1997). "Molecular reconstruction of Sleeping Beauty, a Tc1-like transposon from fish, and its transposition in human cells". *Cell* **91**: 501–510. doi:10.1016/S0092-8674(00)80436-5. PMID 9390559.

[37] Ivics Z., Izsvak Z. (2005). "A whole lotta jumpin' goin' on: new transposon tools for vertebrate functional genomics". *Trends Genet* **21**: 8–11. doi:10.1016/j.tig.2004.11.008. PMID 15680506.

[38] Carlson C.M., Largaespada D.A. (2005). "Insertional mutagenesis in mice: new perspectives and tools". *Nature Rev. Genet* **6**: 568–580.

[39] Hackett P.B., Largaespada D.A., Cooper L.J.N. (2010). "A transposon and transposase system for human application". *Mol. Ther.* **18** (4): 674–683. doi:10.1038/mt.2010.2. PMC 2862530. PMID 20104209.

[40] Gibbs, W. Wayt (1997). "Critters on a Chip" (http://www.sciam.com/article.cfm?id=critters-on-a-chip). *Scientific American*. . Retrieved 2 Mar 2009.

[41] Christensen, Bill (2009). "'Cellborg' Humidity Gauge First Bacterial Cyborg" (http://www.technovelgy.com/ct/Science-Fiction-News.asp?NewsNum=480). Technovelgy.com. . Retrieved 2 Mar 2009.

[42] "Strengthened magnets from bacteria could be used to target cancer" (http://www.nanotech-now.com/news.cgi?story_id=28535). 7thWave, Inc.. 2009. . Retrieved 2 Mar 2009.

[43] ETC Group Extreme Genetic Engineering: ETC Group Releases Report on Synthetic Biology (http://etcgroup.org/upload/publication/602/01/synbioreportweb.pdf)

[44] Schmidt M, Ganguli-Mitra A, Torgersen H, Kelle A, Deplazes A, Biller-Andorno N (2009). "A priority paper for the societal and ethical aspects of synthetic biology" (http://www.synbiosafe.eu/uploads/pdf/Schmidt_etal-2009-SSBJ.pdf) (PDF). *Systems and Synthetic Biology* **3** (1–4): 3–7. doi:10.1007/s11693-009-9034-7. PMC 2759426. PMID 19816794. .

[45] Schmidt M. Kelle A. Ganguli A, de Vriend H. (Eds.) 2009. "Synthetic Biology. The Technoscience and its Societal Consequences". (http://www.springer.com/biomed/book/978-90-481-2677-4) Springer Academic Publishing.

[46] Kelle A (2009). "Ensuring the security of synthetic biology—towards a 5P governance strategy" (http://www.synbiosafe.eu/uploads/pdf/Kelle-2009-SSBJ.pdf) (PDF). *Systems and Synthetic Biology* **3** (1–4): 85–90. doi:10.1007/s11693-009-9041-8. PMC 2759433. PMID 19816803. .

[47] http://arep.med.harvard.edu/SBP/Church_Biohazard04c.htm

[48] http://www.jcvi.org/cms/fileadmin/site/research/projects/synthetic-genomics-report/synthetic-genomics-report.pdf

[49] http://diybio.org/

[50] http://biopunk.org/

[51] http://biohack.sf.net/

[52] Schmidt M (2008). "Diffusion of synthetic biology: a challenge to biosafety" (http://www.markusschmidt.eu/pdf/Diffusion_of_synthetic_biology.pdf) (PDF). *Systems and Synthetic Biology* **2** (1–2): 1–6. doi:10.1007/s11693-008-9018-z. PMC 2671588. PMID 19003431. .

[53] Report of IASB "Technical solutions for biosecurity in synthetic biology" (http://www.ia-sb.eu/tasks/sites/synthetic-biology/assets/File/pdf/iasb_report_biosecurity_syntheticbiology.pdf), Munich, 2008.

[54] Marliere P (2009). "The farther, the safer: a manifesto for securely navigating synthetic species away from the old living worldy" (http://www.synbiosafe.eu/uploads/pdf/Marliere-SSBJ-2009.pdf) (PDF). *Systems and Synthetic Biology* **3** (1–4): 77–84. doi:10.1007/s11693-009-9040-9. PMC 2759432. PMID 19816802. .

[55] http://www.synbiosafe.eu/forum

[56] http://www.synbiosafe.eu/uploads///pdf/SSBJ-SYNBIOSAFE%20e-conference.pdf

[57] http://sites.nationalacademies.org/PGA/stl/PGA_050738

[58] Schmidt M (2008). "Diffusion of synthetic biology: a challenge to biosafety" (http://www.synbiosafe.eu/uploads///pdf/ Diffusion_of_synthetic_biology.pdf). *Systems and Synthetic Biology* 2 (1–2): 1–6. doi:10.1007/s11693-008-9018-z. PMC 2671588. PMID 19003431. .

[59] http://synberc.org/content/articles/human-practices

[60] http://synberc.org/

[61] http://www.synbiosafe.eu

[62] Organisation for International Dialogue and Conflict Management (IDC) Biosafety Working Group (http://www.idialog.eu/index. php?page=biosafety-working-group)

[63] WWCIS 2009 Ethical Issues in Synthetic Biology. An Overview of the Debates (http://www.synbioproject.org/library/publications/ archive/synbio3/)

[64] Parens E., Johnston J., Moses J. Ethical Issues in Synthetic Biology. (http://www.thehastingscenter.org/News/Detail.aspx?id=3022) 2009.

[65] http://www.synbio.at

[66] Kronberger, N; Holtz, P; Kerbe, W; Strasser, E; Wagner, W (2009). "Communicating Synthetic Biology: from the lab via the media to the broader public" (http://www.springerlink.com/content/r170x43868877p68/fulltext.pdf) (PDF). *Systems and Synthetic Biology* 3 (1–4): 19–26. doi:10.1007/s11693-009-9031-x. PMC 2759424. PMID 19816796. .

[67] Cserer A, Seiringer A (2009). "Pictures of Synthetic Biology" (http://www.springerlink.com/content/r170x43868877p68/fulltext.pdf) (PDF). *Systems and Synthetic Biology* 3 (1–4): 27–35. doi:10.1007/s11693-009-9038-3. PMC 2759430. PMID 19816797. .

[68] http://www.synbiosafe.eu/DVD

[69] "Presidential Commission on Bioethics Calls for Enhanced Federal Oversight in Emerging Field of Synthetic Biology" (http://www. bioethics.gov/cms/sites/default/files/PCSBI-Synthetic-Biology-Report-Press-Release-12.16.10.pdf). Presidential Commission for the Study of Bioethical Issues. December 16, 2010. . Retrieved August 29, 2011.

External links

- Transgenics & Artificial Biosystems (http://www.sysbioeng.com/wabse) Genbrain Biosystem Network since 1999.
- syntheticbiology.org community site (http://syntheticbiology.org)
- ETC Group resources on Synthetic Biology (http://www.etcgroup.org/en/issues/synthetic_biology)
- Synthetic Biology Project (http://www.synbioproject.org) Synthetic biology news, events, publications and more.
- Applied BioDynamics Laboratory: Boston University (http://www.bu.edu/abl/)
- Handbook - Synthetic Biology for Beginners - CEMA, Srishti, Bangalore (http://hackteria.org/wiki/images/a/ a1/Handbook.pdf)
- Hastings Center synthetic biology issue page (http://www.thehastingscenter.org/Issues/Default.aspx?v=2392) contains research and resources on the ethical issues in synthetic biology.
- Synthetic Biology Engineering Research Center (SynBERC) (http://www.synberc.org) A NSF-funded multi-university effort to lay the foundations for synthetic biology.
- Pier Luigi Luisi's synthetic biology group (http://www.plluisi.org)
- SYNBIOSAFE: Safety and ethical aspects of synthetic biology (http://www.synbiosafe.eu)
- Ars Synthetica (http://www.ars-synthetica.net) A multimedia forum for engaging specialists and non-specialists in an informed, ethical, and democratic dialogue on the emerging field of synthetic biology.
- Article on applications of synthetic biology (http://web.rollins.edu/~tlairson/tech/synlife5.html)
- Art& Synthetic Biology (http://2009.igem.org/Team:ArtScienceBangalore)
- GenoCAD (http://genocad.org): a web-based open source CAD application for synthetic biology
- SynbioSS (http://synbioss.sourceforge.net): The Synthetic Biology Software Suite. Open license software for modeling synthetic gene regulatory networks
- TinkerCell (http://www.tinkercell.com): A desktop CAD software for synthetic biology
- Biobuilder.org (http://www.biobuilder.org/) an educational website to engage and inform a wider audience of synthetic biology enthusiasts
- International Association Synthetic Biology (http://www.ia-sb.eu)
- Collection of newspaper articles on SB (http://www.synbiosafe.eu/index.php?page=popular-press)

- A review on Human Practices and Synthetic Biology (http://2009.igem.org/wiki/images/0/0d/Sins,_Ethics_and_Biology.pdf)
- The Centre for Systems and Synthetic Biology, India (http://www.cssb.res.in)

Multimedia

- Creation of an artificial virus by a Brazilian University (UFPE) members: it can be the beginning of realization of a vaccine against AIDS. (http://g1.globo.com/jornal-nacional/noticia/2010/05/pesquisadores-anunciam-criacao-do-virus-hiv-artificial.html)
- Public 'Long Now' Debate on Synthetic Biology between Jim Thomas and Drew Endy (http://fora.tv/2008/11/17/Drew_Endy_and_Jim_Thomas_Debate_Synthetic_Biology)
- Video interviews with synthetic biology experts, NGOs and funding institutions (http://www.synbiosafe.eu/index.php?page=expert-interviews)
- Documentary Film on synthetic biology and its societal aspects (DVD) (http://www.synbiosafe.eu/DVD)
- Synthetic Biology & Design (http://www.youtube.com/watch?v=2ZVs29mtQEg) – "Speculative Designer" James King presents his work at The Hastings Center, a nonpartisan bioethics research center
- Synthetic Biology (http://acdis.illinois.edu/students/courses-current/focal-point-seminar/Blanke-syntheticbio.html/)- video of lecture by Steven Blanke, Professor of Microbiology at the University of Illinois, hosted by the Program in Arms Control, Disarmament, and International Security (ACDIS), November 19, 2009. Topics include: definitions and principles of synthetic biology; BioBricks; Internationally Genetically Engineered Machine (iGEM) competition; applications for commercial use, biosecurity; risk assessments; Biological and Toxin Weapons Convention; models of institutional governance.

Systems biology

Systems biology is a term used to describe a number of trends in bioscience research, and a movement which draws on those trends. Proponents describe systems biology as a biology-based inter-disciplinary study field that focuses on complex interactions in biological systems, claiming that it uses a new perspective (holism instead of reduction). Particularly from year 2000 onwards, the term is used widely in the biosciences, and in a variety of contexts. An often stated ambition of systems biology is the modeling and

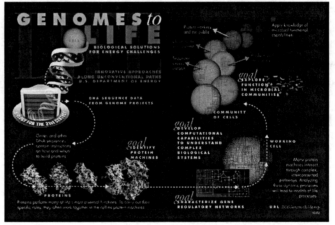

Example of systems biology research.

discovery of emergent properties, properties of a system whose theoretical description is only possible using techniques which fall under the remit of systems biology. These typically involve cell signaling networks, via long-range allostery.

Overview

Systems biology can be considered from a number of different aspects:

- As a **field of study**, particularly, the study of the interactions between the components of *biological systems*, and how these interactions give rise to the function and behavior of that system (for example, the enzymes and metabolites in a metabolic pathway).[1] [2]

- As a **paradigm**, usually defined in antithesis to the so-called reductionist paradigm (biological organisation), although fully consistent with the scientific method. The distinction between the two paradigms is referred to in these quotations:

  > *"The reductionist approach has successfully identified most of the components and many of the interactions but, unfortunately, offers no convincing concepts or methods to understand how system properties emerge...the pluralism of causes and effects in biological networks is better addressed by observing, through quantitative measures, multiple components simultaneously and by rigorous data integration with mathematical models"* Sauer et al[3]

  > *"Systems biology...is about putting together rather than taking apart, integration rather than reduction. It requires that we develop ways of thinking about integration that are as rigorous as our reductionist programmes, but different....It means changing our philosophy, in the full sense of the term"* Denis Noble[4]

- As a series of **operational protocols used for performing research**, namely a cycle composed of theory, analytic or computational modelling to propose specific testable hypotheses about a biological system, experimental validation, and then using the newly acquired quantitative description of cells or cell processes to refine the computational model or theory.[5] Since the objective is a model of the interactions in a system, the experimental techniques that most suit systems biology are those that are system-wide and attempt to be as complete as possible. Therefore, transcriptomics, metabolomics, proteomics and high-throughput techniques are used to collect quantitative data for the construction and validation of models.

- As the application of dynamical systems theory to molecular biology.

- As a **socioscientific phenomenon** defined by the strategy of pursuing integration of complex data about the interactions in biological systems from diverse experimental sources using interdisciplinary tools and personnel.

This variety of viewpoints is illustrative of the fact that systems biology refers to a cluster of peripherally overlapping concepts rather than a single well-delineated field. However the term has widespread currency and popularity as of 2007, with chairs and institutes of systems biology proliferating worldwide.

History

Systems biology finds its roots in:

- the quantitative modeling of enzyme kinetics, a discipline that flourished between 1900 and 1970,
- the mathematical modeling of population growth,
- the simulations developed to study neurophysiology, and
- control theory and cybernetics.

One of the theorists who can be seen as one of the precursors of systems biology is Ludwig von Bertalanffy with his general systems theory.[6] One of the first numerical simulations in biology was published in 1952 by the British neurophysiologists and Nobel prize winners Alan Lloyd Hodgkin and Andrew Fielding Huxley, who constructed a mathematical model that explained the action potential propagating along the axon of a neuronal cell.[7] Their model described a cellular function emerging from the interaction between two different molecular components, a potassium and a sodium channel, and can therefore be seen as the beginning of computational systems biology.[8] In 1960, Denis Noble developed the first computer model of the heart pacemaker.[9]

The formal study of systems biology, as a distinct discipline, was launched by systems theorist Mihajlo Mesarovic in 1966 with an international symposium at the Case Institute of Technology in Cleveland, Ohio entitled "Systems Theory and Biology".[10] [11]

The 1960s and 1970s saw the development of several approaches to study complex molecular systems, such as the Metabolic Control Analysis and the biochemical systems theory. The successes of molecular biology throughout the 1980s, coupled with a skepticism toward theoretical biology, that then promised more than it achieved, caused the quantitative modelling of biological processes to become a somewhat minor field.

However the birth of functional genomics in the 1990s meant that large quantities of high quality data became available, while the computing power exploded, making more realistic models possible. In 1997, the group of Masaru Tomita published the first quantitative model of the metabolism of a whole (hypothetical) cell.[12]

Around the year 2000, after Institutes of Systems Biology were established in Seattle and Tokyo, systems biology emerged as a movement in its own right, spurred on by the completion of various genome projects, the large increase in data from the omics (e.g. genomics and proteomics) and the accompanying advances in high-throughput experiments and bioinformatics. Since then, various research institutes dedicated to systems biology have been developed. For example, the NIGMS of NIH established a project grant that is currently supporting over ten Systems Biology Centers [13] in the United States. As of summer 2006, due to a shortage of people in systems biology[14] several doctoral training programs in systems biology have been established in many parts of the world. In that same year, the National Science Foundation (NSF) put forward a grand challenge for systems biology in the 21st century to build a mathematical model of the whole cell.[15] In 2011, V. A. Shiva Ayyadurai and C. Forbes Dewey, Jr. of Department of Biological Engineering at the Massachusetts Institute of Technology created CytoSolve, a method to model the whole cell by dynamically integrating multiple molecular pathway models.[16] [17]

Associated disciplines

According to the interpretation of Systems Biology as the ability to obtain, integrate and analyze complex data sets from multiple experimental sources using interdisciplinary tools, some typical technology platforms are:

- Phenomics: Organismal variation in phenotype as it changes during its life span.

- Genomics: Organismal deoxyribonucleic acid (DNA) sequence, including intra-organisamal cell specific variation. (i.e. Telomere length variation etc.).

- Epigenomics / Epigenetics: Organismal and corresponding cell specific transcriptomic regulating factors not empirically coded in the genomic sequence. (i.e. DNA methylation, Histone Acetelation etc.).

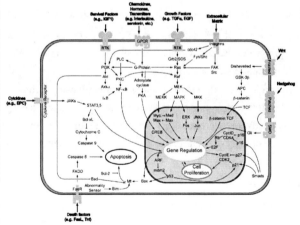

Overview of signal transduction pathways

- Transcriptomics: Organismal, tissue or whole cell gene expression measurements by DNA microarrays or serial analysis of gene expression

- Interferomics: Organismal, tissue, or cell level transcript correcting factors (i.e. RNA interference)

- Translatomics / Proteomics: Organismal, tissue, or cell level measurements of proteins and peptides via two-dimensional gel electrophoresis, mass spectrometry or multi-dimensional protein identification techniques (advanced HPLC systems coupled with mass spectrometry). Sub disciplines include phosphoproteomics, glycoproteomics and other methods to detect chemically modified proteins.

- Metabolomics: Organismal, tissue, or cell level measurements of all small-molecules known as metabolites.
- Glycomics: Organismal, tissue, or cell level measurements of carbohydrates.
- Lipidomics: Organismal, tissue, or cell level measurements of lipids.

In addition to the identification and quantification of the above given molecules further techniques analyze the dynamics and interactions within a cell. This includes:

- Interactomics: Organismal, tissue, or cell level study of interactions between molecules. Currently the authoritative molecular discipline in this field of study is protein-protein interactions (PPI), although the working definition does not pre-clude inclusion of other molecular disciplines such as those defined here.
- NeuroElectroDynamics: Organismal, brain computing function as a dynamic system, underlying biophysical mechanisms and emerging computation by electrical interactions.
- Fluxomics: Organismal, tissue, or cell level measurements of molecular dynamic changes over time.
- Biomics: systems analysis of the biome.

The investigations are frequently combined with large-scale perturbation methods, including gene-based (RNAi, mis-expression of wild type and mutant genes) and chemical approaches using small molecule libraries. Robots and automated sensors enable such large-scale experimentation and data acquisition. These technologies are still emerging and many face problems that the larger the quantity of data produced, the lower the quality. A wide variety of quantitative scientists (computational biologists, statisticians, mathematicians, computer scientists, engineers, and physicists) are working to improve the quality of these approaches and to create, refine, and retest the models to accurately reflect observations.

The systems biology approach often involves the development of mechanistic models, such as the reconstruction of dynamic systems from the quantitative properties of their elementary building blocks.[18] [19] For instance, a cellular network can be modelled mathematically using methods coming from chemical kinetics and control theory. Due to the large number of parameters, variables and constraints in cellular networks, numerical and computational techniques are often used.

Other aspects of computer science and informatics are also used in systems biology. These include:

- New forms of computational model, such as the use of process calculi to model biological processes (notable approaches include stochastic π-calculus, BioAmbients, Beta Binders, BioPEPA and Brane calculus) and constraint-based modeling.
- Integration of information from the literature, using techniques of information extraction and text mining.
- Development of online databases and repositories for sharing data and models, approaches to database integration and software interoperability via loose coupling of software, websites and databases, or commercial suits.
- Development of syntactically and semantically sound ways of representing biological models.

References

[1] Snoep, Jacky L; Westerhoff, Hans V (2005). "From isolation to integration, a systems biology approach for building the Silicon Cell". In Alberghina, Lilia; Westerhoff, Hans V. *Systems Biology: Definitions and Perspectives*. Topics in Current Genetics. **13**. Berlin: Springer-Verlag. pp. 13–30. doi:10.1007/b106456. ISBN 978-3-540-22968-1.

[2] "Systems Biology: the 21st Century Science" (http://www.systemsbiology.org/Intro_to_Systems_Biology/ Systems_Biology_--_the_21st_Century_Science). Institute for Systems Biology. . Retrieved 15 June 2011.

[3] Sauer, Uwe; Heinemann, Matthias; Zamboni, Nicola (27 April 2007). "GENETICS: Getting Closer to the Whole Picture". *Science* **316** (5824): 550–551. doi:10.1126/science.1142502. PMID 17463274.

[4] Noble, Denis (2006). *The music of life: Biology beyond the genome*. Oxford: Oxford University Press. pp. 176. ISBN 978-0-19-929573-9.

[5] Kholodenko, Boris N; Sauro, Herbert M (2005). "Mechanistic and modular approaches to modeling and inference of cellular regulatory networks". In Alberghina, Lilia; Westerhoff, Hans V. *Systems Biology: Definitions and Perspectives*. Topics in Current Genetics. **13**. Berlin: Springer-Verlag. pp. 357–451. doi:10.1007/b136809. ISBN 978-3-540-22968-1.

[6] von Bertalanffy, Ludwig (28 March 1976) [1968]. *General System theory: Foundations, Development, Applications*. George Braziller. pp. 295. ISBN 9780807604533.

[7] Hodgkin, Alan L; Huxley, Andrew F (28 August 1952). "A quantitative description of membrane current and its application to conduction and excitation in nerve". *Journal of Physiology* **117** (4): 500–544. PMC 1392413. PMID 12991237.

[8] Le Novère, Nicolas (13 June 2007). "The long journey to a Systems Biology of neuronal function". *BMC Systems Biology* **1**: 28. doi:10.1186/1752-0509-1-28. PMC 1904462. PMID 17567903.

[9] Noble, Denis (5 November 1960). "Cardiac action and pacemaker potentials based on the Hodgkin-Huxley equations". *Nature* **188** (4749): 495–497. Bibcode 1960Natur.188..495N. doi:10.1038/188495b0. PMID 13729365.

[10] Mesarovic, Mihajlo D (1968). *Systems Theory and Biology*. Berlin: Springer-Verlag.

[11] Rosen, Robert (5 July 1968). "A Means Toward a New Holism". *Science* **161** (3836): 34–35. doi:10.1126/science.161.3836.34. JSTOR 1724368.

[12] Tomita, Masaru; Hashimoto, Kenta; Takahashi, Kouichi; Shimizu, Thomas S; Matsuzaki, Yuri; Miyoshi, Fumihiko; Saito, Kanako; Tanida, Sakura et al. (1997). "E-CELL: Software Environment for Whole Cell Simulation" (http://web.sfc.keio.ac.jp/~mt/mt-lab/publications/ Paper/ecell/bioinfo99/btc007_gml.html). *Genome Inform Ser Workshop Genome Inform* **8**: 147–155. PMID 11072314. . Retrieved 15 June 2011.

[13] http://www.systemscenters.org/

[14] Kling, Jim (3 March 2006). "Working the Systems" (http://sciencecareers.sciencemag.org/career_magazine/previous_issues/articles/ 2006_03_03/noDOI.15936087948366349051). Science. . Retrieved 15 June 2011.

[15] The American Association for the Advancement of Science (http://www.sciencemag.org/content/314/5806/1696.full)

[16] National Center for Biotechnology Information (http://www.ncbi.nlm.nih.gov/pmc/articles/PMC3032229/)

[17] Massachusetts Institute of Technology (http://cytosolve.mit.edu/)

[18] Gardner, Timothy S; di Bernardo, Diego; Lorenz, David; Collins, James J (4 July 2003). "Inferring Genetic Networks and Identifying Compound Mode of Action via Expression Profiling". *Science* **301** (5629): 102–105. doi:10.1126/science.1081900. PMID 12843395.

[19] di Bernardo, Diego; Thompson, Michael J; Gardner, Timothy S; Chobot, Sarah E; Eastwood, Erin L; Wojtovich, Andrew P; Elliott, Sean J; Schaus, Scott E et al. (March 2005). "Chemogenomic profiling on a genome-wide scale using reverse-engineered gene networks". *Nature Biotechnology* **23** (3): 377–383. doi:10.1038/nbt1075. PMID 15765094.

Further reading

- Kitano, Hiroaki (15 October 2001). *Foundations of Systems Biology*. MIT Press. pp. 320. ISBN 978-0-262-11266-6.

- Werner, Eric (29 March 2007). "All systems go". *Nature* **446** (7135): 493–494. doi:10.1038/446493a. provides a comparative review of three books:

  - Alon, Uri (7 July 2006). *An Introduction to Systems Biology: Design Principles of Biological Circuits*. Chapman & Hall. pp. 301. ISBN 978-1-584-88642-6.

  - Kaneko, Kunihiko (15 September 2006). *Life: An Introduction to Complex Systems Biology*. Springer-Verlag. pp. 371. ISBN 978-3-540-32666-3.

  - Palsson, Bernhard O (16 January 2006). *Systems Biology: Properties of Reconstructed Networks*. Cambridge University Press. pp. 334. ISBN 978-0-521-85903-5.

Systems Biology Ontology

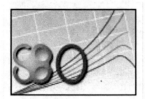

The **Systems Biology Ontology** (SBO) is a set of controlled, relational vocabularies of terms commonly used in Systems Biology, and in particular in computational modeling. SBO is part of the BioModels.net [1] effort.

Motivation

The rise of Systems Biology, seeking to comprehend biological processes as a whole, highlighted the need to not only develop corresponding quantitative models, but also to create standards allowing their exchange and integration. This concern drove the community to design common data format such as SBML and CellML. SBML is now largely accepted and used in the field. However, as important as the definition of a common syntax is, it is also necessary to make clear the semantics of models. SBO is an attempt to provide the means of annotating models with terms that indicate the intended semantics of an important subset of models in common use in computational systems biology.[2] [3] The development of SBO was first discussed at the 9th SBML Forum Meeting in Heidelberg Oct. 14–15, 2004. During the forum, Pedro Mendes mentioned that modellers possessed a lot of knowledge that was necessary to understand the model, and more importantly to simulate it, but this knowledge was not encoded in SBML. Nicolas Le Novère proposed to create a controlled vocabulary to store the content of Pedro Mendes' mind before he wandered out of the community.[4] The development of the ontology was announced more officially in a message from Le Novère to Michael Hucka and Andrew Finney on October 19.

Structure

SBO is currently made up of seven different vocabularies:

- systems description parameter (catalytic constant, thermodynamic temperature, …)
- participant role (substrate, product, catalyst, …)
- modelling framework (discrete, continuous…)
- mathematical expression (mass action rate law, Hill-type rate law, …)
- occurring entity representation (biochemical process, molecular or genetic interaction, …)
- physical entity representation (transporter, physical compartment, observable, …)
- metadata representation (annotation)

Resources

To curate and maintain SBO, a dedicated resource has been developed and the public interface of the SBO browser can be accessed at http://www.ebi.ac.uk/sbo [5]. A relational database management system (MySQL) at the back-end is accessed through a web interface based on Java Server Pages (JSP) and JavaBeans. Its content is encoded in UTF-8, therefore supporting a large set of characters in the definitions of terms. Distributed curation is made possible by using a custom-tailored locking system allowing concurrent access. This system allows a continuous update of the ontology with immediate availability and suppress merging problems.

Several exports formats (OBO [6] flat file, SBO-XML [7] and OWL [8]) are generated daily or on request and can be downloaded from the web interface.

To allow programmatic access to the resource, Web Services have been implemented based on Apache Axis [9] for the communication layer and Castor [10] for the validation.[11] The librairies, full documentation, samples and tutorial are available online [12].

The sourceforge project can be accessed at http://sourceforge.net/projects/sbo/ [13].

SBO and SBML

Since Level 2 Version 2 [14] SBML provides a mechanism to annotate model components with SBO terms, therefore increasing the semantics of the model beyond the sole topology of interaction and mathematical expression. Modelling tools such as SBMLsqueezer use SBO terms to .Simulation tools can check the consistency of a rate law, convert reaction from one modelling framework to another (e.g., continuous to discrete), or distinguish between identical mathematical expressions based on different assumptions (e.g., Henri-Michaelis-Menten Vs. Briggs-Haldane). Other tools such as semanticSBML [15][16] can use the SBO annotation to integrate individual models into a larger one. The use of SBO is not restricted to the development of models. Resources providing quantitative experimental information such as SABIO Reaction Kinetics [17] will be able to annotate the parameters (what do they mean exactly, how were they calculated) and determine relationships between them.

Organization of SBO development

SBO is built in collaboration by the Computational Neurobiology Group [18] (Nicolas Le Novère, EMBL-EBI, United-Kingdom) and the SBMLTeam (Michael Hucka, Caltech, USA).

Funding for SBO

SBO has benefited from the funds of the European Molecular Biology Laboratory and the National Institute of General Medical Sciences.

References

[1] http://www.biomodels.net/

[2] Le Novère N. BioModels.net, tools and resources to support Computational Systems Biology. Proceedings of the 4th Workshop on Computation of Biochemical Pathways and Genetic Networks (2005), Logos, Berlin, pp. 69-74.

[3] Le Novère N., Courtot M., Laibe C. Adding semantics in kinetics models of biochemical pathways. Proceedings of the 2nd International Symposium on experimental standard conditions of enzyme characterizations (2007), 137-153. Available online (http://www.beilstein-institut.de/index.php?id=196)

[4] Nicolas Le Novère, personal communication

[5] http://www.ebi.ac.uk/sbo

[6] http://www.godatabase.org/dev/doc/obo_format_spec.html

[7] http://www.ebi.ac.uk/sbo/docs/sboxml_schema.xsd

[8] http://www.w3.org/TR/owl-features/

[9] http://ws.apache.org/axis/

[10] http://www.castor.org/

[11] Li C, Courtot M, Le Novère N, Laibe C (November 2009). "BioModels.net Web Services, a free and integrated toolkit for computational modelling software" (http://bib.oxfordjournals.org/cgi/pmidlookup?view=long&pmid=19939940). *Brief. Bioinformatics* 11 (3): 270–7. doi:10.1093/bib/bbp056. PMC 2913671. PMID 19939940. .

[12] http://www.ebi.ac.uk/sbo/SBOWSLib/ws.html

[13] http://sourceforge.net/projects/sbo/

[14] http://sourceforge.net/project/showfiles.php?group_id=71971&package_id=76633

[15] http://www.semanticsbml.org/

[16] Krause F, Uhlendorf J., Lubitz T., Schulz M., Klipp E., Liebermeister W. (2010), Annotation and merging of SBML models with semanticSBML, Bioinformatics 26 (3), 421-422

[17] http://sabio.villa-bosch.de/SABIORK/

[18] http://www.ebi.ac.uk/compneur

External references

- www.biomodels.net (http://biomodels.net)
- Hucka M, Finney A, Sauro HM, *et al.* (March 2003). "The systems biology markup language (SBML): A medium for representation and exchange of Biochemical Network Models" (http://bioinformatics.oxfordjournals.org/cgi/pmidlookup?view=long&pmid=12611808). *Bioinformatics* **19** (4): 524–31. doi:10.1093/bioinformatics/btg015. PMID 12611808.
- Lloyd CM, Halstead MD, Nielsen PF (2004). "CellML: its future, present and past" (http://linkinghub.elsevier.com/retrieve/pii/S007961070400015X). *Prog. Biophys. Mol. Biol.* **85** (2-3): 433–50. doi:10.1016/j.pbiomolbio.2004.01.004. PMID 15142756.

Systems biomedicine

Systems Biomedicine is the application of Systems Biology to the understanding and modulation of developmental and pathological processes in humans, and in animal and cellular models. Whereas Systems Biology aims at modeling exhaustive networks of interactions (with the long-term goal of, for example, creating a comprehensive computational model of the cell), Systems Biomedicine emphasizes the multilevel, hierarchical nature of the models (molecule, organelle, cell, tissue, organ, individual/genotype, environmental factor, population, ecosystem) by discovering and selecting the key factors at each level and integrating them into models that reveal the global, emergent behavior of the biological process under consideration. Such an approach will be favorable when the execution of all the experiments necessary to establish exhaustive models is limited by time and expense (e.g., in animal models) or basic ethics (e.g., human experimentation). In the year of 1992, a paper on system biomedicine by Kamada T. was published (Nov.-Dec.), and an article on systems medicine and pharmay by Zeng B.J. was also published (April) in the same time period.

In 2009 one of the first research centers specialized on systems biomedicine was founded by Rudi Balling. The Luxembourg Centre for Systems Biomedicine [1] is an interdisciplinary center of the University of Luxembourg [2].

Landes Bioscience will launch the peer-reviewed journal, Systems Biomedicine, in January 2012 http://www.landesbioscience.com/journals/systemsbiomedicine/

References

[1] http://wwwde.uni.lu/lcsb
[2] http://wwwen.uni.lu/

Systems immunology

Systems immunology is a recent research field that, under the larger umbrella of systems biology, aims to study the immune system in the more integrated perspective on how entities and players participate at different system levels to the immune function.

The immune system has been thoroughly analyzed as regards to its components and function by using a very successful "reductionist" approach, but its overall functioning principles cannot easily be predicted by studying the properties of its isolated components because they strongly rely on and arise from the interactions among these numerous constituents. Systems immunology represents a different approach for the integrated comprehension of the immune system structure and function based on complex systems theory, high-throughput techniques, as well as on mathematical and computational tools.

Bibliography

Articles

- Christophe Benoist, Ronald N. Germain, Diane Mathis, Immunological Reviews, Volume 210, Number 1, April 2006, pp. 229-234 (6) A *Plaidoyer* for 'Systems Immunology' [1]
- Steven H. Kleinstein, PLoS Comput Biol. 2008 Aug 29;4(8):e1000128. Getting started in computational immunology [1]
- Charlotte Schubert, Nature 473 (7345), 5 May 2011, pp. 113–114, Systems immunology: Complexity captured [2]

References

[1] http://www.ingentaconnect.com/content/mksg/imr/2006/00000210/00000001/art00015
[2] http://www.nature.com/naturejobs/2011/110505/full/nj7345-113a.html

T-Coffee

T-Coffee

Developer(s)	Cédric Notredame, Centro de Regulacio Genomica (CRG) - Barcelona
Stable release	8.99 / 25 January 2011
Operating system	UNIX, Linux, MS-Windows
Type	Bioinformatics tool
Licence	GPL
Website	http://www.tcoffee.org [1]

T-Coffee (Tree-based Consistency Objective Function For alignment Evaluation) is a multiple sequence alignment software using a progressive approach.[2] It generates a library of pairwise alignments to guide the multiple sequence alignment. It can also combine multiple sequences alignments obtained previously and in the latest versions can use structural information from PDB files (3D-Coffee). It has advanced features to evaluate the quality of the alignments and some capacity for identifying occurrence of motifs (Mocca). It produces alignment in the aln format (Clustal) by default, but can also produce PIR, MSF and FASTA format. The most common input formats are supported (FASTA, PIR).

Comparisons with other alignment software

While the default output is a Clustal-like format, it is sufficiently different from the output of ClustalW/X that many programs supporting Clustal format cannot read it; fortunately ClustalX *can* import T-Coffee output so the simplest fix for this issue is usually to import T-Coffee's output into ClustalX and then re-export. Another possibility is to request the strict Clustalw output format with the option `"-output=clustalw_aln"`

An important specificity of T-Coffee is its ability to combine different methods and different data types. In its latest version, T-Coffee can be used to combine protein sequences and structures, RNA sequences and structures. It can also run and combine the output of the most common sequence and structure alignment packages. For a complete list see: tclinkdb.txt [3]

T-Coffee comes along with a sophisticated sequence reformatting utility named seq_reformat. An extensive documentation is available from t_coffee_technical.htm [4] along with a tutorial t_coffee_tutorial.htm [5]

Variations

M-Coffee

M-Coffee is a special mode of T-Coffee that makes it possible to combine the output of the most common multiple sequence alignment packages (Muscle, ClustalW, Mafft, ProbCons, etc.). The resulting alignments are slightly better than the individual one, but most important the program indicates the alignment regions where the various packages agree upon. Regions of high agreement are usually well aligned.

Expresso and 3D-Coffee

These are special modes of T-Coffee making it possible to combine sequence and structures in an alignment. The structure based alignments can be carried out using the most common structural aligners such as TMalign, Mustang, and sap.

R-Coffee

R-Coffee is a special mode of T-Coffee making it possible to align RNA sequences while using secondary structure information.

References

[1] http://www.tcoffee.org
[2] Notredame C, Higgins DG, Heringa J (2000-09-08). "T-Coffee: A novel method for fast and accurate multiple sequence alignment". *J Mol Biol*. **302** (1): 205–217. doi:10.1006/jmbi.2000.4042. PMID 10964570.
[3] http://www.tcoffee.org/Resources/tclinkdb.txt
[4] http://www.tcoffee.org/Documentation/t_coffee/t_coffee_technical.htm
[5] http://www.tcoffee.org/Documentation/t_coffee/t_coffee_tutorial.htm

External links

- T-Coffee Home Page (http://www.tcoffee.org)
- T-Coffee Aligner Server (http://tcoffee.crg.cat)
- T-Coffee download page (http://www.tcoffee.org/Projects_home_page/t_coffee_home_page.html)
- Technical documentation (http://www.tcoffee.org/Documentation/t_coffee/t_coffee_technical.htm)
- Tutorial (http://www.tcoffee.org/Documentation/t_coffee/t_coffee_tutorial.htm)
- List of third party aligners supported by T-Coffee (http://www.tcoffee.org/Resources/tclinkdb.txt)

Template Modeling Score (bioinformatics)

The **Template Modeling Score** or **TM-score** is a measure of similarity between two protein structures with different tertiary structures. The TM-score is intended as a more accurate measure of the quality of full-length protein structures than the often used RMSD and GDT measures. The TM-score indicates the difference between two structures by a score between $(0, 1]$, where 1 indicates a perfect match between two structures[1]. Generally scores below 0.20 corresponds to randomly chosen unrelated proteins whereas structures with a score higher than 0.5 assume roughly the same fold[2]. A quantitative study [3] shows that proteins of TM-score = 0.5 have a posterior probability of 37% in the same CATH Topology family and of 13% in the same SCOP Fold family. The probabilities increase rapidly when TM-score >0.5. The TM-score is designed to be independent of protein lengths.

The equation

$$\text{TM-score} = \max \left[\frac{1}{L_{\text{target}}} \sum_i^{L_{\text{aligned}}} \frac{1}{1 + \left(\frac{d_i}{d_0(L_{\text{target}})} \right)^2} \right]$$

where L_{target} and L_{aligned} are the lengths of the target protein and the aligned region respectively. d_i is the distance between the i th pair of residues and

$$d_0(L_{\text{target}}) = 1.24 \sqrt[3]{L_{\text{target}} - 15} - 1.8$$

is a distance scale that normalizes distances.

References

[1] Zhang Y and Skolnick J (2004). "Scoring function for automated assessment of protein structure template quality". *Proteins* **57** (4): 702–710. doi:10.1002/prot.20264. PMID 15476259.

[2] Zhang Y and Skolnick J (2005). "TM-align: a protein structure alignment algorithm based on the TM-score". *Nucleic Acids Res* **33** (7): 2302–2309. doi:10.1093/nar/gki524. PMC 1084323. PMID 15849316.

[3] Xu J and Zhang Y (2010). "How significant is a protein structure similarity with TM-score=0.5?". *Bioinformatics* **26** (7): 889–895. doi:10.1093/bioinformatics/btq066. PMC 2913670. PMID 20164152.

External links

- TM-score webserver (http://zhanglab.ccmb.med.umich.edu/TM-score/) — by the Yang Zhang research group. Calculates TM-score and supplies source code.

The Genomic HyperBrowser

The Genomic HyperBrowser [1] is a web-based system for statistical analysis of genomic annotation data. The primary focus is on statistical inference on relations between genomic tracks, though simpler descriptive statistics and analysis of individual tracks is also supported. An example of analysis is to investigate the relationship between histone modifications and gene expression, using ChIP-based tracks of histone modifications versus tracks of genes marked with expression values from a microarray experiment. The web server includes a sizable collection of annotation tracks, and also supports user-uploaded tracks. The Genomic HyperBrowser runs as a stand-alone system, but is tightly integrated with the Galaxy system for handling of genomic data, especially at the user interface side.

History

The Genomic HyperBrowser has been developed since early 2008 in Oslo, Norway, and went public in December 2010.

References

[1] Geir K Sandve, Sveinung Gundersen, Halfdan Rydbeck, Ingrid Glad, Lars Holden, Marit Holden, Knut Liestol, Trevor Clancy, Egil Ferkingstad, Morten Johansen, Vegard Nygaard, Eivind Tostesen, Arnoldo Frigessi and Eivind Hovig: The Genomic HyperBrowser: inferential genomics at the sequence level. Genome Biology 2010, 11:R121 (http://genomebiology.com/2010/11/12/R121)

External links

HyperBrowser web server (http://hyperbrowser.uio.no)

Threading (protein sequence)

Protein threading, also known as **fold recognition**, is a method of protein modeling (i.e. computational protein structure prediction) which is used to model those proteins which have the same fold as proteins of known structures, but do not have homologous proteins with known structure. It differs from the homology modeling method of structure prediction as it (protein threading) is used for proteins which do not have their homologous protein structures deposited in the Protein Data Bank (PDB), whereas homology modeling is used for those proteins which do. Threading works by using statistical knowledge of the relationship between the structures deposited in the PDB and the sequence of the protein which one wishes to model.

The prediction is made by "threading" (i.e. placing, aligning) each amino acid in the target sequence to a position in the template structure, and evaluating how well the target fits the template. After the best-fit template is selected, the structural model of the sequence is built based on the alignment with the chosen template. Protein threading is based on two basic observations: that the number of different folds in nature is fairly small (approximately 1300); and that 90% of the new structures submitted to the PDB in the past three years have similar structural folds to ones already in the PDB (according to the CATH release notes [1]).

Classification of protein structure

The Structural Classification of Proteins (SCOP) database provides a detailed and comprehensive description of the structural and evolutionary relationships of known structure. Proteins are classified to reflect both structural and evolutionary relatedness. Many levels exist in the hierarchy, but the principal levels are family, superfamily and fold, as described below.

Family (clear evolutionary relationship)

> Proteins clustered together into families are clearly evolutionarily related. Generally, this means that pairwise residue identities between the proteins are 30% and greater. However, in some cases similar functions and structures provide definitive evidence of common descent in the absence of high sequence identity; for example, many globins form a family though some members have sequence identities of only 15%.

Superfamily (probable common evolutionary origin)

> Proteins that have low sequence identities, but whose structural and functional features suggest that a common evolutionary origin is probable, are placed together in superfamilies. For example, actin, the ATPase domain of the heat shock protein, and hexakinase together form a superfamily.

Fold (major structural similarity)

> Proteins are defined as having a common fold if they have the same major secondary structures in the same arrangement and with the same topological connections. Different proteins with the same fold often have peripheral elements of secondary structure and turn regions that differ in size and conformation. In some cases, these differing peripheral regions may comprise half the structure. Proteins placed together in the same fold category may not have a common evolutionary origin: the structural similarities could arise just from the physics and chemistry of proteins favoring certain packing arrangements and chain topologies.

Method

A general paradigm of protein threading consists of the following four steps:

The construction of a structure template database

> Select protein structures from the protein structure databases as structural templates. This generally involves selecting protein structures from databases such as PDB, FSSP, SCOP, or CATH, after removing protein structures with high sequence similarities.

The design of the scoring function

> Design a good scoring function to measure the fitness between target sequences and templates based on the knowledge of the known relationships between the structures and the sequences. A good scoring function should contain mutation potential, environment fitness potential, pairwise potential, secondary structure compatibilities, and gap penalties. The quality of the energy function is closely related to the prediction accuracy, especially the alignment accuracy.

Threading alignment

> Align the target sequence with each of the structure templates by optimizing the designed scoring function. This step is one of the major tasks of all threading-based structure prediction programs that take into account the pairwise contact potential; otherwise, a dynamic programming algorithm can fulfill it.

Threading prediction

> Select the threading alignment that is statistically most probable as the threading prediction. Then construct a structure model for the target by placing the backbone atoms of the target sequence at their aligned backbone positions of the selected structural template.

Comparison with homology modeling

Homology modeling and protein threading are both template-based methods and there is no rigorous boundary between them in terms of prediction techniques. But the protein structures their targets are different. Homology modeling is for those targets which have homologous proteins with known structure(usually/may be of same family), while protein threading is for those targets with only fold-level homology found. In other words, homology modeling is for "easier" targets and protein threading is for "harder" targets.

Homology modeling treats the template in an alignment as a sequence, and only sequence homology is used for prediction. Protein threading treats the template in an alignment as a structure, and both sequence and structure information extracted from the alignment are used for prediction. When there is no significant homology found, protein threading can make a prediction based on the structure information. That also explains why protein threading may be more effective than homology modeling in many cases.

In practice, when the sequence identity in a sequence sequence alignment is low (i.e. <25%), homology modeling may not produce a significant prediction. In this case, if there is distant homology found for the target, protein threading can generate a good prediction.

More about threading

Fold recognition methods can be broadly divided into two types: **1**, those that derive a 1-D profile for each structure in the fold library and align the target sequence to these profiles; and **2**, those that consider the full 3-D structure of the protein template. A simple example of a profile representation would be to take each amino acid in the structure and simply label it according to whether it is buried in the core of the protein or exposed on the surface. More elaborate profiles might take into account the local secondary structure (e.g. whether the amino acid is part of an alpha helix) or even evolutionary information (how conserved the amino acid is). In the 3-D representation, the structure is modeled as a set of inter-atomic distances, i.e. the distances are calculated between some or all of the atom pairs in the structure. This is a much richer and far more flexible description of the structure, but is much harder to use in calculating an alignment. The profile-based fold recognition approach was first described by Bowie, Lüthy and Eisenberg in 1991.[2] The term *threading* was first coined by Jones, Taylor and Thornton in 1992,[3] and originally referred specifically to the use of a full 3-D structure atomic representation of the protein template in fold recognition. Today, the terms threading and fold recognition are frequently (though somewhat incorrectly) used interchangeably.

Fold recognition methods are widely used and effective because it is believed that there are a strictly limited number of different protein folds in nature, mostly as a result of evolution but also due to constraints imposed by the basic physics and chemistry of polypeptide chains. There is, therefore, a good chance (currently 70-80%) that a protein which has a similar fold to the target protein has already been studied by X-ray crystallography or nuclear magnetic resonance (NMR) spectroscopy and can be found in the PDB. Currently there are nearly 1300 different protein folds known (see CATH database statistics [4] for latest view), but new folds are still being discovered every year due in significant part to the ongoing structural genomics projects.

Many different algorithms have been proposed for finding the correct threading of a sequence onto a structure, though many make use of dynamic programming in some form. For full 3-D threading, the problem of identifying the best alignment is very difficult (it is an NP-hard problem for some models of threading). Researchers have made use of many combinatorial optimization methods such as Conditional random fields, simulated annealing, branch and bound and linear programming, searching to arrive at heuristic solutions.

It is interesting to compare threading methods to methods which attempt to align two protein structures (protein structural alignment), and indeed many of the same algorithms have been applied to both problems.

Protein threading software

- HHpred is a popular threading server which runs HHsearch, a widely used software for remote homology detection based on pairwise comparison of hidden Markov models.
- RAPTOR (software) is an integer programming based protein threading software. The original developer of RAPTOR has designed a new protein threading program RaptorX / software for protein modeling and analysis, employing a very different methodology[5] [6] [7]. RaptorX significantly outperforms RAPTOR and is especially good at aligning proteins with sparse sequence profile. The RaptorX server is free to public at RaptorX [45].
- Phyre is a popular threading server combining HHsearch with *ab initio* and multiple-template modelling.
- MUSTER [8] is a standard threading algorithm based on dynamic programming and sequence profile-profile alignment. It also combines multiple structural resources to assist the sequence profile alignment.[9]

References

[1] http://www.cathdb.info/wiki/doku.php?id=release_notes1
[2] Bowie JU, Lüthy R, Eisenberg D (1991). "A method to identify protein sequences that fold into a known three-dimensional structure". *Science* **253** (5016): 164–170. doi:10.1126/science.1853201. PMID 1853201.
[3] Jones DT, Taylor WR, Thornton JM (1992). "A new approach to protein fold recognition". *Nature* **358** (6381): 86–89. doi:10.1038/358086a0. PMID 1614539.
[4] http://www.cathdb.info/wiki/doku.php?id=release_notes
[5] Peng, Jian; Jinbo Xu (2011). "RaptorX: exploiting structure information for protein alignment by statistical inference" (http://onlinelibrary. wiley.com/doi/10.1002/prot.23175/abstract). *Proteins*: n/a. doi:10.1002/prot.23175. .
[6] Peng, Jian; Jinbo Xu (2010). "Low-homology protein threading" (http://bioinformatics.oxfordjournals.org/content/26/12/i294.abstract). *Bioinformatics* **26** (12): i294–i300. doi:10.1093/bioinformatics/btq192. PMC 2881377. PMID 20529920. .
[7] Peng, Jian; Jinbo Xu (April 2011). "A multiple-template approach to protein threading". *Proteins* **79** (6). doi:10.1002/prot.23016/pdf.
[8] http://zhanglab.ccmb.med.umich.edu/MUSTER/
[9] Wu S, Zhang Y (2008). "MUSTER: Improving protein sequence profile–profile alignments by using multiple sources of structure information". *Proteins* **72** (2): 547–56. doi:10.1002/prot.21945. PMC 2666101. PMID 18247410.

Further reading

- Lathrop RH (1994). "The protein threading problem with sequence amino acid interaction preferences is NP-complete". *Protein Eng* **7** (9): 1059–1068. doi:10.1093/protein/7.9.1059. PMID 7831276.
- Jones DT, Hadley C (2000). "Threading methods for protein structure prediction". In Higgins D, Taylor WR. *Bioinformatics: Sequence, structure and databanks.* Heidelberg: Springer-Verlag. pp. 1–13.
- Xu J, Li M, Kim D, Xu Y (2003). "RAPTOR: Optimal Protein Threading by Linear Programming, the inaugural issue". *J Bioinform Comput Biol* **1** (1): 95–117. doi:10.1142/S0219720003000186. PMID 15290783.
- Xu J, Li M, Lin G, Kim D, Xu Y (2003). "Protein threading by linear programming". *Pac Symp Biocomput*: 264–275. PMID 12603034.

Top-down proteomics

Top-down proteomics is a method of protein identification that uses an ion trapping mass spectrometer to store an isolated protein ion for mass measurement and tandem mass spectrometry analysis.[1] [2] The name is derived from the similar approach to DNA seqencing.[3] Proteins are typically ionized by electrospray ionization and trapped in a Fourier transform ion cyclotron resonance (Penning trap)[4] or quadrupole ion trap (Paul trap) mass spectrometer. Fragmentation for tandem mass spectrometry is accomplished by electron-capture dissociation or electron-transfer dissociation.

Recently, a top-down approach has been developed for mapping the connectivity of the disulfide-rich peptide hedyotide B2 [5] . This method allows rapid characterization of the disulfide pattern of cystine-knot miniproteins such as cyclotides, conotoxin, knottin and plant defensins.

References

[1] Sze SK, Ge Y, Oh H, McLafferty FW (2002). "Top-down mass spectrometry of a 29-kDa protein for characterization of any posttranslational modification to within one residue". *Proc. Natl. Acad. Sci. U.S.A.* **99** (4): 1774–9. doi:10.1073/pnas.251691898. PMC 122269. PMID 11842225.

[2] Kelleher NL (2004). "Top-down proteomics". *Anal. Chem.* **76** (11): 197A–203A. doi:10.1021/ac0415657. PMID 15190879.

[3] Smith CL, Cantor CR (1989). "Evolving strategies for making physical maps of mammalian chromosomes". *Genome* **31** (2): 1055–8. PMID 2698822.

[4] Bogdanov B, Smith RD (2005). "Proteomics by FTICR mass spectrometry: top down and bottom up". *Mass spectrometry reviews* **24** (2): 168–200. doi:10.1002/mas.20015. PMID 15389855.

[5] Nguyen GK, Zhang S, Wang W, Wong CT, Nguyen NT, Tam JP: Discovery of a linear cyclotide from the bracelet subfamily and its disulfide mapping by top-down mass spectrometry. J Biol Chem. http://www.jbc.org/content/early/2011/10/06/jbc.M111.290296.abstract

Bibliography

- Borchers CH, Thapar R, Petrotchenko EV, *et al.* (2006). "Combined top-down and bottom-up proteomics identifies a phosphorylation site in stem-loop-binding proteins that contributes to high-affinity RNA binding". *Proc. Natl. Acad. Sci. U.S.A.* **103** (9): 3094–9. doi:10.1073/pnas.0511289103. PMC 1413926. PMID 16492733.
- Han X, Jin M, Breuker K, McLafferty FW (2006). "Extending top-down mass spectrometry to proteins with masses greater than 200 kilodaltons". *Science* **314** (5796): 109–12. doi:10.1126/science.1128868. PMID 17023655.
- Whitelegge J, Halgand F, Souda P, Zabrouskov V (2006). "Top-down mass spectrometry of integral membrane proteins". *Expert review of proteomics* **3** (6): 585–96. doi:10.1586/14789450.3.6.585. PMID 17181473.

TRANSFAC

TRANSFAC

Content		
Description	Transcription Factor Database	
Data types captured	Eukaryotic transcription factors, their binding sites and binding profiles	
Organism(s)	eukaryotes	
Contact		
Research center	Helmholtz Centre for Infection Research; BIOBASE GmbH	
Primary Citation	Wingender (2008)[1]	
Release date	1988	
Access		
Website	[2]	
Tools		
Miscellaneous		

TRANSFAC (TRANScription FACtor database) is a manually curated database of eukaryotic transcription factors, their genomic binding sites and DNA binding profiles. The contents of the database can be used to predict potential transcription factor binding sites.

Introduction

The origin of the database was an early data collection published 1988.[3] The first version that was released under the name TRANSFAC was developed at the former German National Research Centre for Biotechnology and designed for local installation (now: Helmholtz Centre for Infection Research).[4] In one of the first publicly funded bioinformatics projects, launched in 1993, TRANSFAC developed into a resource that became available on the Internet.[5]

In 1997, TRANSFAC was transferred to a newly established company, BIOBASE, in order to secure long-term financing of the database. Since then, the most up-to-date version has to be licensed, whereas older versions are free for non-commercial users.[6] [7]

Content and Features

The content of the database is organized in a way that it is centered around the interaction between transcription factors (TFs) and their DNA binding sites (TFBS). TFs are described with regard to their structural and functional features, extracted from the original scientific literature. They are classified to families, classes and superclasses according to the features of their DNA binding domains.[8] [9] [10] [11]

Binding of a TF to a genomic site is documented by specifying the localization of the site, its sequence and the experimental method applied. All sites that refer to one TF, or a group of closely related TFs, are aligned and used to construct a position-specific scoring matrix (PSSM), or count matrix. Many matrices of the TRANSFAC matrix library have been constructed by a team of curators, others were taken from scientific publications.

Availability

The usage of an older version of TRANSFAC is free of charge for non-profit users. Access to the most up-to-date version requires a license.

Applications

The TRANSFAC database can be used as an encyclopedia of eukaryotic transcription factors. The target sequences and the regulated genes can be listed for each TF, which can be used as training sets for new TFBS recognition algorithms. The TF classification enables to analyze such data sets with regard to the properties of the DNA-binding domains.[12] Another application is to retrieve all TFs that regulate a given (set of) gene(s). In the context of systems-biological studies, the TF-target gene relations documented in TRANSFAC were used to construct and analyze transcription regulatory networks. [13] [14] By far the most frequent use of TRANSFAC is the computational prediction of potential transcription factor binding sites (TFBS). A number of algorithms exist which either use the individual binding sites or the matrix library for this purpose:

- Patch – analyzes sequence similarities with the binding sites documented in TRANSFAC; it is provided along with the database.[15] [16]
- SiteSeer – analyzes sequence similarities with the binding sites documented in TRANSFAC.[17] [18]
- Match – identifies potential TFBS using the matrix library; it is provided along with the database.[19] [20]
- TESS (Transcription Element Search System) – analyzes sequence similarities with binding sites of TRANSFAC as well as potential binding sites using the matrix libraries of TRANSFAC and three other sources.[21] [22] TESS also provides a program for the identification of cis-regulatory modules (CRMs, characteristic combinations of TFBSs), which uses TRANSFAC matrices.[23]
- PROMO – matrix-based prediction of TFBSs with aid of the commercial database version[24] [25]
- TFM Explorer – Identification of common potential TFBSs in a set of genes[26] [27]
- MotifMogul – matrix-based sequence analysis with a number of different algorithms[28]
- ConTra – matrix-based sequence analysis in conserved promoter regions[29] [30]
- PMS (Poly Matrix Search) – matrix-based sequence analysis in conserved promoter regions [31] [32]

Comparison of matrices with the matrix library of TRANSFAC and other sources:

- T-Reg Comparator[33] to compare individual or groups of matrices with those of TRANSFAC or other libraries.
- MACO (Poly Matrix Search)[34] [35] – matrix comparison with matrix libraries.

A number of servers provide genomic annotations computed with the aid of TRANSFAC.[36] [37] Others have used such analyses to infer target gene sets. [38] [39]

Similar Data Sources

The following resources offer contents that are related to or partially overlapping with TRANSFAC:

- JASPAR – collection of transcription factor binding profiles (matrices) and sequence analysis program
- PLACE – cis-regulatory DNA elements in plants; until February 2007
- PlantCARE – cis-regulatory elements and transcription factors in plants (2002)
- PRODORIC – a similar concept as TRANSFAC for prokaryotes
- RegulonDB – focus on the bacterium *Escherichia coli*
- SCPD – specific collection of data- and tools for yeast (*Saccharomyces cerevisiae*) (1998)
- TFe – the transcription factor encyclopedia
- TRDD – Transcription Regulatory Regions Database, mainly about regulatory regions and TF-binding sites

References

[1] Wingender, E. (2008). "The TRANSFAC project as an example of framework technology that supports the analysis of genomic regulation". *Briefings in Bioinformatics* **9** (4): 326–32. doi:10.1093/bib/bbn016. PMID 18436575.

[2] http://www.gene-regulation.com/pub/databases.html

[3] Wingender, Edgar (1988). "Compilation of transcription regulating proteins". *Nucleic Acids Research* **16** (5): 1879–902. doi:10.1093/nar/16.5.1879. PMC 338188. PMID 3282223.

[4] Wingender E, Heinemeyer T, Lincoln D (1991). "Regulatory DNA sequences: predictability of their function". *Genome Analysis - from Sequence to Function; BioTechForum - Advances in Molecular Genetics (J. Collins, A.J. Driesel, eds.)* **4**: 95–108.

[5] Wingender, E; Dietze, P; Karas, H; Knüppel, R (1996). "TRANSFAC: A database on transcription factors and their DNA binding sites". *Nucleic Acids Research* **24** (1): 238–41. doi:10.1093/nar/24.1.238. PMC 145586. PMID 8594589.

[6] *TRANSFAC Public* (http://www.gene-regulation.com/pub/databases.html#transfac) on the gene regulation portal of BIOBASE

[7] *Access to TRANSFAC Public via TESS* (http://www.cbil.upenn.edu/cgi-bin/tess/tess?RQ=NBqt) at the Computational Biology and Informatics Laboratory (CBIL) of University of Pennsylvania (Penn)

[8] Wingender, E (1997). "Classification of eukaryotic transcription factors". *Molekuliarnaia biologiia* **31** (4): 584–600. PMID 9340487.

[9] Heinemeyer, T; Chen, X; Karas, H; Kel, AE; Kel, OV; Liebich, I; Meinhardt, T; Reuter, I et al. (1999). "Expanding the TRANSFAC database towards an expert system of regulatory molecular mechanisms". *Nucleic Acids Research* **27** (1): 318–22. doi:10.1093/nar/27.1.318. PMC 148171. PMID 9847216.

[10] Stegmaier, P; Kel, AE; Wingender, E (2004). "Systematic DNA-binding domain classification of transcription factors". *Genome informatics* **15** (2): 276–86. PMID 15706513.

[11] Wingender, E: *The classification of transcription factors* (http://www.edgar-wingender.de/TFclass.html)

[12] Narlikar, L.; Gordan, R.; Ohler, U.; Hartemink, A. J. (2006). "Informative priors based on transcription factor structural class improve de novo motif discovery". *Bioinformatics* **22** (14): e384–92. doi:10.1093/bioinformatics/btl251. PMID 16873497.

[13] Goemann, Björn; Wingender, Edgar; Potapov, Anatolij P (2009). "An approach to evaluate the topological significance of motifs and other patterns in regulatory networks". *BMC Systems Biology* **3**: 53. doi:10.1186/1752-0509-3-53. PMC 2694767. PMID 19454001.

[14] Kozhenkov, Sergey; Dubinina, Yulia; Sedova, Mayya; Gupta, Amarnath; Ponomarenko, Julia; Baitaluk, Michael (2010). "BiologicalNetworks 2.0 - an integrative view of genome biology data". *BMC Bioinformatics* **11**: 610. doi:10.1186/1471-2105-11-610. PMC 3019228. PMID 21190573.

[15] *Patch* (http://www.gene-regulation.de/Patch/) on the free portal of BIOBASE

[16] Matys, V. (2006). "TRANSFAC(R) and its module TRANSCompel(R): Transcriptional gene regulation in eukaryotes". *Nucleic Acids Research* **34** (90001): D108. doi:10.1093/nar/gkj143.

[17] *SiteSeer* (http://www.chick.manchester.ac.uk/SiteSeer/) of the University of Manchester

[18] Boardman, P. E.; Oliver, SG; Hubbard, SJ (2003). "SiteSeer: Visualisation and analysis of transcription factor binding sites in nucleotide sequences". *Nucleic Acids Research* **31** (13): 3572–5. doi:10.1093/nar/gkg511. PMC 168918. PMID 12824368.

[19] *Match* (http://www.gene-regulation.de/Match/) on the free portal of BIOBASE

[20] Kel, A.E.; Gössling, E; Reuter, I; Cheremushkin, E; Kel-Margoulis, OV; Wingender, E (2003). "MATCHTM: A tool for searching transcription factor binding sites in DNA sequences". *Nucleic Acids Research* **31** (13): 3576–9. doi:10.1093/nar/gkg585. PMC 169193. PMID 12824369.

[21] *TESS (Transcription Element Search System)* (http://www.cbil.upenn.edu/cgi-bin/tess/) at CBIL of the University of Pennsylvania

[22] *Site Search bei TESS* (http://www.cbil.upenn.edu/cgi-bin/tess/tess?RQ=SEA-FR-Query)

[23] *AnGEL CRM Searches* (http://www.cbil.upenn.edu/cgi-bin/tess/tess?RQ=AnGEL-SearchForm) in the TESS system

[24] *PROMO* (http://alggen.lsi.upc.es/cgi-bin/promo_v3/promo/promoinit.cgi?dirDB=TF_8.3) on the ALGGEN server of the Polytechnic University of Catalonia (UPC)

[25] Messeguer, X.; Escudero, R.; Farre, D.; Nunez, O.; Martinez, J.; Alba, M.M. (2002). "PROMO: Detection of known transcription regulatory elements using species-tailored searches". *Bioinformatics* **18** (2): 333–4. doi:10.1093/bioinformatics/18.2.333. PMID 11847087.

[26] *TFM Explorer* (http://bioinfo.lifl.fr/TFM/TFME/index.php) on the bioinformatics software server of the SEQUOIA group

[27] Tonon, L.; Touzet, H.; Varre, J.-S. (2010). "TFM-Explorer: Mining cis-regulatory regions in genomes". *Nucleic Acids Research* **38** (Web Server issue): W286–92. doi:10.1093/nar/gkq473. PMC 2896114. PMID 20522509.

[28] *MotifMogul* (http://xerad.systemsbiology.net/MotifMogulServer/) of the Institute for Systems Biology in Seattle

[29] *ConTra* (http://bioit.dmbr.ugent.be/ConTra/index.php) of the Ghent University

[30] Hooghe, B.; Hulpiau, P.; Van Roy, F.; De Bleser, P. (2008). "ConTra: A promoter alignment analysis tool for identification of transcription factor binding sites across species". *Nucleic Acids Research* **36** (Web Server issue): W128–32. doi:10.1093/nar/gkn195. PMC 2447729. PMID 18453628.

[31] *PMS* (http://mcube.nju.edu.cn/jwang/lab/?type=software&softname=PMS), developed at the Nanjing University

[32] Su, G; Mao, B; Wang, J (2006). "A web server for transcription factor binding site prediction". *Bioinformation* **1** (5): 156–7. PMC 1891680. PMID 17597879.

[33] *T-Reg Comparator* (http://treg.molgen.mpg.de/) on the server of the Max Planck Institute for Molecular Genetics

[34] *MACO* (http://mcube.nju.edu.cn/jwang/lab/?type=software&softname=MACO), developed at Nanjing University

[35] Su, G; Mao, B; Wang, J (2006). "MACO: A gapped-alignment scoring tool for comparing transcription factor binding sites". *In silico biology* **6** (4): 307–10. PMID 16922693.

[36] *PReMOD* (http://genomequebec.mcgill.ca/PReMod/explore/initmodule.do?method=initSearch): Human and mouse genome of the years 2004 & 2005; IRCM / McGill University, Montreal

[37] *PRIMA* (http://acgt.cs.tau.ac.il/prima/PRIMA.htm): Human genome of 2004; Tel-Aviv University

[38] *MSigDB* (http://www.broadinstitute.org/cancer/software/gsea/wiki/index.php/MSigDB_v3. 0_Release_Notes#Transcription_factor_targets_.28TFT.29): Mammalian transcription factor target gene sets; GSEA wiki server of Broad Institute of MIT and Harvard, Cambridge, MA

[39] Xie, Xiaohui; Lu, Jun; Kulbokas, E. J.; Golub, Todd R.; Mootha, Vamsi; Lindblad-Toh, Kerstin; Lander, Eric S.; Kellis, Manolis (2005). "Systematic discovery of regulatory motifs in human promoters and 3′ UTRs by comparison of several mammals". *Nature* **434** (7031): 338–45. doi:10.1038/nature03441. PMC 2923337. PMID 15735639.

External links

- History of the TRANSFAC database (http://www.edgar-wingender.de/TRANSFAC.html) on the homepage of Edgar Wingender
- What is the TRANSFAC database? (http://lane.stanford.edu/howto/index.html?id=2697) at Lane Medical Library, Stanford University School of Medicine

Translational research informatics

Translational Research Informatics (TRI) is a sister domain to or a sub-domain of Biomedical informatics or Medical Informatics concerned with the application of informatics theory and methods to translational research. There is some overlap with the related domain of Clinical Research Informatics, but TRI is more concerned with enabling multi-disciplinary research to accelerate clinical outcomes, with clinical trials often being the natural step beyond translational research.

Translational Research as defined by the National Institutes of Health [1] includes two areas of translation. One is the process of applying discoveries generated during research in the laboratory, and in preclinical studies, to the development of trials and studies in humans. The second area of translation concerns research aimed at enhancing the adoption of best practices in the community. Cost-effectiveness of prevention and treatment strategies is also an important part of translational research.

Overview of Translational Research Informatics

Translational Research Informatics can be described as "An integrated software solution to manage the: (i) logistics, (ii) data integration, and (iii) collaboration, required by translational investigators and their supporting institutions." It is the class of informatics systems that sits between and often interoperates with: (i) Health Information Technology/Electronic Medical Record systems, (ii) CTMS/Clinical Research Informatics, and (iii) statistical analysis and data mining.

Translational Research Informatics is relatively new, with most CTSA [2] awardee academic medical centers actively acquiring and integrating systems to enable the end-to-end TRI requirements. One advanced TRI system is being implemented at the Windber Research Institute in collaboration with GenoLogics [3] and InforSense. Translational Research Informatics systems are expected to rapidly develop and evolve over the next couple of years.

Systems in Translational Research Informatics

System Type	Description of System
Translational Study Management	Systems to manage investigator lead biomarker validation studies / outcomes / observational studies.
Electronic Patient Questionnaires	Web based forms for capturing participant demographic, condition, treatment, and outcomes information.
Clinical Information Management	Systems to integrate clinical annotations extracted from various sources systems, like HL7 Electronic Medical Records, Cancer Registries, Clinical Data Management Systems, and Clinical Data Warehouses.
Biorepository Management Systems	Manage biospecimens derrived from study participants, operating rooms, etc.
Laboratory Information Management Systems	Systems to manage clinical, analytical, and life sciences core technology laboratories - often conducting genomics, proteomics, metabolomics, molecular imaging, peptide synthesis, flow cytometry, etc.
Systems Biology / Science Data Management	A data base and content management system to archive raw instrument files and database science results data.
Research Collaboration System	A software solution to enable investigators and their research teams to share project information, results data, and insights.

CTRI Dedicated WIKI

Further discussion of this domain can be found at the Clinical Research Informatics Wiki (CRI Wiki) [4], a wiki dedicated to issues in Clinical and Translational Research Informatics.

Related Web Sites

ResearchInformatics.org [5]
NIH Roadmap [2]
Clinical and Translational Science Awards [6]
American Medical Informatics Association (AMIA) [7]

References

[1] http://www.nih.gov/
[2] http://www.ctsaweb.org/
[3] http://www.genologics.com
[4] http://www.researchinformatics.org/index.php?option=com_mambowiki&page=Main_Page&page_heading=CRI%20Wiki&show_pageheading=1&allowanonymoususers=0
[5] http://www.researchinformatics.org
[6] http://ctsaweb.org/
[7] http://www.amia.org

Ubuntu-Med

The **Ubuntu-Med** project is a Kubuntu-based operating system customization created to provide a co-ordinated operating system and collection of available free software packages that are suited to the requirements of medical practices and research.

Packages

Ubuntu-Med includes packages in the categories:

- Electronic health record (electronic medical record) server / client systems:
  - OpenVistA EHR
- Medical practice and patient management
- Medical imaging
- Documentation and research
- Other software:
  - Website software (Drupal)
  - Wiki software (MediaWiki)
  - Group calendaring server (DAViCal)
  - Teleconferencing server (BigBlueButton)
  - Patient education / online teaching server (Moodle)

All software and packages are open-source, with a goal of GPL-licensure.

This system has been in use by some medical practitioners.[1]

Availability

Ubuntu-Med is available as a self-installing Live CD image (which is a Kubuntu remaster) or as a Filesystem Archive. Both are available from the project website [2] at Sourceforge.

References

[1] "Ubuntu Doctors Guild: Community Portal" (http://www.ubuntudoctorsguild.org/public/index.php/
    Ubuntu_Doctors_Guild:Community_Portal). Ubuntu Doctors Guild (Jan 2010). .
[2] http://sourceforge.net/projects/ubuntu-med/

External links

- **Ubuntu-Med** – Homepage of the Project (http://kubuntuguide.org/Ubuntu-Med_FAQ/)

Related projects

- Debian-Med - a collection of packages intended for use in medical situations for Debian-based operating systems
- Project **EU Spirit** (http://www.euspirit.org/) – European portal for open-source based software in medicine
- **Open Med** (http://www.openmed.org/) – Support for free medical software (German)

UCSC Genome Browser

The UCSC Genome Browser

Content	
Description	The UCSC Genome Browser
Contact	
Research center	University of California Santa Cruz
Laboratory	Center for Biomolecular Science and Engineering, Baskin School of Engineering,
Primary Citation	Fujita & al. (2011)[1]
Access	
Website	http://genome.ucsc.edu
Tools	
Miscellaneous	

The University of California, Santa Cruz (UCSC) Genome Browser [2] [3] [4] is an up-to-date source for genome sequence data from a variety of vertebrate and invertebrate species and major model organisms, integrated with a large collection of aligned annotations. The Browser is a graphical viewer optimized to support fast interactive performance and is an open-source, web-based tool suite built on top of a MySQL database for rapid visualization, examination, and querying of the data at many levels. The Genome Browser Database, browsing tools, downloadable data files, and documentation can all be found on the UCSC Genome Bioinformatics website [2].

History

Initially built and still managed by Jim Kent, then a graduate student, and David Haussler, professor of Computer Science (now Biomolecular Engineering) at the University of California, Santa Cruz in 2000, the UCSC Genome Browser began as a resource for the distribution of the initial fruits of the Human Genome Project. Funded by the Howard Hughes Medical Institute and the National Human Genome Research Institute, NHGRI (one of the US National Institutes of Health), the browser offered a graphical display of the first full-chromosome draft assembly of human genome sequence. Today the browser is used by geneticists, molecular biologists and physicians as well as students and teachers of evolution for access to genomic information.

Genomes

In the years since its inception, the UCSC Browser has expanded to accommodate genome sequences of all vertebrate species and selected invertebrates for which high-coverage genomic sequences is available,[5] now including 46 species. High coverage is necessary to allow overlap to guide the construction of larger contiguous regions. Genomic sequences with less coverage are included in multiple-alignment tracks on some browsers, but the fragmented nature of these assemblies does not make them suitable for building full featured browsers. (more below on multiple-alignment tracks). The species hosted with full-featured genome browsers are shown in the table.

primates	non-primate mammals	non-mammal chordates	invertebrates
human	mouse	chicken	lancelet
chimpanzee	rat	zebra finch	sea squirt
orangutan	guinea pig	lizard	sea urchin
rhesus macaque	rabbit	frog (*Xenopus tropicalis*)	*11 Drosophila* flies
marmoset	cat	zebrafish	mosquito
	dog	Tetraodon (pufferfish)	honey bee
	panda	Fugu (pufferfish)	*C. elegans* + 5 other worms
	horse	stickleback	Aplysia (sea hare)
	pig	medaka	yeast
	cow	lamprey	
	elephant		
	opossum		
	platypus		

Browser Functionality

The large amount of data about biological systems that is accumulating in the literature makes it necessary to collect and digest information using the tools of bioinformatics. The UCSC Genome Browser presents a diverse collection of annotation datasets (known as "tracks" and presented graphically), including mRNA alignments, mappings of DNA repeat elements, gene predictions, gene-expression data, disease-association data (representing the relationships of genes to diseases), and mappings of commercially available gene chips (e.g., Illumina and Agilent). The basic paradigm of display is to show the genome sequence in the horizontal dimension, and show graphical representations of the locations of the mRNAs, gene predictions, etc. Blocks of color along the coordinate axis show the locations of the alignments of the various data types. The ablitiy to show this large variety of data types on a single coordinate axis makes the browser a handy tool for the vertical integration of the data.

To find a specific gene or genomic region, the user may type in the gene name, (e.g., BRCA1 [6]) an accession number for an RNA, the name of a genomic cytological band (e.g., 20p13 for band 13 on the short arm of chr20) or a chromosomal position (chr17:38,450,000-38,531,000 for the region around the gene BRCA1)

Presenting the data in the graphical format allows the browser to present link access to detailed information about any of the annotations. The gene details page [7] of the UCSC Genes track provides a large number of links to more specific information about the gene at many other data resources, such as Online Mendelian Inheritance in Man (OMIM) and SwissProt.

Designed for the presentation of complex and voluminous data, the UCSC Browser is optimized for speed. By pre-aligning the 55 million RNAs of GenBank to each of the 81 genome assemblies (many of the 46 species have more than one assembly), the browser allows instant access to the alignments of any RNA to any of the hosted species.

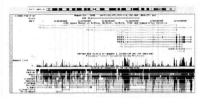

Multiple gene products of FOXP2 gene (top) and
evolutionary conservation shown in multiple
alignment (bottom)

The juxtaposition of the many types of data allow researchers to display exactly the combination of data that will answer specific questions. A pdf/postscript output functionality allows export of a camera-ready image for publication in academic journals.

One unique and useful feature that distinguishes the UCSC Browser from other genome browsers is the continuously variable nature of the display. Sequence of any size can displayed, from a single DNA base up to the entire chromosome (human chr1 = 245 million bases, Mb) with full annotation tracks. Researchers can display a single gene, a single exon, or an entire chromosome band, showing dozens or hundreds of genes and any combination of the many annotations. A convenient drag-and-zoom feature allows the user to choose any region in the genome image and expand it to occupy the full screen.

Researchers may also use the browser to display their own data via the Custom Tracks tool. This feature allows users to upload a file of their own data and view the data in the context of the reference genome assembly. Users may also use the data hosted by UCSC, creating subsets of the data of their choosing with the Table Browser tool (such as only the SNPs that change the amino acid sequence of a protein) and display this specific subset of the data in the browser as a Custom Track.

Any browser view created by a user, including those containing Custom Tracks, may be shared with other users via the Saved Sessions tool.

Variation data

Many types of variation data are also displayed. For example, the entire contents of each release of the dbSNP database from NCBI are mapped to human, mouse and other genomes. This includes the fruits of the 1000 Genomes Project, as soon as they are released in dbSNP. Other types of variation data include copy-number variation data (CNV) and human population allele frequencies from the HapMap project.

The Genome Browser offers a unique set of comparative-genomic data for most of the species hosted on the site. The comparative alignments give a graphical view of the evolutionary relationships among species. This makes it a useful tool both for the researcher, who can visualize regions of conservation among a group of species and make predictions about functional elements in unknown DNA regions, and in the classroom as a tool to illustrate one of the most compelling arguments for the evolution of species. The 44-way comparative track on the human assembly clearly shows that the farther one goes back in evolutionary time, the less sequence homology remains, but functionally important regions of the genome (e.g., exons and control elements, but not introns typically) are conserved much farther back in evolutionary time.

Analysis tools

More than simply a genome browser, the UCSC site hosts a set of genome analysis tools, including a full-featured GUI interface for mining the information in the browser database (the Table Browser [8]), a fast sequence alignment tool (BLAT [9] [10]) that is also useful for simply finding sequences in the massive sequence (human genome = 2.8 billion bases, Gb) of any of the featured genomes. A liftOver tool uses whole-genome alignments to allow conversion of sequences from one assembly to another or between species. The Genome Graphs [11] tool allows users to view all chromosomes at once and display the results of genome-wide association studies (GWAS). The Gene Sorter [12] displays genes grouped by parameters not linked to genome location, such as expression pattern in tissues.

Creating spreadsheet links to UCSC Genome Browser views

Many users of the Genome Browser gather data of their own in Excel spreadsheets and would like to create links to the Browser using data in the spreadsheet. For example, a clinical geneticist may have lists of regions for a patient that are duplicated or deleted, as determined by comparative genomic hybridization (CGH). These regions can be the source information for a browser view allowing access to each region with a single click.

Click to download the spreadsheet: ucscLinks.xls [13]

* chrom	start	end	hg18 links	hg19 links	
3	12000000	15000000	ucsc	ucsc	
chr3	12000000	15000000	ucsc	ucsc	
*NOTE: Different chromNames require different excel link					
chrN is standard ucsc format					
		gene			
		FGFR1	ucsc	ucsc	
		EGFR	ucsc	ucsc	
		position			
		15q11	ucsc	ucsc	
chr3:12000000-15000000			ucsc	ucsc	

Careful use of Excel's "copy" and "move" functions should allow the links on this sheet to be used without modification.

Customizing the links

The contents of the last cell in the image above (cell G22 in the actual spreadsheet) are as follows:

```
=HYPERLINK("http://genome.ucsc.edu/cgi-bin/hgTracks?db=hg19&position="&E22&"&dgv=pack&knownGene=pack&omimGene=pack","ucsc")
```

This example shows how to create a link that turns on specific tracks of interest. In this case, three tracks are explicitly turned on:

```
Database of Genomic Variants (table: dgv)
UCSC Genes (table: knownGene)
OMIM Genes (table: omimGene)
```

Each track is set to "pack" in the link as follows:

```
dgv=pack
knownGene=pack
omimGene=pack
```

Any track that has been open in a session will remain in the view when the new browser window opens.

A new track can be added using the tableName and a visibility of choice:

```
&snp131=dense
```

Simply add to the end of the url any other desired tableName=visibility, connected to the url by an ampersand (&). The simplest way to learn the name of the table underlying a track is to do a mouseover in a Genome Browser image and read the url at the bottom of the browser page. The table is shown in the url as

```
g=tableName
```

Visibility options include:

```
hide
dense
squish
pack
full
```

Open Source / Mirrors

The UCSC Browser code base is open-source for non-commercial use, and is mirrored locally by many research groups, allowing private display of data in the context of the public data. The UCSC Browser is mirrored at several locations world-wide, as shown in the table.

mirror sites
Medical College of Wisconsin [14]
Cornell University [15], NY
Duke University [16], NC
University of Copenhagen [17], Denmark
Queensland Facility for Advanced Bioinformatics [18] (QFAB), Australia

The Browser code is also used in separate installations by the UCSC Malaria Genome Browser and the Archaea Browser [19].

References

[1] Fujita, Pauline A; Rhead Brooke, Zweig Ann S, Hinrichs Angie S, Karolchik Donna, Cline Melissa S, Goldman Mary, Barber Galt P, Clawson Hiram, Coelho Antonio, Diekhans Mark, Dreszer Timothy R, Giardine Belinda M, Harte Rachel A, Hillman-Jackson Jennifer, Hsu Fan, Kirkup Vanessa, Kuhn Robert M, Learned Katrina, Li Chin H, Meyer Laurence R, Pohl Andy, Raney Brian J, Rosenbloom Kate R, Smith Kayla E, Haussler David, Kent W James (Jan 2011). "The UCSC Genome Browser database: update 2011" (in eng). *Nucleic Acids Res.* (England) **39** (Database issue): D876-82. doi:10.1093/nar/gkq963. PMID 20959295.

[2] http://genome.ucsc.edu

[3] Kent WJ, Sugnet CW, Furey TS, Roskin KM, Pringle TH, Zahler AM, Haussler D. The human genome browser at UCSC (http://genome. cshlp.org/content/12/6/996.abstract). Genome Res. 2002 Jun;12(6):996-1006.

[4] Kuhn, RM, Karolchik D, Zweig AS, Wang T, Smith KE, Rosenbloom KR, Rhead B, Raney BJ, Pohl A, Pheasant M, Meyer L, Hsu F, Hinrichs AS, Harte RA, Giardine B, Fujita P, Diekhans M, Dreszer T, Clawson H, Barber GP, Haussler D, Kent WJ. The UCSC Genome Browser Database: update 2009 (http://nar.oxfordjournals.org/cgi/content/full/gkn875?ijkey=BfMrx3EebvOa1Wb&keytype=ref). Nucleic Acids Res. 2009 Jan; 37:D755-D761

[5] "High-coverage" here means 6x coverage, or six times more total sequence than the size of the genome.

[6] http://genome.ucsc.edu/cgi-bin/hgTracks?position=chr17:38449840-38530657&knownGene=pack&hgFind.matches=uc002ico.1& db=hg18

[7] http://genome.ucsc.edu/cgi-bin/hgGene?hgg_gene=uc002ico.1&hgg_prot=P38398&hgg_chrom=chr17&hgg_start=38449839& hgg_end=38530657&hgg_type=knownGene&db=hg18

[8] http://genome.ucsc.edu/cgi-bin/hgTables

[9] http://genome.ucsc.edu/cgi-bin/hgBlat

[10] Kent WJ. BLAT - the BLAST-like alignment tool (http://genome.cshlp.org/content/12/4/656.abstract). Genome Res. 2002
        Apr;12(4):656-64.
[11] http://genome.ucsc.edu/cgi-bin/hgGenome
[12] http://genome.ucsc.edu/cgi-bin/hgNear
[13] http://genomewiki.ucsc.edu/images/0/01/UcscLinks.xls
[14] http://genome.hmgc.mcw.edu/
[15] http://genome-mirror.bscb.cornell.edu/
[16] http://genome-mirror.duhs.duke.edu/
[17] http://genome-mirror.binf.ku.dk/
[18] http://genome.qfab.org
[19] http://archaea.ucsc.edu/

External links

- UCSC Genome Browser (http://genome.ucsc.edu)
- UCSC Genome Browser Tutorials sponsored by the UCSC Group (http://www.openhelix.com/ucscintro)

Uniform Sequence Address

In the Bioinformatics EMBOSS software package, a **Uniform Sequence Address** (USA) is a string defining how the software accesses a biological sequence.

References

- Sourceforge [1] Documentation

References

[1] http://emboss.sourceforge.net/docs/themes/UniformSequenceAddress.html

UniFrac

UniFrac is a method to calculate a distance measure between bacterial communities using phylogenetic information, and is widely used in metagenomics. The method was devised by Catherine Lozupone and Rob Knight of the University of Colorado at Boulder in 2005.[1]

The distance is calculated between pairs of samples (each sample represents a bacterial community). All taxa found in one or both samples are placed on a phylogenetic tree. A branch leading to taxa from both samples is marked as "shared" and branches leading to taxa which appears only in one sample are marked as "unshared". The distance between the two samples is then calculated as (the sum of "shared" branch lengths)/(the sum of all tree branches (= shared+unshared)), i.e. the fraction of shared branch length. This definition satisfies the requirements of a distance metric, being non-negative, zero only when entities are identical, transitive, and conformant to the triangle inequality.

If there are several different samples, a distance matrix can be created, by making a tree for each pair of samples and calculating their UniFrac measure. Later, standard multivariate statistical, methods such as data clustering and principal co-ordinates analysis can be used.

Unifrac also enables to determine if two samples differ significantly, by using Monte Carlo simulations. Namely, randomizing the sample classification of each taxa on the tree (leaving the branch structure unchanged) and creating a distribution of UniFrac distance values. Having a distribution of UniFrac values, a p-value can be given to the actual distance.

References

[1] Lozupone, C; Rob Knight (2005). "UniFrac: a New Phylogenetic Method for Comparing Microbial Communities". *APPLIED AND ENVIRONMENTAL MICROBIOLOGY* **71** (12): 8228–8235. doi:http://aem.asm.org/cgi/content/full/71/12/8228?view=long& pmid=16332807. PMID 16332807.

External links

- UniFrac Online (http://bmf.colorado.edu/unifrac/)

UniProt

UniProt

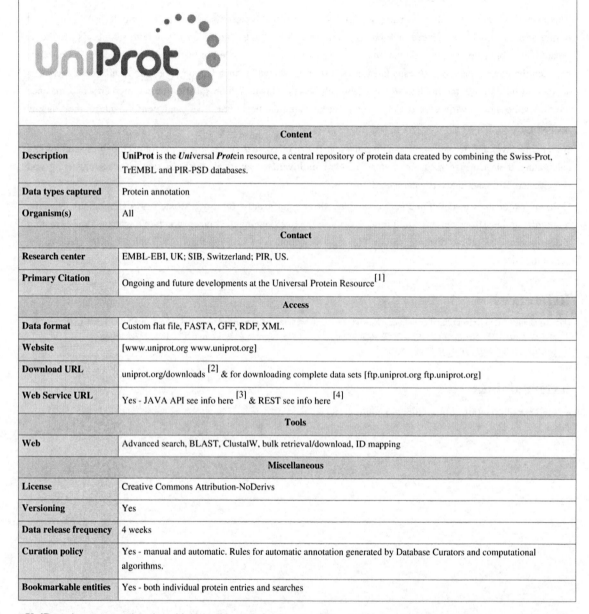

Content	
Description	**UniProt** is the *Uni*versal *Prot*ein resource, a central repository of protein data created by combining the Swiss-Prot, TrEMBL and PIR-PSD databases.
Data types captured	Protein annotation
Organism(s)	All
Contact	
Research center	EMBL-EBI, UK; SIB, Switzerland; PIR, US.
Primary Citation	Ongoing and future developments at the Universal Protein Resource[1]
Access	
Data format	Custom flat file, FASTA, GFF, RDF, XML.
Website	[www.uniprot.org www.uniprot.org]
Download URL	uniprot.org/downloads [2] & for downloading complete data sets [ftp.uniprot.org ftp.uniprot.org]
Web Service URL	Yes - JAVA API see info here [3] & REST see info here [4]
Tools	
Web	Advanced search, BLAST, ClustalW, bulk retrieval/download, ID mapping
Miscellaneous	
License	Creative Commons Attribution-NoDerivs
Versioning	Yes
Data release frequency	4 weeks
Curation policy	Yes - manual and automatic. Rules for automatic annotation generated by Database Curators and computational algorithms.
Bookmarkable entities	Yes - both individual protein entries and searches

UniProt is a comprehensive, high-quality and freely accessible database of protein sequence and functional information, many of which are derived from genome sequencing projects. It contains a large amount of information about the biological function of proteins derived from the research literature.

The UniProt Consortium

The UniProt Consortium comprises the European Bioinformatics Institute (EBI), the Swiss Institute of Bioinformatics (SIB), and the Protein Information Resource (PIR). EBI, located at the Wellcome Trust Genome Campus in Hinxton, UK, hosts a large resource of bioinformatics databases and services. SIB, located in Geneva, Switzerland, maintains the ExPASy (Expert Protein Analysis System) servers that are a central resource for proteomics tools and databases. PIR, hosted by the National Biomedical Research Foundation (NBRF) at the Georgetown University Medical Center in Washington, DC, USA, is heir to the oldest protein sequence database, Margaret Dayhoff's Atlas of Protein Sequence and Structure, first published in 1965.[5] In 2002, EBI, SIB, and PIR joined forces as the UniProt Consortium.[6]

The roots of UniProt databases

Each consortium member is heavily involved in protein database maintenance and annotation. Until recently, EBI and SIB together produced the Swiss-Prot and TrEMBL databases, while PIR produced the Protein Sequence Database (PIR-PSD).[7] [8] [9] These databases coexisted with differing protein sequence coverage and annotation priorities.

Swiss-Prot was created in 1986 by Amos Bairoch during his PhD and developed by the Swiss Institute of Bioinformatics and subsequently developed by Rolf Apweiler at the European Bioinformatics Institute.[10] [11] [12] Swiss-Prot aimed to provide reliable protein sequences associated with a high level of annotation (such as the description of the function of a protein, its domain structure, post-translational modifications, variants, etc.), a minimal level of redundancy and high level of integration with other databases. Recognizing that sequence data were being generated at a pace exceeding Swiss-Prot's ability to keep up, TrEMBL (Translated EMBL Nucleotide Sequence Data Library) was created to provide automated annotations for those proteins not in Swiss-Prot. Meanwhile, PIR maintained the PIR-PSD and related databases, including iProClass, a database of protein sequences and curated families.

The consortium members pooled their overlapping resources and expertise, and launched UniProt in December 2003.[13]

Organization of UniProt databases

UniProt provides four core databases:

UniProtKB

UniProt Knowledgebase (**UniProtKB**) is a protein database curated by experts, consisting of two sections. **UniProtKB/Swiss-Prot** (containing reviewed, manually annotated entries) and **UniProtKB/TrEMBL** (containing unreviewed, automatically annotated entries).[14] In release 2010_09 of 10 August 2010, UniProtKB/Swiss-Prot contained 519,348 entries, and UniProtKB/TrEMBL contained 11,636,205 entries.[15] [16]

UniProtKB/Swiss-Prot

UniProtKB/Swiss-Prot is a high-quality, manually annotated, non-redundant protein sequence database. It combines information extracted from scientific literature and biocurator-evaluated computational analysis. The aim of UniProtKB/Swiss-Prot is to provide all known relevant information about a particular protein. Annotation is regularly reviewed to keep up with current scientific findings. The manual annotation of an entry involves detailed analysis of the protein sequence and of the scientific literature.[17]

Sequences from the same gene and the same species are merged into the same database entry. Differences between sequences are identified, and their cause documented (for example alternative splicing, natural variation, incorrect initiation sites, incorrect exon boundaries, frameshifts, unidentified conflicts). A range of sequence analysis tools is used in the annotation of UniProtKB/Swiss-Prot entries. Computer-predictions are manually evaluated, and relevant results selected for inclusion in the entry. These predictions include post-translational modifications, transmembrane domains and topology, signal peptides, domain identification, and protein family classification.[17] [18]

Relevant publications are identified by searching databases such as PubMed. The full text of each paper is read, and information is extracted and added to the entry. Annotation arising from the scientific literature includes, but is not limited to:[13] [17] [18]

- Protein and gene names
- Function
- Enzyme-specific information such as catalytic activity, cofactors and catalytic residues
- Subcellular location
- Protein-protein interactions
- Pattern of expression
- Locations and roles of significant domains and sites
- Ion-, substrate- and cofactor-binding sites
- Protein variant forms produced by natural genetic variation, RNA editing, alternative splicing, proteolytic processing, and post-translational modification

Annotated entries undergo quality assurance before inclusion into UniProtKB/Swiss-Prot. When new data becomes available, entries are updated.

UniProtKB/TrEMBL

UniProtKB/TrEMBL contains high-quality computationally analyzed records, which are enriched with automatic annotation. It was introduced in response to increased dataflow resulting from genome projects, as the time- and labour-consuming manual annotation process of UniProtKB/Swiss-Prot could not be broadened to include all available protein sequences.[13] The translations of annotated coding sequences in the EMBL-Bank/GenBank/DDBJ nucleotide sequence database are automatically processed and entered in UniProtKB/TrEMBL. UniProtKB/TrEMBL also contains sequences from PDB, and from gene prediction, including Ensembl, RefSeq and CCDS.[19]

UniParc

UniProt Archive (**UniParc**) is a comprehensive and non-redundant database, which contains all the protein sequences from the main, publicly available protein sequence databases.[20] Proteins may exist in several different source databases, and in multiple copies in the same database. In order to avoid redundancy, UniParc stores each unique sequence only once. Identical sequences are merged, regardless of whether they are from the same or different species. Each sequence is given a stable and unique identifier (UPI), making it possible to identify the same protein from different source databases. UniParc contains only protein sequences, with no annotation. Database cross-references in UniParc entries allow further information about the protein to be retrieved from the source databases. When sequences in the source databases change, these changes are tracked by UniParc and history of all changes is archived.

Source databases

Currently UniParc contains protein sequences from the following publicly available databases:

- EMBL-Bank/DDBJ/GenBank nucleotide sequence databases [21]
- Ensembl [15]
- European Patent Office (EPO) [22]
- FlyBase [10]
- H-Invitational Database (H-Inv) [23]
- International Protein Index (IPI) [24]
- Japan Patent Office (JPO) [25]
- PIR-PSD [26]
- Protein Data Bank (PDB) [3]
- Protein Research Foundation (PRF) [27]
- RefSeq [4]
- Saccharomyces Genome database (SGD) [25]
- TAIR Arabidopsis thaliana Information Resource [13]
- TROME [28]
- USA Patent Office (USPTO) [29]
- UniProtKB/Swiss-Prot, UniProtKB/Swiss-Prot protein isoforms, UniProtKB/TrEMBL [30]
- Vertebrate Genome Annotation database (VEGA) [31]
- WormBase [11]

UniRef

The UniProt Reference Clusters (**UniRef**) consist of three databases of clustered sets of protein sequences from UniProtKB and selected UniParc records.[32] The **UniRef100** database combines identical sequences and sequence fragments (from any organism) into a single UniRef entry. The sequence of a representative protein, the accession numbers of all the merged entries and links to the corresponding UniProtKB and UniParc records are displayed. UniRef100 sequences are clustered using the CD-HIT algorithm to build **UniRef90** and **UniRef50**.[32] [33] Each cluster is composed of sequences that have at least 90% or 50% sequence identity, respectively, to the longest sequence. Clustering sequences significantly reduces database size, enabling faster sequence searches.

UniMes

The UniProt Metagenomic and Environmental Sequences (**UniMES**) database is a repository specifically developed for metagenomic and environmental data.[34] The predicted proteins from this dataset are combined with automatic classification by InterPro to enhance the original information with further analysis.

UniProtKB contains protein sequences from known species, data arising from metagenomics studies is from environmental (i.e. uncultured) samples and as such the species may not be known/identified. UniMES was developed for this data. Data from UniMES is not included in UniProtKB or UniRef, but is included in UniParc.[34] UniMES includes data from the Global Ocean Sampling Expedition (GOS).[35]

UniMES is available from the UniProt FTP site [36]

Funding for UniProt

UniProt is funded by grants from the National Human Genome Research Institute, the National Institutes of Health (NIH), the European Commission, the Swiss Federal Government through the Federal Office of Education and Science, NCI-caBIG, and the Department of Defense.[14]

References

[1] Uniprot, C. (2010). "Ongoing and future developments at the Universal Protein Resource". *Nucleic Acids Research* **39** (Database issue): D214–D219. doi:10.1093/nar/gkq1020. PMC 3013648. PMID 21051339.

[2] http://www.uniprot.org/downloads

[3] http://www.ebi.ac.uk/uniprot/remotingAPI/

[4] http://www.uniprot.org/faq/28

[5] Dayhoff, Margaret O. (1965). *Atlas of protein sequence and structure*. Silver Spring, Md: National Biomedical Research Foundation.

[6] http://www.genome.gov/page.cfm?pageID=10005283

[7] O'Donovan, C.; Martin, M. J.; Gattiker, A.; Gasteiger, E.; Bairoch, A.; Apweiler, R. (2002). "High-quality protein knowledge resource: SWISS-PROT and TrEMBL". *Briefings in bioinformatics* **3** (3): 275–284. doi:10.1093/bib/3.3.275. PMID 12230036.

[8] Wu, C. H.; Yeh, L. S.; Huang, H.; Arminski, L.; Castro-Alvear, J.; Chen, Y.; Hu, Z.; Kourtesis, P. et al. (2003). "The Protein Information Resource". *Nucleic Acids Research* **31** (1): 345–347. doi:10.1093/nar/gkg040. PMC 165487. PMID 12520019.

[9] Boeckmann, B.; Bairoch, A.; Apweiler, R.; Blatter, M. C.; Estreicher, A.; Gasteiger, E.; Martin, M. J.; Michoud, K. et al. (2003). "The SWISS-PROT protein knowledgebase and its supplement TrEMBL in 2003". *Nucleic Acids Research* **31** (1): 365–370. doi:10.1093/nar/gkg095. PMC 165542. PMID 12520024.

[10] Bairoch, A.; Apweiler, R. (1996). "The SWISS-PROT protein sequence data bank and its new supplement TREMBL". *Nucleic Acids Research* **24** (1): 21–25. doi:10.1093/nar/24.1.21. PMC 145613. PMID 8594581.

[11] Bairoch, A. (2000). "Serendipity in bioinformatics, the tribulations of a Swiss bioinformatician through exciting times!". *Bioinformatics* **16** (1): 48–64. doi:10.1093/bioinformatics/16.1.48. PMID 10812477.

[12] Séverine Altairac, " Naissance d'une banque de données: Interview du prof. Amos Bairoch (http://expasy.org/prolune/pdf/prolune018_fr. pdf)". *Protéines à la Une* (http://expasy.org/prolune/), August 2006. ISSN 1660-9824.

[13] Apweiler, R.; Bairoch, A.; Wu, C. H. (2004). "Protein sequence databases". *Current Opinion in Chemical Biology* **8** (1): 76–80. doi:10.1016/j.cbpa.2003.12.004. PMID 15036160.

[14] Uniprot, C. (2009). "The Universal Protein Resource (UniProt) in 2010". *Nucleic Acids Research* **38** (Database issue): D142–D148. doi:10.1093/nar/gkp846. PMC 2808944. PMID 19843607.

[15] UniProtKB/SwissProt release statistics (http://www.expasy.org/sprot/relnotes/relstat.html)

[16] UniProtKB/TrEMBL release statistics (http://www.ebi.ac.uk/uniprot/TrEMBLstats/)

[17] Annotation of UniProtKB (http://www.uniprot.org/faq/45)

[18] Apweiler, R.; Bairoch, A.; Wu, C. H.; Barker, W. C.; Boeckmann, B.; Ferro, S.; Gasteiger, E.; Huang, H. et al. (2004). "UniProt: The Universal Protein knowledgebase". *Nucleic Acids Research* **32** (90001): 115D–1119. doi:10.1093/nar/gkh131. PMC 308865. PMID 14681372.

[19] Where do UniProtKB sequences come from (http://www.uniprot.org/faq/37)

[20] Leinonen, R.; Diez, F. G.; Binns, D.; Fleischmann, W.; Lopez, R.; Apweiler, R. (2004). "UniProt archive". *Bioinformatics* **20** (17): 3236–3237. doi:10.1093/bioinformatics/bth191. PMID 15044231.

[21] http://www.insdc.org/

[22] http://www.european-patent-office.org/

[23] http://www.h-invitational.jp/

[24] http://www.ebi.ac.uk/IPI/

[25] http://www.jpo.go.jp/

[26] http://pir.georgetown.edu/pirwww/search/textpsd.shtml

[27] http://www.prf.or.jp/index-e.html

[28] ftp://ftp.isrec.isb-sib.ch/pub/databases/trome

[29] http://www.uspto.gov/

[30] http://www.uniprot.org/uniprot

[31] http://vega.sanger.ac.uk/

[32] Suzek, B. E.; Huang, H.; McGarvey, P.; Mazumder, R.; Wu, C. H. (2007). "UniRef: Comprehensive and non-redundant UniProt reference clusters". *Bioinformatics* **23** (10): 1282–1288. doi:10.1093/bioinformatics/btm098. PMID 17379688.

[33] Li, W.; Jaroszewski, L.; Godzik, A. (2001). "Clustering of highly homologous sequences to reduce the size of large protein databases". *Bioinformatics (Oxford, England)* **17** (3): 282–283. doi:10.1093/bioinformatics/17.3.282. PMID 11294794.

[34] Uniprot, C. (2007). "The Universal Protein Resource (UniProt)". *Nucleic Acids Research* **36** (Database issue): D190–D195. doi:10.1093/nar/gkm895. PMC 2238893. PMID 18045787.

[35] Yooseph, S.; Sutton, G.; Rusch, D. B.; Halpern, A. L.; Williamson, S. J.; Remington, K.; Eisen, J. A.; Heidelberg, K. B. et al. (2007). "The Sorcerer II Global Ocean Sampling Expedition: Expanding the Universe of Protein Families". *PLoS Biology* **5** (3): e16. doi:10.1371/journal.pbio.0050016. PMC 1821046. PMID 17355171.

[36] ftp://ftp.uniprot.org/pub/databases/uniprot/current_release/unimes/

External links

- UniProt (http://www.uniprot.org)
- neXtProt (http://beta.nextprot.org)
- EBI (http://www.ebi.ac.uk/)
- SIB (http://www.isb-sib.ch/)
- PIR (http://pir.georgetown.edu/)

UPGMA

UPGMA (**U**nweighted **P**air **G**roup **M**ethod with **A**rithmetic **M**ean) is a simple agglomerative or hierarchical clustering method used in bioinformatics for the creation of phenetic trees (phenograms). UPGMA assumes a constant rate of evolution (molecular clock hypothesis), and is not a well-regarded method for inferring relationships unless this assumption has been tested and justified for the data set being used. UPGMA was initially designed for use in protein electrophoresis studies, but is currently most often used to produce guide trees for more sophisticated phylogenetic reconstruction algorithms.

The algorithm examines the structure present in a pairwise distance matrix (or a similarity matrix) to then construct a rooted tree (dendrogram).

At each step, the nearest two clusters are combined into a higher-level cluster. The distance between any two clusters A and B is taken to be the average of all distances between pairs of objects "x" in A and "y" in B, that is, the mean distance between elements of each cluster:

$$\frac{1}{|\mathcal{A}| \cdot |\mathcal{B}|} \sum_{x \in \mathcal{A}} \sum_{y \in \mathcal{B}} d(x, y)$$

The method is generally attributed to Sokal and Michener.[1] Fionn Murtagh found a time optimal $O(n^2)$ time algorithm to construct the UPGMA tree.[2]

References

[1] Sokal R and Michener C (1958). "A statistical method for evaluating systematic relationships". *University of Kansas Science Bulletin* **38**: 1409–1438.

[2] Murtagh F (1984). "Complexities of Hierarchic Clustering Algorithms: the state of the art". *Computational Statistics Quarterly* **1**: 101–113.

External links

- UPGMA clustering algorithm implementation in Ruby (AI4R) (http://ai4r.rubyforge.org)
- Example calculation of UPGMA using a similarity matrix (http://books.google.de/books?id=KBoHuoNRO5MC&pg=PA319&lpg=PA319&dq=UPGMA+clustering&source=bl&ots=9t_4R2kFgr&sig=c4jHFEouGm-KCxbg9lwKQZNnWcQ&hl=de&ei=G7kqSo_wFc2Rsga86MyeDA&sa=X&oi=book_result&ct=result&resnum=3)
- Example calculation of UPGMA using a distance matrix (http://www.southampton.ac.uk/~relu06/teaching/upgma/)

VADLO

Life in Research, LLC.

VADLO	
Type	Private
Industry	Life Sciences Search Engine
Founded	Chicago, Illinois (May 4, 2008)
Headquarters	Chicago, Illinois, US
Area served	Worldwide
Website	www.vadlo.com [1]

VADLO is a life sciences search engine, privately owned by Life in Research, LLC., based in Illinois, USA. VADLO caters to life sciences and biomedical researchers, educators, students, clinicians and reference librarians. In addition to providing focused search on biology research methods, databases, online tools and software, VADLO is also a resource for powerpoints on biomedical topics,[2] mainly for which, VADLO was named one of the top 10 Health Search Engines of 2008 by AltSearchEngines.[3]

Search Categories

VADLO offers search within four categories:

- **Protocols** - for molecular biology and other life sciences methods, techniques, and how to make reagents.
- **Online Tools** - for bioinformatics tools such as gene prediction, sequence manipulation, PCR primer design etc.
- **Seminars** - for powerpoint lectuers in biology and medical fields.
- **Software** - for bioinformatics software.

Search Relevance

VADLO is a vertical search engine, geared towards biomedical researchers. VADLO indexes only the webpages that have relevance to biomedical research; categorizes them in one of the five search categories, and returns results according to its relevance-rank algorithm . This process filters out non-research websites and makes the search results more specific in comparison to general-purpose search engines. VADLO index is built by supervised crawling of the web as well as by moderated user-submission. VADLO powerpoint index is built incorporating only the powerpoint files, with subject such as biology research, academia matters such as grants and funding,bioinformatics, biostatistics, biology education, medical topics such as diseases, treatment, literature, library topics relevant to biomedical reference librarians, and biotechnology and pharmaceutical industry related topics.[4]

Life in Research Cartoons

VADLO website also displays cartoons that generally touch upon the lives of researchers. The cartoon themes center upon Postdoc life, journal publications, research organisms, organizations and clinical topics.

References

[1] http://www.vadlo.com/
[2] Search engine Vadlo caters to life sciences (http://www.altsearchengines.com/2008/09/01/search-engine-vadlo-caters-to-life-sciences/)
[3] The Top 10 Health Search Engines of 2008 (http://www.altsearchengines.com/2008/12/29/the-top-10-health-search-engines-of-2008/)
[4] Medicine PowerPoint: Focus on Vadlo (http://www.medicineppt.com/notes/2008/08/focus-on-vadlo.html)

Variant Call Format

The Variant Call Format (**VCF**) is a specification for storing gene sequence variations. The format has been developed with the advent of large-scale genotyping and gene sequencing projects, such as the 1000 Genomes Project. Existing formats for genetic data, such as GFF, stored all of the genetic data, much of which is redundant because it will be shared across the genomes. By using the variant call format only the variations need to be stored along with a reference genome.

The standard is currently in version 4.0,[1] [2] although the 1000 genomes project has developed their own specification for structural variations such as duplications, which are not easily accommodated into the existing schema.[3] A set of tools are also available for editing and manipulating the files[4].

Example

```
##fileformat=VCFv4.0

##fileDate=20110705

##reference=1000GenomesPilot-NCBI37

##phasing=partial

##INFO=<ID=NS,Number=1,Type=Integer,Description="Number of Samples With Data">

##INFO=<ID=DP,Number=1,Type=Integer,Description="Total Depth">

##INFO=<ID=AF,Number=.,Type=Float,Description="Allele Frequency">

##INFO=<ID=AA,Number=1,Type=String,Description="Ancestral Allele">

##INFO=<ID=DB,Number=0,Type=Flag,Description="dbSNP membership, build 129">

##INFO=<ID=H2,Number=0,Type=Flag,Description="HapMap2 membership">

##FILTER=<ID=q10,Description="Quality below 10">

##FILTER=<ID=s50,Description="Less than 50% of samples have data">

##FORMAT=<ID=GQ,Number=1,Type=Integer,Description="Genotype Quality">

##FORMAT=<ID=GT,Number=1,Type=String,Description="Genotype">

##FORMAT=<ID=DP,Number=1,Type=Integer,Description="Read Depth">

##FORMAT=<ID=HQ,Number=2,Type=Integer,Description="Haplotype Quality">

#CHROM POS     ID      REF ALT    QUAL FILTER INFO                          FORMAT        Sample1         Sample2         Sample3

2    4370    rs6057 G      A        29   .    NS=2;DP=13;AF=0.5;DB;H2        GT:GQ:DP:HQ 0|0:48:1:52,51 1|0:48:8:51,51 1/1:43:5:.,.

2    7330    .      T      A        3    q10  NS=5;DP=12;AF=0.017           GT:GQ:DP:HQ 0|0:46:3:58,50 0|1:3:5:65,3    0/0:41:3

2    110696 rs6055 A      G,T      67   PASS NS=2;DP=10;AF=0.333,0.667;AA=T;DB GT:GQ:DP:HQ 1|2:21:6:23,27 2|1:2:0:18,2    2/2:35:4

2    130237 .      T      .        47   .    NS=2;DP=16;AA=T               GT:GQ:DP:HQ 0|0:54:7:56,60 0|0:48:4:56,51 0/0:61:2

2    134567 microsat1 GTCT  G,GTACT 50   PASS NS=2;DP=9;AA=G               GT:GQ:DP    0/1:35:4       0/2:17:2        1/1:40:3

(...)
```

References

[1]   "VCF Specification" (http://vcftools.sourceforge.net/specs.html). . Retrieved 1 February 2011.

[2]   "VCF (Variant Call Format) version 4.0 | 1000 Genomes" (http://www.1000genomes.org/wiki/Analysis/Variant Call Format/
      vcf-variant-call-format-version-40). . Retrieved 1 February 2011.

[3]   "Encoding Structural Variants in VCF (Variant Call Format) version 4.0 | 1000 Genomes" (http://www.1000genomes.org/wiki/Analysis/
      Variant Call Format/VCF (Variant Call Format) version 4.0/encoding-structural-variants). . Retrieved 1 February 2011.

[4]   "VCFtools from SourceForge.net" (http://vcftools.sourceforge.net/). . Retrieved 21 April 2011.

Vector NTI

Vector NTI

Developer(s)	Invitrogen
Stable release	11.5.1 (Windows), 7.1 (OS X) / October 15, 2010
Operating system	Mac OS X, Windows
Type	Molecular biology toolkit
License	Academic and commercial software licenses.
Website	Vector NTI home [1]

Vector NTI is a bioinformatics software package. The current versions are v11.5.1 for Windows/PCs and v7.1 for Macs, but only supporting Mac OS X v10.3 (Panther).

Features

- create, annotate, analyse, and share DNA/protein sequences
- perform and save BLAST searches
- design primers for PCR, cloning, sequencing or hybridisation experiments
- plan cloning and run gels *in silico*
- align multiple protein or DNA sequences
- search NCBI's Entrez, view, and save DNAs, proteins, and citations
- edit chromatogram data, assemble into contigs

External links

Description of software

- Vector NTI homepage at Invitrogen.com [1]
- Vector NTI at openwetware.org [2]
- Vector NTI v10 (only PC) [3]

Tutorials

- Vector NTI tutorial at NorthWestern.edu [4]

Other

- description of Vector NTI Viewer [5]

Other Software

- ApE -A Powerful Multipurpose DNA Engineering Software, Donationware/Freeware [6]
- CLC Main Workbench [7]
- Clone_manager
- Discovery Studio [8]
- DNADynamo [9]
- Gene Designer - A free gene design software suite with a range of design and cloning tools
- Geneious
- GENtle [25]
- Lasergene [10] - by DNASTAR, Inc.
- MacVector
- pDRAW32 [11]
- QuickGene - Actively developed, intuitive DNA analysis software with extensive restriction enzyme information. Particularly useful for cloning. Mac OSX and Windows with a Beta version for Linux coming [12]
- Serial Cloner - A DNA editing and manipulating software for MacOS and Windows, Donationware/Freeware [13]
- SimVector [14] - by Premier Biosoft
- UGENE

References

[1] http://www.invitrogen.com/site/us/en/home/LINNEA-Online-Guides/LINNEA-Communities/Vector-NTI-Community/vector-nti-software.html
[2] http://openwetware.org/wiki/VectorNTI
[3] http://bioinformatics.unc.edu/software/nti/index.htm
[4] http://www.basic.northwestern.edu/VectorNTI/Documentation/VectorNTI/
[5] http://register.informaxinc.com/solutions/vectornti/molecular_viewer.html
[6] http://www.biology.utah.edu/jorgensen/wayned/ape/
[7] http://www.clcbio.com/main
[8] http://www.csc.fi/english/research/sciences/bioscience/programs/ds
[9] http://www.bluetractorsoftware.co.uk/
[10] http://www.dnastar.com/
[11] http://www.acaclone.com/
[12] http://www.crimsonbase.com/
[13] http://www.serialbasics.com/Serial_Cloner.html
[14] http://www.premierbiosoft.com/plasmid_maps/index.html

Vertebrate and Genome Annotation Project

The **Vertebrate and Genome Annotation** (Vega) project provides manual curation of vertebrate genomes for the scientific community.[1] The Vega data repository is publicly available, regularly updated and includes annotations of several finished vertebrate genome sequences: human, mouse, zebrafish, pig and dog.[2]

The Vega website is built upon the Ensembl codebase.[3] The Vega database is run and developed by the Wellcome Trust Sanger Institute.

References

[1] Ashurst JL, Chen CK, Gilbert JG, *et al.* (January 2005). "The Vertebrate Genome Annotation (Vega) database". *Nucleic Acids Research* **33** (Database issue): D459–65. doi:10.1093/nar/gki135. PMC 540089. PMID 15608237.

[2] Loveland J (June 2005). "VEGA, the genome browser with a difference". *Briefings in Bioinformatics* **6** (2): 189–93. doi:10.1093/bib/6.2.189. PMID 15975227.

[3] Searle SM, Gilbert J, Iyer V, Clamp M (May 2004). "The otter annotation system". *Genome Research* **14** (5): 963–70. doi:10.1101/gr.1864804. PMC 479127. PMID 15123593.

External links

• Vega homepage (http://vega.sanger.ac.uk)

Victorian Life Sciences Computation Initiative

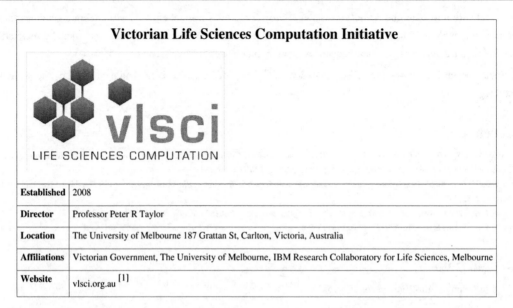

Victorian Life Sciences Computation Initiative

Established	2008
Director	Professor Peter R Taylor
Location	The University of Melbourne 187 Grattan St, Carlton, Victoria, Australia
Affiliations	Victorian Government, The University of Melbourne, IBM Research Collaboratory for Life Sciences, Melbourne
Website	vlsci.org.au [1]

The **Victorian Life Sciences Computation Initiative** is an initiative of the government of Victoria in partnership with the University of Melbourne and the IBM Research Collaboratory for Life Sciences, Melbourne. It exists for all Victorian researchers, and aims to be one of the top 5 life science computation facilities by 2013.

Background

The VLSCI is considered a part of the Victoria government's plans to support biotechnology, and is listed as a key infrastructure projects in the Victorian Biotechnology Action Plan 2011. [2] The VLSCI is a $100m initiative of the Victorian Government in partnership with The University of Melbourne and the IBM Life Sciences Research Collaboratory, Melbourne. Other major stakeholders include key Victorian health and medical research institutions, major Universities and public research organisations.

Key resources

The VLSCI's-high performance computation facility is accessible to all Victorian Life Sciences researchers by operating from three research hubs based in Melbourne's Central (Parkville), South East (Clayton) and North (Bundoora) Precincts. Technical experts are on staff to maximise the user experience, meet the skills gaps in research  teams, build the necessary cross-disciplinary research collaborations, and provide skills to scale up projects to efficiently use the processing power being delivered. Ongoing skills development and training is provided in computational biology, computational imaging and bioinformatics.

The Computers

As of 2011, VLSCI's Peak Computing Facility is at Stage 1, operating at 46 teraflops. Stage 2, scheduled to begin in 2013, will delivering petascale computing in 2013. The systems include 'Bruce', an SGI Altix x86, 'Merri', an IBM iDataplex x86 and 'Tambo', the largest IBM Blue Gene/P supercomputer installation devoted to the Life Sciences in the Southern Hemisphere.

Peak Computing Facility

The VLSCI Peak Computing Facility (PCF) provides high-performance compute infrastructure and computational expertise to Life Sciences researchers across Victoria. The PCF has tightly-coupled clusters with very fast disk subsystems, currently operating at a peak capacity of 46 teraflops and building to petascale computing by 2013. To help researchers maximize their use of compute time and get the most out of their allocated resources, the PCF has a team of system administrators, programmers and application specialists accessible through its help request system.

Life Sciences Computation Centre

The VLSCI Life Science Computation Centre (LSCC) is a cross-institution centre composed of hubs in three research precincts: Central (Parkville), South-East (Clayton) and North (Bundoora), physically housed at the Universities of Melbourne, Monash and La Trobe respectively. The LSCC can be seen as a distributed pool of expertise and infrastructure for computational life science research, servicing life science research institutions across Victoria. It aims to foster research collaboration and support to a relatively small number of specific external projects; act as a source of common resources, software platforms and expertise to support life science researchers; offer research training, education, and career development for bioinformaticians and computational biologists, to support the advancement of the Victorian computational life sciences research community; and support the advancement of life science computation as a whole in Victoria.

IBM Collaboratory for Life Sciences, Melbourne

Co-located at VLSCI is the first IBM Research Collaboratory for Life Sciences. The IBM Research Collaboratory for Life Sciences - Melbourne enables collaboration between the 10,000 world-class life sciences and medical researchers in the Melbourne area, and IBM's computational biology experts.

Scientists from the VLSCI and IBM Research are working to accelerate the translation of theoretical biological knowledge into practical improvements in medical care and health outcomes

References

[1] http://www.vlsci.org.au.html
[2] http://www.business.vic.gov.au/BUSVIC/STANDARD/PC_64131.html

Virtual screening

Virtual screening (VS) is a computational technique used in drug discovery research. It involves the rapid *in silico* assessment of large libraries of chemical structures in order to identify those structures which are most likely to bind to a drug target, typically a protein receptor or enzyme.[1] [2]

Virtual screening has become an integral part of the drug discovery process. Related to the more general and long pursued concept of database searching, the term "virtual screening" is relatively new. Walters, *et al.* define virtual screening as "automatically evaluating very large libraries of compounds" using computer programs.[3] As this definition suggests, VS has largely been a numbers game focusing on questions like how can we filter down the enormous chemical space of over 10^{60} conceivable compounds to a manageable number that can be synthesized, purchased, and tested. Although filtering the entire chemical universe might be a fascinating question, more practical VS scenarios focus on designing and optimizing targeted combinatorial libraries and enriching libraries of available compounds from in-house compound repositories or vendor offerings.

The purpose of virtual screening is to come up with hits of novel chemical structure that bind to the macromolecular target of interest. Thus, success of a virtual screen is defined in terms of finding interesting new scaffolds rather than many hits. Interpretations of VS accuracy should therefore be considered with caution. Low hit rates of interesting scaffolds are clearly preferable over high hit rates of already known scaffolds.

Method

There are two broad categories of screening techniques: ligand-based and structure-based.[4]

Ligand-based

Given a set of structurally diverse ligands that binds to a receptor, a model of the receptor can be built based on what binds to it. These are known as pharmacophore models. A candidate ligand can then be compared to the pharmacophore model to determine whether it is compatible with it and therefore likely to bind.[5]

Another approach to ligand-based virtual screening is to use chemical similarity analysis methods[6] to scan a database of molecules against one active ligand structure.

Structure-based

Structure-based virtual screening involves docking of candidate ligands into a protein target followed by applying a scoring function to estimate the likelihood that the ligand will bind to the protein with high affinity.[7] [8]

Computing Infrastructure

The computation of pair-wise interactions between atoms, which is a prerequisite for the operation of many virtual screening programs, is of $O(N^2)$ computational complexity, where N is the number of atoms in the system.

Because of the exponential scaling with respect to the number of atoms, the computing infrastructure may vary from a laptop computer for a ligand-based method to a mainframe for a structure-based method.

Ligand-based

Ligand-based methods typically require a fraction of a second for a single structure comparison operation. A single CPU is enough to perform a large screening within hours. However, several comparisons can be made in parallel in order to expedite the processing of a large database of compounds.

Structure-based

The size of the task requires a parallel computing infrastructure, such as a cluster of Linux systems, running a batch queue processor to handle the work, such as Sun Grid Engine or Torque PBS.

A means of handling the input from large compound libraries is needed. This requires a form of compound database that can be queried by the parallel cluster, delivering compounds in parallel to the various compute nodes. Commercial database engines may be too ponderous, and a high speed indexing engine, such as Berkeley DB, may be a better choice. Furthermore, it may not be efficient to run one comparison per job, because the ramp up time of the cluster nodes could easily outstrip the amount of useful work. To work around this, it is necessary to process batches of compounds in each cluster job, aggregating the results into some kind of log file. A secondary process, to mine the log files and extract high scoring candidates, can then be run after the whole experiment has been run.

References

[1] Rester, U (July 2008). "From virtuality to reality - Virtual screening in lead discovery and lead optimization: A medicinal chemistry perspective". *Curr Opin Drug Discov Devel* **11** (4): 559–68. PMID 18600572.

[2] Rollinger JM, Stuppner H, Langer T (2008). "Virtual screening for the discovery of bioactive natural products". *Prog Drug Res*. Progress in Drug Research **65** (211): 213–49. doi:10.1007/978-3-7643-8117-2_6. ISBN 978-3-7643-8098-4. PMID 18084917.

[3] Walters WP, Stahl MT, Murcko MA (1998). "Virtual screening – an overview". *Drug Discov. Today* **3** (4): 160–178. doi:10.1016/S1359-6446(97)01163-X.

[4] McInnes C (2007). "Virtual screening strategies in drug discovery". *Curr Opin Chem Biol* **11** (5): 494–502. doi:10.1016/j.cbpa.2007.08.033. PMID 17936059.

[5] Sun H (2008). "Pharmacophore-based virtual screening". *Curr Med Chem* **15** (10): 1018–24. doi:10.2174/092986708784049630. PMID 18393859.

[6] Willet P, Barnard JM, Downs GM (1998). "Chemical similarity searching". *J Chem Inf Comput Sci* **38** (6): 983–996. doi:10.1021/ci9800211.

[7] Kroemer RT (2007). "Structure-based drug design: docking and scoring". *Curr Protein Pept Sci* **8** (4): 312–28. doi:10.2174/138920307781369382. PMID 17696866.

[8] Cavasotto CN, Orry AJ (2007). "Ligand docking and structure-based virtual screening in drug discovery". *Curr Top Med Chem* **7** (10): 1006–14. doi:10.2174/156802607780906753. PMID 17508934.

Further reading

• Melagraki G, Afantitis A, Sarimveis H, Koutentis PA, Markopoulos J, Igglessi-Markopoulou O (2007). "Optimization of biaryl piperidine and 4-amino-2-biarylurea MCH1 receptor antagonists using QSAR modeling, classification techniques and virtual screening". *J. Comput. Aided Mol. Des.* **21** (5): 251–67. doi:10.1007/s10822-007-9112-4. PMID 17377847.

• Afantitis A, Melagraki G, Sarimveis H, Koutentis PA, Markopoulos J, Igglessi-Markopoulou O (2006). "Investigation of substituent effect of 1-(3,3-diphenylpropyl)-piperidinyl phenylacetamides on CCR5 binding affinity using QSAR and virtual screening techniques". *J. Comput. Aided Mol. Des.* **20** (2): 83–95. doi:10.1007/s10822-006-9038-2. PMID 16783600.

• Eckert H, Bajorath J (2007). "Molecular similarity analysis in virtual screening: foundations, limitations and novel approaches". *Drug Discov. Today* **12** (5–6): 225–33. doi:10.1016/j.drudis.2007.01.011. PMID 17331887.

• Willett P (2006). "Similarity-based virtual screening using 2D fingerprints". *Drug Discov. Today* **11** (23–24): 1046–53. doi:10.1016/j.drudis.2006.10.005. PMID 17129822.

• Fara DC, Oprea TI, Prossnitz ER, Bologa CG, Edwards BS, Sklar LA (2006). "Integration of virtual and physical screening". *Drug Discov. Today: Technologies* **3** (4): 377–385. doi:10.1016/j.ddtec.2006.11.003.

• Muegge I, Oloffa S (2006). "Advances in virtual screening". *Drug Discov. Today: Technologies* **3** (4): 405–411. doi:10.1016/j.ddtec.2006.12.002.

External links

• ZINC (http://blaster.docking.org/zinc/) — a free database of commercially-available compounds for virtual screening.
• Virtual Screening Methods (http://barryhardy.blogs.com/cheminfostream/2006/09/virtual_screeni.html)
• Free service to screen for GPCR ligands, ion channel blockers and kinase inhibitors (http://www.molinspiration.com/cgi-bin/properties)
• Brutus (http://www.visipoint.fi/brutus.php) — a similarity analysis tool for ligand-based virtual screening.
• NovaMechanics Cheminformatics Research (http://www.novamechanics.com) Combined structure & ligand based chemistry driven virtual screening.

Volcano plot (statistics)

In statistics, a **volcano plot** is a type of scatter-plot that is used to quickly identify changes in large datasets composed of replicate data [1]. It plots significance versus fold-change on the y- and x-axes, respectively. These plots are increasingly common in omic experiments such as genomics, proteomics, and metabolomics where one often has a list of many thousands of replicate datapoints between two conditions and one wishes to quickly identify the most-meaningful changes. A volcano plot combines a statistical test (e.g., p-value, ANOVA) with the magnitude of the change enabling quick visual identification of those data-points (genes, etc) that display large-magnitude changes that are also statistically significant.

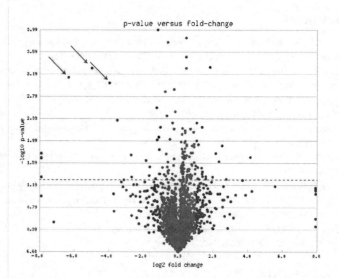

Volcano plot showing metabolomic data. The red arrows indicate points-of-interest that display both large-magnitude fold-changes (x-axis) as well as high statistical significance (-log10 of p-value, y-axis). The dashed red-line shows where p = 0.05 with points above the line having p < 0.05 and points below the line having p > 0.05. This plot is colored such that those points having a fold-change less than 2 (log2 = 1) are shown in gray.

A volcano plot is constructed by plotting the negative log of the p-value on the y-axis (usually base 10). This results in datapoints with low p-values (highly significant) appearing towards the top of the plot. The x-axis is the log of the fold change between the two conditions. The log of the fold-change is used so that changes in both directions (up and down) appear equidistant from the center. Plotting points in this way results in two regions of interest in the plot: those points that are found towards the top of the plot that are far to either the left- or the right-hand side. These represent values that display large magnitude fold changes (hence being left- or right- of center) as well as high statistical significance (hence being towards the top).

Additional information can be added by coloring the points according to a third dimension of data (such as signal-intensity) but this is not uniformly employed.

References

[1] Cui X, Churchill GA (2003). "Statistical tests for differential expression in cDNA microarray experiments". *Genome Biol.* **4** (4): 210. doi:10.1186/gb-2003-4-4-210. PMC 154570. PMID 12702200.

External links

- NCI Documentation describing statistical methods to analyze microarrays, including volcano plots (http:// discover.nci.nih.gov/microarrayAnalysis/Statistical.Tests.jsp)
- Description of volcano plots at MathWorks (http://www.mathworks.com/access/helpdesk/help/toolbox/ bioinfo/ref/mavolcanoplot.html)
- Description of volcano plots in Agilent's Genespring software (http://www.chem.agilent.com/en-US/Support/ FAQs/Informatics/GeneSpring GX/Views/Pages/KB001112.aspx)

WAVe

WAVe stands for Web Analysis of the Variome is a next-generation web-based bioinformatics tool for the human variome research domain.

WAVe logo

Availability

WAVe is available for public usage at [1] and enables gene-centric navigation over miscellaneous resources in a modern and agile web interface.

Funding

WAVe is being developed for the European GEN2PHEN Project by the UA.PT Bioinformatics and Computational Biology [2] group at the University of Aveiro.

Architecture

WAVe is based on a lightweight integration architecture[3] and uses Arabella web crawler[4] combined with a Java-based data gathering engine to aggregate multiple resources in a centralized database.

References

[1] http://bioinformatics.ua.pt/WAVe
[2] http://bioinformatics.ua.pt
[3] http://issuu.com/pedrolopes/docs/linkintegrator
[4] http://issuu.com/pedrolopes/docs/arabella

External links

- WAVe (http://bioinformatics.ua.pt/WAVe)

Webtag (Software)

Webtag[1] is an on-line bioinformatics tool providing oligonucleotide sequences (usually called tags or anchors) that are absent from a specified genome. These tags can be appended to gene specific primers for reverse transcriptase polymerase chain reaction (RT-PCR) experiments, circumventing genomic DNA contamination.

Background

Due to its very high sensitivity, RT-PCR[2] is an extensively used technique for the detection of even very low copy mRNA transcripts. This remarkable sensitivity is also its major shortcoming – RT-PCR is extraordinarily susceptible to DNA contamination. Since PCR is unable to distinguish between cDNA targets and genomic DNA contamination, false positives and/or erroneous quantitative results are possible[3] [4].

In order to overcome genomic DNA contamination in transcriptional studies, reverse template-specific polymerase chain reaction, a modification of RT-PCR is used. The possibility of using tags whose sequences are not found in the genome further improves reverse specific polymerase chain reaction experiments. The use of anchors, or tags, in the 5' region of a gene specific primer or poly-T tail allows for RNA-specific amplification, and constitutes a viable strategy. Techniques such as RS-PCR[5] and (EXACT) RT-PCR are based on the integration of such tags (unique sequences not present in genomic DNA) in the 5' end of the first strand cDNA, permitting RNA-specific amplification without loss of sensitivity.

Webtag

This web based service builds on the Tagenerator[6] tool, but is very fast because all tags are pre-generated and stored in a database. It is also a significant improvement since Webtag takes into account the interactions of the tag with the primers to be used in the experiment. Having it as a web based service also means that the molecular biologist doesn't have to download and install software with all the dependencies on their own computer.

Webtag generates tags that combine genome absence with good priming properties for RT-PCR based experiments. The use of such tags will deliberately not result in PCR amplification of genomic DNA, permitting the exclusive amplification of cDNA, therefore circumventing the effects of genomic DNA contamination in an RNA sample.

References

[1] Lopes Pinto, Fernando; Håkan Svensson, Peter Lindblad (2007-10-25). "Webtag: a new web tool providing tags/anchors for RT-PCR experiments with prokaryotes" (http://www.biomedcentral.com/1472-6750/7/73). *BMC Biotechnology* 7: 73. doi:10.1186/1472-6750-7-73. PMC 2147000. PMID 17961214. . Retrieved 2007-11-06.

[2] Chelly, Jamel; Jean-Claude Kaplan, Pascal Maire, Sophie Gautron, Axel Kahn (1988-06-30). "Transcription of the dystrophin gene in human muscle and non-muscle tissues" (http://www.nature.com/nature/journal/v333/n6176/abs/333858a0.html). *Nature* 333 (6176): 858–860. doi:10.1038/333858a0. PMID 3290682. . Retrieved 2007-11-06.

[3] Borst, A.; A. T. A. Box, A. C. Fluit (2004-03-09). "False-Positive Results and Contamination in Nucleic Acid Amplification Assays: Suggestions for a Prevent and Destroy Strategy". *European Journal of Clinical Microbiology & Infectious Diseases* 23 (4): 289–299. doi:10.1007/s10096-004-1100-1. PMID 15015033.

[4] Martel, Fatima; Dirk Grundemann, Edgar Schöig (2002-03-31). "A simple method for elimination of false positive results in RT-PCR". *J Biochem Mol Biol* 35 (2): 248–250. doi:10.5483/BMBRep.2002.35.2.248. PMID 12297038.

[5] Shuldiner, Alan R.; Ajay Nirula, Jesse Roth (1990). "RNA template-specific polymerase chain reaction (RS-PCR): a novel strategy to reduce dramatically false positives". *Gene* 91 (1): 139–142. doi:10.1016/0378-1119(90)90176-R. PMID 1698167.

[6] Lopes Pinto, Fernando; Håkan Svensson, Peter Lindblad (2006-06-05). "Generation of non-genomic oligonucleotide tag sequences for RNA template-specific PCR" (http://www.biomedcentral.com/1472-6750/6/31). *BMC Biotechnology* 6: 31. doi:10.1186/1472-6750-6-31. PMC 1526424. PMID 16820068. . Retrieved 2007-11-06.

External links

- Official webpage (http://www.egs.uu.se/software/webtag/)
- Tagenerator (http://www.egs.uu.se/software/tagenerator/)

World Health Imaging, Telemedicine, and Informatics Alliance

World Health Imaging, Telemedicine and Informatics Alliance

Founder(s)	Mike Hoaglin, Dave Kelso, Matt Glucksberg, Michael Diamond[1]
Type	501(c)(3) Non-profit Organization
Founded	Chicago, IL, US
Location	Chicago, Illinois United States
Key people	Newton N. Minow, Chair of the Board Michael W. Ferro, Jr., Vice Chair[2] Ivy Walker, CEO [3]
Area served	Worldwide
Focus	Low-cost medical imaging, X-ray, Health Information technology, sustainability
Motto	One digital image can save a life
Website	worldhealthimaging.org [4]

The **World Health Imaging, Telemedicine and Informatics Alliance** (WHITIA) is a non-profit global health technology and social venture established in 2006 by affiliates of Northwestern University near Chicago, Illinois.[1] [5] WHITIA cultivates high-level strategic relationships with non-governmental organizations, imaging industry innovators and academic institutions in order to integrate and deliver meaningful, sustainable, diagnostic technology to underserved communities worldwide. WHITIA's vision is to facilitate the deployment of thousands of digital medical imaging systems worldwide, providing one billion people with access to diagnostic imaging.[6] WHITIA was formerly known as the World Health Imaging Alliance (WHIA) until it formally expanded its scope in June 2009.

WHITIA's first formal public launch was in April 2009 at the Healthcare Information and Management Systems Society (HIMSS) Annual Conference & Exhibition in Chicago, Illinois. WHITIA announced strategic partners including SEDECAL, Carestream Health and Merge Healthcare, receiving extensive coverage in Health IT magazines and publications.[7] [8] At the 2009 Annual Conference of the Society for Imaging Informatics in Medicine (SIIM) in Charlotte, North Carolina, WHITIA announced its partnership with SIIM, which will allow both organizations to collaborate on specific initiatives.[9] [10] WHITIA was recently ranked #15 of the top 25 most influential people, institutions, and organizations in the radiology industry.[11]

At the 2009 RSNA Annual Meeting, WHITIA launched, **Remi-d**, a remote-operated screening X-ray system for use in the developing world. Its strengths in these areas stem from the higher burden of Human Immunodeficiency Virus (HIV) and Tuberculosis (TB) co-infection, high incidences of Black Lung disease, or outbreaks of other infectious respiratory diseases. The teleradiology and remote-controlled features of Remi-d allow resource-limited areas such as sub-Saharan Africa, South and Central America and Southeast Asia, where radiologists and technologists are in short supply to have a functioning X-ray service.[12]

WHITIA currently has pilot integrated digital X-ray sites in South Africa and Guatemala at established clinics in need and is expanding to new qualified sites in partnership with NGOs such as Rotary International while cooperating with the local and national governments.[13]

Guatemala clinics

The Guatemala pilot sites in urban Guatemala City and rural Río Hondo provide essential healthcare technology to thousands of people in the communities served. They are designed to be models for the wider expansion of the WHITIA network throughout the clinics in need in urban and rural Guatemala. The system's specific design for Guatemala City is an integration of some of WHITIA's partners' strengths and generosity:

- SEDECAL provides the X-ray generator and controls
- Carestream Health donates the computed radiography (CR) digital scanner and plates
- Kane X-ray donates personnel to perform installation and set up of the CR and PACS

This project was largely funded by several US and Guatemalan Rotary clubs along with the key resource support of the Guatemalan municipal and national governments.[14]

References

[1] "McCormick students and faculty tackle health care challenge in the developing world" (http://magazine.mccormick.northwestern.edu/ FA2007/Xray.html). Robert R. McCormick School of Engineering and Applied Science, Northwestern University. . Retrieved 2009-07-02.

[2] "Board of Directors" (http://www.worldhealthimaging.org/board.html). . Retrieved 2009-07-02.

[3] "Personnel" (http://www.worldhealthimaging.org/personnel.html). . Retrieved 2009-07-02.

[4] http://www.worldhealthimaging.org

[5] "World Health Imaging Alliance Partners For X-Rays in Developing World" (http://www.mccormick.northwestern.edu/news/articles/ 494). McCormick School of Engineering. . Retrieved 2009-07-04.

[6] http://www.worldhealthimaging.org/

[7] "Not-for-Profit Has a Vision to Help a Billion People" (http://www.reuters.com/article/pressRelease/idUS111037+06-Apr-2009+ BW20090406). Reuters. 2009-04-06. . Retrieved 2009-07-02.

[8] "World Health Imaging Alliance Poised to Bring Imaging Diagnostics and Data to the Developing World" (http://finance.yahoo.com/ news/Merge-Healthcare-Commits-1-bw-14855801.html?x=1&.v=1). Yahoo Finance. . Retrieved 2009-07-02.

[9] "World Health Imaging Alliance (WHIA) Announces Support From The Society for Imaging Informatics in Medicine (SIIM)" (http://www. businesswire.com/news/home/20090605005136/en). Business Wire. . Retrieved 2009-07-02.

[10] "World Health Imaging Alliance poised to bring imaging diagnostics and data to the developing world" (http://www.imagingeconomics. com/news/2009-06-17_01.asp). Imaging Economics. . Retrieved 2009-07-02.

[11] "25 Most Influential in Radiology" (http://www.rt-image.com/ 25_Most_Influential_in_Radiology_Recognizing_the_movers_and_shakers_in_the_radio/ content=9004J05E48B6A084409698724488B0441). rt Image. . Retrieved 2009-10-22.

[12] "WHITIA launches digital medical X-ray device for screening infectious diseases in developing countries" (http://www.news-medical.net/ news/20091130/WHITIA-launches-digital-medical-X-ray-device-for-screening-infectious-diseases-in-developing-countries.aspx). THE MEDICAL NEWS. . Retrieved 2009-12-01.

[13] "SIIM to Support World Health Imaging Alliance" (http://www.healthtechwire.com/The-Industry-s-News-unb.146+M5a262949a06.0. html). HealthTech Wire. . Retrieved 2009-07-02.

[14] "WHITIA Announces the Completion of Digital X-ray Pilot Sites in Urban and Rural Guatemala" (http://www.businesswire.com/news/ home/20110104006502/en/WHITIA-Announces-Completion-Digital-X-ray-Pilot-Sites). Business Wire. . Retrieved 2011-01-09.

External links

- Official webpage (http://www.worldhealthimaging.org/)
- Video interview with WHITIA staff and overview of mission. Shown at Rotary International Convention 2008 (http://www.youtube.com/watch?v=sv0q0hD-fIM)
- (http://www.medicalnewstoday.com/articles/145456.php)
- (http://www.healthtechwire.com/The-Industry-s-News-unb.146+M5a262949a06.0.html)
- (http://www.dotmed.com/news/story/8681/)
- (http://www.cnbc.com/id/31121000/)
- (http://www.tradingmarkets.com/.site/news/Stock News/2362104/)
- (http://www.smartbrief.com/news/aaaa/industryBW-detail. jsp?id=CCB30F65-E324-4325-8B5C-15C061C926F1)
- (http://www.newsrx.com/article.php?articleID=1554620)
- WHITIA Announces the Completion of Digital X-ray Pilot Sites in Urban and Rural Guatemala Press Release (http://www.worldhealthimaging.org/WHITIA Guatemala_01-04-2011press_release.pdf)

WormBase

WormBase

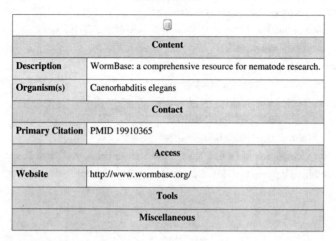

Content		
Description	WormBase: a comprehensive resource for nematode research.	
Organism(s)	Caenorhabditis elegans	
Contact		
Primary Citation	PMID 19910365	
Access		
Website	http://www.wormbase.org/	
Tools		
Miscellaneous		

WormBase is an online bioinformatics database of the biology and genome of the model organism *Caenorhabditis elegans* and related nematodes.[1] [2]

It is used by the *C. elegans* research community both as an information resource and as a mode to publish and distribute their results. The database is constantly updated and new versions are released on a monthly basis.

WormBase is one of the organizations participating in the Generic Model Organism Database (GMOD) project.

Contents

WormBase comprises the following main data sets:

- The annotated genomes of *Caenorhabditis elegans*, *Caenorhabditis briggsae*, *Caenorhabditis remanei*, *Caenorhabditis brenneri*, *Caenorhabditis cangaria*, *Pristionchus pacificus*, *Haemonchus contortus*, *Meloidogyne hapla*, *Meloidogyne incognita*, and *Brugia malayi*;
- Hand-curated annotations describing the function of ~20,500 *C. elegans* protein-coding genes and ~16,000 *C. elegans* non-coding genes;
- Gene families;
- Orthologies;
- Genomic transcription factor binding sites
- Comprehensive information on mutant alleles and their phenotypes;
- Whole-genome RNAi (*RNA interference*) screens;
- Genetic maps, markers and polymorphisms;
- The *C. elegans* physical map;
- Gene expression profiles (stage, tissue and cell) from microarrays, SAGE analysis and GFP promoter fusions;
- The complete cell lineage of the worm;
- The wiring diagram of the worm nervous system;
- Protein-protein interaction Interactome data;
- Genetic regulatory relationships;
- Details of intra- and inter-specific sequence homologies (with links to other model organism databases).

In addition, WormBase contains an up-to-date searchable bibliography of *C. elegans* research and is linked to the WormBook project.

Tools

WormBase offers many ways of searching and retrieving data from the database:

- WormMart [3] - a tool for retrieving varied information on many genes (or the sequences of those genes). This is the WormBase implementation of BioMart [4],[5]
- Genome Browser [6] - browse the genes of *C. elegans* (and other species) in their genomic context
- TextPresso [7] - a search tool that queries published *C. elegans* literature (including meeting abstracts)

Sequence Curation

Sequence curation at WormBase refers to the maintenance and annotation of the primary genomic sequence and a consensus gene set.

Genome Sequence

Even though the *C. elegans* genome sequence is the most accurate and complete eukaryotic genome sequence, it has continually needed refinement as new evidence has been created. Many of these changes were single nucleotide insertions or deletions, however several large mis-assemblies have been uncovered. For example, in 2005 a 39 kb cosmid had to be inverted. Other improvements have come from comparing genomic DNA to cDNA sequences and analysis of RNASeq high-throughput data. When differences between the genomic sequence and transcripts are identified, re-analysis of the original genomic data often leads to modifications of the genomic sequence. The changes in the genomic sequence pose difficulties when comparing chromosomal coordinates of data derived from different releases of WormBase. To aid these comparisons, a coordinate re-mapping program and data are available from: http://wiki.wormbase.org/index.php/Converting_Coordinates_between_releases

Gene structure models

All the gene-sets of the WormBase species were initially generated by gene prediction programs. Gene prediction programs give a reasonable set of gene structures, but the best of them only predict about 80% of the complete gene structures correctly. They have difficulty predicting genes with unusual structures, as well as those with a weak translation start signal, weak splice sites or single exon genes. They can incorrectly predict a coding gene model where the gene is a pseudogene and they predict the isoforms of a gene poorly, if at all.

The gene models of *C. elegans*, *C. briggsae*, *C. remanei*, and *C. brenneri* genes are manually curated. The majority of gene structure changes have been based on transcript data from large scale projects such as Yuji Kohara's EST libraries, Mark Vidal's Orfeome project (worfdb.dfci.harvard.edu/) Waterston and Hillier's Illumina data and Makedonka Mitreva's 454 data. However, other data types (e.g. protein alignments, *ab initio* prediction programs, trans-splice leader sites, poly-A signals and addition sites, SAGE and TEC-RED transcript tags, mass-spectroscopic peptides, and conserved protein domains) are useful in refining the structures, especially where expression is low and so transcripts are not sufficiently available. When genes are conserved between the available nematode species, comparative analysis can also be very informative.

WormBase encourages researchers to inform them via the help-desk if they have evidence for an incorrect gene structure. Any cDNA or mRNA sequence evidence for the change should be submitted to EMBL/GenBank/DDBJ; this helps in the confirmation and evidence for the gene model as WormBase routinely retrieve sequence data from these public databases. This also makes the data public, allowing appropriate reference and acknowledgement to the researchers.

When any change is made to a CDS (or Pseudogene), the old gene model is preserved as a 'history' object. This will have a suffix name like: "AC3.5:wp119", where 'AC3.5' is the name of the CDS and the '119' refers to the database release in which the change was made. The reason for the change and the evidence for the change are added to the annotation of the CDS – these can be seen in the Visible/Remark section of the CDS's 'Tree Display' section on the

WormBase web site.

Gene Nomenclature

Genes

In WormBase, a Gene is a region that is expressed or a region that has been expressed and is now a Pseudogene. Genes have unique identifiers like 'WBGene00006415'. All C. elegans WormBase genes also have a Sequence Name, which is derived from the cosmid, fosmid or YAC clone on which they reside, for instance **F38H4.7**, indicating it is on the cosmid 'F38H4', and there are at least 6 other genes on that cosmid. If a gene produces a protein that can be classified as a member of a family, the gene may also be assigned a **CGC** name like **tag-30** indicating that this is the 30th member of the **tag** gene family. Assignment of gene family names is controlled by WormBase [8] and requests for names should be made, before publication, via the form at: http://tazendra.caltech. edu/~azurebrd/cgi-bin/forms/gene_name.cgi

There are a few exceptions to this format, like the genes **cln-3.1**, **cln-3.2**, and **cln-3.3** which all are equally similar to the human gene **CLN3**. Gene GCG names for non-elegans species in WormBase have the 3-letter species code prepended, like **Cre-acl-5**, **Cbr-acl-5**, **Cbn-acl-5**.

A gene can be a Pseudogene, or can express one or more non-coding RNA genes (ncRNA) or protein-coding sequences (CDS).

Pseudogenes

Pseudogenes are genes that do not produce a reasonable, functional transcript. They may be pseudogenes of coding genes or of non-coding RNA and may be whole or fragments of a gene and may or may not express a transcript. The boundary between what is considered a *reasonable* coding transcript is sometimes subjective as, in the absence of other evidence, the use of weak splice sites or short exons can often produce a putative, though unsatisfactory, model of a CDS. Pseudogenes and genes with a problematic structure are constantly under review in WormBase and new evidence is used to try to resolve their status.

CDSs

Coding Sequences (CDSs) are the only part of a Gene's structure that is manually curated in WormBase. The structure of the Gene and its transcripts are derived from the structure of their CDSs.

CDSs have a Sequence Name that is derived from the same Sequence Name as their parent Gene object, so the gene 'F38H4.7' has a CDS called 'F38H4.7'. The CDS specifies coding exons in the gene from the START (Methionine) codon up to (and including) the STOP codon.

Any gene can code for multiple proteins as a result of alternative splicing. These isoforms have a name that is formed from the Sequence Name of the gene with a unique letter appended. In the case of the gene **bli-4** there are 6 known CDS isoforms, called K04F10.4a, K04F10.4b, K04F10.4c, K04F10.4d, K04F10.4e and K04F10.4f.

It is common to refer to isoforms in the literature using the CGC gene family name with a letter appended, for example **pha-4a**, however this has no meaning within the WormBase database and searches for **pha-4a** in WormBase will not return anything. The correct name of this isoform is either the CDS/Transcript name: **F38A6.1a**, or even better, the Protein name: **WP:CE15998**.

Gene transcripts

The transcripts of a gene in WormBase are automatically derived by mapping any available cDNA or mRNA alignments onto the CDS model. These gene transcripts will therefore often include the UTR exons surrounding the CDS. If there are no available cDNA or mRNA transcripts, then the gene transcripts will have exactly the same structure as the CDS that they are modelled on.

Gene transcripts are named after the Sequence Name of the CDS used to create them, for example, **F38H4.7** or **K04F10.4a**.

However if there is alternative splicing in the UTRs, which would not change the protein sequence, the alternatively-spliced transcripts are named with a digit appended, for example: **K04F10.4a.1** and **K04F10.4a.2**. If there are no isoforms of the coding gene, for example **AC3.5**, but there is alternative splicing in the UTRs, there will be multiple transcripts named **AC3.5.1** and **AC3.5.2**, etc. If there are no alternate UTR transcripts the single coding_transcript is named the same as the CDS and does not have the .1 appended, as in the case of K04F10.4f.

Operons

Groups of genes which are co-transcribed as operons are curated as Operon objects. These have names like **CEOP5460** and are manually curated using evidence from the SL2 trans-spliced leader sequence sites.

Non-coding RNA genes

There are several classes of non-coding RNA gene classes in WormBase:

- tRNA genes are predicted by the program 'tRNAscan-SE'.
- rRNA genes are predicted by homology with other species.
- snRNA genes are mainly imported from Rfam.
- piRNA genes are from an analysis of the characteristic motif in these genes.
- miRNA genes have mainly been imported from mirBASE. They have the primary transcript and the mature transcript marked up. The primary transcript will have a Sequence name like **W09G3.10** and the mature transcript will have a letter added to this name like **W09G3.10a** (and if there are alternative mature transcripts, **W09G3.10b**, etc.).
- snoRNA genes are mainly imported from Rfam or from papers.
- ncRNA genes that have no obvious other function but which are obviously not protein-coding and are not pseudogenes are curated. Many of these have conserved homology with genes in other species. A few of these are expressed on the reverse sense to protein-coding genes.

There is also one scRNA gene.

Transposons

Transposons are not classed as genes and so do not have a parent gene object. Their structure is curated as a Transposon_CDS object with a name like **C29E6.6**.

Other Species

The non-elegans species in WormBase have genomes that have been assembled from sequencing technologies that do not involve sequencing cosmids or YACs. These species therefore do not have sequence names for CDSs and gene transcripts that are based on cosmid names. Instead they have unique alphanumeric identifiers constructed like the names in the table below.

Genes names

Species	Example Gene name
C. briggsae	CBG00001
C. remanei	CRE00001
C. brenneri	CBN00001
C. japonica	CJA00001
Pristionchus pacificus	PPA00001

Proteins

The protein products of gene are created by translating the CDS sequences. Each unique protein sequence is given a unique identifying name like **WP:CE40440**. Examples of the protein identifier names for each species in WormBase is given in the table, below.

Genes names

Species	Example Protein name
C. elegans	WP:CE00001
C. briggsae	BP:CBP00001
C. remanei	RP:RP00001
C. brenneri	CN:CN00001
C. japonica	JA:JA00001
Pristionchus pacificus	PP:PP00001
Heterorhabditis bacteriophora	HB:HB00001
Brugia malayi	BM:BM00001
Meloidogyne hapla	MH:MH00001
Meloidogyne incognita	MI:MI00001
Haemonchus contortus	HC:HC00001

It is possible for two CDS sequences from separate genes, within a species, to be identical and so it is possible to have identical proteins coded for by separate genes. When this happens, a single, unique identifying name is used for the protein even though it is produced by two genes.

WormBase Management

WormBase is a collaboration among the European Bioinformatics Institute, Wellcome Trust Sanger Institute, Ontario Institute for Cancer Research, Washington University in St. Louis, and the California Institute of Technology. It is supported by the grant **P41-HG02223** from the National Institutes of Health and the grant **G0701197** from the British Medical Research Council .[9]

References

[1] Harris, TW; et al. (2009-11-12). "WormBase: a comprehensive resource for nematode research." (http://nar.oxfordjournals.org/cgi/
     content/abstract/38/suppl_1/D463). *Nucleic Acids Res* **38** (Database issue): D463–7. doi:10.1093/nar/gkp952. PMC 2808986.
     PMID 19910365. . Retrieved 2010-04-26.

[2] Williams, G. W.; Davis, P. A.; Rogers, A. S.; Bieri, T.; Ozersky, P.; Spieth, J. (2011). "Methods and strategies for gene structure curation in
     WormBase". *Database* **2011**: baq039–baq039. doi:10.1093/database/baq039. PMC 3092607. PMID 21543339.
[3] http://www.wormbase.org/biomart/martview
[4] http://www.biomart.org
[5] http://www.wormbase.org/wiki/index.php/Data_mining:WormMart
[6] http://www.wormbase.org/db/gb2/gbrowse/c_elegans/
[7] http://www.textpresso.org/cgi-bin/wb/tfw.cgi
[8] "WormBase Gene Nomenclature" (http://wiki.wormbase.org/index.php/UserGuide:Nomenclature). Wormbase. .
[9] http://www.wormbase.org/wiki/index.php/WormBaseWiki:Copyrights

External links

- WormBase (http://www.wormbase.org/)
- The WormBook website (http://www.wormbook.org/), the online textbook companion to WormBase.
- Textpresso (http://www.textpresso.org/), search engine for C. elegans and other biological literature.
- WormBase Wiki (http://www.wormbase.org/wiki/index.php/Main_Page)
- Release notes (http://www.sanger.ac.uk/Projects/C_elegans/WORMBASE/current/release_notes.txt), details of the latest WormBase release
- WormBase: better software, richer content (http://www.pubmedcentral.gov/articlerender.fcgi?tool=pubmed& pubmedid=16381915) Nucleic Acids Research article describing WormBase (2006).
- WormBase (http://twitter.com/wormbase) on Twitter

WormBook

[[Image:WormBook 1.png|thumb|www.WormBook.org [1]] **WormBook** is an open access, comprehensive collection of original, peer-reviewed chapters covering topics related to the biology of *Caenorhabditis elegans* (*C. elegans*). WormBook also includes WormMethods, an up-to-date collection of methods and protocols for *C. elegans* researchers.

WormBook is the online text companion to Wormbase, the *C. elegans* model organism database. Capitalizing on the World Wide Web, WormBook links in-text references (e.g. genes, alleles, proteins, literature citations) with primary biological databases such as WormBase and PubMed. C. elegans was the first multi-cellular organism to have its genome sequenced. It is a model organism for studying developmental genetics and neurobiology.

Contents

The content of WormBook is categorized into the sections listed below, each filled with a variety of relevant chapters. These sections include:

- Genetics and genomics
- Molecular biology
- Biochemistry
- Cell biology
- Signal transduction
- Developmental control
- Post-embryonic development
- Sex determination
- The germ line
- Neurobiology and behavior
- Evolution and ecology

- Disease models and drug discovery
- WormMethods

External links

- The WormBook website [2]
- WormBase [11], the database companion to WormBook
- The WormBook Discussion Forum [3]

References

[1] http://www.wormbook.org
[2] http://www.wormbook.org/
[3] http://www.wormbase.org/forums/index.php?board=31.0/

Z curve

The **Z curve** (or **Z-curve**) method is a bioinformatics algorithm for genome analysis. The Z-curve is a three-dimensional curve that constitutes a unique representation of a DNA sequence, i.e., for the Z-curve and the given DNA sequence each can be uniquely reconstructed from the other.[1] The resulting curve has a zigzag shape, hence the name Z-curve. The Z-curve method has been used in many different areas of genome research, such as replication origin identification,[2] [3] [4] [5] *ab initio* gene prediction,[6] isochore identification,[7] genomic island identification[8] and comparative genomics.[9]

References

[1] Zhang CT, Zhang R, Ou HY (2003). "The Z curve database: a graphic representation of genome sequences". *Bioinformatics* **19** (5): 593–99. doi:10.1093/bioinformatics/btg041. PMID 12651717.
[2] Zhang R, Zhang CT (2005). "Identification of replication origins in archaeal genomes based on the Z-curve method". *Archaea* **1** (5): 335–46. doi:10.1155/2005/509646. PMC 2685548. PMID 15876567.
[3] Zhang R, Zhang CT (September 2002). "Single replication origin of the archaeon *Methanosarcina mazei* revealed by the Z curve method". *Biochem. Biophys. Res. Commun.* **297** (2): 396–400. doi:10.1016/S0006-291X(02)02214-3. PMID 12237132.
[4] Zhang R, Zhang CT (March 2003). "Multiple replication origins of the archaeon *Halobacterium* species NRC-1". *Biochem. Biophys. Res. Commun.* **302** (4): 728–34. doi:10.1016/S0006-291X(03)00252-3. PMID 12646230.
[5] Worning P, Jensen LJ, Hallin PF, Staerfeldt HH, Ussery DW (February 2006). "Origin of replication in circular prokaryotic chromosomes". *Environ. Microbiol.* **8** (2): 353–61. doi:10.1111/j.1462-2920.2005.00917.x. PMID 16423021.
[6] Guo FB, Ou HY, Zhang CT (2003). "ZCURVE: a new system for recognizing protein-coding genes in bacterial and archaeal genomes". *Nucleic Acids Research* **31** (6): 1780–89. doi:10.1093/nar/gkg254. PMC 152858. PMID 12626720.
[7] Zhang CT, Zhang R (2004). "Isochore structures in the mouse genome". *Genomics* **83** (3): 384–94. doi:10.1016/j.ygeno.2003.09.011. PMID 14962664.
[8] Zhang R, Zhang CT (2004). "A systematic method to identify genomic islands and its applications in analyzing the genomes of Corynebacterium glutamicum and Vibrio vulnificus CMCP6 chromosome I". *Bioinformatics* **20** (5): 612–22. doi:10.1093/bioinformatics/btg453. PMID 15033867.
[9] Zhang R, Zhang CT (2003). "Identification of genomic islands in the genome of Bacillus cereus by comparative analysis with Bacillus anthracis". *Physiological Genomics* **16** (1): 19–23. doi:10.1152/physiolgenomics.00170.2003. PMID 14600214.

External links

- The Z curve database (http://tubic.tju.edu.cn/zcurve/)
- "Origin of Replication in Circular Prokaryotic Chromosomes" (http://www.cbs.dtu.dk/services/GenomeAtlas/ suppl/origin/). Center for Biological Sequence Analysis. — a free, open source program for predicting "origins of replication" using Z-curves.

Article Sources and Contributors

Bioinformatics *Source*: http://en.wikipedia.org/w/index.php?oldid=456426420 *Contributors*: 124Nick, 168..., 16@r, 3mta3, APH, Acerperi, Adenosine, Aetkin, Agemoi, Agricola44, AhmedMoustafa, Ahoerstemeier, Ajkarloss, Akpakp, Akriasas, Alai, Alan Au, Alansohn, Alex Kosorukoff, Amandadawnbesemer, Ambertk, Amoghb, Andersduck, Andkaha, Andreas C, AndriuZ, Angelsh, Ansell, ArglebargleIV, Artgen, Arthena, Asasia, Ashalatha.jangala, Ashcroft, Asidhu, AstarothCY, AuGold, Avenue, Azazello, Bact, Badanedwa, Banazir, Banus, Barticus88, Bcheng23, Beetstra, Bffo, Bill.albing, Bill37212, Bio-ITWorld, Bioinformaticsguru, Bioinformin, Biovini, Blastwizard, Bm richard, Bmeguru, Bmunro, Bob, Bobblewik, Bonio05, Bonnarj, Bonus Onus, Bookandcoffee, Bornslippy, Bradenripple, Brona, Burner0718, Burningsquid, CRGreathouse, CWenger, Can't sleep, clown will eat me, Carey Evans, Cavrdg, Cbergman, Cbock, Chameleon, Chasingsol, Cholling, Chopchopwhitey, Christopherlin, Ckuanglim, Colin gravill, Colonialdirt, CommodiCast, ConceptExp, Conversion script, Counsell, Cquan, CryptoDerk, Cyc, Cyde, DIG, Dan198792, Danger, Darkwind, Dave Messina, David Ardell, David Gerard, Dcoetzee, Deflective, Dismas, Dmb000006, Dod1, Don G., DonSiano, Donarreiskoffer, Dr02115, Dtabb, Dullhunk, Duncan.Hull, Dysprosia, EALacey, EdGl, EdJohnston, Edgar181, Edward, Edward Gordon Gey, Efbfweborg, Ehheh, El C, Ensignyu, Epbr123, Eramesan, FTasc, Fcrozat, FireBrandon, Foscoe, Fotinakis, Frap, FreeKill, G716, GLHamilton, Ganeshbio1, Garvind95, Gaurav, Gazpacho, Gene s, Generalboss3, Genometer, Genypholy, Giftlite, Girlwithglasses, Glen, Gonfus, Googed, Gordon014, GraemeL, GrahamColm, Gscshoyru, Gulan722, Gzur, Gökhan, Hawksj, HenkvD, Henriettaminge, Hike395, Hillarivallen, HoopyFrood, Huji, Imjustmatthew, Imtechchd, Iwaterpolo, JHunterJ, Jamelan, Jameslyonsweiler, Jamiejoseph, Jchusid, Jcuticchia, Jebus989, Jedgold, Jengeldk, Jethero, Jimmaths, Jjron, Jjwilkerson, Jkbioinfo, Joconnol, Joelrex, Joeoettinger, Joerg Kurt Wegner, JonHarder, Jorfer, JosephBarillari, Josephholsten, Joychen2010, Kamleong, Karol Langner, Kayvan45622, Keesiewonder, Kevin B12, Kevin.cohen, Kiwi2795, Kjramesh, Kkmurray, Kku, Kotsiantis, Kpengboy, Kwamikagami, L Kensington, Larry laptop, LeeWatts, Lennonr2, Leofer, Leptictidium, Lexor, Littlealien182, LukeGoodsell, Lynx8, MER-C, MacGyverMagic, Macha, Madeleine Price Ball, Malafaya, Malcolm Farmer, Malkinann, Marashie, Marco.caminati, Marcoacostareyes, Martin Jambon, Martin.jambon, Mateo LeFou, Materialscientist, MattWBradbury, Mattigatti, Mauriceling, Mav, Maxmans, Mayumashu, Mazi, Mbadri, MertyWiki, Metahacker, Michael Hardy, MicroBio Hawk, Mike Yang, Mikemoral, Mimihitam, Mindmatrix, Minho Bio Lee, Minimac, Minimice, Mobashirgenome, Mootros, MrOllie, Mstrangwick, Muchness, Muijz, Mxn, My walker 88, Nabeelbasheer, Narayanese, Natalya, Natarajanganesan, Navigatorwiki, Neksa, Nervexmachina, Nihiltres, Nivix, No snow, Nono64, Ohnoitsjamie, Oleg Alexandrov, Oleginger, Opabinia regalis, Orphan Wiki, Otets, P-O limhamn, P99am, PDH, PJY, Parakkum, Pascal.hingamp, Pawyilee, Pdcook, Pde, Peak, Peccoud, Perada, Perfectlover, Peter Znamenskiy, Ph.eyes, Phismith, Piano non troppo, Porcher, Postdoc, Ppgardne, Praveen pillay, Protonk, Prunesqualer, Pselvakumar, Pseudomonas, Quadell, Qwertyus, Qwfp, RaoInWiki, Raul654, Redgecko, Reinyday, Remi0o, Renji143, Rgonzaga, Rhys, Rich Farmbrough, Rifleman 82, Rintintin, Rjwilmsi, Rmky87, RobHutten, Rror, Ruud Koot, Rvencio, S177, Schutz, Scilit, Scottzed, Seglea, Senator Palpatine, SexyGod, Shadowjams, Shawnc, Sherell.jones, Shire Reeve, Shortliffe, Shubinator, Shyamal, Sjoerd de Vries, Smjc, Smoe, Spencerk, Spin2cool, Steinsky, Stewartadcock, Stinkbeard, Strife911, Subhashis.behera, Supten, Surajbodi, Susurrus, Tapir Terrific, Tarcieri, Tdhoufek, Tedder, Tellyaddict, Template namespace initialisation script, Ternto333, Terrace4, TestPilot, Thenothing, Thermochap, Thomaswgc, Thorwald, Thumperward, Tim@, TimVickers, Tincup, Tintenfischlein, Tmccrae, Tombadog, Tompw, Tony1, Tpvipin, Tupeliano, Turnstep, U 06111976, User A1, Vanka5, VashiDonsk, Vasundhar, Vawter, Vegasprof, Venus Victorious, Veterinarian, Vietbio, Vina, Viriditas, Vishnugaikwad, Vizbi, W09110900, Walshga, Warren.cheung, Wavelength, WhatamIdoing, Whoknew.dat, Wieghardt, Wik, Wiki1forall, WilliamBonfieldFRS, Willking1979, Winhide, Wmahan, Wojcz, Woohookitty, Xlnc1706, Yeturukalidas, Ymei, Ymichel, Yoni-vL, Youssefsan, Yves.lussier, Zashaw, ZayZayEM, Zhuozhuo, Zoicon5, Zorozorozoro123, Zzuuzz, आशीष भटनागर, 621 anonymous edits

Gene prediction *Source*: http://en.wikipedia.org/w/index.php?oldid=446464744 *Contributors*: Aciel, Alexbateman, Antonov86, BD2412, Bluezy, Brona, Chaos, El C, Erwinser, Fba 1367, Ffaarr, Fyrael, Herr blaschke, Jbening, Kku, Maurice Carbonaro, Meisterflexer, Michael Hardy, PDH, Pinethicket, Ppgardne, RDBrown, Shaileshtripathy, Shalom Yechiel, Shyamal, Skittleys, Sophus Bie, SteinbDJ, SteveChervitzTrutane, Theo10011, Thorwald, Veryhuman, Virusprobe, Wenhan, Woohookitty, 63 anonymous edits

Premier Biosoft *Source*: http://en.wikipedia.org/w/index.php?oldid=409552888 *Contributors*: Akradecki, Alice Davidson, Daniel Cliff, Ewin Thakur, Latischolar, Materialscientist, Sandstein, Tassedethe, Wikimickeymouse, Wilson trace, 2 anonymous edits

3D-Jury *Source*: http://en.wikipedia.org/w/index.php?oldid=364860341 *Contributors*: Emw, Rich Farmbrough

ABCD Schema *Source*: http://en.wikipedia.org/w/index.php?oldid=449203790 *Contributors*: AvicAWB, Biochemza, Egpetersen, GregorB, Gullivier, Kku, Koavf, NormanGray, Od Mishehu

ABCdb *Source*: http://en.wikipedia.org/w/index.php?oldid=420813256 *Contributors*: Stone geneva

Accession number (bioinformatics) *Source*: http://en.wikipedia.org/w/index.php?oldid=423684512 *Contributors*: A. B., Angela, Ceyockey, Cometsong, Duncan.Hull, PTaschner, Rjwilmsi, Shinwachi, TubeWorld, Widefox, 2 anonymous edits

Accomplishment by a Senior Scientist Award *Source*: http://en.wikipedia.org/w/index.php?oldid=433185263 *Contributors*: Alexbateman, Duncan.Hull, Hut 8.5

Syed I. Ahson *Source*: http://en.wikipedia.org/w/index.php?oldid=455327837 *Contributors*: Fang Aili, Necrothesp, Pcmanish, Sadads, ScottSteiner, Shailwe007, Wayne Slam, 5 anonymous edits

Align-m *Source*: http://en.wikipedia.org/w/index.php?oldid=272485946 *Contributors*: Thorwald, 2 anonymous edits

ANOVA-simultaneous component analysis *Source*: http://en.wikipedia.org/w/index.php?oldid=440666808 *Contributors*: Biochemza, Dj.science, JackSchmidt, Melcombe, Michael Hardy, 4 anonymous edits

Archaeopteryx (evolutionary tree visualization and analysis) *Source*: http://en.wikipedia.org/w/index.php?oldid=408169727 *Contributors*: Funandtrvl, JaGa, Lotje, Rcomplexity, 1 anonymous edits

Arlequin *Source*: http://en.wikipedia.org/w/index.php?oldid=409870942 *Contributors*: Horoporo, Kane5187, Triwbe, Victor Lopes, Willisis2, 7 anonymous edits

ArrayTrack *Source*: http://en.wikipedia.org/w/index.php?oldid=445857878 *Contributors*: D4a8, Markdask, MatthewVanitas

Astrid Research *Source*: http://en.wikipedia.org/w/index.php?oldid=393212220 *Contributors*: Syrthiss, Theresa knott, Zckovacs

Aureus Sciences *Source*: http://en.wikipedia.org/w/index.php?oldid=450743514 *Contributors*: Maladmental, Wilhelmina Will

Automated species identification *Source*: http://en.wikipedia.org/w/index.php?oldid=454635597 *Contributors*: Ademarius, Adhemarius, CutOffTies, Foooobaarbar, John of Reading, Jvhertum, KenBailey, Psyxonova, Riana, 24 anonymous edits

Bayesian inference in phylogeny *Source*: http://en.wikipedia.org/w/index.php?oldid=423015443 *Contributors*: Ben Skála, Elonka, Keinstein, Melcombe, Michael Hardy, Pacaro, Sanjay Tiwari, Skapur, Skittleys, Themfromspace, 7 anonymous edits

Benjamin Franklin Award (Bioinformatics) *Source*: http://en.wikipedia.org/w/index.php?oldid=428757744 *Contributors*: Andorsch, Demize, Duncan.Hull, Jac16888, Plindenbaum, Ppgardne

Biclustering *Source*: http://en.wikipedia.org/w/index.php?oldid=455330211 *Contributors*: Ahsan1010, Akhil 0950, Beefyt, Bunnyhop11, Charles Matthews, Chenopodiaceous, Chire, Cobi, David Eppstein, Delirium, Everyking, Fnielsen, Gwernol, Hazyhxj, Innar, Jonsafari, Linas, Muhandes, Radagast83, Rjwilmsi, SMasters, Seemu, Smadeira, Toninowiki, Took, Xiaowei JIANG, Yhchung, Ykluger, Zeno Gantner, Zy26, 54 anonymous edits

Biochip *Source*: http://en.wikipedia.org/w/index.php?oldid=443251475 *Contributors*: Aleks-eng, Andrew c, Appraiser, AuroraSinclair, Automated Patch Clamp, Buzwad, CPMcE, Ceyockey, Chowbok, Chrislk02, Chrismiceli, Christopherlin, Clicketyclack, Deli nk, Denisetse105, Edward, Gail, Gilligan mark, Gneimer, Haiching, Hede2000, Htaylor-ebuckley, J04n, JOK, JesseW, Joechao, John, Jondel, Kcordina, Kkmurray, Lantonov, Loren.wilton, Lucky 6.9, M-le-mot-dit, Michael Hardy, Mushin, Nmedard, NubKnacker, Nv8200p, Odie5533, Philip Trueman, Rhobite, Rich Farmbrough, Robinmolinier, Robma, Ronbo76, Skittleys, Sole Soul, TexasAndroid, Touchstone42, Yaser hassan 2006, 0, 55 anonymous edits

Bioclipse *Source*: http://en.wikipedia.org/w/index.php?oldid=452597972 *Contributors*: AxelBoldt, Ebyabe, EgonWillighagen, Egonw, Giftlite, JLaTondre, Joerg Kurt Wegner, Leolaursen, Michael Hardy, Pansanel, Prius 2, Progdev, Twas Now, 10 anonymous edits

Bioconductor *Source*: http://en.wikipedia.org/w/index.php?oldid=445150215 *Contributors*: Aaronbrick, Aboyoun, Avenue, Bachrach44, Ben Ben, Den fjättrade ankan, Elwikipedista, Enkrates, Farmanesh, Frap, Gcm, Glenn, Iml, Jacj, JonHarder, Karnesky, Kathleen.wright5, Kl4m-AWB, Koolabsol, Movado73, Ph.eyes, Rb05793, Rich Farmbrough, Smoe, TheParanoidOne, Zven, Пика Пика, 45 anonymous edits

BioCreative *Source*: http://en.wikipedia.org/w/index.php?oldid=443287170 *Contributors*: Alexmorgan, BorgQueen, Ceyockey, Duncan.Hull, EncycloPetey, GregAsche, Kanabekobaton, Kcordina, Kelapstick, Kevin.cohen, Lquilter, Robomanx, TheParanoidOne, 5 anonymous edits

Biocurator *Source*: http://en.wikipedia.org/w/index.php?oldid=433034214 *Contributors*: Alexbateman, Amb sib, Jkbioinfo, Mai-tai-guy, Rich Farmbrough, Segerdell, 3 anonymous edits

Bioimage informatics *Source*: http://en.wikipedia.org/w/index.php?oldid=362098297 *Contributors*: EagleFan, Fabrictramp, Hanchuanpeng, JaGa, Katharineamy, Mephiston999, Nikkimaria, PMDrive1061, Pdcook

Bioinformatic Harvester *Source*: http://en.wikipedia.org/w/index.php?oldid=430850331 *Contributors*: Akriasas, Alan Liefting, Alksub, Ceyockey, D6, Dmb000006, Hobophobe, Ivo, Lwc, Natarajanganesan, OccamzRazor, PigFlu Oink, R'n'B, RDBrown, Rainer Wasserfuhr, Reinyday, Rjwilmsi, Rockpocket, Themfromspace, Tikiwont, Tillalb, UnitedStatesian, Venullian, Widefox, 35 anonymous edits

Bioinformatics (journal) *Source*: http://en.wikipedia.org/w/index.php?oldid=423805029 *Contributors*: Crusio, Dsp13, Duncan.Hull, Narayanese, 2 anonymous edits

Bioinformatics workflow management systems *Source*: http://en.wikipedia.org/w/index.php?oldid=456207555 *Contributors*: Abduallah mohammed, Ansell, Arch dude, Audriusa, Beetstra, Bistline, Denny, DI2000, Doug.jennewein.usd, Duncan.Hull, Ffangs, Firsfron, Grid.man, Gudeldar, Iefremov, Iwaterpolo, JLaTondre, Jethero, Jinnai, Jodi.a.schneider, John of Reading, Jph, Kdn1982, Mbjones.89, Mmreich, MrOllie, Paulmkgordon, Ph.eyes, Rjwilmsi, Ronz, Rwwww, Scattley, Siegele, Skaj, Srjefferys, Tnabtaf, U 06111976, VilleSalmensuu, Vriend, Xuul, 28 anonymous edits

BioJava *Source*: http://en.wikipedia.org/w/index.php?oldid=447100308 *Contributors*: Abduallah mohammed, Alex.g, Alison9, Bact, Bluemoose, Doug Bell, Grunt, Hydkat, Iridiumcao, Lexor, Mike Yang, RedWolf, Reinyday, SHL-at-Sv, Stuartyeates, TheParanoidOne, Trevor Wennblom, 5 anonymous edits

BioLinux *Source*: http://en.wikipedia.org/w/index.php?oldid=444328912 *Contributors*: Asparagus, Chris the speller, ChrisHodgesUK, D6, Davepntr, Dswan, GregorB, Intgr, JHMM13, Jovianeye, Knirirr, Kozuch, Marco.caminati, Markds, Matthew Yeager, Peak, Pearle, Perspectoff, Ricky, SF007, Stephan Leeds, Tillea, Vermiculus, Yworo, Z00zax, 36 anonymous edits

Biological data visualization *Source*: http://en.wikipedia.org/w/index.php?oldid=412983127 *Contributors*: Chris Capoccia, Clayrat, JimProcter, Plindenbaum, RHaworth, Vizbi, WereSpielChequers, 4 anonymous edits

Biological database *Source*: http://en.wikipedia.org/w/index.php?oldid=446593961 *Contributors*: 0dimensional, Akriasas, Amosfolarin, Asasia, Ashgene, AutumnSnow, AxelBoldt, BD2412, Bananab, Beetstra, Bunnyhop11, Camera-PR, Can't sleep, clown will eat me, Cdinesh, Cjc22, Cyberix, Dalloliogm, DarthVader, DarylThomasUCSC, Ddove, Dmb000006, Dnaphd, Dongilbert, Dramamezzo, Duncharris, Fetchcomms, Fratrep, FreeKill, Frifishfry, Frogzrcoolkelsey, GHeckler, Genypholy, Giardine, Gparikh, GregorB, Hodja Nasreddin, Inocinnamon83, Ipatrol, Itskkumaran, Ivo, JSMCD, JimHu, John Vandenberg, Jthangiah, Karasneh, Kbradnam, Kpjas, Kuleebaba, Lerdthenerd, Lexor, Linsalrob, Mai-tai-guy, Maikfr, Mais oui!, Manuelcorpas, Mayankkumar8, Meisterflexer, Merope, MikeHucka, Minimac, MitraE, Mjharrison, MrOllie, Mystere, NCsciencewriter, Nnkalnin, Nurg, Pengo, Physicistjedi, Pisaadvocate, Pkarp11, Plindenbaum, R. S. Shaw, RE73, Rdasari, Researchadvocate, Secretlondon, Shinwachi, Siegele, SpNeo, Speaker to wolves, Stensonpd, Stevenhwu, Thorwald, Tnabtaf, Tomtheeditor, U0171912, Walter Görlitz, WatsonCN, Wclathe, ZayZayEM, 109 anonymous edits

Biological network inference *Source*: http://en.wikipedia.org/w/index.php?oldid=449209893 *Contributors*: Anaxial, BabbaQ, Biochemza, Gdrahnier, Gregbard, Headbomb, J04n, JPG-GR, Jncraton, Jvhertum, RJFJR, Rjwilmsi, Rtaylor pnnl, Thorwald, 6 anonymous edits

Biomax Informatics AG *Source*: http://en.wikipedia.org/w/index.php?oldid=429859357 *Contributors*: Chris Capoccia, Edward, Homebrew70, Rwwww, Trident13, 3 anonymous edits

Biomedical text mining *Source*: http://en.wikipedia.org/w/index.php?oldid=456642261 *Contributors*: BorgQueen, Chenli, D-rew, Facopad, GregAsche, Jkbioinfo, Johnfravolda, Kevin.cohen, Martingenetech, Mayflower3, Mugebirlik, Ph.eyes, RDBrown, Radova, Rjwilmsi, Shastasheen123, ShelfSkewed, Sleuth21, Ste1n, TexMurphy, Thompson paul, Weaddon, Xicouto, Xtisths, Yudhis97, 19 anonymous edits

BioMOBY *Source*: http://en.wikipedia.org/w/index.php?oldid=441882576 *Contributors*: Caerwine, Calaka, Chris the speller, Grid.man, Lawilkin, Mwilkinson, Paulmkgordon, Thorwald, Welsh, 6 anonymous edits

BioPAX *Source*: http://en.wikipedia.org/w/index.php?oldid=433214656 *Contributors*: 4th-otaku, Alexbateman, Bioashok, CuriousOliver, Erkan Yilmaz, IgorRodchenkov, Itskkumaran, Mdd, Peter Karlsen, SHL-at-Sv, Sean Heron, 5 anonymous edits

BioPerl *Source*: http://en.wikipedia.org/w/index.php?oldid=455842122 *Contributors*: Arareko, Ashcroft, Bact, Bluemoose, Carbonrodney, Cariaso, Cjfields, Dave Messina, Duncan.Hull, Emw, Enrobsob, Jongbhak, Joy, Karol Langner, Lexor, Logan, Mild Bill Hiccup, Mindmatrix, Ph.eyes, Reinyday, Rich Farmbrough, Saluce65, Sendu, Senthil, Soumyasch, SteveChervitzTrutane, TheParanoidOne, Thorwald, Wickethewok, 7 anonymous edits

Biopunk *Source*: http://en.wikipedia.org/w/index.php?oldid=452808992 *Contributors*: AaronTAB, Afitillidie13, Al Lemos, Anarchia, Anville, Apeloverage, Apostrophe, Atechi, BD2412, Belovedfreak, Bisected8, Bjones, Bobryuu, CP\M, Cabe6403, Cast, Cburket, Chaetognatha, Colonies Chris, Cometstyles, Commander Keane, Cpesacreta, CyberSkull, Cyde, DH85868993, Dakinijones, DarkJake, Der Hans, Draon, Drat, DryaUnda, Elyu, Emperor, Fmralchemist, Fram, Fred Bradstadt, Fredgoat, Gaius Cornelius, Gnrlotto, Gobonobo, Grutness, Henry Spencer 07, Hmains, Idot, Inoesomestuff, J Milburn, JDspeeder1, Jackson McArthur, Junius49, JustAGal, Kanzure, Kevinalewis, Killridemedly, Kookyunii, Kuralyov, Kuzjrinx, Lightmouse, LilHelpa, Loremaster, Macowell, Magnius, MakeRocketGoNow, Mani1, Martarius, Memespace, Mike40033, Mschock, Museumfreak, Nono64, Oversandal, PeggyK, Pengo, Pharos, Pictureuploader, Piecraft, Piotrus, Plumbago, Prezbo, RPBnimrod, Razorbelle, Reinoutr, Remuel, RepublicanJacobite, Rich Farmbrough, Rjwilmsi, Robocoder, SMcCandlish, Sabretooth, Sbacle, Selfsimilar, Snailwalker, Soetermans, Spike Wilbury, StN, Stevietheman, Summershafer, The little neutrino, TheCyanid, Thecheesykid, Vanished User 03, Waxsin, Wikiborg4711, Wolf ODonnell, Yashas, Yashgaroth, Yobmod, Ziggurat, 163 anonymous edits

Biopython *Source*: http://en.wikipedia.org/w/index.php?oldid=439397957 *Contributors*: Abduallah mohammed, Bact, Bluemoose, Caerwine, Frap, Jovianeye, Karol Langner, Lexor, Maubp, Meenupriya, Michael Devore, Modster, Pegship, Peterrice, Stemonitis, Tevildo, TheParanoidOne, Thorwald, Z00zax, 7 anonymous edits

BIOSCI *Source*: http://en.wikipedia.org/w/index.php?oldid=422966591 *Contributors*: Alan Liefting, Appraiser, Aua, Basawala, Dongilbert, Melaen, Merope, Rjwilmsi, SimonP, Uthbrian, Vespristiano, 5 anonymous edits

bioSearch *Source*: http://en.wikipedia.org/w/index.php?oldid=425194107 *Contributors*: Aditya987, CommonsDelinker, Falcon8765, Gaurav, Kakodkar.aditya, Shyamsunder, Tassedethe, Topbanana, 3 anonymous edits

Biositemap *Source*: http://en.wikipedia.org/w/index.php?oldid=424807214 *Contributors*: 4th-otaku, Aua, Bethalyssa, Chaosdruid, Colincbn, Dendodge, Diannaa, H3llkn0wz, Iwaterpolo, Mdd, PirateMink, Polly, Qwfp, RDBrown, Rjwilmsi, Unused0030, 9 anonymous edits

Biostatistics *Source*: http://en.wikipedia.org/w/index.php?oldid=456598425 *Contributors*: APH, Aboluay, Agricola44, Alansohn, Altenmann, Andycjp, Angusmclellan, AubreyEllenShomo, BigDaddy84, Bigjam01, Boffob, Bryan Derksen, Ceyockey, Chimpex, Conversion script, CountingPine, Cpt ricard, Dekimasu, Deltaseeker, Den fjättrade ankan, Dick Beldin, Dim Grits, Dj Capricorn, Dolovis, Doncram, Drgarden, Drinkybird, EJVargas, EarthPerson, El C, EncMstr, Epipelagic, Eramesan, Free Software Knight, G716, Gfdowney, Giftlite, Graham87, Hhbruun, Hu12, Huangdi, IronChris, Isnow, IvanLanin, Jacob.jose, Jimfbleak, Jose77, Jtsai, Katonal, LiDaobing, Mack2, Magioladitis, Manik762007, MarkSweep, Melcombe, Mgiganteus1, Mike Serfas, Museumfreak, Mzabduk, NERIUM, Narayanese, NeilN, NickBarrowman, Northamerica1000, Nuno Tavares, Oleg Alexandrov, Pep Roca, Phillip J, Pjacobi, Plommenspiser, Poor Yorick, Porcher, Qwfp, RekishiEJ, Richard001, Rjwilmsi, SQL, Saturn star, Sbarnard, Shaile, Shyamal, Sladen, Slant, Sunur7, TedE, Thefellswooper, Thruston, Uncle G, Wikid, Wikiklrsc, Willking1979, World, Zfr, Zuck3434, كاشف عقيل, 110 anonymous edits

BISC (database) *Source*: http://en.wikipedia.org/w/index.php?oldid=426885528 *Contributors*: Boghog, Plindenbaum, Tony1

BLOSUM *Source*: http://en.wikipedia.org/w/index.php?oldid=449721630 *Contributors*: Alan Liefting, Asasia, Brighterorange, Camrn86, Carstensen, Clicketyclack, Epolk, Finiteyoda, Grouse, Hannes Röst, Hossein.bargi, Iridescent, Lvzon, Mollykjones, OliverMay, Quantling, Rajah, Thorwald, Whosasking, Winterschlaefer, XApple, 18 anonymous edits

BMC Bioinformatics *Source*: http://en.wikipedia.org/w/index.php?oldid=437881905 *Contributors*: Fences and windows, Free Software Knight, Hendrik Fuß, Narayanese, 3 anonymous edits

Boolean network *Source*: http://en.wikipedia.org/w/index.php?oldid=445432043 *Contributors*: Adelpine, Amosfolarin, Balpo, Betacommand, Bloodshedder, Chris Bainbridge, Delaszk, EAderhold, Ehamberg, Ekr, Everyking, Gamewizard71, Iluso, Ojii-san, Philip Trueman, Roy W. Wright, Salix alba, Sandrobt, Zargulon, 17 anonymous edits

Bottom-up proteomics *Source*: http://en.wikipedia.org/w/index.php?oldid=451745510 *Contributors*: KathrynLybarger, Kkmurray, MagnusPalmblad, Zchgh, 3 anonymous edits

Brain mapping *Source*: http://en.wikipedia.org/w/index.php?oldid=443168514 *Contributors*: A314268, Afterwriting, Arcadian, Brewhaha@edmc.net, Clicketyclack, CommonsDelinker, Crystallina, DigitalCatalyst, FSHL, Flowanda, Grubber, HamburgerRadio, Hordaland, Indon, Iwaterpolo, Jazzmen301, Jogers, John.d.van.horn, Jponnoly, Just H, Kndiaye, Kpmiyapuram, Kslays, Looie496, Louislemieux, Mange01, MarkSCohen, Mdd, Medlat, Michael Hardy, Mietchen, Minerva2, Radagast83, Richmeister, Roryethanr, Sannse, Woohookitty, Xezbeth, 38 anonymous edits

Briefings in Bioinformatics *Source*: http://en.wikipedia.org/w/index.php?oldid=436824591 *Contributors*: Duncan.Hull

c⁺-probability *Source*: http://en.wikipedia.org/w/index.php?oldid=449910296 *Contributors*: Melcombe, Michael Hardy, SsmdZhang

CaBIG *Source*: http://en.wikipedia.org/w/index.php?oldid=453993810 *Contributors*: AceCoachTheLintier, Attagirl202, Celtics77, Chowbok, Chris Capoccia, Dnaber, FitzColinGerald, Iridescent, Jhspeakman, Jweisen, Kherm, Nafisto, PassingStranger, Ph.eyes, Retired username, Ruebrylla, VNonesuch, W Nowicki, Wallet55, 38 anonymous edits

CAFASP *Source*: http://en.wikipedia.org/w/index.php?oldid=320531100 *Contributors*: Opabinia regalis, Rror, Xp54321

caGrid *Source*: http://en.wikipedia.org/w/index.php?oldid=453977891 *Contributors*: Bnynms, Chowbok, Dervin82, Jweisen, Kherm, Rjwilmsi, Rwwww, TubularWorld, W Nowicki, 15 anonymous edits

Canadian Bioinformatics Workshops *Source*: http://en.wikipedia.org/w/index.php?oldid=436045130 *Contributors*: Bffo, Hut 8.5, Mbrazas, Mr Sheep Measham, Psquared2

CASP *Source*: http://en.wikipedia.org/w/index.php?oldid=438190581 *Contributors*: Antelan, Ben D., Blastwizard, Bluemoose, CasperO, Dcrjsr, Dekisugi, Emw, EncycloPetey, Hodja Nasreddin, MayDoris, MichaK, Miguel Andrade, MindZiper, Mndoci, NuclearWarfare, Piways, Protein314, Proteinstructure, QTCaptain, RDBrown, Rjwilmsi, Roo1812, S.Seymour, Salsb, Shikoten, Soren.harward, Stewartadcock, TestPilot, Thorwald, 39 anonymous edits

CAZy *Source*: http://en.wikipedia.org/w/index.php?oldid=446455759 *Contributors*: 564dude, Alexbateman, Boghog

Cellular model *Source*: http://en.wikipedia.org/w/index.php?oldid=440541043 *Contributors*: Egmontaz, Gautamdey, Gene Nygaard, Nick Number, Noanator10, Spencerk, Squidonius, Wakebrdkid, Wpoeop

Center for Bioinformatics and Computational Biology *Source*: http://en.wikipedia.org/w/index.php?oldid=311808110 *Contributors*: Dpuiu, Eastmain, Jussen, McWomble, Tassedethe, Waacstats

ChEMBL *Source*: http://en.wikipedia.org/w/index.php?oldid=454222237 *Contributors*: Alexbateman, Bearcat, Christian75, Dcirovic, DesiLady, EgonWillighagen, Kazebi, Louisajb, Rangoon11, Rockpocket, Taugei, WikiDan61, Woohookitty, Wrelwser43, 2 anonymous edits

Chemical library *Source*: http://en.wikipedia.org/w/index.php?oldid=452177238 *Contributors*: Aushulz, Cacycle, JaGa, Jason Quinn, Michael Hardy, Rjwilmsi, RotartSinimda, ShelfSkewed, Tassedethe, Theoriste, Woohookitty, Xezbeth, 6 anonymous edits

Chemistry Development Kit *Source*: http://en.wikipedia.org/w/index.php?oldid=432988503 *Contributors*: AngelHerraez, Dockingman, EgonWillighagen, Egonw, Frap, Gaius Cornelius, Gioto, Isilanes, Joerg Kurt Wegner, Kl4m-AWB, Linus M., Pansanel, RDBrown, RossPatterson, Steinbeck, Tassedethe, 19 anonymous edits

ChIP-on-chip *Source*: http://en.wikipedia.org/w/index.php?oldid=451122422 *Contributors*: Ascendedalteran, BillyBobPedant, Ctaplin85, DO11.10, Darked, Dashtheman, David Schaich, Edward, Grouse, Jeangabin, Lantonov, MBCF, Miguel Andrade, Mlupien, Onsetuntil, Pdcook, ScienceGuy5555, Skittleys, Thomas.Hentrich, Waggers, Woohookitty, Yijunw, 45 anonymous edits

Chou–Fasman method *Source*: http://en.wikipedia.org/w/index.php?oldid=443403995 *Contributors*: BillThorne, Lenov, Opabinia regalis, Rjwilmsi, Thorwald, Tripodian, 2 anonymous edits

CIT Program Tumor Identity Cards *Source*: http://en.wikipedia.org/w/index.php?oldid=425266405 *Contributors*: Chowbok, Fabienpetel, Jonkerz, 3 anonymous edits

CLC bio *Source*: http://en.wikipedia.org/w/index.php?oldid=382417057 *Contributors*: Bio-ITWorld, Cbrown1023, Cesium 133, Daen, Don G., ElsevierRogersK, Gogo Dodo, Hmains, JonHarder, MBisanz, Mackensen, WOSlinker, 5 anonymous edits

Clone manager *Source*: http://en.wikipedia.org/w/index.php?oldid=448754422 *Contributors*: CharlieEchoTango, DGG, Johnuniq, KConWiki, Laurawgenesyn, Mrzaius, Peter Drake, Petkraw, Radiant chains, Seans Potato Business, Springbok26, 3 anonymous edits

Clustal *Source*: http://en.wikipedia.org/w/index.php?oldid=436295471 *Contributors*: Alexbateman, Amalas, Aranae, AutumnSnow, BenJWoodcroft, Blastwizard, C-hankel, Christo07, Edward, Flyguy649, Frenkmelk, Johnuniq, MegaSloth, MicroBio Hawk, MrDolomite, MrOllie, Nono64, Onco p53, Opabinia regalis, Ph.eyes, Progeniq, RecursiveMake, Rodrigoluk, Samsara, Skyliner34, Smh.oloomi, Smith609, Springbok26, Stevenhwu, Thorwald, Timrb, Trevor Wennblom, Wzhao553, 23 anonymous edits

CodonCode Aligner *Source*: http://en.wikipedia.org/w/index.php?oldid=434736673 *Contributors*: Alexbateman, Genomesequencer, MegaSloth, MuffledThud, Rjwilmsi

Community Cyberinfrastructure for Advanced Marine Microbial Ecology Research and Analysis *Source*: http://en.wikipedia.org/w/index.php?oldid=406531706 *Contributors*: Dicklyon, Genkuro, Levineps, Patfla, Plindenbaum, Sadads, 14 anonymous edits

Complex system biology *Source*: http://en.wikipedia.org/w/index.php?oldid=452675422 *Contributors*: Bci2, Dolovis, Epipelagic, Michael Hardy, Muxxxa, Rjwilmsi, 1 anonymous edits

Computational biology *Source*: http://en.wikipedia.org/w/index.php?oldid=455080659 *Contributors*: 12 Noon, Agricola44, Auntof6, AvicAWB, Bci2, Bio-ITWorld, Biochaos, CWenger, Corvus Kolk, D-rew, Dicklyon, Disavian, Dratman, Duncan.Hull, Fram, Gaurav, Gogo Dodo, Harihsh, Ideogram, JASONKEIL, Jethero, Joe3600, Karin.van.haren, Kevin k, Lordmetroid, Manuelcorpas, Marcoacostareyes, Meduz, Michael Hardy, Narayanese, Opabinia regalis, Peccoud, Ph.eyes, PhCOOH, Ppgardne, Quantling, Ronz, Sa'y, Sitotorres, Snie007, Spencerk, Sunur7, Tarcieri, Tarinth, Themfromspace, Venus Victorious, Vezzi, Vianello, Wavelength, Whiteh12, Zuck3434, 50 anonymous edits

Computational epigenetics *Source*: http://en.wikipedia.org/w/index.php?oldid=421880515 *Contributors*: 2over0, Asasia, Cbock, Chemberlen, D.M.N., Dnacond, Mr Adequate, Rjwilmsi, TastyPoutine, Tinwee, Tongjoochuan, 4 anonymous edits

Computational genomics *Source*: http://en.wikipedia.org/w/index.php?oldid=402127371 *Contributors*: Appraiser, Blastwizard, Bluemoose, Cbock, D6, Genometer, Ian Henty Holmes, Jethero, Jongbhak, LeaveSleaves, Meredyth, Michael Hardy, Pearle, Rebooted, Skittleys, Tarinth, Tim@, Twooars, Will Beback Auto, 9 anonymous edits

Computational immunology *Source*: http://en.wikipedia.org/w/index.php?oldid=415108564 *Contributors*: Addshore, Andreas Kaufmann, Francescopappalardo, GDonato, Moxon, NerdyNSK, The Transhumanist, 4 anonymous edits

Computational Resource for Drug Discovery (CRDD) *Source*: http://en.wikipedia.org/w/index.php?oldid=454525108 *Contributors*: Avicennasis, Chris Capoccia, Eumolpo, Imtechchd, Ironholds, KuwarOnline, LilHelpa, N5iln, Nightkey, Rich Farmbrough, Rjwilmsi, Tony1, Vgy7ujm, 3 anonymous edits

Consed *Source*: http://en.wikipedia.org/w/index.php?oldid=389084277 *Contributors*: Docu, Genomesequencer, Speleo3, 3 anonymous edits

Consensus sequence *Source*: http://en.wikipedia.org/w/index.php?oldid=456226046 *Contributors*: Can't sleep, clown will eat me, Charles Matthews, Christian75, Eef (A), Everyking, Firsfron, Headbomb, Hoffmeier, Informationtheory, Jay2uk, Jfdwolff, Marshallsumter, Open scientist, Peak, Ricochet17, Rjwilmsi, Srlasky, Temporaluser, 10 anonymous edits

Conserved sequence *Source*: http://en.wikipedia.org/w/index.php?oldid=447224923 *Contributors*: A. B., Arthuc01, BlackPhoenix369, Boghog, ChrisStyan, Clicketyclack, Ebyabe, EliF, Fang Aili, Formerly the IP-Address 24.22.227.53, Jebus989, Julesd, K.murphy, MOF, Mahue, Mccready, Melæn, Open2universe, Philip Trueman, R. S. Shaw, Rich Farmbrough, Smartse, TheProject, Xyzzyplugh, 16 anonymous edits

Contact order *Source*: http://en.wikipedia.org/w/index.php?oldid=445300123 *Contributors*: Herr blaschke, Opabinia regalis, Orenburg1, SirHaddock, 5 anonymous edits

CS-BLAST *Source*: http://en.wikipedia.org/w/index.php?oldid=452178846 *Contributors*: Docu, Rjwilmsi, Soeding, Vanished User 1004, 3 anonymous edits

CSHALS *Source*: http://en.wikipedia.org/w/index.php?oldid=424530559 *Contributors*: Stemonitis, Tedslater, 1 anonymous edits

Darwin Core *Source*: http://en.wikipedia.org/w/index.php?oldid=442095483 *Contributors*: AbsolutDan, Doering73, G.Hagedorn, GTBacchus, Gaurav, Kaldari, Pigsonthewing, R'n'B, Regiov, Sallyrenee, Tassielee, Tucotuco, Vieglais, 12 anonymous edits

Darwin Core Archive *Source*: http://en.wikipedia.org/w/index.php?oldid=405409322 *Contributors*: Doering73, Wayne Slam

Data curation *Source*: http://en.wikipedia.org/w/index.php?oldid=445148331 *Contributors*: Alexbateman, Amb1networks, Carly805, Gracetupelo, Jodi.a.schneider, Xezbeth, 7 anonymous edits

Databases for oncogenomic research *Source*: http://en.wikipedia.org/w/index.php?oldid=434265838 *Contributors*: Alexbateman, Biotechp, Crusio, Michipanero, Patho, Plindenbaum

DAVID (bioinformatics tool) *Source*: http://en.wikipedia.org/w/index.php?oldid=455668503 *Contributors*: Alexbateman, Angusmclellan, CarstenWLederer, Chris Capoccia, Narayanese, PyromaniacTom, Qinatan, Rjwilmsi, Rwwww, Thorwald, Undead warrior, 13 anonymous edits

User:Davidweisss/InSilico DB *Source*: http://en.wikipedia.org/w/index.php?oldid=444060848 *Contributors*: Davidweisss

De novo protein structure prediction *Source*: http://en.wikipedia.org/w/index.php?oldid=455461144 *Contributors*: Biochemza, Charliepeck, Emw, Ideal gas equation, Lcarsdata, Lfh, Maja3141, P99am, Rbonneau, Tabletop, WillowW, 凌海, 7 anonymous edits

Debian-Med *Source*: http://en.wikipedia.org/w/index.php?oldid=434257909 *Contributors*: Dawynn, Jfdwolff, Kathleen.wright5, Kychot, Perspectoff, Physadvoc, Rjwilmsi, Sgpsaros, Smoe, Tillea, Z00zax, 3 anonymous edits

Demographic and Health Surveys *Source*: http://en.wikipedia.org/w/index.php?oldid=453304278 *Contributors*: ElKevbo, Healtheconomist, Jeffdaro, JohnsHopkinsCCP, Measuredhs, Mightymights, Mschiffler, Open2universe, 16 anonymous edits

Dendroscope *Source*: http://en.wikipedia.org/w/index.php?oldid=448805962 *Contributors*: Blechnic, Huson, Jghyt, XCalPab, 4 anonymous edits

Diseases Database *Source*: http://en.wikipedia.org/w/index.php?oldid=456368334 *Contributors*: Alexbateman, Arcadian, Asfreeas, Bemoeial, Borgx, Davidruben, Husond, Jackie, Mentifisto, SDY, Sedmic, WJetChao, Ziga, 26 anonymous edits

Distance matrix *Source*: http://en.wikipedia.org/w/index.php?oldid=432521260 *Contributors*: Abdull, AndrewWatt, Arthur Rubin, BAxelrod, Booyabazooka, CBM, Charles Matthews, Clovis Sangrail, ComplexZeta, Dr. Strangelove, Edward, Fallschirmjäger, FghIJklm, Giftlite, Jaraalbe, Jheiv, Jqshenker, Kevyn, LachlanA, Lemann, Mairi, MarSch, Matt.smart, MrOllie, Oli Filth, Phils, Selket, Talgalili, Tbackstr, Thorwald, Van helsing, 27 anonymous edits

Distributed Annotation System *Source*: http://en.wikipedia.org/w/index.php?oldid=451357765 *Contributors*: Cacolantern, Dmb000006, Makeyourownmaker, Malcolma, Matt J Wood, Nnq2603, Pcingola, Ppgardne, Sezzyboy, Toniher, 3 anonymous edits

Distributed Annotation System/Clients *Source*: http://en.wikipedia.org/w/index.php?oldid=373634268 *Contributors*: ChristoWV, Dmb000006, Kuleebaba, T@nn, 1 anonymous edits

DNA barcoding *Source*: http://en.wikipedia.org/w/index.php?oldid=456316995 *Contributors*: Abduallah mohammed, Aranae, Arga Warga, Ary29, Bagworm, Banus, Bataplai, Beetstra, BoathouseBob, CapitalR, Carlosp420, Ceyockey, Charles Matthews, Cmdrjameson, David Gale, Dratman, Dyanega, Dysmorodrepanis, Earthsky, Evolver, Florentino floro, G Colyer, Gioto, Gj7, HamburgerRadio, Hoffmeier, Horatio, Isilanes, Jlittlet, JoJan, Josh Grosse, Jyril, Kadoo, Kembangraps, Kingdon, Lexor, Mdhowe, Michael Hardy, Nbocs, Omarabid, Onco p53, One more night, Pengo, Physicistjedi, Pjvpjv, Plantsurfer, Pseudomyrmex, RDBrown, Rich Farmbrough, Rjwilmsi, Ronhjones, Samsara, Seglea, Shreth, Shyamal, Springbok26, Squids and Chips, StephenWeber, TastyPoutine, Tedernst, Toytoy, 59 anonymous edits

DNA binding site *Source*: http://en.wikipedia.org/w/index.php?oldid=452194620 *Contributors*: Alexbateman, Augustulus2, Baaphi, Edward, Gnomehacker, Kupirijo, Mlupien, Plindenbaum, Rjwilmsi, Sophus Bie, 9 anonymous edits

DNA microarray *Source*: http://en.wikipedia.org/w/index.php?oldid=454996364 *Contributors*: 168..., 198.143.250.xxx, 3 Löwi, Abductive, Aciel, AdamRetchless, Adenosine, Afluegel, AlastairM3754, Albinpaulxavier, Amar kamath, Amarilla858, Amosfolarin, Andrew73, Andrewericoleman, Angr, AnnaJune, Apers0n, Arcadian, Aremith, Artgen, Aurelduv, AxelBoldt, Barticus88, Bender235, Bensaccount, Big Bird, Bioinformin, Blacksun, Brian Crawford, Brooke618, Calmargulis, Carlsbad, Cathleenmrocco, Ceyockey, Chemist234, Ciar, Cmungall, Cobalt137cc, Conversion script, Crissmyass, DGG, Dacharle, Darkwind, Davidweisss, Daviwrng, Denix13, Dicklyon, Discospinster, DoctorDNA, Dr. William Jacobs, Drdaveng, Duncharris, Effeietsanders, Elagatis, Environmatt, Ewin Thakur, Fawcett5, Figma, GV wiki, Gak, GeeJo, Geno-Supremo, Giftlite, GiollaUidir, Glane23, Glashedy, GoingBatty, GoldenTorc, Graham87, Gurmukh.s, Gustavocarra, HankMansion, Hephaestos, Hgfernan, Hraefen, Hu12, Hydkat, Iidnormal, Ilovemicroarrays, Ipodamos, Jack-A-Roe, Jackhynes, Jafield, Jahiegel, Jeff Marks, Jethero, Jfdwolff, Jgreene1305, Jgruszynski, JonHarder, Jonathan Hall, Jondel, Jorisparmentier, JosephBarillari, Jotomicron, Jubal, Kantokano, Karin sandby, Katieh5584, Khalid hassani, KirbyRandolf, Klamber, Kurykh, La goutte de pluie, Lantonov, Larssono, Lassefolkersen, Lea Cleary, Lexor, Lfrench, Lightmouse, Lindsay658, Lisa230579, Lord.lucan, Luwo, Malljaja, Marj Tiefert, MatthewBChambers, Mattpope, Maxlittle2007, Meddoc13, Mgiganteus1, Michael Hardy, Miguel andrade, Movado73, Mxn, Natarajanganesan, NicolasStransky, Nieselt, NoQuarter, Nrhoads, Nuptsey, Olympos, Orlyal, PCAexplorer, Panoramix303, Paphrag, Parijata, Parkinson, Patrick Maitland, Peipei, PeterCanthropus, Peterish, Pgan002, Phix7, Pixelface, Postglock, Prunesqualer, Pvosta, Qinatan, Quartertone, R'n'B, Radagast83, RainbowOfLight, Raul654, Rebut, Rich Farmbrough, Rjwilmsi, Rlockner, Robert Thyder, Ruud no1, Sandrauesugi, Schutz, Scott.spillman, Sentausa, Shabd sound, Shaggyjacobs, Shamrocktuesday, Skittleys, Slustbader, Speedyboy, Spongebobsqpants, Squidonius, Srlasky, SteveChervitzTrutane, Suffusion of Yellow, SunCreator, Tameeria, Terrace4, TestPilot, Thdog42, The Sunshine Man, TheiNhibition, Thingg, Thomas.Hentrich, Thomas81, Thripsi, Thumperward, Tide rolls, Tijfo098, TimShell, Toddmartinsky, Tombadog, Toniosky, Tstokes, Tstrobaugh, Tuskaloosa, Twisp, Typochimp, Tysi, Unint, Vegetarianrage, Venullian, Vladimír Pilný, Vrr, WAS 4.250, WMod-NS, Wavelength, Webridge, West Brom 4ever, Whosasking, Willia, Wk muriithi, Wleizero, Wli625, Woohookitty, WriterHound, Yaki-gaijin, Zoolium, Zven, 404 anonymous edits

DNA microarray experiment *Source*: http://en.wikipedia.org/w/index.php?oldid=455964768 *Contributors*: Afluegel, Alidev, Cambrasa, Mgiganteus1, Michael Hardy, Mlocolm, Nihiltres, Nneonneo, Nono64, Orchidee3, Skittleys, Squidonius, 10 anonymous edits

Peak calling *Source*: http://en.wikipedia.org/w/index.php?oldid=428127087 *Contributors*: Jebus989, Nachocab, Rjwilmsi

DNA sequencing theory *Source*: http://en.wikipedia.org/w/index.php?oldid=456662454 *Contributors*: Agricola44, Antony-22, BaChev, Bobo192, Jaredroach, Jebus989, Rjwilmsi, Ulner, Wet dog fur, 3 anonymous edits

Docking (molecular) *Source*: http://en.wikipedia.org/w/index.php?oldid=455767133 *Contributors*: Agilemolecule, Altenmann, Anikosimon, Anton Gutsunaev, ArvindRamanathan, Aurelieng, Ben.c.roberts, Bernarddb, Bikadi, Biohuang, Boghog, Bspahh, CanadianLinuxUser, Chaos, Clicketyclack, Dana boomer, Dhatz, Dockingman, Edgar181, Fintler, Frietjes, Gael.even, HollyAtkinson, Horacius.rex, Jir322, Karol Langner, Karthik.raman, Kjaergaard, Kwiki, Logasim, Michael Hardy, Mild Bill Hiccup, Nihiltres, Nscerqueira, P99am, ProteusCoop, Rainman v84, RikB, Rockpocket, S, Smoe, Squidonius, Stewartadcock, Sureshbup, Taw, Tbalius, Thingg, Thorwald, Trevyn, Van helsing, Vgy7ujm, Vincent Vivien, Vipul, Vizbi, Vzoete, WildCowboy, Zarkos, 80 anonymous edits

Dot plot (bioinformatics) *Source*: http://en.wikipedia.org/w/index.php?oldid=439612539 *Contributors*: Alexbateman, Blantstand, Boolstring;, Gparikh, Grafen, Gringer, Herr blaschke, Hoffmeier, Hossein.bargi, Mdd, Mfursov, Oleg Godovykh, Piano non troppo, Pucicu, Qwerty Binary, Rurom, Schutz, Springbok26, Thorwald, 17 anonymous edits

Dry lab *Source*: http://en.wikipedia.org/w/index.php?oldid=448767776 *Contributors*: Betacommand, Bradenripple, Davepntr, Dominic, Kkmurray, Mdd, Michael Hardy, Ph.eyes, Photomart, Saehrimnir, 44 anonymous edits

Dual-flashlight plot *Source*: http://en.wikipedia.org/w/index.php?oldid=442477155 *Contributors*: Michael Hardy, SsmdZhang, Wikiglobaleditor

EC number *Source*: http://en.wikipedia.org/w/index.php?oldid=447442464 *Contributors*: Anypodetos, Arcadian, AxelBoldt, Boghog, Borgx, Bryan Derksen, Christopherlin, Dcirovic, Deviator13, Docu, Eastlaw, Hendrik Fuß, Hichris, Imnotminkus, Jbom1, Jmkim dot com, KaiAdin, MiPe, Peak, Rodasmith, Schneelocke, Slucas, Stepa, Suidafrikaan, Thorwald, Tristanb, Unyoyega, Wikiborg, Zvika, Zzuuzz, 37 anonymous edits

EMAGE *Source*: http://en.wikipedia.org/w/index.php?oldid=427776596 *Contributors*: Alexbateman, Eo313, Rjwilmsi, Rockpocket, Svick

EMBOSS *Source*: http://en.wikipedia.org/w/index.php?oldid=446034108 *Contributors*: Babuganesh32, Beetstra, BenJWoodcroft, Elf, Endithon, Grid.man, Headbomb, Iridiumcao, JonHarder, Karnesky, Mahmutuludag, MrOllie, Peterrice, Pierocielo, Retama, Rjwilmsi, Rotyx, Spoon!, Springbok26, Thorwald, 7 anonymous edits

EMBRACE *Source*: http://en.wikipedia.org/w/index.php?oldid=451047056 *Contributors*: Akriasas, Black Kite, Stuartyeates, Utcursch, Vriend

Ensembl *Source*: http://en.wikipedia.org/w/index.php?oldid=449123953 *Contributors*: 121a0012, Aliekens, Andkaha, Aparker13, Ashgene, CanisRufus, Charles Matthews, Dcirovic, Dnaphd, Dr baggy, Endomion, Genypholy, Grouse, Ivo, JavierHerrero, KnightRider, Lexor, Manuelcorpas, Meisterflexer, Mild Bill Hiccup, Natarajanganesan, Ntsimp, Pansesus, Ph.eyes, Plindenbaum, Ppgardne, Rangoon11, Reinoutr, Rockpocket, Smoe, TheParanoidOne, Thumperward, Vclaw, Widefox, 33 anonymous edits

Eukaryotic Linear Motif resource *Source*: http://en.wikipedia.org/w/index.php?oldid=454974430 *Contributors*: Alexbateman, Ciar, Malcolma, Smoe, 5 anonymous edits

Eurocarbdb *Source*: http://en.wikipedia.org/w/index.php?oldid=409351241 *Contributors*: Mjharrison, Nono64

European Data Format *Source*: http://en.wikipedia.org/w/index.php?oldid=421849091 *Contributors*: Arcadian, Betacommand, Bob Kemp 1951, Borgx, Ebyabe, Ghettoblaster, Jolivan, MrOllie, Naraht, Pjacobi, RDBrown, Theo177, 18 anonymous edits

EVA (benchmark) *Source*: http://en.wikipedia.org/w/index.php?oldid=417986985 *Contributors*: Anders johrn, Opabinia regalis, R'n'B, 1 anonymous edits

Evolution@Home *Source*: http://en.wikipedia.org/w/index.php?oldid=371543633 *Contributors*: Alleborgo, Bovineone, Copysan, Disavian, GastonRabbit, Hurax, Samsara, SuperMidget, 3 anonymous edits

ExPASy *Source*: http://en.wikipedia.org/w/index.php?oldid=453700074 *Contributors*: A Nobody, BroodKiller, Chris Capoccia, Dcirovic, Natarajanganesan, PDH, Professor marginalia, Rjwilmsi, Rror, Schutz, Widefox, 5 anonymous edits

Fast statistical alignment *Source*: http://en.wikipedia.org/w/index.php?oldid=434736777 *Contributors*: Alexbateman, Destard, MegaSloth, RHaworth

FASTA *Source*: http://en.wikipedia.org/w/index.php?oldid=452655560 *Contributors*: Anna Lincoln, Asfarer, BaChev, Blainster, Blastwizard, Bobblewik, Bovineone, Brim, Chris Capoccia, Colonies Chris, Dmb000006, Dvavasour, Dysmorodrepanis, Elagatis, Eyreland, Fedra, GLHamilton, Guitpicker07, Hendrik Fuß, Hydkat, Isoxyl, Japanese Searobin, Kjio, Mandarax, Martin Jambon, Natarajanganesan, Nickj, Ppgardne, Qwerty0, Reinyday, Rich Farmbrough, Rodrigoluk, Sentausa, Slowking Man, Szquirrel, That Guy, From That Show!, Thorwald, Tikiwont, Turnstep, Vietbio, Wrpearson, Wzhao553, 47 anonymous edits

FASTA format *Source*: http://en.wikipedia.org/w/index.php?oldid=453079333 *Contributors*: A. B., Abduallah mohammed, Akriasas, Alchemistmatt, Andrewrp, Applyalert1, Ascha, Augman85, BaChev, Beetstra, Blastwizard, Capricorn42, Cyrius, Dmb000006, Dongilbert, Ehamberg, Fedra, Grub, Gu margaret, Hydkat, J. Finkelstein, Jaredme, Lskatz, Lukaskoz, MHuyck, Maasha, Mandarax, Menat22, Mfursov, Miguel Andrade, Mikhail Dvorkin, Mirc007, Nihiltres, Nowak2000, Paulmkgordon, Ph.eyes, Ppgardne, Quuxplusone, Qwerty0, Reinyday, Rich Farmbrough, Rjwilmsi, SiobhanHansa, Spellsinger180, SteveChervitzTrutane, The Anome, TheObtuseAngleOfDoom, TheTweaker, ToddDeLuca, Torst, Versageek, Wzhao553, 92 anonymous edits

FastContact *Source*: http://en.wikipedia.org/w/index.php?oldid=366931784 *Contributors*: Closeapple, Mild Bill Hiccup, Thorwald

FASTQ format *Source*: http://en.wikipedia.org/w/index.php?oldid=456098905 *Contributors*: Cjfields1, Dmb000006, Drilnoth, Hallows AG, Jeberle, Jourdren, Komich, Magioladitis, Minimac, Narayanese, Peak, Sanders muc, Sealox, Simul, Torst, 51 anonymous edits

FlowJo *Source*: http://en.wikipedia.org/w/index.php?oldid=348429188 *Contributors*: Bejnar, Biochemza, EEMIV, Fabrictramp, Grey Shadow, Lars T., RJFJR, Ryanklose, Sylvie66, Tassedethe, Tfranks, Whpq, Yewlongbow, 7 anonymous edits

Flux balance analysis *Source*: http://en.wikipedia.org/w/index.php?oldid=452246058 *Contributors*: Abhishek Dasgupta, BenJWoodcroft, Btball, Chowbok, Deskana, Dhaluza, Dondegroovily, Feizi, Grenavitar, Jbergquist, JubalHarshaw, Karthik.raman, Mattisse, Michael Hardy, Oleg Alexandrov, Patrikd, Pearle, Rhodydog, Srleffler, Thomasf2811, Vloody, Welsh, YassineMrabet, Zafiroblue05, 25 anonymous edits

Folding@home *Source*: http://en.wikipedia.org/w/index.php?oldid=456763208 *Contributors*: -Majestic-, 7im, 7sagan, AMK1211, Abdullahazzam, Akata, Alfio, Ali@gwc.org.uk, Alton, Amire80, AncientToaster, Ank0ku, Anonymous Dissident, Antisora, Arrenlex, Auntof6, B Fizz, BPinard, Badwolf415, Balmung0731, Bash, Bdesham, BebopBob, Beltz, Bender235, Bensin, Bigboehmboy, Biggins, Bmecoli, Bobo192, Bongle, BrOnXbOmBr21, Brian Kendig, Brickwall04, Bucetass, Burrito, Calle, Cardsplayer4life, Ccson, Ceyockey, ChimpanzeeUK, Chirags, Chowbok, Chris6zep, ClementSeveillac, Clicketyclack, CloudNine, CoMePrAdZ, Codernaut, Colonies Chris, Compotatoj, Considerinfo, CopperKettle, Copysan, Corti, Cowb0y, Credema, CyberShadow, CyberSkull, DMay, DOSGuy, Dan100, Dancinginblood, Darkstar1st, Daveswagon, David Cat, Davidmec, Defsac, Deglr6328, Demonkey36, DerHexer, DevastatorIIC, Dfsghjkgfhdg, Discospinster, Donald Goldberg, Donarreiskoffer, Drakaal, Drbreznjev, Drektor2oo3, Drkameleon, Dungeonscaper, Dust Filter, Dwaipayanc, El C, Elapsed, EliasAlucard, Eliot1785, Emw, EoGuy, Eouw0o83hf, Epbr123, Eskimo, Evaders99, Ewlyahoocom, Extropian314, Eyu100, Falcor84, FayssalF, FearTec, Feureau, Ffgamera, FirefoxRocks, Foundby, Fourchannel, Gaius Cornelius, GalliasM, GastonRabbit, Gibbsjoh, Glenn, Goodone121, Gpearson2, GraemeL, Gravitan, GregorB, Groovenstein, Guroadrunner, Guul, Hellbus, Hellisp, Highwind, Histrion, Hyad, Hyperfusion, IcyStorm, Ida Shaw, Ideal gas equation, Imgaril, InnocentIII, Intangir, InverseHypercube, Irdepesca572, Ixfd64, J.delanoy, Jac16888, Jackster, Jafet, Jaganath, Jaycrabo, Jecowa, Jeff3000, Jerryobject, Jessemv, Jfmantis, Jjhat1, Joel7687, Joffeloff, John Reaves, Johnnaylor, Joshk, Jsbillings, KConWiki, Kaleb zero, Karl-Henner, KaySL, Kbh3rd, Keesiewonder, Kieff, Kiio, Konsumkind, Leevanjackson, Lightmouse, Lionelbrits, Liontamer, Luckrider7, MaGa, Makelelecba, Maraimo, MassKnowledgeLearner, Matey, Mattscool01, MegamanX64, Merlinsorca, Michael Daly, Michaelas10, Migpi, Mikkow, Minghong, Morte, Msavidge, MukiEX, Mvas, Mxn, Myscrnnm, Nebulousity, Neilc, Neodarksaver, Neutrality, Nikola Smolenski, Nitrodist, Nitya Dharma, Nkayesmith, Nonagonal Spider, Noodlez84, Ofbarea, Otvaltak, OuterHeaven, P99am, PS2pcGAMER, Pascal.Tesson, Password, Pathoschild, Pavel Vozenilek, Peripitus, Peter17, Planetary, Pmj, Poolboy8, Possum, PrimeHunter, Quelloquialism, Rada, Radagast, Ratsbew, Raysonho, Rebroad, Records, Reinis, Remember the dot, Rhobite, Ricky81682, Rjwilmsi, Rmallins, Rohedin, Rory096, RoyBoy, Roybb95, Ryan256, Ryanhnelson, Ryk, SDBR39952, SF007, SYSS Mouse, Sahkuhnder, Sam Korn, Samsara, Scepia, Scott Paeth, Sgeo, Shadowstar, Shaggorama, Shaissasas, Shello, SidP, Sietse Snel, Silvershades76, SirGrant, Slammer111, Sligocki, Snowolf, Socby19, Sparky132, Spaully, Steverapaport, StoptheDatabaseState, Strait, Stunt, Tagus, Tarcieri, Techdawg667, TeeEmCee, Tempshill, The Anome, The Fat Guy, Thistledowne, Thomasda, Thumperward, Timwi, Tintazul, Tizio, Tommstein, Trevyn, Tumpy119, VAcharon, Vie ascenseur, ViveCulture, Voyagerfan5761, Wapcaplet, WhosAsking, Wiccalrish, WikHead, WipEout!, Wrightbus, Ww.ellis, Wwoods, Xuenay, Yarmo81, Youlikeyams?, ZachPruckowski, Zagen30, Zak.estrada, Zodon, Zomic13, Ásgeir IV., Александр Мотин, 虞海, 448 anonymous edits

Foldit *Source*: http://en.wikipedia.org/w/index.php?oldid=456175793 *Contributors*: 4th-otaku, ALiEN, Acdx, Ari Rahikkala, Biehl, Bolo1910, ChiZeroOne, Christoph hausner, Djsasso, Duncan.Hull, Eclipsed, Falcon48x, Fiftyquid, Foldmere, Gurch, Gurchzilla, Guyinblack25, Ideal gas equation, Jodi.a.schneider, KConWiki, KellyCoinGuy, Kozmefulanito, Lucien leGrey, M4gnum0n, Micru, Mika1h, MikeCapone, Mindmatrix, Nurg, Oraggagga, Ost316, P99am, RJFJR, Rjwilmsi, Scientizzle, Szquirrel, Tripodian, Tristanlbailey, U-D13, WhatamIdoing, Xofc, 虞海, 22 anonymous edits

FoldX *Source*: http://en.wikipedia.org/w/index.php?oldid=451529804 *Contributors*: Alexbateman, Jvdurme, Protein Chemist, RadioFan, 9 anonymous edits

Foundational Model of Anatomy *Source*: http://en.wikipedia.org/w/index.php?oldid=377091426 *Contributors*: Linforest, OnardFMA, Rror

Full genome sequencing *Source*: http://en.wikipedia.org/w/index.php?oldid=456580537 *Contributors*: Anna Lincoln, Aspstren, BD2412, Belovedfreak, Blaxthos, Boghog, Chowbok, Chstdu, Craig Pemberton, Cros13, Dabomb87, Dandv, Deli nk, DoctorDNA, Dpdimmock, Dragon 280, Emw, Flyskippy1, Fudahik, Gary King, George Church, Gloriamarie, GregRM, Headbomb, Hoffmeier, Intelligentsium, Jahub, John Vandenberg, Ktpickard, Macowell, Mandarax, Maralia, Medical geneticist, MediumBoris, Michael Devore, Mild Bill Hiccup, Narayanese, New299, Night w, Nono64, Off-shell, Optimist on the run, OrangeDog, Ost316, Peak, Pgan002, Player 03, RDBrown, Raul654, Rjwilmsi, RodC, Rokfaith, ScienceGeekling, Shyamal, Solntsa, Sp33dyphil, Squids and Chips, The Elves Of Dunsimore, TimVickers, Tpbradbury, Virtualerian, Wayne Slam, Woohookitty, Xasodfuih, Yablochko, 123 anonymous edits

Gap penalty *Source*: http://en.wikipedia.org/w/index.php?oldid=436300292 *Contributors*: A1kmm, Dr d12, Fba 1367, Gilliam, Popnose, Thorwald, Ubiquity, Useight, Wzhao553, 11 anonymous edits

Gemini Somatics *Source*: http://en.wikipedia.org/w/index.php?oldid=431757964 *Contributors*: Aboutmovies, Midnight2034, Wilhelmina Will

Gene Designer *Source*: http://en.wikipedia.org/w/index.php?oldid=432870329 *Contributors*: Jjron, Laurawgenesyn, Thecheesykid, 9 anonymous edits

Gene nomenclature *Source*: http://en.wikipedia.org/w/index.php?oldid=416992941 *Contributors*: Boku wa kage, Dendrid, Eperotao, Granitethighs, Happy B., Lantonov, Pwb, Rjwilmsi, Segerdell, 31 anonymous edits

Gene Ontology *Source*: http://en.wikipedia.org/w/index.php?oldid=455657712 *Contributors*: Alan Au, Awp-wsu-sl, Bio-ont, Boghog, Bunnyhop11, Calimo, Ceyockey, Cmdrjameson, CopperKettle, DividedByNegativeZero, Drmies, Easelpeasel, Erick.Antezana, Farmanesh, GirlWithGlasses, Girlwithglasses, Headbomb, Ian Pitchford, Jag123, Jiu9, Johannesvillavelius, Kerowyn, Kevin.cohen, Kkmurray, Lalvers, Larry.europe, Low-frequency internal, Mai-tai-guy, Miguel Andrade, Modify, Nnemo, Pgan002, Phismith, Qinatan, Rich Farmbrough, RickiRich, Rjwilmsi, Rror, Sgsfak, Smartse, Suzi.lewis, TestPilot, TheParanoidOne, Tnabtaf, Wavelength, Weaddon, Widefox, 42 anonymous edits

Genenetwork *Source*: http://en.wikipedia.org/w/index.php?oldid=454990197 *Contributors*: Bearian, RETMX, Robwwilliams, Sadads, Tassedethe, 12 anonymous edits

General Data Format for Biomedical Signals *Source*: http://en.wikipedia.org/w/index.php?oldid=384461456 *Contributors*: Icairns, Jfdwolff, Lexor, TheParanoidOne, Theo177, 7 anonymous edits

GeneReviews *Source*: http://en.wikipedia.org/w/index.php?oldid=422793847 *Contributors*: Chris Capoccia, Eubulides, Grook Da Oger

GeneRIF *Source*: http://en.wikipedia.org/w/index.php?oldid=395716082 *Contributors*: Alexbateman, Bobblehead, Bodil, EagleFan, Fnielsen, Kevin.cohen, Kwb778, Lantonov, Obli, PJM, R'n'B, RDBrown, Rror, TheTito, Velella, 1 anonymous edits

GeneSilico *Source*: http://en.wikipedia.org/w/index.php?oldid=370943443 *Contributors*: Bearcat, Jerzyo, Rettetast, Venustas 12

GenMAPP *Source*: http://en.wikipedia.org/w/index.php?oldid=378298567 *Contributors*: AlexanderPico, Frap, Free Software Knight, GenMAPP, JamesCrook, Rich Farmbrough, SaddleAdam, Trevor Wennblom, Veinor, WazzaMan, 9 anonymous edits

GenoCAD *Source*: http://en.wikipedia.org/w/index.php?oldid=453952737 *Contributors*: GMcArthurIV, Rjwilmsi

Genomatix *Source*: http://en.wikipedia.org/w/index.php?oldid=430961354 *Contributors*: Corvus Kolk, Emeraude, Green Giant, Khazar, Klausmay, Koppas, Malcolma, 9 anonymous edits

Genome survey sequence *Source*: http://en.wikipedia.org/w/index.php?oldid=388346993 *Contributors*: GeorgeLouis, Tamariki, Tekkaman

Genome-Based Peptide Fingerprint Scanning *Source*: http://en.wikipedia.org/w/index.php?oldid=429031001 *Contributors*: Bearcat, BillThorne, Frijole, Xenophon777, Xezbeth, ZayZayEM

Genome@home *Source*: http://en.wikipedia.org/w/index.php?oldid=414309688 *Contributors*: 7im, Bobdoe, Bovineone, Ceyockey, Cyrius, Darkness Productions, Elapsed, Kerowyn, Minghong, PS2pcGAMER, Samsara, TheParanoidOne, Wikiacc, 2 anonymous edits

Genostar *Source*: http://en.wikipedia.org/w/index.php?oldid=402838467 *Contributors*: Pierocielo, WOSlinker, 1 anonymous edits

GENSCAN *Source*: http://en.wikipedia.org/w/index.php?oldid=432385187 *Contributors*: Duncan.Hull, EastTN, Fabrictramp, FghIJklm, Neurogem, TubularWorld, 1 anonymous edits

GFP-cDNA *Source*: http://en.wikipedia.org/w/index.php?oldid=425293047 *Contributors*: AEMoreira042281, Ivo, Mak17f, MegaJoule, Pdcook, Rmky87, Spook`, Stone, Widefox, Xaxafrad, 12 anonymous edits

GLIMMER *Source*: http://en.wikipedia.org/w/index.php?oldid=414951905 *Contributors*: EdGl, Genometer, Howardjp, Kku, Melcombe, Michael Hardy, NeilEvans, Rajah, Skittleys, 11 anonymous edits

Global distance test *Source*: http://en.wikipedia.org/w/index.php?oldid=420842752 *Contributors*: Carstensen, DanielPenfield, Opabinia regalis, RasF, Rjwilmsi, Thorwald, 5 anonymous edits

Global Infectious Disease Epidemiology Network *Source*: http://en.wikipedia.org/w/index.php?oldid=405754099 *Contributors*: Altenmann, Artfog, Hbdragon88, J04n, JIP, JonHarder, Lunawisp, Melcombe, MithrandirMage, Nono64, SteinbDJ, Useknowledge, 15 anonymous edits

Global Public Health Intelligence Network *Source*: http://en.wikipedia.org/w/index.php?oldid=449011729 *Contributors*: Lquilter, MLWilson, Pxma, Skier Dude, 2 anonymous edits

Glycoinformatics *Source*: http://en.wikipedia.org/w/index.php?oldid=409387072 *Contributors*: Alex.muller, Hodja Nasreddin, Mjharrison, Nick Number, Nono64, RaoInWiki, Skittleys, Slgcat, Spitfire, Walrus heart, 2 anonymous edits

User:GMcArthurIV/GenoCAD *Source*: http://en.wikipedia.org/w/index.php?oldid=443554662 *Contributors*: GMcArthurIV

GoPubMed *Source*: http://en.wikipedia.org/w/index.php?oldid=440494573 *Contributors*: Artw, AxelBoldt, Kedisi, Lalvers, Medzk, Michelvoss, Radagast83, Venullian, 19 anonymous edits

GOR method *Source*: http://en.wikipedia.org/w/index.php?oldid=429663065 *Contributors*: Andymukhrj, BarryRobson, GreatWhiteNortherner, J04n, Mahmutuludag, Melcombe, Mild Bill Hiccup, Opabinia regalis

Haar-like features *Source*: http://en.wikipedia.org/w/index.php?oldid=449167022 *Contributors*: Alcbwiki, Amiruchka, Biochemza, Bogey4, Bruyninc, Gidoca, Grokmenow, Hadrianheugh, HooHooHoo, Jac16888, Jiuguang Wang, Jperl, Justin W Smith, Kku, Melcombe, Michael Hardy, Mrwojo, Redgecko, Sorry40times, Whpq, 13 anonymous edits

HB plot *Source*: http://en.wikipedia.org/w/index.php?oldid=424511373 *Contributors*: Bikadi, Clicketyclack, EagleFan, Fang Aili, Hodja Nasreddin, Joe.alger, Nick Number, Tabletop, Tbone762, Thorwald, Twirligig, 28 anonymous edits

Heat map *Source*: http://en.wikipedia.org/w/index.php?oldid=444248971 *Contributors*: AndrewHowse, Calle lund LTH, Chimpex, Dancter, Dekisugi, Drjagan, Dzonileon, Encapsul, Gabbe, George Halt, Gervasecb, Hellod85, Jamesscottbrown, Jmrnasdaq, John of Reading, Jonobennett, Jpg, Lbeaumont, Mat the w, Math31, Medialyst, Michael Hardy, Miguel Andrade, Modify, MrOllie, Officiallyover, Onertipaday, Pete142, Philosophistry, Polydeuces, Pzoot, Rebranding, Rjwilmsi, Stevemorr, Sunng87, Supermeshi, V.Rajeswaran, Xanzzibar, Михаυло Анђелковић, 53 anonymous edits

Hidden Markov model *Source*: http://en.wikipedia.org/w/index.php?oldid=455817378 *Contributors*: A Train, Alquantor, Altenmann, Andresmoreira, Anshuldby, Aresgram, Arkanosis, Bender235, Benwing, Borgx, Captainfranz, Casiciaco, Cinexero, Ciphergoth, Cometstyles, DAGwyn, David z 1, DavidCBryant, Ddxc, Delaszk, Dhirajjoshi16, Dratman, Duncan.Hull, Duncharris, Etxrge, Fnielsen, Francis Tyers, FrancisTyers, Gauss, Gene s, Giftlite, Gioto, Glopk, Hakeem.gadi, II MusLiM HyBRiD II, J kabudian, J.delanoy, JA(000)Davidson, Jay Page, Jcarroll, JeDi, Jeltz, Jiali, JIdurrieu, Joel7687, KYN, KYPark, Kingpin13, Kku, Kmcallenberg, Kowey, LDiracDelta, La comadreja, Linas, Loam, Luke Maurits, MacBishop, Marek69, MarkSweep, Maximilianh, Maximus Rex, Melcombe, MichaK, Michael Hardy, Minamti, Mmernex, Mmortal03, Mnemosyne89, MrOllie, Mxn, Neo1942, Nova77, Oleg Alexandrov, Olivier, PDH, Pgan002, Philthecow, Pintaio, Pjmorse, Popnose, Progeniq, Qef, Quantling, Qwfp, Rich Farmbrough, Richwiss, Rjwilmsi, Romanm, Saria, Schutz, SciCompTeacher, Seabhcan, Sergmain, Shotgunlee, Shreevatsa, Skaakt, Skittleys, Smh.oloomi, Snowolf, Soeding, Sraybaud, Stevertigo, Tdunning, TeaDrinker, The Anome, Thorwald, Tomixdf, Tsourakakis, U1024, Uncle Dick, User 1439, Variance3, Vecter, Waldir, WikiLaurent, Wile E. Heresiarch, Yephraim, Zeno Gantner, 257 anonymous edits

HMMER *Source*: http://en.wikipedia.org/w/index.php?oldid=456059337 *Contributors*: Alexbateman, Duncan.Hull, Free Software Knight, Iefremov, La comadreja, LouScheffer, MrOllie, Oleg Alexandrov, Pierocielo, Ppgardne, Quantling, Skittleys, Thorwald, Wanaguna, 4 anonymous edits

HomoloGene *Source*: http://en.wikipedia.org/w/index.php?oldid=386141283 *Contributors*: (aeropagitica), CardinalDan, Clfalcao, JLaTondre, Jamoche, Lithoderm, Szquirrel, Tenawy, Tillalb, Venullian, Widefox, 44 anonymous edits

Homology modeling *Source*: http://en.wikipedia.org/w/index.php?oldid=454963020 *Contributors*: Aesopos, Blastwizard, Boghog, Crambin, Cs30109, DARTH SIDIOUS 2, DanielPenfield, Dcirovic, Dewatson, Hemmingsen, Hodja Nasreddin, Indygent26, John of Reading, Materialscientist, MichaK, Opabinia regalis, Outriggr, P99am, Poccil, QuiteUnusual, R'n'B, R:128.40.76.3, Reach Out to the Truth, Rings969, Temiz, Tony1, Vriend, WillowW, 45 anonymous edits

Horizontal correlation *Source*: http://en.wikipedia.org/w/index.php?oldid=271068127 *Contributors*: Chrispounds, Lsbeeler, Megapixie, 2 anonymous edits

HubMed *Source*: http://en.wikipedia.org/w/index.php?oldid=398924086 *Contributors*: AbsolutDan, Brandon, Cmdrjameson, FirstAuthor, Hubpedia, Pegship, Yanksox, 5 anonymous edits

Haplogroup M (mtDNA) *Source*: http://en.wikipedia.org/w/index.php?oldid=454713020 *Contributors*: Andrew Lancaster, Barbaking, Brambleshire, Brout8, Bulliphant, Cadenas2008, Causteau, Colincbn, Cosmos416, Ebizur, Editor2020, Fedderm, In the government, IvanShim, J.delanoy, JWB, Jheald, John D. Croft, Kalimpa, Kintetsubuffalo, LilHelpa, M arpalmane, Maarifa90, Maulucioni, Mayasutra, Moxy, Mtdna77, Muntuwandi, Pashalamu, RebekahThorn, Reinyday, Rich Farmbrough, Rjwilmsi, Saforrest, Satyadasa, Siddiqui, Smoggyrob, Sugaar, Tomato or tomayto, Tompw, Wafry, Wapondaponda, We used to sit, WikHead, William M. Connolley, Woohookitty, Yom, 34 anonymous edits

Human Proteinpedia *Source*: http://en.wikipedia.org/w/index.php?oldid=404675872 *Contributors*: Anaxial, CWii, Centrx, Chrisisinchrist, Gary King, GregorB, Itskkumaran, Kiradi, Kkmurray, Mathisuresh, My very best wishes, Nandinip08, PigFlu Oink, 20 anonymous edits

Hypothetical protein *Source*: http://en.wikipedia.org/w/index.php?oldid=452065592 *Contributors*: Alexbateman, Am Rathamon, Clicketyclack, Crystallina, Dilipgore123, DragonflySixtyseven, Draicone, Kkmurray, Last Lost, Rjwilmsi, 4 anonymous edits

Imaging informatics *Source*: http://en.wikipedia.org/w/index.php?oldid=413190587 *Contributors*: Fabrictramp, Guangleixiong, Icarus3, Jsfouche, Oddharmonic, Open2universe, Pnagy, Roentgenradiologue, Rsabbatini, 8 anonymous edits

Information Hyperlinked over Proteins *Source*: http://en.wikipedia.org/w/index.php?oldid=442648912 *Contributors*: ACP, Alexbateman, AndreasJS, B, CDN99, CopperKettle, ESkog, Gleason80, Hoffmann, Ivo, Jfdwolff, Khalid hassani, MeltBanana, Mtking, Panopticonopolis, PaulHanson, RDBrown, Rmky87, Shell Kinney, Stephan Leeds, 1 anonymous edits

Integrated Genome Browser *Source*: http://en.wikipedia.org/w/index.php?oldid=417732688 *Contributors*: Aloraine, Kuleebaba, LouriePieterse, Shadowjams, 9 anonymous edits

Integrated Microbial Genomes System *Source*: http://en.wikipedia.org/w/index.php?oldid=375846788 *Contributors*: Bubullito, Kimchi.sg, NebuchadnezzarN, 27 anonymous edits

Integrative bioinformatics *Source*: http://en.wikipedia.org/w/index.php?oldid=389481386 *Contributors*: Bearcat, Danski14, Goxcell, Jonasalmeida, Jweile, Malcolma, Naw3, Talia ali

Intelligent Systems for Molecular Biology *Source*: http://en.wikipedia.org/w/index.php?oldid=446300387 *Contributors*: Alexbateman, Duncan.Hull, Kevin.cohen, Manuelcorpas, Pegship, Quantling, Rost11, Yi-Ping Phoebe Chen, 8 anonymous edits

Interaction network *Source*: http://en.wikipedia.org/w/index.php?oldid=317939748 *Contributors*: Abduallah mohammed, Bci2, Jongbhak, Pichpich, Ronz, 3 anonymous edits

Interactome *Source*: http://en.wikipedia.org/w/index.php?oldid=456632298 *Contributors*: Aejohnst, AlistairMcMillan, AnteaterZot, Ashgene, Augustulus2, Billgordon1099, Ceyockey, CopperKettle, Hodja Nasreddin, Jebus989, Jheppner, Jong, Jongbhak, Kkmurray, Lantonov, Maja3141, Minnsurfur2, Nagelfar, Nardojacq, Navratil vincent, Niteowlneils, Ph.eyes, PhilipNRees, Pindb, Plindenbaum, Rajah, Rholton, Rjwilmsi, Rofl, Saint Aardvark, Shinwachi, Shureg, T4exanadu, Teledildonix314, Thedjatclubrock, Thorwald, Tony1, Vimes656, 52 anonymous edits

Interactomics *Source*: http://en.wikipedia.org/w/index.php?oldid=454594730 *Contributors*: Bci2, Bdevrees, EagleFan, Ediacara, Erick.Antezana, Erodium, J04n, Jong, Jongbhak, Karthik.raman, Lexor, Llull, Michaeldsuarez, Niteowlneils, PDH, Pekaje, Rajah, Tucsontt, 8 anonymous edits

Interferome *Source*: http://en.wikipedia.org/w/index.php?oldid=429990718 *Contributors*: Bender235, Khazar, Kingpin13, LeaveSleaves, Plindenbaum, Rjwilmsi, Sadads, Smartse, Soloxian, Tassedethe, Thrane, 2 anonymous edits

International Protein Index *Source*: http://en.wikipedia.org/w/index.php?oldid=449124233 *Contributors*: Bearcat, Cander0000, Ivo, Marin1978

Interolog *Source*: http://en.wikipedia.org/w/index.php?oldid=449599516 *Contributors*: Abclaybon, Biochemza, Ceolas, CordeliaNaismith, Logan, Malcolma, Peter Grey, Sven1977, Szquirrel, Yisrael.chai, 5 anonymous edits

Ionomics *Source*: http://en.wikipedia.org/w/index.php?oldid=404501087 *Contributors*: Desalt, Gary King, J04n, Leolaursen, Nick Number, Nono64, R'n'B, Woohookitty, 15 anonymous edits

iTools Resourceome *Source*: http://en.wikipedia.org/w/index.php?oldid=442981819 *Contributors*: Alan Liefting, Iwaterpolo, Mdd, Pengyanan, Unused0030, 1 anonymous edits

k-mer *Source*: http://en.wikipedia.org/w/index.php?oldid=449308789 *Contributors*: 7, Goldenrowley, K-merd, Kku, Krievs, Lpantano, Michael Hardy, 6 anonymous edits

KOBIC *Source*: http://en.wikipedia.org/w/index.php?oldid=447920816 *Contributors*: Akriasas, Bwpach, D6, Dmb000006, Dopefiend81, Jongbhak, Mean as custard, Plindenbaum, Tikiwont, Viroid97, 6 anonymous edits

LabKey Server *Source*: http://en.wikipedia.org/w/index.php?oldid=454396427 *Contributors*: 1w1k1wr1ter, Airplaneman, Chowbok, Glenn, Headbomb, JLaTondre, Mo ainm

Legume Information System *Source*: http://en.wikipedia.org/w/index.php?oldid=456048505 *Contributors*: Chris Capoccia, Mr legumoto, Visik, 1 anonymous edits

Arthur M. Lesk *Source*: http://en.wikipedia.org/w/index.php?oldid=439915243 *Contributors*: Akonagurthu, Apoc2400, Binf9010, Chriswiki, Dmb000006, Duncan.Hull, Evb-wiki, Jebus989, John of Reading, Johnpacklambert, Jusjih, Mdeea, Open2universe, Rich Farmbrough, Rich257, Shalom Yechiel, The Sanctuary Sparrow, Tomixdf, Waacstats, Welsh, Zargulon, 10 anonymous edits

List of bioinformatics companies *Source*: http://en.wikipedia.org/w/index.php?oldid=455685646 *Contributors*: Aftabkhan23, Alice Davidson, Allende13, Angusgen, Apalmer.pathways, BD 1141, Beetstra, Betacommand, Bhumity, Biker Biker, Bio09, Bose subrato, Briandurwood, Cche213, ChemSpiderMan, Clovis Sangrail, Colonialdirt, DNAmessenger, Edward, Empty Buffer, Ewin Thakur, Favonian, Fergycool, Gaurav4thareja1983, GeneGo, GeneGo Inc, Gonfus, Gwolber, Hellod85, Ipowersolutions, IvanK100, Jkbioinfo, JonHarder, KdOlivier, Knomeinc, Ksanjeev 2008, Kurt Shaped Box, Lakshmikanth.katrapati, Lectonar, LilHelpa, Logasim, M.Modano, MartinMcRiley, Mayankkumar8, MediSapiens, Mfursov, Mikaela.gabrielli, Mocklert, Mootros, MrOllie, Nivekkagicom, Nnkalnin, Nono64, Oleginger, Olitek, Orange Suede Sofa, P-O limhamn, Patho, Pierocielo, Ppgardne, Prahalad ha, Priyaveera, Qwyrxian, RL0919, Ranjeevhs, Rcawsey, Regisbates, Sbradley4133, Spellcast, Springbok26, Star Mississippi, Syrthiss, Tbhotch, Tortoise-egg, UnitedStatesian, ValKulkov, Velella, Vrenator, Waasu dev, Wieghardt, Wikimickeymouse, Wilson trace, Woohookitty, Zckovacs, 63 anonymous edits

List of bioinformatics journals *Source*: http://en.wikipedia.org/w/index.php?oldid=455322880 *Contributors*: Bubblehead74, Crusio, DGG, Dima.fedorov, Doopa, Emerson7, Harej, John Vandenberg, Kangueane, Kevin k, Krishnaprasath, Lenticel, Mauriceling, Michael Hardy, Movado73, Pavlov123, Pds001979, Peccoud, Pgan002, Philip Trueman, Popnose, Quantling, Rajah, Rich jj, Rvencio, Sanduo, Scientizzle, Sean.hoyland, TanveerBeg, 35 anonymous edits

List of biological databases *Source*: http://en.wikipedia.org/w/index.php?oldid=454721292 *Contributors*: Aliekens, Augustulus2, Biotechp, Crusio, Denisarona, Erxnmedia, Gmadey, Inocinnamon83, Latimeria iv ka, Manuelcorpas, Michipanero, Plindenbaum, Ppgardne, Rjwilmsi, Rockpocket, Yannickwurm, 3 anonymous edits

List of molecular graphics systems *Source*: http://en.wikipedia.org/w/index.php?oldid=454993370 *Contributors*: ASM, Aclark.xyz, Alberto148, Allouchear, Annulen, Anthony66888, Ascha, Chowbok, Chris Capoccia, EVTarau, Egallois, ElaineMeng, Headbomb, Itub, JLaTondre, Kiluk, Nephersir7, Nerdseeksblonde, P99am, Ph.eyes, Rich Farmbrough, Topbanana, Vizbi, Vriend, Williamseanohlinger, Woohookitty, Xcalllibur, Yayahjb, 16 anonymous edits

List of omics topics in biology *Source*: http://en.wikipedia.org/w/index.php?oldid=450183946 *Contributors*: Alan Liefting, Eynar, Fabrictramp, Headbomb, Hodja Nasreddin, Kbradnam, Kingdon, Kkmurray, Miguel Andrade, Nurg, Quiddity, Skittleys, Stevage, Thorwald, TropicalFruits63, Woohookitty, 11 anonymous edits

List of open source bioinformatics software *Source*: http://en.wikipedia.org/w/index.php?oldid=454263218 *Contributors*: 1w1k1wr1ter, 5 albert square, Aboyoun, Arto B, ClifKussmaul, DGG, Frap, Glenfarclas, Graeme Bartlett, JLaTondre, Jjron, Kuleebaba, Mfursov, N5iln, P99am, Peccoud, Ph.eyes, SHL-at-Sv, Tedickey, Tnabtaf, Whoknew.dat, 3 anonymous edits

List of phylogenetic tree visualization software *Source*: http://en.wikipedia.org/w/index.php?oldid=453725218 *Contributors*: Davidmkidd, Jason Quinn, JimProcter, MattOates, Mfursov, Quarkbs, Sgj67, Springbok26, XCalPab, 9 anonymous edits

List of phylogenetics software *Source*: http://en.wikipedia.org/w/index.php?oldid=451978625 *Contributors*: Carden24, Cche213, Eyal Privman, Fred Hsu, Ian Henty Holmes, Jason Quinn, JimProcter, Joerg Kurt Wegner, Katharineamy, Ling.Nut, Locogato, Mfursov, Mlr3703, MrDolomite, Oleg Godovykh, Opabinia regalis, Ramesan, Rasmuss, Rich Farmbrough, Sergios, Thorwald, XCalPab, Zbled, 37 anonymous edits

List of Y-DNA single-nucleotide polymorphisms *Source*: http://en.wikipedia.org/w/index.php?oldid=419121428 *Contributors*: Atysn, Epic77777, Gazzzz, Jheald, Matt1111111, Michael Hardy, Nagelfar, RebekahThorn, Rich Farmbrough, Swid, 2 anonymous edits

LiveBench *Source*: http://en.wikipedia.org/w/index.php?oldid=352813160 *Contributors*: Opabinia regalis, R'n'B

Loop modeling *Source*: http://en.wikipedia.org/w/index.php?oldid=240405982 *Contributors*: Opabinia regalis, WillowW, 2 anonymous edits

Louis and Beatrice Laufer Center for Physical and Quantitative Biology *Source*: http://en.wikipedia.org/w/index.php?oldid=446549487 *Contributors*: Alexbateman, Racklever, Tbalius, Wayne Slam

LSID *Source*: http://en.wikipedia.org/w/index.php?oldid=433423138 *Contributors*: Benjamgo, Cryptoid, DARTH SIDIOUS 2, DBooth, Dr Shorthair, Fernercc, Jeodesic, John Vandenberg, Kaldari, KirbyRandolf, Lenov, Lsidrock, Luna Santin, Maurobio, Mdd4696, Mwilkinson, Paulmkgordon, Plindenbaum, Pvosta, Qidane, Stemonitis, Supposed, Tizio, Venullian, 4 anonymous edits

Macromolecular docking *Source*: http://en.wikipedia.org/w/index.php?oldid=451250836 *Contributors*: A1kmm, Asasia, Baaphi, Biohuang, Blastwizard, Boghog, Clicketyclack, Cowsandmilk, Jurqeti, Kazkaskazkasako, Lfh, Nscerqueira, RG2, Rjwilmsi, Robert K S, Sadads, TestPilot, TheParanoidOne, Tony1, Trevyn, Uthbrian, Zargulon, 29 anonymous edits

MacVector *Source*: http://en.wikipedia.org/w/index.php?oldid=447830534 *Contributors*: AlistairMcMillan, Docu, Fergycool, Laurawgenesyn, Springbok26, 5 anonymous edits

MAGMA (Molecular Animation, Graphics and Modeling Application framework) *Source*: http://en.wikipedia.org/w/index.php?oldid=421452223 *Contributors*: AlphaPyro, Arminms, Auntof6, Belovedfreak, Jeff3000, Kenchikuben, Melnakeeb, Muhandes, P99am, R'n'B, Woohookitty, 2 anonymous edits

MaMF *Source*: http://en.wikipedia.org/w/index.php?oldid=367581665 *Contributors*: A1kmm, Andreas Kaufmann, D6, Kku, Woohookitty

MANET database *Source*: http://en.wikipedia.org/w/index.php?oldid=434519239 *Contributors*: Chris the speller, Frogzrcoolkelsey, Jbom1, Noah Salzman

Multiple displacement amplification *Source*: http://en.wikipedia.org/w/index.php?oldid=448412456 *Contributors*: BD2412, Chris Capoccia, ClockworkSoul, Dansmith01, Fratrep, Ground Zero, Hoffmeier, Michael Hardy, Mixtrak, Qianlim, Rich Farmbrough, Rjwilmsi, Station1, Woohookitty, 26 anonymous edits

Multiple EM for Motif Elicitation *Source*: http://en.wikipedia.org/w/index.php?oldid=383006789 *Contributors*: Aentchen, Biochemza, Drpickem, MiloszD, Payzahh2, Ricky81682, Robofish, Thorwald, XApple, 2 anonymous edits

Multiple sequence alignment *Source*: http://en.wikipedia.org/w/index.php?oldid=454276637 *Contributors*: Alevchuk, Alexbateman, Amkilpatrick, Azazello, Blastwizard, Cpeditorial, Cyfal, Destynova, Effeietsanders, Emw, Fba 1367, Gparikh, Gribskov, Guestjdt, Iefremov, Jezhotwells, JimProcter, John of Reading, Kcomplexity, Ketil, Luuva, Mahmutuludag, Materialscientist, MegaSloth, Miguel Andrade, Miyagawa, MrOllie, NCurse, Opabinia regalis, Quantling, Rajah, Rich Farmbrough, Rjwilmsi, Rodrigoluk, Sadads, SiggyDood, Skittleys, Soeding, Thorwald, Ueberzahl, Ulfada, WereSpielChequers, Wiki1forall, Wzhao553, XApple, Xmlizer, Yamla, 32 anonymous edits

Multiscale Electrophysiology Format *Source*: http://en.wikipedia.org/w/index.php?oldid=422087000 *Contributors*: Benbrinkmann, BrianY, Cwmhiraeth, Diannaa, FiachraByrne, Rd232, Ttonyb1

myGrid *Source*: http://en.wikipedia.org/w/index.php?oldid=421004666 *Contributors*: Alaninmcr, David Edgar, Dder, Duncan.Hull, FisherQueen, Geni, Geoffspear, Gnfnrf, Grid.man, PigFlu Oink, Rettetast, Stuzart, 11 anonymous edits

N50 statistic *Source*: http://en.wikipedia.org/w/index.php?oldid=445140317 *Contributors*: Alexbateman, Alvin Seville, Pcingola, Rotcaeroib, SHL-at-Sv, Veryhuman, 2 anonymous edits

National Center for Genome Resources *Source*: http://en.wikipedia.org/w/index.php?oldid=438051551 *Contributors*: Evaders99, Mr legumoto

National Institute for Mathematical and Biological Synthesis *Source*: http://en.wikipedia.org/w/index.php?oldid=348429110 *Contributors*: A More Perfect Onion, Dr Gangrene, JHunterJ, Nimbios, Sciencetalk09, Tkoosman, 1 anonymous edits

Shamkant Navathe *Source*: http://en.wikipedia.org/w/index.php?oldid=427822685 *Contributors*: CommonsDelinker, Disavian, Discospinster, Griseum, JayJasper, Jwoodger, Karlapalem, LeilaniLad, Maxime.Debosschere, Priyankaprabhu, Raymie, Rjwilmsi, RobinK, Salih, VernoWhitney, 22 anonymous edits

Netherlands Bioinformatics for Proteomics Platform *Source*: http://en.wikipedia.org/w/index.php?oldid=430736846 *Contributors*: Nono64, Peter.Silverstone, Rwalker, Vipinhari

NeuroLex *Source*: http://en.wikipedia.org/w/index.php?oldid=430893576 *Contributors*: Edcolins, Fnielsen, Giancarlo Rossi, Hodja Nasreddin, Jgrethe, LeadSongDog, Quiddity, Slarson, Yaron K.

Newbler *Source*: http://en.wikipedia.org/w/index.php?oldid=426481942 *Contributors*: JLaTondre, Subanark, Torst, WhatamIdoing

Nextbio *Source*: http://en.wikipedia.org/w/index.php?oldid=450137739 *Contributors*: Aminoacid91, Bender235, Brijsethi, COMPFUNK2, Hmains, IW.HG, IanManka, Jkrivoch, Movado73, Nubiatech, Skoch3, TubularWorld, Tzu Zha Men, Y.golovko, 35 anonymous edits

NeXtProt *Source*: http://en.wikipedia.org/w/index.php?oldid=426056595 *Contributors*: Amb sib

Nexus file *Source*: http://en.wikipedia.org/w/index.php?oldid=443633654 *Contributors*: Glenjarvis, Iachimo, Jameblo, Ling.Nut, Onco p53, Quarkbs, Rcomplexity, Stevenhwu, Synergy, Thorwald, Tsiaojian lee, 12 anonymous edits

NIAID ChemDB *Source*: http://en.wikipedia.org/w/index.php?oldid=451611817 *Contributors*: Boghog

NoeClone *Source*: http://en.wikipedia.org/w/index.php?oldid=428402547 *Contributors*: Alvin Seville, E Wing, GoingBatty, Jdtyler, Jjron, LilHelpa, Noegen

NoePrimer *Source*: http://en.wikipedia.org/w/index.php?oldid=428402630 *Contributors*: Andyzweb, Cmcnicoll, Dawynn, Jdtyler, Jjron, LilHelpa, Noegen, Pdcook

Nuclear Receptor Signaling Atlas *Source*: http://en.wikipedia.org/w/index.php?oldid=454490977 *Contributors*: Boghog, Njmk1798

Ontology engineering *Source*: http://en.wikipedia.org/w/index.php?oldid=445763673 *Contributors*: Clay Woolam, DadaNeem, Erkan Yilmaz, Foobarnix, Khalid hassani, Kostmo, Linforest, Mdd, Mjarrar, ProteoPhenom, Recardona, RobertBurrellDonkin, Robykiwi, SheepNotGoats, Sisotani, Wavelength, 9 anonymous edits

Ontology for Biomedical Investigations *Source*: http://en.wikipedia.org/w/index.php?oldid=386417340 *Contributors*: Earle Martin, Elshawkestrel, Mcourtot, Modify, Rojoxiii, SteveChervitzTrutane, 12 anonymous edits

Open Biomedical Ontologies *Source*: http://en.wikipedia.org/w/index.php?oldid=441838683 *Contributors*: 0dimensional, Aa2-2004, Ceyockey, Duncan.Hull, Erick.Antezana, Fernercc, Hamidtirmizi, Khalid hassani, Phismith, Plantontology, Rror, Sgt Pinback, Spark202, SteveChervitzTrutane, Venullian, Weaddon, 10 anonymous edits

Open Regulatory Annotation Database *Source*: http://en.wikipedia.org/w/index.php?oldid=375846892 *Contributors*: Cbergman, Clicketyclack, Obiwan777, RHaworth, Sesameball, Stephen.b.montgomery, 11 anonymous edits

OpenMS *Source*: http://en.wikipedia.org/w/index.php?oldid=449568833 *Contributors*: Magnus Manske, St.aiche

The OpenMS Proteomics Pipeline *Source*: http://en.wikipedia.org/w/index.php?oldid=449647498 *Contributors*: DragonflySixtyseven, GrahamHardy, Nono64, St.aiche

Overton Prize *Source*: http://en.wikipedia.org/w/index.php?oldid=435101829 *Contributors*: Duncan.Hull, Ebe123

Ovid Technologies *Source*: http://en.wikipedia.org/w/index.php?oldid=414525340 *Contributors*: Cherubino, Clifflandis, Gnusmas, Janetfeeney, Joseph Solis in Australia, Jsfouche, Karnesky, Lquilter, Nurg, Pegship, Qwfp, R'n'B, Ray3055, Wikwire, 3 anonymous edits

Paola Sebastiani *Source*: http://en.wikipedia.org/w/index.php?oldid=444642091 *Contributors*: Avicennasis, BD2412, Bwilkins, Crusio, DGG, Epbr123, G716, Giotto 2116, Ktr101, Michael Hardy, Ponyo, Rjwilmsi, Rursus, Salih, 4 anonymous edits

Patrocladogram *Source*: http://en.wikipedia.org/w/index.php?oldid=453791186 *Contributors*: Bearcat, Berton, Katharineamy, Melchoir, Olivier speciel

Peptide sequence *Source*: http://en.wikipedia.org/w/index.php?oldid=428031424 *Contributors*: Chino, Christopherlin, DavidLevinson, Enix150, Eyreland, Ferengi, Hasek is the best, Icairns, Ideal gas equation, Isoxyl, Kim Bruning, L0b0t, Mikael Häggström, Mtiffany71, Murzun, Nina, Noca2plus, SteveChervitzTrutane, Uthbrian, Victor D, Wli625, 處海, 20 anonymous edits

Peptide-mass fingerprint *Source*: http://en.wikipedia.org/w/index.php?oldid=446199475 *Contributors*: Bearcat, BillThorne, Katharineamy, Steven Walling

Personal genomics *Source*: http://en.wikipedia.org/w/index.php?oldid=456294752 *Contributors*: Adam543, Bio-ITWorld, Blanchardb, Chowbok, DoctorDNA, Flightcontroltower, Fnielsen, George Church, Gogo Dodo, GregRM, Ground Zero, Grow60, ImperfectlyInformed, Jahub, Jcuticchia, Jongbhak, Kasjanek21, Kkmurray, Larrymacphail, Medical geneticist, Metzenberg, Michael Hardy, Nbarth, New299, Nono64, Ohconfucius, Rich Farmbrough, Rossburnett, Skittleys, Stevertigo, Swid, Wet dog fur, Woohookitty, 80 anonymous edits

Pfam *Source*: http://en.wikipedia.org/w/index.php?oldid=451129751 *Contributors*: A Train, Antonov86, Anypodetos, Asasia, Asiantuntija, Beetstra, Bunnyhop11, Dcirovic, Dgg32, EncycloPetey, Giancarlo Rossi, Hodja Nasreddin, Iefremov, Miaohehe, Michael Hardy, Miguel Andrade, Mjuarez, MrOllie, Nina Gerlach, Oleg Alexandrov, Pierocielo, Ppgardne, Prodego, Qchristensen, Rangoon11, RobFinn, Rockpocket, Skittleys, Smoe, TheParanoidOne, Thorwald, Thumperward, Widefox, 11 anonymous edits

Phenome *Source*: http://en.wikipedia.org/w/index.php?oldid=429530666 *Contributors*: 12Minutes to 10pm on May 9th,08, AlistairMcMillan, Ameliorate!, Antandrus, BradBeattie, Ceyockey, Colonel Warden, CopperKettle, Crusio, Dryman, EagleFan, Favonian, Firebat08, IstvanWolf, JongPark, Jongbhak, Karthik.raman, Kkmurray, Lexor, Lysdexia, MER-C, MarkBuckles, Nihiltres, Niteowlneils, Nuujinn, PDH, Patho, Pearle, Pekaje, Pfjoseph, Rjwilmsi, Sgaran, Stevage, 16 anonymous edits

Phrap *Source*: http://en.wikipedia.org/w/index.php?oldid=440099606 *Contributors*: A.K.Nole, Drilnoth, Genomesequencer, The Thing That Should Not Be, Welsh, 2 anonymous edits

Phylogenetic profiling *Source*: http://en.wikipedia.org/w/index.php?oldid=410185015 *Contributors*: D6, DanHaft, Daniel haft, Inoesomestuff, Lissajous, Luk, Ntsimp, Rajah, RayAYang, Reywas92, 11 anonymous edits

Phyloscan *Source*: http://en.wikipedia.org/w/index.php?oldid=382121843 *Contributors*: Quantling

PhyloXML *Source*: http://en.wikipedia.org/w/index.php?oldid=417117272 *Contributors*: Dogface, Kaldari, Rcomplexity, 2 anonymous edits

Point accepted mutation *Source*: http://en.wikipedia.org/w/index.php?oldid=455011218 *Contributors*: Aciel, David Eppstein, Dwilke, Lskatz, M-le-mot-dit, Parap110, Qwerty0, Rajah, Rajgadu, Smoe, Thorwald, Tizio, Tony1, Whosasking, Winterschlaefer, Ynhockey, مانی, 12 anonymous edits

Position-specific scoring matrix *Source*: http://en.wikipedia.org/w/index.php?oldid=451220613 *Contributors*: BenFrantzDale, Gnomehacker, Hsiaut, IradBG, Kbradnam, Ketil, Michael Hardy, Montanabw, Opabinia regalis, Ormium, RlyehRising, Sandve, Thorwald, Troels.M, Verne Equinox, 25 anonymous edits

Power graph analysis *Source*: http://en.wikipedia.org/w/index.php?oldid=451036779 *Contributors*: Aervanath, Andreas Kaufmann, David Eppstein, McLar eng, Michael Hardy, Rjwilmsi, Royerloic, Winterschlaefer, Woohookitty, 5 anonymous edits

Precision and recall *Source*: http://en.wikipedia.org/w/index.php?oldid=455363874 *Contributors*: Anypodetos, Benwing, BirgerH, Bovlb, Chriki, Dfrankow, Dirk Riehle, Emma li mk, Fastily, Gustavb, Huwr, Iridescent, Jbom1, Keltus, Krauss, Melcombe, Michael Hardy, Mikipedian, Mild Bill Hiccup, Nichtich, OZJ, Ox thedarkness, RHaworth, Sepreece, Smokybreak, St73ir, Tobi Kellner, UKoch, Vaughan Pratt, WDavis1911, Yago.salamanca, 33 anonymous edits

PRINTS *Source*: http://en.wikipedia.org/w/index.php?oldid=445145833 *Contributors*: Alexbateman, Biochemza, Mqbssis2, Trusilver, Widefox, 1 anonymous edits

ProbCons *Source*: http://en.wikipedia.org/w/index.php?oldid=434736443 *Contributors*: Alexbateman, MegaSloth, Thorwald, 1 anonymous edits

PROSITE *Source*: http://en.wikipedia.org/w/index.php?oldid=454182074 *Contributors*: DMG413, Dcirovic, Dogface, Karol Langner, Last Lost, Malljaja, Peak, Plindenbaum, Rjwilmsi, Shrike, Stone geneva, Thorwald, Widefox, Woohookitty, ZayZayEM, 6 anonymous edits

ProtCID *Source*: http://en.wikipedia.org/w/index.php?oldid=453467042 *Contributors*: Chris Capoccia, Last Lost, Math-ghamhainn, Plindenbaum, Rklawton

Protein family *Source*: http://en.wikipedia.org/w/index.php?oldid=445149443 *Contributors*: Aeonx, Alexbateman, Allen3, Bryan Derksen, Chandres, Dcirovic, Dmb000006, EncycloPetey, Fabiform, Fritol, Gribskov, Hodja Nasreddin, JWSchmidt, JaGa, Javanbakht, K. Annoyomous, Lexor, Macha, Mietchen, Mild Bill Hiccup, Minnsurfur2, Rjwilmsi, Smoe, Sournick3, Tirkfl, Twas Now, Wavelength, Ziounclesi, 17 anonymous edits

Protein fragment library *Source*: http://en.wikipedia.org/w/index.php?oldid=386720822 *Contributors*: Indygent26, Lfh, Xezbeth

Protein function prediction *Source*: http://en.wikipedia.org/w/index.php?oldid=430405133 *Contributors*: Malcolmxl5, Racklever, Rich Farmbrough, Stormbay, Yunesj

Protein Information Resource *Source*: http://en.wikipedia.org/w/index.php?oldid=436645000 *Contributors*: A.bit, Betacommand, Clicketyclack, Duncan.Hull, Hoffmeier, Kjaergaard, Lantonov, Manukahn, PDH, PIR, RDBrown, Thorwald, Weyes, Widefox, 15 anonymous edits

Protein structure prediction *Source*: http://en.wikipedia.org/w/index.php?oldid=456632683 *Contributors*: 168..., 4twenty42o, Agilemolecule, Aiminy, Alex.g, Amr alhossary, Antelan, Antony-22, Aroopsircar, Asasia, Auntof6, Bannerzone, BarryRobson, Blastwizard, Bsiraptor, Chad.davis, Ched Davis, Christo07, CityOfSilver, CommodiCast, Davjon, Dcooper, Dcrjsr, De728631, DerHexer, Dhatz, Dmb000006, DoctaDontist, Dulcet86, Emw, Figureskatingfan, Fvasconcellos, Gaius Cornelius, Gasqw, Giflite, Gschizas, Herr blaschke, Hodja Nasreddin, Il MusLiM HyBRiD II, Icarus3, Ideal gas equation, Indygent26, Intangir, Itub, JWSchmidt, JaGa, JavierMC, Jinboxu, Jrtayloriv, KaHa242, Kaare, Kevyn, Kierano, Kjaergaard, Kku, LawrenceAKelley, Lexor, Lfh, Lionfish0, Maja3141, Malcolm Farmer, Math-ghamhainn, MayDoris, MichaK, Minghong, Nsaa, Opabinia regalis, P99am, Password, Piano non troppo, Pol098, Pro crast in a tor, Q31245, Queenmomcat, RDBrown, Randommouse, RexNL, Rjwilmsi, Samohyl Jan, Selain03, Smuskal, Snowmanradio, SnowyDay, Soeding, Spencerk, Stewartadcock, Superbatfish, TenOfAllTrades, TestPilot, Thorwald, Tomixdf, Tony1, Tregoweth, WhiteDragon, Wik, WillowW, Yuedongyang, Zargulon, 處海, 103 anonymous edits

Protein subcellular localization prediction *Source*: http://en.wikipedia.org/w/index.php?oldid=448448340 *Contributors*: Alan Au, Boghog, Fences and windows, Fionabrinkman, Garion96, Imtechchd, Jasjitbioinfo, Jkhwang, Low-frequency internal, Miguel Andrade, NSH001, Nereful, Pearle, Ragesoss, Rajah, Rjwilmsi, Rostl1, T-borg, Tassedethe, 20 anonymous edits

Protein-DNA interaction *Source*: http://en.wikipedia.org/w/index.php?oldid=422496464 *Contributors*: Alexbateman, Miguel Andrade

Protein–protein interaction *Source*: http://en.wikipedia.org/w/index.php?oldid=455657917 *Contributors*: 56869kltaylor, 7bd1, A wandering 1, AManWithNoPlan, Alboyle, Alexbateman, Apfelsine, Ashcroft, Baaphi, Bci2, Bellu82, Biosci, Clicketyclack, CommonsDelinker, Cowsandmilk, Cpichardo, D-rew, DarkSaber2k, Darnelr, Dcirovic, Delldot, Djstates, Drpickem, Dsome, Emw, Felix Folio Secundus, FreeKill, Gifllite, GracelinTina, Hendrik Fuß, Hodja Nasreddin, Hotheartdog, Jeandré du Toit, Jebus989, Jkbioinfo, Jkwaran, Jn3v16, Jongbhak, Keesiewonder, Kkmurray, Kuheli, Kyawtun, Lafw, Lemchesvej, Lenticel, Lfh, Longhair, Marqueed, Meb025, Michael Hardy, MichaelMcGuffin, Miguel Andrade, Nick Number, NickelShoe, Ninjagecko, Nnh, OlinkBi, OlinkBio, Plindenbaum, Potcherboy, Rajah, Riana, Rich Farmbrough, Rjwilmsi, Ronz, Sangak, Seans Potato Business, Snowolf, Sperandioal, Tassedethe, TheParanoidOne, Thorwald, Tony1, Uthbrian, Victor D, Wenzelr, Whosasking, Wintrag, Wstraub, مانی, 104 anonymous edits

Protein–protein interaction prediction *Source*: http://en.wikipedia.org/w/index.php?oldid=456342536 *Contributors*: A.bit, Antony-22, Baaphi, Bdhuang, Blackcat100, Blastwizard, Bookofjude, Daniel haft, GracelinTina, Harianto, Hodja Nasreddin, Iefremov, J04n, Jakob Suckale, Kjaergaard, Lemmio, Luk, Maja3141, Math-ghamhainn, Opabinia regalis, Pearle, RB972, Rajah, Retired username, Rory096, Sr.kheradpisheh, Ssteinz13, TheParanoidOne, Thorwald, Tim@, Tony1, Weerayuthk, Woohookitty, Zargulon, 41 anonymous edits

Protein–protein interaction screening *Source*: http://en.wikipedia.org/w/index.php?oldid=429979290 *Contributors*: Headbomb, Hotheartdog, Tony1, 2 anonymous edits

Proteogenomics *Source*: http://en.wikipedia.org/w/index.php?oldid=451777421 *Contributors*: Fionammccarthy, Kkmurray, Mcmatter, Nitiniitk, 4 anonymous edits

Proteome *Source*: http://en.wikipedia.org/w/index.php?oldid=455690370 *Contributors*: 137.131.4.xxx, Aa77zz, AlistairMcMillan, Alpha 4615, Andre Engels, Braeden, Centrx, Ceyockey, CharonZ, Clicketyclack, Conversion script, Cyclopia, DIG, Dmb000006, Drbreznjev, Everyking, Finn-Zoltan, Gurch, Hemanshu, Hodja Nasreddin, JOK, JWSchmidt, JackWasey, Johannesvillavelius, JongPark, Kkmurray, Lexor, Mav, Metzenberg, Mikael Häggström, Mintleaf, Misull, N2e, Nbarth, Nina Gerlach, Niteowlneils, Nsaa, Nsolo12, Pgan002, Pion, PlayBike, Plindenbaum, PranoyG, Pvosta, R. S. Shaw, Rich Farmbrough, Rjwilmsi, Rushtong, Schneelocke, Takauji, Tedtoal, TestPilot, Tosendo, Tycho, Wavelength, WhatamIdoing, 40 anonymous edits

Proteomics *Source*: http://en.wikipedia.org/w/index.php?oldid=454257475 *Contributors*: 2over0, Aiko, Akriasas, Alan Liefting, AlistairMcMillan, Apfelsine, ArazZeynili, Aymatth2, Baaphi, Babbage, Bdekker, Bezapt, Bill.albing, Blake-, Borgx, Boy in the bands, BrainOfMorbius, Bryan Derksen, CLW, CWenger, Calimo, CathCarey, Chaos, Chris the speller, Cjb88, Clicketyclack, Cpiggee, DVdm, Dancter, Dave Nelson, Ddon, Dfornika, Dhart, Dicklyon, Djstates, Dmb000006, Download, El C, FTasc, Flowanda, Freezeregister, Gacggt, Gaius Cornelius, GeneExplorer, GraemeLeggett, Graham87, Hadal, Iamunknown, IlyaHaykinson, Iridescent, Itub, Jambell, Janbrogger, Jason.nunes, JeLuF, Jfdwolff, Johannesvillavelius, JonHarder, Jóna Þórunn, Kbelhajj, Kevyn, Kjaergaard, Kkmurray, Kku, Kopfleisch, Kosigrim, Kukini, Lexor, LiDaobing, Lights, Long Live Life, Lupin, Lysdexia, MStreble, Maartenvdv, Mani1, Manyanswer, Mariuspauling, Masquerade001, Mathisuresh, Mav, Mjensen@nas.edu, N2e, Nick Y., Nina Gerlach, Nitiniitk, Nwbeeson, Oddwick, Oleginger, Ottava Rima, PDH, Paul Drye, Pcarvalho, Perissinotti, Petiatil, Pgan002, Pganas, Plumbago, ProteoPhenom, Proteomicon, Provelt, Pscott22, Pvosta, Quintote, RDBrown, Raymond Hui, Remi0o, Rich Farmbrough, Rjwilmsi, Roadnottaken, Sadads, Sater, Schutz, Senski, Sethmrubin, Shizhao, Smcarlson, Someguy1221, Sp3000, Springatlast, Srlasky, StevieNic, Systemfolder, Template namespace initialisation script, TestPilot, Tim@, Tony1, Tregonsee, Trevor MacInnis, Triwbe, Tstrobaugh, Versus22, Voyagerfan5761, Vrenator, Wavelength, Whosasking, Wisdom89, Xeaa, Zashaw, Zchgh, ZimZalaBim, आशीष भटनागर, 251 anonymous edits

Protomap (proteomics) *Source*: http://en.wikipedia.org/w/index.php?oldid=360555419 *Contributors*: Roadnottaken, 1 anonymous edits

PubGene *Source*: http://en.wikipedia.org/w/index.php?oldid=404793380 *Contributors*: FisherQueen, Fnielsen, Johnfravolda, Nurg, 5 anonymous edits

Pubget *Source*: http://en.wikipedia.org/w/index.php?oldid=450143065 *Contributors*: Aimeevanzile, BD2412, Commodore2012, DGG, Geoffspear, Headbomb, Ivo, Ph.eyes, Rjwilmsi, Ryanmjones00, Ryanpubget, Tassedethe, 19 anonymous edits

PubMed Annual Reload Tester *Source*: http://en.wikipedia.org/w/index.php?oldid=413040285 *Contributors*: Dkueter, Ttonyb1

John Quackenbush *Source*: http://en.wikipedia.org/w/index.php?oldid=433428204 *Contributors*: Duncan.Hull, Jenks24, MatthewVanitas, Mkalamaras

Quertle *Source*: http://en.wikipedia.org/w/index.php?oldid=453272352 *Contributors*: Alpha Quadrant, Crusio, Greggelvin, Jimmy Pitt, Kwamikagami, Nanderie, Researchadvocate, Rjwilmsi, Sleuth21, Stone

Regulome *Source*: http://en.wikipedia.org/w/index.php?oldid=364092595 *Contributors*: AlistairMcMillan, Ceyockey, Dekimasu, Dominic, JongPark, Karthik.raman, Kcordina, Lexor, Madbehemoth, Miguel Andrade, Niteowlneils, Nuno Tavares, Pvosta, Skittleys, Who, Woohookitty, 9 anonymous edits

Representative sequences *Source*: http://en.wikipedia.org/w/index.php?oldid=332202878 *Contributors*: Clicketyclack, Dmb000006, Drstuey, Duncharris, Icairns, Poccil, TheParanoidOne, 3 anonymous edits

RNA integrity number *Source*: http://en.wikipedia.org/w/index.php?oldid=450319877 *Contributors*: Lantonov, Vobios, 4 anonymous edits

Rosetta@home *Source*: http://en.wikipedia.org/w/index.php?oldid=456278184 *Contributors*: A More Perfect Onion, Adam McMaster, AdjustShift, Akriasas, Alberthuang2, Ali@gwc.org.uk, Amccaf1, Amire80, Andy00001, Anonymous Dissident, Appraiser, Art LaPella, Bender235, Benjicharlton, Biovolatile, BorgHunter, Bovineone, Bradenripple, C-randles, Capricorn42, Christoph hausner, Claronow, Coneneo, Conformations, Dcdc, Dhatz, Dreish, EdgeOfEpsilon, Elapsed, Emw, Endingkey, Epbr123, Eyreland, Faradayplank, Fartinghippo, Fashnek, FayssalF, Galoubet, Gamer007, Gamingmaster125, Gfn111, Gobonobo, Gogo Dodo, GrahamColm, GregorB, Guul, Hydrogen Iodide, Inmancrk, Irdepesca572, Itai, JaGa, Jacobyoder, Jamelan, Jbmurray, Jemecki, Jennavecia, Jessemv, Jimbreed, JohnCD, Johnnaylor, JustinMullins, K. Aainsqatsi, Kinhull, Laddiebuck, Laver@Taiwan, Law, Lerdsuwa, Lightmouse, Longhair, M.nelson, Malafaya, Mattisse, Mazca, Michael Devore, MikeCapone, MindZiper, MiniZiper, My Wife Saved My Life, Myscrnnm, Nnickn, NostinAdrek, Nv8200p, Opabinia regalis, Orangemarlin, Persian Poet Gal, Pgalioni, Piotrus, Placeneck 55, Possum, PrimeHunter, RJHall, RedKiteUK, Remember the dot, Requen, Rich Farmbrough, Rjmooney, Rjwilmsi, Robert Skyhawk, SandyGeorgia, Sanjayhari, Scray, Search255, ShadowHntr, Shizhao, Shujaaf, Shyamal, Sitonera, Smith609, Sneakers55, Srich32977, Starghost, Stwainer, Svick, Sylvain05, Team4Technologies, TehPh1r3, TestPilot, The Famous Movie Director, TheKMan, Thunderbird2, Tilaye, Tony1, Tribaal, Tsange, Tyro, Usualseven, Vgy7ujm, Visor, WDavis1911, Wikieditor06, Willarveschoug, Wolfgang8741, Wpedzich, Ww.ellis, Xaosflux, ^demon, 135 anonymous edits

SCHEMA (bioinformatics) *Source*: http://en.wikipedia.org/w/index.php?oldid=417166437 *Contributors*: Alan Liefting, Emw, Rjwilmsi, 1 anonymous edits

Scoring functions for docking *Source*: http://en.wikipedia.org/w/index.php?oldid=419751182 *Contributors*: Altenmann, Anikosimon, ArvindRamanathan, Bernarddb, Boghog, Clicketyclack, Jbom1, Ramatata, SamuelTheGhost, WadeSimMiser, 9 anonymous edits

Searching the conformational space for docking *Source*: http://en.wikipedia.org/w/index.php?oldid=455685566 *Contributors*: Altenmann, ArvindRamanathan, Avalon, Boghog, Lfh, Logasim, Ragesoss, Tbalius, Vgy7ujm, 6 anonymous edits

Semantic integration *Source*: http://en.wikipedia.org/w/index.php?oldid=439453819 *Contributors*: Adoligno, Ansell, Artw, Bethmanj, Cainej, Conscious, Daveh1, Dawnseeker2000, Dmccreary, Edward, Fawsy, Fparreiras, Gagsie, Hillarivallen, Hu12, HumanCyclist, Jdatsoton, John of Reading, Kevin.cohen, Kimleonard, Kku, Krlis1337, MER-C, Mdd, Michael Slone, MilerWhite, Minnaert, Morgaladh, Neverclear, Robykiwi, Rogerd, Ronz, Ruud Koot, SchuminWeb, Triadic2000, Veinor, 25 anonymous edits

Sensitivity and specificity *Source*: http://en.wikipedia.org/w/index.php?oldid=449887858 *Contributors*: 3mta3, Akiezun, Arcadian, Az919, Ben Ben, Btyner, CWenger, Calimo, Chaldor, Cmglee, CopperKettle, Craigjob, DMacks, DRosenbach, Decltype, Donjarjar, Eigenclass, Epbr123, Fangyiwiki, Feline Hymnic, Frederic Y Bois, G716, Genista, Giftlite, Herr blaschke, Humbefa, James Cantor, Jaredroach, Jbom1, Jjjjjjjjj, Juansempere, Kaihsu, Kingpin13, Kyle1278, Levineps, MER-C, MaSt, Madhuperiasamy, Maximilianh, Mcstrother, Melcombe, Michael Hardy, Michael93555, Mikael Häggström, Qwfp, R'n'B, Rayccwong, Rmostell, Rod57, Sepreece, Snalwibma, Speciate, Tpsibanda, Umdolofia, Valar, Wawot1, Wifione, Wine Guy, Wjastle, Wolfmankurd, Yt95, ZuluPapa5, 92 anonymous edits

SeqCorator *Source*: http://en.wikipedia.org/w/index.php?oldid=428402652 *Contributors*: Andyzweb, Jdtyler, Jjron, LilHelpa, Noegen

Sequence alignment *Source*: http://en.wikipedia.org/w/index.php?oldid=456503871 *Contributors*: A1kmm, Akriasas, Alevchuk, Alexbateman, Alteripse, Ap, Aranae, Avillia, BaChev, BigT27, Blimblamboom, Bornhj, Bovineone, Brighterorange, Brona, CWenger, CanisRufus, Chaos, CharlotteWebb, ColdFusion650, Cyrius, Dabomb87, DanielPenfield, Danielsundfeld, DeansFA, Delirium, Diannaa, Dmb000006, Dogface, Dreamcarrior, Dvdpwiki, Dysprosia, Edward, Egmontaz, Epolk, Erebus555, Fedra, FelineAvenger, FerralMoonrender, Forluvoft, Fritol, Gaius Cornelius, Giftlite, GravityIsForSuckers, Hahnchen, Heracles31, Heron, Hongooi, I committed suicide last night, JHMM13, Jheppner, Jonathunder, Kilo-Lima, KimvdLinde, Kkumpf, Kotha arun2005, Kozuch, Lambiam, Laurawgenesyn, Leg cream, Lexor, LilHelpa, Madrigal12, Magioladitis, Mahmutuludag, Materialscientist, Mattisse, Mav, MaxSem, Maximus Rex, Michael Hardy, Mietchen, Mike Lin, Milek pl, MisfitToys, MockAE, Mpulier, Mwazzap, Mxater, Narayanese, Natarajanganesan, Niels, Opabinia regalis, P lucio2000, Pgan002, Polyhedron, Popnose, Ppgardne, Pschemp, Quantling, RDBrown, Reimelt, Richard Taylor, Rjwilmsi, Rmky87, Roadsoap, Rsm99833, Rwwww, SallyForth123, Samsara, Sboehringer, Schutz, Sciurinæ, Shadowjams, Shyamal, SiobhanHansa, Skal, Smh.oloomi, Splette, Stephenb, Stevenhwu, Stw, Symon Perriman, Szquirrel, The Anome, Theuser, Thorwald, Thunderboltz, Timwi, Tony1, Tooto, Tosendo, Traminer, Txomin, Ucanlookitup, Whosasking, Wik, Wzhao553, XApple, ^demon, 155 anonymous edits

Sequence analysis *Source*: http://en.wikipedia.org/w/index.php?oldid=454097095 *Contributors*: 168..., AhmadH, Alexbateman, Ap, Bobthefish2, Dcirovic, Duncan.Hull, Dvdpwiki, EncycloPetey, Fergycool, Ground Zero, Kjlewis, Lexor, Luebeck rules, Madeleine Price Ball, Mandarax, MegaSloth, Michael Hardy, MichaelGensheimer, Miguel Andrade, Mike Rosoft, Mild Bill Hiccup, Ph.eyes, Phoinix, Rich Farmbrough, Rjwilmsi, TakuyaMurata, Taufito, That Guy, From That Show!, The Anome, TheParanoidOne, Thorwald, Transfinity, Uthbrian, 30 anonymous edits

Sequence assembly *Source*: http://en.wikipedia.org/w/index.php?oldid=452648282 *Contributors*: A. B., Aaron D. Ball, Aestover, Asasia, Avilella, BaChev, Beetstra, Benjamin.haley, Beroe, DabMachine, Dayarian, Daz10000, Dekisugi, DougBryant, Fedra, Fergycool, Flehmen, Genomesequencer, Genometer, GeorgeVacek, GoneAwayNowAndRetired, Hoffmeier, Imtechchd, Iridescent, Jhannah, Ketil, Käsekroketten, Madrigal12, Mahmutuludag, Mandarax, Mchaisso, Nealmcb, Patrick Dekker, Procho, RDBrown, Rjwilmsi, Romalar, Rwintle, Saintrain, Sequentix, SimonP, SiobhanHansa, Springbok26, Torst, Versageek, Wk master editor, Yard05er, 100 anonymous edits

Sequence clustering *Source*: http://en.wikipedia.org/w/index.php?oldid=432435191 *Contributors*: AnAj, Delirium, Dmb000006, Graham87, Ketil, Lexor, Liwz, Math-ghamhainn, Michael Hardy, Oleg Alexandrov, Pearle, Robertcedgar, The Anome, TheParanoidOne, WatsonCN, 35 anonymous edits

Sequence database *Source*: http://en.wikipedia.org/w/index.php?oldid=446593913 *Contributors*: AlistairMcMillan, Barklund, Bunnyhop11, Eric119, Eyreland, Farmanesh, Hoffmeier, Last Lost, Lexor, MichaelGensheimer, Mikael Häggström, Stone geneva, The Anome, 4 anonymous edits

Sequence logo *Source*: http://en.wikipedia.org/w/index.php?oldid=441666236 *Contributors*: Biehl, Cacycle, Cogiati, Crystallina, Gnomehacker, Informationtheory, Jbening, Melcombe, Peak, Schutz, Talgalili, The Anome, Thorwald, TransControl, WalkinDownThirtyThree, Я, 12 anonymous edits

Sequence mining *Source*: http://en.wikipedia.org/w/index.php?oldid=434310392 *Contributors*: Alexbateman, Andreas Kaufmann, Darklilac, Ikhono, Infrangible, Jj98, Joerg Kurt Wegner, John b cassel, Michael Hardy, Natarajanganesan, Niksab, Rp, ZimZalaBim, 4 anonymous edits

Sequence motif *Source*: http://en.wikipedia.org/w/index.php?oldid=452194755 *Contributors*: 168..., Augustulus2, AxelBoldt, Bensaccount, Cntras, Darked, Ducky, Eef (A), Ekspiulo, GLHamilton, Gerardw, Hsiaut, Karl-Henner, Kdau, Laurawgenesyn, Maximilianh, Meltedsmurf, Merilius, Michael Hardy, Nibbithedog, Peak, Ppgardne, Quantling, RE73, Rjwilmsi, Sandve, Smartse, Thorwald, WilliamH, ZayZayEM, Zundark, 70 anonymous edits

Sequence Ontology *Source*: http://en.wikipedia.org/w/index.php?oldid=451376571 *Contributors*: Boghog

Sequence profiling tool *Source*: http://en.wikipedia.org/w/index.php?oldid=449932702 *Contributors*: Akriasas, Alan Au, Amandadawnbesemer, Austrian, Chaosdruid, Cpichardo, Diderot, Francs2000, Grouse, Ivo, Kkmurray, Lexor, Natarajanganesan, Oleg Alexandrov, Opabinia regalis, RDBrown, RandomP, Szquirrel, Thorwald, Yomangani, 14 anonymous edits

Sequence Read Archive *Source*: http://en.wikipedia.org/w/index.php?oldid=451546611 *Contributors*: Bearcat, Dmb000006, Katharineamy, Narayanese, Plindenbaum

Sequential structure alignment program *Source*: http://en.wikipedia.org/w/index.php?oldid=435431291 *Contributors*: Alexbateman, Martijn Hoekstra, RasF

Sequerome *Source*: http://en.wikipedia.org/w/index.php?oldid=446594771 *Contributors*: Allmightyduck, Bunnyhop11, Gioto, Kkmurray, Mboverload, Natarajanganesan, Patrick O'Leary, Rjwilmsi, SteinbDJ, Thorwald, 6 anonymous edits

Short Oligonucleotide Analysis Package *Source*: http://en.wikipedia.org/w/index.php?oldid=437044237 *Contributors*: Bluky999, Chuunen Baka, Nono64, Sadads, Santryl, 3 anonymous edits

Shotgun proteomics *Source*: http://en.wikipedia.org/w/index.php?oldid=417525032 *Contributors*: CWenger, Kkmurray, 9 anonymous edits

Shredding (disassembling genomic data) *Source*: http://en.wikipedia.org/w/index.php?oldid=413464785 *Contributors*: Malcolma, Sabin126

Silverquant *Source*: http://en.wikipedia.org/w/index.php?oldid=310108737 *Contributors*: Mel81, Skittleys

Sim4 *Source*: http://en.wikipedia.org/w/index.php?oldid=413480565 *Contributors*: Alvin Seville, Azazello, D6, Kerowyn, 3 anonymous edits

Similarity matrix *Source*: http://en.wikipedia.org/w/index.php?oldid=422266690 *Contributors*: A1kmm, BenFrantzDale, Brighterorange, Canadaduane, Charles Matthews, Giftlite, Jim.belk, Kku, Melcombe, Michael Hardy, Phoxhat, PresN, Pucicu, Rajah, Saforrest, Taggard, Wajahatmeister, Whosasking, Wzhao553, 8 anonymous edits

Simulated growth of plants *Source*: http://en.wikipedia.org/w/index.php?oldid=399247966 *Contributors*: Mandarax, Mild Bill Hiccup, Mizuno, Spencerk, Updatehelper, 1 anonymous edits

Single molecule real time sequencing *Source*: http://en.wikipedia.org/w/index.php?oldid=442046702 *Contributors*: Bio-ITWorld, ElizChun, Everyking, Gigacephalus, Gogo Dodo, Homero.rey, KimvdLinde, Kkmurray, Kmcallenberg, Krobison13, Owlmonkey, Rwintle, Snapperman2, Synchronism, Vcrist, Ziggy1964, 4 anonymous edits

Snagger *Source*: http://en.wikipedia.org/w/index.php?oldid=328074304 *Contributors*: Bradv, Ground Zero, Swede1127, Tedickey

SNP array *Source*: http://en.wikipedia.org/w/index.php?oldid=450097498 *Contributors*: Apers0n, CWenger, Flyguy649, Frietjes, Gwern, Hairy Dude, Huybk, Jhagenk, Klamber, Lantonov, Optigan13, PaleWhaleGail, Pgan002, Ph.eyes, Radagast83, Rich Farmbrough, Seb951, Skittleys, St3vo, Wlodarski, Ybit, Zven, 15 anonymous edits

Society for Mathematical Biology *Source*: http://en.wikipedia.org/w/index.php?oldid=426679133 *Contributors*: 1ForTheMoney, Bci2, Crusio, Dolovis, R'n'B, Schmloof, SmokeyJoe, Tamariki, 2 anonymous edits

Software for protein model error verification *Source*: http://en.wikipedia.org/w/index.php?oldid=425221050 *Contributors*: Crambin, Miguel Andrade

Software for protein structure visualization *Source*: http://en.wikipedia.org/w/index.php?oldid=450464053 *Contributors*: Ascha, Bearian, Dawynn, ElaineMeng, Gvitaly, Miguel Andrade, Scivis, Springbok26, 6 anonymous edits

SOSUI *Source*: http://en.wikipedia.org/w/index.php?oldid=415297532 *Contributors*: Dijxtra, Edgar181, FelixP, Ivo, Pinzo, Rmky87, TayaBugs, Tillalb, U9f85, Widefox, 2 anonymous edits

Staden Package *Source*: http://en.wikipedia.org/w/index.php?oldid=455712952 *Contributors*: Dantes Warden, Genomesequencer, Rjwilmsi, 1 anonymous edits

Statistical coupling analysis *Source*: http://en.wikipedia.org/w/index.php?oldid=385697292 *Contributors*: Emw, Rich Farmbrough, 1 anonymous edits

Statistical potential *Source*: http://en.wikipedia.org/w/index.php?oldid=449359721 *Contributors*: Andraaide, Bioinfo177, Boardhead, Hodja Nasreddin, Knordlun, Koumz, Opabinia regalis, Resathakan, Tomixdf, 8 anonymous edits

Stochastic context-free grammar *Source*: http://en.wikipedia.org/w/index.php?oldid=452006252 *Contributors*: Adoniscik, AgarwalSumeet, Burschik, Colonies Chris, Comhreir, Diomede, Ettrig, Gogo Dodo, Gregbard, Headbomb, ILikeThings, Ian Henty Holmes, Jeargle, Jonsafari, Jshadias, Melcombe, MementoVivere, Mouhaned99, Mukerjee, One-dimensional Tangent, Prakash Nadkarni, Qwertyus, RDBrown, Rjwilmsi, Silly rabbit, Smh.oloomi, Squash, Taugold, Veryhuman, Z4r4thustr4, Zashaw, Zeman, 19 anonymous edits

Stockholm format *Source*: http://en.wikipedia.org/w/index.php?oldid=397079766 *Contributors*: D6, Ian Henty Holmes, Iefremov, PigFlu Oink, Ppgardne, 2 anonymous edits

Structural bioinformatics *Source*: http://en.wikipedia.org/w/index.php?oldid=456592401 *Contributors*: Bunnyhop11, Dcrjsr, Docu, EVTarau, Free2city, Graik, Jhjensen, Lexor, Martin.jambon, Math-ghamhainn, Mdd4696, Mfursov, Michael Hardy, Occhanikov, P99am, PDH, Ph.eyes, Rjwilmsi, S014djs, Stemonitis, TallFreak, Wmclaughlin, Yeturukalidas, Ymichel, 11 anonymous edits

Substitution matrix *Source*: http://en.wikipedia.org/w/index.php?oldid=456174498 *Contributors*: AdamRetchless, Bueller 007, Chris Capoccia, Epolk, Evercat, FlyHigh, Frenkmelk, Grouse, Hebrides, Hoffmeier, Jkleinj, Kku, LedgendGamer, MichaelGensheimer, Okted, Quantling, Rajah, Reetep, Rjwilmsi, Sanjay Tiwari, Sebhtml, Skittleys, Smmurphy, Soeding, Szquirrel, Tbackstr, Thorwald, Wild8oar, Winterschlaefer, Ycl6, Zashaw, 36 anonymous edits

Substitution model *Source*: http://en.wikipedia.org/w/index.php?oldid=437286153 *Contributors*: A1kmm, Aranae, Bakerccm, Bernhard Bauer, Brighterorange, Charles Matthews, Cletushenry, Comrade jo, Dbeatty, Interchange88, JHunterJ, Jebus989, Jpgordon, Khazar, Melcombe, Michael Hardy, Pratik.mallya, Quantling, RDBrown, Samsara, Stevenhwu, Thorwald, Tjunier, Trebor, Wickey-nl, Wild8oar, Wzhao553, 47 anonymous edits

Sulston score *Source*: http://en.wikipedia.org/w/index.php?oldid=425950885 *Contributors*: Agricola44, RDBrown, StaticGull

Suspension array technology *Source*: http://en.wikipedia.org/w/index.php?oldid=432979523 *Contributors*: Alpha Quadrant, Armbrust, Mandarax, Taosui

Synteny *Source*: http://en.wikipedia.org/w/index.php?oldid=449554849 *Contributors*: Abductive, Andy Dingley, Ausinha, Colincbn, Corinne68, Dimitrio1980dts, EncycloPetey, Esthurin, EtherealPurple, GLHamilton, Independovirus, Isoxyl, Jamesfong, Jedgold, Marysunshine, Mat8989, Michael Hardy, Mike Lin, MrOllie, Mystman666, OlEnglish, Pratik.mallya, Richard001, Rl, Stemonitis, Stillnotelf, Stretchcat, Thorwald, UW, WDario, Zashaw, ZayZayEM, 44 anonymous edits

Synthetic biology *Source*: http://en.wikipedia.org/w/index.php?oldid=455687121 *Contributors*: Aciel, Aircorn, Al Lemos, Andy J G, Andycjp, Antony-22, Avocadoman333, AxelBoldt, Backin72, Beland, BerserkerBen, Bever123, Beyaz Rus, Bfjf, Bparent, Brian Boyd, Brice one, Bryan Derksen, Bubme, Buhmanator, Ccgrimm, Cerajewski, Cgustafsson, Cmdrjameson, Constantine, Dandv, David Latapie, EME44, Eceleste, Eleassar, Endy, Entelechon, Evercat, Flyguy649, Freemarket, FrostyBytes, GVnayR, George Church, Giraffedata, Gobonobo, Grafen, GregorB, Hans Dunkelberg, Hulagutten, J04n, Jadavies, Jafet, Jameshfisher, Jasonk, John Vandenberg, JonHarder, Jonkerz, Jpbowen, Jweis, KMM, Kane5187, Kanzure, Kardemumma, Karthik.raman, Kevin Costa, Kieran Mace, Lifeboatpres, Linding, Lofikisope, Loremaster, Macowell, Magister Mathematicae, Massbiotech, Matthew Stannard, Mikael Häggström, N2e, NiteSensor23, Nv8200p, Ohnoitsjamie, OlEnglish, Omnipaedista, Orangemike, Paraschopra, Peccoud, Perryhackett, Pilgrimhawk, PointOfPresence, Psykl, RDBrown, RNAgirl, Radowell, Rangoon11, Redwoodseed, Retornaire, Rhodydog, Rjwilmsi, RoyBoy, Rpshetty, Salis, Scorpion451, Ser Amantio di Nicolao, Smartse, Smelissali, Sophos II, Squidonius, Stako, Surfindna, Synbio87, TenPoundHammer, Thrust 4, Timreid, Tlr20, Touchatou, Trevyn, Triplestop, Vespristiano, Viriditas, Voldemore, Wakeford, Wangi, Wufgang, Yobmod, ماني, 165 anonymous edits

Systems biology *Source*: http://en.wikipedia.org/w/index.php?oldid=455080550 *Contributors*: APH, Aciel, Alan Liefting, AlirezaShaneh, Amaher, Amandadawnbesemer, Amirsnik, Andreas td, Arthena, Arthur Rubin, Asadrahman, Aua, Bad Cat, Bamess, BatteryIncluded, Bci2, Benedict Pope, Benjamin Barenblat, Betacommand, Bio-ITWorld, Biochaos, Biophysik, Blueleezard, Boku wa kage, CRGreathouse, CX, Can't sleep, clown will eat me, Cantor, Captain-tucker, Ceolas, Charlenelieu, CharonZ, Ckatz, Claronow, Clayrat, ColinGillespie, Cquan, Crodriguel, D6, DFRussia, DGRichard, DanielNuyu, Dirk Hans, Dmb000006, Drgarden, Droyarzun, Duelist135, Edaddison, Edward, Electric sheep, Erick.Antezana, Erkan Yilmaz, Eveillar, FLeader, Favonian, Fences and windows, Fenice, Fletcher04, Foggy29, Fredrik, GabEuro, Garychurchill, Gauravsjbrana, Gcm, Gdrahnier, Ggonnell, Giftlite, Giovannistefano35, GlenBrydon, Gwolfe, Halx, Heisner, HexiToFor, IPSOS, Insouciantfiend, JRSocInterface, JaGa, Jdegreef, Jethero, Jondel, Jongbhak, Jpbowen, JulioVeraGon, Jwdietrich2, Kane5187, Karthik.raman, Kcordina, Kieran Mace, KirbyRadolf, Kku, Klenod, Klipkow, Lauranrg, Lenov, Lietranova, Lexor, Lilia Alberghina, Linkman21, Lkathmann, Massbiotech, Mbadri, Mdd, Michael Fourman, Michael Hardy, Miguel Andrade, MikeHucka, Mkotl, Mkuiper, Mmxx, Mobashirgenome, Molelect, MrOllie, N2e, NBeale, NIH Media, Narayanese, Natelewis, NavarroJ, Nbaliga, Neilbeach, Nemenman, Netsnipe, Nick Green, Nono64, O RLY?, Oddleik, Ohnoitsjamie, Ombudsman, Opertinicy, OrcaMorgan, Patho, PaulGarner, Pkahlem, PointOfPresence, Pvosta, Quarl, RDBrown, Rajah, Reggiebird, Rich Farmbrough, Rjwilmsi, Robnpov, Rvencio, Rwcitek, Satish.vammi, SeeGee, Senu, Seuss01, Sholto Maud, Skittleys, Slon02, Smythph, Srlasky, Steinsky, Stewartadcock, Strife911, Sunur7, Svick, Synthetic Biologist, Tagishsimon, Template namespace initialisation script, The Bald Russian, TheoThompson, Thomas81, Thorwald, Triamus, U+003F, Unauthorised Immunophysicist, Urselius, Vangos, Versus22, Vonkje, WLU, Waltpohl, Wavelength, Whosasking, Xeaa, Zargulon, Zlite, Zoicon5, Zuck3434, سعي, 406 anonymous edits

Systems Biology Ontology *Source*: http://en.wikipedia.org/w/index.php?oldid=435018323 *Contributors*: Chenli, Clayrat, Clicketyclack, ColinGillespie, Ghundt, Lantonov, Lenov, MBisanz, Mcourtot, MikeHucka, Nehle, Oddbod92, Perkeo, RDBrown, Rich Farmbrough, Tabletop, Tikiwont, UKER, Valoem

Systems biomedicine *Source*: http://en.wikipedia.org/w/index.php?oldid=436016849 *Contributors*: DarthVader, Dirk Hans, Karthik.raman, Ragesoss, TheParanoidOne, YvesMoreau, 3 anonymous edits

Systems immunology *Source*: http://en.wikipedia.org/w/index.php?oldid=450296148 *Contributors*: Alan Liefting, Jfdwolff, Unauthorised Immunophysicist, Ymei, 3 anonymous edits

T-Coffee *Source*: http://en.wikipedia.org/w/index.php?oldid=446727590 *Contributors*: A2Kafir, Blastwizard, Bobthefish2, Dawynn, Frenkmelk, KrakatoaKatie, Mandarax, Marudubshinki, R'n'B, Tabletop, TheParanoidOne, Thorwald, Trevor Wennblom, Warnname, 11 anonymous edits

Template Modeling Score (bioinformatics) *Source*: http://en.wikipedia.org/w/index.php?oldid=385312384 *Contributors*: RasF, Thorwald, 5 anonymous edits

The Genomic HyperBrowser *Source*: http://en.wikipedia.org/w/index.php?oldid=445138629 *Contributors*: Alexbateman, Jørdan, Sandve, 1 anonymous edits

Threading (protein sequence) *Source*: http://en.wikipedia.org/w/index.php?oldid=455981519 *Contributors*: Betastrand, CityOfSilver, Davjon, Dr ST MolecularModelling, EgonWillighagen, Emw, Jinboxu, Kkmurray, Kmcallenberg, LawrenceAKelley, Lfh, Lidentur, Miguel Andrade, Opabinia regalis, P99am, Proteinstructure, Quickos, Resurrection achiever, Smoe, TheParanoidOne, Thecheesykid, Thorwald, 25 anonymous edits

Top-down proteomics *Source*: http://en.wikipedia.org/w/index.php?oldid=455956346 *Contributors*: CWenger, EmaKelly, Kkmurray, Nono64, Rich Farmbrough, 2 anonymous edits

TRANSFAC *Source*: http://en.wikipedia.org/w/index.php?oldid=453934785 *Contributors*: Alpha Quadrant, Augustulus2, Chris Capoccia, Perspeculum

Translational research informatics *Source*: http://en.wikipedia.org/w/index.php?oldid=413190794 *Contributors*: Biochemza, Infomd, Jdegreef, Mr.moyal, Prpayne, R'n'B, RHaworth, 4 anonymous edits

Ubuntu-Med *Source*: http://en.wikipedia.org/w/index.php?oldid=367149464 *Contributors*: Physadvoc

UCSC Genome Browser *Source*: http://en.wikipedia.org/w/index.php?oldid=432561213 *Contributors*: Dnaphd, Ph.eyes, Plindenbaum, Tassedethe, Wclathe, 5 anonymous edits

Uniform Sequence Address *Source*: http://en.wikipedia.org/w/index.php?oldid=214725794 *Contributors*: BenJWoodcroft, Delicious carbuncle, Hut 8.5, Nikkimaria

UniFrac *Source*: http://en.wikipedia.org/w/index.php?oldid=414482508 *Contributors*: MatthewVanitas, OsnatRA, Racklever, Rich Farmbrough, Rotcaeroib

UniProt *Source*: http://en.wikipedia.org/w/index.php?oldid=444058513 *Contributors*: Alexbateman, Amb sib, Brian0918, Bunnyhop11, Chris, Chris the speller, Dcirovic, Duncan.Hull, EncycloPetey, Everyking, Fergycool, Ivo, JHunterJ, Kim Bruning, Marin1978, PDH, RE73, Rjwilmsi, Rmky87, Schutz, Tikiwont, Widefox, Xuul, 17 anonymous edits

UPGMA *Source*: http://en.wikipedia.org/w/index.php?oldid=453586108 *Contributors*: AdamRetchless, Alan filipski, Aranae, Archy33, BroodKiller, Chire, Cyan, Dave noise, Djamesb, Dysmorodrepanis, Edward, Fixtgear, Johnuniq, Jonsafari, Lexor, Lynxoid84, Minority Report, Paalexan, Rajah, Samsara, Springbok26, TheParanoidOne, Thorwald, Wzhao553, 19 anonymous edits

VADLO *Source*: http://en.wikipedia.org/w/index.php?oldid=411829403 *Contributors*: Alan Liefting, Chuunen Baka, DGG, DeSalted, DragonflySixtyseven, EdJohnston, Edward, Kkmurray, Mike, Regisbates, Rjwilmsi, Ronz, Safatracos, 6 anonymous edits

Variant Call Format *Source*: http://en.wikipedia.org/w/index.php?oldid=442637749 *Contributors*: Ardalby, Auton1, Bearcat, Epbr123, KenBailey, Plindenbaum, Tjunier

Vector NTI *Source*: http://en.wikipedia.org/w/index.php?oldid=428402380 *Contributors*: Akriasas, Bkanders, Bmainou, Discospinster, Don G., Excirial, Fergycool, Franckperez, Iefremov, Jabuzzard, Jakob Suckale, Jjron, Kurtzam, Laurawgenesyn, Longhair, MadraghRua, Petkraw, Ph.eyes, Stone, Wilson trace, Xtothel, 23 anonymous edits

Vertebrate and Genome Annotation Project *Source*: http://en.wikipedia.org/w/index.php?oldid=375847107 *Contributors*: Chris Capoccia, DGG, RDBrown, Reinoutr, Rich Farmbrough, SteveChervitzTrutane, Thingg

Victorian Life Sciences Computation Initiative *Source*: http://en.wikipedia.org/w/index.php?oldid=451969295 *Contributors*: DragonflySixtyseven, Lsc187, 1 anonymous edits

Virtual screening *Source*: http://en.wikipedia.org/w/index.php?oldid=451876641 *Contributors*: 32X, Agent 86, Anikosimon, Basingwerk, Ben.c.roberts, Bobbymoo159, Boghog, Brammers, Cander0000, Jaccos, Jir322, Mijuva, Moleecool, Niksab, Sztracsek, TheAlmightyEgg, Thorwald, WhatamIdoing, 19 anonymous edits

Volcano plot (statistics) *Source*: http://en.wikipedia.org/w/index.php?oldid=444675079 *Contributors*: Difu Wu, Hooperbloob, Ironholds, Melcombe, MichaK, Michael Hardy, Rjwilmsi, Roadnottaken

WAVe *Source*: http://en.wikipedia.org/w/index.php?oldid=393976411 *Contributors*: Kudpung, Pdrlps, Umar1996

Webtag (Software) *Source*: http://en.wikipedia.org/w/index.php?oldid=453486441 *Contributors*: Kolindigo, Mr45acp

World Health Imaging, Telemedicine, and Informatics Alliance *Source*: http://en.wikipedia.org/w/index.php?oldid=425217552 *Contributors*: CliffC, CommonsDelinker, Drbreznjev, L Kensington, Mechanistic, Mhoaglin, Rsabbatini, TexasAndroid, TreasuryTag, 4 anonymous edits

WormBase *Source*: http://en.wikipedia.org/w/index.php?oldid=452518116 *Contributors*: Dmb000006, Duncan.Hull, Foobarnix, GWW57, Gareth.williams57, Pablointhebox, Plindenbaum, Rangoon11, Rockpocket, 8 anonymous edits

WormBook *Source*: http://en.wikipedia.org/w/index.php?oldid=447331987 *Contributors*: BioData11724, Delirium, Edward, Marudubshinki, NoraBG, Phoenix-forgotten, Piet Delport, Radagast83, Rich Farmbrough, ZayZayEM, 12 anonymous edits

Z curve *Source*: http://en.wikipedia.org/w/index.php?oldid=373132502 *Contributors*: Black Falcon, Chessor, Editsalot, Hermann.tropf, Kku, Milo03, RDBrown, Rich Farmbrough, Thorwald, Who then was a gentleman?, 5 anonymous edits

Image Sources, Licenses and Contributors

Image:Genome viewer screenshot small.png *Source*: http://en.wikipedia.org/w/index.php?title=File:Genome_viewer_screenshot_small.png *License*: Public Domain *Contributors*: -

Image:Speakerlink.svg *Source*: http://en.wikipedia.org/w/index.php?title=File:Speakerlink.svg *License*: Creative Commons Attribution 3.0 *Contributors*: Woodstone. Original uploader was Woodstone at en.wikipedia

Image:Pbi.png *Source*: http://en.wikipedia.org/w/index.php?title=File:Pbi.png *License*: Fair Use *Contributors*: User:PhilKnight, User:Wikimickeymouse

Image:PD-icon.svg *Source*: http://en.wikipedia.org/w/index.php?title=File:PD-icon.svg *License*: Public Domain *Contributors*: -

Image:ArrayTrackLogo.jpg *Source*: http://en.wikipedia.org/w/index.php?title=File:ArrayTrackLogo.jpg *License*: Public Domain *Contributors*: U.S. Food and Drug Administration

Image:Biochip.jpg *Source*: http://en.wikipedia.org/w/index.php?title=File:Biochip.jpg *License*: Creative Commons Attribution-Sharealike 2.0 *Contributors*: Argonne Laboratory's Flickr page

image:Biochip platform.jpg *Source*: http://en.wikipedia.org/w/index.php?title=File:Biochip_platform.jpg *License*: GNU Free Documentation License *Contributors*: -

File:Sarfus.DNABiochip.jpg *Source*: http://en.wikipedia.org/w/index.php?title=File:Sarfus.DNABiochip.jpg *License*: Creative Commons Attribution-Sharealike 3.0,2.5,2.0,1.0 *Contributors*: Nanolane

Image:BioClogo.gif *Source*: http://en.wikipedia.org/w/index.php?title=File:BioClogo.gif *License*: Fair Use *Contributors*: Debresser, Frogzrcoolkelsey

Image:harvester-kit.JPG *Source*: http://en.wikipedia.org/w/index.php?title=File:Harvester-kit.JPG *License*: unknown *Contributors*: -

File:Genome_viewer_screenshot_small.png *Source*: http://en.wikipedia.org/w/index.php?title=File:Genome_viewer_screenshot_small.png *License*: Public Domain *Contributors*: -

File:Tree_of_life_SVG.svg *Source*: http://en.wikipedia.org/w/index.php?title=File:Tree_of_life_SVG.svg *License*: Public Domain *Contributors*: Ivica Letunic: Iletunic. Retraced by Mariana Ruiz Villarreal: LadyofHats

File:Signal transduction v1.png *Source*: http://en.wikipedia.org/w/index.php?title=File:Signal_transduction_v1.png *License*: GNU Free Documentation License *Contributors*: Original uploader was Roadnottaken at en.wikipedia

File:CaMKII.png *Source*: http://en.wikipedia.org/w/index.php?title=File:CaMKII.png *License*: Creative Commons Attribution-ShareAlike 3.0 Unported *Contributors*: en:User:Diberri (me)

File:Kinetochore.jpg *Source*: http://en.wikipedia.org/w/index.php?title=File:Kinetochore.jpg *License*: Public Domain *Contributors*: Original uploader was Afunguy at en.wikipedia

File:DTI-sagittal-fibers.jpg *Source*: http://en.wikipedia.org/w/index.php?title=File:DTI-sagittal-fibers.jpg *License*: Creative Commons Attribution-ShareAlike 3.0 Unported *Contributors*: Thomas Schultz

Image:Biomax Informatics Logo.png *Source*: http://en.wikipedia.org/w/index.php?title=File:Biomax_Informatics_Logo.png *License*: Fair Use *Contributors*: -

Image:BioPerlLogo.png *Source*: http://en.wikipedia.org/w/index.php?title=File:BioPerlLogo.png *License*: Fair Use *Contributors*: -

Image:Ribofunk cover.gif *Source*: http://en.wikipedia.org/w/index.php?title=File:Ribofunk_cover.gif *License*: unknown *Contributors*: Yobmod

Image:Biositemap iTools NCBC.png *Source*: http://en.wikipedia.org/w/index.php?title=File:Biositemap_iTools_NCBC.png *License*: Public Domain *Contributors*: User:Iwaterpolo

File:Database.png *Source*: http://en.wikipedia.org/w/index.php?title=File:Database.png *License*: Creative Commons Attribution 2.5 *Contributors*: -

Image:BLOSUM62.gif *Source*: http://en.wikipedia.org/w/index.php?title=File:BLOSUM62.gif *License*: Creative Commons Attribution-Sharealike 3.0 *Contributors*: Hannes Röst

File:Temporal evolution of random boolean network.png *Source*: http://en.wikipedia.org/w/index.php?title=File:Temporal_evolution_of_random_boolean_network.png *License*: unknown *Contributors*: Carlos Gershenson

Image:Bottom-up vs top down.svg *Source*: http://en.wikipedia.org/w/index.php?title=File:Bottom-up_vs_top_down.svg *License*: Creative Commons Attribution-Sharealike 3.0 *Contributors*: MagnusPalmblad

Image:CaBIGLogo.JPG *Source*: http://en.wikipedia.org/w/index.php?title=File:CaBIGLogo.JPG *License*: Public Domain *Contributors*: Original uploader was aflattes

Image:CaGrid.gif *Source*: http://en.wikipedia.org/w/index.php?title=File:CaGrid.gif *License*: Public domain *Contributors*: Original uploader was Jweisen at en.wikipedia

Image:CaGrid Portal 2022.png *Source*: http://en.wikipedia.org/w/index.php?title=File:CaGrid_Portal_2022.png *License*: GNU Free Documentation License *Contributors*: -

Image:bioinformatics_ca.jpg *Source*: http://en.wikipedia.org/w/index.php?title=File:Bioinformatics_ca.jpg *License*: Creative Commons Attribution 3.0 *Contributors*: Francis Ouellette

Image:Target3dsmRib 354predictedModels CASP8.jpg *Source*: http://en.wikipedia.org/w/index.php?title=File:Target3dsmRib_354predictedModels_CASP8.jpg *License*: Creative Commons Attribution 3.0 *Contributors*: Jane Richardson (Dcrjsr) & Dan Keedy

Image:CASP PredCtr cumCalpha plot T0398.jpg *Source*: http://en.wikipedia.org/w/index.php?title=File:CASP_PredCtr_cumCalpha_plot_T0398.jpg *License*: Creative Commons Attribution 3.0 *Contributors*: Dcrjsr

Image:Signal transduction v1.png *Source*: http://en.wikipedia.org/w/index.php?title=File:Signal_transduction_v1.png *License*: GNU Free Documentation License *Contributors*: Original uploader was Roadnottaken at en.wikipedia

Image:Cell cycle bifurcation diagram.jpg *Source*: http://en.wikipedia.org/w/index.php?title=File:Cell_cycle_bifurcation_diagram.jpg *License*: Creative Commons Attribution-Sharealike 3.0 *Contributors*: Squidonius (talk)

Image:chembl logo.png *Source*: http://en.wikipedia.org/w/index.php?title=File:Chembl_logo.png *License*: Creative Commons Attribution 3.0 *Contributors*: Chemblgroup

File:Flag of the United Kingdom.svg *Source*: http://en.wikipedia.org/w/index.php?title=File:Flag_of_the_United_Kingdom.svg *License*: Public Domain *Contributors*: -

Image:Cdklogo.svg *Source*: http://en.wikipedia.org/w/index.php?title=File:Cdklogo.svg *License*: Public Domain *Contributors*: EgonWillighagen (talk). Original uploader was EgonWillighagen at en.wikipedia

Image:ChIP-on-chip workflow overview.png *Source*: http://en.wikipedia.org/w/index.php?title=File:ChIP-on-chip_workflow_overview.png *License*: Public Domain *Contributors*: -

Image:ChIP-on-chip wet-lab.png *Source*: http://en.wikipedia.org/w/index.php?title=File:ChIP-on-chip_wet-lab.png *License*: Public Domain *Contributors*: -

Image:ChIP-on-chip dry-lab.png *Source*: http://en.wikipedia.org/w/index.php?title=File:ChIP-on-chip_dry-lab.png *License*: Public Domain *Contributors*: -

Image:CIT-Tumor-Samples-20100507.png *Source*: http://en.wikipedia.org/w/index.php?title=File:CIT-Tumor-Samples-20100507.png *License*: Creative Commons Attribution-Sharealike 3.0 *Contributors*: Fabien PETEL

File:Complex-adaptive-system.jpg *Source*: http://en.wikipedia.org/w/index.php?title=File:Complex-adaptive-system.jpg *License*: GNU Free Documentation License *Contributors*: User:Acadac

image:Seawifs global biosphere.jpg *Source*: http://en.wikipedia.org/w/index.php?title=File:Seawifs_global_biosphere.jpg *License*: unknown *Contributors*: -

File:ADN animation.gif *Source*: http://en.wikipedia.org/w/index.php?title=File:ADN_animation.gif *License*: Public Domain *Contributors*: brian0918™

File:Telomerase illustration.jpg *Source*: http://en.wikipedia.org/w/index.php?title=File:Telomerase_illustration.jpg *License*: Creative Commons Attribution 3.0 *Contributors*: Sierra Sciences, LLC

File:MAPKpathway.png *Source*: http://en.wikipedia.org/w/index.php?title=File:MAPKpathway.png *License*: GNU Free Documentation License *Contributors*: Original uploader was JWSchmidt at en.wikipedia

Image:Conserved residues.svg *Source*: http://en.wikipedia.org/w/index.php?title=File:Conserved_residues.svg *License*: Public Domain *Contributors*: Original uploader was Bensaccount at en.wikipedia

Image:Zinc-finger-seq-alignment2.png *Source*: http://en.wikipedia.org/w/index.php?title=File:Zinc-finger-seq-alignment2.png *License*: Public Domain *Contributors*: Opabinia regalis

File:Flag of Afghanistan.svg *Source*: http://en.wikipedia.org/w/index.php?title=File:Flag_of_Afghanistan.svg *License*: Public Domain *Contributors*: -

File:Flag of Albania.svg *Source*: http://en.wikipedia.org/w/index.php?title=File:Flag_of_Albania.svg *License*: Public Domain *Contributors*: User:Dbenbenn

File:Flag of Armenia.svg *Source*: http://en.wikipedia.org/w/index.php?title=File:Flag_of_Armenia.svg *License*: Public Domain *Contributors*: User:SKopp

File:Flag of Angola.svg *Source*: http://en.wikipedia.org/w/index.php?title=File:Flag_of_Angola.svg *License*: Public Domain *Contributors*: User:SKopp

File:Flag of Azerbaijan.svg *Source*: http://en.wikipedia.org/w/index.php?title=File:Flag_of_Azerbaijan.svg *License*: Public Domain *Contributors*: SKopp and others

File:Flag of Bangladesh.svg *Source*: http://en.wikipedia.org/w/index.php?title=File:Flag_of_Bangladesh.svg *License*: Public Domain *Contributors*: User:SKopp

File:Flag of Botswana.svg *Source*: http://en.wikipedia.org/w/index.php?title=File:Flag_of_Botswana.svg *License*: Public Domain *Contributors*: User:Gabbe, User:Madden, User:SKopp

File:Flag of Burundi.svg *Source*: http://en.wikipedia.org/w/index.php?title=File:Flag_of_Burundi.svg *License*: unknown *Contributors*: User:Pumbaa80

File:Flag of Benin.svg *Source*: http://en.wikipedia.org/w/index.php?title=File:Flag_of_Benin.svg *License*: Public Domain *Contributors*: Drawn by User:SKopp, rewritten by User:Gabbe

License